ISBN 978-0-265-78065-7
PIBN 10968058

1 MONTH OF
FREE
READING

at
www.ForgottenBooks.com

By purchasing this book you are eligible for one month membership to ForgottenBooks.com, giving you unlimited access to our entire collection of over 1,000,000 titles via our web site and mobile apps.

To claim your free month visit:
www.forgottenbooks.com/free968058

English
Français
Deutsche
Italiano
Español
Português

www.forgottenbooks.com

Mythology Photography **Fiction**
Fishing Christianity **Art** Cooking
Essays Buddhism Freemasonry
Medicine **Biology** Music **Ancient
Egypt** Evolution Carpentry Physics
Dance Geology **Mathematics** Fitness
Shakespeare **Folklore** Yoga Marketing
Confidence Immortality Biographies
Poetry **Psychology** Witchcraft
Electronics Chemistry History **Law**
Accounting **Philosophy** Anthropology
Alchemy Drama Quantum Mechanics
Atheism Sexual Health **Ancient History**
Entrepreneurship Languages Sport
Paleontology Needlework Islam
Metaphysics Investment Archaeology
Parenting Statistics Criminology
Motivational

THE JUSTICE OF THE PEACE

FOR

IRELAND.

John C. Guise

THE JUSTICE OF THE PEACE

FOR

IRELAND:

GIVING, IN AN ABRIDGED AND ALPHABETICAL FORM AND ORDER,

THE SEVERAL OFFENCES AND OTHER CAUSES OF COMPLAINT;
THE SUBJECTS OF *SUMMARY ADJUDICATION*;
THE STATUTES RELATING THERETO;
THE EXTENT OF JURISDICTION;
AND WHETHER TRIABLE BY ONE OR MORE JUSTICES.

AND, IN LIKE ALPHABETICAL ORDER,

AN EPITOME OF THE CRIMES AND OFFENCES *TRIABLE BY INDICTMENT.*

AND, AS AN

APPENDIX,

"THE PETTY SESSIONS (IRELAND) ACT, 1851,"

(*With Notes pointing out to what extent it is applicable to or affected by prior and subsequent Legislation*);

THE FINES (IRELAND) ACTS; THE LICENSING (LIQUOR) LAWS;
SMALL PENALTIES (IRELAND) ACT; SMALL DEBTS ACT;
PROTECTION OF JUSTICES ACT;
LAW OF EVIDENCE ACTS;
ABSTRACTS OF OTHER USEFUL AND IMPORTANT STATUTES;
FORMS TO BE USED IN PARTICULAR CASES, AND UNDER SPECIAL ACTS;
CIRCULAR LETTERS ISSUED FROM DUBLIN CASTLE FOR THE DIRECTIONS AND
GUIDANCE OF THE MAGISTRATES AND THE CLERKS OF PETTY SESSIONS, &c.

BY

HENRY HUMPHREYS.

EIGHTH EDITION.

DUBLIN :

PRINTED AT THE UNIVERSITY PRESS,

BY PONSONBY AND WELDRICK.

PREFACE

TO THE EIGHTH EDITION.

————◦◦◦————

...ublication of this, the eighth edition of the Justice of
...ace, is in response to the many calls for it made on the
...r and his Publishers.

...e work has for some time been out of print.

...ttle more than five years have elapsed between this edition
...e last preceding one. During this short intervening space
...legislative changes will be noticeable, both in the law and
...lministration of it.

...e "Faculty", or Special Jurisdiction, conferred by the
...inal Law and Procedure (Ireland) Act, 1887", is at
...i graft on, and modification of, the general Petty Sessions
...ure, when this latter is employed in working out that
...l jurisdiction.

...e Courts so constituted, commonly known as "Crimes
...ourts', have, from the nature of things, met with stern
...tion, the entire chain of procedure challenged and con-
...step by step—of course under such a strain the strength
...whole chain is always just that of the weakest link.

...rliament, the Bar, and the public Press were not silent
...tors, all eagerly took part and took sides.

...nerable statutes—ancient precedents of almost forgotten
...were re-furbished and had new life added to them.

...e Act of 1360-1 (the 34th of King Edward III.) proved
...a right Damascus blade, keen of edge and of wonderful
...lity. The King's Bench, too, as the great conservator
...peace of the realm, brought forth to like purpose from
...moury an original inherent jurisdiction anterior to any
...statutes. It is true that in determining some questions

the Divisions of the Supreme Courts were not always of one mind, nor indeed were the judges of each Division at all times so with one another, still much solid and abiding instruction was imparted, much light thrown on summary jurisdiction in general.

To recur to the legislative changes during this period, amongst others briefly may be noticed—the "Criminal Law Amendment Act, 1885", for the protection of women and girls from those who compass, "procure", and bring about their ruin; to prevent outrages on public decency, with summary power to suppress brothels. The "Prevention of Cruelty to and Protection of Children Act, 1889", as the title indicates, to punish those who ill-treat them, and protect them from cruelty, whether practised by Parents, Guardians, or Employers; and to provide for their future safety.

There are others, such as the "Truck Act", now extended to Ireland, with amendments protecting Artisans and Workmen from that species of dealing or barter which interferes in the laying out of their earnings to the best advantage; and imposing heavy penalties on the offending employers. The summary power to award "alimony" to wives deserted by their husbands. The punishment for frauds in the Sale of Butter, where "Margarine" is substituted for that article. Summary punishment for obtaining pay and pensions by personation or fraud. Important amendments in the Railway Acts. In the Weights and Measures Acts, especially as to fraud in the sale or delivery of coal. Amendments in the "Excise" Acts. An Act dealing summarily with indecent advertisements: the exhibition of obscene prints on highways, in windows, &c. The Registration of Shops dealing in horseflesh as an article of food; protection of purchasers, &c. The "Public Bodies' Corrupt Practices Act, 1889", subjecting bribery and corruption in office to punishment by indictment, and to other disabilities. A General Interpretation Act as to terms used in Acts of Parliament. Some important amendments in the law as to Oaths and Affirmations, and on the subject of newspaper libels. Nor should a most important

Statute, the "Probation of First Offender's Act", be over-looked: an Act in harmony with our reforming institutions, the complement of them, and in keeping with the march of civilization generally. Justices getting this extension of discretionary power should make themselves acquainted with the Act, recognise the intentions of the Legislature, and on fitting occasions employ its salutary provisions.

The volume of the Statutes of the last Session was not issued by the Queen's Printers sufficiently early to admit of all being set out in their fitting places in the alphabetical an-alysis, but the few standing over will be found in the *Addenda*.

The bringing of crimes and offences within the range of the Summary Jurisdiction Courts, wherever the latitude given these Courts in the measure of punishment will meet the case, continues to be favoured by the Legislature; and on the grounds that it saves expense and delay in the administration of criminal justice. The method of procedure is at once swift and certain.

Additional notes are added in the proper places throughout the work; whatever experience suggested to be useful and practical are introduced: everything calculated to perplex is excluded.

The Author repeats his endeavour to forecast what the least experienced Magistrate may need to have pointed out to guide his first timid steps, and so afford him ready facile help.

To this end he would, in the first instance, point attention to the "Preliminary Outline", or review, where he will obtain some general idea of his office and duties. Perhaps some of the things there set down will be found serviceable to the more seasoned Members of the Bench.

The Author now asks that the indulgence and favour with which the former editions were received may be extended to this, which, in the ordinary course of things, probably cannot but be the last to come from his pen.

H. H.

BALLINTEMPLE, BLACKROCK,
　　CORK, *February*, 1890.

CORRECTIONS.

THE following case just decided to be read in connexion with "Assaults," Summary Index and Notes :—

Effect of a previous conviction—Case of Miles, Court of Crown Cases reserved (E.), Feb. 1890, before Lord Coleridge, Mr. Baron Pollock, Sir Henry Hawkins, Mr. Justice Grantham, and Mr. Justice Charles.

The question was whether a conviction for an assault without any sentence beyond merely entering into recognizance to keep the peace is a bar to an indictment for the same assault as a misdemeanour in maliciously wounding and inflicting grievous bodily harm without any felonious intent to inflict such harm. The 24 & 25 Vic., c. 100, s. 45, provides that if a person is summarily convicted of an assault, and shall have suffered his sentence, this shall be a bar to any case or proceeding for the same cause. He was convicted that he did assault and beat. He was upon other evidence *indicted* for unlawfully and maliciously wounding and inflicting grievous bodily harm. The Recorder before whom he was tried stated the case. It was now, after mature deliberation decided that at Common Law, apart from the Statute, if not by the Statute, that the previous conviction was a bar. The giving security for good behaviour places defendant in the same position as if he had suffered punishment. On an established rule of law, whenever a person has been convicted and punished for an offence by a Court of competent jurisdiction, the conviction shall be a bar to all further proceedings for the same offence, and he shall not be punished again for the same matter. Where a party accused of a minor offence is acquitted or convicted he shall not be again charged on the same facts in a more aggravated form. Conviction set aside.

Page 79.—"*Encouraging, &c.*" animals to fight, &c.—*for* "assent" in 3rd line *read* "assist."

TABLE OF CONTENTS.

———◆◦◆———

THE JUSTICE OF THE PEACE.

PRELIMINARY OUTLINE.

THE GENERAL SCOPE OF A MAGISTRATE'S JURISDICTION AND DUTY.

It is not readily that one can select a standpoint whence to pass in review before a newly appointed Justice of the Peace—supposing him to have had no previous insight and experience in the business—the manifold subjects of which he shall have to take cognizance.

The author can only, in the first place, recommend that he endeavour to form some *general* idea of the subjects that will now be referred to, and will then proceed to point out how he is to exercise in respect to them the jurisdiction conferred on him. His integrity, discretion, and good sense he is never once to relinquish. His knowledge of the people around him, acquaintance with their habits, dispositions, feelings, and their folk-lore, will greatly aid him in the proper administration of justice: without these sober, solid qualities, any flippancy and mere superficial acquaintance with Acts of Parliament will fall short —but this is by the way.

It has somehow come to be thought by many persons that our ordinary laws might, had not lawyers interposed, have been reduced to a code not exceeding in scope and extent the Decalogue, and not unlike it in simplicity and comprehensiveness—or, at all events, that they may be so consolidated and classified as without difficulty and uncertainty to be readily turned to and consulted. Well, to people in a rude state, laws few and simple in character may answer their purposes, but then there would be needed unlimited liberty or discretion in their Judges to say what offences the laws meant or did not mean to punish, and such discretion, varying as it must with temper and disposition, would be the law of tyrants. Such simplification is not possible. Not that our jurists and legislators have remained unmindful of the necessity for some codification both as to our Statute and Common Law.

A Bill to establish a code of *Indictable Offences* and the procedure relating thereto was printed so far back as 1878. Eminent lawyers were not agreed as to its principles and details, and Parliament has not to the present, in any serious mood, ventured to discuss its principles. Still, in a modified form, groupings of crimes, amendments in the criminal law, and in the administration of criminal law, gradually progress, as must be apparent to any watchful observer.

There have been passed some important consolidating Statutes of the Criminal Law during the present reign—this was in the twenty-fourth and twenty-fifth years of the Queen.

First, as to *Larceny and similar Offences*.—And as these offences are set out in the Analysis of the Statutes given in the Indictable Offences and Summary Index of this work, they need not be here recapitulated. It embraces crimes, from robbery with violence, and burglary, to the purloining of any cultivated plant, and the stealing of an oyster from its park or bed—almost everything in which one can be said to have a property : 24 & 25 Vic., c. 96.

Malicious Injuries to Property.—These offences are likewise set out in the Analysis, and include all mischief from the firing of buildings, by explosives or other means, destruction of machinery, manufactures—all works of usefulness or of art, with a general provision as to injuries to any real or personal property not specially named : 24 & 25 Vic., c. 97.

with their several distinctions—rape, abduction, defilement of women and children, child stealing, bigamy, attempts to procure abortion, concealing birth. Unnatural offences, abominable crimes (sins against nature being crimes against mankind). Making explosives of any kind to commit offences whereby life is endangered, with other provisions, &c. &c. : 24 & 25 Vic., c. 100. Now, under these heads will be found a great collection of crimes and offences.

There are, in addition to the foregoing, many other crimes under Statute and against the Common Law that are indictable; with all these Magistrates have to do in taking the evidence and sending the accused for trial before a higher tribunal. Some of the offences, those of a minor sort, are allowed to be summarily dealt with in Petty Sessions, notably so those committed by children and young persons. Amendments in these Statutes referred to have been since made almost every Session of Parliament, the exigencies of civilization, locomotion, and commerce so requiring.

Summary Jurisdiction.—A very limited attempt was made in the fourteenth and fifteenth year of Her Majesty to consolidate and amend the Acts relating to certain offences and other matters as to which Justices of the Peace exercise *Summary Jurisdiction* in Ireland. Several of the provisions of this Statute have been repealed or displaced by others; those that remain will be found dispersed through and repeatedly quoted in the Summary Jurisdiction Analysis. Under it are still dealt with—frauds as to provisions, trespass of persons, injuries to public roads, &c., nuisances on public roads, regulations as to stage carriages, carts, cars, &c., and the conduct of drivers. *Civil Jurisdiction* as to possession of small tenements in market towns, &c., disputes in fairs and markets, impounding animals, pound fees and duties as to the animals, trespass of animals, rates of trespass: 14 & 15 Vic., c. 92.

In addition to the above there are many matters respecting which the law has been consolidated, and that are subjects of Summary or Petty Sessions Jurisdiction as those relating to children and young persons, where punishment may in most cases take the form of restraint and reformation. Again, the protection of the young from cruelty on the part of parents, guardians, employers, and others—all of the first importance to the present and future generations—evincing at once the wisdom and beneficence of the Legislature; the "probation of first offenders," generally. There are others: as those relating to the revenue, customs, employers and workmen, fisheries, licensing liquor laws, public health and sanitary regulations, prevention of crime by convicts on licence, &c. &c.

These all, with others both of a public and private nature, form the subject of the Analysis and Abridgment set forth in alphabetical order in this work.

It would be more curious than useful to enter fully into the origin of this branch of the Magisterial office.

The "Magistracy," for whom supplication is so often made that they may be given "grace to execute justice and maintain truth," includes the Sovereign, the Great Officers of the State, &c., Chancellor and Justices of the Queen's Bench, &c., Sheriffs, and those to whom the Commission is assigned. But unless it exist as incident to an office or by direct commission, no Duke, Earl, Baron, as such, has any greater authority to keep the peace than a mere private person.

The present mode of appointing Justices superseded an earlier form of choosing "Conservators of the Peace," as they were called, and which took place before the Sheriff by the freeholders in open Court, the writ directing that they should be chosen from the most respectable and influential people of the county. The violence which terminated the reign of Edward the Second, by the deposal and murder of that monarch, followed by the elevation of Edward the Third, then a minor, to the throne, occasioned the appointment of new officers in whom the Court could have more trust than in the common conservators. Under the 1 Ed. iii., s. 2, c. 16, E. & I., it was enacted that, for the better keeping and maintaining of the peace in every county, good men and lawful, that were no maintainers of evil, or barrators, should be assigned to keep the peace. But even after this they were styled only conservators, wardens, or keepers of the peace, until the Statute 34 Ed. iii., c. 1, E. & I., gave them the power of trying felonies, and then they acquired the more honourable appellation of Justices. This important Statute, amongst other things, directed them "to take of all such as were not of good fame, wherever they were found, sufficient surety and mainprise of their good behaviour, towards the king and his people, and to duly punish others to the intent that people, merchants, and other travellers might not be endangered by such rioters and rebels." This was the first authority they had to take surety for good behaviour, and indeed the first mention of it in any Statute or law book—and, as Dr. Burn remarks, "there is no other which hath received such a largeness of interpretation." The necessity for this Statute seems chiefly to have been the disbanding of the soldiers who served in King Edward's army in his French wars, and of those camp followers that returned with the victorious army to this kingdom; and, in its own words, "that have been pillors and robbers in the parts beyond the sea, and he now come again, and go wandering, and will not labour," &c. I give this Statute a little further on. It is then under this Statute, and their commission, that the Justices of the present day are empowered to hold unruly persons to bail to keep the peace and be of good behaviour." The clause in the commission runs thus:—"And to cause to come before you, or any of you, all these persons who shall threaten any of our people in their person, or with burning their houses, to find sufficient security for the peace, and for their good behaviour towards us and our people;

and if they shall refuse to find such security, then to cause them to be safely kept in our prison until they shall have found security. For further readings on this subject, see "Sureties of the Peace," &c., in the Summary Index to this work.

There are others appointed by different Statutes, such as Stipendiary or Resident Magistrates (6 and 7 Wm. iv., c. 13, s. 31); Justices in virtue of their office, as Mayors, Recorders of Boroughs (3 & 4 Vic., c. 108, ss. 84 & 116; and 14 & 15 Vic., c. 93, s. 44); Chairmen of Quarter Sessions (14 & 15 Vic., c. 57, s. 2; and 21 & 22 Vic., c. 88, s. 3); the Inspector-General, Deputy and Assistant Inspector-General, Royal Irish Constabulary (6 & 7 Wm. iv., c. 13, s. 6).

His power as a Justice of the Peace now depends upon his commission and upon the several Statutes which create the objects of his jurisdiction; and having taken the oaths of office—that is, the oath of allegiance and the judicial oath, and returned same, with the *dedimus*, to the Hanaper Office—he is fully accoutred to exercise his functions and begin operations.

Supposing him to have had no previous experience, he will need to be cautious as he walks abroad armed with these formidable edged tools. He will avoid Quixotically going in search of adventures, redressing wrongs, and like the Don, tilting against windmills; nor, although some of Sancho Panza's decisions, when he became Governor, were inimitable in their way, will he follow the rulings of that great authority, though joking does sometimes decide great things better than earnest can.

It is not improbable that the first perplexities of an inexperienced Magistrate will attend some of those formal matters brought before him out of Petty Sessions; it may happen on the highway or at his house, and it is not unlikely that his inexperience will lead to his being so selected.

Attesting Recruits.—This public duty must be attended to: he should see that the recruit is sober; understands what he is doing; that he is acting under no coercion, as our army is composed of volunteers. He should read to him the questions in the Attestation-paper; receive his answers *seriatim*, and not merely saying in a hurried way "has all this been read over to you—is it all true?" The recruit repeats after the Magistrate the *declaration* that the answers are true; and also repeats and takes the *oath* of allegiance. If the recruit, on appearing before the Justice, dissents from the enlistment, there is an end to it—he is free to walk away. And so the recruiting sergeant is not now, as in former years he was, the dread of mothers, when he appears in the county town or quiet village. Military officers can now attest recruits.

Voluntary Oaths, Declarations, &c.—In former years, when accusations were made against, or suspicions whispered about tending to blacken the reputation of individuals as to their honesty, their chastity, &c., it was not an uncommon practice to have all made clear, straight and pure, on the door-steps of the village Justice, by an oath solemnly and openly taken : all this was of course highly irregular. Such voluntary and extrajudicial oaths are abolished, and the 5 & 6 Wm. iv., chap. 62, enables a Justice to take voluntary declarations, but he must not indiscriminately receive and affix his signature to all voluntary declarations presented to him ; for he may by this means be giving publicity to libels, and that under his signature. If it be in the shape of an accusation tending to blacken the character of an individual, living or dead, he should not receive it ; unless it be a declaration, in substitution for an oath, by a person whose religious belief qualifies him to make declaration in lieu of an oath, for some judicial purpose, and upon which some proceedings are to be taken by warrant or summons. There are some extrajudicial declarations allowable : declarations as to births, deaths, marriages, ages, &c., either for insurance or other purposes ; declarations as to loss or injury to bank-notes ; half-pay and pension declarations ; as to loss of pawnbrokers' duplicates. For declarations liable to bear a shilling Petty Sessions Stamp, *see* Petty Sessions Stamps Act, *Appendix ;* and for those liable to 2*s.* 6*d.* revenue stamp, *see* title " Stamp Act, 1870," Summary Index.

Vagrancy.—Persons found wandering abroad and begging may be brought before a Justice out of Petty Sessions ; and on the charge being proved, he can deal with it as pointed out under the head " Begging," or " Vagrancy," in the Summary Index.

Fraud in Sale of Goods.—This offence, on being proved, he can also deal with out of Petty Sessions—*see* title " Frauds as to Provisions," Summary Index.

Disputes between Buyer and Seller, as to goods sold in fairs and markets, may also be dealt with, but in the manner and under the conditions in such cases provided—for which see title " Fairs and Markets."

Drunk on Highways.—Persons found drunk on highways may also be summarily dealt with out of Petty Sessions ; but the Justice ought not to try the case while the person is drunk ; and, as the constable is, under the Licensing Act, authorized to detain him until sober, then discharge and summon him, there appears no reason why the charge should not be brought regularly forward at the Petty Sessions ; and whenever any case is decided out of Petty Sessions, the Justice shall, as directed by section 21 of the Petty Sessions Act, enter it in the Order Book, or send a certificate of the case to the Clerk of the Petty Sessions.

Excise Cases.—Offences against the Illicit Distillation Act, 1 & 2 Wm. iv., c. 55, where the Revenue Officers apprehend offenders, and bring them before any Justice of the Peace ; and the Justice may at once convict on the case being proved, or confessed by the party charged (1 & 2 Wm. iv., c. 55, s. 34). In these cases the officer generally produces to the Justice the Act and section which provides the penalty.

Summonses and warrants, and the informations on which same are founded, may be signed and taken out of Petty Sessions, but this belongs to the jurisdiction generally in receiving information and complaint, and will come under review in the epitome of Magistrates' duties, which I now proceed to give.

☞ The Petty Sessions (Ireland) Act, 1851, which is set out in the *Appendix*, is to be considered as the general machinery for carrying out and enforcing the provisions of the several other statutes conferring jurisdiction on Magistrates. In some few instances, as in Revenue cases, it is departed from. The Author, by marginal notes to this Act, gives a tolerably full synopsis of it.

Local Jurisdiction.—A Justice for any county may act in all matters within such county, although he may at the time happen to be in an adjoining county, provided that he be also a Justice for such adjoining county. He may also act in matters *arising within his county* although he be at the time in any city, town, or place, being a county of itself, and situated within or adjoining his county, and whether he be Justice of such city, town, or place or not; but unless he be also a Justice of the city, town, or place, he is not to intermeddle in matters *arising therein*. The Inspector-General of Constabulary and the Deputy-Inspectors, being Justices of any county, may act in all matters arising therein, wherever they may be.

The Place for hearing Cases.—Cases of *Summary Jurisdiction* shall, as a rule, be heard or determined in Petty Sessions, except in such instances as before referred to; but if two Justices meet together, and see fit to do so, they may hear and determine a summary case out of Petty Sessions, where the offender is unable to find bail for his appearance at the Petty Sessions; and although the section appears to leave the discretion with the Justices, yet if the offender should select that the case stand adjourned to the Petty Sessions where he may have his witnesses, and if he (being unable to find bail) submits to remain in custody, the request may in reason be complied with, and the Justices ought "to see fit" so to do. It is quite settled that he should be allowed opportunity of giving bail.

Open Court and Publicity of Proceedings.—The place of hearing all *summary* cases shall be deemed to be an open Court, to which the public, so far as they can be accommodated, shall have access; and the parties, by and against whom any complaint is heard, shall be admitted to conduct their cases and make their defence: this they can do themselves, or by their counsel or solicitors on their behalf; but the Justices should not allow the parties and their solicitors to speak at same time as advocates : *see* title "Court," Summary Index.

If the proceeding is of an indictable character, and there are features in the case which lead the Justices to consider that *it should not* be conducted in the

b

public Court, they may in their discretion exclude the general public, that is, where they think that the ends of justice will thereby be best answered. Of course this is limited to preliminary inquiries, and where they are not about to summarily adjudicate on the case.

Contempt of Court or insult to Justice.—The Justices have full power to require that decorum shall be observed wherever they are hearing or investigating a case. No contempt shall be offered to the Court, nor personal insult to the Justices, or any of them; where such takes place, the offender may be removed from the Court or place, or may be fined for the contempt or insult : *see* title "Contempt of Court" in the Summary Index. Until this enactment by sect. 9 of Petty Sessions (Ireland) Act, 1851, it was doubted whether Magistrates had a summary power so to punish for such insult and contempt, although indictable as a misdemeanour. It appears that Justices of the Peace may order a person to find security for his good behaviour who, in making his defence before them as to a specific charge, had been guilty of contempt of the Court by wilfully abusive and insulting language to the Court while acting in discharge of their duty as Justices ; and that the power to punish by the summary method given in the Petty Sessions Act does not take away the power to order the offender to find sureties also. The two things are cumulative : Exchequer Division (Ireland), August, 1889—on motion in behalf of Dr. Tanner, M.P., to make absolute a conditional order for writ of *habeas corpus*; before Lord Chief Baron, Mr. Baron Dowse, and Mr. Justice Andrews.

Jurisdiction (generally) in receiving Information and Complaint.—The 10th section of the Petty Sessions Act fully and clearly points out to the Justice his authority to entertain and receive information in treasons, felonies, misdemeanours, and other offences which arise within his jurisdiction, or where committed elsewhere out of his jurisdiction, or on British waters, or land beyond the seas where an indictment can be preferred and that the offender is suspected to be within his jurisdiction in the United Kingdom, and in all summary cases arising within his jurisdiction. On any question therefore arising as to how far he has power to intermeddle, the Justice is referred to this section and the notes at foot in the *Appendix*. These notes will also point out how offences are dealt with when committed at sea by *British subjects* on board *British ships*, or by those not being British subjects in said ships ; and also when committed by foreigners on board foreign ships within Her Majesty's dominions, but in this last instance the certificate of the Secretary of State is necessary.

Proceedings to be taken.—Where it is intended that a *summons* shall issue in the first instance requiring the attendance of the accused, the complaint may be a verbal one and without oath ; but if a warrant is to issue, the complaint in the form of an information *must be on oath and in writing*, and the party making it may be bound over to prosecute. It will be sufficient if the complaint be on oath and in writing at any time before the signing and issuing of the warrant. It must be made by the complainant or by some one on his behalf.—Sect. 10, sub-sect. 2.

Limitation of Complaints.—In indictable crimes there does not appear to be a limit fixed for making the complaint—although of course this will be a question for the consideration of the Justice ;—how far the delay, if considerable, is accounted for, and may guide him in the step to be taken, whether it shall be a warrant or a summons. In summary proceedings there is a limitation as to time of making complaints: in poor or county rate, or public tax, complaint may be at any time after the date of the warrant to collect; in wages within a year, trespass within two months, in other cases six months.—Sect. 10, sub-sect. 4. Subsequent Acts may extend the time. The Militia Act (sect. 43) provides that offending militiamen may be dealt with within two months after offence becomes known to his officer, or after he is apprehended.

Process to enforce Appearance.—In indictable offences a warrant may, on sworn information, issue in the first instance ; but if the Justice thinks it will meet the ends of justice, he may issue summons ; but the issuing of the summons need not prevent the Justice issuing a warrant if he sees fit, either before or after the time for appearance mentioned in the summons. In *summary cases* a summons should issue in the first instance ; but if defendant fail to appear, on proof that he has been personally served, or that he is keeping out of the way, a warrant may issue (on sworn information). Neither summons nor warrant shall be signed in blank.

Service of Summons.—The 12th section of Petty Sessions Act directs how summonses are to be served, but this does not affect any special mode of services under certain Acts.

Witnesses.—The 13th section points out how the attendance of witnesses may be compelled. And the Justice must mark the distinction in the section, that in *Indictable Offences* it is only the witnesses for the prosecution who can be compelled to appear and give evidence. In cases of *Summary Jurisdiction* the witness for complainant or defendant, after service of summons proved, and no just excuse offered for the non-attendance, the warrant may issue. In all cases before warrant to arrest is issued the complaint must be on oath and in writing, and the witness shown to be material. Before issuing these warrants for witnesses, the Justice or the officers of the Court should see that all the requirements of the section are complied with fully and to the letter. The process of the Court is not to be employed to worry and bring at inconvenience, perhaps at loss and from a distance, persons who may know nothing of the complaint. This plainly is shown by the cautious language of this section, *i. e.* that he will not voluntarily appear for the purpose of being examined ; that he neglects or refuses to appear ; that no just excuse is offered ; that the summons was personally served, or that it is proved he is keeping out of the way; that he is able to give material evidence in the case; and that there is on oath, and in writing, a substantial cause of complaint calling for all this, and for sending the officers of justice in pursuit.

Depositions, manner of taking them in Indictable Offences.—The 14th section directs how the Justice is to proceed in taking depositions; they are to be taken in presence of the accused, who shall be at liberty to put questions to the witnesses. They are to be read over to and signed by witnesses, and by the Justice; they are to be read over to the accused; and he being first cautioned in the form directed by the section that he need not say anything. If he make a statement it should be taken down, read over to him (to be signed by the accused, if he will), then to be signed by the Justice. All material facts bearing on the case should be taken down; they should not be overladen with irrelevant matter, nor with anything unfair to the accused, or what is clearly inadmissible; for where the deposition may on the trial be called for on the part of the accused to contradict a witness's former statement, the accused thereby puts in the deposition as his evidence, and perhaps to his disadvantage. Confessions of the accused are received upon the principle upon which admissions in civil suits are—the presumption that a person will not make an untrue statement against his own interest. But where promises and inducements are held out by anyone in authority, the confessions ought not to be received. It appears now to be settled that, if the inducement is not held out by a person in authority, it is clearly admissible. It seems to be the duty of the Magistrate who presides at the examination to advise the prisoner not to make any statement before the evidence is concluded and the caution administered. By the 30 & 31 Vic., c. 35 (Eng.), which is not extended to Ireland, the accused in criminal cases is to be asked by the Justice if he desires to call witnesses; and if the accused call any, their depositions, if at all material to the case, or tending to prove the innocence of the accused, shall be returned, and the witnesses bound by recognizance to attend at the trial. In Ireland the witnesses for the accused cannot be compelled to give evidence; but if tendered, their evidence should be taken down and returned.

The Depositions shall be taken of those who "know the facts of the case."— Sec. 14. It is laid down as a general rule in all cases, criminal and civil, that the evidence should be confined to the point in issue: that is, the transaction which forms the subject of the (indictment) inquiry, and matters relating thereto. In criminal it has been observed that the necessity is stronger, if possible, than in civil cases, of the strictly enforcing this rule; but that the evidence discloses other offences cannot, on this ground, be excluded, where on general grounds it is admissible—evidence not only of the guilty act itself, but acts so closely connected with it as form the chain of facts, which could not be excluded without rendering the evidence unintelligible.

Examination-in-Chief.—Leading questions which suggest to the witness the answer he is to give must not be put: but it is necessary to a certain extent to lead the mind of the witness to the subject of the inquiry; and even for the purpose of identification a particular prisoner may be pointed out to witness, who may be asked whether he is the man.—*R.* v. *Beranger* (1 Stark On Evidence, 125).

Cross-Examination.—Leading questions are admitted on cross-examination, much larger powers being given than in the original or direct examination. Mr. Justice Buller says:—"You may lead a witness upon cross-examination to bring him directly to the point as to the answer, but you cannot go the length of putting into the witness's mouth the very words he is to echo back again." —*R.* v. *Hardy* (24 How. St. Tr., 755). Baron Alderson says:—"I apprehend you may put a leading question to an unwilling witness on the examination-in-chief, at the discretion of the Judge, but you may always put a leading question in cross-examination, whether a witness be unwilling or not."—*Parker* v. *Moon* (7 C. & P. 405).

The Caption.—Where the charge is a lengthy one, and is set out at the head of the first deposition, the depositions which follow need not so fully set out the offence or charge. They may briefly refer to, or even after the words of the caption—"Taken in presence and hearing of *C. D.*, who stands charged as aforesaid."

Where the depositions were on separate sheets, but under the one caption— "Examination of J. J. Hill and others, taken in the presence of the prisoner, &c."—and the whole were attached together, not at the time of the signature, but subsequently by the Magistrate's clerk, Pollock, C. B., admitted them in evidence.—*R.* v. *Lee* (4 F. & F. 65).

Remands—From absence of witnesses or other *reasonable cause*, the Justice may remand the accused for a term not exceeding eight days at a time—that is where a case justifying a remand has been made out. No order of remand should be made unless the accused be brought before the Justice. On this subject of remands in general the matter is very clearly set out for the guidance of the Justices in the Circular of 24th July, 1879, *Appendix*.

The Justice should carefully mark the distinction between the indictable offences where the remand shall not exceed eight days, under the Criminal Justice Act (18 & 19 Vic., c. 126, s. 5), and where they remand to next Petty Sessions. Attention should also be given to the 3rd paragraph of the Circular as to summary cases. See also sec. 10 of Petty Sessions Act.

Disposal of the Prisoner in Indictable Cases.—When the evidence has been completed, if the Justice be of opinion that the evidence is not sufficient to put the accused on his trial, he is to discharge him; but if, on the other hand, he thinks that the evidence is sufficient to put him on his trial, or that it raises a "strong or probable presumption of guilt," he is to commit the accused for trial, or admit him to bail. The admitting to bail of persons charged with indictable offences—those that are not bailable, those that are bailable in the discretion of the Justice, and those misdemeanours where persons charged are bailable as a matter of right, are fully set out in the 16th section of the Petty Sessions Act.

Taking Depositions of Persons who receive Dangerous Wounds.—Where any person receives a wound such as is likely to endanger life, it is the duty of the constabulary to acquaint a Magistrate of the fact; and if able to make a deposition, and that the accused be in custody, the Magistrate should without delay proceed to take it. He will be careful to do so in the manner prescribed for taking depositions, in this instance especially, calmly, noiselessly, and with patience and precision, as the injured person is able to give the evidence. The accused, or his counsel, or solicitor, may cross-examine; but the Justice should not permit unnecessary noise, nor the injured man to be needlessly worried or disturbed. The accused should be fully at liberty to elicit what may be in his favour at a future time, but any attempt to render it impossible for the injured person to give the evidence should be suppressed. And to this end the Justice should in this cross-examination take down the *question* in writing first, then the answer. This can be quietly done. There is often much meaning in the question; it brings out the evidence correctly, and it also prevents a number of running questions being put without waiting for an answer, besides it will generally be found to shorten cross-examination. A prudent counsel will be careful how he puts questions that are taken down.

Dying Declarations.—When a person finds himself dying of a mortal injury, and is not able to make a deposition, or that the offender may not happen to be then in custody, a Magistrate, or, in his absence, any person, may take the dying declaration. The mode of taking such is fully pointed out under the head "Dying Declarations," in the Indictable Offence Index in this work.

Adjudicating in Cases of Summary Jurisdiction.—The 20th and 21st sections of the Petty Sessions Act contain, with the notes at foot (see *Appendix*), all that is necessary on this subject, and need not here be repeated; and the *general powers in adjudicating and other matters, as to enforcing penalties, &c.,* are given in each case throughout the work.

Orders and Convictions.—I shall not on this subject enter into minute questions which tend more to perplex than to help in a simple duty. A few observations will not be out of place. "Order," as the more expansive term, includes "Conviction," by the interpretation clause to Petty Sessions Act. Yet there are many well-recognised distinctions, as in the case of intervening orders. Under the Sanitary or Public Health Acts, where Justices "order" nuisances to be abated, structural works, &c., done; where Justices "order" public-houses to be closed when a riot is apprehended. These orders must be drawn up and made known to the parties, and the disobedience may be followed up by other proceedings, conviction, fine, &c. The *Forms* in Petty Sessions Act (including the form of "Order Book") are to be deemed good and valid, but no departure from these forms shall vitiate or make void the proceeding, if the form used be in other respects sufficient in substance and effect. This being the prescribed form, it is safe as it is sufficient in all instances to follow it. And it does seem that by fairly attending to the explicit directions of the printed headings which are part of and to be read with each "Order," the procedure is greatly simplified· The Privy Council form of Order Book (that in use) directs more and fuller entries than that prescribed by the Statute.

Where the Order and the Warrant founded on it are Informal—Where the Order is Regular and the Warrant is Informal.—If a Justice make an order in a matter in which he has no jurisdiction, he should, if possible on the same day, get the parties to attend and make known the fact, and make an entry on the Order Book accordingly—*coram non Judice.* Where he acts without or in excess of jurisdiction, and the prisoner has passed into the hands of the gaoler, it would be his duty to point out the error, and, if necessary, communicate the fact to the Lord Lieutenant, and have him discharged. But the gaoler would, of course, see it to be his duty not to carry out the punishment. Where the Justice had duly convicted the defendant, but the conviction had been improperly drawn up, or the warrant founded upon the good conviction is in excess of the Justice's powers, it does appear that the matter can be corrected by drawing up a proper conviction on proper warrant, as the case may be, and returning or sending it to the gaoler in lieu of the former warrant. "Where a warrant of commitment under which the defendant is taken is found to be defective, the error may be amended by a second warrant *if the facts admit of it,* and the prisoner may be lawfully detained under the latter, and, if it is not too late, to lodge an amended warrant, though a writ have already issued for a *habeas corpus.*"—Stone's Practice for Justices, p. 176, citing the following cases as authorities: *Ex parte Cross,* 26 L. J. M. C., 28; *Temple* v. *Cross,* 26 L. J. M. C., 207; *Ex parte Smith,* 27 L. J. M. C., 186; *R.* v. *Richards,* 5 Q. B., 926.

"Where an *informal* conviction has been signed and handed over to the defendant, and even carried into execution by distress or imprisonment, it has been held by the Queen's Bench Division that Justices may, at any time before the trial of an action of trespass for the distress or commitment, draw up and sign a more formal conviction, so that it agree with the actual proceedings as they occurred before the convicting Justices."—Stone, *ut supra,* p. 155.

Disqualification.—A Justice is not at liberty to sit or act in any case in which he is an interested party; and when he is so, and whether sitting alone or with others, the Court is not properly *constituted.* He should not be found speaking to nor sitting with the members of the Bench during the hearing. He should avoid all suspicion of partiality. Still it appears the convictions or orders made in such cases are not absolutely void, as that would lead to great confusion and inconvenience ; but "they are voidable—may be quashed on being removed by *certiorari*, and the Superior Court will do complete justice in that respect." *Dimes* v. *Grand Junc. Canal Co.*, 3 H. L. Cas., 759–786 ; *R.* v. *Recorder of Cambridge*, 27 L. J. M. C., 160.)

But there are exceptions, as if he be assaulted or abused when acting as a Justice, and no other Justice be with him—see "Contempt of Court," Summary Index. It appears, however, that if a party in the case knows of the Justice's interest, and consents to his acting, he cannot afterwards object on this ground : and a party who objects to the conviction on the ground that the Justices were personally interested must satisfy the Court that both he and his attorney were ignorant of the fact at the time of the conviction or they would have objected. But apart from all this it is indiscreet and improper, and the Lord Chancellor, on complaint to him, would be sure to call for the Justice's explanation. Certain disqualifications are removed by Act of Parliament, where, as a ratepayer, he may be interested in proceedings taken by corporations, local boards, &c. See Act, *Appendix*, p. 648. So where a Justice is subpœnaed as a witness in a case, but having no interest in it, he is not thereby disqualified from taking part in the adjudication. This question came before the Queen's Bench in England in Easter Term, 1884, and the Judges held that the request that the Justice should leave the Bench and take no part in adjudicating was a preposterous request, remarking that, if it possessed any ground in law, a suitor might, by subpœnaing the Judge who was to try the case, or for that matter all the Judges, evade any trial of an action. However, where a Justice witnesses an offence, he will necessarily prejudge the case, and if he give evidence he will do well to take no part in adjudicating, at all events while other Justices can be had. Where the disqualification exists it must be from an interest in the case, or created by statute. Under the Irish Bankrupt and Insolvency Acts, (35 & 36 Vic., c. 57, s. 21), where, if he is adjudged bankrupt, or makes any arrangement with his creditors under these Acts, he shall be and remain incapable of acting as a Justice of the Peace until a commission be newly assigned him ; and Mayors and *ex-officio* Justices are included in the provision ; and also included with Town Councillors in the provisions of section 20. See Index, p. 467.

Summary Jurisdiction ousted where Questions of Title arise.—The Justices cannot summarily decide any case where a *bond fide* question of title arises. But it must be *bond fide*, not fictitious, just invented in order to stop the exercise of the jurisdiction. But if even a colourable title exists, and the individual acted under the belief that he had that title, or supposed right, however weak the claim may be, it will oust the summary jurisdiction. Other questions of title exist where justices are asked to interpose, as where property is illegally withheld, but not so as to constitute larceny, and civilly he has no jurisdiction. Where the manifestly rightful owner, in asserting his right, is assaulted, and the goods forcibly taken from him, the Justice can send the case of assault for trial. Where lodging-house keepers and others unlawfully detain the clothing of seamen; pawnbrokers knowingly take in pledge from washerwomen clothes sent to be washed; workmen, tradesmen, &c., unlawfully withhold or make away with materials entrusted to them to work on or make up, the Justice can summarily deal with the complaints. See titles "Merchant Shipping," "Pawnbrokers," "Workmen," Summary Index.

Forms of Procedure, Variance, Defects, &c., how corrected.—Of course in all proceedings before Justices accuracy in the forms is to be observed; where this is not attended to advantage is sure to be taken of any informality, so as thereby, if possible, to embarrass the Court. Section 36 provides that the forms in Schedule to the Petty Sessions Act shall be valid in law, even in cases where different forms are provided by particular Acts; but no departure from them, or the use of other words than those indicated in the forms, shall vitiate or make void the proceedings if the Form used be otherwise sufficient in substance and effect. And then section 39 provides that, in summary proceedings, variance between complaint and the evidence in support of it, as to time and place, shall not avail if the complaint be brought within the limited time, and the offence be shown to have been committed or to have arisen within the jurisdiction of the Justices. *And no objection shall be taken or allowed in any proceedings to the form of procedure under this Act for any alleged defect therein in substance or in form, unless the variance or defect, in the opinion of the Justices, has misled the defendant.* The meaning of all which is, if the defendant knows the charge he has to meet, and that the form of words employed clearly indicate what it is, he is to meet it on its merits. But if the complaint be brought for a specific offence under one Act, although the form of words employed may be adequate to bring it under a different statute by expunging some aggravating circumstance, it would be unfair at the conclusion to surprise the defendant by convicting of an offence and under an Act to which he had not applied either what he may have "had to say," or the "evidence he adduced." Indeed on this the words of the Petty Sessions Act (section 21) seem to be sufficiently explicit, for the Justices having heard what each party shall have had to say, and the evidence adduced by each, "shall either make such order as shall be authorized by the Act under which the complaint shall be made, or shall dismiss it," &c. Where there is an appeal from his order, power is also given to the Court of Appeal to cure defects, so that the case shall be heard on its merits. The Court should not hesitate to act on these powers conferred by the statute:

see sections 36 and 39 Petty Sessions Act (27 & 28 Vic. c. 99, s. 49 ; 40 & 41 Vic. c. 56, s. 76). These are given in the notes on the subject of "Appeal," section 24 of Petty Sessions Act, *Appendix.*

Issuing of Warrants.—This is the step which is generally attended with danger; and whenever a Justice issues a warrant to arrest, he should be careful to see that the sworn information warrants the accusation, and that the charge is one for which a warrant should issue to apprehend the person charged.

Search Warrant.—A warrant to search and overturn everything in a house, dig up floors, &c., is a serious affair. It should clearly appear on the information, in case of stolen property, that there is reasonable cause to suspect that the person referred to has in his possession or on his premises the property in respect to which *an offence punishable either by indictment or upon summary conviction* in virtue of the Act (Larceny Act, 24 & 25 Vic., c. 96, s. 103), and that there is reasonable ground to suspect that it will be found on the person or the place intended to be searched. On close examination of the person seeking the warrant, it may turn out that there is no concealment whatever, that it is property the title to which is disputed. The form of the search-warrant is given in the Schedule to the Petty Sessions Act. It may be altered to suit the case, as to whether the property is likely to be concealed on the person or in a place. For the Acts which authorize the issuing of search-warrants, see title "Search-warrant" and note at foot, Summary Index.

Sunday.—In indictable offences a Justice can issue his warrant on a Sunday. —14 & 15 Vic. c. 23, sec. 1.

Appeals.—The Justice in giving his decision should not be influenced by the fact that it may be appealed from. The punishment ought not to be made more or less on that account. If his conviction be wrong it is all the better that there should be the right of appeal: it is to all parties, including perhaps the Justice, the easier and less expensive course to have it set right. A Justice must not take part at the Quarter Sessions in the hearing of an appeal from an order in which he took part at the Petty Sessions.—40 & 41 Vic., c. 56, s. 73.

Case Stated.—This in an appeal in another form, where, if after the Justices determine any complaint which they have power to determine in a summary way, either party considers the decision to be erroneous *in point of law*, may require them to state a case for the opinion of one of the Superior Courts.—20 & 21 Vic., c. 43. See "Case Stated," Summary Index.

Certiorari.—The Court of Queen's Bench, where *want of jurisdiction* in the Justices is shown, issues this writ on an affidavit, showing sufficient grounds, at any time within six months after the conviction, it is directed to the Justices hearing the record; it is also usual to direct it to the Petty Sessions Clerk; it stays from the time it is received all proceedings by the Justices, and it is their duty in obedience to it to return all records and proceedings which it commands to be returned. If after the return is made the Court of Queen's Bench rule that the Justices are right and that the *certiorari* should be quashed, a *procedendo* may be moved for, and will be granted, allowing the original order of the Justices to be carried out.

Where Magistrates hear a complaint within their jurisdiction, the proceedings being regular, the offence clearly set out in the summons, and the conviction set out that the defendant was guilty of the offence charged, the Court of Queen's Bench Division refused a conditional order for a *certiorari* to quash a conviction, and not being a Court of Appeal, would not examine into or hear evidence or enter into an inquiry as to whether the Magistrates were right or wrong in their decision.—*The Queen* v. *Sullivan*, Q.B. (Ir.), Hilary Term, 1888.

But in this same case and Term the Court of Exchequer Division subsequently granted a *habeas corpus*, and ordered the discharge of the prisoner, it appearing to the Court on the general question of jurisdiction that there was no evidence to sustain the conviction. The offence charged being one of "Conspiracy" under the Criminal Law and Procedure (Ireland) Act, 1887, conferring a special Summary Jurisdiction, but requiring that the evidence be taken as depositions in indictable offences. The Chief Baron and Baron Andrews held that the depositions did not substantiate or prove the offence; Baron Dowse dissenting.

Mandamus.—This writ issues from the Queen's Bench, when Justices without sufficient reason decline a jurisdiction where in point of law they ought not to decline or refuse to act; but if on the facts they merely come to a wrong conclusion the Court will not grant the *mandamus* requiring them to act. "Where Justices or others, on a *mistaken view of the law*, refuse to hear on a point on which jurisdiction depends, we call upon them to go into the inquiry; but when they have heard and determined, we do not review their decision."—*R.* v. *Goodwich*, 19 L. J. Q. B. 413. So that while Magistrates should not easily be frightened from the path of duty by lawyers' threats of bringing these terrible writs down on them, they will do well not to invite them by acts of unreasonable obstinacy.

Riots, &c.—This is another important duty which, as a conservator of the peace, the Magistrate may be called on to perform—the suppressing of riots and unlawful assemblies. He has authority at Common Law, and by Statute (the 3 Geo. iii., c. 19, and 27 Geo. iii., c. 15). On notice of riots and unlawful assemblies every Justice of the Peace, Sheriff, &c., within their jurisdictions, shall take all necessary force and may press into this service all Her Majesty's subjects to disperse and apprehend the offenders, under the 27 Geo. iii., c. 15, called the Riot Act; the Justice is to go as near to the rioters as he safely can, and make proclamation in the words of this Act: *see* form of proclamation under "Riot," Indictable Offences Index. In addition to the constabulary force, if it becomes necessary, the military may be called out; they act under the Civil Magistrate, although the military evolutions and movements are to be under the military officer. The duty of the military, although intended to be against our foreign foes, is not out of place in suppressing civil commotion. Their presence tends to check the riot, "like powder, asleep but ready."

The duties of Justices under the Licensing Liquor Acts, as to granting of licences, transfers, renewals, &c., will all be found under this head in the Summary Index.

It is not deemed necessary here to enter into the duties of Magistrates at Quarter Sessions, Special, or Presentment Sessions.

Protection of Justices.—A Justice is amply protected while acting "*bonâ fide* and under the belief that he is acting in the execution of his duty and in a manner within his jurisdiction." He is not protected when he assumes to do that which under no circumstances can be justified by his authority : *see* Protection of Justices Act, 12 Vic., c. 16, *Appendix.*

February, 1890.—H. H.

PRINCIPLES AND ESTABLISHED MAXIMS TO BE OBSERVED IN THE CONSTRUING OF STATUTES AND ADMINISTRATION OF THE LAW. (a)

Where a Statute directs the doing of a thing for the sake of justice or the public good, the word *may* is the same as the word *shall.*

The rules even of grammar and logic are overlooked, when the *intention* of the parties is evident, but opposed to the compliance with these rules; this also applies to the construing of Acts of Parliament, *mala grammatica non vitiat chartam.*

If the expression be dubious, the sense may be derived from the intent; and if the intent be dubious, it must be derived from the express words. If both be dubious, no rational interpretation can be formed; but if both be clear, but adverse to each other, the intent shall prevail.

The meaning and intention of the law should be collected from the several parts of the Act taken together, or from a single part when not opposed to the collected sense. Also from the occasion of enacting it, ascertained by the history

---

(a) Maxims or established principles are said to be of use in bringing disputes to a conclusion by silencing obstinate wranglers and cavillers, whom anyone is excused from longer arguing with, when they deny these general principles that are received by all reasonable men. But men are allowed to oppose and resist evident truth till they are baffled, *i. e.* till they are reduced to contradict themselves, or some established principle which they themselves cannot but own to be true, and cannot be receded from by either side.

of the times, and an attentive retrospect of previous regulations relative to the same object, as well as of the nature of the Act, whether it be remedial or penal, and other circumstances. (b)

The law presumes a man to be innocent until the contrary is proved, or appears from some stronger presumption.

When a man commits an unlawful act, unaccompanied by any circumstances justifying its commission, it is a presumption of law that he has acted advisedly; and with an intent to produce the consequences which have ensued.

Motives and Intentions.—The plain and fundamental rule is that a man's motives and intentions are to be inferred from the means which he uses and the acts which he does.

The law of England respecteth the effect and substance of the matter, and not every nicety of form or circumstances.

The law compels no man to impossible things.

An excuse cannot be founded on an ignorance of the law, which every man is supposed to know.

All crimes have their inception in a corrupt intent, and their consummation and issuing in a particular fact, which, though it be not the fact at which the intention of the malefactor was levelled, yet the law giveth him no advantage of the error. "It would be infinite," says Lord Bacon, "for the law to judge the causes of causes, and their impulsions, one upon another; it therefore contenteth itself with the immediate cause, and judges of acts by that alone, without looking to any further degree."

Justice shall be preferred to generosity.

Customs.—The evidence of every particular custom must be proved before the Court will take notice of it; and when proved the next inquiry is into the legality of it, for *malus usus abolendus est.* To make a particular custom good

---

(b) "The interpretation of the statute law is not different from the interpretation of every other thought expressed in language : as for instance is expressed in Philology. But its particular character shows itself when we decompose it into its constituent parts. Thus we may distinguish in it four elements—a grammatical, a logical, an historical, and a systematical. The grammatical element of interpretation has for its object the words which procure the passage or transition of the thought of the legislator into our thought, it consists, therefore, in the explanation of the language of the statute used by the legislator. The logical element proceeds upon the dismemberment or decomposition of the thought, and also upon the logical relation in which its individual parts stand to each other. The historical element has for its object the state or condition of the rules of law existing at the time of the statute enacted for the legal relation in question. Finally, the systematical element refers to the internal connecting-link which binds together all the institutions and rules of law into one grand vast unity This connected whole had hovered or floated before the eyes of the legislator, as well as the historical, and we shall know his thoughts then only completely when we make it clear to ourselves in what relation this Statute stands to the whole system of law, and how it will eventually act upon the system. With these four elements the investigation into the contents and import of the statute is complete."—*Savigny System, Reddie's Science of Law.*

it must be ancient, that is, in use so long that the memory of man runneth not to the contrary, uninterrupted, peaceably acquiesced in, reasonable, certain, compulsory, and consistent.

The law constrains no man to accuse himself of a crime, and every oath of testimony is imposed with this tacit reservation. It is a general rule that no one is bound to answer so as to subject himself to legal punishment, in whatever manner that punishment may arise, or whatever may be the nature of the punishment. *Accusare nemo se debet nisi coram Deo.*

No private contract or agreement prejudicial to common right, or repugnant to the general interests of the commonwealth, shall prevail in law.

Where a Statute directs or prohibits the doing of any act, and no other penalty or punishment is provided, any disobedience is punishable by indictment at Common Law. It is said that the law never speaks but to command, nor commands but where it can compel.

A Statute which treats of persons or things of an inferior rank cannot by any *general words* be extended to those of a superior.

Remedial Statutes are made to supply defects in the Common Law, whether arising from the general imperfection of human laws, or the mistakes and unadvised determinations of unlearned Judges; and this is done by *enlarging* or *restraining* Statutes.

An Act of Parliament that imposes a penalty or inflicts a punishment is called a Penal Statute.

Penal Statutes are to be construed *strictly*, and *Remedial Statutes* are to be expounded *liberally*.

When it is said that Penal Statutes are to be construed *strictly*, the meaning is that they shall not be *extended* by doubtful and ambiguous words, and that the punishment shall not be increased beyond what the law requires.

An Affirmative Statute does not take away the Common Law—a negative does so completely, so that it cannot be afterwards made use of upon the same subject.

What the Laws of England are.—The laws of England are of two kinds: the Statute or written Law, and the Common or unwritten Law. The Statute Law depends upon the will of the legislature of the kingdom.

Common Law is a *rule of justice* throughout the kingdom, and is constituted of the laws of nature, of nations, and of religion—certain general customs, principles, &c.; they are called *unwritten* Laws, because the authority for them is not expressed and published in the same manner as the Acts of the Legislature, but they are not to be considered as merely oral, and handed down from age to age by word of mouth, for there are monuments or memorials of their existence in writing, either by established maxims, declaratory Statutes, pleadings, reports, &c. They have grown into use, and have acquired their binding force and power by immemorial usage and general reception. (a)

The Common Law is the same in Ireland as in England.

THE DISCRETIONARY POWER POSSESSED BY JUSTICES OF THE PEACE.

A Justice of the Peace is invested with sufficiently large discretionary powers. Positive laws define the offences and prescribe the degree or extent of punishment. The limits are fixed, but within these he is *free* to exercise his discretion; that is, he is solemnly *bound* without fear or favour to do "equal right to the poor and to the rich, after his cunning, wit and power, and after the laws and customs of this realm and the Statutes thereof made." This is the scope of his commission and the extent of his power, which it is expected he will exercise with proper discernment and a sound, distinguishing judgment, within the bounds of Statute and Common Law, and the *Common Law* is said to be *reason.* Here he will need discretion, firmness, and a knowledge of his duty; here he must endeavour to get rid of those scruples and doubts that are based on no solid reason, but arise from false delicacy or a dubious and irresolute conscience influenced by slight and frivolous difficulties. He is also bound to administer the law as he finds it; and therefore, although the will of the Legislature may not always correspond with his own, it does not become him, or indeed any Judge, to set up in a hasty or inconsiderate manner his own will or ethical superiority to override the jurisprudence of the country.

In looking over the following analysis it will, perhaps, be observed that punishment does not always seem proportionate to guilt. To instance some cases:—For the offence of open and profane cursing and swearing the penalty is 1s. (if of the degree of gentleman, 2s.). For hawking and selling (without licence) the smallest measure of spirits the penalty is up to £100. For *stealing*

(a) *The Common Law.*—Lord Bacon says that our laws are as mixed as our language, compounded of British, Roman, Saxon, Danish, and Norman customs; and as our language is so much the richer, so the laws are the more complete. Sir Matthew Hale says that the origin of the Common Law is as undiscoverable as the head of the Nile. Mr. Hallam, however, is of opinion that our Common Law is not of that high antiquity which is generally supposed. "Our English lawyers, prone to magnify the antiquity, like the other merits of their system, are apt to carry up the date of the Common Law till, like the pedigree of an illustrious family, it loses itself in the obscurity of an ancient time. Even Sir Matthew Hale does not hesitate to say that its origin is as undiscoverable as that of the Nile. But though some features of the Common Law may be distinguishable in Saxon times, while our limited knowledge prevents us from assigning many of its peculiarities to any determinable *period,* yet the general character and most essential parts of the system were *of much later growth.*"—*Middle Ages,* vol. ii., chap. 8.

a turkey, a goose, or any barn-door fowl, the penalty is not to exceed 20s. For *taking* or even *pursuing* (without licence) a *snipe* in the "wild common of nature," where one would suppose it capable of asserting its independence by its swiftness, the penalty is £20; and so on. The Magistrate may consider that the penalties in such cases are unequal and should be inverted; but though no other answer be requisite than that such is the expressed will of the Legislature, which on the principle of general utility has a right to erect certain acts into offences—to prohibit and punish them—that it is not contrary to any of the great original foundations upon which all human laws depend—that the law is to govern him and not he the law, still it may for his satisfaction further be remarked that the guilt of the offender is not *always* to be the measure of punishment; the proper end of punishment is the prevention of crime. The Legislature will take into account the ease and facility with which offences can be committed; the difficulty of detecting, preventing, and prosecuting; the indifference of the greater portion of the community respecting some offences, *created by law*, while with respect to others all are ready to become detectives, and to rise in armed hostility to take summary vengeance on the malefactor. "The more deficient in certainty a punishment is, the severer it should be," but always proportioned to age, sex, condition, fortune, individual habits, and many other circumstances. The rule that should be impressed upon the mind of every Judge and Justice of the Peace is that, when anything is left to be done according to his discretion, the law intends it must be done with sound discretion and according to Law. "*Discretion*," says Lord Coke, "is to discern between right and wrong, shadow and substance, equity and colourable gloss, and not to do according to our will and private affections." It is proper also to observe that the discretion allowed by the law to a Magistrate is to be exercised within prescribed bounds, and in matters clearly defined and within his jurisdiction; for, as Dr. Paley observes—"This is the alternative: either the law must define beforehand, and with precision, the offences which it punishes, or it must be left to the *discretion* of the Magistrate to determine upon each particular accusation whether it constitutes that offence which the law designed to punish or not; which is, in effect, leaving to the Magistrate to punish or not to punish, at his pleasure, the individual who is brought before him; which is just so much tyranny. Where, therefore, the distinction between right and wrong is of too subtile or of too secret a nature to be ascertained by any preconcerted language, the law of most countries, especially of free states, rather than commit the liberty of the subject to the discretion of the Magistrate, leaves men in such cases to themselves."—*Law of the Land,* chap. iii. And of the danger likely to result from a judicial licence or discretion of this nature in the hands of any Judge, the following picture is drawn by Lord Camden:—"The discretion of a Judge is the law of tyrants; it is always unknown; it is different in different men; it is casual, and depends upon constitution, temper, passion. In the best it is oftentimes caprice; in the worst, it is every vice, folly, and passion to which human nature is liable.

"*Discretion*," says Lord Mansfield, "when applied to a Court of Justice, means sound discretion, *guided by law*. It must be governed by rule, not by humour: it must not be arbitrary, vague, and fanciful, but legal and regular."

INTERPRETATION ACT, 1889, 52 & 53 VIC., CHAP. 63, AS TO CON-
STRUCTION OF, AND FOR SHORTENING LANGUAGE USED
IN, ACTS OF PARLIAMENT.*

Rules as to *gender and number*. In Acts passed after 1850, words importing the masculine gender, shall include females, and words in the singular shall include the plural, and words in the plural shall include the singular.

Application of Penal Acts to Bodies Corporate.

Meaning of certain words in Acts, since 1850.

"Month," shall mean Calendar Month.

Sections in Acts to be substantive enactments, without introductory words.

Acts passed since 1850, to be Public Acts, and judicially noticed as such, unless contrary expressly provided by Act.

Official definitions in past and future Acts, Sec. 12.

Judicial definitions in past and future Acts, Sec. 13, of "Supreme Court," "Court of Appeal," "High Court," "Court of Assize," &c. &c.

Summary Jurisdiction (Ireland) Act, shall mean, as respects Dublin Metropolitan Police District, the Acts regulating the powers and duties of Justices of the Peace, or of the Police, of that district, and as respects any other part of Ireland, the Petty Sessions (Ireland) Act, 1851 (14 & 15, Vic., c. 93), and any Act, past or future, amending the same.

"Court of Summary Jurisdiction," shall mean any Justice or Justices of the Peace, or other Magistrate, by whatever name called, to whom jurisdiction is given by, or who is authorized to act under, the Summary Jurisdiction Acts, and, whether acting under the Summary Jurisdiction Acts, or any of them, or

---

* Most of the rules of construction and interpretation given in above Act are merely re-enactments of existing rules, interspersed throughout this work. The Act should, however, be carefully perused. Care should also be taken that the expressions and terms be not strained or misapplied. That the expressions "Summary Jurisdiction (Ir.) Acts," and "Summary Jurisdiction Acts," be rightly understood. That the expression "Court of Summary Jurisdiction" be not taken as giving to a Justice a jurisdiction not given him by other Acts: *see* the additional power given by 37 & 38 Vic., c. 72, s. 5, to a single Justice, where particular Acts direct, that Penalties may be reserved, &c., in a "*Summary manner*."

under any other Act, or by virtue of his commission, or under the Common Law.

"Borough," meaning of, s. 15.

"Person," meaning of, in future Acts, s. 19.

"Writing," meaning of, in past and future Acts, s. 20.

"Statutory Declaration," meaning of, in past and future Acts.

"Service by post," meaning of, s. 26.

"County Court," meaning of, in future Irish Acts, s. 29.

This Act repeals the 13 Vic., c. 21, for shortening the language used in Acts of Parliament.

For further interpretations and definitions, see Act.

PENALTIES RECOVERABLE IN A SUMMARY MANNER.

What is meant when Acts of Parliament state that Penalties are recoverable in a *summary manner*—

"Where by any Act now in force or hereafter to be passed, it is enacted that penalties, offences, or proceedings thereunder may be recovered, prosecuted, or taken in a summary manner, and no further provision with respect thereto is contained in such Act, then such penalties, offences, and proceedings, shall be recoverable, may be prosecuted, or taken with respect to the Police District of Dublin Metropolis, subject and according to the provisions of any Act regulating the powers and duties of Justices of the Peace for such district, or of the Police of such district; and with respect to other parts of Ireland, before a Justice or Justices of the Peace sitting in Petty Sessions, subject and according to the provisions of 'The Petty Sessions (Ireland) Act, 1851,' and any Act amending the same."—37 & 38 Vic., c. 72, s. 5.

For general interpretation of terms in Petty Sessions (Ireland) Act, 1851, see 14 & 15 Vic., c. 93, sec. 44.

All statutes made in England before 10 Hen. vii., c. 22 (Poynings' Act), are by that statute declared to be in force in Ireland.

The people of Ireland are not bound by Acts passed in the Parliament of England subsequent to Poynings' Act, save in respect of those mentioned in 21 & 22 Geo. iii., c. 48 (Irish). From the Union (1800) all Acts extend to Ireland unless expressly or impliedly excepted.

34 EDWARD III.

SURETIES OF GOOD BEHAVIOUR, &c.

The following is a copy of the translation of the 34 Edward III., as it appears in the Second Revised Edition of the Statutes. The notes under the asterisks are those in this Edition :—

"34 EDWARD III. A.D. 1360–1.

"These be the things, which our lord the King, the prelates, lords and the Commons have ordained in this present Parliament, holden at Westminster, the Sunday next before the Feast of the Conversion of St. Paul, to be holden and published openly through the realm.

1. "First, that in every County of England shall be assigned for the keeping of the peace, one lord, and with him three or four of the most worthy in the county, with some learned in the law, and they shall have power to restrain the offenders, rioters, and all other barators, and to pursue, arrest, take and chastise them according their trespass or offence ; and to cause them to be imprisoned and duly punished according to the law and customs of the realm, and according to that which to them shall seem best to do by their discretions and good advisement ; and also to inform them, and to inquire of all those that have been pillors and robbers in the parts beyond the sea, and be now come again, and go wandering, and will not labour as they were wont in times past ; and to take and

arrest all those that they may find by indictment, or by
suspicion, and to put them in prison ; and to take of all
them that be [not*] of good fame, where they shall be
found, sufficient surety and mainprise of their good behaviour towards the king and his people, and the other
duly to punish ; to the intent that the people be not by
such rioters or rebels troubled nor endangered, nor the
peace blemished, nor merchants nor others passing by
the highways of the realm disturbed, nor [put in the
peril which may happen*] of such offenders."

This Statute was in French, as the Statutes continued to be
so for more than a century later, although, in 1362, the thirty-
sixth year of Edward III., an Act was passed (also in French)
ordering that all trials should be conducted in English—the
language understood by the people.   In this Edition of the
Statutes the exact words of the Great Roll and the translation
appear in parallel columns.   The Norman-French is written in
abbreviated form.   The following are the exact words of the one
sentence as it appears on the Great Roll, of which so much use
is still made :—

"& de prendre de touz ceux qi‡ sont de bone fame,
ou ils seront trovez souffisant seurete & meinprise de
lo' bon port, devers le Roi & son poeple, & les autres
duement punir."

---

* " All translations read thus."
* " Put in fear by peril which might happen."
‡ The translations supply the negative as above pointed out.

THE JUSTICE OF THE PEACE

FOR

IRELAND.

SUMMARY JURISDICTION.

In the "Jurisdiction" column, to save lengthy repetitions, where the penalty does not exceed £5, the words "in default of payment, imprisonment, &c.," will mean that under the "Small Penalties Act" the defendant may be at once imprisoned without distress warrant. Where the penalty exceeds £5, the words "in default, &c.," will mean in default of payment and of distress, &c., H.L., hard labour. 1 J. or 2 J. denotes whether one or two Justices may hear the case. (a)

Where the words are "fine or imprisonment," omitting the words "in default, &c.," it will be found that the words of the Statute are followed, which leaves it in the discretion of the Justice either to impose the fine or to inflict the punishment without a fine.

Offence, or cause of Complaint.	Statute.	Extent of Jurisdiction.
ABETTORS: Aiders or abettors in offences of simple larceny, where the age of offender does not exceed 14 years.	14 & 15 Vic. c. 92, s. 6.	Punishable as the principal offender. See "Larceny by Juvenile Offenders."
In offences punishable on summary conviction under the Larceny Act.	24 & 25 Vic. c. 96, s. 99.	Punishable as the principal offender. See "Larceny."

(a) *Number of Justices requisite.*—It will be seen that two Justices are sufficient to try any case to be decided in Petty Sessions; in most instances one is only requisite. Indeed it will, perhaps, in general be found that the decision of one or two affords less ground for objection than that of a greater number. On this subject a moral and political philosopher has sharply observed—"Judges, when they are numerous, *divide* the shame of an unjust determination; they shelter themselves under one another's example; each man thinks his own character hid in the crowd: for which reason, the Judges ought always to be so few as that the conduct of each may be conspicuous to public observation; that each may be responsible in his separate and particular reputation for the decisions in which he concurs."

Jurisdiction.—The Justice should be satisfied that the complaint upon which

B

Offence, or cause of Complaint.	Statute.	Extent of Juris
ABETTORS—*continued*. In offences on summary conviction, under the Malicious Injuries Act.	24 & 25 Vic. c. 97, s. 63.	Punishable as cipal offend "Malicious I
In Misdemeanours. — Whosoever shall aid, abet, counsel, or procure the commission of any misdemeanour, whether same be a misdemeanour at Common Law, or by virtue of any Act passed, or to be passed—	24 & 25 Vic. c. 94, s. 8.	Shall be liabl tried, indict punished as a offender.
Under Petty Sessions Act.—Every person who shall aid, abet, counsel, or procure the commission of any offence, which is or shall be punishable on summary conviction—	14 & 15 Vic. c. 93, s. 22.	Shall be liable, viction, to s feiture and pu to which the offender shall liable ; but wh tor's ago ex years, ho shall to same pur &c., to which cipal offender

Offence, or cause of Complaint.	Statute.	Extent of Jurisdiction.
ADULTERATION : (a) *Adulteration of Food and Drugs.* *Repeals.*—23 & 24 Vic. c. 84; 31 & 32 Vic. c. 121, s. 24; 33 & 34 Vic. c. 26, s. 3; 35 & 36 Vic. c. 74; except as to appointments made under them.	38 & 39 Vic. c. 63.	— .
Food, shall include every article used for *food* or *drink* by man, other than drugs or water. *Drug*, shall include medicine for internal or external use. *County*, shall include county of a city or county of a town, not being a borough. *Justices*, shall include Divisional Justices in Ireland.	s. 1.	
Offences as to Food and Drink.—No person shall mix, colour, stain, or powder any article of food with any ingredient or material so as to render the article injurious to health, with intent that the same may be sold in that state, and no person shall sell any such article so mixed, coloured, &c., under a penalty—	s. 3.	Penalty in each case not exceeding £50 for the first offence ; in default, &c., imprisonment by scale. 1 J. Every offence after a conviction for first offence shall be a misdemeanour (indictable) ; imprisonment not exceeding 6 months' H. L.
Offences as to Drugs.—No person shall, except for the purpose of compounding, as in Act described, mix, colour, stain, or powder, or order or permit any other person so to do, so as to affect injuriously the quality or potency thereof, with intent that same may be sold in that state, and no person shall sell any such, &c.; for offending—	s. 4.	Same penalty in each case, respectively, as in the preceding section, for a first and second offence.
Proviso.—Exemption in case of proof of absence of knowledge.	s. 5.	

(a) The sale of unwholesome provisions (as when a baker sells bread in which pernicious and noxious materials or alum, in a shape which renders it noxious, is mixed) is a misdemeanour, as it affects the public.—*R.* v. *Treeve*, 2 *Ea*., *P.C.*, 821 ; *R.* v. *Dixon*, 3 *M. & S.*

Offence, or cause of Complaint.	Statute.	Extent of Jurisdict
ADULTERATION—*continued*. *Sale of Food and Drugs not of proper quality, &c.*—No person shall sell, to the prejudice of the purchaser, any article of food or any drug which is not of the nature, substance, and quality of the article demanded by such purchaser; for offending—	38 & 39 Vic. c. 63, s. 6.	Penalty not exc £20; in default imprisonment by
Proviso.—Offence not deemed to be committed— (1) Where ingredient not injurious, necessary in the preparation, and no fraud intended. (2) Where same is a proprietary medicine, &c., is the subject of a patent, and supplied accordingly. (3) Where the drug or food is compounded as in Act mentioned. (4) Where it is unavoidably mixed with some extraneous matter, in process of collection or preparation.	,,	
No person shall sell any compound article of food, or compounded drug, which is not composed of ingredients in accordance with demand of the purchaser.	. 7.	Penalty not exc £20; in default imprisonment by
Proviso.—No offence where article not injurious, no fraud intended, and labelled to the effect that same is mixed.	s. 8.	
No person shall, with intent that the same may be sold in its altered state without notice, abstract from an article of food any part of it, so as to affect injuriously its quality, substance, or nature, and no person shall sell any article so altered without disclosing the alteration; for offending—	s. 9.	Penalty in each ca exceeding £20; fault, &c., imp ment by scale.
Appointment of Analysts—	s. 10.	
Town Council of Borough may engage the Analyst of another borough or county.	s. 11.	
Power of purchaser of an article of food to have it analysed.	s. 12.	
Provisions as to samples—the obtaining and dealing with same.	ss. 13–15.	

Offence, or cause of Complaint.	Statute.	Extent of Jurisdiction.
ADULTERATION—*continued.* Person refusing to sell any article to any officer, inspector, constable, &c., as in Act.	38 & 39 Vic. c. 63, s. 17.	Penalty not exceeding £10; in default, &c., imprisonment by scale. 1 J.
Proceedings.—Where from certificate of Analyst it appears that an offence has been committed, the person causing the analysis to be made may proceed for penalties before Justices of the district, in Petty Sessions.	s. 20.	
Proceedings in Dublin under local Acts; elsewhere, under "Petty Sessions (Ireland) Act, 1851," and any Act amending the same.		
Certificate of Analyst to be *prima facie* evidence for prosecution, but Analyst to be called if required.	s. 21.	
Defendant and his wife are competent witnesses.		
Power to Justices before whom complaint or appeal heard, to have articles of food and drug analysed.	s. 22.	
Appeal to Quarter Sessions, under Petty Sessions Act. If Sessions held within 10 days, Appellant may appeal to the following Sessions.	s. 23.	
In prosecutions, defendant to prove that he is protected by exemption or provision.	s. 24.	
Defendant to be discharged if he prove that he bought the article in same state as sold, and with a warranty; but defendant shall be liable to costs unless he shall have given notice that he will rely on above defence.		
Application of Penalties.—To officers, &c., who appoint Analyst, and to be by him paid to authority for whom he acts. In other cases, as directed by "Fines (Ireland) Act, 1851."	s. 26.	
Any person forging, or uttering, knowing same to be forged, certificate or warranty.	s. 27.	Indictable misdemeanour; imprisonment not exceeding 2 years.
Wilful misapplication to articles of food or drug of warranty given for other articles.	"	Penalty not exceeding £20; in default, &c., imprisonment by scales. 1 J.

Offence, or cause of Complaint.	Statute.	Extent of Jurisdiction.
ADULTERATION—*continued*.		
Person giving false warranty in writing to any purchaser, in respect of an article of food or drug sold by him, as principal or agent.	38 & 39 Vic. c. 63, s. 27.	Penalty not exceeding £20; in default, &c., imprisonment by scales. 1 J.
Person wilfully giving false label with article sold by him.	,,	Like. 1 J.
Proceedings by indictment and contracts not to be affected.	s. 28.	
Expenses of executing Act: in counties by Grand Jury cess; in boroughs by borough fund or rate.	s. 29.	
Tea.—Special provisions as to tea. Tea to be examined by the Customs on importation. *Form of Certificate*, in Schedule to Act.	s. 30.	
Food and Drugs Amendment Act, 1879.—In sale of adulterated articles it shall be no defence to allege that purchaser having bought only for analysis was not prejudiced by sale.	42 & 43 Vic. c. 30, s. 2.	
Officer, inspector, or constable may obtain a sample of milk at the place of delivery to submit to Analyst.	s. 3.	
The seller or consignor of any person or persons entrusted by him for the time being with the charge of such milk, if he shall refuse to allow officer, inspector, or constable to take the quantity required for the purpose of analysis.	s. 4.	Penalty not exceeding £10; in default, &c., imprisonment by scale. 1 J.
Any street or open place of public resort shall be held to come within the meaning of sec. 17 of principal Act.	s. 5.	
Reduction allowed to the extent of 25 degrees under proof for brandy, whiskey, or rum, and 35 degrees for gin.	s. 6.	

Offence, or cause of Complaint.	Statute.	Extent of Jurisdiction.
ADULTERATION—*continued.*		
Proceedings.—In proceedings under the principal Act and this Act summons shall be served within a reasonable time; and in the case of a perishable article not exceeding 28 days from the time of the purchase, and particulars of the offence and also name of prosecutor shall be stated on summons, and summons shall not be returnable in less than 7 days from day of service.	42 & 43 Vic. c. 30, s. 10.	
Adulterating corn, meal, flour, &c., or selling or offering same for sale, not being equal to sample; or practising any fraud to increase the weight of same.	1 & 2 Vic. c. 28, s. 8. (14 & 15 Vic. c. 93, s. 22. 36 & 37 Vic. c. 82.)	Penalty not exceeding £10 nor less than 40s.; in default, &c., imprisonment according to the scales, with H. L.; and shall also forfeit the corn, &c. 1 J.
Similar offence under . . .	14 & 15 Vic. c. 92, s. 7.	Penalty not exceeding 40s., or imprisonment not exceeding 1 month, and shall also forfeit the article.
Adulteration of Seeds.—Any person who, with intent to defraud, or enable others to do so, kills or dyes, or causes to be, or sells, or causes to be sold, &c., any killed or dyed seeds.	32 & 33 Vic. c. 112, s. 34. (14 & 15 Vic. c. 93, s. 22. 36 & 37 Vic. c. 82.)	First offence, penalty not exceeding £5; second or subsequent offences, not exceeding £50; in default, &c., imprisonment by the scales. 1 J.
In second, &c., offences, Court may cause offender's name, &c., and punishment to be published in newspapers or otherwise.		
Intent to defraud particular person need not be alleged.		
Power of Appeal to Quarter Sessions.		
Other criminal or civil proceedings not to be affected by this Act.		
Proceedings under this Act shall be commenced within twenty-one days from offence.		
Adulteration of Seeds Act, 1869, amends 32 & 33 Vic. c. 112, sec. 2.		
The term "to dye seeds" means to apply to seeds any process of colouring, dyeing, or sulphur smoking.	41 Vic. c. 17. s. 2.	

Offence, or cause of Complaint.	Statute.	Extent of Jurisdiction.
AFFIRMATION: In criminal proceedings may be received where witness, from conscientious motives, refuses to be sworn. (a)	24 & 25 Vic. c. 66, s. 1.	
AFFRAY: See "Fighting."		
AGRICULTURAL PRODUCE: Assaulting, threatening, &c., with intent to obstruct the sale of grain, &c., or its free passage. See "Assault."	24 & 25 Vic. c. 100, s. 39. (25 & 26 Vic. c. 50, s. 2.)	Imprisonment at H. L. for any term not exceeding 3 months. 1 J.
AIDERS: See "Abettors."		
ALIENS: See "Naturalization."		
AMENDMENTS: In proceedings before Justices in Petty Sessions, and on appeal. See 14 & 15 Vic. c. 93, sec. 39; 27 & 28 Vic. c. 99, s. 49; 40 & 41 Vic. c. 56, s. 74.		

(a) 24 & 25 Vic. c. 66. s. 1.—"If any person called as a witness in any Court of Criminal Jurisdiction in England or Ireland, or required or desiring to make an Affidavit or Deposition in the course of any criminal proceeding, shall refuse or be unwilling, from alleged conscientious motives, to be sworn, it shall be lawful for the Court or Judge, or other presiding Officer or Person qualified to take Affidavits or Depositions, upon being satisfied of the sincerity of such objection, to permit such person, instead of being sworn, to make his or her solemn Affirmation or Declaration in the words following, viz.—(This Act extended to Jurors by 31 & 32 Vic c. 75.)

"'I, A. B., do solemnly, sincerely, and truly affirm and declare, that the taking of any oath is, according to my religious belief, unlawful; and I do also solemnly, sincerely, and truly affirm and declare, &c.'

Which solemn Affirmation and Declaration shall be of the same force and effect as if such person had taken an oath in the usual form."

Sec. 2.—If wilfully false, &c., punishable as for perjury.

For the Oath of Allegiance, Official Oath, and Judicial Oath, see "Promissory Oaths Act," 31 & 32 Vic. c. 72; and where Affirmation or Declaration may be substituted, see section 11 of same Act (and Appendix).

Offence, or cause of Complaint.	Statute.	Extent of Jurisdiction.
ANIMALS: See "Cruelty to Animals." "Larceny." "Malicious Injuries." "Nuisance on Roads." "Contagious Diseases of."		
APPEAL: Where an order is made under the 14 & 15 Vic. c. 92, for the payment of a penal or other sum exceeding 20s.; or for an imprisonment exceeding one month; or for doing anything at a greater expense than 20s.	14 & 15 Vic. c. 92, s. 23.	In cases of a civil nature, either party may appeal; in other cases, the party against whom the order is made may appeal to Quarter Sessions.
General Right of Appeal.—A general right of appeal is given under the 14 & 15 Vic. c. 93, where the order is made for payment of any penal or other sum exceeding 20s., or for any term of imprisonment exceeding one month; or for the doing of anything at a greater expense than 40s.; or for estreating a recognizance to a greater amount than 20s.; *but in no other case.* (a)	14 & 15 Vic. c. 93, s. 24.	In cases of a civil nature, either party may appeal; in other cases the party against whom the order is made may appeal to Quarter Sessions.
The general form of appeal is given in forms in Schedule to	14 & 15 Vic. c. 93.	
In revenue and game prosecutions under the particular Acts.	—	A special power of appeal is given under the Poaching Act of 1862, 25 & 26 Vic. c. 114.

(a) The two Acts above referred to were passed in the same Session; they differ in some particulars as to the conditions, or penalties, &c., which will give a right of appeal. The power of right of appeal given by chap. 92 appears merely to apply to orders made under it. Chap. 93 applies generally to orders made under all previous Statutes, except the cases under chap. 92, and also Customs, Excise, Stamps, Taxes, Post-office, and Game Prosecutions, exempted in sec. 42 of chap. 93; these must be regulated by the conditions and forms of appeal specially appointed for themselves. Chap. 93 will also apply to all convictions under all previous Acts, and will take away the right of appeal given by them unless the penalty or punishment be such as under its (chap. 93) provisions will give that right, for the words of the section "*in no other case*" appear sufficiently strong to have that effect. It will also apply to summary orders under all *subsequent* Acts of Parlia-

Offence, or cause of Complaint.	Statute.	Extent of Jurisdiction.
APPEAL—*continued.* In excise and customs cases, &c., see schedule to Act.	40 Vic. c. 13.	
Where Magistrates refuse Publicans their annual certificate.	18 & 19 Vic. c. 62, ss. 1 & 2	Special power of appeal and form of recognizance given.
Under the Small Debts Act.	22 Vic. c. 14.	Special power of appeal given.
Under Larceny Act, where sum adjudged to be paid exceeds £5; or the imprisonment exceeds one month; or where the conviction takes place before one Justice only.	24 & 25 Vic. c. 96, s. 100.	Special power and conditions of appeal.
By Malicious Injuries Act, under like circumstances.	24 & 25 Vic. c. 97, s. 68.	Special power and conditions of appeal.
Under Towns Improvement Act, where the penalty exceeds 20*s.*	17 & 18 Vic. c. 103, s. 93.	
Under Reformatory Act, where offender is ordered to be sent to Reformatory School.	31 & 32 Vic. c. 59, s. 12.	Offender, parent, or guardian may appeal. (See "Reformatory" and notes thereon.)
Under Public Health Act.	41 & 42 Vic. c. 52, s. 269.	—
Under "Conspiracy and Protection of Property" Act. Under Licensing Act, 1872–74. In other cases, see the particular head.	38 & 39 Vic. c. 86.	
Amendments.—In form of recognizances in appeals from Petty Sessions.	40 & 41 Vic. c. 56, s. 72, &c.	

ment to which the provisions of this Act are extended. *Appeal* can alone be given by Statute, and never lies unless where it is expressly given.—*R.* v. *Recorder of Ipswich,* 8 *Dowl.,* 103. The rule with regard to a *certiorari* is the reverse. It always lies unless expressly taken away, *R.* v. *Abbott, Dougl.,* 553, and it requires very strong words to do so; for even where a Statute gives an appeal to the Sessions, and directed that it should be finally determined there, and no other Court should intermeddle with the causes of appeal, it was held that a *certiorari* lay after the appeal.—*R.* v. *Morley,* 1 *W. Bl.,* 231; *R.* v. *Justices of West Riding of Yorkshire,* 1 *Ad. & Ell.,* 575; *R.* v. *Fell,* 1 *B. & Ad.,* 380; *R.* v. *Justices of Lancashire,* 11 *Ad. & Ell.,* 144. "An appeal from a conviction is not a matter of right, it can only be given by special enactment, and the right will not be extended by any equitable construction."—*Paley on Convic.*

ice, or cause of Complaint.	Statute.	Extent of Jurisdiction.
—continued.		
rho takes part in hearing at Sessions not to take part e hearing on appeal at r Sessions.	40 & 41 Vic. c. 56, s. 73.	
ents may be made and cured on appeal.	27 & 28 Vic. c. 99, s. 49, 40 & 41 Vic. c. 56, s. 74.	.
so Petty Sessions Act, *dix* as to *Appeals*.)		
ΓICE: er head " Employers and nen."		
ace Preservation (Ireland) 881." " Arms " and " Whiteboy indictable offences.		
ЭT, 1881. *nt.*—Justice not to proceed enlistment if he considers to be under the influence or.	44 & 45 Vic. c. 58, s. 80.	
t does not assent to be en- attestation not to be pro- with. (*a*)	,,	
ents, Justice to caution him consequence of giving false s, &c. And as to further of Justice in attesting.	,,	
ig errors in attestation paper.	,,	
ttestation.	,,	
if recruit to purchase his rge.	s. 81.	
ms of masters to apprentices.	s. 96.	
for unlawful recruiting, &c.	s. 98.	

t of Recruit.—If he does not appear before a Justice or, on appearing, ent to be enlisted, no further proceedings shall be taken, nor shall the eed with the enlistment if he considers the recruit under the influence Sec. 77.

on.—Officer *duly authorised may attest* recruits. See 46 Vic. c. 6, s. 6.

Offence, or cause of Complaint.	Statute.	Extent of Ju
ARMY ACT, 1881, &c.—*continued*. Recruit knowingly making false answers to questions in attestation paper, read or put to him by, or by direction of, Justice before whom he appears for the purpose of being attested.	44 & 45 Vic. c. 58, s. 99.	Imprisonment without H. 1 ceeding 3 m 2 J
At the discretion of military authority may be tried by court-martial.	,,	
Billets.—Justice's powers in respect to.	s. 108.	
Offences by constables in respect to billets.—If a constable commits any of the offences following, that is to say:—		
(1) Billets any officer, soldier, or horse on any person not liable to billets without the consent of such person; or	s. 109.	Penalty not le and not exc 2 J
(2) Receives, demands, or agrees for any money or reward whatsoever to excuse from liability to billets, &c.; or	,,	
(3) Billets or quarters on any person or premises without consent of such person or the occupier of such premises any person or horse not entitled to be billeted; or	,,	
(4) Neglects or refuses after sufficient notice is given to give billet demanded for any officer, soldier, or horse entitled to be billeted.	,,	
If keeper of a victualling house commits any of the offences following:—	s. 110.	Penalty not le and not exc 2 J
(1) Refuses or neglects to receive officer, soldier, or horse billeted in pursuance of Act, or furnish accommodation required by Act.	,,	
(2) Gives or agrees to give money to constable to be relieved, &c.	,,	

Offence, or cause of Complaint.	Statute.	Extent of Jurisdiction.
ARMY ACT, 1881, &c.—*continued.* (3) Gives or agrees to give officer or soldier billeted any money or reward in lieu of accommodation, &c.	44 & 45 Vic. c. 58, s. 110.	
Offences by officers or soldiers in respect to billets contrary to Act.	ss. 30–111.	
Punishment for personating.—Any person who falsely represents himself to any military, naval, or civil authority to belong to or to be a particular man in the regular reserve or auxiliary forces, shall be deemed to be guilty of personation.	s. 142. sub-s. (2).	Shall be liable on summary conviction to imprisonment, with or without H. L. for a term not exceeding 3 months, or to a fine not exceeding £25. 2 J. or 1 Stip.
Personating in respect of military service, or to any money or property in the possession of the military authorities—		
Or is guilty of personation under this section.	sub-s. (3).	
Exemption of soldiers in respect to *civil process.*	s. 144.	
Liability of soldier to maintain wife and children. (Not liable to arrest or punishment for neglecting to do so.) And see also 46 Vic. c. 6, s. 7.	s. 145.	
Any person who falsely confesses himself to be a deserter from H. M regular forces.	s. 152.	Imprisonment not exceeding 3 months, with or without H. L. 2 J. or 1 Stip.
Any person who by any means (1) procures or persuades soldiers to desert; or attempts to procure or persuade, &c.; or	s. 153.	Imprisonment with or without H. L., not exceeding 6 months. 2 J. or 1 Stip.
(2) Knowing that a soldier is about to desert, aids or assists him in deserting; or	,,	

Justice may issue warrant to arrest person reasonably suspected to be a deserter. 47 Vic. c. 8, s. 6.

Offence, or cause of Complaint.	Statute.	Extent of J...
ARMY ACT, 1881, &c.—*continued*. (3) Knowing any soldier to be a deserter, conceals or aids in concealing him or aids or assists in his rescue.	44 & 45 Vic. c. 58, s. 153.	
Deserters.—Apprehending, remanding, and reporting deserters. (*a*)	s. 154.	May be rem... indictable o...
Purchasing Soldier's necessaries.— (*a*) Every person who buys, exchanges, takes in pawn, detains, or receives from a soldier, or any person acting on his behalf, on any pretence whatsoever; or	s. 156.	*First offence.* ... exceeding £ ... with trebl... the propert... offender be ... sessed by n... offence.
(*b*) Solicits or entices any soldier to sell, exchange, pawn, or give away; or	,,	*Second offence* ... exceeding ... less than : ... prisonment, ... without H. ... ceeding 6 n... 2 ...
(*c*) Assists or acts for a soldier in selling, exchanging, pawning, or making away with any arms, ammunition, equipments, instruments, regimental necessaries, or clothing or any military decorations of an officer or soldier, or any furniture, bedding, blankets, sheets, utensils, and stores in regimental charge, or any provisions or forage issued for officer, soldier, or horse employed in H. M. service, shall, unless he proves either that he acted in ignorance of the same being such property as aforesaid, or of the person with whom he dealt being or acting for a soldier, or that the same was sold by order of a Secretary of State or some competent military authority.	,,	Where money ... posed in d... imprisonme...

(*a*) Where the Justice causes the deserter to be handed over to mil... or commits him to prison he shall send the descriptive return to th... There is a fee of 2*s.* payable to the Justice's clerk for making the re...

Offence, or cause of Complaint.	Statute.	Extent of Jurisdiction.
ARMY ACT, 1881, &c.—*continued.* (2) *Found in possession.*—Where such property as above is found in possession or keeping of any person, such person may be taken or summoned before a Court of summary jurisdiction, and if Court have reasonable ground to believe that the property so found was stolen or was bought, exchanged, taken in pawn, obtained or received in contravention of section, then, if such person does not satisfy the Court that he came by the property so found lawfully and without any contravention of this Act—	44 & 45 Vic. c. 58, s. 156.	Penalty not exceeding £5 ; in default, &c., imprisonment by scale. 2 J. or 1 Stip.
(3) The person charged and husband or wife competent witnesses.	,,	
(4) Power to apprehend person found committing offence. (a)	,,	
(5) Power to grant *warrant to search.* (b)	,,	

(a) (4) A person found committing an offence against this section may be apprehended without warrant, and taken, with the property which is the subject of the offence, before a Court of Summary Jurisdiction ; and any person to who many such property as above mentioned is offered to be sold, pawned, or delivered, who has reasonable cause to suppose that the same is offered in contravention of this section, may, and if he has the power shall, apprehend the person offering such property, and forthwith take him, together with such property, before a Court of summary jurisdiction. (And see also 24 & 25 Vic. c. 96, s. 103.)

(b) (5) A Court of Summary Jurisdiction, if satisfied on oath that there is reasonable cause to suspect that any person has in his possession, or on his premises, any property in or with respect to which any offence in this section mentioned has been committed, may grant a warrant to search for such property, as in the case of stolen goods, and any property found on such search shall be seized by the officer charged with the execution of such warrant, who shall bring the person in whose possession the same is found before some Court of Summary Jurisdiction, to be dealt with according to law.

(6) For the purposes of this section property shall be deemed to be in the possession or keeping of a person if he knowingly has it in the actual possession or keeping of any other person, or in any house, building, lodging, apartment, field, or place, open or inclosed, *whether occupied by himself or not, and whether the*

Offence, or cause of Complaint.	Statute.	Extent of Ju
ARMY ACT, 1881, &c.—*continued.* *Evidence.*—Regulation as to.	44 & 45 Vic. c. 58, s. 163.	
Attestation paper to be evidence of the answers, &c., contained in it. And as to other official entries, extracts, copies, descriptive returns, &c., which are to be received as evidence. See Section.	„	
Civil conviction.—Certificate signed by clerk of Court (for which a fee of 3*s.* is to be paid) to be evidence.	s. 164.	
Prosecution of offences, recovery and application of fines. (*a*)	s. 166.	
Canteens.—Any two Justices may grant or transfer canteen licences without regard to time of year, and without requirement as to notices, &c.	s. 174.	
Pay and Pensions :—*Punishment for obtaining Pay and Pensions by fraudulent means.* (*b*)—If any person, by means of false certificate, false representation, false document, false statement, or other fraudulent means, obtains, or attempts to obtain, for himself or any other person, the grant, increase, or pay-	47 & 48 Vic. c. 55, s. 3.	On conviction *ment* be lial prisonment, without H. term not exc years. On conviction *of Summar§ tion*, impriso

same is so had for his own use or benefit or for the use or benefit (And see also 38 & 39 Vic. c. 25.)

(7) Articles which are public stores within the meaning of the P Act, 1875, and are not included in the foregoing description, shall no to be stores issued as regimental necessaries or otherwise within the section 13 of that Act. (And see 38 and 39 Vic. c. 25.)

(*a*) *Fines and forfeitures* to be recovered under 14 & 15 Vic. c. 93, amending same.

Court may, if it seem fit, award half fine to informer, remainder to g by Fines Act (Ireland), 1851, and any Acts amending same.

Court to be constituted of *two* or more Justices or *one* Justice for th empowered by law to do alone any act authorized to be done by mo Justice of the Peace.

(*b*) Although by the Index this Statute appears to be limited to I Scotland, manifestly by the sections of the Army Act incorporate applicable to Ireland.

Offence, or cause of Complaint.	Statute.	Extent of Jurisdiction.
ARMY ACT, 1881, &c.—*continued*. ment of any pay or pension payable, or any privilege or advantage obtainable in pursuance of any warrant order, &c., made in pursuance of this Act, or otherwise.		or without H. L. not exceeding 3 months, or to a fine not exceeding £25. 2 J. or 1 Stip.
Army Act, 1881 (44 & 45 Vic. c. 58, s. 142) shall be applicable.	47 & 48 Vic. c. 55, s. 3.	
When prosecuted before a Court of *Summary Jurisdiction* may be prosecuted and fine recovered, as provided by section 166 Army Act, 1881, as if in terms made applicable to this Act.		
For other branches of the service, see " Militia, Reserve Forces," &c.		
ARSENIC: Particulars of sale to be entered in a book, and all sales to be subject to the conditions and restrictions set forth in Act.	14 Vic. c. 13, ss. 1, 2, 3.	—
For selling otherwise than as authorized, or for offending against the provisions of this Act.	s. 4.	Penalty not exceeding £20, recoverable under Petty Sessions Act. 2 J.
And see " Poisons."		
ARTIFICER: Any artificer, workman, journeyman, apprentice, servant, or other person, who shall unlawfully dispose of, or retain in his possession, without the consent of the person by whom he shall be hired, retained, or employed, any goods, wares, work, or materials committed to his care or charge (value not exceeding £5)—	25 & 26 Vic. c. 50, s. 7.	Shall pay such compensation as the Justices shall think reasonable, and shall also be liable to a fine not exceeding £2, or to be imprisoned not exceeding 1 month. 1 J.
See also " Employer and Workman."		

C

Offence, or cause of Complaint.	Statute.	Extent of Jurisdiction
ASSAULT: Under	24 & 25 Vic. c. 100.	—
As amended by	25 & 26 Vic. c. 50	—
Common Assault. (*a*)—Any person who shall assault or beat any other person, shall, upon conviction, be liable to— (Assaults under this section may, if Justices think fit, be proceeded with, although party aggrieved declines to prosecute, 25 & 26 Vic. c. 50, s. 9.) (*b*)	24 & 25 Vic. c. 100, s. 42. (25 & 26 Vic. c. 50, s. 2.)	Imprisonment not ceeding 2 months, or without H. L.; (at the discretion of Justices) fine not ceeding, together costs (if ordered), in default of paym imprisonment as ab unless amount be so paid.

(*a*) *Common Assault* may be by striking at another, with or without a wea holding up one's fist at him, or by any other rash act done in an angry or thre ing manner (1 *Hawk.*, c. 62, s. 1). So advancing in a threatening attitude, with intention to strike, so that the blow would have immediately reached, h not been stopped; and although when stopped he was not near enough fo blow to take effect; this was held to be an assault in point of law.—*T C. J.; Stephens v. Meyers, 4 Car. & P.*, 349.

Battery.—A battery is an injury, however trifling, actually done to the p of another, in an angry, revengeful, rude, or insolent manner, as by spitting i face, or in any way touching him in anger, violently jostling him out of the or the like.—*Hawk.*, c. 62, s. 2.

Trifling Assaults.—But in either case if the Justice finds the assault or ba to be so trifling as not to merit any punishment, he may dismiss the complai Sec. 44. *De minimis non curat lex.* The law does not concern itself about t

Retaliation.—Though fully justified in retaliating, the party must not carr resentment to such a length as to become the assailant in his turn, as by contin to beat the aggressor after he has been disabled, or has submitted, or by us lethel or ponderous weapon, as a knife, poker, hatchet, or hammer, against or cane, or in general pushing his advantage in point of strength or weapon t uttermost. In such cases the defence degenerates into aggression, and the ori assailant is entitled to demand punishment for the new assault committed on after his original attack had been duly chastised.—*Alison.*

Appeal.—The Assault Act itself gives no right of appeal, but the 25 & 26 c. 50, in addition to other modifications, by sec. 2 directs that the hearing *determination* of complaints referred to Justices under the Assaults Act shall accordance with the provisions of the Petty Sessions (Ireland) Act, and this conceived includes the right of appeal given in the latter.

(*b*) Where a constable witnessed an assault and arrested the assailant but not discover the name of person assaulted, the Law Adviser held that the cons could proceed and the Justices could hear case. No. 29463. 1 December, 1

Offence, or cause of Complaint.	Statute.	Extent of Jurisdiction.
ASSAULT—*continued.* *On Females and Boys.*—Assault or battery upon any male child whose age shall not, in the opinion of the Justices, exceed 14, or upon any female, upon complaint of the party aggrieved or otherwise, if the offence be of such an aggravated nature that it cannot, in the opinion of the Justices, be sufficiently punished under above section (42) as to common assaults. (a)	24 & 25 Vic. c. 100, s. 43. (25 & 26 Vic. c. 50, ss. 2, 3.)	Imprisonment not exceeding 6 months, with or without H. L.; or to pay a fine not exceeding (together with costs) £20; and in default, &c., imprisonment not exceeding 6 months, unless amount sooner paid: and, if Justices think fit, be bound to the peace and good behaviour for any time not exceeding 6 months from expiration of such sentence. 1 J.
With Intent to Prevent Sale of Grain, &c.—Whoever shall beat, or use any violence or threat of violence to any person with intent to deter or hinder him from buying, selling, or otherwise disposing of, or to compel him to buy, sell, or otherwise dispose of, any wheat or other grain, flour, meal, malt, or potatoes, in any market or other place, or shall beat, or use any such violence or threat to any person having the care or charge of any wheat, &c., &c., whilst on the way to or from any city, market, town, or other place, with intent to stop the conveyance of same, shall, on conviction, be liable to— See also "Conspiracy and Protection of Property" for *Intimidation.*	24 & 25 Vic. c. 100, s. 39. (25 & 26 Vic. c. 50, s. 2.)	Imprisonment with H. L., not exceeding 3 months. 1 J. Persons punished under this section shall not be punished under any other law for same offence.
On Seamen, &c.—Unlawfully and forcibly hindering any seaman, keelman, or caster from working; or using violence, with intent to hinder or prevent him from working at his trade or business.	24 & 25 Vic. c. 100, s. 40. (25 & 26 Vic. c. 50, s. 2.)	Imprisonment, with H. L., not exceeding 3 months. 1 J. Persons punished under this section shall not be punished under any other law for same offence.

(a) When Justices convict under this section (43), it should be made to so appear on the Order Book and in the committal.

Offence, or cause of Complaint.	Statute.	Extent of J[
ASSAULT—*continued.*		
On Peace Officers, &c.—Assaulting any peace officer in the due execution of his duty, or any person acting in aid of such officer ; or assaulting any person, with intent to resist or prevent the lawful apprehension or detainer of himself, or of any other person, for any offence.	24 & 25 Vic. c. 103, s. 38. (25 & 26 Vic. c. 50, s. 10.)	Imprisonmen' ing 2 mont without H. the discreti Justices) fi ceeding, to costs (if on in default, sonment by
(If the Justices consider the offence so trivial as not to require being dealt with by a superior tribunal.)		
(And for severer punishment for *assault* on Constables, provided under " Prevention of Crime Act," See titles " Crime " and " Constables," Summary Index.)	34 & 35 Vic. c. 112, s. 12.	
Certificate.—Where common assaults and assaults on females and boys (under ss. 42 & 43, 24 & 25 Vic. c. 100), are heard on the merits, and the Justices deem the offence not proved, or to be justifiable, or so trifling as not to merit punishment—	24 & 25 Vic. c. 100, s. 44.	Justices shal make out to defendan cate of the
Certificate of dismissal, or having been convicted, shall have paid penalty, or suffered imprisonment, —to be released from all further proceedings *civil or criminal,* for same cause. (*a*)	s. 45.	
Felonious Assaults ; or where Questions of Title, &c., arise.—Justices shall abstain from adjudicating summarily where assaults are accompanied with attempt to commit felony ; or where, from any other circumstance, it appears to them a fit subject to be tried by indict-	s. 46.	These cases returned f Quarter S Assizes.

(*a*) *Certificate of Dismissal.*—Under the former Summary Jurisd. dismissal by the Magistrates did not protect defendant, or deprive of his right to proceed *civilly.* Under the present Act (sec. 45) a the merits will have that effect.

Offence, or cause of Complaint.	Statute.	Extent of Jurisdiction.
ASSAULT—*continued*. ment; (*a*) or where questions of title arise; or as to bankruptcy, insolvency, or execution under process of any Court of Justice.		
No *certiorari*—nor shall warrant be quashed for want of form.	24 & 25 Vic. c. 100, s. 72.	
For not providing apprentices or servants with necessary food, &c., and felonious assaults on persons under 16, on certificate of two Justices, Guardians, or Overseers, to conduct prosecution.	s. 73.	
For indictable assaults, see "Offences against the Person," Indictable Offences Index. And for assaults on "Water Bailiffs," see Fisheries.		
ASSEMBLY—UNLAWFUL.		
Any person who shall take part in any riot or unlawful assembly—	50 & 51 Vic. c. 20, s. 2, sub-s. (3).	Imprisonment, with or without H. L., not exceeding 6 months. 2 Res. Mag.

(*a*) The Magistrates are to be the judges as to whether or not the offence is a fit subject to be tried by indictment; nor should they yield to the application of either party on the point. If the evidence be concluded, and they are satisfied that it may be dealt with summarily, they can and ought to do so. But where the accused appears on summons or is brought up by warrant charged with an assault attended with grievous bodily harm, or where from the nature of the charge it can only be dealt with by indictment, and during the inquiry it turns out to be of a character that it may be dealt with summarily, it would not be proper there and then to deal with it summarily, unless the defendant shall express himself to be ready with his defence and consent to the summary adjudication; for a defendant may come prepared to meet a summary charge where he may be advised not to disclose his evidence or defence for the present, if it be brought solely in an indictable form.

Common Assault.—Where Magistrates deal summarily with a *common assault*, as such, should any blow given or injury inflicted afterwards become so serious as to endanger life, they may take the depositions and return the offender for trial by indictment; for they did not, and could not, deal summarily with this offence.

Offence, or cause of Complaint.	Statute.	Extent of Jur
AUCTIONEERS: (a)		
Persons exercising the business of an auctioneer to take out an annual licence.	8 Vic. c. 15, s. 4.	
Sales in which auctioneer's licence not necessary specified in—	s. 5.	—
Auctioneer before sale commences shall suspend or affix ticket or board containing his full Christian and surname and place of residence. For default—	s. 7.	Excise penalty
At time of sale, on demand of officer of excise, customs, stamps, and taxes, he shall produce licence, or shall deposit with such officer £10 in default.	s. 8.	May be ap and brought Justice; a1 convicted, m prisoned for ceeding 1 m Not to affect p for penalty without licer
BAIL:		
Indictable offences wherein bail is not allowed to be taken; and where the admitting to bail is in the discretion of the Justices; and where the accused is admitted to bail as of right. See also "Sureties to keep the Peace." For form of bail-bond, see "Appendix of Forms." And for estreating, see to the "Recognizance."	See Petty Sessions Act, 14 & 15 Vic. c. 93, s. 16. Appendix.	It will be see Justices have to admit to sons charged son or of fe the 11 & 12 In the other cified in the is in their and in any of indictabi meanour, th as of right, i to bail. The is set out in t dix; and see a Indictable Off follows the Jurisdiction :

(a) *Fees.*—In sales of Distress made under the 9 & 10 Vic. c. 111, by to said Act, 1s. in the pound to cover all expenses of sale, commission, a To this extent the person distrained is bound to pay; but he is not to to pay more, either *directly* or *indirectly;* and he does pay it *indi* goods are sold on the terms that the purchaser is to pay auctioneer's fees. and that 5 per cent. is also deducted from the proceeds of the sale. See

(b) The Justices may require *one* or *more* sureties. It is the duty of to inquire into and ascertain the solvency of the persons tendered a:

Offence, or cause of Complaint.	Statute.	Extent of Jurisdiction.
BAILIFF : (Appointed under Civil Bill Act, 27 & 28 Vic. c. 99). Extorting, to be guilty of misdemeanour. See title, "Sheriff."	s. 18.	Fine or Imprisonment.
BAKER : See "Bread and Flour."		
BAKEHOUSE, see "Public Health," and "Factories."	26 & 27 Vic. c. 40, s. 3.	Penalty not exceeding £2 ; in default, &c., imprisonment not exceeding 1 month. 1 J.
BASTARDY : See "Poor Law."		
BATHING (*in public*) : See "Towns Improvement Act," which makes provision for preventing indecent exposure by bathers. Also, "Police Clauses Act." And for offences against public decency, see "Indecent Exposure."	17 & 18 Vic. c. 103, s. 77. 10 & 11 Vic. c. 88, s. 28.	
BEAST : See "Nuisance on Roads," &c.		
BEER-HOUSES : See "Licensing Acts."		
BEGGING : Every person wandering abroad and begging, or placing himself in any public place, street, highway, court, or passage to beg or gather alms, or causing or procuring any child so to do— The case may be heard out of Petty Sessions. See also "Vagrancy."	10 & 11 Vic. c. 84, s. 3. 14 & 15 Vic. c. 93, ss. 8, 22.	Shall, if the Justice think fit, be committed to gaol for any time not exceeding 1 month, at H. L. 1 J.

having agreed to admit to bail, they ought not to dissuade persons from becoming sureties.—*R.* v. *Saunders* (2 *Cox, c.* 249). Although it is stated that a married woman, or a minor, cannot be bound, but that the recognizance may be entered into by their sureties alone, the Justice will do well not to dispense with their signing the recognizance. The sureties should qualify in double the amount. For form of oath, see the 57 Geo. iii. c. 56; but it will be found printed on the form of recognizance in general *use.*

Offence, or cause of Complaint.	Statute.	Extent of Juris
BETTING ACTS: See "Gaming Houses."		
BILLET: See title "Army Act."		
BIRD: Stealing. See "Larceny." Injury. See "Malicious Injuries," "Wild Birds," &c.		
BLASPHEMING (*in public streets*): See "Police Clauses Act," for offence of "using *profane* or *obscene* language in any public street." .For offence of profane cursing, &c., in presence of a Justice, see "Swearing."	10 & 11 Vic. c. 89, s. 28.	Penalty not ￡ 40*s.*, or may prisoned for ceeding 14 day (But the Justic first see if this force in his di
BOAT: Taking, using, or employing any cot, barge, boat, or vessel, without owner's permission. See "Fisheries."	5 & 6 Vic. c. 106, s. 72. (36 & 37 Vic. c. 82.)	Penalty not ￡2; in defa imprisonment ceeding 1 mon
BOILER EXPLOSION ACT, 1882: Notice of boiler explosion to be sent to Board of Trade within 24 hours; in default— Board of Trade may direct inquiry.	45 & 46 Vic. c. 22.	Penalty not exce
BONFIRES: Making, or assisting in making, bonfires, or any other kind of fire upon any public road, or within 60 feet of the centre thereof. Making bonfires in streets, see "Towns Improvement Act." And under "Police Clauses Act." For offence of throwing Fireworks on streets, &c., see "Gunpowder."	14 & 15 Vic. c. 92, s. 10. (36 & 37 Vic. c. 82.) 17 & 18 Vic. c. 103, s. 72. 10 & 11 Vic. c. 89, s. 28.	Fine not exceed in default, &c sonment not 7 days. The Justice will of these Acts i in his district.
BOOKS: For provisions of the "Copyright Amendment Act," and penalties incurred by publishers for neglecting to deliver copies at British Museum and specified public libraries, see—	5 6 Vic. c. 45.	

Offence, or cause of Complaint.	Statute.	Extent of Jurisdiction.
BOOTHS AND TENTS: See "Tents."		
BOUNDARIES OF LAND: High Constable of each barony and half-barony, within 10 days after being required by surveyor, shall deliver to surveyor lists of all townlands, &c., and collectors of cess, &c., within the barony, in default—	6 Geo. iv. c. 99, s. 9.	Penalty, £10, by distress; in default, &c., imprisonment by scales. 2 J.
Removing or altering situation of boundary-stone, post, or mark set up for the purposes of this Act; or wilfully defacing, breaking, or destroying same.	s. 12.	Penalty not exceeding £10, and not less than £2, by distress; in default, &c., imprisonment by scales. 2 J.
Wilfully obstructing surveyer in execution of his duty, in ascertaining and marking out boundaries under Act; assaulting or otherwise resisting him, obstructing, or assaulting collector, or any workman, &c., acting in aid of surveyor.	s. 13.	Penalty not exceeding £10; and not less than £2, by distress; in default, &c., imprisonment by scales. 2 J.
And like under, ...	6 & 7 W. iv. c. 84, s. 55.	
BOWL-PLAYING (*on roads*): Playing at any game on road or street to the danger of passengers.	14 & 15 Vic. c. 92, s. 10. (36 & 37 Vic. c. 82.)	Penalty not exceeding 10*s.*; in default, &c., imprisonment not exceeding 7 days. 1 J.
"BOYCOTTING": (*a*) See "Conspiracy and Protection of Property"—Sum. Index, and see also "Assault, &c., with intent to prevent sale of Grain," &c., title "Assaults"—Sum. Index.		

(*a*) "*Boycotting*."—This term, now employed as a synonyme to express by a word an act of intimidation, coercion, or conspiracy of some unlawful kind, took its name from a *Captain Boycott*, a landlord and land-agent in the West of Ireland, against whom a species of social interdict issued in 1880. Where crimes or acts of open violence are not committed the offences would generally partake of the nature of those referred to in the Acts above quoted, 38 & 39 Vic. c. 86, s. 17; 24 & 25 Vic. c. 100, s. 39, and other offences against the Peace by threats of injury to persons or property.

Offence, or cause of Complaint.	Statute	Extent of Ju
BREACH (*Sudden*) **IN ROADS, BRIDGES,** &c. See "Roads."		
BREAD AND FLOUR : (*a*) Selling bread in any other manner than by weight (except French or fancy bread).	1 & 2 Vic. c. 28, s. 4.	Penalty not 40*s.* ; in de imprisonmen ceeding 1 m or without F
Using any other weight than avoirdupois weight, of 16 ounces to the pound.	s. 5.	Penalty not 40*s.*, nor less in default, sonment by or without F
Bakers or sellers of bread shall cause to be fixed in some conspicuous part of shop, on or near the counter, a beam and scales with proper weights, &c., and shall weigh bread if required ; for omitting to do so, or having or using any false or incorrect weights, or refusing to weigh—	s. 6.	Penalty not £5 ; in det imprisonmen not exceedin with or with
Adulterating bread, or using any mixture or ingredient whatsoever in the making other than and except as stated in said Act—	ss. 2 & 7.	Penalty not £5, nor less in default, prisonment with or with and may fender's nam lished in nev

(*a*) *Bread, Weighing, &c.*—A baker was in the habit of weighing o 2lb., 4lb., and 8lb. loaves before putting them into the oven, allowi shrinking of a 4lb. loaf, which is the understood weight of a "quarter he did not weigh the loaves afterwards unless required by the custom tomer bought a "quartern" loaf, and the current price of a 4lb. loaf w paid ; he did not require to have the loaf weighed, and it never was we was baked ; it turned out 2 ozs. 9 drachms short of 4lbs. ; held, that tl rightly convicted. (*Jones* v. *Huxtable*, *L. R.*, 2 *Q. B.*, 460 ; 8 *B. & L. T. N. S.*, 381 ; 36 *L. I. M. C.*, 122 ; 31 *J. P.*, 534 ; and see *Deggan*, 16 *L. T. N. S.*, 492 ; 31 *J. P.*, 807 ; and *Milton* v. *Troke*, 20 563 ; 33 *J. P.*, 821.)

A baker was in the habit of selling loaves of bread at 6*d.*, varyin of the loaf with the price of corn, when he proposed to sell a 3¼lb. custom was to put into the oven 4 lbs. of dough, but the loaf was 'er baking. Having sold at 6*d.* each 6 loaves which varied in w

Offence, or cause of Complaint.	Statute.	Extent of Jurisdiction.
BREAD AND FLOUR—*continued.* Adulterating corn, meal, flour, in grinding, &c., or putting therein any ingredient or mixture, not being the genuine produce of the corn or grain so ground; or selling flour of one sort as flour of another sort, or not equal to sample; or practising any deceit or fraud whereby it may be increased in weight.	1 & 2 Vic. c. 28, s. 8.	Shall forfeit the article, and also a penalty not exceeding £10, nor less than 40*s.*; in default, &c., imprisonment, with or without H. L., by scales. 1 J.
Similar offence under (*a*), . .	14 & 15 Vic. c. 92, s. 7.	Forfeiture of article, and penalty not exceeding 40*s.*; or imprisonment not exceeding 1 month. 1 J.
If ingredients for adulteration of meal or bread are found in any premises of millers, factors, &c. (And for adulterating Seeds, see title "Adulteration.")	1 & 2 Vic. c. 28, s. 11.	Penalty not exceeding £10, nor less than 40*s.*; second offence, £5; every subsequent offence, £10; in default, &c., imprisonment with or without H. L., not exceeding 4 months (by scale); and may order offender's name to be published. 1 J.
Wilfully obstructing search authorized to be made under Act, or the seizure of ingredients for adulteration, &c.	s. 12.	Penalty not exceeding £10; in default, &c., imprisonment by scale, with or without H. L. 1 J.
Act provides remedies by masters, where offences are occasioned by wilful default of journeymen and servants.		

but one weighed over 3½ lbs., he was convicted of selling bread otherwise than by weight, and the conviction was upheld. (*Hill* v. *Browning, L. R. 5 Q. B.,* 453; 22 *L. T. N. S.,* 584; 34 *J. P.* 774.) Though the baker is not bound to weigh in the presence of the customer, unless requested to do so, he is bound to weigh at some time or other; and where a customer asked for a 4lb. loaf, which was found to be substantially deficient in weight; held, that it must be taken as against the baker that he had never weighed it. The conviction was upheld. (*R.* v. *Kennett*; *R.* v. *Saunders, L. R.* 4 *Q. B.,* 565; 10 *B. & S.,* 545; 20 *L. T. N. S.,* 656; 33 *J. P.* 824.) The foregoing decisions in the analogous English Bread Act, 6 & 7 Wm. iv. c. 37, will be found in "Whiteley's Weights and Measures."

(*a*) The offence is the same in both Statutes, the penalties differ, and under the latter the Justice may imprison *without imposing pecuniary* penalty.

Offence, or cause of Complaint.	Statute.	Extent of Juris
BREAD AND FLOUR—*continued.* Against baking on Sundays, . . Opposing persons employed in due execution of Act. See also "Public Health." "Adulteration."	1 & 2 Vic. c. 28, s. 13. s. 15. (36 & 37 Vic. c. 82.)	Penalty not e £5; in defaɪ imprisonment ceeding 2 monʈ or without H.
BRICKS: Clay used in making bricks for public sale must be dug and turned before November preceding the burning, the upper soil to be stripped, and proper and natural brick earth to be used. Clay to be tempered again after November and before February, and picked clear of stones. Clay must be free of limewash ; and bricks shall not be moulded after 25th November, and before 25th March. Bricks shall not be less than 9½ inches long, 4½ inches broad, and 2¼ inches thick ; and clay shall not be formed or moulded unless it be of such a consistence that it will stick together if taken up with a common pitchfork of two prongs or tangs ; and bricks shall not be moulded or burned at any other time than between 1st March and 1st November, unless for the private use of the maker, and not for public sale ; and if made contrary to Act—	3 Geo. ii. c. 14, ss. 11, 12, 13. (Ir.)	Penalty 20s. ɟ sand, and so iɪ tion, for a grea quantity, by in default, &c.,ː ment by scale.
BRIDEWELL— See "Gaols."		
BRIDGES: Any two Justices at Petty Sessions may order a sum not exceeding £20 for repairing sudden damages to bridges.	6 & 7 W. iv. c. 116, s. 49.	
For power of Justices respecting crossings and bridges over Railways see "Railway Clauses Consolidation Act, 1845." *Sudden Breach in,* see "Roads."	8 Vic. c. 20.	

Offence, or cause of Complaint.	Statute.	Extent of Jurisdiction.
BRITISH SEAMEN: See title "Merchant Shipping Act."		
BROTHELS: (Criminal Law Amendment Act, 1885).	48 & 49 Vic. c. 69.	
Suppression of Brothels by Summary Proceedings.—Any person who (1) keeps, or manages, or acts, or assists in the management of a brothel, or (2) being the tenant, lessee, or occupier, of any premises, knowingly permits such premises, or any part thereof, to be used as a brothel, or for the purposes of habitual prostitution, or (3) being the lessor or landlord of any premises, or the agent of such lessor or landlord, lets the same or any part thereof with the knowledge that such premises, or some part thereof are, or is to be, used as a brothel, or is wilfully a party to the continued use of such premises, or any part thereof, as a brothel— *Appeal.* — Defendant may appeal from any summary conviction under this section to general Quarter Sessions. *In Dublin.*—Proceedings to be under Acts regulating the powers and duties of Justices of the Peace of such district, or of the Police of such district :—	s. 13.	Shall, on summary conviction, be liable to a penalty not exceeding £20, or in the discretion of the Court to imprisonment for any term not exceeding 3 months, with or without H. L. *Second, or subsequent conviction.*—Penalty not exceeding £40, or in the discretion of the Court, to imprisonment for any term not exceeding 4 months, with or without H.L. In case of *third or subsequent conviction* may, in addition, be required by the Court to enter into recognizance, with or without sureties, as to the Court seems meet, to be of good behaviour for any period not exceeding 12 months, in default may be imprisoned for any period not exceeding 3 months, in addition to any such term of imprisonment as aforesaid.　　1 J.

Brothels.—It will be seen that the above Act gives summary and extensive power to Justices in Petty Sessions to suppress this nuisance, by dealing with all who take part in the infamous trade, and those who let or permit their houses, &c., to be used for the purpose.

The summary conviction may be before *one Justice*. See 37 & 38 Vic. c. 72, s. 5, and set out on front page of this work.

Offence, or cause of Complaint.	Statute.	Extent of Jurisd
BORTHELS—*continued.* *Elsewhere in Ireland.*—The Petty Sessions J. Act, 1851, and the Acts amending the same.	48 & 49 Vic. c. 69, s. 14.	
Saving.—Not to exempt offender from proceedings at Common Law, or under other Act of Parliament, so that he be not punished twice for same offence.	s. 16.	
Competent Witnesses.—*Persons charged* with offence under this Act, *and the husband or wife* of the person charged shall be competent (but not compellable) witnesses.		
BUILDING: Houses within thirty feet of centre of public road.	14 & 15 Vic. c. 92, s. 9.	Penalty not e£10, and 10s. in default, &c. sonment accor scale.
BURNING LAND: (a) Where affidavit is made before J. P. by landlord, &c., or person acting on his behalf, that there exists probable and just grounds to suspect that any tenant, servant, caretaker, or other person, who has detained possession from any such tenant, &c., is about to *burn*, &c., the soil, surface, or subsoil of the land, or that he is in the act of doing such—	23 & 24 Vic. c. 154, s. 35.	Justice to issue in form in Sch to the Act, to tinue the was the matter of formation be into at next Pe sions.
Punishment for disobedience of precept. See title "Landlord and Tenant."	s. 36.	Imprisonment r ceeding 1 mont ceedings as ir Sessions.

(a) *By sec.* 30.—Tenants holding under instruments conferring any int than a perpetual estate or interest are liable to a penalty not exceeding acre, and so in proportion, for burning or permitting to be burned the so face of the land, recoverable by Civil Bill.

All former Acts, giving Justices the Summary power to enforce pena burning land, are by the above Act repealed.

ce, or cause of Complaint.	Statute.	Extent of Jurisdiction.
ITING: ᵒ Animals Act, . . ielty to Animals,"	12 & 13 Vic. c. 92, s. 3.	Penalty not exceeding £5; in default, &c., imprisonment not exceeding 2 months. 1 J.
irchyard."		
brands, packing, &c.; see hts and Measures."		
TTERS: grancy where offenders are ith as Rogues and Vaga- '		
:ERS: s, servants, &c., refusing to possession of premises on L idlord and Tenant."		
D CARTS: iver."		
ermitting children under 13 f age to drive.	s. 13. (36 & 37 Vic. c. 82.)	Penalty not exceeding 10s. (against owner); in default, &c., imprisonment not exceeding 7 days. 1 J.
as to Nuisances, Towns 'ement Act, Appendix.)		
offences on "Roads, &c.," ᵉᵃ "Driver," "Nuisance on &c.," and the "Towns Im- ient Act," sec. 17, for of- in streets of towns where it 'e, and also "Police Clauses 10 & 11 Vic. c. 89, s. 28.		

Offence, or cause of Complaint.	Statute.	Extent of Jurisdict
CASE:— Stated for opinion of Superior Court.	20 & 21 Vic. c. 43, ss. 2, 4.	
In cases of summary adjudication either party to the proceeding, if dissatisfied with the determination as being erroneous in point of law, may apply as therein, to have a case stated for opinion of Superior Court. See sec. (a)	—	The Justice or J before whom cas shall, unless of c that the applica merely frivolous, a case according
Before case is stated, the appellant shall enter into recognizance, serve notice, and pay fees, as set forth in—	s. 2.	—
Where Justices refuse, Court of Queen's Bench may, by rule, order a case to be stated.	s. 5.	
Persons appealing under this Act, precluded from appealing to Quarter Sessions.	s. 14.	

(a) Section 2.—" After the hearing and determination by a Justice or Jur the Peace of any information or complaint which he or they have power to mine in a summary way, by any law now in force or hereafter to be made party to the proceeding before the said Justice or Justices may, if dissatisfi the said determination as being erroneous in point of law, apply in writing three days after the same to the said Justice or Justices, to state and sign setting forth the facts and the ground of such determination for the opinion of one of the Superior Courts of Law, to be named by the party applyin such party, hereinafter called 'the appellant,' shall, within three day receiving such case, transmit the same to the Court named in his applicati giving notice in writing of such appeal, with a copy of the case, so sta signed, to the other party to the proceeding in which the determination was hereinafter called the 'respondent.'"

In *Stanhope, Appellant, Thorsby ; Respondent, Common Pleas, England, Term*, 1866, it was decided that the recognizance required to be given appellant on a case stated by Justices under 20 & 21 Vic. c. 43, s. 3, need given within the three days mentioned in sec. 2. It is enough if this i before the case is given out by the Justices.

Form of Case.—The form or statement of the case may be simple ; bu are matters to be strictly complied with, so as that it shall come properly the cognizance of the Superior Court. It should be *headed* with the Sessions Court from which it comes ; the title "appellant" and "respon⟨ " Case stated for the opinion of the Court of —— (*as named by the applic⟨ the instance and request of ——, pursuant to the 20 & 21 Vic. c. 43, entitl of Act.*" Set out the copy of summons and information, if any, wherel brought before the Petty Sessions ; the evidence as fully as can be collect⟨ any legal objections raised ; the order of the Justices fully, and the Act

Offence, or cause of Complaint.	Statute.	Extent of Jurisdiction.
CATTLE DISEASES ACTS:	11 & 12 Vic. c. 107.	—
Extended and continued by, . .	16 & 17 Vic. c. 62.	
Further amended by, . . .	29 Vic. c. 4.	—
Further amended by, . . .	33 & 34 Vic. c. 36.	—
Further amended by, . . .	37 & 38 Vic. c. 6.	
Power to Lord Lieutenant in Council to make rules, &c., for all the purposes mentioned in Acts.	29 Vic. c. 4, s. 2. 33 & 34 Vic. c. 36, s. 2.	—
Provides for cleansing of steamboats, railway companies providing water and food; landing animals in contravention of Orders.	33 & 34 Vic. c. 36.	
Sec. 7 enumerates seven classes of offences for which offender is liable, on conviction, to punishment.	s. 7.	.

which made; copy of notice, stating when it was served. State also that the bond has been duly entered into: indeed it may be proper to copy the bond—the Court above may require to see that the Statute is strictly complied with. The case should be dated and signed, and the person delivering it to the appellant ought to indorse on it the date of doing so. The Court of Exchequer has directed that "special cases" under the 20 & 21 Vic. c. 43, should be prepared on "Judicature" paper, which is prescribed by order of the Court. See Circular, December 16, 1868.

Notice may be to following effect:—

(Title of Case, and Petty Sessions Court.)

GENTLEMEN,

Take notice that I, the undersigned (the complainant or defendant, as case may be), in this case being dissatisfied with your determination of the said (Information or Complaint) as being erroneous in point of Law, do hereby call upon and require you, ... pursuant to the provisions of the 20 & 21 Vic. c. 43, entitled "An Act to improve the Administration of the law so far as respects summary proceedings before Justices of the Peace," to state and sign a case setting forth the facts and the grounds of such determination, for the opinion thereon of Her Majesty's Court of Queen's Bench (or other Superior Court to be named,—Com. Pleas or Exchequer).

(Dated)
(Signed)

To

A. B., *C. D.*, the Justices who heard and determined such Complaint.

D

Offence, or cause of Complaint.	Statute.	Extent of Jurisdicti
CATTLE DISEASES ACT—*cont.* For contravening provisions of 29 Vic. c. 4, or any Order of Council made in pursuance thereof, or for contravening provisions of 33 & 34 Vic. c. 36, or Orders in Council made in pursuance thereof—	29 Vic. c. 4, s. 6. 33 & 34 Vic. c. 36, s. 8.	Penalty not exce £20 ; and where mitted with respe more than 4 ani not exceeding £5 may be imposed in of the £20 recove under P. S. Act. Or, for offences in of 33 & 24 Vic. may, in the disc of the Justice, be i soned for not exce 3 months, with or out H. L. See part of sec. 7.
Orders purporting to be signed by Clerk of Privy Council to be evidence.	s. 6.	—
Application of Penalties.—Not exceeding one-third to Informer, the rest to Her Majesty, in aid of the fund for purposes of Acts.	29 Vic. c. 4, s. 5. 33 & 34 Vic. c. 36, s. 9.	— —
CATTLE-WEIGHING : Person appointed by market authority to weigh cattle sold in market or fair ; refusing or neglecting to weigh when required, or to deliver ticket of true weight, or giving false ticket or account—	50 & 51 Vic. c. 27, s. 6.	Penalty not exce 40*s.*, nor less tha 6*d.* ; imprisonmer scale.
Persons knowingly acting or assisting in committing fraud as to weighing, &c. Act gives schedule of fees for weighing.	s. 7.	Penalty not exce £5 ; in default of ment, imprisonme scale.
CERTIFICATE : To be given by Justices when assault dismissed. Under Criminal Justice Act.	24 & 25 Vic. c. 100, s. 44. 18 & 19 Vic. c. 126.	—
Of refusal to state case for opinion of Superior Court.	20 & 21 Vic. c. 43, s. 3.	—

Offence, or cause of Complaint.	Statute.	Extent of Jurisdiction.
CERTIFICATE—*continued.* Of character to servant, when refused by master without sufficient cause. See title "Discharge."	2 Geo. i. c. 17, s. 4.	—
To publicans for renewal of licences.	17 & 18 Vic. c. 89, s. 11.	
Certificate of order made out of Petty Sessions, to be sent to the clerk by the Justices.	14 & 15 Vic. c. 93, s. 21.	
Certificate of any order made in Petty Sessions to be given to either party demanding it.	„	—
Certificate for occasional licence to sell spirits, &c., at athletic sports, &c. See Titles "Army Act" and "Militia," as to convictions thereunder.	25 Vic. c. 22, s. 13.	See "Tents."
CHARACTER TO SERVANT : See "Discharge."		
CHILDREN AND YOUNG PERSONS : "Summary Jurisdiction over Children (Ireland) Act, 1884." Where a *child* (age 7 to 12) is charged before a Court of Summary Jurisdiction with *any indictable offence other than homicide*, if the parent or guardian, when informed by the Court of his right to have the child	47 & 48 Vic. c. 19, s. 4.	May inflict the *same description of punishment* as if tried by indictment, that is— May imprison for not exceeding 1 month.

Sec. 4. "*Child.*"—In the opinion of the Court must be between 7 and 12 years, and of sufficient capacity to commit crime, and, under the circumstances in the section, may be dealt with summarily for any offence other than homicide. It is in the case of a *child*, the parent or guardian is to be addressed and consulted, if practicable, and the Court thinks fit, before the case is summarily dealt with.

A child under 12, and who has not been convicted of *felony* may, under sec. 13 of the Industrial Schools Act, be sent to an Industrial School, although charged with an offence punishable by imprisonment, if the Justices consider that the circumstances of the case render it desirable. See "Industrial School," sum. index.

The restricted punishment in sec. 6 is confined to a *child.*

Offence, or cause of Complaint.	Statute.	Extent of Jurisdi
CHILDREN AND YOUNG PER-SONS—*continued.* tried by a jury, does not object to the child being dealt with summarily, Court may deal summarily with the offence.		Where a fine is the amount shall ceed 40s. If a *male* child, in other punishmei be whipped wi more than 6 str a birch rod by stable, in pres Inspector, or ot ficer of Police o rank than a Co and also of pa guardian (if he to be present) child.
Charge to be reduced to writing, and parent or guardian to be asked, "Do you desire the child to be tried by a jury, and object to the case being dealt with summarily?" explaining if necessary what this means.	47 & 48 Vic. c. 19, s. 4.	By sec. 7, if Cou the offence proved) to be o fling nature, a punishment is dient, or any otl nominal puni
Where parent or guardian not present, Court in its discretion may remand and cause it to be notified to him in case he desires to be present.	,,	Court may, proceeding to tion, dismiss th mation, and if
Not to prejudice right of Court to send child to Reformatory or Industrial School.	,,	fit may order charged to pay not exceeding
In the opinion of the Court the child must be above the age of 7, and of sufficient capacity to commit crime.	,,	costs, or either or, upon convicti discharge him tionally on his
☞ On summary conviction of a *child* under this or any other Act, past or future, the imprisonment shall not exceed 1 month, nor a fine be larger than 40s.	s. 6.	security with or sureties to appea tence when call or to be of goo viour, and eithe
Convictions in the case of a child shall contain a statement as to the consent or otherwise of parent or guardian to child being tried summarily. Guardian includes person having charge or control of child.	s. 8.	out payment of and costs, or su the payment damages and c either of them, thinks reasonabl

Offence, or cause of Complaint.	Statute.	Extent of Jurisdiction.
CHILDREN AND YOUNG PERSONS—*continued.* *Young Persons* (12 to 16). Where a young person is charged before a Court of Summary Jurisdiction with any indictable offence specified in the schedule to this Act, the Court, if they think it expedient so to do, having regard to the character and antecedents of the person charged, the nature of the offence, and all the circumstances of the case, and if the young person charged, when informed by the Court of his right to be tried by a jury, consents to be dealt with summarily, the Court may deal summarily with the offence, and if found guilty— *Caution.* Charge to be reduced to writing, and the Court, on being satisfied that it is expedient to try the case, shall address to the young person a ques-	47 & 48 Vic. c. 19, s. 5.	In the discretion of the Court, either to pay a fine not exceeding £10, *or* to be imprisoned with or without hard labour for any term not exceeding 3 months; and if a male, and in the opinion of the Court under the age of 14, if the Court think it expedient, may either in substitution for or in addition to any other punishment under this Act, adjudge him to be as soon as practicable privately whipped with not more than 12 strokes of a birch rod in presence of an Inspector, or

Young Persons.—That is, of the age of 12 and under 16, can be dealt with under the conditions in the Act, as above, and if he consents, in a summary way, but only for the offences named in the *Schedule.*

The young person is himself to be addressed as to the charge being summarily dealt with. A young person convicted of an offence may be sent to a Reformatory; but to send a child to an Industrial School, or a young person to a Reformatory, two Justices must make the order; in Dublin one Justice can send child to an Industrial School.

Schedule of Indictable Offences which can be dealt with summarily under this Act, young persons consenting.—1. Simple Larceny. 2. Offences declared by any Act for the time being in force to be punishable as Simple Larceny. 3. Larceny from or stealing from the person. 4. Larceny as a clerk or servant. 5. Embezzlement by a clerk or servant. 6. Receiving stolen goods. 7. Aiding, abetting, counselling, or procuring the commission of any of the offences, Nos. 1, 2, 3, 4. 8. Attempting to commit any of said offences, Nos. 1, 2, 3, 4. Act shall also apply to—(1) young persons committing offences in relation to railways and railway carriages mentioned in secs. 32 & 33 of 24 & 25 Vic. c. 100, relating to " Offences against the Person." (2) to offences relating to railways mentioned in sec. 35 of 24 & 25 Vic. c. 97, "Malicious Injuries." (3) Indictable offences under Post-office Laws, or prosecuted by Postmaster-General; Post-office Laws having same meaning as in 7 Wm. iv., and 1 Vic. c. 36, and the Acts amending the same. And now offences under the Post-office Protection Act, 1884, shall be deemed to be indictable offences, and included in the above Schedule (see 47 & 48 Vic. c. 76, s. 12, sub-s. 4), and may be dealt with under the above Act as to children and young persons.

Offence, or cause of Complaint.	Statute.	Extent of Jurisdiction.
CHILDREN AND YOUNG PER-SONS—*continued*. tion to the following effect :—"Do you desire to be tried by a jury, or do you consent to the case being dealt with summarily ?"—with a statement, if the Court think such necessary, of the meaning of being tried summarily, and of the Assizes or Sessions at which he will be tried by a jury. Not to prejudice the right of a Court to send a young person to a Reformatory or Industrial School. *Appeal.*—In Dublin under enactments there in force. Elsewhere under P. Sessions (Ir.) Act, 1851, extended to cases under this Act. Convictions in the case of a *young person* shall contain a statement of his consent or otherwise to be tried summarily. Guardian includes person having charge or control of child or young person.	47 & 48 Vic. c. 19, s. 5. s. 8.	other Officer of Police of higher rank than a Constable, and in presence, if he desires to be present, of parent or guardian. 1 J. If Court deem the offence, though proved, to be of a trifling nature, and that punishment is inexpedient, or any other than nominal punishment, Court may, without proceeding to a conviction, deal with a *young person* precisely as in the case of a *child*, under sec. 7, for which see above.
Children liable to maintain parents (according to ability), and if parents relieved by Union—	1 & 2 Vic. c. 56, s. 57.	Justices may make order for payment of relief given ; recoverable as a penalty. 2 J.
Husband wilfully neglecting to maintain wife or children, so as they shall become destitute, and receive relief in or out of any workhouse.	10 & 11 Vic. c. 84, s. 2.	Imprisonment not exceeding 3 months' H. L.
Aggravated assault on male child not more than 14 years, where the Justice is of opinion that the punishment prescribed for "common assault" is not adequate. See "Assault."	24 & 25 Vic. c. 100, s. 43. (25 & 26 Vic. c. 50, s. 23. 36 & 37 Vic. c. 82.)	Imprisonment not exceeding 6 months, or fine not exceeding (with costs) £20 ; and may be bound to the peace for 6 months from expiration of sentence. 1 J.

Sec. 8. *Appeal.*—The appeal here is given only in such cases as from the amount of penalty, &c., it is given under Petty Sessions Act, and in Dublin the Special Act.

Sec. 8. (*b*) This statement as to consent, &c., should be set out on the P. Sessions "Order Book"; and it would be desirable to do so in any warrant, committal, or proceeding founded on the order or conviction.

Offence, or cause of Complaint.	Statute.	Extent of Jurisdiction.
CHILDREN AND YOUNG PER-SONS—*continued.* Exposing children under two years, whereby life endangered.	24 & 25 Vic. c. 100, s. 56.	Indictable misdemeanour.
Stealing or enticing away child under 14, with intent to deprive parent or guardian of the possession.	—	Felony.
Illegitimate children under 14 supported in workhouse, or out of poor-rates.	26 Vic. c. 21, ss. 2, 3.	Guardians may recover cost from putative father by civil-bill process. Mother to make oath before a J. P. in Petty Sessions.
Children in exhibitions, &c.—Any person who shall cause any child under 14 to take part in public exhibition or performance, whereby, in opinion of Court, life or limb endangered, and the parent or guardian or person having custody of the child who shall aid or abet in same—	42 & 43 Vic. c. 34, s. 3.	Penalty not exceeding £10; in default, &c., imprisonment by scale. 2 J. In Dublin according to Local Acts.
Where exhibition or performance is in its nature dangerous and that bodily harm occurs to child. See also " Chimney Sweeps," " Poor Law," " Factories," and " Workshops," " Industrial Schools," " Reformatories." And for offences on girls, see " Criminal Law Amendment Act, 1885." Indictable Offence Index. See also " Prevention of Cruelty to Children," Summary Index.	,,	Employer liable to be indicted as for assault, and Court may award compensation on behalf of child, not exceeding £20.
CHIMNEY SWEEPS: Any person who shall compel or knowingly allow any child under age of 21 years to ascend or descend a chimney, or enter a flue, to sweep or clean same, or extinguish a fire therein—	3 & 4 Vic. c. 85, s. 2 (27 & 28 Vic. c. 37, ss. 9 & 11).	Penalty not exceeding £10; in default, &c., imprisonment not exceeding 2 months; or in lieu of penalty, may be imprisoned with or

Offence, or cause of Complaint.	Statute.	Extent of Jurisdictio
CHIMNEY SWEEPS—*continued.* Indentures on, if under the age of 16 years, null and void. Section 6 regulates the construction of chimneys.		without H.L., not ceeding 6 months.
Chimney Sweepers Act, 1864.—This Act to be construed with the preceding one of 1840. (a)		
Chimney Sweeper not to employ a child under 10 to do or assist in doing any work or thing in or about the trade or business of a chimney sweeper elsewhere than in his own house, &c.	27 & 28 Vic. c. 37, s. 6.	Penalty not excee £10; in default, imprisonment not ceeding 2 months.
Chimney Sweeper entering house or building for purpose of sweeping, &c., or for extinguishing fire therein, who causes or knowingly allows a person under 16 in his employment or under his control to enter before, with, or after him therein, or to be therein while chimney sweeper continues therein for purposes aforesaid.	s. 7.	Like.
Police Clauses Act, 10 & 11 Vic., c. 89, ss. 30 and 31, provides punishment for the wilfully or accidentally setting fire to chimneys.	—	The Justice will a the Act be in for his district.

(a) These Acts have been so interwoven as now to become a little intricate latter (sec. 4) provides that the two shall be construed together as one A the expression "this Act" in the former shall include the latter. The latt imposes two penalties for offences against ss. 6 & 7, but does not say what i the imprisonment in default of payment. It abolishes the minimum pen £5, and in lieu of any penalty enables the Justices to give up to 6 montl prisonment for contravening section 2 of the first Act. Now, reading tl Acts as they stand as one Act, it is considered that where the Justices re the pecuniary penalty in sec. 2 of the former Act, the imprisonment f penalty is not to exceed 2 *months*, and that is also to be the maximum imp ment to be proportioned to ss. 6 & 7 of latter Act. The offence in sec. 2 Act appears to be the most aggravated, and it would seem that the Justi empowered, if they see fit, to put aside the pecuniary penalty, and impriso 6 months, and as low as they please, but that, having named the pecuniary p they cannot exceed 2 months. Secs. 2 and 11 of the 27 & 28 Vic. c. 37 r by Statute Law Revision Act, 38 & 39 Vic. c. 66.

Offence, or cause of Complaint.	Statute.	Extent of Jurisdiction.
CHIMNEY SWEEPS—_continued._ _Chimney Sweepers Act_, 1875 (a), .	38 & 49 Vic. c. 70.	
Certificates.—Sub-Inspector in each police district (Commissioner in Dublin) to issue certificates to chimney sweeps, authorizing them to carry on their business in the district.	s. 5.	
Chimney sweep shall also take out certificate for journeymen, apprentice, &c.	s. 6.	—
Application for form of application, &c.	s. 7.	
Certificate of partners, . . .	s. 8.	
Journeyman and assistant exempted.	s. 9.	
Fee on certificate, 2s. 6d., to be applied as penalties under the Act.	s. 10.	—
Certificate to hold for one year, and Lord Lieutenant may direct that they expire yearly on the same day.	ss. 12, 22.	—
Indorsing certificates in another district, and register of certificates, &c.	ss. 13, 14.	

(a) This Chimney Sweepers Act of 1875, and which comes into force on 1st January, 1876, is similar in its provisions to that relating to peddlers. It is the object of both Acts to bring under supervision these itinerant traders and tramps or hire, whether they go about from place to place for the purpose of vending their wares or their skilled labour. The control over their certificates operates as kind of guarantee for their conduct, and the facilities thereby given for their recovery is about equal to what would arise from their having known and fixed habitations. Their trading, too, must be _bona fide_, not mere pretext, and they will not be exempt from the Acts relating to idle or disorderly persons, or to rogues and vagabonds, by reason _only of their having certificates._

Offence, or cause of Complaint.	Statute.	Extent of Jurisdiction.
CHIMNEY SWEEPS—*continued.* *Offences.*—Every person carrying on such trade or business of chimney sweeper, as in Act specified, without having such certificate, on conviction—	38 & 39 Vic. c. 70, s. 15.	First offence, penalty not exceeding 10s.; in default of payment imprisonment not exceeding 1 week. 1 J. For every subsequent offence, penalty not exceeding 20s.; in default of payment imprisonment not exceeding 14 days. 1 J.
Name and Address.—Every person carrying on the business of a chimney sweeper, as aforesaid, shall, when required by any person for whom he acts or offers to act as chimney sweeper, or by any Justice, constable, or peace officer, give his name and address, and for failing to do so, or giving false one, &c.—	s. 16.	Penalty not exceeding 10s.; in default of payment imprisonment not exceeding 1 week. 1 J.
Producing Certificate.—Where such person carries on the business of a chimney sweeper, as aforesaid, he shall, on demand, produce and show his certificate (if any) to any person for whom he acts or offers to act as a chimney sweeper, and to any Justice, or constable, or peace officer, and allow it to be read and copied by the person to whom it is produced; if he fails to do so, he shall be guilty of an offence against Act, and on conviction—	s. 17.	First offence, penalty not exceeding 10s.; in default of payment imprisonment not exceeding 7 days. Every subsequent offence, penalty not exceeding 20s.; in default of payment imprisonment not exceeding 14 days. 1 J.
Lending Certificate, &c.—It shall not be lawful to lend or transfer certificate, or to borrow, accept, or use such; for contravention—	s. 18.	Penalty not exceeding 20s.; in default of payment imprisonment not exceeding 14 days. 1 J.
False Representations— (1) If any person makes, procures to be made, or aids in making false statement, knowingly, in any application for certificate— (2) Fabricates, counterfeits, or alters, or procures to be, &c., or aids, &c., in so doing, knowingly—	s. 19.	First offence, penalty not exceeding 40s.: in default of payment imprisonment not exceeding 1 month. Every subsequent offence to the like penalty, with

Offence, or cause of Complaint.	Statute.	Extent of Jurisdiction.
CHIMNEY SWEEPS—*continued.* Every person so offending shall, on conviction—	38 & 39 Vic. c. 70, s. 19.	or without imprisonment, for a term not exceeding 6 months, with or without H. L., or to such imprisonment alone, with or without H. L. 1 J.
If person having certificate is convicted of offence against Chimney Sweepers and Regulation Acts, 1840 and 1864, or either of them, Court may deprive him of certificate for residue of current year.		
Person not having certificate, so convicted, may be disqualified to hold certificate for any time not exceeding one year; but such order to be suspended pending appeal under the Chimney Sweepers Regulation Act, 1840, and to be in discretion of Court of Appeal, if conviction be confirmed.	s. 20.	
Duty of police to enforce the Chimney Sweepers Acts, &c., 1840, 1864, without prejudice to the right of others so to do.	s. 21.	
Penalties to be applied according to Fines (Ireland) Act, 1851, or any Act amending the same.	s. 23.	—
Saving.—Certificate under this Act shall not exempt from the provisions of Acts relating to idle or disorderly persons, or to rogues and vagabonds.		
Saving as to local Acts and local authorities, and not to abridge or take away powers under any general or local Act.	s. 25.	
Proceedings.—In Dublin under local Acts; elsewhere, under Petty Sessions (Ireland) Act, 1851, and any Acts amending the same,	Sch., part 2.	—

Offence, or cause of Complaint.	Statute.	Extent of Jurisdic
CHURCH: *Disturbance in Churches, Church-yards, &c.*—Any person guilty of riotous, violent, or indecent behaviour in any church or chapel of any religious denomination, whether during the celebration of Divine Service or at any other time, or in any church-yard or burial-ground, or who shall molest, let, disturb, vex, or trouble, or by any other unlawful means disquiet, or misuse any preacher duly authorized to preach therein, or any clergyman in Holy Orders, ministering or celebrating any sacrament or Divine Service, rite, or office in any cathedral, church, or chapel, or in any church-yard or burial-ground, liable on conviction for each offence—	23 & 24 Vic. c. 32, s. 2.	Penalty not exc £5; or imprisonm exceeding 2 mont
Offenders may be immediately apprehended by constable or church-warden, and taken before a Justice to be dealt with according to law. (a) *Appeal.*—Persons convicted may appeal to next Quarter Sessions (to be held next after 12 days).	s. 3.	
CHURCH-YARD: Allowing animals to graze in.	19 & 20 Vic. c. 98, s. 13.	Fine not exceedir nor less than 1s., levied as trespa distress.
Burying in private grave without consent of relative. (See also Public Health Act, 1878, sec. 167, &c.)	s. 12.	Penalty not exc £10; in default imprisonment ne ceeding 3 months And may order ex tion and re-inter

(a) *Disturbing Worship.*—This statute gives Justices the power to su1 dispose of such offences as heretofore were subjects of indictment, causin vexation and delay. Such offences do not often take place in this co1 present, and, when they do, can be adequately dealt with in Petty Session

But it requires two Justices to dispose of the case, so that the Justic whom offender brought should merely take measures to secure his atten1 Petty Sessions, &c.

Offence, or cause of Complaint.	Statute.	Extent of Jurisdiction.
CHURCH-YARD—*continued.* Act relating to consecration of church-yards.	30 & 31 Vic. c. 133.	
Where burials of persons not belonging to United Church of England and Ireland take place in burial-ground of such church, priest, &c., of other denominations may perform service, giving twenty-four hours' previous notice.		
Lord Lieutenant in Council may exempt certain church-yards.		
CLERK OF PETTY SESSIONS: (a) Mode for appointing.	21 & 22 Vic. c.100,ss.6,7.	
Prescribed duties.	s. 8, and 14 & 15 Vic. c. 93, s. 5.	.

(a) *Election of Petty Sessions Clerk.*—The chairman at the election has no casting vote. Magistrates being father and son, though they may be prohibited sitting together in Petty Sessions, may yet both vote in the appointment of Clerk. Magistrate non-resident and not attending Petty Sessions, though having property in the district, may not vote. As to the number of attendances which qualifies a Justice to vote, the general rule is subject, however, to be modified where exceptional circumstances exist. A Magistrate cannot be considered as having been in the habit of attending the Petty Sessions Court who has not attended at least *four times* in each of the *three years* next preceding the election, if he has been so long in the Commission of the Peace. Where a Magistrate has been appointed within the three years, he must have put in proportionate attendance.

Petty Sessions Clerk.—Is directed by Lord Lieutenant not to interfere on behalf of candidates at elections ; but it seems he may exercise the franchise, by voting, if he thinks fit. When the office becomes vacant the Magistrate should inform the Registrar of Petty Sessions Clerks, Dublin Castle, when they will be made acquainted with the salary to be paid his successor (Circular, 11th April, 1868). Petty Sessions Clerks to be between ages of 21 and 40, and Lord Lieutenant will not sanction the appointment until the Clerk presents himself at the Registrar's Office, Dublin Castle, and satisfies the Registrar that he is qualified for the office. Practising barrister or attorney, or clerk of an attorney, of not less than 10 years' standing, or conducting clerk of an attorney of not less than 7 years' standing, will be eligible for the office, up to age of 50 years, and after appointment must discontinue practising (Circular, 20th November, 1869). Newspaper editor not to be eligible for the office (Lord Lieutenant's Order, 4th January, 1870). Clerk is required, on pain of dismissal, to cancel all stamps issued by him, by writing his

Offence, or cause of Complaint.	Statute.	Extent of Ju
CLERK OF PETTY SESSIONS— *continued.* Shall not practise as a barrister or attorney, clerk of attorney, clerk of union, collector of public tax, tavern-keeper, &c., or occupation which the Lord Lieutenant shall prohibit. (For circulars as to duties passing accounts, &c., see Appendix.) These circulars are preserved in each Petty Sessions Court.	21 & 22 Vic. c. 100, s. 8.	Exception as holding app the passing
Amending scale of salaries. All fees payable to clerks under any Act to be taken by stamps. Act in other respects amends the law regulating the office of Clerk of Petty Sessions, and law relating to fines.	41 & 42 Vic. c. 69, s. 2 ; s. 7.	

name and the date thereon. (But he must not deface a stamp befc under a penalty of £5, Stamp Act, 33 & 34 Vic. c. 98, s. 25.)

By the 33 & 34 Vic. c. 64, the Lord Lieutenant is empowered to r for the amalgamation of Petty Sessions districts.

The duties of this officer may not here be fully set out ; they are e responsible. In England the office, being in general a most valuable by gentlemen of very high respectability, by whom standard works on Magistrates have been compiled. In Ireland they are paid by Goveri fund created by fines, and the stamps used on the proceedings. The fees, so that so far as these ancient and important Courts are concern tice will not justify the common resemblance of Courts of Justice tc the fable, whereunto, while the sheep flies for defence from the weathe to lose part of the fleece.

The appointment is vested in the Magistrates, but is subject to the the Lord Lieutenant. By the present regulations every Magistrate re Petty Sessions district, and being Magistrates of that district or of t which the district is, although not attending the Petty Sessions, i vote, and so is every Magistrate of the county in which the district attends the Petty Sessions of that district, the attendances averaging four

As the office of Law Adviser in Ireland has been discontinued, anc pected that the Magistrates conferring with the Clerk on any questic practice that may arise, it is expected, and it is of the first importai Magistrates should select persons of intelligence and respectability efficiently performing the duties, and with whom they may with safe many subjects connected with their office ; and while it is not pro authority of the Judge should in the least degree be delegated to the

, or cause of Complaint.	Statute.	Extent of Jurisdiction.
? PETTY SESSIONS— *continued.* ale of fees to be paid sum-rver. :, power of said Lieutenant d form of.	Sch. s. 11.	
iages."		
ls, slack, culm, or cannel, ure and not by weight.	5 & 6 Wm. iv. c. 63, s. 9. (36 & 37 Vic. c. 82).	Penalty for each sale not exceeding 40s.; in default, &c., imprisonment not exceeding 1 month. Mayor or 2 J.
[ES REG. ACT, 1887: nt of women and children	50 & 51 Vic. c. 58.	
HTING: lty to Animals."	12 & 13 Vic. c. 92, s. 3.	Penalty not exceeding £5; in default, &c., imprisonment not exceeding 2 months. 1 J.
nces relating to) : (*a*) —Whosoever shall deface he Queen's current gold, r copper coin, by stamping any names or words, whe-h coin shall or shall not be diminished or ligthened.	24 & 25 Vic. c. 99, s. 16.	As amended by 25 & 26 Vic. c. 50. Indictable misdemeanour.

(*experienced*) clerk, skilful in precedents, wary in proceedings, and g in the business of the Court, is an excellent figure of a Court, and doth)oint the way to the Judge himself."—Bacon's *Essay on Judicature.* *\een's Current Coin.*—"Shall include any coin coined in any of Her ints, or lawfully current, by virtue of any proclamation or otherwise,)f Her Majesty's dominions, and whether made of gold, silver, copper, ixed metal."—Sec. 1. See also 33 Vic. c. 10. *ll be Possession.*—"It shall include, not only the having of it by s personal custody or possession, but also the knowingly and wilfully the actual custody or possession of any other person; and also the od wilfully having it in any dwelling-house, or other building, lodging, eld, or other place, open or enclosed, whether belonging to or occupied 'r not, and whether such matter shall be so had for his own use or 'r that of any other person."—Sec. 1. in to a greater amount than 12d. is not a legal tender, nor silver to a int than 40s.—*33 Vic. c. 10, s. 4.*

Offence, or cause of Complaint.	Statute.	Extent of Jurisd
COIN—*continued*. No tender of payment in money made in any gold, silver, or copper coin so defaced shall be allowed to be a legal tender ; and whosoever shall tender, utter, or put off any coin so defaced— (Proceedings under this section cannot be taken without the consent of the Attorney-General.)	24 & 25 Vic. c. 99, s. 17. (36 & 37 Vic. c. 82).	Forfeiture not ex 40s. The section does vide imprisonm default ; but it according to sca
No person shall make or counterfeit any copper coin, or any other coin made of any metal or mixed metals of less value than the silver coin of any foreign prince, state, or country.	24 & 25 Vic. c. 99, s. 22.	Misdemeanour.
And whosoever, without lawful authority or excuse (the proof whereof shall lie on the party accused), shall have in his custody or possession any greater number of pieces than five pieces of false or counterfeit coin, resembling or apparently intended to resemble or pass for any gold or silver coin of any foreign prince, state, or country, or any such copper or other coin as in last preceding section mentioned—	24 & 25 Vic. c. 99, s. 23. (36 & 37 Vic. c. 82).	Shall, on convict feit and lose : false and co coin, which : cut in pieces stroyed by orde Justice ; and f such offence sl feit and pay a exceeding 40 less than 10s., : such piece of f counterfeit coi in such person's or possession ; default of payn be imprisoned months (or by sc
Where any coin shall be tendered as the Queen's current gold or silver coin to any person who shall suspect the same to be diminished otherwise than by reasonable wearing, or to be counterfeit, it shall be lawful for such person to cut, break, bend, or deface such coin ; and if any coin so cut, &c., shall appear to be diminished otherwise than by	s. 26.	It shall be he finally determii summary man any Justice of tl who is hereby ered to exami oath as well as ties as any othe in order to the of such dispute

(*s*) This appears to be merely an *award* which the Magistrates may m in or out of Petty Sessions, and of course he can enforce his order by v distress. It is not an "offence," and therefore does not require two Ji

Offence, or cause of Complaint.	Statute.	Extent of Jurisdiction.
COIN—*continued.* reasonable wearing, or to be counterfeit, the person tendering same shall bear the loss thereof; but if the same shall be of due weight, and shall appear to be lawful coin, the person cutting, &c., is hereby required to receive the same at the rate it was coined for; and if any dispute shall arise, whether the coin so cut, &c., be diminished in manner aforesaid, or counterfeit—		
Search Warrant.—Where it shall be proved on the oath of a credible witness that there is reasonable cause to suspect that any person has been concerned in counterfeiting the Queen's current gold, silver, or copper coin, or any foreign or other coin, as in this Act mentioned, or has in his possession any such, or any instrument, tool, or engine whatsoever, adapted and intended for the making or counterfeiting of such coin, or any machine used or intended to be used for making or counterfeiting any such coin, or any filings, clippings, or bullion, or any gold or silver in dust, solution, or otherwise, &c.	24 & 25 Vic. c. 99, s. 27.	J. P., by warrant, to cause any place whatsoever belonging to, or in occupation, or under the control, of such suspected person, to be searched either in the day or in the night, and if any such instruments be found, to be brought before him, and, if necessary, secured, to be produced on the trial.
Making or issuing as a coin or token for money any gold, silver, copper, or bronze, or other metal. See also "Indictable Offences Index": title, "Coin."	33 Vic. c. 10. s. 5.	Penalty not exceeding £20; recoverable under Petty Sessions Act; in default, &c., imprisonment by scale.　2 J.

pointed out in the 41st section. The cases, however, of frequent occurrence, and a reference to which the assistance of the Magistrates is sought, is not that provided for in the section, where the dispute may be as to the fact of coin being current or base; but where, after it is discovered to be base and counterfeit, the person who passed it altogether denies that it is the coin which he put off, and disputes the identity. In this latter case the Magistrate has no power to make a summary award; it is purely a civil question for the Quarter Sessions or County Court.

Proof of Coin being Counterfeit.—"Where, upon the trial of any person charged with any offence against this Act, it shall be necessary to prove that any coin produced in evidence against such person is false or counterfeit, it shall not

E

Offence, or cause of Complaint.	Statute.	Extent of Jurisdiction.
COMBINATION OF WORKMEN: See "Conspiracy and Protection of Property."		
COMMON LODGING-HOUSES: (a) See "Public Health Act."		
COMMONS: Skinning or destroying surface.	29 Geo. iii. c. 30, s. 1.	Penalty £5; in default &c., imprisonment n exceeding 2 months, n less than 1 month t scale. 1
Like offence under 31 Geo. iii., for every square yard destroyed.	31 Geo. iii. c. 38, s. 1.	Penalty not exceedi £5, nor less than 5s recovered as in form Act. 1
Pigs without rings in noses therein (if owner not known)— And see "Pound."	29 Geo. iii. c. 30, s. 5.	May be impounded unt payment of 5s. each.
CONSPIRACY AND PROTECTION OF PROPERTY: "Conspiracy and Protection of Property Act, 1875."	38 & 39 Vic. c. 86.	
Trade Disputes. *Conspiracy and Protection of Property.*—An agreement or combination by two or more persons to do, or procure to be done, any act in contemplation or furtherance of a trade dispute between employers and workmen shall not be indictable as a conspiracy, if such act committed by one person would not be punishable as a crime. (b)	s. 3.	

be necessary to prove the same to be false or counterfeit by the evide moneyer or other officer of Her Majesty's Mint; but it shall be sufficie the same to be false or counterfeit by the evidence of any other credibl —Sec. 29.

(a) *Lodging Keeper.*—A boarding-house keeper or lodging-house keepe imposed upon him by law to take care of his lodger's goods.—*Dansey* v. 3 E. & B., 144, 26 & 27 Vic. c. 41, ss. 1, 2, 3. See *Taylor's Law of*

(b) *Combination in furtherance of Trade Disputes.*—By this secti no offence merely to combine to do an act in furtherance of trade dis

Offence, or cause of Complaint.	Statute.	Extent of Jurisdiction.
CONSPIRACY AND PROTECTION OF PROPERTY—*continued*. (Not to exempt from punishment persons guilty of conspiracy for which a punishment is awarded by any Act of Parliament.	38 & 39 Vic. c. 86, s. 3.	
Not to affect law relating to riot, unlawful assembly, breach of peace, sedition, or any offence against the State or Sovereign.	,,	
Crime defined.—A crime, for the purposes of this section, means an offence punishable by indictment, or an offence punishable summarily, and where the offender by statute is liable to be imprisoned absolutely, or at the discretion of the Court, as an alternative for some other punishment.)	,,	
Where a person is convicted of any such agreement or combination as aforesaid, to do, or procure to be done, an act which is punishable on summary conviction, and is sentenced to imprisonment—	,,	The imprisonment shall not exceed 3 months, or such longer time, if any, as may have been prescribed by the statute for the punishment of the said act when committed by one person. 2 J. In Dublin, one or more divisional Justices.
Breach of Contract by Persons employed in Gas- or Water-works.—Where a person employed by municipal authority, or any company or contractor for the supply of gas or water, wilfully and maliciously	s. 4.	Either to pay a penalty not exceeding £20, or to be imprisoned for a term not exceeding 3 months, with or without H. L. 2 J.

the act when actually committed by any one person be punishable as a crime. Thus it must now be a combination to do an *unlawful act*. Heretofore the authorities laid it down that at common law all *combinations* to effect alterations in the rate of wages were illegal conspiracies, except where a statute interposed to protect them. So that what an individual may have lawfully endeavoured to effect, to attempt to effect it by combination would have been an indictable conspiracy.

The section provides that persons guilty of a conspiracy, for which a punishment is awarded by Act of Parliament, shall not be exempt from punishment.

Where the persons who so combine to do an unlawful act actually do commit that act, the offence is indictable.

E 2

Offence, or cause of Complaint.	Statute.	Extent of Jurisdiction.
CONSPIRACY AND PROTECTION OF PROPERTY—*continued.* breaks a contract of service with his employers, knowing or having reasonable cause to believe that the probable consequences of his so doing, either alone or in combination with others, will be to deprive the inhabitants wholly or to a great extent of their supply of gas or water ; and being thereof convicted—		In Dublin, one or more divisional Justices. Like punishment if convicted on indictment. (Accused may elect to be tried by indictment, as in sec. 9.)
("Maliciously," as used above, is to be construed by the 58th section of 24 & 25 Vic. c. 97, Malicious Injuries to Property Act.) (*a*)	38 & 39 Vic. c. 86, s. 15.	
Municipal authority, company, or contractor, as above mentioned, shall cause to be posted up at the gas-works or water-works a printed copy of this section, in some conspicuous place where same may be conveniently read by the employed, and shall renew same when necessary, &c. ; for default—	s. 4.	Penalty not exceeding £5 a day during default, &c. 2 J. In Dublin, one or more divisional Justices.
Defacing Notice.—Every person who unlawfully injures, defaces, or covers up any such notice so posted in pursuance of this Act—	,,	Penalty not exceeding 40s. ; in default of payment, imprisonment not exceeding 1 month. 2 J. In Dublin, one or more divisional Justices.
Breach of Contract involving Injury to Persons or Property.—Where any person wilfully and maliciously breaks a contract of service or of hiring, knowing or having reasonable cause to believe that the probable consequences of his so doing, either alone or in combina-	s. 6.	Either to pay a penalty not exceeding £20, or to be imprisoned for a term not exceeding 3 months, with or without H. L. 2 J. In Dublin, one or more divisional Justices.

(*a*) *Malice.*—24 & 25 Vic. c. 97, s. 58, "Every punishment and forfeiture by this Act imposed on any person maliciously committing any offence, whether the same be punishable upon indictment or upon summary conviction, shall equally apply and be enforced, whether the offence shall be committed from malice conceived against the owner of the property in respect of which it shall be committed otherwise."

Offence, or cause of Complaint.	Statute.	Extent of Jurisdiction.
CONSPIRACY AND PROTECTION OF PROPERTY—*continued.* tion with others, will be to endanger human life, or cause serious bodily injury, or to expose valuable property, whether real or personal, to destruction or serious injury; on conviction— (Accused may elect to be tried by indictment.)		(Accused may elect to be tried by indictment, as in sec. 9.)
Master's neglect to provide Food, Clothing, &c., for Servant or Apprentice.—Where a master, being legally liable to provide for his servant or apprentice necessary food, clothing, medical aid, or lodging, wilfully and without lawful excuse refuses or neglects to provide the same, whereby the health of the servant or apprentice is or is likely to be seriously or permanently injured, he shall on summary conviction be liable—(a) (See also 24 & 25 Vic. c. 100, s. 26, 73.)	38 & 39 Vic. c. 86, s. 6.	Either to pay a penalty not exceeding £20, or to be imprisoned for a term not exceeding 6 months, with or without H. L. 2 J. In Dublin, one or more divisional Justices. (Accused may elect to be tried by indictment, as in sec. 9.)
Intimidation, Annoyance, &c. (b)— Every person who with a view to compel any other person to abstain from doing or to do any act which such other person has a legal right to do or abstain from doing, wrongfully and without legal authority—	s. 7.	

(a) A master is not liable upon an implied promise to pay for medical attendance on a servant who has met with an accident in his service.—*Wennal v. Adney,* 3 *Bos. & P.,* 247; *Newby v. Wiltshire,* 4 *Dougl.,* 284; *S. C.,* 2 *Esp.,* 739; *Sellen v. Norman,* 4 *C. & P.,* 80; *Cooper v. Phillips, ibid.,* 581. These cases, it should seem, must be understood as having overruled the decision of Lord Kenyon in *Scarman v. Castell,* 1 *Esp.,* 270 (cited by Lord Eldon in *Simmons v. Wilmott,* 3 *Esp.,* 91).

(b) *Intimidation.*—While it is most probable that the main object of this section 7 was to prevent that system of intimidation and annoyance in respect to trade disputes called "picketing," resorted to by workmen on strike, there is nothing in the section to confine it to such disputes; and it may be made available to prevent annoyances or intimidation of other kinds, whether in agricultural disputes or otherwise. It is to be observed that to bring the offences mentioned in the five sub-sections under this Act, and its exemplary punishment, it must be

Offence, or cause of Complaint.	Statute.	Extent of Juris
CONSPIRACY AND PROTECTION OF PROPERTY—*continued.* (1) Uses violence to or intimidates such other person or his wife or children, or injures his property ; or, (2) Persistently follows such other person about from place to place ; or, (3) Hides any tools, clothes, or other property owned or used by such other person, or deprives him of or hinders him in the use thereof ; or, (4) Watches or besets the house or other place where such other person resides, or works, or carries on business, or happens to be, or the approach to such house or place ; (Attending at or near residence, place of business, &c. &c., in order merely to obtain or communicate information, shall not be deemed a watching or besetting within the section) ; or (5) Follow such other person with two or more other persons in a disorderly manner, in or through any street or road.	38 & 39 Vic. c. 86, s. 7.	Either to pay not exceeding to be impriso term not ex months, with out H. L. In Dublin, one divisional Jus (Accused may tried by indic in sec. 9.)

shown that, in each case, the act is done *wrongfully and without lega* *and with the view to compel a person to abstain from doing, or to has a right to do, or to abstain from doing.* Nor will it be sufficie annoyance is given in consequence of something already done. It clear that a clamorous creditor dunning or "besetting" an unfortu could not be brought within this Act, for the "wrongful" act of persistently demanding, and the legal right of the other to abstain f may be satisfactorily made out. There is evident labour and difficul legislating on these matters, and that by reason of attempting to detach the cause and the object of it all, namely, trade disputes. The must endeavour to discover the spirit and meaning of the enactments. See also the special provisions of "Criminal Law and Procedure (I '' where jurisdiction is given to two R. M.'s in proclaimed distr

Offence, or cause of Complaint.	Statute.	Extent of Jurisdiction.
CONSPIRACY AND PROTECTION OF PROPERTY—*continued.* *Reduction of Penalties.*—Where in any Act relating to employers or workmen a pecuniary penalty is imposed, and no power is given to reduce it, Justices may mitigate to one-fourth.	38 & 39 Vic. c. 86, s. 8.	
Legal Proceedings.—Where offender is charged with any offence the penalty for which amounts to £20, or imprisonment is imposed, the accused may, on appearing, declare his objection to summary adjudication, and thereupon the case shall be dealt with as if charged with an offence triable by indictment.	s. 9.	
Summary Jurisdiction.—Every offence punishable by Court of Summary Jurisdiction to be dealt with under Petty Sessions (Ireland) Act.	ss. 10, 21.	—
Regulations as to Evidence.—On hearing, or indictment, or information under sections 4, 5, 6, the parties to the contract, husbands and wives, to be competent witnesses. (a)	s. 11.	
Appeal.—Any party feeling aggrieved by conviction of Court of Summary Jurisdiction, on determining any information under Act, may appeal to Quarter Sessions holden in not less than 15 days. Within 7 days give notice to Court and opposite party. Immediately after notice enter into recognizance, with or without sureties, to try appeal, abide the judgment, and pay costs. Where appellant is in custody, Justice	s. 12.	

(a) *Evidence.*—Thus the accused in indictable offences of this nature does not stand in the dock, but as of right enters the witness-chair to give his account of the transaction, if such right can be always considered of advantage to the accused. To be sure it must be at his own request that the charge becomes the subject of trial by indictment.

Offence, or cause of Complaint.	Statute.	Extent of Jurisdiction.
CONSPIRACY AND PROTECTION OF PROPERTY—*continued.* may, if he think fit, on appellant entering into recognizance, release him. Court of Appeal may adjourn appeal, confirm, reverse, or modify decision, or remit same with opinion of Court thereupon, or make such order as Court thinks just. If remitted, the Justices may re-hear and decide in accordance with opinion of Court of Appeal.		
Definitions.—"Maliciously," &c., in Act (defined as in 24 & 25 Vic. c. 97).	38 & 39 Vic. c. 86, s. 14.	
Saving Clause.—Act shall not apply to seamen or apprentices to sea service.	s. 16.	—
Repeal Clause.—Amongst others, "Master and Servant Act, 1867," and enactments in first Schedule to that Act.	s. 17.	—
Excepts sub-sections 1, 2, 3, 5, of sec. 16 of Summary Jurisdiction (Ireland) Act, 1871, relating to disputes between employers and the persons employed by them.	,,	—
Proviso.—That any order for wages, or further sum of compensation in addition to wages, made in pursuance of sec. 16 of Summary Jurisdiction (Ireland) Act, 1851 (14 & 15 Vic. c. 92), may be enforced as if it were an order made by a Court of Summary Jurisdiction in pursuance of Employers and Workmen Act, 1875, and not otherwise.		—
Application to Ireland, with Modifications.—"Summary Jurisdiction Act" shall mean "Petty Sessions (Ireland) Act, 1851," and any Acts amending same.		

Offence, or cause of Complaint.	Statute.	Extent of Jurisdiction.
CONSPIRACY AND PROTECTION OF PROPERTY—*continued.* *Constitution of Court.*—In Dublin, of one or more divisional Justices; elsewhere in Ireland of 2 Justices in Petty Sessions. "Municipal Authority" means Town Council under Municipal Corporation Act, 3 & 4 Vic. c. 108, and Commissioners under local Acts for improving, lighting, &c., &c. See also "Employers and Workmen."		
CONSTABLES :		
Constables neglecting to pay over amounts received or levied under warrant, or to duly account for same.	14 & 15 Vic. c. 90, s. 8.	Penalty not exceeding £20, to be reported and levied according to regulations of the "Force." 2 J.
Wilful neglect in returning any unexecuted warrant at time required by Justices; or wilful default in respect to the execution of the same.	14 & 15 Vic. c. 93, s. 35.	Penalty not exceeding £5, reported and levied as above. 2 J.
Neglecting or refusing to obey and execute warrant; or guilty of any neglect or violation of duty in his office. (a)	6 Wm. iv. c. 13, s. 19.	Penalty not exceeding £5, to be reported and levied off salary. 2 J.

(a) *Constables are bound to execute all warrants directed to them by Magistrates*, and they incur a penalty for any neglect or disobedience. The warrant should on the face of it appear to be a lawful warrant. Warrant or process set aside for irregularity will still protect the officer, as will likewise process founded on a judgment which is void for want of jurisdiction, of which he has no notice.—*Andrews* v. *Marris*, 1 Q. B. (E.), 1. Yet even the officer is not protected where he has notice of the defect of jurisdiction.—*Watson* v. *Bowdell*, 14 M. & W., 57 (England); see notes on *Scott* v. *Sheppard*, *Smith's Leading Cases.* In *indictable crimes* and offences the constable is authorized to execute his warrant on a Sunday (15 & 15 Vic. c. 93, s. 11). The arrest may in all cases be made by night, as well as by day—9 *Co.*, 66; 1 *East*, *P. C.*, 324. But it is recommended that unless it be urgent and necessary the day should be chosen for the purpose. There are numerous cases in which the constable is authorized to *arrest without warrant*, as, for instance, when a felony is committed in his view he is not to wait for a warrant, but use his utmost exertion to arrest, and is punishable for neglect; but this even private persons are bound to do. He is authorized to arrest for felony upon the charge of another, if he considers the charge to be well founded, but in

Offence, or cause of Complaint.	Statute.	Extent of Jurisdiction.
CONSTABLES—*continued.* Constables dismissed to deliver up arms, accoutrements, clothing, &c.; in default—	6 Wm. iv. c. 13, s. 20.	Imprisonment not exceeding 2 months' H. L. 2 J.

this a discretion is left to him, and much will depend upon the character of the person making the charge; but when a constable is required to make an arrest on the charge of another, such person is bound to accompany the constable. He may make the arrest also on his own suspicion, if he has good and reasonable grounds for his suspicion, and he is authorized to detain the party until inquiry can be made.—*Lord Tenderden*, 6 B. & C., 638; *Best, J.*, 5 Bing., 363. He is also authorized to arrest persons about to commit felony, or even a breach of the peace. —1 *Hawk.*, c. 63, ss. 11, 14 (1 *Curw.*, 490); or doing any act which manifestly endangers the life of another, or where a man in a passion threatens the life of another, or where under any such circumstances his immediate interference is called for, or where a lunatic seems disposed to do mischief to himself or any other. And it is held that in all cases where the arrest is made to *prevent* crime, the constable may confine the party in some secure place, until the heat of passion subsides, or until he can be conveniently brought before a Justice. He may arrest without warrant where a dangerous wound has been given, although not in his presence. He may arrest persons loitering at night and suspected of felony, under the Malicious Injuries Act, 24 & 25 Vic. c. 97, sec. 57; persons loitering or lying in highways, yards, or places, by night, suspected of committing or about to commit any felony against the Larceny Act, 24 & 25 Vic. c. 96, s. 104. He is also empowered and bound to prevent and arrest persons committing or taking part in a riot or affray, or who are assembled with such intent. He may apprehend a person who threatens to kill another, upon complaint made forthwith to the constable, and take such person before a Justice: this is, as laid down by *Mr. East*, grounded on the duty of the officer to prevent a probable felony.— 2 *Hale*, 88, 1 *East, P. C.*, 306. He may also interpose and arrest persons about to commit an affray, as where persons are armed and provided with weapons, ready to fight, or where from other circumstances they appear openly preparing to do so, not only where large numbers are engaged, but likewise between individuals; but after the affray is ended and peace restored, and no dangerous wound inflicted, he ought not to arrest on the charge of another.—*Cooke* v. *Nethercote*, 6 C. & P. 741; *Clifford* v. *Brandon*, 2 *Camp.*, 371. There are other offences for which the constable is authorized to arrest without warrant; but when the ends of justice can be otherwise attained, he will act discreetly in allowing the charge to be brought by summons.

It is sometimes asserted that once the constable makes arrest, no matter what the offence, and whether rightly or wrongly, he has no power to release the accused unless directed by a Magistrate. This is not so. To be sure when a Magistrate is at hand it is most proper to consult him, that constables be not open to the charge of acting capriciously. But if he has acted unlawfully or in error, the sooner he sets himself right the better.

Where a person is found drunk on a highway, the constable's duty is to arrest and remove him, or bring him before a Magistrate. If near his home he can allow

Offence, or cause of Complaint.	Statute.	Extent of Jurisdiction.
CONSTABLES—*continued*. Resigning or withdrawing without leave. (Acts authorising expenses of conveying prisoners, 14 & 15 Vic. c. 85, s. 4, 40 & 41 Vic. c. 49, s. 21).	6 Wm. iv. c. 13, s. 21.	Penalty not exceeding £10; in default, &c., imprisonment not exceeding 3 months' H.L. (and by scale).　　　2 J.

him to go home, and can help him to do so. If friends are quietly removing him it is better to allow them, or even when in custody, if they offer to do so, the constable will have power to hand him over to their care. The arrest of drunkards leads to many collisions; and where such is at all apprehended, if there be no urgent necessity, it is better to allow the offender to be removed by his friends. In all such cases the constable can bring forward his complaint by summons, when the punishment will be more certain and effectual. And as to the power to detain and subsequently discharge, to be summoned, persons found drunk and incapable, see 37 & 38 Vic. c. 69, s. 25, "Licensing Acts."

Where a constable is authorized by warrant to arrest in criminal cases, to search for stolen goods, to enter shebeen houses, &c., he may force outer doors. Even without warrant, where a serious affray takes place, or dangerous wound has been given, or a felony has been committed, he may do so in pursuit of the offender; but bare suspicion as to the guilt of the party will not justify this course, unless the officer comes armed with a Magistrate's warrant. "And let it be remembered that not only in this, but in every case where doors may be broken open, there must be a notification, demand, and refusal, before proceeding to this extremity."—*Semayne's Case, Smith's Leading Cases.* And as "every man's house is his castle," it never should be forcibly entered to make arrest, unless the arrest cannot be otherwise effected. So the maxim extends only to the dwelling-house and not to out-houses. In *civil* suits the constable cannot justify breaking open an outward door or window to execute civil process; if he do so he is a trespasser. But finding the outward door open, or that it is opened for him and he enters, he may break inner doors if he finds it necessary to do so. As to cautioning prisoners after arrest, see notes on sec. 14, "Petty Sessions Act"—*Appendix.*

In summary proceedings before Justices in Petty Sessions, the constable (being the complainant) may conduct his own case, and examine and cross-examine witnesses. In indictable offences of a public nature he may take up and conduct the case before Magistrates, and examine and cross-examine witnesses, although he be not the complainant. As to the constable's duty in giving in evidence the statements of prisoners, see notes on sec. 15, "Petty Sessions Act"—*Appendix.*

Constables should not give up or disclose Names of Informers.—It is a rule of evidence, applicable to criminal cases, that a witness is not permitted to disclose privileged communications brought to his knowledge for the furtherance of justice. "This is not the privilege of the witness, but may be justly called a public privilege, and is observed as a principle of public policy and from regard to public interests."—(1 *Phil. Ev.*, 272.) "Those questions which tend to the discovery of the channels by which the disclosure was made to the officers of justice are not permitted to be asked." "If the name of the Informer were to be disclosed, no man would make a discovery, and public justice would be defeated.—(*Rex* v. *Hardy, Buller, J.*) It has been held that a witness for the Crown could not be asked, 'Did you give the *information?*'"—(15 *M. & W.*, 169.)

Offence, or cause of Complaint.	Statute.	Extent of Jur
CONSTABLES—*continued*. Persons unlawfully in possession of arms, &c., supplied to constables; assuming the dress, name, designation, &c., of constables, so as thereby to obtain admission into houses or places—	6 Wm. iv. c. 13, s. 25.	Penalty not £10; in def imprisonment L. (by scale) Besides being the punishme awarded for false name o.
Assaults, &c., on Peace Officers.—Whosoever shall assault any person with intent to commit felony, or shall assault, resist, or wilfully obstruct any peace officer in the due execution of his duty, or any person acting in aid of such officer, or shall assault any person with intent to resist or prevent the lawful apprehension or detainer of himself or any other person, for any offence—	24 & 25 Vic. c. 100, s. 38.	Indictable mis imprisonment ceeding 2 yea without H. L
But if the Justices consider the offence of assault so trivial as not to require being dealt with by a	25 & 26 Vic. c. 50, s. 10.	Imprisonment ceeding 2 mc or without

A police constable was dismissed in consequence of a censure passe by a Magistrate. He brought an action against the Magistrate. Lo Chief Justice, held that it was necessary to prove malice, for it was the Magistrate to express his opinion upon the conduct of police constables. v. *Maltby*, 2 M. & Rob., 438. Where the Magistrates impose a pecun on a constable for any offence, they should not immediately issue enforce payment: a report of the conviction should be sent forward officer.

General Duties.—It is not here deemed necessary to set forth the vari of which constables are by law and their code of regulations bound to sance, and that come within the range of their duties. The paramoun the preservation of the public peace and the detection of offenders. Tl tively minor, but still important, ones have reference to the following Inquests, Nuisances on Highways, Public-houses, Drunkenness on. roughfares, Vagrancy, Illicit Distillation, Unlicensed Houses, called Houses,'' seizing Smuggled Goods, Fishery Laws, Poaching, Gu Peddlers, Weights and Measures, dangerous keeping of Gunpowder, a Deserters, Billeting of Soldiers, execution of Magistrates' Warrants, on Magistrates at their Sessions, occasional duties under Poor Laws, But, as already observed, all must be subservient to the preservation o peace, and the speedy detection of offenders, the prosecution of those trate outrages, and those who harbour them. These are all set out in ᵐᵃry admirable code compiled for the guidance and regulation of the F

Offence, or cause of Complaint.	Statute.	Extent of Jurisdiction.
CONSTABLES—*continued*. superior tribunal, they can try it summarily under the 42nd sec. of 24 & 25 Vic. c. 100.		(at discretion of Justices) fine not exceeding (together with costs, if ordered) £5; in default of payment, either immediately or within such period as the Justices at the time of conviction appoint, imprisonment as above, unless amount be sooner paid. . 2 J.
Assaults on Constables.—Where any person is convicted of an *assault* on any constable when in the execution of his duty, such person shall be guilty of an offence against the Act (Prevention of Crimes Act, 1871), and shall in the discretion of the Court be liable—(*a*)	34 & 35 Vic. c. 112, s. 12.	Either to pay a penalty not exceeding £20, and in default of payment to be imprisoned, with or without H. L., for a term not exceeding 6 months, or to be imprisoned for not exceeding 6 months, or in case such person has been convicted of a similar assault within 2 years, 9 months, with or without H. L. 2 J. or 1 Stip.

(*a*) *Assaults on Constables, &c.*—The offences against the Person Act, 24 & 25 Vic. c. 100, s. 38, makes the offence of *assaulting, resisting, or wilfully obstructing* any *peace officer* an indictable misdemeanour. The 25 & 26 Vic. c. 50, s. 10, gives Justices the summary power to deal with the assault where it is of a trivial nature; but it is to be noticed that, doubtless through negligence or oversight, when giving the summary power and referring to the first Act it merely quotes and refers to *assaults;* consequently it gives no power to deal with *resisting* or *obstructing* unless they amount to an *assault*. These must therefore remain indictable misdemeanours still.

The following is the 10th section of 25 & 26 Vic. c. 50 :—

"And whereas by the Act of 24 & 25 Vic. c. 100, s. 38, certain assaults therein specified on peace officers and others are made misdemeanours, and punishable with imprisonment for a term not exceeding two years, with or without hard labour, and it is desirable also to give a summary jurisdiction in petty cases for the same offence : be it enacted that two Justices of the Peace shall have a concurrent jurisdiction to punish such assaults under the 42nd section of the said Act, if they shall consider the offence so trivial as not to require being dealt with by a superior tribunal."

The Prevention of Crimes Act, 1871, as above set out, gives an additional summary power to deal with *assaults* on constables. The punishment is severer than

Offence, or cause of Complaint.	Statute.	Extent of J
CONSTABLES—*continued*. *Special Constables.*—Where tumult or riot has taken place, or is apprehended, 2 Justices may swear in. For penalty for obtaining Pension, &c., by fraud, 46 Vic. c. 14, s. 9. For duties of R. I. Constabulary to assist Sheriff in execution of writs, &c., see "Sheriff."	2 & 3 Wm. iv. c. 108.	
CONTAGIOUS DISEASES (ANIMALS) ACT, 1878, Repeals previous Act. As to Ireland, the 11 & 12 Vic. c. 105; 11 & 12 Vic. c. 107; 16 & 17 Vic. c. 62; 33 & 34 Vic. c. 36; 35 & 36 Vic. c. 16; 37 & 38 Vic. c. 6; 39 & 40 Vic. c. 41; 47 Vic. c. 13; 49 & 50 Vic. c. 32.	41 & 42 Vic. c. 74.	
Recovery of penalties and summary proceedings to be according to 14 & 15 Vic. c. 93, the Petty Sessions (Ireland) Act, and any Act amending same; as to Dublin, the Acts regulating the powers and duties of Justices for that district.	s. 86.	
CONTEMPT OF COURT: If any person shall wilfully insult any Justice or Justices sitting in any such Court or place, or shall commit any other contempt of any such Court—(a)	14 & 15 Vic. c. 93, s. 9.	May by verl rect remove Court or pl imprisoned ing 7 days, not exceedi default, &c ment, by so
(As to Dublin Metropolis, see also 34 & 35 Vic. c. 76, s. 6.)	—	Like power.

that in any previous Act. Being the last, wherever it is applicable, it
one to use. This also is confined to *assaults*. The former Act say
officer; this last, *any constable*. Peace officer will include any officer
the constabulary force, but constable may not include every peace offi
gives no definition of "constable." It will doubtless take in all r
and including head- and other constable.

(a) The section provides for punishing the offence when committ

nce, or cause of Complaint.	Statute.	Extent of Jurisdiction.
ACTOR (*Road*): ting Contractor in execution of luty. eglect in performing contract, " Roads."	14 & 15 Vic. c. 92, s. 7.	Penalty not exceeding £10, or imprisonment not exceeding 3 months. 1 J.

or "any place" wherein they may be holding private examinations in
offences.

e case of an insult to the Judge himself, it is not indeed on his account
law thus arms him with the authority to fine and imprison the party, for
consideration which should never enter into his mind; but though he
rise the insult, it is a duty which he owes to the station to which he
ot to suffer those things to pass which will make him despicable in the
thers. It is his duty to support the dignity of his station and uphold the
hat in his own presence at least it shall not be infringed."—*Holroyd, J.;*
ld., 329.

ustice should feel satisfied that the offence amounts to a contempt of Court,
insult, and that in punishing he is solely acting in the "*execution of his
Justice.*" And in any action brought against him, the plaintiff must, in
ration, expressly allege that such act was done "maliciously and without
e and probable cause"; and if on the trial he fail to prove such allega-
hall be nonsuited, or a verdict shall be given for the defendant.—12 Vic.
1.

s Magistrates have a general apprehension, and not without some reason,
r judgment and authority are more likely to be contemned by those who
ne extent "learned in the law" than by the common people. Professional
n are allowed considerable latitude, and the Magistrate should not hastily
that because his judgment, and his reasons for it, on legal points may be
ted and disputed, an insult is thereby offered him, or contempt of Court
d. Nothing is more becoming in a Judge than patience; but timidity is
substituted for that quality. Nor is he, when his opinions or views may
id, and convincing reasons offered to show that he is wrong, to substitute
· for firmness. About a deliberate insult, or contempt of Court, there
rcely be a doubt, and when such takes place it should by no means be
d; but the Magistrate would perhaps do well to let some short time elapse
aling with it. If not of an aggravated or unpardonable nature, by just
the offending party "not to leave the Court," he would thereby convey
uld be expected to follow; and the probability is, that an ample apology
ty expression in the heat of the moment would at once vindicate the dig-
e Court, and save the Magistrate what must in all such cases be a very
ble duty.

two or more Justices are present, and the insult is offered to one, it becomes
of the others to interpose.

there is only one he can deal with it. The Justice may also prosecute by
ion or Indictment anyone who assaults or insults him in the execution of

Offence, or cause of Complaint.	Statute.	Extent of Jur
COPYRIGHT: Act for amending the law relating to copyright in works of the fine arts, and for repressing the commission of fraud in the production and sale of such works, providing penalties for fraudulent productions and sales.	25 & 26 Vic. c. 68, ss. 7&8.	Pecuniary pe offences in verable befo by action.
CORN: Assault with intent to prevent sale of grain.	—	See "Assault."
Offering adulterated corn for sale.	14 & 15 Vic. c. 92, s. 7.	Forfeiture of o nalty not exc or imprisonm ceeding 1 mo
Winnowing on Roads, &c., or within 30 feet of the centre.	s. 10.	Penalty not 10s.; in del imprisonment ceeding 7 day
CORONER: See "Inquest."		
COSTS: Justices have power to award costs in all cases of summary adjudication to the party in whose favour the order, whether of conviction or dismissal, is made.	14 & 15 Vic. c. 93, s. 22.	Not to exceed
COTTIER TENANTS: See "Landlord and Tenant."		
COURT (*Petty Sessions*): In summary proceedings to be deemed an open Court, and public to have right of access; in indictable offences to be in discretion of Justices. (a)	14 & 15 Vic. c. 93, s. 9.	

(a) Those cases are indeed but few where Justices will need to sit w doors." If, however, in preliminary investigations, where they act n they consider "that the ends of justice will be thereby best answered,'

Offence, or cause of Complaint.	Statute.	Extent of Jurisdiction.
COURT (*Petty Sessions*): Contempt of Court, or wilfully insulting Justice. See "Contempt;" and for additional powers, see "Sureties of the Peace."	14 & 15 Vic. c. 93, s. 9.	Removal or committal for not exceeding 7 days, or fine not exceeding 40*s.*; in default, &c., imprisonment, by scale. 1 J.
Forging or altering, or putting off, knowing same to be forged, &c.; any summons, conviction, order, warrant, recognizance, deposition, declaration, &c.	24 & 25 Vic. c. 98, s. 32.	Felony.
CRIME: (THE PREVENTION OF CRIMES ACT, 1871.) *Licensed Convicts.*—Any constable in any police district may, if authorised in writing by the Chief Officer of Police of the district, without warrant take into custody any convict who is holder of a licence granted under the Penal Servitude Acts (1853, 1857, 1864), if it appears to such constable that such convict is getting his livelihood by dishonest means, and may bring him before Court of Summary Jurisdiction for adjudication.	34 & 35 Vic. c. 112, s. 3, and s. 17, sub-s. 4.	If it appears from the facts proved that there are reasonable grounds for believing that the convict is getting his livelihood by dishonest means, he shall be deemed guilty of an offence against this Act, and his licence shall be forfeited, and the convict may be committed to any prison, within juris-

may be excluded. In summary proceedings, when acting judicially, the place is to be deemed an open Court.

An Open Court.—A French philosopher (Montesquieu) has dared to remark, that whatever is *secret* must be *doubtful;* and that even our natural horror of vice may be abused as an engine of tyranny.

"In the constitution of a Court of Justice, an equivalent to many checks upon the discretion of Judges is, that its proceedings be carried on in public, *apertis foribus;* not only before a promiscuous concourse of bystanders, but in the audience of the whole profession of the law. The opinion of the Bar concerning what passes will be impartial, and will commonly guide that of the public. The most corrupt Judge will fear to indulge his dishonest wishes in the presence of such an assembly; he must encounter, what few can support, the censure of his equals and companions, together with the indignation and reproaches of his country."—*Paley's Philosophy, chap.* 8, on "*Administration of Justice.*"

A Petty Sessions Court is a Court of record, and Magistrates acting judicially therein are Judges of record. In Petty Sessions, Magistrates elect their chairman, but he has no casting vote.

F

Offence, or cause of Complaint.	Statute.	Extent of Jur
CRIME—*continued.*		diction, until conveniently some prison convicts unde of penal serv be lawfully there to un term to wh liable. Pers mitted may H. L. .2 J.
Breach of Licence.—Where in any licence granted under the Penal Servitude Acts, any conditions besides those in Schedule A of the Act of 1864 are inserted, if the holder break such conditions by an act *not punishable by indictment or summarily,* he shall be deemed guilty of an offence against this Act.	34 & 35 Vic. c. 112, s. 4.	Imprisonment ceeding 3 mo or without H 2 J.
Convict to notify Residence, &c.— Holder of licence under Penal Servitude Acts, who is at large, shall notify his place of residence to police of the district where he resides, and every change of residence; and when changing from one district to another, to the police officer of both. If a male, he shall once a month report himself at such time, and to such person, and either personally or by letter, as officer directs. And any holder of a licence at large, who remains at any place for 48 hours, without so notifying his place of residence, or fails to comply with the requisitions of this section as to change of residence and reporting himself once a month—	s. 5.	Shall, unless h the satisfacti Court that 1 best to act in with the law of an offen Act, and h may, in the of the Cour feited; or, if conviction h penal servi expired, may soned, with H. L., for a exceeding on if term of p tude unexpir than a year, prisonment i

Notifying Residence.—42 & 43 Vic. c. 55, s. 2, amends above, further provision as to reporting by holder of licence under s. 5, and pe to supervision under s. 8, notifying residence and change of residence b presenting himself to chief officer of police, who may direct the report at particular stations, and such directions signed by officer to be eviden

Offence, or cause of Complaint.	Statute.	Extent of Jurisdiction.
CRIME—*continued.*		
Section 6 provides for the register and photographing of criminals.		with or without H. L., as will not exceed one year. (*a*) 2 J. or 1 Stip.
Special offences by Persons twice Convicted.—When any person is convicted on indictment of a crime, and a previous conviction of a crime is proved against him, he shall, at any time within 7 years immediately after expiration of the sentence for the last crime, be guilty of an offence against this Act, under any of the following circumstances :—(*b*)	34 & 35 Vic. c. 112, s. 7.	
First—If on being charged by a constable with getting his livelihood by dishonest means, and being brought before a Court of Summary Jurisdiction, it appears to such Court that there are	,,	Imprisonment, with or without H. L., for a term not exceeding one year. 2 J. or 1 Stip.

(*a*) *Offences against Licence.*—For certificate of conviction, see 27 & 28 Vic. . 47 (schedule to Act) ; 27 & 28 Vic. c. 47, "Act to Amend the Penal Servide Acts." Sec. 8, Where holder of licence is summarily convicted, convicting Iagistrate shall forward certificate of fact to Lord Lieutenant.
The *Form* is as follows :—

SCHEDULE B.
Form of Certificate of Conviction of Holder of Licence.

I do hereby certify, that A. B., the holder of a Licence under the Penal Servide Acts, was on the   day of   , in the year   , duly convicted
r   of the offence of   , and sentenced to
C. D.
Clerk to the said Justices.

(*b*) *Crime, &c.*—The expression "Crime" means (sec. 20) any felony ; or the fence of uttering false or counterfeit coin ; or of possessing counterfeit gold or lver coin ; or obtaining goods or money by false pretences ; or of conspiracy to fraud ; or any misdemeanour under 58 sec. 24 & 25 Vic. c. 96. (See section 58 ider "Larceny"—Indictable Offences.)
Offence.—The expression "Offence" means (sec. 20) any act or omission which not a crime as defined by this Act, and is punishable on indictment or summary nviction.
The above provisions of sec. 7 should be borne in mind when such suspected rsons are apprehended *under the circumstances pointed out.*

Offence, or cause of Complaint.	Statute.	Extent
CRIME—*continued.*		
reasonable grounds for believing that the person so charged is getting his livelihood by dishonest means; or,	34 & 35 Vic. c. 112, s. 7.	
Secondly—If on being charged with any offence punishable on indictment or summary conviction, and on being required by a Court of Summary Jurisdiction to give his name and address, he refuses to do so, or gives a false name or a false address; or	,,	Imprisonn without term not year.
Thirdly—If he is found in any place, whether public or private, under such circumstances as to satisfy the Court before whom he is brought that he was about to commit, or to aid in the commission of, any offence punishable on indictment or summary conviction, or was waiting for an opportunity to commit, or to aid in the commission of, any offence punishable on indictment or summary conviction; or,	,,	Like.
Fourthly—If he is found in or upon any dwelling-house, or any building, yard, or premises, being parcel of or attached to such dwelling-house, or in or upon any shop, warehouse, counting-house, or other place of business, or in any garden, orchard, pleasure-ground, or nursery-ground, or in any building or erection in any garden, orchard, pleasure-ground, or nursery-ground, without being able to account to the satisfaction of the Court before whom he is brought for his being found on such premises.	,,	Like.
Arrest.—Offence against Act as is *first* in this section mentioned, offender may be arrested by any		

Offence, or cause of Complaint.	Statute.	Extent of Jurisdiction.
CRIME—_continued._ constable without warrant, if authorized to do so by Chief Officer of Police of district. ("Chief Officer of Police" means, in Dublin, either of the Commissioners of Police; elsewhere in Ireland, in any other police district, the Sub-Inspector, Royal Irish Constabulary.)	34 & 35 Vic. c. 112, s. 7.	
In case of any offence as is _thirdly_, in the section mentioned, by any constable without warrant, although not specially authorized so to do.		
Also, for offence _fourthly_ in section, may be apprehended without warrant by any constable, or the owner or occupier of property on which offender is found, or their servants or persons authorized by owner or occupier, and detained until given into custody of a constable.		
Police Supervision.—Persons convicted on indictment of crime, and a previous conviction of crime is proved against him, in addition to other punishment, Court may direct offender to be subject to police supervision for any period not exceeding 7 years from expiration of sentence.	s. 8.	
Persons subject to police supervision and who are at large shall notify place of residence, &c., to constabulary (such persons are subject to the same supervision, regulations, and requisitions, in all respects, as set forth for convicts holding licences under section 5, before mentioned); upon conviction—	,,	Unless such person proves to the satisfaction of the Court before whom he is tried that he did his best to act in conformity with the law, be guilty of an offence against this Act, and be subject to be imprisoned, with or without H. L., for any period not exceeding one year. 2 J. or 1 Stip.

Offence, or cause of Complaint.	Statute.	Extent of Jurisdict
CRIME—*continued.*		
Harbouring Thieves, &c.—Every person who occupies or keeps any lodging-house, beer-house, public-house, or other house or place where intoxicating liquors are sold, or any place of public entertainment or public resort, and knowingly lodges, or knowingly harbours, thieves, or reputed thieves, or knowingly permits, or knowingly suffers them to meet or assemble therein, or knowingly allows the deposit of goods therein, having reasonable cause for believing them to be stolen, shall be guilty of an offence against this Act.	34 & 35 Vic. c. 112, s. 10.	Penalty not exc £10, and in defa payment impriso not exceeding 4 m with or without : and if Court thin may, in addition in lieu of penalty, r him to enter into : nisance, with or w sureties, for keepi peace, or being o behaviour durin months. The imprisonment, fault of finding ties, shall not exc months. The security re from a surety sh exceed £20. 2 J. or 1
Licence for sale of intoxicating liquors, or keeping places of public entertainment or resort, may, in the discretion of Court, be forfeited on first conviction; on second conviction it shall be forfeited, and the person disqualified for licence for two years. Two convictions within three years for same premises, whether the person be the same or not, the Court shall direct that, for a term not exceeding one year, the premises shall be disqualified.		
Licensed person shall produce licence, for examination, and if forfeited shall deliver it up altogether.	,,	Penalty not exc £5; in default, &c prisonment, by se
For wilfully neglecting or refusing to produce licence, in addition to any other penalty under section, be liable to—		2 J. or 1
Appeal.—Persons convicted under this section (10) shall have a right to appeal in same manner in all respects as in Licensing Act, 1872 (35 & 36 Vic. c. 94, s. 52).	39 & 40 Vic. c. 20, s. 5.	

Offence, or cause of Complaint.	Statute.	Extent of Jurisdiction.
CRIME—*continued.*		
Brothel Keepers.—Every person who occupies or keeps a brothel, and knowingly lodges or knowingly harbours thieves or reputed thieves or knowingly permits or knowingly suffers them to meet or assemble therein, or knowingly allows the deposit of goods therein, having reasonable cause for believing them to be stolen, shall be guilty of an offence against this Act.	34 & 35 Vic. c. 112, s. 11.	Penalty not exceeding £10, and in default of payment to be imprisoned, not exceeding 4 months, with or without H. L. And Court may, in addition to or in lieu of penalty, require him to enter into recognizance as in this Act described. (See order as to sureties, sec. 10.)　2 J. or 1 Stip.
Assaults on Police.—Where any person is convicted of an assault on any constable when in the execution of his duty, such person shall be guilty of an offence against this Act, and shall be liable—	s. 12.	In the discretion of the Court shall be liable either to a penalty not exceeding £20 (in default of payment to be imprisoned, with or without H.L., for a term not exceeding 6 months), or to be imprisoned for any term not exceeding 6, or in case such person has been convicted of a similar assault within 2 years, 9 months, with or without H. L.　2 J. or 1 Stip.
Dealers in Old Metals, &c.—Any Dealer in Old Metals (a) who either personally or by his servant or agent, purchases, receives, or bargains for any metal mentioned	s. 13.	Penalty not exceeding £5 ; in default of payment, imprisonment not exceeding 2 months.　2 J. or 1 Stip.

(a) *Dealer in Old Metals* means, for the purposes of this section, any person dealing in, buying and selling, old metal, scrap metal, broken metal, or partly manufactured metal goods, or defaced or old metal goods, and whether such person deals in such articles only, or *together with* second-hand goods or marine stores.

Offence, or cause of Complaint.	Statute,	Extent of Jurisd
CRIME—*continued*. in first column of schedule (*a*) annexed to Act, whether new or old, in any quantity at one time of less weight than the quantity set opposite each such metal in the second column annexed to Act, shall be guilty of an offence against this Act.	34 & 35 Vic. c. 112, s. 13.	
As to Children of Women Convicted.—Where any woman is convicted of a crime, and a previous conviction of a crime is proved against her, her children under 14, under her care or control at the time of last conviction, and who have no visible means of support or proper guardianship, provisions of Industrial Schools Act to be applicable.	s. 14.	
Vagrancy Act, 5 Geo. iv. c. 83, for punishment of rogues and vagabonds, extended to Ireland, with amendments, &c. (See this important section below.) (*b*)	s. 15.	

(*a*) *Schedule above referred to :—*

C
Q
n

COLUMN 1.

Lead, or any composite the principal ingredient of which is lead, .
Copper, or any composite the principal ingredient of which is copper,
Brass, or any composite the principal ingredient of which is brass,
Tin, or any composite the principal ingredient of which is tin, .
Pewter, or any composite the principal ingredient of which is pewter,
German silver or spelter, or any composite the principal ingredient of which is German silver or spelter, ...

(*b*) *Rogues and Vagabonds*, sec. 15, 34 & 35 Vic. c. 112.—"Where fourth section of the Act passed in the fifth year of the reign of King G Fourth, chapter 83, intituled, 'An Act for the punishment of idle and persons and rogues and vagabonds, in that part of great Britain called it is amongst other things provided that every suspected person or rep frequenting any river, canal, or navigable stream, dock, or basin, or wharf, or warehouse near or adjoining thereto, or any street, highway, leading thereto, or any place of public resort, or any avenue leading there street, highway, or place adjacent, with intent to commit a felony, shall a rogue and vagabond, and may be apprehended and committed to p hard labour for any time not exceeding three calendar months : An

Offence, or cause of Complaint.	Statute.	Extent of Jurisdiction.
CRIME—*continued.* *Power to Search for Stolen Property.* —Any constable may, under the circumstances in section and hereinafter mentioned, be authorized, in writing, by a chief officer of police (*Dublin, one of the Commissioners; elsewhere in Ireland, the Sub-Inspector, Royal Irish Constabulary*) to enter any house, shop, warehouse, yard, or other premises, in search of stolen property, and search, seize, and secure any property he may believe to have been stolen, in the same manner as he would be authorised to do if he had a search warrant, and the property seized, if any, corresponded to the property described in such search warrant. (*a*) Where property is seized in pursuance of this section, the person on whose premises it was at the time of seizure, or the person from whom it was taken, if other than the person on whose premises it was, shall, unless previously charged with receiving the same, knowing it to have been stolen, be summoned before a Court of Summary Jurisdiction to account for his possession of such property. Court may make	34 & 35 Vic. c. 112, s. 16.	

oubts are entertained as to the construction of the said provision, and as to the nature of the evidence required to prove the intent to commit a felony: Be it enacted, firstly, the said section shall be construed as if instead of the words highway or place adjacent;' there were inserted the words 'or any highway or any place adjacent to a street or highway;' and, secondly, that in proving the intent to commit a felony it shall not be necessary to show that the person suspected was guilty of any particular act or acts tending to show his purpose or intent, and he may be convicted if from the circumstances of the case and from his own character as proved to the Justice of the Peace or Court before whom or which he is brought, it appears to such Justice or Court that his intent was to commit a felony, and the provisions of the said section, as amended by this section, shall be in force in Scotland and Ireland.'' See '' Vagrancy.''

(*a*) That is, acting under this authority he has the same power to search for, seize, and secure any property which he *believes* to be stolen, as he would have in respect to property *particularly named,* when acting under a Magistrate's warrant. His belief becomes *his authority and his duty in this case.*

Offence, or cause of Complaint.	Statute.	Extent of Juri
CRIME—*continued*. order as to property, and award such costs as the justice of the case may require. Police officer may give such authority in either of the following cases :— *First*—When the premises to be searched are, or within the preceding twelve months have been, in the occupation of any person who has been convicted of receiving stolen property or of harbouring thieves ; or, *Second*—When the premises to be searched are in the occupation of any person who has been convicted of any offence involving fraud or dishonesty, and punishable by penal servitude or imprisonment. Police officer need not on giving authority specify any particular property, but he may give such authority if he has reason to believe generally that such premises are being made a receptacle for stolen goods. (*a*)	34 & 35 Vic. c. 112, s. 16.	
Legal Proceedings.—Offences may be prosecuted before a Court of summary jurisdiction. In Dublin police district, before a divisional Justice at a police court, under the Acts regulating the powers and duties of Justices of the Peace for such district. Elsewhere in Ireland, under Petty Sessions (Ireland) Act, 1851, and any Act amending the same, before a Stipendiary Magistrate alone or with others, or any two or more Justices in Petty Sessions.	s. 17.	

(*a*) Where the premises come within either of the two classes, it seem although the officer may not have *reason to believe generally* that the made a receptacle for stolen goods, still if he believes that any particul stolen will be found therein, he may also give the order. That is, belief is not necessary where he entertains a belief or suspicion tha property may be found there. The officer need only give the authorit the Act supplies the rest.

Offence, or cause of Complaint.	Statute.	Extent of Jurisdiction.
CRIME—*continued*. Description of offence in words of Act shall be sufficient. Exemptions, excuses, qualifications, &c., may be proved by Defendant, but need not be negatived in information or complaint, and if so negatived need not be proved. Where offence involves forfeiture of licence under Penal Servitude Acts, offender may be committed to any prison in jurisdiction until removal, &c. Any person accused of offence against this Act may be remanded from time to time to obtain evidence, or for any other just cause. Warrants or conviction not to be quashed for want of form. Court before which question brought may amend, if of opinion that there was evidence at first hearing to justify the order or warrant. Penalties to be applied according to Fines Act (Ireland), 1851.	34 & 35 Vic. c. 112, s. 17.	
Evidence of previous conviction may be by producing record or extract, and identifying the accused as the person therein referred to. As to certifying by officers in indictable and summary offences, see sec. 18. To be in addition to, and not in exclusion of, other authorized mode of proving convictions.	s. 18.	
Evidence in cases of Stolen Goods.— Where person charged with having received goods knowing them to be stolen, or having in possession stolen property, evidence may be given at any stage of proceedings that other stolen property was found in his possession within 12 months.	s. 19.	This evidence is not of itself to be taken as sufficient proof of guilt in the case under consideration, but "may be taken into consideration for the purpose of proving that the person accused knew the property to be stolen."
Where person charged with receiving or having in possession stolen pro-	—	This evidence would seem to be proper to be given

Offence, or cause of Complaint.	Statute.	Extent of Juri
CRIME—*continued.* perty, as above, and evidence has been given that the stolen property has been found in his possession, evidence may be given at any stage of proceedings, of a conviction within 5 years of any offence involving fraud or dishonesty. Not less than 7 days' notice to be given accused that proof will be offered of previous conviction. (*a*)	34 & 35 Vic. c. 112, s. 19.	before the M: and set out o positions to g and the Grand well as before and Jury on t
Definitions of expressions in Act.	s. 20.	
Repeals "Habitual Criminals Act, 1869." So much of section 4 of "Penal Servitude Act, 1864," as requires the holder of a licence to report himself.	s. 21.	—
Saving as to capital punishment under any other law or statute.	s. 22.	—
Registering and Photographing Criminals.—The Lord Lieutenant may place restrictions on the obligations in reference to the registry and photographing of criminals to which the Prevention of Crimes Act, 1871, applies.	39 & 40 Vic. c. 23.	

(*a*) The presumption of law may still be that the prisoner is inn proved to be guilty, but certainly where the accused are placed in th above mentioned, the law now inclines to the conclusion that the stronge tion is the other way.

This Act for the prevention of crime contains many important provisi fully and strictly carried out would tend to hold those disposed to become who are, habitual offenders in check. It does not appear that the Ma the country are as yet so fully acquainted with all its provisions as readily to apply them when the cases arise. The Act is supplied to the lary with their code. They are also furnished with the photographs and of those likely to come within its operation, but then the tracing out of th and identifying them with previous convictions, are attended with c difficulty. Add to this the unusual character of the legislation, the intricate subjects introduced, and the consequent difficulty of callin memory even when the proper objects fall into their hands. The Act mastered by persistent and careful study. This it should receive at th all who are in any way concerned in its administration.

Appeal.—The Act itself gives no right of appeal. Offences, it stat *prosecuted* under the Petty Sessions Act, but this it is conceived so incor Petty Sessions Act as to take in its appeal and all other provisions.

Offence, or cause of Complaint.	Statute.	Extent of Jurisdiction.
"CRIMINAL LAW AND PROCE-DURE (Ir.) ACT, 1887." (a)		
Preliminary inquiries by order of Attorney-General as to offences committed in proclaimed districts.	50 & 51 Vic. c. 20, s. 1.	
Extension of summary jurisdiction in respect to persons taking part in any riot or unlawful assembly anywhere in Ireland.	,,	In Dublin the Court of Summary Jurisdiction shall be a divisional Magistrate, and else-where shall be two re-sident Magistrates ap-pointed under 6 & 7 Wm. iv. c. 13, one of whom shall possess legal know-ledge to the satisfaction of Lord Lieutenant.
And in respect to certain other speci-fied offences committed in Pro-claimed Districts.	ss. 2 & 11.	
Special jury, and removal of trial.	ss. 3 & 4, 9 & 10.	The punishment for each offence is imprisonment, with or without H. L., for a term not exceeding 6 months.
Proclamation of districts as to the preceding enactments.	s. 5.	
Dangerous associations, and Special Proclamation in reference thereto.	s. 6.	
Prohibition of dangerous associations.	s. 7.	
Continuance of Peace Preservation Act and extending power of Search for Arms.	s. 8.	
Punishment, procedure, and defini-tions.	ss. 11 to 19.	
CRIMINAL JUSTICE ACT:		
See "Larceny."	18 & 19 Vic. c. 126.	

(a) The jurisdiction given by above Act, being of a limited character, it is thought sufficient to make the above reference to its principal parts in this work. The summary jurisdiction section, with notes thereon, will be found in the Appendix.

Offence, or cause of Complaint.	Statute.	Extent of Jurisdiction.
CRUELTY TO ANIMALS: (a) Repeals 5 & 6 Wm. iv., c. 59; 7 Wm. iv.; and 1 Vic. c. 66.	12 & 13 Vic. c. 92.	
If any person shall cruelly beat, ill-treat, over-drive, abuse, or torture, or cause or procure such to be done to, any animal, every such offender for every such offence shall be liable to—	s. 2.	Penalty not exceeding £5 a-day; in default of payment, &c., imprisonment not exceeding 2 months, with or without H. L. (b) 1 J.

(a) The legislation for preventing cruelty to animals is modern, the most important being that introduced by Mr. Martin, an Irish Member of the House of Commons. It is limited to those animals which are useful to man, and others which have come under his dominion, and that are of a domestic nature.   Some have hitherto drawn but little advantage from it; amongst them is the ass, his "uncomplaining slave." From the days of Balaam to the present there seems to have been "no law for her."   There is a large class outside these which may be tortured with impunity. They "testify with one sad voice that man is a cruel master."

"Liveth there one amongst a million that shall not bear witness against him!
From the elephant toiling at a launch, to the shrew-mouse in the harvest-field;
From the whale which the harpooner had stricken, to the minnow caught
     upon a pin;
From the albatross, wearied in its flight, to the wren in her covered nest;
The verdict of all is unanimous in finding their master cruel."
Proverbial Philosophy.

(b) *Extent of Punishment.*—Under sec. 18, it is provided that if conviction takes place before *two Justices or before one of the Police Magistrates* sitting at any Police Court within the Metropolitan Police District, they or he, instead of imposing pecuniary penalty, may forthwith commit for any time not exceeding 3 *calendar months, with or without hard labour.*

Animal.—By sec. 29, will mean horse, mare, gelding, bull, ox, cow, heifer, steer, calf, mule, ass, sheep, lamb, hog, pig, sow, goat, dog, cat, or any other domestic animal.

Dishorning of Cattle.—In the Common Pleas Div., Ireland, *June,* 1885, *Society for Prevention of Cruelty to Animals* v. *Callaghan and Others,* on case stated by Magistrates of Meath, Court held that the dishorning of cattle, if performed with ordinary care and skill, is not unlawful, and not subject to penalties under Acts for preventing cruelty to animals.   Court also held that it was not bound by the decision of the Exchequer Division in the case of *Brady* v. *Mardle.* But in *Ford* v. *Wiley,* Q. B. Division, England, Crown Cases Reserved, *May,* 1889, before Lord Coleridge and Mr. Justice Hawkins, the question was whether the Magistrates should have *convicted* instead of *acquitted* the defendant in the case.   The Irish and Scotch cases were referred to.   The Judges delivered written judgments.   It was proved by skilled witnesses that the pain is most excruciating, and lasts for months. *Held,* "that it was *cruel, unnecessary,* and *illegal;* that the Magistrates ought to have convicted; and that the case be remitted to them to deal with in accordance with what we hold to be the law."

Offence, or cause of Complaint.	Statute.	Extent of Jurisdiction.
CRUELTY TO ANIMALS—*con.* *Keeping places for Bull-dog- Cock-fighting, &c.*—Person who shall keep or use or act in the management of any place for purpose of fighting or beating any bull, bear, badger, dog, cock, or other kind of animal, whether of a domestic or wild nature, or shall permit or suffer any place to be so used. (Person receiving money for admission deemed to be the keeper.)	12 & 13 Vic. c. 92, s. 3.	Penalty not exceeding £5 a-day; in default, &c., imprisonment not exceeding 2 months, with or without H. L. 1 J.
Encouraging, &c.—Every person who shall in any manner encourage, aid, or assent at the fighting or baiting of any bull, bear, badger, dog, cock, or other animal as aforesaid.	,,	Penalty not exceeding £5 a-day; in default, &c., imprisonment not exceeding 2 months, with or without H. L. 1 J.
As to Damage.—If any person shall by cruelly beating, ill-treating, over-driving, abusing, or torturing any animal, do any damage or injury to such, or shall thereby cause any damage or injury to be done to any person or to any property, he shall pay to the owner of such animal (if offender be not the owner)— The payment of compensation or imprisonment in default shall not prevent or affect punishment for the offence. Nor shall it prevent proceeding by action where compensation not sought under this Act.	s. 4.	Such compensation, not exceeding £10, as shall be ascertained and determined by the Justice by whom person convicted; in default, &c., imprisonment not exceeding 2 months, with or without H. L.
Food and Water in Pounds.—Every person who shall impound or confine, or cause to be, &c., in any pound or receptacle of the like nature any animal, shall provide sufficient and wholesome food and	s. 5.	Penalty 20s.; in default, &c., imprisonment not exceeding 14 days, with or without H. L. 1 J.

Offence, or cause of Complaint.	Statute.	Extent of Jurisd
CRUELTY TO ANIMALS—*con.* water for such; and for refusal or neglect—		
Where necessary, any person may supply such, and may recover therefor as in manner provided for penalties.	12 & 13 Vic. c. 92, s. 6.	
Slaughter Houses, &c.—For regulations to be observed in places used for slaughtering horses, &c., see sections 7, 9, 10, and title "Knacker."		
Persons licensed to slaughter horses not to be licensed as horse dealers at same time.	,,	
Improperly Conveying Animals.—If any person shall convey or carry, or cause to be, &c., in or upon any vehicle, any animal in such a manner or position as to subject such to unnecessary pain or suffering—	s. 12.	Penalty not e: £3 for first offen a penalty of £5 second and ever quent offence; in &c., imprisonm scale, not exce months, with or
Complaints to be made within one calendar month after offence committed.	s. 14.	H. L.
Where warrant may issue without summons. (*a*)	s. 16.	
Justice may compel attendance of witnesses and commit for refusing to give evidence.	s. 17.	
Using dogs for purposes of draught,	17 & 18 Vic. c. 60, s. 2.	Penalty 40*s.*; in &c., 1 month's sonment, by sca
Second offence, ...	,,	Penalty £5; in &c., 2 months' in ment, by scale. (

(*a*) Some provisions as to procedure, appeals, application of Fines, &c now regulated by the Petty Sessions Act, the Fines Act, Small Penalties other Acts amending same.

(*b*) The above Act states that the penalty is to be recovered under 12 & It means chap. 70, which is repealed by the substituted Petty Sessions Act Vic. c. 93.

Offence, or cause of Complaint.	Statute.	Extent of Jurisdiction.
CRUELTY TO ANIMALS—*con.* *Experiments on Living Animals.* *Cruelty to Animals Act,* 1876.—A person shall not perform on a living animal any experiment calculated to give pain, except subject to the *restrictions imposed by Act*—for offending or acting in contravention— Sec. 2 sets out restrictions.	39 & 40 Vic. c. 77, s. 2.	First offence, penalty not exceeding £50 ; in default, &c., imprisonment by P. S. scale. Second or subsequent offence, at the discretion of Court, shall be liable to penalty not exceeding £100, or imprisonment not exceeding 3 months. 2 J.
Special restrictions on painful experiments on dogs and cats.	s. 5.	
Absolute prohibition of public exhibition of painful experiments.—And any person performing or aiding in performing such shall be deemed guilty of offence against Act.	s. 6.	Same penalty as preceding in respect to first or any subsequent offence.
Publishing any notice of such intended exhibition in newspaper, placard, &c. Person punished under section 6 shall not be punished for same offence under any other section of this Act.	s. 6.	Penalty not exceeding £1. 2 J.
Registry of place for performance of experiments.	s. 7.	
Licence by Secretary of State.	s. 8.	
Reports to Secretary of State.	s. 9.	
Inspection by Secretary of State.	s. 10.	
Certificate of scientific bodies for exceptions to general regulations.	s. 11.	
Entry on warrant by Justice.	s. 13.	
Any person who refuses admission in demand to Police Officer or Constable so authorised, or obstructs him in his duty. Refusing name and address or giving false one— Petty Sessions (Ireland) Act, to be applicable. In Dublin, special Acts.	,,	Penalty not exceeding £5 ; in default of payment, &c., imprisonment, by scale. 2 J.

G

Offence, or cause of Complaint.	Statute.	Extent of Jurisd
CRUELTY TO ANIMALS—*con.* *Fines.*—To be applied as directed by Fines (Ireland) Act, 1851, and any Act amending same. Where penalty exceeding £5 can be imposed offender may elect, on appearing before Court, to be tried by indictment.	39 & 40 Vic. c. 77.	
A prosecution under this Act against a licensed person shall not be instituted except with assent of Chief Secretary.	ss. 20, 21.	
Act shall not apply to invertebrate animals.	s. 22.	
CURRENCY: Currency of Great Britain and Ireland assimilated by—(*a*)	6 Geo. iv. c. 79.	
CUSTOMS: Customs Consolidation Act, 1876.	39 & 40 Vic. c. 36.	
Amended by Revenue Act, 1883.	46 & 47 Vic. c. 45.	
Officers on board ships to have free access to all parts. May seal or secure goods and open locks, and if seal be broken, or goods conveyed away, or hatchways opened—	s. 47.	Master shall forf

(*a*) In convictions and orders under statutes of the Irish Parliament, th
should be entered and set forth in the present currency. For, in entering
of "£10 Irish," it will mean £10 British, both now being the same, an
viction will be improper as being excessive. It would be desirable, and t
safety of the Magistrate, were a short Act passed, providing that penal
the Irish Acts should henceforward be taken to be penalties in the present
It need not interfere with fines provided for in deeds, renewals of leases,
  Customs.—See Schedule to Revenue Act, 1883 (46 & 47 Vic. c. 55), re
part the Customs Act of 1876.

Offence, or cause of Complaint.	Statute.	Extent of Jurisdiction.
CUSTOMS—*continued.*		
Officers may put seals upon stores inwards, and if such seals be broken, or the stores secretly conveyed away—	39 & 40 Vic. c. 36, s. 47.	Master shall forfeit £20. 1 J.
True account of bullion or coin to be delivered to officers of Customs by importer, owner, or consignee. For default—	s. 49.	Shall forfeit £20. 1 J.
Report of Cargo.—Master to report within 24 hours after arrival, according to form No. 1, Schedule B, and for failure or making false report—	ss. 50, 51.	Master shall forfeit £100. 1 J.
Persons in charge of commissioned ships, British or Foreign, having goods on board shall deliver an account of same; in default—	s. 52.	Shall forfeit £100. 1 J.
Masters of ships arriving from parts beyond the seas shall, when making report, answer all questions, &c. Bulk shall not be broken or stowage altered, and if done, unless sufficient cause shown—	s. 53.	Master shall forfeit £100. 1 J.
Packages shall be reported; "Contents unknown" may be opened and examined; prohibited goods shall be forfeited.	s. 54.	
Entries generally.—Persons fraudulently importing goods to evade duty.	s. 67.	Goods shall be forfeited, and person offending shall for every such offence forfeit £100, or treble value. 1 J.
Importer or agent failing to comply with regulations—	s. 72.	Shall forfeit £20. 1 J.

Offence, or cause of Complaint.	Statute.	Extent of Ju
CUSTOMS—*continued.* *Unshipping, landing, examination, &c.*—Warehouse-keeper neglecting to stow goods properly—	39 & 40 Vic. c. 36, s. 81.	Shall forfeit £
Warehouse-keeper neglecting to produce goods deposited, when required—	s. 82.	Shall forfeit £
Persons clandestinely opening warehouse or gaining access to goods therein—	s. 84.	Shall forfeit £
Taking goods out of warehouse without payment of duty.	s. 85.	Misdemeanour
Exportation.—Masters of vessels outward to deliver certificate of clearance of last voyage, and to make entry outwards : Form No. 6, Schedule B ; for default—	—	Shall forfeit £
Clearance, &c.—Drawback goods not agreeing with the Shipping Bill shall be forfeited, and person claiming more drawback than is due—	s. 106.	Shall forfeit treble amoun back claimed of Customs.
No drawback on tobacco not properly manufactured, and for fraudulent attempt to obtain drawback—	s. 108.	Shall forfeit tr of drawback £200 at elect toms, and bacco.
Shipment of Stores.—Victualling bill for stores, stores illegally re-landed forfeited, and master or owner shall be liable.	s. 126.	Penalty of tre stores, or £1 tion of Custo
Clearance outwards.—Short shipment of goods to be notified to proper officer, and if goods be not re-warehoused or re-entered, &c., under bond—	s. 130.	Shall forfeit £
Goods unshipped without sanction of proper officer, from ship entered outwards.	,,	Goods shall b and master concerned s £100 or tre goods, &c.

Offence, or cause of Complaint.	Statute.	Extent of Jurisdiction.
CUSTOMS.—*continued.*		
Boarding of Ships.—If officers put seals upon stores from the warehouse outwards, and such seals be broken—	39 & 40 Vic. c. 36, s. 135.	Master to forfeit £20. 1 J.
Ships not bringing to at stations—	s. 136.	Master shall forfeit £20. 1 J.
Departing from port with Customs Officer on board, without his consent—	„	Master shall forfeit £100. 1 J.
Coasting trade.—Unshipping from ship arriving coastwise, or shipping to be carried coastwise, on Sundays or holidays, or unless in presence of Customs Officer, or unless at times and places appointed by him—	s. 143.	Master shall forfeit £50. 1 J.
Master of coasting vessel to keep a cargo-book, and failing to correctly keep or to produce same, or making any false entries, &c., therein—	s. 144.	Master shall forfeit £20. 1 J.
Account previous to departure to be delivered to Collector in the form No. 11 in Sched., and Master failing to deliver a correct account— (Proviso.—Commissioners may grant general transires.)	s. 145.	Shall forfeit £20.
Transire to be delivered within 24 hours after arrival. Goods subject to Excise duty not to be unladen without permission of Excise Officer. Regulations as to goods from Isle of Man, and for unloading goods contrary to section—	s. 146.	Master shall forfeit £20. 1 J.
Officer may board and examine coasting ship, demand documents, which ought to be on board, to be produced, &c., and for disobedience, &c.—	s. 147.	Master shall forfeit £20. 1 J.
Channel Islands.—Regulations as to arrival at and departure from Channel Islands. And penalty for shipping prohibited goods from or sailing therefrom without clearance.	ss. 156, 157, 158.	

Offence, or cause of Complaint.	Statute.	Extent of Jurisdict
CUSTOMS—*continued.* *Smuggling.*—Ships and boats not bringing to when required— (And for not bringing to may be fired into.)	39 & 40 Vic. c. 36, s. 181.	Master shall forfeit
Persons may be searched if officers have reason to suspect smuggled goods are concealed upon them. And attempting to prevent seizure of such goods or obstructing officer.	s. 184.	Penalty £100. (See also sec. 187.)
Persons before search may require to be taken before a Justice or Officer of Customs. Females to be searched only by females, and if any officer without reasonable ground cause any person to be searched—	s. 185.	Penalty not exc £10.
Persons denying having foreign goods on person or in possession, &c., and if such be afterwards found on person or in baggage, &c.—	s. 185.	Shall forfeit £100 o value, at electi Commissioners.
Illegally importing, being concerned in, &c., unshipping, removing from quay, wharf, &c., carrying goods into warehouse without authority, removing from warehouse, harbouring, carrying, evading customs duties, &c.— (As to how penalties enforced, &c., see secs. 232, 236, 237, footnotes.)	s. 186.	Shall for each offer feit either treble of goods, includ: duty payable the £100, at the ele Commissioners o toms. (a)
Rescuing goods, rescuing person, assaulting, or obstructing officers, &c. &c., assisting in such, &c. (And see also sec. 184.) And for form of information see Sched. C, count 11.	s. 187.	Penalty £100.

Smuggling Cases. Onus of Proof.—In questions as to whether duty p be on Defendant, sec. 259. *Vivâ voce* evidence may be given as to offic sec. 261. What shall be proof of orders of Treasury or Customs, o Revenue, &c., sec. 262.

(a) *Treble Value, including the Duty.*—Will mean treble the value of which duty has been paid, and not treble the value (without duty), and s such a *single* duty. In estimating value it may be according to the rate of best quality upon which duty paid, sec. 214.

Offence, or cause of Complaint.	Statute.	Extent of Jurisdiction.
CUSTOMS—*continued*. Persons to number of three or more assembled, or having assembled to unship, land, run, conceal, &c., &c., spirits, tobacco, or prohibited, restricted, or uncustomed goods—	39 & 40 Vic. c. 36, s. 188.	Shall each forfeit a penalty not exceeding £500, nor less than £100. 1 J.
Procuring or hiring persons to assemble or run goods. Persons armed or disguised, with goods, within five miles of coast.	s. 189.	Imprisonment, with or without H. L., for any term not exceeding 3 years. (This does not appear to be within summary jurisdiction.)
Signalling.—Persons after sunset and before sunrise, between 21 September and 1 April, and after 8 p. m., and before 6 a. m. at other times, signalling smuggling vessels, &c. (Proof that signal not intended, to lie on Defendant.)	s. 191.	Misdemeanour, triable by indictment.
Shooting at boats belonging to navy or revenue service, &c.	s. 193.	Felony.
Where persons are taken before Justices for offences under the Customs Acts, such Justices may order them to be detained or admitted to bail.	s. 197.	
Persons offering goods for sale on pretence of being smuggled, &c.	s. 201.	Shall forfeit treble value. 1 J. And the goods, although not liable to duty, shall be forfeited.
Collusive Seizures.—Officers and persons making collusive seizures, or taking bribes, &c., and on persons—	s. 217.	Officers shall forfeit £500, and persons offering bribes, &c., £200. 1 J.
Penalties, how to be sued for.—And see footnotes.	s. 218, &c.	

The above analysis is to be taken merely as an index to the sections, and in each case the section itself should be consulted in order to have an adequate knowledge of what constitutes the offence.

For powers of R. I. Constabulary in reference to Customs, see 20 & 21 Vic. c. 40, s. 5.

Scale of Penalty and Punishment for Offences. Sec. 233.—Where any person shall be brought before a Justice for any offence against the Customs Acts, for

Offence, or cause of Complaint.	Statute.	Extent of Jurisdiction.
CUSTOMS—*continued*. Customs and Inland Revenue Act, 1878.—Where, in the opinion of Commissioners of Customs, the deficiency in stores on board ship shall be in excess of the quantity which might fairly have been consumed, having regard to time, &c., between clearing for foreign voyage and return to port, whether driven to port by stress of weather, want of repair, or other cause—	41 Vic. c. 15, s. 4.	Master shall forfeit, besides duties on such excess of deficiency at the rate chargeable on importation of goods the subject of such excess, a penalty not exceeding £20, recoverable by information and summons. 1 J.

which a pecuniary penalty is thereby imposed, if the goods in respect of which he shall have been so brought shall not consist of spirits or tobacco, or being spirits or tobacco shall not exceed 5 gallons of spirits or 20 pounds weight of tobacco, such Justice may proceed summarily upon the case without information or direction of the Commissioners of Customs; and if such person shall be convicted, such Justice may adjudge that he shall, in lieu of any other penalty, forfeit a sum not less than the single nor more than the treble value of such goods, including the duty of importation thereof (sec. 214 regulates how value is to be estimated), and in default of payment, commit such person to any of Her Majesty's gaols for any period not less than 14 days nor more than 1 month; and if such spirits or tobacco shall exceed 5 gallons, but not exceed 20 gallons of spirits, or shall exceed 20 pounds weight of tobacco, but not exceed 80 pounds weight, such person shall forfeit a sum equal to treble the duty paid value of such spirits or tobacco, or £100, at the election of the Commissioners of Customs; and if proceeded against for the latter, and convicted, such Justice may mitigate the penalty to any sum not less than one-fourth, and, in default of payment of the penalty or mitigated penalty as imposed, may commit the offender to any of Her Majesty's gaols until the same be paid; and if such spirits shall exceed 20 gallons, or such tobacco shall exceed 80 pounds weight, such person shall forfeit a sum equal to treble the value of such spirits or tobacco, or £100, at the election of the Commissioners of Customs, and shall, upon conviction, forthwith pay without any mitigation the penalty imposed, and in default thereof the said Justice shall commit the person so convicted to any of Her Majesty's gaols, there to remain until such penalty shall be paid.

Sec. 236.—Person committed in default of payment of penalty less than £100 to be discharged by gaoler in 6 months, if not duly released.

Sec. 237.—Where penalty adjudged to be paid exceeds £100, Court may, in case of first offence, commit for not less than 6 nor more than 9 months; and if for a subsequent offence may order that offender shall, in lieu of payment of the penalty, be imprisoned, with or without hard labour, for not less than 6 nor more than 12 months.

Justices may commit to nearest Gaol or House of Correction, if none in their jurisdiction (s. 238).

Hard Labour.—Justices may commute H. L. where offender is a female or infirm.

If prisoner convicted of offence for which liable to imprisonment with hard labour, if it be made to appear, while he is in prison that he had before been con-

Offence, or cause of Complaint.	Statute.	Extent of Jurisdiction.
DEBTS : Small Debts Act (under £2) (a). It shall be lawful for the Justice or Justices at Petty Sessions to hear and determine causes for the recovery of debts, between party and party, under the value of £2, where the right to recover such debts shall have accrued within 12 calendar months before the day of the date of the process issued. (Power of appeal given to Plaintiff	22 Vic. c. 14, s. 5.	"The Justice or Justices shall either make an order for the payment of the sum claimed, or shall dismiss the complaint, either upon the merits, or without prejudice, and with or without costs not exceeding 5s. ; and shall direct execution by the

victed of a similar offence, imprisonment may be extended, and warrant may be amended accordingly (sec. 240).

(a) *Jurisdiction.*—" The Act applies to debts in the usual sense of that term ; no demand for anything in the nature of damages, as breach of warranty, false representation, or deceit, falls within it ; cases between master and apprentice are not within the Act. The original debt must have been contracted within twelve months. The amount recovered must be under £2, if it has been reduced by payments, and the balance sought to be recovered is under £2, the case is within the Act ; but if the debt were originally contracted more than twelve months ago, a subsequent reduction of the debt by payments made within twelve months will not bring the case within the Act. The Magistrates may enforce the attendance of witnesses, as pointed out by the 14 & 15 Vic. c. 93, s. 13. No decree can be issued against the person ; only 5s. costs can be awarded in any case."—*Castle Circular, 12th August,* 1859.

Where the account is settled within the year, and is under £2, there would be the right to recover, and the process may be on foot of "settled account " : see printed form of process.

Decree to hold good for a year.—*Circular, 25th Sept.,* 1865.

Law Officers' opinion, dated 10th Sept., 1866 :

1st. Small debts for rent contracted within the year—such as rent due on weekly holdings, or for use and occupation—are " Debts " within the statute.

2nd. So is an Attorney's bill for costs, if under 40s.

3rd. If a debt single in its nature—for example, £5 lent at one time—is proved to be due, the Plaintiff cannot, before the Justices, abandon the excess and take an order for a sum less than £2. It is different if the debt has been, before the process, reduced by payments to less than 40s.—The Magistrates then have jurisdiction.

4th. If the process is for a sum within the jurisdiction—for example, for £1 15s.—and it is proved that only £1 is due, the Magistrates can give a decree or order for the lesser sum.

5th. The service of the process need not be personal, but may be in the manner prescribed by 14 & 15 Vic. c. 93, sec. 12, and 22 Vic. c. 14, sec. 9.

Stamps.—There are two distinct classes of stamp duties imposed on the proceedings, viz. stamp duties, properly so called, payable to Her Majesty, under sec. 6 (Schedule A) ; and fees denoted by stamps under sec. 7 (Schedule C).—*Circular, 17th November,* 1859.

Stamped forms of process, and the others in Schedule A, may be had of any stamp

Offence, or cause of Complaint.	Statute.	Extent of Jur
DEBTS—*continued.* and Defendant.) See Act and Schedules in Appendix.	22 Vic. c. 14, s. 5.	seizure and i Defendant's tiff's goods."
Wearing apparel and bedding, and the tools and implements of trade of debtor, not exceeding in the whole the value of £5, exempt from execution under decree.	51 & 52 Vic. c. 47, s. 4.	·—
Small Debts.—Defendant may be sued at any Petty Sessions within Petty Sessions district in which he resides, whether it be within or without the county in which he resides.	34 & 35 Vic. c. 76, s. 3.	
Infants.—Contracts by infants, except for necessaries, to be void. No action to be brought on such contract upon promise or ratification made after full age.	37 & 38 Vic. c. 62, s. 1. s. 2.	
DECLARATIONS: Solemn declarations are taken by J.P., under Act for suppression of voluntary and extrajudicial oaths; and see "Dying Declarations" in Indictable Offence Index.	5 & 6 Wm. iv. c. 62. (a)	And wilfully false decla an indictab meanour. "Affirmation
Title of this Act repealed by Stat. Law Rev. Act.	51 & 52 Vic. c. 57.	

distributor. Schedule C are the Petty Sessions Stamps. A 6d. stam put on the *entry of the case* in the book, and a 6d. stamp on the *entry*

Justice's Order.—The words of the Act, it will be observed, are " make an order for the payment of the sum claimed, or shall dism plaint," from which it would appear that there is no power to make a less sum, unless by Plaintiff's consent; but see Law Adviser's op contrary above given.

The complaint should be brought in Petty Sessions district wher resides.

(a) May be entitled the "Statutory Declarations Act, 1835 (4· c. 41, sec. 68)."

Mames, or cause of Complaint.	Statute.	Extent of Jurisdiction.
: Larceny."		
LISHING (*Buildings, &c.*) : Landlord and Tenant."		
ITED TENEMENTS : ng and certifying by Justices, purposes of ejectment.	23 & 24 Vic. c. 154, s. 79.	Form of certificate in Schedule to Act; and see Appendix. 2 J.
ITERS : H. M.'s service, when brought re Justices— int to arrest may issue—	Army Dis- cipline Act. 47 Vic. c. 8, s. 6.	To be committed to gaol, or to depôt, if convenient. Justice to report to War Office, without delay. 1 J.
RTING WIFE OR CHILD : at they become destitute and ive relief in or out of work- se. 'Poor Law" and "Married men."	10 & 11 Vic. c. 84, s. 2.	Imprisonment not ex- ceeding 3 months', H. L. 1 J.
'IDATION : Landlord and Tenant."		
IARGE (*Servant*) : r refusing discharge and certifi-) of behaviour to servant, if no icient cause shown, J. P. may e certificate accordingly. Employers and Workmen."	2 Geo. i. c. 17, s. 4.	1 J.
IARGE FROM FIRST CON- ION. First Offence."		

Offence, or cause of Complaint.	Statute.	Extent of Juri
DISCRETION : In admitting to bail for certain offences.	See 14 & 15 Vic. c. 93, s. 16.	—
In discharging offender from his first offence, under—	14 & 15 Vic. c. 92, s. 21.	—
Like under "Larceny Act."	18 & 19 Vic. c. 126, s. 1.	—
Like Probation of "First Offenders Act."		
And see Introductory Remarks.		
DISORDERLY CONDUCT : Drunk or disorderly in public-house or refreshment house, and refusing to quit.	23 & 24 Vic. c. 107, s. 42.	Penalty not 40s.; in def imprisonment ceeding 1 mon
Riotous or indecent behaviour in any street, police office, Petty Sessions Court, or police station-house within the town. (See first if this Act in force in district.) For other acts of misconduct in streets, though not called by name "Disorderly," see section 72 of the Towns Improvement Act, Appendix ; and see also "Vagrancy" and "Blaspheming" in the streets.	(Towns Improvement Act.) 17 & 18 Vic. c. 103, s. 72.	Penalty not 40s.: in def imprisonment or, in discretio tice, may be i for not exc days.

DISPUTES :
  Between buyer and seller.—See "Fairs and Markets."
  Trade disputes.—See "Employers and Workmen," and "Conspiracy and Protection of Property."		

DISTILLATION (*Illicit*) : See "Excise."		

Offence, or cause of Complaint.	Statute.	Extent of Jurisdiction.
DISTRESS (*For Rent, &c.*): No person making any distress for rent, taxes, rates, &c. (where the same due shall not exceed £20), to take other charges than those mentioned in Schedule to Act, and in no case to charge for any matter not really done. (*s*)	9 & 10 Vic. c. 111, s. 15.	—
Any person who shall levy or take from any person, or retain from the produce of goods sold for rent, taxes, &c., any greater costs or charges than are set forth in the Schedule to this Act; or who shall make any charge for any matter or thing not having been really done—	s. 16.	Justice to award treble the amount so unlawfully taken, to be repaid by the person so acting to the party complaining, with full costs, by distress; in default, &c., imprisonment, by scale. 2 J.

(*s*) *Schedule of the limitation of costs and charges on distress for small rents or rates, taxes, impositions, or assessments not exceeding £20:*

	s.	*d.*
Levying distress, ...	2	0
Man in possession, per day, each (but not exceeding two in number, unless upon information sworn before a Justice, that a rescue or violence is apprehended), . . .	2	0
All expenses of advertisements, if any such, ...	5	0

    Catalogues, sale and commission, and delivery of goods, 1*s.* in the pound on the net produce of the sale, if sold by a licensed auctioneer; otherwise, 6*d.* in the pound on the net produce of the sale.

Auction Fees.—In a distress made for rates, where the auctioneer deducted from the proceeds of the sale 5 per cent., having also charged the purchaser 5 per cent., the following opinion was given by the Law Adviser:—

    "This not being one of the excepted cases in the 8 & 9 Vic. c. 15, s. 5, I think it was necessary to have a licensed auctioneer. The statute 9 & 10 Vic. c. 111, Schedule B, has fixed 1*s.* in the pound to cover all expenses of sale, commission, and delivery; to this extent the farmer is bound to pay, but he is not to be called on to pay more, either directly or indirectly: and he does pay it *indirectly* if his goods are sold on the terms that the purchaser is to pay auctioneer's fees, for he will then give so much less. If that 5 per cent. has already been paid by the purchaser to the auctioneer, pursuant to previous arrangement, I think it ought not to be again deducted from the farmer by the collector."

    Growing crops, plants, &c., are not to be seized under Civil Bill decrees or Justices' orders, 26 & 27 Vic. c. 62; and see also 51 & 52 Vic. c. 47, s. 4, exempting wearing apparel, bedding, tools, &c., under value of £5.

    For Civil Bill Court fees, and expenses of executing decrees, &c., see 27 & 28 Vic. c. 99, s. 17.

Offence, or cause of Complaint.	Statute.	Extent of Jurisdiction.
DISTRESS—*continued.* Witnesses disobeying summons, or refusing to give evidence.	9 & 10 Vic. c. 111, s. 17.	Penalty not exceeding 40s. ; recoverable as above. 2 J.
If complaint unfounded, Justices may give costs, not exceeding 20s., to party complained against.	s. 18.	
No judgment to be given against any Landlord, unless he personally levies the distress.	,,	—
Parties not to be barred of other legal remedies.		
Bailiffs and others who shall levy any distress whatsoever shall, on demand of the party distrained, give a copy of his charges, and of the costs and charges of distress, signed by him ; in default—	s. 20. (36 & 37 Vic. c. 82.)	Shall be liable to forfeit not exceeding 40s. ; in default, &c., imprisonment, by scale. 2 J.
Printed copy of clauses of Act to be hung up in Petty Sessions House.	9 & 10 Vic. c. 111, s. 21.	—
DISQUALIFICATION of Justices in certain cases, Act to remove. See "Appendix."	30 & 31 Vic. c. 115.	—
DOGS : Setting on dogs to attack or worry persons or animals in roads or streets. (*a*)	14 & 15 Vic. c. 92, s. 10. (36 & 37 Vic. c. 82.)	Penalty not exceeding 10s. ; in default, &c., imprisonment not exceeding 7 days. 1 J. Like.
Any person who shall keep or suffer to be at large within fifty yards of any public road any dog without being muzzled, or without a log of sufficient weight to prevent such dog from being dangerous. (*b*)	,,	

(*a*) But if the dog so set on should bite a person, the offence may be dealt with as an assault.

(*b*) It is said that if a dog be out in presence and under control of its master or other person, although unlogged and unmuzzled, and on a public road, it will not be considered *at large* within the meaning of the above section. Were it otherwise, sporting dogs, or a pack of hounds, may be brought within it.

The suffering a mastiff or other furious dog to go about unmuzzled is a public nuisance, and the owner may be indicted.

Offence, or cause of Complaint.	Statute.	Extent of Jurisdiction.
DOGS—*continued*. Justices may, by warrant, direct constables to seize and kill any dangerous dog so kept at large.	14 & 15 Vic. c. 92, s. 10.	—
Injury to Sheep by Dogs.—Owner of dog shall be liable for damages done by such dog to any sheep, where the damages claimed shall not exceed £5. Mischievous propensity of dog, or of owner's knowledge thereof, of owner's neglect, need not be proved. Occupier of house or apartment, as case may be, where the dog was at time of the injury permitted to live, or remain, to be deemed the owner, unless the contrary (or that the dog were allowed there without his sanction or knowledge) be proved.	25 & 26 Vic. c. 59, s. 1.	Owner of sheep may obtain order for damages not exceeding £5, recoverable by distress under Petty Sessions Act. 1 J.
Stealing dogs, &c., see "Larceny." Killing or maiming, see "Malicious Injuries;" also "Cruelty to Animals." For game dogs, see "Game."	"	
Dogs' Regulation Act, 1865. *Licence.*—Person having in his possession or custody any dog or dogs shall, on or before 31st March in each year, take out	28 Vic. c. 50. ss. 6, 20.	Penalty not exceeding £2; in default, &c., imprisonment not exceeding 1 month. 1 J.

Dogs.—The object of the Act as set out in the Preamble is not, as sometimes supposed, to realise a *duty;* it is to "prevent ravages by dogs; to regulate their keeping, and identify their owners." Still it does not appear that for a dog brought into Ireland after 31st March a licence is required at any time before 31st March following. So dogs pupped after 31st March do not require to be licensed before 31st March, following year.

In England, by 30 Vic. c. 5, the annual Excise duty on every dog is 5s. It is not chargeable on any dog under 6 months old.

Owners of dogs kept on board ship lying in harbour are not required to take out licence.—Law Adviser's opinion, 17th April, 1869.

If the dog is destroyed after the order to take out a licence has been made, and before any further proceedings are taken, no other summons need or can be issued.—Law Adviser's opinion, 30th March, 1869.

Justice cannot dismiss the case and order licence to be taken out.—*Circular*, 21 Oct., 1867.

Offence, or cause of Complaint.	Statute.	Extent of Jurisdic
DOGS—*continued.* licence from Petty Sessions Clerk of the district, in default—		
Where owner and person having the custody reside in different Petty Sessions districts, the latter shall take out the licence.	28 Vic. c. 50. ss. 6, 20.	And Justice shall such person for to take out licen for keeping afte without licence
Liability.—Occupier of house or premises where dog kept, or permitted to live or remain, liable to licence duty, unless proof given that he is not owner or that dog remains in premises without his knowledge. Where there are joint occupiers, the occupier of that °part where dog so kept, or permitted to remain, shall be liable. Clerk to enter all licences in book to be kept for the purpose—to be open for inspection of Constabulary, Justices, &c.	s. 7.	in addition to the ties imposed for and subsequent of pay a sum not ing 1s. a-day f day so kept licence.
Transfer.—Where licensed dog transferred by sale or gift, a new licence for that year not necessary, but transferee shall obtain certificate (Form D in Schedule), and within 15 days register the transfer in his district; in default—	s. 9.	Like penalty, above. To be as a person keepi licensed dogs.
Person having in his possession or custody any dog or dogs shall produce licence when required by a Justice or any member of Constabulary force, and for refusal he shall, if licensed, be liable to—	s. 21.	Penalty not exc 5s.: in default, imprisonment n ceeding 1 week.
No penalty where the failure accidental, not wilful.	s. 23.	
List of licences to be annually publicly posted by 15th April.		
Penalties recoverable by Petty Sessions Act—in Dublin by the Local Act.		

Offence, or cause of Complaint.	Statute.	Extent of Jurisdiction.
DOGS—*continued*. Act provides mode of accounting for stamps, &c. The licence duty on each dog is 2s. A 6d. fee denoted by Petty Sessions Stamp, to be paid on each Certificate of Registry. Justice empowered to enforce such fee.	28 Vic. c. 50. s. 23.	
Surplus moneys for stamps, after payment of expenses, to be paid over to Treasurers of Boroughs and Counties. And what is meant by "Boroughs" for such purpose, see—	30 & 31 Vic. c. 116.	
Stray dogs, where owner not known, may be detained, sold, or destroyed, by Constabulary.	34 & 35 Vic. c. 56, s. 1.	—
On complaint that a dog is dangerous and not kept under proper control, and when the Court is satisfied of the fact—	s. 2.	May order dog to be kept under proper control, or destroyed.
Failing to comply with order of Justices.	,,	Penalty not exceeding 20s. a-day during disobedience; imprisonment, by scale; in default, &c. 2 J. or 1 Stip.
Local authority may, if a mad dog is suspected to be found within their jurisdiction, place restrictions such as they think expedient on all dogs not being under control. Due notice to be published. For acting in contravention of order—	s. 3.	Penalty not exceeding 20s.; in default of payment, imprisonment not exceeding 14 days, by scale. 2 J. or 1 Stip.
Not to affect powers in local or other Acts.	s. 6.	
DRAINAGE: Acts in relation to Drainage Works: Unauthorized persons opening loughs, sluices, or canals, made under authority of Act, or wilfully or maliciously letting off the water of any of the reservoirs, rivers, canals, or drains.	5 & 6 Vic. c 89, s. 132. (36 & 37 Vic. c. 82.)	Penalty not exceeding £20, by distress, &c.; in default, imprisonment by scale. 1 J.

H

Offence, or cause of Complaint.	Statute.	Extent of
DRAINAGE—*continued*.		
Persons depositing gravel, &c., so as to obstruct navigation or free passage of the water in the rivers, &c., improved under Act.	5 & 6 Vic. c. 89, s. 134. (36 & 37 Vic. c. 82.)	Penalty n £10 ; in imprisonn ceeding : scale.
Assaulting Commissioners and others engaged on the works.	5 & 6 Vic. c. 89, s. 135. (36 & 37 Vic. c. 82.)	Penalty n £5 ; in c sonment 2 months.
Wilfully causing obstructions in streams or rivers, by depositing stones or materials therein.	5 & 6 Vic. c. 89, s. 152.	Penalty n £5 (in c property, party ag default, ment not months, out H.L.
Justices empowered to investigate complaints where aqueducts, culverts, and tunnels are not kept thoroughly cleansed.	9 & 10 Vic. c. 4, s. 42.	
For drainage in towns, &c., see 10 & 11 Vic. c. 34, and title "Public Health."		
DRIVERS (*Cars, Carts, and Carriages*) :		
Public Stage Carriages.—Driver, owner, or guard, permitting more passengers to be carried than the number for whom seats shall be provided, inside or outside, allowing at least 16 inches for each passenger, not including children under 7 years.	14 & 15 Vic. c. 92, s. 11.	Penalty n 40s. ; im imprisonn ceeding 1
Allowing passengers to sit on top of luggage, or any part not intended for passengers, or permitting luggage exceeding 2 feet in height above the roof on carriage carrying inside passengers.	,,	Like.
Omitting to paint on doors, &c., as therein, the number of passengers to be conveyed.	,,	Penalty n 40s. ; in imprisonn ceeding 1

Offence, or cause of Complaint.	Statute.	Extent of Jurisdiction.
DRIVERS—*continued.* Driver or guard misspending time, insulting passengers, becoming incapacitated by drink, or demanding more than legal fare.	14 & 15 Vic. c. 92, s. 11.	Like penalty as above, and in addition may order repayment of any sum so exacted, or compensation for damage caused; in default, &c., imprisonment not exceeding 1 month. 1 J.
Drivers of such stage carriages (in places where assistance may be procured) quitting horses or box of carriage until proper persons stand at their head, or hold reins to prevent their running away, or any such last-mentioned person not remaining at horses' heads or holding reins until driver has returned; or any driver who shall entrust reins to others to drive; or any person who shall so take the reins and drive.	,,	Penalty not exceeding 40*s.*; in default, &c., imprisonment not exceeding 1 month. 1 J.
Carts and Cars (Names).—Any owner of any cart, car, dray, or other such carriage used for the conveyance of goods, who shall use or allow same to be used on any public road or street without having his name and residence painted upon some conspicuous part of the right or off side, in legible letters, not less than an inch in height, in different colour from the ground on which painted, and in words at length; or who shall paint or cause to be painted false or fictitious name thereon.	s. 12.	Penalty not exceeding 10*s.*; in default, &c., imprisonment not exceeding 7 days, by scale. 1 J.
Driver taking charge of more than one Cart, &c.—Person who shall act as the driver, or have the sole charge of more than one such carriage as last aforesaid, on any public road or street, unless in the	,,	Like.

Punishment, &c.—The section providing penalties for these several offences by drivers of carriages, cars, &c., expressly states that such shall be in addition to any civil action to which he may *subject himself.*

H 2

Offence, or cause of Complaint.	Statute.	Extent of Juris
DRIVERS—*continued.* cases where two of such carriages, and no more, shall be drawn, each by one horse only, and the hinder horse attached by sufficient rein to back of foremost carriage.	14 & 15 Vic. c. 92, s. 12.	Penalty not 10s.; in defa imprisonment ceeding 7 days,
Driver Riding on Carts, &c.—Person having care or charge of any such carriage as last aforesaid, who shall ride upon the same, or upon any horse drawing the same, on any public road or street, except accompanied by some other person on foot or horseback, to guide the same; or where such carriage shall be driven with reins, and be conducted by some person holding the reins of all the horses.	,,	Like.
Driver Leaving Horse, &c.—Driver of such carriage who shall negligently or wilfully be at such distance or in such situation that he cannot have direction of the horse or horses drawing same, or who shall leave such carriage on such road or street, so as to obstruct passage.	,,	Like.
Refusing to tell Owner's Name, &c.—Driver of such carriage as last aforesaid, not having owner's name legibly thereon as required, refusing to tell true Christian and surname and residence of owner. (See special provisions, sec. 13 hereafter, where offender refuses name.)	,,	Like.
Rules of the Road.—Person driving any carriage whatsoever, or riding, who, meeting any other carriage or horse, or other animal, shall not keep on the left or near side of the road or street; or if passing carriage, horse, &c., going in same direction, shall not, where it is practicable, go to the right or off side. (a)	s. 13.	Like.

(a) This rule of the road is not to be followed when manifestly c accident would be occasioned, and which by acting otherwise may be *Turley Thomas*, 8 C. & P., 103.

Offence, or cause of Complaint.	Statute.	Extent of Jurisdiction.
DRIVERS—*continued.* *Passing with led Horse.*—Person riding any horse, and leading any other horse, who shall not keep such led horse on the side farthest away from any carriage or person passing on any public road or street of a town—	14 & 15 Vic. c. 92, s. 13.	Penalty not exceeding 10*s.*; in default, &c., imprisonment not exceeding 7 days, by scale. 1 J.
Obstruction, &c.—Any person who shall in any manner, wilfully or by negligence or misbehaviour, prevent or interrupt the free passage of any person or carriage on any public road or street or crossing.	,,	Penalty not exceeding 20*s.*; in default, &c., imprisonment not exceeding 14 days, by scale. 1 J.
Furious or Negligent Driving.—Any person riding horse or other animal, or driving any sort of carriage, who shall ride or drive same furiously on any public road or street, so as to endanger any passenger or person, or who shall by carelessness or wilful misbehaviour cause any injury to any person or property on any public road or street. (*a*)	,,	Like.

(*a*) *Furious Driving.*—By the "*Offences against the Person Act,*" 24 & 25 Vic. c. 100, s. 35—"Whosoever having the charge of any carriage or vehicle shall by wanton or furious driving or racing, or other wilful misconduct, or by wilful neglect, do or cause to be done any bodily harm to any person whatsoever, shall be guilty of a misdemeanour; and being convicted thereof, shall be liable, at the discretion of the Court, to be imprisoned for any term not exceeding two years, with or without hard labour." Triable by indictment.

If a coachman or driver (being a servant) do any damage to a passenger on the road by negligent driving, his master will be liable for the injury done, and the rule is not that any negligence on the Plaintiff's part will preclude him from recovering; but though there has been negligence on the Plaintiff's part, still he may recover, unless he could by ordinary care have avoided the consequence of the Defendant's negligence. A man who had improperly left an ass fettered on the highway was, nevertheless, held entitled to recover against one who negligently drove over it.—*Davies* v. *Mann*, 10 *M. & W.*, 546. If two drunken stage coachmen were to drive their respective carriages against each other and injure the passengers, each would have to bear the injury to his own carriage, and it has been considered unreasonable that each set of passengers should by a fiction of law be identified with the coachmen who drove them, so as to be restricted for remedy to actions against their own driver or his employer. This appears to be the result of the decision in *Thorogood* v. *Bryan*, 8 *C. B.*, 115 (England). But the reasoning of the Court, and its consistency with other cases, has been questioned. The doctrine of contributory negligence applies to the case of tort in the execution of a

Offence, or cause of Complaint.	Statute.	Extent of Jurisd
DRIVERS—*continued.* *Children under* 13 *not to drive.*—No cart, dray, waggon, or other such carriage, and no hackney car or carriage, or car or carriage let on hire, travelling on any public road or street, shall be driven by any person not fully 13 years of age—(owner liable).	14 & 15 Vic. c. 92, s. 13.	Owner liable to not exceeding default, &c., i ment not exce days, by scale.
Special Provisions as to Proceedings for Road Offences, &c.—Constabulary are to take cognizance of all such offences, and where offender can be discovered summon him to Petty Sessions where offence committed or he resides. Any person may complain.	—	—
If Offender not Known.—Where name and residence of offender unknown, and cannot be ascertained, he may be arrested; and if such offender refuse to discover his name, it shall be lawful for the Justice before whom he shall be taken, or to whom any such complaint made— (*a*)	14 & 15 Vic. c. 92, s. 14.	To commit him t not exceeding or to entertain ceeding against the penalty afo a description of son and offen without addi name or de but expressing proceeding tha fused to disc name.
Horse, &c., and cart, &c., in charge of such offenders may be detained in place of safe custody as security for penalty, and may be sold for payment of the penalty and expenses.	,,	—

contract. Where a man carelessly left his cart and horse unattended in and a young child climbed into it and received a severe fall, the horse forward by a boy, the owner was held responsible, on the ground th thrown temptation in the child's way, he could not be allowed to object yielded to it.—*Lynch* v. *Nurden*, 1 *Q. B.*, 29 (England); and in *Lygo* v 9 *Exch.* 302.

(*a*) This power in the section seems to be conferred on the Justice, al may not happen at the time to be sitting in Petty Sessions. The pow by reason of the offender refusing to discover his name; and on this this case, it is consistent with the 8th section of Petty Sessions Act, v not include this offence in the cases which may be tried out of Pett The Justice should be careful to see that an offence has been committed

Offence, or cause of Complaint.	Statute	Extent of Jurisdiction.
DRIVERS—*continued*. Justice may, by writing, order removal of such obstructions on roads; and Justices at Petty Sessions may issue distress warrant for expense of removal.	14 & 15 Vic. c. 92, s. 14.	
Compensation to Parties injured.—Where any hurt or damage caused by any of the said offences, the Justices on the hearing may, in addition to penalty, order offender, or—where the offence is by the driver of any carriage—the owner of such, forthwith to pay for compensation to party aggrieved a sum not exceeding 40s. (where so much damage proved). And any sum so paid by owner may in like manner be recovered by him from the driver. (*a*)	,,	
Summons for driver of stage carriage may be left with bookkeeper, or with person in care of office.		
Commissioners under 9 Geo. iv. c. 82, and Commissioners under Local Acts, and Justices in Petty Sessions in other than Corporate towns, may appoint car-stands and make regulations as to thoroughfares and markets, to prevent nuisance and obstructions, &c., and persons offending against provisions or breaking through regulations.	s. 17.	See section for regulations and scale of penalties for their violation.
For other offences on Roads, &c., see titles "Nuisances on Roads;" "Roads." And for offences in towns, &c, see "Towns Improvement Act," sec. 17; and sec. 28 of "Police Clauses Act," 10 & 11 Vic. c. 89.		

se of those in the sections as to Road Nuisances; that the offender's name is not sown; that it cannot be ascertained, and that he refuses to disclose it.

(*a*) *Compensation.*—Where the compensation is ordered against the offender it ill be recovered with the penalty imposed, and by the same means; but where it against the owner, the mode is not pointed out. Certainly it cannot be by iprisonment; and assuming, as seems to be the case, that it is by distress, some mmons or notice should be *given the owner* of the intention to make him

Offence, or cause of Complaint.	Statute.	Extent of Ju
DRUNKENNESS: (a) *Drunkenness.*—Every person found drunk in any highway or other public place, whether a building or not, or on any licensed premises.	35 & 36 Vic. c. 94, s. 12. (36 & 37 Vic. c. 82.)	*First Offenc* not exceedi default of p prisonment ing 1 wee without H.
Second Conviction within 12 months.	,,	*Second Cos* Penalty no 20s.; in def ment impri exceeding 1 or without
Third or subsequent conviction within such period of 12 months.	,,	*Third Cos* Penalty no 40s.; in dea ment impri exceeding month, with H. L.
Drunk and Disorderly, or Drunk in Charge of Horse, Carriage, &c.—Every person who in any highway or other public place, whether a building or not, is guilty while drunk of riotous or disorderly behaviour, or who is drunk while in charge on any highway or other public place of any carriage, horse, cattle, or steam engine, or who is drunk when in possession of any	,,	Penalty not 40s.; in def ment impri exceeding month, with H. L.; *or*, cretion of imprisonme without E exceeding month. 2

chargeable. If the damage be done through any misconduct or mis the master's service, the servant may, at master's prosecution, be pi section 16 of above Act. The remedy will be under Employers and V 38 & 39 Vic. c. 90.

(a) By the 24 & 25 Vic. c. 49, s. 2, it is enacted that—"In every any Justice of the Peace shall order any person to be committe drunkenness for a period not exceeding 48 hours, such committal n local or neighbouring bridewell, although the same may not be a distr bridewell."

Drunkenness.—See notes on this subject under "Licensing Acts."

Penalties.—The provisions of the Small Penalties (Ireland) Act, 1 Vic. c. 82, as to enforcing penalties, will apply to small penalties und ing Acts. Where the Towns Improvement Act, 1854, is in force, for offence of drunkenness against above section 12 shall be enforce by the Towns Improvement Act (17 & 18 Vic. c. 103).—See section Act, 1874.

Offence, or cause of Complaint.	Statute.	Extent of Jurisdiction.
DRUNKENNESS—*continued.* loaded firearms, may be apprehended, and shall be liable to a penalty, &c. (As to constable's power to detain drunkards, discharge and summon them, traders permitting drunkenness, and their power to exclude drunkards—see Licensing Acts," Summary Index.)	34 & 35 Vic. c. 94, s. 12. (36 & 37 Vic. c. 82.)	
Drunk or Disorderly Persons refusing to Quit, &c.—Any person who shall be drunk, riotous, quarrelsome, or disorderly in any licensed premises for sale of beer, wine, or spirituous liquors by retail to be consumed on the premises, or for refreshment, resort, or entertainment, under Refreshment Houses Act, *and* shall refuse or neglect to quit on being requested by the manager, &c., or his agent or servant, or by any constable.	23 & 24 Vic. c. 107, s. 42. (36 & 37 Vic. s. 82.)	Penalty not exceeding 40s.; in default of payment imprisonment not exceeding 1 calendar month.　　1 J. And constables on being required are to assist in expelling such disorderly persons.
DWELLINGS OF THE POOR: Tenements held under, and having the requisites set forth in this Act, consisting of house with not more than half an acre, if any, of land, as garden, or cultivated allotment; tenure by the year, half-year, quarter, month, or week; rent not exceeding 12s. by the month, and held under a written agreement of the form in the Act.	19 & 20 Vic. c. 65.	The summary power of ejectment in the 15th section of the Summary Jurisdiction (Ireland) Act, 1851, to be applicable (for which see "Landlord and Tenant").
EGGS: Destroying eggs of wild fowl. See "Game."	23 Geo. iii. c. 35, s. 4. (36 & 37 Vic. c. 82.)	Penalty not exceeding £5; in default, &c., imprisonment not exceeding 2 months, by scale.　　1 J. Prosecution under "Game Laws."
ELECTRIC TELEGRAPH: Injuries to, see "Malicious Injuries."		

Offence, or cause of Complaint.	Statute.	Extent of Jurisdict
EJECTMENT: Of small tenements in city, town, borough, or village, in which fair or market usually held; term not exceeding 1 month; rent not exceeding at rate of £1 a-month. See "Landlord and Tenant."	14 & 15 Vic. c. 92, s. 15.	Justice in Petty Se may order posses not less than 7, no than 10 clear days
EMBEZZLEMENT: For power to summarily dispose of before Justices in Petty Sessions— see title "Larceny," Summary Index.		
EMIGRATION: See "Passenger Ships."		
EMPLOYERS AND WORKMEN: (a) EMPLOYERS AND WORKMEN ACT, 1875. The object of this Act is to enlarge the powers of County Courts in respect of disputes between employers and workmen, and to give	38 & 39 Vic. c. 90, ss. 3, 4.	Court may order pa of any sum which find to be due as or damages, or wise, and

(a) *Employer and Workman*.—Henceforward all disputes between the em and the workman arising out of the contract or incidental to the relation l the parties are to be determined as matters of a purely *civil nature*, and th shall be deemed to be a Court of *Civil Jurisdiction*. Where, however, tn putes arise, and that in contemplation or furtherance of these disputes combine to commit some act made criminal by law, or where any individua advantage of his position or employment wilfully breaks his contract of foreseeing that a large population will by his act be deprived of gas or wi that the probable consequences of his act will be to endanger life or to valuable property to destruction; this is dealt with and punished as an *off* under a distinct statute, called the "Conspiracy and Protection of Prope 1875" (38 & 39 Vic. c. 86). This legislation may be said to be brought a the inquiry and report made by a Royal Commission. The report of the C sion reproduced all the past legislation on the labour question from the times, some of it being of a very curious character, exceptional and one-sid nature. Parliament, having so far deferred to the feelings and wishes of th man, proceeds further to confer on the County Courts, and the Summary Juri Courts, the unusual powers of "rescinding contracts;" adjusting and set "unliquidated" claims. The Justices' powers are ample: the procedure is The steps taken are those to enforce any civil order under the provision Petty Sessions Act, adopting the simple rules and forms the Lord Chance prescribed; and, where necessary, the powers conferred by the "Debtors' (Act, 1872," section 6. Domestic servants are excluded from the provision Employers and Workmen Act.—*See Lord Chancellor's Rules and Forms, A*

Offence, or cause of Complaint.	Statute.	Extent of Jurisdiction.
EMPLOYERS AND WORKMEN— *continued.* other Courts a limited *civil juris-diction in respect of such disputes.* *Summary Jurisdiction.* *A dispute between an employer and a workman (a) arising out of or in-cidental to their relation as such,* is a dispute under this Act. Any proceeding in relation to any such dispute may be heard and deter-mined by a Court of Summary Jurisdiction— Provided that in any proceeding in relation to any such dispute the Court of Summary Jurisdiction— (1) Shall not exercise any juris-diction where the amount claimed exceeds £10 ; and (2) Shall not make an order for any sum exceeding £10, exclusive of the costs incurred in the case ; and (3) Shall not require security to an amount exceeding £10 from any Defendant or his surety or sureties.	38 & 39 Vic. c. 90, ss. 3, 4.	(1) It may adjust and set off the one against the other all such claims on the part of the em-ployer or of the work-man, arising out of or incidental to the re-lation between them, as the Court may find to be subsisting, whether such claims are liqui-dated or unliquidated, and are for the wages, damages, or otherwise ; and (2) If, having regard to all the circumstances of the case, it thinks it just to do so, it may rescind any contract between the employer and the workman upon such terms as to the apportionment of wages or other sums due there-under, and as to the

(a) "*Workman*" defined, sec. 10.—The expression "workman" does not include a domestic or menial servant, but save as aforesaid, means any person who being a labourer, servant in husbandry, journeyman, artificer, handicraftsman, miner, or otherwise engaged in manual labour," whether under the age of 21 years or above that age, has entered into or works under a contract with an employer, whether the contract be made before or after the passing of this Act, be express or implied, oral or in writing, and be a contract of service, or a contract personally to execute any work or labour. An omnibus conductor is not a "workman," or person "engaged in manual labour" within the meaning of the Employers and Workmen Act, 1875, s. 10. *Q. B.* England, 1884 : *Morgan* v. *The London General Omnibus Co., coram* Brett, M. R., Bowen, L. J., and Fry, L. J. The Court in this case goes very fully into the method of reading the statute, and the use to be made of a general know-ledge of things, so as justly to interpret the intentions of the Legislature.

Extent of Summary Jurisdiction.—It will be observed by a careful perusal of the Act that sect. 4, after making the Summary Jurisdiction Court, for the purposes of this Act, a Court of Civil Jurisdiction, then confers on it that power which the County or Civil Bill Court always possessed, and is still retained, to make an order for payment for any sum found to be due as wages, damages, or otherwise, and then proceeds to confer on it all the additional powers by this Act conferred on the County or Civil Bill Court by sec. 3, sub-sections 1, 2, 3, &c.

Offence, or cause of Complaint.	Statute.	·Extent o
EMPLOYERS AND WORKMEN— *continued.*	38 & 39 Vic. c. 90, ss. 3, 4.	payment damages, due, as and (3) Whei might ot damages of contr the defer to give satisfacti for the him of contract performe consent accept and ord of the c ingly, i of the damages otherwis awarded, of such The secur undertak fendant surety o the defe form his ject on ance to a sum in the ui Any sum on behal in respe under th with all by such spect of shall be a debt d the de where si

Mence, or cause of Complaint.	Statute.	Extent of Jurisdiction.
OYERS AND WORKMEN— *continued.* ASTER AND APPRENTICES.		
	38 & 39 Vic. c. 90, ss. 3, 4.	been given in or under the direction of a Court of Summary Jurisdiction, that Court may order payment to the surety of the sum which has so become due to him from the defendant. How money orders enforced — see footnote, and section in full. 2 J. (In Dublin one or more divisional Justices.)
ispute between an apprentice to an this Act applies (a) and his ter, arising out of or incidental heir relation as such (which ute is hereinafter referred to as spute under this Act), may be rd and determined by a Court Summary Jurisdiction.	ss. 5, 6.	The Court of Summary Jurisdiction shall have the *same powers as if the dispute were between an employer and a workman,* and the master were the employer and the apprentice the workman, and the instrument of apprenticeship a contract between an employer and a workman. (b)
cation of Act. (a)—This Act o far as relates to apprentices l apply only to an "*Apprentice he business of a 'Workman' as usd by this Act*" (that is, to	s. 12.	

Apprentices to whom Act applies, &c."—There does not appear to be any scription of apprentice than those above spoken of, in respect to whose Justices in Petty Sessions could exercise summary jurisdiction, unless person se mentioned in the saving clause, section 13. The Irish statute of 31 c. 53, under which Justices heretofore punished them for eloping, runy, or refusing to learn, &c., speaks of them as "persons bound by indenuny *trade or mystery.*" Mystery did not here mean any thing beyond comprehension, but merely some art or handicraft.

sters to whom Act applies.—While part of the definition of "workman" *personally* to execute any work;" and apprentice is "apprentice to the of a workman, as defined by the Act," it does not follow from this that ntice's master must be one who "personally" executes his work. This he definition refers rather to the nature of the workman's *contract,* the a dispute.

iction and powers of the Justices in respect to Apprentices.—Sec. 6 says, Court shall have the *same powers* as if the dispute were between an emd workman, &c., &c. Yet, it does *not* appear that the provisoes in

Offence, or cause of Complaint.	Statute.	Extent of Jurisdiction.
EMPLOYERS AND WORKMEN— MASTERS AND APPRENTICES—*con.* the business of a labourer, servant in husbandry, journeyman, artificer, handicraftsman, miner, or otherwise engaged in manual labour); upon whose binding either no premium is paid, or the premium, if any, paid does not exceed £25, and to an apprentice bound under the provisions of the Acts relating to the Relief of the Poor.	38 & 39 Vic. c. 90, s. 12.	(See order in case of workmen before mentioned), *and shall also have the following powers:—* (1) It may make an order directing the apprentice to perform his duties under the apprenticeship; and, (2) If it rescinds the instrument of apprenticeship it may, if it thinks it just so to do, order the whole or any part of the premium paid on the binding of the apprentice to be repaid. Where an order is made directing an apprentice to perform his duties under the apprenticeship, the Court may from time to time, if satisfied after the ex-

section 4, sub-sections 1, 2, 3, limiting the jurisdiction in "workmen's" disputes, at all attach themselves to the jurisdiction intended to be given in the case of apprentices. Were it intended that they should, the limitation would have appeared in sec. 5, which really gives the jurisdiction; but in addition, the latter part of sec. 7 seems, indirectly, not to recognize the limitations set by the provisoes of sec. 4.

Effect of the Indenture.—Although a deed indented and under seal, the indenture may, by the Court of Summary Jurisdiction, be rescinded, and be treated as of no more binding force than any ordinary workman's contract that may be express or implied, oral or in writing; see secs. 6 and 10. And under these same sections, although an indenture may be informal, it still may be received as some evidence of a contract express or implied, and upon which the Justices may make some order.

Failing to appear.—An apprentice failing to appear and answer a complaint under this Act may be apprehended and brought forward, sec. 9.

Order to imprison Apprentice.—It would seem from the words of the section and the Lord Chancellor's form of order to commit the apprentice, that Magistrates may in his absence hear proofs of his having disobeyed the order; still if the Justices consider it more satisfactory that the apprentice shall be present, or have an opportunity of rebutting the charge, there is nothing to prevent such opportunity by summons or notice being afforded him.

Offence, or cause of Complaint.	Statute.	Extent of Jurisdiction.
EMPLOYERS AND WORKMEN— MASTERS AND APPRENTICES—*con.*	38 & 39 Vic. c. 90, s. 12.	piration of not less than 1 month from the date of the order, that the apprentice has failed to comply therewith, order him to be imprisoned for a period not exceeding 14 days. —
Order against Surety, &c.—Where any person is liable, under the instrument of apprenticeship, for the good conduct of apprentice, that person may, if Court so direct, be summoned as if he were a defendant, and the Court may, in addition to or in substitution for any order which the Court is authorised to make against the apprentice, order the person so summoned to pay damages for any breach of the contract of apprenticeship to an amount not exceeding the limit, if any, to which he is liable under the instrument of apprenticeship.	s. 7.	—
The Court may, if the person so summoned, or any other person, is willing to give security to the satisfaction of the Court for the performance by the apprentice of his contract of apprenticeship, accept such security instead of, or in mitigation of, any punishment which it is authorized to inflict upon the apprentice.	,,	
PROCEDURE. *Mode of giving Security.*—May be by oral or written acknowledgment, &c., and the sum for which bound, in form prescribed by *Rules*, &c.	s. 8.	Where security is so given, Court where given may order payment of any sum which may become due in pursuance of such security. 2 J.
Rules as to Security.—Lord Chancellor may, from time to time, make rules with respect *to giving security under this Act.*	,,	(In Dublin, one or more divisional Justices.)

Offence, or cause of Complaint.	Statute.	Extent of Jurisdiction.
EMPLOYERS AND WORKMEN— PROCEDURE—*continued.* *Procedure.* (*a*)—Disputes in respect to which jurisdiction is given to Court of Summary Jurisdiction shall be deemed to be matters on which orders may be made under Petty Sessions (Ireland) Act, 1851, and any Acts amending same, but shall not be deemed to be a criminal proceeding. And the powers conferred by this Act shall be deemed to be in addition to, and not in derogation of, powers given by Petty Sessions Act, &c.: except that—warrant shall not issue for apprehension of any person other than an apprentice, for failing to appear to answer complaint under this Act. And that an order made for payment of any sum of money under this Act shall not be enforced by im-	38 & 39 Vic. c. 90, ss. 9 and 15.	

(*a*) *Procedure.*—That is, the Petty Sessions Act is to be the machinery for carrying out the provisions of the above Act; but having at the same time regard to the fact that it is carrying out orders in a *civil* and not in a *criminal* proceeding. And being a civil proceeding, of course both parties to the suit, plaintiff and defendant, may give evidence. And notwithstanding that the proceeding is a civil one, it appears that under the above sec. 9 an apprentice failing to appear to answer complaint may be brought forward by warrant. The Petty Sessions Act requires that the information or complaint in all such cases shall be on oath, and in writing.

Money Orders, how enforced. —Sec. 9. "An order made by a Court of Summary Jurisdiction under this Act for the payment of any money shall not be enforced by imprisonment, except in the manner and under the conditions by this Act provided; and no goods or chattels shall be taken under a distress ordered by a Court of Summary Jurisdiction, which might not be taken under an execution issued by a County Court.

"Any sum payable by any person under the order of a Court of Summary Jurisdiction in pursuance of this Act shall be deemed to be a debt due from him in pursuance of a judgment of a competent Court within the meaning of the Debtors' Act: sec. 6 Debtors' (Ireland) Act, 1872; see definitions, and may be enforced accordingly; and as regards any such debt, a Court of Summary Jurisdiction shall be deemed to be a Court within the meaning of the said section."

The substance of sec. 6 of the Debtors' Act (Ireland) 1872, for the purposes of the Summary Jurisdiction Court is as follows:—

Any Court may commit to prison for a term not exceeding six weeks, or until

Offence, or cause of Complaint.	Statute.	Extent of Jurisdiction.
EMPLOYERS AND WORKMEN—		
PROCEDURE—*continued.*		
prisonment, except in the manner and under the conditions by this Act provided.	38 & 39 Vic. c. 90, ss. 9 and 15.	
Instalments.—Court may direct that sums of money be paid by instalments, and may rescind or vary such order.	s. 9.	
Sum ordered to be paid shall be deemed to be a debt and enforced as such.	,,	
Rules as to Jurisdiction, Costs, &c.— The Lord Chancellor may make rules for carrying the summary jurisdiction into effect, and for regulating costs, with power to provide that costs shall not exceed what would in a similar case be incurred in a County Court, &c.	,,	
(*See Rules and Forms—Appendix.*)		

syment of the sum due, any person who makes default in payment of any debt, or stalment of any debt due from him, in pursuance of an order of the Court. Such urisdiction shall only be exercised where it is proved to the satisfaction of the Court at the person making default either has, or has had, since the date of the order, is means to pay the sum in respect of which he has made default, and has refused or neglected, or refuses or neglects to pay same. Proof of the means of the urison making default may be given in such manner as the Court thinks just, and, r the purpose of such proof, the debtor and any witnesses may be summoned and ramined on oath, according to the prescribed rules. The Court may direct the dbt to be paid by instalments, and may from time to time rescind or vary such rder. No imprisonment under this section shall operate as a satisfaction or extinguishment of any debt or demand, or cause of action, or deprive any person of ny right to take out execution against the lands, goods, or chattels, of the person mprisoned, in the same manner as if such imprisonment had not taken place. Any urson imprisoned under this section shall be discharged out of custody upon a urtificate signed in the prescribed manner, to the effect that he has satisfied the debt r instalment of a debt in respect of which he was imprisoned, together with the eescribed costs (if any).

The Magistrate's warrant may be issued as any other warrant, to enforce an rder, in the form, and subject to the provisions of the Petty Sessions (Ireland) kct. It may be addressed to the Constabulary.

The Lord Chancellor may make rules in relation to the exercise of jurisdiction, uder this section of the Debtors' Act.

I

Offence, or cause of Complaint.	Statute.	Extent of Jurisdiction.
EMPLOYERS AND WORKMEN— *continued.*		
Definitions of "Workman," &c., .	38 & 39 Vic. c. 90, s. 10.	—
Set-off in case of young persons and women in factories, under Factory Acts, 1833 to 1874 ; forfeiture on the ground of absence or leaving work shall not be set off against wages due before such absence.	s. 11.	—
Saving Clause.—Nothing in Act shall take away or abridge any *local* or *special* jurisdiction touching apprentices.	s. 13.	—
Seamen.—As to application of Act to "Seamen," see "Merchant Shipping Act," 43 & 44 Vic. c. 16.		
Modifications in application of Act to Ireland.	s. 15.	
"County Court" means "Civil Bill Court." Court of Summary Jurisdiction shall, in Dublin, be constituted of one or more divisional Justices ; elsewhere, two or more Justices in Petty Sessions.	,,	
APPRENTICES.		
Ill-behaviour.—Apprentice guilty of any misdemeanour, miscarriage, or ill-behaviour in service, and upon whose binding no larger sum than £5 fee paid. (*a*)	25 Geo. ii. c. 8, s. 4. 29 Geo. ii. c. 8, s. 13 (Irish).	Imprisonment not exceeding 1 month's H.L.; or Justices may discharge the apprentice. 1 J. (But see note at foot.)
Eloping, &c.—Apprentice eloping, running away, or wilfully refusing to learn or work (*a*)	31 Geo. iii. c. 23, s. 3 (Irish).	Imprisonment not exceeding 3 months. 1 J. (But see note at foot.)

(*a*) *Apprentices Eloping, &c. &c.*—Any dispute between an apprentice to whom this Act applies and his master, "arising out of or incidental to their relation as such," will be a dispute within the *jurisdiction* given by this "Employers and Workmen Act, 1875 ;" and being so, may be dealt with according to the powers conferred by this Act (secs. 5, 6). It may be said that "eloping, running away," &c., cannot be properly called "disputes," but are breaches of unrepealed statute law. Well, after all, the terms employed, whether applied to a workman or an apprentice, do not amount to anything more than a breach of the agreement or indenture, and arise out of and are incidental to the relation subsisting between the parties. And if in England or in Ireland such behaviour on the part of the apprentice may be dealt with under the "Employers and Workmen Act, 1875," then it becomes (sec. 9) a "dispute or matter in respect of which jurisdiction is given by

Offence, or cause of Complaint.	Statute.	Extent of Jurisdiction.
EMPLOYERS AND WORKMEN— APPRENTICES—*continued.* *Cruelty.*—With whom only £5 paid, on complaint against master for misusage, refusal of necessary provision, cruelty, or other ill-treatment. (But see also 38 & 39 Vic. c. 86, s. 6.)	25 Geo. ii. c. 8, s. 3. 29 Geo. ii. c. 8, s. 13 (Irish).	Justice may, by warrant or certificate under his hand, discharge the apprentice. 1 J.
With whom not exceeding £10 (fee) paid on complaint against master for ill-usage. (Repealed by "Master and Servant Act, 1867.")	59 Geo. iii. c. 92, s. 5.	
Cruelty to Apprentices.—Whosoever, being legally liable, either as master or mistress, to provide for any apprentice or servant necessary food, clothing, or lodging, shall wilfully and without lawful excuse refuse or neglect to provide the same; or shall unlawfully and maliciously	24 & 25 Vic. c. 100, s. 26.	Indictable misdemeanour, for which offender may be sentenced to 3 years' penal servitude, or to imprisonment not exceeding 2 years. And guardians or overseers of the poor may

this Act to a Court of Summary Jurisdiction, and shall be deemed to be a matter on which that Court has authority by law to make an order on complaint (in pursuance of the Petty Sessions, Ireland, Act, 1851), *but shall not be deemed to be a criminal proceeding.*" If then the complaint or dispute at all comes within the "*jurisdiction*" given by this Act, it is difficult to see how the same tribunal could deal with it "*criminally*" under the powers given under the Irish Acts above referred to. The Irish Acts have not been repealed, and there may be apprenticeships to *trades*, &c., to which by reason of the amount of the fee, or by their being incorporated with some *local or special* Act as to apprentices, they may still be applicable; but as has been shown, where the dispute or complaint comes within the jurisdiction of the "Employers and Workmen Act, 1875," there are strong reasons for concluding that the provisions of this Act have been substituted for the criminal jurisdiction of the former Acts. Sec. 13 provides that nothing in this Act shall take away or abridge any *local or special* jurisdiction touching apprentices. This can hardly refer to more than particular localities and particular trades, &c. Indeed the saving clause and exceptions (sec. 13) may rather go to point out the general rule intended. The apprentice failing to appear may be compelled under warrant (sec. 9), and as in Petty Sessions (Ireland) Act. The power (sec. 6) to punish the apprentice by imprisonment would appear to be for his contempt or disobedience of the Justices' order, which directed him to perform his duties. This order places his acts in a new light. And it does not even appear that the force of their order becomes spent by each infraction and imprisonment that may follow, or that after each subsequent act of disobedience of it proved against him, a month must elapse. Of course the order and the instrument of apprenticeship may at any time be rescinded.

Apprentices differ in many respects from other domestic servants. "Apprentices

I 2

Offence, or cause of Complaint.	Statute.	Extent of Jurisdiction.
EMPLOYERS AND WORKMEN— APPRENTICES—*continued.* do, or cause to be done, any bodily harm to any such apprentice or servant, so as to endanger life ; or that the health of such apprentice or servant shall have been, or shall be likely to be, permanently injured. (*a*)	24 & 25 Vic. c. 100, s. 26.	be required to prosecute. See s. 73 ; and see title " Prevention of Cruelty to Children."
Apprentice unlawfully disposing or retaining possession, without em- ployer's consent, of goods, work, or materials committed to his care (value not exceeding £5).	25 & 26 Vic. c. 60, s. 7.	Compensation to ag- grieved, and also liable to fine not exceeding 40s.; or to be impri- soned not exceeding 1 month. 1 J.
Apprentice to bakers, by their wilful act, neglect, or default, injuring, damaging, destroying, or adul- terating materials or property of employers.	1 & 2 Vic. c. 28, s. 12.	To pay a reasonable sum as recompense for the money master may have been obliged to pay under the Act, or for

(from the French *apprendre*, to learn) are a species of servants who are usually bound for a term of years, by deed *indented*, or by indenture, to serve their masters, and be maintained and instructed by them."—*Black. Com.*

By 8 & 9 Vic. c. 106, deeds are made effectual as indentures, though not indented.

Exemptions from Stamp Duty.—1. Instrument relating to any poor child apprenticed by, or at the sole charge of any parish or township, or by or at the sole charge of any public charity, or pursuant to any Act for the regulation of parish apprentices. 2. Instrument of apprenticeship in Ireland, where the value of the premium or consideration does not exceed £10. (" The Stamp Act, 1870," 33 & 34 Vic. c. 97.)

(*a*) *Cruelty, and Failure in Trade, &c.*—By 2 Geo. i. c. 17, s. 16 : " Whereas apprentices employed in handicraft trades are often by the failure or death of their master left without employment or instruction in the trade to which they were bound, and others often by the severity of their masters or mistresses have been cruelly used, for remedy whereof, it may be lawful for any two Justices of the Peace of any county, county of a city or town, to hear and determine all such complaints of apprentices who are or shall be employed in any handicraft, trade or manufacture, and to displace and remove such apprentice, if they shall find just cause for so doing, from such service, by order under their hands and seals ; and by the like order, to turn over such apprentice to some other master or mistress of the same trade, for the remainder of the term of such apprenticeship." Master or mistress, feeling aggrieved, may appeal to Quarter Sessions, s. 17.

"Apprentices ought to be employed entirely in the profession or trade which they are intended to learn. Instruction is their hire, and to deprive them of the opportunities of instruction by taking up their time with occupations foreign to their business, is to defraud them of their wages."

Offence, or cause of Complaint.	Statute.	Extent of Jurisdiction.
EMPLOYERS AND WORKMEN— APPRENTICES—*continued.*	1 & 2 Vic. c. 28, s. 12.	the injury he might have otherwise sustained; in default, &c., imprisonment not exceeding 1 month. 1 J.
Enlisting.—Mode of reclaiming apprentice who has enlisted. See form of oath and certificate of Justice in Schedule to Army Act. See also titles: "Merchant Shipping," "Chimney Sweeps."	Army Act.	To be entitled to reclaim, oath, as in schedule to the Act, must be made within 1 month. The binding must be for 5 years at least, and the apprentice not above 16 years when bound. 1 J.
WORKMEN. *Making away with or detaining Goods, &c.*—Any artificer, workman, apprentice, servant, or other person who shall unlawfully dispose of or retain in his possession, without consent of the person by whom he shall be hired, &c., any goods, wares, work, or materials, committed to his care or charge (the value not exceeding £5)—	25 & 26 Vic. c. 50, s. 7.	Shall pay such compensation as the Justice shall think reasonable, and a fine not exceeding £2; or to be imprisoned not exceeding 1 month. 1 J.
Employers' offences in hiring.—If any master-workman or any person whatsoever for him or by his direction, or with his privity, shall knowingly receive, employ, or entertain any artificer, journeyman, manufacturer, workman, or labourer already employed or retained by another, during the time such artificer, &c., shall be so employed or retained, without leave of the person or persons by whom such artificer, &c., shall be so employed or retained, and being thereof convicted.	43 Geo. iii. c. 86, s. 7.	Penalty not less than £5, nor more than £20; in default, &c., imprisonment, by scales; or, in discretion of Justices, to some house of correction, to be kept to H. L., for not exceeding 3 months. 2 J. One moiety (half) of the penalty to party aggrieved (but Fines Act, 14 & 15 Vic. c. 90, sec. 13, allows only one-third to complainant).
All undertakers or contractors for work in Ireland shall be considered as masters under this Act, so far as relates to the journeymen, artificers, workmen, and labourers employed by them.	s. 9.	—

Offence, or cause of Complaint.	Statute.	Extent of Jurisdiction.
EMPLOYERS AND WORKMEN— WORKMEN—*continued.* Summons to be served, at the least, 24 hours before hearing, personally, or to person above 16 years of age resident at defendant's abode.	43 Geo. iii. c. 86, s. 11.	
Master in the particular trade not to act as Justice of Peace.	s. 12.	—
Informer or prosecutor to be a competent witness to prove the offence; and informers giving evidence indemnified from prosecution for the same matter.	s. 14.	—
DOMESTIC SERVANTS, &c. (a) *Discharges, &c.*—Master refusing to give a discharge and certificate of behaviour to servant, servant may apply to Justice, who shall write to master, &c., requiring a reason for such refusal, and if no reply in five days, or no sufficient cause shown for such refusal, &c.	2 Geo. i. c. 17, s. 3 (Irish).	The Justice shall give certificate of such refusal, or of the reason assigned for such refusal, as the case may be, in order that the person about to hire may judge thereof.

(a) *Domestic Servants* are excluded from the provisions of the Employers and Workmen Act, 1875; indeed, so great is the difference between domestic servants as members of or about the household, and outside workmen or servants in husbandry, that the application of this Act could hardly be of advantage. What may be a sufficient reason for speedily determining the hiring or contract with the former would not always be allowed to be so with the latter class. The policy and aim of recent legislation is that questions of contract shall be subjects of civil rather than of criminal law. Some of the early Irish statutes dealing with domestic servants have not been expressly repealed, and portions of them as given in the above analysis continue in force; other portions are regulated by modern criminal legislation. The Irish statute, 2 Geo. i. c. 17, s. 2, empowered one Justice to imprison for not exceeding ten days at hard labour a servant guilty of drunkenness, disorderly conduct, or quitting the service during the hiring. The 25 Geo. 2, c. 8, s. 2 (Irish), as amended by 29 Geo. ii. c. 8, s. 3, and made perpetual by 5 Geo. iii. c. 15, s. 32, enabled one Justice to punish servants, artificers, and labourers guilty of ill-behaviour in service, by imprisonment not exceeding one month at hard labour, or by discharging from the employment, and abatement of wages. The offences just referred to were afterwards in clear and comprehensive language dealt with by the Summary Jurisdiction (Ireland) Act, 1851 (14 & 15 Vic. c. 92, s. 16, sub-section 4). This was therefore the Act under which these particular offences continued to be dealt with up to the passing of the Master and Servant Act, 1867. This Summary Jurisdiction Act, 1851, is introduced as an Act to "*Consolidate and Amend*" several Acts, &c., and at section 16, sub-sect. 4, it fully deals with questions between masters and servants, workmen, &c., and embraces the offences just quoted from the Irish Acts, but the

Offence, or cause of Complaint.	Statute.	Extent of Jurisdiction.
EMPLOYERS AND WORKMEN— Domestic Servants, &c.—*con.*		
Counterfeiting Certificate.—Servant convicted of counterfeiting or producing a counterfeited certificate shall on conviction be—(but see below).	2 Geo. i. c. 17, s. 4 (Irish).	Imprisonment for 3 months' H.L. 2 J.
Hiring under forged Discharge.— Any servant or other person who shall hire or engage with any master or other person, under any false or forged discharge or certificate of character— (This has reference to where the hiring actually takes place on forged discharge).	14 & 15 Vic. c. 92, s. 16.	Shall be liable to forfeit all wages due at the time of conviction, and a penalty not exceeding £5 ; in default, &c., imprisonment not exceeding 2 months' H.L. 1 J.

penalties differ in kind and in degree, so that the Acts in this respect could not well run together, and were *inconsistent.* But this statute (1851), after repealing several enactments by name, also repeals "any other Act *or parts of Acts inconsistent with its provisions.*" The "Master and Servant Act, 1867," adopts (as to Ireland) for its purposes sec. 16 of the Summary Jurisdiction Act, 1851, and from 1867 to 1875 the substituted remedies and procedure were solely applicable. The 'Master and Servant Act, 1867," is now, by 38 & 39 Vic. c. 86, repealed, and with it the sub-sect. 4, sec. 16 of the Summary Jurisdiction Act. If, then, the actions of the Irish Acts be so repealed in the manner stated, they would seem to come under the 5th sec. of 13 Vic. c. 21, as not to be revived by the removal and abrogation of the statutes which repealed them, and, perhaps, not the less so for being penal enactments.

Of course there still remains to the parties the right of civil action in the County Court—the right at either side by a month's notice to terminate the contract, and the master's by paying a month's wages—the forfeiture of wages for misconduct or improperly leaving, and, if the power be fairly and honestly carried out, the just denial of a discharge or certificate of character will in general be a punishment to a domestic servant who values character. Sec. 5 of "The Conspiracy and Protection of Property Act, 1875" (38 & 39 Vic. c. 86), applies to any servant who wilfully and maliciously breaks a contract, having reason to know that in doing so life will be endangered or valuable property injured. There does not appear to be in England any Act in force to punish domestic servants criminally for breaches of contract, never has been, and the English authorities held that the 'Master and Servant Act, 1867," did not apply to domestic servants in England. *Certificate of Character, &c.*—When certificate of character is refused a servant the Superior Court cannot interfere, the common law gives no remedy, the statutory remedy is exclusive. Where, by the Act itself which creates the right, a remedy is given to the party injured, that remedy is the only one open to him,—*Handley v. Moffat,* Com. Pleas (Ireland), 1872. This action it appeared was the only one of the kind brought into the Superior Court since the Act (2 Geo. i. c. 17) was passed. *Masters not bound to give a Character.*—In an action on the case to which defendant pleaded not guilty, on opening the pleadings Lord Kenyon, C.J., addressing

Offence, or cause of Complaint.	Statute.	Extent of Jurisdiction.
EMPLOYERS AND WORKMEN— DOMESTIC SERVANTS, &c.—*con.* *Nurses.*—Nurse hiring herself as such, knowing that she is with child, or continuing to nurse after she knows herself to be with child, without giving notice to parents; or having any foul or infectious disease, Justice may appoint two or more physicians, chirurgeons, or mid-wives, to examine her, and report on oath; on conviction—	2 Geo. i. c. 17, s. 7.	To forfeit all sums due her, and all sums already paid her on account of such nursing to the person informing, same to be recovered as servant's wages, and also to be imprisoned for 3 months' H. L. 1 J.
Firing Houses.—Menial or other servant or servants who, through negligence or carelessness, shall fire or occasion the burning of any dwelling-house or out-house—	2 Geo. i. c. 5, s. 4 (Irish).	To pay and forfeit for the sufferers £50; in default, &c., imprisonment for 18 months' H. L. 2 J.

himself to plaintiff's counsel, said, "Can you make anything of this action? I have read an abstract of the record—it is impossible to support this action." Upon the plaintiff's counsel replying that he had no case, his lordship proceeded to observe: "There is no case; there is no foundation in law for this action. What one's real feeling would dictate is one thing; but can you say that there is a legal obligation on one to give a servant a character at all? I am confident that this action cannot be maintained."—*Carroll* v. *Bird*, Sittings at Westminster after T. T., 40 Geo. iii.—3 *Esp.* 201, S. C. (and see *Ashouer* v. *Brampton*, *Cald.* 11.

Who are Servants within the Statute.—The word "servant" in the phraseology of lawyers has a very extended meaning. It, in strictness, includes every person who is engaged for a consideration to perform any service for another—it matters not how honourable or exalted the office may be; ofttimes it includes gratuitous and friendly services. This definition does not accord with the terms used in the section. The words, "or other person" where they so occur (sec. 16), are generally taken to mean "other *such* person" or persons of the class already named. Accountants, &c., warehousemen, travellers, editors, reporters, actors, ushers, governesses, and the like, do not seem to come within the section, as not being so classified, so as that the Justices could determine claims made by them for wages.

As to Hiring.—If a servant be hired generally, without any stipulation as to time, the law presumes the hiring to have been for a year, unless there are circumstances tending to remove this presumption. In the case of domestic servants, the hiring may at any time be determined by a calendar month's warning, or on payment of a month's wages.—*Turner* v. *Mason*, 14 *M. & W.*, 116. The servant may end the hiring by a like notice, but has not the option of doing so by payment of a sum equal to a month's wages. The notice may be verbal. So that if the master without reasonable cause turn the servant away, the latter will be only entitled to a month's wages. Other servants, such as clerks, &c., may by action recover their wages for the remainder of the year. But in the case of clerks, governesses, warehousemen, editors, reporters, actors, and the like, the law raises no inflexible presumption of an indefeasible yearly hiring, from the mere fact of a hiring for an indefinite period; but in all such cases the jury must determine the

Offence, or cause of Complaint.	Statute.	Extent of Jurisdiction.
EMPLOYERS AND WORKMEN— DOMESTIC SERVANTS, &c.—*con.* *Debts due by Servants to Publicans.*— Retailers of beer or spirits giving credit to servants, day labourers, and other persons who usually work or ply for hire or wages, beyond the amount of 1s., shall have no remedy for the sum due, and securities for such debts shall be void.	9 Geo. ii. c. 8. 1 Geo. iii. c. 17, s. 14.	—
When any pledge is received for such, Justice by warrant to compel restoration to owner, or to make satisfaction for the loss or abuse thereof.	,,	Mayor or 1 J. may make the order.

question for themselves after weighing the circumstances, if possible ascertaining the usages in the particular business to which the hiring relates.—*Baxter* v. *Nurse, 6 M. & Gr.* 935, *Taylor's Ev.*

Parol Agreement.—Under the section giving Magistrates jurisdiction to make the parol agreement binding, the service must be entered upon. Such parol agreement is binding for one year. By the Statute of Frauds, 29 Chas. ii., "No action shall be brought on any agreement that is not to be performed within a year from the making thereof, unless the agreement on which such action shall be brought, or some memorandum or note thereof, shall be in writing, and signed by the party to be charged therewith or some other person by him thereunto lawfully authorized." Where, under the section above quoted, the agreement is in writing, signed by both parties, it is binding, although the service be not entered on. So that a servant may be engaged by parol for a year from to-day, but it must be in writing if it is to commence from to-morrow. An agreement, whether written or verbal (unless it be by deed), may be put an end to by word of mouth, both parties so agreeing.

Infants, or persons under age, may enter into contracts of service if fair in the terms and suitable to their circumstances; but although no action will lie against them for breach of contract, still they may under the statute be punished for misconduct or unlawfully quitting the service, and the servant can, under the statute, enforce his claim for wages. A servant is bound to conform to the general rules of the master's establishment, and to do all that reasonably belongs to the kind of service which he has undertaken.

Master's Liability for acts of Servant.—Master is civilly answerable for the acts of his servant, if done by his command, either expressly or impliedly given. Whatever a servant is *permitted* to do in the usual course of his business is equivalent to a general command. In general, where a servant is guilty of negligence in driving his master's carriage, the latter is answerable in an action on the case; and an allegation that the defendant negligently drove, &c., is supported by evidence that his servant was the driver.—*Brucker* v. *Fromont*, 6 *T. R.*, 659. There are some cases and instances of the master's liability wherein the determinations are said to stand rather upon the authority of the law than any principle of natural justice. However, though the master be liable for the injudicious acts of his servant, he is not answerable for his wilful and malicious acts.—*M'Manus* v. *Crickett*, 1 *East*, 106.

Offence, or cause of Complaint.	Statute.	Extent of Jurisdiction.
EMPLOYERS AND WORKMEN— *Making away with Employer's Goods.* —Workman, servant, &c., disposing of, or retaining possession of, without employer's consent, any goods, ware, work, or materials, committed to care or charge (value not exceeding £5)—	25 & 26 Vic. c. 60, s. 7.	Shall pay such compensation as the Justices shall think reasonable, and a fine not exceeding £2, or to be imprisoned not exceeding 1 month. 1 J.
Breach of Contract of Service or Hiring involving injury to Persons or Property.—Where any person wilfully and maliciously breaks a contract of service or of hiring, knowing or having reasonable cause to believe that the probable consequences of his so doing, either alone or in combination with others, will be to endanger human life, or cause serious bodily harm, or to expose valuable property, whether real or personal, to destruction or serious injury, on conviction—	38 & 39 Vic. c. 68, s. 5.	Penalty not exceeding £20, or to be imprisoned for a term not exceeding 3 months, with or without H. L. 2 J.
Accused may, on appearing, object to being tried summarily, and thereupon it may be dealt with as an indictable offence.	s. 9.	
Servants' Wages. (a)—Justices in Petty Sessions are empowered to hear and determine any disputes concerning any sums which shall be due for wages by any master to his apprentice, or by any employer to any artificer, labourer, servant, or other person employed by him	14 & 15 Vic. c. 92, s. 16, 38 & 39 Vic. c. 86, s. 17.	Justices to make such order as they shall see fit for payment of such sums as shall appear to be justly due; and may award a further sum as compensation (not exceeding 40s.) for loss

(a) Under this statute 14 & 15 Vic. c. 92, s. 16, sub-sections 1, 2, 3, 5, perpetuated by the 38 & 39 Vic. c. 86, Justices are empowered to determine disputes as to *wages*. It is applicable to the claims of *domestic servants*, but it is not limited to their claims. The orders made under it cannot be enforced as orders under the "Employers and Workmen Act, 1875," and not otherwise. That may be by distress warrant, and under sec. 6 of the Debtors' (Ireland) Act, 1872, of which *see* extract under title "Employers and Workmen."

Month's Notice.—As to domestic servants, it is an established rule that a hiring for a year may be dissolved on reasonable notice, as a month's warning or a month's wages.—*Robinson* v. *Hindman*, 3 *Esp.*, 235; *Beeston* v. *Collyer*, 4 *Bing.*, 313. *See* also *Nowlan* v. *Ablett*, 2 *Crompt.*, *Mees. & R.*, 54, where this rule was applied to a head gardener residing in a house in his master's domain, but apart from his sion-house.

Offence, or cause of Complaint.	Statute.	Extent of Jurisdiction.
EMPLOYERS AND WORKMEN— for day's work, task, job, or contract, hire of horses, cars, &c. (not being for the carriage of passengers), and to schoolmaster for tuition, where the demand does not exceed £10.— See section in full, *infra*. (a)	14 & 15 Vic. c. 92, s. 16, 38 & 39 Vic. c. 86, s. 17.	of time, &c., in recovering wages; recoverable under Petty Sessions Act, and *enforced* as orders made in pursuance of "Employers and Workmen Act, 1875," and not otherwise. 2 J.
Limitation.—Complaint shall be made within one year from the termination of the term or period in respect of which it shall be payable.	,,	In Dublin, one or more divisional Justices.

(a) 14 & 15 *Vic. c.* 92, *s.* 16—*Wages.*—" It shall be lawful for the Justice to hear and determine any disputes concerning any sums which shall be due for wages by any master to his apprentice, or by any employer to any artificer, labourer, servant, or other person employed by him to do any species of work or labour whatsoever (whether he shall find materials for the performance of the same or not, and whether such wages shall be due in respect to any day's work or to any labour done or performed by task, job, or contract) ; or which shall be due by any person for the hire of any horse, ass, mule, bullock, or other animal for draught, or of any cart, dray, car, plough, harrow, or vehicle drawn by any such animal, for the purpose of any labouring work (and not being for the carriage of any passenger or passengers), and whether such hire shall be by the day or by contract, or otherwise, or which shall be due to any schoolmaster or teacher for the teaching of any child in any school or other place, and whether the engagement shall be for payment by the day or for any other period, or in any other manner (provided that the amount of the demand for such wages, hire, or tuition, in any of such cases, whether originally greater or not, shall not exceed £10) ; and to make such order as they shall see fit for payment of such sums as shall appear to be justly due to the complainant by his master or employer, or in case of any sum claimed for the teaching of any child, by the parent or other person who shall have engaged the complainant to teach such child." Sub-section 2 provides compensation (not exceeding 40s.) for loss of time, &c., in recovering wages.

Where Employers are absent.—Sub-section 3—" In every case where any such master or employer shall intrust his business to the management and superintendence of any steward, agent, bailiff, foreman, or manager, it shall be lawful for the Justices to summon such steward, &c., to appear at Petty Sessions, and to hear and determine the matter of the complaint in such and the like manner as complaints of the like nature against any master or employer, and to make an order for the payment by such steward, agent, &c. In case of refusal or non-payment, it shall be lawful to issue warrant to levy same by distress and sale of the goods of such master or employer."

Finding Materials.—Where the workman supplies the materials for the "contract" work, as a mason providing the materials for a building, or a tailor the cloth,

Offence, or cause of Complaint.	Statute.	Extent of Jurisdiction.
ENLISTMENT (*Offences connected with*): See titles "Army Act," "Militia," "Naval Coast Volunteers," "Navy," "Reserves."		
ESTREATING RECOGNIZANCE: See "Petty Sessions Act," 14 & 15 Vic. c. 93, ss. 24 and 34, Appendix, and notes thereon.		
EVIDENCE: Law of, see "Appendix."		
EXCISE: *Wholesale Beer Dealers.*—Every person who shall sell *beer*, *cider*, or *perry*, by retail, that is to say, in any quantity less than four and	26 & 27 Vic. c. 33, s. 3.	Penalty £20. "To be sued for and recovered under Laws of Excise." This would be by dis-

he cannot recover the amount before the Justices as "wages"; but where the materials are of trifling value, and merely ancillary to the labour, such as a tailor providing thread, the Magistrates may make the order.

The existence of a legal obligation to pay wages is a necessary preliminary condition to Justices having any authority to enforce such payment, and if no such obligation exists the Magistrate acts without jurisdiction, and he is liable in trespass.—*Newbold* v. *Coltman*, 20 *L. J.*, 149, *M. C.*

Married Women may maintain actions for wages, &c., declared to be her separate property under the "Married Woman's Property Act, 1870," 33 & 34 Vic. c. 93.

Exemption from Stamps.—Agreement or memorandum for the hire of any labourer, artificer, manufacturer, or menial servant, exempt from stamp duty. Stamp Act, 33 & 34 Vic. c. 97. See title "Stamps" and notes thereon.

"*Passenger Cars.*"—In certain towns, where special Acts are in force, there is a power to make a summary order for the fares of hackney cars and cabs. This power is given in the Police Clauses Act, 10 & 11 Vic. c. 89.

Prosecutions under Excise Laws.—The particular laws relating to the "Excise" are almost as numerous as the commodities liable to the tax. Its original establishment was in 1643. It is, as it has always been, an unpopular tax; and when, in 1642, "aspersions were cast by malignant persons upon the House of Commons that they intended to introduce excises, the House, for its vindication therein, did declare that these rumours were false and scandalous, and that their authors should be brought to condign punishment."—*Encyclop. Brit.*, title *Excise*. Before the passing of the 4 Geo. iv. c. 23, there were distinct Excise Boards in Ireland, England,

Offence, or cause of Complaint.	Statute.	Extent of Jurisdiction.
a-half gallons, or in less than two dozen reputed quart bottles at one time, without having an Excise retail licence in force authorizing him so to do, shall for every such offence— Superintendent or Inspector of Police in Dublin, Sub-Inspector, Head or other Constable elsewhere in Ireland, may sue without any order of the Commissioners of Inland Revenue for that purpose, as well as by and in the name of an officer	25 & 26 Vic. c. 33, s. 3.	tress warrant, and in default to be committed until fine paid. 2 J. Although by the section the penalty is fixed at £20, still where the penalty is sued for under the Excise Laws, it would appear that the general power given by 7 & 8 Geo. iv. chap. 53, sec. 78, to mitigate to one-fourth would apply.

and Scotland. The laws for imposing the duties and for their collection and management have been consolidated.

The general law for imposing the duties and for granting Excise Licences is the 6 Geo. iv. c. 81 *(to which others have since been added)*. This Act gives a schedule of licence duty for the sale of beer and other commodities. See also 43 & 44 Vic. cc. 20 & 21.

Excise Procedure.—The General Act for consolidating the laws as to the collection and management of the Excise throughout Great Britain and Ireland is the 7 & 8 Geo. iv. c. 53, *amended by* 4 & 5 Wm. iv. c. 51 ; 4 Vic. c. 20. *As to the summary proceedings before Justices, instituted by authority of the Commissioners,* information may be exhibited before 1 J.P. (s. 65), within ;four calendar months. Summons to be served ten days before hearing ; service need not be personal (4 & 5 Wm. iv. c. 51, s. 19). Two or more Justices to assemble every three months, or oftener, to hear cases (7 & 8 Geo. iv. c. 53, s. 67). Providing for death or absence of Justice or prosecuting officer (same, and 4 & 5 Wm. iv. c. 51, s. 22). General powers of Justices extended to Excise cases (7 & 8 Geo. iv. c. 53, s. 67). No Excise trader, in any case relating to his trade, to act as Justice (s. 68). Justice not to regard defects of form (s. 73). Compelling witnesses (s. 74). If defendant in prison, judgment may be given after summons (s. 77). Power to mitigate penalties to one-fourth (s. 78), except the penalty of double duty and on immediate arrest (4 & 5 Wm. iv. c. 51, s. 20). Board may further remit (7 & 8 Geo. iv. c. 53, s. 78). Summonses may be served by any person (4 Vic. c. 20, s. 31). Persons aggrieved by judgment of Justices may appeal to Quarter Sessions. (For conditions of *appeal* under Excise Acts, *see* notes on the Illicit Distillation Act, under title " Excise," hereafter.)

Form of Appeals.—For forms of appeals in Excise and Customs cases, see 40 Vic. c. 13. Form of conviction or of acquittal to be lodged in County Peace Office. For forms see Schedule to Act.

Traders to put up over their premises their names and trades.—Penalty for not so doing £20 (6 Geo. iv. c. 81, ss. 25, 26, and 27). Penalty for not taking out licences required by Act (s. 26) :—Distillers, &c., £500 ; tobacco or snuff manufacturers, £200 : auctioneers, dealers in spirits (not being retailers), retailers of spirits being licensed to trade in, vend, and sell coffee, tea, &c., dealers in foreign wine, £100 ; retailers of beer, cider, perry, by retail, £50 ; trading in tea, coffee, &c., dealers in tobacco or snuff, £50.

Offence, or cause of Complaint.	Statute.	Extent of Jurisdiction.
EXCISE—*continued*. of Excise under the order of the said Commissioners (*a*)—*see* also " Licensing Acts." SHEBEEN HOUSES — *Warrant to search.*—It shall and may be lawful for any Justice of the Peace, upon being satisfied by the personal examination on oath of a credible witness, that there is reasonable ground for suspecting that spirits are sold, kept for sale, or exposed for sale in any house or place within the county, not licensed for the sale thereof, or by some person not having a licence to sell spirits in or at such house or place, or that illicit spirits are kept for sale in or at any house or place, to grant warrant, authorizing any of the Constabulary (in Dublin, Superintendent or Inspector of Police), with his assistants, to enter such house or place at all times (within one month), to search for spirits; and if any spirits shall be found therein exceeding one gallon, without a permit, or any spirits in any quantity whereon duty shall not have been duly paid, to seize such spirits, together with the vessel in which the same is contained: and the person on whose premises same shall be found shall, on conviction, be liable to— *Selling without a Licence.*—Every person not being duly licensed to	17 & 18 Vic. c. 89, s. 2. s. 3. (*c*)	For first offence :—Fine not exceeding £5, nor less than £2 ; or to be imprisoned, with or without H. L., for any term not exceeding 3 months, nor less than 1 month. Second and every subsequent offence :—Fine not exceeding £10, nor less than £5 ; or to be imprisoned, with or without H. L., for any term not exceeding 6 months, nor less than 3 months, and forfeiture of the spirits and vessel containing same. (*b*) 1 J. First offence :—Fine not exceeding £2, nor less

(*a*) The Constabulary may sue under Licensing Acts, as for selling without licence, &c., 35 & 36 Vic. c. 94, s. 3 ; 37 & 38 Vic. c. 69, s. 34. The penalty is not exceeding £50, and under the mitigating power in the latter Act, section 20, that the penalty could not be less than £5, the minimum under the Excise Acts.

(*b*) Proceedings are directed to be taken under the Petty Sessions (Ireland) Act, 1851. It is not clearly stated whether convictions under sections 2 and 3 must be before one or two Justices ; but by 37 & 38 Vic. c. 72, s. 5, it would as a summary procedure be triable by one Justice in Petty Sessions.

(*c*) Now by 27 & 28 Vic. c. 35, s. 7, unlicensed persons selling beer for consumption on premises, like penalty ; where the Excise prosecute under 6 Geo. iv. c. 81, ss. 26 and 27, penalty £50, and occupiers are liable.

Offence, or cause of Complaint.	Statute.	Extent of Jurisdiction.
EXCISE—*continued.* sell wine, spirits, beer, ale, cider, or perry, who shall sell, or keep for sale, or expose for sale any such, and for every such offence shall be liable— And for the purpose of any such conviction, it shall be sufficient to prove that wine, spirits, beer, ale, cider, or perry was kept for sale, or exposed for sale by such person, or on his premises, or had been illegally consumed on such premises at any time within two months preceding such alleged offence; and if any person shall be found drunk in such house, or having the appearance of having been recently drinking, it shall be deemed evidence of his having been drinking in such house, and of the unlawful consumption of wine, spirits, beer, &c., unless the contrary be proved.	17 & 18 Vic. c. 89, s. 3.	than 5s.; or to be imprisoned, with or without H. L., for not exceeding 1 month, nor less than 1 week. 2 J. Second and every subsequent offence :—Fine not exceeding £5, nor less than 20s; or to be imprisoned, with or without H. L., not exceeding 3 months, nor less than 1 month. 1 J.
Warrant to enter unlicensed houses. —If any member of the Constabulary force, or other credible witness, shall make oath before a Justice of the Peace, that such person has good reason to believe that wine, spirits, beer, ale, cider, or perry are retailed or sold without licence, or kept for sale without licence, in any room, house, or other place, it shall be lawful for such Justice to grant a warrant authorizing any of the Constabulary (in Dublin, any Superintendent, Inspector, or Sergeant of Police), with his assistants, to enter such place at all times (within one month from date of warrant); and if any person shall be found to be drinking or tippling, or having the appearance of having been recently drinking or tippling therein, he may be summoned before Petty Sessions or (divisional Justices, Dublin); or may be law-	s. 4.	*Penalty on persons found therein.*—First offence : —Fine not exceeding 5s., nor less than 2s. 6d.; or to be imprisoned, with or without H. L., not exceeding 24 hours, nor less than 12 hours. 1 J. Second and every subsequent offence :—Fine not exceeding 10s., nor less than 5s.; or to be imprisoned, with or without H. L., not exceeding 1 week, nor less than 3 days. 1 J. And where persons found drinking, &c., or having appearance of having been recently drinking, &c., all wine, spirits, beer, ale, cider, or perry, found therein, and all

Offence, or cause of Complaint.	Statute.	Extent of Jurisdiction.
EXCISE—*continued.* fully apprehended, and brought, as soon as conveniently may be, before a Justice, to be dealt with according to law; and on conviction—	17 & 18 Vic. c. 89, s. 4.	vessels, jugs, or glasses used in the sale thereof, may be seized, and on conviction of persons found therein as aforesaid shall be forfeited.
Delaying or refusing admittance.—If any person occupying any house or place, or any person aiding or assisting such occupier, on demand made of entrance by any Justice of the Peace, Superintendent, Inspector, or Sergeant of Police, Sub-Inspector, Head or other Constable respectively, and on his stating that he seeks to enter by virtue of his office as a Justice of the Peace, or by the authority of a warrant from a Justice of the Peace (which warrant he shall produce when required so to do, shall delay or refuse to admit such Justice of the Peace, &c. &c., into such house or place for the purpose of executing such warrant as aforesaid— (And see also "Licensing Acts," as to warrant and entry.)	s. 5.	Penalty not exceeding £2, nor less than 10s.; or to be imprisoned not exceeding one fortnight, nor less than one week, unless proof shall be made to the satisfaction of the Justice or Justices who may hear the complaint, that there was reasonable cause for giving such delay or refusal. 1 J. "Provided always that, for the purpose of such conviction as last aforesaid, proof to the satisfaction of the Justice who may hear the complaint, that spirits were sold, or kept, or exposed for sale in such house, &c., where such person was so found therein, shall be sufficient evidence that no licence then existed for selling spirits, unless the contrary be proved."
Spirits in transitu without permit.—It shall and may be lawful for any	s. 6. (a)	First offence: Penalty not exceeding £5, nor

(a) Section 8 directs that all proceedings under this Act shall be conducted, and all penalties imposed and costs awarded shall be sued for, levied, and recovered, &c., as by the Petty Sessions (Ireland) Act, 1851, is directed, provided, and enacted. But *see* 24 & 25 Vic. c. 91, s. 19, which prescribes the conditions upon which appeal shall be allowed to either party feeling aggrieved by Justice's order on complaints, under 1 & 2 Wm. iv. c. 55; 17 & 18 Vic. c. 89; and 20 and 21 Vic. c. 40.

Offence, or cause of Complaint	Statute.	Extent of Jurisdiction.
EXCISE—*continued.* County Inspector, Sub-Inspector, Head or other Constable, to demand from any person having in his custody or possession any spirits in any quantity whatsoever exceeding one gallon, a proper permit authorizing the removal of such spirits: and in case no permit shall be produced, or any permit the limitation of which shall have expired, it shall be lawful for such Inspector, &c. &c., to seize such spirits, with the vessel containing same, and the horse or other cattle, and cart or other carriage used in the removal thereof, and to arrest the person in whose possession or custody the same shall have been found, and to convey him, as soon as conveniently may be, before a Justice of the Peace, to be dealt with: and shall be liable to—	17 & 18 Vic. c. 89, s. 6.	less than 20s.; or be imprisoned, with or without H. L., for a term not exceeding 3 months, nor less than 1 month. Second and every subsequent offence. Penalty not exceeding £10, nor less than 40s.; or to be imprisoned, with or without H. L., for a term not exceeding 6 months, nor less than 2 months. 1 J.
Disposal of seizures and penalties. (*a*)	18 & 19 Vic. c. 103.	
Illicit Distillation Act. (*b*)	1 & 2 Wm. iv. c. 55.	—

(*a*) 18 & 19 Vic. c. 103, s. 1, repeals so much of the 2nd and 4th sections of 17 & 18 Vic. c. 89 as directs that any goods seized under the provisions of the said sections respectively shall be delivered to some Revenue Officer.

Section 2 enacts—that, on the conviction of any person in relation to whose offence any goods shall have been seized under the provisions of the said sections respectively, such goods shall be absolutely forfeited; or if any such goods as aforesaid shall not, within 14 days after the making thereof, be claimed by application in writing to the Inspector or Superintendent of Police, or to the County Inspector or Sub-Inspector by whom or within whose district such goods shall have been seized, then, although no conviction shall have taken place, such goods shall be absolutely forfeited: provided always that if any such claim shall be made in the manner and within the time herein directed and limited in that behalf, and no such conviction as aforesaid shall have been or shall be made, then such goods so seized shall be proceeded upon to condemnation by information before any Justice or Justices of the Peace, in like manner as in the case of goods seized under the provisions of any Act relating to duties of Excise. (*See*, as to disposal of seizures, &c., 20 & 21 Vic. c. 40, ss. 2 and 3.)

(*b*) *Procedure and Recovery of Penalties.*—By the 20 & 21 Vic. c. 40, officers of

K

130 THE JUSTICE OF THE PEACE.

Offence, or cause of Complaint.	Statute.	Extent of Jurisdiction.
EXCISE—*continued.* *Stills.*—Chemists, or other persons, not to use stills without licence; such licence to contain certain particulars, and the capacity of such stills to be limited as therein, unless specially authorized by the Commissioners of Excise.	1 & 2 Wm. iv. c. 55, ss. 9 & 10.	Penalty £50, and not less than £6; and in default, &c., imprisonment not less than 3, nor more than 12 months. **2 J.**
Still-maker to permit officer of Excise to enter his premises in the daytime; and such maker shall stamp his name and the content on each still as therein; and within three days after finishing any still, less than 200 gallons, give notice to officer that same is ready to be gauged and stamped; for neglect—	s. 11.	Penalty £60, and not less than £6; and in default, &c., imprisonment not less than 3, nor more than 12 months. **2 J.**
Every person importing any still into *Ireland* of less content than 200 gallons to give notice to officer of the district; in default—	s. 12.	Like. **2 J.**
Still found not gauged may be seized and forfeited, and the owner or person in whose possession same shall be found shall be liable to—	s. 13.	Like. **2 J.**
Brazier, or other person, who shall send or convey any still, still-head, or worm, to any person, or from one part of *Ireland* to another, without permit, shall be liable to—	s. 14.	Forfeit article, and penalty of £100, and not less than £6; and in default, &c., imprisonment not less than 3, nor more than 12 months. **2 J.**

the Constabulary Force in Ireland are empowered to put in force the powers and authorities of the Illicit Distillation Act (1 & 2 Wm. iv. c. 55). Section 6 directs that all penalties and costs shall be sued for and recovered as by the Petty Sessions (Ireland) Act, 1851, is directed. 24 & 25 Vic. c. 91, s. 18, provides that the authority to proceed under the Petty Sessions Act shall not supersede or repeal the 31st section of the Illicit Distillation Act, and that it shall be lawful for *two or more Justices in Petty Sessions* to hear any offence against the Illicit Distillation Act. But where Excise Officers prosecute, the jurisdiction given by 31st sec. of Illicit Distillation Act still exists and can be exercised by one Justice.

Offence, or cause of Complaint.	Statute.	Extent of Jurisdiction.
EXCISE—*continued.* *Illicit Stills.*—Every person, other than a licensed distiller, brewer, or vinegar-maker, who shall brew, make, or have in his possession any worts, wash, or pot-ale (*a*) (except for purposes of being made into beer for private use, proof whereof shall lie on such person), and who shall distil or have in his possession any low wines or singlings; and every person not being duly licensed to keep or use a still, who shall have or keep any still, still-head, or worm of a still; and every person who shall, without being lawfully authorized thereto, have in his possession, or in any dwelling-house, out-building, place, or premises, occupied by him, any such (except as aforesaid), whether same shall or shall not be the property of such person—	1 & 2 Wm. iv. c. 55, s. 16.	Forfeit articles, and a penalty of £100, and not less than £6; and in default, &c., imprisonment not less than 3, nor more than 12 months. 2 J.

(*a*) **Wash** means the liquor in a fermented state before distillation; pot-ale the refuse after distillation; and see definitions, 43 & 44 Vic. c. 24, s. 2.

By 15 & 16 Vic. c. 61, s. 3, officers of Inland Revenue may conduct prosecutions in Revenue cases before Justices.

Constables' Powers.—By the 20 & 21 Vic. c. 40, s. 5, Constabulary shall have and exercise the powers, authorities, and privileges granted to officers of Excise, in relation to any offence against the Illicit Distillation Act, 1 & 2 Wm. iv. c. 55; and of the officers of Customs, under the "Customs Consolidation Act, 1853," or any Act to be passed in relation to the Customs, as far as relates to any seizure, detention, or prosecution, to be made or had under any such Act or Acts, and shall be deemed and considered to be officers of Customs for such purposes so long as they belong to the Constabulary Force. (Constabulary officer shall mean Head or other Constable, s. 8.)

Recovery of Penalties.—Penalties to be sued for, levied, and recovered, as by Petty Sessions (Ireland) Act, 1851, is directed and provided.

Disposal of Seizures and Penalties, 20 & 21 Vic. c. 40, s. 2.—All seizures to be made under 17 & 18 Vic. c. 89 by the Constabulary shall (except in the cases in this clause hereinafter provided for, and except also in cases of seizures made under the Customs Consolidation Act, 1853, hereinafter referred to) be destroyed or otherwise disposed of, as the Inspector-General of Constabulary shall direct in that behalf: provided always that all seizures which may be made under the powers or directions of the 6th sec. of 17 & 18 Vic., of spirits *in transitu*, or process of removal from place to place, where the same shall be sent or removed from or by any licensed distiller or rectifier of, or dealer in or retailer of spirits, shall be

K 2

Offence, or cause of Complaint.	Statute.	Extent of Jurisdiction.
EXCISE—*continued.* *Concealing Illicit Spirits.*—Every person who shall harbour, keep, or conceal, or knowingly permit to be harboured, kept, or concealed; or shall give aid, or assistance, or reward to any person to harbour, keep, or conceal, any spirits, unlawfully made or distilled, or the full duties whereon shall not have been fully paid.	1 & 2 Wm. iv. c. 55, s. 22.	Penalty £100, and not less than £6; and in default, &c., imprisonment not less than 3, nor more than 12 months.　　2 J.
Persons having in possession any spirits in any quantity, the full duty whereon shall not have been fully paid; or any spirits in any quantity exceeding one gallon, without a proper permit, unless due proof shall be made that the duty has been duly paid, or that same was bought from a licensed distiller, or licensed dealer, or that same were attended with a proper permit to such defendant.	s. 23.	Like.　　　　　2 J.

disposed of in such manner as the Commissioners of Inland Revenue may direct or authorize in that behalf. Section 3 directs that penalties recovered by officers of Constabulary, by virtue of the powers conferred, or to be conferred on them, under the authority of the said last-mentioned Act and of this Act, and also the proceeds of the sale of any seizure to be made by them under the said powers, where such seizure may, at the discretion of the Inspector-General of Constabulary, be sold, shall, after deducting and paying thereout all reasonable expenses, be handed over to the Commissioners of Inland Revenue, or to such person as they shall appoint, for the use of Her Majesty: anything contained in any former Act to the contrary notwithstanding.

Where the Excise prosecute, all penalties under these Acts go to the Revenue of Excise, under 16 & 17 Vic. c. 107, s. 282, and so of Customs. Now all fines and penalties, forfeitures, &c., recovered under Revenue Acts, shall be paid to the Commissioners.—31 & 32 Vic. c. 124, s. 1. Penalties under 1 & 2 Wm. iv. c. 55; 23 & 24 Vic. c. 107; 23 & 24 Vic. c. 114; 25 Vic. c. 22; 26 & 27 Vic. c. 33; 29 & 30 Vic. c. 64; 33 & 34 Vic. c. 57, are all to be so paid whether recovered at the instance of Royal Irish Constabulary or not.—See Circular, *Appendix.*

Appeal (24 & 25 Vic. c. 91, s. 19).—Persons aggrieved by the judgment of Justices on any information or complaint exhibited by any officer of Inland Revenue, of any proceedings at the instance of any officer, Head, or other Constable, under the 1 & 2 Wm. iv. c. 55; 17 & 18 Vic. c. 89; 20 & 21 Vic. c. 40, either party, whether complainant or defendant, shall be at liberty to appeal therefrom to the next Quarter Sessions for the county, shire, division, city, town, or place, next after the expiration of 20 days from the giving of such judgment, upon giving such

Offence, or cause of Complaint.	Statute.	Extent of Jurisdiction.
EXCISE—*continued.* Every person who shall sell or deliver any spirits which shall have been illicitly distilled, or the full duty whereon shall not have been fully paid, unless proved to have been received from a licensed distiller or licensed dealer.	1 & 2 Wm. iv. c. 55, s. 24.	Like. 2 J.
Officer empowered to stop and detain any person found removing or carrying any still, still-head, worm, or any spirits of any kind whatever, and to examine same, and to demand production of permit accompanying such still, &c., or such spirits, if amounting to a quantia for which permit is required; and every person so found removing any still, &c., or any spirits for	s. 25.	Penalty of £100, and not less than £6, and forfeit articles; and officer shall arrest and convey offender and articles seized before one or more Justices of the Peace, near to the place, to be dealt with; and in default, &c., to commit offender for not less than 3 months,

notices, and upon such terms, conditions, and regulations as are prescribed in cases of appeals by 7 & 8 Geo. iv. c. 53; 4 & 5 Wm. iv. c. 51; and 4 Vic. c. 20.

The conditions and requirements of these statutes are:—7 & 8 Geo. iv. c. 53, s. 83.—No appeal shall be allowed unless appellant, immediately upon the giving of the judgment appealed against, give notice in writing of such appeal to the presiding Justices and the opposite parties, and also lodging such notice with the Clerk of the Peace, for the Justices at Quarter Sessions; and, within three days after the judgment appealed against, lodging with the Collector or Supervisor of the district the amount of the penalty.

By 4 & 5 Wm. iv. c. 51, s. 23—If there shall not be 20 days between giving the notice of appeal and the next Quarter Sessions, the appeal shall be to the following Quarter Sessions.

By the 4 Vic. c. 20, s. 30—Seven clear days' notice previous to the day on which the appeal is to be heard must be given to the opposite party.

Defects of form, either in the information or any part of the proceedings relating thereto, shall be amended and cured on appeal.—7 & 8 Geo. iv. c. 53, s. 82.

Form of Appeal.—By 40 Vic. c. 13—On notice given of appeal from decision of Justices in Ireland, a record of conviction or acquittal to be lodged with the Clerk of the Peace. Form of conviction or acquittal given in Schedule to Act. Justices' Clerks are directed by Circular from Lord Lieutenant to see that such conviction or acquittal, when necessary or required, be duly lodged.

By 24 & 25 Vic. c. 91, s. 22—The powers given to officers of Excise by 1 & 2 Wm. iv. c. 55, as to search for private stills, making of malt, &c., in Ireland, are extended to officers of Customs.

It will be observed that the powers and duties of the Constabulary are defined, and that they have not, as Excise Officers have, the power of inspecting houses and premises duly " entered " with the Excise.

Offence, or cause of Complaint.	Statute.	Extent of Jurisdiction.
EXCISE—*continued*. which permit is required, who shall refuse to produce such permit or permits as aforesaid, or shall be found removing or carrying any still, &c., or such spirits without a lawful permit; or removing in any quantity spirits illegally distilled, or the duties whereon shall not have been paid; or any cask or vessel which shall have contained illicit spirits, shall for every such offence severally be liable to—	1 & 2 Wm. iv. c. 55, s. 25.	nor more than 12 months. 2 J.
Persons forcibly opposing officers in execution of this Act; or found armed, to the number of two or more ; or masked or disguised ; or assembled for the purpose of aiding and assisting illicit stills, malt, or spirits, &c.	s. 29.	Felony, triable by indictment.
Penalties may (besides other remedies) be recovered in name of *Excise Officer* before *any one or more Justices of the Peace*. (*See* footnote as to "Procedure and recovery of Penalties," *ante*.)	s. 31.	
Persons arrested and brought before Justice may be dealt with immediately, on his own confession, or on proof of the offence, on the oath of one or more credible witnesses, unless he find bail—self £20, and two sureties £10—to appear at next Petty Sessions.	ss. 34, 36.	Under Petty Sessions Act, 2 J. are requisite to decide out of Petty Sessions.
Persons liable to arrest, not detained at the time, may be afterwards arrested.	s. 37.	—
Mitigation of Penalties.—Penalties not to be mitigated to less than £6 ; imprisonment, in default, not to be less than 3, nor more than 12 months.	ss. 39 & 40.	

Offence, or cause of Complaint.	Statute.	Extent of Jurisdiction.
EXCISE—*continued.* *Second Conviction.*—Where person convicted shall be guilty of a subsequent offence, mitigation not to be less than double former penalty or punishment, but in no case is the penalty or punishment to exceed that imposed by the statute for the offence.	1 & 2 Wm. iv. c. 55, s. 40.	
Penalties and imprisonment to be proportioned, and defendants may pay part of the penalty to be released from a portion of the imprisonment, but not to be less than £2 for each calendar month; or if imprisoned 6 months in default of payment of £18, the proportion shall be taken as £3 for each month, and so in proportion, reckoning each month's imprisonment equal to a payment of a monthly proportion of the penalty; and gaoler shall, on receipt of such payment, discharge prisoner.	s. 42.	—
Seizures, if not claimed within 14 days, to be forfeited; and if claimed, proceedings to be taken as for other Excise penalties. Proof of payment of duties, or of a permit, to be made by the defendants.	s. 46.	
Penalties under this Act may be sued for in the Court of Exchequer, or before one or more Justices of the Peace where offence committed. This power is still preserved by the 24 & 25 Vic. c. 91, s. 18. See note hereon as to "recovery of penalties." See also " Licensing Acts (I.), 1872–74."	s. 31.	—

Offence, or cause of Complaint.	Statute.	Extent of Jurisdiction.
EXCISE—*continued.*		
Gun Licences:—"The Gun Licence Act, 1870." (a)	33 & 34 Vic. c. 57.	
Every person who shall use or carry a gun, elsewhere than in a dwelling-house or the curtilage thereof, without having a licence in force under this Act; and it shall lie upon defendant to prove that he is a person not incurring the penalty.	s. 7.	Penalty £10 ; recoverable on Excise prosecution. 2 J. The Excise Act, 7 & 8 Geo. iv.,c. 53, empowers the *Justices* to mitigate penalty to *one-fourth*.
Proviso.—The penalty shall not be incurred by the following persons, namely :—		They may recommend to the Commissioners a further reduction.
1. Person in the naval, military, or volunteer service, or in the Constabulary or other police force, using or carrying any gun in the performance of his duty, or when engaged in target practice.		
2. Persons having a game certificate in force.		
3. Person carrying for or by order of person having game certificate, and for his use, and by giving, on demand, his own and owner's name and address.		

(a) This is an "Act to grant a duty of Excise on licences to use guns." "Gun" includes a fire-arm of any description, and an air-gun or any other kind of gun from which any shot, bullet, or other missile can be discharged. Licence not required to use or carry in a "dwelling-house or the curtilage thereof." *Curtilage* "signifies a court-yard, backside, or piece of ground lying near or belonging to dwelling-house—as the yard, garden, and in short everything that is within the homestall or fence by which the mansion-house is surrounded."—6 *Co.* 64.

The definition of "*Gun*" is now generally taken to include pistols and revolvers. The Excise prosecute where persons are found to be carrying these "weapons," and Justices without question convict. The Act, as its preamble states, is "to raise supplies and increase the public revenue." It is an *Excise Act.* The policy and object of this Act in the first instance seemed to be a supplement to the Game Licences, and to compel persons carrying guns for shooting purposes to take out, if not a Game Licence, some Licence. And the term "gun" appeared to be so well

Offence, or cause of Complaint.	Statute.	Extent of Jurisdiction.
EXCISE—*continued*.		
4. Occupier of lands using to scare birds or kill vermin thereon; or person on any lands, by order of the occupier thereof, who shall have a game certificate or licence under this Act.	33 & 34 Vic. c. 57, s. 7.	
5. Gunsmith or his servant in course of trade, or testing quality in places set apart for the purpose.		
6. Person carrying in course of his trade as a common carrier.		
Where a gun is carried in parts by two or more persons in company, each and every one shall be deemed to carry the gun.	s. 8.	
Officers of Inland Revenue and constables authorized to demand production of licence.	s. 9.	
If person, on demand, shall not produce licence, and permit officer to read same, officer may immediately require name and residence; and for refusing to declare name and residence he shall, for such refusal—	,,	Forfeit penalty of £10 (over and above any other penalty he may be liable to under this or any other Act), or mitigate portion thereof, not being less than one-fourth; and if not

understood that the definition was not viewed as carrying it further than so generally understood, and the bringing into the definition the "air-gun" rather helped to so fix and limit the meaning. It was not thought to be applicable to those arms secreted on the person for the protection of life and property.

All Acts relating to Excise duties and penalties to be applicable to this Act—s. 4. Licence not transferable—s. 5. Licence expires 31st July, by 41 Vic. c. 10, s. 6. The penalty under s. 9 is for refusing to declare name and residence, and the summary power given to one Magistrate seems to be where the offender is brought before him in custody, when the Justice is required to deal with the offence, although he be not sitting in Petty Sessions. If the person give his name and residence he incurs no penalty under s. 9, nor will he under s. 7, unless there be no licence in force. The Act gives no power to seize the gun. Magistrates, constables, and licensed persons are at liberty to inspect the register of licences—s. 6.

Offence, or cause of Complaint.	Statute.	Extent of Jurisdiction.
EXCISE—*continued.*		
Officer may arrest person so refusing, and convey him before a Justice having jurisdiction where offence committed; who, upon proof of offence, or on confession of accused, shall convict in the penalty aforesaid.	33 & 34 Vic. c. 57, s. 9.	immediately paid into the hands of officer or constable, to be committed to hard labour for not exceeding 1 month, nor less than 7 days.　　　　1 J.
Inland Revenue officers and Constabulary who may see person carrying a gun, may enter on lands (other than dwelling-house or the curtilage thereof) for the purpose of making the demand in section 9.		
Licences to be void if person be convicted under 1 & 2 Wm. iv. c. 32, s. 30, or 2 & 3 Wm. iv. c. 68. (These are English Acts, and have reference to trespasses in pursuit of game.)		
Not to interfere with any other Act requiring authority to keep fire-arms.		
Act to amend the law relating to the manufacture and sale of spirits, "The Spirits Act, 1880."	43 & 44 Vic. c. 24.	
Fines and penalties under Act may be sued for, and recovered, &c., under any Act in force relating to the revenue of Excise or Customs.	s. 156.	
"Inland Revenue Act," 1888: (Repeals as to duties several previous Acts set out in a schedule.)	43 & 44 Vic. c. 20.	
Part iii. Gives new scale of duties on licences, &c.	,,	
Part iv. As to income tax.	,,	
Part v. As to certain stamps. Schedule repealing in whole or in part certain previous enactments.	,,	

Offence, or cause of Complaint.	Statute.	Extent of Jurisdiction.
EXCISE—*continued*. Repeals of 1 & 2 Wm. iv. c. 55. ("The Illicit Distillation Act") sections 1 to 8 inclusive, and sections 17 to 21 inclusive, 26, 27, 28, 30, 38, 48, and 51, so far as they relate to malt, or corn or grain making into malt.	43 & 44 Vic. c. 20.	
Spirits Act, 1880. (a) *This Act is to consolidate and amend the Law relating to the manufacture and the sale of Spirits.* Section 3 gives a table of definitions.	43 & 44 Vic. c. 24.	
Part i. Provides Excise penalties for contravening the Law, and regulations as to distilling, brewing, warehousing, &c. &c., and applies to Spirits, &c., other than methylated Spirits.	ss. 1–115.	
Part ii. Applies to methylated Spirits.	ss. 117–132.	
Part iii. Is supplemental, and applies to providing scales, measures, locks, &c. &c., and confers general powers on officers.		
Unlawfully removing Spirits.—Any officer, or any officer of customs or peace officer having commissions from Commissioners, may detain person removing Spirits and demand permit.	s. 145.	
If any person is found carrying or removing any Spirits exceeding one gallon of same denomination and for same person, and shall not produce permit— Any officer may arrest offender.	,,	Penalty £100 and forfeiture of Spirits, and shall not be mitigated to less than £10 ; in default of payment, imprisonment not less than 1 nor more than 6 months, with or without H. L.

(a) This "Spirits Act, 1880," provides a number of heavy penalties for the various offences connected with distillation, &c.

Offence, or cause of Complaint	Statute.	Extent of Jurisdiction.
EXCISE—*continued.* *Unlawful hawking and sale of Spirits.*—If any person hawks, sells, or exposes to sale, any Spirits otherwise than in premises for which he is licensed to sell Spirits—	43 & 44 Vic. c. 24, s. 146.	Penalty £100, and the Spirits shall be forfeited ; shall not be mitigated to less than £6. In default of payment, imprisonment, with or without H. L., not less than 2 nor more than 3 months. 2 J.
Actual sale.—If any person knowingly sells or delivers, or causes to be sold or delivered, any Spirits to the end that they may be unlawfully retailed or consumed or carried into consumption—	s. 147.	Shall, in addition to any other penalty, incur a fine of £100. 2 J.
Purchaser.—If any person receives, buys, or procures any Spirits from a person not having authority to sell or deliver the same.	s. 148.	Penalty £100. 2 J.
Illicit Spirits.—Any person who knowingly buys, receives, or has in possession Spirits unlawfully removed, or before duty thereon has been charged and paid or secured, or where the Spirits have been condemned or forfeited—	s. 149.	Shall forfeit the Spirits, and incur a fine equal to treble value. 2 J.
Forcibly opposing execution of Act.	s. 150.	Penalty £100. 2 J.
For misconduct and collusion with officers.	s. 151.	Penalty £500. 2 J.
Any officer of the Peace who wilfully refuses or neglects to aid in the execution of Act.	s. 153.	Penalty £25. 2 J.
Recovery of Fines, &c.—According to Acts relating to Revenue of Excise or Customs. Repeals 23 & 24 Vic. c. 114.	s. 156.	
"Customs and Inland Revenue Act, 1887."	50 & 51 Vic. c. 15.	
Tobacco.—As to duties and drawback on, &c.		

Offence, or cause of Complaint.	Statute.	Extent of Jurisdiction.
EXCISE—*continued.* *Moisture in.*—If any manufacturer of tobacco shall have in his custody or possession (except process of treatment before fit for sale), or if dealer or retailer shall have tobacco, and if such tobacco shall on being dried at a temperature of 212 degrees (Fahrenheit) be decreased in weight by more than 35 per centum—	50 & 51 Vic. c. 15, s. 4.	Excise penalty £50, and tobacco shall be forfeited. Power to mitigate to one-fourth. 2 J.
Hawkers' Act, 1888. Duty of £2 on Hawker's annual Excise Licence. Hawker's licence shall not be granted (otherwise than by way of renewal of previous year's licence) except on production of certificate of clergyman and two householders of the parish, or a Justice of the Peace.	51 & 52 Vic. c. 33.	
Forging, or producing forged or counterfeit certificate knowingly.	s. 4.	Penalty £50 (which may be mitigated to one-fourth), and licence shall be void. In default of immediate payment, imprisonment, with or without H. L., for any term not exceeding 1 month. 1 J.
"Licensed Hawker" shall be legible on every box, package, vehicle used, &c., and on every room, shop, &c., where goods sold, and on every handbill, &c. He shall	s. 5.	Shall for every offence incur penalty of £10 (which may be mitigated to one-fourth); and in default of immediate

"*Hawker*" means any person who travels with a horse or other beast, bearing or drawing burden, and goes from place to place, or to other men's houses, carrying to sell or exposing for sale any goods, wares, or merchandize, or exposing samples or patterns of any goods, wares, or merchandize to be afterwards delivered; and includes any person who travels by any means of locomotion to any place in which he does not usually reside or carry on business, and there sells or exposes for sale any goods, wares, or merchandize in or at any house, shop-room, booth, stall, or other place whatever, hired or used by him for the purpose.

"*Exemptions.*"—Licence under Act not necessary in the following cases:—

    (a) By any person selling or seeking orders for goods, wares, &c., to or from persons who are dealers therein, and who buy to sell again.

    (b) By the real worker or maker of any goods, wares, &c., and his children, apprentices, and servants usually residing in the same house with him,

Offence, or cause of Complaint.	Statute.	Extent of Jurisdiction.
EXCISE—*continued.* not let or lend his licence to any person, provided that a servant may travel and trade with it for his master's benefit. For contravening any of these provisions—	51 & 52 Vic. c. 43, s. 5.	payment, imprisonment, with or without H. L., for any term not exceeding 1 month. **1 J.**
Person not having in force a licence in his own real name; who uses the words "licensed hawker," or words importing that he carries on the trade of hawker, or that he is licensed so to do; or trades with or under colour of a licence granted to any person other than his master—	,,	Shall for every offence incur a penalty of £10 (which may be mitigated to one-fourth); and in default of immediate payment, imprisonment, with or without H. L., for any term not exceeding 1 month. **1 J.**
Offences under sec. 6, how described.— It shall be sufficient to allege that "defendant did trade as a hawker without having in force a proper licence."	s. 6.	
No further description necessary.		
Jurisdiction to arrest, &c.—Inland Revenue officer, or peace officer, may arrest offender, and bring him before a Justice of the Peace of place where offence committed; and in default of immediate payment, upon conviction, of the fine, or of the sum to which it may be mitigated (which mitigation is hereby authorized), offender may be imprisoned, with or without H. L., for any term not exceeding one month.	,,	
Provisions in other Excise Acts to be applicable to licences and fines under this Act.		
Schedule given of enactments repealed.		

selling or seeking orders for goods, wares, &c., made by such real worker or maker.
(c) By any person selling fish, fruit, victuals, or coal.
(d) By any person selling or exposing for sale goods, wares, &c., in any public mart, market, or fair legally established.

Offence, or cause of Complaint.	Statute.	Extent of Jurisdiction.
EXPENSES (*Witnesses*): Justice may order expenses to witnesses in civil cases, not exceeding 2s. 6d.	14 & 15 Vic. c. 93, s. 13.	1 J.
In summary cases, under the Criminal Justice Act, Justices may order expenses of prosecution, and for loss of time, &c., by order on Treasurer of County.	18 & 19 Vic. c. 126, s. 14.	2 J.
EXPLOSIVES—See "Gunpowder," Sum. Index, and see "Explosives," Indictable Index.		
EXTRADITION ACTS: As to duties of Magistrates, see "Extradition," Indictable Offence Index.		
FACTORY AND WORKSHOP ACT, 1878.	41 Vic. c. 16.	For penalties, compensation, &c., for offences
Sanitary Provisions as to the condition of factories and workshops.	ss. 3, 4.	against Act, see sections 81 to 88.
Safety with respect to the fencing of machinery in factories.	ss. 5–9.	Restraint on Cumulative Fines, s. 88.
Employment and meal hours.—Period of employment of children, young persons, and women, time for meals, &c.	ss. 10–21.	2 J. or 1 Stip. Recoverable under P. S. Act, and any Act amending. In Dublin, under
Holidays, ...	s. 22.	local or special Acts, s. 106.
Education of Children.—Attendance at school of children employed in factory or workshop.	ss. 23–26.	
Certificate of fitness for employment of children and young persons under 16 in factories.	ss. 27–30.	
Accidents.—Notice to be given of accidents causing death or bodily injury, &c.	ss. 31, 32.	
Special provisions for health in certain factories and workshops.	ss. 33–37.	
Special restrictions as to employment, meals, and certificates of fitness.	ss. 38–41.	
Special exceptions relaxing general law in certain factories and workshops, &c., as to meal hours, overtime.	ss. 42–57.	

Offence, or cause of Complaint.	Statute.	Extent of Jurisdiction.
FACTORY AND WORKSHOP ACT, 1878—*continued.*		
Nightwork.—As to employment of male young persons at *night.*	41 Vic. c. 16. ss. 58–60.	For penalties, compensation, &c., for offences against Act see sections 81 to 88.
Special exception for domestic and certain other factories and workshops from certain provisions of Act.	ss. 61, 62.	Restraint on Cumulative Fines, s. 81.
Supplemental.—As to special provisions requirement of sanitary provisions as condition of special exceptions.	ss. 63–66.	2 J. or 1 Stip. Recoverable under P. S. Act, and any Act amending. In Dublin,
Inspection, ...	ss. 67–80.	under local or special
Definitions, ...	ss. 93–96.	Acts, s. 106.
Special exemption of certain trades in private houses, rooms, &c., by family, and exemption of certain home work.	ss. 97, 98.	
Ireland.—Application and modification of Act as to Ireland.	s. 103.	
And definitions, &c., terms, &c., as to Ireland.	s. 106.	
Application of Petty Sessions Act, 14 & 15 Vic. c. 93. Fines Act, 14 & 15 Vic. c. 90. In *Dublin,* the special Acts therefor.	s. 106.	
Repeal of previous Acts, Schedules, &c.	s. 107.	
FACTORY AND WORKSHOP ACT, 1883.		
Provides rules for carrying on white lead factories, and penalties for carrying on without certificate.	46 & 47 Vic. c. 53, ss. 6, 7.	
Explains certain provisions of the Factory Act, 1878, as to calculating overtime, &c. ; and amends as to period of employment of children in certain cases.	ss. 13, 14.	
Bakehouses.—Provides regulations as to bakehouses, and as to the closets, drainage, &c. ; and gives penalties for contravention against those who let for the purpose, and those who carry on the trade, &c.	ss. 15, 16.	
Enforcement of law as to bakehouses by sanitary authorities.	s. 17.	
Amendment of 41 & 42 Vic. c. 16, s. 105.	51 & 52 Vic. c. 22.	

Offence, or cause of Complaint.	Statute.	Extent of Jurisdiction.
FAIRS AND MARKETS: Disputes between buyer and seller relating to the terms of sale, delivery, price, or payment for any article, matter, or thing which shall be exhibited for sale in any fair or market (and which shall not be of a greater value than £5). (a) This may be heard out of Petty Sessions. (b)	14 & 15 Vic. c. 92, s. 17.	Justice to make an award in writing thereon, according to the merits of the case. Award to have the like force and effect as any order made at Petty Sessions. 1 J.
FALSE WEIGHTS: See " Weights and Measures."		
FAT (Stolen): See " Larceny."		
FEMALES (Assaults on): See " Assault," and for other provisions for the " Protection of Women and Girls," the " Suppression of Brothels"—see " Offences against the Person," Indictable Offences, " Criminal Law Amendment Act, 1885."		

(a) The goods or article in dispute must be exhibited for sale in a *fair* or *market*. The value must not exceed £5. It will not be sufficient to give jurisdiction that the amount *in dispute* be under £5. The Justice may hear the case out of Petty Sessions. He can make his order if he be present in the market or fair. It must be in writing. If he award a sum to be paid, he may issue a warrant of distress forthwith. This is really a Court of *Pipowders*. That was a Court incident to every fair and market, and called *Curia Pedis Pulverisate*, because for contracts or injuries done concerning the fair or market, justice shall be done as speedily as the dust can fall from the foot. " Its jurisdiction consists herein, that the contract or cause of action be in the same time of the same fair or market, and not before, or in former, it must be for some matter concerning the same fair or market, done, complained on, heard and determined the same day within the precinct of the same fair or market."—*Bacon's Abr.* But in exercise of the jurisdiction above given as to these disputes, there seems to be no reason why the Justice, if he find it more convenient, should not adjourn to some tent or neighbouring alehouse. The dispute may be also heard in Petty Sessions.

(b) In ordinary disputes of this nature the Justice ought not verbally to order either party to be arrested and brought before him (11 Ir. L. T. Rep. 1).

L

Offence, or cause of Complaint.	Statute.	Extent of Jurisdiction.
FENCE : Altering on road without consent of surveyor.	14 & 15 Vic. c. 92, s. 9.	Penalty not exceeding ... s.; in default, &c., imprisonment not exceeding 14 days, by scale. 1 J.
On complaints for trespass, Justices may order repairs of fences; on refusal, they may authorize repairs by the person aggrieved, to whom they may order payment at not exceeding 2s. a-perch. Stealing Fence : see "Larceny." Injuring : see "Malicious Injuries."	s. 20.	Amount awarded to be recovered by distress. 1 J.
FIGHTING : Persons who break the peace in presence of a peace officer, or are about to do so— Two or more persons fighting in a public place, to the terror of the Queen's subjects. (a) See "Sureties of the Peace," and see also "Prize Fighting," Indictable Offence Index.	34 Edw. iii. c. 1, and Commission. Common Law.	May be ordered to find sureties to keep the peace. 1 J. Indictable misdemeanor. Fine and Imprisonment.
FINDING (*Property*) : See "Treasure-trove," Indictable Offences.		

(a) This is called an affray, from the French "Affrayer" (Effraier), to frighten or terrify. If it be in private it is no affray, but an assault. Any person present may suppress an affray. The principals and seconds in a prize-fight were indicted in one count for a riot, and in another for an affray. The evidence was that the two first prisoners had fought together amidst a great crowd of persons, and that the others were present aiding and abetting ; that the place where they fought was at a considerable distance from any highway, and when the officers made their appearance the fight was at an end. The prisoners, on being required to do so, quietly yielded. Baron Alderson said, " It seems to me that there is no case against these men. As to the affray it must occur in some public place, and this is to all intents and purposes a private one. As to the riot, there must be some sort of resistance made to lawful authority to constitute it, some attempt to oppose the constables who are there to preserve the peace. The case is nothing more than this : Two persons choose to fight, and others look on, and the moment the officers present themselves, all parties quietly depart. The defendants may be indicted for an assault, but nothing more."—*R.* v. *Hunt*, 1 *Cox, C. C.*, 177 (*Roscoe.*)

Offence, or cause of Complaint.	Statute.	Extent of Jurisdiction.
FINES ACT: Fines Amendment Act, ...	14 & 15 Vic. c. 90.	
FIREARMS AND FIREWORKS: Discharging on roads, or within 60 feet of centre, or on streets.	14 & 15 Vic. c. 92, s. 10.	Penalty not exceeding 10s.; in default, &c., imprisonment not exceeding 7 days. 1 J.
Throwing fireworks on any thoroughfare or public place.	23 & 24 Vic. c. 139, s. 9.	Penalty not exceeding £5, recoverable as in Petty Sessions Act. 2 J.
Selling fireworks without licence, or to persons apparently under 16 years of age. See "Gunpowder," and as to Licences to carry, see "Excise" and "Peace Preservation" Act.	s. 8.	Like. 2 J. Imprisonment, by scale.
FIRST CONVICTION: (a) Justices may discharge offenders from conviction for first offence, on making satisfaction to party aggrieved for damages and costs.	14 & 15 Vic. c. 92, s. 21.	Applies only to offences against this Act. 1 J. And as to Lord Lieutenant's power to remit, see 14 & 15 Vic. c. 92, s. 22; and 22 Vic. c. 32.
See also in "Larceny" under Criminal Justice Act. Malicious Injuries Act, ..	18 & 19 Vic. c. 126. 24 & 25 Vic. c. 97, s. 66.	—
Larceny Act, ...	24 & 25 Vic. c. 96, s. 108.	
As to children and young persons,	47 & 48 Vic. c. 19.	
And see now "Probation of First Offenders Act."	50 & 51 Vic. c. 25.	

(a) *Conviction for first offence.*—It is most reasonable that Justices shall be allowed this discretionary power in certain cases. There are some trivial offences of which children may be convicted, but for which it would be extremely harsh and imprudent to send them to the common gaol. The horror of a gaol is to a child greater in the imagination, perhaps, than it is found to be in reality. An acquaintance with a prison is not likely to improve the young. Moreover, it may prove a source of considerable anguish to a respectable man when he is aware that his name is registered in a prison book for some disgraceful act committed in his years of indiscretion. Since this note was written the Act 47 & 48 Vic. c. 19, as to Children, &c., and "Probation of First Offenders Act," 50 & 51 Vic. c. 25, have been passed.

Offence, or cause of Complaint.	Statute.	Extent of Jurisdiction.
FISH : Offering unwholesome fish for sale. (See also "Nuisance and Public Health Act.")	14 & 15 Vic. c. 92, s. 7.	Forfeit article; and also a penalty nor exceeding 40s., or imprisonment not exceeding 14 days, by scale. 1 J.
FISHERIES : (a) Statutes 5 & 6 Vic. c. 106; 7 & 8 Vic. c. 108; 8 & 9 Vic. c. 108; 9 & 10 Vic. c. 114; 11 & 12 Vic. c. 92; 13 & 14 Vic. c. 88; 26 & 27 Vic. cc. 10 and 114; 29 & 30 Vic. c. 97; 32 & 33 Vic. c. 92; 33 & 34 Vic. c. 33; 46 & 47 Vic. cc. 22 and 26.	—	
Persons, to the number of three or more, intimidating or obstructing any other in the lawful prosecution of any fishery, may be apprehended and brought before a Justice, and on conviction—	5 & 6 Vic. c. 106, s. 88.	Penalty not exceeding £20; in default, &c., imprisonment not exceeding 3 months, and by scale. 1 J.
Nets.—Using nets whereby unsizable or young fish may be taken, except dredging for shell-fish.	s. 9.	Forfeit net, and penalty not exceeding £10; in default, &c., imprisonment not exceeding 3 months. 1 J.

(a) For powers of officers and men in Naval and Coast Guard Service to enforce fishery laws, subject to fishery regulations, see 5 & 6 Vic. c. 106, s. 86.

No public right of fishing exists in an inland river above the point in which the tide ebbs and flows.—*Murphy and Others* v. *Ryan, Com. Pleas* (*Ireland*), *Hilary,* 1868. The trespass complained of in this case was committed on the river Barrow, at a place above and beyond the point at which the sea ceases to ebb and flow; and the question to be decided was whether in such a place, though the river be navigable for the purposes of communication, and in that sense may properly be called a navigable river, the public can legally assert a right of fishing. For the plaintiff it was contended that above the point of the tidal flux and reflux the bed and soil of a river are vested in the riparian proprietors—those on either bank possessing it *usque ad medium filum aquæ;* and this not the less because it is navigable, and has been immemorially navigated for commercial and other purposes, and that above the flux and reflux of the tide the right to the fishing is private and exclusive, and cannot be legally claimed by the public, even though they have been allowed the immemorial use of it. The Court held with this view of the case. And further, that no river has been ever held navigable so as to vest in the Crown its bed and soil, and in the public the right of fishing, merely because it has been used as a general highway for the purpose of navigation, and

Offence, or cause of Complaint.	Statute.	Extent of Jurisdiction.
FISHERIES—*continued.* Herring or other nets (except as therein) left shot or floating between sunrise and sunset.	5 & 6 Vic. c. 106, s. 7, and 7 & 8 Vic. c. 108, s. 7.	(Forfeit); and penalty not exceeding £10; in default, &c., imprisonment not exceeding 3 months. 1 J.
Neglecting to haul up and remove such prohibited nets before sunrise, unless prevented by stress of weather, &c.	5 & 6 Vic. c. 106, s. 8.	(Forfeit); and penalty not exceeding £5; in default, &c., imprisonment not exceeding 2 months, 1 J.
Using trawl or trammel nets where prohibited by any by-law.	s. 9.	(Forfeit); and penalty not exceeding £20; in default, &c., imprisonment not exceeding 3 months. 1 J.
Setting nets across entrance to bays, &c., contrary to by-laws.	s. 10.	Penalty not exceeding £5; in default, &c., imprisonment not exceeding 2 months. 1 J.
Suffering stake nets, &c., to extend further than from high to low water-mark, or so placing bag nets as that leaders cannot be raised.	s. 26.	Penalty not exceeding £10; in default, &c., imprisonment not exceeding 3 months. 1 J.

that beyond the point to which the sea ebbs and flows—even in a river so used for public purposes—the soil is *prima facie* in the riparian owners, and the right of fishing private. The ruling referred to *Gatewood's Case*, 6 *Rep*, 59 *a*, where the distinction was taken between "an interest or profit in another's soil and an easement in another's soil;" and it was determined that for an easement there might be a good custom, but not for a profit. A right of way upon the land, a right of passage upon the water, a right for the people of a parish to dance upon a particular field: all these may be established by usage, because they are mere easements which may be enjoyed consistently with the interest of the owner of the land; but no usage can establish a right to take a profit in another's soil, which might involve the destruction of his property, and such a profit would be the taking of fish. The precise point is decided both as to the general law and the particular case of profit by fishing, in *Bland* v. *Lipscombe*, 4 *El. & Bl.*, 713 *n*; and the principle of that case in affirmation of the ancient doctrine is sustained by the judgments in *Lloyd* v. *Jones*, 6 *C. B.*, 89; *Race* v. *Ward*, 4 *El. & Bl.*, 702; *Hudson* v. *M'Crae*, 4 *B. & S.*, 585, and other recent decisions. That principle is beyond controversy. "Therefore the usage relied on in the defence cannot sustain the claim of the right in the public to fish in a river the soil of which is not *publici juris*, but private property." From the many important points decided, this may be considered a *leading case on the subject.*

Offence, or cause of Complaint.	Statute.	Extent of Jurisdic
FISHERIES—*continued*. Nets for taking salmon not to be used at mouths of narrow rivers, nor to be stretched across the mouths of any other parts of rivers (saving as to proprietors, &c.)	5 & 6 Vic. c. 106, s. 27.	Penalty not ex £10; in default imprisonment n ceeding 3 month
For assaulting or obstructing person fishing in a legal manner, or maliciously placing nets or engines to prevent fish entering nets legally used.	s. 28.	Penalty not exceed in default, &c prisonment by and net or engir forfeited.
Ballast.—Discharging in improper places, or unless where allowed by harbour regulations.	s. 14.	Penalty not ex £10; in defaul imprisonment n ceeding 3 month
Obstructing.—Assaulting or opposing authorized persons, &c., or if master of fishing vessel refuse on demand to produce his certificate—	s. 90.	Penalty not ex £10; in defaul imprisonment r ceeding 3 month
Annual Close Season.—Fishing for salmon or trout in close season, or aiding in so doing. (*a*)	5 & 6 Vic. c. 106, s. 36. and 11 & 12 Vic. c. 92, s. 42.	Forfeit fish and and penalty n ceeding £10, n than 10s.; in &c., imprisonm exceeding 3 mon
Buying, selling, or having in possession any salmon or trout, or part thereof, so caught in close time, and having in possession to be *primâ facie* evidence of being caught in close time. (*b*)	13 & 14 Vic. c. 88, s. 35, 5 & 6 Vic. c. 106, s. 36.	(Forfeit); and not exceeding fish, nor less tha in default, &c., sonment, by sca
Neglecting in close season wholly to remove machinery, nets, &c., for taking salmon, &c., in salmon	s. 37.	(Forfeit); and not exceeding in default, &c.,

(*a*) *Close Season*.—The Inspectors of Fisheries are empowered by 44 & c. 66, to alter the close season.

(*b*) The 13 & 14 Vic. c. 88, s. 35, provides the penalty for offence o *part* or *portion* of *salmon* or *trout* in possession, &c. Previous to this Act were made to evade the law by cutting the fish into parts.

Unlawfully taking or destroying fish in water running through land t to a dwelling-house: see 24 & 25 Vic. c. 96, s. 24, and title "Larceny,' after.

Offence, or cause of Complaint.	Statute.	Extent of Jurisdiction.
FISHERIES—*continued.* weirs, or other fixed engines (stress of weather excepted, and also rights by patent, &c., for eel fishing).	5 & 6 Vic. c. 106, s. 37.	sonment not exceeding 3 months (or may be by scale). 1 J.
Neglecting to remove all bag, stole, fly, or stake nets, and other engines for catching salmon in tideway during close season (stress of weather excepted); and see also 26 & 27 Vic. c. 114, as to bag nets, &c.; and all obstructions to free passage of fish to be removed within 36 hours after close season.	s. 38.	(Forfeit); and penalty not exceeding £50; and not exceeding £5 a-day while unremoved; in default, &c., imprisonment not exceeding 3 months. 1 J.
Neglecting to remove nets from banks and vicinity of rivers during yearly close season. (And see "Salmon Fishery Act, 1863," hereafter.)	13 & 14 Vic. c. 88, s. 34.	(Forfeit; and penalty not exceeding £10, and not less than £2; in default, &c., imprisonment not exceeding 2 months. 1 J.
Licence.—Using nets, engines, &c., subject to licence duty, without licence. (Rods used singly for trout, perch, pike, or any fish, except salmon, not subject to licence duty.) Licence to be produced to authorized officers on demand. (Licence only protects person named therein, 32 & 33 Vic. c. 92, s. 17.)	11 & 12 Vic. c. 92, ss. 8. 21, 22, 29. 13 & 14 Vic. c. 88, s. 12.	Penalty not less than double, nor more than treble the duty, and engine forfeited; recovered as penalties. 1 J.
Illegal Nets.—Seized, if such cannot be legally used,	5 & 6 Vic. c. 106, s. 103.	To be destroyed by Justice's order.
And legal nets, if used illegally, .	,,	To be sold, and proceeds applied as penalties. 1 J.
Spears, &c.—Using otter, spear, strokehaul, &c.	13 & 14 Vic. c. 88, s. 40.	Penalties not less than £4, nor exceeding £10; in default, &c., imprisonment not exceeding 3 months. 1 J.

Offence, or cause of Complaint.	Statute.	Extent of Jurisdi
FISHERIES—*continued*.		
Fry.—Wilfully having, taking, or attempting to take fry and spawn of salmon, trout, or eels, or in any way wilfully obstructing the passage of smelts or fry, or injuring or disturbing spawn or fry, &c., wherever same may be.	5 & 6 Vic. c. 106, s. 73.	Penalty not ex £10 each offen gines forfeite default, &c., in ment not exce months. (a)
Unclean Fish.—At any time wilfully taking, killing, &c., exposing to sale, or having in possession any red, black, foul, unclean, or unseasonable salmon or trout. *Proviso.*—If accidentally caught, and immediately returned to the water without injury, no penalty.	s. 74.	Penalty not ex £2 for each default, &c., in ment, by scale.
Weirs—Queen's share.—No obstruction to be placed near Queen's share, nor shall any person fish in or near same (occupancy or ownership *prima facie* evidence)..	s. 57.	Penalty not ex £30; in defau imprisonment ceeding 3 montl
Taking fish within 200 yards of weir used for supplying water to mills, &c., above or below, save with rods and lines (saving right of person possessed of several fishery for 20 years before Act.)	13 & 14 Vic. c. 88, s. 37.	Forfeit nets, & penalty not le £2, nor more th in default, &c. sonment not e 3 months, by s
Fish Passages.—While mills, &c., not working, a wheel, &c., not repairing, waste gates, &c., to be closed in dry seasons, so as to force surplus through fish-pass; for non-observance—	5 & 6 Vic. c. 106, s. 63.	Penalty not e £5; in defau imprisonment ceeding 3 mont
Fishing at or near fish passages, deterring fish, or obstructing fishpass.	s. 64.	Penalty not e £20; in defa imprisonment ceeding 3 mont
Mills and Sluices.—Mills and sluices to be opened or shut as by law required at all times when mills are out of use. (Proviso as to machinery or water power.)	13 & 14 Vic. c. 81, s. 39.	Penalty not le £2, nor more th in default, &c sonment not e 3 months, by s

(a) *Salmon* shall extend to and include grilse, peal, sea trout, samlets, and the spawn and fry thereof.—13 & 14 Vic. c. 88, s. 1.

Offence, or cause of Complaint.	Statute.	Extent of Jurisdiction.
FISHERIES—*continued.* *Mill-dams and Watercourses.*—Taking or attempting to take fish or fry in works appurtenant to mills, &c., or in watercourses diverted from rivers for such purposes.	5 & 6 Vic. c. 106, s. 75.	Forfeit engine, &c., and penalty not exceeding £10; in default, &c., imprisonment not exceeding 3 months. 1 J.
Night.—Between sunset and sunrise having or using light or fire of any kind, or spear, gaff, strokehaul, or other such instrument, with intent to take salmon or other fish in or on the banks of any lake or river.	s. 78.	Forfeit instruments, and penalty not exceeding £10; in default, &c., imprisonment not exceeding 3 months. 1 J.
Disturbing Spawning Fish.—At any time chasing, injuring, or disturbing spawning fish, or fish on the spawning beds, or attempting to catch fish in such places (except with rod and flies only within the lawful period).	,,	Like penalty, &c. 1 J.
Damming River.—Damming, teeming. or emptying any river or mill-race, for the purpose of taking or destroying salmon or trout, or the fry thereof.	,,	Like penalty, &c. 1 J.
Poisonous Matter (a)—Allowed to flow into inland rivers.	5 & 6 Vic. c. 106, s. 80.	Penalty not exceeding £10; in default, &c., imprisonment not exceeding 3 months. 1 J.
Poisoning river for the purpose of taking fish.	13 & 14 Vic. c. 88, s. 36.	Penalty not less than £5, nor more than £10; in default, &c., imprisonment not exceeding 3 months, by scale. 1 J.
Trespass.—Person entering upon lands for the purpose, or under pretence of fishing, without permission. (Fishing with nets where no several fishery exists: see sec. 65.)	5 & 6 Vic. c. 106, s. 71.	Penalty not exceeding £2; in default, &c., imprisonment not exceeding 1 month, by scale. 1 J.

(a) Maliciously putting lime or noxious material into fish-pond to destroy fish—indictable misdemeanour—24 & 25 Vic. c. 97, s. 32.

Offence, or cause of Complaint.	Statute.	Extent of Jurisd:
FISHERIES—*continued.* *Exporting unclean Salmon.*—No unclean or unseasonable salmon, and no salmon caught during time at which sale of is prohibited in district where caught, shall be exported to parts beyond the seas. And person exporting or entering same for exportation, shall be liable to—	26 Vic. c. 10, s. 3. 33 & 34 Vic. c. 33, s. 3.	Penalty not e: £5 each salm default, &c., ir ment, as in s exceeding 3 and forfeiture o
THE SALMON FISHERY ACT, 1863. *As to fixed Engines.*—After the passing of this Act, no bag net shall be placed or allowed to continue in any river, or the estuary of any river, as such river or estuary has been or shall be defined by the Commissioners, or within less than 3 statute miles from mouth of river so defined; for contravention of this section— *Proviso.*—No bag net now legally existing shall be liable to be removed, or deemed illegal under Act, by reason of its being within 3 miles of the mouth of a river, in the whole of which, including all tributary rivers and lakes upon its course, the proprietor of net has the exclusive right of catching salmon.	26 & 27 Vic. c. 114, s. 3. "	To be deemed a nuisance, and taken possessio destroyed, and s any salmon tak by shall be fi and owner of i for each day continued incu: nalty not less i and not exceedi in default, &c. sonment not e: 3 months.
New fixed Nets.—No fixed net that was not legally erected for catching salmon or trout during the open season of 1862 shall be placed or used for catching salmon or trout in any inland or tidal waters. And any net so placed or used in contravention of this section— Commissioners shall abate and remove all fixed salmon or trout nets that, in their judgment, are injurious to navigation; and if satisfied of their illegality, remove all other fixed nets that are contrary to law.	s. 4. s. 5.	Liable to be de in all respects ceding, and like

Offence, or cause of Complaint.	Statute.	Extent of Jurisdiction.
FISHERIES—The Salmon Fishery Act, 1863—continued. Commissioners, subject to certain conditions, may give certificate as to certain fixed nets erected in pursuance of 5 & 6 Vic. c. 106. Certificate, if unappealed from, to be evidence of the right of person named therein.	26 & 27 Vic. c. 114, s. 6.	But not to render a net legal that would be illegal by being injurious to navigation, a common nuisance to public right of fishing, or contrary to common or statute law.
Weirs.—Commissioners shall inquire into legality of all fishing weirs, and as to free gaps, &c.	s. 7.	—
Persons unlawfully erecting or keeping up any fishing weir upon a river after notice from owner or occupier of any grounds on bank of such river—	s. 8.	Liable to forfeit £50, and costs, by action of debt.
Section 9 provides for the construction and regulation of *free gaps.*	s. 9.	—
Section 10 provides for the construction of boxes and cribs in fishing weirs and fishing mill-dams. And owner shall bring any box or crib, attached to weir in contravention of Act, into conformity with Act within 6 months after commencement of Act; in default—	s. 10.	For each day, after expiration of the 6 months, he so fails, penalty not less than £5, and not exceeding £20 ; in default, &c., imprisonment, by scale, and not exceeding 3 months. 1 J.
And any owner failing so to maintain same shall for each day of failure be liable to—	,,	Penalty not less than £1, and not exceeding £5 a-day ; in default, &c., imprisonment in proportion, by scale, and not exceeding 3 months. 1 J.
(Commissioners may extend weekly close time 24 hours, when inexpedient to require a free gap in a particular river.)	s. 11.	
Free Gaps in Weirs.—Rules to be observed for enforcing free gaps. Weir without free gaps, at commencement of Act, owner shall, within 12 months, make same; and for each day after expiration, &c., in default—	s. 12.	Penalty not less than £5, and not exceeding £50 a-day ; in default, &c., imprisonment, by scale, not exceeding 3 months. 1 J.
Where free gap made, but not maintained, in accordance with Act.	,,	Penalty not exceeding £5 a-day ; in default, &c., like imprisonment. 1 J.

Offence, or cause of Complaint.	Statute.	Extent of Jurisdiction.
FISHERIES—The Salmon Fishery Act, 1863—*continued.* No alteration shall be made in the bed of any river in such manner as to reduce the flow of water through a free gap; if it is, person so making shall incur—	26 & 27 Vic. c. 114, s. 12.	Penalty not less than £5, and not exceeding £50, and a further penalty of £1 a-day, until bed restored to original state; in default, &c., imprisonment, in proportion, not to exceed 3 months. 1 J.
Scaring Salmon from Free Gap.—No person shall place obstruction, use contrivance, or do an act whereby fish may be scared, deterred, or in any way prevented from freely entering and passing up and down free gap at all periods of the year, or shall use any nets or other engines within 50 yards above or below free gap—	,,	Penalty not less than £5, and not exceeding £20, for first offence, and not less than £10, and not exceeding £50, for each subsequent offence; in default, &c., imprisonment, in proportion, not to exceed 3 months. 1 J.
Proceedings before Commissioners for abatement of illegal nets and weirs.	s. 13.	—
Mode of appeal from decision of Special Commissioners.	s. 14.	—
Mill-Dams.—No person shall use any box, crib, net, &c., or other instrument for taking fish (save and except rods and lines only) at or within 50 yards either above or below a mill-dam, unless there is attached a fish pass as may be approved by Commissioners, nor unless such pass has constantly running such flow of water as that fish may pass up and down; for offending—	s. 16.	Penalty not less than £5, and not exceeding £20 (recoverable by any one who will sue); in default, &c., imprisonment, in proportion, not exceeding 3 months. 1 J.
Power to Commissioners to define estuaries and mouths of rivers.	s. 17.	—
Boat.—If proved to satisfaction of Justices that boat, cot, or curragh found on or near waters frequented by salmon or trout, has been used for capture of salmon or trout, during any part of annual or weekly close time; person proved to have used same—	s. 18.	Penalty not exceeding £5; in default, &c., imprisonment, not exceeding 2 months. 1 J.

Offence, or cause of Complaint.	Statute.	Extent of Jurisdiction.
FISHERIES—THE SALMON FISHERY ACT, 1863—*continued.* Second, or any subsequent offence— Boat not to be forfeited where proved to be used without knowledge or consent of owner.	26 & 27 Vic. c. 114, s. 18.	Like penalty, and boat may be seized and forfeited. 1 J.
Weekly Close Time.—6 *o'clock p. m. Saturday, to* 6 *o'clock a. m. Monday.* In inland lakes or rivers salmon or trout not to be taken in any traps, nets, or fixed engines, or by any nets of what nature or kind soever; nor in the sea, estuaries, or tide ways to fish by stake, flood, ebb, or head weir, stake net, bag net, fixed net, or other net whatsoever, during the weekly close season (except fishing by single rod and line).	5 & 6 Vic. c. 106, s. 40.	Penalty not less than £5, nor exceeding £50 ; in default, &c., imprisonment not exceeding 3 months. 1 J.
Persons occupying or using cribs, boxes, &c. &c., stake, flood, ebb, head weir, stake net, bag net, or other fixed net or engine, &c., for catching fish, failing to remove or open same as required by the Act (5 & 6 Vic. c. 106), or scaring fish from passing through, or taking therein any salmon or trout— (And see sec. 25, 26 & 27 Vic. c. 114, as to scaring or impeding in any manner free passage of salmon in weekly close time hereafter.)	5 & 6 Vic. c. 106, s. 40. 13 & 14 Vic. c. 88, s. 46. 26 & 27 Vic. c. 114, s. 20.	For every such offence, penalty not less than £10, and not exceeding £50. And when any salmon or trout is taken at any fishing weir in contravention of Acts, or when box, crib, or cruive, left unopened, or otherwise left not in conformity with said Acts, *penalty* of not less than £10, nor exceeding £50, for *each* box, crib, or cruive, in the weir in which any fish so illegally taken, or left unopened, as aforesaid, or not in conformity with said Acts (and net or other instrument, or the

(e) The last Act, 26 & 27 Vic. c. 114, s. 20, alters the weekly close season, and in other respects alters and amends the former Acts. To properly understand the nature of the offences above comprised, a careful reading of the three sections is indispensable, together with the Interpretation Clause, sec. 1, 13 & 14 Vic. c. 88, as to "fixed nets," "fixed engines," &c., "close season," "fisheries," &c.

Offence, or cause of Complaint.	Statute.	Extent of Jurisdiction.
FISHERIES—THE SALMON FISHERY ACT, 1863—*continued.*		inscales or gates and rails of cribs, &c., so used, to be forfeited); in default, &c., imprisonment not exceeding 3 months. 1 J.
Proviso.—No penalty where satisfactory proof by such person that he was prevented by floods, storm, or stress of weather from removing such leaders or making openings during such prevention, but no longer.	13 & 14 Vic. c. 88, s. 46.	—
In freshwater portion of inland river and lakes, sec. 66 (5 & 6 Vic. c. 106) prescribes size of meshes, and regulations as to nets and their use, and prohibits persons from laying, drawing, or fishing with any nets whatsoever, except nets for the taking of eels, as by Act provided, or taking salmon or trout in any way during weekly close time except by single rod and line: for offending—	5 & 6 Vic. c. 106, s. 46. 26 & 27 Vic. c. 114, s. 20.	Forfeit net or instrument used, and penalty not exceeding £10; in default, &c., imprisonment not exceeding 3 months. 1 J.
Annual close season for salmon shall not comprise fewer than 168 days, except when taken for artificial propagation.	26 & 27 Vic. c. 114, ss. 21 and 22.	
For single rod and line, close season from 1st November to 1st February in each year.	s. 23.	—
Nets in Rivers.—No net, except landing net, to be used for capture of salmon or trout in fresh water portion of any river, as defined by Commissioners, between 8 p.m. and 6 a.m., except so far as same may have heretofore been used within the limits of a several fishery next above the tidal flow, and held under Grant or Charter, or by immemorial usage.	s. 24.	Penalty not exceeding £10; in default, &c., imprisonment not exceeding 3 months. And forfeiture of boats, nets, and gear. 1 J.

Offence, or cause of Complaint.	Statute.	Extent of Jurisdiction.
FISHERIES—The Salmon Fishery Act, 1863—*continued.*		
Scaring, &c., Salmon.—No person shall in any manner scare, impede, or obstruct the free passage of salmon or trout during weekly close time; for contravening— (Not to apply to legally taking with rod and line.)	26 & 27 Vic. c. 114, s. 25.	Forfeiture of fish, and net or instrument used, and also penalty not less than £2, and not exceeding £10; in default, &c., imprisonment by scale, and not exceeding 3 months. 1 J.
Licence duties for fixed engines.	s. 26.	—
Hydraulic Machines.—In salmon rivers, to prevent salmon being injured in descent to the sea, owners shall, during time of descent, provide grating or other sufficient means to prevent fish passing into machine; in default—	s. 30.	Penalty not exceeding £50; and also, not exceeding £5 a-day while injury to fry continues; in default, &c., imprisonment, in proportion, and not exceeding 3 months. 1 J.
Recovery of Penalties.—Penalties under this Act recovered and applied in like manner as penalties under previous Acts (5 & 6 Vic. c. 106. s. 94).	45.	—
As to imprisonment, which is in default of payment or of sufficient distress, sec. 94, 5 & 6 Vic. c. 106, directs that where fine does not exceed £5 the imprisonment shall not exceed 2 months, and shall not exceed 3 months in any case. Proceedings may be as in "Petty Sessions Act," and see also Small Penalties Act, and *scale.*		
OYSTERS : Close season between 1st May and 1st September—dredging for, taking, buying, selling, or having in possession— OYSTER FISHERY ACT, 1866. Persons other than licencees or their assigns, their agents, servants, and workmen, within the limits of any oyster-bed, laying, knowing, or doing any of the following things :	5 & 6 Vic. c. 106, ss. 32–36; and 11 & 12 Vic. c. 92, s. 42.	Penalty not exceeding £5, nor less than 10s.; in default, &c., imprisonment not exceeding 2 months. 1 J.

Offence, or cause of Complaint.	Statute.	Extent of Jurisdiction.
FISHERIES—OYSTER FISHERY ACT —*continued.* To use any implement of fishing except a line and hook, adapted solely for catching floating fish, and so used as not to disturb or injure in any manner any oyster-bed or oysters, or the oyster fishery. To dredge for any ballast or other substance except under a lawful authority for improving navigation. To deposit any stone, ballast, rubbish, or other substance.	29 & 30 Vic. c. 97, s. 13.	First offence:—Penalty not exceeding £2. Second:—Penalty not exceeding £5. Third and subsequent offence:—Penalty not exceeding £10 ; in default, &c., imprisonment, by scales. 1 J. And may be sued for compensation for damage sustained.
To place any implement or thing prejudical, or likely to be so, to oyster-bed or oysters, brood, or spawn thereof, or to the oyster fishery, except lawful purpose or navigation or anchorage.		
To disturb or injure in any manner, except as last aforesaid, any oyster-bed or oysters, brood, spawn, or fishery.		
To interfere with or take away any of the oysters from such bed, without consent of licencees, owners, or occupiers. (*a*)	,,	Like.
Proceedings to be under Petty Sessions Act.		
This Act to be construed with former Acts.	s. 16.	—
* Act to promote cultivation of Oysters.	47 & 48 Vic. c. 47.	

(*a*) Stealing oysters or brood from oyster-bed, &c., felony ; and unlawfully dredging in oyster-beds, &c., of another, and known as such, or being sufficiently marked out, 24 & 25 Vic. c. 96, s. 26. See also "Oyster Preservation Act, 1867," 30 Vic. c. 23.

* Provides penalty for wilful trespass on oyster fishery beds or layings, &c., or breach of regulations. Applies Act to mussel-beds and mussel fisheries. Secs. 13 & 19.

Offence, or cause of Complaint.	Statute.	Extent of Jurisdiction.
FISHERIES—*continued.* **FISHERIES ACT, 1869.** (*b*) Persons picking up at sea any fishing boat, gear, rigging, &c., thereof, net, buoy, float, or fishing implement shall, soon as possible, deliver up same at nearest coastguard station; in default—	32 & 33 Vic. c. 92, s. 11.	Penalty not exceeding £10; in default, &c., imprisonment not exceeding 2 months. 1 J.
Licence to fish with rod and line only to entitle person named therein to fish, and for fishing without same, penalty as under sec. 12.— 13 & 14 Vic. c. 88, s. 12.	s. 17.	Penalty not less than double nor more than treble the duty, and the engine to be forfeited; recovered as penalties. 1 J.
This Act provides for appointment of inspectors—the making of byelaws—agreements between owners and crews—oyster-beds—appointing the angling season. Sec. 16 provides penalty for using fixed engine without certificate of Commissioners or inspectors.		
Complaint.—May be verbal or otherwise; triable by one or more Justices.	5 & 6 Vic. c. 106, s. 94.	
Application of Penalties.—One-third to informer, two-thirds to conservators of the district.	11 & 12 Vic. c. 92, s. 35; 21 & 22 Vic. c. 100, s. 28; 32 & 33 Vic. c. 92, s. 19.	
Private Grounds.—For fishing in waters running through private grounds, see "Larceny," Summary Index, ss. 24, 25.		
Crabs, Lobsters.—Prohibition on sale of edible crabs and lobsters, under certain size, and for penalties, see Act—	40 & 41 Vic. c. 42, ss. 8 and 9.	
Power on local application to restrict the taking of crabs and lobsters in certain areas, and to vary, &c.	s. 10.	
Penalties recoverable under Petty Sessions Act.	ss. 11 and 13.	

(*b*) The above Act, called the "Fisheries (Ireland) Act, 1869," incorporates the several previous *Fishery Acts.*

M

Offence, or cause of Complaint.	Statute.	Extent of Jurisdiction.
FISHERIES—*continued.* *Dynamite, &c.*—Any person who uses dynamite or other explosive substance to catch or destroy fish in a public fishery—	40 & 41 Vic. c. 65, s. 2.	Penalty not exceeding £20; in default, &c., imprisonment, by P. S. scale; *or in discretion* of Court, imprisonment not exceeding 2 months, with or without H. L. 2 J.
Act empowering Inspectors of Fisheries to alter close season. **Sea Fisheries Act, 1883:** Sea fishery officer protected as officer of Customs.	44 & 45 Vic. c. 66.	
Obstructing sea fishery officer, neglecting to comply with lawful directions, &c. &c.	46 & 47 Vic. c. 22.	Penalty not exceeding £50; or imprisonment not exceeding 3 months, with or without H. L. 1 J.
Provision as to compensation for damage caused by the offence.	s. 15.	
Appeal—where sum exceeds £5, or where imprisonment is awarded without option of fine.		
Petition for prohibition of trawling, and proceedings thereon.	51 & 52 Vic. c. 29.	
Appeals from Dismiss.—See 40 & 41 Vic. c. 56, s. 74, &c. (*a*) For Constabulary and Coastguard powers under Acts, see 5 & 6 Vic. c. 106, s. 86; 7 & 8 Vic. c. 108, s. 1; 8 & 9 Vic. c. 108, s. 10; 11 & 12 Vic. c. 92, s. 29.		

(*a*) *Appeal from Dismiss under Fishery Acts.*—In case any Justice or Justices shall, after the passing of this Act, dismiss any complaint made under the provisions of the Act 5 & 6 Vic. c. 106, or of any Act altering or amending same, either on the merits or without prejudice, if any person prosecuting shall feel aggrieved by such order of dismissal, such person may appeal against such order, and the several provisions of the 24th sec. of the Petty Sessions (Ireland) Act, 1851, as amended by this Act, shall extend, and may be applied to such appeal : provided that the amount of the recognizance to be entered into by such appellant shall be such as to the Justice shall seem reasonable.—40 & 41 Vic. c. 56, sec. 74. For amendments by this Act in appeals, &c., see ss. 72, 73, 75, 76, 78. Sec. 72 amends recognizance. Sec. 73, Justice at original hearing shall not take part in appeal. Sec. 75 provides for the estreating of the recognizances. Sec. 76 provides that convictions shall not be quashed on the ground of error in complaint. Sec. 78 provides that exceptions need not be negatived. And see notes on *Appeals*, Petty Sessions (Ireland) Act, 1851, *Appendix.*

Offence, or cause of Complaint.	Statute.	Extent of Jurisdiction.
FLAGS (*Party*) : See "Licensing Acts."		
FLAX : Beating on road or street, or within 30 feet of centre.	14 & 15 Vic. c. 92, s. 10. (36 & 37 Vic. c. 82.)	Penalty not exceeding 10s.; in default, &c., imprisonment not exceeding 7 days. 1 J.
FLEECE (*Stolen*) : See "Larceny." Frauds—See "Weights and Measures."		
FLOUR : See "Adulteration."		
FOOD AND DRUGS : See "Adulteration."		
FORCIBLE ENTRY : See "Entry," Indictable Offences Index; and when in proclaimed district, see "Criminal Law and Procedure (Ireland) Act, 1887."		
FOREIGN ENLISTMENT ACT : See "Indictable Offences."		
FOREIGN (SHIP) DESERTERS : Upon application of Consul, &c., Justices shall aid in recovering deserters from ships of foreign powers, and may apprehend them and send them on board.	15 Vic. c. 26, s. 2.	Complaint on oath, warrant to issue for apprehension; may order him to be put on board or delivered over to master or owner. 1 J.
Protecting or harbouring such deserters knowingly—	s. 3.	Penalty not exceeding £10; in default, &c., imprisonment, by scale. (a) 2 J.

(a) *Foreign Deserters Act*, 1852.—To the present the Foreign Powers brought within the provisions of the *Act by orders in Council*, and communicated to the

M 2

Offence, or cause of Complaint.	Statute.	Extent of Jurisd
FORTUNE-TELLERS : See "Vagrancy," where they are punishable as "Rogues and Vagabonds."		
FRAUDS AS TO PROVISIONS ; (a) *Grain.*—Any person who shall sell or offer for sale any wheat, rye, meslin, pease, beans, barley, bere, oats, shillin, cutlings, meal, flour, malt, or other corn, in whole or in part spoiled or adulterated by wetting or mixtures of dirt, &c., or damaged corn or other stuff, or which shall not be equal to sample, or using any fraud to increase weight, &c.	14 & 15 Vic. c. 92, s. 7.	Forfeit articles, a fine not e 40s. ; *or* may b soned, not exc month.
Meat, Fish, &c.—Exhibiting for sale unwholesome or fradulently prepared meat, fish, or other provisions or food of any kind, for man or beast, or shall practise any deceit or fraud in respect to the quality of any such meat, fish, or other provisions. (b) See also "Adulteration," and "Weights and Measures." "Public Health Act."	,,	Forfeit articles, a fine not e 40s. ; *or* may t soned, not exc month. The Justice m the case at may adjourn it Petty Sessions

Magistrates are :—Austria, Belgium, Brazil, Chili, Columbia, Denmark, France, German Empire, Greece, Hawaii, Italy, Madagascar, Morocco Netherlands, Nicaragua, Ottomon Porte, Peru, Russia, Salvador, Siar Sweden and Norway, Tunis, Uruguay, Paraguay, Zanzibar, Dominion of Independent State of Congo, Empire of Brazil, United States of Mex section states that such penalties shall be recovered as penalties for h deserters from British merchant ships ; and these, by the Merchant Act, are directed to be recovered under the Petty Sessions (Ireland) .

(a) May be heard out of Petty Sessions.

(b) It is an indictable offence at Common Law to sell unwholesome mix noxious ingredients in provisions which are offered for sale and sold. *Case,* 3 M. & Selw. 11.

There are many instances of convictions by indictment having bee selling unwholesome food (meat or grain), not fit to be eaten by man.— on the above sections, "*Coppinger's Practice,*" p. 699.

Offence, or cause of Complaint.	Statute.	Extent of Jurisdiction.
FRIENDLY SOCIETIES: Act to consolidate and amend the Law relating to Friendly and other Societies.	38 & 39 Vic. c. 60.	—
Definition of "terms, &c."	s. 4.	
Societies that may be registered under this Act :— (1) Friendly Societies ; (2) Cattle Insurance Societies ; (3) Benevolent Societies ; (4) Working Men's Clubs ; (5) Specially authorized Societies. (For definitions of each of these classes, see Act.)	s. 8.	
Offences by societies to *be also offences by officers* thereof. (a)	s. 14.	
Documents that are exempt from Stamp Duty.	s. 15.	
After decease of member, payment to persons apparently entitled to be valid.	„	
Investment of funds, . . .	s. 16.	—
Frauds, Misappropriation.—If any person obtains possession by false representation or imposition of any property of a society, or having the same in his possession withholds or misapplies the same, or wilfully applies any part thereof to purposes other than those expressed or directed in the rules of the society and authorized by this Act, he shall on the complaint of the society or of any member authorized by it, or the	s. 16. (sub-sec. 9.)	Penalty not exceeding £20 and costs, and to be ordered to deliver up all such property, or to repay all moneys applied improperly ; and in default of such delivery or repayment, or of the payment of such penalty and costs aforesaid, to be imprisoned, with or without H. L., for any

(a) As to quinquennial returns, see 45 & 46 Vic. c. 35.

The above Act occupies a very considerable space in the Statutes for the year. It appears to have been prepared with great care and attention, and with a full knowledge of the evils that grew up under the former system by the want of any proper legal control. There seems to be ample provision to prevent frauds ; and where it is found that an offence by a society becomes an offence by every officer, or member of committee, who does not take steps to prevent its commission, or who cannot bring evidence of innocence by *proving* his ignorance of the transgression, dishonest practices must be less frequent than heretofore.

Offence, or cause of Complaint.	Statute.	Extent of Jurisdiction.
FRIENDLY SOCIETIES—*con.*		
trustees or committee of management of same, or by the central office, or the Chief Registrar, or Assistant Registrar by his authority, be liable on summary conviction to—	38 & 39 Vic. c. 60, s. 16. (sub-sec. 9).	time not exceeding 3 months. 2 J. Nothing herein prevents the offender being proceeded against by indictment, if not previously convicted of the offence summarily.
Trustees of society not liable to make good deficiencies; only liable for money actually received by them, respectively, on account of society.	s. 16.	—
What loans may be made to members.	s. 18.	—
Disputes shall be decided in manner directed by the rules of the society, and the decision so made shall be binding and conclusive on all parties, without appeal, and shall not be removable into any Court of Law or restrainable by injunction; and application for the enforcement thereof may be made to the County Court (in Ireland, the Civil Bill Court).		
Proviso, as to references of disputes and the procedure before referee. Where rules direct disputes to be referred to Justices, the disputes shall be determined by Court of Summary Jurisdiction. Proviso —that it shall be lawful for the parties to consent to its being determined by County Court.	s. 22. and 48 & 49 Vic. c. 27.	
Where rules contain no direction as to disputes, or where within 40 days after application to society for a reference under rules, no decision is made thereon, aggrieved may apply either to County Court or Summary Jurisdiction Court to hear and determine dispute. The Court, Chief or other Registrar, may, at request of either party,		

Offence, or cause of Complaint.	Statute.	Extent of Jurisdiction.
FRIENDLY SOCIETIES—*con.* state a case for opinion of superior Court of Law on any question of law, and may also grant to either party such discovery as to documents and otherwise, or inspection of documents. Discovery to be made on behalf of society by such officer of same as Court or Registrar may determine.		
Unlawful Dissolution.—Officer or person aiding or abetting in dissolution of a society otherwise than as in Act provided—	38 & 39 Vic. c. 60, s. 25. (sub-sec. C.)	Imprisonment not exceeding 3 months' H. L. 2 J.
Provisions as to Friendly Societies and Insurance Companies receiving contributions by Collectors— (Sub-section 10 of this section)—	s. 30. and 42 Vic. c. 9. ,,	—
Disputes between society and person injured, or persons claiming through member or person insured, or other rules, may, notwithstanding provisions of rules to the contrary, apply to County or Summary Jurisdiction Court to settle disputes.		
Notices under this section may be sent through post (sub-sec. 11).	,,	
Money payable by members to be recoverable as a debt in County Court.	38 & 39 Vic. c. 60, s. 31.	
Falsification.—If any person wilfully makes, orders, or allows to be made any entry, erasure, omission from balance-sheet of registered society, or contribution or collecting-book, or return or document required for the purposes of Act, with intent to falsify same, or evade the provisions of Act—	s. 32.	Penalty not exceeding £50, recoverable at suit of Registrar or Assistant, or aggrieved; in default of payment, imprisonment not exceeding 3 months. 2 J.
Ordinary Offences.—Every society officer, or member of a society, or other person, guilty of an offence under this Act for which no penalty is expressly provided herein, shall be liable to—	,,	Penalty not less than £1, and not more than £5; in default of payment, imprisonment not exceeding 3 months. 2 J.

Offence, or cause of Complaint.	Statute.	Extent of Jurisdic
FRIENDLY SOCIETIES—*con.* *Recovery of Penalties.*—All penalties imposed by Act, or to be imposed by regulations or rules, &c., recoverable in a Summary Jurisdiction Court.	38 & 39 Vic. c. 60, s. 32.	—
Offences and penalties may be prosecuted and recovered under Summary Jurisdiction Act (Petty Sessions, Ireland, Act; Definition, sec. 4). In Dublin, before a divisional Justice; elsewhere, before two Justices.	s. 33.	—
Description of Offence may be in words of Act. No exception, proviso, excuse, &c., need be specified or negatived.	,,	—
Legal Proceedings.—(1) Trustees of society or branch, or other officers authorized by rules, may bring or defend actions, &c., and may sue and be sued in their proper names without other description than the title of their office.	s. 21.	
(2) In proceedings by member or person claiming through him, society may also be sued in the name, as defendant, of any officer or person who receives contributions or issues notices, &c., within the jurisdiction of the Court, with the addition of the words "on behalf of the society" (naming the same).	,,	
(3) Proceedings shall not abate by death, resignation, removal, &c., or by any act of officer after commencement of proceedings.	,.	
(4) *Service of Summons, &c.*—Summons, process, &c., against officer sued on behalf of society may be personally served on him, or leaving copy at registered office of society, &c., within jurisdiction, or, if office closed, by posting; but where not served personally or by leaving at	,,	

Offence, or cause of Complaint.	Statute.	Extent of Jurisdiction.
FRIENDLY SOCIETIES—*con.* registered office, a copy shall be transmitted by post to committee of management at the registered office, by registered letter, posted at least six days before any further step taken thereon.	38 & 39 Vic. c. 60, s. 21.	
Appeals, from order or conviction made by Court of Summary Jurisdiction, to Quarter Sessions, held not less than 15 days nor more than 4 months after decision.	s. 33.	—
Appellant shall within 7 days after decision give notice of appeal to other party, and to the Court of Summary Jurisdiction, of intention to appeal, and of ground thereof.		
Immediately after notice he shall enter into recognizance, himself in £10, and two sufficient sureties in £10 each, *personally to try appeal, abide the judgment, and pay costs, if awarded.*		
Where appellant is in custody, the Justice may, on his entering into recognizance, release him.	,,	
Court of Appeal may adjourn appeal, reverse, modify, &c., decision, or remit the matter back, with opinion of Court thereon, or make such other order as the Court thinks just.		
If remitted, the Court of Summary Jurisdiction shall thereupon rehear and decide in accordance with the opinion of Court of Appeal.(*a*)		
Regulation of proceedings in County Courts.	s. 34.	

(*a*) *Rehearing the Matter Remitted.*—This course, not quite new in England, is becoming general now in Ireland, under the Acts giving right of appeal. The only thing strange about it is that, where the Court of Appeal neither confirms, reverses, amends, or alters decision, but expresses an opinion on the matter, and remits it back with that opinion, the Court of Summary Jurisdiction shall again, with grave countenances, "*rehear the matter,*" but *shall decide* in accordance with the opinion of the Court of Appeal. The meaning would, however, appear to be that the decision of the Justices shall be governed by a view of the law, or the equity in relation to some particular facts in the case, of which they might not have been before cognizant.

Offence, or cause of Complaint.	Statute.	Extent of Jurisdiction.
FRIENDLY SOCIETIES—*con.* *Documentary Evidence*, . . .	38 & 39 Vic. c. 60, s. 39. s. 33.	—

Where offences triable, and how.—Under Summary Jurisdiction Acts (Petty Sessions, Ireland, Act), as respects prosecutions against Society or its officers, where registered office is, or offence committed ; against others, where offender resides or offence committed.
Schedules to Act—
  Sch. 1.—Acts and Enactments repealed.
  Sch. 2.—Matters to be provided for by the rules of societies registered under this Act.
  Sch. 3.—Form of bond, receipts, acknowledgments, &c.		

FRIENDLY SOCIETIES AMENDMENT ACT, 1876.	39 & 40 Vic. c. 32.	
Conversion of registered societies into branches.	s. 3.	
Registered societies may contribute to funds of other societies. Forms, &c., term "Society." As to deaths at sea. Amendment in fees payable on certificates of births or deaths.	s. 4. s. 8.	
What shall be sufficient distribution of annual return.	s. 9.	
Amends sub-sections 3 and 6 of principal Act. Notice of proceedings or order to set aside dissolution. Corrects misprint in schedule 2 of principal Act. Where 5000 shall read 10,000.	s. 10.	
Act to extend the power of nomination in Friendly and Industrial, &c., Societies, and to make further provision for cases of intestacy, in respect of personal property of small amount.	46 & 47 Vic. c. 47.	

Offence, or cause of Complaint.	Statute.	Extent of Jurisdiction.
FRIENDLY SOCIETIES—*con.* Interpretation and amendment of sec. 22 of the "Friendly Societies Act, 1875" (38 & 39 Vic. c. 60), and the section shall read as if the following words were inserted after the word "thereof" in the third line of the section :—"Or between any registered branch under the Friendly Society Acts, or an officer thereof, of any registered Society or registered branch, and the registered Society or branch of which the other party to the dispute is a registered branch, or an officer thereof, or between any two or more registered branches of any registered Society or branch, or any officers thereof respectively."	48 & 49 Vic. c. 27, s. 1.	
FRUIT : See "Larceny," or "Malicious Injuries," as case may be.		
FRUIT-TREES : See "Larceny," or "Malicious Injuries," as case may be.		
FURIOUS DRIVING : Riding or driving furiously on any public road or street, so as to endanger any passenger ; or by carelessness or wilful misbehaviour causing any injury to any person or property thereon. For compensation, where injury is done by the driver of any carriage, see "Drivers." Furious driving of cattle, &c., in streets, see "Towns Improvement Act," and "Police Clauses Act," *Appendix.*	14 & 15 Vic. c. 92, s. 13. (36 & 37 Vic. c. 82.)	Penalty not exceeding 20*s.*; in default, &c., imprisonment not exceeding 14 days. 1 J. If bodily harm be done to any person thereby, the offender may be indicted for a misdemeanour under 24 & 25 Vic. c. 100, s. 35.

Offence, or cause of Complaint.	Statute.	Extent of Jurisdiction.
GAME : (a) Qualification to Shoot.—Persons not having freehold estate of £40 a-year, or personal estate to value of £1000, shooting, killing, or taking game, &c. (a)	10 Wm. iii. c. 8, s. 8 (Irish).	Penalty 10s. ; in default, &c., imprisonment, by scale, 1 week. 1 J. (But now the Excise game certificate would seem to make up this qualification.) See footnote (b).

(a) It has been observed that Ireland never felt the extreme severities of the Forest Laws, although replenished with all sorts of game from the most remote era ; yet the existing statutes regulating the right of killing, &c., and the preservation of game, are consequences of the same original causes which produced the English Game Laws, and which, to a certain extent, give a property in game. "Property is the power that a man hath over any other thing for his own use, and the ability that he has to apply it to the sustenance of his being ; when the power ceases his property is lost ; and by consequence, an animal of this kind which, after my seizure, escapes into the wild common of nature, and asserts its own liberty by its swiftness, is no more mine than any other creature in the Indies. because I have it no longer in my power or disposal."—Bacon's Abr.   Still many reasons concurred for the making of these constitutes :—" First, for the encouragement of agriculture and improvement of lands, by giving every man an exclusive dominion over his own soil.   Secondly, for the preservation of the several species of these animals, which would soon be extirpated by a general liberty.   Thirdly, for prevention of idleness and dissipation in husbandmen, artificers, and other persons of lower rank, which would be the unavoidable consequence of universal licence."—Black. Com.

(b) Qualification.—Some provisions in the early statutes as to distinctions and qualifications under the Game Laws, and the penalties and disabilities that follow ; although not expressly repealed, they have so far become obsolete, as that attempts to enforce them after the dominant manner which the Acts in some instances prescribe would now be highly dangerous, and to do so by any means would be invidious, perhaps useless.   The power to enforce the penalties is very uncertain, and even the liability to them extremely doubtful.   The decisions, and rulings of the Superior Court Judges show that the proceedings in all these instances are regarded with disfavour.   This being so, there may not be much difficulty in showing that these laws have been gradually and imperceptibly displaced by more modern legislation, such as the Excise Game Laws and licences, gun licences, dog licences, destruction of dogs that do injury, &c.   The ample laws to prevent trespasses in pursuit of game, the employment of the Constabulary to put down poaching, and the bringing into the Larceny Act the offences of unlawfully killing, hunting, snaring, or pursuing game (beasts and birds, &c.) on lands the property of another.   These things, added to improved knowledge and altered circumstances, help to push such laws into the background, and silently to repeal them. Magistrates should therefore proceed with caution, and in all cases decline a jurisdiction involved in doubt.

Offence, or cause of Complaint.	Statute	Extent of Jurisdiction.
GAME—*continued*. *Dogs.*—Persons not duly qualified (by at least £100 a-year freehold, or personal estate value of £1000) or licensed by Justices as trainers, keeping any SETTING dog or bitch, pointer, hound, beagle, greyhound, or land-spaniel, except whelps at nurse.	10 Wm. iii. c. 8, s. 10. 27 Geo. iii. c. 35, s. 8 (Irish).	Penalty £5 (recoverable by distress) (*a*), and now by scale may in default be imprisoned, not exceeding 2 months. 1 J. (See notes.)
Deer.—Hunting, killing, &c., any male deer before 10th June, or male fallow, after Michaelmas, unless in one's own ground.	10 Wm. iii. c. 8, s. 6.	Penalty £5 ; in default imprisonment not exceeding 2 months, by scale. 1 J.
Pheasant.—Taking, killing, selling, or buying any pheasant or wild turkey between 1st February and 1st October.	27 Geo. iii. c. 35, s. 4 (Irish), and 28 & 29 Vic. c. 54.	Penalty not exceeding £5 a-head ; in default, &c., imprisonment not exceeding 1 month, or by scale in 36 & 37 Vic. c. 82, when not exceeding £5. 1 J.
Grouse, Partridge, &c.—Taking, killing, &c.; selling, buying, or having in possession moor-game, heath-game, or grouse, between 10th December and 12th August ; or partridge, landrail, or quail, between 10th January and 20th September.	37 Geo. iii. c. 21, s. 2 (Irish). 27 Geo. iii. c. 35, s. 4 (Irish). (37 & 38 Vic. c. 11, s. 1).	

(*a*) The section provides no penalty for so keeping a setting dog or bitch, and the Court of Queen's Bench has so decided in a recent case—but it would appear that the offender is liable to be indicted. The law never commands but to compel, and wherever a statute enjoins or prohibits any act, the person disobeying is liable to be indicted at Common Law. Indeed, there being no power to enforce several of these penalties by imprisonment, the law is in most cases rendered nugatory with respect to them. The Court of Queen's Bench also decided that there was no power to imprison for this £5 penalty, and refused a *mandamus* to compel the Justices of Cork to issue imprisonment warrant. The 36 & 37 Vic. c. 82, now provides a remedy.

The *forms* given in Petty Sessions Act may be used in game prosecutions, but in other respects the Act is not extended to proceedings under the Game Laws. 14 & 15 Vic. c. 93, s. 42.

Offence, or cause of Complaint.	Statute.	Extent of Jurisdiction.
GAME—*continued.* *Sunday.*—Using gun, net, &c., to take, kill, or destroy game as aforesaid, or other wildfowl, hare, or rabbit, on Sunday.	27 Geo. iii. c. 35, s. 4.	Penalty not exceeding £5; in default, &c., imprisonment, by scale.
Tracing game in snow, if not qualified, or on own lands.		Like penalty, recoverable as above.
Destroying eggs or nest of game or wildfowl.	„	Penalty not exceeding £5; in default, &c., imprisonment not exceeding 1 month. 1 J.
Trespass in Pursuit of Game.—No person or persons not being duly authorized shall go or enter upon the land of any other person or persons to hunt for, set, spring, start, follow, shoot, course, hunt, hawk, or otherwise pursue, take, or destroy any sort of game, woodcock, snipe, duck, teal, or widgeon, and that every person so offending in any of the particulars herein set forth shall for every such offence—	s. 10. (36 & 37 Vic. c. 82.)	Forfeit a sum not exceeding £10; in default, &c., imprisonment not exceeding 1 month. (*a*) 1 J.
Landlord or lessor, having reserved right of game, shall, for the purpose of prosecuting persons trespassing in pursuit of game, be deemed the legal occupier. And any person who shall enter or be upon the said land, without his consent, shall be deemed a trespasser. (*b*)	27 & 28 Vic. c. 67.	Penalty not exceeding 40*s.* and costs; in default, &c., imprisonment not exceeding 1 month.

(*a*) But if a penalty of £5 be imposed, the imprisonment by the scale in **36 & 37** Vic. c. 82 may be 2 months, whereas if £10 be imposed it cannot exceed 1 month.

(*b*) *Trespass in pursuit of Game.*—"No person shall be construed to be within the meaning of this Act, as looking for game, unless such person shall appear to be provided with a dog or dogs, net or nets, or some other implements for taking or destroying game."—27 Geo. iii. c. 35, s. 11. It is also provided (s. 12) that nothing herein contained shall subject any person or persons *duly qualified* to take or kill game, his or their servants, or necessary attendants, to any of the penalties hereby inflicted for following or pursuing their four-footed game into the lands of other persons. Section 13 preserves to the owners or occupiers their legal civil rights for any actual damage done by persons so following their game.

Not having proper authority or consent, he shall be deemed a Trespasser.— The 30th sec. of the English Act, 1 & 2 Wm. iv. c. 32, is very similar in terms to the 10th sec. of 27 Geo. iii. c. 35, and upon the former it was held that it was not necessary, in order to support a conviction, that the defendant should have intended

Offence, or cause of Complaint.	Statute.	Extent of Jurisdiction.
GAME—*continued.* Prosecutions to be under Petty Sessions Act and Petty Sessions Clerks Act. "Game," in this Act, shall include hares, pheasants, partridges, grouse, heath or moor game, black-game, woodcocks, snipe, quails, landrails, wild-ducks, widgeon, and teal.	27 & 28 Vic. c. 67.	—
Night Poaching.—Persons by night unlawfully taking or destroying any game or rabbits in any land, or entering upon any land with gun, net, or other instrument, for the purpose of taking game. (Extended to the destruction of game, &c., on public roads, by 7 & 8 Vic. c. 29.)	9 Geo. iv. c. 69, s. 1.	First offence : Imprisonment not exceeding 3 months' H. L., and at expiration to find sureties, self in £10, and two sureties in £5, for not again offending; in default of finding sureties, to be recommitted for 6 months' H. L.

to commit or have been conscious that he was committing a trespass. Trespass in pursuit of game is of a civil rather than a criminal character, and is *punishable as an agnes,* for the sake of protecting property.—*Morden* v. *Porter,* 7 *C. B.,* N. S., 641. And upon a question submitted for opinion of the Law Adviser, Dublin Castle, as to whether the entering upon another's land through inadvertence, and in mistake, conceiving that it was part of the property to which an authority extended, he, in reply, quotes the decision as given above, and adds—"I fear that in this case the Magistrates must convict."—13,568, 5th Oct., 1874.

Appeal.—If any person shall think him or herself aggrieved by anything done in pursuance of the laws relative to the game, by any Justice of the Peace, such person may appeal to next General Sessions for the county. Justices at Sessions authorized, if need be, to impannel a jury. Power to give costs to the party *appealed against,* as they shall think reasonable, appellant first entering into recognizance before some Justice of the county, with two sufficient sureties conditioned to try such appeal, and to abide the order of, and to pay such costs as shall be awarded by the Justices.—27 Geo. iii. c. 35, s. 23. There is no appeal given from convictions or orders under 10 Wm. iii. c. 8. There is a power of appeal given by 9 Geo. iv. c. 69, s. 6, to persons convicted under that Act for poaching, &c., to next Sessions (not less than twelve days after the conviction). Notice in writing of appeal, and cause and matter thereof, to be given complainant three days after conviction, and at least seven clear days before Sessions, and either remain in custody or within such three days enter into recognizance with a sufficient surety, conditioned personally to appear, try the appeal, abide the judgment, and pay such costs as shall be awarded ; Court of Appeal to enforce the judgment. The requirements of these appeals should be strictly complied with. In the notice of appeal the party should state that *he feels aggrieved.* The Petty Sessions Act

Offence, or cause of Complaint.	Statute.	Extent of Jurisdiction.
GAME—*continued.* Owners, occupiers, or servants, may apprehend, and offenders assaulting or offering violence with any offensive weapon shall, though it be a first offence, be guilty of a misdemeanour.	9 Geo. iv. c. 69, s. 1.	Second offence : Imprisonment not exceeding 6 months' H.L. ; at expiration to find sureties, self in £20, and two in £10, or one in £20, not to offend for 2 years ; in default to be recommitted for 1 year. 2 J. Third offence : Indictable misdemeanour, penal servitude 5 to 7 years, or imprisonment not exceeding 2 years. (a)
Assaulting with offensive weapon any person so authorized to apprehend offenders.	s. 2.	Misdemeanour, penal servitude 5 to 7 years, or imprisonment with H.L. not exceeding 2 years.
Three or more persons armed unlawfully entering or being found on lands at night for the purpose of taking or killing game or rabbits.	s. 9.	Misdemeanour, penal servitude 5 to 14 years, or imprisonment, with H. L. not exceeding 3 years.
General Act against poaching at any time.—Constable or peace officer authorized on any highway, street, or public place to search any person whom he may have cause to suspect of coming from land where he shall have been unlawfully in search or pursuit of game ; (b) or persons aiding, &c., and having in	*25 & 26 Vic. c. 114, s. 2.	Penalty not exceeding £5 ; in default, &c., imprisonment not exceeding 2 months. 2 J. Game and engines to be forfeited, sold, or destroyed ; proceeds of sale and penalty to be

is made applicable to some of the latter offences in reference to game. In such cases the appeal directions in this Act will be followed.

Application of Penalties.—For application of penalties or forfeitures under the Game Laws (not being Excise penalties), see Fines Act, 14 & 15 Vic. c. 90.

Penalties, how enforced.—Penalties under the Game Laws, not being Excise penalties, may be enforced under the Small Penalties Act, 36 & 37 Vic. c. 82, where the sum imposed does not exceed £5.

(a) The Act says from 3 to 7 years, but now, by 27 & 28 Vic. c. 47, penal servitude is not to be less than 5 years in any case.

(b) *Game*, for the purpose of this Act, shall include hares, pheasants, partridges, eggs of pheasants and partridges, woodcocks, snipe, rabbits, grouse, black or moor game, and eggs of grouse, black or moor game.—Sec. 1.

Offence, or cause of Complaint.	Statute.	Extent of Jurisdiction.
GAME—*continued*. possession any game unlawfully obtained, or any gun, net, engine, &c., used for killing or taking game, and to stop and search any conveyance suspected of having such things therein; and if any game, gun, engines, &c., found, constable may seize and detain same, and shall summon the person to appear before two Justices at the Petty Sessions for the division; and if such person shall have obtained such game by unlawfully going on any land in search or pursuit of game, or shall have used any such article or thing as aforesaid, for unlawfully killing or taking game, or shall have been accessory thereto.	25 & 26 Vic. c. 114, s. 2.	paid to Treasurer of County or Borough where conviction takes place. If no conviction, the property to be restored to owner. (Proceedings to be under Petty Sessions Act.)
Appeal.—Appeal to Quarter Sessions (to be held next after twelve days) from Justices' conviction under this Act. For offence of stealing or setting engines for deer, &c., resisting keepers, or killing hares or rabbits in a warren—see title "Larceny," in the Summary and Indictable Offences Index.	s. 6.	
Excise Penalties (5 & 6 Vic. c. 81, continued in force by 23 & 24 Vic. c. 90, s. 17).—Every person, not acting as a gamekeeper duly deputed or appointed, who shall keep or use any *dog*, gun, net, or engine for destruction of game, shall take out an excise certificate authorizing him to kill game. Gamekeeper shall register his deputation or appointment with Excise officer, and take out annual certificate. (*a*) (By whom licence and certificates	5 & 6 Vic. c. 81, s. 2.	

(*a*) *Gamekeeper*.—There would appear to be no penalty now for acting as a gamekeeper without certificate. The offence for which he would be punished would be for having, with dog or gun, &c., *taken game* contrary to section 5. The duty

N

Offence, or cause of Complaint.	Statute.	Extent of Jurisdic
GAME—*continued.* shall be granted, and form thereof, see 23 & 24 Vic. c. 90, s. 16.)		
Person who shall have, keep, or use any (*greyhound*) (*b*) hound, pointer, setting-dog, spaniel, lurcher, or other dog, or any gun, net, or other engine, for taking, &c., of hare, pheasant, partridge, woodcock, snipe, heath fowl (commonly called black game), or grouse (commonly called red game), or any other game whatsoever ; or if any person shall have or obtain any deputation or appointment as a gamekeeper, without having taken out or renewed a certificate, &c., every such person respectively so offending—	5 & 6 Vic. c. 81, s. 5.	Penalty £20, reco as Excise penalt (As to *Mitigatio* note.)
Demanding Certificate.—If any person be found using dog, gun, net, or other engine for the taking or destruction of game, it shall be lawful for any Officer of Excise, or for the occupier of the land, or any owner, proprietor, or person having any estate therein, &c., whether in possession, reversion, &c., or for any person having a	s. 8.	Excise penalty £5 (See note as to *A tion*, under " Ex

upon the certificate of having registered a deputation, under which certif gamekeeper was authorized to kill game, was repealed by 23 & 24 Vic. c. It is considered, however, with reference to sections 17 and 18 of that Ac gamekeepers' deputation (which should bear a 10*s.* stamp, see 33 & 34 Vi may still be registered with the supervisor, and the person deputed be des a gamekeeper in the certificate to kill game ; if so described, the game employer would be allowed the benefit of the provision in section 7 (5 & 6 Vi on a change of keeper, and be placed upon the same footing as the empl gamekeeper in Great Britain, and this was no doubt the intention of the Leg —See note " *Bell & Dwelly's Excise Laws*," p. 634.

(*b*) *Greyhound, &c.*—Coursing with greyhound, beagles, or other hou cepted and exempted from game certificate, 23 & 24 Vic. c. 90, s. 5. Bu trespass committed, see 27 Geo. iii. c. 35, s. 10 ; and for taking, killing, also offences under Larceny Act, sections 12 to 22, title " Larceny," S Index.

Offence, or cause of Complaint.	Statute.	Extent of Jurisdiction.
GAME—*continued*. certificate then in force, producing the same, to demand and require from the person so using such gun, &c., as aforesaid, to produce, and show a certificate then in force, and such person shall produce same to be inspected, and if such person wilfully refuse to produce a certificate then in force, or shall decline to produce or show the same, or shall refuse, on being required so to do, to give and declare his name and surname, and the place of his residence, or shall give false or fictitious name or address. (a)	5 & 6 Vic. c. 81, s. 8.	
Person refusing to produce certificate, or to declare his name and surname and residence, may be apprehended by any person entitled to demand same, or any person then present, and conveyed forthwith before any Justice of the Peace within whose jurisdiction offence committed, and such Justice shall proceed to the conviction of the offender in the same manner as if he had been summoned on information for such offence—	,,	It would appear that there is nothing in this case of arrest and summary adjudication out of Petty Sessions to take away the power to mitigate, as except that is neither information or summons, the proceedings would, in other respects, be under 7 & 8 Geo. iv. c. 53. (See note at foot on *Mitigation*.)

(a) The offence of refusing to produce the certificate is not complete unless the person of whom the demand is made also refuses to tell his name and place of abode (*Melton* v. *Rogers*, 4 *Esp.* 214); but it is to be noticed that the wording of the analogous section in 23 & 24 Vic. c. 90, s. 10, is so drawn as to fully and clearly warrant this decision being founded on it. The section in the Irish Act given above is more strictly drawn, and would seem to imply that either the *wilful refusal, &c.*, to produce the certificate, *or* the refusal to give the name and address, would render the party liable to the penalty. The 23 & 24 Vic. c. 90, is applicable to the United Kingdom, but from the 6th to the 11th sections appears to be limited to *Great Britain*. Section 17 provides that the 5 & 6 Vic. c. 81, relating to game certificates in *Ireland*, shall continue in force.

Mitigation.—Where penalties are sued for by Excise, the proceedings are under 7 & 8 Geo. iv. c. 53; and unless the Act creating the offence direct that no mitigation shall be made by the Justices, section 78 of that Act authorizes and empowers them to mitigate the penalty, but not to reduce it to less than one-fourth.

N 2

Offence, or cause of Complaint.	Statute.	Extent of Juris
GAME—*continued.* *Exceptions and Exemptions from Licence Duties.* *Greyhounds, &c.*—Pursuing and killing hares, or hunting with beagles or other hounds.	23 & 24 Vic. c. 90, s. 5.	—
Deer.—The pursuing and killing of deer by hunting with hounds.	,,	—
The taking and killing of deer in any enclosed lands by the owner or occupier of such lands, or by his directions or permission.	,,	—
Exemptions as to person aiding or assisting a licensed person in his company and for his use, &c., such *licensed* person not being a deputy or appointee.	,,	
Game certificate not necessary for killing rabbits. (But may be prosecuted for poaching, under 25 & 26 Vic. c. 114, s. 2.)	23 & 24 Vic. c. 113, s. 43.	—
Dealers in Game, licensed by Justices, neglecting to take out Excise licence before dealing.	23 & 24 Vic. c. 90, s. 14.	Penalty £20 ; rec as Excise penal

(*a*) Section 13 of the 23 & 24 Vic. c. 90, extends the 1 & 2 Wm. iv. 2 & 3 Vic. c. 35, relating to granting of licences by Justices to deal in Ireland. Justices can hold Sessions for the purpose at any time, and fro time, from July to December inclusive. Seven days' notice previous t Sessions should be given to each Justice of the district. For licence to l by Justices, see form in *Appendix.* Any two Divisional Magistrates in D grant licence.—28 Vic. c. 2.

A person must take out an Excise licence in order to be at liberty to to a dealer.—23 & 24 Vic. c. 90, s. 13.

Live game is within the meaning of the 1 & 2 Wm. iv. c. 32, s. 4, and is required for the sale thereof.—*Loome, appellant,* v. *Bailey, respondent,* N. S., 406. No licence is required to *deal* in woodcock, snipe, quail, landr or deer.—"*Bell's Excise Laws.*"

Enforcing Penalties under Game Laws.—The *Small Penalties Act,* 36 c. 82, applies to all penalties recoverable in a summary way under a Parliament, the only exception being section 7, "that it shall not app penalties recoverable by or on behalf of the *Commissioners of Inland* . And this Act provides a scale of imprisonment for every penalty that exceed £5. See Act and scale, *Appendix.*

Offence, or cause of Complaint.	Statute.	Extent of Jurisdiction.
GAME—*continued*. Persons dealing in game without Excise licence shall be liable to the penalty, whether licensed by the Justices or not.	24 & 25 Vic. c. 91, s. 17.	Persons selling, under written order of Justices, forfeited game, on conviction under 25 & 26 Vic. c. 114, s. 2, not liable to penalty. —
Hares.—So much of sec. 4, 27 Geo. iii. c. 35, as enacts that any person buying or selling any hare between first Monday in November and first Monday in July following shall forfeit £5 for each hare, repealed by 26 Vic. c. 19, s. 1. Hares Preservation (Ireland) Act, 1879.	42 & 43 Vic. c. 23.	
Close Time.—Any person who shall wilfully kill, wound, or attempt to kill or wound, or take any hare or leveret, or use any gun, net, snare, or dog for the purpose, &c., or shall have in his possession any hare or leveret, killed, wounded, or taken, between 20th April and 12th August in any year, on being convicted—	s. 3.	Shall forfeit and pay for every such hare or leveret taken, wounded, killed, or attempted to be, &c., or in his possession; penalty not exceeding £1, with costs of conviction; in default, &c., imprisonment, not exceeding 14 days. 1 J.
Lord Lieutenant may vary close time.	s. 4.	
Fines to be applied as directed by Fines Act, 14 & 15 Vic. c. 90.		
Poisoned Grain.—As to penalty for selling, and for placing same on ground or exposed place, see—	26 & 27 Vic. c. 113, ss. 1 and 2.	
Poisoned Flesh.—For penalty for placing poisoned flesh on lands, see— Not to apply to occupiers placing poisoned preparation for destruction of vermin.	27 & 28 Vic. c. 115, s. 2.	
Offences under Larceny Act.—For the stealing, coursing, taking, snaring, &c., of deer, hares, rabbits, dogs, birds, pigeons, &c., see Larceny Act, under title "Larceny," Summary Index.	24 & 25 Vic. c. 96, ss. 12 -24.	

Offence, or cause of Complaint.	Statute.	Extent of Jurisdiction.
GAME—*continued*. GROUND GAME ACT, 1880. *Act for the better protection of occupiers of land against injury to their crops from ground game.*	43 & 44 Vic. c. 47.	
Occupier to have a right inseparable from his occupation to kill ground game concurrently with any other person entitled to kill the same on land in his occupation.	s. 1.	
Occupier entitled to kill ground game on land in his occupation not to divest himself wholly of such right. All agreements in contravention of right of occupier to destroy ground game void.	s. 2.	
Exemption from game licence, but not from provisions of Gun Licence Act, 1870.	s. 4.	
Prohibition of Night-shooting, Spring Traps above Ground, or Poison.—No person having a right of killing ground game under this Act or otherwise shall use any fire-arms for the purpose of killing ground game between the expiration of the first hour after sunset and the commencement of the last hour before sunrise; and no such person should for the purpose of killing ground game employ spring traps except in rabbit holes, nor employ poison; and any person acting in contravention of this section shall on summary conviction be liable to—(*a*)	s. 6.	Penalty not exceeding £2; in default, &c., imprisonment not exceeding 1 month. 1 J.
Ground Game.—For purposes of Act shall mean hares and rabbits.	s. 8.	
A person acting in accordance with Act shall not thereby be subject to proceedings or penalties in pursuance of any law or statute.	s. 9.	

(*a*) Act says that offence may be dealt with by summary conviction, and so is, by 37 & 38 Vic. c. 72, s. 5, triable by one Justice in Petty Sessions.

Offence, or cause of Complaint.	Statute.	Extent of Jurisdiction.
GAME—*continued.* *Saving Existing Prohibitions*—Nothing in Act shall authorize killing or taking ground game on any days or seasons or by any methods prohibited by any Act of Parliament in force at the time of the passing of this Act.	43 & 44 Vic. c. 47, s. 10.	
GAMES (*on Roads*): See "Nuisances on Roads."		
GAMING-HOUSES : (*a*) Upon complaint on oath, that there is reason to suspect any house to be used as a common gaming-house, Justice may issue warrant to enter and to bring before him persons found therein.	8 & 9 Vic. c. 109, s. 3.	1 J.
Keeping a common gaming-house ; acting as a banker therein, &c.	,,	Penalty not exceeding £100, or imprisonment not exceeding 6 months. 2 J. Or may be tried by indictment.
Cheating at play or in betting punishable by indictment, as obtaining money under false pretences.	s. 17.	—

(*a*) *Gaming-houses.*—Keeping and maintaining a common gaming-house for lucre and gain, and causing and procuring idle and evil-disposed persons to come there and play for large sums of money, is an indictable offence at Common Law, and it seems that an indictment for such an offence merely charging the defendant with keeping a common gaming-house would be good.—*R.* v. *Taylor, 3 B. & C.,* 502. Winning money, &c., by "fraud, unlawful device, or ill-practice," is deemed to be obtaining same by false pretences, with intent to cheat or defraud such person of the same.—8 & 9 Vic. c. 109, s. 17.

Gaming and Betting-houses.—This Act, 17 & 18 Vic. c. 38, by the index initial letter to the statute indicates that it is limited in its application to England. And indeed some of the sections, such as those dealing with the application of penalties and the appeal, would lead to the supposition that Ireland was not quite in view. However the authorities have, advisedly, directed its enforcement. The Betting-house Act here given (16 & 17 Vic. c. 119), which the index also limits to England, is enforced in Ireland.

Offence, or cause of Complaint.	Statute.	Extent of Jurisdiction.
GAMING-HOUSES—*continued*. Wagers not recoverable at law (not to apply to plates, prizes, or money won in lawful games or exercises).	8 & 9 Vic. c. 109, s. 18.	—
So much of Henry viii. c. 33, *s.* 9, as declares games of mere skill—as bowling, quoiting, tennis, or the like—unlawful, repealed.		
ACT FOR THE FURTHER SUPPRESSION OF GAMING-HOUSES. Person wilfully preventing constable or officer authorized under 8 & 9 Vic. c. 149, or by any means of contrivance, prevent, obstruct, or delay the entry of constable or officer—	17 & 18 Vic. c. 38. s. 2.	Penalty not exceeding £100, with such costs attending conviction as to Justices seem reasonable ; and on non-payment, or in the first instance, if Justices think fit, may be committed for not exceeding 6 months. 2 J.
Wilfully obstructing or preventing as aforesaid constables, to be evidence of house being a common gaming-house.	s. 1.	—
Persons found in house or place by constable refusing to give names or address, or giving false ones—	s. 3.	Penalty not exceeding £50, with costs ; and on non-payment, or in the first instance, if Justices think fit, may be committed for not exceeding 1 month. 2 J.
Person being owner or occupier, or having use of any *house, room, or place*, who shall open, keep, or use the same for the purpose of unlawful gaming being carried on therein ; knowingly permitting same to be so used ; person having management or assisting in conducting, &c. ; persons advancing money for the purpose of gaming with persons frequenting house or place, &c.—	s. 4.	Penalty not exceeding £500, with costs ; and on non-payment, or in the first instance, if Justices see fit, may be committed for not exceeding 12 calendar months. 2 J.
Justice may require persons found in house or place, &c., under authority of 8 & 9 Vic., and brought before them, to be sworn and give evidence touching any act done as to delaying entry of constables, &c., and	s. 5.	Shall be subject to be dealt with in all respects as any witness appearing on summons or subpœna. 2 J.

Offence, or cause of Complaint.	Statute.	Extent of Jurisdiction.
GAMING-HOUSES—*continued.* shall not be excused on the ground that his evidence will tend to criminate himself.	17 & 18 Vic. c. 38, s. 5.	
Persons examined as witnesses, and making a full discovery, to be freed from penalties.	s. 6.	
Penalties and costs may be levied by distress; and where person has been committed in default of payment of penalty and costs, then the costs alone may be levied by distress.	s. 7.	
On neglect to prosecute any summons, Justices may authorize some other person to proceed.	s. 9.	—
Appeal, right of, ...	s. 10.	
BETTING-HOUSES, &c. *No House or Place to be kept for the purpose of Owner or Occupier Betting with other Persons.*—No house, office, room, or other place shall be opened, kept, or used for the purpose of the owner, occupier, or keeper thereof, or any person using the same, or any person acting on behalf of such owner, &c., or person conducting same, &c., betting with persons resorting thereto. (See section.)	16 & 17 Vic. c. 119, s. 1.	Every house, office, room, or place opened, kept, or used for such purposes is declared to be a common nuisance.
Betting-houses, &c., shall be deemed to be gaming-houses, within the 8 & 9 Vic. c. 109.	s. 2.	
Owners or Occupiers of Betting-houses or Places. (a)—Any person who, being the owner or occupier of any house, office, room, or other	s. 3.	Penalty not exceeding together with such costs attending conviction as to the Justices shall

(a) *Betting-houses or Places.*—In *Eastwood* v. *Miller*, Q.B., *England, T.T.*, 1874, the following case came before the Court on appeal from a conviction before the Magistrates of Dewsbury. The proprietor of a field of about three acres, used for the purpose of pigeon-shooting, on information charging him with permitting the said to be used for the purpose of betting on the occasion of pigeon-shooting, two book-makers being present when bets were made by certain bystanders, the Magistrates convicted. The Court affirmed the conviction, holding that the field was a *place* within the meaning of the section.

It has somehow come to be imagined that these Acts, bearing on gamesters and betters, are only properly applicable to *cheats, thimblers,* and *swindlers,* but are

Offence, or cause of Complaint.	Statute.	Extent of Jurisdiction.
GAMING-HOUSES : BETTING-HOUSES—*continued.* place, or a person using the same, shall open, keep, or use the same for the purposes hereinbefore mentioned, or either of them ; and any person who, being the owner or occupier of any house, room, office, or other place shall knowingly and wilfully permit the same to be opened, kept, or used by any other person for the purposes aforesaid, or either of them ; and any person having the care or management of same, or assisting in conducting the business in such house, place, &c. (See section.)	16 & 17 Vic. c. 119, s. 3.	seem reasonable, and on non-payment of penalty and costs, or in the first instance, if to the Justices it shall seem fit, may be committed with or without H. L., for any time not exceeding 6 calendar months. 2 J.
Receiving Money on condition of paying on event of any Bet.—Person, being owner or occupier of any house, place, &c., kept or used for purposes aforesaid, or acting on behalf of owner or occupier, receiving directly or indirectly money or deposit on bet, on condition of paying money, &c., on the event of horse race or other race, fight, game, exercise, &c., or as consideration, undertaking, &c., express or implied, to pay or give thereafter any money or valuable thing on any such event or contingency ; and any person giving acknowledgment, note, security, &c., on receipt of money, &c. (See section.)	s. 4.	Penalty not exceeding £50, and such costs as Justices deem reasonable, and on non-payment of penalty and costs, or in the first instance, if to the Justices it shall seem fit, may be committed, with or without H. L., for any time not exceeding 3 calendar months. 2 J.

quite out of place in associations where the habits of good society and the codes of honour regulate the game. On this subject a writer of some merit observes :— " To those who soberly and fairly appreciate the real nature of human actions, nothing appears more inconsistent than that societies of men who have incorporated themselves for the express purpose of gambling should disclaim fraud or indirection, or affect to drive from their assemblies those among their associates whose crimes would reflect disgrace on them. Surely this, to a considerate mind, is as solemn and refined a banter as can well be exhibited. For when we take into view the vast latitude allowed by the most upright gamesters, when we reflect that, according to their specious casuistry, every advantage may be legitimately taken of the young, the unwary, and the inebriated, which superior coolness, skill,

Offence, or cause of Complaint.	Statute.	Extent of Jurisdiction.
GAMING-HOUSES :		
BETTING-HOUSES—*continued*.		
Money received, as in sec. 4, may, with costs, be recovered in the proper Court, from person receiving same.	16 & 17 Vic. c. 119, s. 5.	
Act not to extend to stakes due to owner of horse winning race.	s. 6.	
Advertising Betting-houses.—Person exhibiting or publishing, or causing to be, &c., any placard, hand-bill, card, writing, sign, advertisement, that house or place is kept [for making bets, or for the purpose of exhibiting lists for betting, or with intent to induce persons to resort thereto for the purpose, &c.—	s. 7.	Penalty not exceeding £30, together with such costs as the Justices shall deem reasonable, and on non-payment, or in the first instance, if to the Justices it seem fit, may be committed, with or without H. L., for not exceeding 2 calendar months. 2 J.
Penalties may also be levied by distress, and although committed in default of payment, the costs alone may be recovered by distress.	s. 8.	
On neglect to prosecute any summons Justices may authorize some person to proceed.	s. 10.	
Justices may authorize search of suspected houses.	s. 11.	
Commissioners of Metropolitan Police may authorize Superintendent of Police to enter and search suspected houses.	s. 12.	
Special form of appeal given, . .	s. 13.	
No objection in matter of form and *certiorari* taken away.	s. 14.	

address, and activity can supply, we must look upon pretences to honesty as a most shameless aggravation of their crimes. Even if it were possible that, in his own practices, a man might be a *fair gamester*, yet to a system necessarily implicated with fraud—to associations of men, a large majority of whom subsist by fraud—to habits calculated to poison the source and principle of all integrity, he gives efficacy, countenance, and concurrence. Even his *virtues* he suffers to be subsidiary to the cause of vice." Or, in the just and pointed language of Sydney Smith, though on another subject, "In such an union of the *amiable* and the vicious (especially if the vices are such, to the commission of which there is no want of natural disposition), the vice will not degrade the man, but the man will ennoble the vice."

Offence, or cause of Complaint.	Statute.	Extent of Jurisdiction.
GAMING-HOUSES :		
BETTING-HOUSES —*continued.*		
Distress not unlawful for want of form.	16 & 17 Vic. c. 119, s. 15.	—
Tender of amends for wrong done, .	s. 16.	—
Limitations of actions, . . .	s. 17.	—
ACT TO AMEND 16 & 17 VIC. c. 119.	37 & 38 Vic. c. 15.	—
This Act to be construed with 16 & 17 Vic. c. 119.	s. 1.	—
Penalty on Persons Advertising as to Betting.—Where any letter, circular, telegram, placard, handbill, card, or advertisement is sent, exhibited, or published— (1) Whereby it is made to appear that any person, either in the United Kingdom or elsewhere, will on application give information or advice for the purpose of or with respect to any such bet or wager, or any such event or contingency as is mentioned in the principal Act, or will make on behalf of any other person any such bet or wager as is mentioned in the principal Act ; or, (2) With intent to induce any person to apply to any house, office, room, or place, or to any person, with the view of obtaining information or advice for the purpose of any such bet or wager, or with respect to any such event or contingency as is mentioned in the principal Act ; or, (3) Inviting any person to make or take any share in or in connexion with any such bet or wager. Every person sending, exhibiting, or publishing, or causing the same to be sent, &c., shall be subject to the penalties provided in the 7th section of the principal Act with respect to offences under that section.	s. 3.	Shall be subject to the penalties provided in the 7th section of the principal Act, 16 & 17 Vic. c. 119.

Offence, or cause of Complaint.	Statute.	Extent of Jurisdiction.
GAMBLERS : See "Thimblers and Swindlers," Towns Improvement Act.	17 & 18 Vic. c. 103, s. 76.	
GAMES (*on Roads, Streets, &c.*): Playing at any game on road or street, to the danger of passengers. And see also " Vagrancy."	14 & 15 Vic. c. 92, s. 10. (36 & 37 Vic. c. 82.)	Penalty not exceeding 10s.; in default, &c., imprisonment not exceeding 7 days. 1 J.
GAOL AND GAOLER : *Prisoner's Offences.*—Prisoner repeatedly offending against prison rules, or guilty of greater offence than gaoler empowered to punish. (*a*)	7 Geo. iv. c. 74, s. 109. Rule 16 of sec. and 40 & 41 Vic. c. 49, s. 55.	May be punished by solitary confinement, on bread and water, for not exceeding 14 days. 1 J.
Prohibited Articles.—Bringing or attempting to bring spirituous liquors into prison.	7 Geo. iv. c. 74, s. 110.	Penalty not exceeding £20; and unless immediately paid, imprisonment not exceeding 3 months; and see scale. 1 J.

(*a*) Prisons Act, 7 Geo. iv. c. 74, s. 109, rule 15.—"The keeper of every prison shall have power to hear all complaints touching disobedience to any of the rules of the prison ; assaults by one person confined in such prison upon another, when no dangerous wound or bruise is given ; profane cursing and swearing ; any indecent behaviour, and any irreverent behaviour at chapel ; breaking windows, or otherwise injuring the prison or any part of the furniture thereof ; absence from chapel without leave ; idleness or negligence in work, or wilful mismanagement of it ; and the keeper may examine any person touching such offences." Limitation of punishment to twenty-four hours. 40 & 41 Vic. c. 49, s. 55.

The duly certifying of gaols and bridewells, &c., is provided for by 7 Geo. iv. c. 74, ss. 6, 92, 94 ; and 19 & 20 Vic. c. 68, s. 26.

Bridewells.—As to imprisonment in district bridewells, and detention in bridewells not being district bridewells, see Prisons Act, 7 Geo. iv. c. 74, s. 94, amended by 19 & 20 Vic. c. 68, s. 26. Prisoners shall not be detained in any bridewell except in district bridewell longer than three days from day of committal, unless by order in writing of 2 Justices. All such persons shall be transmitted to county gaol or district bridewell. Prisoner may be detained in any bridewell other than a district bridewell, which shall be distant more than fifteen miles from county gaol or from district bridewell, who has been committed for any period not exceeding one week, provided such bridewell is duly certified as suitable in manner provided in s. 26 of 19 & 20 Vic. c. 68, in part repealing s. 94 of Prisons Act, 7 Geo. iv., c. 74.

Offence, or cause of Complaint.	Statute.	Extent of Jurisdiction.
GAOL AND GAOLER—*continued.* Bringing or attempting to bring into prison, by throwing over walls or otherwise, any letters, tobacco, or any article prohibited by the rules of the prison. (Penalties under this section go to Board of Superintendence.)	19 & 20 Vic. c. 68, s. 34. (36 & 37 Vic. c. 82.)	Penalty not exceeding £5, nor less than 40s.; in default, &c., imprisonment not exceeding 2 months, by scale. 1 J.
Gaoler, or any officer of any gaol, &c., who shall sell, use, lend, or give away any spirits, or knowingly permit or suffer any spirits to be sold, used, lent, or given away in such gaol, &c., except as medicinally prescribed.	23 & 24 Vic. c 114, s. 193.	Penalty £100, by Excise prosecution. Second offence to be deemed a forfeiture of his office.
Warrants of committal need not be addressed to gaoler.	14 & 15 Vic. c. 93, s. 25.	
Committals, Remands.—In cases of adjournments or remands, gaoler *shall* bring the prisoner at the time and place fixed by the warrant for that purpose.	,,	
Gaoler to give receipt for prisoners committed, stating therein whether *sober* or not. (Form of receipt, Schedule F in Act.)	s. 22.	
Bailing.—Prisoners committed for trial, where committing Justice certifies on back of commitment his consent to bail, and the amount.	s. 16.	Any Justice of the county attending such gaol may admit to bail (on production of certificate) at any time before first day of the sitting of the Court.
Where sureties cannot attend the gaol, Justice may take recognizance of sureties in conformity with certificate, and transmit recognizance to gaoler.	,,	Any Justice attending gaol (before such time as aforesaid) may take recognizance of accused, and Justice shall give the gaoler warrant to discharge—E. *d.* in Schedule, if detained in no other case. (*a*)

(*a*) The *Habeas Corpus* Act, 21 & 22 Geo. iii. c. 11, s. 4, enacts, that if any officer or his under-officer, under-keeper, or deputy, in whose custody the prisoner

Offence, or cause of Complaint.	Statute.	Extent of Jurisdiction.
GAOL AND GAOLER—*continued.* *Fines.*—Keeper of gaol or bridewell, to whom fines shall be paid, shall endorse on warrant amount and date of payment; and within 14 days (or as directed by Chief or Under Secretary) pay over amount to officer of Court.	14 & 15 Vic. c. 90, ss. 5 and 8.	Penalty, in default, not exceeding £20, recoverable before 2 J.
Excise.—In convictions under the "Illicit Distillation Act," gaolers to allow prisoners for time spent, and accept fines in proportion to unexpired term. See title "Excise."	1 & 2 Wm. iv. c. 55, s. 42.	
Customs.—Where persons are committed by Justices for non-payment of any penalty incurred against the Customs Laws— See title "Customs."	16 & 17 Vic. c. 107.	The Act requires that the gaoler shall discharge the offender at the end of 6 months' imprisonment. (*a*).
Seamen.—Seamen undergoing imprisonment for desertion, absence, or breach of discipline against provisions of Merchant Shipping Act. , See title "Merchant Shipping."	17 & 18 Vic. c. 104, s. 248.	May, by order of Justices, be sent on board before the expiration of their sentence, on application of master or owner. (*b*)

is committed or detained, upon demand made by the prisoner or any other person in his behalf, shall refuse to deliver, or within six hours after demand, shall not deliver to the person so demanding it, a true copy of the warrant or warrants of commitment and detainer of such prisoner, he shall forfeit to the prisoner or party aggrieved, for the first offence £100, and for the second offence £200, and shall also be deprived of his office.

(*a*) There are offences in this Act for which the Justices are not empowered to measure the term of imprisonment, but merely to direct in their warrant that the prisoner shall "remain in custody until the penalty be paid." If no other authority interfere, the Act limits the time for the gaoler.

(*b*) The Magistrate, in giving the order, should refer the gaoler to the authority of the Act, for it is the Act of Parliament which could alone give the Magistrate the power to take the prisoner out of custody. As a *rule*, once a prisoner is committed, the Magistrate has no power either to order his release or to alter the sentence; and the gaoler, acting on any such illegal order, may be held liable, as if he had allowed the prisoner to escape.

Offence, or cause of Complaint.	Statute.	Extent of Jurisdiction.
GAOL AND GAOLER—*continued*. *Deserters.*—Gaolers may pay Justices' Clerk fee on committal, and also fee of Medical Practitioner, not being a Military Medical Officer; and notify the fact to Secretary at War; and forward copy committal.	See Army Act.	
Royal Navy.—Gaoler, without lawful excuse, refusing to receive prisoners convicted under the "Act for Government of the Navy."	24 & 25 Vic. c. 115, s. 72.	Penalty not exceeding £100, by distress, recoverable before 2 J.
Reformatory.—Governor of gaol in the first instance to pay for transmission of juvenile offenders from prison to reformatory school.	21 & 22 Vic. c. 103, s. 10.	—
He shall also forward with the offender original duplicate (if any) of warrant, or a copy of warrant, and at foot thereof a memorandum signed by him, stating that the "juvenile offender named therein, and sent therewith, is identical with the person delivered with the warrant."	s. 11.	
Escape.—*Negligently* permitting the escape of a prisoner in custody for criminal offence.	Common Law.	Indictable misdemeanour.
Voluntarily or knowingly causing or permitting escape.	"	Amounts to same crime of which prisoner was guilty, and for which he was in custody.
THE GENERAL PRISONS (IRELAND) ACT, 1877. Power of entry into Prisons by Justices of the Peace. (*a*)	40 & 41 Vic. c. 49, s. 26.	

(*a*) *Power of entry into Prisons by Justices of the Peace.*—By sec. 26 of the General Prisons (Ireland) Act, 1877 (40 & 41 Vic. c. 49), section 5 of the Act passed in the Session of Parliament held in the seventh year of the reign of King George iv. c. 74, is hereby repealed, and instead thereof the following enactment shall take effect, viz. :—"Any Justice of the Peace having jurisdiction in the place in which a prison is situate, or having jurisdiction in the place where the offence in respect

Offence, or cause of Complaint.	Statute.	Extent of Jurisdiction.
GARDEN : Destroying fruit or vegetable productions in garden, &c. See "Malicious Injuries." For offence of stealing same, see "Larceny."		
GAS : Gas-works Clauses Act, 1847, Powers as to laying pipes, Penalties for fraudulently using gas. Wilfully damaging pipes, pillars, lamps, &c., of company. Satisfaction for accidental damage, Nuisance from gas, . . . Recovery of penalties, . .	10 Vic. c. 16. s. 18. s. 19. s. 20. s. 21, &c. s. 40.	Penalties under 10 Vic. c. 15, recoverable as in Railway Clauses Consolidation Act, 1845—that is, before two Justices, by distress, and in default, &c., imprisonment. This 10 Vic. c. 15, is incorporated with 34 & 35 Vic. c. 41.
Act regulating measure in sale of, . Power to enter houses, inspect. Penalties for obstructing, &c. Counterfeiting stamps, &c. Act to amend last-mentioned Act, .	22 & 23 Vic. c. 66. 23 & 24 Vic. c. 146.	Penalties under 22 & 23 Vic. c. 66, and 23 & 24 Vic. c. 146, recoverable in like manner, before two Justices, or the Mayor or Chief Magistrate in towns, &c.

of which any prisoner may be confined in prison was committed, may, when he thinks fit, enter into and examine the condition of such prison, and of the prisoners therein, and he may enter any observations he may think fit to make in reference to the condition of the prison or abuses therein in the Visitors' Book, to be kept by the Governor; and it shall be the duty of the Governor to draw the attention of the Visiting Committee, at their next visit to the prison, to any entries made in the said book; but he shall not be entitled, in pursuance of this section, to visit any prisoner under sentence of death, or to communicate with any prisoner, except in reference to the treatment in prison of such prisoner, or to some complaint that such prisoner may make as to such treatment." Nothing in this section shall apply to convict prisons.

Lock-ups.—The Commissioners of Public Works in Ireland shall, when required by the Lord Lieutenant, provide and maintain, in connexion with all such Constabulary barracks as the Lord Lieutenant shall order, such proper accommodation for the temporary detention of prisoners, being unconvicted or unsentenced prisoners, as the Lord Lieutenant shall direct.—40 & 41 Vic. c. 49, s. 23.

O

Offence, or cause of Complaint.	Statute.	Extent of Jurisdiction.
GAS—*continued.*		
Meters not to be connected or disconnected without notice to company; for contravening this section consumer shall be liable to—	34 & 35 Vic. c. 41, s. 15.	Penalty not exceeding 40s.; in default, &c., imprisonment by scale. 2 J.
Officers of the undertakers (or company) empowered to enter buildings for ascertaining quantities of gas consumed, at reasonable times; for hindering, &c.—	s. 21.	Forfeit to gas undertakers a sum not exceeding £5; in default, &c., imprisonment by scale. 2 J.
Summary power to recover before Justices in Petty Sessions, on summons, sums due for gas. (And see also sections 40 and 41.)	s. 23.	One Justice may make order for the amount, together with costs, including costs of cutting off gas, if it be cut off, recoverable by distress warrant. 1 J.
Where no gas examiner is appointed, or where testing is improperly attended to, two Justices may, on application of consumers, not being less than five, appoint a competent and impartial person to be gas examiner.	s. 30.	—
Undertakers shall allow examiner and his assistants, and to the local authority and their agents, access to the testing place, and afford facilities, &c.; for default—	s. 34.	Penalty not exceeding £5 to the local authority, or to the persons making the application. 2 J.
Undertakers shall furnish to local authority annual statement of account; for default—	s. 35.	Penalty not exceeding 40s. for each day default continues. 2 J.
Neglecting or refusing to supply gas to owners or occupiers entitled to same, within limits of special Act under the prescribed pressure.	s. 36.	Penalty 40s. each day during default. 2 J.
Undertakers neglecting to supply gas to public lamps in accordance with provisions of Act, for each default—	,,	Penalty not exceeding 40s. for each default. Distress warrant. 2 J.
If proved to the satisfaction of any two Justices, not being shareholders in the undertaking, after hearing the parties that on any day the gas supplied by the undertakers is under less pressure, or less illuminating power, or of less	,,	The undertakers shall, in every such case, forfeit and pay to the local authority, or other persons making application for testing the gas, such sum not exceeding £20,

Offence, or cause of Complaint.	Statute.	Extent of Jurisdiction.

GAS—*continued*.
    purity than it ought to be according to provisions of Act—
    (Penalties for same offence under different Acts shall not be cumulative.)
	34 & 35 Vic. c. 41, s. 36.
	
	,,
		as the Justice shall determine. Distress warrant. 2 J.

Where examiner appointed by Justices costs of experiment and remuneration and proceedings shall be ascertained by Justices, and in the event of any penalty being imposed on undertakers, shall be paid with penalty, but where no penalty imposed, costs shall be in discretion of Justices.	s. 37.	
Every person who wilfully, fraudulently, or by culpable negligence injuries, or suffers to be injured, any pipes, meter, fittings belonging to undertakers, alters index, &c., prevents meter duly registering, or fraudulently consuming gas, shall (without prejudice to other rights or modes of punishment) for each offence— Undertakers may in addition recover any damages sustained. Where injury is wilful or fraudulent, or index altered or meter prevented registering, undertakers may refuse, until remedied, to continue to supply gas.	s. 38.	Forfeit and pay to undertakers a sum not exceeding £5. Distress warrant. 2 J.
Gas Rents.—Incoming tenants not liable to pay arrears due by preceding tenant for gas rent unless he has undertaken with former tenant to do so, &c.	s. 39.	
If any person supplied with gas, or with meter or fittings by undertakers neglects to pay the rent due for gas, or the rent or money due for hire or fixing of meter, or expense incurred in cutting off gas—	s. 40.	Sums so due may be recovered in like manner as a *penalty* under Act. 2 J. (*Note.*—Sec. 22 provides that amounts due for gas supplied shall be recovered as a civil debt before the Justice by distress and sale of defendant's goods, while
Whenever any person neglects to pay any rent or sum due and payable by him to the undertakers, they may recover sums with costs	s. 41.	

Offence, or cause of Complaint.	Statute.	Extent of Jurisdiction.
GAS—*continued.* of suit in any court of competent jurisdiction. The remedy under this enactment shall be in addition to their other remedies for recovery, &c.	34 & 35 Vic. c. 41, s. 41.	here under sec. 40, what is called the *rent* for gas and meter rent is recoverable as a *penalty*. The one appears to refer to the ordinary custo-
Legal Proceedings. — Summons or warrant may contain several names and several sums.	s. 42.	mer's account of gas *consumed*, the other to the completion of fit-
Warrant of distress for recovery of money shall include costs to be ascertained by the Justice.	s. 43.	tings and laying on gas, for which a more ready and certain remedy is provided.)
All offences and penalties under this Act, and all money forfeited, and all money and costs directed to be recovered as penalties may be prosecuted and recovered as directed by "The Gas Works Clauses Act, 1847," with respect to the recovery of penalties.	s. 44.	The Gas Works Clauses Act, 1847 (10 & 11 Vic. c. 15, s. 40), directs that all penalties shall be recovered as in the Railway Clauses Consolidation Act, 1845 (8 Vic. c. 20, s. 154). And this
Justice or Judge of County Court or Quarter Sessions shall not be disqualified to act in execution of Act by reason of his being liable to gas rent.	s. 46.	Railway Act referred to directs that (except as to transient offenders, whose names and residences are not known, and who may be ap-
The Gas Act, 23 & 24 Vic. c. 146, s. 2, directs that all penalties under it, and under the Act of 22 & 23 Vic. c. 66, shall be recoverable before two Justices, or the Mayor, or Chief Magistrate of towns, &c.		prehended and brought before Justices) parties may be summoned, two Justices may hear the case, issue distress warrant, and in default of distress imprisonment. Now where the penalty does not exceed £5, see power and scale of imprisonment in 36 & 37 Vic. c. 82—the Act relating to small penalties.
Gas and Water Works Facilities Act, 1870, Amendment Act, 1873. Act applies where amendment of any special Act in force is required, or by local authority, &c. As to the illuminating power, price, and pressure of gas.	36 & 37 Vic. c. 89.	—

Offence, or cause of Complaint.	Statute.	Extent of Jurisdiction.
GATE: Damaging or destroying—see "Malicious Injuries." Stealing—see "Larceny."		
GOOSE: Stealing, or injuring with intent to steal (value not exceeding 5s.).	25 & 26 Vic. c. 50, s. 8.	Penalty not exceeding 20s., or imprisonment not exceeding 14 days. 1 J.
GRAIN: Frauds in sale of—see "Frauds in Sale of Provisions."		
GRAND JURY ACT, . . .	6 & 7 Wm. iv. c. 116.	
Grand Jury Amendment Act, . .	19 & 20 Vic. c. 63.	—
Grand Jury Cess recoverable under	6 & 7 Wm. iv. c. 116, s. 152.	Before Justices in Petty Sessions. 1 J.
Hindering applotter entering on lands for purpose of making applotment.	5 & 6 Vic. c. 77, s. 10.	Penalty £5; in default, &c., imprisonment not exceeding 2 months. 1 J.
Treasurer to applot according to last rate made under Poor Relief Act; publish notice, &c.; for neglect, or refusing extracts to be taken, or refusal to furnish extracts on tender made of the fees therein—	6 & 7 Vic. c. 32, s. 5. (36 & 37 Vic. s. 82.)	Penalty not exceeding £5; in default, &c., imprisonment by scale, not exceeding 2 months. 2 J.
Personal service of notice requiring payment of Grand Jury Cess, to be deemed good service, without prejudice to other remedies provided by law. See also "Roads."	19 & 20 Vic. c. 63, s. 15.	

Offence, or cause of Complaint.	Statute.	Extent of Jurisdiction.
GREENHOUSE: Destroying plants, &c., in — see "Malicious Injuries." Stealing—see "Larceny."		
GUN: Discharging on public road, or within 60 feet of the centre, or in any street.	14 & 15 Vic. c. 92, s. 10. (36 & 37 Vic. c. 82.)	Penalty not exceeding 10s., in default, &c., imprisonment not exceeding 7 days. 1 J.
Setting spring-guns, . . .	24 & 25 Vic. c. 100, s. 31.	Indictable.
For carrying gun in proclaimed district—see title "Peace Preservation Act;" and for "Gun Licences," see under head "Excise," Summary Index.		
GUNPOWDER: Act sets out regulations for making gunpowder, percussion caps, &c. Making loaded percussion caps; making or keeping ammunition contrary to Act.	23 & 24 Vic. c. 139. s. 7.	Forfeiture and penalty not exceeding £10, by distress; in default, &c., imprisonment not exceeding (by Petty Sessions scale) 3 months. 2 J.
Selling fireworks without licence, or to persons apparently under 16 years.	s. 8. (36 & 37 Vic. c. 82.)	Penalty not exceeding £5; in default, &c., imprisonment not exceeding 2 months. 2 J.
Throwing fireworks on thoroughfares.	23 & 24 Vic. c. 139, s. 9.	Like. 2 J.
Section 18 limits the quantity to be kept by others than manufacturers.	s. 18.	
Smoking on board vessel laden with, except as therein, or having or using matches, &c.	s. 22.	Penalty not exceeding £5; in default, &c., imprisonment not exceeding 2 months. 2 J.
Undue delay in loading or unloading,	s. 23.	Penalty not exceeding £10; recoverable as above. 2 J.

Offence, or cause of Complaint.	Statute.	Extent of Jurisdiction.
GUNPOWDER—*continued.*		
Power to Justices to issue warrants to search for gunpowder suspected to be made or kept contrary to Act.	23 & 24 Vic. c. 139, s. 25.	Extended to other explosive compositions by 25 & 26 Vic. c. 98, s. 1. 1 J.
Repeals 9 & 10 Wm. iii. c. 7 ; 5 Geo. ii. c. 12 (I.) ; 12 Geo. iii. c. 61. Not to affect or repeal Local Police Acts.		
The foregoing Act amended by the	24 & 25 Vic. c. 130.	
Powers of granting licences to dealers in gunpowder transferred to Justices in Petty Sessions, who shall hold special Petty Sessions for the purpose.	s. 1.	
Justices with the sanction of one of the principal Secretaries of State, may regulate the mode in which applications for licences shall be made, and fix the scale of fees in respect to them.	24 & 25 Vic. c. 100, s. 2.	
Provided that section 18 of the first Act shall apply to manufacturers of safety fusees.	s. 4.	
Explosives Act, 1875, . . .	38 Vic. c. 17.	
Gunpowder and explosives defined, .	s. 3.	
PART 1.—Law relating to manufacture and keeping of gunpowder, and provides penalty for breach of general rules of factory, &c.	s. 10.	
General rules for stores and penalties for breaches of rules.	s. 17.	
Retail of gunpowder and registration and regulation of registered premises, and penalties for breach of rules. (a)	s. 21.	
Sale of Gunpowder.—Hawking, selling, or exposing, for sale on thoroughfares, &c.	s. 30.	Penalty not exceeding 40s. ; in default of payment, imprisonment not exceeding 1 month, and gunpowder forfeited. 2 J.

(a) From the number and variety of rules to be observed and for the breach of which penalties are provided, it is conceived that a reference to the subject in this abstract is sufficient.

Offence, or cause of Complaint.	Statute	Extent of Jurisdiction.
GUNPOWDER—*continued.* *Children.*—Selling to children apparently under age of 13.	38 Vic. c. 17, s. 31.	Penalty not exceeding £5 ; in default of payment, imprisonment not exceeding 2 months. 2 J.
Sales exceeding one pound in weight to be in closed packages and labelled as in section, for contravening—	s. 32.	Penalty not exceeding 40s. ; in default of payment, imprisonment not exceeding 1 month. Gunpowder so exposed for sale forfeited.　2 J.
By-laws.—Harbour authority, with sanction of Board of Trade, may make by-laws as to conveyance, loading, &c.	s. 34.	—
Like by railway and canal companies,	s. 35.	—
PART 2.—Law relating to other explosives and application of Part 1 of Act thereto.	s. 39.	
Specially dangerous explosives, ．	s. 43.	
Provisions in favour of certain manufacturers and dealers.	s. 44.	
Provision in favour of gunmakers, &c., making cartridges.	s. 46.	
Provisions in favour of owners of mines and quarries as to making charges for blasting.	s. 47.	—
Provision in favour of small firework manufacturer who may obtain licence from local authority.	s. 48.	
Licensing by local authority and regulation of small firework factories.	s. 49.	
Proviso as to percussion-caps, safety-fuzes for blasting, fog-signals by railway companies, &c.	s. 50.	
As to existing factories, magazines, stores, &c.	s. 51.	

cause of Complaint.	Statute.	Extent of Jurisdiction.
—*continued.*		
ministration of the law ment supervision.	38 Vic. c. 17, s. 53, &c.	
n-compliance with no- by Government In-	s. 56.	
ents, notices thereof, quests, &c.	s. 63.	
sion, ...	s. 67.	
l authority to provide id magazines.	s. 71, &c.	
r *of search* by persons orized, for explosives ace in contravention of	s. 73.	
pplemental Provisions, iceedings, Exemptions, ions.	s. 77.	
d removal of trespassers , &c.	,,	
ut warrant of persons : dangerous offences.	s. 78.	
t for wilful act or ne- gering life or limb.	s. 79.	
s.—If any person throw, any fireworks in or in- way, street, thorough- blic place—	s. 80.	Penalty not exceeding £5; in default of pay- ment, imprisonment not exceeding 2 months. 2 J.
otices.—Every person ut due authority, pulls ures, or defaces any of rules, or document ed in pursuance of Act	s. 82.	Penalty not exceeding £2; in default, &c., im- prisonment not exceed- ing 1 month. 2 J.
by-laws, notices, &c.,	s. 84.	

Offence, or cause of Complaint.	Statute.	Extent of Jurisdiction.
GUNPOWDER—*continued.* *Legal Proceedings,*	38 Vic. c. 17, s. 87.	
Penalty where other than the occupier is in fact the real offender.	,,	
Exemption of carriers, owners of ships, &c., where consignee, &c., in fault.	s. 88.	—
As to forfeiture of explosives.	s. 89.	
Jurisdiction in tidal waters or on boundaries.	s. 90.	
Prosecution for offences under Act may be either summarily or by indictment.	s. 91.	—
Proviso.—Penalty imposed by Court of Summary Jurisdiction shall not exceed £100, exclusive of costs, and exclusive of forfeiture or penalty in lieu of forfeiture, and the term of imprisonment shall not exceed 1 month.	,,	—
Power of summary Court to prohibit acts, &c., and punishment for disobedience.	,,	—
Power to Elect.—Where penalty, exclusive of forfeiture, exceeds £100, accused may elect to be tried by indictment.	s. 92.	
Appeal to Quarter Sessions from conviction where amount ordered exceeds £20, on terms in 24 & 25 Vic. c. 96, s. 110.	s. 93.	
Constitution of Court, . . .	s. 94.	
Power in certain cases to distrain ship, &c., for penalty, &c.	s. 95.	
Application of penalties and disposal of forfeitures on prosecutions by Government Inspector.	s. 96.	

Offence, or cause of Complaint.	Statute.	Extent of Jurisdiction.
GUNPOWDER—*continued.*		
In other cases, ...	38 Vic. c. 17, s. 121.	—
Exemptions and saving clauses, .	ss. 97–192.	—
Definitions, ...	ss. 104–108.	—
Application of Act to Ireland, with modifications.	s. 116.	—
Definition and power of local authority, "Summary Jurisdiction Acts," shall mean "Petty Sessions (Ireland) Act, 14 & 15 Vic. c. 93, and any Acts amending same.	"	
Repeal of certain Acts.	s. 122, and schedules 4 and 5.	—
Schedule 1 of Act relates to gunpowder factories and stores. Schedule 2 relates to arbitration. Schedule 3.—Fees for licences granted by Secretary of State. Schedule 4.—Repeal of certain Acts. See also "Explosives," Indictable Index.		
HABITUAL DRUNKARDS : Act to facilitate the control and cure of habitual drunkards.	42 & 43 Vic. c. 19.	
Establishing and licensing retreats for such.		
Provides penalties for offences by licences of retreats, officers, servants, &c., recoverable before Justices in Petty Sessions, &c.		
Power of appeal, &c., . . .	s. 36.	
Section 10—Points out how habitual drunkard, desirous of being admitted to retreats, can do so. Act gives forms in Schedule.		

Offence, or cause of Complaint.	Statute.	Extent of Jurisdiction.
HACKNEY CARS: See "Towns Improvement Act." "Police Clauses Act." In towns where these Acts are in force, and the "By-laws" regulating fares—	17 & 18 Vic. c. 103. 10 & 11 Vic. c. 80.	Justice may enforce payment of hack-car fare as a penalty. 10 & 11 Vic. c. 89, s. 66. 1 J.
HARD LABOUR: In offence cases, where the Act authorizes Justices to order imprisonment, they may order it to be with or without hard labour, as they shall see fit. (a)	14 & 15 Vic. c. 93, s. 82.	—
HARE: Taking or killing hares or rabbits in a warren in the night time. Taking or killing hares or rabbits in a warren in the daytime. See also "Game."	24 & 25 Vic. c. 96, s. 17. "	Indictable misdemeanour. Forfeiture not exceeding £5; in default, &c., imprisonment not exceeding 2 months. 1 J.
HAWKERS: See "Peddler," and for those requiring Excise Licence, see *Hawkers*, "Excise."		
HEALTH (ACT): See "Public Health."		
HEDGES: Surveyor or contractor, by ten days' notice, may require owners of land to prune hedges or trees injurious to road between last day of September and last day of March. See "Roads."	14 & 15 Vic. c. 92, s. 9.	Justice may order that the person liable shall do the work; in default, that contractor may do it, and Justice may issue warrant of distress for the expense. 1 J.

(a) This will be applicable to offences under statutes previous to the above Act. Where subsequent Acts do not add hard labour to the punishment, the Justice should not add it.

Offence, or cause of Complaint.	Statute.	Extent of Jurisdiction.
HORSE: Turning loose on roads or streets.	s. 10.	Penalty not exceeding 10s.; in default, &c., imprisonment not exceeding 7 days. 1 J.
Exposing for show or hire in roads or streets, except in fairs or lawfully appointed places.	,,	Penalty not exceeding 40s.; in default, &c., imprisonment not exceeding 1 month. 1 J.
For regulations to be observed in places used for slaughtering horses —see " Knacker," and	12 & 13 Vic. c. 92, ss. 7–10.	—
HOTHOUSE: Stealing plants, &c., in—see "Larceny."		
HOUSES: Building within 30 feet of centre of road, except in streets of corporate or market towns, or where house now stands.	14 & 15 Vic. c. 92, s. 9.	Penalty not exceeding £10; in default, &c., imprisonment not exceeding 3 months; and also 10s. a-week until removed. 1 J.
HUSBAND: Deserting wife or child so as that they become destitute, and receive poor-law relief in or out of workhouse. See "Poor Law."	10 & 11 Vic. c. 84, s. 2.	Imprisonment not exceeding 3 months' H. L. 1 J.
ICE: Making slides on ice or snow on roads or streets.	14 & 15 Vic. c. 92, s. 10. (36 & 37 Vic. c. 82.)	Penalty not exceeding 10s.; in default, &c., imprisonment not exceeding 7 days. 1 J.
IDIOTS: See "Lunatics."		
IDLE AND DISORDERLY PERSONS: See "Vagrancy."		

Offence, or cause of Complaint.	Statute.	Extent of Jurisdiction.
ILLICIT DISTILLATION : See "Excise."		
IMPOUNDING : See "Pound."		
IMPRISONMENT : In offence cases may be with or without H. L., as Justices may see fit.	14 & 15 Vic. c. 93, s. 22.	See notes on this Section 22, of Petty Sessions Act, Appendix.
May order, in second offence, that it commence on expiration of the first.	,,	
General scale of imprisonment in proportion to penalty.	,,	
Under Larceny Act, . . .	24 & 25 Vic. c. 96, s. 107.	—
,, Malicious Injuries Act, .	24 & 25 Vic. c. 97, s. 65.	
General scale where penalty does not exceed £5.	36 & 37 Vic. c. 82.	
See "Scale," &c.		
INCOME TAX, ...	16 & 17 Vic. c. 34, s. 17.	Recoverable in Petty Sessions before 1 J.
INDECENT CONDUCT (in Streets, &c.) : Every person who wilfully and indecently exposes his person, or commits any act contrary to public decency—see "Towns Improvement Act."	17 & 18 Vic. c. 103, s. 82. (36 & 37 Vic. c. 82.)	Penalty not exceeding 40s.; in default, &c., imprisonment not exceeding 2 months. 1 J.
Like offence under the "Police Clauses Act." (a) And see "Nuisance," Indictable Offences. See also "Rogues and Vagabonds," title "Vagrancy."	10 & 11 Vic. c. 89, s. 28.	Penalty not exceeding 40s., or 14 days' imprisonment. 1 J. The Justice shall first ascertain which Act, if either, be in force in his district.
As to Dublin Metropolis, for acts contrary to public decency, see	34 & 35 Vic. c. 7, s. 5.	—

(a) *Indecency* in public, by exposing the naked person, is an indictable misdemeanour at Common Law, punishable by fine or imprisonment, or both. Bathing in an indecent manner near a highway, or where a man can be distinctly seen from neighbouring houses, is indictable.

Offence, or cause of Complaint.	Statute.	Extent of Jurisdiction.
INDUSTRIAL SCHOOLS: (*b*) Any person may bring before two Justices (*in Petty Sessions, or a Police Magistrate in Dublin*) any child *apparently under the age of 14 years* that comes within any of the following descriptions, namely :		
1. That is found begging or receiving alms (whether actually, or under pretext of selling, or offering for sale anything), or being in any street or public place for the purpose of so begging or receiving alms :	31 Vic. c. 25, s. 11.	The Justices before whom brought as coming within one of those descriptions, if satisfied on inquiry of the fact, and that it is expedient to deal with him under this Act, may order him to be sent to a certified Industrial School.
2. That is found wandering and not having any house or settled place of abode, or proper guardianship, or visible means of subsistence :		2 J. (or 1 Police Magistrate in Dublin). The Justices may (by writing) order temporary detention in workhouse, not exceeding 7 days, while inquiry is being made as to the child, or as to the school.
3. That is found destitute, either being an orphan, or having a surviving parent who is undergoing penal servitude or imprisonment :		
4. That frequents the company of reputed thieves.		

(*b*) *Industrial Schools.*—This Act meets a class of cases which the Reformatory Act does not meet. The latter waits for the commission of some crime or offence, and for which a punishment must be inflicted. The above Act relieves the little sufferer and the community, without waiting until vice and crime shall have effaced all innocence and moral goodness. There will doubtless be cases coming under the Reformatory Act, but manifestly where the above meets the case, it is the proper and the merciful remedy, and excels the other by, at least, as much as prevention is better than cure. The application of the Act will require careful inquiry and discrimination on the part of the Justices that they may clearly comprehend the intentions of the Legislature, and the class of cases it is intended to meet. It goes as far as it reasonably could without encroaching on parental claims or superseding parental responsibility.

Cases within the Act.—There are four classes pointed at in the section, with some circumstances respecting each, to show the Magistrates the intention of the Legislature, and the state of facts that will warrant interference. It is not to be an inducement to the poor to get rid of their children, nor does it warrant their being deprived of them, under the plea that they will be " better off," for as Montesquieu observes, " even our natural horror of vice may be abused as an engine of tyranny." The children *being found* (such is the term used in three of the classes), and brought before the Magistrates as coming within one of the descriptions, if satisfied on inquiry of the fact, and that it is expedient, &c., may send them to the Industrial

Offence, or cause of Complaint.	Statute.	Extent of Jurisdiction.
INDUSTRIAL SCHOOLS—*con.* That is lodging, living, or residing with common or reputed prostitutes, or in a house resided in or frequented by prostitutes for the purposes of prostitution. That frequents the company of prostitutes. (*a*)	43 & 44 Vic. c. 15, s. 1.	
Children under 12 *years.*—Where a child apparently under the age of 12 years is charged before two or more Justices in Petty Sessions (or Police Magistrate in Police Court in Dublin), with an offence punishable by imprisonment, or a less punishment, but has not been convicted of felony, and the child ought, in their opinion (regard being had to his age, and to the circumstances of the case), to be dealt with under this Act. (*b*)	31 Vic. c. 25. s. 13.	The said Justices or Police Magistrate may order him to be sent to a certified Industrial School. Form of detention order in Act shall be in writing, duly signed by the Justices, and shall specify the name of the school, and the time, and shall not extend beyond time that child will attain age of 16 years. 2 J. (in Dublin, 1 Police Magistrate).

School.   Certainly, where the child appears to be a fit subject, the Magistrates should have no hesitation in availing of the salutary provisions of this statute. With respect to the *second class*, "*found wandering, and without proper guardianship,*" some English Justices entertained a doubt as to the meaning of the words, "proper guardianship," and having applied to the Secretary of the Home Department, they received a reply to the following effect :—"The point left to the judgment of the Magistrate is not whether the child is or is not under any guardianship, but whether it is under *proper* guardianship.   If the child's parents are habitual drunkards, or of known vicious or criminal character, or tramps, or if they continually ill-use or *neglect* the child, and are thus the cause of its wandering and destitution, and are leaving it to grow up in the habits of vice and beggary, they cannot be said to be proper guardians of it, and it would be in full accordance with the intention and object of the Act, and for the *advantage* of the public, that the child should be withdrawn from their control, and placed under the corrective training of an Industrial School, the parents being ordered to contribute, in proportion to their means, towards the expense of its maintenance."

(*a*) This amended Act is, as it states, to withdraw children from contaminating influences, and to extend to them the benefits of Industrial School training.

(*b*) This would bring the child under the provisions of the Reformatory Act; but if from the tender age (under 12) and other circumstances, and not having been convicted of *felony*, the Justices consider the Industrial School the proper place, they may send him there.

Detention Order.—For form of order, as amended by Lord Lieutenant, see Appendix, where forms under Industrial Schools Act are given.

Offence, or cause of Complaint.	Statute.	Extent of Jurisdiction.
INDUSTRIAL SCHOOLS—*con.* The school shall be some certified Industrial School, whether situate within jurisdiction of the Justices or not, the managers of which are willing to receive the child, &c. The school shall be presumed to be certified until contrary shown.	31 Vic. c. 25. s. 14.	
Religious Persuasion.—Proviso: child to be sent to school under management of persons of same religious persuasion as parents; or where not known, then of the guardians; and where that not known, the child shall be considered as of religion in which baptized; or that not appearing, to which he professes to belong. (*a*)	,,	
Power to parent, &c., to apply to remove child to a school conducted in accordance with child's religious persuasion. Application to be made before, or within 30 days after child sent to such school, and to be shown that managers of school named are willing to receive child.	s. 15.	Same Justices who made original order, or any others having like jurisdiction, shall, upon proof as therein, comply with request.
Rules.—Any child (apparently above 10 years) so sent, and whether lodging in school or not, wilfully	s. 25.	Justices in Petty Sessions may order him to be imprisoned for not less

(*a*) *Industrial School and Reformatory.*—The rightful guardian of an illegitimate child, the mother being dead. Queen's Bench Division, Novr., 1888; on Habeas Corpus motion before the Lord Chief Justice, Justices O'Brien, Johnson, and Gibson. The motion was on behalf of Joseph Kerr for writ of *habeas corpus* to obtain custody of a boy named Kerr, otherwise M'Ilwrath. A woman named Kerr was the mother; she was a Roman Catholic; the reputed father was M'Ilwrath, a Presbyterian. The child was baptized a Protestant. Subsequently was, without father's knowledge, baptized a Catholic. The mother died. The Court held that thenceforward the father became the rightful guardian. The Lord Chief Justice, in concurring in the decision, quoted Lord Justice Jessel, who laid down that blood relationship gave a right to the custody of the child, against the claim of persons having no higher rights, in this instance no right at all, and with the death of the mother all her rights ended. The conditional order for Habeas Corpus was accordingly discharged, Mr. Justice O'Brien dissenting.

P

Offence, or cause of Complaint.	Statute.	Extent of Jurisdiction.
INDUSTRIAL SCHOOLS—*con.* neglecting, or wilfully refusing to conform to rules of school—	31 Vic. c. 25, s. 25.	than 14 days, and not more than 3 months, with or without H. L.; and at expiration of imprisonment may order him to be sent to a *Reformatory School.* 2 J. (in Dublin, 1 Police Magistrate.)
Escaping.—Child under detention, whether in school itself or not, escaping therefrom, or neglecting to attend, may at any time before expiration of period of detention be apprehended without warrant, and brought before a Justice where school situate, or where he is apprehended.	s. 26.	One Justice may order him back to school. If apparently above ten years, then on summary conviction, he shall be liable at the discretion of the Justices, instead of being sent back to school, to be imprisoned, with or without H. L., for any term not less than 14 days, and not exceeding 3 months, and may order him to be sent, at expiration of imprisonment to a *Reformatory School,* to be there detained according to the provisions of 21 & 22 Vic. c. 103. (*a*) 2 J. (or in Dublin, 1 Police Magistrate.)
Inducing Escape.—Any person who knowingly assists, directly or indirectly, child to escape from school; who directly or indirectly induces such child so to escape; who knowingly harbours or conceals a child who has so escaped; or prevents or knowingly assists in preventing him in returning to school.	s. 27.	Penalty not exceeding £20, or at the discretion of the Justices, to be imprisoned for not exceeding 2 months, with or without H. L. 2 J. (or in Dublin, 1 Police Magistrate.)

(*a*) But this 21 & 22 Vic. c. 103, is repealed by the 31 & 32 Vic. c. 59, s. 32, the Reformatory Act. Still the Justices could, under the Reformatory Act, and for the offence stated in sec. 26 above, now order a child to be detained in a Reformatory, first convicting and imprisoning him for the offence.

Offence, or cause of Complaint.	Statute.	Extent of Jurisdiction.
INDUSTRIAL SCHOOLS.—*con.* *Contribution by Parent.* (a)—The parent, step-parent, or other person for the time being legally liable, shall, if of sufficient ability, contribute to maintenance, &c., a sum not exceeding 5s. a-week.	31 Vic. c. 25, s. 29.	—
Who may Sue.—On complaint of Inspector of Schools, or his agent, or any constable acting under directions of Inspector of Schools, summons to issue to parent, step-parent, or other person liable as aforesaid.	s. 30.	Justices to examine into ability to maintain, and if they think fit, make an order or decree for payment to Inspector or his agent of a weekly sum not exceeding 5s. a-week during whole or part of the time of detention. 2 J. (or in Dublin, 1 Police Magistrate.)
Chief Secretary may remit payment in whole or in part. Justices may from time to time vary order according to circumstances, either party giving 14 days' notice to the other.		Order may specify time during which payment is to be made, or may direct it to be until further order. (b)
Child shall not be detained after 16 years except with own consent in writing.	s. 31.	—
Chief Secretary may order transfer to other school, or may discharge.	ss. 32 & 33.	

(a) This power to enforce contribution from parents, &c., will have the effect of preventing parents, who may be so disposed, throwing their children on the Institution. The Justices will, of course, take care that it shall not be a profitable course for such to desert their children or neglect their education.

Children of Convicts.—The provisions of "The Industrial Schools Act, 1861 (the English Act), shall apply to all the children, under the age of 14 years, of any woman who shall be convicted for the second time of any offence specified in the first schedule of 'Habitual Criminals Act, 1869,' when such children shall, at the time of the conviction, be under her care and control, and have no visible means of subsistence."—32 & 33 Vic. c. 99, s. 16; and see title "Habitual Criminals."

Stamps.—The order on the book and the warrant or order of detention should bear *Sixpenny* stamps.

(b) Although the schedule to the Act gives a form of committal in default of payment, the Act itself does not give the power to commit. It would not be difficult to point out how this oversight and mistake occurred.

P 2

Offence, or cause of Complaint.	Statute.	Extent of Jurisdiction.
INDUSTRIAL SCHOOLS—*con.* *Forms.*—Proceedings not to be invalidated for want of form.	31 Vic. c. 25. s. 39.	Forms in Schedule to Act, or to like effect may be used. See Forms in Appendix to this work.
Petty Sessions Act, 1851.—Shall apply to all offences, payments, and orders under Act. Act provides for inspection and certifying of schools.	s. 41.	—
Grand Juries of Counties, and Town Council in *Dublin, Cork, and Limerick*, may contract with managers for reception of children in schools. See also title "Reformatory."	s. 9.	
INFANTS ; (Relief Act from debts contracted during infancy except as to necessaries.)	37 & 38 Vic. c. 62.	
INFANTS (*Life Protection*) : It shall not be lawful for any person to retain or receive for hire or reward in that behalf more than one infant, and in case of twins more than two infants under the age of one year, for the purpose of nursing or maintaining such infants apart from their parents for a longer period than 24 hours, except in house registered as provided by Act.	35 & 36 Vic. c. 38, s. 2.	Imprisonment not exceeding 6 months, with or without H.L., or penalty not exceeding £5 ; in default of payment, imprisonment by scale. 2 J. (or 1 Stipendiary Magistrate.)
Register of names and houses to be kept by local authority. Every person who receives or retains any infant in contravention of Act.	s. 3.	—
Persons whose names and houses are registered to keep a register of infants, with particulars as in Act, and to produce it when lawfully required, &c.; for non-compliance—	s. 5.	Penalty not exceeding £5 ; in default of payment, imprisonment by scale. 2 J. (or 1 Stipendiary Magistrate).

Offence, or cause of Complaint.	Statute.	Extent of Jurisdiction.
INFANTS—*continued*.		
Person making any false representation with a view to be registered under this Act, or forge any certificate, or using forged certificate knowing it to be forged, or falsifying register.	35 & 36 Vic. c. 38, s. 7.	Imprisonment not exceeding 6 months, with or without H. L., or penalty not exceeding £5 ; in default of payment, imprisonment by scale. 2 J. (or 1 Stipendiary Magistrate.)
Person registered within 24 hours after death of infant shall give notice to the Coroner of the district ; for neglect— Expenses in execution of Act shall be paid out of the local rate.	s. 8.	Imprisonment not exceeding 6 months, with or without H. L., or penalty not exceeding £5 ; in default of payment, imprisonment by scale. 2 J. (or 1 Stipendiary Magistrate.)
Offences may be prosecuted under Summary Jurisdiction Acts (in Ireland means Petty Sessions Act, 1851).	s. 10.	—
Description of offence in words of Act, or as near thereto as may be, shall be sufficient in law.	s. 11.	
Exceptions, &c., may be proved by defendant, but need not be negatived in information, and if negatived, need not be proved.	. 11.	
Penalties may be applied to local rates.		
Provisions of this Act shall not apply to relative or guardians of infants retained as aforesaid, nor to institutions established for their care, nor to persons receiving infants to nurse under Poor Law Acts.		
Act to amend the law relating to the guardianship and custody of infants.	49 & 50 Vic. c. 27.	
On death of father, mother to be guardian alone, or jointly with others.	s. 2.	
Mother may appoint guardian in certain cases.	s. 3.	—
Powers of guardian.	s. 4.	

Offence, or cause of Complaint.	Statute.	Extent of Jurisdiction.
INFANTS—*continued*. Court may make orders as to custody, and in its discretion remove guardian. Guardianship in case of divorce or judicial separation. As to removing proceedings, and as to appeals from County Court to High Court of Justice. *Court* shall mean High Court of Justice or the County Court of district in which respondents or any of them may reside. See also " Prevention of Cruelty to Children."	49 & 50 Vic. c. 27, ss. 5 and 6. s. 7. s. 10. s. 9.	—
INJURY (*to Property*) : See " Malicious Injuries." *To the Person*—See " Assault."		
INNKEEPERS : See " Publicans."		
INOCULATION : Persons inoculating or producing small-pox.	3 & 4 Vic. c. 29, s. 8.	Imprisonment not exceeding 1 month. 2 J.
INQUESTS : (*a*) In the absence of the Coroner, if a dead body be found, and in case no inquest shall be held on it within two days— For duties of the Constabulary, mode of holding the inquest, taking the evidence, fining for non-attendance, granting expenses, &c., see the Act. And for expenses allowed, see Schedule C to Act.	9 & 10 Vic. c. 37, s. 14.	Justices of the district can hold such inquest and do all other acts which the Coroner is empowered to do. 2 J.

(*a*) The jury shall view the body. The Schedule to 9 & 10 Vic. c. 57, gives the amounts which Justices or Coroner may allow as expenses to witnesses, &c. ; and see now 44 & 45 Vic. c. 35.

Offence, or cause of Complaint.	Statute.	Extent of Jurisdiction.
INQUESTS—*continued.*		
Act providing remuneration for Coroners.	44 & 45 Vic. c. 35.	
Coroner or Justices holding inquest may order payment to witnesses, and for removal of dead body to inquest.	s. 5.	
Coroner or the Justices before whom inquest held may admit to bail persons charged by verdict with manslaughter to appear at Assizes.	s. 7.	
For fee and recognizance and for copies of the depositions.	ss. and 9.	
Act not to include Dublin.		
INSECTS :		
Act for preventing the introduction and spreading of insects destructive to crops, and as to powers of Lord Lieutenant to make orders for preventing, &c.	40 & 41 Vic. c. 68.	
Application of Penalties, &c.	s. 7.	
INSULTING (*Magistrate*): See " Contempt."		
INTOXICATING LIQUOR LICENSING ACTS : See " Licensing Acts."		
JOURNEYMAN :		
Wilfully spoiling goods or work committed to his care. See " Malicious Injuries."		
Unlawfully disposing or retaining possession of work or materials committed to his care (under value of £5) without consent of employer.	25 & 26 Vic. c. 50, s. 7. (36 & 37 Vic. c. 82.)	Reasonable compensation, and fine not exceeding 40s. ; in default, &c., imprisonment by scale ; *or* to be imprisoned not exceeding 1 month. (*a*)
And see " Employer and Workmen."		

(*a*) But the fine and compensation being named, and not exceeding £5, may be enforced by the scale.—36 & 37 Vic. c. 82.

Offence, or cause of Complaint.	Statute.	Extent of Jurisdiction.
JURISDICTION : General Jurisdiction of Justices in offence cases.	14 & 15 Vic. c. 93, ss. 7 and 10.	—
JUSTICES (*Protection Act*): Act to remove disqualification of Justices in certain cases.	12 Vic. c. 16 30 & 31 Vic. c. 115.	See Appendix. See Appendix.
JUVENILE OFFENDERS : See "Children and Young Persons."		
KITE : Flying on road or street to the danger of passengers.	14 & 15 Vic. c. 92, s. 10. (36 & 37 Vic. c. 82.]	Penalty not exceeding 10s. ; in default, &c., imprisonment not exceeding 7 days. 1 J.
KNACKER : Persons keeping place for the slaughter of horses or other cattle neglecting or refusing to affix names over doors.	12 & 13 Vic. c. 92, s. 7.	Penalty not exceeding £5 a-day ; in default, &c., imprisonment not exceeding 2 months. 1 J.
Horses or cattle brought to be slaughtered (not intended for butchers' meat), to have the hair cut off the neck and killed within three days ; meantime to be supplied with wholesome food and water. For neglect—	s. 8.	Penalty not exceeding £5 ; in default, &c., imprisonment not exceeding 2 months. 1 J.
For offence of using or employing cattle so brought to be slaughtered.	s. 9.	Penalty not exceeding 40s. a-day ; in default, &c., imprisonment not exceeding 2 months, and by scale. 1 J.
Neglecting to enter full and correct description of cattle so brought to be slaughtered in a book. (Two Justices or one Metropolitan Police Magistrate, may, if they or he think fit, commit offender for 3 months, without pecuniary penalty.)	s. 10.	Penalty not exceeding 40s. a-day; in default, &c., imprisonment not exceeding 2 months, and by scale. 1 J.

Offence, or cause of Complaint.	Statute.	Extent of Jurisdiction.
LABOURER: See "Employer and Workman." LABOURERS' COTTAGES, &c. (IRELAND), ACT, 1882. Power to Land Commission, where agreement and declaration as to fair rent of holding is filed, to make order as to accommodation of labourers employed on the holding.	45 & 46 Vic. c. 60, ss. 3 and 4.	For non-compliance, penalty £1 a-week for every week during which order is not complied with. Justices shall award the penalty to the Guardians of the Union. Recoverable under Petty Sessions Act. 2 J.
Power to Land Commission to relieve from penalty or from Justices' order. Power to sanitary authority, and their duty to make complainant and proceed for penalty before Justices.	s. 5. 46 & 47 Vic. c. 60, s. 11.	
LAMB (*stolen*) : Found in possession, or the head, skin, fleece, or any part thereof, and not satisfactorily accounted for.	25 & 26 Vic. c. 50, s. 6. (36 & 37 Vic. c. 82).	Imprisonment not exceeding 3 months, *or* fine not exceeding £5 ; in default, &c., imprisonment by scale. 1 J.
LANDLORD AND TENANT: *Small Tenements.*—House, or part of a house, in any city, town, borough, or village, in which any fair or market is usually held, (a) the term not exceeding 1 month, rent not	14 & 15 Vic. c. 92, s. 15.	Upon proof of summons being served personally, or left at his usual abode, *four clear days* before hearing, or where

(a) Act is made applicable to Police District, Dublin Metropolis, "although no fair or market be held therein."—34 & 35 Vic. c. 76, s. 10.

"*Artisans' and Labourers' Dwellings Act*, 1868." 31 & 32 Vic. c. 130. As to orders of Justices and duties of local authorities in towns, &c., where dwellings are dangerous to health, unfit for habitation, &c., see Act.

"*Legal Notice to Quit.*"—It is usual in case of a monthly tenancy to give a month's notice, and of a weekly, a week's notice ; it may be written or printed, although it has been decided that a verbal notice is sufficient ; however, these same authorities recommend the written notice as most advisable and prudent. The words of the section are :—"Where the term shall have ended, or be *duly determined by a legal notice to quit*." The wording of the section in the Civil Bill Act

Offence, or cause of Complaint.	Statute.	Extent of Jurisdiction.
LANDLORD AND TENANT—*con.* exceeding at rate of £1 a month, where the term shall have ended or be duly determined by a legal notice to quit, where the tenant or occupier refuses to give up possession, the landlord, his agent, or receiver, may cause summons to issue to show cause why possession shall not be delivered up. Summons to be served 4 clear days before the hearing ; to be given to defendant personally, or left at his residence. Where service cannot be effected, summons may be posted on the premises. Warrant not to be executed on Sunday, Good Friday, or Christmas Day, nor at any time except between 9 A.M. and 4 P.M.	14 & 15 Vic. c. 92, s. 15.	such service cannot be effected, then by posting on the premises; unless cause be shown, Justices may, upon proof of the holding, and termination of the tenancy, issue warrant to give up possession in not less than 7 or more than 10 clear days from date of warrant. 1 J. (*Justices* are spoken of in this section ; but sec. 1 shows that 1 J. may try the case.)

is different; it reads :—" Where the interest had determined, and that notice to quit (in cases where such notice is by law necessary) had been duly served."—14 & 15 Vic. c. 57, s. 72.

The notice shall be signed by the landlord, or by his agent duly authorized. The relation of landlord and tenant subsists up to the expiration of the notice, and the landlord may demand and accept rent up to that date, but acceptance of rent which accrues afterwards, will be a waiver of the notice. But rent received under circumstances showing it to be paid merely as compensation for the use of the premises overheld, and where the intention to proceed to evict has been expressed, will not be a waiver of the notice. The question seems to be, did the lessor receive rent *eo nomine* as rent due under the lease, &c. ? See per *Park, J.; Doe v. Pritchard*, 5 *B. & Ad.*, under *Dumper's Case* (*Leading Cases*).

A demand of possession on the day on which it is stated that the demise is determined is premature.—By Sergeant Greene : *Griffith* v. *Boland, Irish C. C.*, 470. The demand ought, therefore, be made on the day following.

Demand of Possession.—It would seem that, under the special provisions of this statute, an informality either in the mode or time of demanding possession will not be sufficient to stay the jurisdiction of the Justices, for that defect can be cured in Court, and is not under sect. 15 (*infra*) made a necessary part of the plaintiff's proof. If the defendant fails to appear, or appearing, "fails to show reasonable cause why possession should not be given, and shall *still refuse to deliver up* the possession," &c., plaintiff need only prove the holding, and end or determination of the tenancy. Of course, if the defendant does *not still refuse to deliver up possession*, there is an end to the defence.

The Warrant is supposed to be signed on the day the order is made. If order made and warrant dated on the 1st, it cannot be executed berore the 9th; if that be a Sunday, &c., then on the 10th, or any day up to the 12th. Where the tenant overholds after the fourteen days, contrary to his *undertaking*, the warrant may be

Offence, or cause of Complaint.	Statute.	Extent of Jurisdiction.
LANDLORD AND TENANT—*con.* If party summoned undertakes to deliver up possession and pay arrears of rent in 14 days, no warrant to issue till the expiration of that period.	14 & 15 Vic. c. 92, s. 15.	
Cottier Tenants Defined.—Tenements consisting of dwelling-house or cottage, without land, or with land not exceeding half an acre, rent not exceeding at the rate of £5 a-year for 1 month, or from month to month or lesser period, and held under written agreement, and landlord undertaking to keep same in repair, such to be deemed a cottier tenancy within meaning of Act. (And as to lettings by Sanitary Authority, see 46 & 47 Vic. c. 60, s. 13.)	23 & 24 Vic. c. 154, s. 81.	— May be evicted as in sec. 86, *infra.*

issued and executed forthwith. Where for any cause the warrant issued has not been executed within the specified time, there would seem to be no legal difficulty in issuing another, more especially if the delay took place in order to accommodate the defendant, or was occasioned by him ; but all difficulty can be obviated by issuing a new summons.

The Jurisdiction.—The Justices should see clearly that as regards *locality*, *nature of the tenure*, and *rent*, they have jurisdiction. A letting at 5*s.* a-week is not within the jurisdiction ; that would exceed £1 a-month. Month means calendar month (see the interpretation clause). As regards "cottier tenants," it is necessary to ascertain that the letting is of the nature prescribed by that particular statute.

Proof.—14 & 15 Vic. c. 92, s. 15. If such tenant or occupier shall not appear at the time and place appointed, or shall appear, but shall not show to the satisfaction of the Justices reasonable cause why possession should not be given, and shall still neglect or refuse to deliver up the possession, &c., it shall be lawful for the Justices, upon proof of the holding and of the end or determination of the tenancy, with the time and manner thereof (and where the title of the landlord shall have accrued since the letting of the premises, upon proof of the right by which he claims the possession), to issue a warrant to the Sub-Inspector, or to special bailiffs, &c. (as above). Sec. 15.

Cottier Tenants.—The principal European example of this tenure is Ireland, and it is from that country that the term cottier is derived. In its original acceptation the word "cottier" designated a class of sub-tenants who rent a cottage and an acre or two of land from the small farmers, but the usage of writers has long since stretched the term to include those small farmers themselves.—*Mill's Political Economy.* The above Act gives its own definition.

The Constabulary execute the warrants under 14 & 15 Vic. c. 92. Under the 23 & 24 Vic. c. 154, they are *executed by special bailiffs only.*

Offence, or cause of Complaint.	Statute.	Extent of Jurisdiction.
LANDLORD AND TENANT—*con.* *Injuring Premises, &c.*—Cottier tenant, or any tenant for shorter period than 1 month, or at will, or by sufferance, wilfully injuring or permitting to be injured or destroyed any part of the premises which the landlord is bound to keep in repair. On proof thereof—	23 & 24 Vic. c. 154, s. 84.	Justices in Petty Sessions shall issue warrant, directed to special bailiff, to deliver up possession to the landlord or owner. 1 J.
Rent in Arrear.—Cottier tenant in arrear for one clear gale of rent for the space of forty days, on being summoned before Justices—	s. 85.	May be summarily evicted; warrant to issue as above. 2 J.
Tenancy ended.—Cottier tenancy ended, or determined by notice to quit, may be summarily evicted. (See section in full, *infra*). (a)	s. 86.	Warrant under hands and seals (to special bailiff) to give up possession in not less than 7 or more than 14 clear days. 2 J.

(a) *Where Cottier Tenancy is ended, and where Permissive Occupants overhold possession*, sec. 86.—In case the term or interest of any tenant in any such cottier tenement shall have ended, or shall have been duly determined by a notice to quit, and such tenant, or any person by whom the premises or any part of them shall be then actually occupied, shall neglect or refuse to deliver up the possession of the same, or in case any person shall have been put, or shall be put into possession of any lands or premises by permission of the owner, as servant, herdsman, or caretaker, and shall refuse or omit to quit and deliver up the possession of the premises on demand made by the owner thereof, or his known agent or receiver, it shall be lawful for the landlord or owner of the said premises, or his heirs, executors, or administrators, or his known agent or receiver to cause the person so neglecting or refusing to quit or deliver up the possession to be served with a summons in writing, signed by a Justice or Justices not interested in the said premises, but having jurisdiction in the place in which the premises shall be situate, to appear before two or more Justices at the Petty Sessions, Town Hall, or Divisional Justice Room, or other place in which such Justices usually meet for the despatch of public business of such city, town, district, or other place, to show cause why possession of the said premises should not be delivered up to such landlord or owner, or his agent or receiver, as aforesaid; and if the said tenant or occupier shall not appear at the time and place appointed, or if such tenant or occupier shall appear, and shall not show to the satisfaction of such Justices reasonable cause why possession should not be given, and shall still neglect or refuse to deliver up possession of the said premises, or such part of them as was in his actual occupation at the time of the service of such summons to the said landlord or owner, or his agent or receiver, it shall be lawful for such Justices, or any two or more of them, not interested, as aforesaid, on proof being made before them of the holding, or permissive possessions, as the case may be, and of its end, or determination, and the time and manner thereof; and where the title of the landlord shall have accrued since the letting of the premises, the right by which he claims the possession to issue a warrant under their hands and seals to any

Offence, or cause of Complaint.	Statute.	Extent of Jurisdiction.
LANDLORD AND TENANT—*con.* Stay of execution of warrant on undertaking to give up possession in 14 days, and to pay all rent and arrears.	23 & 24 Vic. c. 154, s. 88.	
Caretakers, &c. (a)—In case any person be put into possession of any lands or premises by permission of the owner, as servant, herdsman, or caretaker, and shall refuse or omit to quit or give up possession on demand made by owner, his agent, or receiver, he may, at instance of owner, &c., be summoned to appear before two or more Justices at Petty Sessions. (Summons to be served 4 clear days, sec. 87.) Not to affect owner's right peace-	s. 86.	Upon proof of such permissive possession, 2 Justices to issue warrant, under hands and seals, to special bailiff to give up possession in not less than 7 or more than 14 clear days, unless reasonable cause shown. 2 J.

person as a special bailiff in that behalf on the part of the landlord or owner, requiring and authorizing him, within a period to be therein named, and not less than 7 or more than 14 clear days from the date of such warrant, to give the possession of the said premises to the said landlord, or his agent or receiver; and such warrant shall be a sufficient authority to the said bailiff to enter upon the said premises, with such assistants as he shall deem to be necessary, and to give possession accordingly: Provided that no entry shall be made under such warrant on any *Sunday, Good Friday,* or *Christmas Day,* or at any time except between the hours of 9 in the morning, and 4 in the afternoon: Provided also, that nothing herein contained shall prejudice or affect the right of any owner of property intrusted to the care of any servant or caretaker peaceably to resume the possession thereof without process of law, if he shall so think fit.

Sec. 87.—Provides for service by posting where person overholding cannot be found, and admission to the premises cannot be obtained, and the place of his abode not known.

Sec. 88.—In the case of *tenants*, an undertaking to give up possession within 14 days, and in meantime to pay all rent and arrears; warrant not to *issue* until after expiration of 14 days; but if he continue afterwards to overhold, warrant may issue to deliver up possession forthwith.

Sec. 89.—Landlord not to be deemed a trespasser merely by any irregularity in mode of proceeding, &c.

Sec. 100.—No action to lie against Justices issuing, or bailiff, &c., executing warrant or precept by reason of want of title in person who obtains same.

There does not appear to be any right of appeal from Justices' orders in possession cases either under the 14 & 15 Vic. c. 92, or 23 & 24 Vic. c. 154. If defendant be aggrieved, he can have civil remedy against complainant for any wrong done him.

(a) Previous to this Act the Magistrates in Petty Sessions had no power to restore to the owner premises in the possession of *permissive* occupants, &c.; they should be evicted at Quarter Sessions, under 14 & 15 Vic. c. 57, s. 82.

Notice to quit not necessary in the case of caretakers, &c.

Offence, or cause of Complaint.	Statute.	Extent of Jurisdiction.
LANDLORD AND TENANT—*con.* ably to resume possession without process of law, if he think fit (*a*), sec. 86, see sec. *ante.*	23 & 24 Vic. c. 154, s. 86.	
Caretakers under the "Land Law (Ireland) Act, 1887."	50 & 51 Vic. c. 38.	
Substitution of written notice for the execution of ejectment, and what such notice shall contain, how same shall be served and posted—	s. 7.	
Upon determination of the tenancy by such notice every person upon whom same is served shall be deemed to be put into possession as a caretaker, and the enactment of the "Landlord and Tenant Law Amendment Act (Ireland), 1860," (23 & 24 Vic. c. 154) relating to persons put into possession of lands by permission of the owner as caretakers, shall apply as if on the date of the service of the notice a Writ of possession had been duly executed, and such person having been removed from possession had been re-admitted as caretaker, and such person may be removed at any time after a month from service of such notice, or sooner by leave of the Court, or at expiration of the period of redemption.	,,	Proceedings may be taken under sec. 86 (23 & 24 Vic. c. 154), for the removal from possession of such caretaker. The Justices may, at request of landlord or owner, issue the warrant to the Sheriff of the county where premises are situated, instead of to special bailiff. The Justices may put a stay upon the issue of the warrant for any time not exceeding one month, if they think fit, by reason of the illness of the caretaker or his family, or any other sufficient reason. Warrant may be executed

(*a*) "Not to affect owner's right peaceably to resume possession." To what extent the exercise of this right can be carried, see notes on title "Entry," Indictable Offence Index.

"Put into Possession," &c.—After the death of husband who, as servant was put into possession, wife continuing is deemed to have been put into possession. Allowing a person to remain in possession is putting into possession.—Q. B. (Ir.), 1884.

All former Acts giving Justices in Petty Sessions summary power to enforce penalties for "burning land," are by the above Act, 23 & 24 Vic. c. 154, repealed.

☞ The several Rules, Orders, &c., of 1887 and 1888 issued by the High Court of Justice under this Land Law (Ir.) Act, 1887, have been supplied to the Justices in Petty Sessions. It may be necessary to refer to these Rules in proceedings before Justices under sec. 7.

Offence, or cause of Complaint.	Statute.	Extent of Jurisdiction.
LANDLORD AND TENANT—*con.*		at any time not less than 7 days, nor more than two months from the issue thereof.* 2 J.
Waste.—Where affidavit is made before Justice by landlord, owner,&c., or his agent, that there exists probable and just grounds of suspicion that any tenant, servant, caretaker, or other person, who has obtained possession from any such tenant, &c., is about to commit or permit unlawful waste, injury, alteration, destruction upon, or removal from any such dwelling-house, outhouse, or other building, or unlawfully to burn, break-up, or remove the soil or subsoil of the lands, unlawfully to cut, lop, or grub trees, woods, or underwoods, or otherwise to use or misuse the premises contrary to agreement, or that he is in the act of doing any such—	23 & 24 Vic. c. 154, s. 35.	Justice to issue precept in form in Schedule A to the Act, to discontinue the waste until the matter of the information be inquired into at the next Petty Sessions of the district. 1 J. To be served in person or posted as directed in the section.
In disobedience to such precept, continuing to do any act prohibited thereby, or wilfully aiding, abetting, or assisting in so doing; on conviction—	s. 36.	Imprisonment not exceeding 1 month; proceedings as in Petty Sessions (Ireland) Act. 2 J.
Superior Courts, Judges of Assize, or Chairman of the County, may, on summary application of party aggrieved, by precept, order, or conviction, annul or vary same.	s. 37.	—

* *Notice to Relieving Officer.*—The 11 & 12 Vic. c. 47 intituled, "An Act for the Protection and Relief of the Destitute Poor evicted from their dwellings in Ireland," shall apply to warrants under this sec. 7 of 50 & 51 Vic. c. 38. The section here referred to is to the effect that where a decree or order is given to give up possession of land on which there is any building inhabited as a dwelling-house, notice of the execution of the writ shall be given by landowner, &c., or his agent to the Relieving Officer of the electoral division in which the land is situate. Not to be less than 48 hours' notice. May be served at dwelling-house or office of Relieving Officer, or may be delivered to Postmaster open and in duplicate, and addressed to Relieving Officer, and on payment to Postmaster of 6d., in addition to postage. Sec. 2, 11 & 12 Vic. c. 47.

Offence, or cause of Complaint.	Statute.	Extent of Jurisdiction.
LANDLORD AND TENANT—*con.* Landlord may enter to inspect waste.	23 & 24 Vic. c. 154, s. 38.	—
Nothing in Act to deprive landlord, owner, &c., of ordinary civil remedies.	s. 39.	
Act provides penalties, recoverable by civil bill, for burning the land, cutting or lopping trees, &c., without authority.	ss. 30, 31.	
Deserted Premises.—Where premises are deserted, or the lands uncultivated, &c., or stock or crop removed, at request of landlord or agent—	s. 79.	Two Justices may view the premises between 10 A.M. and 4 P.M., and give certificate as in Schedule to Act. 2 J. See form in Appendix.
Unroofing dwelling-house for purpose of expelling occupier.	11 & 12 Vic. c. 47, s. 7.	Misdemeanour.
LARCENY: (a) As to Larceny and other offences by children and young persons, see "Children and Young Persons," Summary Index.		

(a) Larceny is the fraudulent taking and carrying away by one person of the personal goods of another from any place, with intent to convert them to the taker's own use, without the owner's consent. This is *simple larceny.* It is termed *compound* when attended by aggravating circumstances, and to which a higher degree of punishment attaches—as larceny from the person, larceny by clerk or servant, or larceny from one's dwelling-house ; and when a taking from the person is accompanied by violence or threats, it is robbery.

For the *taking*, or, as the lawyers term it, the *asportavit*, any removal is sufficient, or the removal of any part, however small. Nor need the taking be by the hand of the party himself ; it may be done through another, as by employing an infant who has not attained the age of discretion to do the act. But there are wrongful *takings* which are not larceny, not being taken with a felonious intent; as where an article of husbandry lying in a field, may be taken, used, and returned ; this is merely a trespass. So if the goods are taken under a *bonâ fide* claim of right, it is not larceny.

The whipping of females is abolished by the 1 Geo. iv. c. 57. The 25 Vic. c. 18, limits the number of strokes, and the instrument to be used.

Offence, or cause of Complaint.	Statute.	Extent of Jurisdiction.
LARCENY—*continued.* **UNDER CRIMINAL JUSTICE ACT.** Committing simple larceny (the value of the whole of the property alleged to have been stolen not exceeding, in the judgment of the Justices, 5s.); or attempting to commit larceny from the person, or simple larceny, provided the accused consents to be tried summarily, or that he pleads guilty, unless the Justices, from the fact of a previous conviction, or from any other circumstance, think it a fit case to be prosecuted by indictment— Justice to ask the accused whether he consents to the charge being summarily determined.	18 & 19 Vic. c. 126, ss. 1 and 2 (*a*)	Imprisonment with or without H. L., not exceeding 3 months. 2 J. (or 1 Stipendiary Magistrate specially appointed). If Justices be of opinion that there are circumstances in the case which render it inexpedient to inflict any punishment, they may dismiss the person charged without proceeding to a conviction.
Simple larceny (the property alleged to have been stolen exceeding 5s. in value), or stealing from the person, or larceny as a clerk or servant, where the accused pleads guilty. (*b*)	s. 3.	Imprisonment, with or without H. L., not exceeding 6 months: or, if Justices think fit, may return informations to Quarter Sessions. 2 J. (or 1 Stipendiary Magistrate).

(*a*) Sec. 2.—"Where the Justices before whom any person is charged, as aforesaid, propose to dispose of the case summarily under the foregoing provisions, one of such Justices, after the examination of all the witnesses for the prosecution have been completed, and before calling upon the person charged for any statement which he may wish to make, shall state to such person the substance of the charge against him, and shall then say to him these words, or words to the like effect: 'Do you consent that the charge against you shall be tried by us, or do you desire that it shall be sent for trial by a jury at the Sessions or Assizes? (as the case may be): and if the person charged shall consent to the charge being summarily tried and determined as aforesaid, then the Justices shall reduce the charge into writing, and read the same to such person, and shall then ask him whether he is guilty or not of such charge; and if such person shall say that he is guilty, the Justice shall then proceed to pass such sentence upon him as may by law be passed, subject to the provisions of this Act in respect to such offence; but if the person charged shall say that he is not guilty, the Justices shall then inquire of such person whether he has any defence to make to such charge, and if he shall state that he has a defence, the Justices shall hear such offence, and then proceed to dispose of the case summarily."

(*b*) Sec. 3.—"Where any person is charged before any Justices at such Petty

Q

Offence, or cause of Complaint.	Statute.	Extent of Jurisdiction.
LARCENY (UNDER CRIMINAL JUS-TICE ACT)—*continued*. *Embezzlement*.—By the 31 & 32 Vic. c. 116, all the provisions of the Criminal Justice Act, 18 & 19 Vic. c. 126, shall extend and be applicable to the offence of embezzlement by clerks or servants; and the said Act shall henceforth be read as if the said offence of embezzlement had been included therein. (*a*)		
Justices to warn accused that he is not obliged to plead.	18 & 19 Vic. c. 126, s. 3.	
Persons accused may have assistance of counsel, &c.	s. 4.	—
Power to remand to next Petty Sessions.	s. 5.	
Convictions and proceedings to be returned to Quarter Sessions.	s. 7.	

Sessions, as aforesaid, with simple larceny (the property alleged to have been stolen exceeding in value 5*s*.), or stealing from the person, or larceny as a clerk or servant, and the evidence, when the case on the part of the prosecution has been completed, is, in the opinion of such Justices, sufficient to put the person charged on his trial for the offence with which he is charged, such Justices, if the case appear to them to be one which may properly be disposed of in a summary way, and may be adequately punished by virtue of the powers of this Act, shall reduce the charge into writing, and shall read it to the said person, and shall then ask him whether he is guilty or not of the charge; and if such person shall say that he is guilty, such Justices shall thereupon cause a plea of guilty to be entered upon the proceedings, and shall convict him of such offence, and commit him to the common gaol or house of correction, there to be imprisoned, with or without hard labour, for any term not exceeding six calendar months; and every such conviction shall be in the Form (C) in the Schedule to this Act, or to the like effect: Provided always that the said Justices, before they ask such person whether he is guilty or not, shall explain to him that he is not obliged to plead or answer before them at all, and that if he do not plead or answer before them, he will be committed for trial in the usual course.''

(*a*) *Embezzlement*.—All the limitations and conditions as to the amount, the consent to be tried, and plea of guilty, giving the jurisdiction in cases of larceny, are le to the embezzlement.

Offence, or cause of Complaint.	Statute.	Extent of Jurisdiction.
LARCENY (UNDER CRIMINAL JUS-TICE ACT)—*continued.*		
Justices may order restitution of property stolen, or obtained by false pretences. (*a*)	18 & 19 Vic. c. 126, s. 8.	—
Proceedings under this Act a bar to further proceedings.	s. 12.	—
Justices empowered to order expenses of prosecution, by order on the Treasury.	s. 14.	—

(*a*) *Larceny and False Pretences.*—Sec. 8, which empowers the Justices, on conviction, to order restitution of the property stolen, taken, *or obtained by false pretences*, &c., may have the effect of misleading ; it is the first mention of *False Pretences* in the Act, and they have not power to deal with this offence, which is an indictable misdemeanour : sec. 24 & 25 Vic. c. 96, s. 88. There is a distinction between larceny and obtaining goods by false pretences, but the line in some instances is so slender as to be merely "length without breadth." Larceny is the wrongful taking from a person *against his will;* and yet if a shopkeeper permits a person to take a piece of goods outside his door, under pretence of taking it to the light to examine the quality, and he runs off with it, although he obtained possession of the property with the will of the owner, yet the purpose for which the owner passed it being different from that in which the prisoner received it, the offence is larceny. Out of the numerous decisions, showing the difference between false pretence, or swindling, and larceny, the following may be taken as a summary :—" In the one case the proprietor has agreed to transfer the property, and therefore he has been only *imposed upon* in the transaction ; and in the other he has never agreed to part with his property, and therefore the subsequent appropriation is theft."—*Alison.* And see note under " *Larceny*," Indictable Offence Index, as to " Possession obtained by Fraud." See " False Pretence," Indictable Offence Index.

The following is conceived to be a ready and useful definition of a felonious taking : " The taking and carrying away are felonious where the goods are taken against the will of the owner, either in his absence or in a clandestine manner ; or where possession is obtained either by force or surprise, or by any device or fraudulent expedient, the owner not voluntarily parting with his entire interest in the goods, and where the taker intends, in any such case fraudulently to deprive the owner of his entire interest in the property against his will."—" *Criminal Law Commissioners.*"

Forms of conviction and certificate of dismissal are given in the Schedule to the Act.

Q 2

Offence, or cause of Complaint.	Statute.	Extent of Jurisdiction.
LARCENY—*continued*.		
UNDER LARCENY ACT.	24 & 25 Vic. c. 96.	—
As proceedings are amended by the (a)	25 & 26 Vic. c. 50.	—
Deer in unenclosed Ground.—Whosoever shall unlawfully and wilfully course, hunt, snare, or carry away, or kill, wound, or attempt, &c., any deer kept or being in the unenclosed part of any forest, chase, or purlieu—	24 & 25 Vic. c. 96, s. 12.	Shall forfeit and pay a sum not exceeding £50; and in default, &c., to be imprisoned, with or without H. L., not exceeding 6 months. 1 J. Second offence, felony, triable by indictment.
If the offence be committed in any enclosed ground.	c. 13.	Felony, triable by indictment.
If any deer, or the head, skin, or part thereof, or any snare or engine for taking deer, be found in possession of any person, or on his premises, with his knowledge, and not satisfactorily accounting—	s. 14.	Shall forfeit and pay a sum not exceeding £20; and in default, &c., to be imprisoned, with or without H. L., not exceeding 6 months. 1 J. In case the person cannot be convicted, Justices may summon all persons through whose hands such deer may have passed: and if

(a) *Procedure.*—The 25 & 26 Vic. c. 50, ss. 2 and 3, provides that offences made punishable on summary conviction, under 24 & 25 Vic. c. 96, may be prosecuted before any one Justice in Petty Sessions, or two Justices out of Petty Sessions (where offender shall be unable to procure bail for his appearance at Petty Sessions) and that the mode of compelling appearance of offenders and witnesses, the hearing and determining of complaints, and the making and executing of orders, shall be subject to the provisions of Petty Sessions (Ireland) Act, 1851, as amended by Petty Sessions Clerk (Ireland) Act, 1858, and to the provisions of Act relating to the Divisional Police Offices, when heard in *Dublin* Metropolis.

Appeal allowed to Quarter Sessions, where the sum adjudged to be paid exceeds £5, or the imprisonment exceeds one month, or where the conviction takes place, before one Justice only.—24 & 35 Vic. c. 96, s. 110.

Convictions to be returned to Quarter Sessions, s. 12. (See General Form of Conviction, *Appendix.*)

Where summary penalties, &c., under this Act, 24 & 25 Vic. c. 96, are not paid, by sec. 107 defendant may be imprisoned, with or without H. L., according to the scale of imprisonment there given. But where the sum is under £5, it should proportion to Small Penalties Scales.—36 & 37 Vic. c. 82.

Offence, or cause of Complaint.	Statute.	Extent of Jurisdiction.
LARCENY (UNDER LARCENY ACT)— *continued.*		
	24 & 25 Vic. c. 96, s. 14.	the person from whom first received, or had possession, shall not satisfactorily account, he shall, on conviction, be liable to the penalty above named.
Setting Snares.—Whosoever shall unlawfully and wilfully set or use any snare or engine whatsoever for the purpose of taking or killing deer in any part of any forest, chase, or purlieu, whether such part be enclosed or not, or in any fence or bank dividing the same from any land adjoining, or in any enclosed land where deer shall be usually kept, or wilfully destroying the fences, &c.	s. 15.	Shall forfeit and pay a sum not exceeding £20; and in default, &c., to be imprisoned, with or without H. L., not exceeding 6 months. 1 J.
Beating or wounding keepers in execution of their duty.	s. 16.	Felony, triable by indictment.
Hares, Rabbits.—Whosoever shall unlawfully and wilfully, between the beginning of the last hour before sunrise and the expiration of the first hour after sunset, take or kill any hare or rabbit in any warren or ground lawfully used for breeding or keeping same, whether enclosed or not, or shall, at any time, set or use therein any snare or engine for the taking of hares or rabbits—	s. 17.	Shall forfeit and pay a sum not exceeding £5; and in default, &c., to be imprisoned, with or without H. L., not exceeding 2 months. 1 J.
Stealing Dogs.—Whosoever shall steal any dog—	s. 18.	Imprisonment with or without H. L., not exceeding 6 months; or shall forfeit and pay (over and above the value) a sum not exceeding £20. 1 J. If it be a second offence, indictable misdemeanour.
Possession of Stolen Dogs.—Whosoever shall unlawfully have in his possession or on his premises any stolen dog or the skin of any	s. 19.	Penalty not exceeding £20; and in default of payment, &c., to be imprisoned, with or

Offence, or cause of Complaint.	Statute.	Extent of Jurisdiction.
LARCENY (UNDER LARCENY ACT)— *continued.* stolen dog, knowing such to have been stolen—	24 & 25 Vic. c. 96, s. 19.	without H. L., not exceeding 6 months. 1 J. Second offence, indictable misdemeanour.
Whosoever shall corruptly take any money or reward, directly or indirectly, under pretence or upon account of aiding any person to recover any dog which shall have been stolen, or which shall be in the possession of any person not being the owner thereof.	s. 20.	Indictable misdemeanour.
Stealing Birds, Animals, &c. (a)— Whosoever shall steal any bird, beast, or other animal, ordinarily kept in a state of confinement, or for any domestic purpose, not being the subject of larceny at Common Law, or shall wilfully kill any such bird, .beast, or animal, with intent to steal the same or any part thereof—	s. 21.	Imprisonment with or without H. L., not exceeding 6 months ; or a penalty (over and above the value) not exceeding £20. 1 J. If it be a second offence, imprisonment, with H. L., not exceeding 12 months. 1 J.
Possession of stolen Birds, Animals, &c.—Any person in whose possession or on whose premises such bird or the plumage thereof, or such beast or the skin thereof, or such animal or any part thereof, shall be so found (knowing same to be stolen)— See also "Poultry."	s. 22.	Shall be liable for the first offence to such forfeiture, and for every subsequent offence to such punishment as any person convicted of stealing same is made liable to under the preceding section. 1 J.
Killing or taking Pigeons.—Whosoever shall unlawfully and wilfully kill, wound, or take any housedove or pigeon under such circum-	s. 23.	Shall forfeit and pay (over and above the value of the bird) any sum not exceeding £2 ;

(a) "*Not being the subject of Larceny at Common Law.*"—Pigeons are subjects of larceny if tame and reclaimed, though not confined.—*R.* v. *Cheafor,* 21 *L. J.*, 43 *M. C.* But see summary power to try, s. 23. All birds, &c., kept in a state of confinement, whose flesh is fit for human food, are the subjects of larceny ; but beasts and birds, though kept in a state of confinement, which are not fit for food by reason of the baseness of their nature, as dogs, cats, ferrets, &c., are not subjects of larceny. See "Stealing Poultry," under title above.

Offence, or cause of Complaint.	Statute.	Extent of Jurisdiction.
LARCENY (UNDER LARCENY ACT)— *continued.* stances as shall not amount to larceny at Common Law—	24 & 25 Vic. c. 96, s. 22.	and in default, &c., to be imprisoned, with or without H. L., not exceeding 2 months. (a) 1 J.
Fish.—Whosoever shall unlawfully and wilfully take or destroy any fish in any water which shall run through or be in any land adjoining or belonging to the dwelling-house of any person being the owner of such water or having a right of fishery therein.	s. 24.	Indictable misdemeanour.
Whosoever shall unlawfully and wilfully take or destroy, or attempt to take or destroy any fish in any water, not being such as hereinbefore mentioned, but which shall be private property, or in which there shall be any private right of fishery—	,,	Shall forfeit and pay over and above the value of the fish taken or destroyed (if any) a sum not exceeding £5; and in default, &c., to be imprisoned, with or without H. L., not exceeding 2 months, if the amount does not exceed £5. 1 J.
Provision as to Anglers.—Provided that nothing hereinbefore contained shall extend to any person angling between the beginning of the last hour before sunrise and the expiration of the first hour after sunset.	,,	—
But whosoever shall, by angling between the beginning of the last hour before sunrise and the expiration of the first hour after sunset, unlawfully and wilfully take or destroy, or attempt to take or destroy any fish in any such water as first mentioned—	,,	Shall forfeit and pay a sum not exceeding £5; and in default, &c., to be imprisoned, with or without H. L., not exceeding 2 months. 1 J.
And if in any such water as last mentioned—	,,	Shall forfeit and pay any sum not exceeding £2; in default, &c., imprisonment, with or without H. L., not exceeding 1 month, by scale. 1 J.

(a) But the amount being less than £5, the imprisonment is to be regulated by the scale.—36 & 37 Vic. c. 82.

Offence, or cause of Complaint.	Statute.	Extent of Jurisdiction.
LARCENY (UNDER LARCENY ACT)— *continued*. *Provision as to Boundaries of Parishes, &c.*—Where same happen to be in or by the side of any such water, as in this section before mentioned, it shall be sufficient to prove that the offence was committed either in the parish named in information, &c., or in any adjoining parish.	24 & 25 Vic. c. 96, s. 24.	
The tackle of persons found fishing against the provisions of this Act may be seized; and if seized or given up, to be exempt from penalty for angling.	s. 25.	
Trees, Shrubs, &c.—Whosoever shall steal, or shall cut, break, root up, or otherwise destroy or damage with intent to steal, the whole or any part of any tree, sapling, or shrub, or any underwood wheresoever growing, the stealing or injury done being to the amount of 1*s.* at the least—	s. 33.	Shall forfeit and pay (over and above the value of articles stolen or injury done) a sum not exceeding £5; and in default, &c., to be imprisoned, with or without H. L., not exceeding 2 months, if the amount does not exceed £5. 1 J.
Second Offence.—Whosoever, having been convicted of any such offence either against this or any former Act of Parliament, shall afterwards commit any of the said offences in this section before mentioned—	,,	To be imprisoned, with H. L., for not exceeding 12 months. 1 J.
Third Offence, ...	,,	Felony triable by indictment; to be punished as in the case of simple larceny.
Fence, &c.—Whosoever shall steal, or shall cut, break, or throw down with intent to steal, any part of any live or dead fence, or any stile or gate, or any part thereof respectively—	s. 34.	Shall forfeit and pay (over and above the value of the articles stolen or the amount of the injury done) any sum not exceeding £5; and in default, &c.,

Offence, or cause of Complaint.	Statute.	Extent of Jurisdiction.
LARCENY (UNDER LARCENY ACT)— *continued.*	24 & 25 Vic. c. 96, s. 34.	to be imprisoned, with or without H. L., not exceeding 2 months, if the amount does not exceed £5. 1 J.
Second Offence.—And whosoever, having been convicted of any such offence either against this or any former Act of Parliament, shall afterwards commit any of the said offences in this section before mentioned—	,,	To be imprisoned, and kept to H. L., not exceeding 12 months. 1 J.
Stolen Wood, &c., in possession.—If the whole or any part of any tree, sapling, or shrub, or any underwood, or any part of any live or dead fence, or any post, pale, wire, rail, stile, or gate, or any part thereof (being of the value of 1s. at least), shall be found in possession of any person or on his premises with his knowledge; and, being taken or summoned before a Justice of the Peace, he shall not be able to satisfy the Justice that he came lawfully by the same—	s. 35.	Shall forfeit and pay (over and above the value of the articles so found) a sum not exceeding £2; and in default, &c., imprisonment not exceeding 2 months (but according to scale), with or without H. L. 1 J.
Stealing Fruit, Vegetables, &c., growing in Gardens, &c.—Whosoever shall steal, or shall destroy or damage with intent to steal, any plant, root, fruit, or vegetable production growing in any garden, orchard, pleasure-ground, nursery-ground, hothouse, greenhouse, or conservatory—	s. 36.	At the discretion of the Justices, either imprisonment, with or without H. L., for any term not exceeding 6 months; or else shall forfeit and pay (over and above the value of the articles stolen or injury done) a sum not exceeding £20. 1 J.
Second Offence.—Whosoever, having been convicted of any such offence, either against this or any former Act of Parliament, shall afterwards commit any of the said offences in this section before mentioned—	,,	Felony; to be punished same as in cases of simple larceny.

Offence, or cause of Complaint.	Statute.	Extent of Jurisdiction.
LARCENY (UNDER LARCENY ACT)—*continued.* *Stealing Vegetables, &c., not growing in Gardens.*—Whosoever shall steal, or shall destroy or damage with intent to steal, any cultivated root or plant used for the food of man or beast, or for medicine, or for distilling, or for dyeing, or for or in the course of any manufacture, and growing in any land open or enclosed, not being a garden, orchard, pleasure-ground, or nursery-ground—	24 & 25 Vic. c. 96, s. 37.	Imprisonment, with or without H. L., not exceeding 1 month; or else shall forfeit and pay (over and above the value of the articles stolen or injury done) a sum not exceeding 20s., with costs (if ordered); in default, &c., imprisonment, where under £5, by scale, with or without H. L. 1 J.
Second Offence.—Whosoever, having been convicted of any such offence, either against this or any former Act of Parliament, shall afterwards commit any of the said offences in this section before mentioned—	,,	Imprisonment, with H.L., not exceeding 6 months. 1 J.
Shipwrecked Goods.—If any goods, merchandize, or articles of any kind, belonging to any ship or vessel in distress, or wrecked, &c., shall be found in the possession of any person, or on his premises with his knowledge, and not being able to satisfy the Justices that he came lawfully by the same.	s. 65.	At the discretion of the Justices, either imprisonment, with or without H. L., for any term not exceeding 6 months; or else shall forfeit and pay (over and above the value of the goods, &c.) a sum not exceeding £20. The goods to be delivered to, or for the use of rightful owner. 1 J.
If any person offer or expose for sale any goods, &c., so unlawfully taken or suspected so to have been taken from any such ship in distress, &c., the person to whom same offered or any officer of Customs or Excise or peace officer, may lawfully seize same, and carry same, or give notice of such seizure to some Justice of the Peace; and if the person who shall have offered or exposed same for sale, being summoned, shall	s. 66.	Justices to order goods to be forthwith delivered over to or for the use of the rightful owner, upon payment of a reasonable reward (to be ascertained by the Justices) to the person who seized same; and the offender, at the discretion of the Justices, to be imprisoned, with or without H. L.,

Offence, or cause of Complaint.	Statute.	Extent of Jurisdiction.
LARCENY (UNDER LARCENY ACT)— *continued.* not appear and satisfy the Justice that he came lawfully by same.	24 & 25 Vic. c. 96, s. 66.	for any term not exceeding 6 months, or to pay (over and above the value of the goods) a sum not exceeding £20. 1 J.
Receivers.—Where the stealing or taking of any property whatsoever is by this Act punishable on summary conviction, either for every offence or for the first and second offence only, any person who shall receive any such property, knowing the same to be unlawfully come by—	s. 97.	Shall be liable for every first, second, or subsequent offence of receiving, to the same forfeiture and punishment to which a person guilty of a first, second, or subsequent offence of stealing or taking such property is by this Act made liable. 1 J.
Abettors.—Whosoever shall aid, abet, counsel or procure the commission of any offence which is by this Act punishable on summary conviction, either for every time of its commission, or for the first and second time only, or for the first time only—	s. 99.	Shall be liable for every first, second, or subsequent offence of aiding, abetting, counselling, or procuring, to the same forfeiture and punishment to which a person guilty of a first, second, or subsequent offence as a principal offender is by this Act made liable.
Apprehending Offenders. — Persons found offending (except for offences of angling in the daytime), may be apprehended without warrant by any person.	s. 103.	—
On information on oath, Justice may grant search-warrant for stolen property.	,,	
Person to whom stolen property offered, if he suspect, &c., is required to detain offender.	,,	

Offence, or cause of Complaint.	Statute.	Extent of Jurisdiction.
LARCENY—*continued.*		
LARCENY UNDER 25 & 26 Vic. c. 50. (*a*) *Trees, Shrubs, Fruit, &c., growing*— Any person who shall steal, cut, break, root-up, or destroy or damage, with intent to steal, the whole or any part of any growing tree, sapling, shrub, or underwood, or any growing fruit or vegetable production, or any growing or cultivated root or plant (the value or amount of injury not exceeding £5)—	25 & 26 Vic. c. 50, s. 4. (36 & 37 Vic. c. 82.)	Shall pay to party aggrieved the value of the property stolen or amount of injury done, and shall also be liable to a fine not exceeding £5, *or* to be imprisoned any period not exceeding 3 months. 1 J. (Where sum does not exceed £5, imprisonment to be by scale.)
The like, severed from the soil ; or any *turf* or *peat* manufactured or partly manufactured for fuel (the value of articles stolen or of injury done not exceeding 40*s.*)—	25 & 26 Vic. c. 50, s. 5.	Shall pay to party aggrieved the value of the property stolen or amount of injury done, and also be liable to a fine not exceeding £5, *or* to be imprisoned for not exceeding 3 months. 1 J. (Where sum does not exceed £5, imprisonment to be by scale.)
Sheep, &c.—On information on oath that there is reasonable cause to suspect that the carcase of any sheep or lamb, or the skin, fleece, or any part, &c., has been stolen, or unlawfully taken, and is to be found in any house or other place—		Justice empowered to issue warrant to search such house or place for such articles of property. 1 J.
The person in whose possession or on whose premises any of said articles of property shall be found under such search-warrant (or by Constabulary in discharge of their duty, &c.), and who shall not satisfy the Justice, before whom he shall be brought, that he came lawfully by the same, or that same was on his premises without his knowledge or consent—	”	May be committed until Petty Sessions, unless he enter into recognizance to appear ; and failing to account to Justices' satisfaction, shall at discretion of Justices, be imprisoned not exceeding 3 months, or be liable to a fine not exceeding £5. 1 J.

(*a*) Convictions under this Act need not be returned to Quarter Sessions, and from convictions will be subject to the provisions of the Petty Sessions Act.

Offence, or cause of Complaint.	Statute.	Extent of Jurisdiction.
LARCENY (UNDER 25 & 26 Vic. c. 50) —continued.		
Workmen making away with goods, &c.—Artificer, workman, journeyman, apprentice, servant, or other person who shall unlawfully dispose of, or retain in his possession, without the consent of the person by whom he shall be hired, retained, or employed, any goods, wares, work, or materials committed to his care or charge (value not exceeding £5)—	25 & 26 Vic. c. 50, s. 7.	Shall pay to party aggrieved such compensation as the Justices think reasonable, and shall also be liable to a fine not exceeding 40s., *or* to be imprisoned not exceeding 1 month. 1 J.
Stealing Poultry.—Any person who shall steal, or injure with intent to steal, any turkey, goose, or other poultry (value of such poultry so stolen or injured not exceeding 5s.).	s. 8.	Fine not exceeding 20s., or to be imprisoned not exceeding 14 days. 1 J.
For other offences, see Indictable Offences Index, title "Larceny." Libels, see Indictable Offences Index.		
LIBELS : See Indictable Offences Index.		
LICENSING (LIQUOR) ACTS: Act under which Quarter Sessions grant certificates for licences.	3 & 4 Wm. iv. c. 68.	
Amends preceding as to penalties, powers of Justices, constables, &c.	6 & 7 Wm. iv. c. 38.	
As to spirit grocers, . . .	8 & 9 Vic. c. 64.	

Offence, or cause of Complaint.	Statute.	Extent of Jurisdiction.
LICENSING (LIQUOR) ACTS—*continued.* Act to amend the Laws for better prevention of the Sale of Spirits by Unlicensed Persons, and Suppression of Illicit Distillation in Ireland ; and amongst other things requires that notice shall be given Constabulary officer of intended application for licence, and that traders before renewing Excise licence shall produce certificate from 2 Justices in Petty Sessions as to character, &c.	17 & 18 Vic. c. 89.	—
Act to amend last preceding, giving right of appeal where Justices refuse certificate.	18 & 19 Vic. c. 62.	—
Act to further amend, and repealing sec. 7, 3 & 4 Wm. iv. c. 68, by which bonds with sureties were required.	18 & 19 Vic. c. 103.	—
Act for Transfer of Public House Licences.	18 & 19 Vic. c. 114.	—
Act to amend 18 & 19 Vic. c. 62, as to appeals from informal order of Justices refusing annual certificate of character, &c.	23 & 24 Vic. c. 35.	—
Refreshment Houses and Wine Licence Act, 1860. (a)	23 & 24 Vic. c. 107.	—
The Beer Houses (Ireland) Act, 1864, under which Justices grant certificates for licence in Petty Sessions annually.	27 & 28 Vic. c. 35.	—
Act to amend last preceding, . .	34 & 35 Vic. c. 111.	—
The Licensing Acts, 1872–1874, .	35 & 36 Vic. c. 94, and 37 & 38 Vic. c. 69.	—

(a) Magistrate's certificate does not seem to be requisite in order to sell in refreshment house. See proviso to sec. 77, Licensing Act, 1872.

Offence, or cause of Complaint.	Statute.	Extent of Jurisdiction.
LICENSING (LIQUOR) ACTS— ILLICIT SALES—*continued.* ILLICIT SALES. Any person selling or exposing for sale by retail any intoxicating liquor which he is not licensed to sell by retail, or selling or exposing for sale any intoxicating liquor at any place where he is not authorized by his licence to sell the same, shall be subject to the following penalties :—(*b*) *Proof.*—As to what will be proof of a sale or consumption, see sec. 62.	35 & 36 Vic. c. 94, s. 3.	*First Offence.*—Penalty not exceeding £50 ; in default of payment and of distress, imprisonment by *scale* (*a*), in Act, s. 51, *or* imprisonment, with or without H. L., not exceeding 1 month. Where the penalty imposed does not exceed £5, may be imprisoned in default of payment, for not exceeding 2 months, with or without H. L., under Small Penalties Act, 37 & 38 Vic. c. 69. 2 J. or 1 Stip. (*c*)

(*a*) *Scale of Imprisonment.*—In many cases under above Act, 35 & 36 Vic. c. 94, the Justices have a discretionary power either to impose a money penalty *or* to imprison without giving the option of paying ; but where they name a penal sum, *exceeding* £5, to be levied by distress, in that case, the imprisonment in default may be regulated by the scale given at Section 51 of that Act. But where the penalty *does not exceed* £5, in default of payment the defendant may, without distress warrant, be imprisoned for not exceeding two months, under the Small Penalties Act, 36 & 37 Vic. c. 82. And this latter is applicable to the Licensing Acts of 1872 and 1874. Where the Towns Improvement Act in force, see sec. 30, 37 & 38 Vic. c. 69, and note thereon, *Appendix.*

Mitigation.—See section 20, 35 & 36 Vic. c. 94. Where wholesale beer dealer is convicted, it would appear that the lowest penalty should be £5, that being the minimum authorized by the Excise Act, 26 & 27 Vic. c. 33, s. 3. See title " Excise," *Wholesale Beer Dealers ;* and see also as to *Beer-houses* under 27 & 28 Vic. c. 35, s. 10, where the mitigation is not to be less than one-fourth and the cause of mitigation to be stated.

(*b*) Where the proprietor of a licensed house sells contrary to the licence in any of the respects specified in this section, the prosecution should be under this section, and not for selling without licence under the Excise Acts.—So decided in Q. B. (Ir.), Nov., 1877.

(*c*) *As to the power of a Resident Magistrate alone to hear cases under the Licensing Act.*—The Law Adviser has given the following opinion, No. 10,250, 11th July, 1879 :—" I am of opinion that a Resident Magistrate alone has no power to hear any cases under the Licensing Act of 1872, except cases where offence charged is that of being found drunk on a highway, or public place, or licensed premises."

Then, of course, if the Resident Magistrate finds by his commission that he is not

Offence, or cause of Complaint.	Statute.	Extent of Jurisdiction.
LICENSING (LIQUOR) ACTS— ILLICIT SALES—*continued.* For second or subsequent offences by holder of a licence, the licence is by the Act forfeited ; and on conviction, under the section, the Court, if it thinks fit, may declare any intoxicating liquor found in possession of any such person as last aforesaid, and the vessels containing the same, to be forfeited.	35 & 36 Vic. c. 94, s. 3.	*Second Offence.*—Penalty not exceeding £100 ; in default of payment and of distress, imprisonment by *scale* in Act, s. 51, *or* imprisonment, with or without H. L., not exceeding 3 months. Where penalty is under £5, may be imprisoned, in default of payment, by *scale* of Small Penalties Act, 37 & 38 Vic. c. 69. **2 J. or 1 Stip.** And may be disqualified to hold a licence for not exceeding 5 years ; and if holder of licence it is forfeited.
Exemption as to heirs and executors of licensed person deceased, sec. 3. As to liability of several occupiers of unlicensed premises privy to sale, &c., see sec. 4.		*Third and any subsequent offence.*—Penalty not exceeding £100 ; in default of payment and of distress, imprisonment by *scale* in Act, s. 51 ; *or* imprisonment, with or without H. L., not exceeding 6 months. Where the penalty is under £5,

the "Stipendiary" Magistrate spoken of in sec. 51, sub-sec. 1, Licensing Act of 1872, he should not act alone. There are "Stipendiary" Magistrates *specially appointed under special Acts,* as in Dublin and other places, quite distinct from Resident or ordinary Stipendiary Magistrates ; still the ordinary "Stipendiary" would seem to be pointed out by the section quoted:—He is a "Stipendiary Magistrate," but should the reading be a "Stipendiary Magistrate empowered by law to do alone *any* act authorized to be done by more than one Justice," &c., he does seem to be in many instances so empowered, viz. :—The Crimes Act, 34 & 35 Vic. c. 112, Peddlers Act, 1871 ; and, lastly Peace Preservation (Ireland) Act, 1881, wherein, however, he now begins to be called a "Resident" Magistrate. And under the "Lodgers' Act," 34 & 35 Vic. c. 79 (for which see "Lodgers"), where there is a Stipendiary Magistrate in the place other Justices are not to meddle with the case. "The Criminal Law and Procedure (Ireland) Act, 1887," more clearly defines Resident Magistrate, for its purposes.

Offence, or cause of Complaint.	Statute.	Extent of Jurisdiction.
LICENSING (LIQUOR) ACTS— Illicit Sales—*continued.*		may be imprisoned, in default of payment, by *scale* of Small Penalties Act, 37 & 38 Vic. c. 69. And Court may order that he be disqualified for a term of years, or for ever, from holding licence; and if the holder of a licence it is forfeited. 2 J. or 1 Stip.
Drinking on premises contrary to Licence.—If the purchaser of intoxicating liquor from a person *not licensed to sell same to be drank on the premises* drinks such liquor on the premises where sold, or on highway adjoining or near such premises, the seller shall, if it appear that the drinking was with his privity or consent, be subject, &c.	35 & 36 Vic. c. 94, s. 5.	*First Offence.*—Penalty not exceeding £10; in default of payment and of distress, imprisonment by *scale* in Act, s. 51. If penalty imposed be not exceeding £5, the imprisonment, in default of payment, to be by Small Penalties *Scale* (37 & 38 Vic. c. 69). *Second and any subsequent Offence.*—Penalty not exceeding £20, enforced according to the *scale* as the preceding. 2 J. or 1 Stip. And Court may direct convictions under the section to be recorded on licence.
Evasion of Law as to Drinking on Premises contrary to Licence.— Where taken elsewhere, by privity and consent of seller, to be sold for his benefit— (As to what is the necessary proof, see section.)	s. 6.	Punishable as under preceding sec. 5. 2 J. or 1 Stip. And Court may direct convictions to be recorded on licence.

R

Offence, or cause of Complaint.	Statute.	Extent of Jurisdiction.
LICENSING (LIQUOR) ACTS— ILLICIT SALES—*continued.* *Sales to Children.*—Every holder of a licence who sells or allows any person to sell, *to be consumed on the premises, any description of Spirits* to any person apparently under the age of 16 years—	35 & 36 Vic. c. 94, s. 7.	*First Offence.*— Penalty not exceeding 20s.; in default of payment imprisonment by Small Penalties *Scale*, not exceeding 14 days. *Second and any subsequent Offence.*—Penalty not exceeding 40s.; in default of payment imprisonment not exceeding 1 month, by Small Penalties *Scale.* 2 J. or 1 Stip.
"Act for the protection of children against the sale to them of intoxicating liquors."	49 & 50 Vic. c. 56.	
Every holder of a licence who knowingly sells, or allows any person to sell any description of intoxicating liquors to any person under the age of 13 years for consumption on the premises by any person under such age— Act to be construed as one Act with the Licensing Acts, 1872–1874.	s. 1.	enalty not exceeding 20s. for *first offence.* Penalty not exceeding 40s. for second and any subsequent offence; in default, &c., imprisonment by Small Penalties *Scale.* 2 J. or 1 R.M.
Standard Measure.—Every person shall sell all intoxicating liquor which is sold by retail and not in cask or bottle, and is not sold in a quantity less than half a pint, in measures marked by the imperial standards; and every person who acts, or suffers any person under his control or in his employment to act in contravention of this section—	35 & 36 Vic. c. 94, s. 8.	*First Offence.*—Penalty not exceeding £10; any subsequent offence—not exceeding £20, by distress; in default, &c., imprisonment by *scale* n Act. But penalty not exceeding £5, enforced by Small Penalties *Scale.* 2 J. or 1 Stip.

Offence, or cause of Complaint.	Statute.	Extent of Jurisdiction.
LICENSING (LIQUOR) ACTS—		
ILLICIT SALES—*continued.*		
Internal Communications between Licensed and other Premises. (a) —Every person who makes, uses, or allows to be, &c., any internal communication between any licensed premises and any unlicensed premises which are used for public entertainment or resort, or as a refreshment house—(b)	35 & 36 Vic. c. 94, s. 9.	Penalty not exceeding £10 for every day during which communication remains open, recoverable as above by *scale.* 2 J. or 1 Stip. If holder of a licence it is forfeited by the Act on conviction.
Illicit Storing of Liquor.—If any licensed person has in his possession on the premises in respect of which the licence is granted any description of intoxicating liquor *which he is not authorized to sell,* unless he shall account for the possession of same to the satisfaction of the Court by which he is tried—	s. 10.	He shall forfeit such liquor and the vessels containing same, and shall be liable to a penalty not exceeding for *first offence* £10, and for any *subsequent offence,* not exceeding £20, recoverable as above by *scale.* 2 J. or 1 Stip.
Licensed Show Boards.—Every licensed person shall cause to be, and shall keep painted or fixed on his licensed premises, in a conspicuous place as the Licensing Justices may direct, his name, and the word "licensed," and for what licence granted, and whether drink is to be *consumed on or off the premises, &c.* Acting in contravention—	35 & 36 Vic. c. 94, s. 11. (37 & 38 Vic. c. 69, s. 26.)	*First Offence.*—Penalty not exceeding £10; *second* and any subsequent offence—not exceeding £20, recoverable as above by *scale.* 2 J. or 1 Stip.

(a) Where conviction takes place under this section and the licence in consequence becomes forfeited, see proviso, sec. 13, 37 & 38 Vic. c. 69.

(b) An internal communication with an ordinary dwelling-house or shop for sale of goods would not seem to come within this section.

See note, page 249, as to "Spirit Grocers," &c.

Offence, or cause of Complaint.	Statute.	Extent of Jurisdiction.
LICENSING (LIQUOR) ACTS— OFFENCES AGAINST PUBLIC ORDER. (a) *Drunkenness.*—Every person found drunk in any highway or other public place, whether a building or not, or on any licensed premises—(b) *Detaining Drunkards* (c)—Person so drunk as to be incapable of taking care of himself, may be detained by constable until he can, with safety to himself, be discharged; but if so detained he shall be duly summoned and be liable to the penalty (37 & 38 Vic. c. 69, s. 25).	35 & 36 Vic. c. 94, s. 12.	*First Offence.*—Penalty not exceeding 10s.; in default of payment imprisonment by Small Penalties *Scale,* not exceeding 1 week, with or without H. L. *Second* conviction within 12 months, penalty not exceeding 20s.; in default of payment imprisonment by Small Penalties *Scale,* not exceeding 14 days, with or without H. L. *Third or subsequent conviction* within such period of 12 months, penalty not exceeding 40s.; in default of payment imprisonment by Small Penalties *Scale,* not exceeding 1 calendar month, with or without H. L. 1 J.

(a) Sec. 12.—Wherever the Towns Improvement Act is in force, the penalties under this section 12 are to be enforced as directed by that Act.—See sec. 30, 37 & 38 Vic. c. 69, and note thereon, *Appendix.*

(b) *Licensed person found drunk on his own licensed premises after the premises are closed.*—The term "licensed premises," as used in the Licensing Act, 1872, s. 12, means licensed premises while they are open to the public for the purposes of the licence; consequently a licensed person who is found drunk on licensed premises in his own occupation after licensed hours, and when the premises are closed to the public, is not liable to a penalty under sec. 12.—*Lester* v. *Torrens, Q. B. D., L. R.,* 1877 *(E.).*

Nor can the licensed person when himself found drunk on licensed premises be convicted under section 13 for *permitting* drunkenness.

(c) *Drunk, and Drunk and Incapable.*—Under the 6 & 7 Wm. iv. c. 38, s. 12, persons found drunk on public thoroughfares may be apprehended and detained until brought before a Justice. Now, under 37 & 38 Vic. c. 69, s. 25, if the person be drunk and incapable, he can be detained until he can be safely discharged. The ——— stages of drunkenness appear to be recognized and punishable; and as the mode ————dure in the greater or advanced stage of the offence is to discharge and ⟶ the offender, in the other case, if detention be not necessary, it may be the able car——— ⟶ the offender's name and summon him also.

———This will include such buildings as are dedicated

Offence, or cause of Complaint.	Statute.	Extent of Jurisdiction.
LICENSING (LIQUOR) ACTS— OFFENCES AGAINST PUBLIC ORDER— *continued.* *Drunk and Disorderly, or Drunk in charge of Horse, Carriage, &c.*— Every person who in any highway or other public place, whether a building or not, is guilty while drunk of riotous or disorderly behaviour, or who is drunk while in charge on any highway or other public place of any carriage, horse, cattle or steam-engine, or who is drunk when in possession of any loaded fire-arms, may be apprehended, and shall be liable to a penalty, &c.—	35 & 36 Vic. c. 94, s. 12.	Penalty not exceeding 40s.; in default of payment imprisonment not exceeding (by Small Penalties *Scale*) 1 calendar month, with or without H. L.; or, in the discretion of the Court, imprisonment, with or without H. L., not exceeding 1 month. 2 J. or 1 Stip.
Trader permitting Drunkenness, &c. —If any licensed person permits drunkenness, or any violent, quarrelsome, or riotous conduct to take place on his premises, *or* sells intoxicating liquor to any drunken person—	s. 13.	*First Offence.*—Penalty not exceeding £10. *Second* and any subsequent offence—Penalty not exceeding £20. In default of payment or of distress, imprisonment by *scale* in Act, s. 51; or where penalty

to the public, or to which, without distinction, there is right of access, as Courts of Justice, Public Market-houses or Places, Museums, &c.

Drunk in Possession of Loaded Firearms.—It would appear by the words of the section that such persons may be apprehended wherever they are, whether public thoroughfare or private place.

Found Drunk on Licensed Premises.—Section 18 gives the trader power to expel the drunken person, and constables are required to do so on being requested by the trader or his servant, &c. If then drunk and incapable on the highway, he may be detained by constable, under the 37 & 38 Vic. c. 69, s. 25, until fit to be discharged as therein.

Sales to Drunken Persons.—Intoxicating liquor is not to be *sold* to a drunken person under any circumstances, either to consume on the premises or to take away.

Permitting Drunkenness to take place.—It seems hard to hold the trader liable for permitting these things to take place. Quarrelsome and riotous conduct may take place in a moment, and a state of drunkenness also unexpectedly come on. The section says he is then not to *sell* drink to a drunken person, nor should it at all be supplied to him to be consumed there; but the trader should also immediately exercise the power of expulsion given him in section 18, with respect to all such persons whose presence would subject him to a penalty.

Brothel.—Keeping a common bawdy house is an indictable offence. Under 3 & 4 Wm. iv. c. 68, s. 8, retailers convicted of indictable offences are liable to have their licences annulled.

Offence, or cause of Complaint.	Statute.	Extent of Jurisdiction.
LICENSING (LIQUOR) ACTS— OFFENCES AGAINST PUBLIC ORDER— *continued*.	35 & 36 Vic. c. 94, s. 13.	named does not exceed £5, in default of payment imprisonment not exceeding 2 months, by Small Penalties *Scale*. 2 J. or 1 Stip. Court may direct convictions under Section to be recorded on licence.
Keeping Disorderly House.—If any licensed person knowingly permits his premises to be the habitual resort of, or place of meeting of, reputed prostitutes, whether the object of their so resorting or meeting is, or is not, prostitution, he shall, if he allow them to remain longer than is necessary for the purpose of obtaining reasonable refreshment, be liable—	s. 14.	*First Offence.*—Penalty not exceeding £10. *Second* and any subsequent offence, not exceeding £20. To be enforced as last preceding. 2 J. or 1 Stip. Court may direct convictions under section to be recorded on licence.
Brothel.—If any licensed person is convicted of permitting his premises to be a brothel, he shall be liable to—	s. 15.	Penalty not exceeding £20, recovered by *scale*, sec. 51; where not exceeding £5, under Small Penalties Act. He shall forfeit licence, and be for ever disqualified from holding one. 2 J. or 1 Stip.
Harbouring Constables.—If any licensed person *knowingly* harbours or *knowingly* suffers to remain on his premises, any constable during any part of the time appointed for such constable being on duty, unless for the purpose of keeping or restoring order, or in execution of his duty; *or* supplies any liquor or refreshment, whether by way of gift or sale, to any constable on duty, unless by authority of some superior officer of such constable; *or* bribes or attempts to bribe any constable—	s. 16.	*First Offence.*—Penalty not exceeding £10. *Second* or any subsequent offence, not exceeding £20; recovered as last preceding penalties. Court may direct convictions to be recorded on licence. 2 J. or 1 Stip.

Offence, or cause of Complaint.	Statute.	Extent of Jurisdiction.
LICENSING (LIQUOR) ACTS— OFFENCES AGAINST PUBLIC ORDER— *continued.* *Gaming.*—If any licensed person suffers any gaming, or any unlawful game to be carried on on his premises; or opens, keeps, or uses, or suffers his house to be opened, kept, or used, in contravention of the Act of 16 & 17 Vic. c. 119—	35 & 36 Vic. c. 94, s. 17.	*First Offence.*—Penalty not exceeding £10. *Second* and any subsequent offence, not exceeding £20. In default of payment and distress, imprisonment by *scale*, sec. 51. Where the penalty named does not exceed £5, in default of payment imprisonment not exceeding 2 months by Small Penalties *Scale.* 2 J. or 1 Stip. Court may direct convictions to be recorded on licence.
Power to exclude Drunkards, &c.— Licensed person may refuse to admit to, and may turn out of licensed premises, drunken, violent, quarrelsome, or disorderly persons, and any person whose presence on his premises would subject him to a penalty under this Act—	s. 18.	
Any such person who upon being requested in pursuance of this section, by such licensed person, his agent, or servant, or any constable, to quit such premises, refuses or fails so to do, shall be liable to, &c.— And requisite force may be used to expel such person.	,,	Penalty not exceeding £5; in default of payment, imprisonment, with or without H. L., not exceeding 2 months by Small Penalties *Scale.* 2 J. or 1 Stip.
REPEATED CONVICTIONS. (*a*) As to forfeiture of licence on repeated convictions, see—	s. 30.	

(*a*) And as to disqualifications, see also 3 & 4 Wm. iv. c. 68, s. 13; and 6 & 7 Wm. iv. c. 38, ss. 2, 3.

Recorded Convictions.—Where *two recorded* convictions are followed by a conviction under the Act, the licence is forfeited. (See note on sec. 30 of principal Act, *Appendix.*)

Offence, or cause of Complaint.	Statute.	Extent of Jurisdiction.
LICENSING (LIQUOR) ACTS— REPEATED CONVICTIONS—*continued.* *Proviso* as to liability for pecuniary penalties, or to imprisonment, although person and premises disqualified.	35 & 36 Vic. c. 94, s. 30.	
As to disqualification of premises on conviction of persons licensed after passing of this Act—	s. 31.	—
Proviso as to notice to owners of premises, &c.	,,	—
Convictions after five years not to increase penalties.	s. 32.	—
Omission to record convictions not to exempt person or premises from penalties or consequences, &c.	s. 33.	—
Defacing records of conviction.—If any person defaces or obliterates, or attempts so to do, any record of a conviction on his licence—	s. 34.	Penalty not exceed £5 ; in default of p ment, imprisonm not exceeding 2 mon by Small Pena Scale.　2 J. or 1 S
Recording Convictions, &c.—As to mode of recording convictions and the discretionary power of the Court in reference to same under the Acts of 1872 and 1874, see—	37 & 38 Vic. c. 69, s. 21.	—
Adulteration.—Recording conviction for—	s. 22.	—
SIX-DAY LICENCES AND EARLY-CLOSING LICENCES. Provisions as to six-day licences, to be closed on Sundays, see—	35 & 36 Vic. c. 94, s. 49.	—
Early-closing licences,　.　.　.	37 & 38 Vic. c. 69, s. 2.	—
Remission of duty in respect to six-day and early-closing licence—	s. 3.	—

Offence, or cause of Complaint.	Statute.	Extent of Jurisdiction.
LICENSING (LIQUOR) ACTS— SPIRIT GROCERS. (a) No renewal of licence to be granted to "Spirit Grocers" without certificate of Justices.	35 & 36 Vic. c. 94, s. 82.	—
If any purchaser of any intoxicating liquor from a spirit grocer drinks same on premises where sold, or on any highway adjoining or near, such spirit grocer shall, if it appear that such drinking was with his privity or consent, be liable to, &c.— (As to meaning of expression "premises where same is sold," see section.)	s. 83.	*First Offence.*—Penalty not exceeding £10. *Second* and any subsequent offence—Penalty not exceeding £20; recoverable by *scale.* 2 J. or 1 Stip. Court may direct convictions to be recorded on licence.
Spirit grocer by allowing liquor to be conveyed elsewhere to be sold for his profit, or to be there drank, &c. (see section), so as to evade conditions of his licence—	s. 84.	Like penalty, and Court may direct convictions to be recorded.
Internal communication.—Every person who makes or uses, or allows to be made or used any internal	s. 85.	Penalty not exceeding £10 a-day during every day communication re-

(a) Licence to sell intoxicating liquor off premises, Licensing Act, 1874 (37 & 38 Vic. c. 49, ss. 3, 9), where grocer's shop and drapery shop communicate. Grocer's shop shut after prohibited hours. The appellant, being licensed to sell by retail intoxicating liquors to be consumed off his premises, was charged with keeping open his premises for the sale of such liquors after 10 o'clock at night. He had two shops, a grocer's and a draper's shop, which formed part of his house, and both shops could be entered from the house at the back as well as by the customers' entrance. The grocery business was carried on in a shop which had an entrance for customers in another street. During the day there were means of going, and customers occasionally passed, from one shop to the other, but after 10 o'clock shutters or partitions were put up and all means of communication, except through the house, prevented. It was proved that the draper's shop was kept open till after 10 o'clock at night, but that before 10 o'clock the openings between the two shops were shut, and the grocer's shop left in darkness. The Justices held the charge proved and convicted the appellant :—*Held*, that the conviction was wrong, as there was no evidence that the house was open for the sale of liquors after 10 o'clock. *Brigden, Appellant; Hughes, Respondent, Q. B., Eng.; L. R.*, 1876. In this case *Mellor, J.*, said:—"The Justices, in order to convict, must be able to find that the house and premises in which intoxicating liquors were sold were not really, although apparently, closed ; that the closing was a sham, and that the premises were really kept open for people who wish to purchase intoxicating liquor."

Offence, or cause of Complaint.	Statute.	Extent of Jurisdiction.
LICENSING (LIQUOR) ACTS— SPIRIT GROCERS—*continued.* communication between the premises of any spirit grocer and any other premises which are used for public entertainment or resort, or as a refreshment house—	35 & 36 Vic. c. 94, s. 85.	mains open; recoverable by *scale*, and the licence is forfeited. 2 J. or 1 Stip.
Limitation of hours during which intoxicating liquor may be sold, to be same as before stated for other licensed retailers, and liable to same penalties.	s. 86.	—
Justices and constables, duly authorized as in section, may enter during prohibited hours, remove persons tippling, &c.; persons resisting or found drunk therein may be apprehended; and for neglecting or refusing to quit premises, resisting Justice, constables, &c. (a)— (And see also "Entry on Premises," 37 & 38 Vic. c. 69, s. 23.)	s. 87.	Penalty not exceeding 20s., nor less than 5s.; in default of payment forthwith, imprisonment not exceeding 1 week.
Provisions as to repeated convictions to apply to spirit grocers, &c., with exceptions as to the disqualification of premises.	s. 88.	—
OCCASIONAL LICENCES.* Occasional licences required for selling intoxicating liquors in booths, tents, or places within the limits of holding lawful and accustomed fairs and races; and persons selling without such shall be deemed to be selling without licence. (Proviso as to the annual licensed premises being situate within limits.)	37 & 38 Vic. c. 69, s. 4.	—
Extension of Time for Closing under occasional licence if so specified by consenting Justice.	37 & 38 Vic. c. 69, s. 5.	
As to liability for offences against public order, under occasional licence—	s. 6.	—

(a) This is a similar power to that given constables by 3 & 4 Wm. iv. c. 68, s. 15, to remove persons found tippling at the prohibited hours in ordinary public-houses.
* 1 J. P. may grant Occasional Licence.—26 & 27 Vic. c. 33, s. 20.

Offence, or cases of Complaint.	Statute.	Extent of Jurisdiction.
LICENSING (LIQUOR) ACTS— OCCASIONAL LICENCES—*continued.* *Theatres.*—Restrictions as to licences, under 5 & 6 Wm. iv. c. 39, s. 7, before and after performances.	37 & 38 Vic. c. 69, s. 7.	
Wholesale Beer Dealers.—Certificates required previously to grant of licence.	s. 8.	
Provisions of sec. 82 of the principal Act extended to transfers, &c.	s. 9.	
Notice required by 3 & 4 Wm. iv. c. 68, to be served on church-wardens, amended.	s. 10.	—
Exemption Order in respect of fairs, markets, and certain trades, and extension of closing hours.	s. 11.	
Holder of exemption order making default in affixing and keeping affixed on a conspicuous part of his premises notice intimating as therein, &c.—	,,	Penalty not exceeding £5; in default of payment, imprisonment not exceeding 2 months, by Small Penalties *Scale*. 2 J. or 1 Stip.
Person affixing on his premises any such notice, when he does not hold exemption order—	,,	Penalty not exceeding £10, recovered by *scale*. 2 J. or 1 Stip.
Times for granting annual certificates, ...	ss. 12–14.	—
Register of licences, . . .	ss. 15–17.	—
Payment of fees, &c., . . .	ss. 18–19.	—
Records of conviction, . . .	ss. 21–22.	—
REGULATIONS AS TO ENTRY BY CONSTABLES. Any constable may, for the purpose of preventing or detecting the violation of any of the provisions of the principal Act (35 & 36 Vic. c. 94), or this Act, which it is his duty to enforce, at all times enter on any licensed premises, and on any premises kept by a *spirit grocer*, and on any premises, in respect of which an occasional licence is in force.		

Offence, or cause of Complaint.	Statute.	Extent of Jurisdiction.
LICENSING (LIQUOR) ACTS— REGULATIONS AS TO ENTRY, &c.—*con.* *Refusing Admittance.* (a)—Every person who, by himself, or by any person in his employ, or acting by his direction, or with his consent, refuses or fails to admit any constable in the execution of his duty demanding to enter in pursuance of this section—	37 & 38 Vic. c. 69, s. 23.	*First Offence.*—Penalty not exceeding £5; in default of payment, imprisonment not exceeding 3 months. *Second* and every subsequent offence, not exceeding £10, recoverable by *scale* of imprisonment. 2 J. or 1 Stip. And Court may (sec. 21) direct conviction to be recorded on licence.
Search Warrant to enter Unlicensed Premises (b)—Any Justice may, on sworn information, grant warrant to enter any place within his jurisdiction, whether a building or not, where there is reasonable ground to believe that intoxicating liquor is sold, or exposed, or kept for sale by retail, and in which such liquor is not authorized to be sold by retail.	s. 24.	—
For duties of constable in execution of warrant, see section.	,,	—
Where constable has entered under warrant, and seized and removed liquor as authorized in section, any person found at the time on the premises, until the contrary is proved, shall be deemed to have	,,	Penalty not exceeding 40s.; in default of payment, imprisonment not exceeding 1 month. 2 J. or 1 Stip. And if the licensed per-

(a) *Refusing Admittance.*—"Every person," that is, every licensed person, &c. In this case the trader is responsible for the act or omission of his servants, that is, the *refusal* or the *failure* to admit. While for any assault on or resistance offered to the constable, the actual offender and offence can be dealt with in another way. The constable should remember that this power to act without warrant is limited to *licensed premises and spirit grocers, &c.*

(b) The powers given by this section for the detection and the prevention of sales in *unlicensed houses* are more full and effective than any hitherto conferred. The seller and the consumer are equally regarded as unlawfully *dealing in intoxicating liquor.* The seller is dealt with under sec. 3 of the "Principal Act." The warrant continues in force for a month, and may, during that time, be repeatedly executed; its force is not spent by having been executed. See also note on the section in Act.

Offence, or cause of Complaint.	Statute.	Extent of Jurisdiction.
LICENSING (LIQUOR) ACTS— REGULATIONS AS TO ENTRY, &C.—*con.* been on such premises for the purpose of illegally dealing in intoxicating liquor, and be liable to—	37 & 38 Vic. c. 69, s. 24.	son be convicted, Court may (sec. 21) direct conviction to be recorded on licence.
Any constable may demand the name and address of any person found on any premises on which he seizes or from which he removes liquor as aforesaid; and failing to give correct name and address, and satisfactorily to answer questions of constable as to same, may convey him before a Justice.	,,	—
Any person required by a constable under this section to give his name and address who fails to give same, or gives a false name and address, or gives false information with respect to such name and address—	,,	Penalty not exceeding £5; in default of payment, imprisonment not exceeding 2 months. 2 J. or 1 Stip.
CLOSING HOURS. (*a*) Any person who sells or exposes for sale, or opens or keeps open any premises for the sale of intoxicating liquors, at any other times than those limited by section 43 of 23 & 24 Vic., c. 107, as the same is amended by this section, or dur-	35 & 36 Vic. c. 94, s. 78.	*First Offence.* — Penalty not exceeding £10; and for any subsequent offence, penalty not exceeding £20; in default &c., imprisonment by *scale* in Act, section 51;

(*a*) *Closing Hours.*—The hours at which retailers may now *keep open* to retail, under 23 & 24 Vic. c. 107, s. 43, as amended by the present Act, 35 & 36 Vic. c. 94, s. 78, are as follows :—In cities or towns where the population exceeds 5000, on Sunday, Christmas Day, Good Friday, Public Fast or Thanksgiving Day, between 2 o'clock, P.M., and 9 o'clock, P.M.; and on other days, between 7 o'clock, A.M., and 11 o'clock, P.M. *In other places*—On Sunday, Christmas Day, Good Friday, Public Fast or Thanksgiving Day, between 2 o'clock, P.M., and 7 o'clock, P.M.; and on other days between 7 o'clock, A.M., and 10 o'clock, P.M. The alteration effected by the last Act being that, in the large towns, retailers should close at 9 P.M. on Sundays and holidays, leaving the week nights as before—11 o'clock. Elsewhere, the closing hours on Sundays and holiday nights will be 7 o'clock, and on the other week nights, 10 o'clock.

Sunday Closing Act.—41 & 42 Vic. c. 72, prohibits sales on Sundays—exceptions as to Dublin, Cork, Limerick, Waterford, Belfast, from 2 P.M. to 7 P.M. This Act will probably be made perpetual, and the places now excepted are likely to be included in its provisions.

Offence, or cause of Complaint.	Statute.	Extent of Jurisdiction.
LICENSING (LIQUOR) ACTS— CLOSING HOURS—*continued.* ing such times as aforesaid allows any intoxicating liquors to be consumed on such premises— *Exemption* as to *bonâ fide* travellers or as to lodgers, and at railway-stations to persons arriving or departing from station by railroad. (*a*)	35 & 36 Vic. c. 94, s. 78.	but where the penalty does not exceed £5, in default of payment, imprisonment not exceeding 2 months, by Small Penalties Scale. 2 J. or 1 Stip. And Court may direct convictions to be recorded on licence.
Proof as to what will be evidence of sale or consumption, see section.	s. 62.	
Persons found on Premises during closing hours.—If during any period during which any premises are required under the provisions of the principal Act to be closed, any person is found on such premises, he shall, unless he satisfies the Court that he was an inmate, servant, or lodger on such premises, or a *bonâ fide* traveller, or that otherwise his presence on such premises was not in contravention of the provisions of the principal Act with respect to the closing of licensed premises and premises kept by a spirit grocer—	37 & 38 Vic. c. 69, s. 27.	Penalty not exceeding 40s.; in default of payment, imprisonment not exceeding 1 month. 2 J. or 1 Stip.
Constable may demand name and address of person found on premises during closing hours, and failing to give evidence of same to the satisfaction of constable, may be taken before a Justice.	,,	
Any person required by a constable under this section to give his name and address who fails to give same, or gives a false name or address, or gives false evidence with respect to such name and address—	,,	Penalty not exceeding £5; in default of payment, imprisonment not exceeding 2 months. 2 J. or 1 Stip.

(*a*) *Privilege of Lodgers at an Inn,* and the guests of such lodgers. See note on above, section 78, in *Appendix.*

Offence, or cause of Complaint.	Statute.	Extent of Jurisdiction.
LICENSING (LIQUOR) ACTS— CLOSING HOURS—*continued.* *Traveller.*—Every person who, by falsely representing himself to be a traveller or a lodger, buys or obtains, or attempts to buy or obtain, at any premises any intoxicating liquor during the period during which such premises are closed in pursuance of the principal Act—	37 & 38 Vic. c. 69, s. 27.	Penalty not exceeding £5; in default of payment imprisonment not exceeding 2 months. 2 J. or 1 Stip.
Saving as to pretended Travellers.—Where Justices are satisfied that the defendant truly believed the purchaser to be a *bonâ fide* traveller, and took all reasonable precautions to ascertain the truth, Justices may dismiss the case. Where the purchaser falsely represented himself to be a *bonâ fide* traveller, Justices may direct him to be proceeded against under sec. 27. (*a*)	,,	—
Bonâ fide *Traveller defined.*—A person, for the purposes of this Act and the principal Act, shall not be deemed to be a *bonâ fide* traveller unless the place where he lodged during the preceding night is at least three miles distant by nearest public thoroughfare from where he demands to be supplied with liquor. (*b*)	,,	
Entertaining bonâ fide *Friends.* (*c*)— Licensed person not liable to pen-	s. 29.	

(*a*) *Pretended Travellers.*—Duty of precaution by trader. See note on sec. 28, *Appendix.*

(*b*) Bonâ fide *Traveller.*—But while it is a *sine qua non* that he shall have lodged three miles off the previous night, this negative language of the statute does not seem to imply that his having done so will of itself establish the incontrovertible fact that he is a *bonâ fide* traveller.

(*c*) *Entertaining Friends.*—The section protects the trader while entertaining his private friends. But does it protect the *bonâ fide* friends? We think it does. For the purposes mentioned it is an extension of the closing hours, and they consequently are not found there in "contravention of the provisions of the principal Act, with respect to the closing of licensed premises." See notes on this, sec. 29, *Appendix.*

Offence, or cause of Complaint.	Statute.	Extent of Jurisdicti
LICENSING (LIQUOR) ACTS— *continued.* alty for supplying liquors after hours to private friends, *bond fide* entertained by him, at his own expense.	37 & 38 Vic. c. 69, s. 29.	
Producing Licence. (a)—Every holder of a licence, excise licence, wholesale beer dealer's licence, or order of exemption, under this Act, failing, on being required by the Court hearing complaint or appeal, to produce same, although not required to do so by summons.—(And see sec. 64, 35 & 36 Vic. c. 94.)	s. 33.	Penalty not exc £10; in default imprisonment acc to *scale.* 2 J. or 1 And Court may (st direct conviction recorded on licenc
MITIGATION OF PENALTIES. Repeals 67 sec. of principal Act, and in lieu enacts, that where any person holding a licence, or excise licence, is convicted of any offence against the principal Act, or this Act, or any Act recited therein, the Court may not, except in the case of a first conviction, reduce the penalty to less than 20s., nor shall the penalty, whether of excise or police, be reduced in any case to less than the minimum authorized by any other Act.	s. 20.	—
Local Acts.—As to Jurisdiction of Justices under "Towns Improvement (Ireland) Act, 1854;" and where Act of 9 Geo. iv. c. 82, is in force; and as to the application of penalties in such place, see sec. and note thereon.	s. 30.	
Appeals.—Amendment of sec. 52 of principal Act, as to release from custody in case of appeal.		

(a) *Producing Licence.*—Now, by 37 & 38 Vic. c. 69, s. 33, the holder of shall, on being so required by the Court, produce and deliver up his licence, a penalty, and although the summons may not have stated that such produc required.

Offence, or cause of Complaint.	Statute.	Extent of Jurisdiction.
LICENSING (LIQUOR) ACTS— *continued.*		
DUBLIN METROPOLIS.		
Summons may issue under any intoxicating liquor Act, in Dublin Metropolis, without complaint on oath or in writing.	37 & 38 Vic. c. 69, s. 32.	
Liability in respect of distinct Licences.—Every holder of any excise licence along with any other licence or licences, and every holder of several licences, shall be subject to the provisions of the principal Act and this Act, in respect of each such licence.	s. 34.	—
Evidence of licences, orders, and convictions, &c.	ss. 35, 36.	—
Definitions, ...	s. 37.	
Repealing clause, ...	s. 38.	
See *Appendix,* where these Licensing Acts, 1872-1874, are given in full.		
Persons obtaining retail licence shall, within 6 days, enter name, residence, &c., with Clerk of the Peace. For default—(a)	3 & 4 Wm. iv. c. 68, ss. 10, 24.	Penalty £10, and not less than £2 10s.; in default, &c., imprisonment by scale. 2 J.
Riots.—Disobeying order of Justices to close in case of riot or tumult, &c. &c.—(b)	s. 21.	Penalty £2, and not less than 10s.; in default of payment, imprisonment by scale. 2 J.
Illegal assemblies.—Retailers shall not permit illegal assemblies in place of sale, &c., or suffer to be displayed flags, emblems, &c., except the usual business sign. For offending— (Not to apply to Freemasons or Friendly Brothers.)	6 & 7 Wm. iv. c. 38, s. 8.	Penalty £2, not less than 10s.; in default of payment, imprisonment by scale. 2 J. And Excise officer not to renew licence without a new certificate from Quarter Sessions.

(a) See further provisions, 37 & 38 Vic. c. 69, s. 15.
(b) So also refreshment-houses where wine is retailed, 23 & 24 Vic. c. 107, s. 30-32. See form of "Order"—*Appendix.*

S

Offence, or cause of Complaint.	Statute.	Extent of Jurisdiction.
LICENSING (LIQUOR) ACTS— *Dublin Metropolis—continued.* On information on oath, Justices (and constables duly authorized) may enter, &c., remove flags, take possession of books; and for opposing, resisting, &c., see—	6 & 7 Wm. iv. c. 38, s. 9.	
Witnesses.—Witness not obeying summons, or refusing to give evidence—(a)	3 & 4 Wm. iv. c. 68, s. 30.	Penalty £2, not less than 10s.; in default of payment, imprisonment not exceeding 1 month. 2 J.
Persons who are disqualified to be licensed, see—	s. 13; and 6 & 7 Wm. iv. c. 38, ss. 2, 3.	—
Offences which Disqualify.—Person convicted of misdemeanour, or offence of a higher nature, upon due notice to such person—	3 & 4 Wm. iv. c. 68, s. 8.	Justices in Quarter Sessions may annul licence.
Annual Certificate.—Justice's certificate of good conduct of retailer, and manner in which house conducted in past year, necessary to obtain renewal of licence. (b)	17 & 18 Vic. c. 89, s. 11. 37 & 38 Vic. c. 69, s. 14.	—

(a) *Witnesses.*—The Licensing Act, 1872, sec. 51, incorporates Petty Sessions Act, of which Act *see* sec. 13, as to compelling attendance of witnesses.

(b) *Justices' Annual Certificates of Renewal.*—Excise officer is not to grant renewal of licence without a certificate, signed by two or more Justices of the Peace, in Petty Sessions, for the district (in Dublin by a Divisional Justice), to the good character of such person, and to the peaceable and orderly manner in which his house has been conducted in the past year.—17 & 18 Vic. sec. 11.

Although the order of refusal to grant a renewal by Justices be not in the words of the Act, the order may be good. On the application for a *certiorari* to bring up order, made by the Dublin Justices and the Recorder, refusing to grant renewal of a spirit grocer's licence on the grounds that the order made by the Justices in the first instance was bad, being for "illicit trading, and keeping a watchman and keeping up a partition in the shop," holding that thereby illict trading had been carried on, the Recorder on appeal altered the Justices' order to the effect that the trader "had not conducted his house in a peaceable and orderly manner." For the trader it was contended that the Recorder had not power to so amend the original order. The Court held that although the Recorder could not affirm an illegal order, and it was a question if he could vary it, in this case the Court upheld the order, and also held that the original order of the Justices was good: *Q. B. Division*, Dublin, Feb., 1884, before Justices O'Brien and Johnston.

Boycotting.—In the *Q. B. Division*, Feb., 1887. In the *Queen (Delany) v. The*

Offence, or cause of Complaint.	Statute.	Extent of Jurisdiction.
LICENSING (LIQUOR) ACTS— *Dublin Metropolis—continued.* Appeal from refusal of certificate to Quarter Sessions or Recorder. (a)	18 & 19 Vic. c. 62, ss. 1 & 2 23 & 24 Vic. c. 35, s. 1.	

Justices of Queen's County, the Court upheld the order of the Justices in Petty Sessions, refusing a publican his annual certificate to enable him to obtain a renewal of his excise licence, on the ground that his house had been conducted in a disorderly manner, he having refused to supply goods at ordinary prices to certain persons who were boycotted. The Chairman on appeal confirmed the order of the Justices, and the case now came up on case stated by the Chairman. In this case the publican not alone refused to supply goods to the boycotted person, but also refused undertaking that in future he would.

It seems that if three Justices be sitting, two of them will be sufficient to sign the certificate, although the third may dissent; but should five be sitting, and two of them be in favour of granting the certificate, and three opposed, it will amount to a *refusal*, and the two Justices in minority ought not to sign.

Where the certificate is refused by one bench of Magistrates, it should not be afterwards granted, or the application entertained by another.

In the case of *R.* v. *Sainsbury*, 4 *T. R.*, 456, where a question arose as to the right of one bench of Magistrates to grant a licence under the English statute, which had been refused at a previous meeting, held specially for the purpose, it was decided that the act of the Magistrates at the subsequent meeting was not only void, but was such a breach of the law as to subject them to an indictment.

Lord Kenyon observed:—"Without entering into the question of the legality of the act, and whether it were legal or otherwise, it could not be doubted by any person that it is not decent or decorous for two different sets of Magistrates, having a concurrent jurisdiction, to run a race in the exercise of any part of their jurisdiction; for it is of infinite importance to the public that the acts of Magistrates shall not only be substantially good, but also that they shall be decorous."

Beer licences expire on the 10th October in each year (24 & 25 Vic. c. 91, s. 14). Magistrates should assemble to grant certificates before that day.

If certificate be refused, an entry of the fact, and of the grounds for refusal, are to be made accordingly.

(a) Quarter Sessions or Recorder shall hear and determine appeal, notwithstanding omission, error, or informality in order of refusal.—23 & 24 Vic. c. 35, s. 1.

Appeal from Order refusing Certificate.—Persons aggrieved may appeal to Quarter Sessions or Recorder, as the case may be, if Sessions not held sooner than fifteen days; if sooner, then to next Sessions. No grounds to be entered on but those stated in order of refusal. Licence to remain in force until appeal heard. Appeal to be according to Petty Sessions (Ireland) Act, 1851. Recognizance to be in form given in special Act quoted, 18 & 19 Vic. c. 62, ss. 1 & 2. Licence duty to be deposited with collector, pending appeal; if order confirmed, a proportion will be refunded.—24 & 25 Vic. c. 91, s. 21.

2 S

Offence, or cause of Complaint.	Statute.	Extent of Jurisdiction.
LICENSING (LIQUOR) ACTS—		
DUBLIN METROPOLIS—*continued.*		
Transfer.—Mode of obtaining before Justices in Petty Sessions. (*a*)	18 & 19 Vic. c. 114, s. 1.	

(*a*) *Transfers, &c.*—It is decided that in applications for transfers of existing licences, the Recorder's or Quarter Sessions Courts cannot refuse the transfer on the ground (3 & 4 Wm. iv. s. 2) of the existing number of licensed houses being in excess of or adequate to the requirements of the locality. It was decided, on a review of all the Acts, that this objection could not lie against a transfer. That the Licensing Authority has, therefore, in respect to transfers no jurisdiction to consider the number of previously licensed houses in the neighbourhood of the licensed house. —The Queen at the instance of *Clithero & Others* v. *the Recorder of Dublin, Q.B. (Ireland),* 1877. The Court evidently put the fullest strain on its powers in so interpreting the several Acts bearing on the question in order to prevent extensive injury and loss to those having vested interests.

In the Queen's Bench Division, England, 1888, before Mr. Justice Field and Mr. Justice Wills—*Sharpe* v. *Wakefield & Others*—Justices of Westmoreland, the question as to the discretion of the Justices in refusing renewal licence to an old established inn came before the Court on case stated by the Quarter Sessions for Westmoreland, on appeal from a refusal by the Licensing Justices to renew the licence. They refused, on the ground of the "remoteness of the house from police supervision, and the character and necessities of the locality and neighbourhood of the inn." The Court was unanimous in upholding the decision of the Justices in Quarter Sessions. The power of granting implied the right to refuse. Their discretion of course meant judicial discretion, and to be exercised in each individual case. In granting or refusing the Justices had an absolute discretion. The Licensing Laws and all previous decisions were referred to, and the appellant's counsel relied on the above decision of the *Queen* v. *The Recorder of Dublin,* and that "licences were matter of property." The Court considered that the Irish cases referred to by Mr. Justice Fitzgerald did not support this view, and adding, however, that the Irish case itself was no authority on the point, Irish and English law being so different.

Upon the death of licensed person, removal, or sale of interest, &c., in the premises, Justices in Petty Sessions may, if they think proper (after examining on oath all necessary parties), transfer the licence by indorsement thereon to person seeking same, not being a person disqualified by law, until the next Quarter Sessions for the district, after expiration of one month.—18 & 19 Vic. c. 114, s. 1.

It will be observed that this permission of the Magistrates has not the effect of transferring the licence from one *place* to *another*, but merely from one *person* to *another*, and that only to enable the party to sell until the certificate is regularly obtained at the Quarter Sessions. Whenever an unobjectionable person for some good reason seeks permission to sell until a licence can be regularly obtained at Quarter Sessions, the proper course will be by memorial to the Lord Lieutenant, and the recommendation of the Magistrates of the district; and if his Excellency approves, the Excise will not object to the party selling until licence obtained at Sessions.

Beer Licence.—The 34 & 35 Vic. c. 111, repeals sec. 14 of the 27 & 28 Vic. c. 35.

Offence, or cause of Complaint.	Statute.	Extent of Jurisdiction.
LICENSING (LIQUOR) ACTS—		
BEER HOUSES.		
This Act refers to houses licensed to sell beer by retail to be drank, &c., elsewhere than on the premises where same is sold.	26 & 27 Vic. c. 33, s. 1. 27 & 28 Vic. c. 35.	—
Excise not to grant licences, or renewals, or transfers, unless the applicant produce the certificate of two Justices of the district as to character and conduct of applicant, and if a new licence, as to suitability of the premises.	27 & 28 Vic. c. 35, s. 3.	
Persons applying shall give 21 days' notice to police officers; and if in the trade before, to state where, &c., and police officer may object.	ss. 4, 5.	—
(*Wholesale Beer Dealers.*—The same regulation as preceding shall be complied with in order to obtain a wholesale beer dealer's licence, under 37 & 38 Vic. c. 69, s. 8.)		
Wholesale beer dealers to be subject to police supervision.	27 & 28 Vic. c. 35, s. 11. 40 Vic. c. 4, s. 3.	
These licences are granted in Petty Sessions at the Annual Licensing Sessions. See 37 & 38 Vic. c. 69, sec. 12, sub-sec. 2.		

This section excepted brewers and other traders from the necessity of obtaining Justices' certificate before Excise could grant licence.

(Sec. 2 of 6 Geo. iv. c. 81, and sec. 6 of 13 & 14 Vic. c. 67, so far as relates to brewers' retail licences repealed.)

The Licensing Act, 35 & 36 Vic. c. 94, sec. 76, under term "licence," includes certificates granted by Justices in Petty Sessions, under 27 & 28 Vic. c. 35, as amended by 34 & 35 Vic. c. 111.

Offence, or cause of Complaint.	Statute.	Extent of Jurisdiction.
LICENSING (LIQUOR) ACTS—		
BEER HOUSES—*continued.*		
Prohibitions, penalties, &c., with respect to houses licensed to sell for consumption on the premises, and the hours at which they may be kept open for sale, and the powers of Justices, constables, &c., under 8 & 9 Vic. c. 64, s. 2, and 17 & 18 Vic. c. 89, s. 12, shall be applicable to houses licensed under this Act.	27 & 28 Vic. c. 35.	
Persons found drinking or tippling, or having the appearance of having been recently drinking or tippling in houses licensed under this Act, but not for consumption on premises, may be apprehended or summoned.	s. 8.	First offence, penalty not exceeding 5s.; second or subsequent offence, penalty not exceeding 10s., nor less than 5s.; in default of payment, imprisonment not exceeding 1 week. 1. J.
Justice may require production of licence upon hearing of complaints, and for neglect or refusal to produce same—	s. 9.	Penalty not exceeding £5; in default of payment, imprisonment not exceeding 2 months. 1. J. (And see 37 & 38 Vic. c. 69, s. 20.)
Wholesale dealers in beer shall not keep open between 7 P.M. and 7 A.M.; for non-observance, to be subject to police supervision same as retailers.	s. 11.	—
Penalties recoverable under Petty Sessions Act and Petty Sessions Clerks Act.	s. 12.	—
Appeal to Quarter Sessions as to granting or refusing certificate to beer dealers.	s. 13.	
Like as to wholesale beer dealers.	27 & 28 Vic. c. 69, s. 8.	—
See Licensing Acts, in full, *Appendix.* See also " Refreshment Houses," " Excise."		

Offence, or cause of Complaint.	Statute.	Extent of Jurisdiction.
LICENSING (LIQUOR) ACTS— BEER HOUSES—*continued.* *Beer Licences.*—No licences, transfers, or renewals, for sale of beer, ale, porter *for consumption elsewhere than* on premises to be granted in respect of premises rated at less than £8, nor in cities, &c., with a population exceeding 10,000, unless premises are rated at £15.	40 Vic. c. 4, s. 2.	
Applicant shall be in exclusive occupation for at least 3 months.		
Application shall be made to Justices in Petty Sessions in manner prescribed by "Beer Houses (Ireland) Act, 1864," as amended by "Licensing Act (Ireland), 1874."	"	
Extension of sec. 11 of 27 & 28 Vic. c. 35, to this Act, so as to apply to person licensed to sell beer by wholesale, to be consumed off the premises, who shall keep open between 7 o'clock A.M. and 7 o'clock P.M.		

Publican's right to recover where Sale unlawful.—As to how far non-compliance with Excise regulations will preclude the trader from recovering the price of goods sold in the course of an irregularly conducted business, the general principle is, that where the Act of Parliament is infringed no contract can be supported arising out of it.—*Forster* v. *Taylor,* 5 B. & Ad., 887. But it is now held that this rule does not apply to Excise regulations which have not for their object the protection of the public but the revenue only. But if the business be altogether unlawful, or if the obvious intention and policy of the Act of Parliament, referring to the particular business, be to protect the public as well as the revenue, the trader cannot recover from his creditors.—*Brown* v. *Duncan,* 10 B. & C., 93, and T. R., 560; *Law* v. *Hodgson,* 2 Camp., 147; 11 East., 300.

Liability to Lodgers, &c.—The word "inn" is interpreted as meaning "any hotel, inn, tavern, public-house, or other place of refreshment, the keeper of which is now by law responsible for the goods and property of his guests.—See *Doe* v. *Laming,* 4 Camp., 76. A boarding-house keeper or lodging-house keeper has no duty imposed upon him by law to take care of his lodgers' goods.—*Dansey* v. *Richardson,* 3 E. & B., 144; 26 & 27 *Vic. c.* 41, *ss.* 1, 2, and 3; and see *Taylor's Evidence.*

Liability of Innkeepers and Guests.—The law obliges an innkeeper to keep the

Offence, or cause of Complaint.	Statute.	Extent of Jurisdiction.
LICENSING (LIQUOR) ACTS— *continued.*		—
Debts due by Servants, Labourers, &c.—Retailers of beer or spirits giving credit to servants, day-labourers, and other persons who usually work or ply for hire or wages, beyond the amount of 1*s.*, shall have no remedy for the sum due, and securities for such debts shall be void.	9 Geo. ii. c. 88. 1 Geo. iii. c. 17, s. 14.	
Receiving pledges from servants or workmen as aforesaid, to secure payment of any sum exceeding 1*s.*, contracted in manner aforesaid.	,,	Chief Magistrate in a corporate town, or Justice in county, county of a city or town, may, by warrant, compel retailer, by distress and sale of his goods, to restore the pledge, or to make satisfaction for the loss or abuse thereof. Mayor, or 1 J.P.
By the 55 Geo. iii. c. 104, s. 15, suits cannot be maintained for spirituous liquors sold in less than two quarts at a time. But by the 37 & 38 Vic. c. 69, s. 38, sub-sec. 4, this right of action is preserved, except as to spirituous liquors which shall be used or consumed in the premises where sold.	,,	
(*Spirituous liquors* would seem to be distilled spirits, and will not include beer or ale.)		

goods of persons coming to his inn *causa hospitandi* safely; but there may be circumstances in which the guest by his own conduct induces the loss, which form exception to the general liability. If the innkeeper gives the key of his chamber to the guest, that will not dispense with his own care or discharge him from general responsibility as an innkeeper. But though in general a traveller who resorts to an inn may rest in the protection which the law casts around him, yet if circumstances of suspicion arise he must exercise ordinary care. The definition of an inn is "a house where the traveller is furnished with everything he has occasion for while on his way."—*Smith's Leading Cases.* As to the lien of innkeepers for their charges, the better opinion seems to be that it attaches to goods brought to the inn by a guest, though they be not his own.—*Turrell* v. *Crawly*, 13 *Q. B.* 197. The innkeeper cannot detain the person of his guest for payment of his bill.—*Simbelf* v. *Alford*, 3 *M. & W.*, 248.

Liability to Supply Refreshment.—In August, 1875, a case was heard at the Brentford County Court, before Mr. Sergeant Wheeler, Judge. Mr. F. J. Jackson, of 89, Wigmore-street, sought to recover the sum of £5 5*s.* from the landlord of the Queen Victoria public-house, Ealing, for refusing to supply him with refreshment, thereby causing him much bodily pain, on the afternoon of Sunday, the 4th July. It was argued for the plaintiff, on the basis of an old edition of *Burns's Justice*, that

Offence, or cause of Complaint.	Statute.	Extent of Jurisdiction.
LICENCE: Where required, see the particular head in each Index, "Arms," "Excise," "Gun Licences," "Game," "Public-houses," "Refreshment-houses," "Peace Preservation," &c. &c.		
LINEN: An Act to prevent frauds and abuses by weavers, sewers, &c. (a)	3 & 4 Vic. c. 91.	
Weavers, sewers, or other persons embezzling, pawning, or fraudulently disposing of any of the ma-	s. 2.	To forfeit full value, with such costs and penalties as shall not together

an innkeeper is in duty bound to furnish a traveller with refreshment whenever application may be made; but, on the contrary, it was urged that the 9th and 10th sections of the Licensing Act, 1874, leaves it optional with the publican to do as he pleases when applied to during prohibited hours. His Honor, however, observed that he did not think the Act intended to vest the option in the publican, as in that case there would be a privilege without a duty. After considerable discussion on this point the evidence of the plaintiff and a friend was taken, and inasmuch as they did not show that they had informed the defendant of their being travellers when they applied for refreshment, His Honor ruled that the case was not proved, and accordingly ordered a nonsuit, thus leaving it open for any further proceedings to be taken.

According to Blackstone and Sergeant Hawkins, inns being intended for the receipt of travellers, may be indicted, suppressed, and the innkeepers fined, if they refuse to entertain a traveller without a very sufficient cause; for thus to frustrate the end of their institution is disorderly behaviour. It is said that the innkeeper may be compelled by the constable of the town to receive and entertain a traveller, and for refusal without sufficient reason it would seem that the innkeeper is liable to be indicted and the house to be suppressed.—See *Burns's Alehouses*, and also *Gabbett's Digest*, title "Disorderly Alehouses," &c.

But it does not appear that a *licensed publican* holding a *six-day licence* could be compelled to sell to a traveller *intoxicating liquor on a Sunday*, nor would he, if so disposed, be at liberty to do so.

(a) The above Act deals fully with questions arising between employers and weavers in the linen trade. The seat of this manufacture being in the North of Ireland, this legislation was then felt to be a necessity. But as mills have absorbed the business of the weavers, the offences of embezzling and purloining materials entrusted to workers have in great measure ceased. The above Act (excepting ss. 18 and 23) is continued by the 46 & 47 Vic. c. 40. The offence of artificers, journeymen, &c., detaining or making away with materials, can in most cases be effectually dealt with under 25 & 26 Vic. c. 50.—See title "Workman," in this Index.

Offence, or cause of Complaint.	Statute.	Extent of Jurisdiction.
LINENS—*continued.* terials specified (linen, hempen, cotton, silk, or woollen yarns, or these materials mixed—tools, &c.), entrusted for the purpose of manufacture, &c.—	3 & 4 Vic. c. 91, s. 2.	exceed £5; in default, &c., imprisonment not exceeding 3 months. 2 J.
Persons knowingly purchasing, receiving, or taking in pawn, such materials, tools, &c., knowing same to be embezzled, or that the persons offering them are fraudulently disposing of same—	s. 3.	Indictable misdemeanour.
Justice empowered to grant warrant to search for embezzled materials, &c.	s. 6.	
Receiving materials to be manufactured in fictitious name, or delivering materials to be manufactured to any other person without owner's consent.	s. 19.	Penalty not exceeding £2; in default, &c., imprisonment, not exceeding 1 month. 2 J.
Frivolous or vexatious complaints, or if it appear that such are made from malicious, vexatious, or improper motives—	s. 24.	Justices may award defendant, in addition to his costs, a further sum not exceeding £20, recoverable by distress. 2 J.
LOAN SOCIETIES (*Charitable*): (n) Act to consolidate and amend the laws for the regulation of Charitable Loan Societies in Ireland.	6 & 7 Vic. c. 91.	—
Loans not to exceed £10 to any one individual at one time.	s. 24.	—
Loan debts under this Act, and all fines incurred—	s. 30.	Recoverable before any 1 Justice having jurisdiction where defendant resides, or the office of the Society is situated; amount to be levied by distress.

(a) This Act does not apply to private loan banks; it is only applicable to banks established for charitable purposes, under the control of the Loan Fund Board. The Constabulary execute the Magistrates' warrants.

Offence, or cause of Complaint.	Statute.	Extent of Jurisdiction.
"THE LOCAL GOVERNMENT (IRELAND) ACT, 1871." "The Local Government Board (Ir.) Act, 1872." These enactments vest in the Local Government Board constituted under them; the powers, &c., of the Poor Law Commissioners and those vested in the Lord Lieutenant and Privy Council by several Sanitary Acts set out in a Schedule to the 35 & 36 Vic. c. 69. These Sanitary Acts are, as to Ireland, repealed by Schedule A of the "Public Health (Ir.) Act, 1878" (41 & 42 Vic. c. 52). And this Act of 1878 is substituted for the enactments so repealed.	34 & 35 Vic. c. 109. 35 & 36 Vic. c. 69.	—
LOCOMOTIVES (*on Roads*): Rules for the manner of working locomotives on highways, propelled by steam, and for non-compliance with rules, owner liable to—	28 & 29 Vic. c. 83.	Penalty not exceeding £10, or in default, &c., imprisonment by scale. 2 J.
If owner proves that the penalty is incurred by neglect or wilful default of person in charge, he may summarily recover from him the whole or part of the penalty.	,,	
Power to local authorities to make orders as to hours, &c., when locomotives may pass through cities, speed, &c., and for acting contrary to rules, &c., on summary conviction of persons in charge—	s. 7.	Penalty not exceeding £10; in default, &c., imprisonment by scale. 2 J.
County surveyor to be deemed conservator of roads in his county, and may proceed for damage done to roads, &c. If under £10 in Petty Sessions, if over £10 in Civil Bill Court.	s. 9.	
Penalties recoverable under Petty Sessions Act. Fines to be applied as in Fines Act. (a)	s. 10.	

(a) *Locomotives.*—Act continued by "Expiring Laws Continuance Act, 1883." Where horses, &c., of ordinary steadiness are frightened, and injury result, the compliance with "Rules" may not still be an answer to Civil actions.

Offence, or cause of Complaint.	Statute.	Extent of Jurisdiction.
LODGERS: (a) *Act to protect goods of lodgers against distresses for rent due to the superior landlord.*	34 & 35 Vic. c. 79.	—
Where superior landlord levies or authorizes to be levied distress on furniture, goods, or chattels of lodger for arrears of rent due by the immediate tenant, lodger may serve landlord, his bailiff, &c., with declaration in writing setting forth that the immediate tenant has no right, property, or beneficial interest in the goods distrained, or threatened to be, but that same are the property of the lodger or in his lawful possession; and also setting forth whether any and what rent and for what period, is due by lodger; and such lodger may pay superior landlord or bailiff the rent (if any) so due by him, or so much thereof as may be sufficient to discharge the claim.	s. 1.	Lodger may apply for an order for the restoration of the goods, &c., to a Stipendiary Magistrate; or in places where there is no Stipendiary Magistrate, to 2 Justices, who shall inquire into the truth of the declaration and inventory, and make such order for the recovery of the goods or otherwise as to them shall seem just. Superior landlord may also be liable to an action.
Declaration to contain an inventory of goods referred to. (Knowingly making false declaration a misdemeanour.)		
If landlord, bailiff, &c., after being served with declaration and inventory, and after payment or tender of the rent (if any) which lodger is authorized to pay, shall levy or proceed with distress, &c., the person so offending shall be deemed guilty of illegal distress.		
Payment made by lodger under sec. 1 to be deemed a valid payment on account of any rent due from him.		

(a) *Lodgers.*—This Act is short and comprehensive. The whole proceeding before the Magistrate is supposed to be *ex parte*, and out of Petty Sessions, and without delay. There seems to be, however, no reason why he may not have all the parties before him, as he has to inquire into the truth of the declaration and inventory.

If there be a Stipendiary Magistrate in the place, other Justices are not allowed to interfere.

Offence, or cases of Complaint.	Statute.	Extent of Jurisdiction.
LODGING HOUSES: See "Common Lodging Houses." "Public Health Act."		
LORD'S DAY:—(See "Sunday.")		
LOTTERY: Lotteries are declared to be public nuisances. See "Lotteries," indictable offences.	11 Anne, c. 6, s. 2. 13 Geo. ii. c. 8, s. 2.	Lotteries are deemed to be public nuisances; and lottery keepers are liable to a penalty of £100, recoverable by information, action, &c., or may be prosecuted as cheats.
LUNATICS: Acts under which Magistrates have power to deal with *dangerous* lunatics. Whenever any person shall be brought before any 2 Justices, and it shall be proved to their satisfaction that such person was discovered and apprehended under circumstances denoting a derangement of mind, and a purpose of committing some crime for which, if committed, such person would be liable to be indicted. (a)	1 Vic. c. 27. 8 & 9 Vic. c. 107. 30 & 31 Vic. c. 118, s. 10.	The Justices shall call to their assistance the nearest available medical officer of the dispensary district in which they shall be, and if not available, then the nearest available medical officer of any neighbouring dispensary district,

(a) The evidence of the witnesses should be taken in writing as other depositions; and if an indictable crime has actually been committed, the depositions should be lodged in the Crown or Peace Office. The authorities at the Castle have taken much pains to point out to the Magistracy the necessity and duty of strictly adhering to the requirements of the law on the subject of dangerous lunatics. Forms of committal of dangerous lunatics can be had of Petty Sessions Clerks, and can be obtained from H. M.'s Stationery Office, Dublin. In the cases of lunatics who do not come within the provisions of the statute, as being "discovered and apprehended under circumstances showing a purpose of committing an indictable crime," &c., but who are, nevertheless, fit subjects for a lunatic asylum, and whose friends are desirous of placing them there, the necessary form of affidavit, &c., for that purpose is also given in the *Appendix.* The Justices should send a copy of the medical certificate to the Registrar of Lunatics, Four Courts.—*Circular,* 15th *June,* 1871; and see 34 Vic. c. 22, s. 4.

Offence, or cause of Complaint.	Statute.	Extent of Jurisdiction.
LUNATICS—*continued.* *Proviso.*—Relation or friend may take lunatic under protection on entering into recognizance for the peaceable behaviour or safe custody of the lunatic, before 2 Justices, the Chairman of Quarter Sessions, or a Judge.	30 & 31 Vic. c. 118, s. 10.	who shall examine such person; and if certified to be a dangerous lunatic or dangerous idiot by warrant under hands and seals, to direct that such person shall be taken to the lunatic asy-
From 1st January, 1868, Justices are not to commit any dangerous lunatic or dangerous idiot to a gaol.	s. 9.	lum, established wholly or in part for the county, city, or town wherein apprehended, there to remain as if removed
On becoming of sound mind the Medical Superintendent or Visiting Physician may discharge, as in the case of lunatic poor (9 & 10 Vic. c. 115, s. 3). This 30 & 31 Vic. c. 117, amends the previous Acts; it provides also for the appointment and the superannuation of officers.	s. 11.	from a gaol to the asylum under Lord Lieutenant's warrant. 2 J.
Officers, attendants, or persons having care of lunatics, abusing, ill-treating, or wilfully neglecting them. (But the general application of this Act appears to be contined to England.)	16 & 17 Vic. c. 96, s. 9.	A misdemeanour triable by indictment, or may be summarily tried by Justices; penalty, not exceeding £20, may be enforced under Petty Sessions Act, and by the scales. 2 J.
If any army pensioner becomes insane, any Justice of the Peace can certify the fact to the Commissioners of Chelsea Hospital, who shall direct payment of the pension to persons having charge of the lunatic.	2 & 3 Vic. c. 51, s. 4.	
Lunacy Regulation, Ireland, Act, provides as to commissions of lunacy; proceedings under same; management or estates of lunatics, visiting, protection of property of lunatics, and other purposes.	34 Vic. c. 22.	
Returns to be made by persons receiving or treating lunatics.	ss. 5, 6.	—

Offence, or cause of Complaint.	Statute.	Extent of Jurisdiction.
LUNATICS—*continued.*		
Persons neglecting to make returns, except where it happens through unavoidable accident. Applies 13 & 24 Vic. c. 60, Trustees Act.	34 Vic. c. 22, ss. 8, 9, 10.	Penalty not exceeding £10; in default, &c., imprisonment by scale. Special Act applicable in Dublin.
Repeals sec. 3, in part, of 15 Chas. i. c. 53 (Irish Parliament) ; 6 Geo. iv. c. 53, inquisitions of lunacy ; 1 Wm. iv. c. 65, in part ; 5 & 6 Wm. iv. c. 17, and secs. 1, 2, 3, of 15 & 16 Vic. c. 48.		Elsewhere before 2 J., under Petty Sessions Act.
Act to amend the laws relating to private and district lunatic asylums.	38 & 39 Vic. c. 67.	
Power to detain lunatics in asylums and to retake them.	ss. 3, 4.	
Justices causing person to be examined by medical officer may, by order on guardians, order payment to medical officer, and all other expenses in or about examination, not exceeding £2.	s. 14.	
Property of lunatic, in district asylum to be available for his maintenance.	s. 16.	
Where patient has no estate applicable for maintenance, persons who under Poor Relief Acts are bound to contribute to maintenance, shall be liable to contribute according to ability to maintenance in asylum.	,,	On application of resident Medical Superintendent, Justices in Petty Sessions may make order for the amount, recoverable as penalties under Poor Law Acts. 2 J.
Idiots.—Act to make better provision for idiots, imbeciles, and other afflicted persons in Ireland.	41 & 42 Vic. c. 60.	
Guardians may provide for reception of certain blind, deaf, dumb, and idiotic paupers in suitable institutions.	ss. 3, 4.	

Offence, or cause of Complaint.	Statute.	Extent of Jurisdiction.
LUNATICS—*continued.* Where bankrupt becomes of unsound mind, see—	20 & 21 Vic. c. 69, s. 239.	
As to special verdict where accused is found guilty but insane at the commission of offence, so as not to be responsible, according to law, for his actions at the time—	46 & 47 Vic. c. 38, s. 2.	
Lunatic Asylum Audit Act.	31 & 32 Vic. c. 97.	Two Justices may enforce by distress warrants sums disallowed by Auditor.
MAGNETIC TELEGRAPH : Injuries to—see "Malicious Injuries."		
MAINTENANCE (*under Poor Law*): See "Poor Law."		
MALICIOUS INJURIES TO PROPERTY (*Act*): As amended by, ...	24 & 25 Vic. c. 97. 25 & 26 Vic. c. 50.	— The amended Act has reference to the mode of procedure, and empowers one Justice to hear the case.
Damaging Trees, &c., to the amount of 1*s.*—Whosoever shall unlawfully and maliciously (*a*) cut, break, bark, root-up, or otherwise destroy or damage the whole or any part of any tree, sapling, or shrub, or any underwood, wheresoever the same may be growing; the injury done being to the amount of 1*s.* at the least. (And see ss. 52 & 53 hereafter.)	24 & 25 Vic. c. 97, s. 22. (25 & 26 Vic. c. 50, ss. 2 and 3.)	At the discretion of the Justices, either to be imprisoned, with or without H. L., for any term not exceeding 3 months, *or else* shall forfeit and pay (over and above the amount of injury done), a sum not exceeding £5, by scale, with or without H.L. 1 J.

(*a*) Malice conceived against owner not necessary to be proved, s. 58. When a man commits an unlawful act, unaccompanied by any circumstances justifying its commission, it is a presumption of law that he has acted advisedly, and with an intent to produce the consequences which have ensued.

Offence, or cause of Complaint.	Statute.	Extent of Jurisdiction.
lALICIOUS INJURIES TO PRO- PERTY—*continued.* *Second Offence.*—Whosoever, having been convicted of any such offence, either against this or any former Act of Parliament, shall afterwards commit any of the offences in this section before mentioned—	24 & 25 Vic. c. 97, s. 22.	To be imprisoned at H. L. for such term, not ex- ceeding 12 months, as the Justices shall think fit. 1 J.
A third offence, ...	,,	Indictable misdemeanour.
Destroying Fruit or Vegetable Pro- ductions in Gardens, &c.—Whoso- ever shall unlawfully and mali- ciously destroy, or damage with in- tent to destroy, any plant, root, fruit, or vegetable production grow- ing in any garden, orchard, nursery- ground, hot-house, green-house, or conservatory—	s. 23.	At the discretion of the Justices, to be impri- soned, with or without H. L., not exceeding 6 months; or else shall forfeit and pay (over and above the amount of the injury done) such sum, not exceeding £20, as to the Justices shall seem meet; in default, &c., imprisonment by scale, with or without H. L. (a) 1 J.
Second Offence.—Whosoever, having been convicted of any such offence, either against this or any former Act of Parliament, shall afterwards commit any of the offences in this section before mentioned—	,,	Felony triable by indict- ment.
Destroying Vegetable Productions not growing in Gardens.—Whosoever shall unlawfully and maliciously destroy, or damage with intent to destroy, any cultivated root or plant used for the food of man or beast, or for medicine, or for dis- tilling, or for dyeing, or for or in the course of any manufacture, and growing in any land, open or	s. 24.	At the discretion of the Justice, to be impri- soned, with or without H. L., for any term not exceeding 1 month, or else shall forfeit and pay, over and above the amount of injury done, a sum not exceeding 20s.; and in default of

(a) *Enforcement of Money Penalty.*—Under this, 24 & 25 Vic. c. 97, where money penalty is not paid, as ordered, sec. 65 gives power (unless where other- wise specially directed) to imprison according to the scale in section, *with or without hard labour.* But where the sum does not exceed £5, the imprisonment should be regulated by " Small Penalties Act," 36 & 37 Vic. c. 82.

T

Offence, or cause of Complaint.	Statute.	Extent of Jurisd
MALICIOUS INJURIES TO PRO-PERTY—*continued.* . enclosed, not being a garden, orch-ard, or nursery-ground.	24 & 25 Vic. c. 97, s. 24.	payment, toget costs (if ordere committed for not exceeding unless payment made. But w sum does not ex imprisonment cording to scal 37 Vic. c. 82.
Second Offence.—Whosoever, having been convicted of any such offence, either against this or any former Act of Parliament, shall afterwards commit any of the offences in this section before mentioned—	,,	To be imprison H.L., for such exceeding 6 m the Justices sh fit.
Injuries to Fences, &c.—Whosoever shall unlawfully and maliciously cut, break, throw down, or in any wise destroy any fence, of any de-scription whatsoever, or any wall, stile, or gate, or any part thereof, respectively—	s. 25.	For a first offer forfeit and pay, above amount done, a sum no ing £5 ; in defi to be imprisor or without H exceeding 2 mo less amount soc
Second Offence.—Whosoever, having been convicted of any such offence, either against this or any former Act of Parliament, shall afterwards commit any of the offences in this section before mentioned—	,,	To be committed to H.L. for su not exceeding l as the Justic think fit.
Injuries to Electric or Magnetic Tele-graphs.—Whosoever shall unlaw-fully and maliciously cut, break, throw down, destroy, injure, or remove, any battery, machinery, wire, cable, post, or other matter or thing whatsoever, being part of, or being used or employed in or about any electric or magnetic	s. 37.	Misdemeanour, t indictment ; ment not exc years' H. L.: that if it appe Justices, on tion of the charged, that expedient to tk

(a) The imprisonment in default of paying this penalty does not a attended with hard labour.

Offence, or cause of Complaint.	Statute.	Extent of Jurisdiction.
MALICIOUS INJURIES TO PRO-PERTY—*continued.* telegraph, or in the working thereof, or shall unlawfully and maliciously prevent or obstruct, in any manner whatsoever, the sending, conveyance, or delivery of any communication by any such telegraph.	24 & 25 Vic. c. 97, s. 37.	justice that same should be prosecuted by indictment, they may proceed summarily; and the offender shall, on conviction, in discretion of Justices, be imprisoned, with or without H. L., for not exceeding 3 months, *or* forfeit and pay such sum, not exceeding £10, as to the Justices shall seem meet; in default, &c., imprisonment by scale, with or without H.L. 1 J.
Attempt.—Whosoever shall unlawfully and maliciously, by any overt act, attempt to commit any of the offences in the last preceding section mentioned—	s. 38.	At discretion of Justices, shall either be imprisoned, with or without H. L., for any term not exceeding 3 months, *or else* forfeit and pay such sum, not exceeding £10, as to the Justices shall seem meet; in default, &c., imprisonment by scale, with or without H. L. 1 J.
Animals, Birds, &c.—Whosoever shall unlawfully and maliciously kill, maim, or wound, any dog, bird, beast or other animal, not being cattle, but being either the subject of larceny at Common Law, or being ordinarily kept in a state of confinement, or for any domestic purpose—	s. 41.	At discretion of Justice, to be imprisoned, with or without H. L., not exceeding 6 months, *or* to forfeit, over and above amount of injury done, any sum not exceeding £20; in default, &c., imprisonment by scale, with or without H. L. 1 J. Second conviction, not exceeding 12 months' H. L. 1 J.

T 2

Offence, or cause of Complaint.	Statute.	Extent of Jurisdiction.
MARGARINE: Person dealing in Margarine, in any capacity, guilty of any offence against the Act.	50 & 51 Vic. c. 29, s. 4.	1st offence, penalty not exceeding £20; 2nd, not exceeding £50; 3rd or subsequent offence, penalty not exceeding £100; in default, &c., imprisonment by scale. 1 J.
How employer may claim exemption from penalty and show that another person is liable.	s. 5.	
How dealers shall mark cases.	s. 6.	
Presumption against Vendor, unless he satisfies the Court that he purchased as butter and had warranty, &c.	s. 7.	
Powers of Customs and Inland Revenue Officers, Officers of Health, Inspectors of Nuisances, Constables, to examine and take samples, &c.	s. 8.	
Registration of Manufactory.	s. 9.	
Officer authorized under " Food and Drugs Act, 1875," may take samples without purchase.	s. 10.	
Application of penalties.	s. 11.	
Proceedings as in " Food and Drugs Act, 1875." Defines "Local Authority," "Butter," "Margarine."	s. 12.	
MARINE STORES: Dealer in, shall have the words " Dealer in Marine Stores " painted distinctly, in letters of not less than six inches in length, on every warehouse or other place of deposit belonging to him; in default—	Merchant Shipping Act, 17 & 18 Vic. c. 104, s. 480.	Penalty not exceeding £20, recoverable as in Petty Sessions Act, and by scale. 2 J.

Offence, or cause of Complaint.	Statute	Extent of Jurisdiction.
MARINE STORES—*continued.* He shall keep entries in books, fairly written, account of stores, the time at which and the person, his business and abode, from whom purchased; in default—	Merchant Shipping Act, 17 & 18 Vic. c. 104, s. 480.	First offence, penalty not exceeding £20; every subsequent offence not exceeding £50, recoverable as above. 2 J.
By himself or his agents purchasing marine stores from person apparently under 16 years—	,,	For first offence not exceeding £5; for every subsequent offence not exceeding £20, recoverable as above. 2 J.
Cutting up cable exceeding five fathoms, or unlaying same without permit, as therein—	,,	First offence, penalty not exceeding £20; every subsequent offence not exceeding £50, recoverable as above. 2 J.
For mode of obtaining permit, advertising same in newspapers, and marking anchors, and penalties in default, see—	ss. 481 and 482.	—
Marine forces while on shore, Act regulating.	(Annual.)	—
And see "Public Stores."		
MARKETS: Disputes in fairs and markets between buyer and seller (where value does not exceed £5).	14 & 15 Vic. c. 92, s. 17.	One Justice may make award; if money ordered to be paid, amount to be levied by distress.
Justice may hear the case out of Petty Sessions.	14 & 15 Vic. c. 93, s. 8.	—
See "Fairs and Markets."		

Offence, or cause of Complaint.	Statute.	Extent of Jurisdiction.
MARRIED WOMEN: *Protecting property of, when deserted by husbands.*—A wife deserted by her husband may apply to Justices in Petty Sessions or Judge of Common Pleas in chamber, for an order to protect any money or property she may acquire by her own lawful industry, and property which she may become possessed of after such desertion, against her husband, his creditors, or any person claiming under him; and Justices, if satisfied of the facts of such desertion, and that the same was without reasonable cause.	28 Vic. c. 43, s. 1. (a)	Justices may make and give wife an order protecting her earnings and property acquired since commencement of desertion from her husband, his creditors, and persons claiming under him. 2 J. Or in Dublin, 1 Police Magistrate.
Copy of Magistrate's order to be lodged with Clerk of the Peace for the county within ten days.	,,	
Husband or his creditors may apply to same Court to discharge the order.		

(a) Some difficult questions will, in all probability, from time to time, arise before Justices under sec. 1 :—As to what will constitute desertion, and without reasonable cause: How long the Protecting Order is to continue: What will be considered sufficient grounds for discharging the order, &c. &c. The order may be in words to the following effect :—

Petty Sessions District of ——
County of ——
Protection Order (28 Vic. c. 43).

A. B., of ——, married woman, having this day appeared before us, the undersigned Justices of the Peace, assembled in Petty Sessions at ——, in the County of ——, and given us to understand that she is now, and has been since the —— day of ——, deserted by her husband, C. D., of —— [*describe*], and having at same time applied to us for an order to protect any money or property she may acquire by her own lawful industry, and property she may become possessed of after such desertion, against her husband or his creditors or any person claiming under him; and we the said Justices have inquired into the matter of said complaint and application, and the grounds thereof, and we being satisfied of the fact of such desertion of his said wife by the said C. D., and that the same was without reasonable cause, and that the said A. B. is maintaining herself by her own industry or property: We do accordingly, and by virtue of the statute in that behalf (28 Vic. c. 43), intituled "An Act to provide for the security of property of married women separated from their husbands in Ireland," make and give to the said A. B. this

Offence, or cause of Complaint.	Statute.	Extent of Jurisdiction.
MARRIED WOMEN—*continued*. Husband or his creditors, &c., seizing or holding property of the wife after notice of such order, shall be liable at her suit to restore same, and also a sum equal to double value. And during continuance of order, she shall with regard to property and courtesy, suing and being sued, be as if she obtained decree or divorce á *mensâ et thoro*.	28 Vic. c. 43, s. 1.	
Sec. 2 provides protection for wife's property after divorce á *mensâ et thoro*.		
Sec. 3. After divorce á *mensâ et thoro* wife to be deemed *feme sole* as to property.		
Sec. 4. Mode of enforcing decree for alimony. (See also " Poor Law.")		
"MARRIED WOMEN'S PROPERTY ACT, 1870." (a)	33 & 34 Vic. c. 93.	It does not appear that a Magistrate's order is required under this Act. The Act gives the protection.

our order, protecting her earnings and property acquired since the —— day of ——, the commencement of such desertion, from her said husband and all creditors and persons claiming under him.

Given under our hands in Petty Sessions, at —— in the County of ——, this —— day of ——, 18   .

To all whom it may concern.

(a) This Act of 1870 provides for securing to a married woman her wages and earnings derived from business in which she is engaged separately from her husband, and also in literary pursuits, &c., her receipts alone to be good discharges, s. 1; securing to her deposits in savings banks, s. 2; as to her property in the Funds, Joint Stocks, &c., ss. 3 and 4; as to her property in benefit societies, &c. Provides against deposits of husband's money in her name in fraud of creditors, s. 6. Personal property not exceeding £200 coming to a married woman to be her own; where it is freehold property, the rents and profits only to be her own. Lord Chancellor, in a summary way, may decide questions of ownership between husband and wife, s. 7. Married woman may effect policy of insurance; secures to her policies effected by the husband for her benefit, but protecting creditors where the intent is to defraud

Offence, or cause of Complaint.	Statute.	Extent of Jurisdiction.
MARRIED WOMEN—*continued.* "MARRIED WOMEN'S PROPERTY ACT (1870) AMENDMENT ACT, 1874.	37 & 38 Vic. c. 93.	—
Husband and wife may be jointly sued for her debts before marriage, where marriage takes place after passing of this Act.		
Extent to which husband liable, .	s. 2.	—
If husband without assets, he shall have judgment for costs.	s. 3.	
Joint and separate judgment against husband and wife for debt.	s. 4.	
Assets for which husband liable, .	s. 5.	
"MARRIED WOMEN'S PROPERTY ACT, 1882." Consolidates and amends 33 & 34 Vic. c. 93 ; 37 & 38 Vic. c. 50.	45 & 46 Vic. c. 75.	
Married woman to be capable of holding property and of contracting, as if she were a *feme sole*, without intervention of Justice.	s. 1.	
Woman married after that entitled to hold property held by her as *feme sole* at time of marriage.	s. 2.	
Property acquired after Act by woman married before Act to be held by her as *feme sole*.	s. 5.	

them. Married women may maintain action, s. 11. Husband not to be liable to his wife's contracts before marriage, s. 12. How far she is liable, under Poor Law, to the parish for husband's maintenance, and also as to the maintenance of her children.

☞ Section 11 enables a married woman to sue civilly and criminally in respect to her separate earnings, property, &c. This Act of 1882 gives remedy to husband and wife against each other, and against all others in respect to their separate property, by criminal proceedings.

And by the 47 Vic. c. 14, husband and wife are *competent* witnesses, and except when defendant, he or she is *compellable* to give evidence.

Offence, or cause of Complaint.	Statute.	Extent of Jurisdiction.
MARRIED WOMEN—*continued*. "MARRIED WOMEN'S PROPERTY ACT, 1882." Remedies for protection of her property by *criminal proceedings* against her husband and others.	45 & 46 Vic. c. 75, s. 12.	
Liability to *criminal proceedings* at husband's prosecution.	s. 16.	
Married woman liable to union for maintenance of husband and children and grandchildren.	ss. 20 & 21.	
As to suits and summary proceedings, see Act.		
Alimony.—Married woman who shall have been deserted by her husband may summon him before Justices in Petty Sessions, and if Justices be satisfied that the husband is able, wholly or in part, to maintain his wife, or his wife and family, and has wilfully refused or neglected so to do, and has deserted his wife—	49 & 50 Vic. c. 52, s. 1.	May order that the husband shall pay to his wife such weekly sum, not exceeding £2, as Justices may consider to be in accordance with his means, and with any means the wife may have for her support and the support of her family. And the payment of any sum so ordered shall be enforced *in same manner as the payment of money under an order of affiliation*, and the same or other Justices may from
Proviso.—No order to be made in favour of a wife who has committed adultery, unless it has been condoned. And where it is proved that adultery has been committed by her after order made, the same or other Justices may discharge the order.	"	time to time vary the order on application of the husband or wife upon proof of the husband's or wife's means having altered since making of original or any subsequent order varying it. (*a*)
Summonses under Act to be granted, &c., in the ordinary way, and in the discretion of Justices as to service, &c., at the instance of the wife to obtain the order, and of the husband to rescind it.	s. 2.	2 J. or 1 Stip. Magistrate.

(*a*) *Alimony.*—This is the first Act we know of which empowers Justices in Petty Sessions to order payment of alimony to a wife deserted by her husband. And, indeed, did it not expressly exclude Scotland from its provisions, one would have doubted its application to Ireland. The means for enforcing the order is in a manner wholly unknown to Justices in Ireland, for they absolutely know nothing of these "Affiliation Orders." And so the Justices have to look to the Acts in

Offence, or cause of Complaint.	Statute.	Extent of Jurisdiction.
MASTERS, SERVANTS, WORK-MEN, &c. : See "Employers and Workmen."		
MEAL: See "Frauds as to Provisions."		
MEAT: See "Frauds as to Provisions."		
MERCHANDISE MARKS ACT (1862): Forging or falsely applying any trade-mark, with intent to defraud, or causing or procuring, &c.—Pecuniary penalties under this Act are, in Ireland, recoverable by Civil Bill.	25 & 26 Vic. c. 88, ss. 2 and 3.	Indictable misdemeanour; and adding to or altering trade-mark, forgery, s. 5.
Patents, Designs, and Trade-marks Act, 1883, provides summary powers for punishing persons falsely representing articles to be patented, and for an unauthorized assumption of the Royal Arms.	46 & 47 Vic. c. 57, ss. 105 and 106.	—
Act to amend the Patents, Designs, and Trade-marks Act, 1883.	51 & 52 Vic. c. 50.	

force in England. Two statutes must be consulted—the 11 & 12 Vic. c. 43, and the 42 & 43 Vic. c. 49. Shortly, then, the procedure appears to be an information of the desertion and of the ability to pay :—a summons ; an order. In case of disobedience, and where there are arrears due, an information of the fact, a summons, or warrant if necessary, to bring up defendant to be further dealt with. If defendant has goods, a warrant of distress ; and if he has no goods, and says so, or shows that a warrant of distress would be ruinous to him and his family, or more injurious than imprisonment, then to be committed according to sec. 5, 42 & 43 Vic. c. 49. The Bill on this subject contemplated provisions for judicial separation and the custody of children ; but it was a session that had not settled down to steady legislation, and these were subjects that required delicate handling. They had to be dropped, and the portion as to alimony hurried through Parliament without method or reference to the Acts in force in Ireland enabling Justices to carry out orders. Hence the Act contains a marginal subject "custody of children," but nothing about it in the provisions. As the Act is in its nature civil, and both parties at liberty to seek to have orders varied, so it would appear that the Justices may allow the complainant and defendant, husband and wife, to give evidence.

Offence, or cause of Complaint.	Statute.	Extent of Jurisdiction.
MERCHANT SHIPPING ACT (*principal Act*) : (*a*) DIVISIONS OF ACT.	17 & 18 Vic. c. 104.	
1. Board of Trade—its functions,	ss. 6–16.	—
2. British ships ; ownership ; measurement ; registry.	ss. 18–108.	—
3. Masters and seamen, ...	ss. 109–290.	—
4. Safety and prevention of accidents,	ss. 291–329.	—
5. Pilotage, ...	ss. 330–388.	—
6. Lighthouses, ...	ss. 389–416.	—
7. Mercantile Marine Fund, ..	ss. 417–431.	—
8. Wrecks, casualties, and salvage,	ss. 432–501.	—
9. Liability of ship-owners, ..	ss. 502–516.	—
10. Legal procedure, ...	ss. 517–543.	—
11. Miscellaneous matters. See Admiralty (Ireland) Act, 1876.	39 & 40 Vic. c. 28.	
Engagement of Seamen.—Unlicensed persons (other than the owner, master, or mate, or the *bond fide* servant, and in constant employ of owner or a shipping master) engaging or supplying seamen or apprentices.	17 & 18 Vic. c. 104, s. 147.	Penalty not exceeding £20 ; recoverable as in Petty Sessions Act, and by scale (*b*) 2 J.
Employing unlicensed persons (other than those excepted as aforesaid) for the purpose of engaging or supplying seamen or apprentices.	,,	Penalty not exceeding £20 ; recoverable as in Petty Sessions Act, and by scale. 2 J.
Knowingly receiving or accepting seamen or apprentices so illegally supplied. (*c*)	,,	Like penalty.

(*a*) Such portions of this important statute are abstracted as are most frequently referred to in Maritime Petty Sessions Courts. To facilitate reference on other matters, the various subjects and divisions of the Act are given above.

Fees, &c.—The Schedule of Fees allowed by Board of Trade for inquiries as to wrecks, &c., see 19 & 20 Vic. c. 75 ; and see schedule in *Appendix*.

(*b*) *Procedure.*—Section 518 directs that offences, where the imprisonment does not exceed six months, nor the penalty £100, shall, in Ireland, be prosecuted summarily, before two or more Justices, as in 14 & 15 Vic. c. 93 (the Petty Sessions Act), and all its provisions applicable thereto. By section 519, one Stipendiary Magistrate has power to act alone. Sec. 520 provides that offences shall be deemed to be committed where they actually take place, or where the offender shall be found.

Application of penalties, &c.—See sec. 524.

(*c*) These provisions, as to shipment and discharge, apply to all seagoing *British* ships, wherever registered (sec. 109). They do not seem to apply to unregistered

Offence, or cause of Complaint.	Statute.	Extent of Jurisdiction.
MERCHANT SHIPPING ACT—*con.* Demanding or receiving, directly or indirectly, from any seaman or apprentice, or from any person on his behalf, any remuneration other than the proper fees for shipping them.	17 & 18 Vic. c. 104, s. 148.	Penalty not exceeding £5; recoverable as above. 2 J.
Wages.—Right to wages commences at the time of commencing work, or at the time specified in agreement for commencing work, or presence on board, whichever first happens.	s. 181.	—.
Mode of recovering Wages. (a)—Any seaman or apprentice, or any person duly authorized on his behalf, may sue in a summary manner before any two Justices of the Peace, acting in or near to the place at which the service has terminated, or at which the seaman or apprentice has been discharged, or at which any person upon whom the claim is made is or resides.	17 & 18 Vic. c. 104, ss. 188 and 523.	Justices may decree amount of wages due, not exceeding £50, and if not paid at the time and in the manner prescribed in the order, may, in addition to any other powers for compelling payment, direct amount to be levied by distress or poinding and sale of the ship, her tackle, furniture, and apparel. 1 J.
Master to have same remedies for recovery of his wages as seaman.	s. 191.	
Master to account for wages and effects of any seaman or apprentice who dies during the voyage. (And see also Amended Act, 25 & 26 Vic. c. 63, s. 21, respecting seamen lost with their ship.)	s. 194.	

vessels. Foreign seamen, as well as British subjects, fall within these terms. Every person, too, who serves in *any* capacity on board, save the master and apprentices (see sec. 2), falls within the term " Seaman."—" *Dowdeswell's Shipping.*"

Exemption from Stamp Duty.—Agreement or memorandum made between the master and mariners of any ship or vessel for wages on any voyage coastwise from port to port in the United Kingdom.—Stamp Act, 1870, 33 & 34 Vic. c. 97 (schedule) ; and see title " Stamps."

(a) These provisions as to *Wages, Protection from Imposition, &c. &c.*, applicable also to colonial ships (sec. 109). See also 43 & 44 Vic. c. 16, hereafter as to wages (sec. 11).

Offence, or cause of Complaint.	Statute.	Extent of
MERCHANT SHIPPING ACT—*con.* Seamen or apprentice desiring to go on shore to make complaint to a Justice, consular officer, or naval officer, against master or any of the crew, he shall, if service of the ship will permit, be allowed to do so. And if master refuse—	17 & 18 Vic. c. 104, s. 232.	Penalty n £10 ; reco Petty Sess
Protection from Imposition (a)— Lodging-house keepers overcharging seaman or apprentice—	s. 235.	Like Penalt
Person detaining money, documents, or effects of any seaman or apprentice, and does not return same or pay the value thereof when required by such seaman, &c., subject to such deduction as may be justly due to him from such seaman, &c., in respect of board or lodging, or otherwise, or absconds therewith—	s. 236.	Penalty n £10 ; and, Justices m amount (such mo ments, or ject to su as afores forthwith seaman or
Unauthorized persons going on board before the final arrival of ship at dock or place of discharge, without permission.	s. 237.	Penalty n £20 ; reco Petty Sess
Person within twenty-four hours after arrival soliciting any seaman to become lodger, or who takes out of ship any effects of any seaman except under his personal direction and with permission of master.	s. 238.	Penalty n £5 ; rec above, and
Discipline.—Misconduct endangering ship, or life or limb of any person on board.	s. 239.	Indictable n

(a) These sections, protecting seamen from imposition, reach all (those who do not belong to the ships of any country, so the remed; powers they confer are held to be applicable to the complaints of sea to foreign ships as well as to those of British and colonial ships ; a not contrary to the 109th section. See also 43 & 44 Vic. c. 16, s. .

And for purchasing, &c., or having clothes or effects of R. N. se vard towns, &c., see 32 & 33 Vic. c. 57, and title "Navy," *post.*

Offence, or cause of Complaint.	Statute.	Extent of Jurisdiction.
MERCHANT SHIPPING ACT—*con.* **Desertion.** (*a*)—Desertion by seaman or apprentice. **N**eglecting or refusing without reasonable cause to join ship or proceed to sea; absent without leave within twenty-four hours before sailing; or for absence at any time without leave, and without sufficient reason, from ship or duty (not amounting to desertion).	17 & 18 Vic. c. 104, s. 243. (43 & 44 Vic. c. 16.)	The power to imprison repealed by 43 & 44 Vic. c. 16, sch. 2, and by sec. 11; the Employers and Workmen Act remains applicable to certain disputes.
Quitting ship without leave after arrival at port of delivery, and before she is placed in security.	,,	Shall forfeit out of wages a sum not exceeding one month's pay. 2 J.
Wilful disobedience to any lawful command.	,,	Imprisonment not exceeding 4 weeks, with or without H. L.; and also, at discretion of Court, to forfeit out of wages not exceeding two days' pay. 2 J.
Continued wilful disobedience to lawful commands or continued wilful neglect of duty.	,,	Imprisonment not exceeding 12 weeks, with or without H. L.; and, at discretion of Court, to forfeit for every 24 hours' continuance of disobedience or neglect either a sum not exceeding six days' pay or expense of substitute. 2 J.
Assaulting master or mate, · ·	,,	Imprisonment not exceeding 12 weeks, with or without H. L. 2 J.

(*a*) *Desertion*, as here used, has been held to mean the abandoning of the ship, *ne animo revertendi.* Inhumanity and ill-treatment on the part of the master and officers, and the repetition of which may be justly apprehended, will justify a seamen in quitting the ship, and form a good answer to any plea, alleging the desertion as a justification for non-payment of wages.—See *Dowdswell,* and see *Dowd on the Shipping Acts.*
For these acts of desertion or refusing to join ship or proceed to sea, see 43 & 44 *s.* c. 16, *hereinafter set out* where imprisonment is abolished; but *power is given have seamen, &c., conveyed on board his ship.*

U

Offence, or cause of Complaint.	Statute.	Extent of Jurisdiction.
MERCHANT SHIPPING ACT—*con.* Combining with any other of the crew to disobey lawful commands, to neglect duty, or to impede the navigation of the ship or the progress of the voyage.	17 & 18 Vic. c. 104, s. 243. (43 & 44 Vic. c. 16.)	Imprisonment not exceeding 12 weeks, with or without H. L. 2 J.
Wilfully damaging ship, embezzling or wilfully damaging stores or cargo.	,,	Forfeit out of wages a sum equal to loss sustained, and also to imprisonment not exceeding 12 weeks, with or without H. L. 2 J. —
Official Log.—Entry of offences in sec. 243 to be made in official log, and to be read over, or a copy given to the offender, and his reply, if any, to be also entered. (And see also from sec. 280 to sec. 287, as to entries in official logs.)	s. 244.	
Deserters may be sent on board, on application of master or owner, and may order offender to pay the expenses or that same be deducted from his wages. (a)	s. 247.	See 43 & 44 Vic. c. 16, s. 10, and sch. 2.
Enticing seaman or apprentice to desert or absent himself.	17 & 18 Vic. c. 104, s. 257.	Penalty not exceeding £10, recoverable as in Petty Sessions Act. 2 J.
Harbouring or secreting knowingly,	,,	Penalty not exceeding £20, recoverable as in Petty Sessions Act. 2 J.
Marine Stores.—Dealers in marine stores and manufacturers of anchors: For regulations to be observed, and penalties for their violation, see— And see title "Marine Stores."	ss. 480–483.	—
Crimes committed on the High Seas and Abroad.—Offences by British seamen at foreign ports (ashore or afloat) to be adjudged as if committed within the jurisdiction of the Admiralty of England.	s. 267.	

(a) Where seaman notifies his intention to be absent, see 43 & 44 Vic. c. 16, s. 10, *post.*

Offence, or cause of Complaint.	Statute.	Extent of Jurisdiction.
MERCHANT SHIPPING ACT—*con.* "MERCHANT SHIPPING ACT AMENDMENT ACT, 1862."	25 & 26 Vic. c. 63.	This Act to be construed as part of the foregoing Act.
Extends certain portions of the third part of first Act to registered sea-going fishing-boats, lighthouse vessels, and pleasure yachts.	s. 13.	
Provides for punishment of embezzlement in shipping offices; and officers, &c., to be deemed clerks or servants.	s. 16.	
Magistrates to have power of cancelling or suspending certificates of master or mate in certain cases, and on conditions in section.	s. 23.	

Incompetency.—As to the Power of the Master to Disrate his Mate for Incompetency.—In *Bothwell* v. *Lindsay*, before the Magistrates at the Thames Police Court, September, 1864, summons by chief mate to recover wages. The defence set up was incompetency. Mr. Partridge, for the mate, argued: So long as he holds a certificate of competency from the Board of Trade, I say he cannot be punished for incompetency; you may proceed for penalties for neglect, drunkenness, absence without leave, or other offences. Mr. Smyth, for the master, declined to take this course, and gave up his case. An order for £50 and one guinea costs was made. The Magistrate was asked, through the Home Office, for his report on the case, and the whole having been submitted to the Law Officers, they gave the following opinion:—

" OPINION.

"1 and 2. That it does not appear necessary to determine what would be the effect of a contract between the master and mate independently of the statute, inasmuch as the form of contract issued by the Board of Trade in pursuance of the statute was in this case adopted. This contract contains the following clause:—' If any person enters himself as qualified for a duty which he proves incompetent to perform, his wages shall be reduced in proportion to his incompetency.' We are of opinion that this clause gives the master power to make a reduction in the wages of the mate proportionate to his incompetency. With reference to the suggested causes of incompetency, we think that, if all or any of them produced permanent or continuing disability to perform his duties, this would be 'incompetency' within the meaning of the contract; but that mere occasional misconduct, though punishable in other ways, would not be 'incompetency.' We understand the term 'disrate' to mean the reduction of the wages of the mate to those of an ordinary seaman, which is all that has been done by the master. In this sense, in any case of proved incompetency, we think that the master has the power to 'disrate.'

"3. We are of opinion that this power to disrate or reduce the wages is not taken away by the effect given by the statute to the certificate of competency of the

U 2

Offence, or cause of Complaint.	Statute.	Extent of Jurisdictic
MERCHANT SHIPPING ACT— AMENDMENT ACT, 1862—*continued.* Wilful default in masters, &c., in observing lights, signals, &c., and regulations. (Equally applicable to foreign ships, sec. 57.)	17 & 18 Vic. c. 104, ss. 25, 26, 27, and 28.	Misdemeanour.
Rules for harbours under local Acts to continue in force, and may be made where none exist.	ss. 31 and 32.	
Surveyed Passenger Steamers.— Drunken or disorderly persons persisting in going on board after refusal.	25 & 26 Vic. c. 63, s. 35.	Penalty not exce 40s.: in default, imprisonment not ceeding 1 month. (
Persons on board molesting passengers after warning.	,,	Like.
Persons forcing way on board ship when full.	,,	Like.

₧nce, or cause of Complaint.	Statute.	Extent of Jurisdiction.
IANT SHIPPING ACT— ₘₑₙₜ ACT, 1862—*continued.* ers under last two sections ₛₑ names and addresses are ₁own) may be apprehended brought before any Justice.	s. 37.	Justice to hear and determine the complaint.
.—Extension and amend- : of eighth part of "Principal " giving summary jurisdiction ro Justices in salvage cases. ieutenant may appoint a rota ₁stices for the purpose.	s. 49. ,,	When no rota appointed, salvor, by notice to Justices' Clerk, may name one Justice, and owner another.
ed Act as to accommodation, cines, diet, &c.	30 & 31 Vic. c. 124.	—
's Clothing.—For purchasing, having in possession, &c., and accounting, see 32 & 33 Vic. 7. (Act applies to dockyard ₛ; in Ireland, to Cork and ₘstown.)		
ₐₙₜ SHIPPING ACT, 1871, ₛ and in part repeals 17 & 18 c. 104, and 18 & 19 Vic. ι.	34 & 35 Vic. c. 110.	
ₐₙₜ SHIPPING AMENDMENT 1873. further provision as to agree- ₛ with seamen. ₛ for survey of ships, &c. (*a*) gnals, &c. tions and penalties for sending ₙgerous goods. ₜription of dangerous goods,	36 & 37 Vic. c. 85.	This Act shall be construed as one with the Merchant Shipping Act, 1854, and the Acts amending the same, and the said Acts, and this Act may be cited collectively as the Merchant Shipping Acts, 1854, to 1873.

ₘₑₙ's complaints as to Ship.—See sec. 7, Merchant Shipping Act, 1871.
) Magistrates of 13th January, 1873, containing list of Port Surveyors,
ſustices may apply.

Offence, or cause of Complaint.	Statute.	Extent of Jurisdiction.
MERCHANT SHIPPING ACT—*con.* MERCHANT SHIPPING AMENDMENT ACT, 1873—*continued.* Power to refuse to carry, and throw overboard same. Forfeiture, &c.	36 & 37 Vic. c. 85.	For procedure for penalties see former Act, 17 & 18 Vic. c. 104, secs. 518, 519, 520.
Amends and in part repeals 17 & 18 Vic. c. 104; 18 & 19 Vic. c. 91; 25 & 26 Vic. c. 63; 34 & 35 Vic. c. 110.		
Applies Court of Admiralty (Ireland) Act, 1867.		
Foreign Jurisdiction Acts.		
UNSEAWORTHY SHIPS—OVERLOADING, &c. This Act may be cited as the "Merchant Shipping Act, 1876."(*a*)	39 & 40 Vic. c. 80.	
Unseaworthy Ships.—Sending or attempting to send, or being a party to sending, &c., a British ship to sea in such unseaworthy state as to be likely to endanger life.	s. 4.	Indictable misdemeanour, unless proof given that reasonable means to her being made seaworthy were used, or that her going in such unseaworthy state was, under the circumstances, reasonable and justifiable; defendant may give evidence.

(*a*) This Act (substituted for a five years' Act which just expires, and by this repealed) is known as *Plimsoll's Act*, a member of the House of Commons, conspicuous for his persistent agitation in behalf of seamen, and his complaints of the overloading and unseaworthiness of ships. Its introduction caused considerable consternation amongst the grain merchants, owners, shippers, and consignees. It was feared that British ships would in this respect be placed at so great a disadvantage that our whole mercantile marine would suffer, and that either the trade would be altogether transferred to foreign ships, or that British owners would be driven to sail under foreign flags. No such results have followed. These precautions are now held to be indispensable, and other countries are rather disposed to avail of the precedent and the humane provisions of Plimsoll's Act.

Survey.—There has been supplied to the different seaport Petty Sessions Courts a list of the ports at which the Board of Trade have appointed surveyors, and the districts within which they perform their duties.

Offence, or cause of Complaint.	Statute.	Extent of Jurisdiction.
MERCHANT SHIPPING ACT— UNSEAWORTHY SHIPS, &c.—*con.* Master of British ship knowingly taking such ship as aforesaid to sea.	39 & 40 Vic. c. 80, s. 4.	Like offence, unless he prove as aforesaid.
A prosecution under this section shall not be instituted except by consent of Board of Trade, &c.		
Obligation of shipowner to crew with respect to use of reasonable efforts to secure seaworthiness.	s. 5.	
Power to detain unsafe ship and procedure for such detention.	s. 6.	
Act provides as to survey.		
Foreign Ships.—Application of provisions as to detention of foreign ships *overloading* or *improper loading.*	s. 13.	
Appeal on refusal of certain certificates to ships.	s. 14.	
Scientific referees	s. 15.	
Passenger steamers and emigrant ships.	s. 16, &c.	
Provision as to food, space, &c., signals of distress, inextinguishable lights, and life-buoys in passenger steamers and emigrant ships.	ss. 20–21.	
Grain Cargoes.—How to be stowed and secured.	s. 22.	For non-compliance (knowingly), managing owner, master, or agent of owner charged with the loading, &c., shall incur a penalty not exceeding £300, to be recovered on summary conviction. 2 J.

Offence, or cause of Complaint.	Statute.	Extent of Jurisdiction.
MERCHANT SHIPPING ACT— UNSEAWORTHY SHIPS, &c.—*con.* *Deck Cargoes.*—Space occupied by deck cargo to be liable to dues, and penalty for carrying deck loads of timber in winter.	39 & 40 Vic. c. 80, ss. 23, 24.	
Deck and load lines.—Marking of load lines on foreign-going and coasting vessels.	ss. 25, 26, 27.	
Investigations into Shipping Casualties.	ss. 29–33.	
Miscellaneous provisions, . . (Repeals sub-sec. (4) of sec. 301; portion of sec. 318, which requires owners to transmit declarations therein; sec. 434; sec. 437, from "and in case he so requires" to end of section; and sec. 449 of 17 & 18 Vic. c. 104; sec. 11 of 34 & 35 Vic. c. 110; sections 11, 12, 13, and 14 of 36 & 37 Vic. c. 85; and repeals the whole of 38 & 39 Vic. c. 88.)	34 to end.	
The several shipping Acts may be cited collectively as "The Merchant Shipping Acts, 1854 to 1876." Part of sec. 39 repealed by 45 & 46 Vic. c. 55.	s. 2.	
Merchant Seamen (payment of Wages and Rating) Act, 1880.	43 & 44 Vic. c. 16.	
Shall be construed as one with Merchant Shipping Acts, 1854 to 1876, and may be cited as The Merchant Shipping Acts, 1854 to 1880.	s. 1.	
Advance Notes.—Conditional advance notes illegal. Amends 17 & 18 Vic. c. 104, s. 169, as to allotment notes.	s. 2.	
Wages.—Rules as to payment of wages.	s. 4.	

Offence, or cause of Complaint.	Statute.	Extent of Jurisdiction.
MERCHANT SHIPPING ACT—*con.* *Boarding ship without permission, &c.*—Where a ship is about to arrive, is arriving, or has arrived at the end of her voyage, every person not being in H. M.'s service, or not being duly authorized, by law for the purpose, who— (1) Goes on board without permission of master, before the seamen lawfully leave the ship at the end of their engagement, or are discharged (whichever last happens); or— (2) Being on board the ship, remains there after being warned to leave by master, or by a police officer, or by any officer of Board of Trade or of Customs.	43 & 44 Vic. c. 16, s. 5.	Shall, for every such offence, be liable on summary conviction to a fine not exceeding £20; or at the discretion of Court to imprisonment not exceeding 6 months; and master of the ship or any officer of Board of Trade may take him into custody, and deliver him up forthwith to a constable, to be taken before Court or magistrates having cognizance of the offence. 2 J.
Provisions contained in this sec. 5 to apply to ships of foreign countries whose government have similar provisions as to British ships, and desire that the above provisions shall apply to their ships within British territorial jurisdiction.	s. 6.	
Power of Court to rescind Contract.—Where a proceeding is instituted in or before any Court in relation to any dispute between an owner or master of a ship, and a seaman or apprentice to the sea service, *arising out of or incidental to their relation as such, or is instituted for the purpose of this section.*	s. 8.	The Court if, having regard to all the circumstances of the case, they think it just so to do, may rescind contract upon such terms as Court thinks just, and this power shall be in addition to any other jurisdiction which the Court can exercise independently of this section. 2 J.
"*Court*" for the purposes of section includes any Magistrate or Justice having jurisdiction in the matter to which proceeding relates.		

Offence. or cause of Complaint.	Statute.	Extent of Jurisdiction.
MERCHANT SHIPPING ACT—*con.* *Desertion and absence without leave.* —A seaman or apprentice to the sea service shall not be liable to imprisonment for deserting, or for neglecting or refusing, without reasonable cause, to join his ship, or to proceed to sea in his ship, or for absence without leave at any time within 24 hours of his ship's sailing from any port, or for absence at any time without leave, and without sufficient reason from his ship or from his duty.	43 & 44 Vic. c. 16, s. 8.	
Whenever, either at the commencement, or during the progress of any voyage, any seaman or apprentice neglects or refuses to join, or deserts from or refuses to proceed to sea in any ship in which *he is duly engaged to serve*, or is found otherwise absenting himself therefrom without leave, the master or any mate, or the owner, ship's husband, or consignee, may, with or without the assistance of the local police officers or constables, who are hereby directed to give the same, if required, convey him on board :	s. 10.	
Provided that if seaman or apprentice so requires, he shall first be taken before some Court, capable of taking cognizance of the matters to be dealt with according to law ; and that if it appears to the Court that he has been conveyed on board or taken before the Court on improper or insufficient grounds, the master, mate, owner, ship's husband, or consignee, as the case may be, shall incur—	,,	Penalty not exceeding £20 ; but such penalty, if inflicted, shall be a bar to any action for false imprisonment. 2 J.
If a seaman or apprentice to the sea service intends to absent himself from his ship or his duty, may give notice to owner or master,	,,	

Offence, or cause of Complaint.	Statute.	Extent of Jurisdiction.
MERCHANT SHIPPING ACT—*con.* not less than 48 hours before time which he ought to be on board; such notice being given, Court shall not exercise powers conferred by 17 & 18 Vic. c. 104, s. 247.	43 & 44 Vic. c. 16, s. 10.	
Subject to foregoing provisions of this section, the powers conferred by sec. 247 of 17 & 18 Vic. c. 104, may be exercised, notwithstanding the abolition of imprisonment for desertion and similar offences and of apprehension without warrant.		
Saving.—Nothing in section shall affect sec. 239 of the 17 & 18 Vic. c. 104.		
Extension to Seamen and Apprentices of Employers and Workmen Act, 1875 (38 & 39 Vic. c. 90).		
Repeals the powers to imprison in 17 & 18 Vic. c. 104, s. 243, sub-secs. (1) and (2). Section 246 of same Act.		
In 'sec. 247, same Act, the words "instead of committing the offender to prison." Sec. 248, same Act. See Schedule 2.		
Grain Cargoes.—Merchant Shipping (carriage of grain) Act, 1880, shall be construed with Merchant Shipping Act, 1854, &c. &c., and together cited as Merchant Shipping Acts, 1854 to 1880.	43 & 44 Vic. c. 43.	Penalty not exceeding £300. 2 J.
Obligations to take necessary precautions to prevent grain cargo from shifting, and in default, the master, and any agent of owner charged with the loading—	s. 3.	Owner shall be liable to same penalty, unless he shows that he took all reasonable means to enforce observance and was not privy to breach of the section.

Offence, or cause of Complaint.	Statute.	Extent of Jurisdiction.
MERCHANT SHIPPING ACT—*con.* As to precautions against shifting of grain cargo laden in port in Mediterranean or Black Sea, or on coast of North America, see—	43 & 44 Vic. c. 43, s. 4.	
For exemption from precautions specified in Act for ships laden in Mediterranean or Black Sea, or on coast of North America, see—	s. 5.	
For notice to be given by master of the kind and quantity of grain cargo and other particulars, and penalty in default, see—	s. 6.	Penalty not exceeding £100. 2 J.
Any master of a ship, who in any notice required by this Act wilfully makes any false statement or wilfully omits any material particular.	s. 7.	Penalty not exceeding £100. 2 J.
Power of Board of Trade for enforcing of Act, inspecting cargo, &c.	s. 8.	
Prosecution of offences and recovery of penalties as under " Merchant Shipping Act, 1854, and Acts amending same."		
Repeals sec. 2 of 39 & 40 Vic. c. 80, s. 22.		
MERCHANT SHIPPING (FISHING-BOATS) ACT, 1883. Repeals certain sections of Merchant Shipping Act, 1854, so far as applicable to fishing-boats. First Schedule—	46 & 47 Vic. c. 41.	
How apprenticeship indentures with boys under 16 is to be entered into, and provisions to be therein, and limit of age.	ss. 4, 5, 6.	
Penalty on persons receiving money for binding apprentice to sea-fishing service.	s. 7.	Misdemeanour.

Offence, or cause of Complaint.	Statute.	Extent of Jurisdiction.
MERCHANT SHIPPING ACT— MERCHANT SHIPPING (FISHING-BOATS) ACT, 1883—*continued.* Indentures, if not entered into before Superintendent of Mercantile Marine, to be void—	46 & 47 Vic. c. 41, s. 8.	
Penalty for taking boy to sea under void indenture or agreement, and power of Superintendent of Marine Office in such case.	s. 9.	
Skippers of fishing-boats' agreements with seamen, and manner of entering into.	s. 14, &c.	
Penalty for shipping men without agreement duly executed.	s. 20.	
Penalty for falsifying or delivering false copy agreement.	s. 23.	
As to wages and discharges.	ss. 24-27.	
As to discipline.—Offences of seamen, apprentices, neglect, absence, disobedience, assault on skipper, &c., combination, damage to cargo, stores, &c., smuggling, &c.	s. 28.	
Deserters.—Seamen and apprentices deserting, disobedience, &c., how dealt with.	ss. 31, 32.	
Boat proceeding to sea without duly certified skipper, penalty, &c.	s. 42.	
Disputes between skippers, owners and seamen, to be decided by Superintendent of Marine Office.	s. 46.	
Miscellaneous. — As to Lodging-Houses.	s. 48.	
Legal Proceedings.—Offences to be deemed offences under Merchant Shipping Acts, 1854 to 1883, and every of them.	s. 51.	
Schedules of indentures, agreements, &c.	,,	

Offence, or cause of Complaint.	Statute.	Extent of Jurisdiction.
MILITIA : Act to consolidate the Act relating to militia (may be cited as "Militia Act, 1882.") Sec. 9 applies to militia recruits the following sections of the "Army Act, 1881," viz. :— Sec. 80—Relating to enlistment and attestation. Sec. 96—Relating to claims of masters to apprentices. Sec. 98—Imposing fine for unlawful recruiting. Sec. 99—Making recruits punishable for *false answers.* Sec. 100—As to validity of attestation and enlistment, &c. Sec. 101—Relating to competent military authority. Sec. 163—So far as to *documentary evidence,* &c., substituting militia in sections, and other alterations as to training, &c. And allowing recruits to be attested before militia officer, &c. *Recruit making false Answers.* (a)—Knowingly making false answer to any question contained in the attestation paper.	45 & 46 Vic. c. 49. 44 & 45 Vic. c. 58, s. 99.	 Imprisonment, with or without H. L., not exceeding 3 months. 2 J. or 1 Stipendiary.

(a) *Prosecution of Militiamen.*—In the above and in other cases where the offender may be dealt with by Military Law or by the Court of Summary Jurisdiction, the Justices before dealing summarily with the case shall require to have the authority of the commanding officer of the militiaman, or of a superior authority signified to the court in writing. See Royal Warrant, dated 27th December, 1882. A copy of the Royal Warrant was sent by Under Secretary, Dublin Castle, to each Petty Sessions to be observed in the case of militiamen and men of the reserve forces. See *Circular* to Magistrates, No. 23, 29th February, ____ ; and see sec. 43, under which regulations are made.

Offence, or cause of Complaint.	Statute.	Extent of Jurisdiction.
MILITIA—*continued.* (Sec. 9 of Militia Act makes sec. 99 of Army Act, 1881, applicable to this offence.)	44 & 45 Vic. c. 58, s. 99.	If offender has been attested as a militiaman, he may be tried by court-martial, or summarily as above.
A person discharged with disgrace from any part of H. M.'s forces, or from the navy enlisting into militia without declaring the fact; or is concerned when subject to military law in the enlistment for service in the militia of any man whom he has reason to believe thereby offends against the Army Act, 1881, or this (Militia) Act; or, wilfully contravenes when subject to military law any enactment, regulations, &c., relating to enlistment or attestation of militiaman.	45 & 46 Vic. c. 49, s. 10.	Imprisonment, with or without H. L., for not less than 2 nor more than 6 months. 2 J. or 1 Stip., or by court-martial.
Desertion, absence from training, &c.—Militiaman who, without leave, or such sickness, or other reasonable excuse as may be allowed in accordance with the regulations, fails to appear at preliminary or annual training or embodiment, shall (a) in the case of embodiment be guilty, according to circumstances, of desertion within meaning of sec. 12, or absenting himself without leave within meaning of sec. 15 of Army Act, 1881; and for offence under this section or under sec. 12 or sec. 15 of Army Act, 1881—	s. 23.	Fine not less than 40s., and not more than £25; and in default of payment, imprisonment with or without H. L., by scale, but not less than 7 days. 2 J. or 1 Stip., or be liable to be tried by court-martial.

(a) *Apprehending, Remanding and Reporting Deserters.*—Sec. 154 of the Army Act, 81, as to apprehending, remanding for necessary evidence, &c., is made by sec. 9 of Militia Act applicable to militiamen. And where the deserter or absentee is handed over to escort, or dealt with summarily, the Justice shall send descriptive form to War Office. There is a fee of 2s. payable to the Justice's clerk for making this report.

Masters claiming their Apprentices.—Sec. 9 makes the 96th section of Army Act, 881, form of oath and certificate in schedule applicable to apprentices entering the militia.

Offence, or cause of Complaint.	Statute.	Extent of Jurisdict
MILITIA—*continued.* Any person who *falsely* represents himself to any military, naval, or civil authority, to be a deserter or absentee without leave from militia—	45 & 46 Vio. c. 49, s. 24.	Imprisonment wit without H. L., n ceeding 3 months 2 J. or 1
Aiding desertion, &c.—Any person who, by any means, procures or persuades or attempts to persuade, &c., militiaman to absent himself, or knowingly aids him, &c., or, knowing him to be an absentee, conceals him or aids in doing so, or employs him, or aids or assists in his rescue— Section applies sec. 153 of the Army Act, 1881, to militia deserters and the punishment to the employers as those aiding in concealing them. (a)	s. 25.	Fine not exceeding in default, &c., sonment by scale. 2 J. or 1
Fradulent enlistment, false answers, by militiamen, &c. :— (1) While belonging to *militia*, without having fulfilled the conditions enabling him to enlist, or enrols in any of the auxiliary or reserve forces, or enters the Royal Navy; or,	s. 26.	Liable to be trie court-martial, dealt with summa imprisonment, wi without H. L., fi less than 1 nor than 3 months ; o
(2) When belonging to the *reserve forces*, or to any of *auxiliary forces*, other than the militia, or to the Royal Navy, without having fulfilled the conditions, &c., enlists or enrols in the militia, if on service as part of the regular forces or embodied as a militiaman at the time, shall be guilty of fraudulent enlistment, and in any other case shall be guilty of making a false answer—	,,	not less than £5 more than £25 ; i fault of payment prisonment, wit without H. L., n than 1 month nor than the maximi P. S. scale ; and i of a *second* or *subs* conviction, imp ment not less t nor more than 6 m with or without E 2 J. or 1

(a) Employers of militiamen or reserve men, who desert or absent then should be aware of the consequences that may follow any contravention section. It is the same offence as harbouring or employing, knowingly, a c from the army.

nce, or cause of Complaint.	Statute.	Extent of Jurisdiction.
\—*continued.* : to commit an offence under ection.	45 & 46 Vic. c. 49, s. 26.	If tried summarily:—As if the terms of imprisonment or amounts of fine were reduced to one-half.
ability of deserter, absentee, iudulent enlister to further e.	s. 27.	
roceedings.—Trial of offences, ery and application of fines Militia Act. 166 of the Army Act, 1881, applicable as to recovery and ation of fines. (*a*).	s. 42.	
tion of Fines.—To be paid to mmanding officer of the part ə militia to which offender ɣs.	,,	
sec. 164 of the Army Act, as to evidence of *civil con-* ı, *&c.*	s. 44.	
sec. 163 as to evidence by ition paper, documents, &c.	,,	
on, &c.—Proceedings against ing militiamen may be taken ıer his service has or has not ıd. and within two months ıffence becomes known to his anding officer, if offender be apprehended, or within 2 ıs after he is apprehended, 3. same time be charged with ıl offences of desertion, frau- ı enlistment, or making false ır, and evidence be given of see sec. 43, sub-sec. (3). Militia Reserve," see " Re-Forces."		

lication of Fines.—Court, if it sees fit, may order portion, not exceeding ormer; remainder to be applied as in Fines Act (Ireland), 1851.

X

Offence, or cause of Complaint.	Statute.	Extent of Jurisdiction.
MINES : THE "COAL MINES REGULATION ACT, 1872." Act applies to mines of coal, stratified ironstone, mines of shale, and mines of fireclay. Regulates employment of women, young persons, and children; protection against injuries, &c., inspection, arbitration, general and special rules. Provides penalties for offences against Act, &c.	35 & 36 Vic. c. 76.	Offences triable before a divisional Justice in Dublin; elsewhere in Ireland, before 2 Justices in Petty Sessions.
Somewhat similar provisions are in the Metalliferous Mines Regulation Act, 1872.	35 & 36 Vic. c. 77.	
MONTH. (a)	14 & 15 Vic. c. 93, s. 44.	—
(Means Calendar Month)	13 Vic. c. 21,	So it should appear in sentence and committal.
MUNICIPAL ELECTIONS: No person who is included in a register for a borough or a ward thereof as a burgess or citizen shall be retained or employed for payment or reward by or on behalf of a candidate at an election for such borough or any ward thereof, as a canvasser for the purposes of the election; and the person so employed, and the candidate or other person by whom he is retained or employed shall, on conviction, be liable to—	35 & 36 Vic. c. 60, s. 7.	Penalty not exceeding £10; in default, &c., imprisonment by scale. 2 J.
Agent or canvasser retained or employed for payment or reward shall not vote at the election; for offending—	,,	Penalty not exceed £10; in default, imprisonment by sc

(a) The word "month" means lunar month, unless interpreted to mean o month by a statute, or by the context of the document in which the word "mo used. So if in a committal the word "month" only is used, the gaoler n it a lunar month. The Magistrate should, therefore, in the document or o use the word "calendar," and also in the Order Book.

Offence, or cause of Complaint.	Statute	Extent of Jurisdiction.
NICIPAL ELECTIONS—*con.* ıy candidate, or agent for candi- iate, who pays or agrees to pay any money on account of the convey- ınce of a voter to or from the poll ıhall, on conviction, be liable to—	35 & 36 Vic. c. 60, s. 8.	Penalty not exceeding £5; in default, &c., im- prisonment by scale. 2 J.
plication of Act to Ireland, and iefinitions. peals 5 & 6 Wm. iv. c. 76, ss. 54 to 56, inclusive; 22 Vic. c. 35, ss. 9 to 14, inclusive; 3 & 4 Vic. c. 108, ss. 90, 91. plies sec. 7 of 26 & 27 Vic. c. 29, Corrupt Practices; 31 & 32 Vic. c. 125, Parliamentary Election Act, 1868.	s. 28.	—
NICIPAL PRIVILEGE (IRE- ɪND) ACT, 1875:	39 & 40 Vic. c. 76.	
ITON (*Stolen*): und in possession unaccounted for. See "Larceny."	25 & 26 Vic. c. 30, s. 6.	
TINY ACT: ə "Army Discipline Act."		
TURALIZATION ACT, 1870: ıtus of aliens in the United King- dom.	33 Vic. c. 14. s. 2.	
ıwer of naturalised aliens to divest themselves of their status in cer- tain cases.	s. 3.	
ɔw British subjects may cease to be such.	s. 4.	
ien not entitled to be tried by jury *de medietate linguæ.*	s. 5.	

Offence, or cause of Complaint.	Statute.	Extent of Jurisdiction.
NATURALIZATION ACT, 1870— *continued.*		
Capacity of British subjects to renounce allegiance to Her Majesty.	33 Vic. c. 14, s. 6.	—
Regulations as to naturalization and resumption of British nationality.	s. 7.	—
NATURALIZATION ACT (1872). Act refers to a Convention between Her Majesty and the United States.	35 & 36 Vic. c. 39.	
As to confirmation of renunciation of nationality under the Convention.	s. 2.	—
Nothing contained in the "Naturalisation Act, 1870," shall deprive any married woman of any estate or interest in real or personal property to which she may have become entitled previously to the passing of that Act, or effect such estate or interest to her prejudice.	s. 3.	
NAVAL COAST VOLUNTEERS: *Fraudulent Enlistment.*—Naval Coast Volunteer offering himself to be enlisted in Her Majesty's regular forces or as a militiaman (or militiaman offering to enrol as volunteer).	16 & 17 Vic. c. 73, s. 18.	Imprisonment not exceeding 6 months. 1 J.
Officer or other person knowingly enlisting or enrolling volunteer into Her Majesty's regular forces or militia, or knowingly entering militiaman to serve as a volunteer; for every such offence—	,,	Penalty not exceeding £20. (a) 1 J. And enlistment to be null and void.

(a) These penalties are recoverable under the English Petty Sessions Act, 11 & 12 Vic. c. 43. It differs but little from the Irish Petty Sessions Act; the form of warrant in the latter will suit. By distress, and in default of distress, imprisonment. Where there are not sufficient goods off which to levy the penalty, the imprisonment may be, with or without H. L., for not exceeding 6 months.

Appropriation.—One moiety of penalty to person who shall inform, or sue for same; residue together with treble value—or, where the offence is proved by the ·····ner, then the whole penalty and treble value shall be applied as the Lord ·····dmiral, &c., shall direct.

Offence, or cause of Complaint.	Statute.	Extent of Jurisdiction.
NAVAL COAST VOLUNTEERS— *continued.*		
Accoutrements, &c.—Volunteer who shall sell, pawn, or lose his arms, clothes, accoutrements, or ammunition, or neglecting, &c., to return same in good order as therein.	16 & 17 Vic. c. 73, s. 19.	Penalty not exceeding £3; in default, &c., imprisonment not exceeding 2 months. 1 J.
Person who shall knowingly and willingly buy, take in exchange, in pledge, or otherwise receive or conceal any arms, &c., of such volunteer.	,,	Penalty not exceeding £10, and treble the value of the articles so received. 1 J.
Absent from Training.—Volunteer (not labouring under infirmity, &c.) who shall not appear at time and place appointed for training and exercise, &c. ; or appearing, if he afterwards deserts or absents himself.	s. 20.	Penalty not exceeding £20. 1 J.
Persons not attending when called into actual service—	s. 21.	May be apprehended and punished as deserters from the navy. See "Navy."
Harbouring, &c.—Any person 'who, by words or other means, shall persuade any volunteer under this Act or officer or man of the coast guard, revenue cruisers, &c., or other person required to serve in the navy under this Act, improperly to absent himself from duty—	s. 22.	Shall forfeit the sum of £20. 1 J.
Assisting or procuring volunteer or man as aforesaid, improperly so to absent himself, or concealing or employing him, knowing him to be so improperly absent— (Offence triable before Justice where offence committed, or where offender may happen to be.)	,,	Shall for every such offence, forfeit and pay the sum of £30.
NAVAL RESERVE: *Reserve Volunteer Force of Seamen.*— If any person shall enter or attempt to enter Royal Naval Volunteers as a new Volunteer more than once during whole or any part of same period of service.	22 & 23 Vic. c. 40, s. 16.	Penalty not exceeding £20; in default, &c., imprisonment by scale. 1 J.

Offence, or cause of Complaint.	Statute.	Extent of Jurisdict
NAVAL RESERVE—*continued.* Enlistment of Volunteers under this Act into H. M. Regular, or Indian or Militia, or Naval Coast Volunteers, and entering Militia as Naval Coast Volunteers under this Act to be void. And the person offending shall be liable to—for enlisting or enrolling, &c., for offering, &c.—	22 & 23 Vic. c. 40, s. 18.	Imprisonment not e ing 6 months.
Officer or person knowingly enlisting or enrolling such person.	,,	Penalty not exe £20; in default, imprisonment by
Necessaries.—Volunteer selling, pawning, losing arms, clothes, necessaries, &c., or articles provided for him under Act, or refusing or neglecting to return same in good order.	s. 19.	Penalty not exc £3; in default o ment, imprisonme exceeding 2 mont'
Person knowingly buying, receiving, or concealing such articles, &c. (Power to grant search warrant as in case of stolen goods.)	,,	Penalty not exc £10 and treble in default, &c. prisonment by sc
Absence from Training.—Volunteer not attending training and exercise, on notice, unless incapacitated by infirmity, &c., as in Act, or who deserts or absents himself during training, &c.	s. 20.	Penalty not exc £20; in default, imprisonment by
Person who by any means persuades Volunteer to desert or absent himself from duty.	s. 22.	Penalty not exc £20; in default, imprisonment by

(a) *Recovery of Penalties,* Sec. 24.—Forfeitures and costs may be enforce pecuniary penalty; and where there are no goods off which to levy pena' offender may be imprisoned, *with or without hard labour, for not exces months.* If the penalty, however, be under £5, the term of imprisonment b Penalties Act should be adopted.

Appropriation of Penalty.—Sec. 25 directs how penalty is to be applied. of penalty or forfeiture (not being treble value) shall go to informer or ˙ɋ; the other half, together with treble value, or (where the offence is pr

Offence, or cause of Complaint.	Statute.	Extent of Jurisdiction.
NAVAL RESERVE—*continued*. Assisting or procuring Volunteer to desert, or to be improperly absent, concealing, or employing him, or continuing to do so knowing him to be a deserter or improperly absent.	22 & 23 Vic. c. 40, s. 22.	Penalty not exceeding £30; in default, &c., imprisonment by scale. 1 J.
NAVY (*Royal*): Deserters or persons improperly absent from duty.	10 & 11 Vic. c. 62, s. 9.	To be committed to prison, and Justice to report the case, and give description of the deserter, and the ship from which he is absent, to chief officer of any of Her Majesty's ships, or if convenient to send him on board ship. 1 J.
Fraudulently confessing to be a deserter, or to be improperly absent from any of Her Majesty's ships.	s. 10.	May be compelled to serve as if he had volunteered; or if rejected, may be imprisoned for not exceeding 3 months' H.L. 2 J.
Every person who, by words or any other means, persuades any person in Her Majesty's Navy to desert, or improperly absent himself from duty. (a)	s. 11.	Penalty £20; in default of payment, imprisonment, with or without H. L., not exceeding 6 months. 1 J.
Every person who shall assist or procure any person in Her Majesty's Navy to desert, or improperly absent himself from his duty, or shall conceal or employ him, knowing him to be a deserter or improperly absent.	,,	Penalty £30; in default of payment, imprisonment, with or without H. L., not exceeding 6 months. 1 J.

· informer) the whole penalty and treble value shall be paid as Lord High Admiral or "Commissioners" shall direct.

Report of Adjudication.—Justice adjudging any penalty shall, within *four days* afterwards, report same to the "Secretary of the Admiralty."

Triable.—Where offence committed, or where offender may happen to be.

(a) One-half to informer or complainant of all penalties; the residue to Commissioners of *Greenwich* Hospital.

Offence, or cause of Complaint.	Statute.	Extent of Jurisdiction.
NAVY (*Royal*)—*continued.* Approaching or hovering about any of Her Majesty's ships or vessels, for the purpose of aiding or assisting any officer, seaman, or marine to desert or improperly absent himself.	16 & 17 Vic. c. 69, s. 12.	Penalty not exceeding £10; in default of payment, imprisonment, with or without H. L., not exceeding 6 months. 1 J.
For attempting to bring spirituous or fermented liquors on board ship, without commander's consent.	,,	Like.
Every person who, upon entering or offering himself to enter Her Majesty's naval service, shall make or give any false statement, whether orally or in writing, with intent to deceive any officer or person authorized to enter or enlist seamen or others for the naval service.	s. 16.	Shall be deemed to be a rogue and vagabond, within the intent and meaning of 5 Geo. iv. c. 83, and punished accordingly. (*a*).
Seamen's Clothing.—Penalty on purchasing, and on dealers found in possession of seamen's clothing in certain dockyard towns.	32 & 33 Vic. c. 57, ss. 4 and 5.	One J. P. may deal with cases. In Ireland Act is limited in its application to Cork and Queenstown (see sch. to Act).
Marines would seem to be included as soldiers of the Regular Forces, although under naval control, and the purchasing of the clothing, &c., to be punishable under section 156 of the Army Act, 1881; and, if so, punishable in places other than those named in the schedule to above Act.		
Act does not interfere with liability to being proceeded against by indictment. Incorporates sections 99, 103, 107 to 113, and 120 of the Larceny Act, 24 & 25 Vic. c. 96.	s. 7.	Act does not provide for the application of penalties; they may be applied as in Fines Act.
Naval reserve force of seamen—offences as to fraudulent enlistment.	22 & 23 Vic. c. 40.	

(*a*) This Act of 5 Geo. iv. c. 83, for the punishing of rogues and vagabonds, is an English Act; but for the punishment of this and several other offences in connexion with the public service, it is extended to Ireland; the punishment is not exceeding imprisonment, H. L.—1 J.

nce, or cause of Complaint.	Statute.	Extent of Jurisdiction.
ENT DRIVING : 'Driver."		.
APERS : gulating the conditions of ng, publishing, and payment ty, &c. Act requiring that copies of papers be kept, &c., and other rs, see 32 & 33 Vic. c. 24. to newspapers containing mable or seditious matter, &c., he forfeiture of same, types, to Her Majesty, see News- Libel and Registration Act, 45 Vic. c. 60, and 51 & 52 c. 64, *Appendix ;* and "In- le Offences," *Index.*	6 & 7 Wm. iv. c. 76.	All penalties not exceed- ing £20 may be re- covered at prosecution of any person before 1 Justice, with power to mitigate penalties. .
ICE ON PUBLIC ROADS, RETS, &c. : loose any horse or cattle on road or street. (a)	14 & 15 Vic. c. 92, s. 10. (36 & 37 Vic. c. 82.)	Penalty not exceeding 10s. ; in default, &c., imprisonment not ex- ceeding 7 days. 1 J.
igence or ill-usage in driving causing any mischief.	,,	Like.
on dog or other animal to or worry any person, horse, imal.	,,	Like.

ill be seen in this same section that for allowing swine or *other beast* on public roads the penalty is 2s. *Beast* is a comprehensive term, and le every irrational animal, while cattle strictly means beasts of pasture. rds " *turning loose* " will perhaps sufficiently point out those animals nerally harnessed or tied up ; while the words " *allowing to wander* " ly apply to the hog, goat, &c., the privileged *roué*, and the chartered

Offence, or cause of Complaint.	Statute.	Extent of Jurisdiction.
NUISANCE ON PUBLIC ROADS, STREETS, &c.—*continued.* Flying kites, playing any game, making slides on ice or snow, throwing fireworks, or discharging firearms on or within 60 feet of centre, or in any street of a town, &c. (*a*)	14 & 15 Vic. c. 92, s. 10. (36 & 37 Vic. c. 82.)	Penalty not exceeding 10*s.*; in default, &c., imprisonment not exceeding 7 days. 1 J.
Leaving plough, harrow, cart, &c., without horse, &c., being harnessed thereto, unless accidentally broken down.	,,	Like.
Slaughtering or leaving dead beast on, or skinning thereon, or within 30 feet of centre, save in enclosed yard, &c.	,,	Like.
Laying stones, timber, dirt, dung, turf, straw, rubbish, or scourings of ditches, or drains, or other object, on public road or street, &c., so as to cause danger, &c., to passengers, or allowing to remain longer than necessary.	,,	Like.
For every cartload of dung, rubbish, scourings, clay, stones, bricks, sand, or lime, or other like materials, allowed to remain thereon more than 24 hours after required by Justice or surveyor to remove—	,,	In addition to the foregoing fine, a further fine not exceeding 2*s.* 6*d.* a day after expiration of the 24 hours. 1 J.
Scalding casks, binding car or cartwheels, beating flax, threshing or winnowing corn on or within 30 feet of centre (save in house or enclosed yard).	,,	Penalty not exceeding 10*s.*; in default, &c., imprisonment not exceeding 7 days. 1 J.
Keeping or suffering dogs at large within 50 yards of public road, without being muzzled or sufficiently logged, to prevent their being dangerous.	,,	Like.
Justices may issue order to Constabulary, directing any dangerous dog, so kept at large, to be seized or killed.	,,	

(*a*) For throwing fireworks on *thoroughfares*, see also title "Gunpowder," where a penalty of £5 is provided for the offence.

Offence, or cause of Complaint	Statute.	Extent of Jurisdiction.
NUISANCES ON PUBLIC ROADS, STREETS, &c.—*continued.* Drying flax, burning bricks, or lime, weeds or vegetables for ashes, making bonfires or any other fire on any public road, or within 60 feet of centre (save in house or enclosed yard).	14 & 15 Vic. c. 92, s. 10. (36 & 37 Vic. c. 82.)	Penalty not exceeding 10s.; in default, &c., imprisonment not exceeding 7 days. 1 J.
Carrying timber or iron crosswise, so as to project more than 2 feet beyond wheels or sides. (a)	,,	Like.
Exposing horse or other animal for show, sale, or hire, except in place appointed.	,,	Penalty not exceeding 40s.; in default, &c., imprisonment not exceeding 1 month. 1 J.
Allowing swine or other beasts to wander on road or street (power to impound if owner not known).	,,	Penalty not exceeding 2s.; in default, &c., imprisonment not exceeding 1 week.* 1 J.
Foregoing provisions not to apply to surveyor or road contractor for acts done in execution of office or contract.	,,	
Surveyor or contractor allowing stones or other matter, &c., to remain on roads at night without due precaution.	,,	Penalty not exceeding £5; in default, &c., imprisonment not exceeding 2 months. 1 J.
Constabulary to take cognizance of offences committed on public roads against the provisions of this Act, and summon offenders; and so may other persons summon offenders.	s. 14 (sub-sec. 1).	

(a) A more extensive jurisdiction is given by the Towns Improvement Act. Under it a penalty of 20s. may be imposed on any person who causes any tree, timber, or iron beam to be drawn without sufficient means of guiding the same—sec. 72. And a similar power is given under the Police Clauses Act, 10 & 11 Vic. s. 89.

* This penalty of 2s. does not appear to mean 2s. per head, but 2s. to cover the whole offence.

Offence, or cause of Complaint.	Statute.	Extent of Jurisdiction.
NUISANCES ON PUBLIC ROADS, STREETS, &c.—*continued.* Where the name and residence of offender cannot be ascertained, he may be arrested; and, for refusing to discover his name, he *shall be liable*—	14 & 15 Vic. c. 92, s. 10. (36 & 37 Vic. c. 82.)	To be committed for any time not exceeding 1 month; or may be proceeded against for the penalty incurred, by description of his person, &c.
Horses, carriages, &c., of offenders taken into custody may be detained.	,,	—
Compensation.—Compensation, not exceeding 40*s.*, for any hurt or damage caused by the commission of offences, recoverable before Justices; in addition to penalty—	,,	Where offence is by the driver of any carriage, the owner shall pay compensation, and he may recover against the driver.
Obstructions generally.—Any person who shall, in any manner, wilfully, or by negligence or misbehaviour, prevent or interrupt the free passage of any person or carriage on any public road, or street, or crossing. For injuries to roads, see "Roads"; for other offences, see "Drivers." For nuisances injurious to health, see "Public Health;" see also as to "Street Nuisances," Towns Improvement Act, *Appendix;* "Steam Whistles."	s. 13. (36 & 37 Vic. c. 82.)	Penalty not exceeding 20*s.*; in default, &c., imprisonment not exceeding 14 days. 1 J.
OATH: In criminal proceedings affirmation may be taken in lieu.—See "Affirmation." See forms of Oaths, *Appendix,* and	51 & 52 Vic. c. 46.	
OBSCENE OR INDECENT BEHAVIOUR IN STREETS: See "Indecent Exposure," "Vagrancy."		

ence, or cause of Complaint.	Statute.	Extent of Jurisdiction.
)CTING STREETS, &c.; rson who shall, in any man- wilfully, or by negligence or ehaviour, prevent or inter- the free passage of any per- ir carriage on any public road, reet, or crossing.	14 & 15 Vic. c. 92, s. 13. (36 & 37 Vic. c. 82.)	Penalty not exceeding 20s.; in default, &c., imprisonment not ex- ceeding 14 days. 1 J. (See also Towns Improve- ment Act, *Appendix*.)
ONAL LICENCE: beer, spirits, &c. Jicensing Acts." P. may grant: 26 & 27 Vic. i, s. 20.	25 Vic. c. 22 s. 13. 37 & 38 Vic. c. 86, s. 4.	
. (in *Petty Sessions*): in Order Book, when signed,) good conviction. ments of, see . . .	14 & 15 Vic. c. 93, s. 21. 27 & 28 Vic. c. 99, s. 49 ; and 40 & 41 Vic. c. 56, s. 76.	Each order to be signed by one of the Justices present. (a)
RD : g fruit in—see "Larceny:" aging or destroying — see alicious Injuries."		

) order is not complete until signed by one of the Justices, and the words ction are mandatory. Nor is it sufficient to sign the book once at the veral cases. "Each order should be signed in the Order Book by a igning his name opposite to it, or immediately after it."—*Circular*, *er*, 1860.

g Order.—"I think the Magistrates who pronounced the order for con- iay, on the same day, and in the presence of the parties, alter their before the book is signed by one of the Magistrates."—*Law Adviser's* *3rd January*, 1854. But at all times where Justices happened to draw ormal conviction they were at liberty—bound—to amend, if warranted by in evidence, and on the proceedings, and to draw up a correct one, and it range they should have no such power over their order.—See now Vic. c. 56, s. 74.

Offence, or cause of Complaint.	Statute.	Extent of Jurisdiction.
OVERHOLDING TENEMENTS : See "Landlord and Tenant."		
OYSTERS : See "Fisheries."		
PALE : Stealing—see "Larceny."		
PALMISTRY : See "Vagrancy."		
PARLIAMENTARY ELECTIONS : *Secrecy.*—Officers, clerks, and agents failing to maintain secrecy at polling station, interfering with voters, or attempting to ascertain number on ballot paper at polling station, or at counting of votes, &c. &c. (see this sec. more fully set out under "Elections," Indictable Index).	35 & 36 Vic. c. 33, s. 4.	Imprisonment for any term not exceeding 6 months, with or without H. L. 2 J.
PASSENGER SHIPS : This Act applies to every " passenger ship " from United Kingdom to any place out of Europe, not being within the Mediterranean Sea.	18 & 19 Vic. c. 119.	—
Persons found on board with intent, fraudulently to obtain passage. (Penalty increased from £5 to £20 by 26 & 27 Vic. c. 51, s. 7.)	18 & 19 Vic. c. 119, s. 18.	Penalty not exceeding £20; in default of payment, imprisonment not exceeding 3 months' H. L. 1 J.
Passengers' Rights.—Where passage not provided according to contract ticket in ship specified, or an equally eligible ship to same port, within 10 days.—	s. 48.	Return of passage money, and not exceeding £10 compensation for each passenger; in default of payment, imprisonment not exceeding 3 months' H. L. 2 J. or 1 Stip.

nce, or cause of Complaint.	Statute.	Extent of Jurisdiction.
GER SHIPS—*continued.* nce in case of detention, d by stress of weather, &c., that passengers are main- l, no subsistence money al-	18 & 19 Vic. c. 119, s. 49.	1s. 6d. a-day each adult for first 10 days; after, 3s. a-day until depar- ture; recoverable as above. 2 J. or 1 Stip.
of wreck or damage, passage provided within certain time eks), and subsistence money n meantime. In default—	s. 51.	Return of all passage money paid; recover- able as above.
; passenger at any other than contracted for, unless with at, or rendered necessary by of the sea. 58 preserves passenger's of action.	s. 56.	Penalty not exceeding £50, nor less than £10; in default of payment, imprisonment not ex- ceeding 3 months' H.L. 2 J. or 1 Stip.
·Brokers' and Agents' Of- . — Passage-broker acting ut licence. not required by passage- r's agent; but broker to be 1sible for agents.	s. 66.	Penalty not exceeding £50, nor less than £20; recoverable as above.
-brokers to employ no agents t expressly appointed by ; and agent to produce his ntment on demand. For ompliance by either—	s. 69.	Penalty not exceeding £50, nor less than £20; in default of payment, imprisonment not ex- ceeding 3 months' H.L. 2 J. or 1 Stip.
, by false representations or , inducing any other to en- passages.	s. 70.	Penalty not exceeding £20; nor less than £5; recoverable as before.
;, inducing persons to part or destroying ticket.	s. 72.	Penalty not exceeding £20; in default of pay- ment, imprisonment not exceeding 3 months. 2 J. or 1 Stip.
lisputes arise touching stipu- s in contract ticket, passenger 1e option of having it heard ecided by Justices, who may :e order, as in recovery of ties.	s. 73.	—

Offence, or cause of Complaint.	Statute.	Extent of Jurisdiction.
PASSENGER SHIPS—*continued.* *Runners.*—Persons acting as "Emigration Runners" without licence, not wearing badge, and passage-broker employing them.	18 & 19 Vic. c. 119, s. 75. (36 & 37 Vic. c. 82.)	Penalty not exceeding £5, nor less than 20s.; in default of payment, imprisonment not exceeding 2 months, recoverable as above.
Permitting any other to wear his badge; persons counterfeiting, or using badges not issued to them.	s. 78. (36 & 37 Vic. c. 82.)	Penalty not exceeding £5; in default of payment, imprisonment not exceeding 2 months. 2 J. or 1 Stip.
Procedure for Penalties.—Penalties to be sued for by emigration officer, or other authorized officers as therein. (a)		
Passage, subsistence, and compensation moneys may be sued for by passenger, or by such officer as aforesaid on his behalf.	18 & 19 Vic. c. 119, s. 84.	—
If information be made on oath, and there is reason to suspect that party is likely to abscond, Justice may issue warrant, in the first instance, without summons.	s. 85.	
For forms to be used in proceedings, see Act, and see Amended Act.	26 & 27 Vic. c. 51.	
STEAM NAVIGATION. Vessel not to proceed on her voyage without certificate. No officer of Customs to clear out, &c., any steam vessels but upon production of certificate. Owners and masters of vessels allowing them to proceed (except mail packets, &c.)—	14 & 15 Vic. c. 79, s. 11.	Owner shall be liable to penalty not exceeding £100. Master to penalty not exceeding £20; in default, &c., imprisonment by scale. 2 J.
Owner, master, or person having charge, carrying more passengers than specified number in certificate.	s. 12.	Penalty not exceeding £20, and also 5s. forfeit for every passenger over and above number so specified; imprisonment by scale, &c. 2 J.

(a) *Application of Penalties.*—To be paid to the emigration officer at whose suit they are recovered.—Sec. 88; and see Circular to Clerks, Petty Sessions: No. 28, 17th June, 1885.

Offence, or cause of Complaint.	Statute.	Extent of Jurisdiction.
PASSENGER SHIPS: STEAM NAVIGATION—*continued.* Persons forcing their way on board when vessel is full, and refusing to leave after the fare (if paid) has been offered or returned.	14 & 15 Vic. c. 79, s. 13.	Forfeit to owner a sum not exceeding 40s.; in default, &c., imprisonment not exceeding 14 days. 2 J.
Not paying Fares.—Persons travelling or attempting to travel without having paid fare, and with intent to avoid payment, or having paid for a certain distance proceeds further without paying and with intent to defraud, or refusing to leave at the point to which fare has been paid.	s. 14.	Forfeit and pay to the owner of vessel a sum not exceeding 5s., in addition to the fare payable by him; in default, &c., imprisonment by scale. 2 J.
Offenders, under sections 13 and 14, refusing on application to give name and address, or giving false ones.	s. 15.	Forfeit to the owner a sum not exceeding £20; in default, &c., imprisonment by scale. 2 J.
Act provides penalties for proceeding on voyage without proper surveys, water-tight partitions, safety-valves, boats, equipments, &c., inspection, and penalties for obstructing inspectors.		
Misdemeanours or offences created by Act may be prosecuted by information or indictment.		
Penalties and other sums of money may be recovered with costs (unless previously punished as misdemeanours) by some appropriate summary proceeding before 2 or more Justices, or Judge exercising maritime jurisdiction.		
For penalties, where ship proceeds on her voyage without Board of Trade certificate, and for carrying passengers in excess of number specified in certificate—see Merchant Shipping Act.	17 & 18 Vic. c. 104, ss. 318, 319.	

Y

Offence, or cause of Complaint.	Statute.	Extent of Jurisdiction.
PAWNBROKERS: May take pledges; must lend in money only.	26 Geo. iii. c. 43 (Irish). ss. 1 and 2.	—
Disputes between persons pledging and pawnbrokers, respecting the re-delivery of pledges or the money to be paid pawnbroker.	s. 4.	In case original sum lent does not exceed 40s. (Irish), to be determined by 1 J. P. Exceeding 40s. (Irish), 2 J. P. To be binding on all parties concerned, and not determined in any other manner.
Entries.—Pawnbroker shall enter fairly and regularly, in a book kept for the purpose, a description of all pledges, the sum advanced, the date, name, and place of abode of persons pawning, and also of owner, according to information of person pawning, give duplicate of copy of entry, charging—where sum does not exceed 10s.—one penny; exceeding 10s. and under 40s.—twopence; exceeding 40s.—fourpence; to be on strong fair writing paper, and large in proportion to the number of articles, with pawnbroker's name, number, sign (if any), and place of abode.	s. 5.	In default of making such entry and giving such duplicate, for every offence shall forfeit the sum of 40s. (Irish); by distress. (a) 1 l.
Persons producing duplicates and paying to receive the pawn unless pawnbrokers have notice from real owners of being stolen, &c., as therein.	s. 6.	
Upon such notice from real owner, or in case duplicates are lost, &c. &c., upon proving property and	s. 7.	The proof to be to the satisfaction of a J. P.; and shall also make affi-

(a) The fines and forfeitures in some cases, under this and other old statutes, are directed to be paid to parish authorities for the use of the poor. Under the Fines Act and Petty Sessions Act the appropriation is provided for in another way. These Acts also provide the means of enforcing the penalties—the section says by distress, but the Petty Sessions Act and scale of imprisonment will apply and may be resorted to in default of distress. This being an Irish Act, the fines and other sums are in that currency. The Justice should name the sum to be paid in present currency. The £1 Irish is 18s. 5½d. British.

Offence, or cause of Complaint.	Statute.	Extent of Jurisdiction.
PAWNBROKERS—*continued.* that goods are unredeemed, pawnbroker shall suffer goods to be redeemed, and is indemnified for so doing.		davit or affirmation of the circumstances. (*a*)
Unlawful Pawning.—Knowingly and designedly pawning, exchanging, or unlawfully disposing of the goods or chattels of any person or persons, not being employed or authorized by owner.	26 Geo. iii. c. 43, s. 8.	Shall, for every such offence, forfeit 20*s.* (Irish); in default, &c., imprisonment 14 days. 1 J. If recovered, to be applied in making satisfaction to aggrieved ; residue to be applied as fines.
Where goods are injured.—If proved to the satisfaction of Justice that goods pawned have become of less value than when pledged, by default, neglect, or wilful misbehaviour of pawnbroker, his clerks, &c.— (*b*)	s. 9.	Justice to award reasonable satisfaction to the owner. Sums so awarded shall be deducted out of principal and interest then due ; and in all such cases it shall be sufficient for the pawners to pay or tender the money due upon the balance after deducting such reasonable satisfaction ; or upon so doing the Justice shall proceed as if the pawner had tendered the whole money due for principal and interest. 1 J.

(*a*) Declaration may be substituted—see 5 & 6 Wm. iv. c. 62, s. 12; and see also Schedule, Petty Sessions Stamps Act, exempting from stamps declarations as to loss of pawnbrokers' duplicates. It would seem also to be within the meaning of declarations, "required by law," referred to in the Stamp Act, and in that case is exempt from stamp duty. See title "Stamps," and notes thereon.

(*b*) But if destroyed by fire or other inevitable accident, or stolen, and there is no neglect on the part of the pawnbroker, the pawner has no redress under the above Act, nor by any other means. If a creditor takes a pawn he is bound to restore it on payment of the debt; but it is sufficient if the pawnee use due diligence, and he will be indemnified in so doing, and notwithstanding the loss. The law requires nothing extraordinary from the pawnee, but only that he shall use ordinary care for restoring the goods.—*Southcote's Case ; Smith's Leading Cases.*

Y 2

Offence, or cause of Complaint.	Statute.	Extent of Jurisdiction.
PAWNBROKERS—*continued.* Knowingly buying or taking in pledge any linen or apparel intrusted to any person to wash, scour, iron, mend, or make up.	26 Geo. iii. c. 43, s. 10.	Forfeit double the sum lent, recoverable as other forfeitures, and to restore the goods to owner in presence of Justices. 1 J.
Persons offering goods in pawn, and unable satisfactorily to account, or where goods are suspected to have been stolen, such persons may be seized and detained.	ss. 11 and 12.	If Justice sees cause to suspect that the goods have been stolen or clandestinely obtained, may remand for 3 days for further examination. 1 J. And the person so detaining the party is indemnified.
Search-warrant.—On oath of goods having been unlawfully obtained, and suspected to have been knowingly taken in pawn— Penalty for hindering search.	s. 13. ,,	Justice may issue search-warrant. (*a*)
Producing books, &c.—On complaint on oath respecting disputes between pawnbroker and person pawning, or respecting any felony or other matter, Justice may summon pawnbroker and require production of books, vouchers, &c., which he ought to have; for neglect, refusal, &c., see section *infra.* (*b*)	s. 29.	Penalty £5 (Irish), by distress; in default, &c., imprisonment according to scale, not exceeding 2 months. 1 J.

(*a*) *Stolen Goods.*—The pawnbroker takes in goods on his own risk. If he suspects the goods to be stolen, his duty is to detain them and give the person offering them into custody, and the Act protects him—(ss. 11 and 12). Where he receives in pledge goods which have been stolen, the Court before whom the offender is tried will order the restoration of the goods to the owner. This also is the case if Justices deal summarily with the larceny in Petty Sessions ; the owner is entitled to have his goods restored to him. Where, however, the pawnbroker exercises reasonable precaution, and aids in bringing the offender to justice, the Court in general will order him fair expenses as *a witness;* and perhaps so' as to mitigate the loss he sustains. The Justices can order expenses where they determine the case (18 & 19 Vic. c. 126, ss. 8 and 14) ; but if the Justices have not the offender before them, and cannot therefore summarily determine the case, they should not by their order deliver the goods to the owner, but should leave him to his civil remedy against the pawnbroker.

(*b*) *Pawnbroker may be compelled to produce Books, &c.*, sec. 29.—" It shall be lawful for any Justice of the Peace, upon complaint made to him on the oath of

Offence, or cause of Complaint.	Statute.	Extent of Jurisdiction.
PAWNBROKERS—*continued.* *Hours of pledging.*—No pledges to be taken in on Sundays, nor on week-days before 10 o'clock, A.M., nor after 4 o'clock, P.M., between 29th September and 25th March; nor before 10 o'clock, A.M., nor after 7 o'clock, P.M., between 25th March and 29th September; for non-observance—*	28 Geo. iii. c. 49, s. 20 (36 & 37 Vic. c. 82.)	Penalty 40*s.* (Irish), for each offence; if not paid within 3 days, distress warrant. 1 J. Or, in default, may be imprisoned by scale.
For rates of interest, see .	28 Geo. iii. c. 49, s. 19.	
For selling pawns, except as directed by Act; appraiser's offence by advancing on pledges; his duties; acting without licence; bonds; dividing loans so as to multiply duplicates, and other offences—see Acts.		

One or more credible witness or witnesses, respecting any dispute between pawnbrokers and the persons who shall have pawned goods, or respecting any felony or other matter, which in the judgment of such Justice shall make the production of any book, duplicate, voucher, or other paper necessary, which shall or ought to be in the hands, custody, or power of any pawnbroker, to summon such pawnbroker before him to attend with any book, duplicate, voucher, or other paper which he or she may have in his or her custody or power relating to the same, and which he or she is hereby required to produce before such Justice, in the state the same was made at the time the pawn or pledge was received, without any alteration, erasement or obliteration whatever; and in case such pawnbroker shall neglect or refuse to attend, or to produce the same in its true and perfect state as aforesaid, such pawnbroker shall forfeit and pay the sum of £5, to be levied by distress."

It would appear that under the above section where a *dispute* may arise between the pawnbroker and the person pawning, and when a charge of *felony*, &c., may be brought against any other person, known or unknown, or in any preliminary inquiry, the pawnbroker is bound under a penalty to produce books, vouchers, &c. But should the pawnbroker himself be charged in the summons with feloniously receiving the property, it can scarcely mean that he would be bound under pecuniary penalty to bring evidence tending to convict himself.

Persons trading as pawnbrokers receiving by way of pawn, pledge, or exchange any goods, &c., for repayment of money lent thereon, without a pawnbroker's licence, penalty £50.—Stamp Act, 5 & 6 Vic. c. 82, s. 17, and continued by subsequent Acts.

* *Hours of Pledging.*—It has come to be questioned whether the 28 Geo. iii. c. 49, s. 20, applies to any place outside Dublin. The Law Officers have advised that it does not, and the Constabulary do not enforce it.

Offence, or cause of Complaint.	Statute.	Extent of Jurisdic
PAWNBROKERS—*continued.* *Returns.*—Neglecting or declining to make monthly returns to *Marshal of Dublin* of sums lent on pawns, on oath, &c. (But declaration substituted for oaths under Pawnbrokers' Act, 5 & 6 Wm. iv. c. 62.) No fine to be imposed on pawnbroker until duly summoned, getting sufficient time. There are several other Acts confined in their application to Dublin.	26 Geo. iii. c. 43, ss. 41, and 42.	Penalty 40*s.* (Iri distress; in defau imprisonment by
PEACE: See "Sureties to keep the Peace."		
PEACE OFFICER: See "Constable."		
PEACE PRESERVATION (IRE-LAND) ACT, 1881. (*a*) *In a proclaimed district* a person shall not carry or have any arms or ammunition, save as authorized in proclamation referred to in Act. Person carrying, or having, or reasonably suspected of, &c., in contravention of Act, may be arrested and brought *before Justice* to be dealt with according to law. (*b*)	44 Vic. c. 5, s. 1. "	— —

(*a*) The Act refers to proclaimed districts.

(*b*) This clause evidently means something more than the actual pos arms or ammunition, openly or secretly, at the time of arrest. It w include previous offences within a reasonable time of which the consta give or produce the necessary evidence, and in which cases it would be th the Magistrate to remand the accused to a future day, to admit him to b known, the Magistrate may in his discretion set him at liberty and direc be summoned to appear at next Petty Sessions. This would seem to b with him according to law. See now Criminal Law and Procedure (Irel 1887, sec. 8, continuing Acts of 1881–1886 for 5 years, extending power of s

Offence, or cause of Complaint.	Statute.	Extent of Jurisdiction.
PEACE PRESERVATION (IRE-LAND) ACT—*continued.* Lord Lieutenant may by warrant direct search, &c.	44 Vic. c. 5, s. 1, and 50 & 51 Vic. c. 20, s. 8.	
How warrant is to be executed as to deposit and safe keeping, of surrendered arms, and proviso for paying value thereof to owners—	44 Vic. c. 5, s. 1.	
Power as to proclamation in respect to arms and ammunition.	,,	
Power as to prohibiting or regulating sale or importation of arms and ammunition.	,,	
Penalties.—Any person acting in contravention of Act shall be liable if convicted— Act may be cited as "Peace Preservation (Ireland) Act, 1881." *Definitions, &c.,* of Lord Lieutenant. "Arms" includes cannon, gun, revolver, pistol, and any description of fire-arms; also any sword, cutlass, pike, and bayonet; also any part of such, &c. "Ammunition" includes bullets, gunpowder, nitro-glycerine, dynamite, gun-cotton, and every explosive substance.	44 Vic. c. 5, s. 5, & 49 Vic. c. 24, s. 2.	Imprisonment not exceeding 3 months; or, at discretion of Court, penalty not exceeding £20. If Court think there are circumstances to render it inexpedient to inflict punishment, it may dismiss charge without proceeding to a conviction. (In *Dublin* may be tried before 1 Divisional Justice; elsewhere in Ireland before two or more Resident Magistrates alone, and in Petty Sessions.)
PEDLARS ACT (1871): (a) Act for granting certificates to pedlars. (Repeals Act of 1870.)	34 & 35 Vic. c. 96.	

(a) *Pedlar* means "any hawker, pedlar, petty chapman, tinker, caster of metals, mender of chairs, or other person, who, without any horse or other beast bearing or drawing burden, travels and trades on foot, and goes from town to town, or to other men's houses, carrying to sell or exposing for sale any goods, wares, or merchandise, or procuring orders for goods, wares, or merchandise immediately to be delivered, or selling or offering for sale his skill in handicraft "—s. 3.

Saving—Nothing in this Act shall render it necessary for certificate to be obtained by the following persons :—

1. . Commercial travellers, or other persons selling or seeking orders for goods,

Offence, or cause of Complaint.	Statute.	Extent of Jurisdiction.
PEDLARS ACT, (1871)—*continued.* Any person who acts as a pedlar without having obtained a certificate under this Act—	34 & 35 Vic. c. 96, s. 4. (44 & 45 Vic. c. 42, s. 2, & schedule).	First offence—penalty not exceeding 10s.; any subsequent offence a penalty not exceeding £1; in default of payment, imprisonment by scale. 2 J. or 1 Stip.
Section 6 contains regulations as to the granting certificates.		
The fee on certificate is 5s.; it holds for one year from date of issue.		
Certificate to be extended by indorsement to other districts than that for which it was granted. (a)	34 & 35 Vic. c. 96, s. 7.	
Register of certificates to be kept in each district, and the entries therein or certified copies thereof to be evidence of the facts therein stated.	s. 8.	—
Any pedlar who lends, transfers, or assigns his certificate to any other person.	s. 10.	For each offence a penalty not exceeding 20s.; in default of payment, imprisonment not exceeding 1 month.
Any person who borrows or makes use of such certificate.	s. 11.	Like penalty, &c. 2 J. or 1 Stip.
1. Any person who makes false representations with a view to obtain certificate under this Act:	s. 12.	First offence—penalty not exceeding £2; in default, &c., imprisonment not exceeding 1 month.

wares, or merchandise to or from persons who are dealers therein and who buy to sell again; or selling or seeking orders for books as agents, authorized in writing by the publishers of such books.

2. Sellers of vegetables, fish, fruit, or victuals.

3. Persons selling or exposing to sale goods, wares, or merchandise in any public mart, market, or fair legally established—s. 23. Act reserves the power of local authorities under local Acts—s. 24.

(a) But see now 44 & 45 Vic. c. 45, s. 2, by which certificate while in force enables the holder to act as a pedlar within any part of the United Kingdom.

Offence, or cause of Complaint.	Statute.	Extent of Jurisdiction.
PEDLARS ACT (1871)—*continued*. 2. Who forges or counterfeits a pedlar's certificate granted under this Act : 3. Who forges or counterfeits an indorsement made under Act on such certificate : 4. Aids in making, or procures to be made, such forged or counterfeited certificate or indorsement : 5. Travels with, produces, or shows any such forged or counterfeited certificate or indorsement.	34 & 35 Vic. c. 96, s. 12.	Any subsequent offence—either instead of or in addition to the penalty, imprisonment for any term not exceeding 6 months, with or without H. L. 2 J. or 1 Stip.
A person shall not be exempt from provisions of any Act relative to idle and disorderly persons, rogues, and vagabonds, by reason only that he holds a certificate under this Act, or assists, or is accompanying a pedlar holding a certificate under this Act.	s. 13.	
Court shall indorse convictions under Act on certificate, which shall be evidence of the fact.	s. 14.	
Appeal. (a)—Right of Appeal to Petty Sessions against refusal of certificate or indorsement, see sec.	s. 15.	

(a) *Appeal to Petty Sessions*—If certificate or indorsement refused, applicant, within a week after refusal, shall give officer notice in writing. The appeal shall be heard at the sitting of the Court which happens next after the expiration of the week, with power to adjourn. Court may make order thereon, and with or without costs to either party, as to the Court seems just—s. 15.

There is no particular *form* of appeal. The applicant may therefore move the Court on his notice of appeal. Of course they will be satisfied that the notice of appeal, which should state the time and place of hearing, has been duly given. It is not usual to give costs against the Constabulary or other public officers. The Justices have the power in the above instance.

Police District means Police District of Dublin Metropolis, or any district, whether city, town, or country, over which is appointed a Sub-Inspector of the Royal Irish Constabulary—s. 3.

Chief Officer of Police means in Dublin either of the Commissioners of Police ; elsewhere in Ireland the Sub-Inspectors of Royal Irish Constabulary. Acts

Offence, or cause of Complaint.	Statute.	Extent of Jus
PEDLARS ACT, (1871)—*continued.* The Court before which a pedlar is convicted of any offence, whether under this or any other Act, may, if he or they think fit, deprive such pedlar of his certificate, and shall do so if convicted of begging, or failing to show that he carries on his business in good faith.	34 & 35 Vic. c. 96, s. 16.	—
Duties of Pedlars.—Any pedlar shall at all times, on demand, produce and show his certificate to any Justice of the Peace, or any constable or officer of police, or any person to whom such pedlar offers his goods for sale, or any person in whose private grounds or premises such pedlar is found ; and for refusal, on demand, to show same, allow it to be read, and a copy thereof to be taken—	s. 17.	Shall for each liable to a p exceeding 5s fault of pay prisonment t exceeding 1 2 J
And any person so authorized, and any other acting by his order, may apprehend and bring such pedlar before a Justice.	s. 18.	
Any pedlar who refuses to allow constable or police officer to open or inspect his pack, box, bag, trunk, or case, or who prevents or attempts to prevent his doing so—	s. 19.	For each offer not exceedin default of pa prisonment b exceeding 14
Certificate while in force authorizes pedlar to act under it in any part of United Kingdom, and alters previous Act as to indorsement.	44 & 45 Vic. c. 45.	

authorized to be done by the Chief Officer of Police may be done by authorized by him.

Court includes Justices or Magistrates to whom jurisdiction is given b

Forms of certificate, &c., given in schedule to Act.

Fees received under Act (meaning. it would seem, the fees on certi shall be applied as the penalties, are applicable. The fines to be applie by the Fines Act.

Procedure.—Penalties recovered in Dublin by the Special Acts, and parts of Ireland by the Petty Sessions (Ireland) Act, 1851.

Depriving Pedlar of Certificate.—The power in section 16, vested i

Offence, or cause of Complaint.	Statute.	Extent of Jurisdiction.
PETROLEUM : Act regulating the safe keeping of petroleum and other similar substances.	34 & 35 Vic. c. 105.	Penalties recoverable before 2 J. or 1 Stip. ; in Dublin, before a Divisional Justice. (Sec. 34 & 35 Vic. c. 105, s. 15.)
Continued and amended—	42 & 43 Vic. c. 47.	
Act regulating the hawking of, and substances of like nature, and provides penalty for contravention.	44 & 45 Vic. c. 67, s. 2.	—
PHARMACY : Persons selling or compounding poisons or assuming the title of pharmaceutical chemist, to be qualified, &c. Acting in contravention of Act—	38 & 39 Vic. c. 57, s. 30.	Penalty £5 ; in default, &c., imprisonment not exceeding 2 months. 1 J.
One-third of penalty to person prosecuting, remainder to treasurer for purposes of Act.		
PIGS : See " Swine " ; " Commons."		
PIGEON : Killing or stealing. See " Larceny."	24 & 25 Vic. c. 96, s. 23.	

to deprive the pedlar of his certificate when convicted of any offence, whether under this or any other Act, seems very arbitrary, and there does not appear to be any right of appeal, and the application of the Petty Sessions Act is only as to the "recovery of penalties." It would further seem that what would justify the Court in depriving him of his certificate would warrant the officer in refusing it, without limiting him to the positive prohibition in section 13, which forbids the granting of a certificate to any person " convicted of felony or of any misdemeanour involving dishonesty." There are not many offences of the latter class of misdemeanours—amongst them would be cheating by false measures, and such means, and obtaining goods, &c., by false pretences. The Excise licence to such hawkers or pedlars has been abolished. The above Act is very important. The extensive control given the constabulary over this itinerant class of traders is for many reasons obvious enough.

Offence, or cause of Complaint.	Statute.	Extent of Jurisdiction.
PLANTS : See "Vegetable Productions." Also titles "Larceny," and "Malicious Injuries."		
PLATE : As to dealers in, and necessity for, Excise licence, see 30 & 31 Vic. c. 90.	33 & 34 Vic. c. 32.	—
PLAYING : At any game on road or street, to the danger of passengers.	14 & 15 Vic. c. 92, s. 10. (35 & 36 Vic. c. 82.)	Penalty not exceeding 10s.; in default, &c., imprisonment not exceeding 7 days. 1 J.
POACHING : See "Game."		
POISONS : Act regulating the sale of, &c.; specifying articles which shall be deemed poisonous; labelling, &c.; and for non-compliance with provisions—	33 & 34 Vic. c. 26, s. 2.	First offence—penalty not exceeding £5; subsequent offence—not exceeding £10, recoverable under Petty Sessions Act, and imprisonment by scale.
Poisoned grain, ...	26 & 27 Vic. c. 113.	
Poisoned flesh, ...	27 & 28 Vic. c. 115.	
Master liable for apprentice or servant. The 23 & 24 Vic. c. 84, as to adulteration of food or drink is by this Act extended to medicines.	33 & 34 Vic. c. 26, s. 3.	
See title "Adulteration."		
See also as to "Arsenic."	14 & 15 Vic. c. 13.	—
POLICE : See "Constables."		
POLICE SUPERVISION : See "Crime."		

Offence, or cause of Complaint.	Statute.	Extent of Jurisdiction.
POLICE CLAUSES ACT : See *Appendix*.	10 & 11 Vic. c. 89.	Applicable in towns, &c., where it is incorporated with a *special Act*.
POOR LAW : *Deserting Wife or Child.*—Every person who shall desert or wilfully neglect to maintain his wife, or any child whom he may be liable to maintain, so that such wife or child shall become destitute, and be relieved in or out of the workhouse of any Union in Ireland. (a) (And as to soldier's liability, see	10 & 11 Vic. c. 84, s. 2.	Imprisonment not exceeding 3 months, and H. L. 1 J.

(a) *Husband's Liability.*—1 & 2 Vic. c. 56, s. 53, enacts, "That *for the purposes of this Act*, every husband shall be liable to maintain his wife, and every child under the age of fifteen, whether legitimate or illegitimate, which she may have had at the time of her marriage with such husband ; and every father shall be liable to maintain his child, and every widow to maintain her child, and the mother of every bastard child to maintain such bastard child, until every such child, respectively, shall attain the age of fifteen years : Provided always, and be it declared, that nothing herein contained shall be taken to remove or lessen the obligations to which any husband or parent is by law liable, in regard to the maintenance of his wife or children, legitimate or illegitimate, respectively, independently of this Act." Under this Act it was held, that even proof of adultery committed by the wife would not exonerate the husband from his liability to the Union *for the purposes of this Act ;* and notwithstanding the decision in the case of *King* v. *Flinton, Bar. & A. Q. B. Reports*, 1830. In this case it is decided that " a wife who has left her husband and lives in adultery, a husband is not legally liable to maintain." Littledale, J. :—" Having rendered herself unworthy of her husband's protection, she returns to the same state as if she were not married." Parke, J. :— "It would be strange if the Court could hold that a man was not liable for the supply of necessaries to his wife, and yet, that not supplying them rendered him a vagrant." Bayly, J. :—" A man is criminally answerable for refusing to maintain any of his family, whom he is legally bound to maintain ; that obligation must be made out, and it is not established in the case of a wife who has left her husband and lives in adultery." The offence is now punishable, as will be seen above, under 10 & 11 Vic. c. 84, s. 2 ; and by this Act, so much of the 1 & 2 Vic. c. 56, as provides for the punishment of persons deserting their wives and children is repealed ; but section 53 of the first Act is not introduced or referred to in the latter statute. So it would now seem that the husband is punishable only in those cases where he is, and always was, legally and civilly liable independently of these Acts.

Evidence that a man and woman lived together, and were reputed to be man and wife, is admissible to prove them to be legally married for purposes of above Act : *per* Rt. Hon. F. Blackburne, Attorney-General (Ir.), 1842.

This is not a prosecution by the wife. It is one at suit of the Guardians against the husband ; and although perhaps she can alone prove the *desertion*, she is not,

Offence, or cause of Complaint	Statute.	Extent of Jurisdiction.
POOR LAW.—*continued.* "Army Act" and "Marine Mutiny" Acts. See also title "Married Women." (a)	10 & 11 Vic. c. 84, s. 2.	
Liability of Children.—Where any poor person shall, through old age, infirmity, or defect, be unable to support himself, every child of such poor person shall be liable, according to his ability, to support or contribute to support such poor person; and if relieved by the Union under this Act—	1 & 2 Vic. c. 56, s. 57.	Justices may make an order for payment of the relief given; recoverable as a penalty.
Refusing to be lodged or maintained in workhouse; or absconding therefrom, while his wife or child receives relief therein.	s. 58.	Imprisonment not exceeding 1 month's H.L. 1 J.
Insubordination. — Persons maintained in workhouse refusing to work, guilty of drunkenness, insubordination to officers, disobedience to prescribed rules, or other misbehaviour therein.	,,	Like.
Spirits, &c.—Introducing, or attempting to introduce, spirituous or fermented liquors, contrary to orders of Commissioners.	,,	Like.
Officers wilfully disobeying the legal and reasonable orders of the Guardians—	s. 100.	Penalty not exceeding £5.

it would appear, a competent witness "for or against her husband." But it may be proved without her. If he is aware of her being in the workhouse and does not look after her, or if he has quit his residence without making provision for her, or sending her relief. In all cases it would be the duty of the relieving officer on admitting a married woman to workhouse relief to make the necessary inquiries, and if the residence of the husband be known, to acquaint him with the fact—of course if he still refuse to support her, the relieving officer could prove the case. Should the wife leave the husband, as is frequently the case, on account of his cruel treatment, and seek relief in the workhouse, this would not be a desertion within the meaning of the Act; for any such ill-treatment she may prosecute herself, and the Magistrates could punish him.

(a) *Wife's Liability.*—As to liability of married women to Guardians of Poor Law Unions for maintenance of husband and children, and grandchildren, see 45 & 46 Vic. "Married Women's Property Act, 1882."

Offence, or cause of Complaint.	Statute.	Extent of Jurisdiction.
POOR LAW—*continued.* Officer purloining, embezzling, wilfully wasting, or misapplying moneys or goods of the Union.	1 & 2 Vic. c. 56, s. 101.	In addition to any other pains and penalties otherwise liable to, shall forfeit a sum not exceeding £20, and treble the value of property misapplied, and loss of office; in default, &c., imprisonment not exceeding 3 months. 2 J.
Wilfully neglecting, or disobeying the sealed or stamped orders of the Commissioners.	s. 102.	Penalty not exceeding £5. Second offence—not exceeding £20, nor less than £5; in default, &c., imprisonment not exceeding 3 months. 2 J. Subsequent offence—indictable misdemeanour.
Rates.—Making and collecting of rates.	1 & 2 Vic. c. 56. 6 & 7 Vic. c. 92, s. 2.	—
Persons having custody of rate, refusing to permit persons affected thereby to take copies of extracts.	1 & 2 Vic. c. 56, s. 70.	Penalty not exceeding 10s., by distress; in default, &c., imprisonment not exceeding 14 days.
Vagrants and Beggars.—Every person wandering abroad, and begging, or placing himself in any public street, highway, court, or passage to beg or gather alms, or children so to do, or going from Union to Union, or from one electoral or relief district to another, for relief—	10 & 11 Vic. c. 84, s. 3.	If Justice think fit, shall be imprisoned not exceeding 1 month's H. L. 1 J. See title " Vagrancy," and note thereon.
Illegitimate Children. — Guardians may recover by civil-bill process costs of maintenance of illegitimate children while under 14 years, and in receipt of relief, from putative father.	26 Vic. c. 21. s. 2.	Mother to make affidavit in form given in Act, before a Justice, stating who is the father before process served.

Offence, or cause of Complaint.	Statute.	Extent of Jurisdiction.
POOR LAW—*continued.* Copy, affidavit, &c., to be served with civil-bill. Mother to be examined before Chairman; her evidence must be corroborated.	26 Vic. c. 21, s. 3.	After decree given, evidence of mother not necessary in subsequent proceedings for recovery
Payment by putative father previous to hearing, to stop proceedings, and such payment to be proof of his being the father.	s. 4.	(The Justice should not receive affidavit unless required by Guardians.)
Poor removal of paupers from England to Ireland regulated by—	24 & 25 Vic. c. 76.	—
The last Act provides punishment (a misdemeanour) for deserting pauper on the journey, and a summary penalty for violating section 6 of 24 & 25 Vic. c. 76.	25 & 26 Vic. c. 113. 26 & 27 Vic. c. 89.	—
Act extending age at which orphan children may be kept out at nurse to 14 years.	39 & 40 Vic. c. 38.	
POOR-RATES: Recoverable under (*a*) . . .	1 & 2 Vic. c. 56. 6 & 7 Vic. c. 92, s. 2, and c. 116, ss. 152, 153; 13 & 14 Vic. c. 82, s. 1.	Before Justices in Petty Sessions. 1 J.

Poor Removal.—As it is the law that Irish poor who have not acquired a settlement in England may, on becoming chargeable on the Unions there, be sent to their homes, the Legislature have in the above Acts provided as far as possible for their wants on the passage.

(*a*) *Rates.*—The Court of Queen's Bench has decided that houses not occupied when a poor-rate is made are not liable to it.—1 *Ir. Law Rep.*, N. S., 76.

Notice of Distress.—If the collector distrains under 1 & 2 Vic. c. 56, s. 78, he should leave the same notice as that given in cases of distress for rent; but where he distrains under his own warrant, under the provisions of the 152nd sec. of the Grand Jury Act, 6 & 7 Wm. iv. c. 116, or under a Justice's warrant, he need not serve such notice. One notice and one summons are sufficient, where rates for several denominations are to be recovered. The six-day notice mentioned in section 152, Grand Jury Act, need not be served by collector in person, it may be served by any person authorized by him. The collector having no direct interest in the rates is competent to serve the notice and to prove the case. The block or counterfoil of the notice is sufficient legal evidence of the contents of the notice, and to witness's memory as to the contents; and it need not be an attested copy.

Offence, or cause of Complaint.	Statute.	Extent of Jurisdiction.
POOR-RATES—*continued.* *Arrears.*—Proceedings for arrears against persons not primarily liable must be taken within two years after rate made.	12 & 13 Vic. c. 104, s. 19.	
Persons liable to poor-rates, . .	1 & 2 Vic. c. 56, s. 71. 6 & 7 Vic. c. 92, s. 1.	Justice to make order for amount proved to be due, and issue distress warrant, if required. 1 J.
For power of appeal against rate, see	1 & 2 Vic. c. 56, s. 106, &c. 12 & 13 Vic. c. 104, s. 22.	—
Appeal against valuation, . .	15 & 16 Vic. c. 63, s. 22.	
Bill of Sale, not to protect chattels against poor and other rates, &c.	46 Vic. c. 7. s. 14.	
POST OFFICE : *Letter Carriers.*—Guilty of drunkenness, carelessness, negligence, or other misconduct, whereby safety of letters may be endangered ; or collecting or delivering otherwise than in the ordinary course of the post ; loitering or misspending time.	1 Vic. c. 36, s. 7. 47 & 48 Vic. c. 76, s. 21 and Schedule.	Forfeiture £20 ; in default, &c., imprisonment not exceeding 4 months by Petty Sessions scale. 1 J.

The Magistrates' warrant has been considered preferable to that of the Guardians', inasmuch as the Guardians' warrant could only be executed on the party's goods *found on the premises,* whereas under the Justices' warrant the goods of the party found anywhere within the county may be distrained, or by its being " backed," may be executed in any other county. The production and proof of Rate-books in Court not necessary, the collector's warrant being sufficient. The Magistrates' summons should issue in name of the collector ; it need not be in the name of the Guardians. Magistrates' warrants to levy the rates may issue to the collectors, they not being the parties interested, although the complainants, under 14 & 15 Vic. c. 93, s. 25 ; or under same section, to any person named by collector, if the Justice issuing same shall see fit.

Limitation.—Where complaint relates to non-payment of poor-rate, county-rate, or other public tax, it may be made at any time after date of warrant authorizing the collection—14 & 15 Vic. c. 93, sec. 10, sub-sec. 4.

Warrant.—Justices, in issuing a distress warrant for recovery of poor-rates have no power to order that there shall be any delay in the execution of the warrant— *R.* v. *Hendsley,* " *English Law Reports,*" 7 *Q. B. D.* 398.

Z

Offence, or cause of Complaint.	Statute.	Extent of Jurisdiction.
POST OFFICE—*continued.* Sums of money due for postage not exceeding £20, or due from any deputy, agent, or letter-carrier, or other person employed, or from sureties— (The 47 & 48 Vic. c. 76, s. 12, extends the Petty Sessions (Ireland) Act, 1851, to penalties not exceeding £20 incurred under previous Post Office Acts.) For embezzling, secreting, or fraudulent detention of letters, &c., which are indictable offences, see Act, and the Indictable Offence Index.	1 Vic. c. 36, s. 43.	Recoverable before 1 Justice of the Peace by distress.
POST OFFICE (PROTECTION) ACT, 1884— Prohibition of placing injurious substances or filth of any kind in or against post office letter-boxes, or doing anything to injure, &c.,	47 & 48 Vic. c. 76, s. 3.	Misdemeanour; triable by indictment; imprisonment not exceeding 12 months, with or without H. L., &c.; on summary conviction to fine not exceeding £10; in default, &c., imprisonment, by scale. 1 J.
Prohibition of sending by post explosive, inflammable, noxious, or deleterious substances, or indecent prints, words, marks, &c. &c.	s. 4.	Misdemeanour; triable by indictment, and punishable as above, &c.; on summary conviction to fine not exceeding £10; in default, &c., imprisonment, by scale. 2 J.
Prohibition of affixing placards, notices, &c. &c., on post offices or letter-boxes, &c. (and notwithstanding anything in sec. 9 of Parliamentary and Municipal Registration Act, 1878), without authority.	s. 5.	Fine not exceeding 40s.; in default, &c., imprisonment not exceeding 1 month. 1 J.
Prohibition of imitation of post office stamps, envelopes, forms, marks, &c. &c., issuing or sending, &c. &c.	s. 6.	Fine not exceeding 40s.; in default, &c., imprisonment not exceeding 1 month. 1 J.

Offence, or cause of Complaint.	Statute.	Extent of Jurisdiction.
POST OFFICE—*continued.* POST OFFICE (PROTECTION) ACT, 1884— Prohibition of fictitious, or facsimile stamps, making, issuing, having in possession without lawful excuse dies, plates, &c.	47 & 48 Vic. c. 76, s. 7.	Fine not exceeding £20 (by Inland Revenue prosecution), and under Petty Sessions Act. 1 J.
Prohibition of false notices as to reception of letters, &c., or falsely indicating places, &c., to be a post office, or postal telegraph office, &c.	s. 8.	Fine not exceeding 40s.; and if offence continued after conviction, 5s. a-day, in default, &c.; imprisonment, by scale. 1 J.
Commission of offences in post office, &c., wilfully obstructing officers, or the course of business therein.	s. 9.	Fine, 40s.; recoverable as above. 1 J.
Offenders so obstructing, refusing to leave, &c. Offender may be removed by officer or any constable.	,,	Fine not exceeding £5; in default imprisonment not exceeding 2 months, by scale.
Surrender of regulation clothing, &c., by officer of post office on ceasing to be officer, or if dead by representative; failing to comply—	s. 10.	Fine not exceeding 40s., and further sum not exceeding 40s. for value, or for damage to clothing; in default, imprisonment, by scale. 1 J.
Telegrams.— Forging, or wilfully and without authority, altering telegram, knowingly uttering same, &c. &c., or what is known not to be a telegram.	s. 11.	Misdemeanour: punishable on indictment by imprisonment not exceeding 12 months, with or without H. L.; or, on summary conviction, fine not exceeding £10; in default, &c., imprisonment, by scale. 1 J.
Employées improperly divulging purport of telegrams. (Section defines telegram.) Act applies Petty Sessions (Ir.) Act, 1851; in *Dublin* the special Acts there applicable.	,,	Misdemeanour; punishable on indictment: imprisonment not exceeding 1 year, with or without H. L., or fine not exceeding £200; or, on summary conviction, fine not exceeding £20; in default, &c., imprisonment, by scale.

Offence, or cause of Complaint.	Statute.	Extent of Jurisdiction.
POST OFFICE—*continued*. POST OFFICE (PROTECTION) ACT, 1884— *Application of Fines, &c.*—Fines and forfeitures go to the *Exchequer*.	47 & 48 Vic. c. 76, s. 14.	
Saving as to indictments at Common Law.	s. 16.	
Definitions, ...	ss. 19 & 20.	
Repeals portions of previous Acts, .	Schedule	
POSSESSION (*of Small Tenements*): See "Landlord and Tenant."		
POULTRY : Any person who shall steal or injure with intent to steal, any turkey, goose, or other poultry (value not exceeding 5s.)	25 & 26 Vic. c. 50, s. 8.	Penalty not exceeding 20s.; or to be imprisoned for not exceeding 2 weeks. 1 J
And see "Larceny," sec. 21-23, and "Malicious Injuries," sec. 41, *ante*.		
POUND : Two or more Justices empowered to license pound-keeper. Pound-keeper to enter into recognizance.	14 & 15 Vic. c. 92, s. 19.	
When owner of straying animal not known, it may be sold after publicity ; proceeds applied as in section.	,,	

Dublin Police Force Act, 5 Vic. c. 24, s. 63, gives power to mitigate penal in Dublin. This 47 & 48 Vic. c. 76, s. 13, extends the power in section 4 of English Summary Jurisdiction Act, 1879, as to mitigation of punishment to offe under Post Office Acts, but makes no special reference to the powers in the Du Act.

Offence, or cause of Complaint.	Statute.	Extent of Jurisdiction.
POUND—*continued.*		
Pound-keeper acting without authority, not entering into recognizance, not keeping pound clean, &c., demanding more than legal fees, omitting to post tables or give notices, or liberating without authority, &c.—	14 & 15 Vic. c. 92, s. 19.	Penalty not exceeding £10; in default, &c., imprisonment not exceeding 3 months. 1 J.
Persons rescuing distresses, or injuring pounds, or liberating distresses—	,,	Compensation for injury; and fine not exceeding £10; in default, &c., imprisonment not exceeding 3 months. 1 J. Or Justice may, if he think fit, send case for trial to Quarter Sessions.
Any person impounding elsewhere than in licensed pound, or omitting to give notice, or overdriving or injuring animals—	,,	Penalty not exceeding £5; in default, &c., imprisonment not exceeding 2 months. 1 J.
Pound-keeper to deliver up animal on authority of Justice, or on being paid trespass, and fees, rates, &c.; neglecting, &c.—	s. 20.	Like penalty.
Pound-keeper's fees, (a) . .	s. 19.	
Rates of trespass, (b) . . .	s. 20.	

(a) *Pound-keeper's Fees.*—14 & 15 *Vic. c.* 92, *sec.* 19.—Every pound-keeper shall be entitled to receive from the person by whom any animal shall be impounded in such pound, or from the owner, when such animal shall be delivered up to such owner by proper authority, the following pound fees:—

	s.	*d.*
For any one horse, mare, mule, or horned beast, for any time not exceeding seventy-two hours, ...	0	6
And for any greater number of same, for same period, each, .	0	3

And if impounded for longer than seventy-two hours, one-half of the above sums for every additional seventy-two hours.

For any one sheep, calf, lamb, goat, or pig, for any period not exceeding seventy-two hours, ...	0	2
And for any greater number of same, for the same period, each, .	0	1

And if impounded for longer than seventy-two hours, one-half the above sums for every additional seventy-two hours.

Sustenance.—He shall also be entitled to demand and receive from the like owner or person, as the case may be, such sum for the sustenance of any such animals, for the time during which they shall be so impounded, as the said Justices shall fix as the proper rates of sustenance for animals impounded in such pound, and which they are hereby required to do by writing under their hands.

(b) *Rates of Trespass.*—14 & 15 *Vic. c.* 92, *sec.* 20.—Where the trespass shall

Offence, or cause of Complaint.	Statute.	Extent of Jurisdic
POUND—*continued*. Any person impounding an animal found trespassing where the owner is known to him, or without giving pound-keeper the required notice.	14 & 15 Vic. c. 92, s. 20.	Penalty not ex £5; in default imprisonment n ceeding 2 month
Fences.—Justices may order repair of, sec. 20, sub.-sec. 4.		

be on any common pasture land, or on any arable uncropped land, the r be :—

For every horse, mare, pony, mule, ass, bull, cow, bullock, heifer, *
    or pig, ... (
For calf, sheep, or lamb, ... (
For every goose, ... (
For every other fowl, ... (
For every goat, ... :

And where the trespass shall be upon any fattening pasture or meadow upon any land cropped with corn, pease, flax, vetches, turnips, rape, green crop, or other cultivated vegetable, or by any goat in a planta rates shall be double the amount of the preceding rates.

When parties are not satisfied, Justices to investigate the case and a legal rates; the principal upon which award shall be made to be the abov the first trespass, double for a second, and treble for subsequent t (whether any actual damage done or not), unless Justice shall be sati trespass was caused by occupier's neglect, or that there are justifying stances, in which case they may declare him to be entitled either to no ra a part only of the rates; but in case of actual damage done, Justices m such additional sum as will amount to compensation.—Sec. 20, sub-sec. :

Where Owner of Cattle is known.—It shall not be lawful to impo animal found trespassing upon any land where the owner of such animal known, but the occupier of such land or the person by whom such anima found trespassing, shall either deliver up such animal to the owner, steward, herdsman, caretaker, or other servant, or he shall show such : the act of trespassing to such owner, steward, &c., and allow such anim taken away by him; and the owner shall thereupon be liable to pay to of such land the rate of trespass fixed by scale (or according to such Justices at Quarter Sessions shall from time to time fix, and which they a authorized to do, if they shall see fit)—14 & 15 Vic. c. 92, s. 20. Th compensation is secured to the occupier of the land for any injury or los sustain, the neighbourly duty of caring for the cattle and delivering ther the rightful owner, or his servant, is at the same time provided for. The templates that the parties shall, in a friendly way, on the basis, and acc the rates in the section, settle the question. When any matter is disp Justices, under sub-sections 3 and 4, can enter into the whole question an and arbitrators at once, and make an *award*, both as to trespass and fen binding on both parties.

ǝnce, or cause of Complaint.	Statute.	Extent of Jurisdiction.
PT (*to restrain Waste*): Landlord and Tenant.''		
ƝTMENT SESSIONS: ʉlating and prescribing duties ᴀgistrates at Special Present-Sessions.—*Grand Jury Act.*	6 & 7 Wm. iv. c. 116.	
ᴤtices of the Peace (not being ᴨdiary Magistrates) of every ᵼy, &c., in Ireland, are re-d to assemble with the cess-rs associated to hold special or ᵰtment sessions at time and appointed by the Grand Jury.	s. 4, and 7 Wm. iv. c. 2, s. 14.	
f presenting for compensation ᴍalicious burnings—	6 & 7 Wm. iv. c. 116, s. 137.	See form of information, &c., *Appendix.*
dings, furniture, goods, &c., d by riots.	16 & 17 Vic. c. 38, s. 1.	
ᴤ of murder or personal injury ᴉoned by agrarian outrage or l combinations—see ''Peace rvation Act, 1870.''	33 Vic. c. 9.	
ᵼTION OF CRUELTY TO ᴣHILDREN, &c. ᵰtion of Cruelty to, and pro-n of, Children Act, 1889.''	52 & 53 Vic. c. 44.	Misdemeanour, and on conviction, on indictment shall be liable at
ᵾent for *ill-treatment and t of Children.*—Any person ᴉ6 years of age who, having ᴉy, control, or charge of a being a boy under 14, or a ᴉnder 16, wilfully ill-treats, ᴄts, abandons, or exposes	s. 1.	discretion of the Court, to a fine not exceeding £100, or alternatively, or in default of payment of such fine, or in addition to payment thereof, to imprisonment with

by *Indictment, or by Summary Conviction,* Sec. 1.—Of course sending on ᴌer to be tried by indictment will indicate that the offence is of an ᴉl character, and that the summary punishment would be inadequate.

Offence, or cause of Complaint.	Statute.	Extent of Jurisdict
PREVENTION OF CRUELTY TO CHILDREN, &c.—*continued.* such child, or causes or procures the same, in a manner likely to cause such child unnecessary suffering, or injury to its health. (Sec. 2 gives power on being convicted on indictment, to increase the fine to £200, where offender is shown to have pecuniary interest in child's death, such interest to be set out in indictment.	52 & 53 Vic. c. 44, s. 1.	or without H.L. term not excee years. *On summary* shall be liable, a tion of Court to not exceeding alternatively, or fault of paym such fine, or in a thereto, to im ment with or H. L. for any te exceeding 3 mon
Restrictions on employment of Children. (*a*) Any person who causes or procures any boy under 14, or girl under 16, to be in any street on the purpose of begging or receiving alms, or of inducing the giving of alms, whether under the pretence of singing, playing, performing, offering anything for sale, or otherwise ; or (*b*) Causes or procures any child, being a boy under 14, or girl under 16, to be in any street, or in any premises licensed for the sale of intoxicating liquor, other than premises licensed according to law for public entertainments, for the purpose of singing, playing, or performing for profit, or offering anything for sale, between 10 p.m. and 5 a.m. ; or	s. 3.	Shall, on convict Court of Su Jurisdiction, be at the discretion Court, to a fine ceeding £25, or tively, or in def payment of the s or in addition to imprisonment or without H. any term not ex 3 months. *Proviso.*—Local ity (that is, S Authority under Health (Ir.) Act, may if they think able by by-law, e restrict the hour tioned in sub.

Alternatively, &c.—(1) Fine; or (2) "alternatively" that is, imprisonme out giving the option of paying a fine; or (3) fine, and in default of paymen sonment ; or (4) fine and imprisonment. But whether dealt with by indic summarily, the imprisonment named in the section, respectively, shoul exceeded.

" *Street* " includes any highway or other public place, whether a thor ': sec. 17.

Offence, or cause of Complaint.	Statute.	Extent of Jurisdiction.
PREVENTION OF CRUELTY TO CHILDREN, &c.—*continued.* (e) Causes or procures *any child under* 10 to be at any time in any street or in any premises licensed for the sale of any intoxicating liquor, or in any premises licensed according to law for public entertainments, or in any circus, or other place of public amusement to which the public are admitted by payment, for the purpose of singing, playing, or performing for profit, or offering anything for sale— Power of Secretary of State to assign duties to Inspectors, &c., as to places of entertainment.	52 & 53 Vic. c. 44, s. 3.	either on every or any specified day or days of the week, and as to the whole or any specified area of their district. *Proviso.*—That in places licensed for public entertainments or circuses, &c., where it is shown to satisfaction to Petty Sessional Court, that proper provision has been made to secure the health and kind treatment of children proposed to be employed thereat, Court may grant licence for such time and hours of the day and on such conditions as Court thinks fit, for any child exceeding 7 years, and being satisfied of the child's fitness, &c., and to take part in the entertainments without injury. With power to vary licence, &c.
Taking offender into custody, and protection of Child.—Where offence is committed within view of constable, constable may take offender into custody where name and residence are not known, or cannot be ascertained. And where the offence is against sec. 1, or sub-sec. (a) of sec. 3, he may take the child to place of safety until child can be brought before Summary Jurisdiction Court. Court may cause child to be dealt with as	s. 4.	

" *Place of Safety,*" includes workhouse and any place certified by local authority by by-law under this Act for purposes of Act.

Offence, or cause of Complaint.	Statute.	Extent of Jurisdiction.
PREVENTION OF CRUELTY TO CHILDREN, &c.—*continued.* circumstances require until charge be determined. Inspector or Constable in charge of station may exercise discretion as to releasing offender so arrested without warrant under this section, on bail, with or without sureties, until the hearing of the charge.	52 & 53 Vic. c. 44, s. 4.	
Disposal of Child by order of Court. —Where person having custody of boy under 14, or of a girl under 16, is convicted under sec. 1 of offence involving bodily injury, and punishable with penal servitude, or sent for trial for the offence, or bound over to keep the peace towards such child, any person may bring child before Petty Sessions Court, and Court may order child to be committed to the charge of a relation or other fit person until the age of 14 if a boy, or 16 if a girl, and to vary order, &c.: provided that no order shall be made unless the parent is sent for trial or proved to be a party to the offence, or bound to keep the peace to the child. Section provides for the control of child, and Court may order parent to contribute to maintenance, provides as to religious persuasion of the child, &c. Where the person has been committed for the offence specified in sub-sec (1) (*b*). No order for maintenance shall be made before the trial, and where there is no conviction the order thenceforward shall be void.	s. 5.	

"*Parent*" includes guardian and every person who is by law liable to maintain the child.

"*Committed for Trial,*" means committed to prison or admitted on bail, as in Petty Sessions (Ir.) Act, 1851.

"*Local Authority*" means Sanitary Authority, within meaning of the Public (Ir.) Act, 1878.

Offence, or cause of Complaint.	Statute.	Extent of Jurisdiction.
PREVENTION OF CRUELTY TO CHILDREN, &c.—*continued*. *Power of Search.*—Where on information it is shown that there is good reason to suspect that a boy under 14, or girl under 16, has been or is being ill-treated or neglected so as to cause unnecessary suffering or injury to health, a Stipendiary or two Justices, or in case of urgency one Justice, may by warrant authorize search for, and detention of, child until case brought before the Summary Court. The warrant may also authorize arrest of the accused. The person named in warrant will be empowered by force to enter house or place specified and to remove the child. The warrant shall be addressed to some superior police officer, and may, unless otherwise directed, be accompanied by person making the information; and the Justices may also direct that he be accompanied by a registered medical practitioner.	52 & 53 Vic. c. 44, s. 5.	
Evidence of Accused.—Person accused of offence is competent, but not compellable, to give evidence. Wife or husband of accused may be required to attend to give evidence as an ordinary witness, and is competent, but not compellable, to give evidence.		
Evidence of Child of tender years.—When the child is of tender years and does not understand the nature of an oath, but in opinion of Court is of sufficient intelligence, and understands the duty of speaking the truth, evidence may be taken	s. 8.	

"*Summary Jurisdiction Acts*," means, as regards Ireland, in Dublin, Acts relating the powers and duties of Justices of the Peace for that district, or of the ice for that district; and elsewhere in Ireland, the Petty Sessions (Ir.) Act, 1, and any Act amending same.

Offence, or cause of Complaint.	Statute.	Extent of Jurisdiction
PREVENTION OF CRUELTY TO CHILDREN, &c.—*continued.* in writing, though not on oath, and in accordance with sec. 14 of Petty Sessions (Ir.) Act, 1851, and shall be deemed to be a deposition thereunder: Provided that (*a*) a person shall not be liable to be convicted unless the testimony admitted under this section, 8, is corroborated by other material evidence, and (*b*) any child whose evidence is so received, who shall give wilfully false evidence, shall be liable to be indicted for the offence, and may be punished under sec. 11, 41 & 42 Vic. c. 49, as in the case of juvenile offenders. *Presumption of age of child.*—Where child appears to the Court to be under any specified age, child shall be deemed to be so, unless contrary is proved.	52 & 53 Vic. c. 44, s. 8.	
Appeal from summary conviction to General or Quarter Sessions.	s. 10.	
Expenses.—Guardians of the poor may pay costs of proceedings directed by them. *By-Laws* under Act to be subject to sec. 221 of the "Public Health (Ir.) Act, 1878."	s. 12.	
Act not to take away right of parent, teacher, &c., to administer punishment to child.	s. 14.	
Saving for proceedings under other laws, so that no person be punished twice for same offence. See also title "Children and Young Persons," *ante.*	s. 15.	

" *Court of Summary Jurisdiction,*" as regards Ireland, means any Ju Justices of the Peace, Police Magistrate or Officer, by whatever name c whom jurisdiction is given by the Summary Jurisdiction Acts or any Acts referred to.

" *Petty Sessional Court,*" as regards Ireland, has same meaning as the ex isdiction as above defined.

Offence, or cause of Complaint.	Statute.	Extent of Jurisdiction.
PRINTERS: Act compelling printers, &c., to keep copies of printed papers, &c.	32 & 33 Vic. c. 24.	
PRISONS: See "Gaol," &c.		
PRISONERS' COUNSEL ACT, .	6 & 7 Wm. iv. c. 114.	
PROBATION OF FIRST OFFEN-DERS: To permit the conditional release of in certain cases. See Act, *Appendix*.	50 & 51 Vic. c. 25.	
PROCLAMATION: (*a*) Under "Riot Act." If persons so unlawfully assembled, or twelve or more of them, shall continue together and not disperse within one hour after proclamation made, they may be apprehended.	27 Geo. iii. c. 15, s. 2. s. 4.	

(*a*) By section 2, "The Justice or other person authorized to make the procla-mation shall, amongst the said rioters, or as near to them as he can safely come, with a loud voice command silence to be kept whilst proclamation is making; and after that shall, with a loud voice, make proclamation with these words, or like in effect: ' Our Sovereign Lord the King chargeth and commandeth all persons being assembled immediately to disperse themselves and peaceably to depart to their habitations, or to their lawful business, upon the pains contained in the Act made in the twenty-seventh year of King George the Third, to prevent tumultuous risings and assemblies.'"

The Magistrate should read the proclamation correctly. For "Our Sovereign Lord the King," he may substitute "Sovereign Lady the Queen."

Offence, or cause of Complaint.	Statute.	Extent of Jurisdiction.
PROSTITUTES : (a) 　Common prostitute or night-walker loitering and importuning passengers for the purpose of prostitution, under Police Clauses Act.	10 & 11 Vic. c. 89, s. 28.	Penalty not exceeding 40s. or imprisonment not exceeding 14 days. 1 J.
For like offence or being *otherwise offensive*, under "Towns Improvement Act."	17 & 18 Vic. c. 103, s. 72. (36 & 37 Vic. c. 82.)	Penalty not exceeding 40s., in default, &c., imprisonment not exceeding 1 month. 1 J. See which Act is in force in district.
PROTECTION OF PROPERTY : 　See " Conspiracy," &c.		
PROVIDENT (*Societies*) : 　See " Friendly Societies."		
PROVISIONS : 　See " Frauds," &c., " Adulteration."		
PUBLIC HEALTH (IRELAND) ACT, 1878 : (b)	41 & 42 Vic. c. 52.	—
PART 1. Sanitary authorities, . . .	ss. 1-14.	
PART 2. Sanitary provisions, . . .	ss. 15-159.	
Sewerage and drainage, . . .	ss. 15-51.	
Regulations as to sewers and drains, &c.	ss. 15-29.	

(a) *Prostitutes.*—Open lewdness, grossly scandalous, is an indictable offence, punishable by fine and imprisonment.—1 *Hawk., C.* 5 ; 1 *East., P. C.* 3 ; and see also " *Sureties for Good Behaviour.*"

(b) *Public Health Act.*—Remedial and restrictive laws dealt with some of the subjects in above Act from a very early date in England. It has been pointed out in a work on the subject by Bazalgette and Humphreys that the Court rolls of Stratford-on-Avon show that in 1552 Shakespeare's father was fined for depositing filth in the public street in violation of the by-laws of the Manor ; and again, in 1558, for not keeping his gutter clean.

Offence, or cause of Complaint.	Statute.	Extent of Jurisdiction.
PUBLIC HEALTH ACT—*continued.*		
Disposal of sewage, . . .	41 & 42 Vic. c. 52, ss. 30-34.	
As to sewage works without district,	ss. 35-37.	—
Regulation of buildings, . .	ss. 38-43.	—
Privies, watercloeets, . . .	ss. 44-51.	
Scavenging and cleansing, . .	ss. 52-60.	—
Regulations as to streets and houses,	ss. 52-57.	—
Offensive ditches, and collections of matter.	ss. 58-60.	
Water supply, ...	ss. 61-79.	—
Powers of sanitary authority in relation to supply of water.	ss. 61-76.	
Provisions for protection of water.	ss. 77-79.	
Gas supply, ...	ss. 80-81.	
Regulation of cellar dwellings and lodging-houses	ss. 82-101.	
Occupation of cellar dwellings, .	ss. 82-86.	
Common lodging-houses, . .	ss. 87-99.	
By-laws as to houses let in lodgings,	ss. 100, 101.	
Clocks.—Urban authority may provide public clocks.	s. 102.	
Markets and slaughter-houses, .	ss. 103-106.	
Nuisances, ...	ss. 107-127.	
Offensive Trades, . . .	ss. 128-131.	
Unsound Meat, &c., . . .	ss. 132-136.	
Infectious Diseases. — Provisions against.	ss. 137-148.	

Offence, or cause of Complaint.	Statute.	Extent of Jurisdiction
PUBLIC HEALTH ACT—*continued.*		
Prevention of the spread of infectious diseases.	41 & 42 Vic. c. 52, ss. 149-156.	
Mortuaries, &c., ...	ss. 157-159.	
PART 3.		
Burial-grounds, ...	ss. 160-199.	
PART 4.		
General provisions, . . .	ss. 200-225.	
Contracts, ...	ss. 200, 201.	
Purchase of lands, ...	ss. 202-204.	
Powers of Board in relation to local Acts.	ss. 205-213.	
Provisional Orders by Board, .	ss. 214, 215.	
Arbitration, ...	ss. 216-218.	—
By-laws, ...	ss. 219-225.	
PART 5.		
Financial, ...	ss. 226-248.	
PART 6.		
Legal Proceedings, ...	ss. 249-269.	
Prosecution of offences and recovery of penalties, &c.	ss. 249-264.	—
Notices, ...	ss. 265-267.	
Appeal, ...	ss. 268, 269.	
PART 7.		
Miscellaneous Provisions, . .	ss. 270-279.	

Offence, or cause of Complaint.	Statute.	Extent of Jurisdiction.
PUBLIC HEALTH ACT—*continued.* • PART 8. *Saving clauses and repeal of Acts,* .	41 & 42 Vic. c. 52, ss. 280-294.	
Drainage, &c.—Causing drain to empty into sewer of sanitary authority in contravention of section.	s. 23.	Penalty not exceeding £20 ; in default, &c., imprisonment by scale. 2 J. or 1 Stip.
Building house or occupying same without drains, &c., prohibited ; and any person who causes house to be erected or rebuilt or any drain to be constructed in contravention of section.	s. 27.	Penalty not exceeding £50 ; in default, &c., imprisonment by scale. 2 J. or 1 Stip.
Without written consent of urban authority (1) causing building to be newly erected over sewer ; or (2) causes any vault, arch, or cellar, to be newly built or constructed under carriage-way of any street.	s. 29.	Forfeit to urban authority £5, and 40s. a-day while continued after notice ; in default, &c., imprisonment by scale. 2 J. or 1 Stip.
Without written consent of urban authority bringing forward house or building, forming part of any street beyond front of buildings on either side, after notice from sanitary authority.	s. 40.	Penalty not exceeding 40s. a-day ; in default, &c., imprisonment by scale. 2 J. or 1 Stip.
As to commencement and removal of work, made contrary to building by-laws, and as to penalties under such.	s. 42.	
Privies, &c.—Newly erecting or rebuilding any house from ground floor, without sufficient water-closet, earth-closet, or privy accommodation, and an ashpit, furnished with proper doors and coverings.	s. 44.	Penalty not exceeding £20 ; in default, &c., imprisonment by scale. 2 J. or 1 Stip.
As to separate privy accommodation in factories where both sexes are employed. Person who neglects or refuses to provide such when required by notice from sanitary authority—	. 48.	Penalty not exceeding £20 ; and further penalty of 40s. a-day, in which default continued ; in default, &c., imprisonment by scale. 2 J. or 1 Stip.

Offence, or cause of Complaint.	Statute.	Extent of Jurisdiction.
PUBLIC HEALTH ACT—*continued.* Neglecting to put in proper order drain, water-closet, earth-closet, privy, ashpit, or cesspool, after notice from sanitary authority—	41 & 42 Vic. c. 52, s. 51.	Penalty not exceeding 10*s.* a-day during default, &c., imprisonment by scale. 2 J. or 1 Stip.
Scavenging, &c.—Removing or obstructing sanitary authority or contractor in removing matters by section authorized to be removed by sanitary authority. (*Proviso*—Where it is produced on premises of occupier and intended to be removed for sale or use and not a nuisance.)	s. 52.	Penalty not exceeding £5; imprisonment by scale. 2 J. or 1 Stip.
Cleansing, &c.—Neglect of sanitary authority to perform "undertaking" to remove house refuse, &c. &c., after notice as in section, &c.	s. 53.	Penalty (payable to occupier of house) of 5*s.* a-day, during default. 2 J. or 1 Stip.
On occupier (under by-laws) for similar neglect, or (urban authority) as to snow, filth, ashes, rubbish, &c.	s. 54.	—
Houses to be purified on certificate of officer of health or of two medical practitioners where any person's health, affected or endangered, or that such would tend to prevent or check infectious disease, for failing to comply with notice accordingly—	s. 56.	Penalty not exceeding 10*s.* a-day during default; imprisonment by scale in default, &c. 2 J. or 1 Stip.
Nuisances in Dwellings, Pigsty, &c.—Any person who in sanitary district—(1), keeps any swine or pigsty in any dwelling-house, or so as to be a nuisance to any person; or (2) Suffers any waste or stagnant water to remain in cellar or place within dwelling-house for 24 hours after written notice from sanitary authority to remove; or (3) Allows the contents of any water-closet, privy, or cesspool to overflow or soak therefrom.	s. 57.	Penalty not exceeding 40*s.*, and further penalty not exceeding 5*s.* a-day during continuance of offence. 2 J. or 1 Stip. Sanitary authority shall abate and may recover from occupier or owner as therein.

Offence, or cause of Complaint.	Statute.	Extent of Jurisdiction.
PUBLIC HEALTH ACT—*continued.* *Manures.*—After public notice for periodical removal of manure or refuse matter from mews, stables, &c., if owner of manure, &c., fails to remove same, or permits further accumulation, and does not continue periodical removal as directed, shall, *without further notice,* be liable to—	41 & 42 Vic. c. 52, s. 60.	Penalty not exceeding 20s. a-day during which matter permitted to accumulate ; imprisonment in default by scale. 2 J. or 1 Stip.
Water.—Wilfully or by culpable negligence injures or suffers to be injured meter or fittings, or fraudulently alters index, or prevents it registering supply, or fraudulently abstracts or uses water, &c. (without prejudice to other remedy) ; and see section as to what shall be evidence of fraud.	s. 70.	Penalty not exceeding 40s. ; in default, &c., imprisonment by scale. 2 J. or 1 Stip.
As to penalties for fouling water by gas washings, &c. see—	s. 77.	
Cellar Dwellings.—Only to be let or occupied on certain conditions. Person who lets, occupies, or knowingly suffers to be occupied, for hire or rent any cellar contrary to provisions of Act shall, for every day's offence after notice, cellar in which person passes the night to be deemed occupation, &c.	ss. 83, 84, 85.	Penalty not exceeding 20s. a-day ; in default, &c., imprisonment by scale. 2 J. or 1 Stip.
Common Lodging-houses — Keeper of neglecting to affix or renew notice of registration when required.	s. 90.	Penalty not exceeding £5, and 10s. a-day during neglect after conviction ; imprisonment by scale. 2 J. or 1 Stip.
Refusing access to officer of sanitary authority to inspect, &c.	s. 96.	Penalty not exceeding £5 ; in default, &c., imprisonment by scale. 2 J. or 1 Stip.
(1) Receiving lodger into unregistered lodging.	s. 97.	Penalty not exceeding £5, and for continuing

Offence, or cause of Complaint.	Statute.	Extent of Jurisdiction.
PUBLIC HEALTH ACT—*continued.* (2) Failing to report to sanitary authority after being furnished with schedules.	41 & 42 Vic. c. 52, s. 97.	the offence, not exceeding 40s. a-day. 2 J. or 1 Stip.
(3) Failing to give notices required by Act, where person therein confined to bed by fever or infectious disease.	,,	
Slaughter-houses.—Failing to affix or renew notice of registration, after written requisition so to do as in section.	s. 106.	Penalty not exceeding £5, and 10s. a-day while continued after conviction; in default, &c., imprisonment by scale. 2 J. or 1 Stip.
Definition of Nuisances, . . .	s. 107.	—
Duties of sanitary authority in respect to duties of householders, officers, or constables, in notifying to sanitary authority.	ss. 108, 109.	—
Notice from sanitary authority to abate.	s. 110.	
Failing to comply with notice may be summoned.	s. 111.	
Justices empowered to make order dealing with nuisance, as to abating, prohibiting recurrence, &c.	s. 112.	—
And Court making order of abatement or prohibition, may also impose penalty, &c.	,,	Penalty not exceeding £5, and may also direct payment of all costs incurred; in default, &c., imprisonment by scale. 2 J. or 1 Stip.
Disobedience of Order of Abatement.—Not obeying order of Court, directing compliance with requisitions of sanitary authority or otherwise to abate nuisance, and failing to satisfy Court that all due diligence used, &c.	s. 114.	Penalty 10s. a-day during default; imprisonment by scale. 2 J. or 1 Stip.

Offence, or cause of Complaint.	Statute.	Extent of Jurisdiction.
PUBLIC HEALTH ACT—*continued*. *Order of Prohibition.*—Person knowingly and wilfully acting contrary to Justices *order of prohibition*.	41 & 42 Vic. c. 52, s. 114.	Penalty not exceeding 20s. a-day during such contrary action; imprisonment by scale. 2 J. or 1 Stip.
Disobeying order of Justices for admission of sanitary authority, &c., as therein.	ss. 118, 119.	Penalty not exceeding £5; imprisonment by scale. 2 J. or 1 Stip.
Recovery of Costs.—Costs and expenses incurred in relation to nuisances shall be deemed to be money paid for the use and at request of person on whom order made, and such (not exceeding one year's rack-rent of premises) may be recovered in a summary way or in Civil Bill Court or Superior Court; and Court shall have power to divide costs, penalties, &c., between persons whose acts or defaults cause the nuisance.	s. 120.	
Offensive Trades.—Without consent of sanitary authority establishing offensive trades enumerated in section, &c.	s. 128.	Penalty not exceeding £50; in default, &c., imprisonment by scale. 2 J. or 1 Stip.
Carrying on offensive trade so established.	,,	Penalty not exceeding 40s. a-day; imprisonment by scale. 2 J. or 1 Stip.
Nuisance arising from offensive trades, &c., unless shown that best means taken to prevent such (offender being owner, occupier, or foreman).	s. 130.	Penalty not exceeding £5, nor less than 40s., and for each subsequent offence previous penalty may be doubled, not to exceed £200; imprisonment by scale. 2 J. or 1 Stip.
Unsound Meat.—Power of sanitary officer to inspect and examine meat, fruit, vegetables, bread, flour, milk, butter, intended for sale and for human food, &c., and to seize, if unfit for human food, demand name, &c., and detain person until name and address known; and any person giving false name or address, &c.—	s. 132.	Penalty not exceeding £5; imprisonment by scale. 2 J. or 1 Stip.

Offence, or cause of Complaint.	Statute.	Extent of Jurisdiction.
PUBLIC HEALTH ACT—*continued*. Power of Justice to order destruction of unsound meat as above when so seized, and the person to whom it belonged at the time of exposure, &c., for sale, or in whose possession or premises found shall be liable. (The Justice who orders the destruction may or may not be the Justice who convicts offender.)	41 & 42 Vic. c. 52, s. 133.	Penalty not exceeding £20 for every animal carcass, fish or piece of such, or any poultry or game, or for the parcel of fruit, vegetables, corn, bread, flour, milk, butter, so condemned; in default, &c., imprisonment by scale. Or, in the discretion of Justice, without fine, to be imprisoned for not more than 3 months. 2 J. or 1 Stip.
For hindering officer entering premises and making inspection, &c., or obstructing such officer when carrying provisions of Act into execution.	s. 134.	Penalty not exceeding £5; in default, imprisonment by scale. 2 J. or 1 Stip.
Search Warrant.—On complaint on oath by officer duly authorized, Justice may grant to officer warrant to search for such diseased and unfit food as aforesaid, and to seize and remove same; and for obstructing such officer in the execution of such warrant, shall, in addition to any other punishment to which he may be subject—	s. 135.	Penalty not exceeding £20; in default, &c., imprisonment by scale. 2 J. or 1 Stip.
Infectious Diseases.—Duty of sanitary officer to cause premises to be cleansed and disinfected; and for non-compliance with sanitary officer's notice and requisition—	s. 137.	Penalty not less than 1s. nor exceeding 20s. each day during default, &c.; imprisonment by scale. 2 J. or 1 Stip.
Removal of.—Provision or removal of infected persons without proper lodging, or lodged in room with persons not suffering, &c., or is on board ship or vessel. On proper medical certificate, and with consent of hospital authority, Justice may address order to constable or sanitary officer directing removal	s. 138.	Penalty not exceeding £10; in default, &c., imprisonment by scale. 2 J. or 1 Stip.

Offence, or cause of Complaint.	Statute.	Extent of Jurisdiction.
PUBLIC HEALTH ACT—*continued*. to hospital. Sanitary authority in like certificate may order removal from common lodging-house. For disobeying or obstructing execution of order—	41 & 42 Vic. c. 52, s. 138.	
Exposure, "*Waking*," *&c.*—Wilful exposure, or entry into "public conveyance" of such persons, &c., sale, disposal, or exposure of infected clothing, bedding, &c., exposure, conveyance, or "waking" of persons who died of infectious disease, &c. Sale, disposal— (*Proviso.*—Where clothing, &c., removed for disinfection.)	s. 142.	Penalty not exceeding £5; imprisonment by scale. 2 J. or 1 Stip. And may be ordered to pay owner of any carriage loss occasioned, where driver had no notice of person being diseased.
Carriages.—Owner or driver failing to disinfect public conveyance, &c., after knowledge, &c., of disease—	s. 143.	Penalty not exceeding £5; imprisonment by scale. 2 J. or 1 Stip.
Knowingly letting house, room, &c., in which infected persons have been, without disinfecting to satisfaction of medical practitioner.	s. 144.	Penalty not exceeding £20; in default, &c., imprisonment by scale. 2 J. or 1 Stip.
Persons letting or showing for the purpose, and persons hiring, &c., making false statement one to the other, on being questioned, as to contagious disease within 3 months previously.	s. 145.	Penalty not exceeding £20; imprisonment in default, &c., by scale; or, in discretion of Court, imprisonment, with or without H. L., not exceeding 1 month. 2 J. or 1 Stip.
Schools.—Person knowingly or negligently sending a child to school who, within 3 months, suffers from any dangerous infectious disorder, or who has been resident in house where such existed within 6 weeks, without certificate of medical practitioner that child is free from infection, and unless clothes disinfected.	s. 146.	Penalty not exceeding 40s.; in default, imprisonment by scale. 2 J. or 1 Stip.

Offence, or cause of Complaint.	Statute.	Extent of Jurisdi—
PUBLIC HEALTH ACT—*continued.* *Vaccination.*—For disobedience of Justice's order for the vaccination of any child under 14, after certificate and notice as therein.	41 & 42 Vic. c. 52, s. 147.	Penalty not ex 20s.; imprisonm scale. 2 J. or
Cholera.—For disobedience, or obstructing regulations of Local Government Board as to cholera, epidemic, endemic, &c.	s. 148.	Penalty not ex £50; in default imprisonment by 2 J. or
Preventing spread of disease.—Violation, &c., of regulations of Local Government Board, or wilfully obstructing execution of such.	s. 154.	Penalty not ex £5; in default imprisonment by 2 J. or
Obstructing Justices' order for removal of dead bodies to mortuary, where death has been by infectious disease, made as in section directed.	s. 158.	Like.
Bodies of persons dying from dangerous infectious disease shall not be removed from hospital, unless removed direct to a mortuary or cemetery. Person so violating, or officer of hospital knowingly permitting violation of regulations.	.,	Like.
Burial-grounds.—Burying in places where interment discontinued, and prohibited by law. (Saving as to certain reserved rights in vaults, s. 168.)	s. 167.	Penalty not ex £10; in default imprisonment by 2 J. or
For burial in private family grave without consent, &c. And any person knowingly assisting, &c.	s. 170.	Penalty not ex £10; in default imprisonment by 2 J. or And Court may exhumation.
Animals.—Allowing animals to graze, or be within limits of sufficiently fenced burial-ground.	s. 171.	Fine not exceedi nor less than 1s. f animal; recovera applied as tresp cattle. 2 J. or

Offence, or cause of Complaint.	Statute.	Extent of Jurisdiction.
PUBLIC HEALTH ACT—*continued.* Power to Local Government Board to make regulations as to burial-grounds, and provide for imposition of penalties.	41 & 42 Vic. c. 52, s. 181.	
Power in sanitary authority to make by-laws under this Act, and provide penalties as therein.	s. 220.	
Legal Proceedings—prosecution of offences and recovery of penalties.—Before Court of Summary Jurisdiction.	s. 249.	
Proceedings to be within 6 months.	s. 250.	
Who may sue for Penalties.—Party aggrieved, or sanitary authority of district; by none others without consent of Attorney-General. Proviso dispensing with such consent in respect to nuisances, or offensive trades, *outside* sanitary district.	s. 251.	
Application of penalties, . .	s. 252.	
Several Persons.—Where nuisance caused by act of, proceedings may be against one or more.	s. 253.	
Rates under Act.—Summary process for recovery of.	s. 154.	
Appeals.—From convictions, orders, rates, &c.	s. 269.	
Schedules to Act to be read as part of it.	s. 279.	
Forms contained in schedule C. to Act, or forms to the like effect, varied as circumstances may require may be used, and shall be sufficient for all purposes. (*a*)		

(*a*) This schedule being part of the Act, and as it gives the forms, such are the safe and proper forms to use. The schedule C. gives the form of notice A., to be signed by sanitary officer to abate nuisance. The form of summons B. and the

Offence, or cause of Complaint.	Statute.	Extent of Jurisdiction.
PUBLIC HEALTH ACT—*continued.* See also the " Public Health (Ireland) Amendment Act, 1879," as to Incorporation of Urban Sanitary Authorities : — Orders made under 19 & 20 Vic. c. 98 (" The Burial Grounds (Ir.) Act, 1856"). Burials of persons whose relatives cannot be required to provide for their interment, certain Acts as to paving, flagging, &c., to be deemed Sanitary Acts, returns as to Burials, &c.	42 & 43 Vic. c. 57.	
" Epidemic and other Diseases Prevention Act, 1883," extending borrowing powers to prevent diseases, and amending clause 150 of " Public Health (Ir.) Act, 1878."	46 & 47 Vic. c. 59.	
" The Cholera Hospitals (Ir.) Act, 1885," to enable Sanitary Authorities to take possession of land for the erection of temporary Cholera Hospitals. See also " Adulteration of Food."	48 & 49 Vic. c. 39.	
PUBLICANS AND PUBLIC-HOUSES : See " Licensing (Liquor) Act."		
PUBLIC PARKS : Governing body empowered to make by-laws for control and management of parks, protection from injury of trees, shrubs, &c., and to appoint a penalty not exceeding £5 for breach, &c.	32 & 33 Vic. c. 28, s. 10.	
Amended Act, ...	35 Vic. c. 6.	—

form C., order for abatement or prohibition of the nuisance ; form D., where Justices direct abatement of nuisance by sanitary authority ; form E., order to permit execution of works by owner ; and form F., Justice's order to admit the officer of sanitary authority.

ance, or cause of Complaint.	Statute.	Extent of Jurisdiction.
STORES :		
ʲBLIC STORES ACT, 1875, .	38 & 39 Vic. c. 25.	
ct refers to Her Majesty's ι.	s. 3.	
le to Act gives the marks on ı.		
tent to conceal Her Majesty's ɑrty, destroying or obliterating s.	38 & 39 Vic. c. 25, s. 5.	Felony: penal servitude not exceeding 7 years, or imprisonment not exceeding 2 years, with or without H. L.
ɔlitan constables, and other ables deputed as in Act, em‑ red on suspicion to search and ɑ vessels, &c., or persons sus‑ d of having Her Majesty's ɩ stolen or unlawfully ob‑ ɪ.	s. 6.	
ul possession of such stores, not satisfactorily accounted	s. 7.	Penalty not exceeding £5; or in discretion of Court, imprisonment not exceeding 2 months, with or without H. L. 1 J.
stores found in possession or ng of any person in Her sty's service, or marine store r, &c., or pawnbroker, and atisfactorily shown that he lawfully by the same.	s. 9.	Penalty not exceeding £5; in default of pay‑ ment, imprisonment not exceeding 2 calendar months. 1 J.
l possession explained, .	s. 10.	
ɔ gives summary penalty of ʳ sweeping, &c., near dock‑ , artillery ranges, &c.		
f Larceny Act, 24 & 25 Vic. incorporated.		

Offence, or cause of Complaint.	Statute.	Extent of Jurisdiction.
PUBLIC WORKS : Obstructing or assaulting Commissioners or their officers in execution of works.	10 Vic. c. 32, s. 58. (36 & 37 Vic. c. 82.)	Penalty not exceeding £5 ; in default, &c., imprisonment not exceeding 2 months. 1 J.
For the settling of disputes between parties, and other matters referred to Justices, see Act.		
RABBITS : Game certificate not necessary for killing rabbits.	23 & 24 Vic. c. 113, s. 43.	But for the purpose of the Poaching Act, 25 & 26 Vic. c. 114, they are to be considered game. See title "Game."
Taking or killing in a warren at night,	24 & 25 Vic. c. 96, s. 17.	Indictable misdemeanour.
Like in the daytime, . . .	"	Penalty not exceeding £5 ; in default, &c., imprisonment not exceeding 2 months. 1 J.
For night poaching, see also title "Game."		
RAIL : Stealing rail set up or used for fence, see "Larceny."		
RAILWAYS : *General Acts for the Regulation of Railways.* Conveyance of mails by, .	1 & 2 Vic. c. 98.	—
General regulation of railways, .	3 & 4 Vic. c. 97.	—
For the better regulation of, .	5 & 6 Vic. c. 55.	—
Act to attach certain conditions to construction of future railways.	7 & 8 Vic. c. 85.	—
Companies Clauses Consolidation Act, 1845.	8 Vic. c. 16.	—
Lands Clauses Consolidation Act, 1845.	8 Vic. c. 18.	—
Railway Clauses Consolidation Act, 1845.	8 Vic. c. 20.	—

Offence, or cause of Complaint.	Statute.	Extent of Jurisdiction.
RAILWAYS—*continued.*		
Railways (Powers and Construction) Act.	33 & 34 Vic. c. 19.	—
Railway Regulation Act, . .	31 & 32 Vic. c. 119.	—
Railway Regulation Amendment Act,	34 & 35 Vic. c. 78.	—
Railway servants, or servants of any traffic company, or persons employed on line, found drunk on line, offending against by-laws or regulations, or doing or omitting any act endangering life, &c., or to impede trains, &c.—	3 & 4 Vic. c. 97, s. 13, and 5 & 6 Vic. c. 55, s. 17.	Offender may be seized and taken before Justice, who is required to act summarily, by imprisonment not exceeding 3 months' H. L., or, in discretion of Justice, to pay a fine of £10; and in default of payment, imprisonment not exceeding 2 months. (*a*) 1 J.
Obstructing Officers, &c.—Wilfully obstructing or impeding any officer or agent of the Company in execution of his duty on the line, stations, or premises; wilfully trespassing on railway, stations, works, or premises, and refusing to quit on being requested.	3 & 4 Vic. c. 97, s. 16.	Offenders and persons aiding or assaulting may be seized and taken before Justice, who is required to act summarily; penalty not exceeding £5; in default of payment, imprisonment not exceeding 2 months. (*a*) 1 J.

(*a*) *Transient offenders.*—It will be seen by 8 Vic. c. 16, s. 156, and 8 Vic. c. 20, 164, "that it shall be lawful for any officer, &c., of the Company, and all persons called by him to his assistance, to seize and detain any person who shall have committed any offence against these Acts or the Special Act, or any Act incorporated therewith, and whose name and residence shall be unknown to such officer, &c., and convey him with all convenient despatch before some Justice, without any warrant or other authority than this or the Special Act, and such Justice shall proceed with all convenient despatch to the hearing and determining of the complaint against the offender."

In addition to this *special* provision, these Acts provide that all penalties imposed by these or the Special Act, or any by-law made in pursuance thereof, the recovery of which is not *otherwise provided for,* may be recovered by summary proceeding before 2 Justices—summons to issue in first instance; distress warrant; and in default of distress, imprisonment.

Now it is very doubtful whether at present any one Justice, out of Petty Sessions, can do the acts above referred to respecting "transient offenders." The Petty Sessions (Ireland) Act, 14 & 15 Vic. c. 93, regulates the powers and duties of Justices in all proceedings both in and out of Petty Sessions. By this Act,

Offence, or cause of Complaint.	Statute.	Extent of Jurisdiction.
RAILWAYS—*continued.* *Gates.*—Any person omitting to fasten gates as soon as he and the carriage, cattle, or other animals under his care shall have passed through.	8 Vic. c. 20, s. 75, (36 & 37 Vic. c. 82.)	Penalty not exceeding 40*s.* ; in default, &c., imprisonment not exceeding 1 month. 2 J.
Milestones, &c.—If any person wilfully pull down, deface, or destroy boards or milestones—	8 Vic. c. 20, s. 95. (36 & 37 Vic. c. 82.)	Forfeiture not exceeding £5 ; for every such offence ; in default, &c., imprisonment not exceeding 2 months. 2 J.
Frauds by Passengers.—Travelling or attempting to travel on railway without having previously paid fare, and with intent to avoid payment ; or having paid fare for a certain distance, knowingly and wilfully proceeding beyond such distance without previously paying the additional fare, and with intent to avoid payment thereof and wilfully refusing to quit carriage, on arriving at the place to which fare has been paid—	8 Vic. c. 20, s. 103. (36 & 37 Vic. c. 82.)	Forfeit to the Company a sum not exceeding 40*s.*; in default, &c., imprisonment not exceeding 1 month ; and railway servants, or any peace officer, may apprehend offender until he can be brought before a Justice. 2 J.

sec. 8, " It shall not be lawful for any Justice or Justices to hear and determine any cases of summary jurisdiction out of Petty Sessions, except cases of drunkenness or vagrancy, or fraud in the sale of goods, or disputes as to sales in fairs or markets ; but it shall be lawful for two Justices, if they shall see fit, to hear and determine out of Petty Sessions any complaint as to any offence when the offender shall be unable to give bail for his appearance at Petty Sessions." This section certainly appears sufficiently strong to prevail over the Railways Acts in deciding the course which the Magistrates should pursue. Nor would the fact of a *Special* Railway Act by being passed *subsequently* to the Petty Sessions Act (and which special Act would of course have incorporated with it the Railways and Companies Clauses Consolidation Acts referred to) be likely to alter the case. As the matter now stands, the Justice would be safe in following the Petty Sessions Act ; he can either take bail for the appearance at the Petty Sessions, with or without sureties, as he may think fit ; or, if name and residence be known, can have a summons served, or two Justices may try the case. But it will be observed that the power of the railway officers to arrest the offender and convey him before a Justice is not taken away, and it is the duty of the Justice to act on the complaint; and if no guarantee can be given that the prisoner will be forthcoming, the Justice can take an information on oath, and commit him until the hearing of the complaint—14 & 15 Vic. c. 93, s. 11. When the penalty is under £5 the imprisonment must be according to the scale in 35 & 36 Vic. c. 82, and under this Act the offender v be committed forthwith if he fail to pay the penalty.

Offence, or cause of Complaint.	Statute.	Extent of Jurisdiction.
RAILWAYS—*continued.* *Dangerous Goods, &c.*—Sending by railway aquafortis, oil of vitriol, gunpowder, lucifer matches, or any other goods which, in the judgment of the Company, may be of a dangerous nature, without marking their nature on the outside of the package, or giving notice in writing at the time of sending to some servant of the Company—	8 Vic. c. 20, s. 105.	Forfeit to the Company £20 ; in default, &c., imprisonment not exceeding 3 months. 2 J.
By-laws.—Company empowered to make by-laws and regulations ; amongst others against smoking of tobacco, and other nuisances, in carriages and stations, or premises. Not to be repugnant to the laws of the kingdom. By-laws to be confirmed and published as therein.	3 & 4 Vic. c.97, ss.7,8,9; 8 Vic. c. 20, ss. 108, 109, 110; and By-laws.	Penalty for breach of any by-law, not exceeding £5, recoverable as other penalties. (a) 2 J.
Justices may detain offender convicted until return made to distress warrant, or take bail for his appearance ; or if it be shown, by his admission or otherwise, that he has no goods, he may be committed.	8 Vic. c. 16, s. 149, and 8 Vic. c. 20, s. 147.	
Transient Offenders.—Company's officers may detain persons committing offences whose name and residence may be unknown to them, and without further warrant convey them before a Justice.	8 Vic. c. 16, s. 156, and 8 Vic. c. 20, s. 154.	" Such Justice shall proceed with all convenient despatch to the hearing and determining of the complaint against the offender." But see note p. 320.

(a) *By-laws not to be repugnant to public law, and should be confirmed as required by the Act.*—" A question arose as to the legality of certain of the by-laws of railway companies, namely, those which contain provisions purporting to impose a penalty upon a passenger in cases where he fails to deliver up his ticket on demand, or uses a ticket for a station other than that for which it is available, without any fraudulent intention on his part being shown. I am accordingly directed by the Board of Trade to acquaint you, for the information of your directors, that the Board of Trade have consulted counsel on the point, and are clearly of opinion that by-laws which contain such provisions are illegal."—*Board of Trade, Railway Department, London, S.W.,* 17th *April,* 1874. The statute law quoted above, as to " Frauds by Passengers," is sufficient where there is *intentional fraud.* The foregoing communication was sent to the several railway companies.

Offence, or cause of Complaint.	Statute.	Extent of Jurisdiction.
RAILWAYS—*continued*. *Criminal Offences.*—Maliciously placing, &c., on railway, any matter or thing, displacing rails, &c., moving or diverting machinery, showing, hiding, or removing signals or lights, or doing, or causing to be done, anything with intent to obstruct or injure engine, tender, carriage, or truck.	24 & 25 Vic. c. 97, s. 35.	Felony, triable by indictment. (Juvenile offenders under age of 16 may be summarily dealt with.) (*a*)
Like offence, with intent to endanger passengers. (*b*)	24 & 25 Vic. c. 100, s. 32.	Felony, triable by indictment.
Neglect.—Whosoever, by any unlawful act, or by any wilful omission or neglect, shall obstruct, or cause to be obstructed, any engine or carriage using on any railway, or shall aid or assist—	24 & 25 Vic. c. 97, s. 36.	Indictable misdemeanour.
Guilty of like offence, where by the safety of passengers may be endangered.	24 & 25 Vic. c. 100, s. 34.	Like.
Maliciously throwing, or causing to fall or strike at, against, into, or upon any engine, tender, carriage, or truck, used upon any railway, any wood, stone, or other matter or thing. with intent to injure or endanger the safety of any person therein, &c.	s. 33.	Felony, triable by indictment.

(*a*) *Juvenile Offenders.*—The Railway Regulation Amendment Act, 34 & 35 Vic. c. 78, s. 12, enacts that the Act of 10 & 11 Vic. c. 82, " for the more speedy trial and punishment of juvenile offenders," and the 13 & 14 Vic. c. 37, for the further extension of summary jurisdiction in cases of "Larceny," shall have effect as if there had been mentioned therein, in addition to the offence of Larceny, the several offences following :—The offences mentioned in sections 32 and 33 of 24 & 25 Vic. c. 100 (Offences against the Person), and the offences mentioned in section 35 of 24 & 25 Vic. c. 97 (Malicious Injuries Act). This Juvenile Offenders, Act, 10 & 11 Vic. c. 82, is an English Act, dealing with cases of larceny. The punishment is not to exceed 3 calendar months; and males (under 14) may be whipped, or to pay, in the discretion of the Justices, a fine not exceeding £3.

(*b*) Section 15 of the 3 & 4 Vic. c. 97, which made this offence an indictable misdemeanour, has been repealed by the 24 & 25 Vic. c. 95. It is now made felony.

It will be seen above that the offences are provided for in the Malicious Injuries Act, and also in the Offences against the Person Act, so as to meet the cases of injuring the property of the Company, or endangering the lives of the passengers.

Offence, or cause of Complaint.	Statute.	Extent of Jurisdiction.
RAILWAYS—*continued.* *Prize Fights.*—Railway company knowingly letting for hire, or otherwise providing special train to convey parties to, or to be present at prize fight, or stopping ordinary trains to accommodate such persons at places not ordinary stations on their line. Summons to be served on secretary of company at his office 10 days before hearing.	31 & 32 Vic. c. 119, s. 21.	Penalty not exceeding £500, and not less than £200 ; case to be heard before 2 Justices of the county, where fight held, or attempted to be held. 2 J. Half penalty to go to party suing, other half to county treasurer in aid of county rate.
Provisions for safety of passengers by communication with guard, &c. ; for penalty on company for neglect, and on passengers using same without causes, see—	s. 22.	Company, for *default*, not exceeding £10 ; passenger, for *offence*, not exceeding £5 ; recoverable as other penalties. 2 J.
Trespasser.—If any person shall be or pass upon any railway, except crossing at authorized crossing, after having once received warning by railway company, (*a*) their agents or servants, not to go or pass thereon.	31 & 32 Vic. c. 119, s. 23. 34 & 35 Vic. c. 78, s. 14.	Penalty not exceeding 40s. ; in default, &c., imprisonment by scale. 2 J.
Trees in danger of falling on railway or obstructing traffic, on complaint of company may be removed.	s. 24.	2 Justices may make the order, and may award compensation to owner.
Provides that returns of signal arrangements (under a penalty) be made to the Board of Trade.	36 & 37 Vic. c. 76.	—
Amends 3 & 4 Vic. c. 97 ; 5 & 6 Vic. c. 55 ; Railway Regulation Act, applies Petty Sessions (Ireland) Act, 1851, &c.		

(*a*) *Trespass after warning.*—The earlier Act quoted had the words "after receiving warning," which implied that a warning was necessary in every case of offending. By the second Act quoted, the same person may be warned once for all.

2 B

Offence, or cause of Complaint.	Statute.	Extent of Jurisdiction.
RATES:		
Poor-rates recoverable in Petty Sessions, under— (And see "Poor Rates.")	1 & 2 Vic. c. 56, and 6 & 7 Vic. c. 92, s. 2.	1 J.
County cess, under—	6 & 7 Wm. iv. c. 146, s. 152.	1 J.
RECEIPT: See "Stamps."		
RECEIVER (of *Stolen Property*): Shipwrecked goods found in possession or premises of any person with his knowledge, and not satisfactorily accounting for same.	24 & 25 Vic. c. 96, s. 65.	Imprisonment, with or without H. L., not exceeding 6 months, or forfeiture (over and above value of goods) not exceeding £20. 1 J.
Receivers of stolen property, where the original offence is, by this Act, punishable by summary conviction.	s. 97.	Liable for every first, second, or subsequent offence, to same forfeiture and punishment to which a person guilty is liable.
RECOGNIZANCE: Estreating—see notes on sec. 22. Petty Sessions Act, and on Fines Act, *Appendix*.		
REFORMATORY SCHOOLS: *Juvenile Offenders.* (a)—Any person convicted of any offence punishable with penal servitude, or imprisonment before Judge of Assize. Justices at Quarter Sessions, Divisional Justice of Dublin	31 & 32 Vic. c. 59, s. 12.	In addition to the sentence of punishment for the offence, may direct offender to be sent, at expiration of sentence, to Reformatory School,

(a) *Juvenile Offenders.*—Previous to the passing of this Act, Justices in Petty Sessions could only cause offender to be detained in a Reformatory when convicted under section 6 of 14 & 15 Vic. c. 92. Now where the juvenile offender is convicted of any offence for which a sentence of at least 14 days' imprisonment can be he sent to a Reformatory. The Act is applicable to females as

Offence, or cause of Complaint.	Statute.	Extent of Jurisdiction.
REFORMATORY SCHOOLS—*con.* Police District, or before any Justice or Justices of the Peace at *Petty Sessions*, whose age shall not, in the opinion of the Court, exceed 16 years.	31 & 32 Vic. c. 59, s. 12.	duly certified under Act, and willing to receive offender, for not less than *two* and not exceeding *five* years. 2 J.
Proviso.—The sentence of punishment for the offence must be one of imprisonment for 14 days at the least. (*a*) The Reformatory to be one of religious persuasion of the parents or guardians of juveniles. Where unknown, to be that in which he appears to have been baptized, or professes.	,,	*Appeal.*—Allowed from order of Divisional Justice or Justices in Petty Sessions sending to Reformatory School. The child, parent, or guardian may appeal to Quarter Sessions of the division, if not held within 15 clear days from date of order. If
Imprisonment to which he shall have been sentenced as a punishment for offence—such to be directed to be spent as far as practicable in strict separation.	,,	held within 15 days, then to next following Quarter Sessions. Notice in writing to Divisional Justice (in Dublin) or Clerk of Petty Sessions, of intention to appeal 7 days
Chief Secretary may order discharge of offender from school,		at least before Sessions. Quarter Sessions may confirm, reverse, or vary order. (*b*)

(*a*) *Fourteen days at the least.*—Why the statute directs that a punishment of 14 days at the least shall be inflicted before the juvenile can be sent to a Reformatory School may be difficult to explain. It does certainly seem to be intended that, excluding all other considerations, the Court should view the offence to be of a magnitude demanding punishment to that extent. It may be that in most cases, if it were merely a matter of punishment, they would not imprison a child for a first offence for so long term. However, where from the confirmed vicious habits of the offender, the hopelessness of reformation by the unfortunate circumstances in which he may be placed, and the object of the Legislature being to reform, the course in such a case could not be considered severe or unjust—*it is a necessity.* The community have a right to protection against crime, and, where he can, the Legislature and the Judge should make reformation of the offender the aid and instrument for securing that protection.

(*b*) *Appeal.*—The appeal here allowed is not from the sentence of *punishment* for the offence, it is from the detaining order in Reformatory School. There is no appeal bond or proceeding beyond the notice mentioned in the section, consequently there is no power in the Justice to allow the offender out on bail until the hearing

2 B 2

Offence, or cause of Complaint.	Statute.	Extent of J...
REFORMATORY SCHOOLS—*con.* The particular Reformatory School may or may not be named when passing sentence; or may be changed for another before expiration of imprisonment. (*a*)	31 & 32 Vic. c. 59, ss. 13 and 14.	—
Expense of conveyance, how paid, .	s. 15.	—
Governor of prison to send duplicate or copy of warrant of commitment with offender to reformatory.	s. 16.	—
What shall be deemed sufficient evidence as to identity of juvenile offenders.	s. 17.	
Power of Treasury to defray costs of maintenance at reformatory.	s. 18.	
Absconding, Insubordination, &c.— Absconding, wilfully neglecting, or refusing to abide by or conform to rules of school.	s. 19.	Justice in Pe or Police where offenc or be recapt time of th upon proof
The imprisonment to be, as far as practicable, in strict separation; and at expiration to be sent back to school, if received, to complete full term.	,,	one credibl may comm for any peri ceeding 6 m or without l

of the appeal. The Clerk of Petty Sessions should take care that t the conviction (see form in Act, and *Appendix*) is before the Court of the sentence of *punishment* be of a nature to give the offender a rig then that appeal will be in the usual form, and the defendant will : his discharge on bail until the hearing.

(*a*) If the Justices can, with sufficient certainty, set forth the reformatory at the time of passing sentence, it will render a supple and the re-assembling of the Justices for the purpose unnecessary; case, the entire order may be set forth in the warrant of commitm "To be imprisoned in the gaol of the county of *Cork* for ——; and, ration of such sentence, to be sent to the *Roman Catholic Reformate in the county of Cork*, to be there detained for the period of —— yea

Offence, or cause of Complaint.	Statute.	Extent of Jurisdiction.
REFORMATORY SCHOOLS—*con.* *Harbouring.*—Person directly or indirectly wilfully withdrawing young person from Reformatory School; or inducing him to abscond; or knowingly harbouring, or concealing, or assisting, or preventing him returning—	31 & 32 Vic. c. 59, s. 20.	Penalty not exceeding £5; in default, &c., imprisonment not exceeding 2 months. 2 J. or 1 Stip.
Officers of reformatory duly authorized, &c., to have powers and privileges of constables in respect to offenders under sentence of detention.	s. 21.	
Power to Treasury to repay half cost of recapture.	s. 22.	
Contribution by Parents.—Court to direct the officer of the Court to issue certificate of sentence, which shall be conclusive evidence thereof, and parent, or step-parent, if able, shall be liable to contribute any sum not exceeding 5s. a-week for maintenance; and upon complaint of any person, authorized by Chief or Under Secretary, to summon parent or step-parent, and on hearing, whether defendant appear or not—(a)	s. 23.	Justices to examine into ability to contribute, and make an order for such *weekly* payment, not exceeding 5s. per week, as shall seem reasonable, during whole or part of detention. 1 J. Payment to be made at such times as directed by order to person authorised to take proceedings, or such other as Chief or Under Secretary appoint.
Case to be heard in Petty Sessions District where party summoned resides.	s. 20.	
Power to remit, reduce, or increase weekly payments (not to exceed 5s.), either side giving at least a week's notice to the other of intended application.	s. 24.	

(a) It does not appear from the words of the section that a summons is necessary to bring up the defendant on each occasion of his being a defaulter. The warrant to levy is on an order already made, and which order continues in force until reversed or varied. There is nothing to prevent the Justice issuing summons or notice if he sees fit.

Offence, or cause of Complaint.	Statute.	Extent of Jurisdiction.
REFORMATORY SCHOOLS—*con.* *Defaulters.*—Where default made for 14 days in payment of sums ordered—	31 & 32 Vic. c. 59, s. 25.	Justice to issue distress warrant. 1 J.
If it appear to Justices, on confession of defendant or otherwise, or if so returned to distress warrant, that sufficient goods cannot be found—	,,	Justice (or any Justice of the district or county, &c.) may commit defendant for any term not exceeding 10 days, unless amount and the costs, charges, and expense of conveying to prison be sooner paid. The whole amount to appear on warrant. 1 J.
Provision for care of offenders when discharged from Reformatory.	s. 26.	—
Offenders absconding from licensed parties to be held to have absconded from school.	,,	
Power to apprentice offenders, .	s. 27.	
Offenders may be removed from one school to another.	s. 28.	—
Rules respecting evidence of schools, the rules thereof, identity of offenders, &c. &c.	s. 29.	—
Notice on managers, or any of them, to be personal or sent by post. Sections 4 to 11 refer to mode of certifying, maintenance, &c., of schools.	s. 30.	—
Forms, &c. (a)—Proceedings not invalidated for want of form. The forms in the schedule to Act to be valid.	,,	For the several forms required by Act, and set forth in the schedule— see *Appendix* to this work.
Repeal.—21 & 22 Vic. c. 103, repealed. Act applies to existing certified schools. For "Industrial School," see this title.	s. 32.	—

(a) The several *Forms* in the Act, applicable in Ireland, are set out in the *Appendix* to this Act.

Offence, or cause of Complaint.	Statute.	Extent of Jurisdiction.
REFRESHMENT HOUSES: All houses, rooms, shops, or buildings kept open for public refreshment resort, and entertainment at any time between the hours of 10 o'clock (a) at night and 7 o'clock in the morning, not being licensed for the sale of beer, cider, wine, or spirits respectively, shall be deemed refreshment houses within the Act; and the resident, owner, tenant, or occupier thereof shall be required to take out licence. (b)	23 & 24 Vic. c. 107, s. 6.	

(a) Extended from 9 o'clock to 10 o'clock by the 24 & 25 Vic. c. 91, s. 8.

(b) *Excise Duties.*—Section 2 enacts that the duties by this Act granted shall be deemed to be Excise duties, and shall be under the management of the Commissioners of Inland Revenue: and the powers, regulations, penalties, &c., contained in Excise Acts in relation to Excise Duties, and not herein expressly provided for, and so far as same are consistent with this Act, shall apply to the duties granted by this Act.

Persons entitled to Licence.—Section 3. Every person keeping a shop for the sale of any goods or commodities other than foreign wine, or having a wine dealer's licence (except disqualified by this Act), shall be entitled, without further authority, to a licence under this Act to retail in quart or pint bottles only, not to be consumed on the premises.

Retailed.—Section 4. Every sale of foreign wine in any less quantity than two gallons or a dozen quart bottles at a time, to be deemed selling by retail.

Evading the Act.—Section 5. Permitting drinking wine in a neighbouring house, shed, &c., with intent to evade the provisions of the Act, to be deemed drinking on the premises, and shall be subject to the penalty accordingly.

Disqualified Premises and Persons.—Section 8. No licence to sell foreign wine by retail to be consumed on the premises shall be granted for any refreshment house which, with the premises belonging thereto and occupied therewith, shall be under the value of £8 a-year; nor for any refreshment house situate in any city, borough, town, or place containing a population exceeding 10,000, according to last census, if such refreshment house, with the premises belonging thereto and occupied therewith, shall be under the value of £15 a-year. No sheriff's officer, Clerk of Petty Sessions, or officer executing the legal process of any Court, shall hold licence to sell wine by retail to be consumed on the premises.

Mode of obtaining Wine Licence.—See sections 13 and 14. By requisition, stating certain particulars, to be forwarded by supervisor of excise, who shall transmit copies to sub-inspector and Clerk of Petty Sessions. Justice may object to granting licence, stating the grounds. Sub-constabulary officer or superintendent of police may object to the granting of such wine licence.

Appeal from Order of Refusal.—Section 15. Persons aggrieved by order of refusal may appear to next Quarter Sessions, not being sooner than 15 clear days.

Offence, or cause of Complaint.	Statute.	Extent of Jurisd
REFRESHMENT HOUSES—*con.* No licence required if the house be not situate within any town or place containing a population exceeding 10,000 according to last Parliamentary census.	23 & 24 Vic. c. 107, s. 6.	
Every person licensed to keep a refreshment house, and who shall pursue therein the business of confectioner, or eating-house keeper (subject to conditions in the Act, and not expressly disqualified thereby), entitled to take out licence to sell wine to be drank on the premises.	s. 7.	—
Every person who shall keep a refreshment house for which a licence is required by this Act without taking out and having in force a proper licence in that behalf granted to him under the authority of this Act—	s. 9.	Excise penalty ceeding £20, able as exci alty. (*a*)
In case complaint made before Justice against any person licensed to sell wine by retail under this Act, for any offence against the tenor of his licence or this Act, the Justice may (if he shall think fit) require such person to produce his licence for examination; and in case of wilful neglect or refusal—	s. 19.	Penalty not e £5, recovera distress; and fault, &c.. i ment according Sessions scale.

Form of Recognizance in schedule to Act to be used. Appeal in other be as an appeal under Petty Sessions (Ireland) Act, 1851.

Transfers, Renewals, &c.—Section 17. Justices may object to renewal of a wine licence if they shall see just cause of objection; and by sec! the death of licensed person, representative, widow, or child may be ar continue for the term for which licence originally granted.

List of Licences.—Section 18. A list of licences to be kept by col supervisors for inspection of the Justices, and copies of the list to be t to the Justices' clerk.

(*a*) *Excise Penalties.*—Section 45. The penalties imposed by this minated "Excise penalties," shall be recovered, levied, mitigated, a by the same ways, means, and methods, and in like manner, as penalt recovered, levied, mitigated, and applied under the laws of excise in th!

(*b*) *Penalties other than Excise.*—Proceedings for recovery of pen the hearing and determination of complaints, to be subject in all resp!

Offence, or cause of Complaint.	Statute.	Extent of Jurisdiction.
REFRESHMENT HOUSES—*con.*		
If person licensed or any person in his service or employ, or by his direction, shall refuse to admit, or shall not admit police officers and constables when they think proper to enter between 9 o'clock at night and 7 o'clock in the morning— (*a*)	23 & 24 Vic. c. 107, s. 20.	Penalty not exceeding £5; and costs of conviction, by distress, &c., and for second offence, may (if Justice think fit) be disqualified for not exceeding 2 years. 1 J. Complaint to be made within 7 days.
Every person who shall sell any wine by retail, whether to be consumed on the premises or not, without having a proper licence in force authorising him in that behalf—	s. 21.	Excise penalty £20 (over and above any other penalty to which he may be liable); recoverable as excise penalties. (*b*) 2 J.
And in addition to any excise penalty to which he may thereby become subject—	s. 22.	Shall forfeit £5 additional, by distress; and in default, imprisonment 2 months 1 J.
Section 23 specifies what shall be deemed to be foreign wine, and what be deemed spirits.		
Persons convicted of felony or of selling spirits without licence to be disqualified; and if such person shall take out or have a licence under this Act, it shall be void, and he shall incur the penalty.	s. 24.	

Petty Sessions (Ireland) Act, 1851, as amended by the Petty Sessions Clerks (Ireland) Act, 1858; and to the Provisions of the Act relating to the Divisional Police Offices, when the same shall be heard in Police District of Dublin Metropolis, so far as is consistent with special provisions of this Act.

Fines to be applied as provided by the Fines Act (Ireland), 1851.

(*a*) By section 8 of the 24 & 25 Vic. c. 91 (amending section 6 of the above Act), a licence is not requisite for a refreshment house not open after *ten o'clock at night*.

(*b*) There are penalties (besides those under sections 21 and 22) provided by other Acts for the offence of selling wine without licence; and under 17 & 18 Vic. c. 89, s. 3, a constable may prosecute for the offence, as in the case of "shebeen houses." The powers of constables, &c., under 17 & 18 Vic. c. 89, are extended to houses licensed under the above Act, and to search for and seize spirits.

Offence, or cause of Complaint.	Statute.	Extent of Jurisdicti
REFRESHMENT HOUSES—*con.* Licensed retailers of wine to make entry, &c., with the excise.	23 & 24 Vic. c. 107, s. 25.	
Excise officers and constables empowered to enter the premises of licensed retailers of wine, and to search for and seize all spirits found therein, and may exercise for the purpose the powers granted them by the 17 & 18 Vic. c. 89.	s. 26.	
Retailers of wine under this Act shall, if required, sell wine (except wine in bottle, and quantities less than half a pint) by the gallon, quart, pint, or half-pint measure, sized or marked according to the standard, and, if required by the guest or customer, retail the same in a vessel sized or marked according to such standard; in default—	s. 28.	Forfeit the measur penalty not exce 40s, with costs of viction; by distres Over and above penalties to whic may be liable any other Act.
Limited Hours for Selling.—7 o'clock, A.M., to 11 o'clock, P.M., in places of a certain population as therein, nor after 10 o'clock elsewhere, nor at prohibited hours on Sundays and holidays, at which public-houses are closed—lodgers excepted—under a penalty.—(See section.)	s. 29.	Penalty £2 for offence; by di &c.
Houses licensed for sale of wine to be closed by order of two Justices in cases of riot, &c.; for refusal—	ss. 30, 32.	To be deemed guilt offence against the of his licence; p not exceeding £1 costs of conviction Second offence, if 12 months—penal exceeding £10. Third offence, if 18 months—£50 costs of conviction distress, &c.

Offence, or cause of Complaint.	Statute.	Extent of Jurisdiction.
REFRESHMENT HOUSES—*con.*		
Permitting Drunkenness or Disorderly Conduct.—Every person licensed under this Act to sell wine by retail, who shall permit any person to be guilty of drunkenness or other disorderly conduct in the house or premises mentioned in such licence, or who shall himself be guilty of any such disorderly conduct, shall, for every such offence, forfeit the respective sums following ; and every person who shall transgress or neglect, or shall be a party in transgressing or neglecting the conditions and provisions specified in such licence, or allow such to be done therein, shall be deemed guilty of disorderly conduct, and shall be liable to a—	23 & 24 Vic. c. 107, s. 31.	Penalty not less than 40*s.*, nor exceeding £5. Second offence—not less than £5, nor more than £10. Third offence—not less than £20, nor more than £50 : and for such second or third offence, may be disqualified for not exceeding five years, if Justice of the Peace think fit. 1 J.
Adulterating Wine.—Person licensed who shall mix, or cause to be mixed, any spirits or any drugs or other pernicious ingredients, with any wine sold in his house or premises, or shall fraudulently dilute or in anywise adulterate any such wine, or shall sell or offer for sale any wine which, to the knowledge of such person, has been so mixed, diluted, or adulterated.	,,	First offence— penalty not less than £10, nor more than £20. Second offence—disqualified from selling wine by retail for five years, or penalty not less than £20, nor more than £50 ; and selling wine by retail in same house or elsewhere while disqualified, penalty not less than £25, nor more than £50 ; by distress, &c. 1 J.
Justices may adjudge premises disqualified for sale of wine on proof that, within two years last preceding such third conviction, two convictions have taken place.	s. 33.	Premises disqualified for three years. Notice to be given to Supervisor of Excise. 1 J.

Offence, or cause of Complaint.	Statute	Extent of Jurisdiction
REFRESHMENT HOUSES—*con.*		
Offences in Refreshment Houses. — Every person licensed to keep a refreshment house under this Act, who shall (without licence for that purpose) sell, or suffer to be sold therein, any intoxicating liquor; or knowingly suffer any unlawful games or gaming therein; or knowingly suffer prostitutes, thieves, or drunken and disorderly persons, or members of an unlawful society, to assemble at or continue in or upon his premises; or do, suffer, or permit any act in contravention of his licence.	23 & 24 Vic. c. 107, s. 34.	Penalty :—First offence not exceeding 4[?] second, not exceeding £5; and every subsequent offence, not exceed £20, or forfeiture licence for one y[?] Penalties recoverable distress, &c.
Witnesses.—On questions touching any objection against granting or renewing of licences, Justices may summon witnesses on behalf of either party, and may order the usual expenses of witnesses and other expenses under the Act.	s. 39.	1 J.
Witnesses summoned neglecting or refusing to appear, without reasonable excuse, or refusing to give evidence.	s. 40.	Penalty not exceed £10 for every offen by distress, &c.; in fault, imprisonment Petty Sessions scale.
Harbouring Constables.—Every person licensed to sell beer, spirits, wine, cider, or any other fermented or distilled liquors, by retail, to be drunk or consumed on the premises, who knowingly habours, or entertains, or suffers to remain in the place wherein he carries on his business, any constable during any part of the time appointed for his being on duty, unless for the purpose of quelling disturbance or restoring order.	s. 41.	Penalty not exceed 20s.; by distress, &[?]

Offence, or cause of Complaint.	Statute.	Extent of Jurisdiction.
REFRESHMENT HOUSES—*con.*		
Drunken or Disorderly Persons refusing to quit. (a)—Any person who shall be drunk, riotous, quarrelsome, or disorderly in any shop, house, premises, or place, licensed for the sale of beer, wine, or spirituous liquors by retail, to be consumed on the premises, or for refreshment, resort, or entertainment, under the provisions of this Act, and shall refuse or neglect to quit on being requested by manager, &c., or his agent or servant, or by any constable.	23 & 24 Vic. c. 107, s. 42.	Penalty not exceeding 40s; by distress; in default, imprisonment by Petty Sessions scale. 1 J. And constables, on being required, are to assist in expelling such disorderly persons.
Penalties other than excise penalties recoverable before a Justice or Justices in Petty Sessions, &c., within three months after offence committed, or such shorter time as may be limited herein with regard to any particular penalty.	s. 32.	
Mitigation.—Justices, if they shall see cause, are empowered to mitigate the penalties incurred; Excise penalties not less than one-fourth.	s. 35.	
Transfer.—Licences granted under this Act may be transferred as other Excise licences in case of the removal of the licensed person; but the Excise shall not transfer the licence unless the assignee be duly licensed to keep a refreshment house, nor unless he shall produce a certificate of a Justice of the Peace that such Justice does not object to the transfer.	25 Vic. c. 22, s. 15.	—

(a) This section is equally applicable to "public-houses."

Appeal.—Party convicted of second or third offence may appeal to the next quarter Sessions of the division (or Recorder, in the city of Dublin), if Sessions held within twelve days, then to next subsequent Sessions. Justice shall also bind the recognizance prosecutor and witnesses. For powers of Court of Quarter Sessions, see sections 36 and 37. Forms of proceedings on appeal as in Petty Sessions Act. Proceedings on appeal may be ordered by Justices to be carried on by the constable, and the expenses of prosecution to be charged on the county—section 38.

Offence, or cause of Complaint.	Statute.	Extent of Jurisdiction.
REGIMENTALS : Purchasing : see title "Army Discipline."		
REGISTRATION (*of Births, Deaths, and Marriages*) : BIRTHS AND DEATHS REGISTRATION (IRELAND) ACT, 1880.	43 & 44 Vic. c. 13.	
Births.—After expiration of three months, next after birth of any child, a Registrar shall not register such birth, except as in section provided, &c. &c. And after expiration of 12 months' birth not to be registered except with written authority of Registrar-General, and for acting in contravention—	s. 5.	Penalty not exceed £10 ; in default, imprisonment not ceeding 3 months.
Deaths.—After expiration of 12 months next after any death, or after finding of any dead body elsewhere than in a house, that death shall not be registered, except with written authority of Registrar-General, and in accordance with prescribed rules, &c., and the fact of authority shall be entered in the register. Every person who registers or causes to be registered in contravention of section—	s. 15.	Like.
Burials.—A person shall not wilfully bury or procure to be buried the body of any deceased child as if it were still-born. A person who has control over, or ordinarily buries bodies in any burial-ground, shall not permit such, and shall not permit the burial of a still-born child before there is delivered to him the medical certificate or declaration as therein particularly mentioned, and where there has been an inquest, an order of coroner, and for acting in contravention—	s. 18.	Penalty not exceed £10 ; in default, imprisonment not ceeding 3 months.

ance, or cause of Complaint.	Statute.	Extent of Jurisdiction.
RATION, &c.—*continued*. notices and particulars re- d to be given where coffin ins`more than one dead body, dy of still-born child; such) as required by section and iting to District Registrar or .egistrar-General, as Local rnment Board may, from to time. appoint. Every n who fails to comply with rements of section shall be	43 & 44 Vic. c. 13, s. 19.	Penalty not exceeding £10; in default, &c., imprisonment not ex- ceeding 3 months. 1 J.
ate of cause of death and ations as to.	s. 20.	
person to whom a medical lcate is given by a registered al practitioner in pursuance ction, shall fail to deliver or to be delivered that certifi- to the Registrar within 5	,,	Penalty not exceeding 40s.; in default, &c., imprisonment not ex- ceeding 1 month. 1 J.
on of errors in Registers of s and Deaths.	s. 27.	
when not evidence of birth or , by reason of non-compliance certain requirements as in n.	s. 28.	
to Register Birth or Death.— person required by the prin- Act or this Act to give in- ition concerning any birth or , or any living new-born or any dead body, who neglect or refuse to give or wilfully refusing to r questions of Registrar re- ; to such, or failing to comply requisitions, &c., and every a who, without reasonable e, refuses or fails to give or ertificate in accordance with pal Act or this Act.	s. 29.	Penalty not exceeding 40s.; for each offence; in default, &c., impri- sonment not exceeding 1 month. 1 J.

Offence, or cause of Complaint.	Statute.	Extent of Jurisdiction
REGISTRATION, &c.—*continued.* Parent of any child who fails to give information concerning the birth of such child as required by principal Act or this Act.	43 & 44 Vic. c. 13, s. 29.	Penalty not excee 40s. for each offe in default, &c., im sonment not excee 1 month.
And a person required by principal Act or this Act to give information concerning a death in the first instance, and not merely in default of some other person shall, if such information as is required by principal Act or this Act be not duly given, be liable to—	,,	Like penalty.
False Statements as to Births or Deaths.—Any person who commits any of the following offences, that is to say—	s. 30.	Penalty not excee £10; in default, imprisonment not ceeding 3 months.
(1) Wilfully makes any false answer to any question put to him by a Registrar, relating to the particulars required to be registered concerning any birth or death, or wilfully gives to a Registrar any false information concerning any birth or death, or the cause of any death ; or		And on conviction indictment, to fine o imprisonment, with without H. L., not ceeding 2 years; or penal servitude, not ceeding 7 years.
(2) Wilfully makes any false certificate or declaration under or for the purposes of this Act ; or forges or falsifies any such certificate or declaration, or any order under this Act ; or knowing any such certificate, declaration, or order to be false or forged, uses the same as true, or gives or sends the same as true to any person ; or		
(3) Wilfully makes, gives, or uses any false statement or representation as to a child born alive having been still-born, or as to the body of a deceased person or a still-born child in any coffin, or falsely pretends that any child born alive was still-born ; or		

Offence, or cause of Complaint.	Statute.	Extent of Jurisdiction.
REGISTRATION, &c.—*continued.*		
(4) Makes any false statement with intent to have the same entered in any register of births or deaths, shall, for each offence, be liable, on summary conviction, to—	43 & 44 Vic. c. 13, s. 30.	And, on conviction on indictment, to fine or to imprisonment, with or without H. L., not exceeding 2 years; or to penal servitude, not exceeding 7 years.
As to sending certificates, &c., by post.	s. 31.	
Penalties recoverable (in Dublin under special Acts), elsewhere in Ireland under Petty Sessions Act (14 & 15 Vic. c. 93), and any Acts amending same.	s. 35.	
Repeals of Principal Act (26 Vic. c. 11) part of section 26, and sections 31, 32, 33, 34, 35, 36, 37, 38, 44, 46, 51, 55.		
And for destroying or falsifying Register-books.	26 Vic. c. 11, s. 56.	Provides that ss. 36 and 37 of the Forgery Act, 24 & 25 Vic. c. 98, shall form part of this Act.
Registrar refusing, or without reasonable cause, omitting to register birth or death, of which he has notice, or to make necessary alterations, and every person having custody of Register-book, or any part thereof, carelessly losing or injuring, or carelessly allowing same to be injured whilst in his keeping, for every such offence—	s. 57.	Penalty not exceeding £10; in default, &c., imprisonment not exceeding 3 months. 1 J.
Neglecting to send Register-books, copies, &c., to Superintendent, Registrar, or Registrar-General for 1 month after being required to do so, or at all refusing to do so—	s. 58.	Penalty not exceeding £10; in default, &c., imprisonment not exceeding 3 months. 1 J.
Persons knowingly registering, or causing to be registered, the birth of any child, otherwise than as by the Act required (s. 32), after the expiration of 3 months following birth, or knowingly registering, or causing to be registered, the birth of any child after 6 months, except born at sea or abroad.	s. 59.	Penalty not exceeding £5; in default, &c. imprisonment not exceeding 2 months. 1 J.

2 C

Offence, or cause of Complaint.	Statute.	Extent of Jurisd
REGISTRATION, &c.—*continued.* *Notice of Birth or Death.*—Parents, or in the event of their death or inability, occupier of house, nurse, or any person present, required to give notice of birth within 21 days to Registrar, and occupier or person present, &c., to give notice of death within 7 days.	26 Vic. c. 11, ss. 31, 36, and 60. (36 & 37 Vic. s. 82.)	Penalty not ex 20s.; in defau imprisonment 1 ceeding 14 days
Information.—Any person required by Act who shall within the period specified therein fail to attend personally at the place specified by the Registrar, and to give particulars required touching birth or death, or refusing to sign register in presence of Registrar.	26 Vic. c. 11, s. 61.	Penalty not ex 40s.; in defau imprisonment 1 ceeding 1 montl
Person finding exposed any new-born child or dead body, forthwith to give notice of the finding, and place where found, to Registrar; in default—	s. 62. (36 & 37 Vic. c. 82.)	Penalty not ex 20s.; in defau imprisonment 1 ceeding 14 days
Where any of the persons required to give notice under the Act shall have done so, penalty not to be exacted from others, and notices may be given by post.	26 Vic. c. 11, s. 63.	—
No penalty to be exacted where the Justice is satisfied that failure to give notice or information has not been wilful.	s. 64.	—
Registration of Marriages.—Every person who shall wilfully make or cause to be made for the purpose of being inserted in any register of marriages any false statement touching any of the particulars	26 & 27 Vic. c. 90, s. 22.	Same fines and p as if guilty of pe

The Act does not say who shall sue for the penalties, but it would seem Registrar-General, Superintendent, or District Registrar, or indeed any or other public officer authorized to do so by the Lord Lieutenant, B General, or Attorney-General, &c., may prosecute in the name of the Schedule of forms given in Act.

Offence, or cause of Complaint.	Statute.	Extent of Jurisdiction.
REGISTRATION, &c.—*continued.* required by the Act to be registered.	26 & 27 Vic. c. 90, s. 22.	
36 & 37 secs. of Forgery Act, 24 & 25 Vic. c. 98, incorporated with Act.		
Every Registrar who shall refuse or without reasonable cause omit to fill certificate of marriage, or to register any marriage of which he shall have received certificate, and every person having custody of any Register-book, or part thereof, who shall carelessly lose or injure same, or carelessly allow to be, &c., whilst in his keeping, for every offence—	s. 24.	Penalty not exceeding £10; in default, &c., imprisonment not exceeding 3 months.
Person who under Act is required to deliver register to Superintendent-Registrar or Registrar-General, after being duly required, refuses, or during one month neglects so to do, shall for every such offence—	s. 25.	Penalty not exceeding £10; in default, &c., imprisonment not exceeding 3 months. 1 J.
Nothing in this Act shall affect the law of marriage in Ireland.		
Acts for Registration of Parliamentary electors—	13 & 14 Vic. c. 69. 31 & 32 Vic. c. 112.	
REMAND (*of Accused*) :	14 & 15 Vic. c. 93, s. 14, sub-s. 2, and s. 20, sub-s. 4.	
REMISSION (*of fine, &c.*): See " First Conviction."		
RESERVE FORCES ACT, 1882 : *Army Reserve.*—Where a man belonging to Army Reserve—		
(a) Fails without reasonable excuse on two consecutive occasions to comply with regulations, &c., in force with respect to payment of the Reserve ; or	45 & 46 Vic. c. 48, s. 6.	Fine not less than 40s., nor more than £25 ; in default of payment, imprisonment with or without H. L., not less than

Offence, or cause of Complaint.	Statute.	Extent of Jurisdicti
RESERVE FORCES ACT, 1882— *continued.*		
(b) When required, in pursuance of orders, &c., to attend at any place, fails, without reasonable excuse, to attend accordingly; or,	45 & 46 Vic. c. 48, s. 6.	7 days nor more according to scale. or 1 Stip. (or m: tried by Court Ma
(c) Uses threatening or insulting language, or behaves in an insubordinate manner to any officer, warrant, or non-commissioned officer in execution of his office, &c.;	,,	Like.
(d) By fraudulent means obtains, or is accessory to the obtaining, of any pay or other sum contrary to the orders or regulations in force under this Act ; or,	,,	Like.
(e) Fails, without reasonable excuse, to comply with regulations, &c.	,,	Like.
Officer may direct offender to be taken before Justices. (a)	,,	
Officer's certificate evidence, &c.	,,	
Army or Militia Reserve-men Deserting or Absenting.—Man belonging to Army or Militia Reserve called out for annul training, or on permanent service, or when a man belonging to Army Reserve Force is called out in aid of the civil power, and such man without leave lawfully granted—sickness or other reasonable excuse—fails to appear or attend, &c., he shall—	s. 15.	Fine not less than nor more than £2 default of paymen: prisonment not less 7 days, nor more according to scale. or 1 Stip. (or m: tried by Court Ma:
(a) If called out on permanent service, or in aid of the civil power,		

(a) *Summary Prosecution.*—As in the case of militiamen, where the offen: be dealt with by military law, or by the Court of Summary Jurisdiction, th tices, before dealing with the case, shall require to have the sanction in wri an officer who has power to direct the offender to be tried by Court Martial, an authority superior to such officer. See Royal Warrant, dated 28th De: 1882. This Warrant accompanied *Circular* of Under-Secretary, addres Magistrates—No. 23, 29th Feb., 1883; and see sec. 26 (1) under which regu: -e made.

Offence, or cause of Complaint.	Statute.	Extent of Jurisdiction.
RESERVE FORCES ACT, 1882— *continued.* be guilty according to the circumstances of deserting within meaning of sec. 12, or if absenting, within meaning of sec. 15 of Army Act, 1881.	45 & 46 Vic. c. 48, s. 15.	
Falsely representing himself to be a deserter or absentee from Army or Militia Reserve—	s. 16.	Imprisonment with or without H. L. not exceeding 3 months. 2 J. or 1 Stip.
Inducing, &c., to Desert.—Any person who by any means—		
(*a*) Procures or persuades Army or Militia Reserve-man to commit offence of absence without leave, or attempts so to do ; or	s. 17.	Fine not exceeding £20 ; in default, &c., imprisonment by scale.
(*b*) Knowing that he is about to commit offence of absence, &c., aids or assists him in doing so ; or,	,,	Like.
(*c*) Knowing him to be an absentee, conceals him, or aids in doing so, or employs or continues to employ him, or aids or assists in his rescue.	,,	Like. 2 J. or 1 Stip.
(2) Meaning of desertion by a soldier in sec. 153, Army Act, 1881, shall be applicable in defining desertion of Reserve-man under this Act.	,,	
Applies section 166 of the Army Act, 1881, as to prosecution of offences, recovery and application of fines. (*a*)	s. 25.	
Limitation, &c., proceedings to be taken against Reserve-man within 2 months after the offence becomes known, or after the offender's apprehension. Same as in case of militiaman.	s. 26.	

(*a*) *Application of Fines.*—If Court sees fit, any portion not exceeding half of fine may be paid to informer ; remainder shall be applied as in Fines Act (Ir.), 1851.

Offence, or cause of Complaint.	Statute.	Extent of Jurisdiction.
RESERVE FORCES ACT, 1882— *continued.* Applies sec. 163 of Army Act as to evidence by attestation paper, documents, &c., and as to civil convictions. See also "Naval Volunteers"— "Naval Reserve." For offences under Militia Act, see "Militia."	45 & 46 Vic. c. 48, s. 27.	
RESTITUTION (*of Stolen Property*): See "Stolen Property."		
REVENUE : See titles "Excise," "Customs," and form of Appeal in sec. 40 Vic. c. 13.		
REVISION : Statute Law Revision Act; and see for "Effects of Year's Legislation" at end of Annual Statutes,	30 & 31 Vic. c. 59.	—
RIOTS : Any person who shall take part in any riot or unlawful assembly—	50 & 51 Vic. c. 20, s. 2. sub-s. 3. (*a*)	Imprisonment not exceeding 6 months, with or without H. L. 2 R. M.
ROADS (*generally*) : *Injuries to.*—Owner or occupier of contiguous lands omitting to scour ditches, or to have drains under passages in and out of roads to allow water to pass away; after notice—	14 & 15 Vic. c. 92, s. 9. (36 & 37 Vic. c. 82.)	Penalty not exceeding 20*s.* ; in default, &c., imprisonment not exceeding 14 days. 1 J.
Building houses within thirty feet of centre, except in streets of corporate or market towns, or where house stood when Act passed.	14 & 15 Vic. c. 92, s. 9.	Penalty not exceeding £10, and 10*s.* a-week, from conviction; in default, &c., imprisonment by scale. 1 J.
Scouring, deepening, widening, or filling ditches or drains, altering fences, building wall, making ditch, drain, &c., digging pits or	" (36 & 37 Vic. c. 82.)	Penalty not exceeding 20*s.* ; in default, &c., imprisonment not exceeding 14 days. 1 J.

Offence, or cause of Complaint.	Statute.	Extent of Jurisdiction.
ROADS—*continued.* hollows on road or within thirty feet of centre (save upon or within any ancient fence adjoining such road) or otherwise breaking surface of road, or footpath, without consent of the county surveyor or authority of presentment. (Centre of road to be deemed the centre of the part made with gravel or stones.)	14 & 15 Vic. c. 92, s. 9. (36 & 37 Vic. c. 82.)	
Any person who shall, without consent of surveyor or contractor, scrape any public road, cut sods or turf on the sides, or take earth, stones, &c., from off it—	,,	Penalty not exceeding 20s.; in default, &c., imprisonment not exceeding 14 days. 1 J.
Drawing timber or stones along road without being supported by wheels from touching.	,,	Like.
Riding or driving horse or other animal wilfully and unnecessarily on any footpath.	,,	Like.
Surveyor, contractor, or other person who shall dig, raise, and carry away any gravel, stones, sand, or other materials from the side of any public road, or from beach or seashore, whereby road, bridges, or land within the fences may be injured. (a)	14 & 15 Vic. c. 92, s. 9.	Penalty not exceeding 5s. a load; in default, &c., imprisonment in proportion to amount as in scale 1 J.
Wilfully destroying any pay or turnpike gate, &c., or rescuing any other person in custody for the offence.	,, (36 & 37 Vic. c. 82.)	Penalty not exceeding 40s., or imprisonment not exceeding 1 month. 1 J.

(a) The Grand Jury Amendment Act, 19 & 20 Vic. c. 63, s. 18, provides a penalty of 40s. against any road contractor or other person who, without the authority of a presentment, or the consent of the county surveyor, shall cut any sods or turf on the sides, fences, or any other part of any public road, or dig, raise, or carry away any sods, turf, earth, clay, stones, gravel, or other materials from the sides, or faces, or any other part of any public road or bridge (notwithstanding anything in section 9 of 14 & 15 Vic. c. 92). But it does not state how the penalty is to be recovered, nor does it expressly refer the matter at all to Justices in Petty Sessions.

Offence, or cause of Complaint.	Statute.	Extent of Jurisdi...
ROADS—*continued.* Assaulting engineers, contractors, &c., or persons laying out line of road; injuring instruments or implements, milestones, posts, fences, erections, &c.	14 & 15 Vic. c. 92, s. 9. (36 & 37 Vic. c. 82.)	Penalty not ex... £10; or impris... not exceeding 3 ...
Using new road for a certain time after making, contrary to notice-board.	,,	Penalty not ex... 20s.; in defaul... imprisonment n... ceeding 14 days
Obstructions, &c.—Surveyor or contractor, by 10 days' notice, may require the removal of obstructions, order to fill drains, or to scour drains, which have been filled without authority, remove obstructions to free passage of water, &c., and may require owners of land to prune hedges or trees, injurious to road, between last day of September and last day of March. For other offences on roads, see "Nuisances on Roads," "Drivers."	,,	Justices may ord... the person liabl... do the work; ... fault, to direct t... tractor may do ... Justices may iss... rant (distress) ... penses.
Contractor's Neglect in Repairing—If the contractor be guilty of neglect in performing his contract, surveyor may summon contractor and his sureties before the Justices of the district, and if the charge of neglect or inattention be established—	19 & 20 Vic. c. 63, s. 17.	Justices to make ... der directing t... tractor and his ... to execute his ... within a period ... stated in such or...
Disobeying Order.—If at the expiration of such order the county surveyor shall still see reason for being dissatisfied with the manner in which the work has been executed, he shall again summon contractor and his sureties before the Justices in Petty Sessions; and the Justices shall thereupon inquire into and finally adjudicate upon the complaint, and if it appear that the work has been	,,	It shall be lawful... Justices, having ... tained the amoun... it may require ... completion of suc... according to t... tract, to author... surveyor to c... same, and to le... amount by war... distress upon th... of such contracto...

Offence, or cause of Complaint.	Statute.	Extent of Jurisdiction.
ROADS—*continued*. insufficiently executed, or contrary to the terms of the contract—	19 & 20 Vic. c. 63, s. 17.	sureties, not exceeding the amount of the recognizance or bond of such sureties. (a) 2 J.
Power to dig for materials to repair roads, &c., and Justice's order. See Grand Jury Acts.	6 & 7 Wm. iv. c. 116, s. 162.	-
Sudden Breaches.—Any three Justices in Petty Sessions may order sums not exceeding £50 for repairing sudden damages to roads, bridges, quays, walls, &c.	30 & 31 Vic. c. 112.	Three Justices may make the Order.
Where the sum needed to repair breach does not exceed £20—	6 & 7 Wm. iv. c. 116, s. 149.	Two Justices may make the Order.
In cases of sudden damage, three Justices and five cesspayers may present memorial to Lord Lieutenant.	30 & 31 Vic. c. 112, s. 2.	
For powers of Lord Lieutenant, mode of presenting, and other requirements, &c., see Act.	ss. 3 to 6.	
ROGUES AND VAGABONDS: See "Vagrancy."		
SALMON: See "Fisheries."		
SALVAGE: See "Merchant Shipping Act."		

(a) It is in the power of the Magistrates to issue the warrant to levy the amount ascertained to be requisite forthwith. They need not wait to have the money expended, for it is supposed that the money to be levied is that which is to be expended in completing the work.

The section does not state the number of Justices requisite. As the plural number is used, it is safe to have at least two in a matter of so much consequence.

Offence, or cause of Complaint.	Statute.	Extent of
SANITARY ACTS: See "Public Health."		
SCHOOLMASTER: Entitled to recover wages for tuition from parents or persons engaging him, not exceeding £10.	14 & 15 Vic. c. 92, s. 16.	
SEA: For Justices' powers and duties in reference to offences committed on high seas, see—	14 & 15 Vic. c. 93, s. 10.	
SEA-BIRDS,' &c.: See "Wild Birds."		
SEAMEN: See title "Merchant Shipping," and "Navy (Royal)."		
SEARCH-WARRANT: (a) For stolen property, . . .	24 & 25 Vic. c. 96, s. 103.	Search-war on inform or solemn

(a) *Search-warrant.*—The form of search-warrant in schedule to
Act directs the search to be made in the daytime; but there is no
seem, to prevent the Magistrates authorizing the search at any tin
shown that the case demands it, and that there is a likelihood that t
be removed before morning. Usual demand should be made before
outer doors; and before breaking boxes, keys should be demanded.
warrant also directs the arrest of the person in whose possession
found. But the stolen property may be found in the house of an ii
and the suspected thief be absent. The Justice, if he sees fit, may
rant in this particular. Indeed there seems no reason why the co
not exercise a discretion in the arrest, particularly if the person ii
sion the goods are found be not the suspected person or defendant :
and that a satisfactory account be given for such possession; bi
though not arrested, should be directed to attend before the Magisti

Offence, or cause of Complaint.	Statute.	Extent of Jurisdiction.
SEARCH WARRANT—*continued.* For paper or implements employed in any forgery, and for forged instruments. For counterfeit coin and coining implements. See also under "Linen Acts"; "Excise"; "Gunpowder."	24 & 25 Vic. c. 98, s. 46. 24 & 25 Vic. c. 99, s. 27.	made by a credible witness, and that there are reasonable grounds to suspect the person or place intended to be searched. 1 J.
SEEDS: See "Adulteration."		
SERVANT: See "Employers and Workmen," &c.		
SHEBEEN HOUSES: See "Excise" and "Licensing Acts."		
SHEEP, &c. (*in possession unaccounted for*): Carcase of any sheep or lamb, or the head, skin, or any part thereof, or the fleece of any sheep or lamb stolen, or unlawfully taken, if found under search-warrant, or any constable, &c., acting in discharge of his duty in the possession or on the premises of any person who shall not satisfy the Justice before whom brought that he came lawfully by same, or that same was on his premises without his knowledge or assent (a)— Stealing deer, &c., see "Larceny." In case of sheep injured by dogs, see "Dogs."	25 & 26 Vic. c. 50, s. 6.	May be committed to gaol until next Petty Sessions for district, unless he shall enter recognizance with one or more sureties to appear; and failing to account for same as aforesaid, shall, on summary conviction, either be committed for a term not exceeding 3 months, or be liable to a fine not exceeding £5 (enforced as in Petty Sessions Act, 1851), and according to scale. 1 J.

(a) But should there be evidence of a *stealing* or *wilfully killing with intent to steal* (these offences being "felony," under 24 & 25 Vic. c. 96, sections 10 and 11), the Justices will of course abstain from summarily adjudicating, and return the case for trial by indictment.

Offence, or cause of Complaint.	Statute.	Extent of Jurisdiction.
SHERIFF : No sheriff can act as a J. P. while sheriff—	7 Wm. iii. c. 13, s. 3.	Under a penalty of £20, and his acts shall be void.
Sheriff or bailiff receiving other than fees allowed by Civil Bill Act—	27 & 28 Vic. c. 99, s. 17.	Liable to £20 to person who shall sue for same by civil-bill.
Bailiff or his assistants extorting, &c.	s. 18.	Misdemeanour. Fine or imprisonment, or both.
By violence, threats, &c., to, when executing, &c., or by force compelling sheriff or bailiff, &c., to abandon seizure of body or goods, or rescuing or attempting to rescue body or goods seized.	s. 26.	Misdemeanour; imprisonment not exceeding 6 months, with or without H. L.
By " The Municipal Privilege, Ireland, Act, 1875," the Councils of Dublin, Cork, Limerick, Waterford, Kilkenny, Drogheda, may annually select three persons qualified to act as sheriff, and submit names to Lord Lieutenant. Lord Lieutenant shall, within 7 days, appoint one of the persons so selected.	39 & 40 Vic. c. 76, ss. 3, 4.	

Sheriff.—Is an officer of very great antiquity in this kingdom, called in Latin *Vice Comes*, as being the deputy of the Earl or *Comes*, to whom the custody of the shire is said to have been committed at the first division of the kingdom into counties. The power and duty of a sheriff are either as a Judge, as a keeper of the King's peace, as a ministerial officer of the Superior Courts of Justice, or as Queen's bailiff. He is to determine the elections of knights of the shire, and return such candidates as he shall determine to be duly elected. As the *keeper of the Queen's Peace*, both by the Common Law and Special Commission, he is the first man in the county, and superior in rank to any nobleman therein, during his office. He may, and is bound *ex officio* to pursue and take all traitors, murderers, felons, and other misdoers, and commit them to gaol for safe custody. He is also to defend his country against any of the Queen's enemies when they come into the land, and for this purpose, as well as for keeping the peace and pursuing felons, he may command all the people of his county to attend him, which is called the *posse comitatus*, or power of the county, which summons every person above 15 years old, and under the degree of a peer, is bound to attend upon warning under pain of fine and imprisonment.

Constabulary are bound to assist at and preserve the peace at the execution of writs of possession and other Queen's writs. A most important, perhaps the most ⁀ortant clear and studied view of the law on this subject, is that delivered by af Baron Palles at the Winter Assizes in Sligo in January, 1887, when sen-

Offence, or cause of Complaint.	Statute.	Extent of Jurisdiction.
SHERIFF—*continued*.		
Lord Lieutenant to appoint sheriffs if Corporations neglect.	39 & 40 Vic. c. 76, s. 5.	
Person appointed may decline, .	s. 7.	
Sheriff may be superseded, . .	s. 8.	
Office not to be deemed one of profit,	s. 10.	
Person convicted of felony not to be qualified.	s. 12.	
SHIPWRECKED GOODS: Found in possession of, &c. See "Larceny."		
SHOWS (*in Towns*): See "Towns Improvement Act."	17 & 18 Vic. c. 103.	

tencing prisoners for obstructing the Sheriff at the "Woodford evictions." The Chief Baron, in a learned and elaborate judgment, referred to the earliest decisions in England and Ireland, going back to authorities as old as the third year of Henry VII.:—"Every one is bound to assist the Sheriff, and to maintain him in his office in the execution of writs, for it is the commandment of the King, and the Bailiff has the same authority as his Master," &c. This was at a time when there was no organized force of Constabulary; and strange would have been the decision that Constables, organized and sworn for the sole purpose of keeping the peace, were relieved from the obligation that had previously lain on private persons.

The Chief Baron adds:—"The execution of the decrees of the justiciary in this country does not depend—as it does not, I believe, in any civilized country—upon the will of the Executive who for the moment may happen to be in office." "It is the province and the bounden duty of Courts of Justice to see that their decrees and judgments of their Courts are executed with the assistance of those who by law are bound to aid in their execution."

The Constabulary, constituted under the Act 6 Wm. iv., are therefore bound to assist the Sheriffs in the execution of the Queen's writs. And when a judgment of a Court of Law is given on this subject—"It is not competent for any one in this kingdom, I care not how high he may be, to prevent those who are bound by law to help in the execution of the writ from giving that aid and assistance which the common law and the Constitution require."

Offence, or cause of Complaint.	Statute.	Extent of Jurisdiction.
SHRUBS : See "Larceny" and "Vegetable Productions."		
SKINS (*Stolen*) · See "Larceny," "Sheep," and "Stolen Property."		
SLAUGHTERING (*on Roads, &c.*) : Any person who shall slaughter any beast, or leave any dead beast or skin, or permit to be skinned any beast on any public road, or within 30 feet of the centre thereof (save in house or enclosed yard)— See also under "Towns Improvement Act."	14 & 15 Vic. c. 92, s. 10. (36 & 37 Vic. c. 82.)	Penalty not exceeding 10*s.* ; in default, &c., imprisonment not exceeding 7 days. 1 J.
SLIDES : Making upon ice or snow, on roads or streets.	,,	Like.
SMALL DEBTS : See "Debts."		
SMALL-POX : Producing or attempting to produce in any person by inoculation with variolus matter, or by wilful exposure to variolus matter, or to any matter, &c., impregnated therewith, or wilfully by any other means producing small-pox in any person. See "Vaccination."	31 & 32 Vic. c. 87, s. 4.	Imprisonment not exceeding 6 months. 2 J.
SMUGGLING : See "Customs." "Excise."		

Offence, or cause of Complaint.	Statute.	Extent of Jurisdiction.
SNARES : Setting for deer—see "Larceny."	24 & 25 Vic. c. 96, s. 15.	—
SOCIETIES : See "Friendly Societies."		
SOLDIERS : See title, "Army Discipline."		
SPIRITS : See titles "Customs," "Excise," "Licensing Acts," "Refreshment Houses," as the case may be.		
"STAMP ACT, 1870 :" Provides for the payment, to the officer of Court, of duty and pe- nalty where unstamped or insuffi- ciently stamped instruments are produced, and for his accounting—	33 & 34 Vic. c. 97, s. 16.	All penalties under this Act shall be sued for in Court of Exchequer in the name of the Attor- ney-General (sec. 26) ; but see as to hawkers
Against frauds in the use of adhesive stamps, &c.	s. 25.	of stamps when appre- hended (sec. 11) and brought before Justice.
"*Affidavit or Statutory Declaration*, made under provisions of 5 & 6 Wm. iv. c. 62," requires a Revenue stamp of 2*s.* 6*d.*—(see exemptions, *infra*.)		

Statutory Declarations, &c., Exemptions.—(1). Affidavit made for the immediate purpose of being filed, read, or used in any Court or before any Judge,
Master, or Officer of any Court. (2). Affidavit or declaration made upon a requisition of the Commissioners of any public Board of Revenue, or any of the officers
acting under them, or required by law, and made before any Justice of the Peace.
(3). Affidavit or declaration which may be required at the Bank of England or the
Bank of Ireland to prove the death of any proprietor of any stock transferable there,
or to identify the person of any such proprietor, or to remove any other impediment to the transfer of any such stock. (4). Affidavit or declaration relating to
the loss, mutilation, or defacement of any bank-note or bank post-bill. (5). De-

Offence, or cause of Complaint.	Statute.	Extent of Jurisdiction.
"STAMP ACT, 1870"—*continued.*		
Agreement, or memorandum of agreement, under hand only, and not otherwise specifically charged with duty, whether evidence of a contract, or obligatory on the parties from its being a written instrument, requires a 6*d.* stamp. (See exemptions, *infra*.)	33 & 34 Vic. c. 97, Schedule.	—
An adhesive stamp may be used, to be cancelled by the person by whom agreement is first executed.	s. 36.	—
Apprentice.—Instrument of apprenticeship where there is no premium or consideration—stamp, 2*s.* 6*d.* In any other case for every £5, and also for fractional part of £5 of the premium or consideration—5*s.* (Exemptions *infra*.)	ss. 39 & 40, and Schedule to Act.	—
Receipt for any sum amounting to £2 or upwards—1*d.*	,,	A receipt for a fine, payable to or for the use of Her Majesty, appears to be exempt.
(There are 14 exemptions, chiefly in reference to bankers' receipts, taxes, &c., the public service, funds and stocks, indorsements on stamped instruments, &c.)		

claration required to be made pursuant to any Act relating to marriages in order to a marriage without a licence.

☞ It will be observed that the *first* class of exemptions refer to *Affidavits*. The second class includes those declarations with which the Justice and officer of the Court may find it more difficult to deal, namely, that are "required by law." And by *required* it would seem is not only meant *compellable*, but will also include voluntary declarations authorized and directed by law as the legal remedy or mode of redress.

The Act or exemptions do not interfere with the Petty Sessions Stamps. One is an Excise or Revenue stamp; the other is a law or Court fund stamp, and the latter must be used as heretofore, when form is prepared by Clerk of Petty Sessions.

Agreement Exemptions.—(1). Agreement or memorandum, the latter whereof is not of the value of £5. (2). Agreement or memorandum for the hire of any labourer, artificer, manufacturer, or menial servant. (3). Agreement, letter, or memorandum made for or relating to the sale of any goods, wares, or merchandise. (4). Agreement or memorandum made between the master and mariners of any ship or vessel for wages on any voyage coastwise from port to port in the United Kingdom.

Apprentice Exemptions.—(1). Instrument relating to any poor child apprenticed by or at the sole charge of any parish or township, or by or at the sole charge

Offence, or cause of Complaint.	Statute.	Extent of Jurisdiction.
"STAMP ACT, 1870"—*continued.* *Dealers.*—Unauthorized person dealing in stamps; or, being licensed, deals in authorized place, &c.	33 & 34 Vic. c. 98, s. 7.	Penalty—£20.
Licensed dealers shall notify the fact on the place of sale in words and by letters as in section; in default—	s. 8.	Penalty—£10.
Unauthorized persons holding themselves out as dealers.	s. 9.	Penalty—£10 a-day.
Hawking Stamps.—Any person, whether a licensed dealer or not, who hawks about, offers for sale or in exchange any stamps—	s. 11.	Penalty—£20, over any penalty incurred for being an unlicensed dealer. 1 J.
Any person may apprehend offender, and convey him before a J. P. of the place, who shall hear and determine the matter.	—	But if not apprehended and proceeded against as in section, then to be recovered in Court of Exchequer.
Persons in service of the Post Office may sell postage stamps in any place.	s. 12.	—
Forging, &c.—Section 18 provides against forgeries of dies, &c., and other frauds relating to stamps—	s. 18.	Felony—penal servitude for life, or not less than 5 years, or imprisonment not exceeding 3 years.
Defacement.—Every person who by any writing in any manner defaces any adhesive stamp before it is used. See also title "Stamps," Indictable Offences Index, as to criminal offences relating to stamps.	s. 25.	Penalty—£25.

of any public charity, or pursuant to any Act for the regulation of parish apprentices. (2). Instrument of apprenticeship in Ireland, where the value of the premium or consideration does not exceed £10.

The proceedings to enforce penalties under the above Act are to be taken in the Court of Exchequer. It is introduced in this work only because the documents referred to are frequently submitted to Magistrates in complaints, &c., brought before them.

Criminal Proceedings.—In all criminal proceedings instruments liable to stamp duty are admissible in evidence, although the stamp required by law may be wanting.—17 & 18 Vic. c. 83, s. 27.

Stamps.—By circular of 16th, May, 1884, from the Comptroller of Stamps and Taxes, Custom-house, Dublin, attention of Petty Sessions clerks is directed to

2 D

Offence, or cause of Complaint	Statute.	Extent of Jurisdiction.
"STAMP ACT, 1870"—*continued.* *Petty Sessions Stamps.*—For the stamps to be used on proceedings before Magistrates, and on the several documents enumerated in the schedule to Act, see—	21 & 22 Vic. c. 100.	See abstract of Act in *Appendix.*
Provisions of the Acts relating to stamps under the management of the Commissioners of Inland Revenue, for preventing frauds, &c., extended to Petty Sessions stamps.	s. 18.	Consequently the provisions and regulations for cancelling or defacing stamps used under the "Stamps Act" will apply to Petty Sessions stamps.
No receipt required to be given under the provisions of the Petty Sessions (Ireland) Act shall be subject to any stamp duty, payable to the Crown.	14 & 15 Vic. c. 93, s. 40.	This provision in the Petty Sessions Act appears to be repealed by the "Stamps Act, 1870," unless where it is a fine or "sum to or for the use of Her Majesty."
Insolvent Debtors.—Affidavits, &c., under Insolvent Debtors' Act, made before Magistrate, exempt from Revenue stamps, and also from Petty Sessions stamps.	1 & 2 Vic. c. 110.	These will also probably be held to come within the exemptions of the "Stamps Act, 1870," or not to be affected by this statute.
STATEMENT (*of Case for Opinion of Superior Court*); See title "Case Stated."	20 & 21 Vic. c. 43.	
STATUTE LAW REVISION ACT. And see end of Annual Statutes for "Effects of Legislation."	30 & 31 Vic. c. 59.	

sections 15 & 16 of Stamp Act, 1870 (33 & 34 Vic. c. 97), with reference to stamp duties and penalties paid in respect of unstamped or insufficiently stamped instruments produced as evidence in Courts of civil judicature. And clerks are required to transmit the duties and penalties paid to them, to the Receiver-General of Irish Stamp Duties, Custom-house, Dublin. Clerks should in all cases consult and attend to this circular. It points out the duties and penalties to be charged, together with a list of those instruments which cannot be stamped after execution, and of those which can only be stamped after execution within a limited period.

Offence, or cause of Complaint.	Statute.	Extent of Jurisdiction.
STEAM NAVIGATION : . .	14 & 15 Vic. c. 79.	—
STEAM WHISTLES: No person shall use or employ in any manufactory or any other place any steam whistle or steam trumpet for the purpose of summoning or dismissing workmen, &c., without sanction of the sanitary authority.	35 & 36 Vic. c. 60, s. 2.	Penalty not exceeding £5, and to a further penalty not exceeding 40s. a-day while offence continues; in default, &c., imprisonment by scale. 2 J.
Sanitary authority may, on a month's notice, revoke authority.	,,	
Local Government Board, on the representation of any person that he is prejudicially affected by the sanction of sanitary authority, may revoke same.	,,	
STOLEN PROPERTY: For the punishment of stealing, &c., see title "Larceny."		
Restoration. (a)—Where juvenile offenders summarily convicted under	14 & 15 Vic. c. 92, s. 6.	Justice may order the property stolen to be restored to owner. 1 J.
So likewise, where case summarily tried under the Criminal Justice Act.	18 & 19 Vic. c. 126, s. 8.	Justice may order the property stolen to be restored to owner. 2 J. or 1 Stip.
Shipwrecked goods found in possession of any person.	24 & 25 Vic. c. 96, s. 65.	Justice may order to be restored to the owner. 1 J.

(a) *Restoration of Stolen Property.*—By the Larceny Act, 24 & 25 Vic. c. 96, sec. 100, the owner of property prosecuting the thief or receiver to conviction *by indictment* shall have restitution of his property, and the Court is empowered to award writs of restitution. There is not a general power to make this order in cases of summary jurisdiction, but there will be found in the Act what will answer the purpose equally well. In the case of shipwrecked goods it is specifically given under section 65 ; in other cases they have power to award compensation for the property taken, and to enforce the order by imprisonment; and where any property has been stolen, the offender and property are to be taken before a Justice ; or where the property is not forthcoming, but is supected to be in any place, the Justice may issue a search-warrant to have it brought before him, that the prisoner and the property may be dealt with according to law ; where property is found on a prisoner not in any way likely to be made the subject of a charge, the Justice, if applied to,

Offence, or cause of Complaint.	Statute.	Extent of Jurisdiction.
STONE-THROWING (in *streets, &c.*): See Towns Improvement Act for offence of throwing stones or other missiles.	17 & 18 Vic. c. 103, s. 72. (36 & 37 Vic. c. 82.)	Penalty not exceeding 10s.; in default, &c., imprisonment not exceeding 7 days.　　1 J.
Similar offence, under the Police Clauses Act.	10 & 11 Vic. c. 89, s. 28. (25 Vic. c. 18.) (36 & 37 Vic. c. 82.)	Penalty not exceeding 40s.; or imprisonment not exceeding 14 days.　　1 J. First see which (if either) Act is in force in the district.
STOWAWAYS: See "Passenger Ships."		
STREET OBSTRUCTIONS: *General Section.*—Any person who shall in any manner wilfully, or by negligence or misbehaviour, prevent or interrupt the free passage of any person or carriage on any public road, street, or crossing. For other offences, see "Nuisances on Road"; "Cars, &c."; "Drivers"; and "Towns Improvement Act."	14 & 15 Vic. c. 92, s. 14. (36 & 37 Vic. c. 82.)	Penalty not exceeding 20s.; in default, &c., imprisonment not exceeding 14 days.　　1 J. (And see also Towns Improvement Act, *Appendix*.)
SUDDEN BREACHES (in *Roads, Bridges, &c.*): See title "Roads."		
SUMMARY JURISDICTION ACT: (a)	14 & 15 Vic. c. 92.	

should order its restoration, particularly if its detention would cause a loss; and where it is money, the prisoner may need it for his defence.

Bank-notes.—Bonâ *fide* holder of a bank-note *for value* is entitled to retain it as against a former owner from whom it has been stolen, the Court applying to a bank-note the rule of law applicable to money, and observing that "after it has been paid away honestly and fairly upon a valuable and *bonâ fide* consideration," the true owner cannot recover it.—*Miller* v. *Race*, and *Raphael* v. *Bank of England.*

(a) This Act consolidated and amended several Acts relating to *offences and other matters*, as to which Justices exercise jurisdiction. The provisions which ain in force are referred to throughout this Index. This title is now in legislation generally transferred to the Petty Sessions (Ir.) Act, 1851. See "Interpretation Act," 1889.

Offence, or cause of Complaint.	Statute.	Extent of Jurisdiction.
SUMMONS AND SUMMONS-SERVER: (a) By whom summons is to be served; fee; what shall be good service.	14 & 15 Vic. c. 93, s. 12.	
Summons not to be signed in blank,	,,	
Justices to appoint summons-server, whose fee for service is not to exceed 6d. (and where distance 4 miles 1s.—41 & 42 Vic. c. 69).	s. 11.	

(a) The general groundwork of Justices' proceedings is by summons or warrant. There are but few cases where a complaint in writing is required before issuing summons. Where there is not some such preliminary proceedings as a summons, the Justice should be cautious and see that the Act of Parliament authorizes what he does before he proceeds to a conviction.—See notes on *Jurisdiction*, first page of Index, and on sec. 20, Petty Sessions Act, *Appendix*. Where a special time or mode of service is in any case required, it will be stated under the particular head in the Index. As to defects in summons, under sec. 39 above, unless where such is calculated to mislead, such objections are not to be allowed. The power given to the Chairman of Quarter Sessions under Civil Bill Act, 27 & 28 Vic. c. 99, s. 48, is somewhat different; it is to *amend* all errors and defects in the process or proceedings, so as that the real question between the parties shall be determined; the Justices do not get a similar power under this section to alter or amend the original proceeding, but they may disallow the objection, and their order and subsequent proceedings may be drawn up according to the facts proved. It is held that, if defendant appears, any irregularity in the summons, or even the want of it becomes immaterial.—*R.* v. *Johnson*, 1 *Str.* 261; *R.* v. *Barrett*, 1 *Salk.* 383; *R.* v. *Stone*, 1 *East.*, 649. But see now 40 & 41 Vic. c. 56, s. 74, where Justices can amend summons, &c. &c. See notes on sec. 24, Petty Sessions Act, *Appendix*. In describing offences several terms or allegations may be used, although the proof of any one may be sufficient.

"*Cumulative allegations*, or such as merely operate in aggravation, are immaterial, provided that sufficient is proved to establish some offence included in the charge on the record." This rule, as applicable to criminal proceedings, is defined by Lord Ellenborough in the case of *R.* v. *Hunt*, 2 *Camp.*, 583; *Taylor on Evidence*. The conjunctive had better be used, although the words of the statute be in the disjunctive; thus where, under the 17 & 18 Vic. c. 89, sec. 3, any person not duly licensed who shall sell, *or* keep for sale, *or* expose for sale, any beer, or spirits, &c.— the best way to state the offence in the summons will be that the defendant did sell *and* keep for sale, *and* expose for sale, &c. For where the nature of the offence is such that it may in part be committed by two or more several methods or means, it is as positive to say it was committed by each of these particular methods as to alledge it to be committed by any one of them. This mode of stating the offence has been objected to as duplicate pleading, that is, charging more than one offence for one penalty, upon the authority of *Newman* v. *Bendyshe*, 10 *B. & Ad.*, 11; but this objection has been overruled in *Lockwood* v. *Attorney General in error*, *T. T.*, 1842, *M.S.*; and it is a rule that nothing which may be rejected as surplusage shall vitiate.—*Wilson* v. *Law*, 1 *Ld. Ray.*, 20. *The same summons may contain*

Offence, or cause of Complaint.	Statute.	Extent of Jurisdiction.
SUMMONS AND SUMMONS-SERVER—*continued*. The Justice signing may in any case direct summons to be served by any person who can read and write.	14 & 15 Vic. c. 93, s. 12.	
Complainant in no case to serve summons.	,,	
In Constabulary prosecutions, summons to be served by one of the Constabulary.	,,	
Summons to be served by delivering a copy; and where defendant cannot be conveniently met with, copy to be left at his last or most usual place of abode, or at office, warehouse, counting-house, &c., or place of business, with some inmate, not being under 16 years of age, a reasonable time before hearing. This to be sufficient service, unless where personal service specially required by this Act. Not to affect provisions of any Act authorizing substitution of service.	,,	
As to summons to enforce appearance of defendants and witnesses in all cases, see—	ss. 11, 12, 13.	
No objection to be allowed to summons for any alleged defect therein, in *form or substance*, unless it be calculated to mislead.	s. 39.	

several distinct offences.—Where there are separate charges or counts in one summons, and the Justices convict as to one charge, but come to no decision on the other—marked as to it "no rule," this does not invalidate the conviction, Exch. Div. (Ir.), Aug., 1889, on motion for Writ of Habeas Corpus in the case of Mr. Conybeare, M.P. The arguments and the decisions in this case go to show that, had the Justices found the second charge proved, they might have convicted of that also. The Lord Chief Baron dissenting. Where the defendant confesses the truth of the charge or complaint in the summons, the Justices may convict, &c. (14 & 15 Vic. c. 93, s. 20); but even where there is a full confession—as the summons is not supposed always to disclose sufficient to enable the Justices to fully estimate and judge of the offence—it is satisfactory, in the administration of these summary powers, if the Justices were to inform their own consciences by ...ting the merits before they pronounce judgment; and to this agree the ...orities.

Offence, or cause of Complaint.	Statute.	Extent of Jurisdiction.
SUMMONS AND SUMMONS-SERVER—*continued*.		
Clerk of Court neglecting or refusing to enter summonses in order.	14 & 15 Vic. c. 93, s. 35.	Penalty not exceeding 40s.; in default, &c., imprisonment not exceeding 1 month. 2 J.
Summons-server making wilful default in service.	,,	Like. 2 J.
Form of summons—see Schedule of forms to Petty Sessions Act, *Appendix*.		
Amend. —Power in Justices to amend summons.	40 & 41 Vic. c. 56, s. 74.	
SUNDAY : (a)		
Tradesmen, labourers, &c., or other such person following ordinary callings on Sunday (except works of necessity or charity), and being upwards of 14 years of age.	7 Wm. iii. c. 17, s. 1. (Irish.)	Penalty 5s. ; in default, &c., imprisonment by scale. (The punishment in the section, in default of distress, is two hours in the stocks.)

(a) *Sunday.*—This clause extends only to work done in the *ordinary calling* of the offender, and includes only persons who have an ordinary calling; but it seems every species of labour, public or private, in their ordinary calling, is within the prohibition.—*Drury* v. *Defontaine*, 1 *Taunt*, 131; *Fennell* v. *Ridler*, 5 *B. & C.*, 408; 8 *D. & R.*, 206. And the words other person, means other person of the kind or class stated, and have been held not to include the driver of a stage-coach.—*Sandiman* v. *Breach*, 9 *D. & R.*, 796 ; 7 *B. & C.*, 96.

The section (7 Wm. iii. c. 17) with pompous piety begins—"All and every person and persons whatsoever shall, on every Lord's day, apply themselves to the observation of the same by exercising themselves thereon in the duties of piety and true religion, publicly and privately; and no tradesman, artificer, workman, labourer, or other person whatsoever, shall do or exercise any worldly labour, business, or work of their ordinary callings, upon the Lord's day or any part thereof, works of necessity and charity only excepted ; and every person being of the age of 14 years and upwards offending shall, for every such offence, forfeit, &c."

Dressing meat in families and in cookshops, and crying of milk or fish before 10 A.M., and after 4 P.M., excepted. Prosecutions shall commence within 10 days. Some portions of the Act could not now be enforced, they have fallen into desuetude.

In indictable offences the Justice may issue his warrant on a Sunday.—14 & 15 Vic. c. 93, s. 11. But warrants to enforce a penalty should not be executed on a Sunday.

Hurling, &c.—This section says, that its object is to prevent *disorderly meetings*, under pretence of hurling and other sports. It is not now enforced.

Offence, or cause of Complaint.	Statute.	Extent of Jurisdiction.
SUNDAY—*continued.*		
Crying or selling wares, fruit, goods, &c.	7 Wm. iii. c. 17, s. 1.	Forfeiture of articles exposed for sale. 1 J.
Carrier, butcher, &c., travelling on Sunday.	s. 2.	Penalty 20s. : in default, &c., imprisonment by scale. 1 J.
Playing at hurling, football, wrestling, and other games and sports.	s. 3.	Penalty 12d., recoverable as above.
Pawnbroker taking in pawns on Sunday—see "Pawnbroker."		
In indictable offences, Justice may issue his warrant on Sunday.	14 & 15 Vic. c. 93, s. 11.	—
Churchwardens' duties in respect to; see—	10 & 11 Vic. c. 89.	
For unlawful sales of beer and spirits on Sundays, see "Licensing Acts."		
SURETIES OF THE PEACE AND GOOD BEHAVIOUR.		
Of the Peace. (*n*)—Wherever a person has just cause to fear that another will do him a corporal hurt, as by killing or beating him, or will procure others to do so, or to burn his house, or threatening to hurt his wife or child; upon satisfying the Justice, by one or more informations on oath, that he is actually under such fear, and that he has just cause to be so, and that he does not require such sureties out of malice or vexation—	Under the Commission of the Peace.	Every Justice of the Peace is bound to grant it, for such *limited* period, and in such amount as in his discretion he may think reasonable ; and, in default, to commit the party for that period, or until he finds the sureties required. 1 J.

(a) *Surety of the Peace*—so called because the party that was in fear is thereby secured—is a recognizance entered into to the King for the keeping of the peace.— *Bac. Abr.*

In *Flower* v. *Dillon*, Q. B. (Ir.), *Dec.* 1886, the Court refused to receive oral evidence to contradict the affidavits of witnesses for the prosecution, or in any way than by writing on affidavit. The ruling in this case, and the exhaustive judgment of Mr. Justice O'Brien, pointing out the law and the practice of the *Superior Courts* from the earliest date, is a valuable synopsis for reference.

The English Amended Petty Sessions Act of 1879 (42 & 43 Vic. c. 49, s. 25) expressly gives Justices in Petty Sessions power to examine witnesses for the defence, including the defendant, and subjects the parties to costs as in other com-. This Act is not applicable to Ireland.

'ty of the peace every Justice may take and command by a twofold lrst, as a minister commanded thereto by a higher authority, as when

Offence, or cause of Complaint.	Statute.	Extent of Jurisdiction.
SURETIES OF THE PEACE AND GOOD BEHAVIOUR—*con.* Justice may, *ex officio*, bind those who in his *presence* make affray, threaten to kill or beat any person, or contend together with hot words, or go about with unusual weapons to the terror of the people, or break the peace, in presence of a constable, or who challenge another to fight.	Under the Commission of the Peace.	Every Justice of the Peace is bound to grant it, for such *limited* period, and in such amount as in his discretion he may think reasonable; and, in default, to commit the party for that period, or until he finds the sureties required. 1 J.

a writ directed out of the Chancery or Queen's Bench is delivered to him; secondly, as a Judge, and by virtue of his office, derived from his commission.

The clause of the commission of the peace referred to runs thus:—"And to cause to come before you, or any of you, all these persons who shall threaten any of our people in their person, or with burning their houses, to find sufficient security for the peace, or for their good behaviour towards us and our people; and if they shall refuse to find such security, then to cause them to be safely kept in our prison until they shall have found security." (But a definite reasonable time should be stated.)—*Q. B. (Ir.), Hil. Term,* 1883, *Attorney-General v. Davitt, Healy, and Quinn,* decided that the Court of Queen's Bench possessed an original and inherent jurisdiction to issue process to bind to the peace and good behaviour, independent of the statute 34 Edw. iii.

The best authorities say that there should be a certain stated time for which the security is required, and in default of finding the sureties, to be *committed for that period.*—*Prickett v. Greatrix,* 8 *Q. B. Reports,* 1021. It is also laid down that the party ought not to be allowed by witnesses to contradict the fact stated in the affidavits on which the application is grounded, that these can only be negatived through the medium of an appropriate prosecution.—*R. v. Stanhope,* 12 *A. & E.* 620; *Ex parte Mallinson* (15 *Jur.,* 746, *per Coleridge, J., Lord Vane's Case*), 13 *East.,* 121. But the constant practice before Magistrates is to allow the defendant to cross-examine the complainant, state his defence, and examine witnesses, dispute the facts and the inferences, and not unfrequently does so successfully. Indeed if it can be considered a summary order, and seeing that it is a *judicial* proceeding, the rule in the Petty Sessions Act as to hearing the defence would seem to regulate this proceeding also. In an application under the statute 34 Edw. iii., c. 1, to bind a party over to be of good behaviour, several distinct instances of misconduct may be alleged and relied on.—*R. v. Queen's County Justices,* 10 *Irish Law Reports,* 294.

A warrant to commit in default of bail, issued by a Magistrate on a Sunday, held to be a "judicial act," and will be void.—*Queen v. Ramsay and Justices County Cork, Q. B. (Ir.), Trin. Term,* 1867. "*Dies dominicus non est juridicus.*"

As the imprisonment is in the nature of restraint rather than punishment, it ought not to be accompanied with hard labour.

No one ought to be bound to be of good behaviour for any rash, quarrelsome, or unmannerly words, unless they directly tend to a breach of the peace, or to scandalize the government, by abusing those intrusted with the administration of justice, or to deter an officer from doing his duty; and that therefore it seems that he who

Offence, or cause of Complaint.	Statute.	Extent of Jurisdiction.
SURETIES OF THE PEACE AND GOOD BEHAVIOUR—*con.* *Of Good Behaviour—of whom required.*—Person whom Justice of the Peace shall have just cause to suspect to be dangerous, quarrelsome, scandalous, common quarrellers, and common breakers of the peace; rioters; those who lie in wait to rob, or are suspected to do so, or who assault or attempt to rob another, or put passengers in	34 Edw. iii. c. 1, and the Commission.	Justice of the Peace has a discretionary power to take sureties of all such, and others whose behaviour may reasonably be intended to bring them within the meaning of the statute, as "persons of evil fame." 1 J.

barely calls another rogue, rascal, liar, drunkard, &c., ought not to be bound.— 1 *Hawk.*, c. 60, *s.* 3.

Lunatics should not be bound, nor should others on their application.

Peers ought only to be bound by a Superior Court: the Q. B. or Chan.—*Bl. Com.* If a man that was bound to keep the peace hath broken his bond, the Justices ought of discretion to bind him anew.—*Lamb.* 78. But not until he be thereof convicted by due course of law, for before conviction he standeth indifferent, whether he had forfeited his recognizance or not.—*Cromp.* 175. So also if the Justice had been deceived as to the solvency of the sureties, he may require new sureties. *Surety for good behaviour* includes surety for the peace, and he that is bound to good behaviour is therein also bound to the peace. The 34 Edw. iii., c. 1, is that which gives power to Justices "to take of all them *that be not of good fame* where they shall be found sufficient surety and mainprize of their good behaviour towards the king and his people." This left in the Justices, taken in connexion with their commission, a discretion not to be found in any other statute; and, certainly, as Dr. Burn remarks, "there is no other which had received such a largeness of interpretation." Yet these are the interpretations which, after a lapse of five hundred years, still regulate the procedure. It is said to have had in view chiefly the disorders to which the country was then liable, from the great numbers of disbanded soldiers who, having served abroad in the wars of that victorious king, were grown strangers to industry, and were rather inclined to live upon rapine and spoil. The principal writers who have collected instances of the application of the statute, and on whose works the modern books are founded, are Mr. Dalton, who wrote towards the latter end of the reign of James I., and Mr. Sergeant Hawkins, who wrote in the reign of George I. Even then it became difficult to define how far the statute should extend, or where it should stop. Mr. Dalton, in order to determine with some kind of certainty how far it may be applied, inserted a number of instances; and these are the cases given by Dr. Burn and all modern text writers. Certainly, in the present day, it would neither be judicious nor discreet in a Justice to bring some of the cases under his jurisdiction. It is justly remarked on the subject, that the Magistrate cannot exercise too much caution, and in matters which the law hath left indefinite, it is better to fall short of than to exceed his authority. Still these ancient mere-stones have not been removed, although, in some instances, the lines have with reason been contracted, and the modern works, in addition to those above enumerated in the text, quote the following instances given by Sergeant Hawkins:—Accusing Justice of ignorance of his duty—*R.* v.

Offence, or cause of Complaint.	Statute.	Extent of Jurisdiction.
SURETIES OF THE PEACE AND GOOD BEHAVIOUR—*con*. · fear or peril; such as be generally feared or suspected to be highway-robbers; night-walkers, who sleep in the day and go abroad at night, that be suspected to be pilferers, or otherwise like to disturb the peace; such as abuse constables, &c., in executing their office; common drunkards, and idle vagabonds. The Local Acts for Dublin and Belfast contain special provisions to punish for using language or conduct calculated to provoke breaches of the peace.	34 Edw. iii. c. 1, and the Commission.	

Burford, 1 *Ventr.*, 16. Exciting discontent in the minds of the people.—*Rudyard's Case*, 2 *Ventr.*, 22. Who poison or destroy the cattle or goods of others.—*Dalt.*, 124. Who keep brothels, or are common frequenters of brothels, common gamesters, women offering money to buy medicine to destroy child in the womb.—1 *Haw.*, c. 61. Obstructing a person on his way to a Court of Justice.—2 *Lill. Rep.*, 649. Being guilty of forcible entry or detainer.—1 *Haw.*, c. 68, *s.* 8. Publishing obscene books.—*Fort.*, 193. Writings containing obscene ribaldry, though no person be referred to, such may be bound as a scandalous person of *evil fame;* and all others whose misconduct may fairly bring them within the purview of the statute as *persons of evil fame.* And Mr. Dalton says, that in general whatsoever act or thing is of itself a misbehaviour, is cause sufficient to bind such an offender to the good behaviour.

In 1889, on a question raised in Parliament, Sir Edward Clarke, Solicitor-General, is reported as follows:—"The jurisdiction of the Magistrates, both under the Commission of the Peace and under the statute 34 Edw. iii., to require sureties against conduct calculated to lead to an offence against the law, or a breach of the peace, is clearly established by a number of cases. These cases show that the jurisdiction in question may be exercised as a precautionary measure, without proof of the commission of crime; or even after acquittal the person accused of the crime may be ordered to find sureties of good behaviour."

In requiring sureties the Justice acts *judicially;* when in obedience to a Superior Court *ministerially.*—*Dalt., J., co.* 116, 123; *Hutt's Case*, 2 *Burr.*, 1039.

The schedule to 14 & 15 Vic. c. 93, gives the form of recognizance; section 34 of that Act points out the particulars which it should contain. The 57 Geo. iii. c. 56, s. 2, gives the form of oath which is to be annexed to or written on the recognizance:—

"I, *A. B.*, do swear that I am a householder, and have a house wherein I usually reside at ——, in the parish of ——, barony (*or* half-barony) of ——, and county of ——, and that I support and maintain myself by ——, and that I am worth the sum of (*here insert double the sum in which he or she is to be bound*), over and above all my just debts. So help me God."

Offence, or cause of Complaint.	Statute.	Extent of Jurisdiction.
"SUSPECTED PERSONS." See "Vagrancy."	50 Geo. iii. c. 102, s. 7.	Repealed by 28 Vic. c. 33. (*a*)
SWEARING: Profane cursing or swearing in presence of Justice. If a servant, labourer, soldier, or seaman— Other person, ...	7 Wm. iii. c. 9, s. 1. ,,	Penalty 1*s.* ; in default, &c., imprisonment by scale. 1 J. Penalty 2*s.* ; in default, &c., imprisonment by scale. 1 J. The punishment in the Act is—adult, 1 hour in the stocks ; youths to be whipped.
See also " Blaspheming in Streets," &c.		

Principals to be sworn only as to residence—sec. 3.

Penalty on Magistrates neglecting to comply with the provisions of this Act, £50—sec. 4.

There is no form of oath given in the form of recognizance in schedule to Petty Sessions Act; and section 34 of that Act states that every recognizance so taken according to the form in the schedule shall be binding and effectual. It would, however, be of little value that the bond shall be " binding and effectual," if the sureties be insolvent. The Justice protects himself when he requires them to qualify on oath.

The practice is to require the sureties to qualify in double the amount of the bond. New sureties cannot be required if the former should die, as their executors and administrators continue liable. It has been decided that if the accused find sureties and be discharged, he cannot, on the ground of their being insufficient, be again arrested, and ordered to find fresh bail. The contrary position, however, rests on the high authority of Sergeant Hawkins. The summary of the decisions seems to be, that if the Justices be misled or imposed upon as to the solvency of the sureties, and that they should, on sufficient sworn information, consider new bail requisite, they may require such. It is said that where a breach of the peace had been committed, and the offender punished by fine or imprisonment, the Justices cannot on that same complaint order him to find sureties. Still, if an assault has been committed, and accompanied then, or followed subsequently, with a threat of further bodily harm, there appears no reason why distinct complaints may not be brought, one for the assault and the other for sureties to keep the peace. For aggravated assaults on females and boys, under the 24 & 25 Vic. c. 100, s. 43, the Justices may, on the same complaint, punish for the offence, and also require sureties. The grounds upon which sureties of the peace are sought should appear on one or more sufficient forms. For form of notice to estreat recognizance, see *Appendix*.

(*a*) Geo. iii. c. 102, s. 7, enabling Justices to compel suspected strangers, to give a satisfactory account of themselves, to find sureties, repealed

of sufficient property. Married women

Offence, or cause of Complaint.	Statute.	Extent of Jurisdiction.
SWEEPS : See "Chimney Sweeps."		
SWINE : Allowing to wander on public road or streets.	14 & 15 Vic. c. 92, s. 10.	Penalty not exceeding 2s. ; in default, &c., imprisonment not exceeding 1 week. 1 J. —
May be impounded if owner not known. See also "Commons."	,,	
TELEGRAPHS : Injuries to electric or magnetic telegraphs, or attempting to injure— see "Malicious Injuries."		
And for sending telegram in contravention of the Telegraph Act, 1868, see—	32 & 33 Vic. c. 73, s. 6.	
All fines and penalties under Telegraph Acts may be recovered by Postmaster-General before Court of Summary Jurisdiction. In Dublin by the Local Acts regulating the duties of Justices ; and elsewhere in Ireland under Petty Sessions (Ireland) Act, 1851, and any Act amending same before any Justice of the Peace—	41 & 42 Vic. c. 76, s. 10.	
Fines shall be paid to the Exchequer.	,,	
TENEMENTS : See "Landlord and Tenant."		
TENTS OR BOOTHS AT FAIRS, RACES, &c.: For the granting of occasional licence to sell thereat, see "Licensing Acts."		

and persons under 21 cannot become sureties ; their bonds would be void. But see now 28 Vic. c. 42, when she obtains a protection order by reason of desertion by her husband, and after which she may sue or be sued.

A form of commitment, in default of finding sureties, &c., is given in the *Appendix*.

Offence, or cause of Complaint.	Statute.	Extent of Jurisdiction.
THEATRE: Summary power is given to Justices in Dublin to punish offensive or riotous conduct in theatres and public places, and in Cork by Local Acts. For sale of spirits in, see " Licensing Acts."	34 & 35 Vic. c. 76, s. 8.	
THIMBLERS AND SWINDLERS: See "Vagrancy."		
THRESHING OR WINNOWING CORN ON ROADSIDE.	14 & 15 Vic. c. 92, s. 10. (36 & 37 Vic. c. 82.)	Penalty not exceeding 10s.; in default, &c., imprisonment not exceeding 7 days. 1 J.
TIMBER: Conveying on public road or street carts with timber, boards, or iron laid across, so that either end project more than 2 feet beyond the wheels or sides thereof. (See "Nuisance on Roads," and note at foot.)	,,	Like.
TOBACCO: See " Customs." Excessive moisture in—see "Excise."		
TOLLS: See "Turnpike."		
TOWNS IMPROVEMENT ACT. (a) See *Appendix*.	17 & 18 Vic. c. 103.	
TOWN COMMISSIONERS' ACT, .	9 Geo. iv. c. 82.	

(a) As this Act is at present limited in its application, to prevent mistakes its provisions are not here introduced. It is of sufficient extent to be specially noticed, and a copious abstract will be found in the *Appendix*.

Offence, or cause of Complaint.	Statute.	Extent of Jurisdiction.
TRADE DISPUTES : See "Conspiracy and Protection of Property," Summary Index.		
TRADE MARKS : See "Merchandise Marks."		
TRADES UNIONS : Trade union not criminal by reason merely of being in restraint of trade.	34 & 35 Vic. c. 31, s. 2.	
Nor be unlawful so as to render void any agreement or trust.	s. 3.	—
Certain trade union contracts (as specified in section) not enforceable in courts of law, although such contracts be not unlawful.		
Provides as to registration, buildings, property, &c., of trades unions, liability of trustees, &c., treasurers' accounts, &c.		
Provides punishment for fraudulently obtaining moneys, books, papers, &c., or fraudulently misapplying same.	s. 12.	Power to order restitution, &c., and a sum not exceeding £20, with costs not exceeding 20s. In default of compliance, imprisonment not exceeding 3 months, with or without H. L. 1 Res. Magistrate.
Not to prevent offender being proceeded against by indictment, but not in addition to summary conviction.		
Provides penalties for not registering office, and transmitting returns, and making false entries, &c.		
Proceedings in Dublin to be under special Acts ; elsewhere in Ireland under Petty Sessions (Ireland) Act, 1851, and any Act amending same.	—	Orders to be enforced before a Divisional Justice in Dublin, and elsewhere in Ireland before a Resident Magistrate. Act gives right of appeal from summary orders, with special conditions.
Circulating false copies of rules, &c., is an indictable misdemeanour. See "Friendly Societies," and also—	34 & 35 Vic. c. 31, s. 18. 32 & 33 Vic. c. 61.	—

Offence, or cause of Complaint.	Statute.	Extent of Jurisdiction.
TREASURE TROVE: See Indictable Offence Index.		
TREES, PLANTS, &c.: See "Larceny," and "Malicious Injuries," as the case may be.		
TRESPASS (*of Persons*) : (*a*) Wilful trespass in field, garden, pleasure-ground, wood, plantation, or other place, and neglecting or refusing to leave when warned—	14 & 15 Vic. c. 92, s. 8.	Penalty not exceeding 10s.; in default, &c., imprisonment not exceeding 1 week. 1 J.
Repetition of trespass within three months after such warning.	,,	Like.
Unauthorized persons entering upon the lands of others to look for, start, shoot, course, hunt, &c., game or wild fowl.	27 Geo. iii. c. 35, s. 10. (Irish).	Penalty not exceeding £10; in default, &c., imprisonment not exceeding 1 month; and where not exceeding £5, in default of payment imprisonment by scale. 1 J.
For trespass of animals, rates of trespass, and pound-keepers' fees, see "Pound."		
In pursuit of game, and fishing—see "Game," and "Fisheries."		
TROUT: See "Fisheries."		

(a) Section does not apply where the person acted under reasonable supposition of right, &c., unintentional trespass in pursuit of game, &c., see 14 & 15 Vic. c. 92, s. 8. The words "other places" will not include a house, only places *ejusdem generis:* Perase, appellant; Murphy and Others, respondents, on case stated.—Q. B. Division, Hilary Term, 1888.

Trespassers.—Posted notice insufficient as warning to trespassers. Complaint of trespass on a Several Fishery.—*Exchequer Division, Dublin, November 23rd,* Baron Dowse and Mr. Justice Andrews. A general notice posted up here was held not to be sufficient.

Offence, or cause of Complaint.	Statute.	Extent of Jurisdiction.
TRUCK ACTS (a), 1831 AND 1887: Shall be construed together as one Act.		
Act to prohibit the payment in certain trades of wages in goods, or otherwise, than in the current coin of the realm: called the "Truck Act, 1831."	1 & 2 Wm. iv. c. 37.	
Truck Amendment Act, 1887.	50 & 51 Vic. c. 46.	
Employers' Offences.—Contracts for the hiring of artificers (which means and includes all workmen, as defined by Employers' and Workmen Act, 1875; 38 & 39 Vic. c. 90) must be made in the current coin of this realm only; and if any part of wages be made payable in any other manner, the contract is *illegal*, null, and void, and employer liable to—	1 & 2 Wm. iv. c. 37, ss. 1, 9; and 50 & 51 Vic. c. 46, s. 18.	The employer who, by himself or the agency of any other, directly or indirectly enters into any contract, or makes any payment hereby declared illegal shall, for 1st offence, forfeit a sum not exceeding £10, nor less than £5. Second offence, not exceeding £20, nor less than £10; in default of payment and distress, imprisonment by Petty Sessions scale. 1 J. Third offence, misdemeanour; but punishable by fine or fines only, not exceeding £100.

(a) *Truck Acts.*—This Act of 1 & 2 Wm. iv. c. 37, has been extended to Ireland by 50 & 51 Vic. c. 46, with certain modifications. The object being that, workmen shall have the full benefit of their contract by being free to get the best value for their money.

Penalties.—Sec. 9. Any employer of any artificer in any of the trades enumerated who shall, by himself or by the agency of any other person or persons, directly or indirectly enter into any contract, or make any payment hereby declared illegal, shall, for the *first offence*, forfeit a sum not exceeding £10, nor less than £5; and for the *second offence*, any sum not exceeding £20, nor less than £10; and in case of a *third offence*, any such employer shall be, and be deemed, guilty of a misdemeanour, and, being thereof convicted, shall be punished by fine only, at the discretion of the Court, so that the fines shall not in any case exceed the sum of £100. But see note on sec. 18, 50 & 51 Vic. c. 46, extending Acts to Ireland; and on sec. 10 of the principal Act.

Offence, or cause of Complaint.	Statute.	Extent of Jurisdiction.
TRUCK ACTS, 1831 AND 1887—*con.* The contract must not, directly or indirectly, contain any stipulation as to the place where, or the manner in which, or the person with whom the wages or any part thereof shall be laid out; such stipulation renders contract *illegal*, null, and void, and employer liable—	1 & 2 Wm. iv. c. 37, ss. 2, 9. 50 & 51 Vic. c. 46, s. 18.	The Employer who, by himself or the agency of any other, directly or indirectly enters into any contract, or makes any payment hereby declared illegal shall, for first offence forfeit a sum not exceeding £10, nor less than £5. Second offence, not exceeding £20, nor less than £10; in default of payment and distress, imprisonment by Petty Sessions scale. 1 J. Third offence, misdemeanour; but punishable by fine or fines only, not exceeding £100.
All wages earned by or payable to the workman must be paid to him in current coin; payment in goods, or otherwise, *illegal*, null, and void, and employer liable, &c.— (*Not to invalidate payment in Banknotes if workman consents.*)	1 & 2 Wm. iv. c. 37, ss. 3, 8. 50 & 51 Vic. c. 46, s. 18.	Like.
Artificer, or workman, may recover wages in usual way, if not so paid—	1 & 2 Wm. iv. c. 37, s. 4.	
In an action brought for wages, no set-off shall be allowed for goods supplied by the employer, or by any shop in which the employer is interested.	s. 5.	
No employer shall have action against *his* artificer or workman for goods supplied to him on account of wages.	s. 6.	
Where workman or wife become chargeable on the parish, the overseers (Guardians of Union) may recover any wages earned within the 3 preceding months, and not cash.	s. 7.	

Offence, or cause of Complaint.	Statute.	Extent of Jurisdiction.
TRUCK ACTS, 1831 AND 1887—*con.* *Bank-notes.*—Not to invalidate the payment of wages in Bank-notes if the employed consents.	1 & 2 Wm. iv. c. 37, s. 8.	
For penalties on employers entering into contracts declared illegal—	s. 9.	
Proviso as to second offence, &c.—Ten days must elapse between the 1st conviction and second conviction; but each *separate offence*, in the meantime, may be punished by separate penalties, but as first convictions; and so in like manner between *second* and *third convictions*. And informant, if unable, or if he sees fit, may forego right to give evidence of previous convictions, and so go for distinct penalties, as though each such offence were a first or second conviction, as the case may be (*a*).	s. 10.	
Partners not to be personally liable for offences of co-partner, but the partnership property to be so liable.	s. 13.	
Convictions not to be quashed for want of form.	s. 17.	
Domestics.—Nothing in Act to extend to Domestic Servant.	s. 20.	
Exceptions.—Supplying, or contracts to supply, medicine and medical attendance, fuel, or materials, tools, implements, where employed	s. 23.	

(*a*) *Second Convictions, &c.*—The meaning of this section seems to be that, no matter how many soever may be the previous convictions, the prosecutor may elect to go for distinct penalties for each offence as if it were a first offence; or in like manner elect to go for distinct second offence penalties. But no person shall be punished as for a *second*, or as for a *third* offence, at the distance of more than *two* years from the commission of the next preceding offence. See proviso to sec. 10.

Offence, or cause of Complaint.	Statute.	Extent of Jurisdiction.
TRUCK ACTS, 1831 AND 1887—con. in mining purposes; provender for horses employed; the letting to workman of tenements at reserved rent; or victuals dressed under employer's roof, and there consumed by workman; nor from making or contracting to make stoppages of such rent, &c. &c., or in respect of money advanced for such purposes: provided that such stoppage shall not exceed the true value, and the agreement in all such cases to be in writing and signed by artificer.	1 & 2 Wm. iv. c. 37, s. 23.	
Employers may advance to artificer money to contribute to Friendly Society, or legally established Savings Bank; money for relief in sickness, for education of children; and may contract to deduct from wages advances for education.	s. 24.	
Definition of Contract.—On the subject of wages any agreement, understanding, device, arrangement, &c., written or oral, direct or indirect, to which parties assent, or are mutually bound, or whereby either of them shall have endeavoured to impose an obligation on the other, shall be deemed a "Contract."	s. 25.	
"Truck Amendment Act, 1887."	50 & 51 Vic. c. 46.	
The provisions of the principal Act (1 & 2 Wm. iv. c. 37) shall extend to "workmen," as defined by "Employers and Workmen Act, 1875" (38 & 39 Vic. c. 90); and the expression "artificer" in the principal Act will include workman; and inconsistent provisions in principal Act with this Act are repealed.	s. 2.	

Offence, or cause of Complaint.	Statute.	Extent of Jurisdiction.
TRUCK ACTS, 1831 AND 1887—*con.* Where by agreement, custom, or otherwise, a workman is entitled to receive, in anticipation of the regular period of the payment of his wages, an advance as part or on account thereof, it shall not be lawful to withhold such advance, or make any deduction in respect of such advance on account of poundage, discount, or interest on any similar charge; for contravening or failing to comply—	50 & 51 Vic. c. 46, s. 3.	First offence—shall forfeit a sum not exceeding £10, nor less than £5. Second offence—not exceeding £20, nor less than £10. In default of payment and of distress, imprisonment by Petty Sessions scale. 1 J.
Husbandmen.— Contracts to give food, drink (not being intoxicating), cottage, allowance, or privileges, in addition to money wages, as remuneration for services of a servant in husbandry, not to be deemed illegal under the principal Act or this Act.	s. 4.	
Order for Goods illegal.—In action by workman for recovery of wages, employer shall not be entitled to set-off goods supplied to workman by any person under order of employer or his agent; nor shall workman be liable to be sued for such. Proviso—nothing in this section shall apply to exceptions in *section* 23 of principal Act before mentioned.	s. 5.	
No employer shall, directly or indirectly, by himself or his agent, impose as a condition, express or implied, any terms as to the place or the manner in which workman shall expend any portion of his wages; nor shall the workman be dismissed on account of the place or manner of his spending his wages; for contravening—	s. 6.	Like penalties as aforesaid. 1 J.

Offence, or cause of Complaint.	Statute.	Extent of Jurisdiction.
TRUCK ACTS, 1831 AND 1887—*con.* *Education.*—Where deduction from wages is made for education, workman on sending child to State-inspected elementary schools (under the inspection of Board of National Education), selected by workman shall be entitled to have the school fees paid at the same rate as the workmen from whose wages deduction is made by employer; for failing to comply—	50 & 51 Vic. c. 46, s. 7.	First offence—shall forfeit a sum not exceeding £10, nor less than £5. Second offence, not exceeding £20, nor less than £10. In default of payment and of distress, imprisonment by Petty Sessions scale. 1 J.
Sharpening Tools.—No deduction shall be made from workman's wages for sharpening tools, except by agreement, not forming part of the condition of hiring; for contravening—	s. 8.	Like penalties. 1 J.
Audit of Deductions.—Where deductions are made from wages for education of children, medicine, medical attendance, or tools, employer shall once a year, by himself or agent, make out correct account of receipts and expenditure in respect of such deductions, and submit same to two auditors appointed by workmen, and produce to auditors books, vouchers, &c., and afford such facilities as are required for such audit; for contravening or failure—	s. 9.	Like penalties. 1 J.
Articles made at workman's home to be paid for in cash and not by way of barter.—Special provision as to articles made by a person at his home, &c., by self and his own family, Acts shall apply as if he were a workman, and the purchaser of such articles in the way of trade as an employer, and the provisions of *this Act with respect to the payment of wages* shall apply. Section applies to articles under	s. 10.	

Offence, or cause of Complaint.	Statute.	Extent of Jurisdiction.
TRUCK ACTS, 1831 AND 1887—*con.* value of £5, and of particular materials; and Queen in Council may suspend operation of section in interest·of workmen in any place, and wholly or in part.	50 & 51 Vic. c. 46, s. 10.	
Offences.—Employer or agent, as case may be, *contravening on failing to comply* with any of provisions of this Act shall be guilty of an offence against the principal Act, and liable to the penalties imposed by sec. 9 of that Act (but see note on sec. 18).	s. 11.	
Provision for fining person committing offence for which employer is liable, and power of employer to exempt himself from penalty upon showing that he used due diligence to carry out Act; and laying information against the actual offender, satisfying Court that offence was committed without his knowledge or connivance. The actual offender shall thereupon be convicted, and the employer be exempt.	s. 12.	
Inspectors of Factories and Workshops empowered to inspect and enforce the provisions of principal Act and this Act.	s. 13. (sub-sec. 2.)	
Application to Ireland. (*a*)—Offences against the principal Act and this Act may be prosecuted and penalties recovered in *Dublin* under the Local Acts. Elsewhere in Ireland under the "Petty Sessions (Ir.) Act, 1851" (14 & 15 Vic. c. 93), and Acts amending same.	s. 18.	

(*a*) *Section* 18. *Application of Acts to Ireland.*—From the wording of this section extending the unrepealed portion of the principal Act and this Act to Ireland, subject to the provisions that *any offence* against either Act may be prosecuted and penalty recovered in a summary way. Then it would seem that the summary jurisdiction is the only method of recovering penalties.

Offence, or cause of Complaint.	Statute.	Extent of Jurisdiction.
TRUCK ACTS, 1831 AND 1887—*con.* Penalties to be applied as directed by the "*Fines (Ir.) Act*, 1851," and the Acts amending same. Schedule to Act repeals in part sections of the principal Act.	50 & 51 Vic. c. 46, s. 18.	
TUITION : See "Schoolmaster."		
TURF : Stealing, or damaging with intent to steal, any turf or peat manufactured or partly manufactured for fuel (value of injury done not exceeding 40*s.*)	25 & 26 Vic. c. 50, s. 5. (36 & 37 Vic. c. 82.)	Shall pay compensation, and also a fine not exceeding £5, or to be imprisoned not exceeding 3 months. (Imprisonment for penalty to be by scale.) 1 J.
TURKEY (*stealing*): See "Poultry."		
TURNPIKE-GATE : Wilfully damaging or destroying any pay-gate or turnpike-gate, post, rail, &c., or fence of any kind used to prevent passengers passing without paying toll, or any toll-house, or rescuing or attempting to rescue person in custody for the offence.	14 & 15 Vic. c. 92, s. 9. (36 & 37 Vic. c. 82.)	Penalty not exceeding 40*s.*; or imprisonment not exceeding 1 month. 1 J.
TURNPIKE ABOLITION ACT, 1857,	20 & 21 Vic. c. 16.	
Persons examined under authority of this Act, giving false evidence, refusing to give evidence, destroying documents, &c.	s. 12.	Penalty not exceeding £10; recoverable under Petty Sessions Act; imprisonment by scale. 1 J.
Power to Justices at Petty Sessions to give possession of toll-house to Commissioners. Act gives schedule of local and personal Acts repealed.	s. 42.	

Offence, or cause of Complaint.	Statute.	Extent of Jurisdiction.
UNION (ACT OF, BETWEEN ENGLAND AND IRELAND, 1800)*	40 Geo. iii. c. 38. (Ir.) 39 & 40 Geo. iii. c. 67.	Ratified in the Parliament of Great Britain, 2nd July, 1800. Came into force 1st January, 1801.
UNLAWFUL ASSEMBLY: Any person who shall take part in any riot or unlawful assembly—	50 & 51 Vic. c. 20, s. 2, sub. sec. (3) (a)	Imprisonment with or without H. L., not exceeding 6 months. 2 Res. Mag.
UNWHOLESOME MEAT: See "Frauds as to provisions."		
VACCINATION: (b) Parents and guardians of children to have such children vaccinated within 3 months after birth. In workhouses or charitable institution, Master or officer of such shall comply with Act.	42 & 43 Vic. c. 70, s. 3.	
Provision for inspection of vaccination—re-vaccination when necessary, and if medical officer sees fit may take lymph from child.	s. 5.	
Certificate of successful vaccination to be given to parent or guardian, and duplicate to be transmitted to Registrar. Provision where medical officer of dispensary district is also Registrar of births and deaths. Rate of payment for successful cases of vaccination.	"	

* By 23 Geo. iii. c. 28, it was declared that the Parliament and Courts of Ireland had exclusive right as to all matters of legislation and judicature in Ireland, and from that to 39 & 40 Geo. iii. c. 67, Ireland is not bound by any Acts of Parliament passed in England. From the Union all Acts of Parliament extend to Ireland, whether expressly mentioned or not, unless expressly or by implication excepted.

(b) Vaccination is not to be considered as parochial relief so as to disqualify, &c.—31 & 32 Vic. c. 87.

Offence, or cause of Complaint.	Statute	Extent of Jurisdiction.
VACCINATION—*continued.*		
Every person who prevents any dispensary medical officer from taking from any child lymph, as provided by section 4, shall be liable to—	42 & 43 Vic. c. 70, s. 7.	Penalty not exceeding 20s.; in default, &c., imprisonment not exceeding 14 days. 1 J.
Parent or person having custody of child, failing to produce such child when required so to do by any summons under the Vaccination Acts shall be liable—	,,	Like penalty. 1 J.
Every parent or person having the custody of a child who neglects to take such child or to cause it to be taken, to be vaccinated, or after vaccination to be inspected according to provisions of Vaccination (Ireland) Acts (21 & 22 Vic. c. 64, 26 & 27 Vic. c. 52, 31 & 32 Vic. c. 87)—and does not render a reasonable excuse for neglect.	,,	Like penalty. 1 J.
Every medical officer, parent, or person, as the case shall require, who shall neglect to transmit any certificate required of him by the provisions of the Vaccination (Ireland) Acts, completely filled up and legibly written, to the Registrar within the time specified by the said Acts, and every medical officer who shall refuse to deliver the duplicate to the parent or other person on request, or who shall refuse to fill up and sign the certificate of successful vaccination—	s. 8.	Like penalty. 1 J.
Person wilfully signing false certificate or duplicate.	,,	Misdemeanour; triable by indictment.
Notice to procure vaccination need not be proved.		
Certificate or register of successful vaccination sufficient defence, save as to certificate, form B., where time of postponement of vaccination has expired.	s. 9.	— —

Offence, or cause of Complaint.	Statute.	Extent of Jurisdiction.
VACCINATION—*continued.*		
Power to guardians of the poor to direct proceedings and remuneration of medical officers of dispensary districts. Justice may certify amount, 21 & 22 Vic. c. 64, 26 & 27 Vic. c. 52, 31 & 32 Vic. c. 87.	42 & 43 Vic. c. 70, s. 10.	
Transmission to medical officer of list of births and deaths—	s. 11.	—
Act gives forms of certificates in schedules.		
Registrar of births and deaths in every district to give notice according to form in schedule, of requirement of vaccination, and on failure of parent or guardian to comply, or neglecting on eighth day after vaccination to take child for inspection; the father or mother or person having the care, nurture, or custody of child so offending—	26 & 27 Vic. c. 52, s. 8. (36 & 37. Vic. c. 82.)	Penalty not exceeding 10s.; in default, &c., imprisonment not exceeding 7 days. 1 J.
Registrar failing to register successful vaccination, or registering vaccination of any child not successfully vaccinated, or certified so to him.	26 & 27 Vic. c. 52, s. 10.	Penalty not exceeding 40s.; in default, &c., imprisonment not exceeding 14 days. 1 J.
Fee for successful vaccination, 1s.		
Fee to Registrar (when he is not the operator), 3d.		
Form of notices and certificates are given in Schedule to Act.		
Inoculating, or by any means wilfully producing small-pox in any person.	31 & 32 Vic. c. 87, s. 4.	Imprisonment not exceeding 2 months.
VAGABONDS. See "Vagrancy."		

Offence, or cause of Complaint.	Statute.	Extent of Jurisdiction.
VAGRANCY: Every person wandering abroad and begging, or placing himself in any public place, street, highway, court, or passage, to beg, or gather alms, or causing or procuring or encouraging any child or children so to do; and every person who, having been resident in any union in Ireland, shall go from such union to some other union, or from one electoral or relief district to another electoral or relief district in Ireland, for the purpose of obtaining relief in such last-mentioned union or district; on conviction—	10 & 11 Vic. c. 84, s. 3.	Shall, if the Justice think fit, be committed for any time not exceeding 1 month's H. L. 1 J.
Cases of vagrancy may be tried out of Petty Sessions, and Justice shall enter same in the Order Book, or send certificate of the fact to the clerk.	14 & 15 Vic. c. 93, ss. 8, 22.	
ROGUES AND VAGABONDS. Every person pretending or professing to tell fortunes, or using any subtle craft, means, or device, by palmistry or otherwise, to deceive and impose on any of His Majesty's subjects.	5 Geo. iv. c. 83, s. 4. 34 & 35 Vic. c. 112, s. 15.	Shall be deemed a rogue and a vagabond within the true intent and meaning of this Act; and it shall be lawful for any Justice of the Peace to commit such offender (being thereof convicted before him by the confession of such offender, or by the evidence on oath of one or more credible witness or witnesses) to the house of correction, there to be kept to hard labour for any time not exceeding 3 calendar months; and every such picklock,
Every person wandering abroad and lodging in any barn or out-house, or in any deserted or unoccupied building, or in the open air, or under a tent, or in any cart or wagon, not having any visible means of subsistence, and not giving a good account of himself or herself.		
Every person wilfully exposing to view in any street, road, highway, or public place, any obscene print, picture, or other indecent exhibition.		

The Vagrancy Act, 6 Anne, c. 11, and the 7 sec. of 50 Geo. iii. c. 102, respecting "suspected persons," repealed by 28 Vic. c. 33. And for "suspected persons," see also "Crime," Sum. Index, s. 7, when apprehended under the circumstances there pointed out.

Offence, or cause of Complaint.	Statute.	Extent of Jurisdiction.
VAGRANCY—ROGUES AND VAGABONDS—*continued*. Every person wilfully, openly, lewdly, and obscenely exposing his person in any street, road, or public highway, or in the view thereof, or in any place of public resort, with intent to insult any female. Every person wandering abroad and endeavouring, by the exposure of wounds or deformities, to obtain or gather alms. Every person going about as a gatherer or collector of alms, or endeavouring to procure charitable contributions of any nature or kind, under any false or fraudulent pretence. Every person running away and leaving his wife, or his or her child or children chargeable, or whereby she or they, or any of them shall become chargeable to any parish, township, or place.	5 Geo. iv. c. 83, s. 4. 34 & 35 Vic. c. 112, s. 15.	key, crow, jack, bit, and other implement, and every such gun, pistol, hanger, cutlass, bludgeon, or other offensive weapon, and every such instrument as aforesaid shall, by the conviction of the offender, become forfeited to the King's Majesty. (*a*) 1 J.

(*a*) The above Act, relating to "Rogues and Vagabonds," is an English Act, and by the "Prevention of Crimes Act," 34 & 35 Vic. c. 112, is now extended to Ireland. It is to be observed that the first paragraph of the section which says, "Every person committing any of the offences hereinbefore mentioned, after having been convicted as an idle and disorderly person," cannot be applicable, as that before-mentioned section referred to, the conviction under which would make an idle and disorderly person, does not apply to Ireland. And for the same reason the last paragraph of the section, "Every person apprehended as an idle and disorderly person, and violently resisting any constable or other peace officer so apprehending him or her, *and being subsequently convicted of the offence for which he or she shall have been so apprehended*," is not applicable to Ireland. The 17 Geo. ii. c. 5, Classified Vagrants:—1st, Idle and disorderly persons; 2nd, Rogues and vagabonds; 3rd, Incorrigible rogues.

Sec. 15 of the "Prevention of Crimes Act," 34 & 35 Vic. c. 112, which extends this Act of 5 Geo. iv. c. 83, s. 4, dealing with rogues and vagabonds to Ireland, is as follows:—"Whereas, by the fourth section of the Act passed in the fifth year of the reign of King George the Fourth, chapter eighty-three, intituled, 'An Act for the punishment of idle and disorderly persons, and rogues and vagabonds, in that part of Great Britain called England,' it is, amongst other things, provided that every suspected person or reputed thief frequenting any river, canal, or navigable stream, dock, or basin, or any quay, wharf, or warehouse near or adjoining thereto, or any street, highway, or avenue leading thereto, or any place of public resort, or any avenue leading thereto, or any street, highway, or place adjacent, with intent to commit felony, shall be deemed a rogue and vaga-

Offence, or cause of Complaint.	Statute.	Extent of Jurisdiction.
VAGRANCY—ROGUES AND VAGA- BONDS—*continued*. Every person playing or betting in any street, road, highway, or other open and public place, at or with any table or instrument of gaming, at any game or pretended game of chance.	5 Geo. iv. c. 83, s. 4. 34 & 35 Vic. c. 112, s. 15.	
Every person having in his or her custody or possession any pick-lock, key, crow, jack, bit, or other implement, with intent feloniously to break into any dwelling-house, warehouse, coach-house, stable, or out-building, or being armed with any gun, pistol, hanger, cutlass, bludgeon, or other offensive wea-pon, or having upon him or her any instrument, with intent to commit any felonious act.	,,	—
Every person being found in or upon any dwelling-house, warehouse, coach-house, stable, or out-house, or in any enclosed yard, garden, or area, for any unlawful purpose.	,,	
Every suspected person or reputed thief frequenting any river, canal, or navigable stream, dock, or basin, or any quay, wharf, or warehouse, near or adjoining thereto, or any street, highway,	,,	

bond, and may be apprehended and committed to prison with hard labour for any time not exceeding three calendar months. And whereas doubts are entertained as to the construction of the said provision, and as to the nature of the evidence required to prove the intent to commit a felony : Be it enacted, firstly, the said section shall be construed as if instead of the words 'highway or place adjacent,' there were inserted the words ' or any highway or any place adjacent to a street or highway ;' and, secondly, that, in proving the intent to commit a felony, it shall not be necessary to show that the person suspected was guilty of any particular act or acts tending to show his purpose or intent, and he may be convicted if from the circumstances of the case, and from his known character, as proved to the Justice of the Peace or Court before whom or which he is brought, it appears to such Justice or Court that his intent was to commit a felony ; and the provisions of the said section, as amended by this section, shall be in force in Scotland and Ireland. For the purposes of this section in Scotland, the word 'felony' shall mean any of the pleas of the Crown, any theft, which, in respect of aggravation, or of the amount in value of the money, goods, or thing stolen, may be punished with penal servitude, any forgery, and any uttering of any forged writing.''

Offence, or cause of Complaint.	Statute.	Extent of Jurisdiction.
VAGRANCY—Rogues and Vaga-bonds—*continued.* or avenue leading thereto, or any place of public resort, or any avenue leading thereto, or any street, (*or any*) highway, or (*any*) place adjacent (*to a street or high-way*), with intent to commit fe-lony. See also "Poor Law"; and see "Crime," sec. 7, Sum. Index.	5 Geo. iv. c. 83, s. 4. 34 & 35 Vic. c. 112, s. 15.	
VEGETABLE PRODUCTIONS: See "Larceny," and "Malicious Injuries," as the case may be.		
VETERINARY SURGEONS: Act providing for registration of, and penalties for false representations.	44 & 45 Vic. c. 62.	
VOLUNTEERS: See "Militia," "Navy," "Naval Coast Volunteers."		
WAGES (*Servants, Workmen, &c.*): Justices in Petty Sessions are em-powered to hear and determine any disputes concerning any sums which shall be due for wages by any master to his apprentice, or by any employer to any artificer, labourer, servant, or other person employed by him for day's work, task, job, or contract, hire of horses, carts, &c. (not being for the carriage of passengers); and to schoolmaster for tuition, where the demand does not exceed £10.* See "Employers and Workmen," and notes thereon.	14 & 15 Vic. c. 92, s. 16. 38 & 39 Vic. c. 86, s. 17.	Justices to make such order as they shall see fit for payment of such sums as shall appear to be justly due, and may award a further sum as compensation (not ex-ceeding 40*s.*) for loss of time, &c., in recovering wages; recoverable by distress. 2 J.

* Under 9 Vic. c. 2, s. 20, contractors for "county work" shall pay wages in *money—not goods*—and at intervals not more than 14 days, and shall not induce him to expend at particular shops, or to take goods in lieu of money, under a penalty not exceeding £5, before Justices.—See "Truck Act."

Offence, or cause of Complaint.	Statute.	Extent of Jurisdiction.
WALL: Maliciously throwing down, breaking, &c., any wall, stile, or gate.	24 & 25 Vic. c. 97, s. 25.	Shall forfeit, over and above the injury done, a sum not exceeding £5; in default, &c., imprisonment not exceeding 2 months. 1 J.
Second or subsequent offence, . .	,,	Imprisonment, with H. L., not exceeding 12 months. 1 J.
WASHERWOMEN: Pawning clothes without owner's consent. (Under Pawnbrokers' Act.)	26 Geo. iii. c. 43, s. 8. (Irish.)	Forfeiture (20s. Irish) 18s. 6½d. British; in default, &c., imprisonment 14 days. 1 J. If paid, to be applied in making satisfaction to the aggrieved, and in costs of prosecution; residue applied as fines.
WASTE: See " Landlord and Tenant."		
WEIGHTS AND MEASURES: *Prevention of Frauds—Brands, Tickets, &c.*— (1) With intent to defraud, counterfeiting, or procuring to be counterfeited, brand or stamp used by authority of owner or lessee of market or fair to denote weight, measure, or quality, or of any cask, firkin, or other vessel, &c., in which such article is sold, or the impression of any such brand or stamp.	25 & 26 Vic. c. 76, s. 14.	Penalty not exceeding £5; in default of payment, imprisonment not exceeding 2 months. 1 J.
(2) Or, with like intent, procuring to be used any such counterfeit brand, stamp or impression.	,,	Like.
(3) Or, with like intent, alter an impression of any such genuine brand or stamp.	,,	Like.
(4) Or, with like intent, having in his possession anything having thereon an impression of any such counterfeit brand or stamp, or a fraudulently altered impression of any such genuine brand or stamp.	,,	Like.

Offence, or cause of Complaint.	Statute.	Extent of Jurisdiction.
WEIGHTS AND MEASURES—*con.*		
(5) Or, with like intent, transferring genuine branded or stamped cask, firkin, &c., to any article other than that for which same was impressed, or in any manner altering the *bonâ fide* application of such brand or stamp.	25 & 26 Vic. c. 76, s. 14.	Penalty not exceeding £5 ; in default of payment, imprisonment not exceeding 2 months. 1 J.
(6) Or knowingly weigh, or cause to be weighed, contrary to provisions of this Act, or assisting or conniving at any fraud respecting weighing or weight or measure of any article, as in Part II. of this Act is mentioned.	,,	Like.
(7) Or, with intent to defraud, alter any ticket specifying the weight of any such article.	,,	Like.
(8) Or, with intent to defraud, make or use, or be privy to the making or using of any such ticket, falsely stating the weight of any such article, or of any covering, cart, or load.	,,	Like.
(9) Or shall dispose of, sell, or cause to be sold, any weight or measure having a false or counterfeit stamp, or a stamp purporting to resemble a genuine stamp.	,,	Like.
Butter—Frauds in Packing.—Any person who shall wilfully pack up, or mix, or cause, &c., with or in any butter contained in any firkin or cask, any salt, pickle, or other substance, with intent to increase the weight, and shall bring or send same so packed, &c., to market for sale.	s. 15.	Penalty not exceeding 40*s.*, or to be imprisoned for any period not exceeding 1 month. 1 J.
Fleeces.—Winding, or causing to be wound in any fleece, any wool not being sufficiently rivered or washed; or winding, or causing to be wound within any fleeces, any deceitful locks, cots, skin, or lamb's wool, or any substance, matter, or thing whereby the fleece may be rendered more weighty, to the deceit and loss of the buyer.	s. 16.	Penalty 2*s.* for every fleece so fraudulently made up; in default, &c., imprisonment by scale. 1 J.

Offence, or cause of Complaint.	Statute.	Extent of Jurisdiction.
WEIGHTS AND MEASURES—*con.* Penalties recoverable under Petty Sessions (Ireland) Act, 1851. In *Dublin*, under special Acts.	25 & 26 Vic. c. 76, s. 16.	—
Penalties to be sued for within three months after commission of offence.	s. 18.	
Nothing to prevent persons being indicted for any indictable offence, in lieu of summary punishment.	s. 19.	
WEIGHTS AND MEASURES ACT, 1878.	41 & 42 Vic. c. 49.	
Repeals 5 & 6 Wm. iv. c. 63; 23 & 24 Vic. c. 119; and 25 & 26 Vic. c. 76, *except sec.* 2, *and part* 3, *and so much of part* 4 *as relates to part* 3; *and several other Acts.* Re-enacts 5 & 6 Wm. iv. c. 63, ss. 9 and 26. *Use of Imperial Weights and Measures.*—Trade contracts, sales, dealings, &c., to be in terms of imperial weights and measures.		
Any person who sells by any denomination of weight or measure, other than one of the imperial weights or measures, or some multiple or part thereof, shall be liable to— *Exception* for contract, &c., in metric weights and measures. *Exception* for sale of article in vessel not represented as being of imperial or local measure.	s. 19.	Fine not exceeding 40*s.* for every such sale; in default, imprisonment not exceeding 1 month, 2 J. or 1 Stip.
Price Lists, &c.—Any person who prints, or any clerk of a market or person who makes any return, price list, prices current, or any journal or other paper containing price list or price current in which the denomination of weights and measures quoted or referred to denotes or implies a greater or less weight or measure than is denoted or implied by the same denomination of the imperial weights and measures under this Act—	s. 23.	Fine not exceeding 10*s.* for every copy of every such return, price list, price current, journal or other paper which he publishes; in default of payment, imprisonment by scale. 2 J. or 1 Stip.

Offence, or cause of Complaint.	Statute.	Extent of Jurisdiction.
WEIGHTS AND MEASURES—*con.* *Possession of unauthorised Weights, &c.*—Every 'person who uses, or has in his possession for use for trade, a weight or measure which is not of the denomination of some Board of Trade standard—	41 & 42 Vic. c. 49, s. 24.	Penalty not exceeding £5; or in the case of a second offence (within 5 years under same section), £10, and the weight or measure shall be liable to be forfeited; in default, &c., imprisonment by scale. 2 J. or 1 Stip.
Possession of unjust Measures, &c.—Every person who uses, or has in his possession for use for trade, any weight, measure, scale, balance, steel-yard, or weighing machine, which is false or unjust—	s. 25. and 52 & 53 Vic. c. 21, s. 3.	Like penalty, not exceeding £5 for first offence, and for second or subsequent offence within 5 years under same section, not exceeding £20, and the weights, measures, weighing instruments, &c., liable to be forfeited. 2 J. or 1 Stip.
Fraud, &c.—Where any fraud is wilfully committed in the using of any weight, measure, scale, balance, steel-yard, or weighing machine, the person committing such fraud, and every person party to the fraud shall be liable to—	s. 26. and 52 & 53 Vic. c. 21, s. 3.	Like penalties as last preceding, and the weight, measure, &c. &c., shall be liable to be forfeited. 2 J. or 1 Stip.
Selling.—A person shall not, wilfully or knowingly, make or sell, or cause to be made or sold, any false or unjust 'weight, measure, scale, balance, steel-yard, or weighing machine, and every person who acts in contravention of this section—	41 & 42 Vic. c. 49, s. 27.	Penalty not exceeding £10, or in case of a second offence (within 5 years, against same section), £50; in default, &c., imprisonment by scale. 2 J. or 1 Stip.
Stamping and verification, &c.—Every weight, except where the small size of the weight renders it impracticable, shall have the denomination of such weight stamped on the top or side thereof in legible figures and letters.	s. 28.	

All Acts in force as to Weights and Measures and inspection, &c., shall extend to Factories and Workshops, and all Weighing Machines therein, 41 Vic. c. 16, s. 80.

Offence, or cause of Complaint.	Statute.	Extent of Jurisdiction.
WEIGHTS AND MEASURES—*con.* Every measure of capacity shall have the denomination thereof stamped on the outside of such measure in legible figures and letters. A weight or measure not in conformity with this section shall not be stamped with such stamp of verification under this Act as is hereinafter mentioned.	41 & 42 Vic. c. 49, s. 28.	
Every measure and weight whatsoever used for trade shall be verified and stamped by an inspector with a stamp of verification under this Act.	,,	
Every person who uses or has in his possession for use for trade any measure or weight not stamped as required by this section, shall be liable to—	s. 29.	Fine not exceeding £5, or in case of a second offence (within 5 years, under same section), £10; in default, &c., imprisonment by scale; and shall be liable to forfeit the said measure or weight; and any contract, bargain, sale, or dealing made by such measure or weight shall be void. 2 J. or 1 Stip.
Lead or Pewter Weights.—A weight made of lead or pewter, or of any mixture thereof, shall not be stamped with a stamp of verification, or used for trade unless it be wholly and substantially cased with brass, copper, and iron, and legibly stamped or marked "cased," provided that nothing in this section shall prevent the insertion into a weight of such a plug of lead or pewter as is *bonâ fide* necessary for the purpose of adjusting it, and of affixing thereon the stamp of verification.		

Offence, or cause of Complaint.	Statute.	Extent of Jurisdiction.
WEIGHTS AND MEASURES—*con.* A person guilty of any offence against or disobedience to the provisions of this section shall be liable to—	41 & 42 Vic. c. 49, s. 30.	Penalty not exceeding £5, or in case of a second offence (within 5 years, under same section), £10; in default, &c., imprisonment by scale. 2 J. or 1 Stip.
Of Coin.—Every coin weight, not less in weight than the weight of the lightest coin for the time being current, shall be verified and stamped by the Board of Trade with a mark of verification under this Act, and otherwise shall not be deemed a just weight for determining the weight of gold and silver coin of the realm.	,,	
Every person who uses any weight declared by this section not to be a just weight, shall be liable to—	s. 31.	Penalty not exceeding £50; in default, &c., imprisonment by scale. 2 J. or 1 Stip.
Forging Stamps, &c.—If any person forges or counterfeits any stamp used for the stamping under this Act of any measure or weight, or used before the commencement of this Act for the stamping of any measure or weight under any enactment repealed by this Act, or wilfully increases or diminishes a weight so stamped—	s. 32, and 52 & 53 Vic. c. 21, s. 1.	Penalty not exceeding £50; in default, &c., imprisonment by scale, and all such measures, weights, and weighing instruments shall be forfeited. 2 J. or 1 Stip.
Any person who knowingly uses, sells, utters, disposes of, or exposes for sale any measure or weight with such forged or counterfeit stamp thereon, or a weight so increased or diminished—	,,	Penalty not exceeding £10; in default, &c., imprisonment by scale, and all such measures, weights, and weighing instruments shall be forfeited. 2 J. or 1 Stip.
If any inspector under this Act stamps a weight or measure in contravention of any provision of this Act, or without duly verifying the same by comparison with a local standard, or is guilty of a breach of any duty imposed upon him by Act, or otherwise misconducts himself in execution of his office—	41 & 42 Vic. c. 49, s. 49.	Penalty not exceeding £5 for each offence; in default, &c., imprisonment not exceeding 2 months. 2 J. or 1 Stip.

Offence, or cause of Complaint.	Statute.	Extent of Jurisdiction.
WEIGHTS AND MEASURES—*con.* *Legal Proceedings.* Application of Act to *Ireland*, with modifications. (*a*)	41 & 42 Vic. c. 49, s.¦56. s. 76.	—
Mode of Weighing.—In *Ireland* every article sold by weight shall, if weighed, be weighed in full net standing beam; and for the purposes of every contract, bargain, sale, or dealing, the weight so ascertained shall be deemed the true weight of the article, and no deduction or allowance for tret or beamage, or on any other account, or under any other name whatsoever, the weight of any sack, vessel, or other covering in which such article may be contained alone excepted, shall be claimed or made by any purchaser on any pretext whatever; for contravention— Providing of local standards and substandards.	s. 77. s. 78.	Penalty not exceeding £5; in default, &c., imprisonment, 2 months. 2 J. or 1 Stip. A proceeding for recovery of a penalty under this section shall be begun within 3 months after offence committed.
Coals.—All coals, slack, culm, and cannel, of every description, shall be ¦sold by weight, and not by measure. Every person who sells such by measure and not by weight—	41 & 42 Vic. c. 49. 6th sch. 2nd part.	Penalty not exceeding 40s. for every such sale; in default, &c., imprisonment by scale. 2 J. or 1 Stip.

(*a*) *Application of Act to Ireland.*—This Act shall apply to Ireland, with the following modifications :—(s. 76). "In Ireland every contract, bargain, sale, or dealing, for any quantity of corn, grain, pulses, potatoes, hay, straw, flax, roots, carcasses of beef or mutton, butter, wool, or dead pigs, sold, delivered, or agreed for; or for any quantity of any other commodity sold, delivered, or agreed for by weight (not being a commodity which may by law be sold by the troy ounce or by apothecaries' weight), shall be made or had by one of the following denominations of imperial weight; namely, the ounce avoirdupois; the imperial pound of 16 ounces; the stone of 14 lbs.; the quarter-hundred of 28 lbs.; the half-hundred of 56 lbs.; the hundred of 112 lbs.; the ton of 20 cwt; and not by any local or customary denomination of weight whatsoever, otherwise such contract, bargain, sale, or dealing, shall be void : Provided always, that nothing in the present section shall be deemed to prevent the use in any contract, bargain, sale, or dealing, of the denomination of the quarter, half, or other aliquot part of the ounce, pound, or other denomination aforesaid, or shall be deemed to extend to any contract, bargain, sale, or dealing, relating to standing or growing crops."

Offence, or cause of Complaint.	Statute.	Extent of Jurisdiction.
WEIGHTS AND MEASURES—*con.* Every person or persons, or body corporate, exercising the privilege of appointing a weighmaster, shall supply him with accurate scales, and with an accurate set of copies of the local standards ; in default— (The accuracy of such set of copies shall be certified under the hand of some inspector of weights and measures.)	41 & 42 Vic. c. 49. 6th sch. 2nd part.	Penalty not exceeding £20; in default, &c., imprisonment by scale. 2 J. or 1 Stip.
Shall also, once at least in every five years, cause such copies to be re-adjusted by comparison with some local standards which have been verified by the Board of Trade; in default—	,,	Penalty £5; in default, imprisonment by scale. 2 J. or 1 Stip.
Such set of copies shall, for the purpose of comparison and verification, be considered local standards, and shall be used for no other purpose whatever, and if so used, the person using same shall be liable—	,,	Penalty £5; recoverable as last preceding. 2 J. or 1 Stip.
Recovery of Fines, &c.—As directed by Petty Sessions (Ireland) Act, 14 & 15 Vic. c. 93, and any Acts amending same.	41 & 42 Vic. c. 49, s. 84.	
WEIGHTS AND MEASURES ACT, 1889—	52 & 53 Vic. c. 21.	
Every person who, after expiration of 12 months from commencement of this Act uses, or has in his possession for use for trade, any weighing instrument not stamped as required by Act—	s. 1.	Fine not exceeding £2; 2nd offence not exceeding £5; in default of payment, imprisonment by scale. (*a*) 2 J. or 1 Stip.

(*a*) *Second and subsequent offences.*—In some modern statutes the economy of words is noticeable. So, in the above Act, in naming the penalty for second and subsequent offences, it may appear that the maximum penalty must be imposed. For the correct reading and true meaning, however, the words "not exceeding," applicable to the penalties for the first offence, seem also fairly applicable to that for the subsequent offences; and this view has been adopted. Of course, to impose the maximum penalties in such cases would be safe and legal.

Offence, or cause of Complaint.	Statute.	Extent of Jurisdiction.
WEIGHTS AND MEASURES—*con.*		
WEIGHTS AND MEASURES ACT, 1889.		
(3) The power of making by-laws, conferred by sec. 53 of the principal Act, shall extend to making by-laws to give effect to this section.	52 & 53 Vic. c. 21, s. 1.	
(4) Section 32 of the principal Act shall apply to weighing instruments in like manner as it applies to weights and measures.		
In cases of Fraud.—Where a person is convicted under any section of the principal Act or this Act of a second or subsequent offence, and the Court is of opinion that there was intent to defraud, offender shall be liable, *in addition to or in lieu of any fine,* to—	s. 4.	Imprisonment with or without H. L., for a term not exceeding 2 months. 2 J. or 1 Stip.
Repeal of sections 16 and 46 of 41 & 42 Vic. c. 49, the principal Act.	s. 5.	
Board of Trade shall cause new denominations of standards to be made and verified.	s. 6.	
Local Authority may provide working standards.	s. 7.	
Power of Board of Trade to take fees on comparison and verification of weights, &c., not being standards for Local Authority, and not being coin weights.	s. 8.	
General regulations may be made by Local Authority with approval of Board of Trade with respect to verifying, stamping, inspection, &c.	s. 9.	
Provision with respect to local inquiries by Board of Trade.	s. 10.	

Offence, or cause of Complaint.	Statute.	Extent of Jurisdiction.
WEIGHTS AND MEASURES—*con.*		
WEIGHTS AND MEASURES ACT, 1889.		
Examination as to qualifications of inspectors of weights and measures.	52 & 53 Vic. c. 21, s. 11.	
Inspector not to be a maker, seller, or adjuster of weights, measures, or weighing instruments.	s. 12.	
Fees for verification and stamping by inspectors.		
Publication of Convictions.—Where a person is convicted under the principal Act or this Act, the Court may, if it thinks fit, cause the conviction to be published in such manner as it thinks desirable.	s. 14.	
Gas Standards.—Application of sec. 66 of 41 & 42 Vic. c. 49 to Gas Standards.	s. 15.	
Provision as to copies of local standards in Ireland.	s. 18.	
Amendment of 41 & 42 Vic. c. 49 as to inspectors in Ireland.	s. 19.	
Sale of Coal.—(1) All coal shall be sold by weight only, except where, by the written consent of the purchaser, it is sold by boat-load, or by waggons, or tubs, delivered from the colliery into the works of the purchaser. (2) If any person sells coal, otherwise than is required by this section, he shall be liable to—	s. 20.	Fine not exceeding £5 for each such sale ; in default, &c., imprisonment by scale. 2 J. or 1 Stip.
(1) Weight ticket or a note, as in schedule shall, on delivery of coal, over two hundred weight delivered by any vehicle to purchaser, be delivered or sent, or caused to be delivered or sent, to purchaser or his servant.	s. 21.	

Offence, or cause of Complaint.	Statute.	Extent of Jurisdiction.
WEIGHTS AND MEASURES—*con.*		
WEIGHTS AND MEASURES ACT, 1889.		
(2) If default is made in complying with requirements of this section with respect to the delivery or sending of ticket or note, or if the quantity of coal delivered is less than the quantity expressed in the ticket or note, the seller of the coal shall be liable to—	52 & 53 Vic. c. 21, s. 21.	Fine not exceeding £5; in default, &c., imprisonment by scale. 2 J. or 1 Stip.
(3) If any person attending on any such vehicle, having received any such ticket or note for delivery to the purchaser, refuses or neglects to deliver it as required by this section, or, on being requested so to do, to exhibit it to any inspector of weights and measures, or other officer appointed for the purpose by the Local Authority, he shall be liable to—	s. 21.	Like.
(1) *Tare weight of vehicle where coal is sold in bulk exceeding 2 cwt.*—The seller shall, unless the vehicle is provided by purchaser, cause weight of vehicle and coal to be ascertained by weighing instrument stamped by inspector, and being near to the place from where the coal is brought, cause the tare weight of the vehicle to be marked thereon in such manner as Local Authority may approve.	s. 22.	
(2) In any such case the seller of the coal shall insert, or cause to be inserted in the ticket, the correct weight of the vehicle, or of the vehicle and animal drawing it, where both are weighed together with the load, as well as the correct weight of the coal contained in the vehicle.		

Offence, or cause of Complaint.	Statute.	Extent of Jurisdiction.
WEIGHTS AND MEASURES—_con._		
WEIGHTS AND MEASURES ACT, 1889.		
(3) Any person failing to comply with requirements of this section, he shall be liable to—	52 & 53 Vic. c. 21, s. 22.	Fine not exceeding £5; in default, &c., imprisonment by scale. 2 J. or 1 Stip.
Frauds by drivers of carts.—If any person in charge of any vehicle in which coal is being carried wilfully makes any false statement as to the tare weight of the vehicle, or wilfully does any act by which either the seller or the purchaser of the coal is defrauded, he shall be liable to—	s. 23.	Like.
Deficient weight on small Sales.—If any person, on the sale of coal in any quantity, not exceeding 2 cwt., fraudulently delivers to the purchaser a less quantity of coal than is agreed to be sold, he shall be liable to—	s. 24.	Like.
Weighing Instrument, &c. : (1) Weighing instrument, duly stamped, to be kept in or near place where coal is sold by retail, and seller shall, if required by purchaser or inspector, &c., weigh before sale or delivery. (2) If any person fails to comply with requirements of this section, he shall be liable to—	s. 25.	_First offence._—Fine not exceeding £2; and for any subsequent offence, not exceeding £5; in default, &c., imprisonment by scale. 2 J. or 1 Stip.
Weighing Instruments : (1) Local Authority may erect weighing instruments at convenient places, &c., and appoint persons to attend. (2) If keeper of any such fixed weighing instrument refuses, without reasonable excuse, to weigh, or re-weigh, any vehicle or coal, or so weighs any vehicle or coal as wilfully to defraud either the seller or the purchaser of coal, he shall be liable to—	s. 26.	Fine not exceeding £5; in default, &c., imprisonment by scale. 2 J. or 1 Stip.

Offence, or cause of Complaint.	Statute.	Extent of Jurisdiction.
WEIGHTS AND MEASURES—con.		
WEIGHTS AND MEASURES ACT, 1889.		
Power to require weighment of coal or vehicle.—Seller or purchaser, person in charge of vehicle, or inspector, &c., may require that coal, or vehicle used for carriage of coal in bulk, be weighed, or re-weighed, by stamped weighing instrument—	52 & 53 Vic. c. 21, s. 27.	
Proviso—(a) Seller or carrier not required to carry beyond such prescribed distance, not exceeding half mile :		
(b) Where weighed at instance of purchaser and found to be just, purchaser liable to expense incurred.		
(2) If any person obstructs any weighing, or re-weighing, authorized by this section, he shall be liable to—	,,	Fine not exceeding £5; in default, &c., imprisonment by scale. 2 J. or 1 Stip.
By-Laws.—Local authorities may make by-laws as to sales under 2 cwt., and as to weighing instruments to be carried with vehicle, prescribing distance beyond which coal is not required to be carried to be weighed in pursuance of Act; fixing fees for use of weighing instruments maintained by local authority. By-laws may impose fines not exceeding £5 for breach of by-law. By-laws to be approved by Board of Trade and published.	s. 28.	
Power to weigh coal in shop or vehicle.—Inspector or officer may, at reasonable times enter place of sale, may stop vehicle carrying coal to purchaser, may test weighing instruments in such place or vehicle, and may weigh load, in sack, &c.	s. 29.	

Offence, or cause of Complaint.	Statute.	Extent of Jurisdiction.
WEIGHTS AND MEASURES—*con.*		
WEIGHTS AND MEASURES ACT, 1889.		
If it appears to Court that any load, sack, or less quantity so weighed is of less weight than that represented by seller, the person selling or keeping, or exposing the coal for sale, or the person in charge of the vehicle, as the case may be, shall be liable to—	52 & 53 Vic. c. 21, s. 29.	Fine not exceeding £5; in default, &c., imprisonment by scale. 2 J. or 1 Stip.
Any person who obstructs or hinders any Inspector acting under this section shall be liable to—	,,	Fine not exceeding £5; or in the case of a second or subsequent offence, not exceeding £10; in default, &c., imprisonment by scale. 2 J. or 1 Stip.
Power to make local exemptions on the application of local authority—	s. 30.	
Saving as to Civil remedy. Not to exempt 'from indictment, but no second punishment for same offence. Court may direct proceedings by indictment.	s. 33.	
Definitions of " Weighing Instrument, &c.," " Measuring Instrument, &c.," " Vehicle," " Inspector." Other expressions shall have same meaning as in principal Act.	s. 34.	
Saving as to rights or privileges conferred on Dublin Corporation by charter or statute.	s. 38.	
Title. — Act may be cited as, " Weights and Measures Act, 1889 "; and principal Act and this Act together as, " Weights and Measures Acts, 1878 and 1889."	s. 39.	

Offence, or cause of Complaint.	Statute.	Extent of Jurisdiction.
WEIGHTS AND MEASURES—*con.*		
WEIGHTS AND MEASURES ACT, 1889.		
Commencement of this Act, 1st January, 1890. In Ireland, where Grand Jury is the Local Authority, so much as concerns duties of Local Authority, and the consequences of exercise of duties, shall come into operation 1st May, 1890.	52 & 53 Vic. c. 21, s. 37.	
Act gives schedules of fees for stamping, &c., form of ticket or consignment note, and of other matters.		
Recovery of fines, &c., as in principal Act, under Petty Sessions (Ir.) Act; 14 & 15 Vic. c. 93, and any Acts amending same.	41 & 42 Vic. c. 49, s. 84.	
WEIGHING CATTLE: See "Cattle."		
WHEAT: See "Adulteration."		
"Frauds in provisions."		
WHIPPING (*of Juvenile Offenders*): *Male* between 7 and 12 years, not exceeding six strokes; and not exceeding 14 years, strokes not to exceed twelve—see title "Children," &c.	47 & 48 Vic. c. 19, ss. 4 & 5.	Justice, when sentencing, to name the number of strokes, and with a birch rod.
WIFE DESERTION: See "Poor Law," and "Married Women;" and as to rights and liabilities in connexion with husband, see title "Wife," Indictable Offences Index.		

Offence, or cause of Complaint.	Statute.	Extent of Jurisdiction.
WILD BIRDS:		
WILD BIRDS PROTECTION ACT, 1880.	43 & 44 Vic. c. 35.	
The words "Wild Birds" shall, for all the purposes of this Act, be deemed to mean all Wild Birds.		
Any person who, between the 1st of March and 1st of August, in any year, shall knowingly and wilfully shoot, or attempt to shoot, or shall use any boat for the purpose of shooting, or causing to be shot, any wild bird; or shall use any lime, trap, snare, net, or other instrument for the purpose of taking any wild bird; or shall expose or offer for sale, or shall have in his control or possession, after the 15th of March, any wild bird recently killed or taken—	43 & 44 Vic. c. 35, s. 3.	*On conviction in the case of any wild bird included on the Schedule to Act.*— Shall forfeit and pay for every such bird in respect of which an offence has been committed, a sum not exceeding £1. And in the case of any other wild bird shall, for a *first offence* be reprimanded and discharged on payment of costs. And for *every subsequent offence* forfeit and pay for every such

Wild Birds.—Schedule referred to in Sections:—American quail, auk, avocet, bee eater, bittern, bonxie, colin, coonish chaugh, coulterneb, cuckoo, curlew, diver, dotterel, dun bird, dunlin, eider duck, fern owl, fulmar, gannet, goatsucker, godwit, goldfinch, grebe, greenshank, guillemot, gull (except blacked gull), hoopoe, kingfisher, kittiwake, lapwing, loon, mallard, marrot, merganser, murre, night-hawk, night-jar, nightingale, oriole, owl, ox-bird, oystercatcher, pewit, petrel, phalurope, plover, ploverspage, pochard, puffin, purre, razorbill, redshank, reeve, or ruff, roller, sanderling, sandpiper, scout, sea-lark, sea-mew, sea-parrot, sea-swallow, shearwater, shelldrake, shoveller, skua, smew, snipe, solan-goose, spoonbill, stint, stone curlew, stonehatch, summer snipe, tarrock, teal, tern, thicknee, tystey, whaup, whimbrel, widgeon, wild-duck, willock, woodcock, woodpecker.

It will be observed that the penalty is greater in respect to wild birds in the Schedule than to those which are not.

☞ The first Statute on this subject was passed in 1869; it extended its protection to sea-birds only, and this during the breeding season: this season passed, the birds were thought to be more capable of protecting themselves. Before the passing of the Act vast numbers of these birds were destroyed for the sake of their plumage, which went to embellish and ornament our female population. So great was the havoc made, that some of the most beautiful birds which adorn our coasts had begun to be extremely scarce, and, with respect to some, it was feared the species would have disappeared altogether. This protection, being only partial, the demand soon extended to the plumage of wild birds in general, and so the present Act extends to all, and more particularly to those in the Schedule which are set out in alphabetical order. The present Act alters the close season and effects other amendments.

Offence, or cause of Complaint.	Statute.	Extent of Jurisdiction.
WILD BIRDS—*continued.* WILD BIRDS PROTECTION ACT, 1880. This section shall not apply to the owner or occupier of any land, or to any person authorized by owner or occupier, killing or taking any wild bird, on such land not included in the schedule to Act. (No conviction under sec. 3 of *exposing for sale*, if he satisfies the Court that the killing was lawful, or that the bird was imported from a place to which Act does not extend : 44 & 45 Vic. c. 51.)	43 & 44 Vic. c. 35, s. 3.	wild bird in respect of which an offence is committed, a sum not exceeding 5s., in addition to the costs, unless such person shall prove that the said wild bird was either killed, or taken, or bought, or received during the period in which it could be legally killed or taken, or from some person residing out of the United Kingdom. In default of payment imprisonment by *scale*. 2 J.
Refusing to give name, &c.—Where any person shall be found offending against this Act, it shall be lawful for any person to require the person so offending to give his christian name, surname, and place of abode ; and for refusing to give same, or giving an untrue name or place of abode, he shall be liable, on being convicted of any such offence—	s. 4.	To forfeit and pay, in addition to the penalties imposed by section 3, such sum of money, not exceeding 10s., as to the Justices shall seem meet. In default, &c., imprisonment by *scale*. 2 J.
Proceedings.—In Dublin, in manner provided by the Acts regulating the duties of the district. Elsewhere in Ireland before 2 Justices in manner provided by the Petty Sessions (Ir.) Act, 1851, and any Act amending same. The *scale* of imprisonment proportioned to penalties where the penalty exceeds £5 is provided by Petty Sessions (Ir.) Act, 1851. Where they do not exceed £5, it will be according to Small Penalties Act, 1873 (36 & 37 Vic. c. 82.)	s. 5.	

Offence, or cause of Complaint.	Statute.	Extent of Jurisdiction.
WILD BIRDS—*continued.* **WILD BIRDS PROTECTION ACT, 1880.** *When offence committed on "high seas."*—Offences committed within jurisdiction of the Admiralty, may be dealt with as if committed on any land in United Kingdom, and may be tried, &c., in any part of the United Kingdom where offender is found, as if offence had been committed in that place—and the offence may be stated to have been committed "on the high seas." Offence committed on waters, forming boundary between two counties, &c., may be prosecuted in either.	43 & 44 Vic. c. 35, s. 6.	
Repeals 32 & 33 Vic. c. 17, 35 & 36 Vic. c. 18, 39 & 40 Vic. c. 29.	s. 7.	
Lord Lieutenant, on application of Justices in Quarter Sessions, extend or vary the close time, &c., and order to be published in *Dublin Gazette.* And in like manner to exempt any county or part of county as to *all* or *any* wild birds from operation of Act.	ss. 8 and 9.	
Persons shall not be convicted under sec. 3 of the Act of 1880 above, *of exposing for sale*, if he satisfies the Court that the killing was lawful, or that the bird was killed at, or imported from, a place to which Act does not extend.	44 & 45 Vic. c. 51.	
Sandgrouse Protection Act, 1888.—Any person who shall knowingly with intent, kill, wound, or take any sandgrouse, or shall expose, or offer for sale any sandgrouse killed or taken in the United Kingdom, between 1st Feb., 1889, and before 1st Jan., 1892—	51 & 52 Vic. c. 55.	Penalty not exceeding £1 for every bird so killed, wounded, or taken, or exposed, or offered for sale. In default imprisonment by scale. 1 J.

Offence, or cause of Complaint.	Statute.	Extent of Jurisdiction.
WILFUL INJURIES TO PROPERTY: See "Malicious Injuries."		
WINNOWING CORN ON ROADSIDE.	14 & 15 Vic. c. 92, s. 10: (36 & 37 Vic. c. 82.)	Penalty not exceeding 10s.; in default, &c., imprisonment not exceeding 7 days.　1 J.
WITNESS: Refusing to be sworn, or to answer when sworn, or to produce documents required by summons (without just excuse)— (See section 13 in *Appendix*, and note thereon.) May be ordered expenses in civil cases not exceeding 2s. 6d. May be ordered expenses in cases of larceny tried under Criminal Justice Act, 18 & 19 Vic. c. 126, and of embezzlement under 31 & 32 Vic. c. 116.	14 & 15 Vic. c. 93, s. 13.	May be committed from time to time until he comply, not exceeding 8 clear days at a time; and (in cases of summary jurisdiction) not exceeding 1 month in the whole.　1 J.
WOMEN AND GIRLS: (Protection of) See "Criminal Law Amendment Act, 1885," Indictable Offences Index.		
WOOD: See "Larceny," and "Malicious Injuries."		

Offence, or cause of Complaint.	Statute.	Extent of Jurisdiction.
WOOL: (Frauds as to) See "Weights and Measures."		
WORKMAN: Artificer, workman, journeyman, apprentice, servant, or other person, unlawfully disposing of or retaining possession (without consent of employer) of any goods, work, or materials, &c., committed to his care (the value not exceeding £5). (a)	25 & 26 Vic. c. 50, s. 7.	Compensation, and also a fine not exceeding 40s., or to be imprisoned not exceeding 1 month. 1 J.
For wilfully spoiling goods or work—see "Malicious Injuries."		
See also "Employer and Workmen."		
Act to establish equitable councils of conciliation to adjust differences between Masters and Workmen—see 30 & 31 Vic. c. 105; and for workmen's strikes see "Conspiracy and Protection of Property," Sum. Index.		
WORKSHOP (*Regulation Act*): Regulating time of labour for children, &c.; and as to schooling &c., 41 & 42 Vic. c. 16. See "Factories."		
Exemption from penalties as to Jews working on Sundays, with proviso as to working on Saturday.	34 Vic. c. 19.	—
See also "Factories."		

(a) A similar provision in 14 & 15 Vic. c. 92 (Ireland), is repealed by 24 & 25 Vic. c. 95.

Offence, or cause of Complaint.	Statute.	Extent of Jurisdiction.
WRECK AND SALVAGE: See Merchant Shipping Acts for investigations to be held before Justices.	17 & 18 Vic. c. 104, ss. 433 &c.; and 25 & 26 Vic. c. 63, s. 49.	See title "Merchant Shipping Act."
Having shipwrecked goods in possession.	24 & 25 Vic. c. 96, s. 65.	
See "Larceny."		
YOUNG PERSONS (Offences by): See "Children and Young Persons."		
Industrial Schools— See "Reformatory," Sum. Index.		
Offences on— See "Assault," Sum. Index.		
Offences on girls— See "Protection of Women and Girls," Indictable Offences Index, and "Prevention of Cruelty to Children," Summary Index.		

INDICTABLE OFFENCES.

INTRODUCTORY REMARKS.

THE ministerial duty of the Magistrate in dealing with indictable crimes and offences is defined and unmistakable. He is, first, to be satisfied on a most important point (and to this end it is conceived the following Index may prove useful), that the offence or cause of complaint brought under his notice is one of which he can take cognizance, and in respect to which he is called upon to put the Criminal Law in motion. Then, if it is intended that a warrant shall issue to apprehend the accused, an information on oath and in writing is requisite; or, if he shall think that the ends of justice will be thereby sufficiently answered, it shall be lawful for him, instead of a warrant, to issue a summons in the first instance; but a summons having been served, will not, if he think fit, prevent his issuing a warrant, either before or after the day stated in the summons for appearance (14 & 15 Vic., c. 93, s. 11). It must always be borne in mind that, for the warrant, an information on oath and in writing, setting forth the offence, is indispensable; for the summons, the complaint may be made either on or without oath, and either in writing or not, according as the Justices shall see fit (sec. 10).

The accused being present, the witnesses shall be sworn, their evidence taken down, and the case proceeded with in the consecutive order pointed out in the statute.—14 & 15 Vic., c. 93, s. 14. (a)

The evidence being concluded, if the Justice shall be of opinion that it is not sufficient to put the accused on his trial, he shall order his discharge; but if he be of opinion that such evidence is sufficient to put him on his trial, or if such evidence "raises a strong or probable presumption of guilt," then he shall commit him for trial or admit him to bail (sec. 15). For the offences which are bailable as of right, those in the discretion of the Justice, and those bailable only by order of the Lord Lieutenant, or Chief Secretary, or Queen's Bench—see sec. 16. These last are cases of treason and treasonable felonies.

It will be seen that the duty of the Magistrate between the Crown and the prisoner is to act according to the best of his judgment and opinion on the evidence before him. It is not the case, as is sometimes asserted, that he ought not to put the accused on his trial unless upon evidence sufficiently clear for a petty jury to convict; he ought to send it forward for inquiry if, "in his opinion, the evidence raises a strong or probable

---

(a) This Act is given in the *Appendix*.

For the taking of "dying declarations," which need not be taken in presence of the accused, see the following Index.

presumption of guilt." It is equally erroneous to assert that, no matter how infamous the witnesses or improbable the case may be, the Justice has no discretion, and should form no opinion, but is bound to send it forward for trial. If such were the fact one cannot easily imagine to what purpose an inquiry by a Magistrate becomes necessary. Upon this subject Justice Bayly says :—"I differ from those authorities which say that the Magistrate has no discretion, and that he is not to judge of the probability of the case, and of the credit of the witnesses who are brought before him, to sustain a charge of felony; I think the Magistrate has a right to exercise his own discretion in such cases, and that he is bound to do it; and he ought not, as it seems to me, to commit the party unless he thinks there is a *prima facie* case made out by witnesses whom he may think entitled to a reasonable degree of credit." The Magistrate ought, therefore, to act on the clear conviction of his own understanding.

H. H.

. The Index contains the crimes and offences given in the late Criminal Law Consolidation Acts, those created by other unrepealed statutes, and the offences punishable at Common Law. It was considered that such a summary would be useful. Although the *extent of punishment* in these cases forms no part of the duty of a Justice in Petty Sessions, it is added for the sake of uniformity.

INDICTABLE OFFENCES—WHERE TRIABLE.

In determining to what Court Justices should return cases for trial, the following are offences which *Recorders'* or *Quarter Sessions Courts* are in general restrained from trying, and should, therefore, be returned to Assizes.—See *Taylor's Evidence*, vol. 2.

Treason, murder; capital felony, or any felony which, when committed by a person not previously convicted of felony, is punishable by penal servitude for life; or any of the following offences :—

1. Misprison of treason.
2. Offences against the Queen's title, prerogative, person, or Government, or against either House of Parliament.
3. Offences subject to the penalties of præmunire.
4. Blasphemy, and offences against religion.
5. Administering or taking unlawful oath.
6. Perjury and subornation of perjury.
7. Making, or suborning any other person to make a false oath, affirmation, or declaration, punishable as perjury or as a misdemeanour.
8. Forgery.
9. Unlawful and malicious setting fire to crops of corn, &c., or any part of a wood, coppice, or plantation of trees, or to any heath, gorse, furze, or fern.
10. Bigamy, and offences against the laws relating to marriage.
11. Abduction of women and girls.

12. Endeavouring to conceal the birth of a child by secret disposal of the dead body.

13. Offences against the laws relating to bankrupts and insolvents.

14. Composing, printing, or publishing blasphemous, seditious, or defamatory libels.

15. Bribery.

16. Unlawful combinations and conspiracies, or combination to commit any offence which such Justice or Recorder respectively have or has jurisdiction to try when committed by one person. (a)

17. Stealing, or fraudulently taking or injuring or destroying records or documents belonging to any Court of Law or Equity, or relating to any proceedings therein.

18. Stealing, or fraudulently destroying or concealing wills or testamentary papers, or any document or written instrument, being or containing evidence of title to any real estate or interest in lands, tenements, or hereditaments.

19. Any misdemeanour against the sections of the Larceny Act of 1861, which relates to frauds committed by bankers, factors, trustees, directors, attorneys, or other agents.

WHAT OFFENCES ARE INDICTABLE.

All offences of a *public* nature, *i. e.* such acts or attempts as tend to the prejudice of the community in general, are indictable. And, therefore, not only all actual breaches of the peace, as riots, affrays, assaults, &c., but also every criminal irregularity that tend to disturb the good order of government, or to endanger or annoy the tranquillity, welfare, or convenience of the public, is punishable by indictment—2 *Haw.*, c. 25, s. 4; 3 *M. S. Sum.*, 28; *et per* Lawrence, J., *R.* v. *Higgins*, 2 *East.*, 21.

The following, therefore, are indictable misdemeanours, viz. :—

1. All open offences against God and religion, or against public decency, that tend to corrupt the morals of the people. Of this sort are blasphemous books, or any profane or obscene publications, bawdy-houses, &c.—*Sir C. Sedley's Case*, 1 *Sid.* 168. *R.* v. *Crunden*, 2 *Camph.*, 89; 1 *Russ.*, 64.

2. All crimes that are *mala in se*, and of evil example.

3. All practices that tend to endanger the Constitution, as bribery at elections, seditious pamphlets, &c.

4. All contempts of the King and his Courts.

5. All attempts to corrupt, mislead, or pervert public justice, or to make it a handle of fraud or oppression.;

6. All acts and designs against the common occasions, necessities, and general commerce of the public, such as unlawful combinations, monopolies, forestalling, engrossing, and regrating, adulteration of victuals, and all public cheats, &c. &c.

In this class are also included the several kinds of common nuisances, both positive and negative, *i. e.* either positive acts that annoy the public,

(a) But assaults in pursuance of unlawful combination to *raise wages or respecting trade*, &c., are not unfrequently tried at Quarter Sessions; nevertheless, if of an aggravated nature, and that many are concerned, the Assizes may be the more proper tribunal, from the larger range of jurors and for other reasons.

or the neglect of some duty which the public have a right to require from the defendant, and by the omission of which a general inconvenience arises.

It is an indictable offence to incite and solicit a servant to steal his master's goods, though the servant do not steal the goods, and no other act be done except the soliciting and inciting—*R. v. Higgins*, 2 *East.*, 5. And such offence is indictable at the Quarter Sessions as falling in with the class of offences which, being violations of the law of the land, have a tendency, as it is said, to a breach of the peace, and are therefore cognizable by that jurisdiction. In the case referred to, Lord Kenyon, in delivering his opinion, said—"Can it be a question in a country professing to have laws subservient to justice and morality whether this be an offence? It would be a slander upon the law to suppose that an offence of such magnitude is not indictable." Lawrence, J., said—"All offences of a public nature, that is, all such acts or attempts as tend to the prejudice of the community, are indictable. Then the question is, whether an attempt to incite another to steal is not prejudicial to the community? of which there can be no doubt. The whole argument for the defendant turns upon a fallacy in assuming that no act is charged to have been done by him: for a solicitation is an act. It is an endeavour to attempt to commit a crime." The doctrine laid down by Lord Mansfield in *R. v. Scofield*, Cald. 397, 403, comprises all the principles of the former decisions that so long as an act rests in bare intention it is not punishable by our laws, but immediately when an act is done, the law judges not only of the act done, but of the motive with which it is done; and if accompanied with an unlawful and malicious intent, though the act itself would otherwise have been innocent, the intent being criminal, the act becomes criminal and punishable.

INDEX

TO

CRIMES AND OFFENCES TRIABLE BY INDICTMENT,

UNDER STATUTE AND AT COMMON LAW.

———◦◦———

☞ In this Analysis, under the head "Punishment," regard is had to the Provisions of the Penal Servitude Act, 27 & 28 Vic., c. 47.

Offence.	Statute.	Punishment.
Abandoning or exposing any child under the age of two years, whereby life may be endangered, &c.	24 & 25 Vic. c. 100, s. 27. (27 & 28 Vic. c. 47.)	Misdemeanour; penal servitude, 5 years (not less than 7 if previously convicted of felony); or imprisonment not exceeding 2 years, with or without H. L.
Abduction of a woman against her will, with intent to marry or carnally know her, or to cause her to be married or carnally known, she having any interest, present or future, &c., in real or personal estate; fraudulently alluring, taking away, or detaining such woman, being under 21, out of possession or against the will of her parents or guardian, with intent to marry or carnally know her, or cause her to be, &c.	24 & 25 Vic. c. 100, s. 53. (27 & 28 Vic. c. 47.)	Felony; penal servitude not exceeding 14 years, nor less than 5 years (not less than 7 if previously convicted of felony; or imprisonment not exceeding 2 years, with or without H. L.
Forcible Abduction of any woman with intent to marry her or cause her to be married, &c.	s. 54.	Like.
Taking any girl under sixteen years of age out of possession, or against will of parents or guardian. And see title, "Criminal Law Amendment Act, 1865," as to protection of women and girls: 48 & 49 Vic. c. 69.	s. 55.	Misdemeanour; imprisonment not exceeding 2 years, with or without H. L.

Abettors in Larceny—		
Punishable as principals in summary convictions.	24 & 25 Vic. c. 100, s. 99.	See also Summary Juris diction Index.
Like in malicious injuries, . .	24 & 25 Vic. c. 97, s. 63.	—
In misdemeanours, . . .	24 & 25 Vic. c. 94, s. 8.	—
Abortion—		
Administering drugs, or using instruments to procure it.	24 & 25 Vic. c. 100, s. 58. (27 & 28 Vic. c. 47.)	Felony; penal servitud for life, or not less tha 5 years (not less than if previously convicte of felony); or imprison ment not exceeding years, with or withou H. L., and solitary con finement.
Supplying or procuring drugs for the purpose.	24 & 25 Vic. c. 100, s. 59. (27 & 28 Vic. c. 47.)	Misdemeanour; pen servitude, 5 years (no less than 7 if previousl; convicted of felony; o imprisonment not ex

Offence.	Statute.	Punishment.
Accomplice. (a)		
Accounts— Falsification of—see "Larceny."		
Accusing— Knowingly sending, or causing to be received, letter threatening to accuse of crime, with intent to extort.	24 & 25 Vic. c. 96, s. 46. (27 & 28 Vic. c. 47.)	Felony ; penal servitude for life, or not less than 5 years (not less than 7 if previously convicted of felony) ; or imprisonment not exceeding 2 years, with or without H. L., and solitary confinement ; and male under 16 years may be whipped.
Accusing or threatening to accuse of crime, with intent to extort.	s. 47.	Like.
Admiralty— Offences within the jurisdiction of, *against the person*, how triable.	24 & 25 Vic. c. 100, s. 68.	
Under the Larceny Act, . . .	24 & 25 Vic. c. 96, s. 115.	
Under the Malicious Injuries Act, .	24 & 25 Vic. c. 97, s. 72.	
In forgeries, ...	24 & 25 Vic. c. 98, s. 50.	
Offences as to the coin, . .	24 & 25 Vic. c. 99, s. 36.	
As to accessories to any felony, .	24 & 25 Vic. c. 94, s. 9.	
Under Foreign Enlistment Act, 1870,	33 & 34 Vic. c. 90.	

(a) *Accomplice* in a felony, although it be intended to call him as a witness, ought not to be discharged or admitted to bail ; it is the duty of the Magistrate to commit him. If on no other evidence, his own will warrant this course. The accomplice is usually committed to a place of confinement separate from the other prisoners, and it is provided by the Prison Act, 7 Geo. iv. c. 74, s. 6, that places of confinement shall be set apart for witnesses intended to be examined on behalf of the Crown. The corroboration of an accomplice should be in a part of his testimony

Offence.	Statute.	Punishment.
Adulterations (of food and drugs), and that are indictable as misdemeanours—see "Adulteration," Summary Index.		
Affray— Two or more persons fighting in a public place, to the terror of the people. See "Fighting," and "Assault," Summary Index.	CommonLaw.	Misdemeanour; punishable by fine or imprisonment, or both.
Aggravated Assault upon woman or boys, and see also title "Criminal Law Amendment Act, 1885," and "Prevention of Cruelty to Children," Summary Index.	24 & 25 Vic. c. 100, s. 43.	See title "Assault," in Summary Jurisdiction Index.
Agricultural Machines— Destroying or damaging—see "Malicious Injuries."		
Aiding — See "Abettors."		
Aliens. (a)		

affecting the prisoner. The untrue denial by a prisoner of his acquaintance with an approver will be allowed to go to the jury as evidence to corroborate approver.— *R. v. Farrelly and Others; Trim Lent Assizes,* 1832.

It is now taken for granted in the administration of justice, and sanctioned by the usage of the Judicial Bench, that the testimony of an accomplice is to be regarded with distrust, unless it be materially confirmed by other evidence. There is no rigid presumption of the common law against such testimony; yet experience has shown that it is little worthy of credit, and on this experience the usage is founded.—*Taylor on Evidence.*

(a) *Aliens.*—By the Naturalization Act, 1870 (33 Vic., c. 14, s. 5), alien shall not be entitled to be tried by a jury *de medietate linguæ,* but shall be triable as if he were a natural-born subject.

As to how far aliens are amenable to our laws for offences on land or sea in the United Kingdom, or within the jurisdiction of the Admiralty—see notes on section 10 of Petty Sessions Act, *Appendix.*

Offence.	Statute.	Punishment.
Allegiance— Malicious endeavouring to seduce soldiers or seamen from their allegiance.	57 Geo. iii. c. 7. 37 Geo. iii. c. 40, s. 1.	Felony; and see also Summary Index; titles "Army," "Navy," and "Militia."
Animals— Stealing—see "Larceny."	—	And see also the Summary Index; title, "Larceny."
Apprehension— Of offenders against Larceny Act, .	24 & 25 Vic. c. 96, s. 103.	—
Of offenders against the Malicious Injuries Act.	24 & 25 Vic. c. 97, ss. 57, 61.	
For assaults and offences against the person.	24 & 25 Vic. c. 100, s. 66.	
For offences relating to the coin, .	24 & 25 Vic. c. 99, s. 31.	—
Wounding, shooting, or attempting to shoot, with intent to prevent lawful apprehension of any person.	24 & 25 Vic. c. 100, s. 18. (27 & 28 Vic. c. 47.)	Felony; penal servitude for life; or not less than 5 years (not less than 7 if previously convicted of felony); or imprisonment not exceeding 2 years, with or without H. L., and solitary confinement.
Of persons loitering at night, and suspected of felony.	24 & 25 Vic. c. 96, s. 104.	—
Apprentices— Persons liable [wilfully refusing or neglecting to provide them with proper food, clothing, lodging, or maliciously doing them bodily harm. See also "Summary Index."	24 & 25 Vic. c. 100, s. 26. (27 & 28 Vic. c. 47.)	Misdemeanour; penal servitude, 5 years (not less than 7 if previously convicted of felony); or imprisonment not exceeding 2 years, with or without H. L.
Approver— See "Accomplice."		

Offence.	Statute.	Punishment.
Arms— Being armed with intent to break and enter a house, &c., at night; or, without lawful excuse, found by night, having in possession any implement of housebreaking, face blackened, or disguised, &c. What shall be deemed to be loaded arms, within meaning of Act of 23 & 25 Vic. c. 100, s. 19.	24 & 25 Vic. c. 96, s. 58. (27 & 28 Vic. c. 47.)	Penal servitude, 5 years (not less than 7 if previously convicted of felony); or imprisonment not exceeding 2 years, with or without H. L.
Drilling.—Attending meeting to train or drill others to use of arms, or the practice of military exercise, &c.	60 Geo. iii. and 1 Geo. iv. c. 1.	Misdemeanour; penal servitude not exceeding 7 years (not less than 7 if previously convicted of felony); or imprisonment not exceeding 2 years.
Attending to be trained or drilled, &c. (a) See also "Peace Preservation Act," Summary Index; and see "Whiteboy Acts," Indictable Offences.	,,	Fine, and imprisonment not exceeding 2 years.

(a) *Illegal Drilling, &c.*—60 Geo. iii., and 1 Geo. iv. c. 1, s. 1 : "All meetings and assemblies of persons for the purpose of training or drilling themselves, or of being trained or drilled to the use of arms, or for the purpose of practising military exercise, movements, or evolutions, without any lawful authority from His Majesty, or the Lord Lieutenant, or 2 Justices of the Peace of any county or riding, or of any stewartry by commission or otherwise for so doing, shall be and the same are hereby prohibited as dangerous to the peace, &c. And every person who shall be present at or attend any such meeting or assembly for the purpose of training and drilling any other person or persons to the use of arms, or the practice of military exercise, movements, or evolutions, or who shall aid or assist therein, being legally convicted thereof, shall be liable to be transported for any term not exceeding 7 years, or imprisonment, &c., at the discretion of Court, not exceeding 2 years. And every person who shall attend or be present at any such meeting or assembly as aforesaid for the purpose of being, or who shall at any such meeting or assembly be trained or drilled to the use of arms, or the practice of military exercise, movements, or evolutions, being legally convicted, &c., fine and imprisonment not exceeding 2 years."

"Sec. 2. Persons assembled may be dispersed or apprehended, or committed for trial unless they find bail."

"Sec. 4. Offenders may be prosecuted as if Act not passed. Prosecutions to be within 6 months."

These offences of illegal drilling, &c., may, in proclaimed districts, be summarily tried before Justices under "Peace Preservation Act"—see title "Peace Preservation," Summary Index.

Offence.	Statute.	Punishment.
Arrest— Under civil process, of a clergyman, when performing, going to, or returning from divine service.	24 & 25 Vic. c. 100, s. 36.	Misdemeanour; imprisonment not exceeding 2 years' H. L.
Arson— See "Malicious Injuries."		
Art— Works of, destroying, &c.—See "Malicious Injuries."		
Assaults— See "Offences against the Person;" and see also title, "Assault," in Summary Index, and for offences on women, girls, &c., see title "Criminal Law Amendment Act, 1885," and on children—see "Prevention of Cruelty to Children," Summary Index.		
Assembly, Unlawful— Any person joining in or giving countenance and support to an unlawful assembly.	Common Law.	Misdemeanour; punishable by fine or imprisonment, or both.
See proclamation under "Riot Act," Summary Index; and see "Riot," hereinafter.		
Any person who shall take part in any riot or unlawful assembly—	50 & 51 Vic. c. 20, s. 2, sub.-s. (3)(a)	Summary Jurisdiction. Imprisonment not exceeding 6 months, with or without H. L. 2 R. M.
Assisting— See "Abettors."		

Offence.	Statute.	Punishment.
Attempt—(a)		
Attempt to choke, suffocate, or strangle any person, so as to render any person insensible or incapable of resistance, with intent thereby to commit, or assist in committing, any indictable offence.	24 & 25 Vic. c. 100, s. 21. (27 & 28 Vic. c. 47.)	Felony; penal servitude for life, or not less than 5 years (not less than 7 if previously convicted of felony); or imprisonment not exceeding 2 years, with or without H. L.
Attempt to do bodily harm, by impeding a person endeavouring to save himself from shipwreck, or impeding any person assisting to save, &c.	24 & 25 Vic. c. 100, s. 17.	Felony; penal servitude for life, or not less than 5 years (not less than 7 if previously convicted of felony); or imprisonment not exceeding 2 years, with or without H. L., and solitary confinement.
Attempt to poison, or by shooting or attempting to shoot, or attempting to drown, suffocate, or strangle, with intent to commit murder, shall, whether bodily injury be effected or not—	s. 14.	Felony; punishment as last preceding.
By poison, or by any means wounding with intent to murder.	s. 11.	Felony; like punishment.
Attempt to have carnal knowledge of a girl under 13, and between 13 years and 16 years. And see "Criminal Law Amendment Act, 1885."	48 & 49 Vic. c. 69, s. 4.	Imprisonment not exceeding 2 years, with or without H. L.
Attempting to set fire to buildings or goods therein, where the offence would (if set fire to) amount to felony.	24 & 25 Vic. c. 97. (27 & 28 Vic. c. 47.)	Penal servitude not exceeding 14 years, and not less than 5 years (not less than 7 if previously convicted of felony); or imprisonment not exceeding 2 years, with or without H. L., and with or without solitary confinement; male under 16 may be whipped.
Attempting to set fire to crops, plantations, furze, heath, turf, &c.; stacks of corn, hay, &c. See "Malicious Injuries."		

(a) *Attempt.*—An attempt can only be when there is such a beginning as if uninterrupted would end in the completion of the act—*Reg.* v. *Collins, L. & C.,* 471. At Common Law every attempt to commit a felony or misdemeanour is in itself a misdemeanour.

Offence.	Statute.	Punishment.
Attorney-General— Where authority required before certain indictments can be preferred, see "Vexatious Indictments."		
Bail— For indictable offences which are *not* bailable, and where it is in the *discretion* of Justices, and where as of right—see Petty Sessions Act.	14 & 15 Vic. c. 93, s. 15.	This Act is given in the *Appendix*.
Bailee— Of any chattel, money, or security, fraudulently converting same to his own use, or to the use of any person other than owner, although he shall not break bulk, &c—	24 & 25 Vic. c. 96, s. 3.	Shall be guilty of larceny. Not to apply to any offence punishable summarily.
Bankers and Bank-notes :— See "Forgery" and "Embezzlement."		
Bankrupt (*Act*)— Member of a joint stock company which shall be adjudged bankrupt, who shall after, and with the knowledge of an act of bankruptcy within the meaning of the Act, or in contemplation of bankruptcy by such company, destroy, falsify, &c., books or papers, &c.	20 & 21 Vic. c. 60, s. 379.	Misdemeanour; imprisonment not exceeding 2 years, with or without H. L.
Bankrupt or insolvent, within three months preceding bankruptcy or insolvency, obtaining goods on credit with intent to defraud, or with such intent disposing of his goods, otherwise than by *bonâ fide* sales in ordinary way of trade.	s. 380.	Like.
Within three months preceding filing of petition, wilfully and actually	s. 381.	Like.

As to the duty of Justices when the bankrupt becomes of unsound mind, see **20 & 21** Vic. c. 69, s. 239.

2 H

Offence.	Statute.	Punishment.
Bankrupt (*Act*)—*continued.* committing any fraud on creditors, or doing any act, or making any false representation, knowing it to be false with intent to defraud.		
Fraudulent Debtors.—Any person adjudged bankrupt, and any person who shall have presented a petition for an arrangement with his creditors, in pursuance of "The Irish Bankrupt and Insolvent Act, 1857," as amended by "The Bankruptcy (Ireland) Amendment Act, 1872," shall in each of the cases following be deemed guilty of a misdemeanour, and on conviction thereof— (Here follows a catalogue of offences, sixteen in number, as to frauds, concealment of property, books, false statements, &c., for which see Act.)	35 & 36 Vic. c. 57, s. 11.	Imprisonment not exceeding 2 years, with or without H. L.
Absconding.—Any person adjudged bankrupt, or who has presented a petition for arrangement after adjudication or presentation respectively, or within four months before such adjudication or presentation, quits Ireland, and takes with him, or attempts or prepares to do so, any part of his property, to the amount of £20 or upwards, which ought by law to be divided amongst his creditors, unless the jury is satisfied that he had no intent to defraud.	s. 12.	elony; imprisonment not exceeding 2 years, with or without H. L.
Fraudulently obtaining Credit.— Any person who— (1) If, in incurring any debt or liability, he has obtained credit under false pretences, or by means of any other fraud— (2) If he has, with intent to defraud his creditors, or any of them, made or caused to be made any gift, delivery, or transfer of any charge on his property—	s. 13.	Misdemeanour; imprisonment not exceeding 1 year, with or without H. L.

Offence.	Statute.	Punishment.
Bankrupt (*Act*)—*continued.*		
(3) If he has, with intent to defraud his creditors, concealed or removed any part of his property since or within two months before the date of any unsatisfied judgment or order for payment of money obtained against him—	35 & 36 Vic. c. 57, s. 13.	Misdemeanour; imprisonment not exceeding 1 year, with or without H. L.
(4) If he has wilfully concealed any real or personal estate of any bankrupt or arranging creditor, and has not, within 42 days after the filing of the petition of bankruptcy or for arrangement, discovered such estate to the Court, or to the assignees, or the trustees or trustee—		
False Claim.—If creditor wilfully and with intent to defraud makes any false claim, or any proof, declaration, or statement of account which is untrue in any material particular.	s. 14.	Like.
As to debtor's continued liability for debts incurred by fraud, and where creditor has not arranged, &c.	s. 15.	—
Bankruptcy Court may order prosecution on report of assignee or trustee.	s. 16.	
Where Court orders prosecution the expense shall be allowed as in prosecutions for felony.	s. 17.	
Act to prevent Vexatious Indictments (22 & 23 Vic. c. 17), as to certain misdemeanours applicable to this Act; and Justices shall take into consideration any evidence adduced tending to show that the act charged was not committed with a guilty intent.	s. 18.	—
As to the disqualification of Mayors, Aldermen, Town Councillors, and Justices, adjudged bankrupt or compounding.	ss. 20 and 21.	
As to Justices.—"If any person being assigned by Her Majesty's Commission to act as a Justice of	s. 21.	•—

Offence.	Statute.	Punishment.
Bankrupt (*Act*)—*continued.* the Peace is adjudged bankrupt, or makes any arrangement or composition with his creditors under the Irish Bankrupt and Insolvent Act, 1857, or the Bankruptcy (Ireland) Amendment Act, 1872, he shall be and remain incapable of acting as a Justice of the Peace, until he has been newly assigned by Her Majesty in that behalf."	35 & 36 Vic. c. 57, s. 21.	
Mayors as ex-officio Justices are included in the provision, of section 20, with members of Town Councils, &c.		
Saving prosecutions under other Acts or at Common Law, punishments not to be cumulative.	s. 22.	
Applies— 20 & 21 Vic. c. 60, ⎫ Bankruptcy 35 & 36 Vic. c. 58, ⎭ (Ireland). 16 & 17 Vic. c. 113, Common Law Procedure (Ireland). 14 & 15 Vic. c. 57, ⎫ Civil Bill Courts 27 & 28 Vic. c. 99, ⎭ (Ireland). 30 & 31 Vic. c. 44, Court of Chancery (Ireland). 23 & 24 Vic. c. 17, Vexatious Indictments. Secs. 88 and 89, 3 & 4 Vic. c. 108, Municipal Corporations (Ireland).		
Repeals sec. 1 of 11 & 12 Vic. c. 28, Imprisonment for Debt (Ireland).		

In "The Debtors Act (Ireland), 1872," section 5, there are, amongst others, the following exceptions:—"With the exceptions hereinafter mentioned, no person shall, after the commencement of this Act, be arrested or imprisoned for making default in payment of a debt contracted after the passing of this Act." There shall be excepted from the operation of the above enactment:—

    1. Default in payment of a penalty, or sum in the nature of a penalty, other than a penalty in respect of any contract.

    2. Default in payment of any sum recoverable summarily before a Justice or Justices of the Peace.

Provided, first, that no person shall be imprisoned in any case excepted from the

Offence.	Statute.	Punishment.
Barking Trees— See "Malicious Injuries."		
Barrator— Common barrator, who excites or maintains suits, &c., or who breeds disputes between neighbours, or spreads false reports.	Common Law.	Misdemeanour; punishable by fine and imprisonment; or may be compelled by Justices to find sureties for good behaviour, as persons of "evil fame." See "Sureties to keep the Peace," Summary Index.
Battery— See "Assault."		
Bawdy House— Persons keeping a common bawdy house, or a disorderly house. (a) And for summary power to suppress, see "Brothels," Sum. Index; and title, "Criminal Law Amendment Act, 1885."	Common Law. 7 Geo. iv. c. 9, s. 1.	Misdemeanour; indictable as a nuisance; fine, imprisonment, or both, and H. L.

operation of this section for a longer period than one year; and, secondly, that nothing in this section shall alter the effect of any judgment, or order of any Court for payment of money, except as regards the arrest and imprisonment of the person making default in having such money.

(a) *Bawdy House.*—A wife may be indicted together with her husband and punished with him for keeping a common bawdy house, for this is an offence as to the government of the house, in which the wife has a principal share; and also such an offence as may generally be presumed to be managed by the intrigues of her sex.—1 *Hawk.*, c. 1, s. 12; 1 *Russ.*, 16. Justices may bind by sureties to the good behaviour, maintainers of houses commonly suspected to be houses of common bawdry; also common whoremongers and common whores; for bawdry is an offence temporal as well as spiritual, and is against the peace of the land—*Dalt. Cases;* and see *Burns' Justice.*

It may be added (though the rule is not enforced) that, under the same authority, "such as are greatly defamed for resorting to houses suspected to maintain adultery or incontinency, may also be held to surety for the good behaviour;" or, in the language of the time, their "good abearing."

As to conditions on which indictment shall be preferred, see title "Vexatious Indictments."

Offence.	Statute.	Punishment.
Beast— Stealing—see " Larceny." Injuring—see "Malicious Injuries."		
Bestiality— See " Unnatural Offences."		
Bigamy— Whosoever, being married, shall marry any other person during the life of the former husband or wife, whether the second marriage shall have taken place in Ireland, or England, or elsewhere— Not to extend to a second marriage contracted out of England and Ireland, or by other than a subject, of Her Majesty; or where husband or wife continually absent for seven years, and not known to be living within that time; or where divorced, &c.	24 & 25 Vic. c. 100, s. 57. (27 & 28 Vic. c. 47.)	Felony; penal servitude not exceeding 7 years, nor less than 5 years (not less than 7 if previously convicted of felony); or imprisonment not exceeding 2 years, with or without H. L. Offender may be dealt with where apprehended.
Birds— See " Larceny," and "Malicious Injuries." Protection of, &c.— See " Wild Birds," Sum. Index.		
Birth— See " Concealing Birth." Forgery, registry of—see "Forgery."		

Offence.	Statute.	Punishment.
Blasphemy (a)— Blasphemous publications, or libels against religion. See "Libels." And see "Blasphemy," in Summary Index.	Common Law.	Misdemeanour; fine and imprisonment.
Boat— Stealing from—see "Larceny." And stealing or taking boat—see Summary Index; title "Boat."		
Bodily Harm— See "Murder"; "Assault"; "Attempt"; "Offence against the Person."		
Bond— Forging—see "Forgery."		
Boy— Under 14 years of age cannot be convicted of a rape. Or of carnally knowing a girl under ten years. Or of an unnatural offence. See also Summary Index—"Juvenile Offenders"; and see title, "Criminal Law Amendment Act, 1885"; 48 & 49 Vic. c. 69.	— — —	R. v. Phillips, 8 Car. and P., 736.

(a) *Blasphemy.*—All blasphemies against God, as denying His being or Providence, and all contumelious reproaches of Jesus Christ; all profane scoffing at the Holy Scriptures, or exposing any part of them to contempt or ridicule; impostures in religion, as falsely pretending to extraordinary commissions from God, and terrifying or abusing the people with false denunciations of judgments, and all open lewdness, grossly scandalous, are punishable by fine and imprisonment.—1 *Hawk.*, c. 5, s. 6; 1 *East, P.*, c. 3.

The statute 9 & 10 Wm. iii., c. 32, has not altered the Common Law as to the offence of blasphemy, but only gives a cumulative punishment. It is, therefore, still an offence at the Common Law to publish a blasphemous libel; and cases cited, 1 *Russ*, 218; *R. v. Richard Carlisle, M.* 60, *G.* 3; 3 *B. & A.* 161; and see *Gab. Cr. Law*, 72.

Offence.	Statute.	Punishment.
Breaking and Entering House, &c. See "Burglary," "Larceny," and "Malicious Injuries."		
Bridge— Damaging—see "Malicious Injuries."		
Broker— See "Frauds by Agents."	24 & 25 Vic. c. 96, s. 75.	—
Brothel— See "Bawdy House."	Common Law.	Keeper may be indicted as for a nuisance.
Buggery— See "Unnatural Offences."	24 & 25 Vic. c. 100, s. 61.	—
Buildings— See "Burglary," and "Malicious Injuries."		
Buoys— See "Malicious Injuries."		
Burglary—(a) Whosoever shall enter the dwelling-house of another with intent to commit any felony therein, or being in such dwelling-house shall commit any felony therein, and shall, in either case, break out of said dwelling-house in the night, shall be deemed guilty of burglary.	24 & 25 Vic. c. 96, s. 51. (27 & 28 Vic. c. 47.)	Penal servitude for life, or not less than 5 years (not less than 7 if previously convicted of felony); or imprisonment not exceeding 2 years, with or without H. L., and solitary confinement.

(a) Burglary is the breaking and entering of the dwelling-house of another in the night-time with intent to commit a felony therein. Any actual or constructive breaking in the night-time is sufficient. If any of the family sleep in the house, it will be considered a dwelling-house. (*Night* shall be deemed to commence at 9 o'clock, P.M., and to conclude at 6 o'clock, A.M.—24 & 25 Vic., c. 96, s. 1.)

A person lawfully in a house as a lodger, &c., unbolting a door, and stealing

Offence.	Statute.	Punishment.
Burial— Person executed for murder shall be buried within the prison in which last ‚confined; the sentence shall so direct. See also "Dead Bodies."	24 & 25 Vic. c. 96, s. 3.	—
Burning— See "Malicious Injuries."		
Calf— See "Larceny."		
Canals— See "Malicious Injuries."		
Cancelling (*written Instruments*)— See "Larceny."		
Carnal Knowledge— Unlawfully and carnally knowing and abusing any girl under 10.	24 & 25 Vic. c. 96, s. 50. (27 & 28 Vic. c. 47.)	Felony; penal servitude for life, or not less than 5 years (not less than 7 if previously convicted of felony); or imprisonment not exceeding 2 years, with or without H. L.
Above 10 and under 12 years.	s. 51.	Penal servitude, 5 years; or imprisonment as above.
Indecent assault upon, . . . And see title "Criminal Law Amendment Act, 1885."	s. 52.	Imprisonment not exceeding 2 years, with or without H. L.

from the house in the night may be convicted of burglary—*R.* v. *Wheeldon*, 8 *C. & P.*, 747. Where by means of fraud an entrance is effected in the night-time, with a felonious intent, it is burglary—*R.* v. *Hawkins*, 2 *East. P. C.*, 585. A breaking may be effected by conspiring with persons within the house, by whose means those without effect an entrance—1 *Hale, P. C.*, 553. Entering by a chimney, though the room be not entered, is held to be a breaking—*R.* v. *Brice*, *Russ. & Ry.*, 451. Any part of the body, hand, or foot within the house will be sufficient proof of entry—*Foster*, 108; and see "*Roscoe's Digest*."

Offence.	Statute.	Punishment.
Cattle— Unlawfully and maliciously killing, maiming, &c. See also " Larceny."	24 & 25 Vic. c. 97, s. 40. (27 & 28 Vic. c. 47.)	Felony; penal servitude not exceeding 14 nor less than 5 years (not less than 7 if previously convicted of felony); or imprisonment not exceeding 2 years, with or without H. L., and solitary confinement.
Certificate— Of marriage—see " Forgery." Of dismissal in assaults—see "Assaults," Summary Index.		
Challenge (*to Fight*)— Sending, or provoking another to send, challenge to fight. (a) For " Prize Fighting," see title. See " Duel."	Common Law.	Misdemeanour; punishable by fine and imprisonment.
Champerty— See " Maintenance."		
Chapel or Church— See " Larceny," " Malicious Injuries," and " Disturbing Divine Worship."		
Cheating— At play, or by any other deceitful and illegal practice which may affect the public.	Common Law.	Punishable by fine and imprisonment.

(a) *Challenging*, or provoking another to send a challenge to duel, or even an endeavour to provoke another to commit the offence of sending a challenge to fight, is held to be a misdemeanour.—*R.* v. *Phillips*, 6 *East.*, 464, 471 ; 1 *Russ.*, 276 ; 5 *E.*, 581 ; *Arch.*, 570. The offence is more generally proceeded with by information exhibited before the Court of Queen's Bench.

Offence.	Statute.	Punishment.
Child—		
Abandoning or exposing under age of two years, whereby life may be endangered or permanently injured.	24 & 25 Vic. c. 100, s. 27. (27 & 28 Vic. c. 47.)	Penal servitude, 5 years (not less than 7 if previously convicted of felony); or imprisonment not exceeding 2 years, with or without H. L.
Aggravated assaults upon, . .	s. 43.	See "Assault," Summary Index.
Stealing.—By force or fraud taking, enticing, or detaining child under 14 from parents or guardian, or with intent to steal any article from the person of such child.	s. 56.	Felony; penal servitude not exceeding 7 nor less than 5 years (not less than 7 if previously convicted of felony); or imprisonment not exceeding 2 years. Male under 16 may be whipped.
Knowingly harbouring or receiving with like intent— Abusing, &c., under 12, and above 12 and under 13, see "Offences against the Person." See also " Concealing Birth."	,,	Like.
Indecent Assaults on Young Persons. —It shall be no defence to a charge or indictment for an indecent assault on a young person under the age of 13 to prove that *he* or *she* consented to the act of indecency.	43 & 44 Vic. c. 45, s. 2.	
And see also title "Criminal Law Amendment Act, 1885," as to protection of girls, &c.	48 & 49 Vic. c. 69.	
And "Prevention of Cruelty to Children," Summary Index.	52 & 53 Vic. c. 44.	
Chloroform—		
Using chloroform or other stupefying drug, or causing same to be taken by any person with intent to commit or enable any other to commit, an indictable offence.	24 & 25 Vic. c. 100, s. 22. (27 & 28 Vic. s. 47.)	Felony; penal servitude for life, or not less than 5 years (not less than 7 if previously convicted of felony); or imprisonment not exceeding 2 years, with or without H. L.

Offence.	Statute.	Punishment.
Choke— Attempting to choke or suffocate, in order thereby to commit, or assist another in committing, an indictable offence.	24 & 25 Vic. c. 100, s. 21.	Felony; like punishment as last preceding.
Church— See "Larceny," and "Malicious Injuries."		
Behaving irreverently in church or churchyard during Divine service. (a) See title "Church," Summary Index.	Common Law.	Misdemeanour; punishable by fine and imprisonment.
Clergyman— Assaulting or obstructing him in discharge of his duty, or arresting under civil process while performing duty, or going to or returning from.	24 & 25 Vic. c. 100, s. 36.	Misdemeanour; imprisonment not exceeding 2 years, with or without H. L.
Clerks— See "Larceny," and for forging records of Court, see "Forgery."		
Coal Mines Registration Act, 1887— As to employment of women and children in Coal Mines, regulations, &c., and as to what offences are made misdemeanours, see also "Coal Mines," Summary Index.		

(a) Where burials of persons not belonging to United Church of England and Ireland take place in burial-grounds of such church, priest, &c., of other denomination may perform service, but not within half an hour of service in such church, &c. Obstructing is misdemeanour.—31 & 32 Vic. c. 103, s. 1.

Offence.	Statute.	Punishment.
Coin (*Offences relating to*)—(*a*) *Gold and Silver Coin.*—Falsely making or counterfeiting any coin resembling or apparently intended to resemble or pass for current gold or silver coin.	24 & 25 Vic. c. 99, s. 2. (27 & 28 Vic. c. 47.)	Felony; penal servitude for life, or not less than 5 years (not less than 7 if previously convicted of felony); or imprisonment not exceeding 2 years, with or without H. L., and solitary confinement.
Gilding, silvering, washing, or colouring genuine coin, with intent to make it pass for a higher coin. (As to gilding medals, &c., so as to counterfeit, &c., see 46 & 47 Vic. c. 45, hereafter.)	s. 3.	Like.
Impairing, diminishing, or lightening the current gold or silver coin.	s. 4.	Felony; penal servitude not exceeding 14 years and not less than 5 years (not less than 7 if previously convicted of felony); or imprisonment not exceeding 2 years, with or without H. L., and solitary confinement.
Unlawfully having in possession any filings, or clippings, dust, solution, or otherwise, produced by impairing or diminishing, &c.	s. 5.	Felony; penal servitude not exceeding 7 and not less than 5 years (not less than 7 if previously convicted of felony); or imprisonment not exceeding 2 years, with or without H. L., and solitary confinement.
Without lawful authority or excuse buying, selling, receiving, or putting off counterfeit gold or silver coin for less than apparent value.	s. 6.	Felony; penal servitude for life, or not less than 5 years (not less than 7 if previously convicted of felony); or imprisonment not exceeding 2 years, with or without H. L., and solitary confinement.

(*a*) All coins, gold, silver, copper, or bronze, of any value whatever, not issued by the Mint, prohibited, and offender liable on summary conviction, to a penalty not exceeding £20.—33 Vic. c. 10, s. 5.

Offence.	Statute.	Punishment.
Coin (*Offences relating to*)—*continued.* *Importing*, without lawful authority, from beyond the seas, any false or counterfeit coin apparently intended to resemble the Queen's current gold or silver coin, knowing same to be false or counterfeit.	24 & 25 Vic. c. 99, s. 7. (27 & 28 Vic. c. 47.)	Felony; penal servitude for life, or not less than 5 years (not less than 7 if previously convicted of felony); or imprisonment not exceeding 2 years, with or without H. L., and solitary confinement.
Exporting any false or counterfeit coin apparently intended to resemble or pass for any of the Queen's current coin, knowing same to be false, &c.	s. 8.	Misdemeanour; imprisonment not exceeding 2 years, with or without H. L., and solitary confinement.
Tendering, uttering, or putting off, false or counterfeit gold or silver coin, knowingly.	s. 9.	Misdemeanour; imprisonment not exceeding 1 year, with or without H. L., and solitary confinement.
Tendering or uttering, &c., knowingly and having in possession at the time of tendering, &c., any other counterfeit gold or silver coin; or either on the same, or within ten days, knowingly tendering any counterfeit gold or silver coin.	s. 10.	Misdemeanour; imprisonment not exceeding 2 years, with or without H. L., and solitary confinement.
Possession.—Knowingly having in possession three or more pieces of counterfeit coin apparently intended to resemble current gold or silver coin, and with intent to put off same.	s. 11.	Misdemeanour; penal servitude 5 years (not less than 7 if previously convicted of felony); or imprisonment not exceeding 2 years, with or without H. L., and solitary confinement.
Second Offence.—If any person, before convicted of offence relating to the coin, shall commit any of the offences in sections 9, 10, 11—	s. 12.	Felony; penal servitude for life, or not less than 5 years (not less than 7 if previously convicted of felony); or imprisonment not exceeding 2 years, with or without H. L., and solitary confinement.

Legal Tenders.—Gold to any amount; silver not exceeding 40s.; bronze not exceeding 1s.—33 Vic. c. 10, s. 4.

Offence.	Statute.	Punishment.
Coin (*Offences relating to*)—*continued.* *Foreign Coin.*—With intent to defraud, tendering or putting off as current gold or silver coin any coin not being such, or medals or metals resembling, and being of less value.	24 & 25 Vic. c. 99, s. 13. (27 & 28 Vic. c. 47.)	Misdemeanour; imprisonment not exceeding 1 year, with or without H. L., and solitary confinement.
Copper Coin.— Counterfeiting the copper coin ; making, mending, or having in possession without lawful authority, tools, or implements for the purpose ; buying, selling, or putting off counterfeit copper coin for less than apparent value.	s. 14.	Felony ; penal servitude not exceeding 7 nor less than 5 years (not less than 7 if previously convicted of felony) ; or imprisonment not exceeding 2 years, with or without H. L., and solitary confinement.
Tendering, uttering, &c., counterfeit copper coin, knowingly ; or having three or more pieces of counterfeit copper coin in possession, knowingly.	s. 15.	Misdemeanour; imprisonment not exceeding 1 year, with or without H. L., and solitary confinement.
Defacing Coin.—Defacing gold, silver, or copper coin by stamping names or words thereon.	s. 16.	Like.
Foreign Coin.—Counterfeiting foreign coin.	s. 18.	Felony ; penal servitude not exceeding 7 and not less than 5 years (not less than 7 if previously convicted of felony) ; or imprisonment not exceeding 2 years, with or without H. L., and solitary confinement.
Importing without lawful authority into United Kingdom counterfeit foreign gold or silver coin.	s. 19.	Felony ; like punishment as last preceding.
Uttering, tendering, &c., counterfeit foreign gold or silver coin, knowingly.	s. 20.	Misdemeanour; imprisonment not exceeding 6 months, with or without H. L.

Offence.	Statute.	Punishment.
Coin (*Offences relating to*)—*continued.* *Second Offence* of uttering as in last section.	24 & 25 Vic. c. 99, s. 21. (27 & 28 Vic. c. 47.)	Misdemeanour; imprisonment not exceeding 2 years, with or without H. L., and solitary confinement.
Third Offence, ...	,,	Felony; penal servitude for life, or not less than 5 years (not less than 7 if previously convicted of felony); or imprisonment not exceeding 2 years, with or without H. L., and solitary confinement.
Counterfeiting any foreign coin of less value than silver.	s. 22.	Misdemeanour; imprisonment not exceeding 1 year.
Second Offence, ...	,,	Penal servitude not exceeding 7 nor less than 5 years (not less than 7 if previously convicted of felony); or imprisonment not exceeding 2 years, with or without H. L., and solitary confinement.
Possession.—Without lawful authority, having more than five pieces of counterfeit foreign gold or silver coin.	s. 23.	Triable before a Justice of the Peace. See "Coin," Summary Index.
Coining Tools.—Making, mending, buying, selling, or having in possession, knowingly, tools or implements for coining, &c.	s. 24.	Felony; penal servitude for life, or not less than 5 years (not less than 7 if previously convicted of felony); or imprisonment not exceeding 2 years, with or without H. L., and solitary confinement.

Offence.	Statute.	Punishment.
Coin (*Offences relating to*)—*continued*. *Mint*.—Without lawful authority, knowingly conveying tools out of Her Majesty's mints, or any coin, bullion, metals, &c.	24 & 25 Vic. c. 99, s. 25.	Felony; penal servitude for life, or not less than 5 years (not less than 7 if previously convicted of felony); or imprisonment not exceeding 2 years, with or without H. L., and solitary confinement.
Coin suspected may be cut, . .	s. 26.	—
Discovery and seizure of coin and tools.	s. 27.	
Proof.—Any moneyer or credible witness may prove coin to be counterfeit.	s. 29.	
Counterfeit complete, although unfinished.	s. 30.	
Apprehension of offenders, . .	s. 31.	—
Accessories, ...	s. 35.	—
The Counterfeit Medal Act, 1883 ("An Act for preventing the Sale of Medals Resembling Current Coin.")	46 & 47 Vic. c. 45.	
If any person without due authority, &c., makes or has in his possession, or offers for sale, or sells, any medal, cast, coin, or other like thing made wholly or partially of metal or any metallic combination, and resembling in size, figure, and colour any of the Queen's current gold or silver coin, or having thereon a device resembling any device on any of the Queen's current gold or silver coin, or being so formed that it can by gilding, silvering, colouring, washing, or other like process be so dealt with as to resemble any of the Queen's current gold or silver coin. See also Summary Jurisdiction Index, "Coin."	s. 2.	Misdemeanour; imprisonment not exceeding 1 year, with or without H. L.
For provisions as to exchange of light pre-Victorian Coins by Mint, see—	52 & 53 Vic. c. 58.	

Offence.	Statute.	Punishment.
Combination— Assault in pursuance of unlawful combination to raise wages, or respecting trade, &c. See also "Conspiracy"; and for "Combination of Workmen," see Summary Index.	24 & 25 Vic. c. 100, s. 41.	Misdemeanour; imprisonment not exceeding 2 years' H. L.
Common Assault— See Summary Index, title "Assault."		
Companies (*Frauds by Public*)— See "Larceny."		
Compounding Offences (a)— Compounding (that is, taking a reward for forbearing to prosecute) any felony or misdemeanour, or even an information, on a penal statute.	Common Law	Misdemeanour; punishable by fine or imprisonment, or both. (See *Gabbet*, 240; 2 *Burn*, 831; 1 *Hawk.*, 59, *s.* 5.)
Compounding offences against the Larceny Act, by corruptly taking reward for helping to restore stolen goods (without bringing offender to trial).	24 & 25 Vic. c. 96, s. 101. (27 & 28 Vic. c. 47.)	Felony; penal servitude not exceeding 7, and not less than 5 years (not less than 7 if previously convicted of felony); or imprisonment not exceeding 2 years, with or without H. L., and solitary confinement. Male under 18 may be whipped.

(a) *Compromise of Offence.*—While it is clearly indictable to *compound offences* as above set forth, it appears that in all offences which involve damage to an injured party for which he may maintain an action, it is competent for him, notwithstanding they are of a public nature, to *compromise* or settle his private damage in any way he thinks fit. "It is said, indeed, that in the case of an assault he may also undertake not to prosecute on behalf of the public. It may be so, but we are not disposed to extend this any further."—*Tindal, C. J., Kier* v. *Seeman*, 9 Q. B., 395. As a rule, the law will not allow offences of a public nature to be compromised.

Offence.	Statute.	Punishment.
Concealing Birth— If any woman shall be delivered of a child, every person who shall, by any secret disposition of the dead body of the said child, whether such child died before, at, or after its birth, endeavour to conceal the birth thereof—	24 & 25 Vic. c. 100, s. 60.	Misdemeanour; imprisonment not exceeding 2 years, with or without H. L.
		Proviso: Person indicted for murder, and acquitted, may (if it appear in evidence) be convicted of concealing.
Concealing Deeds, &c.— See "Larceny."		
Conspiracy (a)— Conspiring, agreeing, soliciting, endeavouring to persuade, or proposing to any person to murder another—	24 & 25 Vic. c. 100, s. 4. (27 & 28 Vic. c. 47).	Misdemeanour; penal servitude, not more than 10 nor less than 5 years (not less than 7 if previously convicted of felony); or imprisonment not exceeding 2 years, with or without H. L. (b)
To charge another with a crime punishable by law, either from vindictive motives or to extort money.	Common Law	Fine or imprisonment, or both.
To wrongfully injure any third person or body of men in any other manner, unless the injury be a mere civil trespass.	,,	Like.
To commit any offence punishable by law.	,,	Like.
To do any act with intent to pervert the course of justice.	,,	Like.
To effect a legal purpose with a corrupt intent, or by illegal means. (*Gab. Crim. Law.*)	,,	Like.
And see "Conspiracy and Protection of Property Act, 1875," Summary Index; and in proclaimed districts, see "Criminal Law Procedure (Ir.) Act, 1887."	50 & 51 Vic. c. 20.	

(*a*) Indictments shall not be preferred unless on conditions in 22 & 23 Vic., c. 17. See title, "Vexatious Indictments."

(*b*) This offence is here made punishable as a misdemeanour, but if convicted as an "accessory," the offence would be felony. (See *Archbold*, p. 24.)

Offence.	Statute.	Punishment.
Constable— Assaulting, resisting, or wilfully obstructing peace officer in execution of his duty or any person acting in his aid, or assaulting any person **with intent to resist** or prevent lawful apprehension for any offence. (a)	24 & 25 Vic. c. 100, s. 38.	Misdemeanour; imprisonment not exceedi years, with or wi H. L.
Larceny or embezzlement by constable—see "Larceny."		
See also Summary Index, titles "Constable," and "**Crime Prevention**;" and in proclaimed districts, see "Criminal Law Procedure (Ir.) Act, 1887."	50 & 51 Vic. c. 20, s. 2 (c).	
Contagion— See "Nuisance."		
Contempts—		

Offence.	Statute.	Punishment.
Convention *Treaty*— See "Extradition."		
Conviction— See Summary Index.		
Convicts— On licence when convicted, &c., see 27 & 28 Vic., c. 47; and see "*Penal Servitude.*"		
Co-partners (*Larceny and Embezzlement by*)— See "Larceny."		
Copper Coin (*Counterfeiting, &c.*)— See "Coin."		
Corn— Crops of, &c.—setting fire to—see "Malicious Injuries."		
Corrosive Fluid— Throwing on the person—see "Offences against the Person."		
Corrupt Practices (*at Elections*)— See "Elections."		

to it the functions of either House of Parliament, or any of them, or having for its object or tendency to bring Parliament into hatred or contempt. This Act shall not exempt any person from any proceeding for an offence punishable at Common Law or under any statute.

The 39 Geo. iii., c. 79 (Eng.), declared the "Societies of United Englishmen, United Scotchmen, United Britons, United Irishmen, and the London Corresponding Society, and all Societies called Corresponding Societies," to be unlawful combinations and confederacies, highly dangerous to the peace and tranquillity of the kingdom, and to the constitution of the Government thereof.

Offence.	Statute.	Punishment.
Counsel— Prisoners' Counsel Act, . . .	6 & 7 Wm. iv. c. 114.	—
In Petty Sessions parties may plead by Counsel or Attorney.	14 & 15 Vic. c. 93, s. 9.	
Counterfeit Coin— See " Coin."		
Cow (*Stealing*)— See " Larceny."		
Crime— The Prevention of Crimes Act, 1871,	34 & 35 Vic. c. 112.	
Amends Penal Servitude Acts; provides for the register and photographing of criminals.		
Persons twice convicted as in section may be subjected to police supervision.	s. 8.	
Incorporation of certain rules of procedure on indictments.	s. 9.	
Amendment of the law of evidence in cases of receiving stolen property. See Summary Index, title " Crime."	s. 19.	
Criminal Law Amendment Act, 1885: *Protection of Women and Girls— Procuration.*—(1) Any person who attempts to procure any girl or woman under 21 years of age, not being a common prostitute, or of known immoral character, to have unlawful carnal connexion, either	48 & 49 Vic. c. 69, s. 2.	Misdemeanour; imprisonment at the discretion of the Court for any term not exceeding 2 years, with or without H. L.

Offence.	Statute.	Punishment.
Criminal Law Amendment Act, 1885—*continued.* within or without the Queen's dominions, with any other person or persons ; or (2) Procures, or attempts to procure, any woman or girl to become, either within or without the Queen's dominions, a common prostitute ; or (3) Procures, or attempts to procure, any woman or girl to leave the United Kingdom, with intent that she may become an inmate of a brothel elsewhere ; or (4) Procures, or attempts to procure, any woman or girl to leave her usual place of abode in the United Kingdom (such place not being a brothel), with intent that she may, for the purposes of prostitution, become an inmate of a brothel within or without the Queen's dominions.	48 & 49 Vic. c. 69, s. 2.	*Proviso :* Conviction not to be on evidence of *one* witness, unless corroborated in some material particular by evidence implicating the accused.
Procurement by threats, fraud, drugs— Any person who—(1) by threats or intimidation procures, or attempts to procure, any woman or girl to have any unlawful carnal connexion, either within or without the Queen's dominions ; or (2) By false pretences, or false representations, procures any woman or girl, not being a common prostitute, or of known immoral character, to have any unlawful carnal connexion, either within or without the Queen's dominions; or (3) Applies, administers to, or causes to be taken by, any woman or girl any drug, matter, or thing, with intent to stupefy or overpower, so as thereby to enable any person to have unlawful carnal connexion with such woman or girl.	s. 3.	Misdemeanour ; imprisonment at the discretion of the Court for any term not exceeding 2 years, with or without H. L. *Proviso :* Conviction not to be on evidence of *one* witness, unless corroborated in some material particular by evidence implicating the accused.

Offence.	Statute.	Punishment.
Criminal Law Amendment Act, 1885—*continued.* *Defilement of girl under 13*— Any person who unlawfully and carnally knows any girl under the age of 13 years.	48 & 49 Vic. c. 69, s. 4.	Felony. Penal servitude for life, or for any term not less than 5 years, or to be imprisoned for any term not exceeding 2 years, with or without H. L.
Attempts.—Any person who attempts to have unlawful carnal knowledge of any girl under the age of 13 years.	,,	Misdemeanour, imprisonment not exceeding 2 years, with or without H. L.
Proviso.—When age of offender does not exceed 16, Court may, instead of imprisonment, substitute whipping, and for this purpose, and so far as circumstances admit, may apply to offence 25 and 26 Vic. c. 18 ; and if, having regard to age and other circumstances, it appear expedient, may, in addition to whipping, order him to be sent to Reformatory School for not less than 2 nor more than 5 years, and for this purpose may order that he be detained in custody for not more than 7 days before he is sent to Reformatory School.	,,	☞ No person shall be liable to be convicted unless the testimony admitted by this section for the prosecution shall be corroborated by some other material evidence in support thereof implicating the accused (sec. 4).
Where child on whom offence charged is committed, or any child of tender years tendered as a witness, does not, in the opinion of the Court or Justices, understand the nature of an oath, evidence may be received without oath where Court is satisfied that the child is of sufficient intelligence, and understands duty of speaking the truth ; and may be prosecuted for perjury, as if sworn.	,,	

Note.—For the offence of *defiling*, or *attempting to defile, girls under* 13 (sec. 4) the evidence admitted by the section must be corroborated by other material evidence implicating the accused. The corroboration would in this case seem to be necessary only where the section admits the testimony of a child who does not

Offence.	Statute.	Punishment.
Criminal Law Amendment Act, 1885—*continued.* *Rape.*—Man who induces married woman to permit him to have connexion with her by personating her husband, deemed to be guilty of rape.	48 & 49 Vic. c. 69, s. 4.	
Defilement of girls between 13 and 16— Any person who—(1) unlawfully and carnally knows, or attempts to have unlawful carnal knowledge of any girl being of or above the age of 13 and under 16; or	s. 5. (sub s. 1.)	Misdemeanour; imprisonment not exceeding 2 years, with or without H. L. *Proviso :* It shall be sufficient defence to any charge under this section—(1) if it appear to Court or jury that the person charged had reasonable cause to believe that the girl was of or above 16. And no prosecution to be commenced under subsec. (1) more than three months after commission of the offence.
(2) *Idiots.*—Unlawfully and carnally knows, or attempts to have unlawful carnal knowledge of, any female idiot, or imbecile woman or girl, under circumstances which do not amount to rape, but which prove that the offender knew at the time that the female was an idiot or imbecile.	(sub s. 2.)	
Householders, &c., permitting defilement of young girl on his premises— Any person who, being the owner or occupier of any premises, or having, or acting or assisting in, the management or control thereof, induces, or knowingly suffers any girl of such age as in this section mentioned to resort to, or be in or upon such premises, for the purpose of being unlawfully and carnally known by any man, whether such carnal knowledge is intended to be with any particular man or generally.	s. 6.	(1) If such girl is under the age of 13, felony. Penal servitude for life, or not less than 5 years, or to be imprisoned for not exceeding 2 years, with or without H. L. (2) If such girl is above 13 and under 16 years, misdemeanour. Imprisonment not exceeding 2 years, with or without H. L. *Proviso :* It shall be sufficient defence to any

understand the nature of an oath. Where the offence is in respect of girls over 13 and under 16 (sec. 5) the section does not require corroboration; but it does provide that no proceedings shall be instituted more than *three months* after the commission of the offence.

Offence.	Statute.	Punishment.
Criminal Law Amendment Act, 1885—*continued.*	48 & 49 Vic. c. 69, s. 6.	charge under this sec. (6) if it appear to the Court or jury that the person charged had reasonable cause to believe that the girl was of or above 16.
Abduction of girl under 18 with intent, &c.— Any person who, with intent that any unmarried girl under the age of 18 years should be unlawfully and carnally known by any man, whether such carnal knowledge is intended to be with any particular man, or generally takes, or causes to be taken, such girl out of the possession, and against the will of her father or mother, or any other person having the lawful care or charge of her—	s. 7.	Misdemeanour. Imprisonment not exceeding 2 years, with or without H. L. *Proviso :* It shall be sufficient defence to this charge if it appear to Court or jury that the person charged had reasonable cause to believe that the girl was above the age of 18.
Unlawful detention with intent, &c.— Any person who detains any woman against her will—(1) in or upon any premises with intent that she may be unlawfully and carnally known by any man, whether any particular man or generally ; or (2) In any brothel. Evidence of unlawful detention for unlawful purposes ; to induce her to remain, detains her clothes, &c.: or threatens her with legal proceedings for taking away clothes lent her. No proceedings shall be taken against female for taking away necessary clothing lent her. Power on indictment for *rape*, or any offence made felony under sec. 4, to convict of an offence under sects. 3, 4, or 5 of this Act, or of an indecent assault, and to acquit of the felony charged in indictment.	s. 8. s. 9.	Misdemeanour. Imprisonment not exceeding 2 years, with or without H. L.

Offence.	Statute.	Punishment.
Criminal Law Amendment Act, 1885—*continued*.		
Power of Justice to issue search warrant when female is detained for immoral purposes.—(See section in full, *infra*.	48 & 49 Vic. c. 69, s. 10.	
Outrages on decency—Sodomy— Any male person who, in public or private, commits, or is a party to the commission of, or procures, or attempts to procure, the commission, by any male person, of any act of gross indecency with another male person—	s. 11.	Misdemeanour. Imprisonment not exceeding 2 years, with or without H. L.

Power of search (sec. 10) *where female is forcibly detained for immoral purposes.*
—" If it appears to any Justice of the Peace on information made before him on oath by any parent, relative, or guardian of any woman or girl, or any other person who, in the opinion of the Justice, is *bonâ fide* acting in the interest of any woman or girl, that there is reasonable cause to suspect that such woman or girl is unlawfully detained for immoral purposes by any person in any place within the jurisdiction of such Justice, such Justice may issue a warrant authorizing any person named therein to search for, and, when found, to take to, and detain in, a place of safety such woman or girl until she can be brought before a Justice of the Peace ; and the Justice of the peace before whom such woman or girl is brought may cause her to be delivered up to her parents or guardians, or otherwise dealt with, as circumstances may permit and require. The Justice of the Peace issuing such warrant may, by the same or any other warrant, cause any person accused of so unlawfully detaining such woman or girl to be apprehended and brought before a Justice, and proceedings to be taken for punishing such person according to law. A woman or girl shall be deemed to be unlawfully detained for immoral purposes if she is so detained for the purpose of being unlawfully and carnally known by any man, whether any particular man or generally, and—

" (*a*) Either is under the age of 16 years ; or

"(*b*) If of or over the age of 16 years, and under the age of 18 years, is so detained against her will, or against the will of her father or mother, or of any other person having the lawful care or charge of her ; or

"(*c*) If of or above the age of 18 years is so detained against her will. Any person authorized by warrant under this section to search for any woman or girl so detained as aforesaid may enter (if need be by force) any house, building, or other place specified in such warrant, and may remove such woman or girl therefrom : Provided always, that every warrant issued under this section shall be addressed to, and executed by, some superintendent, inspector, or other officer of police, who shall be accompanied by the parent, relative, or guardian or other person making the information, if such person so desire, unless the Justice shall otherwise direct."

Offence.	Statute.	Punishment.
Criminal Law Amendment Act, 1885—*continued.*		
Custody of girls under 16.—Court may transfer the custody of girl under 16 until she attains an age not exceeding 21, when the Court is satisfied that parents, guardians, &c., encouraged or favoured her prostitution.	48 & 49 Vic. c. 69, s. 12.	
Brothels.—As to suppression of brothels by summary proceedings (sec. 13) see Summary Index, title " Brothel."		
Saving.—Not to exempt offender from proceedings at Common Law, or under other Act of Parliament, so that he be not punished twice for same offence.	s. 16.	
Indictable misdemeanour under Act to be subject to provisions of 22 & 23 Vic. c. 17, as to Vexatious Indictments, and Acts amending same.	s. 17.	
Costs. In indictable misdemeanour, or cases of indecent assault, Court	s. 18.	

Offence.	Statute.	Punishment.
Crops (*Setting fire to*)— See " Malicious Injuries."		
Cruelty— To children, apprentices, &c.—See " Offences against the Person ;" " Child."		
Customs— See Summary Index.		
Damage (*Wilful*)— See " Malicious Injuries."		
Dangerous Goods— Delivering, or causing to be delivered, to any carrier, warehouse, ship, railway, &c., goods which are specially dangerous, without being specially marked, &c., as by Act required. (Proviso as to absence of knowledge.) See also " Explosives."	29 & 30 Vic. c. 90, s. 3.	Penalty not exceeding £500 ; or imprisonment with or without H. L., not exceeding 2 years.
Dead Bodies— Obstructing a clergyman in the discharge of his duty reading the burial service.	Common Law.	Misdemeanour ; fine and imprisonment.
Burying the body of one who has died a violent death, without sending for the coroner, or before inquest held.	,,	Like.
Although larceny cannot be committed of a dead body, no one having any right of property therein, yet it is an offence to remove a body without lawful authority.	,,	Indictable misdemeanour ; punishable by fine and imprisonment.
So to take it from a burial-ground without lawful authority the offence is indictable, as being highly indecent and *contra bonos mores*.	,,	
It is not clear that, where from motives of filial affection the body is removed from the burial-ground, the act is indictable as above, but is merely a trespass against the owner of the soil of the burying-place. See Roscoe, title " Dead Bodies."		

Offence.	Statute.	Punishment.
Debtors (*Fraudulent*)— See "Bankrupt."		
Declaration— Wilfully making false statements in declarations, substituted for oaths under— See also "Dying Declarations."	5 & 6 Wm. iv. c. 62.	Misdemeanour.
Deer (*Stealing*)— See title "Larceny," in this and also in the Summary Index.		
Defacing Coin— See "Coin."		
Defamatory Libel— See "Libel."		
Defilement (*of Girls*)— Procuring—see "Offences against the Person, and see title "Criminal Law Amendment Act, 1885."	48 & 49 Vic. c. 69.	
Demanding Money (*with Menaces*)— See "Larceny from the Person."		
Demolishing Buildings— By rioters—see "Malicious Injuries." By tenants—see "Landlord and Tenant," Summary Index. Unroofing dwelling-house, for pur- pose of expelling occupier.	11 & 12 Vic. c. 47, s. 7.	Misdemeanour.
Depositions— Mode of taking, and other duties in respect to same, by Justices and Officers. See also Prisoners' Counsel Act,	14 & 15 Vic. c. 93, s. 14. &c. 6 & 7 Wm. iv. c. 114, s. 3.	For Act, see *Appendix.*
Disfigure— See "Offences against the Person."		

Offence.	Statute.	Punishment.
Disorderly House— See " Bawdy House."		
Disturbing (*Public Worship*)— Disturbing the public worship of any congregation assembled according to law.	Common Law.	Misdemeanour (see *Gab. Cr. L.*, 294).
Maliciously and contemptuously to enter any church, chapel, or congregation of Protestant Dissenters, and disturb same, or misuse any teacher. And see title " Church," Summary Index. See also " Offences against the Person," and " Malicious Injuries."	6 Geo. i. c. 5.	Penalty £20, recoverable at Quarter Sessions.
Documentary (*Evidence Act*, 1868)— As to admitting Proclamations, Gazettes, &c., in evidence. See *Appendix*.	31 & 32 Vic. c. 37.	
Dogs— See " Larceny of Animals "; and in Summary Index, see " Dogs," and " Cruelty to Animals."		
Duelling (*where Death ensues*)— See " Offences against the Person," and " Challenging," &c.		
Challenging to fight a duel, or provoking to send challenge, or acting as messenger in conveying any challenge to fight a duel.	Common Law.	Indictable Misdemeanour.
Drilling (*Illegal*)— See " Arms."		
Driving (*Furious*)— See " Offences against the Person "; and see also Summary Index.		

Offence.	Statute.	Punishment.
Drugs (*Adulteration of*)— See "Adulteration," Summary Index.		
Dwelling-House— See "Burglary," and "Malicious Injuries."		
Dying Declarations, (*a*) . . .	—	May be taken by a Magistrate or any other person, when the person making it is dying from a mortal injury.

(*a*) The depositions of witnesses who have died, in order to have same read on the trial of the accused, it must clearly appear that they have been taken, as directed by the statute (14 & 15 Vic. c. 93, s. 14), in presence and hearing of the accused ; and that he or his counsel had an opportunity of cross-examining the witness. The reading of a dying declaration on the trial is an exception ; and the principle upon which it is received as evidence is the awful solemnity of the situation under which it is delivered, when all hope of this world is gone, when every motive to falsehood is silenced, and the mind is induced by the most powerful considerations to speak the truth. It need not be in the presence of the accused, nor is it to be on oath ; for the situation of a dying man is considered by the law as creating an obligation equal to that which is imposed by an oath administered in Court. It is very desirable that it should be in writing, but it is admissible although not committed to writing. It may be taken down by any person, but it is most likely that a Magistrate will be called in ; and, if it be at all practicable, it is his duty to commit it to writing. The proceeding is simple, but demands caution and close attention. It should not alone appear to others that he is dying, but it should be collected from his own statements, or other circumstances, that he is aware of the extremity of his situation, and impressed with the hopelessness of his recovery. The Magistrate will, with caution and delicacy, inquire into this, collecting the facts from circumstances, and from the dying man, according to the best of his judgment. He will closely watch and attend to the whole conduct of the person making the statement, the state of his mind, his recollection and understanding, although naturally these must be impaired by the decay of nature, and, above all, that he feels he is at the time dying of the wounds received. The Magistrate, or whoever takes the declaration, will in the first instance acquaint the party with his awfully solemn situation, and admonish him from these considerations to speak the truth. It will be for the Court afterwards, on hearing the declaration read, and examining the Magistrate or person who took it, to say whether or not it is admissible. It is proper to observe that if the injured person does not feel that he is dying, and that he is able to make his statement on oath, and if the accused can be brought forward, the deposition should be regularly taken as directed by the statute. If the *deposition* of the deceased has been taken under any of the statutes on that

Offence.	Statute.	Punishment.
Elections (*Parliamentary*) (a)— Bribery, undue influence, personation, &c. &c.	31 & 32 Vic. c. 125.	Misdemeanour; and punishable by fines and imprisonment.
BALLOT ACT, 1872. Every person who— (1) Forges, or fraudulently defaces, or fraudulently destroys, any nomination paper, or delivers to the returning officer any nomination paper knowing the same to be forged; or,	35 & 36 Vic. c. 33. s. 3.	Misdemeanour; and shall be liable, if he is a returning officer, or an officer or clerk in attendance at a polling station, to imprisonment

subject, and is inadmissible as such for want of compliance with some of the legal formularies, it seems that it may still be treated as a dying declaration, if made *in extremis.*

The declaration must have been made by a person who, if alive, would have been a competent witness. Thus, on an indictment for the murder of a girl aged 4 years, it was held that she could not have had that idea of a future state which is necessary in order to make her dying declaration admissible—*R.* v. *Pike*, *3 C. & P.* 598. But when the child is of an intelligent mind, impressed with the nature of an oath and expecting to die, the declaration is receivable. It is no objection that the facts have been elicited by questions put to the deceased.

(*s*) *Elections.*—Summary of what will amount to bribery, &c., under the Act :—

I.—All "bribery" is prohibited. Bribery includes the following :—

1. Giving, lending, or agreeing to give, lend, or obtain money or other valuable consideration to or for a voter, or anyone else, either before the poll, in order to induce such voter to vote or refrain from voting, or after poll, in consideration of a vote given or withheld.

2. Giving, procuring, or agreeing to give or procure employment for a voter or any other person, either before poll, in order to induce such voter to give or withhold his vote, or after poll, in consideration of a vote given or withheld.

3. Any kind of bargain, direct or indirect, with any person whatsover, with the view of inducing him to endeavour to procure the return of a candidate or the vote of an elector.

4. Payment or causing payment in any manner of money with the intent of its being used for bribery, or the repayment to any person of money already so expended, wholly or in part.

Persons found guilty of any of the above-mentioned acts, as well as the voter or other person with or for whom they are all done, are liable to fine and imprisonment and a penalty.

Vide " The Corrupt Practices Prevention Act, secs. 2 and 3.

II.—All "Treating" is prohibited. Treating means any payment for, or providing in any manner, meat, drink, entertainment, or other provision, directly or indirectly, on the part of a candidate or anyone else on his behalf, for the

2 K

Offence.	Statute.	Punishment.
Elections (*Parliamentary*)— BALLOT ACT, 1872—*continued.* (2) Forges or counterfeits, or fraudulently defaces, or fraudulently destroys any ballot paper, or the official mark on any ballot paper ; or, (3) Without due authority, supplies any ballot paper to any person ; or,	35 & 36 Vic. c. 33, s. 3.	for any term not exceeding 2 years, with or without H. L. And if he is any other person not exceeding 6 months, with or without H. L.

purposes of election or of corruptly influencing the giving or withholding of a vote, whether before, during, or after an election.

This offence involves liability to penalties, and the voter who accepts any such provision loses his vote.

Vide "The Corrupt Practices Prevention Act, 1854," sec. 4.

III.—All "Undue Influence" is prohibited. This term includes the direct or indirect use or threat by any person, either personally or through others, of any violence, force, or restraint, or the infliction or threat to inflict any injury, damage, harm, or loss, or the practice in any manner of intimidation upon or against any person in order to induce him to give or withhold his vote, or on account of his having given or withheld his vote ; also the interfering with the free exercise of the franchise by means of abduction, confinement, or any kind of fraudulent device or contrivance.

A threat to withdraw custom from a tradesman unless he voted in a particular manner has been decided to amount to "undue influence."

This offence involves liability to fine and imprisonment and a penalty.

Vide "The Corrupt Practices Prevention Act, 1854," sec. 5.

Note.—Offences against the above provisions will, if proved against a candidate or his agents, be sufficient to unseat him after election, in addition to other penalties.

IV.—All marks of distinction are prohibited. These include cockades, ribbons, and all other such marks ; and all payments for " chairing" or marks of distinction, and for music, flags, or banners, are illegal.

Vide "The Corrupt Practices Prevention Act, 1854," sec. 7.

An offence against this provision involves a penalty.

V.—Conveyance of voters to the poll at borough elections at the expense of a candidate, or anyone on his behalf, is illegal.

Vide "The Representation of the People Act, 1867," sec. 36.

VI.—The giving of refreshments to voters, or of money, or tickets to enable them to procure refreshments, on the nomination or polling days, on account of their having polled or being about to poll, is illegal, and involves a liability to a penalty.

Vide "The Corrupt Practices Prevention Act, 1854," sec. 23.

VII.—*Employment of Electors.*—No elector employed for payment in connexion with the election as agent, clerk, canvasser, messenger, or other like employment, must vote. If anyone so employed tenders a vote he is liable to fine and imprisonment.

Vide "The Representation of the People Act, 1867," sec. 11.

Offence.	Statute.	Punishment.
Elections (*Parliamentary*)— BALLOT ACT, 1872—*continued.* (4) Fraudulently puts into any ballot-box any paper other than the ballot paper which he is authorized by law to put in ; or, (5) Fraudulently takes out of the polling station any ballot paper; or, (6) Without due authority, destroys, takes, opens, or otherwise interferes with, any ballot-box or packet of ballot papers then in use for the purposes of the election.	35 & 36 Vic. c. 33, s. 3.	
Secrecy.—Every officer, clerk, and agent in attendance at a polling station, shall maintain and aid in maintaining the secrecy of the voting in such station, and shall not communicate, except for some purpose authorized by law, before the poll is closed, to any person, any information as to the name or number on the register of voters of any elector who has or has not	s. 4.	Triable summarily. Imprisonment for any term not exceeding 6 months, with or without H. L. 2 J.

VIII.—Payment of rates on behalf of voters, for the purpose of inducing them to give or withhold votes, by whomsoever and however made, exposes all persons privy to such payments to the penalties of bribery.

Vide "The Representation of the People Act, 1867," sec. 49.

IX.—"Personation," or knowingly and falsely assuming to vote in the name of another person whose name is on the Register of Voters, whether such other person be living or dead, or the name be a fictitious one, exposes the person found guilty of it to the penalties of a misdemeanour. This liability extends to all aiders and abettors as principal offenders.

Vide Act 6 Vic., cap. 18, sec. 3, 1843.

The Ballot Act.—In the *Queen* v. *Unkles*, *Q. Bench* (before *Whiteside, C. J., O'Brien, Fitzgerald*, and *Barry, JJ.*), on a Case Stated by the Justices of Cork, appealing from a conviction under the 4th sec., it was held that the 21st sec. of the Petty Sessions (Ireland) Act, 1851, is prospective, and applies to the offences created by sec. 4 of the Ballot Act; therefore that a "dismiss without prejudice" is not a bar to a subsequent proceeding for the same offence. It was contended on the part of defendant that any dismiss was equivalent to an acquittal, and that it is against the general principle of law to try a man, once acquitted of a criminal charge, a second time.

2 K 2

Offence.	Statute.	Punishment.
Elections (*Parliamentary*)— BALLOT ACT, 1872—*continued*. applied for a ballot paper or voted at that station, or as to the official mark. And no such officer, clerk, or agent, and no person whosoever, shall interfere or attempt to interfere with a voter when marking his vote, or otherwise attempt to obtain in the polling station information as to the candidate for whom any voter in such station is about to vote or has voted ; or communicate at any time to any person any information obtained on a polling station as to the candidate for whom any voter in such station is about to vote or has voted, or as to the number on the back of the ballot paper given to any voter at such station. Every officer, clerk, and agent in attendance at the counting of the votes shall maintain and aid in maintaining the secrecy of the voting, and shall not attempt to ascertain at such counting the number on the back of any ballot paper, or communicate any information obtained at such counting as to the candidate for whom any vote is given in any particular ballot paper. No person shall, directly or indirectly, induce any voter to display his ballot paper, after he shall have marked the same, so as to make known to any person the name of the candidate for or against whom he has so marked his vote. For contravention of the provisions of this section—	35 & 36 Vic. c. 33, s. 4.	
Ballot.—Every returning officer, presiding officer, and clerk, guilty of any wilful malfeasance, act, or omission in contravention of Act, shall, in addition to other penalties, be liable to forfeit to the aggrieved a penal sum not exceeding £100.	s. 11.	

Offence.	Statute.	Punishment.
Elections (*Parliamentary*)—		
"Corrupt and Illegal Practices Prevention Act, 1883."	46 & 47 Vic. c. 51.	
Act to Prevent Corrupt and Illegal Practices at Parliamentary Elections. (*a*)		
Corrupt Practices.—Defines "treating," and extends sec. 4 of Corrupt Practices Prevention Act, 1854.	s. 1.	
Defines "undue influence."	s. 2.	
Defines "corrupt practice."	s. 3.	
Punishment of person convicted on indictment of corrupt practices.	s. 6.	
Punishment on summary conviction of illegal practice.	s. 10.	
Punishment on summary conviction of illegal payment, employment, or hiring.	s. 21.	
Legal Proceedings.—As to trial by indictment.	s. 50.	
Limitation of time for prosecution of offence.	s. 51.	
Persons charged with corrupt practice may be found guilty of illegal practice.	s. 52.	
Application of certain other enactments in prosecutions for bribery.	s. 53.	
Husband or wife of accused may be examined.	,,	
Appeals—right of, in summary cases.	s. 54.	

(*a*) Act continued by 50 & 51 Vic., c. 63.

For Bribery, &c., by Public Officers, see 52 & 53 Vic. c. 69, and title, "Public Bodies," &c.

Offence.	Statute.	Punishment.
Embezzlement— Clerk or servant who shall fraudulently embezzle any chattel, money, or valuable security delivered to, or received by him for, or on account of his master, shall be deemed to have feloniously stolen same. (a) And for summary power to try before Justices, see title "Larceny," Summary Index.)	24 & 25 Vic. c. 96, s. 48. (27 & 28 Vic. c. 47.)	Penal servitude not exceeding 14 years, and not less than 5 years (not less than 7 if previously convicted of felony) ; or imprisonment not exceeding 2 years, with or without H. L., and solitary confinement.
Persons employed in the Queen's service, or the police, who shall embezzle any chattel, money, &c., or shall in any manner fraudulently apply or dispose of same for any other than the public service. Committal or indictment may lay the property in Her Majesty.	24 & 25 Vic. c. 96, s. 70.	Shall be deemed to have feloniously stolen same. Penal servitude not exceeding 14 years, and not less than 5 years (not less than 7 if previously convicted of felony) ; or imprisonment not exceeding 2 years, with or without H. L.
If, upon trial for embezzlement, it turn out to be larceny, defendant not to be acquitted ; and *vice versa*.	s. 72.	—
Officers of Bank of England or Ireland secreting, embezzling, or running away with bonds, notes, moneys, or effects, &c. (For embezzlement by copartners, see title "Larceny.")	s. 73. (27 & 28 Vic. c. 47.)	Felony; penal servitude for life, or not less than 5 years (not less than 7 if previously convicted of felony) ; or imprisonment not exceeding 2 years, with or without H. L., and solitary confinement.

(a) *Embezzlement* is a specific term. The offence is of the same nature as Larceny. The possession of the servant is said to be the possession of the master. The wrongful appropriation by the servant of goods, money. &c., given him by the master, is larceny, but when given him by another for his master, the wrongful appropriation is embezzlement. A proper understanding of the terms *Possession* and *Property* is requisite. *Possession* extends to those things under our control, or under the control of our servants, and even further. *Property* is the right to that ssion, with an ability to exercise that right. In larceny the owner is deprived property in the thing taken. Embezzlement, then, is the fraudulent misap-

Offence.	Statute.	Punishment.
Embezzlement.—*continued*. Knowingly receiving goods, moneys, &c., where the stealing, obtaining, embezzling, &c., amounts to felony by this Act, or at Common Law. See also "Larceny."	24 & 25 Vic. c. 96, s. 91.	Felony; penal servitude not exceeding 14 years, or not less than 5 years (not less than 7 if previously convicted of felony) ; or imprisonment not exceeding 2 years, with or without H. L., and solitary confinement. Male under 16 may be whipped.
Engine (*Obstructing*)— See "Offences against the Person," and "Malicious Injuries."		
Enlistment— See "Foreign Enlistment," and see "Army Discipline, &c., Act," Summary Index.		

plication by clerk or servant of any chattel, &c., received by him for his master—and, in the words of the section, "he shall be deemed to have *stolen* the same."

It is clearly settled that a prisoner, by making an admission in his accounts that he has received the money, does not thereby necessarily free himself from the charge of embezzlement, if there be other circumstances from which the jury may infer that the money was fraudulently appropriated—*R.* v. *Lister, Dears & B., C. C.* 118, *Roscoe.*

Employment.—Where a servant who was not authorized to receive money was standing near a desk in his master's counting-house, and a person who owed money to the master paid it to the servant, who appropriated it, this was held to be no embezzlement—*R.* v. *Hawker,* 7 *C. & P.* 281. It is not, however, necessary that the servant should have been acting in the ordinary course of his employment when he received the money, provided that he was employed by his master to do so on that particular occasion—*R.* v. *Smith, Russ. & Ry.,* 516. So although it may not have been part of the servant's duty to receive money in the capacity in which he was originally hired, yet if he has been in the habit of receiving money for his master, he is within the statute—*R.* v. *Barker, Dow. & Ry. N. P. C.* 19. For further readings and decisions, see *Roscoe* and *Archibald.*

Offence.	Statute.	Punishment.
Entry (*Forcible*) (*a*)— Forcible possession, entry, or detainer, of lands or tenements, without due process or authority of law.	Common Law Also 5 Rich. ii. c. 8. 15 Rich. ii. c. 2. 8 Hy. vi. c. 9. 10 Car. 1. st. 3, s. 13 (Ir.)	Misdemeanour, punishable by fine and imprisonment.
Forcibly, and without due process of law, taking possession of a house, land, or tenement, or holding such possession, or resisting process for giving quiet possession. **Entry** in burglary—see "Burglary."	26 Geo. iii. c. 24. ss. 64, 65. 25 Geo. ii. c. 12. (Ir.) 40 Geo. iii. c. 96. (Ir.)	Felony; but the offence is generally indicted as a misdemeanour at Common Law.
Escape— Negligently permitting prisoner to escape.*		Misdemeanour.
Voluntarily permitting prisoner to escape. See Summary Index "Gaol," &c.		Felony; punishable as offence for which prisoner in custody. (1 *Russ.*, 370.)

(*a*) *Forcible Entry.*—There seems now to be no doubt that a party may be guilty of a forcible entry by violently and with force entering into that to which he has a legal title—*Newton* v. *Harland*, 1 *M. & G.*, 644, 1 *Russ. by Grea.*, 305 ; see *Roscoe.*

Right of Entry, how exercised.—"It is true that persons having only a right are not to assert that right by force ; if any violence be used it becomes the subject of a criminal prosecution. But the question is, whether a person having a right of possession may not peaceably assert it, if he do not transgress the laws of his country. I think he may ; for a person who has a right of entry may enter peaceably, and being in possession may retain it, and plead that it is his soil and freehold. And this will not break in upon any rule of law respecting the mode of obtaining possession of lands."—*Lord Kenyon.* No person who has a right of entry into lands can be considered as a trespasser for asserting that right, unless it be attended with such acts of violence as will subject him to a criminal prosecution. The common plea of *liberum tenementum* proves it—*Ashurst, J., Taylor* v. *Cole, England, reported* 3 *Term Rep.* 299, *Smith's Leading Cases.* It is not necessary that there should be anyone assaulted to constitute a forcible entry ; for if persons take or keep possession of either house or land with such numbers of persons and show of force as are calculated to deter the rightful owner from sending them away and resuming his own possession, that is sufficient in point of law to constitute a forcible entry, or a forcible detainer.—*Milner* v. *Maclean*, 2 *C. & P.* 18, per *Abbott, C. J.*

* *Escape.*—An escape by a person who is in custody on a criminal charge may be either with or without force, or with or without the consent of the officer or other

Offence.	Statute.	Punishment.
Evidence (*Law of*)— See *Appendix*.		
Explosive Substances (*a*)— EXPLOSIVE SUBSTANCES ACT, 1883.		
Causing Explosion, &c.—Any person who unlawfully and maliciously causes by any explosive substance an explosion of a nature likely to endanger life, or causes serious injury to property, shall, whether any injury to person or property has been actually caused or not, be guilty of—	46 Vic. c. 3.	Felony; penal servitude for life, or for any less term (not less than the minimum term allowed by law), or to imprisonment with or without H. L., for a term not exceeding 2 years.
Attempt, Intent, &c.—Any person who within or (being a subject of Her Majesty) without Her Majesty's dominions unlawfully and maliciously— (*a*) Does any act with intent to cause by an explosive substance an explosion in the United Kingdom of a nature likely to endanger life, or to cause serious injury to property; or,	46 Vic. c. 3.	Felony; penal servitude for a term not exceeding 20 years, or imprisonment with or without H. L., for a term not exceeding 2 years; and explosive substance shall be forfeited.
(*b*) Makes or has in his possession or under his control any explosive substance, with intent by means thereof to endanger life or cause serious injury to property in the United Kingdom, shall, whether any explosion does or not take place, and whether any injury to person or property has been actually caused or not, be guilty of—		Like.

person who has him in custody. All persons are bound to submit themselves to the judgment of law, and therefore if anyone, being in custody, frees himself from it by any artifice, he is guilty of a high contempt, punishable by fine and imprisonment—2 *Hawk. P. C.*, c. 17, s. 5. It must be proved that the party was in custody on a criminal charge, otherwise the escape is not a criminal offence: 1 *Russ.* by Greaves, 416—*Roscoe.*

(*a*) *Explosive Substance* includes materials for making same; also any apparatus, machine, implement, or materials used, or intended to be used or adapted, for causing, aiding, &c., explosion, &c., sec. 9.

Offence.	Statute.	Punishment.
Explosive Substances— EXPLOSIVE SUBSTANCES ACT, 1883— *continued.* *Unlawful Possession, &c.—* (1) Any person who makes, or knowingly has in his possession, or under his control, any explosive substance, under such circumstances as to give rise to a reasonable suspicion that he is not making it, or does not have it in his possession or under his control for a lawful object, shall, unless he can show that he made it, or had it in his possession or under his control for a lawful object, be guilty of—	46 Vic. c. 4. s. 4.	Felony : penal servitude for not exceeding 14 years, or to imprisonment for not exceeding 2 years, with or without H. L., and explosive substance shall be forfeited.
(2) Accused and wife, or husband, may give evidence under this section 4.	,,	
Accessories.—Any person who, within or (being a subject of Her Majesty) without Her Majesty's dominions, by the supply of or solicitation for money, the providing of premises, the supply of materials, or in any manner whatsoever procures, counsels, aids, abets, or is accessory to the commission of any crime under this Act—	s. 5.	Felony ; and shall be liable to be tried and punished for that crime as if he had been guilty as a principal.
Attorney-General (a) may direct inquiry before Justices, where he has reason to believe that crime has been committed against Act, and although no person be charged ; and Justice may in any Petty Sessional or occasional Court, or Police Station, as in Act, compel attendance of witnesses, &c., witness not excused on ground that answer may criminate himself. Justice taking part in preliminary inquiry	s. 6.	

(a) *Attorney-General.*—In case of inability or vacancy in the office, includes "Solicitor-General."

Offence.	Statute.	Punishment.
Explosive Substances—		
EXPLOSIVE SUBSTANCES ACT, 1883—*continued.*		
not to take part in committing persons for trial of crime under Act. Power to apprehend absconding witnesses, &c.	46 Vic. c. 6.	
(1) No prosecution, beyond remand for safe custody, &c., of person charged, without the leave of Attorney-General. (*a*)	s. 7.	
(2) Regulations as to framing indictment.	,,	
Applies secs. 73, 74, 75, 89, and 96 of Explosives Act, 1875 (38 & 39 Vic. c. 17) as to seizure and disposal of explosives.	s. 8.	
Power of masters or owners of vessels to search, &c.	,,	
This Act not to exempt offender from being tried by Common Law, or by any other Act of Parliament, but not to be twice punished for the same offence.	s. 7.	
And see " Offences against the Person," " Malicious Injuries."		
Exposing (*Child*)—		
See " Offences against the Person," and " Child."		

(*a*) *Where triable.*—For all purposes of and incidental to arrest, trial, and punishment, a crime for which a person is liable to be punished under this Act, when committed out of the United Kingdom, shall be deemed to have been committed in the place in which such person is apprehended, or is in custody, sec. 7 .

Offence.	Statute.	Punishment.
Extortion—		
Letter threatening to accuse of crime, with intent to extort, &c.	24 & 25 Vic. c. 96, s. 46. (27 & 28 Vic. c. 47.)	Felony; penal servitude for life, or not less than 5 years (not less than 7 if previously convicted of felony); or imprisonment not exceeding 2 years, with or without H. L., and solitary confinement; and male under 16 may be whipped.
Knowingly receiving goods, &c., obtained by extortion.	s. 91.	May be convicted as an accessory after the fact, or for a substantive felony.
The unlawful taking of money or thing of value by any officer by colour of his office; exacting a greater fee than is due, or where none is due, or before it is due.	Common Law	Misdemeanour; fine and imprisonment. (1 *Hawk.*, c. 68, ss. 1, 5; *Hayes*, 349.)
Extortion by Sheriff's bailiff, . .	27 & 28 Vic. c. 99, s. 18.	Misdemeanour.
For extortion by officers of bankruptcy, &c., see—	20 & 21 Vic. c. 60, s. 395.	To forfeit on conviction £500.
Extradition of Criminals (a)— EXTRADITION ACT, 1870, . .	33 & 34 Vic. c. 52.	
As to Orders in Council: The restrictions on surrender of criminals, when the offence is only of a political nature, or where he is accused of or undergoing sentence for offence in United Kingdom.	s. 3.	
Fifteen days must elapse between committal to prison and surrender.	,,	

(a) "*Extradition Crime*" means a crime which, if committed in England or within English jurisdiction, would be one of the crimes described in the *first schedule* to this Act, s. 26. The crimes enumerated in the *first schedule* to Act are—murder, and attempt and conspiracy to murder; manslaughter; counterfeiting and altering money, and uttering counterfeit or altered money; forgery; counterfeiting, and altering, and uttering what is forged or counterfeited or altered; em-

Offence.	Statute.	Punishment.
Extradition of Criminals— **EXTRADITION ACT, 1870—*continued*.** 1. *Warrant* to apprehend fugitive criminal may be issued by a Police Magistrate on receipt of order from Secretary of State, and on such evidence as would justify the warrant if offence committed in England. 2. Warrant may be issued by Police Magistrate or any Justice of the Peace in any part of the United Kingdom, on such information or complaint and evidence as would justify the issuing of warrant if the crime were committed within his jurisdiction. When criminal arrested and brought before a Magistrate authorized to issue warrant, he shall, by warrant, authorize him to be brought before police Magistrate.	33 & 34 Vic. c. 52, s. 8. "	Where the warrant is issued without authority of Secretary of State, report of the fact, and the evidence, &c., or certified copies thereof, to be forthwith transmitted to Secretary of State.

bezzlement and larceny, obtaining money or goods by false pretences; crimes by bankrupts against bankruptcy law; fraud by a baillie, banker, agent, factor, trustee, or director, or member, or public officer of any company—made criminal by any Act for the time being in force; rape; abduction; child-stealing; burglary and housebreaking; arson, robbery with violence; threats by letter or otherwise with intent to extort; piracy by law of nations; sinking or destroying a vessel at sea, or attempting or conspiring to do so; assaults on board a ship on the high seas, with intent to destroy life or to do grievous bodily harm; revolt or conspiracy to revolt by two or more persons on board a ship, on the high seas, against the authority of the master. The previous Convention Acts, as enumerated in the third schedule, are repealed. For forms of warrants, &c., see Act. If the Police Magistrate commits a fugitive criminal to prison, he shall inform such criminal that he will not be surrendered until after the expiration of 15 days, and that he has a right to apply for a writ of *Habeas Corpus*, s. 11. For receiving as authentic foreign warrants, depositions, &c., see sec. 15. The Justice, before issuing his warrant, should be satisfied of the authenticity of the warrant and documents produced to him; that they are brought by an accredited officer; that the charge against the criminal fugitive be clearly set forth in the warrant produced, and that the crime is one for which the accused should be surrendered: *Reg.* v. *Maurer* (or *Ex parte Maurer*), *L. R.* 10 *Q. B. D.*, 513; 52 *L. J.*, *M. C.*, 104; 31 *W. R.*, 609 (1883).

Where a fugitive criminal has been committed by a Police Magistrate under the provisions of the Extradition Act (33 & 34 Vic. c. 52, ss. 9, 10), it is not competent for the Court, upon an application for a writ of *Habeas Corpus*, to examine the weight of the evidence, provided there was reasonable evidence of an extradition crime for the Magistrate to act upon.

Offence.	Statute.	Punishment.
Extradition of Criminals—		
EXTRADITION ACT, 1870—*continued*.		
As to duties of Police Magistrate; hearing case and evidence; committal, discharge, or surrender of criminal, see—	33 & 34 Vic. c. 52, ss. 8 and 9.	
Receiving in evidence authenticated depositions, &c., in foreign state—	ss. 14 and 15.	
As to crimes committed at sea by such fugitive criminals, and where ship comes into the United Kingdom, certain powers of Police Magistrates to be exercised by Stipendiary Magistrates.	s. 16.	
EXTRADITION ACT, 1870, AMENDMENT.	36 & 37 Vic. c. 60.	
Explains sec. 6 of 33 & 34 Vic. c. 52,	s. 2.	
Liability of accessories to surrender,	s. 3.	
Explanations of sec. 14 of 33 & 34 Vic. c. 52, as to statements on oath, including affirmations.	s. 4.	
Power of taking evidence in United Kingdom for foreign criminal matters.	s. 5.	
Explanation of sec. 16 of 33 & 34 Vic. c. 52.	s. 6.	
Explanation of diplomatic representative and consul. Section 8 provides that the principal Act shall be construed as if there were included in the first schedule to that Act the list of crimes contained in the schedule to this Act. (See list at foot). (*a*) As to fugitive offenders in H. M. dominions, see title "Fugitive Offenders."	s. 7.	

(*a*) *List of Crimes above referred to.*—The following list of crimes is to be construed according to the law existing in England or in a British possession (as the

Offence.	Statute.	Punishment.
Factors (*Frauds by*)— See "Larceny," "Frauds by Agents," &c.		
False Entries (*in Register*)— See " Forgery."		
False Lights or Signals (*to Ships*)— See "Malicious Injuries."		
False Imprisonment— Every confinement of the person is an imprisonment, whether in a common prison or in a private house, or even a forcible detainer in the public streets. 2 *Inst.*, 589.	Common Law	Misdemeanour ; fine and imprisonment.

case may be), at the date of the alleged crime, whether by common law or by statute made before or after the passing of this Act :—

Kidnapping and false imprisonment.

Perjury and subornation of perjury, whether under common or statute law.

Any indictable offence under the " Larceny Act, 1861," or any Act amending or substituted for the same, which is not included in the first schedule to the principal Act.

Any indictable offence under the Act of the Session of the twenty-fourth and twenty-fifth years of the reign of Her present Majesty, chapter ninety-seven, " To consolidate and amend the Statute Law of England and Ireland, relating to Malicious Injuries to Property," or any Act amending or substituted for the same, which is not included in the first schedule to the principal Act.

Any indictable offence under the Act of the Session of the twenty-fourth and twenty-fifth years of the reign of Her present Majesty, chapter ninety-eight, " To consolidate and amend the Statute Law of England and Ireland, relating to Indictable Offences by Forgery," or any Act amending or substituted for the same, which is not included in the first schedule to the principal Act.

Any indictable offence under the Act of the Session of the twenty-fourth and twenty-fifth years of the reign of Her present Majesty, chapter ninety-nine, " To consolidate and amend the Statute Law of the United Kingdom against Offences relating to the Coin," or any Act amending or substituted for the same, which is not included in the first schedule to the principal Act.

Any indictable offence under the Act of the Session of the twenty-fourth and twenty-fifth years of the reign of Her present Majesty, chapter one hundred, " To consolidate and amend the Statute Law of England and Ireland relating to Offences against the Person," or any Act amending or substituted for the same, which is not included in the first schedule to the principal Act.

Any indictable offence under the laws for the time being in force in relation to bankruptcy which is not included in the first schedule to the principal Act.

Offence.	Statute.	Punishment.
False Personation— See "Personation."		
False Pretences (a)— By false pretence obtaining from any person any chattel, money, or valuable security, with intent to defraud. (The *attempt* to obtain, &c., with intent to defraud, is sufficient under this section). (b)	24 & 25 Vic. c. 96, s. 88. (27 & 28 Vic. c. 47.)	Misdemeanour; penal servitude 5 years (not less than 7 if previously convicted of felony); or imprisonment not exceeding 2 years, with or without H. L., and solitary confinement; and if on the trial it be found to be larceny, prisoner shall not be acquitted of the misdemeanour.
By false pretence causing or procuring money to be paid, or any chattel or security to be delivered to any other person with intent to defraud.	24 & 25 Vic. c. 96, s. 89.	Offence to be within the meaning of the preceding section.

(a) *False Pretence.*—In taking depositions for "False Pretences," it is important to give as nearly as possible the words used which constitute the offence. But it is not always necessary that the false pretence should be in words ; there may be a sufficient false pretence within the meaning of the Act, to be implied from the acts and conduct of the party, without any verbal representation of a false or fraudulent nature.—*Archbold, False Pretences*, page 305.

When a man represents as an existing fact that which is not an existing fact, and so gets the money or chattels of another, that is a false pretence. It is for the jury to say whether or not the pretences used were the means of obtaining the property.—*2 Russ., Cr.*, 3rd ed., 289, n. (g). So it is a false pretence—Where money is obtained by means of a begging letter, setting forth false statements as to the name and circumstances of the accused.—*Reg.* v. *Jones*, 1 *Den. C. C.*, 551. Or, where the accused falsely represents that he is connected with B, a person of known opulence, and on the faith of such representation obtains for himself property.— *Reg.* v. *Archer, Dearsl.*, 449. Or, where C, by fraudulently pretending that a genuine £1 Irish bank-note is a £5 note, obtains from D the full value of a £5 note in change.—*R.* v. *Jessop, Dearsl. & B.*, 442. It is not necessary that the false pretence should be in words, it may be evidenced by the conduct and acts of the accused, as by the fact of the prisoner going to a shop in Oxford or Cambridge, dressed in the academical costume, and ordering goods, although not being a member of the university : for this would be evidence whence a jury might infer a pretence that he was such a member.—*R.* v. *Barnard*, 7 *Car. & P.*, 784. (See also notes on "Larceny," Summary Index.)

(b) In the proviso at the end of the above section, it will be seen that the *attempt* to obtain the property, with intent to defraud, is sufficient for the purposes of the indictment.

As to conditions on which Bills of Indictment shall be sent to Grand Jury, see 22 & 23 Vic. c. 17, and title "Vexatious Indictments."

Offence.	Statute	Punishment.
False Pretences—*continued.* By false pretence fraudulently causing or inducing any other person to execute, make, accept, indorse, or destroy any valuable security, or to execute deeds, &c. And see "Bankrupt Act"; see also "Personation."	24 & 25 Vic. c. 96, s. 90. (27 & 28 Vic. c. 47.) 35 & 36 Vic. c. 57, s. 13.	Misdemeanour; penal servitude, 5 years (not less than 7, if previously convicted of felony); or imprisonment not exceeding 2 years, with or without H. L., and solitary confinement.
False Weights— Cheating by means of false weights, See Summary Index—"Weights and Measures."	Common Law	Misdemeanour; fine and imprisonment.
Falsification of Accounts— See "Larceny."		
Felony—(*Assault with intent to Commit*— See "Offences against the Person." And for Act abolishing forfeitures for treason or felony, and otherwise amending the law relating thereto; the disqualification of persons convicted for certain offences from exercising Franchise, &c., see— As to *costs* in cases of felony, the 55 Geo. iii. c. 91, repealed by "The Statute Law Revision Act, 1873," is revived by 37 & 38 Vic. c. 35. As to sentence of penal servitude, where offender previously convicted of felony, see "Penal Servitude."	33 & 34 Vic. c. 23, s. 32.	
Fences— See Summary Index—"Larceny," and "Malicious Injuries."		
Filings— See "Coin."		

Offence.	Statute.	Punishment.
Fire— See " Malicious Offences."		
Firing (*at Person*)— See " Offences against the Person."		
First Offenders— To permit the conditional release of in certain cases when before Superior and Summary Courts.	50 & 51 Vic. c. 25.	See Act, *Appendix.*
Fish (*taking in water belonging to a dwelling-house*)— See Summary Index ; title, " Larceny." See also " Fisheries."		
Fish-ponds— See " Malicious Injuries."		
Fixtures— See " Larceny " ; " Malicious Injuries." Also Summary Index ; title, " Landlord and Tenant," for precept to prevent waste.		
Food (*not providing Apprentices, &c., with*)— See " Offences against the Person " and " Public Health." Adulteration of—see " Adulteration," Summary Index.		
Forcible Abduction— See " Abduction" and " Offences against the Person" ; and see also title, " Criminial Law Amendment Act, 1885."		
Forcible Entry— See " Entry."		

Offence.	Statute.	Punishment.
Forcibly demanding Money— See "Larceny," &c. ; and see also "Conspiracy and Protection of Property," Summary Index.		
Foreign Enlistment Act, 1870— (Repeals the former Act, 59 Geo. iii. c. 69.) This Act is to regulate the conduct of Her Majesty's subjects during hostilities between foreign States with which Her Majesty is at peace.	33 & 34 Vic. c. 90.	
Prohibits enlistment by British subjects, or inducement by others of British subjects in Her Majesty's dominions to enlist in foreign service.	s. 4.	Misdemeanour; punishable by fine and imprisonment, or either of such punishments, at the discretion of the Court; imprisonment may be with or without H. L., but the term of imprisonment (sec. 13) shall not exceed 2 years; and all ships, munitions, &c., used in such expeditions, shall be forfeited to Her Majesty. Penalties not to extend to persons entering into military service in Asia.
Leaving Her Majesty's dominions with intent to serve foreign State.	s. 5.	
Embarking under false representations; taking illegally enlisted persons on board ship, &c.	ss. 6 and 7.	
Prohibits illegal ship-building, and illegal expeditions.	33 & 34 Vic. c. 90, s. 8.	
Aiding in warlike equipment of foreign ships.	s. 10.	
Fitting out naval or military expeditions without licence.	s. 11.	
Accessories punishable as principals.	s. 12.	
Provides for the disposal of illegal prizes.		
Procedure.—Offences deemed to be committed where wholly or partly committed, or where offender may be.		
As to power of Lord Lieutenant, &c., Customs and Naval Officers and local authority to seize and detain ships, and for general provisions, see Act.		
Foreign Coin— See "Coin."		

Offence.	Statute.	Punishment.
Forgery (a) *Of Her Majesty's seals*, sign-manual, &c., or uttering documents so forged.	24 & 25 Vic. c. 98, s. 1. (27 & 28 Vic. c. 47.)	Felony; penal servitude for life, or not less than 5 years (not less than 7 if previously convicted of felony); or imprisonment not exceeding 2 years, with or without H. L., and solitary confinement.
Public Funds. (b)—Forgery of transfer of stock, or powers of attorney, &c.	s. 2.	Felony; penal servitude for life, or not less than 5 years (not less than 7 if previously convicted of felony); or imprisonment not exceeding 2 years, with or without H. L., and solitary confinement.
Personating owner of stock, &c., .	s. 3.	Like.
Forging attestation of power of attorney for transfers.	s. 4.	Felony; penal servitude from 5 to 7 years (not less than 7 if previously convicted of felony); or imprisonment as preceding.
Making false entries in the books of the public funds, &c.	s. 5.	Felony; penal servitude for life, or not less than 5 years (not less than 7 if previously convicted of felony); or imprisonment as above.

(a) *Forgery at Common Law.*—At Common Law the offence of forgery was punished as a misdemeanour. It is defined by *Blackstone* as "the fraudulent making or alteration of a writing to the prejudice of another man's right," and by *Mr. East* as "a false making *malo animo* of any written instrument for the purpose of fraud and deceit."—2 *East, P. C.* 852.

(b) *Stocks, Certificates, Coupons, &c.*—The Forgery Act, 1870, further provides against the forgery, &c., of stock, certificates, coupons, &c., issued in pursuance of Part V. of the National Debt Act, 1870, or of any former Act; against the personation of owners of stock, &c.; the unlawfully engraving of plates, &c., for stock, certificates, &c.; and the forgery of certificates of transfer of stocks from England to Ireland, &c.

Offence.	Statute.	Punishment.
Forgery—*continued.* **Making** out or delivering false dividend warrants.	24 & 25 Vic. c. 98, s. 6. (27 & 28 Vic. c. 47.)	Felony; penal servitude from 5 to 7 years (not less than 7 if previously convicted of felony); or imprisonment not exceeding 2 years, with or without H. L., and solitary confinement.
India Bonds.—Forging, uttering, altering, &c.	s. 7.	Felony; penal servitude for life, or not less than 5 years (not less than 7 if previously convicted of felony); or imprisonment as preceding.
Exchequer Bills, &c.—Forging, uttering, altering, &c., or any receipts for interest.	s. 8.	Felony; like punishment.
Plates.—Without lawful authority, making, or causing to be made, or knowingly having in possession, frames or instruments, plates, seals, or dies, &c., in imitation.	s. 9.	Felony; penal servitude 5 to 7 years (not less than 7 if previously convicted of felony); or imprisonment not exceeding 2 years, with or without H. L., and solitary confinement.
Paper, &c.—Making, causing to be made, or having in possession, intended to imitate.	s. 10.	Like.
Possession of paper manufactured under directions of Commissioners, &c., for Exchequer bills, bonds, &c., before issue for public use, or any plates or seals as in two preceding sections, without lawful authority.	s. 11.	Misdemeanour; imprisonment not exceeding 5 years, with or without H. L.
Bank-notes.—Forging, uttering, &c., notes of Bank of England or Ireland, or any bank notes, bills of	s. 12.	Felony; penal servitude for life, or not less than 5 years (not less than 7

Offence.	Statute.	Punishment.
Forgery—*continued.* exchange, bank post bills, &c., with intent to defraud. (a)	24 & 25 Vic. c. 98, s. 12. (27 & 28 Vic. c. 47.)	if previously convicted of felony) ; or imprisonment not exceeding 2 years, with or without H. L., and solitary confinement.
Purchasing, receiving, or having in possession, knowingly, and without lawful excuse.	s. 13.	Felony ; penal servitude 14 years, and not less than 5 years (not less than 7 if previously convicted of felony) ; or imprisonment not exceeding 2 years, with or without H. L.
Making or knowingly having in possession mould or instrument for making paper with the words "Bank of England," or "Bank of Ireland," or with curved lines, or selling such paper. And see exceptions.	s. 14.	Felony ; like punishment.
Plates, &c.—Engraving plates, &c., for notes of Bank of England or Ireland, or other banks ; or having paper upon which a blank banknote, &c., is printed.	s. 16.	Felony ; like punishment.
Engraving resembling part of a banknote, or paper on which any such part is impressed, having same in possession, &c.	s. 17.	Felony ; like punishment.
Making, using, or having in possession, mould for paper, with the name of any banker, or having paper in possession.	s. 18.	Felony ; like punishment.
Making plates for foreign bills, or paper upon which any part of such bill is printed, or knowingly having in possession.	s. 19.	Felony ; penal servitude not exceeding 14 years, nor less than 5 (not less than 7 if previously convicted of felony) ; or imprisonment not exceeding 2 years, with or without H. L.

(a) It has been decided that the forgery may be proved by any of the bank inspectors or by any person acquainted with the handwriting of the signing clerk, without calling the latter.—*Archbold*, 457.

Offence.	Statute.	Punishment.
Forgery—*continued.* *Deeds, Wills, Bills of Exchange, Orders, &c.*—With intent to defraud, forging, altering, uttering, &c., any deed, bond, or assignment, or forging witnesses' names, &c.	24 & 25 Vic. c. 98, s. 20. (27 & 28 Vic. c. 47.)	Felony; penal servitude for life, or not less than 5 years (not less than 7 if previously convicted of felony); or imprisonment not exceeding 2 years, with or without H. L., and solitary confinement.
Forging, altering, uttering *Wills, &c.,* knowingly. (a)	s. 21.	Like offence and punishment.
Forging, altering, uttering, &c., knowingly, bills of exchange, acceptances, promissory notes, or assignments, &c,, with intent to defraud.	s. 22.	Like offence and punishment.
Forging, uttering, &c., knowingly, undertaking, warrant, order, &c., for payment of money, delivery or transfer of goods, &c., or for procuring or giving credit, &c., with intent to defraud.	s. 23.	Like offence and punishment.
Making or accepting, &c., bill, note, undertaking, order, &c., by procuration or otherwise, in the name of any person, without lawful authority, and with intent to defraud.	s. 24.	Felony; penal servitude not exceeding 14 years, and not less than 5 years (not less than 7 if previously convicted of felony); or imprisonment not exceeding 2 years, with or without H. L., and solitary confinement.
Obliterating bankers' names, or crossings on cheques or drafts, or adding to, altering, uttering, &c.,	s. 25.	Felony; penal servitude for life, or not less than 5 years (not less than

(a) Forgery may be committed of the will of a person who is alive, or the will f a person who never existed; nor will a probate (unrevoked) of the forged will e an answer to the charge.—*Arch. Forg.*, p. 465.

Offence.	Statute.	Punishment.
Forgery—*continued.* same, knowingly, and with intent to defraud. (See extension of this section for purposes of the "Revenue Act, 1883," 46 & 47 Vic. c. 55, s. 17.)	24 & 25 Vic. c. 98, s. 25. (27 & 28 Vic. c. 47.)	7 if previously convicted of felony); or imprisonment not exceeding 2 years, with or without H. L., and solitary confinement.
Debentures.—Forging, altering, uttering debentures issued under lawful authority in Her Majesty's dominions or elsewhere.	s. 26.	Felony; penal servitude not exceeding 14 nor less than 5 years (not less than 7 if previously convicted of felony); or imprisonment not exceeding 2 years, with or without H. L., and solitary confinement.
Records of Courts, &c.—Forging, altering, uttering knowingly, records, writs, returns, panel, process, rule, order, warrant, interrogatory, deposition, affidavit, affirmation, recognizance, *cognovit actionem*, warrant of attorney, or any original document of Courts of Record or proceedings of Courts of Equity or Admiralty, or copies of documents to be used as evidence.	s. 27.	Felony; penal servitude not exceeding 7 nor less than 5 years (not less than 7 if previously convicted of felony); or imprisonment not exceeding 2 years, with or without H L., and solitary confinement.
Clerk or officer altering false copies or certificates of records knowingly; persons other than officers, &c., signing as such officer; and any person forging or altering, or knowingly uttering forged copies or certificates of records; forging seals of Courts of Record, or forging processes of any other Courts than those in section before mentioned, serving or enforcing forged process, or acting thereunder.	s. 28.	Felony; like punishment.
Forging or uttering, &c., knowingly, instruments made evidence by statute.	s. 29.	Felony; like punishment.

Offence.	Statute.	Punishment.
Forgery—*continued*. *Court Rolls.*—Forging,altering,uttering, &c., knowingly, with intent to defraud.	24 & 25 Vic. c. 98, s. 30. (27 & 28 Vic. c. 47.)	Felony; penal servitude for life, or not less than 5 years (not less than 7 if previously convicted of felony); or imprisonment not exceeding 2 years, with or without H. L., and solitary confinement.
Proclamations, &c.—Forging proclamations, orders, or regulations, falsely purporting to be printed by Government printer, knowingly tendering same in evidence, &c., see—	31 & 32 Vic. c. 37.	Felony; penal servitude 5 years (not less than 7 if previously convicted of felony); or imprisonment not exceeding 2 years, with or without H. L.
Registers of Deeds, &c.—Forging, altering, uttering, &c., knowingly, forged or fraudulently altered memorial, affidavit, &c., or writing made or issued under Acts relating to registry of deeds, seals, stamps, or names of persons, &c.	24 & 25 Vic. c. 98, s. 7. (27 & 28 Vic. c. 47.)	Felony; penal servitude not exceeding 14 years, nor less than 5 years (not less than 7 if previously convicted of felony); or imprisonment not exceeding 2 years, with or without H. L., and solitary confinement.
Orders, &c., of Justices of the Peace.—With intent to defraud, forging, altering, uttering, &c., summons, conviction, order, warrant, recognizance, examination, deposition, affidavit, affirmation, solemn declaration.	s. 32.	Felony; penal servitude for 5 years (not less than 7 if previously convicted of felony); or imprisonment not exceeding 2 years, with or without H. L., and solitary confinement.
Accountant-General, &c.—With intent to defraud, forging or altering certificate, instrument, writing, &c., of Accountant-General, officers of Courts of Chancery, officers of Banks of England or Ireland, or their names, or uttering, &c.	s. 33.	Felony; penal servitude not exceeding 14 years, nor less than 5 years (not less than 7 if previously convicted of felony); or imprisonment not exceeding 2 years, with or without H. L., and solitary confinement.

Offence.	Statute.	Punishment.
Forgery—*continued.* *Recognizances, &c.*—Acknowledging, without lawful authority, recognizance, bail, cognovit, or instrument, &c., in name of another.	24 & 25 Vic. c. 98, s. 34. (27 & 28 Vic. c. 47.)	Felony; penal servitude not exceeding 7, nor less than 5 years (not less than 7 if previously convicted of felony); or imprisonment not exceeding 2 years, with or without H. L., and solitary confinement.
Marriage Licences or Certificates.—Forging altering, &c.	s. 35.	Like.
Forging Registers of Births, Marriages, Deaths, or Burials, authorized or required by Law, or certified copies thereof, inserting false entries, &c., or giving false certificates, or certifying false copies, seals, &c., or uttering.	s. 36.	Felony; penal servitude for life, or not less than 5 years (not less than 7 if previously convicted of felony); or imprisonment not exceeding 2 years, with or without H. L., and solitary confinement.
Knowingly and wilfully inserting false entries in copies of register required by law, relating to baptism, marriage, burial, certifying false copies, fraudulently destroying, removing, or concealing copies, &c.	s. 37.	Like.
Forging Signature of Commissioner or Officers of Court of Matrimonial Causes, or Commissioner of Court of Chancery, or counterfeiting seals, &c., or tendering in evidence forged documents, &c.	34 & 35 Vic. c. 49, s. 15.	Felony; penal servitude for life, or not less than 7 years; or imprisonment not exceeding 3 years, with or without H. L.
Forging trade-marks, by addition or alteration, see—	25 & 26 Vic. c. 88.	Misdemeanour; and for penalty and punishment see Act.
Demanding Property upon Forged Instruments.—With intent to defraud, demanding, receiving, obtaining, or causing to be, &c., any chattel, money, or property whatsoever, under or by virtue of any forged or altered instrument, letters of administration, &c., knowing will, &c., to be forged—	24 & 25 Vic. c. 98, s. 38. (27 & 28 Vic. c. 47.)	Felony; penal servitude not exceeding 14 years, nor less than 5 years (not less than 7 if previously convicted of felony); or imprisonment not exceeding 2 years, with or without H. L., and solitary confinement.

Offence.	Statute.	Punishment.
Forgery—*continued.*		
Other Matters.—Forging, altering, or uttering, knowingly, any instrument or writing, however designated, which shall be in law a will, deed, bond, bill, note, &c.	24 & 25 Vic. c. 98, s. 39. (27 & 28 Vic. c. 47.)	May be indicted as an offender against this Act, and punished accordingly.
Forging in England or Ireland documents purporting to be made out of England and Ireland. Forging, &c., in England or Ireland bills of exchange, &c., purporting to be payable out of England or Ireland.	s. 40.	Shall be deemed an offender against this Act, and punishable as if the money were payable in England and Ireland.
Forgers, &c., may be tried in the county where they are apprehended, or in custody.	s. 41.	
In indictment, instruments may be described under the name usually known by.	s. 42.	
So in indictments for engraving.	s. 43.	—
Intent to defraud particular persons need not be alleged or proved.	s. 44.	—
Criminal Possession shall mean personal custody or possession, or knowingly in actual custody or possession of another, or knowingly in any place, &c., and whether for own use or that of another.	s. 45.	
Search-warrant.—On information on oath, Justice may grant warrant to search for paper and implements employed in forgery, and for forged instruments.	s. 46.	
Punishments substituted for those of 5 Eliz. c. 14, which have been adopted in other Acts.	s. 47.	
All forgeries which were capital before the 1 Wm. iv. c. 66, and are not otherwise punishable under this Act, shall be punishable with—	s. 48.	Penal servitude for life, or for not less than 5 years (nor less than 7 if previously convicted of felony); or imprisonment not exceeding 2 years, with or without H. D., and solitary confinement.
Principals, &c.—In felony, principals in second degree, and every accessory before the fact—	s. 49.	Punishable as principal in first degree.

Offence.	Statute.	Punishment.
Forgery—*continued.* Accessory after the fact to felony.	24 & 25 Vic. c. 98, s. 49. (27 & 28 Vic. c. 47.)	Imprisonment not exceed- ing 2 years, with or without H. L., and soli- tary confinement.
Aiders and abettors in misdemean- ours.	,,	Punishable as principal offenders.
Solitary confinement, when awarded.	s. 53.	Not to exceed a month at a time, and not to ex- ceed 3 months in a year.
Stamps.—As to forgeries of dies or stamps, and criminal offences re- lating to, see "Stamps," and	33 & 34 Vic. c. 98, s. 18.	
Customs.—Forging, counterfeiting, or causing, &c., name or hand- writing of Commissioner of Cus- toms, Accountant- or Comptroller- General, &c., in order to obtain money from Bank of England, &c., or uttering, &c., with intent—	34 & 35 Vic. c. 104, s. 8.	Felony.
"*Documentary Evidence Act*, 1882." —Applies Documentary Evidence Act, 1868, as amended by this Act, to Ireland, as to certain procla- mations, orders, regulations, &c., issued by Lord Lieutenant.	45 Vic. c. 9.	
If any person prints any copy of any Act, proclamation, order, regula- tion, Royal Warrant, circular, list, gazette, or document, which falsely purports to have been printed under the superintendence of Her Majesty's Stationery Office, or tenders in evidence any copy which falsely purports to have been printed as aforesaid, knowing that the same was not so printed—	s. 3.	Felony; penal servitude not exceeding 7 years; or imprisonment not ex- ceeding 2 years, with or without H. L.
Frauds (*By Bankers, Agents, &c.*)— See "Larceny."		

Offence.	Statute.	Punishment.
Fugitive Offenders Act, 1881— As to apprehension of fugitive offenders accused of offences committed in any part of Her Majesty's dominions, the issue of provisional warrants, &c., and how offender to be dealth with, see sections 2 to 11.	44 & 45 Vic. c. 69.	
Offences to which this part of Act applies.—Treason, piracy, and to every offence whatever called felony, misdemeanour, crime, or by any other name which is for the time being punishable in any part of Her Majesty's dominions in which it was committed, either by indictment or information, by imprisonment with H. L. (*a*). For extradition criminals see "Extradition."		
Furious Driving (*Bodily Harm by*)— See "Offences against the Person," and Summary Index.		
Furze (*Setting Fire to*)— See "Malicious Injuries."		
Fraudulent Debtors— See "Bankrupt."		
Game (*Night Poaching*)— See Summary Index; title, "Game."	9 Geo. iv. c. 69.	Where third offence, becomes indictable misdemeanour.

(*a*) *Fugitive Offenders.*—The Justice who issues warrant should see that the evidence which accompanies the demand for the arrest should contain distinct allegations that the offence is punishable in England by H. L., for a term of 12 months or more (sec. 9). Magistrates should also attend to the circular on the subject, No. 27, 9th January, 1884, forwarding communications from the Secretary of State and the Solicitor's Department to the Treasury. Act applies to fugitive offenders from one part to another part of Her Majesty's dominions.

Offence.	Statute.	Punishment.
Gaming Houses— See Summary Index; title, "Gaming Houses," and see "Vexatious Indictments."		
Garden— See "Larceny" and "Malicious Injuries."		
Gazette (*Proclamations, &c., as to given in evidence*).	31 & 32 Vic. c. 37.	
Girl— Abusing, &c., "Offences against the Person," and see title, "Criminal Law Amendment Act, 1885."		
Glycerine— See "Nitro-Glycerine."		
Gunpowder (*having*)— To commit offences—see "Malicious Injuries," and "Offences against the Person," and see "Gunpowder," Summary Index. See also "Explosives," Indictable Index.		
Habeas Corpus Act (*a*)—	31 Car. ii. c. 2. 21 & 21 Geo. iii. c. 11. 56 Geo. iii. c. 100.	

(a) *Habeas Corpus Act.*—This celebrated statute did not introduce any new principle, but only confirmed and rendered more available a remedy which had long existed. The great charter had provided against arbitrary imprisonment, and the Petition of Right renewed and extended the principle; but some provisions were still wanting to render it complete, and prevent all evasion or delay from Ministers and Judges. By the Act of *Habeas Corpus* it is prohibited to send any one to prison beyond the sea: no Judge, under severe penalties, must refuse to any ner a Writ of *Habeas Corpus*, by which the gaoler is directed to produce in

Offence.	Statute.	Punishment.
Harbouring— Harbouring or concealing a felon in house, or affording him assistance in order to prevent his apprehension, trial, or punishment, or employing another person to harbour him.	—	Such person thereby becomes an accessory after the fact to a felony.
Hard Labour— Offenders may be sentenced to, in certain misdemeanours. (a)	14 & 15 Vic. c. 100, s. 29.	

Court the body of the prisoner (whence the writ had its name), and to certify the cause of his detainer and imprisonment. Every prisoner must be indicted the first term after his commitment, and brought to trial in the subsequent term; and no man, after being enlarged by order of Court, can be recommitted for the same offence. The writ appears to have been framed in conformity with one of the essential clauses of Magna Charta, which says: "No freeman shall be taken or imprisoned or be disseised of his freehold, or liberties of free customs, or be outlawed, or exiled, or any otherwise destroyed; nor will we pass upon him, nor send upon him, but by lawful judgment of his peers or by the law of the land. We will sell to no man, we will not deny or delay to any man justice or right." These are the words of the 4th chap. of Henry III.'s Charter, which is the existing law. They differ only slightly from those in John's Charter. "It is obvious," adds Mr. Hallam, "that these words, interpreted by any honest Court of Law, convey an ample security for the two main rights of civil society. Whether Courts of justice framed the writ of *Habeas Corpus* in conformity to the spirit of this clause, or found it already in their register, it became from that era the right of every subject to demand it. That writ, rendered more actively remedial by the statute of Charles the Second, but founded upon the broad basis of Magna Charta, is the principal bulwark of English liberty; and if ever temporary circumstances, or the doubtful plea of political necessity, it shall lead men to look on its denial with apathy, the most distinguishing characteristic of our Constitution will be effaced." —*Hallam's Middle Ages*, vol. ii. c. 1.

The Act has been suspended on many occasions, the last being by the Session of 1881, Coercion (Ireland) Act.

(a) 14 & 15 Vic. c. 100, s. 29.—"Whenever any person shall be convicted of any one of the offences following, as an indictable misdemeanour, that is to say—any cheat or fraud punishable at Common Law; any conspiracy to cheat or defraud, or to extort money or goods, or falsely to accuse of any crime, or to obstruct, prevent, pervert, or defeat the course of public justice; any escape or rescue from lawful custody on a criminal charge; any public and indecent exposure of the person; any indecent assaut, or any assault occasioning actual bodily harm; any attempt to have carnal knowledge of a child under 12 years of age; any public selling, or exposure for public sale, or to public view, of any obscene book, print, picture, or other indecent exhibition; it shall be lawful for the Court to sentence the offender to be imprisoned for any term now warranted

Statute.

Homicide—
See " Offences against the Person."

Horse—
Stealing—see " Larceny."
Injuries to—see " Malicious In-
juries."

House—
See " Larceny " and " Malicious
Injuries."

Husband and Wife—
See " Wife ; " and see also " Married Women," Summary Index.

Importing (*Counterfeit Coin*)—
See " Coin."

Offence.	Statute.	Punishment.
Infamous Crime— Letter threatening to accuse of, with intent to extort—see "Larceny," &c.; also "Offences against the Person."		
Infant— Abandoning, exposing, concealing birth, &c.—see "Offences against the Person."		
Infanticide— See "Offences against the Person" (*Homicide*).		
Kidnapping (*Stealing, Carrying Away or Secreting any Person*). (And see "Child Stealing," "Offence against the Person" Act—24 & 25 Vic. c. 100, s. 56; and for protection of Girls, see title, "Criminal Law Amendment Act, 1885."	Common Law	Fine and imprisonment.
Larceny, and Offences of that nature (*a*)— (Under this head will be included the other criminal offences:—*Stealing, Robbery, Burglary, Embezzlement, Frauds, &c., False Pretences, Receiving Stolen Property*.)	24 & 25 Vic. s. 96.	In case, wherein Magistrates exercise summary jurisdiction—see Summary Index; title, "Larceny."

(*a*) *Property*.—Shall include every description of real and personal property, money, debts, and legacies, and all deeds and instruments evidencing title, &c.—sec. 1.

Night.—Shall be deemed to commence at 9 o'clock, P.M., and to conclude at o'clock, A.M., on the succeeding day.—Sec. 1.

Larceny generally.—Every larceny, whatever be the value of the property stolen, shall be deemed to be of the same nature, and shall be subject to the same incidents in all respects as grand larceny was before 21st June, 1827.—Sec. 2.

Bailee.—Whosoever being a bailee of any chattel, money, or valuable security shall fraudulently take or convert the same to his own use, or the use of any

2 M

Offence.	Statute.	Punishment.
Larceny—*continued.* Simple larceny after a previous con- viction for felony, whether such conviction shall have taken place upon an indictment or under the provisions of 18 & 19 Vic. c. 126, shall be liable to— (This statute 18 & 19 Vic. c. 126, called the Criminal Justice Act, enables Justices in Petty Sessions to try cases of larceny—see Sum- mary Index.)	24 & 25 Vic. c. 96, s. 7. (27 & 28 Vic. c. 47.)	Penal servitude not ex- ceeding 10 years, and not less than 5 (not less than 7 if previously con- victed of felony) ; or imprisonment not ex- ceeding 2 years, with or without H. L., and solitary confinement. Male under 16 may be whipped.

person other than the owner thereof, although he shall not break bulk or otherwise determine the bailment, shall be guilty of larceny, and may be convicted thereof upon an indictment for larceny ; but this section shall not extend to any offence punishable on summary conviction—Sec. 3.

Punishment generally—"Whosoever shall be convicted of simple larceny, or of any felony hereby made punishable like simple larceny, shall (except in the cases hereinafter otherwise provided for) be liable, at the discretion of the Court, to be kept in penal servitude for the term of three (now five) years, or to be imprisoned for any term not exceeding two years, with or without hard labour, and with or without solitary confinement ; and if a male under the age of 16 years, with or without whipping."—Sec. 4. And where offender has been previously convicted of felony, not less than seven years.—27 & 28 Vic. c. 47.

Indictment.—"It shall be lawful to insert several counts in the same indictment against the same person for any number of distinct acts of stealing, not exceeding three, which may have been committed by him against the same person within the space of six months from the first to the last of such acts, and to proceed thereon for all or any of them."—Sec. 5. (It is the same in embezzlement—see sec. 71.)

Possession obtained by Fraud.—"It is clear that if the possession of goods be obtained by fraud, this is a taking possession of the goods so as to constitute larceny. The difficulty in these cases has arisen in discovering what was the intention of the prisoner at the time that he obtained the possession ; as the question, whether or not he was guilty of larceny, turned formerly entirely on this point. If his intention was originally fraudulent, then it was larceny ; if it was originally innocent, then he was merely a *bailee*, and a subsequent fraudulent appropriation was not necessarily larceny. Now, however, inasmuch as every fraudulent appropriation by a bailee is (by 24 & 25 Vic. c. 96, s. 3) a larceny, and the prisoner in this case would be at least a bailee, the distinction is of less importance."—*Roscoe*. See note *Bailee, supra*. But it must be borne in mind that if the owner of the goods part with the *property* as well as the *possession*, the offence is not larceny. "The point aimed at by the expressions *animo furandi*, and *lucri causâ*, the meaning of which has been much discussed, seems to be this—that the goods must be taken into the possession of the thief with the intention of depriving the owner of his property in them."—*Roscoe*.

Offence.	Statute.	Punishment.
Larceny—*continued.* Simple larceny, or any offence so punishable, after a previous conviction of any indictable misdemeanour under this Act.	24 & 25 Vic. c. 96, s. 8. (27 & 28 Vic. c. 47.)	Penal servitude not exceeding 7 years, and not less than 5 years (not less than 7 if previously convicted of felony); or imprisonment not exceeding 2 years, with or without H. L., and solitary confinement; and male under 16 may be whipped.
Simple larceny or any offence hereby so punishable, after being twice summarily convicted of any of the offences punishable upon summary conviction under 7 & 8 Geo. iv. cc. 29 and 30; 9 Geo. iv. cc. 55 and 56; 10 & 11 Vic. c. 82; 11 & 12 Vic. c. 59; or in sections 3, 4, 5, and 6 of 14 & 15 Vic. c. 92; or under this Act, or the Malicious Injuries Act, c. 97, whether or not each of the convictions shall be in respect to an offence of the same description, or whether the convictions be before or after this Act.	s. 9.	Felony; penal servitude not exceeding 7, and not less than 5 years (not less than 7 if previously convicted of felony); or imprisonment not exceeding 2 years, with or without H. L., and solitary confinement; and male under 16 may be whipped.
Larceny of Animals.—Stealing any horse, mare, gelding, colt, or filly; or any bull, cow, ox, heifer, or calf; or any ram, ewe, sheep, or lamb.	24 & 25 Vic. c. 96, s. 10.	Felony; penal servitude not exceeding 14, and not less than 5 years (not less than 7 if previously convicted of felony); or imprisonment not exceeding 2 years, with or without H. L., and solitary confinement.
Wilfully killing any animal with intent to steal the carcass, skin, or any part of the animal so killed.	s. 11.	Felony; punishable as for stealing, provided the stealing of the animal so killed would have amounted to felony.
Whosoever shall unlawfully and wilfully course, hunt, snare, or carry away, or kill or wound, or attempt to kill or wound, any *deer* kept or being in the *unenclosed* part of any forest, chase, or purlieu—	s. 12.	Triable summarily. See Summary Index; title, "Larceny."

Offence.	Statute.	Punishment.
Larceny—*continued.* *Second offence* as above enumerated, and whether of same description as the first or not—	24 & 25 Vic. c. 96, s. 12.	Felony; imprisonment not exceeding 2 years, with or without H. L., and solitary confinement. Male under 16 may be whipped.
Whoever shall unlawfully and wilfully course, hunt, snare, or carry away, or kill or wound, or attempt, &c., any deer kept or being in the *enclosed* part of any forest, chase, or purlieu, or in any enclosed land where deer shall be usually kept—	s. 13.	Like punishment as last preceding.
Suspected persons in possession of venison, &c., or snare or engine, &c.	s. 14.	Summary Index; title, "Larceny."
Setting engines for taking deer, or pulling down fences.	s. 15.	Like.
Deer-keepers may seize the guns, dogs, &c., of offenders; and for beating or wounding any person who may be intrusted with the care of deer, or his assistants—	s. 16.	Felony; imprisonment not exceeding 2 years, with or without H. L., and solitary confinement; and Male under 16 may be whipped.
Killing hares or rabbits in a warren between expiration of first hour after sunset and beginning of last hour before sunrise, whether enclosed or not.	s. 17.	Misdemeanour.
Killing at other times, . . .	,,	See Summary Index; title, "Larceny."
Whosoever shall steal any dog, .	s. 18.	Like.
Second offence, ...	,,	Misdemeanour.
Corruptly taking money or reward, directly or indirectly, under the pretence of aiding in the recovery of stolen dog.	s. 20.	Misdemeanour; imprisonment not exceeding 18 months, with or without H. L.
Stealing beasts or birds ordinarily kept in a state of confinement, &c.	ss. 21, 22, 23.	See Summary Index; title, "Larceny."

Offence.	Statute.	Punishment.
Larceny—*continued.* *Fish.*—Unlawfully and wilfully taking and destroying any fish in any water which shall run through or be in any land adjoining or belonging to the dwelling-house of any person being the owner of such water, or having a right of fishery therein.	24 & 25 Vic c. 96, s. 24.	Misdemeanour; and see also Summary Index; title, "Larceny."
Stealing any oysters or oyster-brood from any oyster-bed, laying, or fishery, being the property of any other person and sufficiently marked out or known as such.	s. 26.	Felony; punishable as simple larceny.
Unlawfully and wilfully dredging for, &c., although none be actually taken. Not to prevent the taking of floating fish.	—	Misdemeanour; imprisonment not exceeding 3 months, with or without H. L., and solitary confinement.
Larceny of Written Instruments.— Stealing, or, for a fraudulent purpose, destroying, &c., any valuable security, other than a document of title to lands.	24 & 25 Vic. c. 96, s. 27. (27 & 28 Vic. c. 47.)	Felony ; punishable as if he had stolen the property or money thereby represented or secured, &c. &c.
Stealing, or, for a fraudulent purpose destroying, &c., or concealing the whole or part of document of title to lands.	s. 28.	Felony ; penal servitude 5 years (not less than 7 if previously convicted of felony) ; or imprisonment not exceeding 2 years, with or without H. L., and solitary confinement.
Stealing, or, for a fraudulent purpose destroying, cancelling, &c.; or concealing the whole or part of any will or codicil, or testamentary writing, during testator's life or after his death.	s. 29.	Penal servitude for life, or for not less than 5 years (not less than 7 if previously convicted of felony); or, imprisonment not exceeding 2 years, with or without H. L., and solitary confinement; and not to take away other remedies.

Offence.	Statute.	Punishment.
Larceny—*continued.* Stealing, &c., writs, documents, or proceedings on suits depending or terminated, &c. ; or from public offices or departments.	24 & 25 Vic. c. 96, s. 30. (27 & 28 Vic. c. 47.)	Felony; penal servitude 5 years (not less than 7 if previously convicted of felony); or imprisonment not exceeding 2 years, with or without H. L., and solitary confinement.
Larceny of things attached to Land. —Stealing, ripping, breaking, with intent to steal, any glass, wood-work belonging to any building ; lead, iron, copper, brass utensils or fixtures fixed in any building ; or anything made of metal, fixed in any land, being private property ; or for a fence to any dwelling-house, garden, or area, square, or street, or place dedicated to public use or ornament, or in any burial-ground.	s. 31.	Felony; punishable as in simple larceny.
Trees.—Stealing, or damaging with intent to steal, any tree, sapling, shrub, underwood, growing in park, pleasure-ground, orchard, garden, avenue, or ground adjoining or belonging to dwelling-house (if the value or injury done exceed £1).	s. 32.	Felony ; punishable as simple larceny.
If growing elsewhere, and the value or injury exceed £5.	,,	Like.
Trees, &c., wheresoever growing, .	s. 33.	See Summary Index; title, " Larceny."
Stealing *fence*, stile or gate, . .	s. 34.	Like.
Stealing fruit or vegetables, . .	ss. 36 and 37.	Like.
Larceny from Mines.—Stealing, or severing with intent to steal, the ore of any metal, lapis calaminaris, manganese, or mundic ; or any wad, black cauk, black lead, coal or cannel coal, from any mine, &c.	s. 38.	Felony ; imprisonment not exceeding 2 years, wich or without H. L., and solitary confinement.
Miners removing ore, with intent to defraud.	s. 39.	Like.

Offence.	Statute.	Punishment.
Larceny—*continued.* *Larceny from the Person.*—Whosoever shall rob any person, or shall steal any chattel, money, or valuable security from the person of another. (*a*)	24 & 25 Vic. c. 96, s. 40. (27 & 28 Vic. c. 47.)	Felony ; penal servitude not exceeding 14, and not less than 5 years (not less than 7 if previously convicted of felony) ; or, imprisonment not exceeding 2 years, with or without H. L., and solitary confinement.
On trial for robbery, the jury may convict of an assault with intent to rob.	s. 41.	
Whosoever shall assault any person with intent to rob.	s. 42.	Felony (save where greater punishment provided by this Act) ; penal servitude 5 years (not less than 7 if previously convicted of felony) ; or imprisonment not exceeding 2 years, with or without H. L., and solitary confinement.
Whosoever shall, being armed with any offensive weapon, rob, or assault with intent to rob, any person ; or, together with one or more others, rob, or assault with intent to rob any person ; or shall rob any person, and at the time, or immediately before or after, shall beat, wound, &c., or use any other personal violence.	s. 43.	Felony ; penal servitude for life, or not less than 5 years (not less than 7 if previously convicted of felony) ; or imprisonment not exceeding 2 years, with or without H. L., and solitary confinement ; and male offender may be whipped —26 & 27 Vic. c. 44. (*b*)

(*a*) Actual force is not essentially necessary to constitute robbery ; if, by the use of threats, by words or gestures sufficient to overcome a mind of ordinary firmness, a man be induced to part with his property to another who has no pretence or claim of right to it, it is as much a robbery as if it had been obtained by actual violence. —*Fost.*, 128 ; *Arch.*, p. 216.

(*b*) The 26 & 27 Vic. c. 44, adds whipping in above case, and also for offences against the 23rd sec. of the 24 & 25 Vic. c. 100 (" Offences against the Person Act"). See title " Offences against the Person," where the Whipping Act is given at foot.

Offence.	Statute.	Punishment.
Larceny—*continued.* Sending, delivering, uttering, or directly or indirectly causing to be received, knowing the contents, any letter or writing demanding with menaces and without probable cause any property, money, or security, &c.	24 & 25 Vic. c. 96, s. 44. (27 & 28 Vic. c. 47.)	Felony; penal servitude for life, or not less than 5 years (not less than 7 if previously convicted of felony); or imprisonment not exceeding 2 years, with or without H. L., and solitary confinement.
With menaces or by force demanding any property, money, &c., with intent to steal.	s. 45.	Felony; penal servitude 5 years (not less than 7 if previously convicted of felony); or imprisonment not exceeding 2 years, with or without H. L., and solitary confinement.
Sending, or directly or indirectly causing to be received, letter accusing or threatening to accuse of any crime punishable with death, penal servitude, or not less than 7 years; or assault with intent to, or attempt to commit rape; or with *infamous* crime, with intent to extort. (Infamous crime by the section means Sodomy or bestiality.)	s. 46.	Felony; penal servitude for life, or not less than 5 years (not less than 7 if previously convicted of felony); or imprisonment not exceeding 2 years, with or without H. L., and solitary confinement. Male under 16 may be whipped.
Accusing, or threatening to accuse, either the person to whom accusation or threat made, or any other, of any of the infamous or other crimes in preceding section mentioned, with the view or intent to extort from person accused, or any other, any money or valuable thing, &c.	s. 47.	Felony; penal servitude for life, or not less than 5 years (not less than 7 if previously convicted of felony); or imprisonment not exceeding 2 years, with or without H. L. Male under 16 may be whipped.
With intent to defraud or injure any person, by unlawful violence or restraint, threat of, &c., accusing, or threatening to accuse, any person	,,	Felony; penal servitude for life, or not less than 5 years (not less than 7 if previously convicted

Offence.	Statute.	Punishment.
Larceny—*continued.*		
of treason, felony, or infamous crime (as before defined); compelling or inducing any person to execute, accept, indorse, alter, or destroy deeds, securities, &c. (Immaterial, whether the threats be of injury, &c., to be caused by offender himself or by any other.)	24 & 25 Vic. c. 96, s. 48. (27 & 28 Vic. c. 47.)	of felony); or imprisonment not exceeding 2 years, with or without H. L., and solitary confinement.
Sacrilege, Burglary, and House-breaking.—Breaking and entering place of *Divine Worship*, and committing felony therein; or, being therein, committing felony and breaking out.	s. 50.	Felony; penal servitude for life, or not less than 5 years (not less than 7 if previously convicted of felony); or imprisonment ¦not exceeding 2 years, with or without H. L., and solitary confinement.
Whosoever shall enter the dwelling-house of another with intent to commit any felony therein, or being therein shall commit a felony therein, and shall in either case break out in the night—	s. 51.	Shall be deemed guilty of burglary.
And whosoever shall be convicted of the crime of *burglary* shall be liable to—	s. 52.	Penal servitude for life, or not less than 5 years (not less than 7 if previously convicted of felony); or imprisonment not exceeding 2 years, with or without H. L., and solitary confinement.
Building within the same curtilage, not to be deemed part of dwelling-house unless communicating therewith.	s. 53.	
Entering dwelling-house at night, with intent to commit any felony therein.	s. 54.	Felony; penal servitude not exceeding 7 and not less than 5 years (not less than 7 if previously convicted of felony); or imprisonment not exceeding 2 years, with or without H. L., and solitary confinement.

Offence.	Statute.	Punishment.
Larceny—*continued.*		
Breaking into building within the curtilage, although not part thereof according to provisions of this Act (as in sec. 53); or being in such building shall commit any felony therein, and break out of the same.	24 & 25 Vic. c. 96, s. 55. (27 & 28 Vic. c. 47.)	Felony; penal servitude not exceeding 14, and not less than 5 years (not less than 7 if previously convicted of felony); or imprisonment not exceeding 2 years, with or without H. L.
Breaking and entering dwelling-house, school-house, shop, ware-house, or counting-house, committing felony therein, and breaking out of same.	s. 56.	Felony; penal servitude not exceeding 14, and not less than 5 years (not less than 7 if previously convicted of felony); or imprisonment not exceeding 2 years, with or without H. L., and solitary confinement.
Breaking and entering dwelling-house, or house or place of Divine Worship, building within the curtilage, school-house, shop, ware-house, or counting-house, with intent to commit felony therein.	s. 57.	Felony; penal servitude not exceeding 7 and not less than 5 years (not less than 7 if previously convicted of felony); or imprisonment not exceeding 2 years, with or without H. L., and solitary confinement.
Found by night armed with dangerous or offensive weapon with intent to break or enter dwelling-house or other building, and to commit felony therein; or having in possession, without lawful excuse, any implement of house-breaking; or face blackened or disguised, or found in dwelling-house or building with intent to commit felony.	s. 58.	Misdemeanour: penal servitude 5 years (not less than 7 if previously convicted of felony); or imprisonment not exceeding 2 years, with or without H. L.
The like, after such previous conviction or a conviction for felony.	s. 59.	Penal servitude not exceeding 10, and not less than 5 years (not less than 7 if previously convicted of felony); or imprisonment not exceeding 2 years, with or without H. L. (*a*)

(*a*) If the previous conviction shall have been for *felony*, the sentence of penal servitude not to be less than 7 years—27 & 28 Vic. c. 47.

Offence.	Statute.	Punishment.
Larceny—*continued*.		
Larceny in the House.—Stealing in any dwelling-house to the value in the whole of £5 or more.	24 & 25 Vic. c. 96, s. 60. (27 & 28 Vic. s. 47.)	Felony; penal servitude not exceeding 14, and not less than 5 years (not less than 7 if previously convicted of felony; or imprisonment not exceeding 2 years, with or without H. L., and solitary confinement.
Stealing in any dwelling-house, and by menace or threat putting any-one being therein in bodily fear.	s. 61.	Felony; like punishment as last preceding.
Stealing to the value of 10s. woollen, linen, hempen, or cotton yarn, or articles of silk, woolen, linen, cotton, alpaca, or mohair, or of these materials mixed, while in progress of manufacture, in building, field, or other place.	s. 62.	Like.
Larceny from Ships, Wharfs, &c.— Stealing goods in vessel or boat, in haven or port, river or canal, &c., or from docks, wharfs, or quays adjacent.	s. 63.	Like.
Plundering or stealing from ship in distress or wrecked.	s. 64.	Like.
Having possession of shipwrecked goods, or offering for sale, &c.	ss. 65, 66.	See Summary Index; title, "Larceny."
Larceny or Embezzlement by Clerks, Servants, or Persons in the Public Service.—Clerk or servant stealing chattel, money, or valuable security belonging to or in possession or power of his master or employer.	s. 67.	Felony: penal servitude not exceeding 14, and not less than 5 years (not less than 7 if previously convicted of felony); or imprisonment not exceeding 2 years, with or without H. L., and solitary confinement. Male under 16 may be whipped.

Offence.	Statute.	Punishment.
Larceny—*continued.*		
Clerk or servant embezzling chattel, money, or security, received into his possession for account of his master, &c., shall be deemed to have feloniously stolen same, although not otherwise received into master's possession than by such clerk, &c.	24 & 25 Vic. c. 96, s. 68. (27 & 28 Vic. c. 47.)	Penal servitude not exceeding 14, and not less than 5 years (not less than 7 if previously convicted of felony); or imprisonment not exceeding 2 years, with or without H. L., and solitary confinement. Male under 16 may be whipped.
Person employed in the public service of Her Majesty, constabulary, or police, stealing chattels or moneys belonging to or in possession or power of Her Majesty, or in possession of such person by virtue of his employment.	s. 69.	Felony; penal servitude not exceeding 14, and not less than 5 years (not less than 7 if previously convicted of felony); or imprisonment not exceeding 2 years, with or without H. L., and solitary confinement.
Person in Queen's service, constabulary, or police, embezzling any money or property received by virtue of his employment, or fraudulently disposing of same, shall be deemed to have feloniously stolen same.	s. 70.	Penal servitude not exceeding 14, and not less than 5 years (not less than 7 if previously convicted of felony); or imprisonment not exceeding 2 years, with or without H. L.
Offender may be dealt with where apprehended or found, or where offence committed ; property may be laid in Her Majesty.		
Indictment may include three distinct acts within six months ; particular coin, &c., need not be specified.	s. 71.	
If, upon trial for *embezzlement*, it turn out to be *larceny*, defendant not to be acquitted, and *vice versâ*.	s. 72.	
Embezzlement by officers of the Bank of England or Ireland.	s. 73.	Felony; penal servitude for life, or not less than 5 years (not less than 7 if previously convicted of felony); or imprisonment not exceeding 2 years, with or without H. L., and solitary confinement.

Offence.	Statute.	Punishment.
Larceny—*continued.* *Falsification of Accounts.*—If any clerk, officer, or servant, or any person employed or acting in the capacity of a clerk, officer, or servant, shall wilfully and with intent to defraud, destroy, alter, mutilate, or falsify any book, paper writing, valuable security, or account, which belongs to or is in the possession of his employer, or has been received by him for or on behalf of his employer, or shall wilfully and with intent to defraud make or concur in making any false entry in, or omit, or alter, or concur in omitting or altering, any material particular from or in any such book, or any document or account—	38 & 39 Vic. c. 24, s. 1.	Misdemeanour; penal servitude not exceeding 7 years, or to be imprisoned, with or without H. L., for any term not exceeding 2 years.
General intent to defraud sufficient in indictment, without naming any particular person, &c.	s. 2.	
Act to be read with 24 & 25 Vic., c. 96.	s. 3.	
Larceny by Tenants or Lodgers.—Stealing chattel or fixture let to be used in or with house or lodging.	24 & 25 Vic. c. 96, s. 74.	Felony; imprisonment not exceeding 2 years, with or without H. L., and solitary confinement; and male under 16 may be whipped.
If the value exceeds 5s.	24 & 25 Vic. c. 96, s. 74. (27 & 28 Vic. c. 47.)	Penal servitude not exceeding 7, and not less than 5 years (not less than 7 if previously convicted of felony); or imprisonment as in last preceding.
Indictment may be in common form, as for larceny, &c.	,,	—
Frauds by Agents, Bankers, or Factors.—Banker, merchant, broker, attorney, or agent, intrusted with money, or security for payment of money, with written directions for	s. 75.	Misdemeanour; penal servitude not exceeding 7, and not less than 5 years (not less than 7 if previously convicted

Offence.	Statute.	Punishment.
Larceny—*continued.* Its application, otherwise and in violation of good faith converting and misapplying same ; and so also as to Stocks or funds, &c. (Exceptions as to trustees, agents, entitled or having liens, &c.)	24 & 25 Vic. c. 96, s. 81. (27 & 28 Vic. c. 47.)	of felony) ; or imprisonment not exceeding 2 years, with or without H. L., and solitary confinement. Triable at Assizes.
Banker, merchant, broker, attorney, or agent, intrusted with property for safe custody, with intent to defraud, selling or converting same to his own use, or otherwise than for the purpose intrusted.	s. 76.	Misdemeanour ;[1] punishable as in last preceding section. Triable at Assizes.
Persons intrusted with power of attorney to sell or transfer property, fraudulently selling, converting, &c.	s. 77.	Like.
Factors or agents intrusted with goods, documents of title, &c., without authority getting advances thereon, &c., consigning or pledging same, &c.	s. 78.	Like.
Clerk or other person knowingly and wilfully assisting. (Exception—where advances do not exceed amount due to agent from his principal.)	,.	Like.
Definition of terms under this head ; see—	s. 79.	
Trustees fraudulently disposing of property—	s. 80.	Like.
Directors, members, or officers of any corporate or public company, fraudulently appropriating property.	s. 81.	Misdemeanour ; punishable as in last preceding section. Triable at Assizes.
Or keeping fraudulent accounts, .	s. 82.	Like.
Or wilfully destroying, falsifying, &c., books, papers, &c., making false entries, or omitting material ones.	s. 83.	Like.
Or publishing fraudulent statements or accounts, knowingly, and with intent to deceive shareholders, or to induce others to become shareholders.	s. 84.	Like.

Offence.	Statute.	Punishment.
Larceny—*continued.* Compulsory disclosures in suits at law or in equity not to subject person making such to prosecution under last ten sections.	24 & 25 Vic. c. 96, s. 85. (27 & 28 Vic. c. 47.)	
Nothing in last eleven sections to affect any remedy at law or in equity.	s. 86.	
Misdemeanours against any of the last preceding twelve sections not to be tried at Quarter Sessions.	s. 87.	To be returned to Assizes.
False Pretences.—By any false pretence obtaining from any person any chattel, money, or valuable security, with intent to defraud any person. (Not to be acquitted if offence proved to be larceny.)	s. 88.	Misdemeanour ; penal servitude, 5 years (not less than 7 if previously convicted of felony) ; or imprisonment not exceeding 2 years, with or without H. L., and solitary confinement.
By false pretence causing or procuring money or property to be paid or delivered to another for benefit of person making false pretence, and of any other person, with intent to defraud.	s. 89.	To be an offence within meaning of last preceding section.
With intent to defraud, by false pretences inducing persons to execute deeds ; indorse, accept, or destroy securities, &c. See also title, "False Pretences."	s. 90.	Misdemeanour; penal servitude, 5 years (not less than 7 if previously convicted of felony) ; or imprisonment not exceeding 2 years, with or without H. L., and solitary confinement.
Receiving Stolen Goods.—Knowingly receiving any chattel, money, or property, &c., the taking or obtaining of which amounts to felony.	s. 91.	Felony (indictable as accessory after, &c., or for a substantive felony) ; penal servitude not exceeding 14, and not less than 5 years (not less than 7 if previously convicted of felony) ; or imprisonment not exceeding 2 years, with or without H. L., and solitary confinement. Male under 16 may be whipped.

Offence.	Statute.	Punishment.
Larceny—*continued.* Indictments for stealing or receiving may contain counts for both. Prosecutor need not elect. If several included, jury may find some guilty of stealing and others of receiving.	24 & 25 Vic. c. 96, s. 92. (27 & 28 Vic. c. 47.)	—
Several receivers may be included in same indictment, although principal felon not yet amenable.	s. 93.	
On such indictment, persons may be convicted of separately receiving.	s. 94.	
Knowingly receiving, &c., where the taking, &c., is a misdemeanour by this Act. (And may be convicted although the principal not amenable.)	s. 95.	Misdemeanour; penal servitude not exceeding 7, and not less than 5 years (not less than 7 if previously convicted of felony); or imprisonment not exceeding 2 years, with or without H. L., and solitary confinement. Male under 16 may be whipped.
Receiving Goods obtained by false Pretences.—Receivers triable in any county where they may have had the property; or where the principal may be tried. Receivers, where original offence is punishable on summary conviction.	s. 97.	Same punishment, &c., to which person guilty of first, second, or subsequent offence of stealing is liable.
Principals in second degree, and accessories before fact, in felonies, punishable as principal in first degree.	s. 98.	—
Accessory after the fact to any felony punishable under this Act (except receiver of stolen property).	,,	Imprisonment not exceeding 2 years, with or without H. L., and solitary confinement.
Aiding, abetting, counselling, or procuring commission of misdemeanour under this Act.	,,	Indicted and punished as principal.
Abettors in offences punishable on summary conviction.	s. 99.	Punishable as principals in cases of first, second, or subsequent offence.

Offence.	Statute.	Punishment.
Larceny—*continued.*		
Restitution of Stolen Property.—The owner, on prosecuting thief or receiver to conviction by indictment—	24 & 25 Vic. c. 96, s. 100. (27 & 28 Vic. c. 47.)	To have restitution of property.
(*Exceptions.*—Securities or negotiable instrument *bona fide* paid, taken, or received for consideration, without notice, or cause to suspect, &c.; factors or agents intrusted with goods.)		
Corruptly taking reward, directly or indirectly, to help in restoring goods, &c., by felony or misdemeanour stolen or obtained (unless due diligence used to bring offender to trial).	s. 101.	Felony; penal servitude not exceeding 7, and not less than 5 years (not less than 7 if previously convicted of felony); or imprisonment not exceeding 2 years, with or without H. L., and solitary confinement. Male under 16 may be whipped.
Advertising reward for recovery of property stolen or lost, and stating that no questions will be asked, &c.; or to repay pawnbroker's money advanced.	s. 102.	Forfeit £50, and costs, recoverable by action of debt to person suing.
Apprehension of Offenders.—Offenders punishable under this Act (except angling in daytime) may be apprehended and brought before Justice.	s. 103.	
Power to issue search-warrant,	,,	Information to be on oath.
Pawnbrokers required to apprehend offenders, &c.	,,	
Constables or peace officers may apprehend persons lying or loitering in any highway, yard, or other place during the night, and suspected of having committed or being about to commit any felony against this Act.	s. 104.	To take such person before a Justice of the Peace, to be dealt with according to law.

Offence.	Statute.	Punishment.
Larceny—*continued.*		
Summary Proceedings, . . .	24 & 25 Vic. c. 96, s. 105. (27 & 28 Vic. c. 47.)	See Summary Index, "Larceny."
Other matters.—Stealers of property in one part of the United Kingdom having it in another may be tried in the latter.	s. 114.	
Offences committed within jurisdiction of Admiralty to be as if committed on land in England or Ireland.	s. 115.	
Form of indictment for subsequent offences.	s. 116.	
In indictable misdemeanours under this Act—	s. 117.	Fine, and sureties of the peace may be required in addition to, or in lieu of, any other punishment.
Solitary confinement, when ordered, not to exceed 1 month at a time, and not exceeding 3 months in the year.	s. 119.	
In whipping, the Court shall specify the number of strokes and the instrument.	,,	
Co-partners (*Larceny by*), (*a*) see— See also "Larceny," Summary Index.	31 & 32 Vic. c. 116.	

(*a*) *Co-partners.*—"If any person, being a member of any co-partnership, or being one of two or more beneficial owners of any money, goods, or effects, bills, notes, securities, or other property, shall steal or embezzle any such money, goods, or effects, bills, notes, securities, or other property of or belonging to any such co-partnership, or to such joint beneficial owners, every such person shall be liable to be dealt with, tried, convicted, and punished for the same as if such person had not been or was not a member of such co-partnership or one of such beneficial owners."—31 & 32 Vic. c. 116, s. 1.

Offence.	Statute.	Punishment.
Letter— Threatening to murder—see "Offences against the Person." Demanding money with menaces, and threatening to accuse of crime, with intent to extort—see "Larceny." Threatening to destroy buildings—see "Malicious Injuries."		
Libels— Blasphemies against God and the Christian religion, or the Holy Scriptures.	Common Law	Punishable by fine and imprisonment, or either.
Indecent Libels, whether by writing or printing, or any sign which is indecent and contrary to public order.	"	Like.
Libels on the Government, by using terms of obloquy or contumely, tending to alienate the affections of the people from the King and his Government, to weaken the ties of allegiance and loyalty, and to bring about sedition or revolution.	"	Like.
Upon the Proceedings of Courts of Justice, by merely using declamation and invective, not to elucidate the truth, but to injure the character of individuals, and to bring the administration of justice into contempt and ridicule.	"	Like.
Libels upon Individuals, by malicious defamation expressed in writing or printing, and tending to blacken the memory of one that is dead, or the reputation of one that is alive, and expose him to hatred, contempt, or ridicule. (a)	"	Misdemeanour; punishable by fine and imprisonment.

(a) *Libels on Individuals.*—Though the words impute no punishable crime, yet if they contain that sort of imputation which is calculated to vilify a man, and to

2 N 2

Offence.	Statute.	Punishment.
Libels—*continued.* Publishing or threatening to publish a libel, or directly or indirectly threatening to print or publish, or directly or indirectly proposing to abstain from printing or publishing, or to prevent the printing or publishing, of matters, with intent to extort money, &c., or to procure appointment or office of profit. (*a*)	6 & 7 Vic. c. 96, s. 3.	Misdemeanour; imprisonment not exceeding 3 years, with or without H. L. And see also "Threatening letter with intent to extort," title, "Larceny."
Maliciously publishing any defamatory libel, knowing same to be false.	s. 4.	To pay such fine as the Court shall award; and also imprisonment not exceeding 2 years.
Maliciously publishing any defamatory libel.	s. 5.	Fine or imprisonment, or both; imprisonment not to exceed 1 year.

bring him into hatred, contempt, and ridicule, an indictment lies.—*Mansfield, C.J.* No man has a right to render the person or abilities of another ridiculous, not only in publications, but if the peace and welfare of individuals or society be interrupted, or even exposed by types or figures, the act, by the Law of England, is a libel.—*Lord Ellenborough.* An information was granted against the printer of a newspaper for a ludicrous paragraph giving an account of the Earl of Clanricarde's marriage with an actress in Dublin, and of his appearing with her in the boxes of the theatre with jewels, &c.—See *Roscoe's Crim. Law.*

Libels on the Dead.—This was an application on the part of the Duke of Vallombroso, a foreign nobleman, calling upon Mr. Labouchere, as the proprietor of *Truth,* to show cause why a criminal information should not be filed against him for a libel published in that newspaper upon the father of the applicant :—*Held,* that the Court, in the exercise of its discretion, must refuse the leave, being guided by the following principles :—The non-residence of the applicant in this country, as rendering it unlikely that any breach of the peace will follow, is a cogent argument, though not conclusive, against the interference of the Court. The fact that the subject of the libel is dead is, upon the weight of the authorities, an objection which the Court will regard as almost conclusive against allowing an information to be filed. To entitle the person to ask the Court for a criminal information he must occupy some public office, and the libel complained of must attack him in relation to such office, not as a private person. A Peer in private matters is not entitled merely as a Peer to the interference of the Court.—The *Queen* v. *Labouchere,* Q. B. E., 1884.

(*a*) *Malice.*—Where a man publishes a writing which upon the face of it is "...ellous, the law presumes that he does so with the malicious intention which ...itutes the offence, and it will be for the accused to show the contrary.
 actions for libel, where the jury give damages under 40*s.,* the plaintiff shall

Offence.	Statute.	Punishment.
Libels—_continued._ _Newspaper Libel and Registration Act,_ 1881, _Appendix._ (a) (See also " Blasphemy " and " Nuisance.")	44 & 45 Vic. c. 60., and 51 & 52 Vic. c. 64.	
Lights— Exhibiting false lights to ships, &c. —See " Malicious Injuries."		
Lime— Putting in fish-ponds—see " Malicious Injuries."		

not be entitled to more costs than damages, unless the Judge, immediately after, certifies on the record that the libel was wilful and malicious.—31 & 32 Vic., c. 69.

Libels on Administration of Justice.—By writing, printing, or other means calumniating the proceedings of a Court of Justice, where such is not discussed with decency and candour, or with a view to elucidate the truth, but to injure the character of individuals, and to bring into hatred and contempt the administration of justice; such publications are indictable.—_Gross, J. R._, v. _White,_ 1 _Campb._, 359.

Indecent Libels.—Obscene and indecent writing or printing, or by any sign or substitute: representations in obscene plays; these, all being against public morals and contrary to public order, are indictable.—_R._ v. _Sedley, Sid._ 168; _R._ v. _Wilkes,_ 4 _Burr._, 25, 30. The 20 & 21 Vic., c. 83, gives power to Magistrates to grant warrant to search for obscene books, pictures, &c., where sold, and to punish summarily the offender. Scotland is expressly exempt; and there is nothing in the Act to show that it does not extend to Ireland, beyond that in the Index the initial letter limits the Act to England. This, added to the necessity for it, certainly led to the conclusion that it is so limited.

(a) _Newspaper Libels.—Privileged Publications._—A fair and accurate report of proceedings publicly heard before any Court exercising judicial authority, if published contemporaneously with such proceedings.

Fair and accurate report of public meetings;—and (public or reporters not being excluded) vestries, public boards, &c., constituted by Act of Parliament; Committees of Parliament, &c.; Justices in Quarter Sessions, &c.; _unless it be proved that the report or publication is made maliciously._

Proviso.—No protection if defendant refuse to publish reasonable contradiction or explanation.

No protection of any publications not of public concern and for public benefit.

No protection to publications of blasphemous or indecent matter.

No abridgment of privileges by Law existing.—51 & 52 Vic., c. 64 (see Act, _Appendix_).

Offence.	Statute.	Punishment.
Linen (*in course of manufacture*)— Damaging—see "Malicious Injuries."	—	And see Summary Index; title "Linen Acts."
Lodgers (*Larceny by*)— See "Larceny."		
Loom (*damaging or destroying*)— See "Malicious Injuries."		
Lotteries— All lotteries and gaming tables are declared to be public nuisances. (*a*) Insuring in lotteries, prohibited by 33 Geo. iii., c. 18.	6 Anne, c. 17, s. 1. 11 Anne, c. 6, ss. 1, 2, 3. 13 Geo. ii. c. 8.	Indictable (keepers and players) as public nuisances; and keepers are liable to penalty of £100, recoverable by information, action, &c., or may be prosecuted as cheats. (Players liable to a penalty of £10.)
Advertising foreign or illegal lotteries.	6 & 7 Wm. iv. c. 66.	Penalty—£50, recoverable in Superior Court. But as coming under the head of gaming, see generally 22 & 23 Vic., c. 17, s. 1.
Voluntary Associations constituted for distribution of works of art deemed legal, provided charter first obtained.	9 & 10 Vic. c. 48.	—
Associations for disposal of works of utility and ornament by chance or otherwise, as prizes, indemnified from suits and penalties; and See "Gaming," Summary Index.	20 & 21 Vic. c. 102.	

(*a*) *Lotteries.*—Whatever the Legislature declares to be a public nuisance is indictable as such.—*R.* v. *Crawshaw*, 9 *W. R.*, 38; *R.* v. *Gregory*, 5 *Barn. and* *'.*, 555.

Offence.	Statute.	Punishment.
Lunatics— Dangerous Lunatics, . . . TRIAL OF LUNATICS ACT, 1883. A special verdict where accused is found guilty, but insane at the commission of offence, so as not to be responsible according to law for his actions at the time.	— 46 & 47 Vic. c. 38, s. 2.	See Summary Index; title, "Lunatics," and *Appendix.*
Machinery— See "Malicious Injuries."		
Maintenance— Unlawfully taking in hands or upholding of quarrels or sides, to the disturbance or hindrance of common right, and not having in the suit any certain or contingent interest. (Exceptions to justify, &c.:—Interest in the suit; master for his servant; affinity; poverty—it being lawful to give money to a poor man to enable him to sue; Counsel and Attorneys.) (*a*) Champerty is a bargain to divide the matter sued for; and the champertor to carry on the suit.—*Black. Com.*	Common Law.	Punishable by fine and imprisonment. There are various old statutes declaratory of the Common Law.
Maiming (*Cattle*)— See "Malicious Injuries."		

(*a*) *Maintenance of Suits.*—A moral philosopher has observed that the rights of the poor are not so important or intricate as their contentions are violent and ruinous; and he may be said to *give* a poor man twenty pounds, who prevents his throwing it away upon law. But in fairness to the "profession," he adds—"I know not a more exalted charity than that which presents a shield against the rapacity or persecution of a tyrant."

Offence.	Statute.	Punishment.
Malicious Injuries— *To Buildings, by Fire.*—Unlawfully and maliciously setting fire to any church, chapel, meeting-house, or other place of divine worship.	24 & 25 Vic. c. 97, s. 1. (27 & 28 Vic. c. 47.)	Felony ; penal servitude for life, or not less than 5 years (not less than 7 if previously convicted of felony); or imprisonment not exceeding 2 years, with or without H. L., and solitary confinement. Male under 16 may be whipped.
Unlawfully and maliciously setting fire to any house, any person being therein.	s. 2.	Felony; like punishment.
Unlawfully and maliciously setting fire to any house, outhouse, &c., manufactory, farm-building, &c., whether in possession of offender or any other, with intent to injure or defraud.	s. 3.	Felony; like punishment.
Unlawfully and maliciously setting fire to any station or building belonging to any railway, port, dock, or harbour, canal or navigation.	s. 4.	Felony; like punishment.
Unlawfully and maliciously setting fire to any public building, other than those before mentioned, belonging to the Queen, county, borough, union, college, &c.	s. 5.	Felony; like punishment.
Setting fire to any building, other than such as are in this Act before mentioned.	s. 6.	Felony ; penal servitude not exceeding 14 years, and not less than 5 years (not less than 7 if previously convicted of felony); or imprisonment not exceeding 2 years, with or without H. L., and solitary confinement. Male under 16 may be whipped.

Offence.	Statute.	Punishment.
Malicious Injuries—*continued.* Setting fire to any goods in a building under such circumstances that, if the building was set on fire, the offence would amount to felony.	24 & 25 Vic. c. 97, s. 7. (27 & 28 Vic. c. 47.)	Felony; like punishment as last preceding.
Unlawfully and maliciously, by any overt act, attempting to set fire to any building or anything in the last section mentioned, under circumstances that, if set fire to, the offence would be felony.	s. 8.	Felony; like punishment.
To Buildings by Explosive Substances.—Unlawfully and maliciously, by explosion of gunpowder or other explosive substance, destroying dwelling-house, any person being therein, or any building whereby life endangered.	s. 9.	Felony; penal servitude for life, or not less than 5 years (not less than 7 if previously convicted of felony); or imprisonment not exceeding 2 years, with or without H. L., and solitary confinement. Male under 16 may be whipped.
Attempting to destroy buildings, machinery, goods, &c., with gunpowder or explosive substance, whether or not damage be caused. (*a*)	s. 10.	Felony; penal servitude not exceeding 14, and not less than 5 years (not less than 7 if previously convicted of felony; or imprisonment not exceeding 2 years, with or without H. L., and solitary confinement. Male under 16 may be whipped.
To Buildings by Rioters.—Persons riotously assembled, with force demolishing, &c., places of divine worship, house, outhouse, &c., farm-building, manufactory, or any public building, &c., machinery, &c.	s. 11.	Felony; penal servitude for life, or not less than 5 years (not less than 7 if previously convicted of felony); or imprisonment not exceeding 2 years, with or without H. L., and solitary confinement.

(*a*) For other offences against Explosives Act, 1883, see "Explosives," this Index.

Offence.	Statute.	Punishment.
Malicious Injuries—*continued.* Rioters, with force, injuring or damaging buildings, &c., in last section mentioned.	24 & 25 Vic. c. 97, s. 12. (27 & 28 Vic. c. 47.)	Misdemeanour; penal servitude not exceeding 7, and not less than 5 years (not less than 7 if previously convicted of felony); or imprisonment not exceeding 2 years, with or without H. L. (and although tried for felony under sec. 11, may be convicted of misdemeanour under this section).
To Building by Tenants.—Tenants unlawfully and maliciously pulling down, demolishing, or beginning to pull down, &c., dwelling-house or building, or to sever fixtures from the freehold.	s. 13.	Misdemeanour. See also Summary Index; title, "Landlord and Tenant."
To Manufactures, Machinery, &c.—Unlawfully and maliciously cutting, damaging, &c., silk, woollen, linen, cotton, hair, mohair, or alpaca goods, &c., in process of manufacture, or the machinery, &c., &c.	s. 14.	Felony; penal servitude for life; or not less than 5 years (not less than 7 if previously convicted of felony); or imprisonment not exceeding 2 years, with or without H. L., and solitary confinement. Male under 16 may be whipped.
Damaging or destroying machines, &c., fixed or movable, used in agricultural operations, or used in any manufacture whatsoever (except in manufacture as in preceding section).	s. 15.	Felony; penal servitude not exceeding 7, and not less than 5 years (not less than 7 if previously convicted of felony); or imprisonment not exceeding 2 years, with or without H. L., and solitary confinement. Male under 16 may be whipped.
To Corn, Trees, Vegetable Productions.—Setting fire to any crop of hay, grass, corn, grain, or pulse, or cultivated vegetable, standing or cut down; wood, plantation, heath, furze, &c.	s. 16.	Felony; penal servitude not exceeding 14, and not less than 5 years (not less than 7 if previously convicted of felony); or imprisonment as in last preceding section.

Offence.	Statute.	Punishment.
Malicious Injuries—*continued.*		
Unlawfully and maliciously setting fire to stacks of corn, grain, pulse, tares, hay, straw, haulm, stubble, cultivated vegetable produce, furze, gorse, heath, turf, wood, &c.	24 & 25 Vic. c. 97, s. 17. (27 & 28 Vic. c. 47.)	Felony; penal servitude for life, or not less than 5 years (not less than 7 if previously convicted of felony); or imprisonment not exceeding 2 years, with or without H. L., and solitary confinement. Male under 16 may be whipped.
Attempting to set fire to crops, stacks of corn, &c., as in last two sections mentioned, under circumstances that, if set on fire, the offence would be felony.	s. 18.	Felony; penal servitude not exceeding 7, and not less than 5 years (not less than 7 if previously convicted of felony); or imprisonment as in preceding section.
Cutting or destroying hop-binds, .	s. 19.	Felony; penal servitude not exceeding 14, and not less than 5 years (not less than 7 if previously convicted of felony); or imprisonment as in last preceding sections.
Trees, Shrubs, &c.—Maliciously cutting or destroying any tree, sapling, shrub, or any underwood, growing in park, pleasure-ground, garden, orchard, or avenue, or in ground adjoining or belonging to dwelling-house (in case the injury exceed £1).	s. 20.	Felony; penal servitude 5 years (not less than 7 if previously convicted of felony); or imprisonment not exceeding 2 years, with or without H. L., and solitary confinement. Male under 16 may be whipped.
Maliciously damaging them, growing elsewhere (in case the injury done exceed £5).	s. 21.	Felony; like punishment.
Damaging them to the amount of 1s. wheresoever growing.	s. 22.	Triable summarily; see Summary Index, "Malicious Injuries."
Destroying fruit in gardens, &c. .	s. 23.	See Summary Index, "Malicious Injuries."
Destroying vegetable productions, .	s. 24.	Like.
To Fences.—Damaging fence, wall, stile, or gate.	s. 25.	Like.

Offence.	Statute.	Punishment.
Malicious Injuries—*continued.* *To Mines.*—Maliciously setting fire to coal, cannel-coal, anthracite, or other mineral fuel.	24 & 25 Vic. c. 97, s. 26. (27 & 28 Vic. c. 47.)	Felony; penal servitude for life, or not less than 5 years (not less than 7 if previously convicted of felony); or imprisonment not exceeding 2 years, with or without H. L., and solitary confinement. Male under 16 may be whipped.
Maliciously, by any overt act, attempting to set fire to any mine, under such circumstances that, if set on fire, the offender would be guilty of felony.	s. 27.	Penal servitude not exceeding 14 years, and not less than 5 years (not less than 7 if previously convicted of felony); or imprisonment not exceeding 2 years, with or without H. L., and with or without solitary confinement. Male under 16 may be whipped.
Maliciously conveying water into any mine, with intent to damage, &c.; destroying or obstructing airway, waterway, &c. (Proviso as to damage by owner of adjoining mine, or by person employed.)	s. 28.	Felony; penal servitude not exceeding 7 and not less than 5 years (not less than 7 if previously convicted of felony); or imprisonment as in preceding section.
Maliciously damaging steam engines used in mines, or apparatus in connexion, &c.; building, bridge, waggonway, or trunk; obstruct or hinder working of steam or other engine, &c., with intent to damage mine, or delay working; cutting tackle, &c.	s. 29.	Felony; penal servitude not exceeding 7, and not less than 5 years (not less than 7 if previously convicted of felony); or imprisonment not exceeding 2 years, with or without H. L., and solitary confinement. Male under 16 may be whipped.
To Sea-banks, Rivers, Canals, Ponds.—Maliciously breaking down, damaging, &c., sea-bank, wall, &c., whereby land or building may be damaged, undermining or destroying quay, wharf, jetty, water-se, &c., or other work belong- river or canal.	s. 30.	Felony; penal servitude for life, or not less than 5 years (not less than 7 if previously convicted of felony); or imprisonment as in preceding section.

Offence.	Statute.	Punishment.
Malicious Injuries—*continued.*		
Removing piles, material, &c., of sea-bank, river, reservoir, canal, &c., opening flood-gates, &c., or otherwise damaging river or canal.	24 & 25 Vic. c. 97, s. 31. (27 & 28 Vic. c. 47.)	Felony; penal servitude not exceeding 7, and not less than 5 years (not less than 7 if previously convicted of felony); or imprisonment as in preceding section.
Maliciously breaking down or destroying the dam, &c., of any fish-pond, or of any water, private property, or in which there shall be private right of fishery, with intent to take or cause destruction of fish; putting noxious materials therein to destroy fish; damaging mill-pond, &c.	s. 32.	Misdemeanour; penal servitude not exceeding 7, and not less than 5 years (not less than 7 if previously convicted of felony); or imprisonment not exceeding 2 years, with or without H. L., and solitary confinement. Male under 16 may be whipped.
To Bridges, Turnpikes, Gates, &c.—Maliciously throwing down any bridge, viaduct, or aqueduct, or doing any act to render same dangerous or impassable.	s. 34.	Felony; penal servitude for life, or not less than 5 years (not less than 7 if previously convicted of felony); or imprisonment not exceeding 2 years, with or without H. L., and solitary confinement. Male under 16 may be whipped.
Maliciously destroying, &c., turnpike gate, toll-house, &c.	,,	Misdemeanour.
Injuries to Railways, Telegraphs, &c.—Maliciously placing upon railway any wood, stone, or other matter; displacing rails, sleepers, &c., diverting machinery, showing or removing signals, &c., or doing anything to obstruct carriages, &c.	s. 35.	Felony; penal servitude for life, or not less than 5 years (not less than 7 if previously convicted of felony); or imprisonment not exceeding 2 years, with or without H. L. Male under 16 may be whipped. (a)

(a) *Railways.*—Offenders under age of 16 may be summarily dealt with for these offences, under 10 & 11 Vic., c. 82, and 13 & 14 Vic., c. 37, as if the above offences had been mentioned therein in addition to the offence of larceny—34 & 35 Vic., c. 78, s. 13. See "Railways," Summary Index; and see also "Children and Young Persons," Summary Index, limiting the age for whipping to 14.

Offence.	Statute.	Punishment.
Malicious Injuries—*continued.* (The like offence, with intent *to endanger passengers, &c.*, is punishable in like manner, under 24 & 25 Vic, c. 100, s. 32. See title "Offences against the Person," in this Index.) By any unlawful act, or by any wilful omission or neglect, shall obstruct or cause to be obstructed any engine or carriage using on any railway, or shall aid or assist therein.	24 & 25 Vic. c. 97, s. 36. (27 & 28 Vic. c. 47.)	Misdemeanour; imprisonment not exceeding 2 years, with or without H. L.
Maliciously injuring or destroying any machinery, wire, post, &c., or other thing employed about electric or magnetic telegraph; obstructing delivery of communications.	s. 37.	Misdemeanour; imprisonment not exceeding 2 years, with or without H. L. But if Justice think it a fit case for summary adjudication, it may be so determined. See Summary Index, "Malicious Injuries."
Attempting to commit offences in last section.	s. 38.	See Summary Index, "Malicious Injuries."
To Works of Art.—Maliciously destroying or damaging books, &c., or any article or thing for the purpose of art, science, literature, or curiosity in museum, library, &c., to which persons are admitted ; or works of art or memorials in places of divine worship, or other public building, or burial ground, or garden, or any public statue or monument, or ornament or fences thereof.	s. 39.	Misdemeanour; imprisonment not exceeding 6 months, with or without H. L. Male under 16 may be whipped. (And not to affect civil remedy for damage done.)
To Cattle and other Animals.—Maliciously killing, maiming, or wounding any cattle.	s. 40.	Felony ; penal servitude not exceeding 14 and not less than 5 years (not less than 7 if previously convicted of felony) ; or imprisonment not exceeding 2 years, with or without H. L., and solitary confinement

Offence.	Statute.	Punishment.
Malicious Injuries—*continued*.		
Maliciously killing, maiming, or wounding any dog, bird, beast, or other animal, not being cattle, but being either the subject of larceny at Common Law, or being ordinarily kept in a state of confinement, as for any domestic purpose.	24 & 25 Vic. c. 97, s. 47, (27 & 28 Vic. c. 47.)	May be summarily tried by Justices. See Summary Index, "Malicious Injuries."
To Ships.—Maliciously setting fire to, casting away, &c., whether complete or in an unfinished state.	s. 42.	Felony; penal servitude for life, or not less than 5 years (not less than 7 if previously convicted of felony); or imprisonment not exceeding 2 years, with or without H. L., and solitary confinement. Male under 16 may be whipped.
Setting fire to, or destroying it, to prejudice the owner of the ship or goods, or the underwriters, &c.	s. 43.	Felony; punishable as in last section.
Attempting to set fire to, or cast away or destroy ship or vessel, under circumstances that, if attempt succeeded, the offender would be guilty of felony.	s. 44.	Felony; penal servitude not exceeding 14, and not less than 5 years (not less than 7 if previously convicted of felony); or imprisonment not exceeding 2 years, with or without H. L., and solitary confinement. Male under 16 may be whipped.
Maliciously placing in or near any ship any gunpowder or explosive substance, with intent to destroy or damage, whether or not it explode, or damage be done.	s. 45.	Felony; like punishment.
Damaging ships otherwise than by fire.	s. 46.	Felony; penal servitude not exceeding 7, or not less than 5 years (not less than 7 if previously convicted of felony); or imprisonment not exceeding 2 years, with or without H. L., and solitary confinement. Male under 16 may be whipped.

Offence.	Statute.	Punishment.
Malicious Injuries—*continued.* Unlawfully masking or removing lights or signals, or exhibiting false ones with intent to bring ship or boat into danger ; or maliciously doing anything tending to the immediate loss or destruction of any ship, vessel, or boat, for which no punishment is hereinbefore provided.	24 & 25 Vic. c. 97, s. 47. (27 & 28 Vic. c. 47.)	Felony ; penal servitude for life, and not less than 5 years (not less than 7 if previously convicted of felony) ; or imprisonment not exceeding 2 years, with or without H. L., and solitary confinement. Male under 16 may be whipped.
Maliciously cutting away, sinking, removing, &c. (or doing act with intent, &c.), or in any other manner maliciously injuring or concealing any boat, buoy, buoy-rope, perch, or mark used for guidance of seamen, or for purpose of navigation.	s. 48.	Felony ; penal servitude not exceeding 7, and not less than 5 years (not less than 7 if previously convicted of felony) ; or imprisonment as in last section.
Maliciously destroying any ship or vessel in distress, or wrecked, or any goods or articles belonging to such ship.	s. 49.	Felony ; penal servitude not exceeding 14, and not less than 5 years (not less than 7 if previously convicted of felony) ; or imprisonment not exceeding 2 years, with or without H. L., and solitary confinement.
Letter threatening to burn or destroy.—Sending, delivering, uttering, or directly or indirectly causing to be received, knowing the contents, letter threatening to burn any house or building, stacks of grain, or other agricultural produce, &c., ship or vessel ; or to kill or wound cattle.	s. 50.	Felony ; penal servitude not exceeding 10, and not less than 5 years (not less than 7 if previously convicted of felony) ; or imprisonment not exceeding 2 years, with or without H. L., and solitary confinement. Male under 16 may be whipped.
Injuries not hereinbefore mentioned.—Malicious injury or spoil to any real or personal property, either of a public or private nature, for which no punishment is hereinbefore provided (the damage or spoil exceeding £5).	s. 51.	Misdemeanour ; imprisonment not exceeding 2 years, with or without H. L.

Offence.	Statute.	Punishment.
Malicious Injuries—*continued*.		
In case such last-named offence be committed between 9 P.M., and 6 A.M.	24 & 25 Vic. c. 97, s. 46. (27 & 28 Vic. c. 47.)	Penal servitude 5 years (not less than 7 if previously convicted of felony); or imprisonment not exceeding 2 years, with or without H. L.
Where the injury does not exceed £5. (Section not to extend to cases where party acts under fair and reasonable supposition of right.)	s. 52.	Triable summarily. See Summary Index, "Malicious Injuries."
Provisions of section 52 extend to malicious injuries to trees, sapling, shrub, or underwood, for which no punishment is before provided.	s. 53.	
Making or having Gunpowder to commit offences.—Manufacturing or knowingly having in possession any gunpowder or other explosive substance or noxious thing, or any instrument or thing, with intent to commit, or enable another to commit, any of the felonies in this Act.	s. 54.	Misdemeanour; imprisonment not exceeding 2 years, with or without H. L., and solitary confinement; and male under 16 may be whipped.
Upon reasonable cause assigned on oath, Justice may issue warrant to search in the daytime for gunpowder and noxious substance, suspected to be kept to commit such offences.	s. 55.	
Other Matters.—In felonies, principal in second degree and accessory before the fact—	s. 56.	Punishable as principal in first degree.
Accessory after the fact to felony .	,,	Imprisonment not exceeding 2 years, with or without H. L., and solitary confinement.
Aiding, counselling, abetting, or procuring commission of misdemeanour—	,,	To be indicted and punished as principal offender.

Offence.	Statute.	Punishment.
Malicious Injuries—*continued.*		
Constables may apprehend persons loitering at night and suspected of felony against this Act.	24 & 25 Vic. c. 97, s. 57.	To be taken before Justice of the Peace as soon as reasonably may.
Malice against owner of property need not be proved.	s. 58.	
Act applies to persons in possession of the property injured, and who do the acts with intent to injure or defraud any other.	s. 59.	
Intent to injure particular persons need not be stated in indictment.	s. 60.	
Persons in the act of committing offences may be apprehended without warrant.	s. 61.	—
For proceedings in respect to summary convictions, &c.	—	See Summary Index; "Malicious Injuries."
Indictable offences committed within jurisdiction of the Admiralty may be tried in England or Ireland, wherever offender may be.	s. 72.	
Solitary confinement, when ordered, is not to exceed 1 month at a time, and not exceeding three months in a year.	s. 75.	
When offender ordered to be whipped, Court to name the number of strokes and the instrument with which they shall be inflicted. See also Summary Index; title, "Malicious Injuries."	,,	
Manslaughter— See "Offences against the Person."		
Mantraps (*Setting*)— See "Offences against the Person."		

Offence.	Statute.	Punishment.
— ed clergyman, or a layman nding to be a clergyman of stablished Church in Ireland, rating marriage between Pro- its, or between Protestant and iist.	12 Geo. i. c. 3, s. 1. 5 Vic. sess. 2. c. 28, ss. 1, 17.	Felony; penal servitude for 7 years; and may also be imprisoned not exceeding 4 years, nor less than one year, previous to transporta- tion, with or without H. L., and solitary con- finement. The latter Act gives the punish- ment.
it special licence solemnizing iage in places other than :h or chapel where same may wfully solemnized according to of United Church of England Ireland, or a certified house or ing appointed pursuant to Act.	7 & 8 Vic. c. 81, s. 45.	Felony; penal servitude for 7 years, or impri- sonment not exceeding 2 years.
izing marriage in registered , &c., in absence of Registrar, ntrary to Act.	,,	Like.
ig licence or publishing banns same shall have been forbid- by some authorized person.	s. 46.	Like.
g marriage licence or register ' Forgery.''	—	(And for other offences see Act.)
o Marriages Amendment Act, ic., c. 27, providing penalties ieglect of duty by Clergymen Registrars, in not registering, &c.	26 Vic. c. 27.	This Act amends 7 & 8 Vic., c. 81.
i knowingly or wilfully ng false declaration or signing false notice required by Acts rocuring any marriage—	s. 15.	Perjury.

Offence.	Statute.	Punishment.
Marriage—*continued.*		
MATRIMONIAL CAUSES AND MARRIAGE LAW (IRELAND) AMENDMENT ACT, 1870.	33 & 34 Vic. c. 110.	—
Empowers the Moderators and Presidents, &c., of certain denominations to grant special licencees to marry.	s. 37.	—
Provides for the legalization of marriages between persons of different religious persuasions, upon the conditions therein.	s. 38.	
Repeals so much of 19 Geo. ii., c. 13, as declares that a "marriage between a Papist and any person who professes being a Protestant within 12 months previously, if celebrated by a Popish Priest, shall be void." (*a*)	s. 39.	
No Protestant Episcopalian Clergyman, and no Roman Catholic Clergyman, shall be subject to any punishment or penalty for solemnizing marriage in accordance with the provisions of this Act.	s. 40.	
Amends sec. 3 of the 26 Vic. c. 27.	s. 41.	
This Act and 7 & 8 Vic, c. 81, and 26 Vic. c. 27, to be construed together.	s. 43.	
Act gives form of licence and of notice of marriage.		
Act applies to Ireland only.		
For registration of marriages—see title " Registration," &c., Summary Index.		

(a) *Marriages.*—The above Act, while thus repealing the partial and exceptionable legislation of 19 Geo. ii., c. 13, s. 1, of which advantage had too frequently been taken to inflict grievous and heartless wrong, makes impartial and reasonable provision against the deceptions that under such circumstances may be practised clandestine marriages. In the same sec. 39 it is enacted—" That any marriage mnized by a Protestant Episcopalian Clergyman, between a person who is a

Offence.	Statute.	Punishment.
Marriage—*continued.*		
MATRIMONIAL CAUSES AND MARRIAGE LAW (IRELAND) AMENDMENT ACT. Amends 33 & 34 Vic. c. 110.	34 & 35 Vic. c. 49.	
Amends sec. 13 of 7 & 8 Vic. c. 81, as to marriage of Jews.		
Provisions as to licences for Roman Catholic marriages and for mixed marriages, and provides punishment for forging signatures and counterfeiting official seals, &c.		
Provisions of 26 & 27 Vic. c. 27, and 7 & 8 Vic. c. 81, to persons one or both of whom shall belong to any such Church or religious community as therein.	36 Vic. c. 16.	
Acts for removing doubts as to validity of certain marriages in foreign countries, where either party is a British subject.	31 & 32 Vic. c. 61.	
Master (*of Ship*)— See Summary Index; "Merchant Shipping Act."		
Merchandize Marks Act—	25 & 36 Vic. c. 88, ss. 2, 3.	Forging trade marks, misdemeanour; and adding to or altering trade marks, forgery.

Protestant Episcopalian and a person who is not, or by a Roman Catholic Clergyman, between a person who is a Roman Catholic and a person who is not, shall be void to all intents, in cases where the parties to such marriage knowingly and wilfully intermarried without due notice to the Registrar, or without certificate of notice duly issued, or without presence of two or more credible witnesses, or in a building not set apart for the celebration of Divine Service according to the rites and ceremonies of the religion of the clergyman solemnizing such marriage.

Offence.	Statute.	Punishment.
Murder. (a) Whosoever shall be convicted of murder— See "Offences against the Person."	24 & 25 Vic. c. 100, s. 2.	Shall suffer death as a felon. The body to be buried within the precincts of the prison in which last confined, and the sentence of the Court shall so direct.
Museum (*damaging Works of Art in*)— See "Malicious Injuries."		
Mutiny— See Summary Index; "Army Discipline."		
Naturalisation Act—	33 Vic. c. 14.	—
Newspaper—Libel and Registration Act. *Appendix.*	44 & 45 Vic. c. 60. 51 & 52 Vic. c. 64.	—
Night (*in Burglaries and other Offences against the Larceny Act*)— Shall be deemed to commence at 9, P.M., and to conclude at 6 A.M.	24 & 25 Vic. c. 96, s. 1.	
Nitro-Glycerine— Manufacturing, carrying, selling, &c., or having in possession without licence, as specified in Act. (Search-warrant may issue—same as for gunpowder under 23 & 24 Vic. c. 139, and both Acts incorporated.)	32 & 33 Vic. c. 113. s. 6.	Misdemeanour; imprisonment with or without H. L., not exceeding 1 year, or penalty not exceeding £500.

(a) *Murder* is homicide, committed "feloniously, wilfully, and of malice aforethought," or prepense. Malice is particular or general, and express or implied.
If a man give another a stroke, which it may be is not in itself so mortal but that with good care it might be cured, yet if he dies within the year and day, it is � � or murder, as the case is.—*Lord Hale.*

Offence.	Statute.	Punishment.
Nuisance. (a)— Annoyance on highways, bridges, and public rivers, &c., by actual obstruction, or want of repair by party liable; offensive and dangerous trades and manufactures; making great noise in the night, or exposing in thoroughfares a person infected with contagious disease; suffering ferocious animals to go at large—as a fierce bull in a field where there is a foothpath, or a ferocious dog unmuzzled; acts of public indecency and such as are injurious to public morals, as bathing in the open sea where plainly visible from the neighbouring houses.	CommonLaw.	Fine and imprisonment, and the Court may order the nuisance to be abated or removed at defendant's cost. If the nuisance has been abated, that being the object of the indictment, the Court will adapt judgment accordingly.
Keeping a common bawdy-house, gaming-house, or a common, ill-governed and disorderly house, and see "Brothel," Summary Index. (For "Nuisances on roads, streets, &c.," see Summary Index; and for offences against Sanitary laws, see "Public Health, &c.," Summary Index.)	CommonLaw, and 7 Geo.iv. c. 9, s. 1.	Fine and imprisonment; and the Court may order the nuisance to be abated or removed at defendant's cost. If the nuisance has been abated, that being the object of the indictment, the Court will adapt judgment accordingly.

(a) A public or common nuisance is such an inconvenient or troublesome offence as annoys the whole community in general, and not merely some particular person, and therefore this is indictable only, and not actionable.—*Black. Com.* If the annoyance be only to a private individual, and not to the public, it can only be the subject of an action, and is not indictable.—1 *Hawk.*, c. 75, ss. 1 & 2. It seems that if a man set up a noxious trade where it has been long established, it is not indictable unless the annoyance is greatly increased; and if it was originally remote from houses, and houses are afterwards built there, it will not be a nuisance, merely for annoying the newcomers. The gist of the offence is that it renders the enjoyment of life and property uncomfortable. It may be both indictable and actionable.—*Rose* v. *Graves*, 5 *M. & Gr.* 613. It is now settled that the circumstance that the thing complained of furnishes upon the whole a greater convenience to the public than it takes away, is no answer to an indictment for a nuisance. It is not necessary that a public nuisance should be injurious to health; if there are smells offensive to the senses, it is enough, as the neighbourhood has a right to pure and fresh air.—*R.* v. *Neill*, 2 *C. & P.*, 485. Keeping large quantities of inflammable or explosive substance in a crowded neighbourhood is a nuisance for which an indictment will lie. No length of time will legitimate a nuisance, and it is immaterial how long the practice has prevailed. Though 20 years' use may

Offence.	Statute.	Punishment.
Obstructing (*Railway Engines, &c.*) —See "Malicious Injuries" and "Offences against the Person."		
Oath— To administer, or cause to be administered, or by threats, persuasion, or other undue means, cause any person to take an unlawful oath, on a book or otherwise; or to take such oath, not being compelled by inevitable necessity.	27 Geo. iii. c. 15, s. 6.	Felony; penal servitude for 7 years.
Administering, tendering, or causing to be, &c., or by undue means causing to be taken, oath or engagement binding to belong to any society formed for seditious purposes, or to disturb the peace, or injure person or property, or to compel any person to do or not to do any act; binding to obey orders of unlawful committee or leader, or to assemble at command, &c.; or not to give evidence against associates, or reveal, &c.; or taking any such oath. Aiders and abettors, though not present, to be deemed principals.	50 Geo. iii. c. 102, ss. 1, 2, and 3.	Felony; penal servitude for life. The taking of any such oath, penal servitude for 7 years. Persons compelled to take oaths excused by giving information on oath within 10 days. If detained by force or sickness, 7 days after such ceases.
Abolition of voluntary and extrajudicial oaths before Justice of the Peace.	5 & 6 Wm. iv. c. 62.	(For "Forms" of oaths, &c.—see *Appendix*,)

bind the right of an individual, yet the public have a right to demand the suppression of a nuisance, though of longer standing.—*Weld* v. *Hornby*, 7 *East*, 199; see *Reeves. Acts of Indecency.*—"Whatever outrages public decency, and is injurious to public morals, is indictable as a misdemeanour."—*Hawk.* Whatever place becomes the habitation of civilized men, there the laws of decency must be enforced.—*R.* v. *Crundin*, 2 *Camp.* 89. But an indecent exposure in a place of public resort, if actually seen only by one person, no other person being in a position to see it, is not a common nuisance. An indecent exposure in an omnibus was considered to be a public place, so as to sustain the indictment. The towns Improvement Act,

Offence.	Statute.	Punishment.
Obscene (*Books, Prints, Conduct, &c.*) —See "Libel," and "Nuisance," and see Summary Index, "Indecent Conduct in Streets," &c.		
Obtaining (*Money, &c., under False Pretences*)—see "Larceny," &c.		
Offences against the Person— *Homicide*—Whoever shall be convicted of murder shall suffer death as a felon.	24 & 25 Vic. c. 100, s. 1. (27 & 28 Vic. c. 47.)	Death as a felon.
Sentence—Court shall pronounce sentence of death.	s. 2.	
Burial—Body shall be buried within precincts of prison in which last confined, and Court shall so direct.	s. 3.	
Conspiracy or solicitation to murder any person, whether a subject of Her Majesty or not, and whether or not within Queen's dominions.	s. 4.	Misdemeanour; penal servitude not more than 10, nor less than 5 years (not less than 7 if previously convicted of felony); or imprisonment not exceeding 2 years, with or without H. L.
Manslaughter, ...	s. 5.	Penal servitude for life, or not less than 5 years (not less than 7 if previously convicted of felony); or imprisonment not exceeding 2 years, with or without H. L., and with or without fine.

17 & 18 Vic., c. 103, gives power to Justices to deal with, in a summary way, acts contrary to public decency.

Bawdy-houses.—The keeping of a bawdy-house, or the keeping of a single room for the purpose of bawdry, is indictable as a common nuisance, on the ground of its corrupting public morals, and endangering the public peace by drawing together dissolute persons.—*Hawk.; R. v. Pierson*, 2 Ld. Raym. These houses being generally managed by intrigues of the female, a married woman may be punished as well as the husband, or as if she were married.—*R. v. Williams.* As to indecent publications and writings, see "Libel."

Offence.	Statute.	Punishment.
Offences against the Person—*con.* *Indictment.*—What it shall contain, for murder and manslaughter.	24 & 25 Vic. c. 100, s. 6. (27 & 28 Vic. c. 47.)	—
For murder—" Feloniously, wilfully, and of his malice aforethought, kill and murder the deceased."	,,	—
Manslaughter—" Did feloniously kill and slay the deceased." Manner or means by which death caused not necessary to be set forth.	,,	
Excusable Homicide.—No punishment or forfeiture shall be incurred by any person who shall kill another by misfortune or in his own defence, or in any other manner without felony.—*Blackstone*, iv., 186, 201 ; *Broom*, 921, &c.	s. 7.	—
Petit treason abolished, . .	24 & 25 Vic. c. 100, s. 8.	
Murder or manslaughter abroad, by subject of Her Majesty, may be tried where offenders apprehended in England or Ireland.	s. 9.	
Where death or cause of death happens in England or Ireland.	s. 10. (27 & 28 Vic. c. 47.)	May be tried in England or Ireland where the death, or cause of death, happens.
Attempts to Murder.—By poison or wounding :—Causing to be administered to, or taken by any person, any poison or destructive thing, or by any means wounding or causing grievous bodily harm, with intent to commit murder. And see also " Explosives Act, 1873," 46 Vic., c. 3.	s. 11.	Felony ; penal servitude for life, or not less than 5 years (not less than 7 if previously convicted of felony) ; or imprisonment not exceeding 2 years, with or without H. L., and solitary confinement.
Gunpowder.—By destroying or damaging any building by gunpowder or explosive substance with intent to murder. (*a*)	s. 12.	Felony ; like punishment as last preceding.

(*a*) For other offences by explosives—see title " Explosives," Act, 46 Vic., c. 3.

Offence.	Statute.	Punishment.
Offences against the Person—*con.*		
By setting fire to or casting a ship away, with intent to murder.	24 & 25 Vic. c. 100, s. 13. (27 & 28 Vic. c. 47.)	Felony; like punishment.
By attempting to poison, or by shooting, or attempting to shoot, or attempting to drown, or strangle, or suffocate, with intent to murder.	s. 14.	Felony; like punishment.
Other means.—By any other means than those specified in preceding sections attempting to commit murder.	s. 15.	Felony; like punishment.
Threatening Letters. — Maliciously sending, delivering, uttering, or directly or indirectly causing to be received, knowing the contents thereof, any letter or writing threatening to kill or murder. (See " Malicious Injuries.")	s. 16.	Felony; penal servitude not exceeding 10 years, and not less than 5 years (not less than 7 if previously convicted of felony); or imprisonment not exceeding 2 years, with or without H. L., and solitary confinement; and male under 16 may be whipped.
Attempt to do Bodily Harm.—By preventing or impeding a person endeavouring to save himself from shipwreck, or preventing any other in his endeavour to save the life of such person.	s. 17.	Felony; penal servitude for life, or not less than 5 years (not less than 7 if previously convicted of felony); or imprisonment not exceeding 2 years, with or without H. L., and solitary confinement.
By any means, or by shooting, or attempting to shoot at a person, with intent to maim, disfigure, disable, or do grievous bodily harm, or prevent lawful apprehension of any person.	s. 18.	Felony; like punishment as last preceding.
Gun, pistol, or other arms, loaded with gunpowder or explosive substance and ball, shot, slug, or destructive material, to be deemed loaded arms.	s. 19.	

Offence.	Statute.	Punishment.
Offences against the Person—*con.* Unlawfully and maliciously wounding, or inflicting any grievous bodily harm, either with or without weapon or instrument.	24 & 25 Vic. c. 100, s. 20. (27 & 28 Vic. c. 47.)	Misdemeanour; penal servitude 5 years (not less than 7 if previously convicted of felony); or imprisonment not exceeding 2 years, with or without H. L.
By attempting to choke, suffocate, strangle, render insensible, &c., with intent to commit, or enable any other to commit, indictable offence.	s. 21.	Felony; penal servitude for life, or not less than 5 years (not less than 7 if previously convicted of felony); or imprisonment not exceeding 2 years, with or without H. L.; and male offender may be whipped. (*a*)
Chloroform, &c.—Administering, or causing to be, &c., to any person, chloroform, &c., or other stupefying drugs, with intent to commit or enable another to commit indictable offence.	s. 22.	Felony; like punishment as preceding.

(*a*) *Whipping.*—26 & 27 Vic., c. 44.—" Where any person is convicted of a crime under either of the said sections (43rd section of Larceny Act, 24 & 25 Vic., c. 96, and 21st section of the above Act), the Court may, in addition to the punishment awarded by said sections, or any part thereof, direct that the offender, if a male, be once, twice, or thrice privately whipped, subject to the following provisions :—

" 1. That in case of an offender whose age does not exceed 16 years, the number of strokes at each whipping do not exceed 25, and the instrument used shall be a birch rod.

" 2. That in the case of any other male offender, the number of strokes do not exceed 50 at each such whipping.

" 3. That in each case the Court, in its sentence, shall specify the number of strokes to be inflicted, and the instrument to be used."

Whipping shall not take place after six months from sentence, and if the person be sentenced to penal servitude it shall be inflicted before he shall be removed to convict prison.

This Act was passed to deter offenders and prevent garrotte robberies which had become alarmingly frequent within the few previous years in London. The Judges did, in almost every case, cause the offenders to be whipped, and the result is that such offences now rarely occur. It is called " An Act for the further security of the persons of Her Majesty's subjects from personal violence."

Offence.	Statute.	Punishment.
Offences against the Person—*con.* *Poison, &c.*—By administering, or causing to be, &c., poison or noxious thing to any person, so as to endanger life or inflict grievous bodily harm.	24 & 25 Vic. c. 100, s. 23. (27 & 29 Vic. c. 47.)	Felony; penal servitude not exceeding 10 years, nor less than 5 (not less than 7 if previously convicted of felony) ; or imprisonment not exceeding 2 years, with or without H. L.
Administering, or causing to be, &c., poison, or noxious thing, with intent to injure, aggrieve, or annoy.	s. 24.	Misdemeanour; penal servitude 5 years (not less than 7 if previously convicted of felony) ; or imprisonment not exceeding 2 years, with or without H. L.
Jury may acquit of the felony under section 23, and convict of the misdemeanour under section 24.	s. 25.	—
Apprentices.—Master or mistress, legally liable, refusing or neglecting, without lawful excuse, to provide for apprentice necessary food, clothing or lodging, or maliciously doing bodily harm, so as to endanger life or health, or cause permanent injury. (And for summary power for neglecting to provide food, lodging, medical aid, &c. &c.—see 38 & 39 Vic. c. 86, s. 6, and "Employers and Workmen," Summary Index). (a)	s. 26.	Misdemeanour; penal servitude 5 years (not less than 7 if previously convicted of felony); or imprisonment not exceeding 2 years, with or without H. L. ; and on certificate of Justices, guardians or overseers shall conduct prosecution. See 73.
Children.—By abandoning or exposing children under two years, whereby life may be endangered, or health permanently injured.	s. 27.	Misdemeanour; like punishment as last preceding.

(a) *Apprentices.*—The Conspiracy and Protection of Property Act, 38 & 39 Vic., c. 86, s. 6, gives Justices a summary power to punish for not providing (where legally liable) food, clothing, medical aid, whereby health of apprentice or servant likely to be seriously or permanently injured.

Offence.	Statute.	Punishment.
Offences against the Person—_con._ By explosion of gunpowder, or other explosive substance, burning, &c., or doing grievous bodily harm.	24 & 25 Vic. c. 100, s. 28. (27 & 28 Vic. c. 47.)	Felony; penal servitude for life, or not less than 5 years (not less than 7 if previously convicted of felony); or imprisonment not exceeding 2 years, with or without H. L., and solitary confinement. Male under 16 may be whipped.
Causing gunpowder or explosive substance to explode; sending to, or causing to be received, explosive or noxious thing; laying at any place, or throwing upon any person, corrosive fluid, destructive or explosive substance, with intent to do bodily harm, &c. See also 46 Vic. c. 3, title "Explosives."	s. 29.	Felony; like punishment as last preceding.
Placing gunpowder or explosive substance on building, vessel, &c., with intent to do bodily injury to any person (and see section 12).	s. 30.	Felony; penal servitude not exceeding 14, and not less than 5 years (not less than 7 if previously convicted of felony); or imprisonment not exceeding 2 years, with or without H. L., and solitary confinement; and male under 16 may be whipped.
Spring-guns, &c.—Setting, or causing to be set, spring-gun, man-trap, or engine, calculated to destroy human life, or inflict grievous bodily harm, with intent, or whereby same may destroy or do bodily harm to trespassers. Permitting same to be or continue set. Not to apply to guns or traps for vermin, or set in houses between sunset and sunrise.	s. 31. "	Misdemeanour; penal servitude 5 years (not less than 7 if previously convicted of felony); or imprisonment not exceeding 2 years, with or without H. L. —
Railways. — Maliciously throwing stones, &c., upon; displacing rails, sleepers, &c.; diverting points, &c.;	s. 32.	Felony; penal servitude for life, or not less than 5 years (not less

Offence.	Statute.	Punishment.
Offences against the Person—*con.* showing, hiding, or removing signals, or doing anything with intent to endanger safety of travellers.	24 & 25 Vic. c. 100, s. 32. (27 & 28 Vic. c. 47.)	than 7 if previously convicted of felony); or imprisonment not exceeding 2 years, with or without H. L., and solitary confinement. Male under 16 may be whipped. (*a*)
(Like offence, with intent to obstruct or upset engine, &c., is punishable under Malicious Injuries Act, 24 & 25 Vic., c. 97, s. 35.)		
Maliciously throwing into or upon railway engine, tender, carriage, truck, &c., wood, stone, or other thing, with intent to endanger any person.	s. 33,	Felony; penal servitude for life, or not less than 5 years (not less than 7 if previously convicted of felony); or imprisonment not exceeding 2 years, with or without H. L. (*a*)
(Like offence, with intent to obstruct engine, or carriage, punishable under Malicious Injuries Act, 24 & 25 Vic., c. 97, s. 36.)		
By any unlawful act, wilful omission, or neglect, endangering, or causing to be, &c., the safety of any passenger, or aiding or assisting therein.	s. 34.	Misdemeanour; imprisonment not exceeding 2 years, with or without H. L.
Persons having charge of any carriage or vehicle, by wanton or furious driving or racing, wilful misconduct or neglect, doing or causing bodily harm to any person.	s. 35.	Like.
Assaults.—Obstructing or preventing *clergyman* or other minister from celebrating divine service; or at any lawful burial, striking or offering violence to; or while so engaged (or to offender's knowledge about to engage) in such duties, arresting under civil process.	s. 36.	Like.

(*a*) *Railways.*—Juvenile offenders under 6 years may be summarily dealt with for these offences, under 10 & 11 Vic., c. 82, and 13 & 14 Vic., c. 37, as if the above offences had been mentioned therein in addition to the offence of larceny—34 & 35 Vic., c. 78, s. 13. See "Railways," Summary Index; and see "Children and Young Persons," Summary Index, where whipping is limited to age of 14.

Offence.	Statute.	Punishment.
Offences against the Person—*con.* Assaulting Magistrate or officer in exercise of his duty, in or on account of his preserving *wreck, &c.*	24 & 25 Vic. c. 100, s. 37. (27 & 28 Vic. c. 47.)	Misdemeanour; penal servitude not exceeding 7 years, and not less than 5 years (not less than 7 if previously convicted of felony); or imprisonment not exceeding 2 years, with or without H. L.
Assault with intent to commit felony; or assaulting or obstructing *peace officer*, or person acting in his aid; or on any person with intent to prevent lawful apprehension.	s. 38.	Misdemeanour; imprisonment not exceeding 2 years, with or without H. L. (But if of a trivial nature may be tried summarily by two Justices. See "Assault." Summary Index.)
Assaulting or threatening with intent to hinder buying, selling, or free passage of *grain, potatoes, &c.*	s. 39.	Misdemeanour. See Summary Index, "Assault."
Assault to prevent seamen or keelmen working.	s. 40.	Summary Index.
Assault in pursuance of unlawful *combination*, or conspiracy to raise wages, or respecting trade, &c.	s. 41.	This section is repealed by 34 & 35 Vic. c. 32.
Common Assault.—Assaulting or beating any other person (but see section 47).	s. 42.	Summary Index; title, "Assault."
Aggravated assaults on females and on boys.	s. 43.	Summary Index; title, "Assault."
Any assault occasioning actual bodily harm.	s. 47.	Penal servitude 5 years (not less than 7 if previously convicted of felony); or imprisonment not exceeding 2 years, with or without H. L.
Common Assault.—Whosoever shall be convicted upon an indictment for a common assault.	,,	Imprisonment not exceeding 1 year, with or without H. L.

Offence.	Statute.	Punishment.
Offences against the Person—*con.* *Rape.*—Person convicted of the crime of. (*Rape is the having carnal knowledge of a woman by force and against her will*—1 *Hawk.*, c. 41, s. 2 ; and see *Archbold.*) (*a*)	24 & 25 Vic. c. 100, s. 48. (27 & 28 Vic. c. 47.)	Felony ; penal servitude for life, or not less than 5 years (not less than 7 if previously convicted of felony) ; or imprisonment not exceeding 2 years, with or without H. L.
Indecent assault upon any female, (*b*) (See amendment of this section ; schedule to 48 & 49 Vic. c. 69.)	24 & 25 Vic. c.100, ss. 8, 52.	Imprisonment not exceeding 2 years, with or without H. L.
Abduction of a woman against her will, with intent to marry or carnally know her, or to cause her to be married or carnally known, she having any interest, present or future, &c., in real or personal estate ; fraudulently alluring, taking away, or detaining such woman, being under 21, out of possession, or against the will of her parents or guardian, with intent to marry or carnally know her, or cause her to be, &c.	s. 53.	Felony ; penal servitude not exceeding 14 years, and not less than 5 years (not less than 7 if previously convicted of felony) ; or imprisonment not exceeding 2 years, with or without H. L. Offender incapable of deriving any interest in her property ; if married, Court of Chancery to settle property.
Forcible abduction of any woman of any age, with intent to marry or carnally know her, or to cause her to be married or carnally known by any other.	s. 54.	Felony ; penal servitude not exceeding 14 years, nor less than 5 years (not less than 7 if previously convicted of felony) ; or imprisonment not exceeding 2 years, with or without H. L.

(*a*) The Criminal Law Amendment Act, 1885 (48 & 49 Vic. c 69, s. 20), makes the accused, and the husband or wife competent witnesses in offences under sections 48, and 52 to 55 inclusive, of the above Act—24 & 25 Vic. c. 100.

(*b*) *Indecent Assaults on Young Persons.*—It shall be no defence to a charge on indictment for an indecent assault on a young person under the age of 13 to prove that *he* or *she* consented to the act of indecency: 43 & 44 Vic. c. 45. It will be observed that males and females are included.

2 P

INDICTABLE OFFENCES.

Offence.	Statute.	Punishment.
Offences against the Person—*con.* Unlawfully taking or causing to be taken, any unmarried girl under 16 out of possession and against the will of her parents or guardian.	24 & 25 Vic. c. 100, s. 55. (27 & 28 Vic. c. 47.)	Misdemeanour; imprisonment not exceeding 2 years, with or without H. L.
Child Stealing.—By force or fraud, taking or enticing away or detaining any child under 14, with intent to deprive parent, guardian, or caretaker of possession of such child, or with intent to steal any article upon such child; and with such intent harbouring such child knowingly. (Exception as to person claiming right to the possession.)	s. 56.	Felony; penal servitude not exceeding 7, and not less than 5 years (not less than 7 if previously convicted of felony); or imprisonment not exceeding 2 years, with or without H. L. Male under 16 may be whipped.
Bigamy.—Marrying any other person during life of former husband or wife, whether the second marriage take place in Ireland or England, or elsewhere. (Not to apply to second marriage contracted elsewhere than in England and Ireland, or by any other than a subject of Her Majesty, or where first husband or wife not known to be living within seven years.)	s. 57.	Felony; penal servitude not exceeding 7, nor less than 5 years, not less than 7 if previously convicted of felony): or imprisonment not exceeding 2 years, with or without H. L.
Abortion.—Administering drugs, &c., or using instruments to procure abortion, or causing to be used, &c.	s. 58.	Felony; penal servitude for life, or not less than 5 years (not less than 7 if previously convicted of felony); or imprisonment not exceeding 2 years, with or without H. L., and solitary confinement.
Supplying or procuring drugs or instruments, for the purpose, knowingly.	s. 59.	Misdemeanour; penal servitude, 5 years (not less than 7 if previously convicted of felony); or imprisonment not exceeding 2 years, with or without H. L.

Offence.	Statute.	Punishment.
Offences against the Person—*con.* *Concealing Birth.*—If any woman be delivered of a child, every person who shall by any secret disposition of the dead body of said child, whether such child died before, at, or after its birth, endeavour to conceal the birth thereof. (Person tried and acquitted of the murder may be convicted of concealing birth.)	24 & 25 Vic. c. 100, s. 60. (27 & 28 Vic. c. 47).	Misdemeanour; imprisonment not exceeding 2 years, with or without H. L.
Unnatural Offences—Sodomy and Bestiality. — Committing the abominable crime of buggery either with mankind or with any animal. (*a*)	s. 61.	Penal servitude for life, or not less than 10 years.
Attempting to commit the said abominable crime, or guilty of assault, with intent, &c., or of any indecent assault upon any male person. *Carnal knowledge, what.*—Not necessary to prove actual emission, but offence shall be complete upon proof of penetration. (*b*)	s. 62.	Misdemeanour; penal servitude, not exceeding 10, and not less than 5 years (not less than 7 if previously convicted of felony); or imprisonment not exceeding 2 years, with or without H. L.
Gunpowder, &c.—Making, having in possession, &c., gunpowder, explosive substance, noxious thing, or instrument to commit, or enable another to commit, any of the felonies in this Act (and now	s. 64.	Misdemeanour; imprisonment not exceeding 2 years, with or without H. L., and solitary confinement. Male under 16 may be whipped.

(*a*) It has been well said that some errors would never have thriven were it not for learned refutation. There are some vices, and the above is certainly one of them, which in its prosecution or punishment should receive as little publicity as possible. It is one of those cases which Magistrates should investigate in private. The Executive, as much as possible, endeavour to prevent its ever being brought before the public. "I touch with reluctance and dispatch with impatience this most odious vice, of which modesty rejects the name, and nature abominates the idea."—*Gibbon's "Decline and Fall."*

(*b*) By the Criminal Law Amendment Act, 1885, 48 & 49 Vic., c. 69, s. 11—Any male person who in public or private commits, or is a party to the commission of, or procures, or attempts to procure, the commission by any male person of any act of gross indecency with another male person shall be guilty of a misdemeanour, and liable to be imprisoned for any term not exceeding 2 years, with or without H. L.

2 P 2

Offence.	Statute.	Punishment.
Offences against the Person—*con.* for the punishment of making, or having in possession any explosive substance, under suspicious circumstances, by the 46 Vic., c. 3, s. 4, is not to exceed 14 years, or imprisonment not exceeding 2 years).	24 & 25 Vic. c. 100, s. 64. (27 & 28 Vic. c. 47.)	
Justice, on oath made, may grant warrant to search.	s. 65.	Search to be made in the daytime.
Other matters.—Persons suspected of intending offences against this Act may be apprehended.	s. 66.	
In felonies under this Act, principal in second degree and accessory before the fact—	s. 67.	Punishable as principal in first degree.
Accessory after the fact to felonies (except murder).	,,	Imprisonment not exceeding 2 years, with or without H. L.
Accessory after the fact to murder,	,,	Penal servitude for life, or not less than 5 years (not less than 7 if previously convicted of felony) ; or imprisonment not exceeding 2 years, with or without H. L.
Whoever shall counsel, aid, or abet, the commission of indictable misdemeanour punishable under this Act— (See also 24 & 25 Vic., c. 94, s. 8 ; and see title " Abettors.''	s. 67.	Punishable as principal offender.
Admiralty — Offences committed within jurisdiction of the Admiralty to be dealt with as if committed upon land in England or Ireland, wherever offender apprehended or in custody.	s. 68.	
Solitary confinement, when awarded, not to exceed 1 month at a time, nor exceeding 3 months in a year.	s. 70.	

Offence.	Statute.	Punishment.
Offences against the Person—*con.* *Whipping*, when awarded, to be private; the Court shall name the number of strokes and the instrument.	24 & 25 Vic. c. 100, s. 70. (27 & 28 Vic. c. 47.)	
Sureties, &c.—Persons convicted of indictable misdemeanour under this Act, if the Court think fit, may, in lieu of punishment—	s. 71.	Fine the offender, and require him to enter into recognizance with sureties, both or either, for keeping the peace and being of good behaviour.
And in case of felony, punishable otherwise than with death, may order—	,,	Offender to enter into recognizance with sureties, both or either, for keeping the peace, in addition to any punishment by this Act authorized. In default of finding sureties, imprisonment not exceeding 1 year.
Assaults on apprentices under section 26; indictable assaults on persons under 16 amounting to, or with intent to commit felony.	24 & 25 Vic. c. 100, s. 73.	*Guardians or overseers* to prosecute on certificate of two Justices.
Costs.—In indictable assaults, with or without battery or wounding.	s. 74.	In addition to sentence, Court may order prosecutor his expenses, and for loss of time; in default of payment, additional imprisonment not exceeding 3 months.
Court may issue distress warrant to levy such costs.	s. 75.	On being levied by distress, the imprisonment awarded in default to cease.
Summary proceedings—how, . .	s. 76.	
In indictable misdemeanour, Court may order costs of prosecutions, as in felonies.	s. 77.	

Offence.	Statute.	Punishment.
Office and Officers—		
Constable or overseer refusing to execute his office.	Common Law	Misdemeanour; fine and imprisonment.
Buying, selling, or bargaining for the sale of, offices (specified in 49 Geo. iii. c. 126, or the 5 & 6 Edwd. vi. c. 16, Eng.); assisting or negotiating, &c.	49 Geo. iii. c. 126, ss. 3 & 4.	Misdemeanour; punishable by fine and imprisonment.
Bribery, extortion, malfeasance, or culpable nonfeasance, of an officer of justice, in relation to his office. See also title, "Public Bodies Corrupt Practices Act, 1889," p. 592. Officers of Courts falsifying records, &c.: see "Forgery."	Common Law	Misdemeanour; fine and imprisonment.
Official Secrets Act, 1889—(a) Act to prevent the disclosure of official documents and information obtained in Her Majesty's arsenals, fortresses, dockyards, ships, &c. &c.	52 & 53 Vic. c. 52.	Some offences against this Act are felony and some misdemeanours; saving also as to prosecutions at Common Law, or by Military or Naval Law.
Paper (*Bank*)— Blank bank-notes or imitation—see "Forgery."		
Parliamentary (*Elections*)— See "Elections."		
Peace Preservation Act— See Summary Index, and *Appendix.*	44 Vic. c. 5.	

(a) *Official Secrets.*—The above Act was passed in consequence of important plans and drawings in Her Majesty's Arsenals having got into the possession of a foreign power. Some of the offences of unlawfully obtaining sketches, drawings, plans, &c., or disclosing them, are misdemeanours; and where it is intended to disclose the information to a foreign power, the offence will amount to felony. The consent of Attorney-General is necessary to the institution of prosecution.

Offence.	Statute.	Punishment.
Penal Servitude— Act substituting penal servitude for transportation.	16 & 17 Vic. c. 99.	—
Where sentence of transportation for 7 years might have been passed, the Court in its discretion may pass sentence of penal servitude for not less than 5 years in any case. (*a*)	20 & 21 Vic. c. 3. 27 & 28 Vic. c. 47.	
The 42 & 43 Vic. c. 55, s. 1, repeals 27 & 28 Vic. c. 47, s. 2, as to the minimum term of penal servitude being 7 years.	42 & 43 Vic. c. 55, s. 1.	
For the recommitting of convicts whose licence has been revoked, see Act (*b*)—	27 & 28 Vic. c. 47, s. 9.	
Perjury (*c*)— Wilful and corrupt perjury, or subornation of perjury.	Common Law 3 Geo. ii. c. 4. 17 & 18 Geo. iii. c. 36.	Misdemeanour; fine and imprisonment; or penal servitude for 7, and not less than 5 years (not less than 7 if previously convicted of felony.)

(*a*) *Sentences of Penal Servitude.*—" Act to amend the Penal Servitude Acts," 27 & 28 Vic. c. 47, s. 2 :—

" No person shall be sentenced to penal servitude in respect to any offence committed after the passing of this Act for a period of less than five years, and where under any Act now in force a period of less than five years is the utmost sentence of penal servitude that can be awarded, a period of five years shall, in respect to any offence committed after the passing of this Act, in such Act be substituted for the less period ; and where under any Act now in force a period of either less or more than five years may be awarded as a sentence of penal servitude, the least sentence of penal servitude that can be awarded under that Act shall, in respect to any offence committed after the passing of this Act, be a period of five years ; and where any person shall, on indictment, be convicted of any crime or offence punishable with penal servitude, after having been previously convicted of felony, or in *Scotland* of any crime (whether such previous conviction shall have taken place upon an indictment, or under the provisions of the Act passed in the Eighteenth and Nineteenth of *Victoria*, chapter one hundred and twenty-six), the least sentence of penal servitude that can be awarded in such case shall be a period of seven years."

(*b*) For certificate of conviction, whereby licence becomes forfeited, see 27 & 28 Vic. c. 47, sec. 8, and see " Crime."—*Summary Index.*

(*c*) *Perjury* at Common Law is defined to be a wilful false oath, by one who, being lawfully required to depose the truth in any proceeding in a Court of Justice, swears

Offence.	Statute.	Punishment.
Perjury—continued. Although Justices may refuse to commit or to hold a person to bail to answer the charge of perjury, they shall, if prosecutor desire it, take his recognizance to prosecute the charge, and transmit any depositions taken as if the accused were committed.	22 & 23 Vic. c. 17.	—
Any Judge or Justice of the Peace may direct any person guilty of perjury in evidence before him to be prosecuted, and commit him unless he enter into recognizance to take his trial; may bind persons to give evidence, and give certificate of prosecution being directed, which shall be sufficient evidence of same. (a)	14 & 15 Vic. c. 100, s. 19, and following.	—

absolutely, in a matter of some consequence, to the point in question, whether he be believed or not.—*Hawk., P. C.* To support the indictment, there must be proved—the authority to administer the oath, the occasion of doing so, the taking of the oath, the substance of it, the materiality of the matter sworn, the falsity, and the corrupt intention. It is a general rule that *two* witnesses should disprove the fact sworn to, for otherwise it would be one oath against another. This is a rule founded on substantial justice; and evidence confirmatory of the one witness in some slight particular only is not sufficient to warrant a conviction; but it is laid down that strong circumstantial evidence in support of the direct testimony of one witness may turn the scale and warrant the conviction.

Perjury.—Mr. Justice Stephen: " If, upon a trial for perjury, the only evidence against the defendant is the statement of one witness contradicting the oath on which the perjury is assigned, and if no circumstances are proved which corroborate such witness, the defendant is entitled to be acquitted. That I believe to be the law of the land; and I may observe that it is stated less favourably to the prisoner than it usually is, because it is usually said that you cannot convict a man for perjury upon the evidence of less than two witnesses. There have been many cases in which a man has been convicted for perjury corroborated by circumstances not directly connected with it, but leading up to it."—Mr. Justice Stephen reading his own dictum from his own book in the case of the Crown by *Cass* v. *Endicott*, Central Criminal Court, Nov., 1887.

Subornation of Perjury at Common Law is the procuring a man to take a false oath, amounting to perjury, the man actually taking such oath; but if he do not actually take it, the person so inciting is not guilty of subornation of perjury, yet he may be punished by fine and corporal punishment.—*Hawk., P. C.*

(a) By the 22 & 23 Vic., c. 17, indictments for perjury, &c., and certain other misdemeanours, shall not be presented to Grand Jury unless the prosecutor or other person presenting such indictment has been bound by recognizance to prosecute or

Offence.	Statute.	Punishment.
Perjury—*continued*. *Bankruptcy Laws.*—Wilfully and corruptly giving false evidence, making false affidavits, &c., upon examination, &c., under Bankruptcy Acts.	35 & 36 Vic. c. 58, s. 123.	Liable to the penalties of wilful and corrupt perjury.
Personation— Falsely personating owner of share or interest in stocks or funds transferable at Banks of England or Ireland, body corporate, or society, and endeavouring to transfer or receive same.	24 & 25 Vic. c. 98, s. 3. (27 & 28 Vic. c. 47.)	Felony; penal servitude for life, or not less than 5 years (not less than 7 if previously convicted of felony); or imprisonment not exceeding 2 years, with or without H. L., and solitary confinement.
Under any Act now in force, falsely personating another, or falsely acknowledging anything in the name of another, or falsely representing any other person than the real party to be such real party. For offences under this Act, see title, "Forgeries;" and see also "False Pretences."	24 & 25 Vic. c. 96, s. 48.	Where same were capital before 1 Wm. iv., c. 66, and not otherwise punishable, under this Act :—Penal servitude for life, or not less than 5 years (not less than 7 if previously convicted of felony) ; or imprisonment not exceeding 2 years, with or without H. L., and solitary confinement.
Personating Parliamentary voters,	13 & 14 Vic. c. 69, s. 93.	Two Justices may commit offender for trial.
With intent to deprive any person of real estate or other property. (a)— If any person shall falsely and de-	37 & 38 Vic. c. 36, s. 1.	Felony; penal servitude for life, or any period not less than 5 years

give evidence against the accused, or unless authorized by a Judge of one of the Superior Courts, or acting under 14 & 15 Vic., c. 100, or the Attorney-General. Where a Justice of the Peace refuses to commit for trial, &c., and the prosecutor desires to prefer an indictment, the Justice shall take the recognizance of the prosecutor to prosecute the charge, and shall transmit same, with the information and depositions (if any) to the Court where indictment is to be preferred.—See title, "Vexatious Indictments."

(a) The above Act, called the "False Personation Act, 1874," was passed in consequence of a person named *Arthur Orton*, a butcher, of Wapping, having personated *Sir Roger Doughty Tichborne*, believed to have been drowned at sea.

...... of property.	
Not to prevent such person being tried or punished under other Acts or at Common Law.	s.
Offences under this Act shall not be tried at Quarter Sessions.	
In all cases not provided for by Statute the offence remains a misdemeanour at Common Law, and the offender is punishable as a cheat.	Comm
Any person who, by false certificate, &c., or other fraudulent means, obtains, or attempts to obtain, the grant, increase, &c., payment of pay, &c., pension, &c.	47 & c. 55,
Offences may be prosecuted before Courts of Summary Jurisdiction	

The suit was perhaps the most extraordinary a
tender having succeeded in imposing himself
Tichborne, and on many persons of charac
positively identified him as Tichborne. But
cross-examination of himself, and lost his suit
into custody for perjury, and the Government
undertook the prosecution—a prosecution to
furnish no parallel, witnesses having been brou
from all parts of the world. The funds at the
....

Offence.	Statute.	Punishment.
Personation—*continued.* in manner provided by sections 166, 167, 168 of Army Act, 1881. See "Army Act," p. 16, Summary Index.	47 & 48 Vic. c. 55, s. 3.	without H. L., not exceeding 3 months, or fine not exceeding £25.
Physician—(*Guilty of malpractice, &c.*)—(*a*)	Common Law	Misdemeanour.
Piracy— Robbery on the high seas is piracy.	Common Law 11, 12, & 13 Jac. i. c. 2. (Ir.) (*b*)	Cognizable by Court of Admiralty, and punishable as if committed on land.
Assaulting with intent to murder, or doing act to endanger life with intent to commit piracy, or at the time of or immediately before or after piracy.	1 Vic. c. 88, s. 2.	Felony; punishable with death; and for punishment of principals and accessories before fact to offence of piracy, see 5 Vic. sess. 2, c. 28, ss. 17, 19.

* Although by the Index to the Statutes the above is noted to be applicable to England and Scotland only, yet the wording of the Act clearly shows that Ireland is included.

(*a*) *Physician.*—*Mala Praxis* in a physician, whether from experiment, curiosity, or neglect, is a misdemeanour, as it affects the public—*Dr. Goenvelt's Case*, 1 *Lord Raym.* 213, and 4 *C. & P.* 398, 423.

(*b*) By 11, 12, 13 *Jac.* i. *c.* 2, *s.* 1 (*Ir.*)—Treason, felonies, robberies, murders, and confederacies committed on sea, or in any other haven, river, creek, or place where the admiral has or pretends to have jurisdiction, shall be tried, &c., as if done on land, according to the Common Law, in such shire as shall be limited by the King's commission, under the great seal of *Ireland*, to be directed to the admiral or his deputy, and three or four others nominated by Chancellor; and by 33 Geo. iii., c. 14, Commissioners under 11 Jac. i., c. 2, or any two, may hear and determine offences in said Act with same power as Justices of *Oyer*, &c., or gaol delivery have as to offences committed on land. The 1 Vic. c. 88, now prescribed the punishment, and repeals several of the English Statutes, but takes no notice of the Irish Act. A pirate is said to be *hostis humani generis*, and therefore every community hath a right to inflict that punishment upon him which every individual would in a state of nature have a right to do for any invasion of his person or personal property.

Offence.	Statute.	Punishment.
Plate— Defacing names or crests on family plate or watches, or employing persons so to do without consent of owner or some person authorized to sell, or unless bought at public auction. (Under Pawnbrokers' Act.)	28 Geo. iii. c. 49, s. 7.	Misdemeanour; same punishment as for receiving stolen goods.
Poisoning— See "Offences against the Person."		
Police Supervision— See "Crime."		
Post Office (a)— Persons employed, opening, wilfully detaining or delaying, or suffering to be opened, &c., any letter.	1 Vic. c. 36, ss. 25, 42. (27 & 28 Vic. c. 47.)	Misdemeanour; fine and imprisonment, or either, with or without H. L., and solitary confinement.
Stealing, or for any purpose embezzling, secreting, or destroying a post letter.	ss. 26, 42.	Felony; penal servitude 7 years, or not less than 5 years (not less than 7 if previously convicted of felony); or imprisonment not exceeding 3 years, with or without H. L., and solitary confinement. (b)

(a) *Post Letter.*—By the 33 & 34 Vic., c. 79, sec. 16, a book-packet, pattern or sample packet, or post card sent by post, shall be deemed a post letter.

(b) See Acts substituting penal servitude for transportation. By the amended Act, 27 & 28 Vic., c. 47, where penal servitude can be awarded, it shall be 5 years at least, and not less than 7 where the offender has been previously convicted of felony.

By 1 *Vic., c.* 90, *s.* 5—Solitary confinement shall not exceed one month at a time, nor exceed three months in a year. Section 5 of this Act is unrepealed.

Offence.	Statute.	Punishment.
Post Office—_continued._ But if such letter contain any chattel, money, or valuable security.	1 Vic. c. 36, ss. 26, 42. (27 & 28 Vic. s. 47.)	Felony; penal servitude for life, or not less than 5 years (not less than 7 if previously convicted of felony); or imprisonment not exceeding 3 years, with or without H. L., and solitary confinement.
Any person stealing chattel, money, or valuable security, out of post letter.	ss. 27, 41, 42.	Felony; penal servitude for life, or not less than 5 years (not less than 7 if previously convicted of felony); or imprisonment not exceeding 4 years, with or without H. L., and solitary confinement.
Stealing post letter bag, or post letter from bag, or from a post office, or from officer of, &c., or from a mail, or to stop a mail, with intent to rob or search.	ss. 28, 41, 42.	Felony : like punishment.
Stealing or unlawfully taking away letter bag sent by post office packet, or a letter thereout, or unlawfully opening such bag.	ss. 29, 41, 42.	Felony; penal servitude for 14, or not less than 5 years (not less than 7 if previously convicted of felony); or imprisonment not exceeding 3 years, with or without H. L,, and solitary confinement.
Knowingly receiving letter, letter bag, chattel, money, security, &c., where the taking, embezzling, &c., amounts to felony under Post Office Acts.	ss. 30, 41, 42.	Felony; penal servitude for life, or not less than 5 years (not less than 7 if previously convicted of felony); or imprisonment not exceeding 4 years, with or without H. L., and solitary confinement.

Offence.	Statute.	Punishment.
Post Office—*continued*. Fraudulently retaining, secreting, or detaining, or after being required by officer of the post office neglecting or refusing to deliver up letter which ought to have been delivered to any other person, or post letter bag, or post letter, by whomsoever found.	1 Vic. c. 36, ss. 31, 42. (27 & 28 Vic. c. 47.)	Misdemeanour; fine and imprisonment, with or without H. L., and solitary confinement.
Officers stealing, destroying, or delaying, &c., printed votes of proceedings in Parliament, newspapers, or other papers, open at the sides.	ss. 32, 42.	Misdemeanour; fine and imprisonment, or either, with or without H. L., and solitary confinement.
Soliciting any other to commit felony or misdemeanour against Post Office Acts.	ss. 36, 42.	Misdemeanour; imprisonment not exceeding 2 years, with or without H. L., and solitary confinement.
Aiders and abettors in misdemeanours, punishable as principals.	,,	—
In felonies, under Post Office Acts, principals in second degree, and accessories before the fact.	ss. 35, 42.	Felony; punishable as principals in the first degree.
Telegraph Messages deemed to be post letters within meaning of 1 Vic. c. 36.	32 & 33 Vic. c. 23, s. 23.	—
Telegraph Act, 1868, and this Act shall be Post Office Laws. For other matters, see Summary Index.	s. 24.	—
For offences of forgery, of crossing of money orders, &c., see—	43 & 44 Vic. c. 33.	
As amended by—	46 & 47 Vic. c. 58 (and Schedule.)	
P. O. (*Protection*) *Act*, 1884, for protection of letters, &c., from explosives, disfiguring letter-boxes, &c., imitating stamps, offences by P. O. officers; and as to forging or disclosing telegrams, &c., see Summary Index.	47 & 48 Vic. c. 76.	Offences are for most part punishable on summary conviction.

Offence.	Statute.	Punishment.
Pound · See Summary Index.		
Pretence—(*False*)— See "Larceny," &c.		
Prisoners' Counsel Act, . . . See also	6 & 7 W. 4. 28 Vic. c. 18.	
Prison— See Summary Index; title "Gaol and Gaoler." Capital punishment within, . .	31 Vic. c. 24.	
Principals (*in Second Degree*)— In "Offences against the Person," "Larceny," "Malicious Injuries," "Forgery," "Coin,"—see these titles.		
Prize-fighting (*a*)— Prize-fighting and boxing matches are unlawful, and if death ensue it is manslaughter—*East*, *P. C.* 270. Seconds and others who encourage and remain during the fight are equally guilty of manslaughter— *R.* v. *Murphy*, 6 *Car.* & *P.*	—	See also title "Fighting," Summary Index.
Probation of First Offenders' Act, 1887.	50 & 51 Vic. c. 25.	See Act, *Appendix*.

(*a*) *Prize-fights.*—For suppressing prize-fights, which are classed among unlawful assemblies, Mr. Justice Bayly suggests—"My advice to Magistrates and constables is, in cases where they have information of a fight, to secure the combatants beforehand, and to take them to a Magistrate, who ought to compel them to enter into securities to keep the Peace till the next Assizes or Sessions, and if they will not enter into such security to commit them to prison."—*Bayly, J., R.* v. *Belling- ham*, 2 *C.* & *P*, 234.

For penalty on Railway Company conveying persons to prize-fights, **see** "Railway," Summary Index.

Offence.	Statute.	Punishment.
Proclamations, Gazettes, &c.— Admitting in evidence.	31 & 32 Vic.	...
Procuration— See title "Criminal Law Amendment Act, 1885."		
Protection of Women and Girls, &c. See title "Criminal Law Amendment Act, 1885."		
Public Bodies Corrupt Practices Act, 1889. *Bribery and Corruption in Office.*		
Act for the more effectual prevention and punishment of Bribery and Corruption of and by members, officers, or servants of Corporations, Councils, Boards, Commissioners, or other Public Bodies.	52 & 53 Vic. c. 69.	Misdemeanour; and on conviction shall, at discretion of the Court, be liable to imprisonment for any period not exceeding 2 years, with or without H.L., or to pay a fine not exceeding £500, or to both imprisonment and fine.
Corruption in office a Misdemeanour; corruptly soliciting or receiving, &c.— (1) Every person who shall, by himself or by or in conjunction with another, corruptly solicit or receive, or agree to receive, for himself, or for any other any gift, loan, fee, reward or advantage whatever as an inducement to or reward for, or otherwise on account of any member, officer or servant of a public body, as in Act defined, doing or forbearing to do anything in respect of any matter or transaction whatsoever, actual or proposed, in which the public body is concerned.	ss. 1, 2.	In addition, shall be liable to pay to such Body and as the Court directs the value of gift, loan, &c., or any part thereof, and to be liable to be adjudged incapable of being elected to any office for 7 years, and to forfeit office held at the time of conviction. *On second conviction for* like offence, in addition to foregoing penalties, shall be liable to be adjudged for ever incapable of holding any public office, and to be

Offence.	Statute.	Punishment.
Public Bodies Corrupt Practices Act, 1889—*continued.* *Corruptly giving or offering—* (2) Every person who shall, by himself or by or in conjunction with any other, corruptly give, promise or offer any gift, &c. &c., for such purposes as aforesaid—	52 & 53 Vic. c. 96, ss. 1, 2.	incapable for 7 years of being registered as an Elector, or voting at an election, &c.; and shall also, at the discretion of Court, be liable to forfeit his claim to any compensation or pension to which he would otherwise have been entitled.
Saving—As to prosecution, &c., under any other enactment or at Common Law; but no second punishment for same offence.	s. 3.	
Invalidity of appointment to office not to exempt from punishment.	,,	
Restriction on prosecution without consent of Attorney- or Solicitor-General.	s. 4.	
Expenses of prosecution to be defrayed, as in case of felony.	s. 5.	
For definition of "Public Body," "Public Office," "Person," "Advantage," "Misdemeanour," "Municipal Borough."	ss. 7, 8.	
Provisions of the "Criminal Law and Procedure (Ireland), Act, 1887" (50 & 51 Vic., c. 20), not to apply to trials under this Act.	s. 9.	
Public Company— Officers of, appropriating property, &c.—See "Larceny."		
Public Worship— See "Disturbing Public Worship."		

Offence.	Statute.	Punishment.
Rabbit— Killing in warren by night—see "Larceny;" and see "Larceny" in Summary Index, and title "Game."		
Railway— See "Offences against the Person," and "Malicious Injuries;" and Summary Index, title, "Railway."		
Rape (a)— Rape is the having carnal knowledge of a woman by force and against her will—see also "Offences against the Person." Where connexion is had by personating husband the offence is rape (48 & 49 Vic., c. 69, s. 4).	24 & 25 Vic. c. 100, s. 48. (27 & 28 Vic. c. 47.)	Felony; penal servitude for life, or not less than 5 years (not less than 7 if previously convicted of felony); or imprisonment not exceeding 2 years, with or without H. L.

(a) *Rape.*—This, as Lord Hale says, is "An accusation easily made and hard to be proved, and still harder to be disproved by the party accused." But whatever all this may mean, it is very certain that the prosecutrix as a witness—and in general the only witness—feels a greater interest in establishing the charge against the accused than in ordinary prosecutions witnesses are supposed to have. Therefore the Magistrate in taking down the evidence cannot be too careful in noting every fact and circumstance detailed, how trifling soever they may at the time seem to be. He should be very precise as to the time and the place, and whether the prosecutrix made an alarm ; and if she immediately, or how soon after, told of the occurrence. Nor should the Magistrate (as is too often the case in the course of investigations) allow seeming or obvious inconsistencies in the details with probability, or with one another, to be pointed out to the witness or observed upon before the evidence is concluded. It is also a case (an exception to the general rule) where the character of the woman bringing the charge of rape, or assault with intent to commit a rape, is permitted to be impeached in respect of her chastity. Where these charges break down it is generally by showing that the complainant's conduct at the time, before and after the affair, is not consistent with outraged innocence and modesty. She will, of course, say she resisted to the utmost, where in truth the resistance may be like that of Donna Julia—

"A little still she strove and much repented,
And whispering, I will ne'er consent—consented."

It is, however, held that the words "against her will" must be taken to mean no more than "without her consent." Some distinction has also been made between

Offence.	Statute.	Punishment.
Receivers (*of Stolen Property*) (*a*)— Whoever shall receive any chattel, money, valuable security, or property whatsoever, the stealing, taking, extorting, obtaining, embezzling, or otherwise disposing whereof, shall amount to a felony, either at Common Law, or by virtue of this Act, knowing the same to have been feloniously stolen, taken, extorted, obtained, embezzled, or disposed of— (Receivers are triable in any county where they may have had the property or wherever the principal is triable.)	24 & 25 Vic. c. 96, s. 91. (27 & 28 Vic. c. 47.)	Shall be guilty of felony (and may be indicted and convicted either as an accessory after the fact, or for a substantive felony; and in the latter case whether the principal felon shall or shall not have been previously convicted); penal servitude not exceeding 14 years, and not less than 5 years (not less than 7 if previously convicted of felony); or imprisonment not exceeding 2 years, with or without H. L., and solitary confinement. Male under 16 may be whipped.
Knowingly receiving property, &c., where the taking, obtaining, &c., is a misdemeanour by this Act; see also title "Larceny."	s. 95.	Misdemeanour; penal servitude not exceeding 7 years, and not less than 5 years (not less than 7 if previously convicted

consent and *submission*, as it by no means follows that every submission involves a consent. And further, where there is a submission, how far it has been superinduced by acting on the fears and helplessness of the prosecutrix.

(*a*) *Receivers.*—The presumption arising from the possession of stolen property is that the party stole the property, not that he received it, unless there be evidence that it was stolen by another.

Proof of Guilty Knowledge.—Evidence must be given to show a guilty knowledge. This is in general to be collected from the facts of the case, and conduct of the accused; buying at under-value, concealment, untrue or contradictory accounts as to how he came by the property will be presumptive evidence of the guilty knowledge. In calling on a person to account for the possession of stolen goods, the length of time that has elapsed must be taken into account, and this will vary with the nature of the property, whether they are of a description that pass from hand to hand readily or otherwise. This being a case where the presumption of guilt or innocence may chiefly depend upon the conduct of the party, it is said that in weighing such evidence "nothing more than ordinary caution is required, and honestly to draw such inferences as experience indicates; this in general will be found a safer guide than a consideration of some of the extreme cases which are related in many of the books on evidence."

In *Dublin* there is a summary power given to punish persons who fail to satisfactorily account for goods suspected to be stolen—5 Vic., c. 24, s. 53.

Offence.	Statute.	Punishment.
Receivers (*of Stolen Property*)—*con.* And as to evidence see "Crime," Summary Index, and Act—	34 & 35 Vic. c. 112, s. 19.	of felony); or imprisonment not exceeding 2 years, with or without H. L., and solitary confinement. Male under 16 may be whipped.
Children.—Harbouring or detaining stolen child under 14, with intent to deprive parents, guardians, &c., of the possession, &c. (See title "Offences against the Person." 24 & 25 Vic., c. 100, s. 56.)		
Rescue— Of distress made for rent, . .	4 Geo. i. c. 5, s. 1 (Ir.)	Misdemeanour; fine, and in default of payment imprisonment with H.L. not less than 6 months.
Of cattle seized for purpose of being impounded, or committing pound breach whereby cattle escape, or injuring pound. (And see "Pound," Summary Index.)	6 Geo. iv. c. 43, s 2.	Misdemeanour; fine and imprisonment.
Rescuing goods seized, and assaulting sheriff or bailiff in execution of their duty.	27 & 28 Vic. c. 99, s. 26.	Misdemeanour; imprisonment not exceeding 6 months, with or without H. L.
Of persons in custody, &c. (a) Rescuing or attempting to rescue out of prison, or going to, or during execution, any person committed for or found guilty of murder.	31 Geo. iii. c. 17, s. 10. 1 Vic. c. 91, ss. 1 and 2. 9 & 10 Vic. c. 24, s. 1. 20 & 21 Vic. c. 3, s. 2. 27 & 28 Vic. c. 47.	Felony; penal servitude for life, or not less than 5 years, or imprisonment not exceeding 2 years.

(a) *Rescue*—Is the forcibly freeing of another from arrest or imprisonment; and whether it be felony or not depends upon the nature of the offence for which the party rescued was in custody; but it seems that although offender in custody for felony, but not convicted, the rescue would be only a misdemeanour.—1 *Russ.*, 385. The allegation must be proved by showing that the act was done forcibly, and against the will of the officer who had the party rescued in custody.

The offence of rescue is said to nearly resemble that of prison-breach. The party rescued being in custody for felony or suspicion of felony, the rescuing from custody will be felony. Where the arrest of a felon is lawful, the rescue of him

Offence.	Statute.	Punishment.
Rescue—*continued.*		
Rescuing from sheriff or officers body of murderer after execution.	31 Geo. iii. c. 17, s. 11. 20 & 21 Vic. c. iii., s. 2. 27 & 28 Vic. c. 47, s. 2.	Felony; penal servitude not exceeding 7 years, and not less than 5 years.
Rescuing, or assisting, &c., therein, any offender from House of Correction, &c., confined under 51 Geo. iii., c. 63, or from custody going thereto.	51 Geo. iii. c. 63, s. 5.	Misdemeanour; imprisonment for same period as person rescued had to serve.
Rescuing from lawful custody any person charged with, or suspected of, or committed for any felony.	1 & 2 Geo. iv. c. 88, s. 1. 20 & 21 Vic. c. 3, s. 2. 27 & 28 Vic. c. 47.	Felony; penal servitude not exceeding 7 years, nor less than 5 years; or imprisonment not exceeding 2 years, nor less than 1 year H. L.
Rescuing any person committed by a magistrate for treason, felony, punishable with penal servitude under Whiteboy Act (1 & 2 Wm. iv., c. 44) before person committed is lodged in gaol.	1 & 2 Wm. iv. c. 44, s. 5. 20 & 21 Vic. c. 3, s. 2. 27 & 28 Vic. c. 47.	Penal servitude for life, or not less than 5 years, or imprisonment not exceeding 2 years H. L.
Aiding prisoner to escape, and thereby obstructing the cause of justice.	Common Law	Felony or misdemeanour, according to the nature of the offence for which prisoner was in custody.
For assaulting or obstructing peace-officers, constables, &c., acting in execution of their duty, and triable by indictment, &c. Summarily—see "Constable," &c., "Crime Prevention," "Offences against the Person."		

will be felony; and where the party is in the custody of a public officer, sheriff or constable, or in prison, the party rescuing will be deemed thereby to have knowledge that he is under arrest for felony. The authorities also hold that the forcible rescue of a person in illegal custody is an indictable offence. And aiding a prisoner to escape may be classed under same head. This is an obstruction of the course of justice; and an offence at Common Law being a felony where the prisoner was in custody on a charge of felony, and a misdemeanour in other cases whether the charge were criminal or not. If the party who is arrested yield himself and make no resistance, but others endeavour to rescue him and he do no act to declare his joining with them, if those who come to rescue him kill any of the bailiffs it is murder in them, but not in the party arrested; otherwise, if he do any act to countenance the violence of the rescuers.—*R.* v. *Stanley*; *Russell* v. *Greaves*, 536; and see Roscoe's *Digest.*

Offence.	Statute.	Punishment.
Restitution (*of Stolen Property*)— See "Larceny."	24 & 25 Vic. c. 96, s. 100.	
Reward— Taking, for helping to return stolen goods, or advertising reward, &c. —see "Larceny."	ss. 101, 102.	
Riot (*a*)—	Common Law	Misdemeanour; fine and imprisonment (unless where made felony by some particular Statute).
Riot Act (*b*)— To the number of 12, or more, riotously remaining for one hour after proclamation.	27 Geo. iii. c. 15 ; 5 Vic. sess. 2, c. 28.	Felony, if disobeyed.
Damage to buildings, &c., by rioters, —see "Malicious Injuries."		
Any party who shall take part in riot or unlawful assembly.	50 & 51 Vic. c. 20 s. 2, sub-s. (3) (*a*).	*Summary Jurisdiction.*— Imprisonment, with or without H. L., not exceeding 6 months; 2 Resident Magistrates.

(*a*) A riot is defined to be a tumultuous disturbance of the peace by three persons or more assembled together of their own authority, with an intent mutually to assist one another against anyone who shall oppose them in the execution of some enterprise of a private nature, and afterwards actually executing the same in a violent and turbulent manner, to the terror of the people, whether the act intended were of itself lawful or unlawful.—*Hawk., P. C., b.* 1, *c.* 65, *s.* 1.

Form of Proclamation.—"Our Sovereign Lord the King (*Lady the Queen may be substituted*) chargeth and commandeth all persons being assembled immediately to disperse themselves, and peaceably to depart to their habitations, or to their lawful business, upon the pains contained in the Act made in the 27th year of King George the Third, to prevent tumultuous risings and assemblies."

(*b*) If the Magistrate finds that the riot cannot be otherwise quelled, he should read aloud the Riot Act. He need not wait until the disturbance has amounted strictly to what the law calls a riot ; if there be such an assembly that there would be a riot if the parties were to carry their purpose into effect, it is enough.—*R. v. Woodcock, C. & P.*, 516. This is a step *in terrorem* and of gentleness, but it is not made a necessary step, as he may instantly repel force by force. All persons who remain riotously assembled, to the number of 12 or upwards, for the space of one hour after proclamation made are guilty of a capital felony.—27 Geo. iii., c. 15, s. 1. When the proclamation has been more than once read the hour will be counted from the first reading. " But it should not be imagined that because the law allows an hour for the dispersion of a mob, the civil power and the Magistracy

Offence.	Statute.	Punishment.
Robbery— See "Offences against the Person," and "Larceny."		
Sacrilege— See "Larceny in place of Worship," &c.		
Sea— Offences committed at—in "Offences against the Person," in "Larceny," "Malicious Injuries," "Forgery," "Coin"—see particular title; and under the "Merchant Shipping Act." see this title in Summary Index.	—	All indictable offences committed against these Acts, within jurisdiction of the Admiralty, shall be deemed to be of the same nature and liable to same punishment as if committed on land in England or Ireland, and may be tried where offender is in custody.
Act to regulate the law relating to the trial of offences committed on the sea, within a certain distance of the coasts of H. M. dominions.	41 & 42 Vic. c. 73.	—
Where offence committed by a foreigner on board a foreign ship, within the territorial waters of H. M. dominions.	s. 2.	
Where such offender is a foreigner, certificate of Secretary of State necessary before proceedings instituted.	ss. 3, 4.	
Saving clauses as to jurisdiction in other respects.		

during that time are disarmed; no such meaning was within view of the Legislature, nor does the operation of the Act warrant any such effect. The civil Magistrates are left in possession of these powers which the law had given them before."—*Lord Loughborough, C. J.*, 21 *St. Tr.*, 493.—*Hayes' Crim. Law.*

Any Magistrate present or called upon is bound to interfere. A Justice having power to interfere for the preservation of the peace, it becomes a criminal offence, punishable on information, if he refuse.—*R. v Kennet*, 5 *C. & P.*, 282.

A Magistrate is not justified in forcibly dispersing a meeting, upon the ground merely that he believes, and has reasonable and probable grounds for believing, that the meeting was held with an unlawful intent, unless the meeting be in itself unlawful.—*O'Kelly* v. *Harvey*, 10 *Irish Law Reports*, 285.

Offence.	Statute.	Punishment.
Search-warrant— See Summary Index.		
Sedition (a)— See "Unlawful Assembly," "Riot."	Common Law	Misdemeanour.
Ship— *Unseaworthy Ships.*—Sending them to sea, being privy thereto, &c. Master knowingly taking such to sea, whereby life endangered, &c. See "Offences against the Person," and "Malicious Injuries:" offering shipwrecked goods for sale, see "Larceny;" masters forcing men ashore, see "Merchant Shipping Act," Summary Index.	39 & 40 Vic. c. 80, s. 4.	Misdemeanour.
Shooting at— See "Offences against the Person."		

(a) *Sedition.*—Attacks, whether by speaking or writing, the object of which is wantonly to calumniate the system of law and government, or indecorously assail the King or Constitution of the country, are indictable as misdemeanours. What will amount to sedition, and what is to be adjudged a legitimate discussion and criticism on the measures of the King and Government is, however, a question of great nicety.—See *Gabbett*, 647, and also "*Report of the Criminal Law Commissioners.*"

"Seditious writings are permanent things, and, if published, they scatter the poison far and wide; they are acts of deliberation, capable of satisfactory proof, and not ordinarily liable to misconstruction, and they are submitted to the judgment of the Court naked and undisguised as they came out of the author's hands."—*Sir Michael Forster on Crown Law.*

In 1868 the present Lord Fitzgerald, in charging the grand jury in the case of *The Queen* v. *Pigott*, used the following words:—"Gentlemen, as such prosecutions are unusual, I think it necessary that I should define sedition, and point out what may be a seditious libel. Sedition is a crime against society nearly allied to treason, and it too frequently precedes it only by a short interval. It is a comprehensive term, and embraces all those practices, whether by word or deed, or writing, which are calculated and intended to disturb the tranquillity of the State, and lead the Queen's subjects to resist or subvert the established Government of the empire. Its objects are to create commotion, and to introduce discontent and disaffection, to stir up opposition to the laws and Government, and to bring the administration of justice into contempt, and its natural and ultimate tendency is to excite the people to insurrection and rebellion. The distance is never great between contempt for the laws and open violation of them. Sedition has been aptly described as 'disloyalty in action,' and the law treats as seditious all those practices which have for their object to excite discontent or disaffection—to create public disturbance or lead to civil war—to bring into hatred or contempt the

Offence.	Statute.	Punishment.
Slander (a)—	Common Law	Misdemeanour.
Slave Trade (Abolition Act)— Conveying, detaining, &c., any person for the purpose of being sold, &c.; or in any way dealing in or being connected with the slave trade.	5 Geo. iv. c. 113.	Felony; and petty officers and seamen knowingly serving in such ship, misdemeanour.
Smuggling— See Summary Index : titles, "Customs," "Excise."		
Sodomy— See "Offences against the Person" and "Unnatural Crimes." And see "Criminal Law Amendment Act, 1885."	48 & 49 Vic. c. 69, s. 11.	
Soliciting (to Murder)— See "Offences against the Person."		

Sovereign or the Government, the laws or Constitution of the realm, and generally all endeavours to promote public disorder. Sedition, being inconsistent with the safety of the State, is regarded as a high misdemeanour, and as such punishable with fine and imprisonment ; and it has been truly said that it is the duty of the Government, acting for the protection of society, to resist and extinguish it at the earliest moment. . . . With respect to articles extracted from American and other newspapers, it was recently contended in argument before the Court of Queen's Bench, by the learned counsel for Mr. Pigott, that even if those articles were of a seditious or treasonable character the defendant was justified, in point of law, in publishing them as foreign news. Gentlemen, I am bound to warn you against this very unsound contention ; and I now tell you, with the concurrence of my learned colleague, that the law gives no such sanction, and does not in the abstract justify or excuse the republication of treasonable articles, no matter from what source they may be taken. In reference to all such republications, the time, the object, and all the surrounding circumstances are to be taken into consideration, and may be such as to rebut any inference of a criminal intention on the part of the Government."

(a) *Slander.*—Mere words spoken of an individual are not generally indictable, unless they tend to a breach of the peace, as if they convey a challenge; but to speak slanderous and contemptuous words of a Magistrate in execution of his office is a misdemeanour.—*Gab.*, 654. Spreading false news, with a mischievous intent, and eavesdropping, with the purpose of propagating slander, are also misdemeanours at Common Law. A woman may also be indicted for being a common scold.—*Gab.*, 319 ; *Black. Com.* (See also "Libel" and "Sureties to keep the Peace," &c.— Summary Index.)

Solitary Confinement— To what extent may be—see "Offences against the Person;" "Larceny;" "Malicious Injuries;" "Forgery;" "Coin."	(24 & 25 Vic. c. 100, s. 70. c. 96, s. 119. c. 97, s. 75. c. 98, s. 53. c. 99, s. 40:	Not exceeding 1 month at a time, and not exceeding 3 months in a year.
And generally under . . .	1 Vic. c. 90, s. 5.	
Spring-guns (*Setting*)— See "Offences against the Person."		
Stamps— *Criminal Offences relating to Her Majesty's Stamps.*—1. Forging a die or stamp. 2. Making an impression upon any material with a forged die. 3. Fraudulently cutting, tearing, or in any way removing from any material any stamp, with the intent that any use should be made of such stamp, or of any part thereof. 4. Frau-	33 & 34 Vic. c. 98, s. 18.	Felony; penal servitude for life, or not less than 5 years (not less than 7 if previously convicted of felony); or imprisonment not exceeding 3 years.

Offence.	Statute.	Punishment.
Stealing— See "Larceny."		
Stolen Property— Receiving and restoring—see "Larceny;" and see "Stolen Property," Summary Index.		
Subornation— See "Perjury."		
Suicide (*Dublin Metropolis*)— In certain cases of attempted suicide, Justice, on confession and consent, may convict summarily. And see "Homicide," "Offences against the Person." *	34 & 35 Vic. c. 76, s. 9.	
Telegraph— Telegraph messages deemed to be post letters within meaning of 1 Vic., c. 36. Telegraph Act, 1868, and this Act shall be Post Office Laws.	32 & 33 Vic. c. 23, s. 23. s. 24.	
Threatening— To accuse of crime; letter, &c., with intent to extort, &c.—see "Larceny." To destroy buildings, ships, &c.—see "Malicious Injuries." To murder—see "Offences against the Person," and see also under "*Whiteboy Acts.*"	 1 & 2 Wm. iv. c. 44, s. 3.	

* *Suicide.—Felo de se*, or self-murder, is a species of felonious homicide. If a person committing some unlawful malicious act cause his own death, it will be suicide. Where the *attempt* to commit suicide is the charge, the Justice takes the depositions, showing the act done, and the likelihood of the means used to cause death, and returns the accused for trial. In *Dublin* there is a limited summary power. If one person persuade another to kill himself, and the other do so, the person persuading is guilty of murder. If two persons mutually agree to commit suicide together, and the means employed to produce death only take effect on one, the survivor will, in point of law, be guilty of the murder of the one who died. —*R.* v. *Allison*, 8 C. & P., 418.

Offence.	Statute.	Punishment.
Transportation— Acts substituting penal servitude for transportation. See "Penal Servitude."	16 & 17 Vic. c. 99; 20 & 21 Vic. c. 3.	—
Treason (a)— Compassing the death of the king, Queen Consort, or eldest son and heir; violating Queen Consort or King's eldest daughter unmarried, or wife of eldest son; levying war against the King; being adherent to, aiding, or comforting the King's enemies; slaying the Chancellor or Judges in execution of their offices; rebelling or conspiring against Lord Lieutenant, or urging the Irish to make war on the English; wishing or practising harm to the King or his heirs, or pronouncing him a heretic, usurper, or detaining his fortresses; by writing or other exterior acts doing anything to the peril of the King's person or disturbing the succession to the Crown of Ireland; maintaining or defending the authority of any foreign prince or prelate; disappointing the succession as directed by the Act of Settlement.	25 Edw. iii. stat. 5, c. 2. 10 Hen. vii. c. 13 (Ir.) 28 Hen. viii. c. 7. (Ir.) 33 Hen. viii. c. 1. (Ir.) 2 Eliz. c. 1, s. 12. 2 Anne, c. 5, s. 1. (Ir.) 54 Geo. iii. c. 146. 33 & 34 Vic. c. 23, s. 32.	Death.
Treasonable Felony (b)— "Act for the better securing the Crown and Government of the United Kingdom."	11 & 12 Vic. c. 12.	

(a) *Treason.*—That part of the sentence, in cases of high treason, which directed that the guilty person should be drawn on a hurdle to the place of execution and there hanged till dead, the head to be then severed from the body, the body to be divided into four quarters, &c., has been repealed by the 33 & 34 Vic. c. 23, s. 32.

For Act to abolish forfeitures for treason and felony, and otherwise amending the law relating thereto, and whereby persons convicted are disqualified for public offices, and from exercising franchise, and when convicted may be condemned in costs—see 33 & 34 Vic. c. 23; and as to how far Act is applicable to Ireland—see s. 32.

(b) Treason, or treasonable felony, are not bailable except by order of Lord Lieutenant, Chief Secretary, or Court of Queen's Bench.—14 & 15 Vic., c. 93, s. 15.

Offence.	Statute.	Punishment.
Treasonable Felony—*continued.* Compassing, imagining, &c., to depose or deprive the Queen, her heirs, or successors, of style, &c., or Crown of United Kingdom, or other dominions; uttering, publishing, &c., such compassing, open speaking, &c., or by overt act. Compassing, &c., to levy war to force a change of measures or counsels, to intimidate or overawe either House of Parliament; or uttering, &c.; or to move foreigners to invade any of Her Majesty's dominions; uttering, or declaring such compassing, &c., or any of them. **Treasure Trove** (a)—	11 & 12 Vic. c. 12, s. 3.	Felony; penal servitude for life, or not less than 7 years; or imprisonment not exceeding 2 years' H. L.

(a) *Treasure Trove.*—A person who finds goods, there being no apparent owner, has a right to take possession of them. If at the time the property be taken possession of, there be no apparent owner, the subsequent discovery of one will not render the original taking unlawful, nor will it render the finder a bailee for the true owner. No conversion of the property, therefore, subsequent to the discovery of the true owner, will render the finder guilty of larceny. "But if a person picks up a thing, and knows that he can immediately find the owner, and instead of restoring it to the owner converts it to his own use, this is felony."—*Park, J.; R.* v. *Pope,* 6 C. & P., 346. A person purchased a bureau at a public auction, in which in a secret drawer, he afterwards discovered a purse containing several sovereigns, and having appropriated the money, he was found guilty of larceny. If the finder knows who the owner of the lost chattel is, or if from any mark upon it, or the circumstances under which it is found, the owner could be reasonably ascertained, then the fraudulent conversion, *animo furandi,* constitutes a larceny.—*Merry* v. *Green,* 7 M. & W., 623. And if under like circumstances he acquire possession and mean to act honourably, but afterwards alter his mind, and open the parcel with intent to embezzle its contents, such unlawful act would render him guilty of larceny.—*R.* v. *Wynne,* 1 Leach., 413.—See cases at length, *Roscoe's Crim. Law.* Of course the moral duty (and this is the only safe course) is to use reasonable diligence to discover the owner, and give publicity to the finding through the constabulary. It is to be observed that no other person has a right to take the property from the finder. For though he does not, by such finding, acquire an absolute property or ownership, yet he has such a property as will enable him to keep it against all but the rightful owner, and consequently may maintain his action of trover. Possession constitutes a sufficient title to enable the party enjoying it to obtain legal remedy against a wrongdoer. There are numerous cases in support of this proposition. The leading case is *Armory* v. *Delamairie,* where the plaintiff, a chimney-sweeper's boy found a jewel, and took it to a goldsmith's to know what it was; the apprentice in the shop, under pretence of weighing it, took out the

Offence.	Statute.	Punishment.
Treaty (*Extradition*)— See "Extradition."		
Trees— See "Larceny," and "Malicious Injuries;" and those titles in Summary Index.		
Unlawful Assembly (*a*)— Joining, countenancing, or supporting. See also "Riot," "Arms." And see "Convention (Ir.) Act Repeal Act, 1879," and "Unlawful Assembly," Summary Index.	Common Law	Fine and imprisonment, or either.

stone, saying that the value was three-halfpence. This was refused, and the stone not having been returned, the goldsmith was held liable in trover for his apprentice. The Chief Justice directed the jury that unless defendant produced the jewels they should presume the strongest case against him, and make the value of the best jewels the measure of their damages, which they accordingly did.—*Smith's Leading Cases.*

(*a*) An unlawful assembly is a disturbance of the peace by persons barely assembling together, with an intention to do a thing which, if it were executed, would make them rioters, but neither actually executing it, nor making a motion towards its execution.—5 *C. & P.*, 154.

Any meeting whatsoever of great numbers of people, with such circumstances of terror as cannot but endanger the public peace, and raise fears and jealousies among the King's subjects, seems properly to be called an unlawful assembly.—1 *Hawk.*, c. 65, *s.* 9.

Any meeting under such circumstances as, according to the opinion of rational and firm men, are likely to produce danger to the tranquillity and peace of the neighbourhood is an unlawful assembly.—*Alderson, B.; Reg.* v. *Vincent,* 9 *C. & P.*, 109.

Proclamation.—As to the effect of an ordinary proclamation prohibiting a meeting. Such a proclamation, although issued by persons in authority, could not make illegal a meeting which would otherwise be legal; but those who oppose such a proclamation of the Lord Lieutenant in Ireland, or of the Home Secretary in England, must be well assured that when holding a meeting in defiance of the proclamation, that such meeting is a legal one, and take the risk of proving on a subsequent occasion that the opinion they had arrived at, knowing all the facts, was an opinion on which a jury, knowing these facts, would arrive at; for if it be reasonably believed in the opinion of fair and rational men it would lead to a breach of the tranquillity of the peace it would be illegal. And so the intent of the promoters and the result of the meeting will have to be considered by the jury in determining the legality or illegality of the meeting. Mr. Justice Gasalee (6 *Carrington & Payne*) states, "The proclamation states it to be an illegal meeting, and commands all constables and others to disperse it. If such notice be given, and a party chooses to treat it as of no effect he does so at his

Offence.	Statute.	Punishment.
Unlawful Oaths— See "Oaths."		
Unnatural Crimes (a)— *Sodomy and Bestiality.*—Committing the abominable crime of buggery, either with mankind or with any animal—	24 & 25 Vic. c. 100, s. 61.	Penal servitude for life; or not less than 10 years.
And see title "Criminal Law Amendment Act, 1885."	48 & 49 Vic. c. 69, s. 11.	
Vagrancy— See Title, Summary Index.		
Vegetable Productions— See "Larceny"and "Malicious Injuries," in this and Summary Index.		
Vexatious Indictments— To prevent vexatious indictments for certain misdemeanours :—perjury, conspiracy, obtaining money under false pretences, keeping gambling-	22 & 23 Vic. c. 17, s. 1.	Bills not to be presented to or found by Grand Jury, unless prosecutor, &c., be bound by re-

own risk." Perhaps the most elaborate and lucid exposition of the law on this subject is that of Chief Baron Palles, given in the action of *Blunt* v. *Byrne*, in the Court of Exchequer (Ir.), February, 1888, tried before the Chief Baron and a Special Jury.

(a) *Unnatural Crimes.*—The Magistrate, if it ever becomes necessary, should take the depositions in private. The Crown seldom finds it necessary to send the case to a jury—the wretched criminal being willing to expatriate himself. Though on the recent statute-book, amongst offences against the person, it is happily of very rare occurrence in this country. But these "vile affections" have prevailed : they formed part of the religious or superstitious system of the Egyptians, and were not unfrequent in the East—

> " Witness the streets of Sodom, and that night
> In Gibeah, when the hospitable door
> Exposed a matron, to avoid worse rape."—*Paradise Lost.*

Mankind will include *womankind ;* and the whole crime seems to take in the act of any person who carnally knows, or permits himself or herself to be carnally known by, any living creature other than a human being. Being a male, carnally knows any man or any woman against the order of nature, or permits himself or herself to be so carnally known. This sin against nature is a crime against society.

Offence.	Statute.	Punishment.
Vexatious Indictments—*cont. and*		
Prefer the charge before indictment presented.	22 & 23 Vic. c. 17. s. 1.	recognizance to prosecute, &c., or unless accused has been committed or bound by recognizance to appear and answer charge: or unless prosecution directed by Judge of Superior Court or Attorney-General, or in case of perjury, by directions of Court, or Judge, &c., where committed.[f]
Where Justice refuses to commit or to bail person charged to appear for any of the offences aforesaid to be tried for same, and if prosecutor desires to prefer bill of indictment for the offence—	—	The Justice is required to take recognizance of the prosecutor to prosecute charge, and transmit any depositions taken, in same manner as if the accused were committed for trial for the offence.
Warrant to Search—		
See "Search-Warrant." Summary Index.	—	For form of search-warrant see Schedule to Petty Sessions Act.
Whiteboy &c.—		
Persons unlawfully armed, or disguised with arms and badge, or any persons armed by night, &c., and seeking the arms of Her Majesty's subjects.	15 & 16 Geo. III. c. 21. s. 1. 4 Geo. IV.	Misdemeanor: fine, imprisonment and whipping, and finding sureties to keep the peace, at the return of the Court.
By day in arms administering oath or engagement.	..	Misdemeanor: fine, imprisonment and whipping, at discretion of Court.

f. *Vexatious Indictments.*—In the preliminary inquiry it is no concern of the Magistrates whether or not the consent of the Attorney-General has been obtained.

g. In proclaimed districts Justices may summarily try these offences in 15 & 16 Geo. III. (Irish) c. 21. s. 1. See "Peace Preservation (Ireland) Act."—Summary Index.

h. *Whiteboy.*—Where a district is in a state of Whiteboy disturbance, under the statute 15 & 16 Geo. III. c. 21. s. 1. and the prisoner in the indictment is charged that he did, with firearms and thus covered and thereby disguised, with other evil-disposed persons unknown, likewise armed and disguised, unlawfully rise, assemble, &c., although the evidence is to the particular act constituting the act pointed only to the prisoner, and the jury convicted, the Court for Crown Cases reserved upheld the conviction.—*Queen v. Sullivan*. 1883.

Offence.	Statute.	Punishment.
Whiteboy (*Act*)—*continued*. By drums, music, fire, signal, &c., knowingly exciting, promoting, &c., unlawful meetings.	15 & 16 Geo. iii. c. 21 (Ir.) 40 Geo. iii. c. 96.	Misdemeanour; fine and imprisonment.
By force or threats attempting to compel persons to quit dwellings, habitations, services, &c.; assaulting dwelling-houses, &c.; breaking into premises forcibly or by threats; maliciously injuring property; taking away cattle or chattels; injuring crops, &c.	1 & 2 Wm. iv. c. 44. s. 2. (27 & 28 Vic. c. 47.)	Misdemeanour; penal servitude for life, or not less than 5 years (not less than 7 if previously convicted of felony); or imprisonment not exceeding 3 years, with or without H. L.; and male may be whipped.
Printing, writing, sending, or causing, &c., notices, &c., tending to excite unlawful meeting or combination; threatening violence, &c.; demanding money, arms, &c.; requiring any person to do or not to do any act.	s. 3.	Penal servitude 7, and not less than 5 years (not less than 7 if previously convicted of felony); or imprisonment not exceeding 3 years. Male may be whipped.
Abetting or encouraging others, See also "Riot;" "Unlawful Assemblies;" "Oaths;" and in Summary Index—"Malicious Injuries by Rioters;" "Arms."	s. 6.	Like.
Wife (*a*)— See "Married Women," Sum. Index.		

(*a*) *Wife.*—A wife shall not be deemed accessory to a felony for receiving her husband who has been guilty of it, as her husband shall be for receiving her, because she is under the power of her husband, and she is bound to receive him.— 1 *Hawk.*, c. 1, s. 10; 1 *Hale*, 47.

But a wife may be indicted together with her husband, and punished with him for keeping a bawdy-house, for this is an offence as to the government of the house, and such an offence as may be generally presumed to be managed by the intrigues of her sex.—1 *Hawk.*, c. 1, s. 12; 1 *Russ.*, 16. And generally a married woman shall answer as much as if she were sole for an offence against the Common Law or Statute; and if it be of a nature that it may be committed by her alone, without concurrence of the husband, she may be punished alone. But if a wife incur the forfeiture of a penal statute, the husband shall be made a party to an action, or information for the same (as he may generally to any suit for a cause of action given by his wife), and shall be liable to answer what shall be recovered thereupon.—1 *Hawk.*, c. 1, s. 13. It will be observed that in these decisions a distinction is made between offences against the criminal law and those against penal statutes. If the wife, apart from the control of her husband,

2 R

Offence.	Statute.	Punishment.
Witness— Refusing to attend or give evidence —see "Petty Sessions Act," 14 & 15 Vic. c. 93, s. 13 (*Appendix*).		
Worship— See " Disturbing Public Worship."		
Wreck and Salvage— See "Merchant Shipping Act,"	17 & 18 Vic. c. 104, part 8, s. 477, &c.	The former Acts (1 Vic. c. 87, and 9 & 10 Vic. c. 99) on this subject are repealed; the first by the Criminal Statutes Repeal Act, 24 & 25 Vic. c. 95, and the latter by the Merchant Shipping Repeal Act, 17 & 18 Vic. c. 120.
And see Summary Index—title "Merchant Shipping Act." Stealing from wreck, . .	24 & 25 Vic. c. 96, s. 64.	
Destroying wrecks, or articles belonging thereto. See " Larceny " and " Malicious Injuries."	24 & 25 Vic. c. 97, s. 49.	
Young Persons (*Offences by*)— See "Juvenile Offenders," Sum-		

APPENDIX.

SCALE OF IMPRISONMENT.

For sums up to £5, under Small Penalties (Ireland) Act, 1873.
(36 & 37 Vic., c. 82.)

For any Penalty,	The imprisonment not to exceed
Not exceeding 10s., ...	Seven days.
Exceeding 10s., and not exceeding £1, . . .	Fourteen days.
Exceeding £1, but not exceeding £2, . . .	One month.
Exceeding £2, but not exceeding £5, . . .	Two months.

(Nothing in this Act contained shall affect the power of imposing hard labour, in addition to imprisonment, in cases where hard labour might, on non-payment of the penalty, have been so imposed if this Act had not passed.)

See this Act in full, and notes thereon, next page.

Under Petty Sessions Act 14 & 15 Vic., c. 93, sec. 22, where the sums exceed £5.

In all cases of summary jurisdiction it shall be lawful for the Justices in adjudicating thereon to exercise the following general powers, whether the same shall be authorized by the Act under which the complaint shall be made, or not :—

In every case of an offence, where they shall order that distress shall be made in default of payment of any penal sum, they may order that in default of the said sum being paid as directed, the said person shall be imprisoned for any term not exceeding the period specified in the following scale :—

For any sum,	The imprisonment not to exceed
Exceeding £5, but not exceeding £10, . . .	Three months.
Exceeding the last, but not exceeding £30, . .	Four months.
Exceeding the last, but not exceeding £50, . .	Six months.
Exceeding the last	One year.

Under the Licensing Act, 35 & 36 Vic. c. 94, s. 51, the scale is the same as in Petty Sessions Act.

Under the Larceny Act, 24 & 25 Vic., c. 96, s. 107, and Malicious Injuries Act, 24 & 25 Vic., c. 97, s. 65, it is provided that, unless where otherwise specially directed, the imprisonment may be with or without hard labour, for not exceeding two months, where forfeiture or penalty or both, and the costs, shall not exceed £5 ; and not exceeding four months where the amount, with costs, shall not exceed £10 ; and not exceeding six months in any other case.

See Small Penalties Act, and notes thereon, next page.
See Petty Sessions Act, sec. 22, and note thereon, Appendix.

A provision in a local Act shall not give a Justice power to mitigate a penalty below that given in the public Act creating the offence ; 27 & 28 Vic., c. 110, s. 1.

SMALL
PENALTIES
ACT.
—

THE SMALL PENALTIES (IRELAND) ACT, 1873.
36 & 37 Vic., c. 82.

"An Act to amend the Law relating to Small Penalties in Ireland."
(5th August, 1873.)

Whereas it is expedient to amend the law relating to small penalties in Ireland : Be it therefore enacted by the Queen's Most Excellent Majesty, by and with the advice and consent of the Lords Spiritual and Temporal, and Commons, in this present Parliament assembled, and by the authority of the same, as follows :—

Short Title. 1. This Act may be cited for all purposes as "The Small Penalties (Ireland) Act, 1873."

Commencement of Act. 2. This Act shall come into operation on the first day of September, one thousand eight hundred and seventy-three.

Definition of "penalty." 3. The word "penalty" in this Act shall include any sum of money recoverable in a summary manner.

Recovery of small penalties. 4. Where upon summary conviction any offender is adjudged to pay a penalty not exceeding five pounds, such offender, in case of non-payment thereof, may, without any warrant of distress, be committed to prison for any term not exceeding the period specified in the following scale, unless the penalty shall be sooner paid :

For any Penalty.	The imprisonment not to exceed
Not exceeding 10s.	Seven days.
Exceeding 10s., and not exceeding £1	Fourteen days.
Exceeding £1, but not exceeding £2	One month.
Exceeding £2, but not exceeding £5	Two months.

Saving as to hard labour. 5. Nothing in this Act contained shall affect the power of imposing hard labour in addition to imprisonment in cases where hard labour might, on non-payment of the penalty, have been so imposed if this Act had not passed.

Small Penalties.—Sec. 3. Definition. "Penalty in this Act shall include any sum of money recoverable in a summary manner " That is, all penal sums inflicted for offences ; as compensation for malicious injuries ; and all sums of money and forfeitures in the nature of penalties ; and sums which, although in the nature of debts, yet are by certain Acts of Parliament made recoverable in a summary way as if they were penalties, such as fares due by travellers under the Railway Acts and By laws, and all sums of money imposed by any statute by way of punishment *on convictions for offences.* Altogether the Act has reference to *penalties,* and the persons liable to imprisonment, it will be observed, are called *offenders.* But cases of a purely civil nature, and in respect to which the statutes creating the jurisdiction have given no authority to imprison the person, do not seem to come within the operation of this Act. The only penalties exempted are those recoverable by or on behalf of the Commissioners of Inland Revenue—section 7. The Act is not confined to Petty Sessions Courts ; any Court having the summary power to convict in a penalty would seem to be within the Act.

Sec. 6. This section employs unusually strong language, and would, as may at first sight appear, attempt to tie up the hands of Parliament against legislating contrary to its provisions ; but, after all, its powers will, perhaps, only go so far as to be applicable to penalties under all Acts previously passed, and, so far, to repeal their contrary provisions, and to all Acts hereafter to be passed which shall not make for themselves other and different provisions. It is parliamentary phraseology.

6. This Act shall apply to penalties, including costs, recoverable in a summary manner in pursuance of any Act of Parliament, whether passed before or after the commencement of this Act, and all provisions of any Act of Parliament authorizing, in the case of non-payment of a penalty not exceeding five pounds, a longer term of imprisonment than is provided by this Act, shall be repealed.

7. This Act shall not apply to any penalties recoverable by or on behalf of the Commissioners of Inland Revenue.

8. This Act shall extend to Ireland only.

THE FINES ACT (IRELAND), 1851.

14 & 15 Vic. c. 90.

"An Act for the better Collection of Fines, Penalties, Issues, Amerciaments, and forfeited Recognizances in *Ireland*."

(7th August, 1851.)

Whereas it is expedient to make provision for the better collection and application of fines, penalties, issues, amerciaments, and forfeited recognizances in *Ireland* : Be it therefore declared and enacted by the Queen's Most Excellent Majesty, by and with the advice and consent of the Lords Spiritual and Temporal, and Commons, in this present Parliament assembled, and by the authority of the same, that—

I. The proper officers to make entries and render accounts of all such penal sums as aforesaid for the several Courts by which such penal sums shall be ordered to be paid shall be the several officers or persons hereinafter mentioned, viz. :

1. The Clerk of the Crown for the Crown Side of the Court of Queen's Bench and for the Crown Court at Assizes;
2. The Clerk of the Rules for the Courts of Common Pleas and Exchequer, and for the Civil Side of the Court of Queen's Bench, and for the Civil Court at Assizes;
. The Clerk of the Peace for Quarter Sessions ;
4. The Chief Clerk or such other Clerk as shall be deputed by the Justices for that purpose for each Divisonal Police Office of *Dublin* Metropolis :
5. The Clerk of Petty Sessons for each Petty Sessions;
6. And the person at any other Court whose duty it shall be to attend and make entries of the proceedings ;

And the provisions hereinafter contained shall severally apply to such respective officers and persons, or their legally authorized deputies

---

This Act was passed in same session as the Petty Sessions Act, chap. 93, and forms part of the same legislation. It provides for the collecting and accounting for all fines, penalties, &c. &c., in the several Courts. It does not appear to confer on Justices in Petty Sessions any additional powers of enforcing penalties, whether they be penalties for *offences*, or the forfeitures under recognizances which are in the nature of penalties, beyond those given by the Petty Sessions Act. The sections as to the collecting and levying deal with them all as penal sums, but it would seem that the nature of the warrant, particularly as to imprisonment, must be governed by the nature of the case. A distress warrant may be used in all cases.— See note on sec. 3.

FINES ACT. (if any) as fully as if the more particular designation of each of such officers, persons, or deputies was repeated in each provision.

Entry of Fines.

II. Whenever an order shall be made by any Court or other authorized person for the imposition or levy of any such penal sum as aforesaid, the said officer of the Court shall proceed as follows:

All fines, &c., to be entered in a book.

1. He shall forthwith enter the particulars of the said order in a book (Form A.) to be by him kept for that purpose, and shall afterwards from time to time make such further entries in the said book as may be necessary for the purpose of accounting for the said sums:

In case of fines upon jurors, officer to send notice.

2. In every case where a fine shall be imposed upon any person for non-attendance as a juror, he shall, within fourteen days after the end of the Term, Assizes, Quarter Sessions, or Sittings of the Court at which such fine shall have been imposed, send a notice by post to such person, addressed to his usual place of residence, informing him of the imposition of such fine, and that if not paid within thirty days from the date of such notice a warrant will be issued for the levy of the same:

Judge's Registrar to certify fines to Clerk of Rules for entry.

And in order to enable the Clerk of the Rules of the Superior Courts the better to discharge the duty required of him under this Act, the Judge's Registrar or other person who shall act as clerk at Nisi Prius at the Nisi Prius Sittings of any of the said Superior Courts, or in the Civil Court at Assizes, shall, within seven days after the termination of the said Nisi Prius Sittings or of the said Assizes, as the case may be, certify under his hand to the Clerk of the Rules of the Superior Courts in which the proceedings in the case shall have been had, the particulars of any penal sum which shall have been imposed or ordered to be levied by the said Court in such case, and said certificate shall be a sufficient authority to the said Clerk of the Rules to do all acts for the entry and levy of the same which he could or ought to do in case such penal sum had been imposed or ordered to be levied by such Superior Court.

Issue of Warrants.

III. In all cases where an order shall have been made for the imposition or levy of any such penal sum as aforesaid, the Court, or the justice, or the officer competent so to act, as the case may be, shall (unless where the same shall have been remitted by the Crown or other proper authority) issue the proper warrant for the execution of such order at the following periods, viz.:

Warrants for the execution of orders to be issued at certain periods.

1. In case of any fine imposed upon any person for non-attendance as a juror, within one week from the expiration of thirty days after notice of same shall have been sent to such person by post as hereinbefore directed:

2. In case of any order for the imposition or levy of any such penal

Sec. 3. *Warrant* to levy distress, and in default of distress to commit for the like period for which the person might be imprisoned *in any late case*, in default of distress under provisions of Petty Sessions Act:—See section 22 of Petty Sessions Act. Its sub-sections and notes thereon; and see section 34 of same Act and notes thereon; and in convictions for offences where penalty does not exceed £5. See power to imprison without issuing distress warrant under Small Penalties Act, 36 & 37 Vic. c. 82 (*Appendix*): and as to forfeited recognizances which, under above Fines Act are in the nature of penal sums, see note on section 1, and form of order to estreat in Schedule C. of above Act, and also secs. 24 & 34 Petty Sessions Act, and notes thereon.

sum by the Justices of the Divisional Offices of Police of *Dublin* Metropolis, within one week from the making of such order:

3. In case of any like order by a Justice at or out of Petty Sessions, at such time as shall be directed by "The Petty Sessions Act, *Ireland*, 1851;"

4. In all other cases, within fourteen days from the making of the order.

And it shall be lawful for the Court or Officer by whom any such warrant shall be issued to use the like form of warrant as is authorized by the said Petty Sessions Act, for any warrant of distress issued by a Justice at Petty Sessions, and also to direct by such warrant, that in default of distress for the sum therein directed to be levied, the person against whose goods such warrant shall be issued shall be committed to gaol for the like period for which any person might be imprisoned in any like case in default of distress under the provisions of the said Petty Sessions Act: Provided always, that after this Act shall come into operation no warrant or process shall be issued to any Sheriff to levy the amount of any forfeited recognizance, or of any other fine or penalty whatsoever, but only to the Constabulary or *Dublin* Metropolitan Police, as the case may be; but in every case where any Court shall impose any fine upon any person for non-attendance as a juror, or shall direct any issues to be levied, the process for levying the same shall be addressed to the Sheriff of the county, and such Sheriff shall account for the same, in like manner as he shall be by law bound to account for any other sums coming into his hands as Sheriff, before the proper Officer of the Court of Exchequer by whom Sheriff's accounts shall be audited and declared, and shall from time to time, when directed so to do by the Chief or under Secretary to the Lord Lieutenant, pay over the amount of any such jurors' fines so to be levied by him to the credit of the same fund, and to be applied to the same purposes to which any fines imposed at Petty Sessions, and awarded to the Crown, shall be by law payable and applicable. (*a*).
(margin: Form, &c., of warrant, and power to imprison in default of distress, to be as in Petty Sessions Act.)
(margin: Sheriffs not to levy fines;)
(margin: but issues to be levied by Sheriffs (but see now 41 & 42 Vic. c. 69, s. 8).)

IV. The manner in which warrants issued to the Constabulary or *Dublin* Metropolitan Police for the levy of any penal sums under this Act shall be addressed shall be subject to the following provisions:
(margin: Addressing Warrants.)

1. All such warrants for the levy of any such penal sums as aforesaid (not being issues), ordered to be levied by any of the Superior or other Courts within the Police District of *Dublin* Metropolis (other than the Divisional Police Offices), shall be addressed to the Commissioners of Metropolitan Police:
(margin: To whom warrants shall be addressed:)
(margin: From Courts in Dublin to the Commissioners of Police:)

2. All such warrants issued from the said Divisional Police Offices shall be addressed to the office sergeant, or such other member of the said police force as the said Commissioners shall appoint for that purpose.
(margin: From Divisional Offices to Office Sergeant:)

3. All such warrants issued from any Court in *Ireland*, not being within the Police District of *Dublin* Metropolis, shall be addressed to the Sub-Inspector of Constabulary who shall act for the place in which such Court shall be situated:
(margin: From other Courts to Sub-Inspector of Constabulary.)

4. All such warrants issued by any Justice or Justices, out of

(*a*) *Fines on Jurors, Issues*, &c.- Warrants to levy all such shall henceforward be issued to Constabulary, 41 & 42 Vic., c 69, s. 8; and as to fines imposed by Masters of High Court of Justice, see sec. 9, 41 & 42 Vic., c. 69.

FINES ACT.

Quarter Sessions shall be addressed as required by the said Petty Sessions Act :

Warrants to be executed, certified, and backed as under Petty Sessions Act.

And the several provisions of the said Petty Sessions Act as to the certifying, indorsing, executing, or returning any warrant issued by a Justice at Petty Sessions, and as to the selling of any distress or otherwise acting thereunder, shall also apply to any like warrant issued by any Court Officer, or Divisional Justice under the provisions of this Act, and to the selling of any distress or otherwise acting thereunder; and in the application of the said provisions of the said Petty Sessions Act to any such warrants issued within the said Police District of *Dublin* Metropolis, whatever may be done by any Head or other Constable in executing any warrant addressed to any Sub-Inspector shall and may be done in any like case by any member of the said police force (to be named by the said Commissioners or Divisional Justices) in executing any such warrant, addressed either to the said Commissioners or to any other member of the said police force; and whatever may be done by any Sub-Inspector in certifying any warrant to the Inspector-General of Constabulary may be done by the office sergeant or other member of the said police force to whom such warrant shall be addressed, in certifying the same to the said Commissioners; and whatever may be done by the said Inspector-General, or by either of the Deputy-Inspectors-General of Constabulary, in indorsing any warrant certified by any Sub-Inspector, may be done by the said Inspector or Deputy-Inspector-General in indorsing any warrant, which shall be so certified to the said Commissioners, or which shall be addressed to the said Commissioners in the first instance : provided that such warrant shall have been first indorsed by one of the said Commissioners, the officer of the Court from which the warrant was issued, in **FINES ACT.** each case in which it shall appear that the person committed was discharged before the expiration of the period for which he was committed, and shall also compare the sum mentioned in such receipt with the amount in the warrant of committal, and shall certify in the said books that such receipt has been produced to him or them, and that such sums correspond, or otherwise, as the case may be:

3. In every case where any such penal sums shall be paid in Court *Officer to* or to the said officer of the Court (before the issue of a warrant), *receive all* or shall be so paid over or transmitted to the said officer of the *fines.* Court (after the issue of a warrant), he shall receive the same, and shall at the time deliver or transmit a receipt for the same in the Form (Ba. or b.) to the person by whom the same shall be so paid or transmitted:

4. The said officer shall out of the sums so received pay to the *Officer to* several parties such portion of the same as shall have been *pay parties.* awarded to them by the Court, and which shall be claimed by them either in Court or at the public office of the said officer, taking from each of such parties a receipt for the same in the Form (B c.):

And it shall not be lawful for any person, other than the said *Penalty on* officers hereinbefore mentioned respectively, or their lawfully autho- *any persons* rised deputies (if any), save the person to whom any warrant shall be *proper* delivered for execution, or the keeper of any gaol or bridewell to *officers or* which the defendant shall be committed, as the case may be, to *their legal* receive any such penal sum as aforesaid, or any part of the same; *receiving* and if any other officer or person than the several officers or persons *fines, &c-* hereinbefore mentioned respectively shall take or receive any such sum, or any part of same, from the person by whom the same shall be ordered to be paid, he shall, on conviction thereof before any two Justices of the County sitting in Petty Sessions, forfeit and pay for every such offence any sum not exceeding ten pounds.

VI. The manner in which all such penal sums as aforesaid shall be *Accounts* accounted for shall be as follows: *of Fines.*

1. It shall be lawful for the said Chief or Under Secretary to *Chief or* make such general regulations as shall seem expedient for carry- *Under Secre-* into effect the provisions of this Act, for the better collection *tary may* of all said sums, and the regular accounting for the same by all *make general* persons into whose hands the same shall come; and such persons *as to* shall keep and render account of said sums in such forms, and *accounts.* shall pay over said sums, and transmit for examination said warrant or receipt, at such times and in such manner as shall be directed by such general regulations, or as shall be at any time specially required by the said Chief or Under Secretary; and it shall also be lawful for the said Chief or Under Secretary to make such general regulations as shall seem expedient for the examination, checking, or countersigning of any of such accounts by any of the Sub-Inspectors, Inspectors, or other members of the Constabulary or Police forces, as the case may be:

2. And to every such account shall be annexed a declaration in *Declaration* writing under the hand of the said officer, to be made before a *that accounts* Justice, affirming the truth and accuracy of such account; and *are correct.*

FINES ACT. every such officer who shall make any such declaration, knowing the said account to be false in any particular, and being thereof convicted, shall, in addition to any penalty to which he may be liable under the provisions of this Act hereinafter contained, be also liable to the penalties of wilful and corrupt perjury:

Mode of enforcing payment of balances or sums. And if default shall at any time be made by any such officer or person in paying over any balance on such accounts, or any of such penal sums received by him, at such times as the said Chief or Under Secretary shall direct, it shall be lawful for the said Chief or Under Secretary to certify such default to any two Justices of the County, who shall thereupon issue the proper warrant for the levy of such balance or sums as shall have been so certified to be due by such officer or person, by distress and sale of his goods and chattels.

Mode of accounting by officers not being officers of Courts of Justice. VII. In every case in which a fine shall not be imposed by any Court of Justice, but by some public officer or person legally authorized in that behalf, such officer or person shall make such entries and render such accounts of same, and shall pay over such fine or balance of fines, according to law, in such manner and at such times as the said Chief or Under Secretary shall from time to time direct and require.

Penal Clause.

Penalties for non-observance of Provisions of Act.

Officers of Courts.
VIII. Any of the officers or persons hereinafter mentioned who shall commit any of the offences or neglects hereinafter mentioned, and who shall be convicted thereof before any two Justices of the County sitting in Petty Sessions, or at one of the said Divisional Police Offices, shall be liable to forfeit for every such offence or neglect any sum not exceeding twenty pounds (that is to say),

1. Any such officer or person who shall at any time make default in making true and correct entries of all such penal sums as

Court or officer as aforesaid, exceeding the sum of forty shillings, and *Fines Act.* in cases of fines upon jurors whatever the amount may be, to appeal for against impo-the reduction or remission thereof by petition to the Court of Assizes sition of fine, which shall be held next after such order shall be made if the same &c., may be. shall be made at Assizes, or to one of the Superior Courts of Law in made to Court of *Dublin* at the next term if the same shall be made by a Superior Court, Assize or or to the Court of Quarter Sessions of the county which shall be held Quarter Sessions, &c.; next after such order shall be made if the same shall have been made at Quarter Sessions, or to the Recorder of *Dublin* at his next Sessions if the same shall have been made at any of the Divisional Police Offices of *Dublin* Metropolis, or to the next Quarter Sessions to be held in the same division of the county where the order shall be made by any Justice or Justices in any Petty Sessions district, or to the Recorder of any corporate or borough town where the order shall be made by any Justice or Justices in such corporate or borough town (unless when any such Sessions shall commence within seven days from the date of any such order, in which case it may be made to the next succeeding Sessions to be held for such division or town); and such appeal, when made against any order by the said Divisional Justices or by any other Justice upon summary conviction, shall be subject in all respects to but subject the provisions of the said Petty Sessions Act, but in every other case to following it shall be made by petition to the Court which shall have power to provisions. entertain the appeal, and shall be subject to the provisions following:

1. The person so entitled to appeal shall not exercise such right Appellant to unless he shall enter into a recognizance (Form C.), with two enter into surveties, in double the amount of the sum ordered to be paid, recognizance to appeal. before any Justice, conditioned for the due prosecution of such To lodge Appeal, and unless he shall also lodge with the officer of the Court certificate of a certificate (Form D.) under the hand of the Justice by whom Justice. such recognizance shall have been taken, and which certificate any such Justice is hereby required to give, that such person has duly entered into such recognizance:

2. In every case where such certificate shall be so lodged with the In such case said officer he shall suspend the issue of any warrant to execute no warrant to the said order until such appeal shall have been decided or until be issued; the appellant shall have failed to prosecute the same, as the case may be, or if such warrant shall have been issued he shall direct or, if issued, the person to whom it was addressed to suspend its execution for not to be the like period; and in every case where such warrant shall have executed until decision been issued the person to whom it was addressed shall, either of appeal. upon being so directed by the said officer, or upon the said certificate being produced to him, suspend its execution for the like period; and in every case where the person against whom Party, if in any such warrant shall be issued shall be in custody, or shall have custody or been committed to gaol under the same, the Court by which the gaol, to be discharged.] order shall have been made, or the officer by whom the warrant shall have been signed, shall upon application being made to him in that behalf, forthwith order his discharge:

3. In every case where an appeal shall be so made the Judges of Court of the said Superior Courts, Judge of Assize, or Assistant-Barrister, Appeal may or Recorder, as the case may be, shall, and are hereby severally entertain appeal. authorized to hear the Matter of the said Petition, and to make such order thereon for confirming the original order, or for reducing or wholly remitting the fine or other penal sum, as may seem

FINES ACT.

Order of Court of Appeal to be certified by its officer.

Execution of order of Court of Appeal.

Execution when Appeal dismissed or not prosecuted.

In case of Jurors' fines, party may have further appeal to Superior Courts.

Not to interfere with the prerogative of Crown, &c.

Extreat of recognizances.

On proof of non-performance of condition. Court may order levy of recognizance so forfeited.

Proof of notice to be first given.

fit under all the circumstances of the case; and the proper officer of such Court of Appeal shall thereupon certify the said order under his hand to the officer of the Court by which the original order shall have been made, who shall forthwith issue a warrant for the execution of same, if no warrant shall have been already issued, or shall indorse the same on the warrant, if a warrant shall have been already issued, and direct the person to whom it shall have been addressed to proceed in its execution, or otherwise according to such indorsement; and in every case where such appeal shall be dismissed, or shall not be duly prosecuted, the said proper officer of the Court of Appeal shall so certify under his hand to the officer of the Court by which the original order shall have been made, who shall thereupon proceed as if no such appeal had been made:

4. In every case where any fine shall be imposed on any person for non-attendance as a juror, and the order imposing such fine shall not be reversed upon any such appeal, it shall be lawful for such person in like manner to make a further appeal to one of the Superior Courts of law in *Dublin*, during the term next after such first-mentioned appeal shall have been decided, and it shall be lawful for such Court to hear and determine such appeal; and the several provisions hereinbefore contained as to the suspension and subsequent execution of any warrant for the levy of such fine shall also apply to such last-mentioned appeal in like manner as to such first-mentioned appeal:

Provided always, that nothing herein contained shall be deemed in any way to limit or restrain the Lord Lieutenant, or the Lords Commissioners of Her Majesty's Treasury, or the Commissioners of Inland Revenue, from reducing or remitting any fine or sum imposed or ordered to be levied which by law he or they may be in any way authorized to reduce or remit.

X. In every case where any person who shall enter into a recognizance to keep the peace, or to appear to answer to any complaint as to an indictable offence, or to prosecute or give evidence in any case of an indictable offence, or to perform the duties of Petty Sessions Clerk, shall in any manner fail to perform the condition of such recognizance, it shall be lawful for the several Assistant-Barristers, Recorders of cities or boroughs, and for the Chairman of Quarter Sessions of the county of *Dublin*, as the case may be, upon conviction of such person of any offence that shall be a breach of the condition of the said recognizance, or upon the production of a certificate thereof signed and attested by the proper officer in that behalf, that the person so bound by recognizance had failed to perform the condition of the same, to order that such recognizance shall be forfeited to such amount as such Assistant-Barrister, Recorder, or Chairman shall think fit, and to direct a warrant to issue to levy such amount in like manner as other penal sums are directed to be levied by this Act: Provided always, that proof shall be first made on oath before such Assistant-Barrister, or Recorder, or Chairman, that notice in writing has been given to or left at the usual place of abode of the party or each of the parties, if there be more than one, against whom it shall be sought to put such recognizance in force, seven days at the least before the commencement of the Sessions at which such application shall be made, and such notice shall state in substance the cause or matter on which it is *Fines Act.* intended to sustain the application (a).

XI. The forms in the Schedule to this Act contained, or forms to *Forms of* the like effect, shall be deemed good, valid, and sufficient in law: *Procedure.* Provided always, that it shall be lawful for the Chief or Under Secre- *Forms in the* tary to the Lord Lieutenant from time to time to alter the said form of *Schedule* Book (A.), so far as to introduce into it such further particulars as *deemed* may be necessary in order to adapt it to any state of facts either new *valid.* or not provided for therein.

XII. No receipt, voucher, document, or instrument required to be *Form of* given, made, or provided in pursuance of the provisions of this Act shall *book may be* be subject to or chargeable with any Stamp Duty payable to the Crown. *extended*

XIII. In every case where the Act under which any penal sum shall *Receipts not* be ordered to be paid as a penalty for an offence (and no sum shall be *to be subject* awarded to the complainant as compensation for damage), it shall be *to stamps.* lawful for the Court to award any sum not exceeding one-third of *Applica-* such penalty to the prosecutor or informer, and the remainder of such *tion of* penalty and all other penalties shall be awarded to the Crown, any *Fines.* Act or Acts to the contrary notwithstanding : Provided always, that nothing herein contained shall be construed to alter the appropriation *Appropria-* or application of any fine or penalty imposed at any of the Divisional *fines and* Police Offices of *Dublin* Metropolis or by the Justices in any Corporate *penalties;* Town, and payable to any Borough Fund, but the same shall continue *but not to* to be appropriated and applied as is now by law authorised, and shall *apply to fines* be paid over to the same purposes from time to time in such manner *police offices.* and at such times as the Chief or Under Secretary to the Lord Lieu- tenant shall direct (b).

XIV. All fines or penalties payable to the Crown, not being fines *Crown fines,* or penalties imposed at any of the said Divisional Police Offices or by *&c., to be* the Justices in any corporate town as aforesaid, and the amount levied *bank.* under any forfeited recognizance, shall be from time to time lodged in the Bank of *Ireland* by the said several officers into whose hands the same shall come, in such manner as shall be from time to time directed by the Chief or Under Secretary to the Lord Lieutenant, to the credit of

(a) This section does not appear to give Assistant-Barristers, Recorders, &c., any larger power for levying the amounts of forfeited recognizances than are given in respect to other " *penal sums* " or penal sums of like character under the Act. The form of estreat against *the goods only* is given at foot of recognizance in schedule to Act. It was doubted whether above section extended to the sureties: the 37 & 38 Vic. c. 72, sec. 2, removes the doubt and extends it to the sureties. Sec. explaining Act next following.

(b) The 21 & 22 Vic., c. 100, s. 28, enacts that fines and penalties under the Fishery Acts shall be applied as directed by 11 & 12 Vic., c. 22; and the 35th sec. of this latter directs that one-third shall go to the informer, the other two-thirds to the conservators of the district.

Section 13, *Appropriation of fines and penalties.*—No fine or portion of a fine or penalty can be paid to a complainant or prosecutor (Constabulary or otherwise), unless the separate and distinct written order made in the " Order Book " in each case so directs; and the clerk is accountable to the Crown for the whole amount of fines levied, unless he can show a legal order for the disposal of a fine, or portion of a fine, to any other than the Crown.—*Circular,* 26 November, 1868, and see *Law Adviser's Opinion,* 30 March, 1867.

It is to be understood that this does not apply to fines where the Act under which they are imposed is mandatory as to their application. but only to such fines as the Act under which they are imposed leaves it discretionary with the Justices whether or not they shall order a portion thereof to the complainant.—*Circular,* 12 January, 1871.

The Crown fines payable to any *Borough fund* should be paid by the clerk or officer of the Court to the Borough Treasurer or other officer authorised to receive and account for same. Other *Crown fines,* &c., shall be lodged in bank, sec. 14.

Fines Act.

Lord Lieutenant to charge expense of audit on the fund.

the same fund and for the same purposes to which all fines and penalties payable to the Crown are now by law directed to be lodged.

XV. It shall be lawful for the Lord Lieutenant to charge the said fund with the payment of such expenses as may be necessarily incurred in the examination of the accounts to be rendered under the provisions of this Act and in the supply of books for the entry of orders at Petty Sessions, and in otherwise carrying the provisions of this Act and of the said Petty Sessions Act into effect.

Miscellaneous Provisions.

Clerks of divisional offices to give security.

XVI. The several Chief Clerks of the said several Divisional Police Offices, or such other clerks as may be deputed as aforesaid at the said Divisional Police Offices, shall give such security for the proper accounting for all fines or other moneys which may pass through their hands, under the provisions of this Act, as the said Chief or under Secretary shall direct, in like form and manner as is required to be given by each clerk of Petty Sessions under the provisions of the said Petty Sessions Act (a).

Annual account to be laid before Parliament.

XVII. An abstract account of all fines and other penal sums accounted for under the provisions of this Act shall be annually laid before both Houses of Parliament as soon as the accounts for each year shall have been examined and declared.

Interpretation of terms.

XVIII. In the interpretation of this Act, save where there is anything in the subject or context repugnant to such construction, the word "County" shall be deemed to include "County of a City," "County of a Town," or "Riding of a County"; the words "Lord Lieutenant" shall include any other "Chief Governor or Governors of Ireland"; the word "Justice" shall mean Justice of the Peace, and include a Justice of the Divisional Police Office of *Dublin* Metropolis; the word "Gaol" shall include any "House of Correction" or "Bridewell" or other legal place of imprisonment of the county; the

SCHEDULE.

FORM (A.)—OFFICERS' FINES ACCOUNT BOOK.

County of ————.　　County of ————.

Month of														
No. in Order Book (for the Month.)	PARTIES. —Plff. v. —Deft.	NATURE OF CASE.	SUMS AWARDED.		If Warrant issued.	For what Amount.	COLLECTION OF FINES, &c.						Act under which Fine imposed.	REMARKS.
			To whom. Crown - Complainant - Costs -	Amount to each. £ s. d.	To whom addressed. If committed, to what Gaol. Date when issued.	£ s. d.	Account by Officer of sums paid in Court, or paid over to him by Constabulary, Gaolers, &c.							
							Receipts.			Payments.				
							From whom.	Date.	Amount. £ s. d.	To whom.	Date.	Amount. £ s. d.		

Form Act.

Form (B.)—Return.

(B a.) Receipt for sums paid to officer of Court by parties.

—— *Plaintiff.* } Court of ——
—— *Defendant.* } County of ——

I have received from *C.D.* the sum of   under an order of the above Court, made on the   day of

Sum. £   ·
Costs. £   :   :   Signed ——
                            Officer of said Court of

                    This   day of   18   .

————

(B b.) Receipt for sums paid to officer of Court by gaoler.

—— *Plaintiff.* } Court of ——
—— *Defendant.* } County of ——

I have received from   keeper of [gaol] at   the sum of stated to be the sum in a warrant under which *C.D.* was committed on the   day of   under the order of the above Court to the said gaol.

Sum. £   :   :
Costs. £   :   Signed ——
                        Officer of said Court.

                    This   day of   18   .

————

(B c.) Receipt for sums paid to parties by Officer of Court.

—— *Plaintiff.* } Court of ——
—— *Defendant.* } County of ——

FORM (C.)—RECOGNIZANCE.

—— *Plaintiff*. } Court of ——
—— *Defendant*. } County of ——

Whereas an order was made on the   day of
by the above Court, That ([1])
The undersigned principal party to this Recognizance hereby binds
himself to perform the following obligation, viz.:

To attend the ([2])
to be held at   on the   day of
at   o'clock in the forenoon, and there to prosecute his Appeal
against the said order.

And the said principal party, together with the undersigned sureties,
hereby severally acknowledge themselves bound to forfeit to the Crown
the sums following, viz. the said principal party the sum of
and the said sureties the sum of   each, in case the said principal
party fails to perform the above obligation.

{ —— Principal Party.
{ —— } Sureties.

Taken before me, this   day of   at

Signed —— Justice.

([1]) Order of Court against which party appeals.

([2]) *the Court of Assizes or Quarter Sessions, or other Court of Appeal.*

———

I certify, that the said   has not performed the above obligation.

Signed ——

This   day of   18 .

Certificate or forfeiture.

———

I order that the sum of   be levied off the goods of the said
principal party, and the sum of   off the goods of each of the said
sureties. (*b*)

Signed ——

This   day of   18 .

Order to estreat

FORM (D.)—CERTIFICATE OF RECOGNIZANCE TO APPEAL.

—— *Plaintiff*. } Court of ——
—— *Defendant*. } County of ——

Whereas an order was made by the Court of   on the
day of   against   of   to the following effect,
viz. ([1])

I certify, that he has duly entered into a recognizance in the sum
of   with two sureties in the sum of   each, conditioned to
prosecute his appeal against the said order.

([1]) Order of Court against which party appeals.

Signed —— Justice.

This   day of   18 .

(*b*) This order to levy off the goods would appear to be the only order the Court
is authorised to make.

2 S

CHAPTER 72.

Fines Act. An Act to explain and amend the Fines Act (Ireland), 1851, and for other purposes relating thereto. [*7th August*, 1874.]

Whereas by section 10 of the Fines Act (Ireland), 1851, provisions were made for the estreat of recognizances, and doubts have arisen as to whether the said provisions extend to sureties as well as to principal parties, and it is expedient to remove the said doubts:

And whereas quarterly and monthly returns of proceedings in Petty Sessions, and of the appropriation of fees, fines, and penalties, are now by law required to be made by Clerks of Petty Sessions in Ireland, and by reason of such monthly returns such quarterly returns are unnecessary, and it is expedient that the same should cease to be made:

And whereas it is expedient to make provision for the recovery of penalties and with respect to offences in certain cases:

Be it therefore enacted by the Queen's Most Excellent Majesty, by and with the advice and consent of the Lords Spiritual and Temporal, and Commons, in this present Parliament assembled, and by the authority of the same, as follows:

Short title.   1. This Act may be cited for all purposes as the Fines Act (Ireland), 1851, Amendment Act, 1874, and the said Act and this Act may be cited together for all purposes as "The Fines Acts (Ireland), 1851–1874."

Meaning of section 10 of Fines Act (Ireland) 1851, explained.   2. It is hereby declared that the provisions of section 10 of the Fines Act (Ireland), 1851, extend and authorize the Assistant-Barrister, Recorder, or Chairman therein mentioned, whenever he orders that any recognizance which shall have been entered into by any person or persons as surety or sureties for any principal party shall be forfeited, in such order to state with respect not only to such principal party, but also to such surety or sureties the amounts of such forfeiture, and to direct a warrant or warrants to issue to levy such amounts respectively from such surety or sureties in like manner as other penal sums are directed to be levied by the said Act.

Repeal of 6 & 7 Wm. iv. c. 34, s. 4.   3. From and after the passing of this Act section 4 of the Act passed in the session of Parliament held in the sixth and seventh years of the reign of His late Majesty William the Fourth, chapter 34, relating to quarterly returns by Clerks of Petty Sessions, shall be and the same is hereby repealed.

Application of penalties to town of Galway.   4. Every penalty recovered in respect of offences committed within the limits of the Galway Town Improvement Act, 1853, against section 12 of the Licensing Act, 1872, as applied to Ireland, shall be applied as follows:—One-half of such penalty shall go to the informer, and the remainder to the Town Commissioners, and if the Town Commissioners be the informers, they shall be entitled to the whole of said penalty.

Mode of recovering penalties, &c. in certain cases.   5. Where by any Act now in force or hereafter to be passed it is enacted that penalties, offences, or proceedings thereunder may be

---

Sec. 2. This section has reference to the powers of Recorders and Quarter Sessions Courts to enforce the amount of forfeited recognizances against *sureties* as well as against principals.—See sec. 10, Fines Act. *ante.*

Sec. 5. There are several such Acts as are referred to in this sec. 5, which merely direct that offences are to be prosecuted in a summary way; but in accordance with

recovered, prosecuted, or taken in a summary manner, and no further provision with respect thereto is contained in such Act, then such penalties, offences, and proceedings shall be recoverable, may be prosecuted, or taken with respect to the Police district of Dublin Metropolis, subject and according to the provisions of any Act regulating the powers and duties of Justices of the Peace for such district, or of the police of such district; and with respect to other parts of Ireland, before a Justice or Justices of the Peace sitting in Petty Sessions, subject and according to the provisions of "The Petty Sessions (Ireland) Act, 1851," and any Act amending the same.

PETTY SESSIONS (STAMPS) ACT.

21 & 22 Vic., c. 100.

"An Act to regulate the Office of Petty Sessions in *Ireland*."
[*2nd August*, 1858.]

Sec. 14. "Every document enumerated in the Schedule (C) to this Act annexed shall, after the first day of January, 1859, be printed or written upon paper bearing a stamp denoting the amount or value set opposite to such document in that Schedule; and where any such document shall consist of more than one sheet, the first sheet only shall be impressed with the stamp; and no fees other than those contained in Schedule (C), nor any stamp duties, shall be payable in respect of any of the documents therein enumerated.

15. Commissioners of Inland Revenue to provide dies for denoting fees, either by impressed or adhesive stamps, &c.

16. Power to Justices to enforce payment of stamps on complaint of Clerk of Petty Sessions, to be enforced under the provisions of the Petty Sessions (Ireland) Act, 1851.

SCHEDULE C.

Forms.	Stamps. s. d.
On every summons and copy, (a)	0 6
On every information or deposition,	1 0
(The recognizance to bind the deponent to prosecute or give evidence may be added at foot without any further stamp duty.)	
On every solemn declaration (not being a declaration as to loss of pawnbrokers' duplicates, or as to the admission of paupers into workhouses), (b)	1 0
On every copy of any written information or complaint in summary proceedings, ...	0 6

the above section they appear in the *Summary Index* of this work as coming within the jurisdiction of Justices in Petty Sessions; and so necessary is it to bear this in mind, that the author has set out the above section in the introductory part of the work.

(a) Stamp to be placed on original summons.
(b) Pensioners' declarations, if taken before a Magistrate (out of Sessions), need not be stamped.—*Circular*, 9 June, 1859. This applies only to pensioners from British Army; all others are liable.

Every solemn declaration, no matter what the subject is, made before a Magistrate, either in or out of Petty Sessions, should have two sixpenny Petty Sessions

SCHEDULE C.—*continued*.

Forms.

	Stamps.
	s. *d.*
On every warrant	0 6
On every recognizance, when not at foot of an information, or deposition, ...	1 0
On the entry of each order, (*a*)	0 6
On every certificate of order, ...	1 0
On every appeal, including the recognizance to prosecute, .	2 0
On every notice of appeal to be served on the respondent, (*b*)	1 0
On every other notice in proceedings by or before Justices, when such notice is drawn by the Petty Sessions Clerk, (*c*)	0 6
On every form, other than the aforesaid, upon which any fee is now payable by law to the Clerks of Petty Sessions, any sum not exceeding	2 6

SMALL
DEBTS
ACT.

SMALL DEBTS ACT. (*d*)

" Act for the abolition of Manor Courts, and the better recovery of Small Debts in *Ireland*." [19*th April*, 1859.]

22 *Vic.*, *c*. 14.

Whereas the continued existence of Manor Courts in *Ireland* has been found prejudicial to the proper administration of justice : And whereas it is expedient that such Manor Courts should be abolished : Be it therefore enacted by the Queen's Most Excellent Majesty, by and with the advice and consent of the Lords Spiritual and Temporal, and Commons, in this present Parliament assembled, and by the authority of the same, as follows :—

Manor Courts abolished, but certain Manorial Rights preserved.

1. From and after the passing of this Act all the said several Manor Courts in *Ireland* shall be abolished, and from and after the passing of this Act no action or suit shall be commenced in any of the said Courts : Provided always, that the abolition of such Manor Courts shall not alter or affect any other franchise or manorial rights, or any right to head money, leet money, or leet silver, or any other right appertaining to any manor which now by law may be exercised or exists, except where the seneschal is the returning officer of any borough within the said manor, in which case it is hereby enacted that the sheriff for the time being of the county in which such borough may be situated shall henceforth be the returning officer in lieu of the said

stamps affixed, unless it is exempted from the duty either by that Act or some other Statute.—*Law Adviser's Opinion*, 19 November, 1877.

Declarations of loss or mutilation of Bank Notes, and of Disclaimer in Bankruptcy, require to be stamped. The intention of the Statute was by these stamps to provide a fund for the remuneration of the Magistrate's Clerk.—*Law Adviser's Opinion*, 14 March, 1877.

Muster rolls and accounts, and pay and pension lists, which are required to be verified by declaration, exempt by Mutiny Act, 22 Vic. c. 4, sec. 100, and *Circular*, 21 April, 1859.

(*a*) The stamp for order is payable by the person at whose instance the case is heard. —*Circular*, 16 March, 1865.

(*b*) Thus, on a party lodging an appeal, the officer of the Court will be entitled to receive 3*s.*, that is 2*s.* on the appeal and recognizance, and 1*s.* on the notice, besides costs of service.

(*c*) For the form of notice required by section 8, par. 6, see Schedule of Forms.

(*d*) For opinions on Acts, see title " Debts," Summary Index.

seneschal: provided also, that all proceedings commenced in the said
Manor Courts before the passing of this Act shall be continued until
decree or dismissal pronounced, as if they had been commenced and
finally determined before this Act passed.

SMALL
DEBTS
ACT.

2. All judgments, orders, or decrees obtained in any of the Courts
hereby abolished shall, notwithstanding the passing of this Act, be
valid and effectual, and capable of being enforced by the process of
the several Courts in *Ireland* held by the Chairmen of Quarter Sessions, in the same manner and by the same process as the decrees pronounced in the said Courts are now by law enforced; and the records,
muniments, and writings of the several courts abolished by this Act
shall, as soon as conveniently may be after the passing of this Act be
placed under the charge and superintendence of the Clerk of the
Peace, and be deposited and kept by him with the other records of
the county.

Existing
Judgments.
Orders, and
Decrees
valid, to be
enforced in
County
Courts by
Chairman of
Quarter
Sessions.

3. It shall be lawful for the respective Chairmen of Quarter Sessions of the several counties in *Ireland*, and the Recorders of *Dublin*,
Cork, *Galway*, and *Londonderry*, within the limits of their respective
jurisdictions, to renew all decrees and dismisses made and pronounced
by the several seneschals or stewards of the said Manor Courts hereby
abolished prior to this Act receiving the Royal assent, and every
such renewed decree or dismiss shall be deemed a renewal, decree, or
dismiss of the said Chairmen and Recorders, as the case may be, and
may be executed as such.

Powers
to renew
Decrees
founded on
Orders of
Seneschals
and
Stewards.

4. Every seneschal, steward, or registrar or marshal of any Manor
Court hereby abolished, in which proceedings have been had according to the course of the Court within one year before the first day of
January, one thousand eight hundred and fifty-nine, and who shall
show that he is legally entitled to such office, shall be entitled to make
a claim for compensation to the Commissioners of Her Majesty's
Treasury within six calendar months after the passing of this Act;
and it shall be lawful for the said Commissioners, in such manner as
they shall think fit, to inquire what was the nature of the office, and
what was the tenure thereof, and what were the lawful fees actually
received in respect of which such compensation should be allowed,
and the Commissioners shall in each case award such gross or yearly
sum, and for such time, as they shall think just, to be awarded, upon
the consideration of the special circumstances of each case, and all such
compensation shall be paid out of such moneys as may be provided by
Parliament for the purpose.

Power to
award com-
pensation to
existing
Seneschals,
Stewards,
&c.

5. And whereas it is enacted by the Fourteenth and Fifteenth
Victoria, Chapter ninety-two, that it shall be lawful for any Justice
or Justices at Petty Sessions to hear and determine certain disputes
concerning any sums due for wages, or for hire of any horse, or for
tuition, and to make such order as they shall see fit, for payment, provided the sum shall not exceed ten pounds: And whereas by Seventeenth Section of the said Act Justices are authorized to make awards
as to disputes at sales in fairs and markets where the value does not
exceed five pounds: And whereas it might be useful and beneficial
to extend the said powers, and to authorize any Justice or Justices at
Petty Sessions in like manner to hear and determine disputes concerning any sums of money which shall be due for small debts between
party and party: Be it therefore enacted, That it shall be lawful for
the Justice or Justices at Petty Sessions to hear and determine causes

Power to
Justices at
Petty
Sessions to
hear and
determine
cases for
recovery of
debts not
exceeding
two pounds.

SMALL
DEBTS.
ACT.
for the recovery of debts between party and party under the value of two pounds, where the right to recover such debts shall have accrued within twelve calendar months before the day of the date of the process hereinafter mentioned, and having heard what each party shall have had to say, and the evidence adduced by each, shall either make an order for the payment of the sum claimed, or shall dismiss the complaint, either upon the merits or without prejudice, and with or without costs, not exceeding five shillings, in the form in Schedule A, and shall direct execution by the seizure and sale of the defendant's

Power to
appeal to
Quarter
Sessions.
or plaintiff's goods : Provided always, that it shall be lawful for either party to appeal from such order or decision of such Justice or Justices to the Chairman of the Quarter Sessions, in the Civil Court at the next General Quarter Sessions held in the same division and district of the county, the said sessions being held next immediately after such decision at Petty Sessions by such Justice or Justices when the order shall be made by the Justice or Justices in any Petty Sessions districts, or to the Recorder at his next Sessions when the order shall be made by the Divisional Justices in the Police District of *Dublin* Metropolis, or to the Recorder of any corporate or borough town : Provided always that no such right of appeal shall exist unless three clear days shall elapse between the time when such order shall be made, and such appeal can be heard ; (a) and if three days do not elapse the appeal shall be made to and heard at the next succeeding Sessions for the division and district, which appeal the said Justice or Justices are hereby required to receive, and stop all proceedings on such order at Petty Sessions, the party appealing, if a defendant,

By lodging
amount or by
recogni-
zance.
first lodging with the Clerk at Petty Sessions the amount ordered to be paid by the said Justice or Justices, or entering into a recognizance of appeal in manner prescribed by the Summary Jurisdiction (*Ireland*) Act, 1851, Section twenty-four ; and if a plaintiff, to deposit the sum of five shillings as and for costs on the hearing of such appeal ; and such Chairmen and Recorders are hereby respectively required and empowered to hear such appeal, and to issue a decree and execution thereon, in like manner and form as if such appeal had been brought before such Chairmen and Recorders as an original Civil Bill, under the Fourteenth and Fifteenth *Victoria*, Chapter fifty-seven, and with like costs, but without further appeal.

Forms of
process as
those in
Schedule A.
6. The process to be served upon the defendant in all cases, requiring him to appear before the Justice or Justices at Petty Sessions, and the orders made thereon shall be in the Forms I. and II. in the Schedule A to this Act annexed, or as near thereto as the nature of the case will permit, and it shall not be necessary that such process shall be signed by any attorney, but it shall be sufficient if the same be signed by the complainant, or any person on behalf of such complainant ; and the said forms shall be severally subject to the following Stamp Duties payable to Her Majesty : that is to say,

	s.	*d.*
For every original process, ...	0	6
For every copy thereof served, ...	0	6
For every certificate on appeal	1	0

(a) *Appeal* to be sent on the next Quarter Sessions after *three clear days shall* have lapsed. This would seem by implication to repeal the necessity of giving the seven days' notice required by par. 5, sec. 24, of the Petty Sessions Act.

7. Every paper or document in respect of which any fee shall be payable at Petty Sessions, under the provisions of this Act, shall bear an impressed or adhesive stamp denoting the amount or value of such fee, as the same is specified in Schedule C of this Act; and such impressed or adhesive stamps shall be supplied and accounted for in the like manner, and shall be subject to the like provisions, rules, and regulations, so far as the same are applicable, as are provided in respect of stamped forms or adhesive stamps by an Act passed in the twenty-first and twenty-second years of the reign of Her Majesty, c. 100.

SMALL DEBTS ACT.

Stamps to be used in lieu of fees at Petty Sessions, and to be accounted for as provided by 21 & 22 Vic. c. 100.

8. The duties by this Act granted shall be denominated and deemed to be Stamp duties, and shall be under the care and management of the Commissioners of Inland Revenue for the time being; and all powers, provisions, clauses, regulations and directions, fines and penalties, contained in or imposed by the several Acts of Parliament relating to duties of the same kind or description in force at the time of the passing of this Act shall respectively be of full force and effect with respect to the duties by this Act granted, so far as the same are or may be applicable, as fully and effectually to all intents and purposes as if the same had been herein repeated and specially enacted with reference to the duties by this Act granted.

Duties granted by this Act to be deemed Stamp duties, and the provisions of the Stamp Acts to apply thereto.

9. The process to appear shall in all cases be served by a process-server, duly authorized by the Justice or Justices at Petty Sessions to serve summonses, *three clear days* before the first day of the Petty Sessions at which the case shall be heard, and in no case whatsoever shall any process be served on *Sundays, Good Friday,* or *Christmas Day,* and service on any of the said days shall be absolutely void; and any such summons-server shall be entitled to be paid by the complainant or person for whom he may be employed, such sum not exceeding the sum of sixpence for the service of each process upon each party as the Justice or Justices shall fix and determine.

Process to be served by process-server authorized by Justices at Petty Sessions.

10. No defendant shall be liable to be sued or proceeded against at Petty Sessions under this Act, or obliged to appear in any cause to be heard and determined at any Petty Sessions held in any other part of the country than at the Petty Sessions held within the county and within the Petty Sessions district of such county in which the defendant or defendants reside or resides: Provided always, that if any defendant or defendants shall have and occupy any house, warehouse, counting-house, shop, factory, or office for the sale of goods, or for carrying on any business, within the district of such Petty Sessions district, he shall be deemed to have a residence within such Petty Sessions district. The several fees as set forth in Schedules B and C shall be the proper fees payable on any proceedings under the provisions of this Act.

Defendant not to be sued, or obliged to appear, except within district of Petty Sessions in which he resides. Occupation of house, &c. deemed a residence.

SCHEDULE A.

(1.)

PROCESS.

Date.

Petty Sessions district of   County of
    A. B., Complainant.   *C. D.,* Defendant.

The defendant is hereby required personally to appear before the Justice [*or* Justices] assembled at the Petty Sessions of
on the   day of   next, to answer the Plaintiff's Bill

SMALL
DEBTS
ACT.
——

in an action for the sum of   , for that the Defendant is indebted to the said Plaintiff in the said sum for [*Goods sold, Money lent, settled Account, &c. &c.*], and in default of such Appearance the said Justices will be required to proceed as to justice shall appertain.

(Signed),   *A.B.*, Plaintiff.

(2.)

Decree founded on Order.

Date.

A. B., Complainant.   *C. D.*, Defendant.

By the Justices assembled at Petty Sessions held for the District of   : It appearing to the Court that process to appear at this present Sessions was duly served on the Defendant [*or* Defendants], and that the Defendant [*or* Defendants] is [*or* are] justly indebted to the Plaintiff [*or* Plaintiffs] in the sum of   Pounds [*here state Cause of Action*], it is therefore ordered by the Court that the Plaintiff do recover the sum of   Pounds, with Costs, and that in default of payment thereof, and the said Defendant not having appealed from such Order, we order that the sum of Pounds and   Pounds be levied off the goods of the said

(Signed),   *A. B.* } Justices.
                       C. D. }

or

E. F. Justice.

Form of Certificate of Appeal.

Petty Sessions District of   , County of

A. B., Plaintiff.   *C. D.*, Defendant.

Whereas an order having this day been made that the Defendant shall pay to the Plaintiff the sum of   Pounds [*or* that the Plaintiff be dismissed, *as the case may be*], and the said Plaintiff [*or* Defendant, *as the case may be*], has appealed from such order, I certify that the said Plaintiff [*or* Defendant, *as the case may be*], paid into Court the Sum of   Pounds [*the sum ordered to be paid, or Five Shillings on the Dismiss*], in compliance with the said Act of

A. B., Clerk of Petty Sessions.

SCHEDULE B.

	s.	d.
To plaintiff's attorney, for attending and taking instructions for and attending the hearing,	2	6
To defendant's attorney, for attending hearing	2	6
To plaintiff's attorney, for attending the hearing of every appeal under this Act,	2	6
To defendant's attorney for same,	2	6
To Clerk of the Peace, upon the entry of every appeal,	0	6
For signing the decree or dismiss on such appeal,	0	6

SCHEDULE C.

	s.	d.
On the entry of every process at Petty Sessions,	0	6
On the entry of every order of the Magistrates in Petty Sessions Book	0	6
On every certificate of appeal,	0	6

THE TOWNS IMPROVEMENT (IRELAND) ACT, 1854.

17 & 18 Vic. c. 103.

TOWNS IMPROVEMENT ACT.

This, though a "Public General Statute," is in force only in towns containing a certain population, who have specially applied to have its provisions carried into execution therein.

Application of Act.

Section 100 states that it shall extend to Dublin, Cork, Limerick, Londonderry and Belfast.

These places have their special local Acts, but to some of them the provisions of the above Act have been since extended. It is so in Limerick and Cork.

Sections

JURISDICTION, ... 29 & 91
 Any one Justice in Petty Sessions, or a Justice specially appointed for the purposes of this Act, may hear and determine complaints.

RECOVERY OF PENALTIES, ... 90
 By distress and sale, &c., and offender may be detained (or recognizance taken for his appearance) until return had to warrant of distress; and if before issuing distress warrant, or upon its return, Justice is satisfied that no sufficient distress can be had within his jurisdiction, he may commit for any term not exceeding three months.

COSTS, ... 90 & 91
 Of proceedings to be in discretion of Justice who hears the case.

APPEAL, ... 93
 To Quarter Sessions in every case where penalty or sum adjudged exceeds 20s.

UNWHOLESOME MEAT, ... 48
 Meat or fish unfit for human food to be kept separate and ticketed as such, in default,
       penalty not exceeding £5.

ADULTERATION OF FOOD, ... 49
 Selling, or exposing for sale, adulterated butter, meal, bread, or other article of food, knowingly,
       penalty not exceeding 40s.

₊ There are two distinct classes of stamp duties imposed on the proceedings viz.:—Stamp duties, properly so called, payable to Her Majesty under sec. 6 (Schedule A. above), and fees denoted by Stamps under sec. 7 (Schedule C, above). —*Circular.* Nov. 17, 1859.

Stamped forms in Schedule A may be had of any stamp distributor. Schedule C are the Petty Sessions stamps. A 6d. stamp should be put on the *entry of the case* in the book, and a 6d. stamp on the entry of the order.

Every person who, in any street, to the obstruction, annoyance, or danger of the residents or passengers, commits any of the following offences, shall be liable to the penalties for each offence as hereinafter mentioned ; and any constable or other officer appointed by virtue of this Act shall take into custody, without warrant, and forthwith convey before a Justice or Justices, any person who, within his view, commits any such offence :

Horse shows. Public shows. Farrying. Turning cattle loose, &c.

Every person who exposes for show, hire, or sale (except in lawfully appointed place) any horse or other animal, or exhibits in a caravan or otherwise any show or public entertainment, or shoes, bleeds, or farries any horse or animal except in cases of accidents or cleans, dresses, trains, or breaks or turns loose any horse or animal, or makes or repairs any part of any cart or carriage (except in cases of accident when repair on the spot is necessary), penalty not exceeding 10s.

Repairs. Dogs at large, or setting on, &c.

Every person who suffers to be at large any unmuzzled ferocious dog, or sets on or urges any dog or other animal to attack, worry, or put in fear any person or animal,

penalty not exceeding 10s.

Rabid, &c.

Every owner of any dog who suffers such dog to go at large, knowing or having reasonable ground for believing it to be in a rabid state, or to have been bitten by any dog or other animal in a rabid state, penalty not exceeding 10s.

Canine madness.

Every person who, after public notice given by any Justice or Justices at Petty Sessions, Chief Magistrate, or Chairman of Commissioners, directing dogs to be confined on account of suspicion of canine madness, suffers any dog to be at large during the time specified in such notice,

penalty not exceeding 10s.

Slaughtering cattle in streets.

Every person who slaughters or dresses any cattle or any part thereof, except in the case of cattle over-driven, which may have met with any accident, and which for the public safety or other reasonable cause ought to be killed on the spot,

penalty not exceeding 10s.

Negligence by drivers.

Every person having the care of any wagon, cart, or carriage, who rides on the shafts thereof, or who, without having reins, and holding the same, rides upon such wagon, cart, or carriage, or on any animal drawing the same ; or who is at such

Section

STREET NUISANCES AND OBSTRUCTIONS, &c.—*continued*. . 72

a distance from such wagon, cart, or carriage, as not to have
due control over the animal drawing the same, or who does
not, in meeting any other carriage, keep his wagon, cart, or
carriage to the left or near side, or who, in passing any other
carriage, does not keep his wagon, &c., on the right or off
side of the road (except in cases of actual necessity or some
sufficient reason for deviation) ; or who, by obstructing the
street, wilfully prevents any person or carriage from passing
him, or any wagon, &c., under his care,
penalty not exceeding 10s.

Keeping
wrong side,

or other
obstruction.

Every person who, at any one time, drives more than two carts
or wagons, and every person driving two carts, &c., who has
not the halter of the horse in the last cart, &c., securely
fastened to the back of the first cart, &c., or has such halter
of a greater length from such fastening to the horse's head
than four feet, penalty not exceeding 10s.

In charge of
two carts, &c.

Every person who rides or drives furiously any horse or carriage,
or drives furiously any cattle, penalty not exceeding 20s.

Furious
driving.

Every person who causes any public carriage, sledge, truck, or
barrow, with or without horses, or any beast of burden, to
stand longer than is necessary for loading or unloading goods,
or for taking up or setting down passengers (except hackney
carriages and horses, and other beasts of draught or burden,
standing for hire in any place appointed, &c.) ; and every
person who by any means of any cart, carriage, &c., or any
animal, or other means, wilfully interrupts any public
crossing, or wilfully causes any obstruction in any public
footpath or other public thoroughfare,
penalty not exceeding 20s.

Loading and
unloading :
delaying.

Obstructing
footways,
crossings, &c.

Every person who causes any tree, or timber, or iron beam to
be drawn in or upon any carriage without having sufficient
means of safely guiding the same,
penalty not exceeding 20s.

Beams,
timber, &c.,
on cars.

Every person who leads or rides any horse or other animal or
draws or drives any cart, &c., upon any footway of any street,
or fastens any horse or other animal so that it stands across
or upon any footway, penalty not exceeding 20s.

Riding on
footways.

Every person who places or leaves any furniture, goods, &c., or
any cask, tub, basket, pail, or bucket, or places or uses any
standing-place, stool, bench, stall, or show-board on any
footway, or who places any blind, shade, &c., or other projection over and along any such footway, unless 8 feet in height
from the ground, penalty not exceeding 20s.

Standings on
and projec-
tions over
footways.

Every person who places, or hangs up, or otherwise exposes
to sale any goods, wares, or thing whatsoever, so that same
project into or over any footway, or beyond shop front, so
as to incommode passenger, &c.,
penalty not exceeding 20s.

Rolling
casks, hoops,
&c.

Every person who rolls or carries any cask, tub, hoop, or wheel,
or any ladder, plank, pole, timber, or log of wood, upon any
footway, except for the purpose of loading or unloading any
cart, &c., or of crossing the footway,
penalty not exceeding 20s.

Towns Improvement Act.

Lines across streets.
Every person who places any line, cord, or pole across any street, or hangs or places any clothes thereon,
penalty not exceeding 20s.

Prostitutes, &c.
Every common prostitute or night-walker loitering and importuning passengers for the purpose of prostitution, or being otherwise offensive, penalty not exceeding 40s.

Obscene conduct.
Every person who wilfully and indecently exposes his person, or who commits any act contrary to public decency,
penalty not exceeding 40s.

Books, songs, &c., &c.
Every person who publicly offers for sale or distribution, or exhibits to public view, any profane, indecent, or obscene, book, paper, or representation, &c., or sings any profane or obscene song or ballad, penalty not exceeding 40s.

Firearms, stone-throwing, bonfires, &c., &c.
Every person who wantonly discharges any firearm, or throws or discharges any stone or other missile, or makes any bonfire, or throws or sets fire to any firework,
penalty not exceeding 10s.

Door-bells, &c., &c.
Every person who wilfully and wantonly disturbs any inhabitant, by pulling or ringing any door-bell, or knocking at any door, or who wilfully and unlawfully extinguishes the light

Extinguishing lamps.
of any lamp, penalty not exceeding 40s.

Kites, slides.
Every person who flies any kite, or who makes or uses any slide upon ice or snow, penalty not exceeding 10s.

Slacking lime, &c.
Every person who cleanses, hoops, fires, washes or scalds any cask or tub ; or hews, saws, bores, or cuts any timber or stone ; slacks lime, &c., penalty not exceeding 10s.

Rubbish or streets.
Every person who throws or lays down any stones, coals, slate, shells, lime, bricks, timber, iron, or other materials (except building materials, so enclosed as to prevent mischief to passengers), penalty not exceeding 10s.

Shaking door-mats.
Every person who beats or shakes any carpet, rug, or mat (except before 9 o'clock, A.M.), penalty not exceeding 10s.

Pots, &c., on window-stools.
Every person who fixes or places any flower-pot or box, or other heavy article in any upper window, without sufficiently guarding the same against being blown down,
penalty not exceeding 10s.

Rubbish from roofs.
Every person who throws from the roof of any part of any house, or other building, any slate, brick, &c., or other thing, except snow, thrown so as not to fall on any passenger, penalty not exceeding 20s.

Leaving cellars or sewers open.
Every person who leaves open any vault or cellar, or the entrance from any street to any cellar, &c., without sufficient fence or handrail, or leaves defective the door of any such, or who does not sufficiently fence any area, pit, or sewer, left open or leaving same without light after sunset, to warn and prevent passengers falling thereinto, penalty not exceeding 10s.

Dirt, offensive matter from manufactory, &c.
Every person who throws, &c., dirt, rubbish, &c. &c., on any street, beach, or strand ; or causes offensive matter to run from manufactory, brewery, slaughter-house, butcher's shop, or dunghill, into any street, except sand, &c., in time of frost or of sickness, to prevent noise, penalty not exceeding 10s.

Section

STREET NUISANCES AND OBSTRUCTIONS, &c.—*continued.* . 72

Every person who keeps any pigsty to the front of any street, not being shut out by sufficient wall or fence, or who keeps any swine in or near any street, so as to be a common nuisance,   penalty not exceeding 40*s.* *Pigsty in streets.*

Every person drunk in any street (*a*) or guilty of any riotous or indecent behaviour in any street, (*a*) Police Office or Petty Sessions Court, or any Police station-house within the town, penalty not exceeding 40*s.*; *or* in discretion of Justice, imprisonment not exceeding 7 days. *Drunk, riotous, &c.*

Every victualler, or public-house keeper, who knowingly suffers common prostitutes, or reputed thieves, to assemble therein, (*b*)   penalty not exceeding £5. 74 *Publicans allowing thieves, prostitutes, &c. to assemble.*

Persons keeping places for baiting animals, penalty not exceeding £5; or in discretion of Justice, imprisonment with or without hard labour not exceeding 1 month. Persons found therein liable to a penalty not exceeding £5, . . 75 *Baiting animals.*

Thimblers, swindlers, &c., found in possession of implements, &c., for practising games of hazard, or exhibiting such to induce persons to play, or cheating, &c., thereat, imprisonment not exceeding 30 days. And to return money or property obtained ; in default, not exceeding an additional 30 days, ... 76 *Thimblers, swindlers, cheats, &c.*

Bathing machines and bathing, ... 77

Hackney carriages, ... 78 to 88

[Act not to extend to cities of Dublin, Cork, Limerick, and Londonderry, the town of Belfast.—Act has since been extended to some of these places.]

POLICE CLAUSES ACT.

10 & 11 *Vic., c.* 89.

The following are the principal sections of this Act, in reference to *Street Nuisances, Obstructions, &c.*

The Justice should be careful to see if the Act be in force in his district.

Sections 6 to 19 have reference to appointment and duties of constables hereunder.

20. Every person who assaults or resists, or who aids or incites any person to assault or resist any constable in the execution of his duty under the provisions of this or the special Act, shall for every such offence be liable to a penalty not exceeding £5, or, in the discretion of the Justice before whom he is convicted, may be imprisoned for any term not exceeding one month, with or without hard labour. *Penalties on persons assaulting constables.*

(*a*) In the Police Clauses Act, 10 & 11 Vic., cap. 89, the offence is "drunk *and* riotous," &c. &c. The Police Clauses Act is in force in Cork and other cities. For simple drunkenness there is no power to imprison without fine—Secs 35 & 36 Vic., cap. 94, sec. 12 ; 37 & 38 Vic., cap. 69, sec. 30.

(*b*) A licensed victualler, or licensed ale-house keeper, is the same as a licensed publican. The term victualler and ale-house keeper are used in England and Scotland. The clause in the Police Clauses Act takes in all refreshment houses.

POLICE CLAUSES ACT.

Obstructions and Nuisances.

And with respect to obstructions and nuisances in the street, be it enacted as follows:

21. Power to prevent obstructions in the streets during public processions, &c.; penalty for offending, 40s.

22. Power to regulate the route of persons driving stage carriages, &c., during divine service, on Sunday, Good Friday, Christmas Day, and public fast-days; for offending, penalty not exceeding 40s.

23. Proprietors of stage carriages deviating from route by order, free from penalty.

Power to impound stray cattle.

24. If any cattle be at any time found at large in any street within the limits of the special Act, without any person having the charge thereof, any constable or officer of police, or any person residing within the limits of the special Act, may seize and impound such cattle in any common pound within the said limits, or in such other place as the Commissioners appoint for that purpose, and may detain the same therein until the owner thereof pay to the Commissioners a penalty not exceeding 40s., besides the reasonable expenses of impounding and keeping such cattle.

Power to sell stray cattle for penalty: and expenses.

25. If the said penalty and expenses be not paid within three days after such impounding, the pound-keeper, or other person appointed by the Commissioners for that purpose, may proceed to sell, or cause to be sold, any such cattle; but previous to such sale seven days' notice thereof shall be given to or left at the dwelling-house or place of abode of the owner of such cattle, if he be known; or if not, then notice of such intended sale shall be given by advertisement; to be inserted seven days before such sale in some newspaper published or circulated within the limits of the special Act; and the money arising from such sale, after deducting the said sums and the expenses aforesaid, and all other expenses attending the impounding, advertising, keeping, and sale of any such cattle so impounded, shall be paid to the Commissioners, and shall be by them paid, on demand, to the owner of the cattle so sold.

Persons guilty of pound breach to be committed for three months.

26. Every person who releases or attempts to release any cattle from any pound or place where the same are impounded under the authority of this or the special Act, or who pulls down, damages, or destroys the same pound or place, or any part thereof, with intent to procure the unlawful release of such cattle, shall, upon conviction of such offence before any two Justices, be committed by them to some common gaol or house of correction for any time not exceeding three months.

Power to provide a pound.

27. The Commissioners may purchase a piece of land within the limits of the special Act, for the purpose of a pound for stray animals, and may erect a pound thereon, and such pound when made shall be kept in repair by the Commissioners.

STREET NUISANCES (a).

Penalty on persons committing any of the offences herein named.

28. Every person, who in any street, to the obstruction, annoyance, or danger of the residents or passengers, commits any of the following offences, shall be liable to a penalty not exceeding 40s. for each offence, or, in the discretion of the Justice before whom he is

---

(a) These offences are very similar to those set out in the "Towns Improvement Act."

STREET NUISANCES—*continued*.

convicted may be committed to prison, there to remain for a period not exceeding fourteen days; and any constable or other officer appointed by virtue of this or the special Act shall take into custody, without warrant, and forthwith convey before a Justice, any person who within his view commits any such offence; (that is to say)—

Every person who exposes for show, hire, or sale (except in a market, or market-place, or fair, lawfully appointed for that purpose), any horse or other animal, or exhibits in a caravan or otherwise any show or public entertainment, or shoes, bleeds, or farries any horse or animal (except in cases of accident), or cleans, dresses, exercises, trains, or breaks, or turns loose any horse or animal, or makes or repairs any part of any cart or carriage (except in cases of accident, where repair on the spot is necessary) : *Exposing cattle for sale; or doing certain works in streets.*

Every person who suffers to be at large any unmuzzled ferocious dog, or sets on or urges any dog or other animal to attack, worry, or put in fear any person or animal : *Dogs at large, setting on, &c.*

Every owner of any dog who suffers such dog to go at large, knowing or having reasonable ground for believing it to be in a rabid state, or to have been bitten by any dog or other animal in a rabid state :

Every person who, after public notice given by any Justice directing dogs to be confined on account of suspicion of canine madness, suffers any dog to be at large during the time specified in such notice : *Canine madness.*

Every person who slaughters or dresses any cattle, or any part thereof, except in the case of any cattle overdriven which may have met with any accident, and which for the public safety or other reasonable cause ought to be killed on the spot : *Slaughtering cattle in street, &c.*

Every person having the care of any wagon, cart, or carriage, who rides on the shafts thereof, or who without having reins, and holding the same, rides upon such wagon, cart, or carriage, or on any animal drawing the same; or who is at such a distance from such wagon, cart, or carriage, as not to have due control over every animal drawing the same; or who does not, in meeting any other carriage, keep his wagon, cart, or carriage to the left or near side; or who in passing any other carriage does not keep his wagon, cart, or carriage on the right or off side of the road (except in cases of actual necessity, or some sufficient reason for deviation), or who, by obstructing the street, wilfully prevents any person or carriage from passing him, or any wagon, cart, or carriage under his care : *Drivers' offences generally.*
Control of, &c.
Wrong side.
Obstructions.

Every person who at one time drives more than two carts or wagons, and every person driving two carts or wagons who has not the halter of the horse in the last cart or wagon securely fastened to the back of the first cart or wagon, or has such halter of a greater length from such fastening to the horse's head than four feet : *Where in charge of several.*

Every person who rides or drives furiously any horse or carriage, or drives furiously any cattle : *Furious driving.*

·POLICE CLAUSES ACT.

STREET NUISANCES—*continued.*

Beasts of burden obstructing streets, except loading, &c.

Every person who causes any public carriage, sledge, truck, or barrow, with or without horses, or any beast of burden, to stand longer than is necessary for loading or unloading goods, or for taking up or setting down passengers (except hackney carriages, and horses and other beasts of draught or burden, standing for hire in any place appointed for that purpose by the Commissioners or other lawful authority), and every person who, by means of any cart, carriage, sledge, truck, or barrow, or any animal, or other means, wilfully interrupts any public crossing, or wilfully causes any obstruction in any public footpath or other public thoroughfare:

Obstructing street, &c.

Carriage of timber, &c.

Every person who causes any tree or timber or iron beam to be drawn in or upon any carriage, without having sufficient means of safely guiding the same:

Horses, &c. on footways.

Every person who leads or rides any horse or other animal, or draws or drives any cart or carriage, sledge, truck, or barrow, upon any footway of any street, or fastens any horse or other animal so that it stand across or upon any footway:

Exhibiting wares on footways.

Every person who places or leaves any furniture, goods, wares, or merchandise, or any cask, tub, basket, pail, or bucket; or places or uses any standing-place, stools, bench, stall, or show-board on any footway; or who places any blind, shade, covering, awning, or other projection over or along any such footway, unless such blind, shade, covering, awning, or other projection is eight feet in height at least in every part thereof from the ground:

Goods hanging from shops, &c.

Every person who places, hangs up, or otherwise exposes to sale any goods, wares, or merchandise, matter, or thing whatsoever, so that the same project into or over any footway, or beyond the line of any house, shop, or building, at which the same are so exposed, so as to obstruct or incommode the passage of any person over or along such footway:

Conveying goods, &c., on footway.

Every person who rolls or carries any cask, tub, hoop, or wheel, or any ladder, plank, pole, timber, or log of wood, upon any footway, except for the purpose of loading or unloading any cart or carriage, or of crossing the footway:

Hanging clothes on.

Every person who places any line, cord, or pole across any street, or hangs or places any clothes thereon:

Prostitutes, &c.

Every common prostitute or nightwalker loitering and importuning passengers for the purpose of prostitution:

Indecency.

Every person who wilfully and indecently exposes his person:

Offering obscene productions, &c., or profane conduct in streets.

Every person who publicly offers for sale or distribution, or exhibits to public view any profane, indecent, or obscene book, paper, print, drawing, painting, or representation, or sings any profane or obscene song or ballad, or uses any profane or obscene language:

Bonfires, &c., and fireworks; throwing missiles.

Every person who wantonly discharges any firearms, or throws or discharges any stone or other missile, or makes any bonfire, or throws or sets fire to any firework:

STREET NUISANCES—*continued*.

Every person who wilfully and wantonly disturbs any inhabitant, by pulling or ringing any door-bell, or knocking at any door, or who wilfully and unlawfully extinguishes the light of any lamp :

Every person who flies any kite, or who makes or uses any slide upon ice or snow :

Every person who cleanses, hoops, fires, washes or scalds any cask or tub, or hews, saws, bores, or cuts any timber or stone, or slacks, sifts, or screens any lime :

Every person who throws or lays down any stones, coals, slate, shells, lime, bricks, timber, iron, or other materials (except building material, so enclosed as to prevent mischief to passengers) :

Every person who beats or shakes any carpet, rug, or mat (except door-mats, beaten or shaken before the hour of eight in the morning :

Every person who fixes or places any flower-pot or box, or other heavy article, in any upper window, without sufficiently guarding the same against being blown down :

Every person who throws from the roof of any part of any house or other building any slate, brick, wood, rubbish, or other thing, except snow, thrown so as not to fall on any passenger :

Every occupier of any house or other building, or other person, who orders or permits any person in his service to stand on the sill of any window, in order to clean, paint, or perform any other operation upon the outside of such window, or upon any house or other building within the said limits, unless such window be in the sunk or basement storey :

Every person who leaves open any vault or cellar, or the entrance from any street to any cellar or room under ground, without a sufficient fence or handrail, or leaves defective the door, window, or other covering of any vault or cellar ; or who does not sufficiently fence any area, pit, or sewer left open ; or who leaves such open area, pit, or sewer without a sufficient light after sunset, to warn and prevent persons from falling thereinto :

Every person who throws or lays any dirt, litter, or ashes, or night soil, or any carrion, fish, offal, or rubbish, on any street, or causes any offensive matter to run from any manufactory, brewery, slaughter-house, butcher's shop, or dunghill into any street : Provided always, that it shall not be deemed an offence to lay sand or other materials in any street in time of frost, to prevent accidents ; or litter, or any other suitable materials to prevent the freezing of water in pipes, or in case of sickness, to prevent noise, if the party laying any such things causes them to be removed as soon as the occasion for them ceases.

Every person who keeps any pigsty to the front of any street not being shut out from such street by a sufficient wall or fence, or who keeps any swine in or near any street, so as to be a common nuisance.

2 T

POLICE CLAUSES ACT.

29. Every person drunk in any street, and guilty of any riotous or indecent behaviour therein, and also every person guilty of any violent or indecent behaviour in any police office or any police station-house within the limits of the special Act, shall be liable to a penalty not exceeding 40s. for every such offence, or in the discretion of the Justice before whom he is convicted, to imprisonment for a period not exceeding seven days.

Penalty on drunken persons, &c.] guilty of riotous or indecent behaviour.

Sections 30 to 33 have reference to fires.

Fires.

Sec. 34 provides penalties for publicans, &c., harbouring constables while on duty.

Places of public resort, &c.

Sec. 35. Keeper of house, shop, room, or other place of public resort within limits of the special Act, for sale or consumption of refreshments of any kind, who knowingly suffers common prostitutes or reputed thieves to assemble at, and continue in his premises, shall for every such offence be liable to a penalty not exceeding £5.

Prostitutes, thieves harbouring.

Cock fighting.

Sec. 36 provides penalties on persons keeping places for bear-baiting, cock-fighting, &c.

Hackney carriages.

Sections 37 to 68 have reference to hackney carriages.

Bathing.

Sections 69 to 72 have reference to public bathing, providing of bathing machines, and preventing of indecent exposure.

Recovery of penalties, &c.

Sec. 73. Clauses of "Railway Clauses Consolidation Act, 1845," with respect to damages not specially provided for, and penalties, and to the determination of any other matter referred to Justices, incorporated with this Act, &c.

(Proceedings may be according to the Petty Sessions Act, and penalties recovered as therein provided.)

PROTECTION OF JUSTICES ACT.

PROTECTION OF JUSTICES ACT.

12th Vic., cap. 16.

                                             Section

" Every action hereafter to be brought against any Justice of the Peace in *Ireland*, in any of Her Majesty's Superior Courts of Law at *Dublin*, for any act done by him in the execution of his duty, as such Justice, with respect to any matter within his jurisdiction as such Justice, shall be an action on the case as for a tort; and in the declaration, it shall be expressly alleged that such act was done maliciously, and without reasonable and probable cause; (a) and if at the trial of any such action, upon the general issue being pleaded, the plaintiff shall fail to prove such allegation, he shall be nonsuited, or a verdict shall be given for the defendant." (b).   1

" And be it enacted, that for any act done by a Justice of the Peace, in a matter of which by law he has not jurisdiction, or in which he shall have exceeded his jurisdiction, any person injured thereby, or by any act done under any conviction, or order made, or warrant issued, by such Justice in such matter, may maintain an action against such Justice in the

---

(a) *Probable cause* is said to be matter for the Court and not for the jury.
(b) This section refers to cases wherein the Justice has jurisdiction; and to sustain an action for any act done in such cases it must be alleged and proved that he acted *maliciously, and without reasonable and probable cause*. It is difficult to imagine how a Magistrate could place himself without the protection above provided.

same form and in the same case as he might have done before the passing of this Act, without making any allegation
in his declaration that the act complained of was done maliciously and without reasonable and probable cause : Provided, nevertheless, that (in any case where a conviction
may be quashed, either upon appeal or upon application to
Her Majesty's Court of Queen's Bench) no such action shall
be brought for anything done under such conviction or order
until after such conviction or order shall have been quashed,
either upon appeal or upon application to Her Majesty's
Court of Queen's Bench ; nor shall any such action be
brought for anything done under any such warrant, which
shall have been issued by such Justice to procure the appearance of such party, and which shall have been followed
by a conviction or order in the same matter, until after such
conviction or order shall have been so quashed as aforesaid ;
or if such last-mentioned warrant shall not have been followed by any such conviction or order, or if it be a warrant
upon an information for an alleged indictable offence, nevertheless if a summons were issued previously to such warrant, and such summons were served upon such person, either
personally or by leaving the same for him with some person,
at his last or most usual place of abode, and he did not appear according to the exigency of such summons, in such
case no such action shall be maintained against such Justice
for anything done under such warrant." (a) . . . 2

If one Justice makes a conviction or order, and another grant
a warrant upon it, the action must be brought against the
former, not the latter, ... 3

No action against Justices for the manner in which they exercise a *discretionary* power, ... 2

After conviction or order confirmed on appeal, no action shall
be brought for anything done under warrant upon that conviction, ... 7

(a) Such protection as this section affords has reference to cases wherein the Justice acts without any jurisdiction whatever, or in which he exceeds his jurisdiction ; the party injured need not allege or prove malice, &c. But if it be a case in
which there exists a right of appeal or of application to Court of Queen's Bench,
these remedies must be availed of to quash the conviction before the action can be
brought. The 20 & 21 Vic., c. 43, gives (in matters of complaint which Justices
have power to determine summarily) a right to the party aggrieved to call upon the
Justices to state a case for opinion of Superior Court, if dissatisfied with the decision
as being " erroneous in point of law."
And as to the protection of persons acting in execution of an office, if a party
believes, with some colour of reason and *bona fide*, in a state of facts which, if they
had existed, would have afforded a defence to the action, he is entitled to protection,
although he may have proceeded illegally or exceeded his jurisdiction.—*Hazeldine
v. Grove*, 3 Q. B., 997 ; *Taylor on Evidence.*
[There are then three accidents of office to be guarded against by the Justice of
the Peace : the first, which must be wilful, is not so much to be feared, as not being
likely to happen. The next is the more dangerous, being the result of inadvertence. The third, though not visited with pecuniary penalty, may be attended by a
still more humiliating consequence, that is, where, by injudiciousness or want of
discretion, he may happen to transgress the conditions of his commission.]
Nor shall action be brought for act done under warrant to compel appearance, if
a summons were previously served and not obeyed. But it is of the utmost importance that the summons and warrant should contain an *offence* which the Justice
has power to entertain, and that the information upon which the warrant issues
discloses such offence.

DOCUMENTARY EVIDENCE. (b)

Railways.—*Evidence* of documents purporting to be stamped, sealed, or signed, as required by any Act to be received in evidence, without proof of stamp, seal, or signature, 8 & 9 Vic., c. 113, sec.1.

Where Defendants compelled to give evidence.—On the trial of any

? trying or enforcing a civil right only, every defendant to such in-
ictment or proceeding, and the wife or husband of any such de-
ndant shall be admissible witnesses, and compellable to give
vidence.—40 & 41 Vic., c. 14.

14 & 15 *Vic.*, *cap.* 99.
"An Act to amend the Law of Evidence."

Repeals a proviso in 6 & 7 Wm. IV., cap. 85.

Section

On the trial of any issue joined, or of any matter or question, or on any inquiry arising in any suit, action, or other
proceeding in any Court of Justice, or before any person
having, by law, or by consent of parties, anthority to hear,
receive, and examine evidence, the parties thereto, and the
persons in whose behalf any such suit, action, or other proceeding may be brought or defended shall, except as hereinafter excepted, be competent and compellable to give evidence
either *viva voce*, or by deposition, according to the practice
of the Court on behalf of either or any of the parties to the
said suit, action, or other proceeding.

Parties to suits, &c., to be competent and compellable to give evidence.

Persons charged with criminal offence not competent or compellable to give evidence to criminate himself.

But nothing herein contained shall render any person who,
in any criminal proceeding, is charged with the commission of any indictable offence, or any offence punishable on
summary conviction, competent or compellable to give
evidence for or against himself or herself, or shall render
any person compellable to answer any questions tending to
criminate himself or herself, or shall, in any criminal proceeding, render any husband competent or compellable to
give evidence for or against his wife, or any wife competent or compellable to give evidence for or against her
husband, ... **3**

No person bound to answer question tending to criminate himself.

Where husband or wife charged with criminal offence, one not competent to give evidence for or against the other.

LAW OF EVIDENCE AMENDMENT. (a)
16 & 17 *Vic.*, *cap.* 83.
"An Act to amend 14 & 15 Vic., cap. 99."

Section

On the trial of any issue joined, or of any matter or question,
or on any inquiry arising in any suit, action, or other proceeding in any Court of Justice, or before any person having
by law, or by consent of parties, authority to hear, receive,
and examine evidence, the husbands and wives of the
parties thereto, and of the persons in whose behalf any such
suit, action, or other proceedings may be brought or instituted, or opposed or defended, shall, except as hereinafter
excepted, be competent and compellable to give evidence
either *viva voce* or by deposition, according to the practice
of the Court, on behalf of either or any of the parties to the
said suit, action, or other proceeding, ... **1**

Husbands and wives of parties to suits to be admissible witnesses.

(a) *Documentary* Evidence Act, as to giving in evidence and making admissible
ertain Government Proclamations, Gazettes, &c.—31 & 32 Vic., c. 37.
Rules of Evidence.—It is the first rule of evidence that the best evidence of which
he case is capable shall be given, otherwise the presumption is that it would tell
gainst the party neglecting to produce it. A written document, where it can be
roduced or its production compelled, should be produced, unless where on physical

LAW OF
EVIDENCE.

Where husband or wife charged with criminal offence, one not admissible as evidence for or against the other.
Husband and wife not compelled to disclose communications made to each other.

Nothing herein shall render any husband competent or compellable to give evidence for or against his wife, or any wife competent or compellable to give evidence for or against her husband in any criminal proceeding, or in any proceeding instituted in consequence of adultery (a) . 2

No husband shall be compellable to disclose any communication made to him by his wife during the marriage, and no wife shall be compellable to disclose any communication made to her by her husband during the marriage, . . .

So much of section 1 of 6 & 7 Vic., cap. 85, as relates to husbands and wives repealed : see now 47 Vic., c. 14, . .

LAW OF EVIDENCE ACT. (b)

" An Act for amending the Law of Evidence and Practice on Criminal Trials."—28 Vic., c. 18.

Whereas it is expedient that the law of evidence and practice on trials for felony and misdemeanour and other proceedings in Courts of Criminal Judicature should be more nearly assimilated to that on trials at Nisi Prius : Be it enacted by the Queen's Most Excellent

grounds, or of privilege, or by reason of other inconvenience, on account of its public nature, or where some other mode of proof is provided. But certain preliminary conditions must be complied with before secondary evidence will be allowed. Payment of money may be proved without producing receipt. So a person who takes notes of a conversation need not produce them: they would not be evidence if produced. A marriage may be proved by witnesses without producing the register. On an indictment for perjury committed in a County Court, witnesses who were present are competent to prove what was sworn to, as a Judge of a County Court is not bound to take notes. It is held that in proving handwriting the evidence of third persons is not inferior to that of the party whose the writing is; and on this ground it is concluded that such evidence is also admissible to disprove it. Where persons act in a public capacity, as Justices, peace officers, &c. &c., evidence of acting in that capacity is sufficient without producing or proving appointment. Where notice has been served to produce a document, it must be served a reasonable time before secondary evidence can be given (what is reasonable time will depend on the circumstances of the case). It is now held that where the party in possession of the document has it in Court, notice to produce is dispensed with.—*Dwyer* v. *Collins*, 7 *Ex. R.*, 639. If a document is known to be lost or destroyed, and can be proved to be so, notice may be dispensed with. Notice to produce may be by parole. *As to presumptive or circumstantial evidence*, it is said "that in many cases it is more to be depended on than living witnesses, who may be mistaken themselves or wickedly intend to deceive others, whereas circumstances and presumptions naturally and necessarily arising out of a given fact cannot lie." —*Mountenoy, B.* Still it is with equal force observed that, " not unfrequently a presumption is formed from circumstances which would not have existed as a ground of crimination but for the accusation itself; such are the conduct, demeanour, and expressions of a suspected person, when scrutinized by those who suspect him. And it may be observed that circumstantial evidence, which must in general be submitted to a Court of Justice through the means of witnesses, is capable of being perverted in like manner as direct evidence, and that, moreover, it is subjected to this additional infirmity, that it is composed of inferences each of which may be fallacious."

Hearsay evidence of what is written or spoken is not admissible ; but there are some exceptions to this rule, viz. : pedigrees, customs, births, deaths, &c. For further readings, see *Roscoe's Digest ; Taylor on Evidence.*

(a) See now 47 Vic., c. 14.

(b) Though this Act is entitled the Law of Evidence and Practice on Criminal *Trials*, sec. 1 declares that from secs. 3 to 8, inclusive, " It shall apply to all Courts of Judicature, as well criminal as all others, and to all persons having, by law or by consent of parties, authority to hear, receive, and examine evidence." Sec. 1 has reference to Courts of Oyer and Terminer.

Majesty, by and with the advice and consent of the Lords Spiritual
aud Temporal, and Commons, in this present Parliament assembled,
and by the anthority of the same, as follows: that is to say,

1. That the provisions of section two of this Act shall apply to Provisions of sect. 2 of this Act to apply to trials commenced on or after July 1, 1865. Secs. 3 to 8 shall apply to all Courts of Judicature. every trial for felony and misdemeanour which shall be commenced
on or after the First day of *July*, one thousand eight hundred and
sixty-five, and that the provisions of sections from three to eight
inclusive, of this Act, shall apply to all Courts of Judicature, as well
Criminal as all others, and to all persons having, by law or by consent of parties, authority to hear, receive, and examine evidence.

2. If any prisoner or prisoners, defendant or defendants, shall be Summing up of evidence in cases of felony and misde- meanour. defended by counsel, but not otherwise, it shall be the duty of the
presiding Judge, at the close of the case for the prosecution, to ask
the counsel for each prisoner or defendant so defended by counsel,
whether he or they intend to adduce evidence, and in the event of
none of them thereupon announciug his intention to adduce evidence,
the counsel for the prosecution shall be allowed to address the jury a
second time in support of his case, for the purpose of summing up the
evidence against such prisoner or prisoners, or defendant or defendants; and upon every trial for felony or misdemeanour, whether
the prisoners or defendants, or any of them, shall be defended by
counsel or not, each and every such prisoner or defendant, or his or
their counsel respectively, shall be allowed, if he or they shall think
fit, to open his or their case or cases respectively; and after the conclusion of such opening or of all such openings, if more than one,
such prisoner or prisoners, or defendant or defendants, or their
counsel, shall be entitled to examine such witnesses as he or they
may think fit, and when all the evidence is concluded, to sum up the
evidence respectively; and the right of reply, and practice and
course of proceedings, save as hereby altered, shall be as at present.

3. A party producing a witness shall not be allowed to impeach his How far witness may be dis- credited by the party producing. credit by general evidence of bad character, but he may, in case the
witness shall, in the opinion of the Judge, prove adverse, contradict
him by other evidence, or, by leave of the Judge, prove that he has
made at other times a statement inconsistent with his present testimony; but before such last-mentioned proof can be given, the
circumstances of the supposed statement sufficient to designate the
particular occasion, must be mentioned to the witness, and he must
be asked whether or not he has made such statement.

4. If a witness, upon cross-examination as to a former statement As to proof of contra- dictory statements of adverse witness. made by him relative to the subject-matter of the indictment or
proceeding, and inconsistent with his present testimony, does not
distinctly admit that he has made such statement, proof may be given
that he did in fact make it; but before such proof can be given, the
circumstances of the supposed statement, sufficient to designate the
particular occasion, must be mentioned to the witness, and he must
be asked whether or not he has made such statement.

5. A witness may be cross-examined as to previous statements Cross- examinations as to previous statements in writing. made by him in writing, or reduced into writing, relative to the
subject-matter of the indictment or proceeding, without such writing
being shown to him; but if it is intended to contradict such witness
by the writing, his attention must, before such contradictory proof
can be given, be called to those parts of the writing which are to be

LAW OF
EVIDENCE.

used for the purpose of so contradicting him : Provided always that it shall be competent for the Judge, at any time during the trial, to require the production of the writing for his inspection, and he may thereupon make such use of it for the purposes of the trial as he may think fit.

Proof of previous conviction of witness may be given.

6. A witness may be questioned as to whether he has been convicted of any felony or misdemeanour, and upon being so questioned, if he either denies or does not admit the fact, or refuses to answer, it shall be lawful for the cross-examining party to prove such conviction ; and a certificate containing the substance and effect only (omitting the formal part) of the indictment and conviction for such offence, purporting to be signed by the Clerk of the Court or other officer having the custody of the records of the Court where the offender was convicted, or by the deputy of such clerk or officer (for which certificate a fee of five shillings, and no more, shall be demanded or taken) shall, upon proof of the identity of the person, be sufficient evidence of the said conviction, without proof of the signature or official character of the person appearing to have signed the same.

As to proof by attesting witnesses.

7. It shall not be necessary to prove by the attesting witness any instrument to the validity of which attestation is not requisite, and such instrument may be proved as if there had been no attesting witness thereto.

As to comparison of disputed writing.

8. Comparison of a disputed writing with any writing proved to the satisfaction of the Judge to be genuine shall be permitted to be made by witnesses ; and such writings, and the evidence of witnesses respecting the same, may be submitted to the Court and jury as evidence of the genuineness or otherwise of the writing in dispute.

" Counsel."

9. The word " counsel " in this Act shall be construed to apply to attorneys in all cases where attorneys are allowed by law or by the practice of any Court to appear as advocates.

Not to apply to Scotland.

10. This Act shall not apply to *Scotland*.

JUSTICES OF THE PEACE ACT, 1867.

JUSTICES OF THE PEACE ACT, 1867.

30 & 31 *Vic.*, *c.* 115.

" An Act to remove Disqualifications of Justices of the Peace in certain cases."

[*20th August*, 1867.]

" In order that Justices of the Peace may act in the execution of Acts in some cases in which they are now incapable of so acting, Be it enacted, &c. :—

" A Justice of the Peace shall not be incapable of acting as a Justice at any Petty, or Special, or General, or Quarter Sessions on the trial of an offence arising under an Act to be put in execution by a Municipal Corporation, or a Local Board of Health, or Improvement Commissioners, or Trustees, or any other local authority, by reason only of his being as one of several ratepayers, or as one of any other class of persons liable in common with the others, to contribute to or to be benefited by any fund, to the account of which the penalty payable in respect of such offence is directed to be carried, or of which it will form part, or to contribute to any rate or expenses in diminution of which such penalty will go." (a).

THE LICENSING ACT.

35 & 36 *Vic., c.* 94.

An Act for Regulating the Sale of Intoxicating Liquors.

[*10th August*, 1872.]

WHEREAS it is expedient to amend the law for the sale by retail of intoxicating liquors, and the regulation of public-houses and other places in which intoxicating liquors are sold, and to make further provision in respect of the grant of new licences for the sale of intoxicating liquors, and the better prevention of drunkenness :
Be it enacted by the Queen's Most Excellent Majesty, by and with the advice and consent of the Lords Spiritual and Temporal, and Commons, in this present Parliament assembled, and by the authority of the same, as follows :

PRELIMINARY.

1. This Act may be cited as "The Licensing Act, 1872."
2. This Act shall not extend to Scotland.

Short title.
Extent of Act.

ILLICIT SALES.

3. No person shall sell or expose for sale by retail any intoxicating liquor without being duly licensed to sell the same, or at any place where he is not authorized by his licence to sell the same.   Any person selling or exposing for sale by retail any intoxicating liquor which he is not licensed to sell by retail, or selling or exposing for sale any intoxicating liquor at any place where he is not authorized

Illicit Sales.

Prohibition of sale of intoxicating liquors without licence.

(a) It is said that "an exception proves the existence of a rule," the meaning of which is, that there is a rule, and that where an exception is made in an Act of Parliament there is not by implication or otherwise any other exception but that specified ; and on the general principle that no man can be a judge in his own case, or in which he has an interest, for

"Where self the wav'ring balance holds,
'Tis rarely right adjusted."

so it requires an Act of Parliament to except that remote interest which Justices may have in the instances above stated.   But supposing the Justice to be a member of a Corporation or public Board, in which case he will be *complainant and Judge,* is he excepted under the above provisions?   Probably it will be allowed that it is his being a ratepayer which gives him the interest requiring the Act to remove the disqualification ; and that in the other character he has no interest in the suit.

Where Justice is a Witness.—A Magistrate subpœnaed in a case, but having no interest in it, is not thereby disqualified from taking part in the adjudication.   The question came before the Q. B., England, in Easter Term, 1864, and Mr. Justice Grove and Mr. Baron Huddleston, on the discussion of the case, held that the request that the Justice who had been subpœnaed should leave the Bench and take no part in adjudicating was a preposterous request, remarking that, if it possessed any ground in law, a suitor might, by subpœnaing the Judge who was to try the case, or for that matter all the Judges, evade any trial of an action.

CENSING ACT, 1872.

Illicit Sales.

by his licence to sell the same, shall be subject to the following penalties, that is to say :—

(1.) For the first offence he shall be liable to a penalty not exceeding fifty pounds, or to imprisonment, with or without hard labour, for a term not exceeding one month : (a).

(2.) For the second offence he shall be liable to a penalty not exceeding one hundred pounds, or to imprisonment, with or without hard labour, for a term not exceeding three months, and he may by order of the Court by which he is tried be disqualified for any term not exceeding five years from holding any licence for the sale of intoxicating liquors :

(3.) For the third and any subsequent offence he shall be liable to a penalty not exceeding one hundred pounds, or to imprisonment with or without hard labour, for any term not exceeding six months, and may, by order of the Court by which he is tried, be disqualified for any term of years, or for ever, from holding any licence for the sale of intoxicating liquors.

In addition to any other penalty imposed by this section, any person convicted of a second or any subsequent offence under this section shall, if he be the holder of a licence, forfeit such licence ; and in the case of a conviction for any offence under this section, the Court may, if it thinks expedient to do so, declare all intoxicating liquor found in the possession of any such person as last aforesaid, and the vessels, containing such liquor, to be forfeited.

No penalty shall be incurred under this section by the heirs, executors, administrators, or assigns of any licensed person who dies before the expiration of his licence, or by the trustee of any licensed person who is adjudged a bankrupt, or whose affairs are liquidated by arrangement before the expiration of his licence, in respect of the sale or exposure for sale of any intoxicating liquor, so that such sale or exposure for sale be made on the premises specified in such licence, and take place prior to the special session then next issuing, or (if special session be holden within fourteen days next after the death of the said person, or the appointment of a trustee in the case of his bankruptcy, or the liquidation of his affairs by arrangement) take place prior to the special session holden next after such special session as last aforesaid.

(a) *Fine or Imprisonment.*—The discretionary power to impose the fine or inflict the punishment is in the Justices ; but where they do impose the fine and it cannot afterwards be levied, the scale of imprisonment need not be that which they might have adopted in the first instance without a fine, but may be regulated by the scale at sec. 51. which is the same as that in Petty Sessions (Ireland) Act, where the sums exceed £5. But where the penalty *does not exceed* £5, the defendant may, in default of payment, and without any distress warrant, be imprisoned for any term not exceeding two months, and for less sums in proportion, under Small Penalties Act, 36 & 37 Vic., c. 82. See *Scale*, pages 541, 542.

Illicit Sales.—The Manager of an institution, carried on *bona fide* as a club (the members paying an entrance fee and subscription, the property being vested in trustees, and intoxicating liquors being supplied to members for consumption on and off the premises, 33 per cent. above cost price being charged for liquors to be consumed off the premises, and the money produced thereby going to the general funds of the club, and the club not being licensed for sale of intoxicating liquors) who supplies a member for consumption off the premises, cannot be convicted under Licensing Act, 1872. s. 3 : *Graff* v. *Evans*, English L. R., 8 Q. B. D., 273 ; 51 L. J., M. C. 25 ; 46 L. T., N. S., 347 ; 30 W. R., 380 ; 46 J. P., 262.

4. The occupier of any unlicensed premises on which any intoxicating liquor is sold, or if such premises are occupied by more than one person, every occupier thereof shall, if it be proved that he was privy or consenting to the sale, be subject to the penalties imposed upon persons for the sale of intoxicating liquors without licence.

5. If any purchaser of any intoxicating liquor from a person who is not licensed to sell the same to be drunk on the premises drinks such liquor on the premises where the same is sold, or on any highway adjoining or near such premises, the seller of such liquor shall, if it shall appear that such drinking was with his privity, or consent, be subject to the following penalties, that is to say :—

For the first offence he shall be liable to a penalty not exceeding ten pounds.

For the second and any subsequent offence he shall be liable to a penalty not exceeding twenty pounds.

For the purposes of this section the expression "premises where the same is sold" shall include any premises adjoining or near the premises where the liquor is sold, if belonging to the seller of the liquor, or under his control, or used by his permission.

Any conviction for an offence under this section shall be recorded on the licence of the person convicted.

6. If any person having a licence to sell intoxicating liquors not to be drunk on the premises, himself takes or carries, or employs or suffers any other person to take or carry any intoxicating liquor out of or from the premises of such licensed person for the purpose of being sold on his account, or for his benefit or profit, and of being drunk or consumed in any other house, or in any tent, shed, or other building of any kind whatever, belonging to such licensed person, or hired, used, or occupied by him, or on or in any place, whether enclosed or not, and whether or not a public thoroughfare, such intoxicating liquor shall be deemed to have been consumed by the purchaser thereof, on the premises of such licensed person, with his privity and consent, and such licensed person shall be punished accordingly in manner provided by this Act.

Any conviction for an offence under this section shall be recorded on the licence of the person convicted.

In any proceeding under this section it shall not be necessary to prove that the premises or place or places to which such liquor is taken to be drunk belonged to, or were hired, used, or occupied by the seller, if proof be given to the satisfaction of the Court hearing the case that such liquor was taken to be consumed thereon or therein with intent to evade the conditions of his licence.

7. Every holder of a licence who sells or allows any person to sell, to be consumed on the premises, any description of spirits to any person apparently under the age of sixteen years, shall be liable to a penalty not exceeding twenty shillings, for the first offence, and not exceeding forty shillings for the second and any subsequent offence. (a)

Side notes: LICENSING ACT. 1872. *Illicit Sales.* Occupier of unlicensed premises liable for sale of liquor. Seller liable for drinking on premises contrary to licence. Evasion of Law as to drinking on premises contrary to licence. Sale of spirits to children.

(a) This applies only to the sale "*spirits to be consumed on the premises.*" He may be supplied with spirits to take away, or with ale ("stunning ale") to be consumed on the premises. But see now 49 & 50 Vic., c. 56, s. 1, p. 242. Summary Index, as to children under 13.

LICENSING ACT, 1872.

Illicit Sales.

8. Every person shall sell all intoxicating liquor which is sold by retail and not in cask, or bottle, and is not sold in a quantity less than half a pint, in measures marked according to the imperial standards.

Sale to be by standard measure.

Every person who acts or suffers any person under his control or in his employment to act in contravention of this section, shall be liable to a penalty not exceeding for the first offence ten pounds, and not exceeding for any subsequent offence twenty pounds, and shall also be liable to forfeit the illegal measure in which such liquor was sold.

Penalty on internal communication between licensed premises and house of public resort.

9. Every person who makes or uses, or allows to be made or used, any internal communication between any licensed premises and any unlicensed premises which are used for public entertainment or resort or as a refreshment house (a) shall be liable to a penalty not exceeding ten pounds for every day during which such communication remains open.

In addition to any penalty imposed by this section any person convicted of an offence under this section shall, if he be the holder of a licence, forfeit such licence.

Penalty on illicit storing of liquor.

10. If any licensed person has in his possession on the premises in respect of which his licence is granted any description of intoxicating liquor which he is not authorized to sell, unless he shall account for the possession of the same to the satisfaction of the Court by which he is tried, he shall forfeit such liquor and the vessels containing the same, and shall be liable to a penalty not exceeding for the first offence ten pounds, and not exceeding for any subsequent offence twenty pounds (b).

Names of licensed persons to be affixed to premises.

11. Every licensed person shall cause to be painted, or fixed, and shall keep painted or fixed on the premises in respect of which his licence is granted, in a conspicuous place and in such form and manner as the Commissioners of Inland Revenue may from time to time direct, his name, with the addition after the name of the word "licensed," and of words sufficient, in the opinion of the said Commissioners, to express the business for which his licence has been granted, and in particular of words expressing whether the licence authorizes the sale of intoxicating liquor to be consumed on or off the premises only, as the case may be; and no person shall have any words or letters on his premises importing that he is authorized as a licensed person to sell any intoxicating liquor which he is not in fact duly authorized to sell. Every person who acts in contravention of the provisions of this section shall be liable to a penalty not exceeding for the first offence ten pounds, and not exceeding for the second and any subsequent offence twenty pounds (c).

(a) An ordinary dwelling-house or shop would not seem to be a place of entertainment or public resort within the meaning of the Act. But where any sale takes place therein, see penalties on occupiers, sec. 4.

(b) He must then be brought to Court to explain the possession. His safest course would be to go and acquaint the authorities that he had a particular liquor for private consumption, or *in transitu*, &c.

(c) *Show-boards.*—The notices to be affixed on licensed premises shall be directed by Licensing Justices, and not, as is above required, by Commissioners.—37 & 38 Vic., c. 69, s. 26.

OFFENCES AGAINST PUBLIC ORDER.

Offences against Public Order.

12. Every person found drunk, in any highway or other public place, whether a building or not, or on any licensed premises, shall be liable to a penalty not exceeding ten shillings, and on a second conviction within a period of twelve months shall be liable to a penalty not exceeding twenty shillings, and on a third or subsequent conviction within such period of twelve months be liable to a penalty not exceeding forty shillings.

Penalty on persons found drunk.

Every person who in any highway or other public place, whether a building or not, is guilty while drunk of riotous or disorderly behaviour, or who is drunk while in charge on any highway or other public place of any carriage, horse, cattle, or steam engine, or who is drunk when in possession of any loaded fire-arms, may be apprehended, and shall be liable to a penalty not exceeding forty shillings, or in the discretion of the Court to imprisonment with or without hard labour for any term not exceeding one month (*a*).

Where the Court commits any person to prison for non-payment of any penalty under this section, the Court may order him to be imprisoned with hard labour.

13. If any licensed person permits drunkenness or any violent, quarrelsome, or riotous conduct to take place on his premises, or sells any intoxicating liquor to any drunken person, he shall be liable to a penalty not exceeding for the first offence ten pounds, and not exceeding for the second and any subsequent offence twenty pounds.

Penalty for permitting drunkenness.

Any conviction for an offence under this section shall be recorded on the licence of the person convicted, unless the convicting Magistrate or Justices shall otherwise direct.

14. If any licensed person knowingly permits his premises to be the habitual resort of or place of meeting of reputed prostitutes, whether the object of their so resorting or meeting is or is not prostitution, he shall, if he allow them to remain longer than is necessary for the purpose of obtaining reasonable refreshment, be liable to a penalty not exceeding for the first offence ten pounds, and not exceeding for the second and any subsequent offence twenty pounds.

Penalty for keeping disorderly house.

Any conviction for an offence under this section shall, unless the convicting Magistrate or Justices shall otherwise direct, be recorded on the licence of the person convicted.

15. If any licensed person is convicted of permitting his premises to be a brothel, he shall be liable to a penalty not exceeding twenty pounds, and shall forfeit his licence, and he shall be disqualified for ever from holding any licence for the sale of intoxicating liquors.

Penalty for permitting premises to be a brothel.

(*a*) " *Whether a building or not.*"—See note on section in Analysis.
It will be noticed that no special direction is given in the first part of section 12 to arrest. The power given in 6 & 7 Wm. iv., c. 38, sec. 12, to arrest persons drunk in public thoroughfares, is not taken away; but where no complaint is made, the constable is not required to enter public buildings and arrest persons who are drunk but not disorderly or riotous. *For being drunk and incapable, drunk in public buildings, on licensed premises, and in possession of loaded firearms,* see notes on sec. 12. Analysis.

LICENSING
ACT, 1872.

*Offences
against
Public
Order.*

Penalty for
harbouring
constable.

16. If any licensed person—

(1.) Knowingly harbours or knowingly suffers to remain on his premises any constable during any part of the time appointed for such constable being on duty, unless for the purpose of keeping or restoring order or in execution of his duty ; or

(2.) Supplies any liquor or refreshment, whether by way of gift or sale, to any constable on duty unless by authority of some superior officer of such constable; or

(3.) Bribes or attempts to bribe any constable,

he shall be liable to a penalty not exceeding for the first offence ten pounds, and not exceeding for the second or any subsequent offence twenty pounds. Any conviction for an offence under this section shall, unless the convicting Magistrate or Justices shall otherwise direct, be recorded on the licence of the person convicted.

17. If any licensed person—

(1.) Suffers any gaming or any unlawful game to be carried on on his premises ; or

(2.) Opens, keeps, or uses, or suffers his house to be opened, kept, or used in contravention of the Act of the session of the sixteenth and seventeenth years of the reign of her present Majesty, chapter one hundred and nineteen, intituled, "An Act for the suppression of betting houses,"

he shall be liable to a penalty not exceeding for the first offence ten pounds, and not exceeding for the second and any subsequent offence twenty pounds.

Any conviction for an offence under this section shall, unless the convicting Magistrate shall otherwise direct, be recorded on the licence of the person convicted.

18. Any licensed person may refuse to admit to and may turn out of the premises in respect of which his licence is granted any person who is drunken, violent, quarrelsome, or disorderly, and any person whose presence on his premesis would subject him to a penalty under this Act. (*a*)

(*a*) It may be a question whether the power to *exclude* should be exercised in respect to persons who by *reputation* are as here described, or those who at the time are *actually* so. Well, it is probable that the power is to *turn out* some, who are actually drunken, violent, quarrelsome or disorderly, and to "refuse to admit" and to "turn out" others, such as prostitutes and reputed thieves, all these being persons whose presence may subject the licensed person to a penalty.

Gaming.—Some wager, however small, would seem to be necessary to constitute "gaming." Billiards, bagatelle, or cards, played for amusement or pastime, only, seems allowable; and see 8 & 9 Vic., c. 109, s. 11. And some evidence should be given that such gaming takes place with sanction or knowledge of the trader or whoever represented him in the place of sale.

Betting Houses.—The Act for the suppression of betting houses, 16 & 17 Vic., c. 119, provides that "No house, office, room, or other place shall be opened, kept, or used for the purpose of the owner, occupier or keeper thereof, or any person using the same, or any person procured or employed by, or acting for or on behalf of such owner, occupier, or keeper, or person using the same, or of any person having the management or in any manner conducting the business thereof, betting with persons resorting thereto, or for the purpose of any money or valuable thing being received by or on behalf of such owner, occupier, keeper, or person as aforesaid, or for the consideration for any assurance, undertaking, promise, or agreement,

Any such person who upon being requested in pursuance of this section, by such licensed person, or his agent or servant, or any constable to quit such premises, refuses or fails so do, shall be liable to a penalty not exceeding five pounds, and all constables are required on the demand of such licensed person, agent, or servant, to expel, or assist in expelling every such person from such premises, and may use such force as may be required for that purpose.

The Court committing any person to prison for non-payment of any penalty under this section may order him to be imprisoned, with hard labour.

(From sections 19 to 22 inclusive, relating to adulteration, are repealed by the 37 & 38 Vic., c. 69.)

REPEATED CONVICTIONS.

30. If any licensed person on whose licence two convictions for offences committed by him against this Act have been recorded is convicted of any offence which is directed by this Act to be recorded on his licence, the following consequences shall ensue : that is to say (a)

(1.) The licence of such licensed person shall be forfeited, and he shall be disqualified for a term of five years from the date of such third conviction from holding any licence ; and

(2.) The premises in respect of which his licence was granted shall, unless the Court having cognizance of the case in its discretion thinks fit otherwise to order, be disqualified from receiving any licence for a term of two years from the date of such third conviction. (b)

Provided that nothing in this section contained shall prevent the infliction by the Court of any pecuniary penalty or any term of imprisonment to which such licensed person would otherwise be liable, or shall preclude the Court from exercising any power given by any other section of this Act of disqualifying such licensed person or such premises for a longer period than the term mentioned in this section.

Marginal notes: LICENSING ACT, 1872. *Offences against Public Order.* Power to exclude drunkards from licensed premises. *Repeated Convictions.* Forfeiture of licence on repeated convictions.

express or implied, to pay or give thereafter any money or valuable thing on any event or contingency of or relating to any horse race or other race, fight, game, sport or exercise, or as or for the consideration for securing the paying or giving by some other person of any money or valuable thing on any such event or contingency as aforesaid ; and every house, office, room, or other place opened, kept, or used for the purposes aforesaid, or any of them, is hereby declared to be a common nuisance and contrary to law."

The holder of an occasional licence shall be deemed to be a licensed person within meaning of sections 12 to 18 inclusive, and the sections giving effect to same, 37 & 38 Vic., c. 69, sec. 6.

(a) As to recording convictions, and as to what is meant by the above words, " directed by this Act to be recorded," see sec. 21, 37 & 38 Vic., c. 69; and where defendant holds several licences, see sec. 34, same Act.

(b) And where he is the holder of several licences, see effect of sec. 34, 37 & 38 Vic., c. 69.

Recorded Convictions.—Where two convictions are recorded on a licence, and are followed by a third conviction under the Act, the licence is thereby forfeited. Neither the Act of 1872 nor 1874 provides for the recording of a third conviction; and under the Act of 1872 it was not necessary that any order should be made by the Justices directing the third conviction to be recorded. It was only in certain cases the Justices could order the conviction not to be recorded : *O'Leary* v. *Justices Co. Cork*, Q. B., Trin. 1882. But the Court may still order (sub-sec. 2) that the premises be not disqualified. And see also sec. 53, as to temporary licence pending appeal from such third conviction.

LICENSING
ACT, 1872.

*Repeated
Convic-
tions.*

Disqualifi-
cation of
premises.

31. The following additional provisions shall be enacted with respect only to convictions of persons who may hereafter become licensed in respect of premises, and shall not apply to a conviction of any person licensed for any premises at the passing of this Act so long as he is licensed in respect of the same premises, viz. : (s)

(1.) The second and every subsequent conviction recorded on the licence of any one such person shall also be recorded in the register of licences against the premises.

(2.) When four convictions (whether of the same or of different licensed persons) have within five years been so recorded against premises, those premises shall during one year be disqualified for the purposes of this Act :

(3.) If the licences of two such persons licensed in respect of the same premises are forfeited within any period of two years, the premises shall be disqualified for one year from the date of the last forfeiture :

Provided that where any premises are disqualified under this section notice of such disqualification shall be served upon the owner of the premises in like manner as an order of disqualification is required to be served under this Act, and the regulations for the protection of the owner of premises in case of an order of disqualification shall, so far as the same are applicable, extend to the case of disqualification under this section.

Conviction
after five
years not to

32. A conviction for any offence under this Act shall not after five years from the date of such conviction be receivable in evidence

SIX-DAY LICENCES.

*Six-day
Licences.*

49. Where on the occasion of an application for a new licence or transfer or renewal of a licence which authorizes the sale of any intoxicating liquor for consumption on the premises, the applicant, at the time of his application, applies to the licensing Justices to insert in his licence a condition that he shall keep the premises in respect of which such licence is or is to be granted closed during the whole of Sunday, the Justices shall insert the said condition in such licence.

Provisions as
to six-day
licences.

The holder of a licence in which such condition is inserted (in this Act referred to as a six-day licence) shall keep his premises closed during the whole of Sunday, and the provisions of this Act with respect to the closing of licensed premises during certain hours on Sunday shall apply to the premises in respect of which a six-day licence is granted as if the whole of Sunday were mentioned in those provisions instead of certain hours only.

The holder of a six-day licence may obtain from the Commissioners of Inland Revenue any licence granted by such Commissioners, which he is entitled to obtain in pursuance of such six-day licence, upon payment of six-seventh parts of the duty which would otherwise be payable by him for a similar licence not limited to six days ; and if he sell any intoxicating liquor on Sunday he shall be deemed to be selling intoxicating liquor without a licence.

The notice which a licensed person is required to keep painted or fixed on his premises shall, in the case of a licence under this section, contain words indicating that such licence is for six days only. In calculating the amount to be paid for a six-day licence any fraction of a penny shall be disregarded. (*a*)

LEGAL PROCEEDINGS.

*Legal
Proceedings.*

51. Except as in this Act otherwise expressly provided, every offence under this Act may be prosecuted, and every penalty and forfeiture may be recovered and enforced, in manner provided by the Summary Jurisdiction Act, 1848 (*b*), subject to the following provisions :

Summary
proceedings
for offences
under this
Act, &c.

(1.) The Court of summary jurisdiction, when hearing and determining any information or complaint, other than in a case where the offence charged is that of being found drunk in any highway or other public place, or any licensed premises, shall be constituted either of two or more Justices of the peace in petty Sessions sitting at a place appointed for holding Petty Sessions, or of a stipendiary Magistrate, or some other officer for the time being empowered by law to do alone any act authorized to be done by more than one Justice of the Peace, and sitting alone or with others at some Court or other place appointed for the administration of justice.

Six-day Licences.—The Justices in Quarter Sessions, or Recorder, as the case may be, will be the authority to make the alteration in existing licences, or grant new ones. And generally, as to six-day licences and early closing licences and the remission of duty on such, see Amended Act, 37 & 38 Vic., chap. 69, secs. 2, 3.

(*a*) The notice to be affixed on premises shall be such as Licensing Justices shall direct ; 37 & 38 Vic., chap. 69, s. 2.

(*b*) "Summary Jurisdiction Act, 1848," shall in Ireland mean the Petty Sessions (Ireland) Act. See Schedule of "modifications," section 77.

2 U

LICENSING
ACT, 1872.

*Legal
Proceed-
ings.*

Scale of
imprison-
ment.

(2.) Where the Court of summary jurisdiction orders that a distress shall be made in default of payment of any penal sum
exceeding five pounds, including under that expression costs actually adjudged in respect of an offence, the Court may order
that in default of the said sum being paid as directed, the person
liable to pay the same shall be imprisoned for any term not exceeding the period specified in the following scale :

For any sum exceeding five pounds, but not exceeding ten
pounds, three months ;

For any sum exceeding ten pounds, but not exceeding thirty
pounds, four months :

For any sum exceeding thirty pounds, but not exceeding fifty
pounds, six months :

For any sum exceeding fifty pounds, one year. (a)

3.) The description of any offence under this Act in the words of
such Act, or in similar words, shall be sufficient in law :

(4.) Any exception, exemption, proviso, excuse, or qualification,
whether it does or does not accompany the description of the
offence in this Act, may be proved by the defendant, but need
not be specified or negatived in the information, and if so specified or negatived, no proof in relation to the matters so specified
or negatived shall be required on the part of the informant or
complainant ; and in all the cases of summary proceedings under
this Act the defendant and his wife shall be competent to give
evidence. (a)

(1. It will be seen that for penalties exceeding £5 the above scale agrees with the
Petty Sessions scale. See note " Scale of imprisonment," in Analysis.
Scale of imprisonment where penalty does not exceed £5.—Where upon summary
conviction any offender is adjudged to pay a penalty not exceeding £5, such
offender, in case of non-payment thereof, may, without any warrant of distress,
be committed to prison for any term not exceeding the period specified in the
following scale, unless the penalty shall be sooner paid.

For any penalty	The imprisonment not to exceed
Not exceeding ten shillings.	Seven days.
Exceeding ten shillings, and not exceeding one pound.	Fourteen days.
Exceeding one pound, but not exceeding two pounds.	One month.
Exceeding two pounds, but not exceeding five pounds.	Two months.

"Nothing in this Act contained shall affect the power of imposing hard labour
in addition to imprisonment in cases where hard labour might, on non-payment of
the penalty, have been so imposed if this Act had not passed."—36 & 37 Vic.,
chap. 93.

Thus where the penalty does not exceed £5 this is the proper scale and remedy
to adopt. But there is nothing to prevent the Justices issuing distress warrants if
they think fit. Where the fine imposed exceeds £5 and the party convicted has
property off which the fine can be levied, the distress warrant should issue in the
first instance, as in Petty Sessions Act, 14 & 15 Vic., chap. 93, sec. 22, directed.
And where Towns Improvement Act, &c., in force, see sec. 30, 37 & 38 Vic., c. 69.
and note thereon.
(a) It is always safe in the original proceedings to negative exemptions, &c.
Husband and wife are competent witnesses, but cannot be compelled to give
evidence.

(5.) All forfeitures shall be sold or otherwise disposed of in such manner as the Court may direct, and the proceeds of such sale or disposal (if any) shall be applied in the like manner as penalties ; but the Court may direct that such proceeds may be applied in the first instance in paying the expenses of and incidental to any search and seizure which resulted in such forfeiture :

(6.) Penalties and forfeitures under this Act shall not, for the purpose of any Act respecting the application of such penalties, or the costs, charges, and expenses attending proceedings for recovery of such penalties or of forfeitures, be deemed to be penalties or forfeitures under any Act relating to the Inland Revenue.

Any officer appointed by the Commissioners of Inland Revenue, may sue for any penalties under this Act, and when so sued for any penalties which may be recovered shall be applied in the manner in which Excise penalties are for the time being applicable by law. (a)

Where under this Act any sum for costs (other than costs upon a conviction or order of dismissal of an information) or for compensation, or both, is ordered or awarded to be paid by any person, the amount thereof shall be recovered in manner directed by "The Summary Jurisdiction Act, 1848," for the recovery of costs awarded upon the dismissal of an information or complaint.

52. If any person feels aggrieved by any order or conviction made by a Court of summary jurisdiction, the person so aggrieved may appeal therefrom, subject to the conditions and regulations following (b) :—

(1.) The appeal shall be made to the next Court of Quarter Sessions for the county or place in which the cause of appeal has arisen, holden not less than fifteen days after the decision of the Court from which the appeal is made :

(2.) The appellant shall, within seven days after the cause of appeal has arisen, give notice to the other party and to the Court of summary jurisdiction of his intention to appeal, and of the ground thereof :

(3.) The appellant, immediately after such notice, shall enter into a recognizance before a Justice of the Peace, with two sufficient sureties, conditioned personally to try such appeal, and to abide the judgment of the Court thereon, and to pay such costs as may be awarded by the Court, or shall give such other security by deposit of money or otherwise as the Justice may allow :

(4.) Where the appellant is in custody the Justice may, if he think fit, on the appellant entering into such recognizance or giving such other security as aforesaid, release him from custody : (c)

(a) The constabulary are also authorized to carry out this Act, this being a graft on existing Public-house Acts, and on the 17 & 18 Vic., c. 89, &c., &c.

(b) The conditions of appeal as above should be attended to. In oth·r respects the procedure is to be under the Petty Sessions (Ireland) Act. It is observable also, that the notice shall state the "ground" of appeal. Of course, general words will be sufficient, such as "Conviction was against weight of evidence," or "Want of jurisdiction," or "Made on evidence which was inadmissible," &c., &c. The lodging of a sum of money in lieu of entering into recognizance is a new and ready mode; it is certainly a safe one.

(c) This sub-section 4 is now repealed, and where appellant completes his recognizances or gives security as by Act provided, the Justice shall release him from custody. 37 & 38 Vic., c. 69, s 31.

(5.) The Court of Appeal may adjourn the appeal, and upon the hearing thereof may confirm, reverse, or modify the decision of the Court of summary jurisdiction, or remit the matter to the Court of summary jurisdiction, with the opinion of the Court of Appeal thereon, or make such other order in the matter as the Court thinks just. The Court of Appeal may also make such order as to costs to be paid by either party as the Court thinks just.

Continuance of licence during pendency of appeal against justices' refusal to renew.

53. Where the Justices refuse to renew a licence, and an appeal against such refusal is duly made, and such licence expires before the appeal is determined, the Commissioners of Inland Revenue may, by order, permit the person whose licence is refused to carry on his business during the pendency of the appeal upon such conditions as they think just; and subject to such conditions, any person so permitted may, during the continuance of such order, carry on his business in the same manner as if the renewal of the licence had not been refused. (a)

Where a licence is forfeited on or in pursuance of a conviction for an offence, and an appeal is duly made against such conviction, the Court by whom the conviction was made may, by order, grant a temporary licence to be in force during the pendency of the appeal upon such conditions as they think just.

Conviction, &c., not to be quashed for want of form, or removed by *certiorari*.

54. No conviction or order made in pursuance of this Act, originally or on appeal, relative to any offence, penalty, forfeiture, or summary order, shall be quashed for want of form, or, if made by a Court of summary jurisdiction, be removed by *certiorari* otherwise, either at the instance of the Crown or of any private party, into any Superior Court. Moreover, no warrant of commitment in any such matter shall be held void by reason of any defect therein, provided that there is a valid conviction to maintain such warrant, and it is alleged in the warrant that the party has been convicted.

As to record of convictions of licensed persons for offences under Act.

55. With respect to the record of convictions of licensed persons for offences under this Act committed by them as such, the following provisions shall have effect in cases where this Act requires the conviction to be recorded on the licence : that is to say,

(1.) The Court before whom any licensed person is accused shall require such person to produce and deliver to the clerk of the Court the licence under which such person carries on business, and the summons shall state that such production will be required : (b)

(2.) If such person is convicted, the Court shall cause the short particulars of such conviction, and the penalty imposed, to be indorsed on his licence before it is returned to the offender :

(a) To make this section intelligible for Ireland, it must mean the Justices in Petty Sessions, and the renewal, their annual certificate. See 18 & 19 Vic., chap. cf, secs. 1 and 2, and Introduction.

(b) *Production of Licence* —The holder of licence shall, on being required by the Court, produce and deliver up his licence under a penalty, although the summons may not state that such production is required. — 37 & 38 Vic., c. 69, s. 33.

(3.) The clerk to the licensing Justices shall enter the particulars respecting such conviction, or such of them as the case may require, in the register of licences, kept by him under this Act:

(4.) If the clerk to the Court be not the clerk to the licensing Justices, he shall send forthwith to the last-mentioned clerk notice of such conviction, and of the particulars thereof. (a)

(5.) Where the conviction of any such person has the effect of forfeiting the licence, or of disqualifying any person or premises for the purposes of this Act, the licence shall be retained by the clerk of the Court, and notice of such forfeiture or disqualification shall be sent to the licensing officer of the district, and if the clerk to the Court is not the clerk to the licensing Justices, to such last-mentioned clerk, together with the forfeited licence.

56. Where any tenant of any licensed premises is convicted of an offence against this Act, and such offence is one the repetition of which may render the premises liable to be disqualified from receiving a licence for any period, it shall be the duty of the clerk of the licensing Justices to serve, in manner provided by this Act, notice of every such conviction on the owner of the premises.

Where any order of a Court of summary jurisdiction declaring any licensed premises to be disqualified from receiving a licence for any period has been made, the Court shall cause such order to be served on the owner of such premises, where the owner is not the occupier, with the addition of a statement that the Court will hold a Petty Sessions at a time and place therein specified, at which the owner may appear and appeal against such order on all or any of the following grounds, but on no other grounds:

(a.) That notice, as required by this Act, has not been served on the owner of a prior offence which on repetition renders the premises liable to be disqualified from receiving a licence at any period; or

(b.) That the tenant by whom the offence was committed held under a contract made prior to the commencement of this Act, and that the owner could not legally have evicted the tenant in the interval between the commission of the offence, in respect of which the disqualifying order was made, and the receipt by him of the notice of the immediately preceding offence which on repetition renders the premises liable to be disqualified from receiving a licence at any period; or

(c.) That the offence in respect of which the disqualifying order was made occurred so soon after the receipt of such last-mentioned notice that the owner, notwithstanding he had legal power to evict the tenant, could not with reasonable diligence have exercised that power in the interval which occurred between the said notice and the second offence.

If the owner appear at the time and place specified, and at such Sessions, or any adjournment thereof, satisfy the Court that he is

Recording Convictions and Penalties.—See secs. 16 and 21, 37 & 38 Vic., c. 69.
(a) The clerk who keeps the "Register of Licences" will now be the clerk to licensing Justices. See Amended Act, sec. 15, and Definitions, sec. 37.

(marginal notes:)
LICENSING ACT, 1872.
Legal Proceedings.

For protection of owners of licensed premises in case of offences committed by tenants.

LICENSING ACT, 1872.

Legal Proceedings.

entitled to have the order cancelled on any of the grounds aforesaid, the Court shall thereupon direct such order to be cancelled, and the same shall be void. (The remainder of this section 56, beginning with the words, " In a county the Justices," to the end, is repealed by Amended Act, 37 & 38 Vic., c. 69, sec. 38.)

As to conviction of licensed persons of more than one offence on same day.

57. Where a licensed person is convicted of more offences than one committed on the same day, the convictions for which are by this Act directed to be recorded on his licence, the Court by whom he is convicted may, in their discretion, order that one or some only of such convictions shall be so recorded. (a)

Evidence of indorsements and register.

58. The registers of licences kept in pursuance of this Act shall be receivable in evidence of the matters required by this Act to be entered therein. Every indorsement upon a licence, and every copy of an entry made in the registers of licences in pursuance of this Act, purporting to be signed by the clerk to the licensing Justices and (in the case of a copy) to be certified to be a true copy, shall be evidence of the matters stated in such indorsement and entry, without proof of the signature or authority of the person signing the same.

Saving for indictments, &c., under other Acts.

59. Nothing in this Act shall prevent any person from being liable to be indicted or punished under any other Act, or otherwise, so that he be not punished twice for the same offence.

Miscellaneous.

MISCELLANEOUS.

Disqualification of Justices to act under this Act.

60. No Justice shall act for any purpose under this Act, or under any of the Intoxicating Liquor Licensing Acts, except in cases where the offence charged is that of being found drunk on any highway or other public place, whether a building or not, or on any licensed premises, or of being guilty while drunk of riotous or disorderly conduct, or of being drunk while in charge on any highway or other public place, of any carriage, horse, cattle, or steam engine, or of being drunk when in possession of loaded fire-arms, who is or is in partnership with or holds any share in any company which is a common brewer, distiller, maker of malt for sale, or retailer of malt or of any intoxicating liquor in the licensing district, or in the district or districts adjoining to that in which such Justice usually acts; and no Justice shall act for any purpose under this Act, or under any of the Intoxicating Liquor Acts, in respect of any premises in the profits to which such Justice is interested, or of which he is wholly or partly the owner, lessee, or occupier, or for the owner, lessee, or occupier of which he is manager or agent.

Any Justice hereby declared not to be qualified to act under this Act who knowingly acts as a Justice for any of the purposes of this Act shall for every such offence be liable to a penalty not exceeding

(a) *Sec. 57.*—The Justices can now exercise a discretion as to recording the convictions (see Amended Act, sec. 21): and although under the above section, as it stood, where there were on the same day more convictions than one directed by the Act to be recorded, they might have limited the number to one record, now it would seem that, under the Amended Act (sec. 21), they may direct that not even *one* shall be recorded. But where he is the holder of several licences he will be subject to the provisions of both Acts in respect of each such licence. (Amended Act, sec. 34). As to effect of a third conviction after two recorded convictions, see sec. 30, and note, " Recorded Convictions," at foot.

one hundred pounds, to be recovered by action in one of Her Majesty's Superior Courts at Westminster :

Provided that—

(1.) No Justice shall be disqualified under this section to act in respect of any premises by reason of his having vested in him a legal interest only, and not a beneficial interest, in such premises or the profits thereof :

(2.) No Justice shall be liable to a penalty for more than one offence committed by him under this section before the institution of any proceedings for the recovery of such penalty.

(3.) No act done by any Justice disqualified by this section shall by reason only of such disqualification be invalid.

61. For all the purposes of this Act any pier, quay, jetty, mole, or work extending from any place within the jurisdiction of any licensing Justices or Court of summary jurisdiction into or over any part of the sea, or any part of a river within the ebb and flow of the tide, shall be deemed to be within the jurisdiction of such Justices and Court.

Extension of jurisdiction of Justices over river or water, &c.

For the purpose of jurisdiction in any proceeding under this Act, any river or water which runs between or forms the boundary of two or more licensing districts, or of the jurisdiction of two or more Courts of summary jurisdiction, shall be deemed to be wholly within each such licensing district and the jurisdiction of each of such Courts.

62. In proving the sale or consumption of intoxicating liquor for the purpose of any proceeding relative to any offence under this Act, it shall not be necessary to show that any money actually passed or any intoxicating liquor was actually consumed, if the Court hearing the case be satisfied that a transaction in the nature of a sale actually took place, or that any consumption of intoxicating liquor was about to take place, and proof of consumption or intended consumption of intoxicating liquor on premises to which a licence under this Act is attached, by some person other than the occupier of, or a servant in such premises, shall be evidence that such liquor was sold to the person consuming, or being about to consume, or carrying away the same by or on behalf of the holder of such licence.

Evidence of sale or consumption of intoxicating liquor.

63. Where a licence is forfeited in pursuance of this Act, or becomes void under any of the provisions of this Act, any licence for the sale of intoxicating liquors granted by the Commissioners of Inland Revenue to the holder of such licence shall be void.

Avoidance of excise licence on forfeiture of licence.

64. Every holder of a licence, or of an order of exemption made by a local authority in pursuance of this Act shall, by himself, his agent, or servant, produce such licence or order within a reasonable time after the production thereof is demanded by a Justice of the Peace, constable, or officer of Inland Revenue, and deliver the same to be read and examined by him. Any person who acts in contravention of this section shall be liable to a penalty not exceeding ten pounds. (a)

Production of licence by holder, and penalty on non-production.

(a) And see also Amended Act, 37 & 38 Vic., c. 69, sec. 33. This latter refers to the production of the licence on hearing of complaints, and on appeals ; and as to " exemption orders," see sec. 11, Amended Act.

65. The population for any area for the purposes of this Act shall be ascertained according to the last published census for the time being.

66. Any part not exceeding a moiety of a penalty recovered under this Act may, if the Court shall so direct, be paid to the superannuation fund of the police establishment within whose jurisdiction the offence in respect of which such penalties are imposed shall have occurred.

67. [This section (67), as to mitigation of penalties, is repealed, and in lieu thereof see Amended Act, 37 & 38 Vic. c. 69, sec. 20.]

68. No person shall sell by retail liqueurs or spirits under the authority of any retail licence which such person shall have obtained as a wholesale spirit dealer from the Commissioners of Inland Revenue. except in premises occupied and used exclusively for the sale therein of intoxicating liquor, and which premises have no communication with the premises of nor are in any way occupied by a person who is carrying on any other trade or business, unless such person shall have first obtained from the licensing Justices a licence authorizing such sale in premises not exclusively so occupied and used.

69. A licence for the sale of liqueurs or spirits by retail not to be consumed on the premises may, where such licence is required by this Act, be granted in the same manner in all respects in which a licence for selling wine not to be consumed on the premises may by law be granted, and an application for such a licence shall not be refused except upon one or more of the grounds on which a certificate in respect of a licence to sell by retail beer, cider, or wine not to be con-

Marginal notes:

Licensing Act, 1872.

Miscellaneous.

Population to be according to last census.

Moiety of penalties may be awarded to police superannuation fund.

Limit of mitigation of penalties.

Regulations as to retail licences of wholesale dealers.

Licences for sale of liqueurs, &c., by retail not to be consumed on the premises.

section, all notices shall be deemed to be duly served if sent to any address which such clerk or other person in the exercise of his discretion believes to be the address of the person to whom the notice was so sent.

Provided that any notice of any offence required by this Act to be sent to the owner of licensed premises shall be either served personally or sent by registered letter.

71. The schedules to this Act shall be construed and have effect as part of this Act.

Saving Clauses.

72. Nothing in this Act shall affect or apply to—

1. The privileges at the date of the passing of this Act enjoyed by any university in England, or the respective chancellors or scholars of the same, or their successors :

2. The privileges at the date of the passing of this Act enjoyed by the mayor and burgesses of the borough of St. Albans, in the county of Hertford, or their successors, or the exemption from the obligation to take out a licence as defined by this Act, or a licence from the Commissioners of Inland Revenue enjoyed by the Company of the Master, Wardens, and Commonalty of Vintners of the city of London :

3. The sale of spruce or black beer.

4. The sale of intoxicating liquor by proprietors of theatres, in pursuance of the Acts in that behalf :

5. The sale of intoxicating liquor in packet boats, in pursuance of the Acts in that behalf :

6. The sale of intoxicating liquor on special occasions, in pursuance of the provisions in that behalf enacted.

7. The sale of spirits in canteens, in pursuance of any Act regulating the same :

8. The sale of medicated or methylated spirits, or spirits made up in medicine and sold by medical practitioners or chemists and druggists :

9. The sale of intoxicating liquor by wholesale :

10. Any penalties recoverable by or on behalf of the Commissioners of Inland Revenue, or any laws relating to the excise.

73. A licence as defined by this Act shall not be required for—

1. The sale of wine by retail, not to be consumed on the premises, by a wine merchant in pursuance of a wine dealer's licence granted by the Commissioners of Inland Revenue ; or

2. The sale of liqueurs or spirits by retail, not to be consumed on the premises by a wholesale spirit dealer whose premises are exclusively used for the sale of intoxicating liquors, in pursuance of a retail licence granted by the Commissioners of Inland Revenue, under the provisions of the twenty-fourth and twenty-fifth of her present Majesty, chapter twenty-one, intituled, "An Act for granting to Her Majesty certain duties of excise and stamps."

APPLICATION OF CERTAIN OF THE PRECEDING PROVISIONS OF THIS
ACT TO IRELAND.

ode of   76. A reference to the words forming a heading to any of the pro-
erence to   visions of this Act shall be deemed to be a reference to all the provi-
  lcular   sions under such heading, unless otherwise specially provided.
visions of
  ?.
plication   77. The preceding provisions of this Act with respect to—1, Illicit
Ireland   sales ; 2, Offences against public order ; 3, Adulteration ; 4, Repeated
  :ertain   convictions ; 5, Entry on premises ; 6, Six-day licences ; 7, Legal
  visions   proceedings ; 8, Miscellaneous ; and 9, Saving Clauses, shall extend
the Act,   to Ireland, with the modifications following :—(a)
th modifi-
  tions.
                  " Intoxicating liquor " shall mean spirits, wine, beer, porter, cider,
                  perry, and sweets, and any fermented, distilled, or spirituous
                  liquor which cannot, according to any law for the time being in
                  force, be legally sold without a licence from the Commissioners
                  of Inland Revenue :

                  " Licence " shall mean a certificate of Justices, under the provisions
                  of the Act passed in the session of Parliament held in the third
                  and fourth years of the reign of his late Majesty King William
                  the Fourth, chapter sixty-eight, or of the Act passed in the ses-
                  sion of Parliament held in the seventeenth and eighteenth years
                  of the reign of her present Majesty, chapter eighty-nine, and any
                  Act amending the same, and shall include a certificate under
                  " The Beerhouses (Ireland) Act, 1864," as amended by " The
                  Beerhouses (Ireland) Act, 1864, Amendment Act, 1871," and
                  any Act or Acts amending the same :

                  " Intoxicating Liquor Licensing Acts " shall include the Acts

"Sale by retail" in respect of any intoxicating liquor means the sale of that liquor in such quantity as is declared to be sale by retail of any Acts relating to the sale of intoxicating liquors :

" Owner of licensed premises " shall mean the person for the time being entitled to receive on his own account, either as mortgagee or other incumbrancer, in possession of the rackrent of such premises :

" Order in Council" or "Order of Her Majesty in Council " shall mean any order made by the Lord Lieutenant of Ireland or the Lords Justices or other chief governor or governors of Ireland for the time being, by and with the advice of Her Majesty's Privy Council in Ireland :

The powers which may be exercised by Her Majesty may be exercised as to Ireland by the Lord Lieutenant or the Lords Justices or other chief governor or governors of Ireland for the time being :

The term " Dublin Gazette " shall be substituted for the term " London Gazette.'

The term "county " shall extend to and include county of a city, county of a town, county of a town and city, city, and county :

The term "register of licences," except in the police district of Dublin metropolis, shall mean the list or register directed to be kept by section eleven of the Act passed in the session of Parliament held in the third and fourth years of the reign of his late Majesty, King William the Fourth, chapter sixty-eight ; and in the police district of Dublin metropolis a list or register to be formed by such person as may be directed by the chief magistrate of the said district in like manner in every respect and containing the like particulars in relation to the said district and the persons licensed therein, as the list or register directed to be kept elsewhere by the said section of the said Act ; and all the provisions of the said section shall, so far as the same are applicable, apply to such list or register within the said district, and the same shall be kept at the head police office of such district.

The term "Clerk to the licensing Justices" in relation to the police district of Dublin metropolis shall mean the person who keeps the register of licenses in such district, and elsewhere in any county or borough shall mean the clerk of the peace for such county or borough : (a)

The term "police authority" shall mean—

In the police district of Dublin metropolis either of the Commissioners of Police for the said district, and

Elsewhere in Ireland, in any other police district, the Sub-Inspector of the Royal Irish Constabulary :

(a) The authority as to granting original licences is thus left as it was in the Act 3 & 4 Wm. iv., ch. 68, at Quarter Sessions. The Justices in Petty Sessions grant the annual certificates for renewal. The latter also grant certificates under the Beerhouses Acts, that is, to enable persons to sell beer to be drunk *elsewhere than on the premises where sold.*

The term "superintendent of police" shall mean—

In the police district of Dublin metropolis any superintendent, inspector, acting-inspector, or sergeant of Dublin metropolitan police, and

Elsewhere in Ireland, in any other police district, any sub-inspector or head-constable of the Royal Irish Constabulary: The term "constable"—

In the police district of Dublin metropolis shall mean constable of the Dublin metropolitan police, and

Elsewhere in Ireland any constable or sub-constable of the Royal Irish Constabulary:

The term "Special Session" shall mean "Petty Sessions":

The term "Summary Jurisdiction Act, 1848," shall mean, as regards the police district of Dublin metropolis, the Acts regulating the powers and duties of Justices of the Peace for such district, and elsewhere in Ireland the Act passed in the session holden in the fourteenth and fifteenth years of the reign of Her Majesty Queen Victoria, chapter ninety-three, intituled, "An Act to "consolidate and amend the Acts regulating the proceedings of "Petty Sessions, and the duties of Justices of the Peace out of "Quarter Sessions in Ireland," and any Acts amending the same: (a)

The term "Court of Summary Jurisdiction" shall mean any Justice or Justices of the Peace or other Magistrate to whom jurisdiction is given by the Summary Jurisdiction Act, 1848; and when hearing and determining any information or complaint under this Act, the said Court shall be constituted in manner prescribed by the said first-mentioned Act:

The expression "Court of Quarter Sessions for the county or place in which the cause of appeal has arisen" shall mean the Court of Quarter Sessions of the division of the county or the Court of the Recorder of the borough (if there be a Recorder in such borough) in which the cause of appeal has arisen, and if the cause of appeal has arisen within the police district of Dublin metropolis the Court of the Recorder of the city of Dublin:

The term "one of Her Majesty's Superior Courts at Dublin" shall be substituted for the term "one of Her Majesty's Superior Courts at Westminster."

Provided always that a licence, as defined by this section, shall not be required for the sale of intoxicating liquor by retail in pursuance of a retail licence granted by the Commissioners of Inland Revenue, in any case which, previous to the passing of this Act, such first-mentioned licence was not required.

(a) "Summary Jurisdiction Act, 1848," and "Court of summary jurisdiction."—One of the above definitions appears necessary to explain the other. It may possibly be a question whether the term "Summary Jurisdiction Act, 1848," means the same under both headings; it it should not, much confusion would follow.

CLOSING HOURS. (a)

*Closing
Hours.*

78. Notwithstanding the provisions of section forty-three of the Act passed in the session of Parliament held in the twenty-third and twenty-fourth years of the reign of Her present Majesty, chapter one hundred and seven, it shall not be lawful for any person to sell or expose for sale, or to open or to keep open any premises for the sale of intoxicating liquors on Sunday, Christmas Day, Good Friday, or any day appointed for a public fast or thanksgiving after nine o'clock at night within any city or town the population of which according to the last parliamentary census shall exceed five thousand, nor elsewhere after seven o'clock at night on such days, and on other days after ten o'clock at night. (b)

Closing of premises at certain hours on Sunday, Christmas Day, Good Friday, &c.

The provisions of all Acts relating to the sale of intoxicating liquors by retail, authorizing or forbidding the doing of any act, matter, or thing at any times during which the sale of intoxicating liquors is by the said Acts prohibited, shall be construed as if the times during which the sale of intoxicating liquors is prohibited by this section were substituted respectively in the said Acts for the times therein mentioned.

Any person who sells or exposes for sale, or opens or keeps open any premises for the sale of intoxicating liquors, at any other times than those limited for such purpose by section forty-three of the Act passed in the session of Parliament held in the twenty-third and twenty-fourth years of the reign of her present Majesty, chapter one hundred and seven, as the same is amended by this section, or during such times as aforesaid allows any intoxicating liquors to be consumed on such premises, shall for the first offence be liable to a penalty not exceeding ten pounds, and for any subsequent offence to a penalty not exceeding twenty pounds.

Any conviction for an offence against this section shall be recorded on the licence of the person convicted, unless the convicting Magistrate or Justices shall otherwise direct.

None of the provisions contained in this section shall preclude a person licensed to sell any intoxicating liquor to be consumed on the premises from selling such liquor to *bona fide* travellers (c) or to persons lodging in his house.

Nothing in this section contained shall preclude the sale at any

---

(a) *Closing Hours.*—The hours at which retailers may now *keep open* to retail, under 23 & 24 Vic., cap. 107, s 43, as amended by the present Act, 35 & 36 Vic., cap. 94, s. 78, are as follows :—In cities or towns where the population exceeds 5000, on Sunday, Christmas Day, Good Friday, Public Fast or Thanksgiving Day, between 2 o'clock, P.M., and 9 o'clock, P.M. ; and on other days, between 7 o'clock, A.M., and 11 o'clock, P.M. *In other places*—On Sunday, Christmas Day, Good Friday, Public Fast or Thanksgiving Day, between 2 o'clock, P.M., and 7 o'clock, P.M. ; and on other days, between 7 o'clock, A.M., and 10 o'clock, P.M.; the alteration effected by the last Act being that in the large towns retailers should close at 9 P.M., on Sundays and holidays, leaving the week nights as before, 11 o'clock. *Elsewhere*, the closing hours on Sunday and holiday nights will be 7 o'clock, and on the other week nights, 10 o'clock. And as to persons found on premises during " Closing Hours," see sec. 27, 37 & 38 Vic., chap. 69.

(b) As to what will be proof of sale or consumption, see sec. 62.
(c) *Bona fide Travellers.*—Defined by 37 & 38 Vic., c. 69, sec. 28.
Privilege of Lodgers at an Inn.—The Superior Courts in Scotland, looking at the hardship and inconvenience likely to result from a too narrow interpretation of the

Licensing Act, 1872.

time at a railway station of intoxicating liquors to persons arriving at or departing from such station by railroad.

Closing Hours.

79. All penalties and forfeitures in respect of offences under the preceding provisions of this Act, as applied to Ireland, shall be in

Recovery and application of penalties.

substitution for and not in addition to penalties and forfeitures (other than penalties recoverable by or on behalf of the Commissioners of Inland Revenue, or any laws relating to the excise) incurred in respect of like offences under any other Act or Acts, and all penalties recovered under the said provisions of this Act shall be applied in manner directed by "The Fines Act (Ireland), 1851," and any Act amending the same. (a)

Repeal of section 4 of 34 & 35 Vic. c. 88.

80. Section four of "The Intoxicating Liquors (Licences Suspension) Act, 1871," shall be and the same is hereby repealed.

81. The following provisions shall apply to Ireland only :

Spirit Grocers.

SPIRIT GROCERS.

Interpretation of "spirit grocer," "excise licence," &c., as applying to Ireland.

The term "Spirit Grocer" in the following provisions of this Act means any person dealing in or selling tea, cocoa-nuts, chocolate, or pepper, and having an excise licence to sell spirits by retail in any quantity not exceeding two quarts at any one time to be consumed elsewhere than on the premises where sold, under the provisions of the Act passed in the session of Parliament held in the eighth and ninth years of the reign of her present Majesty, chapter sixty-four, which licence is in the following provisions referred to as an "excise licence," and, save as aforesaid, terms

exceptions in the Licensing Act, as to lodgers at an inn, and their guests, who may not be lodgers or travellers, have, by virtue of their inherent right, determined to uphold ancient privileges and Common Law principles, until removed by more explicit legislation.

High Court of Justiciary (Scotland), 27th Oct., 1882. (Before Lord Justice Clerk, Lords Young and Craighill) On appeal, *Gemmell* v *Fleck.* Appellant was Procurator-Fiscal Lord of Haddington, and the Respondent a hotel-keeper in North Berwick. The appeal was from a dismissal by the Justices, the charge being that persons not lodgers or travellers were found consuming liquors during the closing hours Lord Young—I learn that the guests of lodgers consume drink between 11 and 12 o'clock. Is that illegal? It is quite new. I never heard it before. Mr. M'Kechnie—The Act makes well-known exceptions as to travellers, and there was no objection to guests remaining in the house. Lord Justice Clerk—Suppose the Court on circuit and sat till 11 o'clock, could they not dine with counsel after that hour? Lord Craighill—How would the law affect a Provost dining with them? There must be a reasonable allowance made in all these matters. The Court dismissed the appeal.

A like view was taken of an appeal in *Murray* v. *M'Dougall,* 7th Feb, 1883. Lord Justice Clerk concluded his judgment by stating that the statute did not prevent a lodger giving a friend refreshment at his own charge and on his own order. It was supplying to a guest of an inmate in the house, whose home the house temporarily was. Unless the Superior Courts in England or Ireland decide the other way, the Justices in Ireland may, with safety, adopt the foregoing views in *bona fide* cases. For, as Lord Craighill observes, "there must be a reasonable allowance made in all these matters."

(a) And see Amended Act, 37 & 38 Vic., c. 69, s. 30, as to towns where Towns Improvement Act, 17 & 18 Vic., c. 103, and 9 Geo. iv., c. 82, are in force, as to penalties under section 12.

"Sunday Closing Act."—Act prohibiting sale of liquor on Sundays, 41 & 42 Vic. c. 72, Dublin, Cork, Limerick, Waterford, Belfast, excepted, during certain hours (2 P.M. to 7 P.M.) Act expires in December, 1882, unless renewed. It will probably be continued, and the places now excepted are likely to be included

used in the following provisions of this Act shall have the same meanings respectively as they have in the preceding provisions of this Act, as applied to Ireland.

82. It shall not be lawful for any officer of excise in Ireland to grant a new excise licence to any person who at any time during the then next preceding two years has been a spirit grocer, or who during such period as aforesaid has held a certificate under "The Beerhouses (Ireland) Act, 1864," or "The Beerhouses (Ireland) Act (1864) Amendment Act, 1871," or to grant to any spirit grocer upon the expiration of his excise licence a renewal of such excise licence, unless such person or spirit grocer produces a certificate signed by two or more Justices of the Peace presiding at the petty sessions of the district in which such person or spirit grocer resides, or if in the Dublin metropolitan police district by a Divisional Justice of the District in which such person or spirit grocer resides, to the good character of such person, and to the peaceable and orderly manner in which his business was conducted during the year next preceding the expiration of his former excise licence or certificate, or, in case of a renewal, during the past year. (a)

No renewal of licence to be granted to spirit grocers without certificate of Justices.

All applications for such certificates shall be made in the manner and subject to the like conditions as to appeals against the same and otherwise (so far as the same are applicable) as are prescribed by "The Beerhouses (Ireland) Act, 1864," in relation to applications for certificates under the said Act.

83. If any purchaser of any intoxicating liquor from a spirit grocer drinks such liquor on the premises where the same is sold, or on any highway adjoining or near such premises, such spirit grocer shall, if it shall appear that such drinking was with his privity or consent, be subject to the following penalties : that is to say,

Penalty on spirit grocer if liquor drunk on or near to the premises.

> For the first offence he shall be liable to a penalty not exceeding ten pounds :
> For the second and any subsequent offence he shall be liable to a penalty not exceeding twenty pounds :
> For the purposes of this section the expression "premises where the same is sold" shall include any premises adjoining or near the premises where the liquor is sold, if belonging to such spirit grocer, or under his control, or used by his permission.

Any conviction for an offence under this section shall be recorded on the excise licence of the spirit grocer convicted.

84. If any spirit grocer himself takes or carries, or employs or suffers any other person to take or carry any intoxicating liquor out of or from the premises of such spirit grocer for the purpose of being sold on his account, or for his benefit or profit, and of being drunk or consumed in any other house or in any tent, shed, or other building of any kind whatever, belonging to such spirit grocer, or hired, used, or occupied by him, or on or in any place, whether enclosed or

Penalty on evasion of law as to drinking on premises of spirit grocer.

(a) *Section 82.*—The provisions of above sec 82, relating to new and renewals of excise licences are by sec. 9 of Amended Act extended to transfers of excise licences.

not, and whether or not a public thoroughfare, such intoxicating liquor shall be deemed to have been consumed by the purchaser thereof on the premises of such spirit grocer, with his privity and consent; and such spirit grocer shall be punished accordingly in manner provided by the next preceding section.

Any conviction for an offence under this section shall be recorded on the excise licence of the spirit grocer convicted.

In any proceeding under this section it shall not be necessary to prove that the premises or place or places to which such liquor is taken to be drunk belonged to or were hired, used, or occupied by such spirit grocer, if proof be given to the satisfaction of the Court hearing the case that such liquor was taken to be consumed thereon or therein with intent to evade the conditions of his excise licence.

Penalty on internal communication between premises of spirit grocer and house of public resort. 85. Every person who makes or uses, or allows to be made or used, any internal communication between the premises of any spirit grocer and any other premises which are used for public entertainment or resort, or as a refreshment house, shall be liable to a penalty not exceeding ten pounds for every day during which such communication remains open.

In addition to any penalty imposed by this section, any person convicted of an offence under this section shall, if he be the holder of an excise licence, forfeit such licence.

Limitation of hours during which spirit grocers may sell intoxicating liquors. 86. No spirit grocer shall have or keep his premises open, nor shall he sell any intoxicating liquor in any such premises at any other times than those limited for the sale of intoxicating liquors by retail to be drunk or consumed on the premises by section forty-three of the Act passed in the session of Parliament held in the twenty-third and

to apprehend and take into custody any such person so offending, and Licensing
Act. 1872.
to carry and convey, or cause to be carried and conveyed, every and
any such person so apprehended before any Justice of the Peace within *Spirit*
Grocers.
whose jurisdiction such premises shall be situate, to be dealt with
according to law ; and every such person who shall so neglect or refuse
to remove from or quit such premises, or shall so forcibly resist such
Justice, superintendent, or constable, being duly convicted of such
offence, shall, thereupon for every such offence forfeit any sum not
exceeding twenty shillings, nor less than five shillings; and if any
offender so convicted shall not forthwith pay the sum so forfeited,
such offender shall be imprisoned for any time not exceeding one
week. (*a*)

88. The preceding provisions of this Act, relating to repeated con-Provisions as
victions, except so much therof as relate to the disqualification of to repeated
convictions
premises, shall apply to spirit grocers, and for the purpose of such to apply to
application the terms "spirit grocer" and excise licence" shall spirit
respectively be therein substituted for the terms licensed person and grocers, &c.
licence. (*b*)

89. The preceding provisions of this Act relating to legal pro-Application
ceedings as the same are applied to Ireland, and to the application of of provisions
as to legal
penalties in Ireland, shall apply to all legal proceedings in respect of proceedings,
any of the special provisions of this Act relating to Ireland, and to penalties, &c.
the application of all penalties recovered in pursuance thereof.

90. In Ireland no licence or excise licence, as respectively defined No licence
in the preceding provisions of this Act in relation to Ireland, shall be to be
granted to
granted under the Intoxicating Liquor Licensing Acts to any person disqualified
or in respect of any persons declared by or in pursuance of any of persons or
the Intoxicating Liquor Licensing Acts or this Act to be disqualified for disquali-
fied premises.
persons or disqualified premises during the continuance of such dis-
qualification. Any licence or excise licence held by any person so
disqualified or attached to premises so disqualified shall be void.

SCHEDULES TO WHICH THIS ACT REFERS.

First Schedule. (*c*)

Deleterious Ingredients.

Cocculus indicus ; chloride of sodium, otherwise common salt;
copperas, opium, Indian hemp, strychnine, tobacco, darnel seed, extract of logwood, salts of zinc, or lead, alum, and any extract or
compound of any of the above ingredients.

(*a*) *Right of Entry.*—Under the Amended Act, 37 & 38 Vic , c. 69, sec. 23, a constable may, on his own authority, now enter at all times into licensed premises, or premises kept by a *spirit grocer;* and for refusing or failing to admit him, the penalty is,
not exceeding five pounds for first, ten pounds for second offence.
    (*b*) The discretionary power in the Justices as to recording the convictions is also
applicable to spirit grocers.
    (*c*) The First Schedule as to Deleterious Ingredients is repealed with the
adulteration clauses in Act, by Amended Act, 37 & 38 Vic., c. 69, sec. 38, sub-
sec. 1.

SECOND SCHEDULE.

Session and Chapter.	Title.	Extent of Repeal.
23 & 24 Vic. c. 113	An Act to grant duties of excise on chicory and on licences to dealers in sweets or made wines, also to reduce the excise duty on hops, and the period of credit allowed for payment of the duty on malt and hops respectively; to repeal the exemption from licence duty of persons dealing in foreign wine and spirits in bond, and to amend the laws relating to the excise.	Section forty-one.
34 & 35 Vic. c. 88.	An Act to restrict during a limited time the grant by Justices of the Peace of new licences and certificates for the sale of intoxicating liquors by retail, and for other purposes.	The whole Act.

NOTE.—There are several other Acts which were in force in England repealed by this Schedule. The above were the only ones affecting Ireland.

EARLY-CLOSING LICENCES, LICENCES, AND EXCISE LICENCES.

Early-closing Licences, Licences, and Excise Licences.

2. Where, on the occasion of any application for a certificate for a new licence, or the transfer or renewal of a licence which authorizes the sale of any intoxicating liquor for consumption on the premises, the applicant applies to the licensing Justices, to cause to be inserted in his licence a condition that he shall close the premises in respect of which such licence is or is to be granted one hour earlier at night than that at which such premises would otherwise have to be closed, the Justices shall cause the said condition to be inserted in such certificate, and the same shall be inserted in any licence granted in pursuance thereof. (a)

Early-closing licences.

The holder of a licence in which such condition is inserted (in this Act referred to as an early-closing licence) shall close his premises at night one hour earlier than the ordinary hour at which such premises would be closed under the provisions of the principal Act, and the provisions of this Act and the principal Act shall apply to the premises as if such earlier hour were the hour at which the premises are required to be closed.

The applicant for an earlier-closing licence may obtain from the Commissioners of Inland Revenue any licence granted by such Commissioners which he is entitled to obtain in pursuance of any such certificate as aforesaid, upon payment of a sum representing six-sevenths of the duty which would otherwise be payable by him for a similar licence not limited to such earlier closing as aforesaid. In calculating, the six-seventh fraction of a penny shall be disregarded.

. The notice which a licensed person is required by section eleven of the principal Act to keep painted or fixed on his premises shall, in the case of an early-closing licence, contain such words as the licensing Justices may order for giving notice to the public that an early-closing licence has been granted in respect of such premises. (b)

3. A person who takes out a licence containing conditions rendering such licence a six-day licence as well as an early-closing licence shall be entitled to a remission of two-sevenths of the duty.

Remission of duty in case of six-day and early-closing licence.

4. Any person selling or exposing for sale any intoxicating liquor in any booth, tent, or place within the limits of holding any lawful and accustomed fair or any races, without an occasional licence authorizing such sale, shall, notwithstanding anything contained in any Act of Parliament to the contrary, be deemed to be a person selling or exposing for sale by retail intoxicating liquor at a place where he is not authorized by his licence to sell the same, and be punishable accordingly.

Occasional licence required at fairs and races.

Provided that this section shall not apply to any person selling or exposing for sale intoxicating liquors in premises in which he is duly authorized to sell the same throughout the year, although such premises are situate within the limits aforesaid.

(a) This condition is to be inserted by the Justices in Quarter Sessions or Recorder, as in cases of six-day licences.

(b) *Notice.*—That is, the notification to the public, as to the early closing, shall be in addition to what is directed under sec. 11 of the principal Act, as amended by sec. 26 of above Act.

LICENSING
ACT, 1874.

*Early-
closing
Licences,
Licences,
and Excise
Licences.*

Occasional
licences—
extension of
time for
closing.

Offences on
premises
with occa-
sional
licence.
Restrictions
as to licences
under
5 & 6 Wm. iv.
c. 39, s. 7.

5. Whereas by the twentieth section of the Act of the session of the twenty-sixth and twenty-seventh years of the reign of her present Majesty, chapter thirty-three, it is provided that the hours during which an occasional licence shall authorize the sale of any beer, spirits, or wine shall extend from sunrise until one hour after sunset : Be it enacted that the said section shall be construed as if in place of the words "sunrise until one hour after sunset " there were inserted the words "such hour, not earlier than sunrise, until such hour, not later than ten o'clock at night as may be specified in that behalf in the consent given by the justice for the granting of such occasional licence."(a)

6. For the purpose of so much of the principal Act as relates to offences against public order, that is to say, sections twelve to eighteen, both inclusive, and the sections for giving effect to the same, a person taking out an occasional licence shall be deemed to be a licensed person within the meaning of the said sections, and the place in which any intoxicating liquors are sold in pursuance of the occasional licence shall be deemed to be licensed premises, and to be the premises of the person taking out such a licence. (b)

7. From and after the passing of this Act it shall not be lawful for any person under the authority of any licence granted under the authority of section seven of the Act of the session of the fifth and sixth years of the reign of his late Majesty King William the Fourth, intituled "An Act to exempt certain retailers of spirits to a small amount from the additional duties on licences, and to discontinue the excise and survey on wine, and the use of permits for the removal thereof" to sell or expose for sale by retail any intoxicating liquors elsewhere than within the part or parts of the theatre or other place

8. It shall not be lawful for any officer of excise in Ireland to grant a wholesale beer dealer's licence, or to grant a renewal or transfer of any such licence to any person unless such person shall produce a certificate to the effect, and as required by section three of "The Beerhouses (Ireland) Act, 1864," with respect to the grant, renewal, or transfer of the licence to sell beer by retail therein mentioned.

All applications for such certificate shall be made in the manner and subject to the like conditions as to appeals against the same and otherwise (so far as the same are applicable) as are prescribed by "The Beerhouses (Ireland) Act, 1864," in relation to applications for certificates under the said Act, as the same are amended by this Act. (a)

9. The provisions of section eighty-two of the principal Act, relating to the grant of new excise licence and of renewals of excise licences to certain persons therein described, shall extend to the transfer of excise licences, and the said provisions so extended shall not be limited to the case of such persons, but shall extend and apply to all such transfers and grants when made to any other persons : Provided always, that in the case of a new excise licence or transfer of an excise licence under this section the certificate shall be to the good character of the person applying for the same and to the suitability of the premises.

10. Every person intending to apply for a new licence or for the transfer of a licence, instead of serving notice, as hitherto required by the Act of the session of the third and fourth years of the reign of King William the Fourth, chapter sixty-eight, section two, upon the churchwardens of the parish or union wherein the premises sought to be licensed are situate, shall, on some day not more than four and not less than two weeks before the intended application is to be heard, cause to be inserted or advertised in some paper circulating in the place in which such premises are situate a notice conformable to the requirements of the said section two. (b)

Marginal notes:

LICENSING ACT, 1874.

Early-closing Licences, Licences, and Excise Licences.

Certificates required, previously to grant of wholesale beer dealer's licence.

Provisions of section 82 of principal Act extended.

Notice of intended application for licence.

---

they are hereby authorized and empowered, to grant retail licences to any person to sell beer, spirits, and wine in any theatre established under a royal patent, or in any theatre or other place of public entertainment licensed by the Lord Chamberlain, or by Justices of the Peace, without the production by the person applying for such licence or licences of any certificate or authority for such person to keep a common inn, ale-house, or victualling-house, anything in any Act or Acts to the contrary notwithstanding."

(a) The Beerhouses (Ireland) Act, 1864, is the 27 & 28 Vic., c. 35. The excise licence under it is " *to sell beer to be consumed elsewhere than on the premises where sold.*" It can only be obtained on the certificate of two Justices in Petty Sessions (Divisional Justice in Dublin) as to good character of the applicant. and the suitability of the premises. Applicant must first give notice to police officer of district. A wholesale beer dealer's licence is defined at sec. 37 of this Act.

(b) *Section* 10.—This notice to be advertised in local paper is in lieu of that required to be served on churchwardens, but does not dispense with the other notices required to be served on Clerk of the Peace, and two next Magistrates, &c., and that required by 17 & 18 Vic., c. 89, a. 9, to be served on constabulary officer.

Exemption Order.—But the place being open, the sales cannot well be confined to those persons having business at the fair. The 78th section of the principal Act allows sale of liquor at any time at railway stations to persons arriving at or departing from such station by railroad. The Justices can limit the order to one particular fair or market day. and on the return of each such day make the renewal of the order necessary, or may give a general order mentioning the particular days. The Justices may at any time vary the order, or withdraw it altogether; but where one bench of Magistrates grant the exemption it would not seem to be in the power of another bench by way of opposition to vary or withdraw it.

TERMS FOR GRANT OF CERTIFICATES.

14. It shall be lawful for the Lord Lieutenant or other chief governor or governors of Ireland at any time within six months after the passing of this Act, by and with the advice and consent of the Privy Council, by order to be published in the Dublin Gazette, to constitute ... of the General or Quarter Sessions of the peace now usually holden

in and for the several divisions of counties or ridings, counties of cities. and counties of towns, cities, towns, and boroughs, to be the annual licensing Quarter Sessions for such divisions of counties and ridings, and for such counties of cities, counti‑s of towns, cities, towns, and boroughs respectively, and with the like advice and consent, by order to be published in the *Dublin Gazette*, to appoint for each Petty Sessions district and for the police district of Dublin metropolis a time for holding annual licensing Petty Sessions for each such district.

(margin: LICENSING ACT, 1874. Times for Grant of Certificates.)

From and after the publication in the *Dublin Gazette* of such orders respectively, and the constitution and appointment thereby of annual licensing Quarter Sessions and of annual licensing Petty Sessions, the provisions following shall apply : (a)

(margin: tenant and Privy Council to fix times for grant of certificate.)

1. Where under the provisions of any Act now in force or hereafter to be passed, the production of a certificate of Justices in Quarter Sessions assembled, or of a Recorder of any city, town, or borough, is required previous to the grant of any licence by an officer of excise, such certificate shall (save as hereinafter provided) not be granted except at an annual licensing Quarter Sessions : Provided always that in case any licence shall, under the authority of the Act of the session of the eighteenth and nineteenth years of the reign of Her present Majesty, chapter one hundred and fourteen, be transferred to any person, and in such other cases as may seem fit to such Justices or Recorder, a certificate may, notwithstanding the preceding provisions, be granted at any general or Quarter Sessions (other than the annual licensing Quarter Sessions), and in like manner as heretofore ; but any licence granted in pursuance of any such last-mentioned certificate shall only continue in force until the annual licensing Quarter Sessions held next after the grant of such certificate, unless at such annual licensing Quarter Sessions such certificate shall be confirmed, and in case such certificate shall not be then confirmed, the licence granted in pursuance thereof shall not be renewed.

(margin: As to Quarter Sessions certificates.)

2. Where under the provisions of this Act, or any Act now in force or hereafter to be passed, the production of a certificate by Justices presiding at Petty Sessions, or of a Divisional Justice in the police district of Dublin, is required previous to the grant or transfer of any licence or of an excise licence, or of a wholesale

(margin: At to Petty Sessions certificate.)

(a) *Times for granting Certificates.*—There will be but *one annual licensing Quarter Sessions* for the granting of certificates, with a special provision for granting certificates where Justices in Petty Sessions grant temporary transfers under 18 & 19 Vic., c. 114, and in any other fit case; but licence granted on such shall only continue in force until the annual licensing Sessions. *As to Petty Sessions certificates* required previous to grant or transfer of any licence, excise licence, or wholesale beer dealers' licence (such as beer dealers under 27 & 28 Vic., c. 35; spirit grocers under 35 & 36 Vic., c. 94, s. 82; wholesale beer dealers under 37 & 38 Vic., c. 69, s. 8); these shall only be granted at the annual licensing Petty Sessions, with a *proviso* that in such cases as may seem fit to the Justices, in all cases of the *transfers of such licences* certificates may be granted at any other time; but licences granted on such shall only continue until the annual licensing Petty Sessions. If certificates be not then confirmed the licences shall not be renewed. The annual certificates required by traders previous to renewal of their licences from the excise, and granted in Petty Sessions under 17 & 18 Vic., c. 89, s 11, and as amended by sec. 14 of the Licensing Act, 1874, are granted as heretofore.

Canteens.—To person holding canteen under War Department, two Justices may at any time grant licence or transfer to such person. See Army Act.

CENSING
OT, 1874.

*imes for
'rant of
Certi-
tes.*

beer dealer's licence by an officer of excise, such certificate shall
not (save as hereinafter provided) be granted except at an
annual licensing Petty Sessions : Provided always, that in such
cases as may seem fit to such Justices sitting in Petty Sessions, or
to such Divisional Justice, and in all cases in which a certificate
is required from such Justice or Justices for the transfer of a
licence, or of an excise licence, or of a wholesale beer dealer's
licence, a certificate may, notwithstanding the preceding provisions, be granted at any time other than that fixed for annual
licensing Petty Sessions, and in like manner as heretofore; but
any licence granted in pursuance of any such certificate shall
only continue in force until the annual licensing Petty Sessions
held next after the grant of such certificate, unless at such
annual licensing Petty Sessions such certificate shall be confirmed,
and in case such certificate shall not be then confirmed, the
licence, or excise licence, or wholesale beer dealer's licence
granted in pursuance thereof shall not be renewed.

porary
ntinuance
licences,
excise
ences,
rfeited
thout dis-
alification
premises.

13. Where any licensed person or spirit grocer is convicted for the
first time of any one of the following offences : (a)

1. Making an internal communication between the premises of
such licensed person or spirit grocer and any unlicensed premises ;

2. Selling spirits without a spirit licence ;

3. Any felony ;

and in consequence either becomes personally disqualified, or has his
licence forfeited, there may be made by or on behalf of the owner of

that where such Quarter Sessions or Petty Sessions shall not be the annual licensing Quarter Sessions, or the annual licensing Petty Sessions, application for a transfer of such licence to some person other than the person convicted may be made and granted or refused in like manner, and on the same conditions, and for the same time, as if the person convicted had removed from such premises, and the person applying for such grant was his assignee.

LICENSING
ACT, 1874.

*Times for
Grant of
Certi-
ficates.*

14. Where a person licensed to sell intoxicating liquors, to be consumed on the premises, applies for a certificate for the renewal of his licence, the following provisions shall have effect :—

Provisions
on annual
renewal of
certificate.

> He need not attend in person at the Court unless he is required by the Justices or police authority so to attend, for some special cause personal to himself.

> The Justices shall not entertain any objection to the signing of such certificate, or receive any evidence with respect to same unless a written notice of intention to oppose be served on the applicant not later than seven days before the holding of such Session, stating in general terms the grounds on which the renewal of such licence is to be opposed.

> The Justices may, notwithstanding that no notice of objection has been served, if objection is made in Court, adjourn the signing of the certificate to a future day, and require the attendance of the applicant.

> The Justices shall not receive any evidence with respect to the signing of such certificate which is not given on oath in open Court. (a)

REGISTER OF LICENCES.

*Register of
Licences.*

15. Whereas by section ten of the Act of the session of the third and fourth years of the reign of His late Majesty King William the Fourth, chapter sixty-eight, provision is made that every person who

Amendment
of sects 10
and 11 of
3 & 4 Wm. iv.
c. 68.

(a) *Section 14.—Renewal Certificate.*—This annual certificate may be refused by the Justices on grounds and for offences different from those in the Licensing Acts. It is as to the character of the trader and the manner in which his place of sale has been conducted in the past year. The convictions under the Licensing Acts speak for themselves, and if they accumulate to a forfeiture there is an end to the licence; still, even one conviction within the year may be of such a nature and committed under such circumstances as that added to the general character of the trade, and the mode in which his place of sale is conducted, may compel the Magistrates to refuse the certificate which as to good character and conduct is positive. The Justices cannot refuse this certificate on the grounds that the applicant is not known to them. He is entitled to it unless sufficient grounds be shown for withholding it. They now hold what amounts to a judicial inquiry, and even though a Justice should be personally aware of objections to the certificate being granted, it will be his duty to judge by evidence offered on oath, and if he has any to offer he ought to leave the bench and give his testimony accordingly. The 17 & 18 Vic. c. 89. s. 11, is that under which Magistrates sit for the granting of certificates to licensed retailers of beer and spirits, &c., to be drunk and consumed on the premises or elsewhere. The 18 & 19 Vic., c. 62, s. 2, as amended by 23 & 24 Vic., c. 55, gives right of appeal from an order of refusal. The 27 & 28 Vic., c. 35, is that which provides for the granting of certificates to retailers of beer to be drunk and consumed elsewhere than on the premises where sold, with right of appeal from order of refusal as above.

Section 15.—The 3 & 4 Wm. iv., c. 68, secs. 10, 24, provides a penalty of £10, and not less than 50s. for omitting to make the entry of the excise licence with the Clerk of the Peace.

LICENSING ACT, 1874.

Register of Licences.

shall obtain a licence shall, within six days next after he shall have obtained such licence, deliver or cause to be delivered to the clerk of the peace of the county, city, or town in which the house mentioned in such licence is situate, a note in writing, signed by him or on his behalf, in which shall be specified the Christian and surname and place of abode of such person, and other the particulars in said section mentioned ; and by section eleven of the said Act provision is made for the entry by such clerk of the peace in a list or register to be kept by him of the particulars specified in every such note, and it is expedient to amend the said sections : Be it therefore enacted that, in addition to the particulars required by said section ten of the said Act, every such note shall contain the name and address of the owner of the house in which intoxicating liquors are licensed to be sold by the person by or on whose behalf such note shall be signed, and the same shall be in the form in the Schedule (A) to this Act annexed, and the clerk of the peace, to whom such note shall be delivered, in the said list or register to be kept by him as aforesaid shall enter the name and address of every such owner in addition to the particulars prescribed by said section eleven.

The clerk of the peace of every county, city, and town shall, from time to time, transmit to the clerk of Petty Sessions of each Petty Sessions district within such county, city, or town, and in Dublin to the chief clerk of the Metropolitan Police Court, a copy of every entry made by him in pursuance of the said Act and this Act relating to any house or place in such district.

Register of licences to

16. There shall be kept in every Petty Sessions district, by the clerk

as hereinafter mentioned, be deemed, for the purposes of the principal Act and this Act, the owner of the premises. *Licensing Act, 1874.*

A Court of summary jurisdiction in any Petty Sessions district may, on the application of any person who proves to the Court that he is entitled to be entered as owner of any premises in such district in place of the person appearing on the register to be the owner, make an order substituting the name of the applicant, and such order shall be obeyed by the clerk of Petty Sessions of such district, and a corresponding correction may be directed to be made on the certificate and licence or excise licence granted in respect of the premises of which such applicant claims to be the owner. *Register of Licences.*

Any ratepayer, any owner of premises to which a licence or excise licence or wholesale beer dealer's licence is attached, and any holder of a licence or excise licence, within any Petty Sessions district, shall, upon payment of a fee of one shilling, and any officer of police and any officer of excise in such district, without payment, shall be entitled at any reasonable time to inspect and take copies of or extracts from any register kept in pursuance of this section ; and the clerk of Petty Sessions and every other person who prevents the inspection or taking copies of or extracts from the same, or demands any unauthorized fee therefor, shall be liable to a penalty not exceeding five pounds for each offence.

The preceding provisions of this section shall apply to the police district of Dublin metropolis : Provided always, that the register in such district shall be kept by the chief clerk of the Dublin Metropolitan Police Court, and that the terms " Petty Sessions District," and " district," and " Clerk of Petty Sessions," shall be construed to mean respectively the police district of Dublin metropolis, and the chief clerk of the Dublin Metropolitan Police Court.

17. From and after the first day of September, one thousand eight hundred and seventy-four, there shall be paid a fee of five shillings upon every certificate given for the grant of a new licence, new excise licence, or new wholesale beer dealer's licence, or for the transfer of any licence, excise licence, or wholesale beer dealer's licence, by a divisional Justice of the police district of Dublin metropolis, or by Justices in Petty Sessions, and no other fee or stamp duty shall be payable in respect of any such certificate or the entry thereof. *Fee upon certificate in certain cases.*

PAYMENT &c., OF FEES.
Payment, &c., of Fees.

18. All fees under this Act payable in Dublin shall be paid to the chief clerk of the Metropolitan Police Court, and shall be paid and accounted for, and payment of the same may be enforced in like manner, subject to the same conditions, and by the like means in *Payment of fees in Dublin.*

Section 17.—Fees on Petty Sessions Certificates.—There is but one Petty Sessions in the year for the *granting* and for the *transferring* of licences (sec. 12). This fee of 5s. will then be payable on the certificate for the original grant of any new licence, new excise licence, new beer dealer's licence, and also on all *certificates of transfers granted* of these and all such licences. It will also be payable on any *provisional certificate* granted under sub-sec. 2, sec. 12, but, it would appear, not again on the *confirmation* of this certificate at the annual Licensing Petty Sessions. The section does not include the annual renewal certificates under 17 & 18 Vic., c. 89, s. 11. The fee is not payable on " Occasional Licences."

<table>
<tr><td>LICENSING ACT, 1874.

Payment &c., of Fees.

Payment of fees in Petty Sessions district.</td><td>every respect as fines payable under the Acts regulating the powers and duties of Justices of the Peace for such district, and the same shall be applied towards defraying the expense of the police establishment of the said district.

19. All fees under this Act payable in any Petty Sessions district shall not be received in money, but by stamps denoting the amount of the fees payable.

Every exemption order under this Act, and every certificate given in any Petty Sessions district, upon which a fee is by this Act made payable, shall be printed or written, or partly printed and partly written, upon paper bearing a stamp denoting the amount of such fee.

All the provisions of "The Petty Sessions Clerk (Ireland) Act, 1858," with respect to the documents enumerated in the Schedule C to the said Act annexed, and to the payment of the fees in respect thereof, and to the stamps denoting the amount of such fees, and to the payment of fees, and to stamps and the providing of and supply of the same, and the payment and accounting for the same, and enforcing the payment thereof, and generally with respect to all matters relating thereto shall extend, and be applicable with respect to all exemption orders under this Act and certificates given in Petty Sessions district upon which fees are by this Act made payable, and to all fees and stamps under this Act, in like manner in every respect as if such exemption orders, certificates, fees, and stamps were included amongst the documents, fees, and stamps mentioned in the said Petty Sessions Clerk (Ireland) Act, 1858.</td></tr>
</table>

RECORD OF CONVICTIONS AND PENALTIES.

<table>
<tr><td>Record of Convictions and Penalties.

Mitigation of penalties.</td><td>20. The sixty-seventh section of the principal Act is hereby repealed; and in lieu thereof be it enacted, that where any person holding a licence or excise licence is convicted of any offence against this or the principal Act, or against any of the Acts recited or mentioned therein, the Court may not, except in the case of a first offence, reduce the penalty to less than twenty shillings, nor shall the penalty, whether of excise or police, be reduced in any case to less than the minimum authorized by any other Act.</td></tr>
<tr><td>Record of convictions on licences.</td><td>21. Where any licensed person or spirit grocer is convicted of any offence against the principal Act which by such Act was to have been or might have been indorsed upon the licence or excise licence, or of</td></tr>
</table>

Section 20.—*Mitigation.*—The minimum penalty to be imposed on licensed persons under sec. 67 of the principal Act was twenty shillings. The Justices are not now, in first offences, bound to that sum; still the giving a power as above, and at same time sending the Justices to consult other Acts, with directions that they shall not reduce the penalty to less than the minimum in other Acts, wherever these other Acts are to be found, is very confusing, and a mistake of their power may render the conviction useless. There are offences dealt with by these Licensing Acts, such as selling without licence, contrary to licence, in places not authorized by licence, without an occasional licence, &c., and under these the minimum penalties under the excise laws are very high, and not less than the "*minimum authorized by any other Act*" would be the highest of the law; so that, to be at the safe side, the Justices may, in some cases reluctantly be driven to take the maximum in the present Acts. With few exceptions the penalties on publicans, under 3 & 4 Wm. iv., c. 68, and 6 & 7 Wm. iv., c. 38, were two pounds, with power to mitigate to ten shillings for sales during the closing hours.

Section 21.—*Records of Convictions.*—These records are henceforward to be made in the "Register of Licences," directed to be kept in sec. 16, and the Justices, before

any offence against this Act, the Court before whom the offender is brought shall cause the register of licences in which the licence or excise licence of the offender is entered, or a copy of the entries therein relating to the licence or excise licence of the offender, certified in manner prescribed by this Act, to be produced to the Court before passing sentence ; and after inspecting the entries therein in relation to the licence or excise licence of the offender, or such copy thereof as aforesaid, the Court shall declare, as part of its sentence, whether it will or will not cause the conviction for such offence to be recorded on the licence or excise licence of the offender, and if it decide that such record is to be made, the same shall be made accordingly.

A declaration by the Court that a record of an offence is to be made on a licence or excise licence shall be deemed to be part of the conviction or order of the Court in reference to such offence, and shall be subject accordingly to the jurisdiction of the Court of Appeal.

A direction by the Court that a conviction for an offence is to be recorded on the licence or excise licence of the offender shall, for the purposes of the principal Act, be deemed equivalent to a direction or requirement by the Act that such conviction is to be recorded ; and all the provisions of the principal Act importing that convictions are required or directed by the Act to be recorded on the licence or excise licence of an offender shall be construed accordingly.

22. Where a licensed person or a spirit grocer is convicted of any offence against the provisions of any Act for the time being in force relating to the adulteration of drink, such conviction shall be entered in the proper register of licences, and may be directed to be recorded on the licence or excise licence of the offender in the same manner as if the conviction were for an offence against the principal Act, and when so recorded shall have effect as if it had been a conviction for an offence against the principal Act.

REGULATIONS AS TO ENTRY ON PREMISES.

23. Any constable may, for the purpose of preventing or detecting the violation of any of the provisions of the principal Act or this Act, which it is his duty to enforce, at all times enter on any licensed premises in respect of which an occasional licence is in force.

Every person who, by himself, or by any person in his employ, or acting by his direction or with his consent, refuses or fails to admit any constable in the execution of his duty demanding to enter in pursuance of this section, shall be liable to a penalty not exceeding for

Marginal notes:
LICENSING ACT, 1874.
Record of Convictions and Penalties.
Record of conviction for adulteration.
Regulations as to Entry on Premises.
Constable to enter on premises for enforcement of Act.

---

passing sentence, are to examine the register. This direction of the statute should be complied with strictly, although the not doing so could not make the conviction bad. Indeed the Justices ought not to look at the register until the offender has been convicted ; they are then to do so in order that the sentence be properly apportioned to the offence taken in connexion with what may appear on the register. The offences that the Justices can order to be recorded are those stated in the principal Act (except that referred to in sec. 22 of the above Act). And also convictions for offences against this Act of 1874.

the first offence five pounds, and not exceeding for the second and
every subsequent offence ten pounds. (a)

*Regula-
tions as to
Entry on
Premises.*

Search
warrant for
detection of
liquors sold
or kept con-
trary to law.

24. Any Justice of the Peace, if satisfied by information on oath
that there is reasonable ground to believe that any intoxicating
liquor is sold by retail, or exposed or kept for sale by retail at any
place within his jurisdiction, whether a building or not, in which
such liquor is not authorized to be sold by retail, may in his discretion grant a warrant under his hand, by virtue whereof it shall be
lawful for any constable named in such warrant, at any time or
times within one month from the date thereof, to enter, and if need be
by force, the place named in the warrant, and every part thereof,
and examine the same and search for intoxicating liquor therein, and
seize and remove any intoxicating liquor found therein which there
is reasonable ground to suppose is in such place for the purpose of
unlawful sale at that or any other place, and the vessels containing
such liquor; and in the event of the owner or occupier of such premises being convicted of selling by retail or exposing or keeping for
sale by retail any liquor which he is not authorized to sell by retail,
the intoxicating liquor so seized and the vessels containing such
liquor shall be forfeited.

When a constable has entered any premises in pursuance of any
such warrant as is mentioned in this section, and has seized and removed such liquor as aforesaid, any person found at the time on the
premises shall, until the contrary is proved, be deemed to have been
on such premises for the purpose of illegally dealing in intoxicating
liquor, and be liable to a penalty not exceeding forty shillings.

MISCELLANEOUS.

Miscellaneous.

25. Every person who, in any highway or other public place, whether a building or not, is so drunk as to be incapable of taking care of himself, may be detained by any constable until he can with safety to himself be discharged ; but if so detained he shall be summoned in due course to answer for such offence, and he shall not by such discharge be relieved from the liability to any penalty to which he is subject.

Drunken person may be detained if incapable of taking care of himself.

26. Whereas by section eleven of the principal Act it is provided that every licensed person shall cause to be painted or fixed, and shall keep painted or fixed on the premises in respect of which his licence is granted, in a conspicuous place and in such form and manner as the Commissioners of Inland Revenue may from time to time direct, his name with such additions as in the said Act mentioned : And whereas it is expedient to substitute in the said section the licensing Justices for the Commissioners of Inland Revenue : Be it therefore enacted :

Substitution of licensing Justices for Commissioners of Inland Revenue as respects certain notices.

> That in the said eleventh section the expression "Licensing Justices" shall be deemed to be substituted for the expression "Commissioners of Inland Revenue," and the word "Justices" for the word "Commissioners."

27. If during any period during which any premises are required under the provisions of the principal Act to be closed any person is found on such premises, he shall, unless he satisfies the Court that he was an inmate, servant, or a lodger on such premises, or a *bonâ fide* traveller, or that otherwise his presence on such premises was not in contravention of the provisions of the principal Act with respect to the closing of licensed premises and premises kept by a spirit grocer, be liable to a penalty not exceeding forty shillings.

Penalty on person found on premises during closing hours.

Any constable may demand the name and address of any person found on any premises during the period during which they are required by the provisions of the principal Act to be closed, and if he has reasonable ground to suppose that the name and address given is false, may require evidence of the correctness of such name and address, and may, if such person fail upon such demand to give his

---

Sec. 25.—Persons drunk and incapable may be detained.—It does not mean that the constable is bound to stand still with him until he becomes perfectly sober. He can do so if he likes ; but he can also remove him to a lock-up or police station. The *safety* of the drunken person becomes an important part of the duty, and he ought not to be set at liberty until it may be done " with safety to himself;" but once a person is so detained he must be summoned. See also notes on offences, " Drunk, and drunk and incapable," sec. 12 of principal Act, "*Analysis.*"

Sec. 27.— Persons found on premises during closing hours.—This section, by dealing with the persons found on the licensed premises, while it does not absolve the trader, it does relieve him in a most effectual way of customers whom he may have wished, but had not the courage, to expel. Their being involved in the consequences, or, in any case, subjected to much inconvenience, must help materially to diminish tippling during the closing hours. By this section persons found on premises of *spirit grocer* during the hours in which the premises should be closed will, unless they can show that their presence there is not in contravention of the Act as to closing, be liable to the penalty.

name and address, or such evidence, apprehend him **without warrant**, and carry him as soon as practicable before a Justice of the Peace.

*Miscel-
laneous.*

Any person required by a constable under this section to give his name and address who fails to give the same, or gives a **false name** or address, or gives false evidence with respect to such **name or address**, shall be liable to a penalty not exceeding five pounds.

Every person who by falsely representing himself to **be a traveller** or a lodger buys or obtains or attempts to buy or **obtain at any** premises any intoxicating liquor during the period during **which such** premises are closed in pursuance of the principal Act, **shall be liable** to a penalty not exceeding five pounds. (*a*)

Saving as to
bona fide
travellers.
28. If in the course of any proceedings which **may be taken against** any person licensed to sell any intoxicating liquor to **be consumed on** the premises for infringing the provisions of the principal Act relating to the closing of premises, such person (in this section **referred to** as the defendant) fails to prove that the person to whom **the intoxi-** cating liquor was sold (in this section referred to as the **purchaser) is** a *bona fide* traveller, but the Justices are satisfied that **the defendant** truly believed that the purchaser was a *bona fide* traveller, **and further** that the defendant took all reasonable precautions to ascertain **whether** or not the purchaser was such a traveller, the Justices **shall dismiss** the case as against the defendant, and if they think that the **purchaser** falsely represented himself to be a *bona fide* traveller, it **shall be law-** ful for the Justices to direct proceedings to be instituted against such purchaser under the next preceding section of this Act. (*b*)

Supply of
intoxicating
A person for the purposes of this Act and the principal Act **shall**

herever "The Towns Improvement (Ireland) Act, 1854," cal Act incorporating the said Act in whole or in part, is in iny town or place, any person empowered for the purposes of Act or of such local Act to act as a Justice of the Peace ie boundaries of such town or place shall, notwithstanding in the principal Act to the contrary, have all and the same on, power, and authority to hear and determine charges for committed within the boundaries of such town or place ection twelve of the principal Act as any Justice of the Peace jurisdiction in that behalf, and may for such purpose sit , in his own Court, together with any Justice or Justices of e, according as the offence against the said section may be one or by two or more Justices, or any Justice or Justices in ssions of the peace.

enalty imposed by such Justice or Justices, or by the Jus-'etty Sessions in every such town or place as aforesaid, and town in which the Act of the Session of the ninth year of of King George the Fourth, chapter eighty-two, is in force nuch offence committed within the boundaries of such town shall be enforced as penalties are by the Towns Improveeland) Act, 1854, or such local Act, or such Act of the ninth King George the Fourth, chapter eighty-two, respectively to be enforced, and shall be applied in manner prescribed by ns Improvement (Ireland) Act, 1854, for the purposes of such id Acts as is in forre within such town or place.

ig in this section shall apply to the police district of Dublin is.

LICENSING ACT, 1874.

Miscellaneous.

As to jurisdiction of Justices under 17 & 18 Vic. c. 108.

LICENSING ACT, 1874.

Miscellaneous.

Amendment of s. 52 of principal Act as to release from custody in case of appeal.

31. Sub-section four of section fifty-two of the principal Act is hereby repealed, and in lieu thereof the following provision shall be substituted, viz. :—

When the appellant is in custody, and shall enter into such recognizances with sureties approved by the Justices in manner by said Act provided, or shall give such other security as by said Act provided, the Justice shall release him from custody. (a)

Summons in police district of Dublin metropolis.

32. In the police district of Dublin metropolis a divisional Justice may issue a summons for any offence under the principal Act or this Act, or any Act relating to the sale of any intoxicating liquor, upon any information or complaint, either on oath or not, or in writing or not, as such Justice shall see fit.

Licence to be produced in Court.

33. Every holder of a licence, excise licence, wholesale beer dealer's licence, or order of exemption made under this Act, who on being required by any Recorder or Court of Quarter Sessions on the hearing of any appeal, or by a divisional Justice or Justice of the Peace on the hearing of any summons or complaint, shall not produce and deliver such licence. excise licence, wholesale beer dealer's licence, or order to be read and examined by such Recorder, Court, or Justice, respectively, shall be subject to a penalty not exceeding ten pounds, whether it shall or shall not be stated in any summons that such production will be required. (b)

Liability in respect of distinct licences.

34. Every holder of any excise licence along with any other licence or licences, and every holder of several licences, shall be subject to the provisions of the principal Act and this Act in respect of each such licence. (c)

Evidence of licences, orders, and convictions.

35. Every entry in any register of licences of any licence, excise licence, wholesale beer dealer's licence, certificate, or exemption order, and of any conviction ordered to be recorded on a licence or on

---

(a) The principal Act seemed to leave it optional with the Justice to discharge the appellant or not, as he thought fit, after entering into recognizances.

(b) *Producing Licence.*—See also sec. 64 of principal Act. And conviction may (sec. 21) be recorded on licence.

Production of Licence in Court.—By the 55th sec. of principal Act the summons should have stated that the production of the licence would be required.

(c) *Sec. 34. Liability in respect of distinct Licences.*—This section, which at first sight appears to be, and for certain purposes is, plain, may give rise also to some difficulties. That the holder of several licences should be " subject to the provisions of these Acts in respect of each such licence " is to be expected : and under the principal Act (sec. 30), where a licence became forfeited, the holder became disqualified from holding any licence, the only thing doubtful being in the case of a " licence " and an " excise licence " being vested in the same person, and on account of the definitions the disqualification to hold any "licence " may not include an " excise licence," and, perhaps, the necessity of legislating for that exception made it necessary in like manner to do so for the " holder of several licences." The other questions that may possibly arise on the section are in the new registry. Supposing the same holder to appear at the head of the account of three licences, and in the event of one recorded conviction taking place for each of his licensed premises, will these disqualify him altogether? That may seem hard. On the other hand, it may be suggested that the intention is to deal with him as though the licences were held by three distinct persons, and that his responsibility as to each should be also distinct and detached, so as that a forfeiture of one licence should not affect the other. The section would hardly bear this interpretation so as to neutralise the effect of sec. 30 of the principal Act.

an excise licence, shall for every purpose be evidence of such licence, excise licence, wholesale beer dealer's licence, certificate, exemption order, and conviction respectively, and every entry in any book kept in a Police Court, or in any Petty Sessions order-book of any conviction or order under the principal Act or this Act, or either of them, and any copy of such entry purporting in every such case (except that of a Petty Sessions order-book) to be signed and certified as a true copy by the person to whose custody such register or book is intrusted, and in the case of a Petty Sessions order book purporting to be certified by a Justice of the Peace, pursuant to "The Petty Sessions (Ireland) Act 1851," section twenty-one, and form (I a) in the schedule thereto (a), shall for every purpose be evidence of such conviction and order respectively; and any such entry or any such copy of such entry of a conviction ordered to be recorded on a licence or excise licence, which licence or excise licence shall not be produced when required by any Recorder, Court of Quarter Sessions, divisional Justice, or Justice of the Peace, shall be conclusive evidence that such conviction was duly recorded on such licence or excise licence.

36. Any copy or certiccate of any licence, or of any excise licence, or of any wholesale beer dealer's licence, purporting to be signed and certified as a true copy or certificate by any officer in that behalf appointed by the Commissioners of Inland Revenue, shall for every purpose be conclusive evidence of such licence or excise licence.

37. In the principal Act and in this Act the following terms have the meanings hereby assigned to them respectively, unless there be something in the subject or context repugnant thereto; namely,

"Town" shall mean and include—

Any parliamentary or municipal borough;

Any town having commissioners under an Act passed in the session of Parliament held in the ninth year of the reign of King George the Fourth, intituled, "An Act to make provision for the lighting, cleansing, and watching of cities and towns corporate, and market towns, in Ireland, in certain cases;"

Any town having municipal commissioners under an Act passed in the session of Parliament held in the third and fourth years of the reign of Her present Majesty Queen Victoria, intituled, "An Act for the Regulation of Municipal Corporations in Ireland."

Any town having town commissioners or commissioners under the Towns Improvement Act, 1854, or under any local and personal Act:

"Licence" shall mean any licence for sale of any intoxicating liquor granted by an officer of excise in Ireland upon production in the police district of Dublin metropolis, of a certificate of the Recorder of the city of Dublin, or of a divisional Justice, and elsewhere of a certificate of any Recorder of a city or borough, or

---

(a) *Form* (I a) *in Schedule thereto.*—This is not the form of order-book in use. (But see sec. 36 of that Act where Lord Lieutenant has power to amend.) Still the section calls for very strict compliance.

Licensing Act, 1874.

Miscellaneous.

of Justices, under the provisions of any Act now or hereafter requiring such certificate, but shall not include an excise licence as defined by section eighty-one of the principal Act, or a wholesale beer dealer's licence, as hereinafter defined : (a)

"Wholesale beer dealer's licence."

" Wholesale beer dealer's licence " shall mean a licence to any person not being a brewer of beer, authorizing the sale of strong beer, only in casks containing not less than four and a-half gallons imperial measure, or in not less than two dozen reputed quart bottles at one time, to be drunk or consumed elsewhere than on the premises of such person :

"Occasional licence."

" Occasional licence " shall mean a licence to sell beer, spirits, or wine granted in pursuance of the thirteenth section of the Act of twenty-fifth and twenty-sixth years of the reign of Her present Majesty, chapter twenty-two, and section five of the Act of the session of the twenty-seventh year of the reign of Her present Majesty, chapter eighteen, and the Acts amending the same in relation to the licences therein mentioned or of any of such Acts :

"New licence," &c.

" New licence," " new excise licence," and " new wholesale beer dealer's licence," shall mean respectively a licence, excise licence, and wholesale beer dealer's licence granted in respect of premises in respect of which a similar licence has not theretofore been granted, or, if granted, has been annulled, or has not been in force during the preceding six months :

"Licensing Justices."

The term " Licensing Justices " shall mean as to licences granted in pursuance of certificates granted at Quarter Sessions, and as to renewals or transfers of such licences, the Justices or authority empowered to grant such certificates at Quarter Sessions, and as to other licences, excise licences, and wholesale beer dealers' licences the Justices or Justice empowered to grant certificates for the same respectively : (b)

"Register of licences."

" Register of licences " shall mean the list or register directed to be kept by this Act : (c)

"Clerk to the Licensing Justices."

The term " Clerk to the Licensing Justices " shall mean the person who keeps the register of licences :

And the principal Act shall be construed as if the meanings by this Act assigned to the terms " licence," " Licensing Justices," " register of licences," and " Clerk to the Licensing Justices" were respectively substituted in the seventy-seventh section of the Licensing Act, 1872, for the respective meanings thereby assigned to the same terms.

(a) *Definitions.*—" Licence," it will 'be observed, here means the excise licence when granted on certificates of Recorder, Justices, &c., or as the case may be, but does not include a spirit grocer's licence or wholesale beer dealer's licence. This last, and also an " occasional licence," are specially defined. One Justice can grant certificate for occasional licence. 26 & 27 Vic., c. 33, s. 20.

(b) *Licensing Justices* are defined to be the Recorder or Justices at Quarter Sessions, and also the Justices at Petty Sessions, as the case may be, and according to the certificates required.

(c) *Register of Licences* means the Register kept by Clerk of Petty Sessions, and he is the " Clerk to the Licensing Justices " of his district.

38. From and after the commencement of this Act there shall be repealed the sections of the principal Act relating to the following matters ; that is to say,

(1). Sections nineteen to twenty-two, both inclusive, relating to adulteration, and the first schedule to the principal Act ;

(2). Section thirty-five, relating to entry on premises by constables ; and

(3). So much of sections five, six, thirteen, fourteen, sixteen, seventeen, seventy-eight, eighty-three, and eighty-four as relates to the records of convictions on licences ;

(4). The last paragraph of section fifty-six, beginning with the words, " In a county the Justices," to the end of a section ; and also section fifteen of the Act of the session of the fifty-fifth year of the reign of King George the Third, chapter one hundred and four, except so far as the same applies to spirituous liquors which shall be used and consumed in the house, shop, or premises in which the same are sold :

Provided that the repeal enacted in this Act shall not affect—

(1). Anything duly done or suffered under any enactment hereby repealed ;

(2). Any right or privilege acquired, or any liability incurred under any enactment hereby repealed ;

(3). Any penalty, forfeiture, or other punishment incurred or to be incurred in respect of any offence against any enactment hereby repealed.

(margin:) LICENSING ACT, 1874. *Miscellaneous.* Repeal.

SCHEDULE (A).

Form of Notice.

To the Clerk of the Peace for the County [*or* city *or* town] of

Take notice, I have obtained a [licence, early-closing licence, *or* six-day licence, *as the case may be*] to sell spirits, beer, and cider by retail, up to the   day of   18   ,

(margin:) *Form of Notice.*

Repeal.—Section 38, *sub-section* 3.—Although the portions of the sections relating to the records of convictions on licences are repealed, still they are to be referred to as the instances in the principal Act wherein convictions were authorized to be recorded in the manner therein, but now in the manner authorized by section 21 of this Act (1874), and being altogether in the discretion of the Justices, and notwithstanding the above repeal of the clauses altogether, they are sufficiently incorporated with section 21 to be resorted to for its purposes. An Act of Parliament being repealed does not necessarily mean that it is expunged from the Statute Book. It lies there still, and may be revived and again employed at the pleasure of the Legislature.

Sub-section 4.—The partial repeal of section 15 of 55 Geo. iii., c. 104, is but justice. That Act provides that suits cannot be maintained for any *spirituous liquors* sold in less than two quarts at a time. Now the debt can be recovered where it is sold to be drunk elsewhere than on the premises where sold. Spirituous liquors would seem to be distilled spirits, and will not include beer or ale.

For original certificate granted by Clerk of the Peace on application or licence, and fee, 2*s.* 6*d.*, payable thereon, see 3 & 4 Wm. iv., c. 68, s. 5. Persons obtaining licences from excise shall make entries with Clerk of the Peace, and pay fee of 2*s.* 6*d.* : 3 & 4 Wm. iv., c. 68, s. 10.

and I require you to enter my name and the description of my house in the Register of Licences as follows:—

Christian name of trader.

Surname of same.

Place of abode of same.

Description or sign of house and premises.

Name of townland [or in cities, towns, or villages name of street and number therein].

Petty Sessions district where house situate.

Christian name of owner of house.

Surname of same.

Address of same.

Dated this   day of   18

Trader's name.

PETTY
SESSIONS
ACT.

PETTY SESSIONS (IRELAND) ACT, 1851. (a)

14 & 15 Vic., c. 93.

"An Act to consolidate and amend the Acts regulating the Proceedings at Petty Sessions, and the duties of Justices of the Peace out of Quarter Sessions in Ireland."

[7th August, 1851.]

Section 1 provides for the formation of Petty Sessions districts, and the times and places for holding Petty Sessions.

Sections 2, 3, 4, which refer to the appointment, fees, &c., of Petty Sessions Clerks, are repealed by the 21 & 22 Vic., c. 100 (the Petty Sessions Clerks Act, 1858).

Section 5 prescribes the duties of the Petty Sessions Clerk: the Petty Sessions Clerks Act, 1858. and Petty Sessions Clerks and Fines (Ireland) Act, 1878, point out additional duties.

Local Jurisdiction.

7. The powers of Justices and others to act in and for different localities shall be subject to the following conditions:

Justice may act for one county whilst being in another adjoining county, of

1. A Justice for any county may act as such in all matters arising within such county, although he may at the time happen to be in an adjoining county, provided he shall be also a Justice for such adjoining county:

2. A Justice for any county may in like manner act as such in all matters arising within such county, although he may at the

---

(a) This Petty Sessions Act is to be considered as the machinery for carrying out and enforcing the provisions of the several other statutes which give jurisdiction to Magistrates; an adequate acquaintance with its powers and requirements is, therefore, of the utmost importance.

For additional powers of Justices in boroughs, see Municipal Corporations Act, 3 & 4 Vic., c 108, s. 161.

☞ *Marginal Readings.*—The marginal readings on this Act have been enlarged to the more readily to discern the subject and meaning of the text.

time happen to be in any city, town, or place, being a county of itself, situated within or adjoining to such first-mentioned county, whether he shall be a Justice of such city, town, or place or not; but nothing herein contained shall extend to empower any Justice for any county, not being also a Justice for any such city, town, or place as aforesaid, or any person acting under him, to act or intermeddle in any matters arising within any such city, town, or place : (a)

PETTY SESSIONS ACT.
—
which he shall also be Justice; or whilst in adjoining county of a city, though not a Justice of same ; but not to act as to matters arising in such county of a city, &c.

3. The Inspector-General, or either of the Deputy-Inspectors-General of Constabulary, being a Justice of any county, may act in all matters arising within such county, wherever he may happen to be at the time:

Inspector-General of Constabulary may act wherever he may be.

4. Whenever any townland belonging to one county shall be included in any petty sessions district of the adjoining county under the provisions of this Act, any Justice having jurisdiction in such petty sessions district shall have the like jurisdiction in such townland, although he may not be a Justice of the county to which such townland belongs; and any committal to any gaol or bridewell of such last-mentioned county, or any other magisterial act done by any such Justice, in any case in which the offence or cause of complaint shall have arisen in such townland, shall have the like force and effect as if such Justice was also a Justice of such last-mentioned county.

Justices for one county may act for annexed townlands of another.

And all constables or other persons apprehending any person whom they lawfully may and ought to apprehend by virtue of their office or otherwise, in any such county or place as aforesaid, may lawfully convey such person before any Justice for such county or place whilst such Justice shall be in such adjoining county or place as aforesaid, and such constables or other persons are hereby authorized and required in all such cases to act in all things as if such Justice were within the county or place for which he shall so act.

Constables, &c., may take offenders before Justice in adjoining county.

8. The places where Justices shall sit in the discharge of their duties shall be subject to the following provisions :—

1. Whenever a public Court-house shall be maintained by county presentment at any place fixed for the holding of petty sessions, the petty sessions shall be held therein, if not inconvenient to the public ; but whenever no such public Court-house shall be

Petty Sessions to be held in Court-house.

(a) *Jurisdiction.*—9 Geo. iv., c. 54, ss. 26 and 27, provides that all offences committed on the boundaries of two or more counties, or within 500 yards of such boundaries, or begun in one county and completed in another, whether they be felonies or misdemeanours, may be dealt with in all respects in any of the said counties as if they had been wholly committed therein : and if the offence has been committed on any person, or with respect to any property, in any coach, waggon, cart, or other carriage, on a journey, or in any vessel on a voyage on any river or canal. it may be dealt with in any county through any part of which such carriage or vessel passed, on the journey or voyage during which the offence was committed ; or if the side, bank, or any part of such road, river, or canal constitute a boundary between two counties, the offences may be treated as if actually committed in either of such two counties.

The power above conferred is now very frequently called into exercise where offences committed in railway carriages cannot be conveniently brought before a Justice until several Petty Sessions districts have been passed over, and the journey has terminated. And see section 10 of Petty Sessions Act, and note thereon.

By the 33 & 34 Vic., c. 64, Lord Lieutenant empowered to rescind order for amalgamation of Petty Sessions districts, to be served by one clerk.

Where no
Court-house,
grand jury
may present
rent of
justice-room.

so maintained, or the holding of petty sessions therein would be
inconvenient to the public, it shall be lawful for the grand jury
of the county to present an annual sum not exceeding ten pounds
for the rent of a public justice-room in which the petty sessions
shall be held, and of a lock-up: provided that such room shall
not be in a house where spirituous or fermented liquors are sold,
or in a constabulary barrack, or in any building maintained in
the whole or in part at the public expense, and that it shall be
proved to the satisfaction of the county presentment sessions,
where application shall be made for such rent, that at least four
meetings of Justices shall have been held in such room during
the four months next preceding such application.

In summary
proceedings
complaint
not to be
heard or
determined
out of petty
sessions
except in
certain cases;
but two Jus-
tices may act
out of petty
sessions
where
offender can-
not find bail.
Proviso.

2. It shall not be lawful for any Justice or Justices to hear and
determine any cases of summary jurisdiction out of petty sessions, except cases of drunkenness or vagrancy, or fraud in
the sale of goods, or disputes as to sales in fairs or markets: but
it shall be lawful for two Justices, if they shall seem fit, to hear
and determine out of petty sessions any complaint as to any
offence, when the offender shall be unable to give bail for his
appearance at petty sessions: (b)

Provided always, that nothing herein contained shall be construed
to prevent any Justice or Justices acting out of petty sessions from
making any order not being in the nature of a conviction, or of an
adjudication upon a complaint, which a Justice or Justices may be
authorized or required by law to make.

*Publicity
of Proceed-
ings.*

9. The right of the public to have access to the place in which
Justices shall sit shall be subject to the following provisions:—(c)

Place in
which Jus-
tices shall sit
to hear sum-
mary pro-
ceedings to
be deemed an
open Court.
Parties to be
allowed to
plead by
counsel or
attorney.

1. In all cases of summary proceedings, the place in which any
Justice or Justices shall sit to hear and determine any complaint
shall be deemed an open Court, to which the public generally
may have access, so far as the same can conveniently contain
them; and the parties by and against whom any complaint or
information shall there be heard shall be admitted to conduct or
make their full answer and defence thereto respectively, and to
have the witnesses examined and cross-examined by themselves
or by counsel or attorney on their behalf:

(a) For the punishment or order in these cases, see the particular title in the
Summary Index.
(b) The latter provision, empowering two Justices to deal with the cases out of
Petty Sessions, when the offender shall be unable to give bail for his appearance at
Petty Sessions, is extended to 24 & 25 Vic., cc. 96, 97, 99, 100, by the 25 & 26 Vic.,
c. 50, s. 2.
(c) The Magistrates are to be judges of what is a convenient number in their
Court; those who have business are first to be accommodated.—See notes on title
"Court," Summary Index.
Place of Hearing.—The hearing of cases in a particular Petty Sessions district is a
question of general convenience, and being so should, as far as practicable, be the
general rule observed. In some few cases it cannot be departed from. This is so
under Small Debts' Act, 34 & 35 Vic. c. 76, s. 3, the defendant is to be sued in the
Petty Sessions district wherein he resides; but where in other cases any exigency
render a departure from the rule necessary or expedient there seems to exist
legal impediment or prohibition to cases being brought to any Petty Sessions in
County, and to compel the attendance there of defendants and witnesses.

2. In all cases of proceedings for indictable offences, the place in which any Justice or Justices shall sit to take any examination or statement relating to any such offence shall not be deemed an open Court for that purpose, but it shall be lawful for such Justice or Justices, in his or their discretion, to order that no person (the counsel or attorney of any person, then being in such Court as a prisoner, only excepted) shall have access to, or be or remain in such place without the consent or permission of such Justice or Justices, if it appear to him or them that the ends of justice will be thereby best answered :

Petty Sessions Act.

Place where examinations in proceedings for indictable offences are taken not to be deemed an open Court without consent of Justice.

And if any person shall wilfully insult any Justice or Justices so sitting in any such Court or place, or shall commit any other contempt of any such Court, it shall be lawful for such Justice or Justices by any verbal order, either to direct such person to be removed from such Court or place, or to be taken into custody, and at any time before the rising of such Court, by warrant to commit such person to gaol for any period not exceeding seven days, or to fine such person in any sum not exceeding forty shillings (a).

Power to commit and fine for contempt of Court.

10. Whenever information shall be given to any Justice that any person has committed or is suspected to have committed any treason, felony, misdemeanour, or other offence, within the limits of the jurisdiction of such Justice, for which such person shall be punishable either by indictment or upon a summary conviction ; or that any person has committed or is suspected to have committed any such crime or offence elsewhere out of the jurisdiction of such Justice, either in *Great Britain* or *Ireland*, or in the Isles of *Man, Jersey, Guernsey, Alderney,* or *Sark,* and such person is residing or being, or is suspected to reside or be, within the limits of the jurisdiction of such Justice ; or that any person has committed or is suspected to have committed any crime or offence whatsoever on the high seas. or in any creek, harbour, haven, or other place in which the Admiralty of *England* or *Ireland* have or claim to have jurisdic-

Informations and complaints.

Justice may receive information or complaint.

As to offences within his jurisdiction :

As to offence out of his jurisdiction :

(a) See title "Contempt," and notes thereon, Summary Index.

General Jurisdiction.—This sec. 10 may be properly divided into four parts on the subject of jurisdiction:—1st. Where any crime or offence, punishable by *indictment* or *summarily,* is committed within the limits of his jurisdiction. 2nd. Where any *such crime or offence* is committed *anywhere* in the United Kingdom or the Channel Islands, and the offender is residing or suspected to be residing within his jurisdiction. 3rd. Crimes, &c., committed on the high seas, triable by indictment in England or Ireland, and the offender is suspected to be within his jurisdiction. 4th. Any other matter arising within the jurisdiction of the Justice in which he has power to make a summary order. It will be observed that under the divisions 1 and 2 the *offence,* whether it be indictable or triable summarily, may be taken cognizance of by a Justice where offence committed or offender found.

The fourth division refers to a class of cases not amounting to crimes or offences, but that are rather of a civil nature, and must therefore *arise* within his jurisdiction. As to the description of the offences in the section, viz. treason, felony, misdemeanour, or other offence, they may be distinguished with sufficient certainty. Misdemeanour is such a crime as, while it does not amount to a felony, is the subject of indictment. *Offence* is a generic term. Any act committed contrary to law is an offence, and in general any warrant which a Justice may issue for a penalty, or for arrest, or imprisonment of the person, is a warrant for an *offence.*

A conviction is good although it may not take place in the Petty Sessions district where offender resides, or offence committed, provided it be in the county. Where it is practicable, and that no failure of justice would ensue, the case should be brought in the proper Petty Sessions district.

tion (a), or on land beyond the seas, for which an indictment can be legally preferred in any place in the United Kingdom of *England* and *Ireland* (b), and such person is residing or being, or is suspected to reside or be, within the limits of the jurisdiction of such justice : or whenever a complaint shall be made to any Justice as to any other matter arising within the limits of his jurisdiction, upon which he

---

(a) *Where Admiralty claims Jurisdiction.*—The extent of the maritime dominion of England seems to consist of two parts, the *profitable* and the *honorary.* The *profitable* regards our own coasts only, to a certain distance from the shore, in the sight whereof foreigners were not usually suffered to catch fish. The *honorary* is that of respect to the British flag, which we claim from all nations, and still support. The boundaries we have established for the purpose are the " British Channel on the South, extending to the shores of France, and to those of Spain as far as Cape Finisterre ; from thence by an imaginary line west twenty-three degrees of longitude from London to the latitude of sixty degrees north, which last is called the Western Ocean of Britain; from thence by another imaginary line in that parallel of latitude to the middle point of the land Van Staten, on the coast of Norway, which is the northern boundary ; and from that point it extends along the shores of Norway, Denmark, Germany, and the Netherlands, to the British Channel again, which last boundary comprehends what is called the Eastern Ocean of Britain." These are the original limits acquired at the time of King Alfred's beating the Danes out of these seas; and from thenceforth the kings of England took on themselves the more peculiar guard and sovereignty of the seas, protecting the traders of all nations from the insults of pirates ; and to answer the expense of keeping fleets at sea, and for protection, all nations who sailed into these seas paid a tribute in proportion to the burden of their ships ; but this tribute is now confined to the ceremony of lowering the flag.

The *Isle of Man* is a distinct territory from England ; no act of Parliament extends to it unless it be particularly named therein. It was anciently governed by its own Lord, who was called the King of the Island, and had a crown of gold, but he was subject to the King of England.

The *Isles of Jersey, Guernsey, Alderney* and *Sark* were all parcels of the Duchy of Normandy, and were united to the Crown of England by the first Princes of the Norman line.

shall have power to make a summary order, it shall be lawful for such Justice to receive such information or complaint, and to proceed in respect to the same, subject to the following provisions :—

PETTY SESSIONS ACT.

1. Whenever it is intended that a summons only should issue to require the attendance of any person, the information or complaint may be made either with or without oath, and either in writing or not, according as the Justice shall see fit : (*a*)

It may be verbal, and without oath in certain cases.

2. But whenever it is intended that a warrant shall issue for the arrest or committal of any person, the information or complaint shall be in writing, and on the oath of the complainant or of some person or persons on his behalf :

It must be in writing, and on oath in certain other cases.

3. Whenever any such information shall have been taken on oath and in writing, that any person has committed or is suspected to have committed any indictable crime or offence (or any offence for which such person shall be punishable upon summary conviction, and for whose arrest the Justices shall issue a warrant), it shall be lawful for the Justice if he shall see fit, to bind the informant or complainant by recognizance (A a.*) or (C.) to appear at the Court or place where the defendant is to be tried or the complaint is to be heard, to prosecute or give evidence, as the case may be, against such person :

Binding the informant to prosecute.

4. In all cases of summary jurisdiction the complaint shall be made, when it shall relate to the non-payment of any poor-rate, county rate or other public tax, at any time after the date of the warrant authorizing the collection of the same ; and when it shall relate to the non-payment of money for wages, hire, or tuition, within one year from the termination of the term or period in respect of which it shall be payable ; and when it shall relate to any trespass, within two months from the time when the trespass shall have occurred ; and in any other case, within six months from the time when the cause of complaint shall have arisen, but not otherwise. But in other cases, under Acts since passed, other limits may be fixed for making complaint.

In summary proceedings complaints must be made for poor-rate, &c., at any time after the date of the warrant; for wages, &c., within one year; for trespass, within two months; in other cases, within six months.

And in all cases of summary jurisdiction, any person against whom any such information or complaint shall have been made in writing shall, upon being amenable, or appearing in person, or by

In summary proceedings defendant entitled to copy of information of complaint when in writing.

---

vessel, and the prisoner an American citizen, the Court had no jurisdiction to try him. Lord Chief Justice Bovill, in delivering judgment, said the prisoner being one of the crew of a British merchant vessel he was under the protection of British law, and also liable to its provisions. The prisoner was an American citizen, and he was, therefore, under the circumstances of this case, subject to American and French jurisdiction for certain purposes, to be within British jurisdiction. If this offence had been committed on the high seas, it would have been within the Admiralty jurisdiction ; and this offence having been committed in a place where the tide ebbed and flowed, the prisoner was amenable to British law. The other learned Judges concurred, and the conviction was affirmed" (1869).—See also "Naturalization," Summary Index.

(*a*) Reckless and disreputable persons frequently bring hasty and groundless charges, sometimes of a very heinous nature ; to set forth these, or indeed any indictable crime, on the face of a summons to be left at a man's residence, is in itself a serious thing to do. The Magistrate will (at all events in some cases) act wisely by requiring that the charge shall be supported by some sworn reliable information, and that there are reasonable grounds for putting the criminal law in motion. Of course *the nature of the charge and the character of the person making it* will influence the Magistrate in exercising his discretion in the matter.

PETTY
SESSIONS
ACT.
———
*Process
to enforce
appear-
ance.*
———
In cases of
indictable
offences,
warrant to
issue in the
first instance.

But in
certain cases
a summons
may issue.

If party
appears or is
arrested,
Justice to
proceed
under sub-
sequent
provisions.

In cases of
summary
jurisdiction,
summons to
issue in the
first instance.

But in
certain cases

counsel or attorney, be entitled to receive from the Clerk of Petty Sessions a copy of such information or complaint, on payment of the sum of sixpence to such clerk; and such clerk shall in no case allow the original information or complaint to be taken out of his possession.

11. The manner in which persons against whom any such informations or complaints as aforesaid shall have been received by any Justice, shall be made to appear to answer to the same shall be subject to the following provisions:—

1. In all cases of indictable crimes and offences (where an information that any person has committed the same shall have been taken in writing and on oath) the Justice shall issue a warrant (B b.) to arrest and bring such person before him, or some other Justice of the same county, to answer to the complaint made in information (and which warrant may be issued or executed on a *Sunday* as well as on any other day); or if he shall think that the ends of justice would be thereby sufficiently answered, it shall be lawful for him instead of issuing such warrant, to issue a summons in the first instance to such person, requiring him to appear and answer to the said complaint; but nothing herein contained shall prevent any Justice from issuing a warrant for the arrest of such person at any time before or after the time mentioned in such summons for his appearance; and whenever such person shall afterwards appear or be brought before any such Justice, he shall proceed according to the provisions hereinafter contained, as to taking the evidence against such person, and committing such person for trial:

2. In all cases of summary jurisdiction the Justice may issue his summons (B a.) directed to such person, requiring him to appear and answer to the complaint, and it shall not be necessary that such Justice shall be the Justice, or one of the Justices by whom the complaint shall be afterwards heard and determined; and in all cases of offences, where such person shall not appear at the required time and place, and it shall be proved on oath either that he was personally served with such summons, or that he is

And each summons or warrant shall be signed by the Justice or one of the Justices issuing the same, and it shall state shortly the cause of complaint, and no summons or warrant shall be signed in blank ; and in every case where the offence shall have occurred or the cause of complaint shall have arisen within the petty sessions district for which the Justice issuing any such summons or warrant shall act, but the party or witness to whom such summons shall be directed, or against whom such warrant shall be issued, shall reside in an adjoining county, it shall be lawful for such Justice to compel the appearance of such party or witness at the hearing of the charge or complaint within such district, in like manner as if such party or witness resided in such district, although such Justice may not be a Justice of such adjoining county. *PETTY SESSIONS ACT.* *Warrant of summons to be signed, but not in blank. Summons or warrant may run into an adjoining county.*

12. The manner in which summonses shall be served shall be subject to the following provisions :— *Service of summonses.*

1. It shall be lawful for the Justices of each petty sessions to appoint some one or more persons, who shall be able to read and write, to act as summons-server or servers of the district during the pleasure of such Justices ; and any such summons-server shall be entitled to be paid by the complainant, or person for whom he may be employed, such sum not exceeding the sum of sixpence for the service of each summons upon each party or witness (or upon any number of parties or witnesses in the same case who shall be served in the same house) as the Justices shall fix : *Justices to appoint a summons-server.*

2. In cases of the offences prosecuted by the constabulary, the summons shall be served by a head or other constable, but in all other cases it may be served by the summons-server of the district, or (if the Justice issuing the same shall so direct or permit) by any other person whom the complainant shall employ, and who shall be able to read and write, but in no case by the complainant himself : *By whom summons to be served.*

3. Every summons shall be served upon the person to whom it is directed by delivering to him a copy of such summons, or if he cannot be conveniently met with, by leaving such copy for him at his last or most usual place of abode, or at his office, warehouse, counting-house, shop, factory, or place of business, with some inmate of the house, not being under sixteen years of age, a reasonable time before the hearing of the complaint ; and such *What shall be due service.* *Proof of service.*

---

committed or cause of complaint has arisen, even though he reside in an adjoining county. Where the witnesses reside in an adjoining county, see sec. 13 and note thereon.

Unlawful Arrest.—If a man maliciously and without probable cause procure the arrest of another either by civil or criminal process, that is the subject-matter of an action on the case, for the wrong consists not in any immediate violence to the plaintiff's person, but in communicating an improper direction to the process of the law. And it is held that trespass will not lie against a man who merely states his case to a Court of Justice in consequence of which it issues process, and this even though he say he will take it at his peril, and even prepare it, provided he take no part in executing it. But if without having recourse to legal process he made the arrest, or assist in making it of his own authority, or direct a constable to make it, the remedy is *trespass*, for in that case he commits an unwarrantable act of violence.— *Stonehouse* v. *Elliott*, 6 T. R., 315.

PETTY
SESSIONS
ACT.
———
But this not
to affect any
special mode
of service.

last-mentioned service shall be deemed sufficient service of such
summons in every case except where personal service shall be
specially required by this Act ; and in every case the person
who shall serve such summons shall endorse on the same the
time and place where it was served, and shall attend with the
same at the hearing of the complaint, to depose, if necessary, to
such service :

Provided always, that nothing herein contained shall be construed
to affect the provisions of any Act authorizing the substitution of
service in particular cases. (a)

Witnesses.
———
Justice may
force wit-
nesses to
attend and
give
evidence.

13. Whenever it shall be made to appear to any Justice that any
person within the jurisdiction of such Justice is able to give material
evidence for the prosecution in cases of indictable offences, or for the
complainant or defendant in cases of summary jurisdiction, and will
not voluntarily appear for the purpose of being examined as a witness,
such Justice may proceed as follows :—(b)

Issue of
summons.

1. He may issue a summons (B a.) to such person requiring him
to appear at a time and place mentioned in such summons, to
testify what he may know concerning the matter of the information or complaint, and (if the Justice shall see fit) to bring
with him and produce for examination such accounts, papers,
or other documents as shall be in his possession or power and as
shall be deemed necessary to such Justice ; but in any case of
an indictable crime or offence, whenever the Justice shall be
satisfied by proof upon oath that it is probable that such person

will not attend to give evidence without being compelled so to do, then (the information or complaint being in writing and on oath), instead of issuing such summons as aforesaid he may issue a warrant (B b.) in the first instance for the arrest of such person :

2. And in any case when any person to whom a summons shall be issued in the first instance shall neglect or refuse to appear at the time and place appointed by such summons, and no just excuse shall be offered for such neglect or refusal, then (the information or complaint being in writing and on oath), after proof upon oath that such summons was personally served upon such person, or that such person is keeping out of the way of such service, and that he is able to give material evidence in the case, the Justice before whom such person should have appeared may issue a warrant (B b.) to arrest such person, and to bring him at the time and place appointed for the hearing of the case, to testify and to produce such accounts, papers, and documents as may be required as aforesaid :

3. In all cases of prosecutions for offences, the evidence of the informer or party aggrieved shall be admissible in proof of the offence : and in all cases of complaints on which a Justice can make an order for the payment of money, or otherwise, the evidence of the complainant shall be admissible in proof of his complaint ; and in cases of wages, hire, or tuition the evidence of the master or employer may, in the discretion of the Justices, be admitted in proof against the complaint : (a)

4. All witnesses shall be examined upon oath, and any Justice before whom any such witnesses shall appear for the purpose of being so examined shall have full authority to administer to every such witness the usual oath : (b)

5. Whenever any person shall appear as a witness, either in obedience to a summons or by virtue of a warrant (or shall be present, and shall be verbally required by the Justice or Justices to give evidence) and he shall refuse (c) to be examined upon oath concerning the matter of the information or complaint, or shall refuse to take such oath. or having taken such oath, shall refuse to answer such questions concerning the said matter as shall then be put to him, or shall refuse or neglect to produce any such accounts, papers, or documents as aforesaid (without offering any just excuse for such refusal), the Justice or Jus-

(marginal notes:)
PETTY SESSIONS ACT.

In cases of indictable offences warrant may issue in the first instance.

If summons be not obeyed, Justices may issue warrant to arrest witness.

What persons shall be competent witnesses:
Prosecutors and complainants in all cases:
Defendants in wages cases.

Witnesses to be examined on oath.

Witnesses refusing to be examined may be committed from time to time till they consent to be examined.

(a) In all civil cases, the plaintiff and defendant are now competent and admissible. See "Law of Evidence," *Appendix.*
(b) But see "Affirmation," and note thereon, page 2.
(c) *Witness—when not compelled to answer.*—First, where the answer would have a tendency to expose the witness, or as it seems the husband or wife of the witness, to any kind of criminal charge, or to a penalty or forfeiture of any nature whatsoever. This rule is of very great antiquity, and was even recognized by Chief Justice Jefferies, when it told against the prisoner.
There are several occasions where the Legislature, by Acts of indemnity, deprive the witness of this privilege.
It is a rule of evidence applicable to criminal cases that a witness is not permitted to disclose privileged communications brought to his knowledge for the furtherance of justice. " This is not the privilege of the witness, but may be justly called a public privilege, and is observed on a principle of public policy, and from regard to public interests."—1 *Phil. Ev.*, 272. Hence "those questions which tend to the

PETTY
SESSIONS
ACT.
—

tices then present may adjourn the proceedings for any period not
exceeding eight clear days, and may in the meantime by warrant
(E b.) commit the said witness to gaol, unless he shall sooner
consent to be sworn or to testify as aforesaid, or to produce such
accounts, papers, or documents, as the case may be ; and if such
witness, upon being brought up upon such adjourned hearing,
shall again refuse to be sworn, or to testify as aforesaid, or to
produce such accounts, papers, or documents, as the case may be,
the said Justices, if they shall see fit, may again adjourn the
proceedings, and commit the witness for the like period, and so
again from time to time, until he shall consent to be sworn or to

But this not
to prevent
case from
being dis-
posed of on
other
sufficient
evidence.

testify as aforesaid or to produce such accounts, papers, or
documents, as the case may be (provided that no such imprisonment shall, in any case of summary jurisdiction, exceed one
month in the whole); but nothing herein contained shall be
deemed to prevent the Justice or Justices from sending any such
case for trial, or otherwise disposing of the same, in the meantime, according to any other sufficient evidence which shall have
been received by him or them :

In cases of
indictable
offences,
witnesses
may be
bound to give
evidence, and
on refusal
may be
committed ;
but if party
is not com-

6. Whenever, in cases of indictable offences, the Justice or Justices
shall see fit, they may bind the witnesses by recognizance (A b*)
or (C.) to appear at the trial of the offender and give evidence
against him ; and whenever any witness shall refuse to be so
bound, it shall be lawful for the Justice or Justices by warrant
(E b.) to commit him to the gaol of the county or place in which
the person accused is to be tried, there to be imprisoned until
the trial of the person accused, unless in the meantime such
witnesses shall duly enter into recognizance (C.) before some

shillings and sixpence, as to such Justices shall seem fit, for his
expenses or loss of time for each day of attending to give evidence, and in default of payment thereof at such time as such
Justice shall appoint, then to issue a warrant to levy the amount
thereof by distress of the goods of such party :

And no person who shall be summoned to attend before any Court
of petty sessions, or before any Justice out of petty sessions, as a
witness, shall be liable to arrest for debt whilst at such Court, or at
the place where such Justice shall sit, or whilst proceeding to or returning from the same, provided he shall proceed and return by the
most direct road without unnecessary delay ; and it shall be lawful
for the Court out of which the writ or process shall have issued to
order the discharge of any person who shall be so arrested. (a)

Petty Sessions Act.

Witnesses to be protected from arrest for debt; and if arrested shall be discharged by the Court.

14. The manner in which the evidence shall be taken in proceedings for indictable offences shall be subject to the following
provisions :—

Taking the evidence—indictable offences.

1. In every case where any person shall appear or be brought before any Justice or Justices charged with any indictable crime
or offence, such Justice or Justices (b), before committing
such person for trial, or admitting him to bail, shall, in
the presence of such person, who shall be at liberty to put ques-

Justices to take deposi- tions.

(a) The Magistrates have no power to order the discharge from the arrest.
(b) The Clerk to the Justices may take down the depositions, &c. : it is his duty to
do so (sec b). The Judge of Assize, or Justices at Quarter Sessions, may fine him £20
for wilful neglect. It seems also that if depositions be carelessly or illegibly written,
it will amount to a contempt of Court. At the Liverpool Assizes, 1862, Mr. Barton
Wilde fined a coroner £10 for depositions which were badly and illegibly written by
him : his lordship remarked that negligence of this kind amounted to contempt of
Court, as it interfered with the operations of justice. The directions of sect 14
should be most attentively followed. See *Circular Letter* of 24th August, 1854
(Appendix), on the subject; and see also suggestions from Law Officers as to taking
of informations, &c. (Appendix)
Should a witness die before the trial, in order to the information or deposition
being allowed to be read in evidence it must be so complete as to point with certainty to the precise offence with which the prisoner is charged. and the witness
being dead no amendment can be made in his evidence. By a reference to the Forms
in the Schedule it will be seen that they begin with the offence, to which the witness
speaks. In the case of a living witness many defects of form may be cured, but in
the case of a deceased witness it is otherwise, the more particularly when the deceased may happen to be the only witness.
The Caption.—The title or caption of the deposition need state no more than that
it is the deposition of the witness, and the particular charge before the Magistrate to
which the deposition had reference   One caption at the head of the body of the
depositions taken in the case is sufficient. and the particular deposition sought to be
given in evidence need not have a separate caption.—*R. v. Johnson,* 2 C. & K. 355.
So where the deposition had one caption which mentioned the names of all the
witnesses, and at the end had one jurat, which also contained the names of all the
witnesses, and to which was the signature of the Magistrate, and each witness signed
his own deposition, Williams, J., was of opinion that they were correctly taken.—
R. v. Young, 3 C. & K., 106.   A deposition without a caption is inadmissible
though otherwise formally taken.—*R. v. Newton,* 1 F. & F. 641 (Roscoe).
As to the Deposition, if it be used, being confined to the technical charge made in it —
It appears that the true guide in each case is, not any technical distinction between
the charge on which the deposition is taken and that on which the prisoner is ulti-
mately tried. but whether the prisoner appears to have had full opportunity to cross-
examine the witness on all points material to one charge as well as the other.—
R. v. Lee, 4 F & F., 63.   This view has been taken in a charge of uttering a forged
note, the original charge having been one of false pretences.—*R. v Williams,* 12 Cox,
C. C. 101.
The information or deposition should be taken in the first person, that is as the
witness speaks, and as if he were writing his own statement.

2 Z

PETTY
ACT.
———

tions
itnesses
have

tions to any witness produced against him, take the depositions (A b.) on oath and in writing of those who shall know the facts of the case, and such depositions shall be read over to and signed respectively by the witnesses who shall have been so examined, and shall also be signed by the Justice, or one of the Justices who shall take the same ; and if upon the trial of the person so accused it shall be proved by the oath of any credible witness that any person whose deposition shall have been so taken is dead, and that such deposition was taken in the presence or hearing of the person accused, and that he or his counsel or attorney had an opportunity of cross-examining such witness, it shall be lawful to read such deposition as evidence on the trial, without further proof thereof, unless it shall be proved that the same was not signed by the Justice purporting to have signed the same : (a)

tement of
soner.

ices to
ion
ner, and
take
his
ent ;

2. Whenever the examination of the witnesses on the part of the prosecution shall have been completed, the Justice, or one of the Justices present shall (without requiring the attendance of the witnesses) read or cause to be read to the person accused the several depositions, and then take down in writing the statement (A c.) of such person (having first cautioned him that he is not obliged to say anything unless he desires to do so, but that whatever he does say will be taken down in writing, and may be given in evidence against him on his trial) ; (b) and whatever

(a) But there are other cases where, although the informant be not dead, his evidence may be read on the trial. It is so under the Whiteboy Act, 1 & 2 Wm. iv. c. 44, s. 8, where the witness may be maimed, carried away, and secreted by, or by some

statement the said person shall then make in answer to the
charge shall, when taken down in writing, be read over to him,
and shall be signed by the said Justice or one of the Justices
present, and shall be transmitted to the Clerk of the Crown
or Peace, as the case may be, along with the depositions, and
afterwards, upon the trial may, if necessary, and if so signed, be
given in evidence against the person accused, without further
proof thereof, unless it shall be proved that it was not signed by
the Justice purporting to sign the same ; but nothing herein
contained shall prevent the prosecutor from giving in evidence
any admission or confession, or other statement made at any
time by the person accused, and which would be admissible by
law as evidence against such person :

Petty Sessions Act — but prosecutor may give any other statement also in evidence.

But if from the absence of any witnesses, or from any other
reasonable cause, it shall become necessary or advisable to defer the
examination or further examination of the witnesses for any time, it
shall be lawful for the Justice before whom the person accused shall
appear or be brought, either to admit such person to bail in manner
hereinafter provided, or by warrant (E b.) from time to time to
remand such person to gaol for such time as the Justice shall deem
expedient, not exceeding eight clear days ; but any such Justice may
order the said person to be brought before him or some other Justice
of the county, at any time before the expiration of the period for
which he shall have been so remanded : Provided always that at any
time after the examinations in any proceedings for an indictable
offence shall have been completed, and on or before the first day of
the Assizes or Sessions, or other first sitting of the Court at which
any person committed to gaol or admitted to bail is to be tried, such

Remanding prisoner. May be remanded for any time not exceeding eight days; but may be ordered up sooner. In cases of indictable offences after the examinations, &c., have been completed, defendant entitled to copies of depositions.

stable tender his evidence, the Magistrate may take it ; its admissibility will be for
the Court, on the trial.
   The English Act (11 & 12 Vic., c. 42, s. 17) makes the deposition evidence if the
witness be so ill as not to be able to travel.
   It too often happens that when a constable proceeds to offer in evidence a voluntary statement of a prisoner, not elicited by any questions or unfair means on the
part of the officer, the Magistrate, or advocate for the accused, at once stops him,
unless he "cautioned the prisoner not to say anything." Now some of the strictest
and most constitutional Judges have only gone the length of saying, that the constable should not interrogate a prisoner on the subject of the charge, and that
answers given to questions put by him, though he had given the prisoner a previous
caution, would not be permitted to be given in evidence, on the ground that no
person ought to be made to criminate himself.—R. v. Hughes, 1 C. & Dix, C. C., 15 ;
and R v. Grey: Lefroy, J. So then the constable's duty is not to interrogate the
prisoner as to the charge. But it is also laid down (R. v. Kerr, 8 C. & P., 176), that
a constable has no business to caution a prisoner not to say anything; whatever the
prisoner says it is the constable's duty to hear. On the whole, it would be a safe
and unobjectionable course for the officer to adopt on arresting the prisoner, and
after stating to him the nature of the charge against him, to add, "You need not
now say anything; whatever you do say may be used against you hereafter." After
that the constable's duty is, to use the words of a learned Judge on a late occasion,
"to keep his ears open and his mouth shut." But whether fairly and voluntarily
made before a constable, or formally and voluntarily made before the Magistrate,
"everything which the prisoner says against himself is proper for the consideration
of the jury, who are to ascribe such weight to it as it may seem to them to deserve."—
1 Russ. on Crimes.
   "Remand not exceeding eight clear days." Unless the gaoler counts the prisoner's
time by hours, the eight clear days will be exclusive of the day on which he is
remanded, and of that on which he is brought up for hearing. If the Magistrate
remand on the 1st to be brought up on the 10th, the authority given by the statute
does not appear to be exceeded. If the gaoler's prison rules be against this
view he will do well to acquaint the Magistrate of the fact. See Circular, p. 699
(Appendix).

PETTY
SESSIONS
ACT.
———

person may require and shall be entitled to receive from the officer or person having the custody (a) of the same, copies of the depositions on which he shall have been committed or bailed (or copies of any depositions taken at any inquest, in case of murder or manslaughter), on payment of a reasonable sum for the same, not exceeding a sum at the rate of three halfpence for each folio of ninety words.

Disposal of the prisoner indictable offences.
———
When evidence has been completed, Justices to discharge or commit, or admit to bail.

15. The manner in which the person accused shall be disposed of when the evidence shall have been taken in proceedings for indictable offences, shall be subject to the following provisions :—

1. Whenever the offence shall have been committed within the jurisdiction of the Justice or Justices present, and he or they shall be of opinion that the evidence is not sufficient to put such accused person on his trial, he or they shall forthwith order such accused person, if in custody, to be discharged as to the information then under inquiry ; but if in the opinion of such Justice or Justices such evidence is sufficient to put such person on his trial, or if such evidence raises a strong or possible presumption of guilt, then such Justice or Justices shall either by warrant (E b.) commit him to gaol, to be there kept until his trial for the said offence, or shall admit him to bail in manner hereinafter provided, according as he or they shall see fit : (b)

Justice of one county may examine as to offence committed in another county, and either commit prisoner or admit him to bail.

If evidence is not sufficient, Justice may send prisoner to county where offence was committed ; but if evidence not 1

2. Whenever any person shall appear or be brought before any Justice charged with an offence alleged to have been committed by him in any county or place in *Ireland* wherein such Justice shall not have jurisdiction, it shall be lawful for such Justice and he is hereby required to examine such witnesses, and receive such evidence in proof of such charge as shall be produced before him within his jurisdiction ; and if in his opinion such evidence shall be sufficient proof of the said charge, such Justice shall thereupon, either by a like warrant (E b.) commit the person accused to the gaol of the county or place wherein the offence shall be alleged to have been committed, or shall admit him to bail, according as such Justice shall see fit ; but if in his opinion such evidence shall not be sufficient to put the accused party on his trial, then such Justice shall bind over the prosecutor, if he shall have appeared, and the witnesses, to give evidence when required so to do, and shall thereupon, by warrant (E c.) order

(a) Although the Magistrates' clerk may, if he think fit, give the copies, strictly speaking the Clerk of the Crown or Peace is the officer who has "custody" of the depositions. The authority in the above section to furnish copies of the depositions, and the fee to be charged, is similar to the provision in the Prisoner's Counsel Act, 6 & 7 Wm. iv., c. 114, s. 3. Prisoners remanded or committed for re-examination are not entitled to have copies of the depositions —*Reg.* v. *the Lord Mayor of London*, 1 *Car., H. & A.*, 40.

A Magistrate is not bound to give copy of an information to a person charged with felony, with a view to bring an action against the person who made it.—*Ex parte West* v. *Plumbtree, a Magistrate of Kent*, 1865, Q. B. *England.*

(b) On charge of perjury, where Justice refuses to commit accused, he still may be required to transmit depositions, &c.—See 22 & 23 Vic., c. 17. See titles "Vexatious Indictments," and " Perjury."

"There should be a separate committal for each prisoner."—*Law Adv. Opinion*, 29th *January*, 1856. Still the gaoler may be justified in receiving more than one under same committal for same offence, unless they be of different sexes, and under Prison Act may not be received in same gaol.

such person to be taken before some Justice of the county in which and near the place where the offence is alleged to have been committed, and shall at the same time deliver to the person having the execution of such warrant the information, depositions, and recognisances (if any), so taken, to be delivered to the Justices before whom the accused person shall be taken in obedience to such warrant, and such information, depositions, and recognizances shall be treated to all intents as if they had been taken before such last-mentioned Justice :— *PETTY SESSIONS ACT. — sufficient, and party not bailed, former recognizance to be void.*

Provided always, that if such last-mentioned Justice shall not think the evidence against such accused party sufficient to put him on his trial and shall discharge him without holding him to bail, any recognizance so taken by the said first-mentioned Justice shall be null and void.

16. The admission to bail of persons charged with indictable offences shall be subject to the following provisions :— *Bailing prisoners— indictable offences.*

1. In every case where any person shall be charged before any Justice in manner aforesaid with any felony (save as hereinafter excepted) or with any assault with intent to commit any felony, or with any attempt to commit any felony, or with an offence against an Act of the first and second years of His late Majesty King William the Fourth, intituled, "*An Act to amend an Act passed in the parliament of Ireland in the fifteenth and sixteenth years of the reign of his Majesty King George the Third, intituled 'An Act to prevent and punish tumultuous Risings of persons within this Kingdom, and for other purposes therein mentioned,'*" or with obtaining or attempting to obtain property by false pretences, or with a misdemeanour in receiving property stolen or obtained by false pretences, or with perjury or subornation of perjury, or with concealing the birth of a child by secret burying or otherwise, or with wilful and indecent exposure of the person, or with riot, or with assault in pursuance of a conspiracy to raise wages, or assault upon peace officer in the execution of his duty, or upon any person acting in his aid, or with neglect or breach of duty as peace officer, or without any misdemeanour for the prosecution of which the costs may be allowed out of the county rate or funds, it shall be lawful either for the Justice before whom such charge shall be made, at any time before such person shall have been committed to gaol, or for the Justice by whom the warrant to commit shall have been signed, at any time afterwards, and before the first day of the sitting of the Court before which he shall have been committed to be tried, if (having regard to the nature of the charge, and the cogency of the evidence adduced in support of it) it appears to him to be a case in which bail ought to be taken, to admit such accused person to bail by recognizance (C.) with one or more sufficient sureties, at the discretion of the Justice, conditioned that he will appear at the time and place when and where he is to be tried for such offence, and that he will then surrender and take his trial, and not depart the Court without leave ; and whenever in any such case the accused person shall not be so admitted to bail, if the committing Justice shall be of opinion that he ought to be admitted *Persons charged with certain felonies and misdemeanours may be admitted to bail, at the discretion of the Justice, before commitment for trial. 1 & 2 Wm. iv. c. 44. Having regard to nature of the charge and cogency of the evidence. In such cases the committing Justice to certify on*

PETTY
SESSIONS
ACT.
___
warrant his
consent to
bail;
and any other
Justice may
admit to bail.

to bail, he shall certify (I c.) on the warrant of commitment his consent to his being bailed, stating also the amount of bail which ought to be required; and any Justice of the county attending or being at the gaol where such accused party shall be in custody, on production of such certificate at any time before the first day of the sitting of the Court before which he shall have been committed to be tried, may admit such accused person to bail in manner as aforesaid.

Persons
charged with
other misde-
meanours
shall be
admitted to
bail at any
time as of
right.

2. In every case where any person shall be charged before any Justice with any indictable misdemeanour other than those herein-before mentioned, such Justice, after taking the examinations instead of committing him to prison shall, upon the application of such person (and upon being satisfied as to the sufficiency of the bail offered), admit him to bail in manner aforesaid; or if he shall have been committed to gaol, and shall apply to any Justice for the same county to admit him to bail at any time before the first day of the sitting of the Court before which he shall have been committed to be tried, such Justice shall admit him to bail in manner aforesaid : (a)

When sure-
ties cannot
attend, Jus-
tice to give
a duplicate
certificate.

And whenever it shall not be convenient for the surety or sureties in any case to attend at the gaol to join with the accused person in the recognizance of bail, then the committing Justice, or the Justice by whom such person can be admitted to bail, as the case may be, shall make a duplicate of such certificate (I c.) as aforesaid, and upon the same being produced to any Justice for the same county, it shall be

When Justice
admits a per-
son to bail

lawful for such last-mentioned Justice, before such time as aforesaid, to take such recognizance of the surety or sureties in conformity with

shall be lawful for the Justice by whom he shall have been bailed, or for any other Justice, if he shall see fit, upon the application of the surety or of either of the sureties of such person, and upon information being made in writing and on oath by such surety, or by some person on his behalf, that the person so bailed is about to abscond for the purpose of evading justice, to issue his warrant for the arrest of such person so bailed, and afterwards, upon being satisfied that the ends of justice would otherwise be defeated, to commit such person, when so arrested, to gaol, until his trial or until he shall produce another sufficient surety or other sufficient sureties, as the case may be, in like manner as before. (*a*).

Petty Sessions Act.

Justice may, upon application of bailsman, order arrest and require new bail.

18. Whenever an indictment shall have been found by the Grand Jury in any Court of Oyer and Terminer or General Gaol Delivery, or at any General or Quarter Sessions of the peace in *Ireland*, against any person who shall then be at large, and who shall not already have appeared and pleaded to such indictment (and whether such person shall have been bound by recognizance to answer to the same or not), the person who shall act as Clerk of the Crown at such Court, or as Clerk of the Peace at such Sessions, shall at any time after the end of the Assizes or Sessions at which such indictment shall have been found, upon application of the prosecutor or of some person on his behalf, and free from charge, grant unto such prosecutor or person a certificate (I b.) of such indictment having been found ; and upon production of such certificate to any Justice for the county in which the offence shall be alledged in such indictment to have been committed, or in which the person thereby indicted shall reside or be, or be suspected to reside or be, such Justice shall issue his warrant to arrest such person and to cause him to be brought before him, or some other Justice for the same county, to be dealt with according to law ; and upon such person being so brought before such Justice, and upon its being proved on oath that the person so arrested is the same person who is charged and named in such indictment, such Justice shall, without further inquiry, either commit him for trial or admit him to bail, in manner aforesaid ; and in any such case as last aforesaid, if the person so indicted shall at the time be confined in any gaol for any other offence than that charged in such indictment, such Justice shall, upon like proof on oath that the person so confined is the same person who is so charged in such indictment, issue his warrant (E b.) to the keeper of such gaol, commanding him to detain such person in his custody until he shall be discharged therefrom by the course of law ; but nothing herein contained shall be deemed to prevent any Clerk of the Crown or Peace or other officer from issuing any warrant in any such case for the arrest of any such person which he might otherwise by law issue.

Warrant to arrest a party against whom an indictment is found.

Party so arrested to be committed for trial or bailed.

If party indicted be in prison for some other offence, Justice to order his detention. But not to interfere with Bench warrants, &c.

19. The manner in which information, examinations, statements of accused parties, and recognizances, in proceedings for indictable

(*a*) It is only on the application of the bailsman that the Justice can issue this warrant, although the information may be made by some other and on behalf of the bailsman. The surety has himself it appears a Common Law right to arrest the person for whom he is bound, and bring him before a Justice, to have him committed, unless he find other sureties.—*2 Hawk.*, c. 15, sec. 3. If it be at all practicable, he will act wisely to obtain the Justice's warrant.

PETTY
SESSIONS
ACT.

Disposal of
the infor-
mations,&c.
Indictable
offences.

Informations,
&c., taken
before Jus-
tice out of
Petty Ses-
sions to be
transmitted
to Petty
Sessions.

Informations,
&c., to be
transmitted
to the Clerks
of the Crown
and Peace; .

offences, shall be disposed of, when taken, shall be subject to the
following provisions:—

1. Every such information, examination, statement, and recognizance sworn, taken, or acknowledged by or before any Justice
not sitting in Petty Sessions shall, with all convenient despatch,
and at the latest before the Petty Sessions then next ensuing for
the district where the case may have arisen, be transmitted by
him to the Justices at such Petty Sessions, except in cases where
the person accused shall not have been committed or shall not be
amenable, and such Justice shall deem it expedient to retain
such documents for a longer period :

2. The Justices at Petty Sessions shall transmit or cause the Clerk
of Petty Sessions to transmit every such information, examination, statement, or recognizance so received from any Justice out
of Petty Sessions, or which shall be sworn, taken, or acknowledged at Petty Sessions to the Clerk of the Crown of the county
where the same shall relate to any matter to be tried by the
Assizes, or to the Clerk of the Peace where same shall relate to
any matter to be tried at Quarter Sessions, with all convenient
despatch, or at latest within seven days from the holding of each
Petty Sessions where the party shall have been committed or
shall be amenable (or at least seven days before the Assizes
or Quarter Sessions, as the case may be, where the party shall
not have been committed or shall not be amenable), except
in cases of indictable offences where the party shall not have
been committed or shall not be amenable, and the Justices shall
deem it expedient to retain such documents for a longer period :

20. In all cases of summary jurisdiction the proceedings upon the hearing of the complaint shall be subject to the following provisions:—

1. Whenever the defendant or his agent (a) shall be present, the substance of the complaint shall be stated to him, and if he thereupon admit the truth of the complaint, then the Justices shall, if they shall see no sufficient reason to the contrary, convict or make an order against him accordingly, but if he do not admit the truth of the complaint, then the Justices shall proceed to hear such evidence as may be adduced in support of the complaint, and also to hear their defence, and such evidence as may be adduced on behalf of the defence, and also such evidence as the complainant may adduce in reply, if such defendant shall have given any evidence other than as to his the defendant's general character; but the complainant or his agent shall not be entitled to make any observations in reply upon the evidence given by the defendant, nor shall the defendant or his agent be entitled to make any observations in reply upon the evidence given by the complainant in reply; and if the information or complaint shall negative any exemption, exception, proviso, or condition in the statute on which the same shall be framed, it shall not be necessary for the complainant to prove such negative, but the defendant may prove the affirmative thereof, if he will have advantage of the same: (c)

Where both parties appear, case to be heard on both sides. (b)

Right of reply.

Proof of a negative.

No second speeches.

(a) *Agent.*—In Petty Sessions (Ireland) Act, 1851, the word "Agent" shall include the father, son, husband, wife, or brother of the complainant or defendant: provided that any such person be thereunto authorized in writing by the complainant or defendant (as the case may be); and to receive no remuneration therefor, and have the leave of the Court to appear and be heard, and that the Court is satisfied that such complainant or defendant is from infirmity, or other unavoidable cause, unable to appear.—45 & 46 Vict., c. 24.

(b) *Case to be heard on both sides.*—No man should be condemned unheard. "The laws of God and man," says Fortescue, J., in *Dr. Bentley's Case*, "both give the party an opportunity to make his defence, if he has any;" therefore Justices should hear what every accused has to say, by himself, or by his witnesses; and by hearing is meant to hear with patience. "Patience in a Judge ought to be considered as one of the chief branches of his duty, as it certainly is of justice. Well, but some unnecessary things are said: true, but it is better that what is unnecessary should be spoken, than that what is necessary should be omitted."—*Pliny's Epistles.*

If defendant admits the truth of the complaint, it should be so stated on the proceedings, and there is then no necessity for evidence; even though the statute direct the conviction to be on the oath of credible witnesses; where the defendant confesses no evidence is necessary.—*R.* v. *Hall,* 1 *T. R.,* 320.

(c) *Proving a Negative.*—Thus, selling beer without licence is an offence, and if the information or complaint state that it was so sold, without licence, the defendant will have to prove a licence. The complainant will have only to prove a sale. It is another question, if the complaint should not negative the exception, will it be sufficient to prove on the hearing that there is no licence? Well, the statutable offence should appear on the face of the complaint or summons. This is the rule, but several statutes, especially Excise Laws, make provision for these defects, and throw the burden of proof on the defendant. There are some exceptions which need not be negatived. Exceptions in the statute creating the offence should be negatived where they appear in the clause creating the offence, though it is otherwise when they appear by way of proviso in subsequent clauses or statutes.— *Cathcart* v. *Hardy,* 2 *M. & S.,* 534.

Proving Exceptions, &c.—In all cases of summary jurisdiction any exception, exemption, proviso, qualification, or excuse, whether it does or does not accompany the description of the offence complained of, may be proved by the defendant, but need not be specified or negatived in the information or complaint, and if so specified or negatived no proof in relation to the matters so specified or negatived shall be required from the complainant unless it shall be given by the defendant concerning the same.—40 & 41 Vict., c. 56, s. 78.

PETTY
SESSIONS ·
ACT.

Where defendant does not appear, hearing may be *ex parte.*

2. Whenever the defendant or his agent shall not appear at the time and place mentioned in the summons, and it shall appear to the Justices on oath that the summons was duly served a reasonable time before the time therein appointed for appearing, and no sufficient grounds shall be shown for an adjournment, the Justices may either proceed *ex parte* to hear and determine the complaint or may adjourn the hearing to a future day : (*a*)

Where complainant does not appear, case to be dismissed or adjourned.

3. Whenever the defendant or his agent shall appear at the time and place appointed in the summons, or shall be brought before the Justices by virtue of any warrant, then, if the complainant (having, in the case of a warrant, had due notice of the defendant's arrest) do not appear by himself or his agent, the Justices may either dismiss such complaint, or may adjourn the hearing to a future day :

Justices to take down evidence in offence cases in writing, if required by party.

4. Whenever any Justices shall proceed to hear and determine any complaint or information as to an offence, they, or one of them, shall, when required so to do by either party, or his agent, take or cause to be taken a note in writing of the evidence, or of so much thereof as shall be material, in a book to be kept for that purpose by the Clerk of Petty Sessions, and which book shall be signed by one of the Justices by whom such information or complaint shall have been heard on the day on which the same shall have been determined :

Justices may adjourn the Court generally, or may adjourn

And whenever all the cases shall not have been heard and determined on any Court day, the Justices then present may adjourn the remaining cases either to the next Court day, or to such other day as they shall see fit ; and whenever, either before or during the hearing of

ance at the time and place to which such hearing or further hearing shall be adjourned. (*a*)

21. In all cases of summary jurisdiction the Justices having heard what each party shall have had to say, and the evidence adduced by each, shall either make such order as shall be authorized by the Act under which the complaint shall be made, or shall dismiss the complaint either upon the merits or without prejudice to its being again made ; and the entry of the order so made shall be as follows :—

1. One of the Justices then present shall thereupon enter or cause the clerk to enter the particulars of such case and the substance of the decision thereon in a book to be kept for that purpose, to be called the " Order Book," according to the form (D), (and shall, in case of a dismissal, state whether the same is upon the merits or without prejudice to a further complaint) ; and such entry, when one of the Justices present shall have signed his name opposite to it or after it (which one of the said Justices is hereby required to do), shall be deemed to all intents and purposes a conviction or order, as the case may be : (*b*)

2. Whenever any Justice or Justices shall have made any such conviction or order out of Petty Sessions, in the cases permitted by this Act to be decided out of Petty Sessions, (*c*) he or they shall either enter the same in the Order Book in manner aforesaid, or shall enter the substance of the decision in the form of certificate (I a.), and shall forthwith, or at furthest before the next Court day, deliver or forward such certificate to the Clerk of the Petty Sessions of the district, who shall enter the same in the proper Order Book (with a special note that he has so done), and shall submit such entry for signature to the Justice or one of the Justices by whom the order shall have been made upon the next day of his attendance at Petty Sessions ; but in case such Justice shall not sign the same, the clerk shall make a special entry to that effect in the Order Book opposite to such case, and shall preserve the original certificate as a record of the proceedings :

3. The Sub-Inspector of Constabulary of the district shall make a return to the Justices at each Petty Sessions of the particulars of any cases of summary jurisdiction in which any Justices or Justices of the said Petty Sessions shall have made an order or issued any

Marginal notes:
PETTY SESSIONS ACT.

Adjudication of cases—Summary jurisdiction.

Justices either to convict, or to dismiss the complaint on the merits or without prejudice. Entry of orders.

If order made out of Petty Sessions.

Return and entry of cases decided out of Petty Sessions in which constabulary prosecute or act.

(*a*) *In Petty Sessions.*—Justices may adjourn Court, or may adjourn a particular case; and in prosecutions for offences, the information being on oath and in writing, may allow defendant to go at large, or *commit, or bind by recognizance* to appear, but in *summary cases, out of Petty Sessions,* it is otherwise. See *Circular* on this subject (*Appendix*).

(*b*) See present form of Order Book, and specimen for entering orders and keeping same, Forms in Schedule hereto.

(*c*) The cases referred to in which he can make the order out of Petty Sessions are drunkenness, vagrancy, fraud in the sale of goods, and disputes as to sales in fairs and markets.—See sec. 8. There are also cases under Excise Laws which may be heard out of Petty Sessions.

Justices who hear a complaint should give the decision.—Where four Justices heard a case of assault, and the case then stood adjourned to a future time for decision, and only two attended and delivered judgment, and notwithstanding the Affidavits of the Magistrates that all four concurred in the judgment, this was held to be fatal to the conviction. *Certiorari* granted to quash the conviction.—*Queen (Sullivan) v. Justices of Bantry, Q. B. Div.,* July, 1885. Probably it would have been otherwise had three of the four attended.

PETTY SESSIONS ACT.

warrant out of Petty Sessions, and in which any head or other constable of such district shall have been engaged, since the next preceding Petty Sessions.

Copies of convictions need not be returned to Quarter Sessions as hitherto; but certificate of order to be given to party; and certificate of a dismissal on the merits to be a bar to future proceedings; and to be good evidence of conviction.

And it shall not hereafter be necessary to return to Quarter Sessions copies of the summary convictions so made and entered at Petty Sessions; but if either party shall require it, a certificate (Form I a.) of any order so made (signed by the Justice who shall have made the same, or by any other Justice of the same Petty Sessions), shall be delivered to him at any time, and such certificate shall operate to all intents as a good form of conviction or order, as the case may be, any purpose for which any form of conviction or order may now by law be required, and in case of a dismissal, where the same shall be stated therein by the Justice to have been a dismissal on the merits, or that any assault was of a trifling or justifiable nature (and which he is hereby required to state if the case be so), such certificate upon being produced shall be a bar to any subsequent information or complaint for the same matter against the same party; and in any such case such certificate shall, on proof of the signature of the Justice to the same, be received as good evidence of the conviction or order in all Courts of Justice. (a)

General powers in adjudicating.

22. In all cases of summary jurisdiction it shall be lawful for the Justices in adjudicating thereon to exercise the following general powers, whether the same shall be authorized by the Act under which the complaint shall be made or not—

Justices may in all cases fix the time and manner of payment.

1. In every case where the Justices shall be authorized to award any penal or other sum, they may order that the same shall be paid either forthwith or at such time as they shall see fit to fix

they may order that in default of the said sum being paid as directed, the said person shall be imprisoned for any term not exceeding the period specified in the following scale : (a)

be ordered in default of distress, according to scale :

For any sum.	The imprisonment not to exceed.
Exceeding £5, but not exceeding £10	Three months.
Exceeding the last, but not exceeding £30	Four months.
Exceeding the last, but not exceeding £50	Six months.
Exceeding the last	One year.

And any such imprisonment shall be determinable upon payment of the said sum and costs, and any costs of the distress, where a distress shall have been made ; and such imprisonment may be directed in the same warrant as such distress; but if the said person shall admit, or if it shall be otherwise proved on oath, that he has no goods, or that a distress would be ruinous to him or his family, they may order that such person shall be imprisoned in the first instance for the like period for which he might be imprisoned in default of distress :

and may be directed by same warrant

So also in like cases in the first instance, where no goods, or the distress would be ruinous.

4. In every case of an offence where the order shall only have directed distress in default of payment of a penal sum, and it shall afterwards be found impossible to execute a warrant of distress, it shall be lawful for the Justices at Petty Sessions to order a warrant to issue to commit the person against whom such order shall have been made to gaol for such period as might have been directed by the original order ; and, in like manner, where

In offence cases Justices at Petty Sessions may substitute distress for committal, and vice versa, on failure of first warrant.

(a) *General powers in adjudicating where penal or other sums ordered.*—A distinction is noticeable in these sub-sections. All sums, penal or otherwise, may be levied by *distress*. A forfeited recognizance is in the nature of a penalty. The surety is amerced for what he never had any equivalent, but not for an offence. It is only under sub-secs. 3 and 4, where penalties are imposed for *offences*, that the power to imprison is here given. It is well to keep this in mind where by this or other Acts of Parliament this section is to be employed in enforcing penalties. The power given by "Small Penalties (Ireland) Act, 1873" (36 & 37 Vic., c. 82), is where the penalties are imposed by *Summary Conviction for Offences.*

Scale.—Up to £5 the scale is now regulated by the "Small Penalties (Ireland) Act, 1873," as follows :—

For any penalty	The imprisonment not to exceed
Not exceeding 10s.	Seven days.
Exceeding 10s., and not exceeding £1	Fourteen days.
Exceeding £1, but not exceeding £2 .	One month.
Exceeding £2, but not exceeding £5 .	Two months.

Up to £5 this Small Penalties Act scale is the proper one to be employed, except as to penalties recoverable by or on behalf of the Commissioners of Inland Revenue (sec. 7). The Militia Act of 1875 also departs from this scale. And as to offences against section 12 of the Licensing Act, 1872 (Drunkenness, &c.), in places where the Towns Improvement (Ireland) Act, 1854, is in force, see section 30 of the Licensing Act, 1874. which directs penalties to be enforced under the Towns Improvement Act.

In convictions under the Larceny Act, 24 & 25 Vic., c. 96, s. 107. and the Malicious Injuries Act, 24 & 25 Vic., c. 97, s. 65, it is enacted that, unless where otherwise specially directed, the Justice may imprison the offender, with or without hard labour, for any term not exceeding two months where the amount of the sum forfeited, or of the penalty imposed, or both (as the case may be), together with the costs, shall not exceed five pounds; and for any term not exceeding four months, where the amount with costs shall not exceed ten pounds; and for any term not

Petty
essions
Act.
—
the order shall have only directed imprisonment, and it shall be
found impossible to execute a warrant of committal, it shall be
lawful for the Justices at Petty Sessions to order a warrant to
issue to levy by distress of the goods of such person such penal
sum as might have been awarded by the original order; and in
all such cases a note of such proceeding shall be made by the
Justices in the Order Book: (a)

wer to
ard hard
ur in
ace cases.
5. In every case of an offence, where the Act shall authorize the
Justices to order imprisonment, they may adjudge by their order
that the said imprisonment shall be either with or without hard
labour, according as they shall see fit: (b)

rison-
t may
mence at
ration of
rison-
t under
ous
viction.
6. In every case of an offence, where the person against whom an
order to imprison shall be made shall then be in prison under-
going imprisonment upon a conviction for any other offence, it
shall be lawful for the Justice issuing the same, if he shall think
fit, to order therein that the imprisonment shall commence at the
expiration of the imprisonment to which such person shall have
been previously sentenced: (c)

r com-
sation
arded
all be paid
party
grieved,
cept in
rtain cases.
7. In every case where any sum shall be awarded under the provisions of any Act as compensation for damage, or as the value of
any article, or as the amount of any injury done, such sum shall
be paid to the party or public body aggrieved; but where the
party aggrieved is unknown, such sum shall be applied in like
manner as any penalties awarded to the Crown; and where

exceeding six months, in any other case: the commitment to be determinable upon
payment of the amount and costs. In all *intermediate* fines up to five pounds, the

several persons join in an offence, and are severally punished, each in the amount of the injury done, no more than one of such sums shall be paid to the party aggrieved, and the rest shall be applied as other penalties awarded to the Crown :

8. In every case where the Act under which any penal sum shall be ordered to be paid as a penalty for an offence (and no sum shall be awarded to the complainant as compensation for damage) it shall be lawful for the Justices to award any sum not exceeding one-third of such penal sum to the prosecutor or informer, and the remainder of such sum and all other penal sums shall be awarded to the Crown, any Act or Acts to the contrary notwithstanding : (a)

9. In all cases the Justices may order that the defendant shall pay to the complainant ; or in case of a dismissal, that the complainant shall pay to the defendant, such sum not exceeding twenty shillings, for costs, as to such Justices shall seem fit, and the same shall be recoverable in the same manner as any penal or other sum adjudged to be paid by the Justices : (b)

Provided always, that every person who shall aid, abet, counsel, or procure the commission of any offence which is or shall be punishable on summary conviction shall be liable to be proceeded against and convicted for the same, either together with the principal offender or before or after his conviction, and shall be liable, on conviction, to the same forfeiture and punishment to which such principal offender shall be by law liable (except where the age of such aider or abettor shall exceed fourteen years, in which case he shall be liable to the same forfeiture and punishment to which any principal offender whose age shall exceed fourteen years shall be liable), and may be proceeded against and convicted either in the county where such principal offender may be convicted, or in that in which such offence of aiding, abetting, counselling, or procuring, may have been committed. (c)

Margin notes: PETTY SESSIONS ACT. — Appropriation of fines and penalties. — Power to award costs in all cases to either party. — Aiders and abettors in the commission of offences to be punishable, on summary conviction, as principals.

(a) This appropriation is overruled by several Acts—"Fishery," "Poaching," "Militia," &c. See "Fines Act," *ante*, and notes thereon.

Revenue.—All penalties under Inland Revenue Acts to belong to Her Majesty and be paid to the Commissioners of Inland Revenue, 31 & 32 Vic., c. 124; and see also Fines Act, 14 & 15 Vic, c. 90. s. 13; and see also the exceptions in section 42 of above Act, and which exceptions do not appear in Fines Act, though passed in same Session.

(b) *Costs in all Cases.*—That is, in all cases of *summary* adjudication. They cannot award costs to either party in indictable offence cases. But the section says, that in all cases of summary adjudication, costs up to 20s. may be given *either party*, and that such costs may be recoverable as *penal or other sums.* Of course it cannot mean that costs in a civil case can be recovered as a penalty. But, then, does it mean that in an *offence* case, where they dismiss the complaint with costs, they can imprison the complainant as if it were a penalty ? I think the meaning to be, that the costs shall have the advantages of the remedy attached to the sums which they follow, but certainly no further. Now, under the *scale* the imprisonment is to be in proportion to the *penal* sum. To be sure, the costs must be paid with it; but there must be some penal sum. however small, to warrant the imprisonment. Costs, if ordered to a defendant, cannot be in the nature of a penalty, and therefore the remedy must be that provided for "other sums," which may be levied by distress, but not by imprisonment.

Where defendant is a married woman, the husband's goods are not liable to be distrained for her penalty.—*R.* v. *Johnson, 5 Q. B.*, 685.

(c) See title "Abettors," Summary Index.

PETTY
Sessions
Act.

Enforce-
ment of
orders.—
Summary
jurisdic-
tion.

In offence
cases warrant
to issue
peremptorily.

In civil cases
warrants to
issue on
application
of party;

but no
execution
of order
pending an
appeal;

except in
certain cases;
or if warrant
issued, not to
be executed;
or if exe-
cuted, party
to be dis-
charged or
distress to be
returned.

23. In all cases of summary jurisdiction, whenever an order shall be made upon the conviction of any person for an offence, the Justice shall issue the proper warrant for its execution forthwith, when the imprisonment is to take place immediately, or at the time fixed by the order for the imprisonment to take place where it is not to be immediate, or directly upon the non-payment of any penal sum or the non-performance of any condition at the time and in the manner fixed by the order for that purpose, or at furthest upon the next Court day (*a*) after the expiration of the time so fixed for the imprisonment, payment, performance of a condition, as the case may be, unless the imprisonment or penal sum shall have been remitted by the Crown or other competent authority in the interval; and whenever an order shall be made in any case of a civil nature, and the same shall not be obeyed, the Justice shall issue the proper warrant for its execution at any time after the time fixed for compliance with its directions, where required so to do by the person in whose favour such order shall have been made, or by some person on his behalf, and it shall not be necessary that the Justice by whom any such warrant shall be issued shall be the Justice or one of the Justices by whom the order shall have been made: Provided always, that in every case where the party being entitled to appeal against any such order shall have duly given notice thereof, and entered into a recognizance to prosecute the same in the manner hereinafter provided, it shall not be lawful for any Justice to issue any warrant to execute the said order until such appeal shall have been decided, or until the appellant shall have failed to perform the condition of such recognizance, as the case may be (except where any Act shall expressly authorize or direct the levy of any sum to be made notwithstanding the appeal); and in any case where the person shall be in custody, or shall have been committed to gaol, or any warrant of distress shall have been issued or executed, under any such order, the Justice by whom the warrant shall have been issued, or any other Justice of the same county shall, upon an application being made to him in that behalf, forthwith order the discharge of such person from custody or from gaol, or that such warrant of distress shall not be executed, or that if executed the distress shall be returned to the owner, as the case may be.

Appeals (*b*)
Summary
jurisdic-
tion.

In what cases
appeals shall
be permitted.

24. In any case of summary jurisdiction, where an order shall be made by the Justices for payment of any penal or other sum exceeding twenty shillings, or for any term of imprisonment exceeding one month, or for the doing of anything at a greater expense than forty shillings, or for the estreating of any recognizance to a greater amount than twenty shillings (but in no other case), either party

---

(a) This is directory, and should be obeyed by the Magistrate and officer of the Court; but the warrant may issue after the time above stated.
The clerk should see that warrants in offence cases are duly issued. He is responsible for the due and regular routine of proceedings.—*Law Adviser's Opinion, 17th Oct., 1867.*
(b) An appeal is given by the Larceny Act, 24 & 25 Vic., c. 96, s. 110, and by the Malicious Injuries Act, 24 & 25 Vic., c. 97, s. 68, where the sum adjudged to be paid shall exceed five pounds, or the imprisonment shall exceed one month, or the conviction shall take place before one Justice only. The following is the section:—
"In all cases where the sum adjudged to be paid on any summary conviction shall exceed five pounds, or the 'imprisonment adjudged shall exceed one month, or the conviction shall take place before one Justice only, any person who shall think himself aggrieved by any such conviction may appeal to the next Court of General or Quarter Sessions, which shall be holden not less than twelve days after the day of

(whether he shall be the complainant or the defendant), in cases of a civil nature, or the party against whom the order shall have been made in other cases, shall be entitled to appeal to the next Quarter Sessions to be held in the same division of the county when the order shall have been made by any Justice or Justices of any Petty Sessions district (or to the Recorder of any corporate or borough town at his next Sessions when the order shall have been made by any Justice or Justices of such corporate or borough town (unless when any such Sessions shall commence within seven days from the date of the order, in which case the appeal may be made to the next succeeding Sessions of such division or town) ; and such appeal shall be subject to the following provisions :— *Petty Sessions Act.*

1. The appellant shall serve notice in writing of his intention to appeal upon the Clerk of Petty Sessions, within three days from the date of the order against which the appeal shall be made :* *Appeal only to next Quarter Sessions of the division.*

2. He shall also within three days after such notice as aforesaid, enter into a recognizance, according to the form (C) with two solvent sureties, conditioned to prosecute such appeal, and the amount of such recognizance shall be double the amount of the *Notice to be given within three days.*

such conviction, for the county or place wherein the cause of complaint shall have arisen : Provided that such person shall give to the complainant a notice in writing of such appeal, and of the cause and matter thereof, within three days after such conviction, and seven clear days at the least before such Sessions, and shall also either remain in custody until the Sessions, or shall enter into a recognizance, with two sufficient sureties, before a Justice of the Peace, conditioned personally to appear at the said Sessions and to try such appeal, and to abide the judgment of the Court thereupon, and to pay such costs as shall be by the Court awarded ; or if such appeal shall be against any conviction, whereby only a penalty or sum of money shall be adjudged to be paid, shall deposit with the Clerk of the convicting Justice such a sum of money as such Justice shall deem to be sufficient to cover the sum so adjudged to be paid, together with the costs of the conviction and the costs of the appeal ; and upon such notice being given, and such recognizance being entered into, or such deposit being made, the Justice before whom such recognizance shall be entered into, or such deposit shall be made, shall liberate such person, if in custody ; and the Court at such Sessions shall hear and determine the matter of the appeal, and shall make such order therein, with or without costs to either party, as to the Court shall seem meet ; and in case of the dismissal of the appeal, or the affirmance of the conviction, shall order and adjudge the offender to be punished according to the conviction, and to pay such costs as shall be awarded ; and shall, if necessary, issue process for enforcing such judgment ; and in any case where, after any such deposit shall have been made as aforesaid, the conviction shall be affirmed, the Court may order the sum thereby adjudged to be paid, together with the costs of the conviction and the costs of the appeal, to be paid out of the money deposited, and the residue thereof (if any) to be repaid to the party convicted ; and in any case where after any such deposit the conviction shall be quashed, the Court shall order the money deposited to be repaid to the party convicted ; and in every case where any conviction shall be quashed on appeal as aforesaid, the Clerk of the Peace or other proper officer shall forthwith endorse on the conviction a memorandum that the same has been quashed : and whenever any copy or certificate of such conviction shall be made, a copy of such memorandum shall be added thereto, and shall be sufficient evidence that the conviction has been quashed, in every case where such copy or certificate would be sufficient evidence of such conviction."

To what Sessions Appeal shall be returned.—" To the next Quarter Sessions, *unless* when such shall be held within seven days from the date of the order." Within seven days will mean in or on the seventh day. If the order be made on the 1st and the Quarter Sessions be held on the 9th (and not sooner), the appeal shall there be sent. This just gives time to comply with par. 5, which directs that at least seven *clear days'* notice shall be given to the opposite party of the intention to prosecute. So that although three days be allowed to serve the notice in par. 1, and three days under par. 2 to enter into recognizance, still this seven days' notice in par. 5 must (in the event of the Quarter Sessions being held as here supposed) be given on the day on which the order is made.

* Where the appeal is under the Licensing Act, 1872, sec. 52, the notice must be given to the " Court of Summary Jurisdiction." *Ex parte* Curtis, Q. B. Div., E., 1877.

3 A

PETTY
SESSIONS
ACT.

Recogni-
zance to
prosecute
appeal.

Amount of
recogni-
zance.

Form of
appeal.

Recogni-
zance to
appeal to be
transmitted
to Clerk of
Peace.

Appellant to
give notice
to opposite
party.

Court of
Quarter
Sessions (or
Recorder)
may decide

sum and costs ordered to be paid, where payment only is ordered, or of such reasonable amount as the Justice shall see fit, where imprisonment is ordered :

3. Whenever the appellant shall have given notice and entered into such recognizance there shall be delivered to him the form of appeal (H) containing a certificate of the order against which he shall appeal (signed by the Justice who shall have made the same, or by any other Justice of the same Petty Sessions) ; and it shall also be therein certified by the Clerk of Petty Sessions that the said notice was duly given, and that the said recognizance was duly entered into, if the fact shall be so :

4. In every case where an appeal shall be so made, the Clerk of Petty Sessions shall transmit the recognizance entered into to prosecute such appeal and all other proceedings in such case to the Clerk of the Peace of the county or to the proper officer of the Recorder's Court at least seven days before the commencement of the Sessions to which the appeal shall be made, or as soon afterwards as may be practicable, in the same manner as hereinbefore provided for the transmission of informations as to indictable offences :

5. The appellant shall give notice in writing to the opposite party of his intention to prosecute his appeal at least seven clear days before the commencement of the Sessions to which the appeal shall be made :

6. Whenever an appeal shall have been so made, and such last-mentioned notice shall have been duly given, it shall be lawful for the said Court of Quarter Sessions (or Recorder, at the case may be) to entertain the same, and to confirm, vary, (a) or

---

(a) *Amendment of Orders, &c., on appeal.*—By the Civil Bill Act, 27 & 28 Vic. c. 99. sec. 49, " If objection made on appeal on account of any omission or mistake in the making or drawing up of convictions or orders pronounced by Justices of the Peace, or any variance between the facts stated in conviction or order and the evidence adduced in support thereof, and it should be shown to the satisfaction of the Court that sufficient grounds were in proof before the Justice or Justices making such conviction or order to have authorized the drawing up thereof free from the said omission or mistake, or that such variance is in some point not material to the merits of the case, it shall be lawful for the Court to amend such conviction or order on such terms as it shall think fit, and to adjudicate thereupon as if no such omission or mistake or variance had existed."

And by 40 & 41 Vic. c. 56, s. 76—No conviction or order made by any Justice or Justices shall be held void, or shall be quashed, by reason of any defect, omission, or variance in the summons, charge, or information upon which the same shall purport to have been made, provided that such defect, omission, or variance shall not have misled or prejudiced the defendant, or have affected the merits of the case ; and the Justice or Justices at the original hearing, or any Court of Appeal or Superior Court before which the decision of any such Justice or Justices shall afterwards come, may, upon such terms as shall appear just, make any amendment in any summons, charge, or information, which shall appear to be requisite for the purpose of making the conviction or order conformable with the same, or of raising the real question at issue, and deciding the case as justice shall require.

And see also secs. 36 and 39 of Petty Sessions (Ireland) Act, 14 & 15 Vic. c. 93. There is thus ample power in the Justices at Petty Sessions in the first instance, and in the Court of Appeal afterwards, to dispose of frivolous objections, and correct mistakes in procedure, so that the merits of the case shall be heard.

Justice who takes part in original hearing at Petty Sessions shall not take part in hearing of appeal from that decision.—40 & 41 Vic. c. 56, s. 73.

The rule in Superior Courts is in general found to be, and has been so expressed by the most eminent Judges of the land, that the order of the inferior tribunal will be upheld when the facts and circumstances will at all warrant it. It will be reversed only when it is decidedly bad and cannot at all be sustained.

reverse the order made by the Justices (as so certified in the form of appeal), and to award to either party any sum not exceeding forty shillings (a) for the costs of such appeal; and whenever the said Court of Appeal shall have decided any such appeal the Clerk of the Peace or proper officer of the Recorder's Court, as the case may be, shall certify such decision at foot of the form of appeal, and return the same and the said proceedings to the Justices of the Petty Sessions at which the order shall have been made, within seven days after such appeal shall have been decided; and whenever any such appeal shall not have been duly prosecuted, the Clerk of the Peace or proper officer of the Recorder's Court, as the case may be, shall so certify upon such recognizance, and return the same to the Justices of the Petty Sessions from which the same shall have been transmitted (in the same manner and subject to the same provisions as are hereinbefore contained as to the transmission of informations for indictable offences), within seven days after the termination of the Sessions at which such appeal ought to have been prosecuted and which certificate shall be free from any charge:

Petty Sessions Act.

appeal and give costs not exceeding 40s.

Clerk of Peace or proper officer of Recorder's Court to certify decision; or certify upon and return recognizance if appeal is not prosecuted.

7. And whenever it shall appear from such certificate that such appeal has not been duly prosecuted, or that the original order has been confirmed upon appeal the Justices who shall have made the original order, or any other Justice of the same Petty Sessions, shall issue the proper warrant for the execution of the same as if no such appeal had been brought; and in every case in which it shall appear from such certificate that the Court of Appeal shall have varied the original order, the said Justices shall forthwith issue the proper warrant for the execution of the order so made by the Court of Appeal, in like manner as they might have issued a warrant for the execution of the original order in case no appeal had been prosecuted; and if upon any such appeal either party shall be ordered to pay costs, it shall be lawful for such Justice to enforce payment of the same, in like manner as any costs awarded by the original order; and in any case where any order by which any person shall be adjudged to be imprisoned shall be confirmed on appeal, such person shall be liable to be imprisoned for the period

If order is not varied on appeal, Justice shall issue warrant for execution of the same.

But where order is varied, warrant to issue for execution of order of Quarter Sessions.

Costs of appeal, how recovered.

Where party has been

Appeal: power to vary.—In the Exchequer Division, May, 1888, before the Lord Chief Baron, Baron Dowse, and Mr.Justice Andrews: *Held*, that the CountyCourt Judge had the power,on appeal, to increase as well as to reduce the sentence passed by the Magistrates, and that the word "vary" in sec. 24 of the Petty Sessions (Ireland) Act (14 & 15 Vic., c. 93), covered this power. The Court further held that the appeal given to the County Court Judge was practically a rehearing. This question came before the Exchequer Division on arguments showing cause against conditional order for writ of *habeas corpus* at suit of the Rev. J. M'Fadden, a prisoner convicted on a charge under the Criminal Law & Procedure (Ireland) Act, 1887, where the County Court Judge had increased the original sentence from 3 to 6 months.

(*a*) In appeals under the Larceny Act and Malicious Injuries Act, these Acts provide that the Court shall "make such order therein, with or without costs to either party, as to the Court shall seem meet."

Application of the Penalty.—In drawing up convictions or orders for appeal, or where convictions are required, it is sufficient in most cases to state that the penalty is to be distributed or paid according to the form of the statute in such case made and provided; but when the statute leaves the application discretionary, the mode in which the discretion was exercised ought to be stated.—*R.* v. *Dempsey*, 2 *T. R.*, 96 (*E.*) Where costs are given they should be mentioned and set out in the conviction.—See notes on "Appeal," Summary Index.

Petty
Sessions
Act.

Imprisoned,
he is only to
be impri-
soned for re-
mainder of
period.

In certain
case, where
party fails to
prosecute ap-
peal, Justice
may estreat
recognizance.

This provi-
sion is re-
pealed by
40 & 41 Vic.,
c. 56, s. 75,
and other
provisions
substi-
tuted. (b)

*Addressing
warrants.*

To whom to
be addressed
in offence
cases;

In other
cases.

adjudged by the original order, where he shall not have been apprehended under the original order, or where he shall have been
so apprehended and discharged, then for such period as, together
with the time during which he shall so have been in custody
shall be equal to the period adjudged by the original order: (a)
Provided always, that whenever the party bound by recognizance to
prosecute an appeal against an order to imprison shall have absconded,
or when the party bound to prosecute an appeal against an order for
payment of any penal or other sum shall have no goods whereon to
levy same by distress, it shall be lawful for the Justices at the Petty
Sessions where the original order was made, and after like proof of
notice to the parties as in estreating other recognizances in summary
proceedings, to make an order for estreating the recognizance in any
such case to such amount as they shall see fit, and for paying out of
such amount such sum as shall have been directed to be paid to any
party by such original order, and thereupon to issue a warrant (E a.)
for the levy of the same upon the goods of the several persons bound
thereby.

25. The persons to whom warrants shall be addressed for execution
shall be as follows:—

1. All warrants in proceedings as to offences punishable either by
   indictment or upon summary conviction, which shall be issued
   in any Petty Sessions district, shall be addressed to the sub-inspector or head constable of constabulary who shall act for the
   place where the Petty Sessions for such district shall be held:

2. All warrants in other cases shall be addressed either to the sub-
   inspector or head constable of constabulary in manner afore-

And it shall not be necessary to address any warrant of committal to the keeper of the gaol, but upon the delivery of such warrant by the person charged with its execution to the keeper of the gaol to which the committal shall be made, such keeper shall receive and detain the person named therein (or shall detain him if already in his custody for such period and in such manner as it shall appear from the warrant that the said person is to be imprisoned; and in cases of adjournments or remands, such keeper shall bring the said person at the time and place fixed by the warrant for that purpose before such Justices as shall be there. *Petty Sessions Act. Committals need not be addressed to gaoler. Gaoler to produce prisoner in case of adjournments or remands.*

26. The execution of warrants so addressed to the sub-inspector or head constable of constabulary shall be subject to the following provisions :— *By whom warrants may be executed.*

1. Whenever the person against whom any warrant so addressed shall have been issued shall be to be found in case of committal, or shall have goods in case of distress, in any place for which such sub-inspector or head constable shall act, it shall be lawful for the sub-inspector, or head constable who shall act for the time being for such place, or for any head or other constable to be appointed by him, to execute the same : *Executing constabulary warrants in the district.*

2. Whenever it shall appear that the said person or his goods, as the case may be, are not to be found in any place for which such sub-inspector shall act, but that they are to be found elsewhere in the same county, said sub-inspector or head-constable shall certify on the warrant, according to the Form (G b.), the place where he believes that the said person or his goods are to be found, and also (having first satisfied himself as to the fact) that he believes the signature to the warrant to be genuine, and shall forthwith transmit the said warrant to the sub-inspector or head constable who shall act for such last-mentioned place, and the same shall be executed in like manner as any warrant addressed to him in the first instance : *Certifying to some other district of same county.*

3. Whenever it shall appear that the said person or his goods, as the case may be, are not to be found in the county to which such sub-inspector or head constable shall belong, but that such person or his goods, as the case may be, are to be found elsewhere out of the said county, the said sub-inspector or head constable shall, as before, certify on the warrant, according to the Form (G b.), and forthwith transmit the same to the Inspector-General of the Constabulary Force, to be backed, as hereinafter mentioned : *Certifying out of the county.*

Provided always, that in any case which shall appear to the Justice by whom any warrant shall be issued to be a case of emergency, he may address such warrant to any constable of the county ; and it shall be lawful for such constable to execute such warrant at any place within the county in which the Justice issuing such warrant shall have jurisdiction, or in case of fresh pursuit of an offender, at any place in the next adjoining county ; but the constable to whom any such warrant shall be so addressed shall, if the time will permit, show or deliver the same to the sub-inspector or head constable under whose command the said constable shall be, who shall proceed *But in case of emergency warrant may be executed by any constable, &c., in the same or adjoining county.*

PETTY SESSIONS ACT.

in respect to the same according to the Acts regulating the constabulary force.

Backing warrants.

27. Whenever any warrant addressed to the sub-inspector of constabulary, or to any head or other constable, shall be so certified and transmitted to the said Inspector-General, the manner in which it shall be backed for execution elsewhere shall be as follows :—

Constabulary warrants :

To any constabulary district in Ireland.

1. Whenever it shall appear that the said person or his goods are to be found in any place in *Ireland* (not being within the police district of *Dublin* metropolis), it shall be lawful for the said Inspector-General or for either of the Deputy Inspectors-General of Constabulary to indorse the said warrant according to the Form (G c.), and to transmit the same to the sub-inspector who shall act for such place, and the same shall be executed in like manner as any warrant addressed to him in the first instance : (*s*)

To the police district of Dublin metropolis.

2. Whenever it shall appear that the said person or his goods are to be found in the police district of *Dublin* metropolis, it shall be lawful for the said Inspector-General or for either of the said Deputy Inspectors-General, to indorse the said warrant according to the Form (G c.), and to transmit the same to the Commissioners of Metropolitan Police, and the same shall be executed in like manner as any warrant addressed to them in the first instance :

To England, &c.

3. Whenever it shall appear that the said person or his goods are to be found in some place in *England* or *Scotland*, or the Isles of *Man*, *Guernsey*, *Jersey*, *Alderney*, or *Sark*, it shall be lawful for the said Inspector-General, or for either of the said Deputy In-

Inspector-General, &c.,

place in *Ireland*, or in any of the places out of *Ireland* hereinbefore mentioned, it shall be lawful for any Justice or other such officer as aforesaid of such place, upon proof on oath of the handwriting of the Justice who shall have signed the warrant, to indorse the same for execution in such place in like manner as is hereinbefore provided as to any warrant indorsed by the Inspector-General of Constabulary.

Petty Sessions Act.

29. Whenever any person against whom any warrant shall be issued by any Justice or other such officer as aforesaid in *England* or *Scotland*, or in the Isles of *Man, Guernsey, Jersey, Alderney,* or *Sark,* for any crime or offence (*a*), shall reside or be, or be suspected to reside or be, in any place in *Ireland*, it shall be lawful for the said Inspector-General or for either of the said Deputy Inspectors-General, or for any Justice of the said last-mentioned place to indorse the same in like manner and upon like proof as aforesaid, authorizing the execution of the same within his jurisdiction.

Backing warrants from England, &c., into Ireland.

30. The aforesaid provisions as to the indorsement of warrants shall equally apply to any warrants for the arrest of any person charged with any indictable crime or offence for which he is punishable by law, whether the same shall be signed or indorsed or issued by a Justice of the Peace, or by a Judge of Her Majesty's Court of Queen's Bench, or Justices of Oyer and Terminer and General Gaol Delivery, in *England* or *Ireland*, or by the Lord Justice General, Lord Justice Clerk, or any of the Lords Commissioners of Justiciary, or by any Sheriff or Steward Depute or Substitute, in *Scotland*, or by the Chief or Under Secretary to the Lord Lieutenant.

The above provisions to apply also to Judges' warrants.

31. Whenever any warrant, addressed either to the constabulary or to any other person, shall be so indorsed by the said Inspector-General or by either of the said Deputy Inspectors-General, or by any Justice or other such officer as aforesaid, it shall be a sufficient authority to the person bringing such warrant, and also to all constables or peace officers of the county or place where such warrant shall be so indorsed, to execute the same by arrest, committal, or levy, as the case may be, within the jurisdiction of the said Justice or officer, and in case of a warrant to arrest any person, to convey him when arrested before the Justice or officer by whom the same was issued, or before some other Justice or officer of the same county or place, to be dealt with according to law : Provided always, that if the prosecutor, or any of the witnesses for the prosecution, in cases of indictable offences, shall then be in the county or place where any person shall have been arrested under any warrant so backed as aforesaid, the constable or other person who shall have arrested such person shall, if so directed by the Justice who shall have indorsed the warrant, bring the person so arrested before him or some other Justice of the same county or place, who may thereupon take the examinations of such prosecutor or witnesses, and proceed in every

Warrants so backed to be valid for execution ; but if the prosecutor or witnesses be on the spot, examinations may be taken

---

(*a*) *Crime* or *Offence* are generic terms. Disobedience of an order which a Magistrate is authorized to make is in itself an *offence*. As a rule, any Magistrate's warrant, authorizing the arrest of the person, may be taken to be a warrant for an offence. These are the terms used in the oldest statutes on the subject, authorizing the pursuit and arrest of persons escaping from one island to the others.

PETTY
SESSIONS
ACT.

respect as hereinbefore directed with respect to persons charged before
a Justice with an indictable crime or offence, alleged to have been
committed in any other county or place than that in which such
person shall have been arrested.

*Execution
of
warrants.*

32. The manner in which distresses and committals under warrants
shall be made shall be as follows :—

When ad-
dressed to
constabu-
lary ;

1. Whenever any warrant to levy any penal or other sum by distress shall be addressed to the constabulary, the sums levied
under it shall be accounted for under the provisions of the
" Fines Act, *Ireland*, 1851 ; " but whenever any such warrant
shall be addressed to any other person than the constabulary,

when
addressed to
other persons.

such person shall pay over the sum levied under it to the person
who shall appear by such warrant to be entitled to the same, or
in such other manner, and subject to such account of the same,
as the Justices shall direct :

Distress may
be sold in a
certain time.

2. In every case where a distress shall be made under any such
warrant, it shall be lawful for the person charged with its execution to sell the said distress within such period as shall be specifically fixed by the said warrant ; or if no period shall be so fixed,
then within the period of three days from the making of the distress, unless the sum for which the warrant was issued, and also
the reasonable charges of taking and keeping the said distress
shall be sooner paid ; and in every case where he shall sell any
such distress, he shall render to the owner the overplus (if any)
after retaining the amount of the said sums and charges : (*a*)

On payment
of penalty,
&c., distress
not to be
levied.

3. In every case where any person against whom any such warrant
shall be issued shall pay or tender to the person having the execution of the same the sum in such warrant mentioned, or shall
produce the receipt of the officer of the Court for the same, and
shall also pay the amount of the expenses of such distress up to
the time of such payment or tender, such person shall refrain
from executing the same :

Distress may
be sold by
auction with-
out licence.

4. In every case where any sub-inspector or member of the
Metropolitan Police Force shall be empowered to distrain any
goods under such warrant, he may and is hereby authorized to
sell or cause the same to be sold by auction by any head constable of the said constabulary force, or by any member of the
said Metropolitan Police Force, as the case may be, without procuring any licence to act as an auctioneer, and may deduct out of
the amount of such sale all reasonable costs and charges actually
incurred in effecting the same.

(*a*) Growing crops, trees, plants, vegetables, &c., not severed from the soil, not
liable to be seized under civil-bill decree or Magistrate's warrant.—26 & 27 Vic.,
c. 62, sec. 2 ; and see also 51 & 52 Vic., c. 47, s. 4, exempting wearing apparel, bedding,
tools, &c., under value of £5.
Warrants under the Towns Improvement (Ireland) Act, 1854.—The provisions of
the Petty Sessions (Ireland) Act, 14 & 15 Vic., c. 93, as to the execution of warrants,
shall extend and may be applied to the execution of warrants issued by Magistrates
appointed under the Towns Improvement (Ireland) Act, 1854 ; and the term "county"
in the Petty Sessions Act shall, for this purpose, include any town within the boundaries of which any such Magistrate shall have the jurisdiction of a Justice of the Peace

5. In every case where any person who shall be apprehended under any such warrant shall pay or cause to be paid to the keeper of the gaol in which he shall be imprisoned the sum in the warrant mentioned, the said keeper shall receive the same, and shall thereupon discharge such person if he be in his custody for no other matter :

PETTY SESSIONS ACT. —— If sum paid after committal, prisoner to be discharged.

6. Whenever the warrant shall be to commit any prisoner to gaol, the head or other constable or other person whose duty it shall be to convey such prisoner to gaol shall deliver over the said warrant and the said prisoner to the keeper of the gaol, who shall thereupon give to such head or other constable or other person a receipt for such prisoner (Form F.), setting forth the state and condition in which he shall have been delivered into the custody of such keeper :

Gaoler to give receipt for prisoners.

7. In any case of summary jurisdiction in which a Justice shall order any person to be committed to gaol for any period, either in default of payment of any sum, or in default of distress, or as a punishment for any offence, such committal shall be to the county gaol, district bridewell, or house of correction of the county in which the party shall be arrested (*a*), unless where such arrest shall be made in any county adjoining to that in which the warrant shall have been issued, in which case the committal shall be to any of the said prisons of such last-mentioned county; and whenever any Justices shall order any person to be committed on account of any adjournment of the hearing, or until the return of a warrant of distress, or for any like temporary purpose, such committal shall be either to the gaol, or house of correction, district bridewell, or to any bridewell or lock-up of the county, built or supported by county presentment, according as shall appear to the Justices most convenient for that purpose.

To what prison offenders shall be committed in summary proceedings.

33. Whenever the person to whom any warrant shall be so addressed, transmitted, or indorsed for execution, shall be unable to find the person against whom such warrant shall have been issued, or his goods, as the case may be, or to discover where such person or his goods are to be found, he shall return such warrant to the Justices by whom the same shall have been issued within such time as shall have been fixed by such warrant (or within a reasonable time where no time shall have been so fixed), and together with it a certificate (G a.) of the reasons why the same shall not have been executed; and it shall be lawful for such Justices to examine such person on oath touching the non-execution of such warrant, and to re-issue the said warrant again, or to issue any other warrant for the same purpose from time to time as shall seem expedient.

Return of unexecuted warrants. Re-issue of warrant.

(*a*) This may be attended with difficulty; the practice is to name in the warrant the gaol of the county in which offender resides and for which the Magistrate acts, and the prescribed form of warrant in the schedule supposes that a particular gaol will be named. And if the arrest take place in a county *not adjoining*, the gaoler of that county may refuse to take the prisoner, finding a different prison named in it. This may be rectified by the Inspector-General or the Magistrate who backs the warrant. If the warrant be bad, informal, or does not give the order correctly, another may be substituted, but taking care that the imprisonment run from date mentioned in former warrant.

See now Prisons (Ireland) Act, 1877, 40 & 41 Vic., c. 49.

34. Whenever any person shall be bound to appear, or to keep the
peace, it shall be done by a separate recognizance (C) ; but whenever
any person shall be bound to prosecute or to give evidence as a witness,
it may be done either by a recognizance at foot of his deposition (A b.)
or by a separate recognizance at the discretion of the Justice ; and
the taking of every recognizance shall be subject to the following
provisions :—(*a*)

1. It shall be in such amount as the Justice shall, in his discretion,
think expedient, except in cases of appeal, in which the amount
shall be as hereinbefore provided :

2. It shall particularly specify the profession, trade, or occupation
of every person entering into the same, together with his Christian and surname, and the name of the parish and townland, or
town, in which he resides ; and if he resides in a town, the
name of the street and the number (if any) of the house in which
he resides, and whether he is owner or tenant thereof, or a lodger
therein :

3. Every recognizance so taken according to the form in the schedule
to this Act, or to the like effect, either at foot of the deposition or
by a separate form, shall have the like force and effect in binding
the lands, tenements, goods, and chattels of the persons acknow-
ledging the same, and in all other respects, which any recognizance now by law has :

And whenever the condition of any such recognizance shall be to
appear at Assizes or Quarter Sessions, or at any place other than before any Justice or Justices, or to perform the duties of Petty Sessions
Clerk, it shall be forwarded to the Clerk of the Crown or Peace as
hereinbefore provided, and shall be liable, upon any breach of the
condition thereof, to be estreated in the same manner as any forfeited
recognizance to appear is now by law liable to be estreated by the
Court before which the principal party thereto shall have been bound
to appear : But whenever the condition of any such recognizance
shall be to keep the peace, or to appear before any Justice out of
Quarter Sessions, or to perform the duties of a pound-keeper, it shall
be deposited with the Clerk of Petty Sessions of the district by the
Justice by whom it shall have been taken, and upon non-performance
of the condition thereof, any Justice who may then be there present

(*a*) *The Recognizance.*—To prevent questions being raised, it is proper that the particulars in this section specified shall appear on the face of the recognizance. The
question has been raised on appeal, and while some hold that these particulars, being
indorsed and sworn to (as directed by 57 Geo. III., c. 56, s. 2), is a sufficient compliance,
and that the indorsement is to be taken and read as part of the recognizance, still
the prevailing opinion is the other way. It is, however, to be observed that sec. 26
(on the subject of *appeal*) states the recognizance is to be in the Form (C) ; and sec.
34 (on the general question of recognizance) refers to the same form, and directs
that the "*taking* of every recognizance" shall be subject to its containing the particulars there specified. Sec. 36 states that the *forms* in the Schedule shall be valid,
and by sec. 34 every recognizance so taken according to Form in Schedule, or "to
the like effect," shall be of force and effect in binding the lands, &c. But although,
as in the case of appeals, the opposite party may object to the recognizance as not
being up to the directions of the statute, the parties to the recognizance may not be
allowed to question it on the same grounds if the omission should be such as would
not vitiate an ordinary bond to the Crown. Still it is the duty of the officer who
prepares it, and of the Magistrate who receives it, to see that the requirements of
sec. 34 and sub-sections 1 and 2 be strictly complied with. See Schedule.

may certify on the recognizance the non-performance of the said condition, and it shall thereupon be lawful for the Justices sitting at the Petty Sessions of the district, and in open Court, upon proof of the non-performance of the said condition, to make an order to estreat such recognizance to such amount as they shall see fit, and thereupon to issue a warrant (E a.) to levy such amount by distress and sale of the goods of the parties who shall have acknowledged the same : Provided always, that in every case where any Justices shall order any such recognizance to be estreated, proof shall be first made on oath that notice in writing (stating the general grounds on which it is intended to sustain the application) was left at the usual place of abode of the party, or of each of the parties, if more than one, against whom it is sought to put such recognizance in force, at least seven days before the day on which the application to estreat such recognizance shall be made. (*a*)

and may be estreated by Justices ; after proof on oath of notice to parties.

(*a*) *Estreating Recognizances.*—On examining this section, three distinct steps will be found necessary in order to estreat the recognizances before the Justices : first the *forfeiture*, which must be certified thereon by " any Justice who may then be there present : " next (and it would seem after the forfeiture), a seven-day notice of the application to estreat : and then the Justices in open Court, "upon proof of the non-performance of the condition," are to make the *order to estreat.* The certificate and the order (which are distinct) will be found at foot of the form in Schedule, and are generally printed on the bond. But what evidence or facts are necessary to be before the Justice in the first instance, to warrant his certifying that the recognizance has been forfeited, the section does not state. It is plain enough where it is a *failure to appear*, or if the principal party be before him, convicted of a breach of the peace, the Justice on that occasion may certify the forfeiture of the recognizance ; and it matters not on what evidence he may act, as proof must afterwards be made in open Court before the order to estreat can be made. On the whole, it would seem to be an irregular and unauthorized proceeding (although it is sometimes done) for a private party to serve notices to *estreat* a Crown bond unless a Justice, acting either on his own knowledge or on some complaint, information, or other evidence, against the principal party, certifies that the recognizance is forfeited. One Justice may certify, two or more make the order to estreat. A Justice, peace officer, or person aggrieved may proceed on the bond —(See Form of Notice to Estreat, *Appendix*.)

How amount of Recognizance estreated is to be levied.—The above section, which gives Justices in Petty Sessions the power to estreat the recognizance, also specially directs that it is to be levied by *distress* and sale of the goods of the parties—nothing more. But see Fines (Ireland) Act passed in same session, chap. 90, notes and opinions thereon, *Appendix*. Of course the *offence* of which the principal party may have been convicted is dealt with on its own merits. The forfeiture of the recognizance as a consequence of that conviction is, as against principal and sureties, another matter. The Justice's power to imprison must be given by very distinct and unequivocal legislation, not drawn from doubtful and ambiguous words.

What will cause a Forfeiture of Recognizance to keep the Peace.—Actual violence to the person of another, whether it be done by the party himself or by others through his procurement, or by any unlawful assembly in terror of the people, and even by words directly tending to a breach of the peace, as by challenging one to fight or in his presence threatening to beat him, or the like.—1 *Hawk.*, c. 60, ss. 20, 21. But if the party threatened be absent, it is otherwise ; and yet if the party so bound shall threaten to kill or beat a person who is absent, *and after shall lie in wait for him* to kill or beat him, this is a forfeiture of the recognizance.—*Dalt.*, c. 121, s. 1. However, it shall not be forfeited by bare words of heat and choler, as calling a man a knave.—1 *Hawk.*, c. 60, s. 22.

What for Good Behaviour.—The rule that whatever will be a cause to bind a man to his good behaviour will forfeit a recognizance for it is now denied : because the statute, in ordering persons of evil fame to be bound in this manner, seems to regard the prevention of that mischief which they may be justly suspected to be likely to do, and in that respect requires them to secure the public from that danger which may be apprehended from their future behaviour, whether any actual crime can be proved upon them or not ; and it would be extremely hard in such cases to make persons forfeit their recognizances who yet may be justly compellable to give one, as those who keep suspicious company, or those who spend much money idly without having any visible means of getting it honestly, or those who lie under the general suspicion of being rogues, or the like.—1 *Hawk.*, 61, c. 5. But he who is bound to his good

35. Any of the officers or persons hereinafter mentioned who shall commit any of the offences or neglects hereinafter mentioned, and who shall be convicted thereof before any two Justices of the county sitting at Petty Sessions, shall be liable to forfeit for every such offence or neglect the penalties hereinafter mentioned : (that is to say),

Any Clerk of Petty Sessions who shall neglect or refuse to enter any summons in the order required under the provisions of this Act shall be liable to a penalty not exceeding 40s.

Any Clerk of Petty Sessions who shall demand or receive any other or different fees, or any greater amount of fees, as to any proceedings in any case than he can legally demand or receive under this Act, shall be liable to a penalty not exceeding £5.

Any person who, whilst he shall hold the office of Petty Sessions Clerk shall practise as an attorney or solicitor in any case at such Petty Sessions or at the Quarter Sessions of the division of the county in which such Petty Sessions shall be situated, or who shall act as the Clerk of any attorney or solicitor so practising, or as the clerk of a Poor Law Union, or as a collector of any public tax, or as a pound-keeper, or as the keeper or partner in keeping any inn or public-house, or who shall engage in any other business or occupation which the Justices or the Lord Lieutenant shall have forbidden as inconsistent with his duties as Petty Sessions Clerk, shall be liable to a penalty not exceeding £20.

Any summons-server or other person who shall make any wilful default in serving any summons shall be liable to a penalty not exceeding 40s.

Any sub-inspector, head or other constable, or other person who shall wilfully neglect to return any unexecuted warrant at the time required by the Justices, or who shall commit any wilful default in respect to the execution of the same, shall be liable to a penalty not exceeding £5.

Any person in whose possession any books, papers, or other effects belonging to the Justices at Petty Sessions, or relating to such Court, shall be upon or after the death, resignation, suspension, or dismissal of any Petty Sessions Clerk, and who shall refuse to deliver up the same to the sub-inspector or head constable, or other person directed by the Justices under the provisions of this Act to demand the same, shall be liable to a penalty not exceeding £10.

Marginal notes:

PETTY SESSIONS ACT.
—
Offences against this Act.
—
Entry of summonses.

Clerk taking more than legal fees.

Clerk engaging in occupation inconsistent with his duties.

Service of summonses.

Constabulary, &c., not returning warrants, or committing any wilful default.

Retaining Petty Sessions books, &c.

---

behaviour ought to demean himself well in his carriage and in his company, not doing anything which shall be a cause of breach of the peace ; or put the people in fear, dread, or trouble ; and so shall be intended of all things which concern the peace, but not in misdoing of other things which touch not the peace.—*Dalt.*, c. 1, 22. s. 14. However, such a recognizance shall not only be forfeited for such actual breaches of the peace, for which a recognizance for the peace may be forfeited, but also for some others for which such recognizances cannot be forfeited—as for going armed with great numbers, to the terror of the people, or speaking words tending to sedition, and the like ; and also for all such actual misbehaviours which are intended to be prevented by such a recognizance; but not for barely giving cause of suspicion of what perhaps may never actually happen.—1 *Hawk.*, c. 61, s. 6 ; *Dalt.*, c. 127, s. 14. See also " Sureties of the Peace," Summary Index.

Any person who shall oppose or hinder any search under any warrant issued by the Justices for the discovery of any such books, papers, or other effects, shall be liable to a penalty not exceeding £5.

Petty Sessions Act.

Hindering search for books, &c.

Any person having any other duty to perform under the provisions of this Act, and who shall wilfully neglect to perform the same, shall be liable to a penalty not exceeding £5.

Any other neglect of duty.

And it shall be lawful for the said Justices to award the said penalties; and if the same shall be imposed upon any member of the constabulary force, the amount shall be deducted from his pay; but if imposed upon any other person, then in default of payment thereof forthwith, or at such time as the Justices shall fix, such person may be committed to prison for the like period, in proportion to the amount of the penalty imposed, for which the Justices are authorized to commit any offender in default of distress for any other penalty under the provisions of this Act.

Justices may award the foregoing penalties.

36. In all proceedings under this Act the several forms in the Schedule to this Act contained, or forms to the like effect, shall be deemed good, valid, and sufficient in law, and shall be the proper forms to be used, even in cases in which other and different special forms shall be or shall have been provided by the particular Act or Acts under which the information or complaint shall be made; but no departure from any of the said first-mentioned forms, or omission of any of the particulars required thereby, or use of any other words than those indicated in such forms, shall vitiate or make void the proceeding or matter to which the same shall relate, if the form used be otherwise sufficient in substance and effect, and the words used clearly express the intention of the person who shall use the same; and it shall be sufficient in any of the forms provided by this Act to state sums of money either in words or figures, according as the person using the same shall see fit: Provided always, that it shall be lawful for the Lord Lieutenant, from time to time, with the advice and consent of the Privy Council, to extend the said form of Order Book (D) (*a*) so far as to adapt it to any like proceedings either new or not provided for therein: Provided also, that the sealing of any warrant or other form of procedure under this Act shall not be necessary in addition to the signature of the Justice by whom the same shall be signed.

Forms of procedure.

Forms in the Schedule to be deemed valid, and the proper forms in all proceedings; but informality not to vitiate any proceeding. Form of Order Book may be extended by Lord Lieutenant in Council.

37. And with a view to simplify forms, the prosecutor or party at whose instance the proceedings shall take place may be termed in such forms the "Complainant," whether he shall be an informant or prosecutor or otherwise; and the matter of the proceeding may be termed the "Complaint," whether founded on an information or

Warrants, &c., need not be sealed.

General terms used in Forms of Procedure.

(*a*) See specimen form in Schedule hereto.

Forms.—This Petty Sessions Act, in the Schedule, provided Forms applicable to all cases, to the great convenience of Magistrates. This rule has been forgotten and disregarded by law officers or bill drawers; the result is that new Forms are being accumulated to an inconvenient extent.

otherwise; and in summary proceedings the decision of the Justices
may be termed their "Order," whether the same shall be a conviction or otherwise.

**Description
of the pro-
perty of part-
ners, &c. ;**

**of the
property of
counties ;**

**of the
property in
goods pro-
vided for the
poor ;**

**of the
property in
materials for
road ;**

**of the
property in
materials for
turnpike
roads, &c. ;**

**of the
property of**

38. It shall be sufficient, in any information or complaint, or the
proceedings thereon, to describe the property belonging to or in the
possession of partners, joint tenants, parceners, or tenants in common,
as the property of any one of such persons who shall be named, and
of another or others, without naming them, as the case may be; and
any work or building made, maintained, or repaired at the expense
of any county or place, or any materials for the making, altering, or
repairing of the same, as the property of the inhabitants of such
county or place respectively ; and any goods provided by guardians
of the poor or their officers respectively for the use of the poor, as
the goods of the guardians of the poor of the Union to which the
same belong, without naming any of them; and any materials and
tools provided for the repair of highways at the expense of baronie
or other districts in which such highways may be situate, as the
property of the county surveyor or surveyors respectively, without
naming him or them ; and any materials or tools provided for making
or repairing any turnpike road, and any buildings, gates, lamps,
boards, stones, posts, fences, or other things erected or provided for
the purpose of any such turnpike road, as the property of the commissioners or trustees of such turnpike road, without naming them;
and any property of any persons described in any Act of Parliament,
or in any charter or letters of incorporation, as commissioners,
directors, trustees, or by any other general designation whatsoever,
as the property of such commissioners, directors, trustees, or persons

the same shall be alleged to have been committed or to have arisen, shall not be deemed material, provided that the said offence or cause be proved to have been committed or to have arisen within the jurisdiction of the Justice or Justices by whom such information or complaint shall be heard and determined ; and no objection shall be taken or allowed in any proceedings to any information, complaint, summons, warrant, or other form of procedure under this Act, for any alleged defect therein in substance or in form, or for any variance between any information, complaint, or summons, and the evidence adduced on the part of the complainant or prosecutor at the hearing of the case in summary proceedings, or at the examination of the witnesses by a Justice or Justices in proceedings for indictable offences : Provided always, that if any such variance or defect shall appear to the Justice or Justices at the hearing to be such that the defendant has been thereby deceived or misled, it shall be lawful for such Justice or Justices, upon such terms as he or they shall think fit, to adjourn the hearing of the case to some future day, and in the meantime, in cases of proceeding for offences, to commit the said defendant to gaol, or to discharge him upon his entering into a recognizance conditioned for his appearance at the time and place to which such hearing shall be so adjourned.

PETTY SESSIONS ACT.

be in time, or offence be actually committed within the jurisdiction.

No objection to be allowed for defect of substance or form in warrant, or for any variance between it and evidence adduced; but if the party charged is deceived by such variation or defect, he may be committed or discharged upon recognizance till adjourned hearing.

40. No receipt required to be given under the provisions of this Act shall be subject to any stamp duty payable to the Crown.

41. Nothing in this Act shall extend to the police district of *Dublin* metropolis, or alter or affect in any manner whatsoever any of the provisions or enactments contained in any Act regulating the powers and duties of Justices of the Peace, or of the police of the district of *Dublin* metropolis, or be deemed applicable in any way to the same, save so far as relates to the backing or executing of any warrants, or to alter the provisions of any Act or Acts whereby any part of any county is annexed for the purpose of criminal proceedings to any other county, or whereby any offences committed in one county are authorized to be tried in any other county.

42. Nothing in this Act shall extend or be construed to extend to any information or complaint or other proceeding under or by virtue of any of the Acts relating to Her Majesty's revenue of excise or customs, stamps, taxes, or post-office, or relating to the preservation

---

complaint ought not to fall short of the necessary legal description of the offence, either in the words of the statute, or in equivalent words. The great point is to clearly see and understand the offence pointed at by the statute, and that the evidence sustains the charge.

"40 & 41 *Vic.*, c. 56, *sec* 76.—No conviction order made by any Justice or Justices shall be held void or shall be quashed by reason of any defect, omission, or variance in the summons, charge, or information, upon which the same shall purport to have been made, provided that such defect, omission, or variance, shall not have misled or prejudiced the defendant, or have affected the merits of the case ; and the Justice or Justices, at the original hearing, or any Court of Appeal or Superior Court, before whom the decision of any such Justice or Justices shall afterwards come, may, upon such terms as shall appear just, make any amendment in any summons, charge, or information, which shall appear to be requisite for the purpose of making the conviction or order conformable with the same, or of raising the real question at issue, and deciding the case as Justice shall require."

of game, except that all proceedings as to the same may be in the
forms of procedure required by this Act, or as near thereto as the
circumstances of the case will admit. (*a*)

Section 43 repeals certain previous Petty Sessions Acts.

Section 44, interpretation clause of the several terms used throughout the Act.*

Title of Act to be "The Petty Sessions (Ireland) Act, 1851."
To extend to *Ireland* only.   Schedule to be part of Act.

(*a*) This Act is applicable (by express provision) to the "Poaching Act," 25 & 26
Vic., c. 114.   In all proceedings instituted by the constabulary for offences against
the Illicit Distillation Act, 1 & 2 Wm. iv., c. 55, the proceedings for recovery of
penalties are to be under this Petty Sessions Act.—See 20 & 21 Vic., c. 40, s. 6, and
title "Excise."   It is also by the 26 & 27 Vic., c. 96, made applicable to the Public
House Acts, 3 & 4 Wm. iv., c. 68, and 6 & 7 Wm. iv., c. 38, doubts having been entertained as to whether these were not Excise Acts.   It is now applicable to the
Licensing Acts, 1872-74.   And for power to amend summons and proceedings, see
also 40 & 41 Vic.. c. 56, s. 76.
* See also "Interpretation Act, 1889," 51 & 52 Vic., ch. 63: "Preliminary".

PETTY SESSIONS ACT.

SCHEDULE.

[The words in the footnotes in *italics*, or words to the like effect, are to be used according to the circumstances of each case.]

₊ In all forms of procedure the name and description of each party is to be specified in like manner and with the same particulars as is required by this Act (section 35) as to any party bound by a recognizance. (a)

FORMS (A)—PROOFS.

(A a.)—*Information.*

—— *Complainant.* } Petty Sessions District of ——, County of ——
—— *Defendant.* } The Information of A.B., of M.N., who saith on his (¹)
that (²)
    Taken before me, this —— day of ——, in the year eighteen hundred and
——, at ——, in the said county.

    (b)   Signed ——, Justice of said County.

(¹) *Oath or Affirmation.*
(²) State cause of complaint, with time and place. Adding :—For the arrest of a witness, *And he further saith that X. Y. can give material evidence, but is not likely to attend voluntarily ;* or (*and is keeping out of the way of personal service of summons*); or, for sureties of the peace *And he makes this information for the safety of his person and property, and not from malice or revenge against the said C. D.*

(A b.)—*Deposition of a Witness.*

—— *Complainant.* } Petty Sessions District of ——, County of ——
—— *Defendant.* } The Deposition of X.Y., of M.N., taken in the presence
and hearing of C.D., who stands charged that (¹)
The said deponent saith on his (²)   that (³
    (b)

(¹) Cause of complaint, with time or place.
(²) *Oath or Affirmation.*
(³) Deposition as nearly as possible in the words of the witness, and to be signed by him if he will.

(a) *What Forms shall contain.*—The above note is given in the statute. By sec. 36 the omission of any of these particulars shall not vitiate the proceedings. Sec. 35 in the above reference was a mistake, it refers to sec. 34.

(b) The informant or witness may be bound to prosecute or give evidence by the following Form of Recognizance at foot of his Information or Deposition :—
" And the said informant (*or* deponent) binds himself to appear at ——, on the ——, to prosecute (*or* to give evidence) against the said C. D. for the said offence, or otherwise to forfeit to the Crown the sum of——.

                         " Signed ——, Informant (*or* Deponent).
" Taken before me, this —— day of ——, in the year eighteen hundred and —— at —— in the said County.
                         " Signed ——, Justice of said County."

(A c.)—*Statement of the Accused.*

—— *Complainant.* } Petty Sessions District of ——, County of ——
—— *Defendant.* }   A charge having been made against C.D., before the undersigned Justice that ([1])
and the said charge having been read to the said C.D., and the witnesses for the prosecution having been severally examined in his presence, and the said C.D., having been first duly cautioned that he was not obliged to say anything, but that whatever he did say might be given in evidence against him upon his trial, saith as follows :—([2])

Taken before me, this —— day of ——, in the year eighteen hundred and ——, at ——, in said County.

Signed ——, Justice of said County.

([1]) Cause of complaint, with time and place.
([2]) Statement of prisoner in his very words, or as nearly so as possible, and to be signed by him if he will.

(A d.)—*Solemn Declaration.* (a)

—— *Complainant.* } Petty Sessions District of ——, County of ——
—— *Defendant.* }   I, A.B., do solemnly and sincerely declare, that ([1])
and I make this solemn declaration conscientiously believing the same to be true, and by virtue of the provisions of an Act passed in the sixth year of the reign of His late Majesty King William the Fourth, chapter sixty-two, for the abolition of unnecessary oaths.

Signed ——

Made and subscribed before me, this —— day of ——, in the year eighteen hundred and ——

Signed ——, Justice of said County.

([1]) Matter of Declaration.

FORMS (B)—PROCESS TO ENFORCE APPEARANCE.

(B a.)—*Summons.* (b)

—— *Complainant.* } Petty Sessions District of ——, County of ——
—— *Defendant.* }   Whereas a complaint has been made to me that ([1])
This is to command you to appear as a —— ([2]) on the hearing of said complaint at ——, on the —— day of ——, at —— o'clock, before such Justices as shall be there.

Signed ——, Justice of said County.
This —— day of ——, 18—

To ·· ——, of ——

([1]) Cause of complaint, with time and place.
([2]) Insert : *defendant* or *witness.*

(a) A to revenue stamps on declarations, see title, " Stamps," Summary Index.
(b) See specimens of Summons hereafter.

(B b.)—*Warrant to Arrest.*

—— *Complainant.* } Petty Sessions District of ——, County of ——,
—— *Defendant.* } Whereas a complaint has been made on oath and in
writing that (¹)
and (²)

This is to command you to whom this warrant is addressed to arrest the
said ——, (³) of ——, and to bring him before me, or some other Justice of the
County, to answer to the said complaint.

Signed ——, Justice of said County.

This —— day of ——, 18—.

To——, (⁴) of ——

(¹) Cause of complaint, with time and place.
(²) If the case be so, add, for the defendant—*Whereas the said C. D. has neglected to appear in
obedience to a summons.* For witness—*Whereas oath has been made that X. Y. can give material
evidence, but will not attend voluntarily; or is purposely keeping out of the way of personal service
of a summons.* If after indictment—*It has been certified to me that* (state as in certificate of Clerk
of Crown or Peace).
(³) Person against whom warrant is issued.
(⁴) ADDRESS—"*The Sub-Inspector of Constabulary,*" or name of person who is to execute the
warrant.

FORM (C) RECOGNIZANCE (TO APPEAR, &c.).

—— *Complainant.* } Petty Sessions District of ——, County of ——.
—— *Defendant.* } Whereas (¹)

The undersigned (²) —— residing (³) —— (⁴) —— the principal party to this
recognizance, hereby binds   self to perform the following obligation, viz.,
to (⁵) ——

And the said principal party, together with (²) —— residing (³) —— (⁴) ——
and (²) —— residing (³) —— (⁴) —— the undersigned sureties, hereby severally

---

•₀• The words in *italics,* or words to the like effect, are to be used according to the circumstances of each case.
(¹) In binding a party, &c., state cause of complaint, with time and place. ¹In binding a
pound-keeper, state fact of his appointment.
(²) Here insert Christian name and surname at full length respectively.
(³) Here insert *in* or *at,* as the case may be.
(⁴) If the person does not reside in a town, here insert the name of the townland, parish,
barony, and county respectively, in which such person resides, and also the profession, trade, or
occupation, of such person, for instance, *the townland of ——, parish of ——, and barony of
——, in the said county of ——, farmer* [or *labourer* or *smith,* &c.], as the case may be. If
the person resides in a town, here insert the number (if any) of the house at or in which such
person resides, and state whether he is owner or tenant thereof, or a lodger therein. and also
insert the name of the street, parish, town, and county, respectively, in which such person

3 B 2

acknowledge themselves bound to forfeit to the Crown the sums following, viz.:—
The said principal party the sum of —— and the said sureties the sum of ——
each, in case the said principal party fails to perform the above obligation. (⁶)

Signed, $\left\{ \begin{array}{l} \text{——} \\ \text{——} \end{array} \right.$ Principal party.
Sureties.

Taken before me, this —— day of —— 18—, at ——,

Signed ——, Justice of said County.

I certify that the said —— has not performed the above obligation. (⁶)

Signed, —— (⁷)

This —— day of —— 18—.

(⁸) I order that the sum of —— be levied off the goods of the said (²) —— and
the sum of —— off the goods of each of the said sureties (²) —— and (³)

Signed, $\left\{ \begin{array}{l} \text{——} \\ \text{——} \end{array} \right.$ Justice of said County.

This —— day of ——, 18—.

---

resides, and the profession, trade, or occupation of such person, for instance, *owner of* [or *tenant of*, or *a lodger in*, as the case may be], *number one* ——, *street* ——, *in the parish of* ——, *in the town of* ——, *in the county of* ——*shopkeeper* [or *tailor*, &c., as the case may be].

(³) OBLIGATION.—*To attend (the Court of Assizes or Quarter Sessions or Petty Sessions), at* ——, *on the* —— *day of* ——, *at* —— *o'clock, and there—To prefer (or prosecute, or give evidence upon) a bill of indictment against the said C. D., for the said offence:* or, *To surrender himself to the keeper of the gaol at F., and plead to any indictment found against him for said offence, and take his trial for the same;* or, *To prosecute (or answer to) said complaint:* or, *To prosecute his appeal against the order made on the* —— *day of* ——, *upon the said complaint, and to abide and perform the Judgment and Order of the Court of Appeal thereon, and to pay such costs as may be awarded by the said Court, and (in case of an Order to imprison) not to abscond pending the execution of the original Order, or of the Judgment, or Order of the Court of Appeal:* or, *To keep the peace (and be of good behaviour) towards all Her Majesty's subjects, and particularly towards A. B., for the space of:* or, *To perform faithfully and diligently the several duties required of him as pound-keeper, under the provisions of the Summary Jurisdiction Act, Ireland, 1851.*

(⁶) FORFEITURE.   (⁷) *Justice or Clerk of the Peace, &c.*

(⁸) ESTREAT.

☞ The above is the form now directed to be used ; the notes supply the additional conditions required by 40 & 41 Vic., c. 56. s. 72 in *appeals.*

Appeals.—For additional conditions necessary in appeal bonds.—See 40 & 41 Vict., c. 56, s. 72, &c. Government has supplied a special form of recognizance to the Petty Session Courts which should be used. It is given above.

FORM (D).—ORDER BOOK, AS APPROVED BY THE LORD LIEUTENANT (WITH THE ADVICE AND CONSENT OF THE PRIVY COUNCIL), PURSUANT TO SECTIONS 21 AND 36, PETTY SESSIONS (IRELAND) ACT, 1851.

1.	2.	3.	4.	5.	6.	7.
No.	Date of Order.	Name or Names of Justice or Justices by whom Order made; and if entry in this book made from a certificate, same to be here stated.	PARTIES.—Complainant and Defendant (Christian, surname, rank, occupation, or other addition, and residence, stating parish and townland, to be given, and the parties to be distinguished by prefixing their appellation, Complainant or Defendant).	Names of Witnesses examined, and whether for Complainant or Defendant.	Cause of Complaint, set forth in Summons.	Particulars of order or dismissal. If dismiss, whether with or without prejudice, and whether with or without costs, &c. In ejectment, when to be evicted, and from what premises, &c. If to be whipped, whether in or out of prison, &c. Where money ordered to be paid by or to any person, the amount to be written in words at full length in this column as well as to be entered in figures in the money column.

8.	9.	10.	11.	12.	AMOUNT ORDERED TO BE PAID. (13.)						14.	14.
					In Civil Cases.		In Penal Cases.					
Act under which Order made.	When and how amount ordered to be paid, and nature of warrant to issue in default, whether distress, committal, or otherwise.	Imprisonment, term of, whether with or without hard labour, in addition to fine, &c., or in default of payment, &c., and name of gaol or bridewell.	Name, description, and residence of person to whom compensation (if any) ordered to be paid.	Name of Defendants against whom order made.	Sum to Complainant.	Costs to Complainant or Defendant.	Fine.	Costs to Complainant or Defendant.	Compensation.	Costs to Complainant or Defendant.	Portion of Fine (if any) awarded to Complainant.	Signature of Justice (if entry in this book from a certificate, and entry not signed by the Justice who made the order, a special note of the circumstance to be made by the Clerk). *Vide* secs. 21 & 22.

" NOTE.—No erasure to be on any account made; and every interlineation or other change to be initialled by the Justice who affixes his signature to the order. The greatest care to be taken that the cases be kept distinct from each other."

The Form (D) Order Book given in the Schedule to the statute is not used. The above is the Form approved by the Lord Lieutenant and Privy Council, pursuant to sec. 36 of the Act. It is much better adapted to the making a complete and legal order than that given in the statute. The Lord Lieutenant and Council have power to alter form of " Order Book."—41 & 42 Vic., c. 69, sec. 11.

The imprisonment may be named and directed in the same warrant that directs a distress to be made, in the event of there being no goods to distrain.—Sub-sec. 3, sec. 27.

Where at the time of making the Order no imprisonment is named in default of payment and of distress, the Justices can name the proper period of imprisonment on the return of the distress warrant; and so, in like manner, where an imprisonment, in default of payment, only is named, and the warrant to commit cannot be executed, the Justices can issue a distress warrant. A note of this proceeding is to be made in the Order Book.—Sub-sec. 4, sec. 22. From column 7 to 10 inclusive should be carefully filled in, so as to contain all the ingredients of a complete Order and the mode of enforcing it. It frequently happens that the Justice pronounces the decision thus:—"To pay a penalty of £——, or to be imprisoned for ——;" and, if so entered on the Order Book it will be bad, for it is indefinite. What is plainly intended, although inaccurately expressed, should be correctly entered by the Chairman or the Clerk in the Order Book, showing that a penalty has been named, and that *in default of payment* the imprisonment is to follow.

In case of second or subsequent offence, and the penalty imposed exceeds that for a first offence, enter on the *Order Book* that it is for a second offence. State so likewise in the warrant, appeals, &c.

☞ In prosecutions under the "Criminal Law and Procedure (Ir.) Act, 1887" (50 & 51 Vic., c. 20), it is the practice, although not necessary in law, to describe the Resident Magistrates and their qualifications, &c., as pointed out in sec. 41 sub-sec. (6) of this Act

FORMS (E)—WARRANTS.

(E a.)—*Warrants of Execution (Summary Jurisdiction).*

—— *Complainant.* ⎱　Petty Sessions District of ——, County of ——.
—— *Defendant.* ⎰　　Whereas upon the hearing a complaint that ([1])
an order was made on the —— day of —— by the Justices present against the
said ——, ([2]) of ——, to the following effect, viz. :—([3])

And whereas ([4])

And whereas the said order has not been complied with. This is to command
you to whom this warrant is addressed to execute the said Order against the said
person as follows :—([5])

And for this the present warrant shall be a sufficient authority to all whom it
may concern.

The sum levied to be paid to ([6])
The warrant to be returned in —— days, if not executed.

　　　　　　　　　　　Signed ——, Justice of said County.

　　　　　　　　　　　This —— day of ——, 18—.

To ——, ([7]) of ——.

([1]) Cause of Complaint, with time and place. In ejectments, *The defendant had refused to give
up to the plaintiff possession of ——, situate at ——, on the termination of his tenancy.*

([2]) Person against whom Order was made.

([3]) ORDER: Imprisonment in addition or default.—Fine or debt.—*To pay for fine* (or *debt*) *the
sum of ——, and for costs the sum of —— (forthwith),* or *(in —— days). And also in addition,* or *And in default of payment* (or *distress*). Imprisonment.—*To be imprisoned for the period
of ——, with* (or *without*) *hard labour.*

Ejectment.—*To be ejected from said premises in —— days, and pay the sum of —— to the
Complainant for costs.* Dismissal.—*That his Complaint be dismissed on the merits* (or *without
prejudice, and that he do pay the sum of —— to the defendant for costs.*

([4]) RECITALS.— After Appeal.—*The Court of Appeal decided on the —— day of —— that
(Order).* No distress.—*He has* (or *admits that he has,* or *it has been returned to a warrant of
distress that he has*) *no goods.* Distress ruinous.—*A distress would be ruinous to him* (or *to his
family*).

([5]) EXECUTION : Committal in addition or default.—To distrain.—*To levy said sums by distress
and sale of his goods. And in addition,* or *And in default of distress.* To commit.—*To lodge him
in the gaol at F., to be imprisoned there for the period of ——, with* (or *without*) *hard labour*
(*unless said sums be sooner paid*).

To eject.—*To enter and give possession of said premises to the complainant or his agent in
—— days.*

([6]) PAYMENT.—In all warrants to Constabulary, insert " *Clerk of Petty Sessions.*" In all other
warrants, insert name of person to whom sum was ordered to be paid, if the Justices so think fit.

([7]) ADDRESS.—" *The Sub-Inspector* (or *Head Constable*) *of Constabulary,*" or name of person
who is to execute the warrant.

(E b.)—*Warrant to commit (or detain) for Trial, &c.*

—— *Complainant.*   Petty Sessions District of ——, County of ——.
—— *Defendant.*   Whereas a complaint was made on the —— day of ——,
on the oath of X. Y., that (^{1})

and (^{2})

This is to command you to whom this warrant is addressed to lodge the said
——, (^{3}) of —— in the gaol at F., there to be imprisoned by the Keeper of said
gaol, as follows :—(^{4})

And for this the present warrant shall be a sufficient authority to all whom it
may concern.

> Signed ——, Justice of said County.
>
> This —— day of ——, 18—.

To ——, (^{5}) of ——

(^{1}) Cause of complaint, with time and place.
(^{2}) RECITALS.—If indictment found.—*Whereas a bill of indictment has been found against the said C. D. for the said offence.* Adjournments.—*Whereas the hearing of the said complaint has been adjourned to the —— day of ——, at ——.* Remands on arrest.—*Whereas the said C. D. has been brought before me under a warrant of arrest, and the said complaint is to be heard on the —— day of ——, at ——.* Refractory Witness.—*Whereas X. Y., a material witness, has without just excuse refused to make oath as a witness (or to answer certain questions) (or to enter into recognisance to give evidence on the trial of the said C. D.) in that behalf.*
(^{3}) Name of person to be committed.
(^{4}) PERIOD OF IMPRISONMENT.—For trial.—*Until his trial for said offence, and he shall be discharged by due course of law.* For witness.—*Until the trial of the said C. D., unless he shall in the meantime enter into such recognisance as required (or until the —— day of ——, unless he shall in the meantime consent to answer as required.)* For adjournments.—*Until the above time of adjournment (or hearing), when he shall have him at the above place.*
(^{5}) ADDRESS.—"*The Sub-Constable (or Head Constable) of Constabulary,*" or name of person who is to execute the warrant.

———————————

(E c.)—*Warrant to convey before a Justice of another County.*

—— *Complainant.*   Petty Sessions District of ——, County of ——.
—— *Defendant.*   Whereas a complaint was made that (^{1})

And whereas I have taken the deposition of X. Y. as to the said offence.

And whereas the other witnesses reside in the County of ——

This is to command you to convey the said ——, (^{2}) of ——, before some Justice
of the last-mentioned County, near the above place, and to deliver to him this
warrant and the said deposition.

> Signed ——, Justice of the first-mentioned County.
>
> This —— day of ——, 18—.

To ——, (^{3}) of ——.

(^{1}) Cause of complaint, with time and place.
(^{2}) Name of accused person.
(^{3}) "*The Sub-Inspector (or Head Constable) of Constabulary,*" or name of person who is to execute the warrant.

(E d.)—*Warrant to discharge from Gaol.*

—— *Complainant.* ⎫   Petty Sessions District of ——, County of ——.
—— *Defendant.* ⎭   Whereas a complaint was made that (¹
and whereas the said ——, (²) of ——, (³)

This is to command you to discharge the said person so committed, unless he shall be in your custody for some other cause.

Signed ——, Justice of said County.

This —— day of ——, 18—.

To the Keeper of the Gaol at ——. (⁴)

(¹) Cause of complaint, with time and place.
(²) Name of prisoner.
(³) RECITALS.—*For accused.*—*Was committed to take his trial for said offence, but has now duly entered into recognizance to appear for that purpose. For witness.—Was committed for refusing to enter into recognizance to give evidence on the trial of C. D. for said offence, but has now done so (or and the said C. D. for want of evidence has not been bailed or committed).*
(⁴) Address.

————————

(E e.)—*Warrant to Search.*

—— *Complainant.* ⎫   Petty Sessions District of ——, County of ——.
—— *Defendant.* ⎭   Whereas it appears on oath of A. B., of M. N., that the
following articles of property, viz. :—(¹)
were stolen, and that there is reason to suspect that the same are concealed in ——
at ——.

This is, therefore, to authorize and require you to enter in the daytime into the said premises, and to search for said property, and to bring the same and the persons in whose possession the same may be found before me or some other Justice.

Signed ——, Justice of said County.

This —— day of ——, 18.

To ——, of ——, (²) of ——.

(¹) Description of articles stolen.
(²) ADDRESS.—" *The Sub-Inspector (or Head Constable of Constabulary,*" or name of person who is to ‑ the warrant.

FORM (F.)—RECEIPT FOR PRISONER.

County of——.

I hereby certify that I have received from A.B. ([1]), of ——, the body of C.D., together with a warrant under the hand of J. S., Esq., Justice for the County of ——, and that the said prisoner was ——→ ([2]) at the time he was so delivered into my custody.

Signed ——, Keeper of the Gaol at ——.

This —— day of ——, 18—.

([1]) Name, rank, &c.
([2]) "*Sober*," or as the case may be.

FORMS (G.)—INDORSEMENTS ON WARRANTS.

(G a.) *Return of no Person or Goods.*

I certify that after diligent search (and for the following reasons):—([1]) against whom the within warrant was issued, cannot be found.

Signed —— { To whom this warrant was delivered for execution.

This —— day of ——, 18—.

([1]) *The person, or sufficient goods of the person.*

(G b.) *Certificate of no Goods or Persons.*

I —— ([1]) that I have reason to believe that the person against whom the within warrant was issued ([2]) at ——, in the County of ——, and that I believe the signature to the within warrant to be in the handwriting of the said Justice.

Signed —— { To whom this warrant was delivered for execution.

To ——, of ——   This —— day of ——, 18—.

([1]) For Constabulary—*Certify*. For bailiff—*Make oath.*
([2]) *Is to be found*, or *has goods.*

(G c.) *Backing by Inspector-General or other Justice.*

It being —— ([1]) to me as above, I hereby indorse the within warrant for execution in said County of —— ([2]) (or Metropolitan District or other place).

Signed ——, Inspector-General (or Deputy, or Justice).

To ——.   This —— day of ——, 18—.

([1]) For Commissioners of Police or Constabulary—*Certified*. For bailiff—*Proved on oath.*
([2]) In backing warrant to arrest, add, if so intended—*And to bring the said person before me or some other Justice of said county.*

FORM (H.)—APPEAL.

—— *Complainant.* }   Petty Sessions District of ——, County of ——.
—— *Defendant.* }   I certify that upon the hearing of a complaint that (¹)
an order was made on the —— day of ——, by the Justices present, against the
said ——, (²) of ——, to the following effect, viz. :—(³)

Signed ——, Justice of the said County.

(*a*)   This —— day of ——, 18—.

(¹) Cause of complaint, with time and place.

(²) Person against whom order was made.

(³) ORDER: Imprisonment in addition or default—Fine or debt.—*To pay the sum of —— to
the Crown, and the sum of —— to the complainant, with —— costs (forthwith*), or (*in ——
days*). *And in addition,* or *And in default of payment* (or *distress*). Imprisonment—*To be imprisoned for the period of ——, with* (or *without*) *hard labour.*

Ejectment—*To be ejected from said premises in —— days, and pay the sum of —— to the
complainant for costs.* Dismissal.—*That his complaint be dismissed on the merits* (or *without
prejudice*), *and that he do pay the sum of —— to the complainant for costs.*

The person against whom said order was made hereby appeals against the same
to the next Court of Quarter Sessions (or Recorder's Sessions) to be held at ——

Signed ——, Appellant.

This —— day of ——, 18—.

FORMS (I.)—CERTIFICATES.

(I a.) *Certificate of Order.*

—— *Complainant.* } Petty Sessions District of ——, County of ——.
—— *Defendant.* }   I certify, that upon the hearing of a complaint that ([1])
an order was made on the —— day of ——, by the Justices present against ([2])
——, of ——, to the following effect, viz. :—([3])

                        Signed ——, Justice of said County.
                              This —— day of ——, 18—.

([1]) Cause of complaint, with time and place. In ejectments—*The defendant had refused to give up to the plaintiff possession of ——, situate at —— on the termination of his tenancy.*
([2]) Person against whom order was made.
([3]) ORDER: Imprisonment in addition or default—Fine or debt—*To pay for fine* (or *debt*) *the sum of ——, and for costs the sum of —— (forthwith),* or *in (—— days).* And *in addition, or And in default of payment* (or *distress*). Imprisonment.—*To be imprisoned for the period of ——, with* (or *without*) *hard labour.*
    Ejectment—*To be ejected from said premises in —— days, and pay the sum of —— to the complainant for costs.* Dismissal—*That his complaint be dismissed on the merits* (or *without prejudice*), *and that he do pay the sum of —— to the defendant for costs.*

(I b.) *Of Indictment being Found.*

County of ——.

    I hereby certify that at the ([1])
held at ——, in the said County, on the —— day of ——, a bill of indictment
was found by the Grand Jury against C. D., therein described as C. D., of N.,
for that on the —— day of ——, at ——,   ([2])   and that the said
C. D. has not appeared or pleaded to the said indictment.

    Dated this —— day of ——,

                      Signed ——, Clerk of Crown (*or* Peace).
                            This —— day of ——, 18—.

([1]) "*Court of Oyer and Terminer, and General Gaol Delivery,*" or *Court of Quarter Sessions.*
([2]) Offence as in indictment.

(I c.) *Of Consent to Bail.*

Petty Sessions District of ——, County of ——.

    Whereas on the —— day of ——, C. D. was committed to the gaol at ——,
charged with ([1])

    I hereby consent to the said C. D. being bailed by recognizance, himself in
the sum of ——, and [two] sureties in the sum of —— each.

                      Signed ——, Justice of said County.
                            This —— day of ——, 18—.

([1]) Offence.

Form of Warrant of Commitment in default of Bail to keep the Peace, &c.

34 Edw. 3, c. 1, and the Commission.

—— *Complainant.* ⎞   Petty Sessions District of —— County of ——.
—— *Defendant.* ⎠   Whereas, upon the hearing of a complaint that on or about the —— day of —— 18—, at and in said District and County, the said Defendant (a) did (*State shortly the threats used, and from which complainant apprehended injury to his person or his property*), an order was made on the —— day of ——, 18—, by the Justices present, against the said ——, to the following effect, viz.:—to enter into recognizance —— in the sum of £ ——, and Two Sureties in the sum of £ —— each, to keep the peace, and be of good behaviour towards all Her Majesty's subjects, and particularly towards ——, for the space of —— months. And whereas the Defendant being present, and although called upon to enter into such recognizance with such Securities as aforesaid failed to do so, and the said Order has not been complied with,—This is to command you to whom this Warrant is addressed to execute the said Order against the said person as follows :—To lodge —— in the —— Gaol of ——, to be imprisoned there for the period of ——, unless —— shall in the meantime enter into such recognizance as aforesaid.—And for this the present Warrant shall be sufficient authority to all whom it may concern.

—— *Justice of said* ——

This —— day of —— 18—.

To the Sub-Inspector and the Head and   ⎞
other Constables acting in and for said —— ⎠

(a) The defendant should be present when the order is made; and if he be summoned and does not appear, a warrant to compel his appearance should issue before the order for committal is made, for he ought not be committed until he has been called; on to enter into recognizance with sureties, and that he fails to do so.

EMPLOYERS AND WORKMEN ACT, 1875.

(38 & 39 Vic., chap. 90.)

RULES.*

1. A person desirous to make a complaint under the "Employers and Workmen Act, 1875," shall deliver to the clerk of the Court particulars in writing of his cause of action, and the clerk of the Court shall enter in the Order Book (Form D), supplied under the Act 14 & 15 Vic., c. 93, the names and the last known places of abode of the parties, and the substance of the complaint ; and thereupon a summons shall be issued according to the form in the Schedule, and be served on the Defendant, not less than two clear days before the day on which the Court shall be holden at which the complaint is to be heard ; and no misnomer or inaccurate description of any person or place in any such plaint or summons shall vitiate the same, so that the person or place be therein described so as to be commonly known.

2. The particulars shall be indorsed upon and be deemed part of the summons.

3. Such summons may issue in any district in which the Defendant or one of the Defendants dwelt or carried on his business or was employed at the time the cause of action arose.

4. Any summons which may be required to be served out of the district of the Court from which the same shall have issued may be served by the summons-server of any other Court of summary jurisdiction, or (if the Justice issuing the same shall so direct or permit), by any other person whom the complainant shall employ, and who shall be able to read and write, but in no case by the complainant himself ; any such service may be proved by affidavit of the person who served the summons ; such affidavit may be made before any Justice of the Peace or other Magistrate.

5. Every summons shall be served upon the person to whom it is directed by delivering to him a copy of such summons, or by leaving such copy for him with some person apparently sixteen years old, at his house or place of dwelling or place of business or employment, or at the office of his employer for the time being.

Hearing.

6. No notice shall be required to be given by a Defendant of any set-off or counter-claim that he may wish to advance at the hearing against the claim of the Plaintiff.

7. If upon the day of the return of any summons, or at any continuation or adjournment of the said Court, the Plaintiff shall not appear, the cause shall be struck out, and the Court may award to the Defendant, by way of costs and satisfaction for his attendance, such sum as it in its discretion shall think fit.

8. If on the day named in the summons, or at any continuation or adjournment of the Court, the Defendant shall not appear, or sufficiently excuse his absence, or shall neglect to answer when called in Court, the Court, upon due

---

* These Rules, Forms, &c., follow those prescribed by the Lord Chancellor Cairns for England. To strictly follow Rule 1 may, in Irish Petty Sessions practice, be attended with some inconvenience. It evidently supposes that there is a Form of Complaint Book (called in the Schedule of Forms (18) here given "Plaint and Minute Book.") The Rule is directory, and it would seem that if the Clerk duly enters the complaint in the Summons or Complaint Book, in the first instance, and in due course enters the case for *hearing* on the Order Book (D), this will be a proper compliance with this Rule, although the case be not entered on the Order Book before summons issued.—H. H.

proof of service of the summons, may either adjourn the cause from time to time or proceed to the hearing of the cause on the part of the Plaintiff only, and the judgment thereupon shall be as valid as if both parties had attended: Provided that the Court in any such case, at the same or any subsequent Court, may set aside any judgment so given in the absence of the Defendant, and the execution thereupon, and may grant a new trial upon such terms (if any) as it may think fit.

Judgment-Summons.

9. No order of commitment under the "Debtors' Act (Ireland), 1872," shall be made unless a summons to appear and be examined on oath, hereinafter called a judgment-summons, shall have been personally served upon the judgment debtor, which service were made out of the district may be proved by affidavit.

10. A judgment-summons may issue although no distress warrant has been applied for.

11. Every judgment-summons shall be according to the form in the Schedule, and be served not less than two clear days before the day on which the judgment-debtor is required to appear, except the judgment-debtor is stated to be about to remove, or is keeping out of the way to avoid service.

12. The hearing of a judgment-summons may be adjourned from time to time.

13. Any witness may be summoned to prove the means of the judgment-debtor, in the same manner as witnesses are summoned to give evidence upon the hearing of a complaint.

14. An order of commitment made under the "Debtors' Act (Ireland), 1872," shall be according to the form in the Schedule, and shall, on whatever day it may be issued, bear date on the day on which the order for commitment was made, and shall continue in force for one year from such date and no longer.

15. When an order of commitment for non-payment of money is issued, the Defendant may, at any time before his body is delivered into the custody of the gaoler, pay to the officer holding such order the amount indorsed thereon as that on the payment of which he may be discharged; and on receiving such amount the officer shall discharge the Defendant, and shall forthwith pay over the amount to the clerk of the Court.

16. The sum indorsed on the order of commitment as that upon payment of which the prisoner may be discharged may be paid to the clerk of the Court from which the commitment order was issued, or to the gaoler in whose custody the prisoner is. Where it is paid to the clerk, he shall sign a certificate of such payment, and upon receiving such certificate by post or otherwise, the gaoler in whose custody the prisoner shall then be shall forthwith discharge such prisoner. And where it is paid to the gaoler, he shall, upon payment to him of such amount, together with costs sufficient to pay for transmitting by post-office order or otherwise such amount to the Court under the order of which the prisoner was committed, sign a certificate of such payment, and discharge the prisoner.

17. A certificate of payment by a prisoner shall be according to the form in the Schedule.

18. All costs incurred by the Plaintiff in endeavouring to enforce an order shall be deemed to be due in pursuance of such order under section 6 of the "Debtors' (Ireland) Act, 1872," unless the Court shall otherwise order.

19. The costs which may be awarded shall not in any case exceed one pound.

Forms.

20. The forms given in the Schedule shall be used, with such variations as may be necessary to meet the circumstances of each case.

                          J. T. BALL, *C.*

SCHEDULE.

1.—*Summons to Appear.*

"Employers and Workmen Act, 1875."

In the County of ——, Petty Sessions District of ——.

Between —— (¹) of ——, Plaintiff; and, (¹) ——, Defendant.

You are hereby summoned to appear on the —— day of ——, 18—, at the hour of —— in the —— noon, at ——, before such Justices as shall be there, to answer the Plaintiff, to a claim the particulars of which are hereon indorsed.

Signed ——, Justice of said County.

This —— day of ——, 18—.

To ——, of ——.

(¹) Here state address and description.

2.—*Summons to Witness.*

"Employers and Workmen Act, 1875."

In the County of ——, Petty Sessions District of ——.

Between ——, Plaintiff ; and ——, Defendant.

You are hereby required to attend at ——, on ——, the —— day of ——, 18—, at the hour of —— in the —— noon, to give evidence in the above cause on behalf of the —— (¹).

Signed ——, Justice of said County.

This —— day of ——, 18—.

To ——, of ——.

(¹) Plaintiff [*or* Defendant], as the case may be.

3.—*Judgment for Plaintiff.*

"Employers and Workmen Act, 1875."

In the County of ——, Petty Sessions District of ——.

Between ——, Plaintiff ; and ——, Defendant.

It is this day adjudged that the Plaintiff do recover against the Defendant the sum of £ —— for —— (¹) and £ —— for costs, amounting together to the sum of ——.

And it is ordered that the Defendant do pay the same to the Plaintiff —— (²) ; and if the same be not paid as ordered, it is hereby further ordered that the same be levied by distress and sale of the goods and chattels of the said Defendant.

Signed, ⎯⎯} Justices of said County.

This —— day of —— , 18—.

(¹) Debt [*or* damages].

(²) On or before the —— day of —— [*or* by instalments of —— for every —— days: the first instalment to be paid on or before the —— day of ——, 18—].

4.—*Judgment for Defendant.*

"Employers and Workmen Act, 1875."

In the County of ——, Petty Sessions District of ——.

Between —— Plaintiff; and ——, Defendant.

Upon hearing this cause this day, it is adjudged that judgment be entered for the Defendant, and that the Plaintiff do pay the sum of £ —— for the Defendant's costs, on or before the —— day of —— ; and if the same be not paid as ordered, it is hereby further ordered that the same be levied by distress and sale of the goods and chattels of the said Plaintiff.

Signed, —— } Justices of said County.

This —— day of ——, 18—.

_____

5.—*Judgment-Summons.*

"Employers and Workmen Act, 1875," and "The Debtors' Act (Ireland), 1872."

In the County of ——, Petty Sessions District of ——.

Between ——, (¹) of ——, in the ——, Plaintiff; and ——, (¹) of ——, in the ——, Defendant.

Whereas the ——, (²) obtained an order against you the above-named —— (³) in this Court, on the —— day of ——, 18—, for the payment of —— pounds —— shillings and —— pence.

And whereas you have made default in payment of the sum payable in pursuance of the said order.

You are therefore hereby summoned to appear personally in this Court, at ——, on the —— day of ——, at the hour of —— in the —— noon, to be examined on oath by the Court touching the means you have or have had since the date of the order to satisfy the sum payable in pursuance of the said order; and also to show cause why you should not be committed to prison for such default.

Signed, ——, Justice of said County.

This —— day of ——, 18—.

_____

	£	s.	d.
Amount of order and costs, ...			
Costs of distress against the goods (if any) . . .			

		£	s.	d.
	Paid into Court, . . .			
Deduct,	{ Instalments which were not required to have been paid before the date of the summons, .			

Sum payable, ...	
Costs of this Summons, ...	

Amount upon the payment of which no further proceedings will be had until default in payment of next instalment, ...

_____

(¹) Here state address and description.
(²) Plaintiff [or Defendant], as the case may be.
(³) Defendant [or Plaintiff], as the case may be.

6.—*Order of Commitment.*

"Employers and Workmen Act, 1875," and "The Debtors' Act (Ireland), 1872."

In the County of ——, Petty Sessions District of ——.

Between ——, Plaintiff; and ——, Defendant.

To ——, (^{1}) and all other peace officers of the county, and to the Governor or Keeper of the gaol at ——.

Whereas the —— (^{2}) obtained an order against the —— (^{3}) in this Court on the —— day of ——, 18—, for the payment of £ ——.

And whereas the —— (^{3}) hath made default in payment of ——, payable in pursuance of the said order :

And whereas a summons was, at the instance of the —— (^{2}) duly issued out of this Court, by which the —— (^{3}) was required to appear personally at this Court on the —— day of —— 18—, to be examined on oath touching the means he had then or had had since the date of the order to satisfy the sum then due and payable in pursuance of the order, and to show cause why he should not be committed to prison for such default :

And whereas, at the hearing of the said summons, the ——, (^{4}) and it has now been proved to the satisfaction of the Court that the —— (^{3}) —— (^{5}) the means to pay the sum then due and payable in pursuance of the order, and —— (^{6}) to pay the same, and the —— (^{3}) has shown no cause why he should not be committed to gaol.

Now, therefore, it is ordered that, for such default as aforesaid, the —— (^{3}) shall be committed to gaol for —— days, unless he shall sooner pay the sum stated below as that upon the payment of which he is to be discharged.

These are, therefore, to require you the said —— and peace officers, to take the —— (^{3}) and to deliver him to the Governor or Keeper of the gaol aforesaid, and you the said Governor or Keeper to receive the —— (^{3}) and him safely keep in the said gaol for —— days from the arrest under this order, or until he shall be sooner discharged by due course of law.

Signed, —— this —— day of ——, 18—.

—— } Justices of said County.

————

	£	s.	d.
Total sum payable at the time of hearing of the judgment summons, ...			
Hearing of summons, and cost of order, ...			
Total sum upon payment of which the prisoner will be discharged, ...			

(^{1}) "The *Sub-Inspector* [or *Head Constable*] of *Constabulary*," or name of person who is to execute the Order of Commitment.
(^{2}) Plaintiff [or Defendant].
(^{3}) Defendant [or Plaintiff].
(^{4}) Defendant or Plaintiff appeared [or the summons was proved to have been personally and duly served].
(^{5}) Now has [or has had since the date of the order].
(^{6}) Has refused or neglected [or then refused or neglected]. .

7.—*Certificate for the Discharge of a Prisoner from Custody.*

"Employers and Workmen Act, 1875," and "The Debtors' Act (Ireland), 1872."

In the County of ——, Petty Sessions District of ——.
Between ——, Plaintiff ; and ——, Defendant.
I hereby certify that the —— (¹), who was committed to your custody by virtue of an order of commitment under the seals of two Justices of this Court, bearing date the —— day of ——, 18—, has paid and satisfied the sum of money for the non-payment whereof he was so committed, together with all costs due and payable by him in respect thereof ; and that the —— (¹) may, in respect of such order, be forthwith discharged out of your custody.

Dated this —— day of ——, 18—.

—— Clerk of the Court.

To the Governor or Keeper of the Gaol at ——.

(¹) Defendant [*or* Plaintiff].

8.—*Warrant of Distress for Payment of Money by Plaintiff.*

"Employers and Workmen Act, 1875."

In the County of ——, Petty Sessions District of ——.
Between —— Plaintiff ; and ——, Defendant.
Whereas at a Court holden at —— on the —— day of ——, 18—, it was ordered by the Court that judgment should be entered for the Defendant, and that the Plaintiff should pay to the Defendant, on or before the —— day of ——, the sum of £——, for the Defendant's costs of suit ; and that if the same were not paid as ordered, it was further ordered that the same should be levied by distress and sale of the goods and chattels of the said Plaintiff :

ordered by the Court that the Defendant should pay the same to the Plaintiff —— ; (¹) and that if the same were not paid as ordered, it was further ordered that the same should be levied by distress and sale of the goods and chattels of the said Defendant.

And whereas default has been made in payment according to the said order : These are therefore to command you forthwith to make distress of the goods and chattels of the Defendant (except the wearing apparel and bedding of him or his family, and the tools and implements of his trade, if any, to the value of five pounds), the sum of £——, being the amount due to the Plaintiff under the said order, together with the reasonable charges of taking and keeping the said distress ; and that you do pay what you shall have so levied to the Clerk of this Court.

Signed this —— day of ——, 18—.

——, Justice of said County,

To the ——, (²) and all other peace officers in the County of ——.

(¹) On the —— day of ——, [or by instalments of —— for every —— days].
(²) " Sub-Inspector (or Head Constable), of Constabulary," or name of person who is to execute the warrant.

Notice.— The goods and chattels are not to be sold until after the end of five clear days next following the day on which they were seized, unless they be of a perishable nature, or at the request of the Defendant.

10.—Undertaking in Writing by Defendant to perform Contract.

"Employers and Workmen Act, 1875."

In the County of ——, Petty Sessions District of ——.
Between ——, Plaintiff ; and ——, Defendant.
Whereas it has been found by this Court on the —— day of ——, 18—, that the Defendant had broken the contract for the breach of which he was summoned :

And whereas the Court would have awarded to the Plaintiff the sum of £—— by way of damages suffered by him in consequence of such breach, and would have ordered him to have been paid such sum, but that the Defendant was willing to give security for the performance by him of so much of the contract as remains unperformed :

Now, therefore, I the undersigned Defendant, and we, —— (¹) do undertake that the said Defendant will perform so much of the said contract as remains unperformed : that is to say ——, (²)

And I the said Defendant, and ——, (³) hereby severally acknowledge ourselves bound to forfeit to A. B., the Plaintiff, the sum of —— pounds and —— shillings, in case the said Defendant fails to perform what he has hereby undertaken to perform :

(Signed, where not taken orally)   C. D., Defendant.
E. F., ⎫
G. H., ⎬ Sureties.

Taken [orally] before me this —— day of ——, 18—.

——, Justice of said County.

(¹) The undersigned sureties [or the —— undersigned surety].
(²) Here set out so much of the contract as remains to be performed.
(³) We [or I] the said sureties [or surety.]

Note.—Where the undertaking is given orally, strike out the words " undersigned" where they occur, and insert the word "orally" after "taken."

3 C 3

11.—*Order on an Apprentice to perform his Duties.*

"Employers and Workmen Act, 1875."

In the County of ——, Petty Sessions District of ——.
Between ——, Plaintiff; and ——, Defendant.
It is ordered that the Defendant do forthwith perform the duties he has con-
tracted to perform under his apprenticeship to the Plaintiff.

Signed this —— day of —— 18—.

$$\left.\begin{array}{c} ——\\ —— \end{array}\right\}$$ Justices of said County.

12.—*Order rescinding a Contract of Apprenticeship.*

In the County of ——, Petty Sessions District of ——.
Between ——, Plaintiff : and ——, Defendant.
It is adjudged that the instrument of apprenticeship made between the Plaintiff and Defendant be rescinded, and that the —— (¹) do pay to M. N., of ——,
the sum of £——, being —— (²) of the premium paid by the said M. N., on the
binding of the —— (³) as apprentice to the —— (³)

Signed this —— day of ——, 18—.

$$\left.\begin{array}{c} ——\\ —— \end{array}\right\}$$ Justices of said County.

(1) Plaintiff [*or* Defendant].　　(2) The whole [*or* a part].　(3) Defendant [*or* Plaintiff].

13.—*Committal of an Apprentice.*

"Employers and Workmen Act, 1875."

In the County of ——, Petty Sessions District of ——.
Between ——, Plaintiff ; and ——, Defendant.
To the —— (¹) and all other the peace officers of ——.
Whereas on the —— day of ——, 18—, it was ordered that the Defendant
should forthwith perform the duties he had contracted to perform under his
contract of apprenticeship to the Plaintiff :
And whereas it hath been made to appear to the satisfaction of the Court, on
the oath of the Plaintiff —— (²) that the Defendant has failed to comply with
the requirements of the said order :
Now, therefore, it is ordered that the said Defendant be committed to prison
for —— days.
These are therefore to require you the said —— and others to take the Defendant and deliver him to the Governor or Keeper of the Gaol at ——, and you the
said Governor or Keeper to receive the Defendant and him safely keep in the said
gaol for —— days from the arrest under this order, or until he shall be sooner
discharged by due course of law.

Signed this —— day of ——, 18—.

$$\left.\begin{array}{c} ——\\ —— \end{array}\right\}$$ Justices of said County.

—— *Inspector* (or *Head Constable*) *of Constabulary,"* or name of person who is to execute
——
of G H., of —— .]

14.—Acceptance of Security for Performance of Contract by an Apprentice.

" Employers and Workmen Act, 1875."

In the County of ——, Petty Sessions District of ——.

Between ——, Plaintiff; and ——, Defendant; and ——, Bondsman under the contract of apprenticeship of the Defendant:

Whereas on the —— day of ——, 18—, it was ordered that the Defendant should forthwith perform the duties he had contracted to perform under his contract of apprenticeship to the Plaintiff.

And whereas it hath been made to appear to the satisfaction of the Court, on the oath of the Plaintiff —— (¹) that the Defendant has failed to comply with the requirements of the said order :

And whereas by the said failure the Defendant hath rendered himself liable to be committed :

And whereas the said —— (²) is willing to give security to the amount of —— pounds for the due performance by the Defendant of his duties under his said contract of apprenticeship :

Now, therefore, the Court doth direct such security to be forthwith given, and doth order that if payment of the said sum be not made, on the Defendant failing to perform his contract, such sum may be levied by distress of the goods and chattels of the said ——, or an application be made to this Court for commitment of the said ——, according to the provisions of this Act.

Signed this —— day of ——, 18—.

—— } Justices of said County.

(¹) [And of G. H., of ——].   (²) [Or R. S., of ——].

———

15.—Application for the Summoning of a Bondsman for an Apprentice.

" Employers and Workmen Act, 1875."

In the County of ——, Petty Sessions District of ——

Between ——, Plaintiff; and ——, Defendant.

The Plaintiff in this case applies to the Court to direct that——, of ——, who is liable under the instrument of the apprenticeship of the Defendant to the Plaintiff for the good conduct of the Defendant as apprentice to the Plaintiff, be summoned to attend at the hearing of the proceeding.

Signed ——, Plaintiff.

It is hereby directed by the Court that —— be summoned accordingly.

Signed this —— day of ——, 18—.

—— Justice of said County.

16.—*Summons to a Bondsman for an Apprentice.*

"Employer and Workmen Act, 1875."

In the County of ——, Petty Sessions District of ——.
Between ——, Plaintiff ; and ——. Defendant.
To ——, of ——.
Take notice that you are hereby summoned to attend at ——, on the —— day of ——, 18—, at —— o'clock in the —— noon, to show cause why the Court should not, in addition to or in substitution for any order to be made against the said Defendant, order you to pay the amount of any damages which it may find that the Plaintiff has suffered in consequence of the breach of the contract of apprenticeship made between you and the Plaintiff and the Defendant.

Signed this —— day of ——, 18—.

——, Justice of said County.

17.—*Order on a Bondsman for an Apprentice to pay Damages.*

"Employers and Workmen Act, 1875."

In the County of ——, Petty Sessions District of ——.
Between ——, Plaintiff ; and ——, Defendant; and ——, Bondsman under the contract of apprenticeship of the Defendant.
It is adjudged that the said bondsman do pay to the Plaintiff, on or before the —— day of ——, 18—, the sum of —— pounds for damages suffered by him in consequence of the breach of the contract of apprenticeship made between the

THE REFORMATORY SCHOOLS (IRELAND).

31 & 32 Vic., c. 50.

FORMS.

(A.)

Conviction.

to wit } Be it remembered, that on the ——day of ——, at ——, in the said [*county*] of ——, *A.B.*, under the age of sixteen years, to wit, of the age of [*thirteen*] years, is convicted before us, two of Her Majesty's Justices of the Peace for the said [*county*], for that, *&c.* [*state offence in usual manner*]: and we adjudge the said *A.B.*, for his said offence to be imprisoned in the [*prison*] at ——, in the said [*county*], [*and to be there kept to hard labour*] for the space of ——.

And that in pursuance of the Irish Reformatory Schools Act, 1868, we also sentence the said *A.B.* (whose religious persuasion appears to us to be ——) to be sent, at the expiration of the term of imprisonment aforesaid, to ——Reformatory School at ——, in the County of —— (the managers whereof are willing to receive him) [or to some certified Reformatory School to be hereafter, and before the expiration of the term of imprisonment aforesaid, named in this behalf), and to be there detained for the period of ——, commencing from and after the —— day of —— [*the date of the expiration of the sentence*].

Given under our hands and seals, the day and year first above mentioned, at ——, in the [*county*] aforesaid.

J.S.   (L.S.)

L.M.   (L.S.)

(B.)

Order of Detention.

to wit. } To the Constable of ——, and to the Governor of the [*prison*] at ——, in the said [*county*] of ——.

Whereas *A.B.*, late of —— [*labourer*], under the age of sixteen years, to wit, of the age of [*thirteen*] years, was this day duly convicted before the undersigned, two of Her Majesty's Justices of the Peace in and for the said [*county*] of ——, for that, *&c.* [*stating the offence as in the conviction*], and it was thereby adjudged that the said *A.B.* for his said offence should be imprisoned in the [*prison*] at ——, in the said [*county*], [*and be there kept to hard labour*] for the space of ——; and in pursuance of the Irish Reformatory Schools Act, 1868, the said *A.B.* (whose religious persuasion appeared to us to be ——) was thereby sentenced to be sent, at the expiration of the term of imprisonment aforesaid, to the —— Reformatory School at ——, in the county of —— (the managers whereof are willing to receive him therein), [*or* to some certified Reformatory School to be before the expiration of the said term named in that behalf], and to be there detained for the period of ——, commencing from and after the —— day of —— [*the date of the expiration of the sentence*].

These are therefore to command you, the said Constable of ——, to take the said *A.B.* and him safely convey to the [*prison*] at —— aforesaid, and there to deliver him to the Governor thereof, together with this precept: And we do hereby command you, the said Governor of the said [*prison*], to receive the said *A.B.* into your custody in the said [*prison*], there to imprison him [*and keep him to hard labour*] for the space of ——: And we further command you, the said Governor, to send the said *A.B.*, at the expiration of his term of imprisonment aforesaid, as and in the manner directed by the Irish Reformatory Schools Act, 1868, to the —— Reformatory School at —— aforesaid [*or* to the Reformatory School named by an order indorsed hereon under the hands and seals of us, or under the hand and seal of one or other of Her Majesty's Justices of the Peace for the said [*county*], being a visiting Justice of the said prison], together with this order. And for so doing this shall be your sufficient warrant.

Given under our hands and seals this —— day of ——, in the year of our Lord ——, at ——, in the [*county*] aforesaid.

J.S.   (L.S.)
L.M.   (L.S.)

(C.)

Nomination of School indorsed on the Order of Detention.

In pursuance of the Irish Reformatory Schools Act, 1868, I, the undersigned, one of Her Majesty's Justices of the Peace for the [*county*] of ——, hereby name the —— Reformatory School at ——, in the county of ——, as the school to which the within-named *A.B.* (whose religious persuasion appears to me to be ——) is to be sent as within provided [*add where required*, in lieu of the school within (*or* above) named].

Given under my hand and seal, this —— day of ——, at ——, in the county of ——.

E.F.   (L.S.)

(D.)

Complaint for enforcing Contribution from Parent, &c.

to wit. } The complaint of the Inspector of Reformatory Schools [*or as the case may be*] made to us, the undersigned, two of Her Majesty's Justices of the Peace for the said County of ——, this —— day of ——, at ——, in the same county, who says that one *A.B.* of (*) the age of —— years, or thereabouts, is now detained in the —— Reformatory School at —— in the county of ——, under the Irish Reformatory Schools Act, 1868, and has been duly ordered and directed to be detained therein until the —— day of ——: [That one *C.B.*, dwelling in the parish of ——, in the county of ——, is the parent *or* step-parent, &c.] of the said *A.B.*, and is of sufficient ability to contribute to the support and maintenance of the said *A.B.*, his son: (*) The said complainant therefore prays that the said *C.B.* may be summoned to show cause why an order should not be made on him so to contribute.

Exhibited before us, C.D.

J.S.
L.M.

(E.)

Summons to Parent, &c.

To *C.B.*, of —— [*Labourer*].

Whereas information hath this day been laid [*or* complaint hath this day been made] before the undersigned [*one, or as the case may be*] of Her Majesty's Justices of the Peace in and for the said [*county*] of ——, for that you [*here state shortly the matter of the information or complaint*]: These are therefore to command you, in Her Majesty's name, to be and appear on ——, at —— o'clock in the forenoon, at ——, before such Justices of the Peace for the said county [*or as the case may be*] as may then be there, to answer to the said information [*or* complaint], and to be further dealt with according to law.

Given under my [*or our*] hand and seal, this —— day of ——, in the year of our Lord ——, at ——, in the [*county*] aforesaid.

J.S. (L.S.)

Warrant where the Summons is disobeyed.

To the [*Head or other*] Constable of ——, and to all other peace officers in the said [*county*] of ——.

Whereas on —— last past, information was laid [*or* complaint was made] before the undersigned [*one*] of Her Majesty's Justices of the Peace in and for the said [*county*] of ——, for that *A.B.* &c. [*as in the summons*]: And whereas [*I*] then issued my summons unto the said *C.B.*, commanding him in Her Majesty's name to be and appear on ——, at —— o'clock in the forenoon, at ——, before such Justices of the Peace for the said [*county*] as might then be there, to answer to the said information [or complaint], and to be further dealt with according to law: And whereas the said C.B. hath neglected to be or appear at the time and place so appointed in and by the said summons, although it hath now been proved to me on oath that the said summons hath been duly served upon the said C.B.: These are therefore to command you, in Her Majesty's name, forthwith to apprehend the said C.B., and to bring him before some one or more of Her Majesty's Justices of the Peace in and for the said [county] to answer to the information [or complaint] and to be further dealt with according to law.

Given under my hand and seal, this —— day of ——, in the year of our Lord ——, at ——, in the [county] aforesaid.

J.S. L.S.

———————

F.

Order in Bastardy, &c., to maintain a weekly sum.

, Be it remembered that on this —— day of ——, at ——, in the to wit.   said [county] ——, a certain complaint of the Inspector of Reformatory Schools [*or the case may be*], for that one A.B. of the [county] the mother of a child named Fred. D., between the defendant * * was heard by and before us, the undersigned two of Her Majesty's Justices of the Peace in and for the said [county] ——, in the presence and hearing of the said C.B. [*or*, in the said C.B. not appearing to the summons duly served and served in this behalf], and we, having duly examined into the ability of the said C.B. and on consideration of all the circumstances of the case, do order the said C.B. to pay to the said Inspector [*or*, an agent of the said Inspector] the sum of —— shillings per week, from the date of this order until the —— day of ——, the same to be paid at the expiration of each [fourteen, *or as the case may be,* days].

Given under our hands and seals, the day and year first above mentioned, at ——, in the [county] aforesaid.

J.S. L.S.
L.M. L.S.

(G.)

Distress Warrant for amount in Arrear.

)   To the Constable of ——, and to all other peace officers in the
to wit. }   said [*county*] of ——.

Whereas on the hearing of a complaint made by the Inspector of Reformatory Schools [*or as the case may be*], that *A.B.* of, &c. [*stating the cause of complaint as in the Form* (D.) *between the asterisks* (*) (*)], an order was made on the —— day of ——, by us, the undersigned [*or by L.M. and J.H.*], two of Her Majesty's Justices of the Peace in and for the said [*county*] of ——, against the said *C.B.*, to pay to the said Inspector [*or as the case may be*] the sum of —— per week, from the date of the said order until the —— day of ——, the same to be paid at the expiration of each [*twenty-eight*] days [*or as the case may be*] (*): And whereas there is due upon the said order the sum of ——, being for [*three*] periods of [*fourteen*] days each, and default has been made therein for the space of fourteen days.

These are therefore to command you, in Her Majesty's name, forthwith to make distress of the goods and chattels of the said *C.B.*, and if within the space of [*five*] days next after the making of such distress the said last-mentioned sum, together with the reasonable charges of taking and keeping the said distress, is not paid, that then you do sell the said goods and chattels so by you distrained, and do pay the money arising from such sale to ——, the Clerk of the Petty Sessions for the district of ——, that he may pay and apply the same as by law directed, and may render the overplus (if any) on demand, to the said *C.B*; and if no such distress can be found, then that you certify the same to us, to the end that such proceedings may be had therein as the law requires.

Given under our hands and seals this —— day of ——, at ——, in the [*county*] aforesaid.

J.S.   (L.S.)

L.M.   (L.S.)

(H.)

Commitment in Default of Distress.

)   To the Constable of ——, and to the Governor of the [*prison*]
to wit. }   at ——, in the said [*county*] of ——.

Whereas, &c. [*as in the Form* (G.) *to the single asterisks* (*), *and then thus*]: And whereas afterwards, on the —— day of —— last, I, the undersigned, together with *L.M.*, Esquire [*or J.S. and L.M.*, Esquires] two of Her Majesty's Justices of the Peace in and for the said [*county*] of ——, issued a warrant to the Constable of —— aforesaid, commanding him to levy the sum of ——, due upon the said recited order, being for [*three*] periods of [*fourteen*] days, by distress and sale of the goods and chattels of the said *C.B.*: And whereas a return has this day been made to me the said Justice [*or the undersigned, one of Her Majesty's Justices of the Peace in and for the said (county) of* ——], that no sufficient goods of the said *C.B.* can be found.

These are therefore to command you, the said Constable of ——, to take the said *C.B.* and him safely to convey to the [*prison*] at —— aforesaid, and there deliver him to the Governor thereof, together with this precept: And I do hereby command you, the said Governor of the said [*prison*] to receive the said *C.B.* into your custody in the said [*prison*] there to imprison him for the term of ——, unless the said sum, and all costs and charges of the said distress, and of the commitment and conveying of the said *C.B.* to the said [*prison*], amounting to the further sum of ——, shall be sooner paid unto you the said Governor; and for your so doing this shall be your sufficient warrant.

Given under my hand and seal this —— day of ——, in the year of our Lord ——, at ——, in the [*county*] aforesaid.

                                          J.S.   (L.S.)

INDUSTRIAL SCHOOLS (IRELAND).

—

FORMS.

(A.)

Order sending Child to Industrial School.

(C.)

Complaint for enforcing contributions from Parent, &c.

         } The complaint of the Inspector of Industrial Schools [*or as the*
to wit.   }   *case may be*] made to us (*a*) the undersigned, two of Her
Majesty's Justices of the Peace for the said [*county*] of ——, this —— day of
——, at ——, in the same [*county*], who says that one *A.B.*, of (*) the age of
—— years, or thereabouts, is now detained in the —— Industrial School at ——,
in the county of ——, under the Industrial Schools (Ireland) Act, 1868, and has
been duly ordered and directed to be detained therein until the —— day of ——:
That one *C.B.*, dwelling in the parish of ——, in the county of ——, is the
parent'[*or* step-parent, &c.] of the said *A.B.*, and is of sufficient ability to contribute to the support and maintenance of the said *A.B.*, his son : (*) The said
complainant therefore prays that the said *C.B.* may be summoned to show cause
why an order should not be made on him so to contribute.

C.D.

        Exhibited before us,

(Signed)   *J.S.*

L.M.

(D.)

Summons to the Parent.

To *C.B.*, of —— [*Labourer*].

    Whereas information has this day been laid [*or* complaint hath this day been
made] before the undersigned [one, *or as the case may be*] of Her Majesty's
Justices of the Peace in and for that said [*county*]of ——, for that you [*here
state shortly the matter of the information or complaint*] : These are therefore to
command you, in Her Majesty's name, to be and appear on ——, at —— o'clock
in the forenoon, at ——, before such Justices of the Peace for the said county
[*or as the case may be*] as may then be there, to answer the said information [*or*
complaint], and to be further dealt with according to law.
    Given under my [*or* our] hand and seal, this —— day of ——, in the year of
our Lord ——, at ——, in the [*county*] aforesaid.

(*a*) Or in Dublin, " to me, a Police Magistrate of the Dublin Metropolitan Police District."

(E.)

Order on Parent, &c., to contribute a Weekly Sum.

to wit. } Be it remembered that on this —— day of ——, at - ——, in the said [county] of ——, a certain complaint of the Inspector of Industrial Schools [*or as the case may be*], for that one *A.B.*, of, *&c.* [*stating the cause of complaint as in the Form* (C.) *between the asterisks* (*) (*)[was duly heard by and before us, the undersigned, two (*a*) of Her Majesty's Justices of the Peace in and for the said [county] of —— (in the presence and hearing of the said *C.B.*, *if so, or* the said *C.B.*, not appearing to the summons duly issued and served in this behalf) ; and we having duly examined into the ability of the said *C.B.*, and on consideration of all the circumstances of the case, do order the said *C.B.* to pay to the said Inspector [*or* to an agent of the said Inspector] the sum of —— shillings per week, from the date of this order until —— day of ——, the same to be paid at the expiration of each fourteen [*or as the case may be*] days.

Given under our hands and seals, the day and year first above mentioned, at ——, in the [county] aforesaid.

L.S.   (L.S.)
L.M.   (L.S.)

(F,)

Distress warrant for Amount in Arrear.

to wit. } To the Head or other Constable of ——, and to all other peace officers in the said [county] of ——.

Whereas on the hearing of a complaint made by the Inspector of Industrial Schools *or as the case way be*], that *A.B.* of, *&c. stating the cause of complaint*

(G.)

Commitment in default of Distress (a)

        } To the Head or other Constable of ——, and to the Keeper of
to wit.   } the [*prison*] at ——, in the said [*county*] of ——.

Whereas, *&c.* [*as in the Form* (F.) *to the single asterisk* (*), *and then thus*]:
And whereas afterwards on the —— day of ——, last, I, the undersigned, together with *L.M.*, Esquire [*or J.S.* and *L.M.*, Esquires], two (*b*) of Her Majesty's Justices of the Peace in and for the said [*county*] of ——, issued a warrant to the Constable of —— aforesaid, commanding him to levy the sum of —— due upon the said recited order, being for [*three*] periods of [*fourteen*] days, by distress and sale of the goods and chattels of the said *C.B.*: And whereas a return has this day been made to me the said Justice [*or the undersigned*, one of Her Majesty's Justices of the Peace in and for the said [*county*] of ——, that no sufficient goods of the said *C.B.* can be found:

These are therefore to command you the said Head Constable of —— to take the said *C.B.*, and him safely to convey to the [*prison*] at —— aforesaid, and there deliver him to the keeper thereof, together with this precept: And I do hereby command you the said keeper of the said [*prison*] to receive the said *C.D.* into your custody in the said [*prison*], there to imprison him for the term of ——, unless the said sum and all costs and charges of the said distress, and of the commitment and conveying of the said *C.D.* to the said [*prison*], amounting to the further sum of ——, shall be sooner paid unto you the said Keeper, and for your so doing this shall be your sufficient warrant.

Given under my hand and seal, this —— day of ——, in the year of our Lord —— at —— in the [*county*] aforesaid.

                                    J.S.   (L.S.)

FORMS.

SHORT FORM OF TRANSFER OF PUBLICANS' LICENCE BY JUSTICES IN PETTY SESSIONS, 18 & 19 VIC., c. 114, s. 1.

Petty Sessions ——. Co. ——.

We, the undersigned Justices in Petty Sessions, after examination on oath of all necessary parties, do hereby transfer the within Licence to ——. This transfer to remain in force until the next Quarter Sessions for the District after the expiration of one month from this date.

Dated——.   *J.P.*
                                        J.P.

Where Excise Licence lost, Justices may grant the transfer on Certificate from the Excise Officer, or on Clerk of Peace's Certificate of such Licence having been registered, and Justices being satisfied that Licence cannot be found or produced: and see now 47 & 48 Vic. c. 29.

(*a*) Although this Form is given in the Schedule to the Act, the Act itself does not give the power to commit. There is no such power.
(*b*) Or in Dublin, "One of the Police Magistrates of the Dublin Metropolitan Police District."

FORM OF NOTICES TO ESTREAT RECOGNIZANCE BEFORE JUSTICES IN PETTY SESSIONS, UNDER 14 & 15 VIC., c. 93, s. 34. (*See notes on sec. 34 of Petty Sessions Act, Appendix.*)

Take notice that the recognizance entered into on the —— day of ——, 18—, by you, the undernamed persons, conditioned that *A.B.*, the principal party to said recognizance (*a*) should keep the peace and be of good behaviour towards *G.H.* and all Her Majesty's subjects for —— months from the date aforesaid, having become forfeited, an application will be made to the Justices at the Petty Sessions, to be holden at ——, (*b*) in the county of ——, on the ——(*c*) day of ——, to estreat the said recognizance so entered into by you and each of you. And it is intended to sustain such application on the following grounds, viz. that the said *A.B.*, the principal party to such recognizance, failed to perform the conditions thereof, and contrary thereto did, on the —— day of ——, at [*state act complained of, time, and place.*]

Dated ——. Signed —— (*d*)

To *A.B.*, principal party : *C.D.* and *E.F.*,
sureties to the said recognizance.

(Indorse on each notice the name and full description of person served.)

NOTICE OF APPEAL. (No. 1.) (*e*)

Under Petty Sessions Act.

——, *Complainant.* | Petty Sessions District of ——, County of ——.
——, *Defendant.* | Take notice that, feeling aggrieved by the order of the

From Convictions under the Larceny and Malicious Injuries Acts, 1861.

——, *Complainant.*) Petty Sessions District of ——, County of ——.
——, *Defendant.*)   Take notice that, feeling myself aggrieved by the order of the Justices (or Justice) made in the above Petty Sessions, on the —— day of ——, 18—, on the hearing of a complaint that [*state shortly offence*], I intend to appeal from the said order to the next General or Quarter Sessions which shall be holden at [*Division and County*], on the —— day of ——, 18—, [*next after twelve days from date of conviction*], and the cause and grounds for such appeal are (*a*) [*set out here*].

Signed ——,   Date ——.

To *A.B.*, the complainant above named.

(No. 2.)

FORM OF NOTICE REQUIRED TO BE GIVEN BY CLERK OF PETTY SESSIONS (UNDER 21 & 22 Vic., c. 100, s. 8) TO THE RESPONDENT, WHEN APPEAL HAS BEEN LODGED, &c.

A.B., *Appellant.*) Petty Sessions District of ——, County of ——.
C.D., *Respondent.*)   Take notice, that the appellant has duly entered into a recognizance to prosecute his appeal from the order made on the —— day of ——, by the Justices presiding in the above Petty Sessions, in which case you were complainant, and the said *A.B.*, defendant ; and such appeal will be heard at the Quarter Sessions, to be holden at ——, in and for the said county, on the —— day of ——, and you are hereby required to attend, with the necessary witnesses, on the hearing of such appeal. (*b*)

Signed ——,
Clerk of the above Petty Sessions.

Date ——.

To *C.D.*, the respondent.   *Stamp* 1s.

(*a*) In appeals under the Larceny and Malicious Injuries Acts above referred to, it is required that notice be given to the opposite party three days after the conviction, and seven days before the Sessions ; and the section directs that the "cause and matter" of appeal be stated. General terms may be used, as, for instance, "the absence of material witnesses ;" "the penalty or punishment being excessive and not in proportion to offence ;" "the order being erroneous in point of law ;" "contrary to the weight of evidence ;" "want of jurisdiction ;" or "exceeding jurisdiction ;" and if the fact be so, it may be added that the conviction took place before one Justice only. There is no time limited for entering into recognizance, but defendant may be kept in custody until he does, or lodges the amount, as in the section. The conviction should, with the recognizance, be returned to Quarter Sessions in due course. Notice is to be served on complainant, not on Clerk of Petty Sessions. See Larceny Act, 24 & 25 Vic., c. 96, s. 110 ; Malicious Injuries Act, 24 & 25 Vic. c. 97, s. 68.
Notice of intention to prosecute the appeal to be served seven days at least before Sessions.
(*b*) It now appears to be the prevailing opinion that this notice does not supersede the necessity for serving the ordinary seven days' notice by appellant on respondent.

3 D

770   APPENDIX.

Forms of Conviction, &c., given in 18 & 19 Vic., c. 126.

(*The Criminal Justice Act.*) (*a*)

Schedule.—Form (A.)

Conviction.

           Be it remembered, that on the —— day of——, in the year of
to wit.   our Lord ——, at ——, in the said [*county*], *A.B.*, being
charged before us, the undersigned, —— of Her Majesty's Justices of the Peace
for the said [*county*], and consenting to our deciding upon the charge summarily,
is convicted before us, for that he the said *A.B. &c.* [*stating the offence and the
time and place when and where committed*] : and we adjudge the said *A.B.*, for
his said offence to be imprisoned in the [*House of Correction*], at ——, in the said
[*county*]. [and there kept to hard labour], for the space of——.
     Given under our hands and seals, the day and year first above mentioned, at
——, in the [*county*] aforesaid.

J.S.   (L.S.)
H.M.   (L.S.)

Form (B.)

Certificate of Dismissal.

           We, —— of Her Majesty's Justices of the Peace for the [*county*]
to wit.   of ——, certify that on the —— day of ——, in the year of
our Lord ——, at ——, in the said [*county*], *A.B.*, being charged before us, and
consenting to our deciding upon the charge summarily, for that [he the said *A.B.*,
*stating the offence charged, and the time and place when and where alleged to be
committed*], we did, having summarily adjudicated thereon, dismiss the said
charge.
     Given under our hands and seals, this —— day of ——, at ——, in the [*county*]
aforesaid.

J.S.   (L.S.)
H.M.   (L.S.)

Form (C.)

Conviction upon a plea of Guilty.

           Be it remembered, that on the —— day of ——, in the year
to wit.   of our Lord ——, at ——, in the said [*county*], *A.B.*, being
charged before us, the undersigned, —— of Her Majesty's Justices of the Peace
for the said [*county*], for that [he the said *A.B.*, *&c.*, *stating the offence, and the
time and place when and where committed*] ; and pleading guilty to such charge,
he is thereupon convicted before us of the said offence ; and we adjudge the said
A.B. for his said offence to be imprisoned in the [*House of Correction*] at ——,
in the said [*county*], [and there kept to hard labour] for the space of——.
     Given under our hands and seals, the day and year first above mentioned, at
——, in the [*county*] aforesaid.

J.S.   (L.S.)
H.M.   (L.S.)

---

ons of this Act extended to embezzlement by clerks or servants.—31 & 32 Vic.

CONVICTION.

The following general Form of Conviction is prescribed by the 3 Geo. iii., cap. 23, to be used in cases where no particular form is directed :—(a)

See 3 Geo. iv., cap. 23, s. 1.

County of ——, ⎰ Be it remembered, that on the —— day of ——, in the year of
to wit. ⎱ our Lord——, at ——, in the county of——, A.B., of——,
in the county of ——, [labourer] personally came before me, J.P., one [or us, J.P. and R.S., two] of Her Majesty's Justices of the Peace for the said county, and informed me, [or us], that G.H., of ——, in the county of ——, on the —— day of ——, at ——, in the said ——, did [here set forth the fact for which the information is laid], contrary to the form of the statute in such case made and provided; whereupon the said G.H., after being duly summoned to answer the said charge, appeared before me [or us, &c.] on the —— day of ——, at ——, in the said ——, and having heard the charge contained in the said information, declared he was not guilty of the said offence [or did not appear before, &c., pursuant to the said summons, or did neglect and refuse to make any defence against the said charge, as the case may happen to be]. Whereupon I [or we, or, nevertheless, I, or we] the said Justice [or Justices] did proceed to examine into the truth of the charge contained in the said information, and on the —— day of ——, aforesaid, at the parish of ——, aforesaid, one credible witness, to wit, A.W., of ——, in the county of ——, upon his oath deposeth and saith, [if G.H. be present say, in the presence of the said G.H.] that within —— months [or, as the case may be,] next before the said information was made before me, [or us] the said Justice [or Justices] by the said A.B., to wit, on the —— day of ——, in the year ——, the said G.H. at —— in the said county of —— [here state the evidence, and as nearly as possible in the words used by the witness; and if more than one witness be examined, state the evidence given by each; or if the defendant confess, instead of stating the evidence, say], and the said G.H. acknowledged and voluntarily confessed the same to be true. Therefore it manifestly appearing to me [or us], &c., that he, the said G.H. is guilty of the offence charged upon him in the said information, I [or we], &c., do hereby convict him of the offence aforesaid, and do declare and adjudge that he, the said G.H., hath forfeited the sum of ——, of lawful money of Great Britain and Ireland, for the offence aforesaid, to be distributed [or paid, as the case may be] according to the form of the statute in that case made and provided.

Given under my hand and seal [or our hands and seals] the ——day of ——, in the year of our Lord ——.

J. P.   (Seal.)
R. S.   (Seal.)

(Stamp.)

(a) While the above Form, changing what ought to be changed, can be made to suit any case, it does not seem necessary, judging from the Forms given in recent statutes (see those in Criminal Justice Act. &c.), to set out or recite the preliminary proceedings and the evidence on the hearing. It is conceived that the simple Form which follows, and that can be easily prepared from the entry in the "Order Book," may be made to answer all purposes.

The Forms in the Schedule to the Petty Sessions Act are proper Forms to be used on all occasions, but it gives no form of conviction, merely the "certificate" of the order. It needs only the addition of a few technical words to make it a "conviction." The Petty Sessions Stamp Act has not in the Schedule any stamp to suit a conviction. However for this purpose the stamp on a "certificate of order," 1s. appears to be the proper one; and the last item in the Schedule would give authority to enforce it.

3 D 2

CONVICTION (NO. 2).

County of —— } Petty Sessions District of ——, County of ——.

to wit. } Be it remembered, that on the —— day of ——, in the year of our Lord ——, at ——, in the county of ——, A.B., of——, is convicted before me [or us] E.F., —— of Her Majesty's Justices of the Peace for the said county [or city, &c.], for that he, the said A.B. [*specify the offence, and the time and place, when and where, and upon whom the same was committed, and on second conviction state the first*], and I [or we], the said E.F., do adjudge the said A.B. for his said offence [*here state fully the order, whether of imprisonment, or of penalty, compensation, and costs, and the imprisonment in default, &c., as fully as is required by Form (H.) in Schedule to Petty Sessions Act, or as required by the Order Book*].

Given under my [or our] hand and seal, the day and year first above mentioned, at ——, in the county aforesaid.

(*Seal.*)
(*Stamp.*)

———— ·

FORMS OF OATHS, &c. (*a*)

As to truth of Information or Affidavit.—You shall true answers make to all such questions as shall be demanded of you touching this (information or affidavit). So help you God.

Oath of a Witness.—The evidence which you shall give to this Court touching this (if a civil proceeding, *this case*; if a crime or offence, *this complaint*, or *this charge*), shall be the truth, the whole truth, and nothing but the truth. So help you God.

Quaker or Moravian, 1 & 2 Vic., c. 77.—I, A.B., having been one of the people called Quakers (or one of the persuasion of people called Quakers, *or of the*

OATH OF ALLEGIANCE, OFFICIAL AND JUDICIAL OATHS.

(31 & 32 Vic., c. 72, called the "Promissory Oaths Act, 1868.")

Oath of allegiance. I, ——, do swear that I will be faithful and bear true allegiance to Her Majesty Queen Victoria, her heirs and successors, according to law. So help me God.

Official Oath. I, ——, do swear that I will well and truly serve Her Majesty Queen Victoria, in the office of ——. So help me God.

Judicial Oath. I, ——, do swear that I will well and truly serve our Sovereign Lady Queen Victoria, in the office of ——, and I will do right to all manner of people after the laws and usages of this realm, without fear or favour, affection or ill-will. So help me God.

OATHS ACT, 1888.

A.D. 1888. 51 & 52 Vic., c. 46: "An Act to Amend the Law as to Oaths."

Be it enacted by the Queen's most Excellent Majesty, by and with the advice and consent of the Lords Spiritual and Temporal, and Commons, in this present Parliament assembled, and by the authority of the same, as follows:

When affirmation may be made instead of oath. 1. Every person upon objecting to being sworn, and stating, as the ground of such objection, either that he has no religious belief, or that the taking of an oath is contrary to his religious belief, shall be permitted to make his solemn affirmation instead of taking an oath in all places and for all purposes where an oath is or shall be required by law, which affirmation shall be of the same force and effect as if he had taken the oath; and if any person making such affirmation shall wilfully, falsely, and corruptly affirm any matter or thing which, if deposed on oath, would have amounted to wilful and corrupt perjury, he shall be liable to prosecution, indictment, sentence, and punishment in all respects as if he had committed wilful and corrupt perjury.

Form of affirmation. 2. Every such affirmation shall be as follows:
"I, A.B., do solemnly, sincerely, and truly declare and affirm," and then proceed with the words of the oath prescribed by law, omitting any words of imprecation or calling to witness.

Validity of oath not affected by 3. Where an oath has been duly administered and taken, the fact that the person to whom the same was administered had, at the time

---

Christians in these islands on the Gospels. The French form is by raising the right hand, and using the same form of words; but they, and all others who profess the Christian religion, most generally, when sworn here, make oath on the Gospels. Quakers and Separatists *affirm*, having conscientious objections to the taking of an oath; and although the forms of their affirmations are prescribed by statute—3 & 4 Wm. iv., c. 82, s. 1. (Separatist), 1 & 2 Vic., c. 77.(Quaker or Moravian).

The Forms of oaths, like other religious ceremonies, have in all ages been various, consisting however, for the most part, of some bodily action, and of a prescribed form of words. It is commonly thought that oaths are denominated *corporal* oaths from the bodily action which accompanies them of laying the right hand upon a book containing the Four Gospels. This opinion, however, appears to be a mistake, for the term is borrowed from the ancient usage of touching on these occasions the *corporale* or cloth which covered the consecrated elements. Whatever be the form, the signification is the same. It is "the calling upon God as witness to take notice of what we say, and it is invoking His vengeance, or renouncing His favour, if what we say be false, or what we promise be not performed." But see now sec. 3 of above Act.

The Consolidated General Orders of the Court of Chancery in England contain an express rule "that oaths shall be administered in a reverent manner."

<table>
<tr><td>absence of religious belief.</td><td>of taking such oath, no religious belief, shall not for any purpose affect the validity of such oath.</td></tr>
</table>

absence of religious belief. of taking such oath, no religious belief, shall not for any purpose affect the validity of such oath.

Form of affirmation in writing. 4. Every affirmation in writing shall commence "I, ——, of ——, do solemnly and sincerely affirm," and the form in lieu of jurat shall be "Affirmed at ——, this —— day of ——, 18—. Before me."

Swearing with up- lifted hand. 5. If any person to whom an oath is administered desires to swear with uplifted hand, in the form and manner in which an oath is usually administered in Scotland, he shall be permitted so to do, and the oath shall be administered to him in such form and manner with- out further question.

Repeal. 6. The Acts mentioned in the schedule to this Act are hereby repealed to the extent in the third column of the schedule men- tioned.

Short title. 7. This Act may be cited as the Oaths Act, 1888.

——

SCHEDULE.

Session and Chapter.	Title.	Extent of Repeal.
17 & 18 Vic., c. 125.	The Common Law Procedure	Section twenty.

INQUEST.—*Foreman's Oath.*—You shall well and truly try, and true presentment make, of all such matters and things as shall be given you in charge on
behalf of our Sovereign Lady the Queen touching the death of A. B., now lying
dead, of whose body you shall have the view. You shall present no person for
hatred, malice, or ill-will, nor spare any through fear, favour, or affection, but a
true verdict give according to the evidence and the best of your skill and knowledge. So help you God.

The same oath which A. B., your foreman on this inquest, hath now taken
before you on his part, you and each of you shall well and truly observe and
keep on your parts. So help you God.

CERTIORARI.

The Justices in making return to a writ of *Certiorari* when served on them,
should set out the proceedings before them on the back of the writ thus :—

" The answer of ——, in the county of ——, Esq., a Justice of the Peace
for said county of ——, being the J.P. (or one of the Justices) who made the
Order at —— Petty Sessions, on the —— day of ——."

The following is a copy of the Complaint and the Order made thereon (here
copy the summons or complaint as before the Court, and the exact Order made
on it, and state the Statute under which the Order was made): and at foot add
these words :—" The execution of this writ appears by a certain Schedule
annexed hereto."

"Signed, ——, J.P."

Then on a separate piece of parchment, about size of the writ, state :—

County of —— ⎫ I, —— one of H. M. Justices of the Peace for the said
   to wit. ⎭ county, by virtue of this writ to me delivered, do hereby
certify unto Her Majesty, in Her Court of Queen's Bench, the conviction of
which mention is made in the same writ, together with all matters touching the
same, as by said writ I am commanded. In witness whereof I, the said ——,
have hereunto set my hand and seal, at ——, in said county, this —— day of
—— , in the year of our Lord, One Thousand Eight Hundred and ——.

Signed, —— .

(Seal.)

The above may be delivered by hand, or by post, addressed to the Clerk of
Crown, Queen's Bench, Four Courts, Dublin.

FORM OF PRECEPT TO RESTRAIN WASTE UNDER LANDLORD AND TENANT ACT,

23 & 24 Vic., c. 154.

County of —— ⎫　　To C. D. and E. F. and all persons whom it may concern.
to wit.　　⎭　　　　Whereas information on oath has been this day laid before
me, being one of Her Majesty's Justices of the Peace for the county of M., that
you, C. D. and E. F., being the occupiers of (or acting under the authority of and
in collusion with one M. N., being the occupier of) a certain dwelling-house (or
farm of land), situated at N., in the barony of O., and county of M. aforesaid, and
held by you as (tenant from year to year, or otherwise as tenant or caretaker, as
the case may be) to A. B., do intend and are about to commit or suffer (or are in
the act of committing or suffering) certain unlawful waste and injury to the
premises by [state the nature of the waste, injury, alteration, or removal which is
apprehended or actually being done], contrary to the statute in that case made
and provided.

These are therefore to command and firmly enjoin you and each of you, and
all other persons whomsoever, not to proceed to [state again the waste, &c., apprehended or being done], or to continue the same, or otherwise to injure the said
premises or any part of them, until special leave, licence, and authority in writing
for that purpose shall be first procured from and given by me the said Justice,
or until the matter of the said information shall be first inquired into at the Petty
Sessions of the Peace to be holden at ——, on the —— day of —— next, and
this my precept lawfully annulled or altered in that behalf (or until the —— day
of ——. next, naming a particular day, or further order).

of M., late in the possession of J. K., as tenant thereof, containing —— acres, —— roods, and —— perches, or thereabouts, on the —— day of ——, between the hours of ten o'clock in the forenoon, and four o'clock in the afternoon of the said day, do certify that the premises aforesaid then appeared to us to be deserted and abandoned by the said J. K., the said lands, or the greater portion of them being left uncultivated or unemployed, contrary to the course of good husbandry, and without sufficient distress to be found therein [or *if the case be*, the stock and crop thereof having been carried off; or *in case the premises consist chiefly of a dwelling-house, say* the dwelling-house being left unoccupied].

Given under our hands and seals this —— day of ——, in the year 18—.

A. B. (*Seal.*)

C. D. (*Seal.*)

To the Assistant-Barrister for the county of M.
Witness present, X. Y.

LICENCE FROM JUSTICES TO DEAL IN GAME.

1 & 2 Wm. iv., cap. 32.

At a Special Session of the Justices of the Peace for the county of ——, acting for the Petty Sessions district of ——, in the said county, holden at ——, in the said district, on the —— day of ——, in the year of our Lord one thousand eight hundred and ——, we, ——, being —— Justices acting for the said —— assembled at the said Special Sessions, do hereby authorize and empower [*here insert the name, description, and place of residence, and if more than one in partnership, say* C. D., *of, &c., and* E. F., *of, &c., being partners*] being a householder [*or householders, or keeper or keepers of a shop or stall, as the case may be*], to buy game from any person authorized to sell game, by virtue of an Act passed in the second year of the reign of King William the Fourth, intituled "An Act to Amend the Laws in England relative to Game;" and we do also authorize and empower the said [A.B., *or* C.D., *and* E.F., *being partners*] to sell at [*his or their*] house [*shop or stall*] any game so bought, provided that the said [A. B., *or* C. D.. *and* E. F., *being partners*] shall affix to some part of the outside of the front of [*his or their*] house [*shop or stall*], and shall there keep a board having thereon, in clear and legible characters, his Christian name and surname [*or their Christian names and surnames*], together with the following words, "Licensed to deal in Game." This licence will expire on ——.

Signed, { ——, Justice of the Peace.
{ ——, Justice of the Peace.

FORM OF INFORMATION, TO BE MADE BEFORE A JUSTICE, OF MALICIOUS INJURY, WHERE IT IS INTENDED TO SEEK FOR COMPENSATION UNDER GRAND JURY ACT, sec. 6, 7 Wm. iv., c. 116.

County of —— } Petty Sessions district of ——, County of ——.
to wit. } The information of A. B., of [*describe fully residence and calling, &c.*], who saith on his oath, that sometime between the hour of eleven o'clock on the night of Thursday, and two o'clock in the morning of Friday, the 12th or 13th day of November instant [*or in any other words that indicate the time or about the time, so far as is known*] on the lands of ——, in the parish of ——, barony of ——, and county of ——, [*here describe the property—so many ricks of hay, straw, &c.*] my property, [*or if made by a steward or servant, state whose property it is*] were wilfully and maliciously [*or if he cannot state positively*, were as I verily believe], set on fire and wholly [*or partly*] destroyed. And I further say that I do not know the person or persons who so committed the said injury, or any of them. [*If he knows or believes who the parties are let him describe them.*]

—— (Informant signs.)

Taken before me, this —— day of ——, 18—, at ——, in the said county.

FORM OF NOTICE.

To A.B., High Constable of the barony of ——, and C.D., and E.F., Church-wardens of the parish of ——, in the said barony, and county of ——.

You and each of you are hereby required to take notice that [*describe the outrage and injury just as in the information, and stating also the value of the property destroyed*]. And that it is my intention to apply to the Presentment Sessions to be held on the —— day of ——, 18—, at ——, for the said barony of ——, and county of ——, for compensation for the loss sustained by me by reason of the said malicious injury to my said property, and that same may be levied off the county at large, or off such barony, parish, district, townland, or subdemonination thereof as the Grand Jury shall direct.

Dated this —— day of ——, 18—. Signed —— [*Name and Residence.*]

This notice is to be served on the Baronial High Constable and the Church-wardens (or if there be no Churchwardens, upon two of the principal inhabitants) of the parish where the offence is committed, and at the nearest police station, within six days at least after the commission of the offence, and lodge with the High Constable or Secretary to the Grand Jury in like manner and time as application for presentments for public works, &c., an application setting forth the loss, damage, time, and place, &c. ; see section 135.

BOARD OF TRADE INQUIRIES AS TO WRECKS, &c.

JUSTICES' CLERKS FEES.

(According to Treasury Chambers Minute F. 10097, 13th Sept., 1877.)

	s.	d.
Taking instructions to hold investigation,	3	4
Convening Justices and Assessors, for each member of the Court convened,	2	6
Summons and duplicate to witnesses, each,	1	6
Service of each summons, (a)	2	6
Taking down examination of witnesses in writing, per folio of 90 words, (b)	0	4
Copy of evidence when required—per folio,	0	2
Drawing report to the Board of Trade—per folio,	0	8
Fair copy thereof—per folio,	0	4
Attending Justices, &c., for their approval and signatures,	3	4
Letter to Board of Trade, with report,	3	6
Attending Court, and taking down examination in writing, for each hour employed,	6	8

(a) These summonses are sometimes served by Custom-house servants, and therefore no fees are payable to any other.

(b) The Board of Trade or Wreck Commissioners sometimes direct (it is so in Ireland at present) that a shorthand-writer shall perform this duty, therefore the clerk cannot charge for it, but it does not interfere with the clerk's fees, attending Court, &c., at 6s. and 8d. per hour.

☞ The Justice is paid three guineas for first day, and two guineas each subsequent day during the inquiry.

Dangerous Lunatics and Idiots.—It was intended to set out the Form used in the committal of dangerous lunatics, and that used in the case of pauper lunatics or idiots whose friends desire to place them in the public asylum, but the forms, certificates, &c., are too lengthy for this work. The forms of committal of dangerous lunatics are to be had from Thom & Co., Her Majesty's Stationery Office, Dublin ; the others can be obtained at the lunatic asylum to which it is intended to send the patient. These forms contain all particulars requiring to be complied with by Magistrates, medical officer, and friends of the lunatic. They ought to be kept in Petty Sessions Courts and police stations.

Fees.—Circular directing new Fees and Penalties are to be paid and disposed of.

Circular to Clerks of Petty Sessions.

*Chief Secretary's Fines and Penalties Audit Office.
Dublin Castle, 1st November, 1852.*

In reference to the Fines Act (Ireland), which comes into operation the 1st of November 1852, Clerks of Petty Sessions are to observe, that on and after that day they will be held accountable as to all moneys received on foot of fines and penalties which shall be imposed subsequent to that date, and as to all proceedings in respect thereto.

All moneys levied by the Constabulary, under warrants, are to be paid over without delay to the clerks, as now all moneys received by rate-payers or received-keepers. The clerks, on receipt of such moneys, are primarily to make all payments thereof which shall be lawfully raised by law, and all moneys payable to the Crown shall forthwith, in manner as the clerks will be hereafter informed.

...the ... of ... ... all moneys received to ... account of the balances ... ... shall ... paid over ... weekly or at such time ... the rules and ... the Fines Act may require.

Forms of the several ... of accounts will be hereafter furnished, and the ... in these accounts, the clerks will be required to provide without trouble ... to the ... to these forms.

Into the ... of ... ... any of fines, or other penal sums to parties in ... will ... ... are to be required.

Tables ... shewing ... ... as to the new scale of fines and the amounts ... to the ... are to be made in the ... at present in hand. The clerk making use ... ... of ... as many shewn as may be required for a full register of ... that have been ... in reference to ... case.

Tables are ... shewing that, with reference to the fines, &c., imposed previous to the 1st of November 1852, the returns are to be furnished to the clerk, ... in all respects as heretofore, who will be the proper party to render account thereof.

In the payments of ... of fines to members ... the Constabulary Force, the payments are to be made in precisely the same manner as payments to any other parties.

Wm. M. Somerville

STAMPS—Revenue Cases not liable to Stamps.

Dublin Castle, 7th March, 1859.

GENTLEMEN,—Referring to the circular addressed to you on the 15th ultimo, I am directed by the Lord Lieutenant to acquaint you that the question whether documents used in proceedings at Petty Sessions, at the instance of the Inland Revenue Department, are liable to the Stamp duty imposed by the 21 & 22 Vic., c. 100, having been submitted to the Law Officers of the Crown, they have given the following opinion thereon :—

" We think that the documents used at Petty Sessions, in proceeding before Magistrates at the prosecution of the Inland Revenue Department, are *not* liable to the Stamp duty imposed by the 21 & 22 Vic., c. 100, s. 14.

"The Petty Sessions Act, 14 & 15 Vic., c. 93 (imposing fees on Forms, &c.), exempted, by the 42nd section, informations and other proceedings relating to Her Majesty's revenue, &c., and this Act is incorporated with the late Act, 21 & 22 Vic., c. 100, and therefore the exemption is continued, unless expressly taken away.

" One of the main objects of the late Act was to pay clerks by salaries from a fund to be derived from stamps and fines, &c., but we think that the 14th section and Schedule C only imposed stamps on such Forms as paid fees under the former Act, and that Revenue cases are not within the purview of either Act.

" An apparent difficulty arises from the 25th section, providing that when a case is prosecuted by the Constabulary, or by any public officer on behalf of the Crown, he may have the stamps remitted by the Registrar ; but there are other public prosecutions which would satisfy the words of the Act, and a giving of new stamps by the Registrar to the Revenue officers, in lieu of stamps used at Sessions, would be of no use to parties not liable to stamps in the first instance.

" We think that the exemption conferred on the Revenue by the first Act has not been taken away by express words, or even by necessary implication (if that were sufficient) in the second, and that to impose a tax or take away a Crown exemption would require stronger words than are contained in the late Act." (a)

I am, Gentlemen, your obedient Servant,

THOMAS A. LARCOM.

——

STAMPS—Committals of Prisoners are to be Stamped.

Dublin Castle, 30th January, 1860.

GENTLEMEN,—It having been represented to the Lord Lieutenant that, in different parts of the country, prisoners have been committed to gaols by warrants of committal not bearing the stamp required by 21 & 22 Vic., c. 100, His Excellency desires to call the attention of the Magistrates to the irregularity of this practice, and trusts that it will be discontinued.

I am, Gentlemen, your obedient Servant,

THOMAS A. LARCOM.

(a) Then it would seem that the clerk may accept of the *fees* payable in Revenue cases, and provided for under previous Acts, as the Acts above referred to do not in any way affect the question.

CIRCULAR TO CLERKS OF PETTY SESSIONS.

Levy Warrants—Clerks to notify to Constable if amount paid after Warrant issued.

Dublin Castle, 10th May, 1852.

Under the provisions of the Act 14 & 15 Vic., c. 93, sec. 5, par. 7, it is ordered by the Lord Lieutenant that the following regulation be observed by all Clerks of Petty Sessions throughout Ireland, viz. :—

In all cases where a warrant shall have been issued for the levy, *by distress alone*, of any sum, whether of a penal or civil nature, and after the issue of such warrant, the amount thereof shall have been tendered to the clerk who shall have received the same, and given his receipt therefor, it shall be the duty of the clerk, *promptly, in writing under his hand*, to notify the fact of such payment to the officer of Constabulary to whom the warrant was directed, and also to the officer in charge of the nearest Constabulary station.

JOHN WYNNE.

CIRCULAR TO THE CLERKS OF PETTY SESSIONS IN IRELAND.

Clerks—Not to interfere at Elections.

Dublin Castle, 30th June, 1852.

The attention of the Lord Lieutenant having been called to the circumstance that possibly several of the persons holding the situation of Petty Sessions Clerk may be induced to engage themselves in various capacities for candidates at the coming election, and His Excellency being of opinion that any such proceeding would interfere with the proper discharge of the duties which belong to their office, I think it right to call your attention to the provisions of the Petty Sessions Act, 14 & 15 Vic., c. 93, sec. 4, and to apprise you that it is His Excellency's positive injunction that you shall not in anywise interfere on behalf of any candidate at the coming elections.

JOHN WYNNE.

CIRCULAR ADDRESSED BY LORD NAAS, CHIEF SECRETARY, TO THE LIEUTENANTS OF COUNTIES IN IRELAND.

Magistrates—Members of the same Family should not act in Conjunction.

Dublin Castle, 28th October, 1852.

I am directed by his Excellency the Lord Lieutenant to inform you that representations have been made to him, that Magistrates nearly related have been in the habit of presiding and acting together at Petty Sessions. The objection to this practice is distinctly intimated by several of the printed questions which Magistrates are required to answer previous to their appointment; and its tendency to prejudice the administration of justice is so obvious, that his Excellency trusts that a mere expression of his disapproval will be sufficient to prevent its continuance.

I am also directed by his Excellency to send you a copy of a Circular Letter which has been brought under his consideration by the Lord Chancellor, and was addressed by order of Lord Normandy to the Lieutenants of Counties ory to a revision of the Magistracy of Ireland. This communication was the result of a conference with the then Lord Chancellor, Lord Plunket, as to the general principles by which that revision was to be guided. His Excellency entirely adopts those principles, and desires me to direct your attention to the objections that exist to the issuing of Commissions to members of the same family, which, though in terms confined to cases where they reside together, is obviously directed against their acting in conjunction.

NAAS.

DEPOSITIONS.

To be taken from *viva voce* Examination and in presence of Accused.

Dublin Castle, 24th August, 1854.

GENTLEMEN,—I am commanded by the Lord Lieutenant to call your particular attention to the provisions contained in the Petty Sessions (Ireland) Act, 1851, 14 & 15 Vic., c. 93, with respect to taking informations against parties accused of indictable offences. His Excellency desires to impress on you the necessity of a strict observance of the provisions of that statute, which requires that in every case where a person shall appear or be brought before any Justice, charged with any indictable crime or offence, the Justice, before committing the person so accused or accepting bail for his appearance, shall take the deposition on oath, and in writing, of the witness or witnesses, according to the form A.B., in the schedule to the said Act annexed, such deposition to be taken on a *viva voce* examination of the informants, in the presence and hearing of the accused person, who may put questions to the witness if he think proper, the answers to such questions to be also taken down, and to form a portion of the deposition. When the deposition, including the answers to the questions put by the accused party, is completed, it is to be read over to the witness, and signed by him, and then signed by the presiding Justices or one of them.

Formerly it was the habit to take the deposition of the witness in the first instance, and then to read it over in the presence of the accused; but this practice is an irregular one, and should not be persevered in, unless the accused expresses himself satisfied with it, and states that he does not wish to put any question to the party to be examined; and even in such a case the more correct practice will be to have the deposition taken down by the clerk from the *viva voce* examination of the witness in the presence of the accused as already stated.

It is also to be observed, that the statute referred to has made provisions that a deposition sworn by a person who may have died may be read as evidence on the trial. But as this most salutary provision can be available only on proof of the death of the witness, and on proof that such deposition was taken in the presence or hearing of the person accused, and that he, or his counsel or attorney, had an opportunity of cross-examining such witness, due care should be taken in every case that the requirements of the statute in this respect have been fulfilled. Great care is also necessary in reference to statements made by the accused party; these should not be received until after such a caution as the statute requires, and should then be taken in the manner prescribed, and be signed by the accused, or with his mark, and duly witnessed and attested.

I am, Gentlemen, your obedient Servant,

THOMAS A. LARCOM.

The Magistrates at Petty Sessions.

CIRCULAR.

Small Debts Act.—Opinion on Clauses.

Dublin Castle, 12*th August,* 1859.

GENTLEMEN,—The Law Officers of the Crown having had under their consideration various inquiries made by Magistrates as to the construction and working of the Act 22 Vic., c. 14, for the "Abolition of Manor Courts, and the better recovery of Small Debts in Ireland," I am directed by the Lord Lieutenant to communicate, for your guidance, their opinion upon the several matters submitted to them, in reference to that Act.

Jurisdictions.—The Act applies to *debts* in the usual sense of that term; no demand for anything in the nature of damages, as breach of warranty, false representation or deceit, falls within it; cases between master and apprentice are not within the Act. The original debt must have been contracted within twelve months. The amount recovered must be under £2; but although the original debt exceeded £2, if it has been reduced by payments, and the balance sought to be recovered is under £2, the case is within the Act; but if the debt were originally contracted more than twelve months ago, a subsequent reduction of the debt by payments made within twelve months will not bring the case within the Act.

Hearing.—The plaintiff may move his own process. The Magistrates may receive evidence of a set-off. No notice of set-off is absolutely necessary, but as a matter of practice the Magistrates ought to require a notice in order to prevent

Stamps.—The stamps to be used may be either impressed or adhesive. The decree is chargeable with a 6*d.* stamp as a warrant.

There is no inconsistency in the Act in reference to the stamp on the certificate of appeal, but the Law Officers are of opinion that only a 6*d.* *stamp* is chargeable on a certificate of appeal, and no fee on its entry. (*a*)

There is a stamp of 6*d.* on the entry of every process, and 6*d.* on the entry of every order.

I am, Gentlemen, your obedient Servant,

THOMAS A. LARCOM.

To Magistrates at Petty Sessions.

(*a*) This was a misapprehension, and is corrected in the next Circular, 17th Nov., 1859.

CIRCULAR.

Small Debts Act.—Further Opinion.

Dublin Castle, 17*th November,* 1859.

GENTLEMEN,—Referring to the Circular addressed to you on the 12th August last, on the subject of the Act 22 Vic., c. 14, I am directed by the Lord Lieutenant to inform you that, doubts having arisen with respect to the construction of the 6th and 7th sections of the Act, the subject has been considered by the Law Officers of the Crown, and that they have come to the conclusion that, on the true interpretation of the Act, two distinct classes of stamp duties have been imposed on proceedings taken under it, viz. stamp duties properly so called, payable to Her Majesty under sec. 6, and fees denoted by stamps, impressed or adhesive, under sec. 7; thus, for instance, the certificate of appeal is subject to a stamp duty of 1*s.* under sec. 6, and a fee of 6*d.*, denoted by an impressed or adhesive stamp, under sec. 7.

The opinion in regard to stamps, conveyed in the last paragraph but one of the above-mentioned Circular, is now considered by the Law Officers to be erroneous, and is superseded by that herein expressed.

I am, Gentlemen, your obedient Servant.

THOMAS A. LARCOM.

To Magistrates at Petty Sessions.

CIRCULARS TO CLERKS OF PETTY SESSIONS.

Copies of Depositions to be sent to Sessional Crown Prosecutors.

Dublin Castle, 11*th April,* 1866.

SIR,—The Lord Lieutenant deeming it necessary for the ends of justice that the Sessional Crown Prosecutors should be supplied as early as possible with copies of the informations in all cases to be prosecuted by them at Quarter Sessions, I am directed to convey to you His Excellency's desire, that you will in all criminal cases returned for trial at Quarter Sessions transmit as early as possible to the Sessional Crown Prosecutor for the county stamped copies of the informations, and that you will after each Quarter Sessions forward to him an account of the copies so furnished, which account, being examined and found correct, will be forwarded by him to the Crown Solicitor for the circuit or district, for payment at the rate of sixpence for each copy.

I am, Sir, your obedient Servant,

THOMAS A. LARCOM.

CIRCULAR TO CLERKS OF PETTY SESSIONS.

Committals in Summary Convictions, Clerk to state therein the Statute.

Dublin Castle, 31*st August,* 1860.

SIR,—I am directed by the Lord Lieutenant to request that, for the future, in all cases of summary conviction, when any person has been committed to gaol, you will state in the committal the statute under which the prisoner was convicted. (*a*)

I am, Sir, your obedient Servant,

THOMAS A. LARCOM.

CIRCULAR.

Order Book.—One of the Justices to sign *each Order.*

Dublin Castle, 31*st October,* 1860.

GENTLEMEN,—Certain Magistrates having applied for the opinion of the Law Adviser, whether it is sufficient that the signature of the Justices presiding at Petty Sessions be affixed to the Order Book once on each day, that is to say, at the end of the cases entered in the Book on that day; I am directed by the Lord Lieutenant to acquaint you, that the Law Adviser is of opinion that each Order should be signed in the Order Book by a Justice signing his name opposite to it, or immediately after it.

I am, Gentlemen, your obedient Servant,

EDWARD CARDWELL.

The Magistrates at Petty Sessions.

CIRCULAR TO MAGISTRATES AT PETTY SESSIONS.

Faction Fights.

Dublin Castle, 18*th June,* 1861.

GENTLEMEN,—The Lord Lieutenant's attention has been called to the fact that, in some counties in Ireland, the offence of faction fighting, which had happily disappeared, is again exhibiting itself.

It is of great importance that this practice should be at once checked, and that those engaged in it should be brought to justice; and his Excellency deems it advisable that, for the future, such cases should be sent to the Assizes for trial.

I am, Gentlemen, your obedient Servant,

THOMAS A. LARCOM.

(*a*) It does not follow that, a particular statute being named, the Justice would therefore be precluded from relying on other statutes, or the Common Law, provided the language describing the offence be clearly set forth in the committal.

3 E 2

Publicans' Annual Certificates.—Justices to hold Sessions before 10th October for granting Certificates.

Dublin Castle, 31st *January,* 1862.

GENTLEMEN,—Representations having been made to the Commissioners of Inland Revenue, that in several districts in Ireland considerable inconvenience has been caused by the certificates required to be signed by Justices in Petty Sessions in order to the renewal of licences for the sale of spirits, &c., not having been signed until long after the proper time for the issue of the renewed licences, I am directed by the Lord Lieutenant to call your attention to the necessity of some arrangements being made in every Petty Sessions district, which shall insure the examination of applications for certificates, and the signing of them, where there is no sufficient objection, on some day previous to the 10th of October, when the licences expire. It will in many cases be advisable to adjourn the Petty Sessions to a day to be fixed for the purpose, of which notice should be published in the district, and when care should be taken that at least two Magistrates should attend.

I am, Gentlemen, your obedient Servant,

THOMAS A. LARCOM.

To Magistrates at Petty Sessions.

———

MEDICAL WITNESSES NOT TO BE PAID UNLESS WHERE EVIDENCE INDISPENSABLE.

Dublin Castle, 28th *August,* 1865.

GENTLEMEN,—Claims of Medical Practitioners for remuneration for attending as witnesses at Petty Sessions having recently become very numerous, and there being reason to believe that their evidence might be dispensed with in many cases in which they are summoned, without detriment to the administration of justice. I am directed by the Lord Lieutenant to inform you that no claim of a medical witness will hereafter be admitted, unless it be satisfactorily shown by a Magistrate that his evidence was indispensable for rightly disposing of the case.

I am also to call the attention of the Magistrates of the district, individually, to another subject connected with medical claims :—Payment has been frequently claimed for surgical attendance on a person severely assaulted, such attendance having been ordered by a Magistrate. In such cases the attendance of the Medical Officer of the Dispensary district should be procured by a visiting ticket ; or if, in any case of extraordinary urgency, such a ticket cannot be procured without dangerous delay, it should be obtained before a second visit is made. Instructions to this effect have long since been issued to the Constabulary ; and I am to state that no claim will be admitted in respect of any case in which the course here indicated has not been taken.

I am, Gentlemen, your obedient Servant,

THOMAS A. LARCOM.

ORDER OF 30TH NOVEMBER, 1866, AS TO THE CANCELLING OF PETTY SESSIONS STAMPS.

ABERCORN,

By virtue and in pursuance of the powers and authorities vested in me by the provisions of the Petty Sessions Clerks (Ireland) Act, 1858, the following general rules are hereby made, for the purpose of carrying into effect the provisions of the said Act :—

1. That the Stamp Duties payable under the provisions of said Act shall be denoted by the use of adhesive Stamps.

2. For this purpose a uniform die has been prepared by the Commissioners of Inland Revenue, bearing on the face thereof the words "Petty Sessions, Ireland," and "Sixpence;" and the requisite amount of Stamp Duty is, in each case, to be denoted by affixing to the document as many of the Stamps struck from said die as will together amount to and denote the sum set opposite to such document in the Schedule to the Act.

3. Whenever any Clerk of Petty Sessions, in the performance of his duty as such clerk, shall affix one or more of said Petty Sessions Stamps to any of the documents enumerated in the Schedule to the said Act, it shall be his duty to cancel such Stamp or Stamps, by writing his name, and the date, conspicuously across it or them ; and any clerk who shall issue any such document without having previously cancelled the Stamp or Stamps thereon in manner aforesaid will be liable to be dismissed, in addition to any proceeding that may be instituted against him under the 18th section of the said Act. (a)

4. Whenever any Magistrate signs or countersigns any of the documents enumerated in the Schedule to the said Act, he shall, in case the Clerk of Petty Sessions has not already done so, cancel the Stamp or Stamps on such document, by writing his name and the date conspicuously across it or them.

5. The four General Orders as to Petty Sessions Stamps, of the 27th December, 1858, are hereby revoked.

Given at Her Majesty's Castle in Dublin, the Thirtieth day of November, One Thousand Eight Hundred and Sixty-six.

By His Excellency's Command,

NAAS.

DOGS REGULATION ACT.

CIRCULAR TO MAGISTRATES AT PETTY SESSIONS.

Dublin Castle, 21st *October,* 1867.

GENTLEMEN,—Numerous cases of prosecutions under the Dogs Regulation (Ireland) Act, 1865, brought at Petty Sessions against parties for keeping dogs without licence, having occurred throughout the country, in which the Justices, while ordering a licence to be taken out, in accordance with the 23rd section of the Act, have at the same time either dismissed the case, or have refused to order costs, or remitted the costs of Court, I am directed by the Lord Lieutenant to draw your attention to the inconvenience of making an order in a case and, at the same time dismissing it ; and to state for your information that the Act of

---

(a) For penalty for *defacing* adhesive stamps before they are *used,* see Stamp Act, 33 & 34 Vic., c. 96, s. 26. And see "Stamps," Summary Index.

Parliament provides that the Justices should convict in all cases in which it is proper to make an order that the defendant take out a dog licence, and that it is not in accordance with the provisions of the statute that Justices should dismiss a case, and then order the defendant to take out the licence. It is obvious that a case having been dismissed, the Justices have no further jurisdiction, and cannot, therefore, direct a licence to be taken out ; but as by the 20th and 23rd sections of the above-mentioned Act, they are directed to order such a licence to be forthwith obtained, it naturally follows that no order of dismissal can be made.

As regards the refusal to order costs, or the remission of the costs of Court, in these cases I am to refer you to sec. 14 of the Petty Sessions Clerks (Ireland) Act, 1858, which requires stamps of a certain value to be affixed to all documents used at Petty Sessions, and to sec. 16 of the same Act, which requires the Justices to enforce the payment of such fees by the person liable thereto in all cases, except where, under sec. 19 of the Act, the Justices are empowered to remit the fees in whole, or in part, on being satisfied of the inability of the parties liable thereto to pay such fees; and as this is the only case in which the Justices have power to remit the cost of the stamps employed in proceedings at Petty Sessions, I have to point out that the costs of the proceedings ought to be enforced against the parties liable, in all cases in which the statutory exemption does not apply.

I have the honour to be, Gentlemen, your obedient Servant.

MAYO.

_____

CIRCULAR TO CLERKS OF PETTY SESSIONS AS TO RENDERING ACCOUNTS.

☞ *Special attention is requested to this Circular.*

As in some instances Clerks of Petty Sessions have neglected to attend to the General Rules issued for their guidance as to the furnishing of the accounts of fines and stamps, and the lodging of the moneys due thereon. I have to call particular attention to these rules, and to state that in future I shall insist on their being strictly adhered to.

No. 1.
A 1,
A 2,
with
Vouchers.

According to the rules referred to, the returns of fines and other penal sums for each quarter, ending respectively the 31st of March, 30th June, 30th September, and 31st December in each year, are to be rendered on or before the close of the month immediately following the end of the quarter. The Crown fines must be lodged before sending in the returns, and all vouchers for sums paid away should accompany the returns.

Form B.

Return Form B, containing lists of warrants issued, should be furnished to the Sub-Inspector as soon as possible after the termination of each quarter. A Nil return B should be sent when no warrants were issued.

Form X.

The accounts of Petty Sessions stamps must be furnished half-yearly, ending respectively the 30th June and 31st December, within the month immediately succeeding the end of the half year; and whenever the amount received for Petty Sessions stamps exceeds the half-year's salary, such excess must be lodged before sending in the accounts.

The accounts of Dog Licence stamps must also be rendered half-yearly, ending respectively 30th June and 31st December, within the month immediately following the half-year, and the whole of the money received for Dog Licence stamps must be lodged from time to time as it is received, and any balance remaining must be lodged, less necessary expenses, before sending in the accounts.

Any returns received without the money having been fully accounted for as above directed shall be sent back to the clerks, be treated as not rendered, and the clerks' sureties written to on the subject.

No salary can be paid until all accounts shall have been furnished; and as credit can only be given in the half-yearly general statement of accounts submitted to each clerk, for the lodgments made up to the close of the month immediately following the termination of the half-year, it is necessary that all such lodgments should be made in sufficient time to appear in the Books of the Bank of Ireland, IN DUBLIN, ON OR BEFORE THE LAST DAY OF THE MONTH.

RICHARD R. WINGFIELD.

Registrar of Petty Sessions Clerks Office,
Dublin Castle, 18th December, 1868.

ACCOUNTS.

CIRCULAR TO CLERKS OF PETTY SESSIONS.

In preparing and furnishing their Quarterly Returns of Fines, Clerks of Petty Sessions are directed to pay particular attention to the following directions:—

I.—1. All fines and other penal sums *imposed during the quarter* (no matter to whom payable), with the compensation and costs, are to be correctly entered in the A 1, and the totals transferred to the No. 1.

(The costs to include the charge for the issue of warrant in all cases where a warrant is issued.)

2. The "Warrant" column must be a complete list of all warrants issued, whether of distress or committal, and must agree with the Form B furnished to the Sub-Inspector of Royal Irish Constabulary; and the total of this column added to the total of the column of "Receipts from Party" must agree in amount with the totals of the columns of fine and costs imposed.

(Clerks are bound to issue warrants in every case where the fine is not paid immediately, unless the order of the Magistrates in the Order Book otherwise directs.)

3. Particular attention must be used to distinguish between moneys received from party, gaoler, and Constabulary.

4. The total of all the columns of payments must agree in amount with the total of all the columns of receipts, both in the A 1, A 2, and No. 1.

5. The dates and amounts of all lodgments on account of fines are to be entered in their proper place on the No. 1.

(It is desirable that the lodgments for each quarter be made separately, so that no balance of a lodgment made on account of the fines appearing in one quarter's return should appear to the credit of the next quarter's account.)

II.—1. The returns of fines and other penal sums for each quarter ending respectively the 31st of March, 30th June, 30th September, and 31st December, in each year, are to be rendered during the month immediately following the close of the quarter. The Crown fines must be lodged before sending in the returns.

2. The return Form B, containing list of warrants issued, must be furnished to the Sub-Inspector as soon as possible after the termination of each quarter. A Nil return should be sent when no warrants were issued. (a)

3. The Forms F are to be rendered in accordance with the Circular of the 30th November, 1866.

4. Vouchers must be furnished in every case where portions of fines, compensation, or costs (where such costs exceed the ordinary costs of Court) are paid to parties other than the Crown.

5. The authority must be furnished with the return where a fine is reduced or remitted by the Lord Lieutenant.

6. The Certificate of the Clerk of the Peace must be furnished with the return, where on appeal the fine is reversed or reduced at Quarter Sessions.

Clerks of Petty Sessions are informed that unless these particulars are attended to their returns cannot be received, and will be treated as unrendered.

RICHARD R. WINGFIELD.

Registrar of Petty Sessions Clerks Office,
Dublin Castle, 8th October, 1870.

(a) At present this form B need only contain list of warrants where amounts have not been paid to the Clerk.

In several instances I have discovered that Clerks of Petty Sessions, either disregarding the directions contained in said Circular, or acting through carelessness, have paid away large sums on a general or verbal order of the Justices, and I was therefore obliged to make them repay the amounts so illegally paid. It will be my duty to act similarly in every case where a like conduct is pursued.

It is to be understood that the said Circular of the 26th November, 1868, does *not* apply to fines where the Act under which they are imposed is mandatory as to their application, but only to such fines as the Act under which they are imposed leaves it discretionary with the Justices whether or not they shall order a portion thereof to the complainant.

III. Instructions have been issued to the Constabulary to pay over to Clerks of Petty Sessions in all cases the produce of the sale of straying animals (after deducting the expenses necessarily incurred in connexion with the impounding and sale of such animals); and I have to call your attention to the Act 14 & 15 Vic., cap. 92, sec. 19, clause 8, as to the manner in which such moneys should be applied. In that section it is directed that such moneys "shall be paid over to the Treasurer of the county to the credit of the county, in any case when the Grand Jury of such county shall have presented any sum for the erection of any pound therein; but when no sum shall have been so presented, such surplus proceeds shall be applied in like manner as any penal sums payable to the Crown, or, with the consent of the Chief or Under Secretary to the Lord Lieutenant, may be applied by the said Justices in the erection or repair of any pounds within the Petty Sessions District."

When any such moneys shall be paid to any Clerk of Petty Sessions, he will enter a record thereof in the Order Book, and ascertain whether the amount is payable to the County Treasurer in accordance with the above section of the Act of Parliament, and if so he will pay it to that officer, taking his receipt therefor; but if the money be not so payable, he will lodge it in bank with the fines for the Crown. In all cases, whether payable to the County Treasurer or to the Crown, the amount is to be included and accounted for by the Clerk in his returns to this office.

RICHARD R. WINGFIELD.

Registrar of Petty Sessions Clerks Office,
Dublin Castle, 12th January, 1871.

SPECIMEN SUMMONS FORMS. (a)

The form of words in each of the following cases may be used in describing the offence in the summons :—

Adulteration of Food, &c.—38 & 39 Vic., c. 63 ; 42 & 43 Vic., c. 30.—That you, the said defendant, did sell to the said complainant, to his prejudice as purchaser thereof, an article of food, to wit :—*Four ounces of coffee which was adulterated with chicory,* and which was not of the nature, substance, and quality of the article demanded by the said complainant as such purchaser, contrary to the statute in such case made and provided, or, *three pints of new milk, the butter (or the total solid matter) in the sample being less than that found*

(a) *Forms of Summons.*—The above are given in the hope that they may be useful to such officers of Courts as have not much experience. It is not to be supposed that the form of words given may not be departed from, or that they may not be abridged. The offence, however, should be clearly and unequivocally stated. See notes on "Summons," Summary Index. It is also proper to add in every case that the defendant did "unlawfully," or "contrary to law," do the act complained of.

in normal milk or milk, of average quality. If the fact set forth in analysis be so, add—*and compared with milk of average quality would have about* —— *per cent. of its cream removed* (*b*), and which was not of the nature, substance, and quality, &c.

Assaults (*Common*).—Did unlawfully assault and beat the said complainant.

Assaults (*Indictable*).—Unlawfully, assault, beat, and inflict grievous bodily harm on the said——(and if by a particular wound, such as stabbing, it may be added).

Assaults (*on Constables*).—Unlawfully assault, resist, and obstruct the said complainant while acting in execution of his duty as a constable. (Where it is merely obstructing by words, or such behaviour, assault may be omitted.)

Animals, cruelty to.—Unlawfully and cruelly beat and ill-use —— (name the animal); or overdrive —— ; or wantonly and cruelly torture ——; or overload —— ; or drive and use, while sore and unable and unfit to work ——; or urge and set on dogs or cocks to fight, &c.

Apprentice (*Misconduct*).—Unlawfully, and contrary to your indentures, misdemean and misconduct yourself in the service of your master, the said complainant.

Apprentice (*Absenting*).—Unlawfully, and contrary, &c., and without leave of your master elope and absent yourself ; or run away from the service of, &c.; or wilfully refuse to learn or work.

Employer and Workman, Apprentice and Master.—After setting forth in the summons the act complained of, add "and such being a dispute coming within the provisions of the 'Employer and Workmen Act, 1875.'"

Drunk.—You, the said defendant, were found drunk on the public road (or street) contrary to law (and where there are previous convictions add, and it being a second offence, or a third offence). Third offence will answer for more than three within 12 months.

Embezzlement.—You, the said defendant, being the clerk or servant of the said complainant, did unlawfully embezzle a sum of £——, received by you from C. D. for the said complainant (or where there are several sums from several persons or customers, may state—several sums of money, amounting to the sum of £——, received by you from the several persons, and of the amounts hereon indorsed, &c. These particulars may be given on back of summons).

Disputes in Markets, &c.—Did unlawfully dispute with and refuse to pay complainant the sum of £—— (under £5), the price of a sheep, pig, &c., sold by him to you in the public market (or fair).

False Pretences.—Did unlawfully and by fraud and false pretences obtain (or attempt to obtain) from complainant the sum of (or whatever it may be).

Landlord and Tenant—Small Tenements in Towns, &c., 14 & 15 *Vic.*, *c.* 92, *s.* 15.—You, the said defendant, continue unlawfully to overhold, and neglect and refuse to deliver up to complainant the possession of (house, room in a house, &c., as case may be), situate in (describe) your weekly (or otherwise) tenancy at 2*s.* a-week, being duly determined by notice to quit (and after the words in summons to answer the said complaint add, "and to show cause why possession of the said premises shall not be delivered up").

Caretakers—You, the said defendant, unlawfully refused and omitted, and still refuse and omit, to quit or to give up to complainant, on demand made, possession of the (describe premises) into the possession of which premises you had been put by permission of the said complainant, the owner thereof, as a caretaker (or *servant*, or *herdsman*), and see 221, 222, Summary Index.

Larceny.—You, the said defendant, did unlawfully steal, take, and carry away from the person (or *possession*) of the said complainant (name property).

Malicious Injury.—You, the said defendant, did unlawfully, wilfully, and maliciously damage, injure, and destroy (name property) the property of the said complainant, to the value of £——, or thereabouts (or under the value of £5).

Breach of Peace, &c.—Unlawfully abuse, and threaten to take the life of complainant (or threaten to do grievous bodily harm to complainant, or threaten to damage, or burn, or injure the property of complainant), for which he seeks to have you bound to keep the peace, &c.

(In this case, where violent threats were used and immediate danger feared. and such is set forth on the information, a warrant may issue.)

Unjust Weights.—Had in your shop (or store or place of sale) several light and unjust weights. If the weights be too heavy, say "unjust weights;" if they be measures, and they are too large or too small, say "unjust measures," contrary to law.

Deserting Wife, &c., under Poor Law Act.—Did unlawfully desert and wilfully neglect to maintain your wife (or your child), whereby she became destitute and was relieved, and continues to be relieved, in the Belfast Union Workhouse.

Licensing Acts.—State time and place.

Illicit Sales.—You, the said defendant, did unlawfully sell and expose for sale by retail intoxicating liquor, that is to say (*beer, spirits, &c., as the case may be*), you not being licensed to sell same by retail.

Selling on Unlicensed Premises.—You, the said defendant, did there unlawfully sell and expose for sale intoxicating liquor, that is to say (*beer, spirits, &c., as the case may be*), same being a place where you are not authorized by your licence to sell the same.

Drinking on Premises contrary to Licence.—That A. B., who then and there purchased intoxicating liquor, that is to say (*beer, &c., as the case may be*), of and from you, the said defendant, being a person not licensed to sell intoxicating liquor to be drunk on the premises, he did drink such liquor on the premises where sold (*or on the highway adjoining or near the premises where sold*), and he so drank same with your privity and consent, and contrary to law.

Permitting Drunkenness, &c.—You, the said defendant, being a person licensed to sell intoxicating liquor, permitted drunkenness to take place on your licensed premises, contrary to law.

Or permitted *violent conduct* to take place, &c.

Or permitted *quarrelsome conduct*, &c.

Or permitted *riotous conduct* to take place, &c.

Gaming.—You, the said defendant, being a person licensed to sell intoxicating liquor, suffered gaming (*at cards, dice, &c., as the case may be*), to be carried on on your licensed premises, contrary to law. *

Unlawful Game.—*Or,* suffered an unlawful game, that is (*roulette, &c.*) to be carried on on your licensed premises, contrary to law.

Closing hours, selling.—You, the said defendant, being a person licensed to sell intoxicating liquor, about (*state about time*) on said (*morning or night*) being (*Sunday night, or as may be*), did sell, and expose for sale on your licensed premises, to persons not being *bona fide travellers*, or lodgers therein, intoxicating liquor, contrary to law.

Or did open your licensed premises for the sale of intoxicating liquor, contrary to law.

Or did keep open your licensed premises for the sale of intoxicating liquor, contrary to law.

Or did allow intoxicating liquor to be consumed on your licensed premises, contrary to law. (*a*)

Persons found on premises during closing hours.—(*After stating the hour of morning or night, as in preceding.*) You, the said defendant, were found on the licensed premises of A. B., where intoxicating liquor is licensed to be sold, and it being during a period during which said premises are required by law to be closed, your presence therein being in contravention of the provisions of the Licensing Act, 1872, with respect to the closing of such premises, you, the said defendant, not being an inmate, servant, or lodger on such premises, or a *bona fide* traveller.

Refusing to admit Constable.—You, the said defendant, did unlawfully (*refuse or fail, or refuse and fail, as the case may be*), to admit complainant to enter your licensed premises, he being a constable, and at the time acting in the execution of his duty, and he having demanded so to enter in pursuance of sec. 23 of the Licensing Act (Ireland), 1874, for the purpose of preventing and detecting the violation of the provisions of the Licensing Acts (Ireland), 1872-1874, which it was his duty to enforce.

(*a*) As to what will be evidence of sale or of consumption, see Licensing Act of 1872, 35 & 36 Vic., c. 94, s. 62.

* The Licensing Act applies to games of *skill* as well as games of *chance* if there be any wager.

SUGGESTIONS FROM THE LAW OFFICERS.

For the Assistance of Clerks of Petty Sessions and others preparing Informations in Criminal Cases returned for Trial.

Each information should contain a full and simple statement of all the material facts to which the witness can depose. It should be taken as nearly as possible in the witness's own words, and in the first person, thus, after the introductory part—"I saw," "I went," &c., instead of "this deponent saw," "this deponent went," &c. The use of technical terms and descriptions, such as "informant," "deponent," "complainant," "defendant," &c., after the merely introductory portion, should be avoided, as likely to mislead both the witness and the subsequent reader. It is not necessary to introduce such words as "feloniously," "maliciously," and the like, it being the province of the Crown Prosecutor, at another stage, to ascertain and determine the class of offence, and the terms to be adopted in the subsequent pleadings. The information should contain a simple but full statement and history of all the facts, in the language used by the witness.

Where several persons are charged with an offence, the several acts done by each should be distinctly set forth, and in what manner each individual took part in it.

Where there are several witnesses, the file of informations should be arranged and pinned together in such manner as may best serve to give a connected account of the transaction, and form a regular chain of evidence.

The examinations, statements, bail-bonds, and recognizances of the accused should be attached at the back of the informations, in the order in which these parties are severally named in the evidence.

A memorandum should invariably be annexed to, or indorsed on, each file of informations, stating whether the accused is in "custody," "bailed," or "at large"—not having been made amenable.

The Christian names and surnames of the informant, and of all persons named in his information, should be stated in full, without any abbreviations or use of initial letters, and also their several places of abode.

Where a woman swears an information, it should be particularly stated whether she is single, married, or a widow.. If married, her husband's name should be also mentioned.

The time and place of the offence should be stated in every information. (a)

☞ When witnesses are produced on the part of the accused, their depositions should, in all cases, be taken and returned. (b)

(a) But where an illiterate witness may not know the dates of the month, so as to give the date of the offence in that way, it should not be put into his mouth, as on the trial afterwards it will be evident that he knows nothing about that date and cannot give it again. The proper way will be to take it down as he best can give it, as—"this day week past;" "last Saturday was a fortnight." The Magistrate should give the date of offence in the caption, and of course the jurat gives the date on which the deposition is made.—H. H.

(b) *Depositions for Defence.*—The 30 & 31 Vic., c. 35 (England), makes provision for taking evidence for defence, and of witnesses dangerously ill, who can give evidence for prosecution or defence. Act is not applicable to Ireland.

The following is a specification of the principal facts material to be particularly stated in the cases of more frequent occurrence, viz. :—

ASSAULTS.

The weapon or weapons used, and the nature and extent of the injuries inflicted. Whether the prosecutor was rendered insensible ; recovery of consciousness; attendance of doctor ; confinement to bed ; endangering of life ; motive of assault, if it appear or has been ascertained.

LARCENY.

An accurate and distinct description of each stolen article by name, not in general words, and the name and description of the owner of each article. In case of animals, the sex and character of the animal—for instance, whether an entire horse, a mare, a gelding, a colt, or a filly ; in horned cattle, whether a bull, cow, ox, heifer, or calf ; in sheep, whether ram, ewe, sheep, or lamb. If the sex is not known, it should be so stated.

STEALING FROM THE PERSON.

The mode in which the goods were taken ; and if any force used, describe it fully, so that it may appear whether the offence was stealing from the person, or robbery with violence. State whether the goods belonged to him from whose person they were taken, or to another.

STEALING IN A DWELLING-HOUSE.

The value of the goods stolen, if it amounts to £5, and whether any person in the house was put in fear.

BURGLARY AND HOUSEBREAKING.

The hour of the day or night at which the offence was committed ; how the entry was effected ; to whom the house belonged ; any goods taken. If in an out-house, describe it, and state whether it communicated with the dwelling-house by any enclosed or covered passage leading from one to the other.

RESCUES.

The authority under which the goods were seized. If as a distress for rent, to whom due, and out of what holding ; if in the execution of a Civil Bill Decree, the names of the parties to the suit, date and place of Sessions, name of Chairman and Sheriff, and date of Sheriff's Warrant at foot. In all cases accurately describe the articles rescued ; state whose property they were, and the nature of the violence used. Retain, and attach to the informations, the Decree Warrant under which the seizure was made.

False Pretences.

Describe the whole conversation and conduct of the prisoner, and the frauds practised, as accurately as possible. If the money or goods have been obtained under a written order, it should be impounded, and affixed to the information, after being marked by the persons whose information refer to it.

Taking Forcible Possession.

Describe the land, messuage, or tenement entered; the amount of force used by the accused to expel those in previous possession; and all threats, words, or acts of his, calculated to inspire them with fear, or apprehension of personal danger.

Arms.

The name of the townland and proclaimed barony in which found, and whether carried out of doors by the accused, or found in his dwelling-house, or out-house.

In other Cases. (a)

If the offence be created or made punishable by statute; a careful perusal of the section relating to it, before taking the information, will suggest to the clerk the facts and particulars necessary to be introduced or stated, to enable a correct and proper bill of indictment to be framed.

☞ The attention of Clerks of Petty Sessions is particularly called to the 19th section of the Petty Sessions Act (14 & 15 Vic., cap. 93), which directs that every information, examination, statement and recognizance shall be transmitted to the Clerk of the Crown or Peace, according as same may relate to Assizes or Quarter Sessions, within seven days from the holding of the Petty Sessions, when the party shall have been committed, or shall be amenable; and also to the fifth section of the same Act, imposing a penalty of £20 for any neglect or default in transmitting the documents within the time stated. Informations taken within the seven days next preceding an Assizes or Sessions should be returned at once, without any delay whatever.

In cases returned for trial at Quarter Sessions copies of the informations should be sent to the Sessional Crown Prosecutor, pursuant to the Government Circular, immediately upon the evidence being completed at Petty Sessions, whether the originals have been then returned to the Clerk of the Peace or not.

(a) See also notes on section 14 of Petty Sessions Act. And see also Circular as to the taking of depositions, ante.

WHITEBOY ACTS.

MEMORANDUM AS TO POWERS AND DUTIES OF MAGISTRATES UNDER THE ACTS 15 & 16 Geo. iii., chap. 21, and 1 & 2 Wm. iv., chap. 44.

1. All persons armed with fire-arms, or any other weapons, or appearing in any disguise, or wearing any unusual uniform or badge, or assuming any name or denomination not usually assumed by ordinary persons in their lawful occasions, who shall assemble, or who shall appear, alone or with others, by day or night, to the terror of Her Majesty's subjects, are guilty of a high misdemeanour, subjecting them to imprisonment and other penalties.

2. All persons who assemble, and unlawfully compel, or by force or threats attempt to compel anyone to quit his dwelling-house, farm, service, or employment, or maliciously assault any dwelling-house, or break into any house or out-house, or cause any door to be opened by threats, or shall carry off any horse or mule, or any gun or other weapon, money, or other property, or shall by threats cause same to be given up to them, or shall maliciously dig up, turn up, cut down, level, demolish, or injure the lands or crops growing or severed, or the walls, paling, hedges, or other fences, or the cattle, goods, or chattels of any other person or persons, are guilty of a misdemeanour subjecting them to penal servitude, imprisonment, and other penalties.

3. Any persons who shall write, post, publish, or give any notice, letter, or message, exciting, or tending to excite, any riot or unlawful assembly, or combination, or threatening any violence to person or property, or demanding arms, ammunition, money, or other property, or requiring any person to quit any employment, is liable to the same punishment as last above mentioned.

4. All persons aiding and abetting others in the commission of any of the above offences are equally guilty, and liable to the punishments above mentioned.

5. All persons who by drum, horn, fire, shouting, or any signal, excite, or promote, or attempt to excite or promote such unlawful meetings, are also guilty of a high misdemeanour, punishable by fine and imprisonment.

6. Any persons who, by force or threats, unlawfully impose on or tender to any person any oath or solemn engagement are guilty of a grave misdemeanour, punishable by fine and imprisonment.

7. All Magistrates and Constables are empowered and bound to apprehend, disperse, and oppose all persons so engaged, and may call upon and command all persons who are not disabled by age or infirmity to assist them in so doing.

8. Any two Magistrates having reasonable cause to suspect any person to be guilty of any such unlawful rising, assembling, or appearing as above mentioned, or of having been at any such unlawful assembly, or of intending so to be, may and are required to summon before them any such person, and bind him over in his own recognizance to appear at the next Assizes, and to be of good behaviour in the meantime; and in case of refusal such Magistrates have power to commit such person to gaol.

9. Every Magistrate has authority to summon any person within his jurisdiction whom he thinks capable of giving material evidence as to any of the offences specified in the 1st, 5th, and 6th paragraphs, and examine him or her on oath, and bind such person in recognizance to appear and give evidence, and on refusal to answer or to enter into recognizance, to commit such person to gaol.

By His Excellency's Command,

W. E. FORSTER.

·lin Castle, 1st December, 1880.

Convicts Holding Licences.

Dublin Castle, 25th March, 1875.

Gentlemen,—The attention of the Lord Lieutenant has been drawn to cases in which convicts holding licences under the Penal Servitude Acts have been summarily convicted of minor offences, and in which the Magistrates, before whom such summary conviction took place, have not forwarded to this office the certificate required by law to be forwarded in such cases, thereby frustrating the intention of the statute with respect to the revocation of licences upon the occurrence of a further conviction.

His Grace desires me, therefore, to call the special attention of the Magistrates to the provisions of section 8 of the Act 27 & 28 Vic., cap. 47, which direct that " where any holder of a licence granted in the form set forth in the Schedule (A) is convicted of an offence punishable summarily under this or any other Act, the Justices, Sheriff, Sheriff Substitute, or other Magistrate convicting the prisoner, shall without delay forward by post a certificate in the Form given in Schedule (B) to this Act annexed, &c., to the Lord Lieutenant or other Chief Governor of Ireland."

Schedule B.

Form of Certificate of Conviction of Holder of Licence.

I do hereby certify that A. B., the holder of a licence under the Penal Servitude Acts, was, on the —— day of ——, in the year ——, duly convicted by —— of the offence of ——, and sentenced to ——.

C. D., Clerk to the said Justices.

I am to add that when the licence holder is convicted under a different name from that appearing in the licence, the fact should appear in the certificate of conviction. It should be stated that A. B., the holder, &c., was, on the —— day of ——, in the year ——, duly convicted, &c., under the name of C. D.

I have the honour to be, Gentlemen,

Your obedient Servant,

T. H. Burke.

The Magistrates at Petty Sessions.

Circular to Magistrates at Petty Sessions as to Orders, Depositions, Recognizances, &c.

Dublin Castle, 6th February, 1878.

Gentlemen,—1. The attention of the Lord Lieutenant has been directed to the irregular manner in which, in some Petty Sessions Courts in Ireland, the Orders of the Justices are entered in the Order Book.

It appears that in many cases the Orders are not signed by a Magistrate, in others they are only signed with initials, and in some instances alterations are made in Orders after they have been regularly signed.

His Grace is advised that each Order should be signed in the Order Book by a Justice signing his name opposite to it or immediately after it; that a signature by initials is not sufficient, that all the terms of the Order should be entered in the Book before the signature is attached, and that afterwards no alteration or amendment of any kind can be made. As Orders made without a proper regard to these legal requirements are irregular, it is the interest and duty of not only the Chairman but also of every Justice present to see that they are duly complied with. It is also the duty of a Magistrate, signing an Order or any other document liable to a stamp by the 14th section of the 21 & 22 Vic., cap. 101, and Schedule (C) annexed thereto, to see that such Order or document is duly stamped before he attaches his signature.

II. It has also been represented to His Grace that some Magistrates, when taking informations in cases of indictable offences, think that it is not necessary to receive more evidence than is sufficient to justify them in sending the defendant for trial, although there may be other witnesses forthcoming and ready for examination.

His Grace is advised that in this class of cases it conduces to the ends of justice for Magistrates to take the informations of all witnesses who can give material evidence, and to make the depositions as complete as circumstances will admit before returning the accused for trial.

It is, moreover, not enough that the depositions should be read over to the witness in the presence of the accused; but it is necessary that the whole of the evidence should be given in his hearing, and that he should have a full opportunity of putting questions to the deponent.

III. His Grace regrets to learn that, notwithstanding the Circular addressed to the Magistrates on the subject on 19th January, 1871, the want of accurate compliance with the provisions of the 14 & 15 Vic., cap. 93, sec. 34, and Schedule (Form C), which in appeals has been altered by 40 & 41 Vic., cap. 56, sec. 72, has not unfrequently led to a miscarriage of justice. I am therefore directed by His Grace to transmit the accompanying Form, which has been prepared, with ample marginal notes for directions and guidance, and he requests that you will be so good as to give special instructions to your Clerk in filling up Recognizances carefully to observe and comply with the provisions of the 34th section and Form C in the Schedule of the Petty Sessions Act (attending to the alteration above referred to in appeals), and that you will make him sign his name at × in the margin opposite this paragraph as his acknowledgment of having received the aforesaid instructions.*

I have the honour to be, Gentlemen,

Your obedient Servant,

T. H. BURKE.

Note.--The above Circular is substituted for that of the 18th ult., which is hereby cancelled.

The attention of Petty Sessions Clerks is directed to the alteration in the Form of Recognizance.

* The Form given in this Appendix complies with above.—H. H.

(No. 3.)

CIRCULAR TO MAGISTRATES AT PETTY SESSIONS AS TO HEARING CASES OUT OF PETTY SESSIONS, REMANDS, &c.

To be substituted for Circular No. 3, issued on the 2nd May, 1879.

11,188. *Dublin Castle, 24th July, 1879.*

GENTLEMEN,—I am directed by the Lords Justices to state that the attention of their Excellencies has been called to the fact that warrants of committal have not unfrequently been issued by a single Justice directing persons to be detained in custody to take their trial at the next Petty Sessions, and that warrants of further remand have not unfrequently being signed by Justices without seeing the party in custody or inquiring into the necessity for such further remand. For the purpose of preventing the recurrence of such in the future, I am directed to forward for your guidance the following instructions :—

1. Where a person charged with an indictable offence is brought up under a warrant before a Justice sitting out of Petty Sessions, the Justice should read the information on which the warrant was issued, and take such further depositions as may be offered. If the depositions have been completed, and a sufficient case has been thereby made out, the Justice should commit the party charged to take his trial at the next Quarter Sessions or Assizes. If the depositions have not been completed and a case has been made justifying a remand, the Justice should remand for a period not exceeding eight days.

2. A Justice should not make any order of remand unless the party charged be produced before him, and a sufficient case made to justify in his opinion such order of remand.

3. When any person is brought under a warrant before any Justice sitting out of Petty Sessions, charged with an offence which in the opinion of such Justice should be disposed of summarily, the Justice may, if he can procure the assistance of another Justice, and if the accused is unable to find bail for his appearance, hear the case with such second Justice out of Petty Sessions ; or he may direct the person so charged to be discharged from custody on his giving sufficient bail to appear at the next Petty Sessions. Cases not coming within the exceptions mentioned in the 8th section of the Petty Sessions Act should not be heard out of Petty Sessions unless where the party charged has been required by the Justice to give bail, and is unable to do so. (a)

4. Where any person brought under warrant, before any summons has been issued, before a Justice sitting out of Petty Sessions, charged with an

(a) But see footnote of section 20, sub-section (4), Petty Sessions Act, where adjournments take place in *Petty Sessions.* The above important Circular is too often overlooked.

3 F 2

offence which, in his opinion may be disposed of summarily should be unable to give bail, and if the case be not disposed of by two Justices sitting out of Petty Sessions, or does not come within the Criminal Justice Act, 18 & 19 Vic., cap. 126, sec. 5, the Justice should discharge him, and inform the prosecutor that a summons may be issued requiring the party charged to attend at Petty Sessions : but in no case should such person be committed to prison to take his trial for such offence at the next or any other Petty Sessions, save where the provisions of the statute 18 & 19 Vic., cap. 126, sec. 5, apply.　In cases coming within this section the Justices may proceed as the statute points out.

Their Excellencies desire me further to inform you that the Circular of the 29th May which refers to the same subject is hereby cancelled, and their Excellencies request that this Circular may be substituted for it.

I am, Gentlemen, your obedient Servant,

T. H. BURKE.

PEACE PRESERVATION (IRELAND) ACT, 1881,

44 Vic., c. 5. (a)

An Act to Amend the law relating to the Carrying and Possession of Arms, and for the Preservation of the Public Peace in Ireland.

[21st March, 1881.]

BE it enacted by the Queen's most Excellent Majesty, by and with the advice and consent of the Lords Spiritual and Temporal, and Commons, in this present Parliament assembled, and by the authority of the same, as follows :

Prohibition on having or carrying arms in proclaimed district, and search. 1. In a proclaimed district a person shall not carry or have any arms or ammunition save as authorized by the conditions set forth in the proclamation hereinafter mentioned.

Any person carrying or having, or reasonably suspected of carrying or having, any arms or ammunition in contravention of this Act may be arrested without warrant by any constable or peace officer, and, as soon as reasonably can be, conveyed before some Justice of the Peace in order to his being dealt with according to law.

The Lord Lieutenant may by warrant direct any person named in such warrant to search in houses, buildings, and places situate in a proclaimed district and specified in the warrant, for any arms or ammunition suspected to be therein in contravention of this Act.

The person named in such warrant, with such constables and other persons as he calls to his assistance, may, within ten days next after

---

(a) The " Peace Preservation (I.) Continuance Act, 1886," 49 Vic., c. 44, amends the above Act as to returns, &c , and provides that elsewhere than in Dublin Metropolis the Court of Summary Jurisdiction, in section 5, shall be constituted of two or more Resident Magistrates sitting alone in Petty Sessions.

the date of the warrant, at any time between sunrise and sunset, enter into any house, building, or place specified in such warrant, and there execute the warrant; and in case admittance shall be refused to the persons aforesaid, or shall not be obtained by them within a reasonable time after it shall have been first demanded, they may enter by force in order to execute such warrant. The person named in such warrant shall, before executing the same, if so desired, produce the said warrant. Any arms or ammunition carried, had, or found under circumstances which contravene this Act shall be forfeited to Her Majesty.

Any arms or ammunition in the possession of persons not entitled to have the same which shall, within a period to be fixed by the pro-clamation hereinafter mentioned, be given up voluntarily or taken under such circumstances as shall prove to the satisfaction of the Lord Lieutenant that they have not been wilfully kept back, shall be deemed to be in the possession of Her Majesty, and provision shall be made in such proclamation for the deposit, registration, valuation, and care of the same; and such arms and ammunition shall be re-turned to the owners thereof whenever the proclamation relating thereto shall cease to be in force: Provided that at any time the Lord Lieutenant may, instead of keeping and returning the arms and ammunition aforesaid, if he think fit, pay to the owners of the same the value thereof as ascertained in the manner provided by the procla-mation, or the owners thereof may demand payment of such value, and such payments may be made out of moneys to be provided by Parliament.

2. The Lord Lieutenant, by and with the advice of the Privy Council in Ireland, may from time to time by proclamation declare this Act to be in force within any specified part of Ireland, and this Act shall thereupon after the date specified in the proclamation be in force within such specified part, and any such specified part of Ireland is in this Act referred to as a "proclaimed district;" and any such proclamation may set forth the conditions and regulations under which the carrying or having of arms or ammunition is authorized, and make provision for the appointment of persons to give effect to the same and the manner of the promulgation thereof. *Power as to proclamation in respect to arms and ammunition.*

3. The Lord Lieutenant, by and with the advice of the Privy Council in Ireland, may from time to time make orders for prohibiting or regulating in Ireland the sale or importation of arms and ammunition, and for the appointment of persons for the purpose of giving effect to such orders, and providing for the manner of the promulgation thereof. *Power as to prohibiting or regulating sale or im- portation of arms and am- munition.*

If any person sell or import, or attempt to sell or import, any arms or ammunition in contravention of any such order, such arms and ammunition shall be liable to be forfeited to Her Majesty, and the person so acting wilfully shall be guilty of an offence against this Act.

4. (1.) The Lord Lieutenant, by and with the advice of the Privy Council, may, by a further proclamation or order, from time to time, alter or revoke any proclamation or order made by him under this Act. *Supple- mental pro- visions.*

Peace
Preserva-
tion (Ire-
land) Act,
1881.
A copy of every proclamation and order under this Act shall be laid before each House of Parliament within fourteen days after the making thereof, if Parliament is then sitting, and, if not, then within fourteen days after the next meeting of Parliament.

(2.) The Lord Lieutenant may from time to time by order prescribe forms for the purposes of this Act, and any form so prescribed shall be valid in law.

(3.) Any warrant or order of the Lord Lieutenant under this Act may be signified under his hand or under the hand of the Chief Secretary to the Lord Lieutenant.

(4.) Any person who may be appointed under any proclamation issued pursuant to this Act to grant licences to have or carry arms, in any district, shall be bound to grant to any occupier of one or more agricultural holdings a licence to have arms, or to have and carry arms upon any specified lands, or a licence to have and carry arms generally, who shall produce to him a certificate signed by two Justices of the Peace for the county, residing within the same Petty Sessions district as the person producing such certificate, that he is, to their own personal knowledge, a fit and proper person to have such licence respectively.

(5.) Every proclamation and order under this Act, and a notice of the promulgation thereof in the manner provided, shall be published in the *Dublin Gazette*, and the production of a printed copy of the *Dublin Gazette* purporting to be printed and published by the Queen's authority, and containing the publication of any proclamation, order, or notice under this Act, shall be conclusive evidence of the contents of such proclamation, order, or notice, and of the date thereof, and that the district specified in such proclamation is a proclaimed district within the meaning of this Act, and that the said proclamation or order has been duly promulgated.

Penalties. 5. Any person acting in contravention of this Act shall be liable if convicted before a Court of summary jurisdiction to be imprisoned for a term not exceeding three months, or, at the discretion of the Court, to a penalty not exceeding twenty pounds; but if upon the hearing of the charge, the Court shall be of opinion that there are circumstances in the case which render it inexpedient to inflict any punishment, it shall have power to dismiss the person charged without proceeding to a conviction. For the purposes of this Act, the Court of summary jurisdiction shall, in the Police district of Dublin metropolis, be constituted of a divisional Justice acting for the said district, and elsewhere in Ireland shall be constituted of two or more Resident Magistrates sitting alone in Petty Sessions.*

Definitions. 6. In this Act the expression "Lord Lieutenant" means the Lord Lieutenant of Ireland, or other Chief Governor or Governors of Ireland for the time being.

The expression "arms" includes any cannon, gun, revolver, pistol,

---

* The Act of 1886, 49 Vic. c. 24, amends above section 5, and provides that the Court be constituted of *two or more R. M.'s* sitting alone in Petty Sessions.

and any description of fire-arms, also any sword, cutlass, pike, and bayonet, also any part of any arms as so defined.

The expression "ammunition" includes bullets, gunpowder, nitro-glycerine, dynamite, gun-cotton, and every other explosive substance whether fitted for use with any arms or otherwise.

7. This Act may be cited as the Peace Preservation (Ireland) Act, 1881.

8. This Act shall continue in force until the first day of June, one thousand eight hundred and eighty-six.

☞ This Act of 1881, and the continuance Act of 1886, are by the "Criminal Law and Procedure (I.) Act, 1887" (50 & 51 Vic. c. 20) continued to 1892, and the end of the then next Session of Parliament.

NEWSPAPER LIBEL AND REGISTRATION ACT, 1881,

44 & 45 Vic., c. 60.

"An Act to Amend the Law of Newspaper Libel and to Provide for the Registration of Newspaper Proprietors."

[*27th August*, 1881.]

Whereas it is expedient to amend the law affecting civil actions and criminal prosecutions for newspaper libel :

And whereas it is also expedient to provide for the registration of newspaper proprietors :

Be it enacted by the Queen's most Excellent Majesty, by and with the advice and consent of the Lords Spiritual and Temporal, and Commons, in this present Parliament assembled, and by the authority of the same as follows :

1. In the construction of this Act, unless there is anything in the subject or context repugnant thereto, the several words and phrases hereinafter mentioned shall have and include the meaning following : (that is to say).

The word "registrar," shall mean in England the registrar for the time being of joint stock companies, or such person as the Board of Trade may for the time being authorize in that behalf, and in Ireland the assistant registrar for the time being of joint stock companies for Ireland, or such person as the Board of Trade may for the time being authorize in that behalf.

The phrase "registry office" shall mean the principal office for the time being of the registrar in England or Ireland, as the case may be, or such other office as the Board of Trade may from time to time appoint.

NEWSPAPER LIBEL AND REGISTRATION ACT.

The word "newspaper" shall mean any paper containing public news, intelligence, or occurrences, or any remarks or observations therein printed for sale and published in England or Ireland periodically, or in parts or numbers at intervals not exceeding twenty-six days between the publication of any two such papers, parts, or numbers.

Also any paper printed in order to be dispersed, and made public weekly or oftener, or at intervals not exceeding twenty-six days, containing only or principally advertisements.

The word "occupation" when applied to any person shall mean his trade or following, and, if none, then his rank or usual title, as esquire, gentleman.

The phrase "place of residence" shall include the street, square, or place where the person to whom it refers shall reside, and the number (if any) or other designation of the house in which he shall so reside.

The word "proprietor" shall mean and include as well the sole proprietor of any newspaper, as also in the case of a divided proprietorship the persons who, as partners or otherwise, represent and are responsible for any share or interest in the newspaper as between themselves and the persons in like manner representing or responsible for the other shares or interests therein, and no other person.

Inquiry by Court of summary jurisdiction as to libel being for public benefit or being true.

4. A Court of summary jurisdiction, upon the hearing of a charge against a proprietor, publisher, or editor, or any person responsible for the publication of a newspaper, for a libel published therein, may receive evidence as to the publication being for the public benefit, and as to the matters charged in the libel being true, and as to the report being fair and accurate, and published without malice, and as to any matter which under this or any other Act, or otherwise, might be given in evidence by way of defence by the person charged on his trial or indictment, and the Court, if of opinion after hearing such evidence that there is a strong or probable presumption that the jury on the trial would acquit the person charged, may dismiss the case.

Provision as to summary conviction for libel.

5. If a Court of summary jurisdiction upon the hearing of a charge against a proprietor, publisher, editor, or any person responsible for the publication of a newspaper for a libel published therein is of opinion that though the person charged is shown to have been guilty the libel was of a trivial character, and that the offence may be adequately punished by virtue of the powers of this section, the Court shall cause the charge to be reduced into writing and read to the person charged, and then address a question to him to the following effect : " Do you desire to be tried by a jury or do you consent to the

---

Sections 2 and 3 have been repealed by 51 & 52 Vic., c. 64

*Sec. 4 —Published without malice, &c.—*Where a man publishes a writing which upon the face of it is libellous, the law presumes that he does so with the malicious intention which constitutes the offence, and it will be for the accused to show the contrary.

case being dealt with summarily?" (a) and, if such person assents to the case being dealt with summarily, the Court may summarily convict him and adjudge him to pay a fine not exceeding fifty pounds.

Section twenty-seven of the Summary Jurisdiction Act, 1879, shall, so far as is consistent with the tenor thereof, apply to every such proceeding as if it were within enacted and extended to Ireland, and, as if the Summary Jurisdiction Acts were therein referred to instead of the Summary Jurisdiction Act, 1848. (b)

6. Every libel or alleged libel, and every offence under this Act, shall be deemed to be an offence within and subject to the provisions of the Act of the session of the twenty-second and twenty-third years of the reign of her present Majesty, chapter seventeen, intituled "An Act to Prevent Vexatious Indictments for Certain Misdemeanours."

7. Where, in the opinion of the Board of Trade, inconvenience would arise or be caused in any case from the registry of the names of all the proprietors of the newspaper (either owing to minority, coverture, absence from the United Kingdom, minute sub-division of shares, or other special circumstances), it shall be lawful for the Board of Trade to authorize the registration of such newspaper in the name or names of some one or more responsible "representative proprietors."

8. A register of the proprietors of newspapers as defined by this Act shall be established under the superintendence of the registrar.

9. It shall be the duty of the printers and publishers for the time being of every newspaper to make or cause to be made to the Registry

---

(a) "Do you consent to the case being dealt with summarily?" When this question is put, defendant must know that he is to be convicted: it is therefore to the punishment the Court may think fit to inflict that he consents.

(b) Summary Jurisdiction Act, 1879 (b). The following is the portion of the section above referred to which becomes applicable to the proceeding:—

27. Where an indictable offence is under, the circumstances in this Act mentioned authorized to be dealt with summarily,—

(1.) The procedure shall, until the Court assume the power to deal with such offence summarily, be the same in all respects as if the offence were to be dealt with throughout as an indictable offence, but when and so soon as the Court assume the power to deal with such offence summarily, the procedure shall be the same from and after that period as if the offence were an offence punishable on summary conviction and not on indictment, and the provisions of the Acts relating to offences punishable on summary conviction shall apply accordingly; and

(2.) The evidence of any witness taken before the Court assumed the said power need not be taken again, but every such witness shall, if the defendant so require it, be recalled for the purpose of cross-examination.

Sec. 6.—Offences under Act shall be subject to the provisions of 22 & 23 Vic., c. 17, "An Act to Prevent Vexatious Indictments for Certain Misdemeanours." Under this Act, when a Justice refuses to commit for trial or hold to bail the person charged with any of the indictable offences in the Act, and that the prosecutor desires to prefer a bill of indictment, the Justice is required to take the recognizance of the prosecutor to prosecute the charge, and transmit any depositions taken, in same manner as if the accused were committed for trial for the offence. (Libels are sent for trial to Assizes.)

NEWSPAPER
LIBEL AND
REGISTRA-
TION ACT.
　— — Office on or before the thirty-first of July, one thousand eight hundred and eighty-one, and thereafter annually in the month of July in every year, a return of the following particulars according to the Schedule A. hereunto annexed : that is to say,

(a) The title of a newspaper :

(b) The names of all the proprietors of such newspaper together with their respective occupations, places of business (if any), and places of residence.

Penalty for
omission to
make annual
returns. 10. If within the further period of one month after the time hereinbefore appointed for the making of any return as to any newspaper such return be not made, then each printer and publisher of such newspaper shall, on conviction thereof, be liable to a penalty not exceeding twenty-five pounds, and also to be directed by a summary order to make a return within a specified time.

Power to
party to
make return. 11. Any party to a transfer or transmission of or dealing with any share of or interest in any newspaper, whereby any person ceases to be a proprietor or any new proprietor is introduced, may at any time make or cause to be made to the Registry Office a return according to the Schedule B hereunto annexed, and containing the particulars therein set forth.

Penalty for
wilful misre-
presentation
in or omission
from return. 12. If any person shall knowingly and wilfully make or cause to be made any return by this Act required or permitted to be made in which shall be inserted or set forth the name of any person as a proprietor of a newspaper who shall not be a proprietor thereof, or in which there shall be any misrepresentation, or from which there shall be any omission in respect of any of the particulars by this Act required to be contained therein whereby such return shall be misleading, or if any proprietor of a newspaper shall knowingly and wilfully permit any such return to be made which shall be misleading as to any of the particulars with reference to his own name, occupation, place of business (if any), or place of residence, then and in every such case every such offender being convicted thereof shall be liable to a penalty not exceeding one hundred pounds.

Registrar to
enter returns
in register,
which shall
be accessible
to parties to
inspect. Sec. 13 directs registrar to enter returns in register.

Sec. 14 provides for the fees to be payable for registrar's services.

Fees payable
for registrar's
services. Sec. 15 provides for making copies of entries in, and extracts from, register to be evidence when certified, or under official seal, as in section.

Copies of
entries in
and extracts
from register
to be evi-
dence. 16 All penalties under this Act may be recovered before a Court of summary jurisdiction in manner provided by the Summary Jurisdiction Acts. (a)

Sec. 12.—Wilful misrepresentation —This penalty of £100 may also be recovered before the Summary Jurisdiction Court under section 16. The Attorney-General's fiat is not necessary to the prosecution.

(a) Recovery of Penalties — By section 17 penalties are to be recovered under Petty Sessions (Ireland) Act, and any Act amending the same.

Summary orders under this Act may be made by a Court of summary jurisdiction, and enforced in manner provided by section thirty-four of the Summary Jurisdiction Act, 1879 ; and for the purposes of this Act, that section shall be deemed to apply to Ireland in the same manner as if it were re-enacted in this Act. (a)

17. The expression "a Court of summary jurisdiction" has in England the meanings assigned to it by the Summary Jurisdiction Act, 1879 : and in Ireland means any Justice or Justices of the Peace, stipendiary or other magistrate or magistrates, having jurisdiction under the Summary Jurisdiction Acts.

The expression " Summary Jurisdiction Acts" has as regards England the meanings assigned to it by the Summary Jurisdiction Act, 1879 ; and as regards Ireland means within the police district of Dublin metropolis the Acts regulating the powers and duties of Justices of the Peace for such district, or of the police of that district, and elsewhere in Ireland the Petty Sessions (Ireland) Act, 1851, and any Act amending the same.

18. The provisions as to the registration of newspaper proprietors contained in this Act shall not apply to the case of any newspaper which belongs to a joint stock company duly incorporated under and subject to the provisions of the Companies Acts, 1862 to 1879.

[margin notes: NEWSPAPER LIBEL AND REGISTRATION ACT. — Definitions. — 14 & 15 Vic. c. 93. — Provisions as to registration of newspaper proprietors not to apply to newspaper belonging to a joint stock company. 25 & 26 Vic. c. 89, &c.]

(a) *Summary* orders are to be enforced by section 34 of the English Summary Jurisdiction Act, 1879; the following is the section :—

34. (1.) Where a power is given by any future Act to a Court of summary jurisdiction of requiring any person to do or abstain from doing any act or thing other than the payment of money, or of requiring any act or thing to be done or left undone other than the payment of money, and no mode is prescribed of enforcing such requisition, the Court may exercise such power by an order or orders, and may annex to any such order any conditions as to time or mode of action which the Court may think just, and may suspend or rescind any such order on such undertaking being given or condition being performed as the Court may think just, and generally may make such arrangement for carrying into effect such power as to the Court seems meet.

(2.) A person making default in complying with an order of a Court of summary jurisdiction in relation to any matter arising under any future Act other than the payment of money shall be punished in the prescribed manner, or if no punishment is prescribed may, in the discretion of the Court, be ordered to pay a sum (to be enforced as a civil debt, recoverable summarily under this Act) not exceeding one pound for every day during which he is in default, or to be imprisoned until he has remedied his default :

Provided that a person shall not, for non-compliance with the requisition of a Court of summary jurisdiction, whether made by one or more orders, to do or abstain from doing any act or thing, be liable under this section to imprisonment for a period or periods amounting in the aggregate to more than two months, or to the payment of any sums exceeding in the aggregate twenty pounds.

☞ This section would appear to refer to such orders as that mentioned at end of section 10, where the Court orders a return within a specified time : if the order be disobeyed, the Court may as above order a sum of money, and that is recoverable as a "civil debt." Section 35 gives the remedy for enforcing "civil debts," but this section is not extended to Ireland, so the Court has to look for the remedy in the Petty Sessions Act, but by distress warrant only.

Court of summary jurisdiction.—It would be desirable that the proceedings should be carried on in the regular Petty Sessions Court from the first, and that it be an open Court. Defendant consenting to the summary jurisdiction would cure many defects.

NEWSPAPER
LIBEL AND
REGISTRA-
TION ACT.

Act not to
extend to
Scotland.
Short title.

19. This Act shall not extend to Scotland.

20. This Act may for all purposes be cited as the Newspaper
Libel and Registration Act, 1881.

Appeal —The Act says nothing as to the right of appeal. be Petty Sessions Act
gives the right where the penalty exceeds 20s. The defendant may claim the right
on the grounds that the penalty imposed is out of proportion to the offence.
The Act is perplexing, and made so by the bringing in of portions of the English
Act. The closer it is examined the more difficulties arise : one does not readily see
why *fine* is used in section 5, *penalty* in sections 10 and 12, and the summary power
in section 6 is to recover *penalties*. *Fine* may mean that it is adjudged to put an end
to all proceedings—civil and criminal. The 49th section of the English Summary
Jurisdiction Act, 1879, interprets fine to include any pecuniary penalty, pecuniary
forfeiture, or pecuniary compensation payable under a conviction. That under
section 5 is a conviction.

THE SCHEDULES TO WHICH THIS ACT REFERS.

SCHEDULE A.

Return made pursuant to the Newspaper Libel and Registration Act, 1881.

Title of the Newspaper.	Names of the Proprietors.	Occupations of the Proprietors.	Places of Business (if any) of the Proprietors.	Places of Residence of the Proprietors.

SCHEDULE B.

Reture made pursuant to the Newspaper Libel and Registration Act, 1881.

Title of Newspaper.	Names of Persons who cease to be Proprietors.	Names of Persons who become Proprietors,	Occupation. of new Proprietors.	Places of business (if any) of new Proprietors.	Places of Residence of new Proprietors.

LAW OF LIBEL AMENDMENT ACT, 1888.

A.D. 1888

51 & 52 Vic., c. 64.

An Act to Amend the Law of Libel.

[*24th December*, 1888.]

WHEREAS it is expedient to amend the law of libel :

Be it therefore enacted by the Queen's most Excellent Majesty, by and with the advice and consent of the Lords Spiritual and Temporal, and Commons, in this present Parliament assembled, and by the authority of the same, as follows :

1. In the construction of this Act the word "newspaper" shall have the same meaning as in the Newspaper Libel and Registration Act, 1881. *Interpretation.*

2. Section 2 of the Newspaper Libel and Registration Act, 1881, is hereby repealed. *Repeal of 44 & 45 Vic. c. 60, s. 2.*

3. A fair and accurate report in any newspaper of proceedings publicly heard before any Court exercising judicial authority shall, if published contemporaneously with such proceedings, be privileged : Provided that nothing in this section shall authorize the publication of any blasphemous or indecent matter. *Newspaper reports of proceedings in court privileged.*

4. A fair and accurate report published in any newspaper of the proceedings of a public meeting, or (except where neither the public nor any newspaper reporter is admitted) of any meeting of a vestry, town council, school board, board of guardians, board or local authority formed or constituted under the provisions of any Act of Parliament, or of any committee appointed by any of the above-mentioned bodies, or of any meeting of any commissioners authorized to act by letters patent, Act of Parliament, warrant under the Royal Sign Manual, or other lawful warrant or authority, select committees of either House of Parliament, Justices of the Peace in Quarter Sessions assembled for administrative or deliberative purposes, and the publication at the request of any Government office or department, officer of State, commissioner of police, or chief constable of any notice or report issued by them for the information of the public, shall be privileged, unless it shall be proved that such report or publication was published or made maliciously : Provided that nothing in this section shall authorize the publication of any blasphemous or indecent matter : Provided also, that the protection intended to be *Newspaper reports of proceedings of public meetings and of certain bodies and persons privileged.*

Sec. 3.—This privilege will not, then, extend to private ministerial inquiries.
Sec. 4.—The definition at end of section applies to the "public meeting" in first clause of section, and where, although called public, the admission thereto may be restricted. The privilege extended to the meetings of other public bodies in the section is where the public *or* a newspaper reporter is admitted, by which, probably, is meant where both are not excluded.

afforded by this section shall not be available as a defence in any
proceedings if it shall be proved that the defendant has been
requested to insert in the newspaper in which the report or other
publication complained of appeared a reasonable letter or statement
by way of contradiction or explanation of such report or other publication, and has refused or neglected to insert the same: Provided
further, that nothing in this section contained shall be deemed or
construed to limit or abridge any privilege now by law existing, or
to protect the publication of any matter not of public concern and
the publication of which is not for the public benefit.

For the purposes of this section "public meeting" shall mean any
meeting bonâ fide and lawfully held for a lawful purpose, and for the
furtherance or discussion of any matter of public concern, whether
the admission thereto be general or restricted.

5. It shall be competent for a Judge or the Court, upon an application by or on behalf of two or more defendants in actions in respect
to the same, or substantially the same, libel brought by one and the
same person, to make an order for the consolidation of such actions,
so that they shall be tried together; and after such order has been
made, and before the trial of the said actions, the defendants in any
new actions instituted in respect to the same, or substantially the
same, libel shall also be entitled to be joined in a common action
upon a joint application being made by such new defendants and the
defendants in the actions already consolidated.

In a consolidated action under this section the jury shall assess the
whole amount of the damages (if any) in one sum, but a separate
verdict shall be taken for or against each defendant in the same way
as if the actions consolidated had been tried separately; and if the
jury shall have found a verdict against the defendant or defendants
in more than one of the actions so consolidated, they shall proceed
to apportion the amount of damages which they shall have so found
between and against the said last-mentioned defendants; and the
Judge at the trial, if he awards to the plaintiff the costs of the action,
shall thereupon make such order as he shall deem just for the appor-
tionment of such costs between and against such defendants.

Power to
defendant to
give certain
evidence in
mitigation of
damages.
6. At the trial of an action for a libel contained in any newspaper
the defendant shall be at liberty to give in evidence in mitigation of
damages that the plaintiff has already recovered (or has brought
actions for) damages, or has received or agreed to receive compensation in respect of a libel or libels to the same purport or effect as the
libel for which such action has been brought.

Obscene
matter need
not be set
forth in
indictment
or other
judicial pro-
ceeding.
7. It shall not be necessary to set out in any indictment or other
judicial proceeding instituted against the publisher of any obscene
libel the obscene passages, but it shall be sufficient to deposit the book,
newspaper, or other documents containing the alleged libel with the
indictment or other judicial proceeding, together with particulars
showing precisely by reference to pages, columns, and lines in what
part of the book, newspaper, or other document the alleged libel is to
be found, and such particulars shall be deemed to form part of the
record, and all proceedings may be taken thereon as though the passages complained of had been set out in the indictment or judicial
proceeding.

8. Section three of the forty-fourth and forty-fifth Victoria, chapter sixty, is hereby repealed, and instead thereof be it enacted that no criminal prosecution shall be commenced against any proprietor, publisher, editor, or any person responsible for the publication of a newspaper for any libel published therein without the order of a Judge at Chambers being first had and obtained.*

Such application shall be made on notice to the person accused, who shall have an opportunity of being heard against such application.

9. Every person charged with the offence of libel before any Court of criminal jurisdiction, and the husband or wife of the person so charged, shall be competent, but not compellable, witnesses on every hearing at every stage of such charge.

10. This Act shall not apply to Scotland.

11. This Act may be cited as the Law of Libel Amendment Act, 1888.

LAW OF LIBEL AMENDMENT ACT, 1888.

Repeal of 44 & 45 Vic. c. 60, s. 3. Order of Judge required for prosecution of newspaper proprietor, &c.

Persons proceeded against criminally a competent witness.

Extent of Act.

Short title.

PROBATION OF FIRST OFFENDERS ACT, 1887.

50 & 51 Vic., c. 25.

An Act to Permit the Conditional Release of First Offenders in Certain Cases. (a)   [8th August, 1887.]

A.D. 1887.

WHEREAS it is expedient to make provision for cases where the reformation of persons convicted of first offences may, by reason of the offender's youth or the trivial nature of the offence, be brought about without imprisonment.

Be it therefore enacted by the Queen's most Excellent Majesty, by and with the advice and consent of the Lords Spiritual and Temporal, and Commons, in this present Parliament assembled, and by the authority of the same, as follows:

1.—(1.) In any case in which a person is convicted of larceny or false pretences, or any other offence punishable with not more than two years' imprisonment before any Court, and no previous conviction is proved against him, if it appears to the Court before whom he is so convicted that, regard being had to the youth, character, and antecedents of the offender, to the trivial nature of the offence,

Power to Court to release upon probation of good conduct instead of sentencing to punishment

---

* Sec. 8.—Judge at Chambers is in this sections substituted for the Attorney-General in the repealed section of the Act of 1881.

(a) The object of this Act, as disclosed by its preamble, deserves attention, i.e. the expediency of bringing about reformation where there is reason to think such can be attained without imprisonment.

Release upon probation, 1st Sec.—This applies to *larceny or false pretences, or any other offence punishable with not more than two years' imprisonment, and where no previous conviction is proved.* The period of probation should be named, by the Court, and appear in the recognizance and in the words of the section.

PROBATION OF FIRST OFFENDERS ACT, 1887.   and to any extenuating circumstances under which the offence was committed, it is expedient that the offender be released on probation of good conduct, the Court may, instead of sentencing him at once to any punishment, direct that he be released on his entering into a recognizance, with or without sureties, and during such period as the Court may direct, to appear and receive judgment when called upon, and in the meantime to keep the peace and be of good behaviour.

(2.) The Court may, if it thinks fit, direct that the offender shall pay the costs of the prosecution, or some portion of the same, within such period and by such instalments as may be directed by the Court.

Provision in case of offender failing to observe conditions of his recognizances.   2.—(1) If the Court having power to deal with the offender in respect of his original offence, or any Court of summary jurisdiction, is satisfied by information on oath that the offender has failed to observe any of the conditions of his recognizance, it may issue a warrant for his apprehension.

(2.) An offender, when apprehended on any such warrant, shall, if not brought forthwith before a Court having power to sentence him, be brought before a Court of summary jurisdiction, and that Court may either remand him by warrant until the time at which he was required by his recognizance to appear for judgment, or until the sitting of a Court having power to deal with his original offence, or may admit him to bail with a sufficient surety conditioned on his appearing for judgment.

(3.) The offender when so remanded may be committed to a prison, either for the county or place in or for which the Court remanding him acts, or for the county or place where he is bound to appear for judgment, and the warrant of remand shall order that he be brought before the Court before which he was bound to appear for judgment, or to answer as to his conduct since his release.

Conditions as to abode of the offender.   3. The Court, before directing the release of an offender under this Act, shall be satisfied that the offender or his surety has a fixed place of abode or regular occupation in the county or place for which the Court acts, or in which the offender is likely to live during the period named for the observance of the conditions.

Definition of "Court."   4. In this Act the term "Court" includes a Court of summary jurisdiction.

Short title.   5. This Act may be cited as the Probation of First Offenders Act, 1887.

CRIMINAL LAW AND PROCEDURE (IRELAND) ACT, 1887. A.D. 1887.

50 & 51 Vict., c. 20.

SUMMARY JURISDICTION.

Section 2. Any person who shall commit an offence mentioned in sub-section 3 (a) of this section anywhere in Ireland, or shall commit any of the following offences in a Proclaimed District may be prose-cuted before a court of summary jurisdiction under this Act:— *Extension of summary jurisdiction.*

(1.) Any person who shall take part in any criminal conspiracy now punishable by law to compel or induce any person or persons either not to fulfil his or their legal obligations, or not to let, hire, use, or occupy any land, or not to deal with, work for, or hire any person or persons in the ordinary course of trade, business, or occupation; or to interfere with the administration of the law:

(2.) Any person who shall wrongfully and without legal authority use violence or intimidation—

(a) to or towards any person or persons with a view to cause any person or persons either to do any act which such person or persons has or have a legal right to abstain from doing, or to abstain from doing any act which such person or persons has or have a legal right to do; or

(b) to or towards any person or persons in consequence, either of his or their having done any act which he or they had a legal right to do, or of his or their having abstained from doing any act which he or they had a legal right to abstain doing:

By sec. 19 the expression "intimidation" includes any words or acts intended and calculated to put any person in fear of any injury or danger to himself, or to any member of his family, or to any person in his employment, or in fear of any injury to or loss of property, business, employment, or means of living.

The expression "writ of possession" includes any decree, warrant, order, or other document issued from any Court directing possession to be given, or authorizing possession to be taken, of any house or land.

The expression "The Summary Jurisdiction Acts" means in the Dublin Metro-politan Police District the Acts regulating the powers and duties of Justices of the Peace and of the police in that district, and elsewhere in Ireland means "the Petty Sessions (Ireland) Act, 1851," and the Acts amending it. *14 & 15 Vict. c. 93.*

The expression "prescribed" means prescribed by rules to be made under this Act.

3 G

(3.)—(*a*) Any person who shall take part in any riot or unlawful assembly; or

(*b*) within twelve months after the execution of any writ of possession of any house or land shall wrongfully take or hold forcible possession of such house or land or any part thereof; or

(*c*) shall assault, or wilfully and unlawfully resist or obstruct, any sheriff, constable, bailiff, process server, or other minister of the law, while in the execution of his duty, or shall assault him in consequence of such execution:

(4.) Any person who shall incite any other person to commit any of the offences hereinbefore mentioned.

Punishment, Procedure, and Definitions.

Section 11.—(1.) A person prosecuted before a court of summary jurisdiction under this Act shall be liable on conviction to imprisonment with or without hard labour for a term not exceeding six months, and shall have the same right of appeal as he would have under the Summary Jurisdiction Acts in the case of any other summary conviction.

(2.) If any person licensed under the Acts relating to intoxicating liquors is convicted under this Act, such conviction shall be entered in the proper register of licences, and may be directed to be recorded on the licence of the offender in the same manner, and when so recorded shall have the same effect as if the conviction were a conviction for an offence against those Acts.

(3.) If an offence is prosecuted summarily under this Act the same shall be prosecuted before a court of summary jurisdiction in manner provided by the Petty Sessions (Ireland) Act, 1851, and subject to the provisions thereof, save so far as they are altered by the provisions of this section.

(4.) The proceedings for enforcing the appearance of the person charged, and the attendance of witnesses for the prosecution shall be the same as if the offence were an indictable offence.

(5.) Upon every proceeding before a court of summary jurisdiction for an offence under this Act, the evidence for the prosecution and defence shall be taken as depositions in the same manner as if the offence were an indictable offence, and such depositions shall be admissible in evidence on any appeal.

(6.) The court of summary jurisdiction shall within the police district of Dublin metropolis be a divisional justice of that district, and elsewhere be two resident magistrates in petty sessions, one of whom shall be a person of the sufficiency of whose legal knowledge the Lord Lieutenant shall be satisfied, and the expression "resident magistrate" means a magistrate appointed in pursuance of the Act of the session of the sixth and seventh years of the reign of King William the Fourth, chapter thirteen, intituled, "An Act to consolidate the laws relating to the constabulary force in Ireland."(a) One resident magistrate may act alone in adjourning or postponing a court, or in doing any other thing antecedent to the hearing of a charge under this Act.

CRIMINAL LAW AND PROCEDURE (IRELAND) ACT.

(a) It is the practice to add this description after the names of the Resident Magistrates in the Order Book, and also in warrants to convict under this Act. Some Judges of the Supreme Court having pointed out that the jurisdiction should clearly appear on the face of the proceedings. On ordinary principles this is not necessary. On the well-known presumption—*omnia rité esse acta.*

Riot.—It is not sufficient to state in *the conviction* that in the words of sub-sec. (3.) the "*defendant took part in a riot.*" Riot here being a Common-law offence, the Exchequer Division held that the terms of the conviction were insufficient. *Ex parte* Latchford, J.P., on application of a *habeas corpus,* August, 1888, before Chief Baron Palles, Baron Dowse, and Mr. Justice Andrews From this decision it would appear that the conviction should describe the offence in such words as will amount to what a riot is defined to be, *i. e.* such as would be set out in a Bill of Indictment, viz. that to the number of (3 or more) they did riotously and tumultuously assemble, and in a violent and turbulent manner, to the terror of the people, &c. (describe what they did, and that the acts were accompanied with force and violence). See Riot, and definition, Indictable Offences Index.

Unlawful Assembly.—Where the Justices dismiss a charge of riot, but on a distinct summons, and on same evidence, convict of the charge of unlawful assembly, the plea of *autre fois acquis* will not be a valid plea.—*Queen* (by Markham) v. *Boyle and Others,* on case stated, Exchr. Div., Nov., 1888.

Execution of Warrant by the Sheriff.—On a case stated it was argued that the sheriff was acting illegally in executing the decree of the County Court Judge, as the service of the six months' notice under the Land Act of 1887 had not been proved to have been served, and that the sheriff should have satisfied himself on this point before executing the writ of possession. The Court held that the sheriff was a ministerial officer, obliged to obey the Court, and could not be expected to exercise judicial discretion. The warrant obliged him to execute the decree to possession, and to obstruct him in this was to obstruct him in the execution of his duty. The Court upheld the conviction of the Resident Magistrates.—*The Queen* v. *Patrick Magrath,* Nov. 1888, Exchr. Div.

SUMMARY OF CIRCULARS.

SUMMARY OF CIRCULARS ADDRESSED TO MAGISTRATES, AND WHICH ARE FILED
IN EVERY PETTY SESSIONS COURT, IN CHRONOLOGICAL ORDER, AND ENTERED
IN AN ALPHABETICAL INDEX. SEVERAL OF THE MOST ESSENTIAL ARE FULLY
GIVEN IN THE *Appendix.*

Oct. 31, 1860. *Signing " Order Book."*—Each order should be signed in the
Order Book by a justice signing his name opposite to it or immediately after it.

Mar. 16, 1865. *Stamps on Orders.*—On the entry of any order the 6d. for the
stamp to be affixed thereto is payable by the person at whose instance the case
has been heard. No sum is payable on the entry of the case for hearing, and
if neither party appears the case should be simply struck out, and no order made.

Aug. 4, 1866. *Cattle Diseases Act.*—Directing attention of magistrates to
the importance of imposing penalties under the Cattle Diseases (Ireland) Act,
1866, &c., suitable to the gravity of the offences.

Jan. 17, 1867. *Spoiled Stamps.*—General rules as to allowance for stamps
improperly or unnecessarily used under Petty Sessions Clerks (Ireland) Act,
1858, and Dogs Registration (Ireland) Act, 1865.

Apr. 16, 1867. *Dog Licences.*—Clerks of Petty Sessions not to issue Dog
Licences after March 31, unless under order of Justices.

Sep. 9, 1867. *Month.*—Where month in Statute means calendar month, the
word "calendar" is to be inserted in the sentence of committal.

Oct. 6, 1868. *Number of persons in the same Summons.*—As to joining
several defendants in the one original summons, and like as to witnesses.

Feb. 1, 1869. *Publicans' Licences.*—Justices to discourage applications to
Government to grant or transfer publicans' licences to other places, unless at
Quarter Sessions, or where some sudden occurrence which could not be provided
against takes place.

May 8, 1869. *Binding to the Peace.*—The power to bind to keep the peace,
&c., after expiration of the sentence of punishment, is limited to cases enumerated in s. 43 24 & 25 Vic. c. 100; but opinion is limited to cases arising under
s. 42, and in no way applies to *ordinary jurisdiction* of the justices in proper
cases to bind persons to keep the peace, &c.

Aug. 29, 1870. *When Constabulary may prosecute.*—In summary cases the
constabulary, being complainants, can conduct their cases, examine and cross-
examine witnesses. In indictable offences, although not the complainants or informants, it is their right and their duty to conduct the case, and examine and
cross-examine witnesses.

Oct. 10, 1870. *Expenses of Conveying Prisoners.*—As to certifying for expenses of conveying prisoners.

Feb. 22 1872, Oct. 24, 1874, and May 24, 1875. *Aggravated Assaults.*—
·ndangering life, or of a felonious or aggravated character, accused
mitted for trial and not summarily dealt with.

Dec. 8, 1870. *Revenue Fines.*—As to the application and payment of Inland Revenue fines, which is to be as directed by 31 & 32 Vic., c. 124, s. 1, whether recovered at the instance of Royal Irish Constabulary or not.

June 15, 1871. *Lunatics.*—Where dangerous lunatic is, under warrant, sent to asylum, copy of the medical officer's certificate to be sent to "Office of the Registrar in Lunacy, Four Courts, Dublin."

Mar. 10, 1874. *Lunatics.*—Class of cases contemplated by the Statute to justify the committal to asylum as dangerous lunatics.

Dec. 24, 1874 and Feb 8, 1875; Order in Council, Feb. 2, 1875. *Licensing Sessions.*—Recommending dates for holding Quarter Sessions and Petty Sessions (for Petty Sessions the last Petty Sessions held in September) for granting publicans' licences.

Jan. 27, 1875. *Tramps.*—Vagrancy, its increase, and outrages committed by "tramps" wandering through the country, and calling magistrate's attention to the summary powers in dealing with such offences.

Mar. 25, 1875. *Convicts holding Licence.*—When summarily punished, the magistrate or clerk to forward certificate of conviction in Act (27 & 28 Vic., c. 47). As this certificate is signed by the clerk to the justices, he should forward it.

Apr. 16, 1875. *Circulars.*—Justices to read and sign his name to circular showing that he has done so.

May 4, 1875. *Transmitting Informations.*—Where offender committal for trial information, &c., to be returned to the Clerk of the Crown and Peace within 7 days.

July 19, 1875. *Lunatics.*—As to their proper treatment in transit to asylum, the suitable conveyance, and that they shall arrive at asylum before night.

June 29, 1875. *Licences.*—Spirit-grocers' and beer-dealers' licences under Revenue Act (38 Vic., c. 23, s. 12) to expire on October 10.

May 2, 1876. *Reformatory Act.*—Parental responsibility. Justices to see that parents contribute in proportion to earnings from time to time, and so indemnify the public.

Sept. 19, 1877. *Industrial School.*—Magistrates can order detention of Protestant boys in Gibraltar Training Ship, Belfast, under sections 11 & 13 of Act, and pointing out the advantages where boys are suited to seafaring life.

Sept. 20, 1877. *Italian Children.*—Suspected to be stolen by persons known as Padroni, and leading vagrant life. To be sent to an industrial school. Italian Consul-General will pay for maintenance until children are transferred to their native country. Royal Irish Constabulary are instructed on this subject by Inspector-General.

Oct. 2, 1877. *Excise Appeals.*—Where excise prosecute, and that appeal is lodged from conviction or decision, the record of such conviction or acquittal to be lodged with Clerk of the Peace three clear days before the Quarter Sessions. The form is given in schedule to Act, s. 10, 40 Vic., c. 13, and is also given in circulars.

May 15, 1878. *Medical witnesses.*—Not to be needlessly summoned, &c., unless in important cases, where their evidence is essential, their attendance can afterwards be procured at Assizes or Quarter Sessions.

May 27, 1878. *Dogs Unlicensed.*—Recommending that substantial penalties be imposed, unless it be shown that the failure to license is occasioned by accident.

Aug. 5, 1878.　*Clerk of Petty Sessions.*—Magistrate before being appointed Clerk of Petty Sessions must first resign his commission.

May 2, 1879.　*Remands.*—General circular on the subject of "Remands." This circular should be attended to. It is in full in the Appendix to this work.

Dec. 8, 1879.　*On the Petroleum Acts*, 1871 & 1879.—The testing of temperature, &c. (42 & 43 Vic., c. 47).

June 16, 1880.　*Reformatory Act. Sentences.*—To be as directed, and within the limits in the Act.

May 10, 1881.　*Habitual Offenders.*—Before summarily dealing with offence of larceny, justices may remand, pending inquiry as to character, previous conviction, &c., and, if advisable, commit the prisoner for trial.

Oct. 5, 1881, Feb. 28, 1883.　*Militia.*—As to necessary authority to be obtained before dealing summarily with offenders under Militia Act, Royal Warrant, &c.

Aug. 12, 1882.　*Canine Rabies.*—As to local authorities, under the Dogs Act, 1871, their duties, and duties of Royal Irish Constabulary.

Jan. 9, 1884.　*Fugitive offenders.*—Instructions and Home Office Circular for information and guidance as to the surrender of criminals under Fugitive Offenders Act, 1881.

May 16, 1884.　*Unstamped Instruments.*—As to the amount of duties and penalties to be received when unstamped or insufficiently stamped instruments are tendered in evidence in Court. Extract from Stamp Act, 1870, 33 & 34 Vic., c. 97.

June 19, 1884.　*Industrial Schools.*—Justices to ascertain before committing child to industrial school if there be a vacancy, &c., and so prevent inconvenience, &c.

July 18, 1884.　*Industrial Schools.*—St. Joseph's Roman Catholic Female Industrial School, Ballinasloe, Co. Galway. will receive Roman Catholic girls committed under s. 11 ; and are specially bound to receive those committed under s. 13 of Act.

May 1, 1885.　*Like.*—As to *Probationary Industrial Schools* at Kilmore, Santry, Co. Dublin, for Roman Catholic boys under 12 years, sentenced under s. 13 of Act, where grand jury has previously contracted with managers. (Calls attention to circulars of July 8, and July 18, 1881, on same subject.)

Feb. 5, 1886.　*Rabies in Dogs.*—Circular as to rabies in dogs, and hydrophobia in persons bitten by them, and pointing out duties of local authorities on the subject, under "The Dogs Act, 1871," and recommending rigorous enforcement of the Act. (Refers to circular of Aug. 12, 1882, as the subject on the fly-leaf).

Feb. 22, 1886.　*Fugitive Offenders.*—Calling attention to the care necessary to be observed in preparing informations and warrants intended to arrest fugitives going abroad.

Feb. 7, 1887.　As to *Convicts, Licence Holders*, convicted of not complying with statutory requirements of licence, &c.—Calling special attention to sentences under s. 5, and irregular convictions under s. 7, "Prevention of Crimes Act, 1871," 34 & 35 Vic., c. 112, ss. 5 & 8, and s. 7.

Mar. 16, 1888.　*Short Sentences, Committals.*—The importance that imprisonment when resorted to should be for a period in keeping with the statutory ʼnts applicable to the particular offence.

Summary of Circulars addressed to Clerks of Petty Sessions.

May 10, 1852.—Circular under 14 & 15 Vic., c. 93, par 7, where after warrant is issued the Clerk of Petty Sessions receives amount from defendant he should, in writing, immediately notify the fact to the constabulary.

Apr. 11, 1860.—Copies of informations, depositions, &c., in cases returned for trial to Quarter Sessions should, as early as possible, be sent to Sessional Crown Solicitor.

Aug. 31, 1861.—Committals on summary conviction to state the Act under which prisoner was convicted.

Nov. 6, 1862.—The clerk should only pay to parties a portion of fine on a special order in each case, and not on a mere general order.

June 4, 1879.—Under Small Debts Act, clerks should provide the printed forms in schedule to Act, and fill up the processes under Act.

July 31, 1879.—Clerk of Petty Sessions to send to Lieutenant of County half-yearly return of attendance of magistrates at Petty Sessions.

Apr. 12, 1880. *No. 8.*—The fees on committals of deserters (2s.) will be paid by paymaster of sub-district. The claim must be certified by a magistrate. Circular gives list of paymasters in Ireland.

Mar. 11, 1881.—Circular from Comptroller of Customs as to necessity of having general duty of 2s. 6d. upon affidavits apart from Petty Session stamps.

Apr. 7, 1881.—As to application of fines for drunkenness in towns under Towns Improvement Act, 1884.

Mar. 24, 1882.—Circular as to the summary prosecution of militia offenders, accompanied by army circular.

Mar. 31, 1882. *No. 14.*—Monthly return to be made of magistrates' attendance.

Nov. 20, 1883.—Where aggrieved party takes no part in prosecution by information or evidence, the constabulary prosecute. The aggrieved party is to get no portion of fine.

Jan. 9, 1884.—Circular and instructions as to "fugitive offenders," their detention, surrender, &c.

Mar. 6, 1882. *No. 18.*—Further circular calling attention to prosecution of militiamen before magistrates.

Dec. 18, 1884. *No. 25.*—As to copies of documents sent to Sessional Crown Solicitor, and the necessity of naming them as they are in Schedule C, 21 & 22 Vic., c. 100.

Mar. 19, 1885. *No. 26.*—Further circular as to sending accounts quarterly, immediately after Quarter Sessions, to Sessional Crown Solicitor.

June 17, 1885. *No. 28.*—Fines under Merchant Shipping Acts, and the unappropriated portions of fines under Passengers' Act, 1885, to be accounted for with Registrar, Petty Sessions Department.

Sept. 17, 1885. *Clerks' Sureties.*—On death, departure from the realm, or insolvency of surety, clerk, without delay, should notify fact to the Petty Sessions Clerk's Office, Castle.

Oct. 13, 1885. *No. 30.*—Militia officers prosecuting for militia offences. Red stamps to be supplied.

July 28, 1887. *No. 33.*—Unless so directed by the justices, clerks of Petty Sessions should not prepare memorials for remission of penalties.

Dec. 11, 1887. *No. 37.* Miscellaneous Circulars :—

Warrants of committal to specify the prison.
Letters addressed to Bank of Ireland to be prepaid.
Witnesses getting orders under 18 & 19 Vic., c. 126 (Larceny), to cash the orders themselves.

Feb. 24, 1888. *No. 38.*—"Probation of First Offenders' Act, 1887," to be attended to and kept before justices.

Mar. 15, 1888. *No. 39.*—Dog Licence money received in March should be lodged within first fortnight in April.

Apr. 6, 1888. *No 40.* Miscellaneous Circulars :—

Claims on Sessional Crown Solicitor for copies, informations, &c., to be to be made after each Quarter Sessions.
As to stamping depositions for the *defence* under 50 & 51 Vic., c. 20, triable before two resident magistrates where the defendant refuses to supply the stamps.
In committals of dangerous lunatics a seal to be affixed opposite signatures of justices.

June 9, 1888. *No. 41.*—Depositions in indictable offences to be returned to Crown and Peace Office without delay.

Nov. 20, 1888. *No. 43.*—All depositions against same offender, taken at *same hearing* for several offences, to be *bound or tied together* for Clerk of the Crown,

ADDENDA.

Offence.	Statute.	Punishment.
Cotton Cloth Factories Act, 1889— To be construed as one with the "Factory and Workshop Act, 1878" (41 & 42 Vic., c. 16).	52 & 53 Vic. c. 62.	
Regulating temperature and humidity of the atmosphere therein.	,,	
The Thermometers to be employed therein.		
Notice of artificial production of humidity to be given; notice of cessation, &c. Provisions for preventing inhalation of dust.		
Acting in contravention of Act after notice from Inspector, &c., or repeating within 12 months after notice. Occupier shall be liable to—	s. 13.	First offence, penalty not less than £5, nor more than £10; for every subsequent offence, penalty not less than £10, nor more than £20. In default, &c., imprisonment by scale. 2 J.
Fisheries (*Steam Trawling*)— Act to enable Inspectors of Irish Fisheries to prohibit Steam Trawling within a certain distance of the coast, and for using any Trawl net or method of fishing in contravention of by-laws of Inspectors. Extension of powers of 5 & 6 Vic., c. 106, as to boarding, seizing, &c.	52 & 53 Vic. c. 74, s. 3.	First offence, fine not exceeding £5, for second or subsequent offence fine not exceeding £20, in default, &c., imprisonment by scale, and forfeiture of nets, ropes, tackle, &c. 1 J.
For landing or selling fish caught in contravention of section, &c.		First offence, fine not exceeding £5; second or subsequent offence not exceeding £20, in default, &c., imprisonment by scale. 1 J.

Offence.	Statute.	Punishment.
Friendly Societies— Exemption from provisions of section 30 of the 38 & 39 Vic., c. 60, in certain cases. **Repeal of 51 & 52 Vic., c. 66.**	**52 & 53 Vic. c. 22.**	
Horse-flesh— Act to regulate **the sale of horse-**flesh for human food.	**52 Vic. c. 11.**	
Signs, &c., to be placed on horse-flesh shops.	s. 1.	
Horse-flesh not to be sold as other meat.	s. 2.	
Power of Medical Officer of Health to inspect meat, &c.	s. 3.	
Power of Justice to grant warrant to search.	s. 4.	
Power of Justice with reference to disposal of horse-flesh.	s. 5.	
Person offending against any of the provisions of Act.	s. 6.	Penalty not exceeding £20, in default, &c., imprisonment by scale. 1 J.
Onus of proving that horse-flesh exposed **was not intended for sale** to lie on person exposing it.		

Offence.	Statute.	Punishment.
Infectious Disease— Act to provide for the notification of Infectious Diseases to Local Authorities.	52 & 53 Vic. c. 72.	
Definition of Infectious Disease.	s. 6.	
Merchant Shipping (Pilotage) Act, 1879—	52 & 53 Vic. c. 68.	
Provides penalty for displaying on ordinary boat a colourable imitation of pilot flag—	s. 10.	
British Merchant Service Act to amend the law relating to the use of Flags, and penalty on ship not showing colours.	52 & 53 Vic. c. 73.	
Railways— "*Regulation of Railways Act*, 1889." Railway Companies shall make returns to Board of Trade of overtime of persons whose duty involves safety of trains, &c., and provides penalties for default.	52 & 53 Vic. c. 57.	
Penalty for avoiding payment of fare. Every passenger shall produce, and when requested, deliver up ticket, showing that fare is paid, or pay fare from the place whence he started, or give officer his name and address, or in default—	s. 5.	Fine not exceeding 40*s.*; in default, &c., imprisonment by scale.* 2 J.
For failing to comply, officer or servant of company, or constable, may detain him until brought before Justice, or discharged by due course of law.		

* See notes as to "Transient Offenders, title "Railways," Summary Index.

Offence.	Statute.	Punishment.
Railways—*continued.*		
If any person—		
(a) Travels, or attempts to travel, on a railway without having previously paid his fare, and with intent to avoid payment thereof; or,—	s. 5.	Fine not exceeding 40s.; in default, &c., imprisonment not exceeding 1 month.
(b) Having paid his fare for a certain distance, knowingly and wilfully proceeds by train beyond that distance without previously paying the additional fare, and with intent to avoid payment thereof; or,—	,,	*Second or subsequent offence.* —Either fine not exceeding £20, or in the discretion of Court, imprisonment not exceeding 1 month.　　　2 J.
(c) Having failed to pay his fare, gives in reply to a request by an officer of a railway company a false name or address, he shall be liable to—	,,	
Punishment under section not to prejudice recovery of fare payable.		
Passenger ticket to have fare printed thereon.		
Every passenger ticket by railway shall bear on its face printed or written, legibly, the fare for the journey, subject to Board of Trade exceptions, &c., and Company acting in contravention shall be liable to—	s. 6.	Penalty not exceeding 40s., for every ticket so issued, in default distress warrant.　2 J.
Power to make bye-laws, &c., for regulating use of stations and the approaches thereto.	s. 7	
This Act and the Regulation of Railways Acts, 1840 to 1871, may be cited collectively as the Regulation of Railways Acts, 1840 to 1889.		

INDEX.

ARREST :
    of clergymen when unlawful under civil process, 463.
    general powers of constables to arrest, &c., 61.
    under the Extradition Act, &c., 508.
    of accused persons and witnesses generally, *see* PETTY SESSIONS ACT, 701.
    unlawful or without probable cause, 701.

ARSENIC :
    regulating sale of, 17.

ARSON :
    see MALICIOUS INJURIES.
    indictable Offences.

ART :
    wilful damage to works of.
    see MALICIOUS INJURIES, INDICTABLE OFFENCES.

ARTIFICER, 17.

ASSAULTS :
    triable summarily, &c., 18.
    indictable, *see* OFFENCES AGAINST THE PERSON, 569, 581.

ASSEMBLY :
    unlawful, 463.

ASSISTING, 463.
    and *see* ABBETTORS, 1, 458.

ATTEMPT :
    to commit indictable offences, 464.

ATTORNEY :
    right to be heard in Petty Sessions, 696.

ATTORNEY-GENERAL.
    indictments, requiring his consent, *see* VEXATIOUS INDICTMENTS, and *see* NEWSPAPER LAW OF LIBEL, Appendix.

AUCTIONEERS, 22.

BACKING WARRANTS, 727.

BAIL :
    to keep the peace, &c., 408.
    in indictable offences, 22, 709.
    mode of binding, 722.
    estreating recognizances, &c., 724, 731.
    notice to estreat, 768.
    bailsman obtaining warrant against absconding principal, 711.

BEER-HOUSES :
 see title LICENSING ACTS, 237, 649.
 and Appendix, Acts in full, &c., 649.

BEGGING IN PUBLIC PLACES, 23, 428.

BEGGING-LETTERS, 430.

BENCH WARRANT, 711.

BESETTING PERSON OR HOUSE, &c., 54.

BESTIALITY AND UNNATURAL OFFENCES, 607.

BETTTING HOUSES, 186.

BIGAMY, 470.

BILLET :
 of soldiers, 12.

BINDING :
 Apprentice, &c., 114.
 informants and witnesses to prosecute, 705.

BIRDS :
 larceny of, 230, 237.
 malicious injury of, 276.
 Sea-birds Preservation Act, 394.
 and *see* GAME.

BIRTHS :
 registration of, 382.
 concealing, 483.
 forging entries in register, 522.

BLASPHEMING, 24, 471.
 and *see* LIBELS.

BOARD OF TRADE (inquiries) FEES, 779.
 and *see* MERCHANT SHIPPING ACT.

BOAT :
 taking without consent, 24.
 stealing from, 539.

BODILY HARM :
 see OFFENCES AGAINST THE PERSON.

BOILER EXPLOSION ACT :
 notice of explosion to be sent to Board of Trade, 24.

3 H

CHARACTER:
to servant, *see* DISCHARGE, 91.

CHEATING:
at play, 474, and *see* GAMING AND BETTING HOUSES, &c., 183.

CHILD under 12 may be summarily dealt with for any indictable offence other
than homicide, 35.
on summary conviction under any Act, shall not be imprisoned longer than
one month, nor fined a larger sum than 40*s*., 36.
and *see* also YOUNG PERSONS.
under 14 taking part in exhibitions, 39.
under 14 where mother convicted of *crime*, 72.
liability to maintain parents, under Poor Law, 38.
offences on, 38, 475.
concealing birth of, 483.
carnally knowing females, and attempts, &c., under 12, 473.
and *see* also REFORMATORY and INDUSTRIAL SCHOOLS, BAKEHOUSE, FAC-
TORIES, WORKSHOPS.

CHILDREN AND YOUNG PERSONS:
summary jurisdiction over, 35.
prevention of cruelty to, 343.

CHIMNEY SWEEPS, 39, 43.

CHLOROFORM:
using, to commit offences, 475.

CHOKE:
attempting to, 476.

CHURCH, CHURCH-YARD, AND BURIAL-GROUND:
disturbances and offences in, 44, 476.
and *see* also LARCENY, and MALICIOUS INJURIES, Indictable Offences.

CIRCULAR LETTERS:
to Magistrates and their clerks, Appendix.

CLAIM OF RIGHT, 276.

CLERGYMAN:
obstructing, in duty, 44.
unlawfully arresting, 476.
offences against and duties under marriage laws, &c., 563.
and *see* also REGISTRATION OF BIRTHS, MARRIAGES, &c., 382.

CLERK:

offences by, *see* titles LARCENY, EMBEZZLEMENT, FORGERY, Indictable Offences.

CLERK OF PETTY SESSIONS, 45.

CLOSING HOURS:

public houses, 253.

COACH:

(stage) offences, 98.

COALS:

how sold, 47.
mode of weighing, 438.

COCK-FIGHTING, 47.

COIN:

offences relating to, 47, 424–429, 477, 481.

COMBINATION:

of workmen, and intimidation by, *see* CONSPIRACY AND PROTECTION OF PROPERTY, 50.
assault in pursuance of combination, 482.
and *see* CONSPIRACY, 483.

COMMAND, OR NOTICE.

under RIOT ACT, 598.

COMMITTALS:

act to be stated in, 787.
to be stamped as warrant, 627.

COMMON ASSAULT, 18.

COMMON LODGING-HOUSES:

see PUBLIC HEALTH.

COMMONS:

injury, &c., 50.

COMPANIES:

frauds by, *see* LARCENY, 542, &c.

COMPENSATION:

to be given party aggrieved, 718.
ting for compensation for malicious burnings, &c., 343.
r FORMS, *see* Appendix.

CONVICTS (Licensed), 66, &c.
offences by, see Larceny.

CO-PARTNERS:
offences by, see Larceny.

COPY INFORMATIONS:
defendant entitled to, 699.

COPPER COIN, see Coin.

COPYRIGHT ACT, 64.

CORN:
frauds in sale of, 3, 64, 164.
assault in preventing sale of, 19.
winnowing, on roads, 64.
malicious injury to, 555.

CORONER, 214.

CORROSIVE FLUID:
throwing on person, 574.

CORRUPT PRACTICES AT ELECTIONS, 497, &c.
Public Bodies Corrupt Practices Act, 1889, 592.

COSTS:
in Petty Sessions, 64, 719.
of Petty Sessions stamps, 627.
under Small Debts Act, 628, &c.

COTTIER TENANTS, 219.

COTTON CLOTH FACTORIES ACT, 825.

COUNSEL:
right to be heard in Petty Sessions, 696.

COUNTERFEIT COIN, 47, 477–481.

COURT OF PETTY SESSIONS:
an open court, 64, 697.
pt of, 62, 484.
f, 45.

ALING, 531.

ELECTRIC TELEGRAPH :
injuries to, 557.

EJECTMENT :
of small tenement in market towns, &c., 106, 217.
cottier tenants, 219.
caretakers, 221.
deserted premises, 224.

EMBEZZLEMENT, 502.
summary power of Justices to try. &c., 226.

EMIGRATION :
laws relating to, *see* PASSENGER SHIPS, 318, &c.

EMPLOYERS AND WORKMEN, 106-123.
apprentices, 109, &c.
domestic servants, 112-123.

ENGINE :
obstructing, and for regulations as to locomotives on highways, *see* 28 & 29
Vic., c. 83, which provides penalties. Act now continued by 43 & 44
Vic., c. 48.

ENLISTMENT :
offences connected with, 11-12, &c., *see* ARMY.
the line, 11, 12, &c.
militia, 302, &c.
Naval Coast Volunteers, 308.
Navy, Royal, 309.
against Foreign Enlistment Act, 515.

ENTRY :
forcible, 504.

ESCAPE OF PRISONER, 504.

ESTREATING RECOGNIZANCE, 614, 731.

EVIDENCE :
how taken in indictable offences, 705.
in summary cases, 714.
" Law of Evidence," 644, &c.
refusing to give evidence, 702.

EXCEPTIONS :
see NEGATIVE, 713.

FOWL (stealing), 340.

FRAUDS:
  as to provisions, 3, 164, 433.
  by bankers, agents, &c., 542.

FRIENDLY SOCIETIES, 165 ; and see *Addenda.*

FRUIT AND FRUIT TREES:
  see LARCENY, and MALICIOUS INJURIES, Summary Index.

FUGITIVE:
  offenders, 525.
  and *see* EXTRADITION, 508.

FURIOUS DRIVING, 101, 103, 575.

FURZE:
  setting fire to, 554.

GAMBLERS:
  thimblers and swindlers, 430.

GAME LAWS, 172–183.

GAMES:
  on roads, &c., 25, 313.

GAMING HOUSES, 183.

GAOL AND GAOLER, 189.

GARDEN:
  see LARCENY and MALICIOUS INJURIES, 234, 272.

GARROTTERS:
  may be whipped, 572.

GAS ACTS, 193.
  breach of contract by persons employed in works, 51.

GATE:
  damaging, 274.
  stealing, 232.

GAZETTE:
  evidence of proclamation, &c., 526, 644.

GIRL:
  abusing girl under age of 12 years, 458.

GLYCERINE:
  offences relating to, 566.

3 L

---

* It was intended to give Form of this Order in Appendix, but it somehow was overlooked. The Form can now be had from the Law Stationers.

POULTRY:
stealing, &c., 340.

POUND, 340.

PRECEPT:
to restrain waste, 223.
form of, 776.

PRESENTMENT:
Sessions, 343.
mode of presenting for malicious injuries, 278, 778.
forms, 778.

PRETENCES:
by false pretences obtaining money, goods, &c., 512.

PREVENTION OF CRIME ACT, 65.

PREVENTION OF CRUELTY TO CHILDREN:
summary index, 343.

PRINCIPAL:
in second degree, 591.

PRISONER:
how disposed of after case heard in Petty Sessions, 708.
when witnesses are in another county, 708.
when about to abscond after being bailed, 710.
prisoner's statement when in custody by constable, 706.
when before Justice, 706.

PRISONERS (COUNSEL ACT, 6 & 7 Wm. iv., c. 114).

PRISONS, 189.
Prisons Act, 1877, 192.

PRIZE-FIGHTING, 146, 695; and see SURETIES TO KEEP THE PEACE, &c.,
408, &c.

PROBATION:
of first offenders, 349; 815.

PROCEDURE GENERAL:
Local jurisdiction of Justices, 694.
When in adjoining county, *ib.*
Place of hearing cases, and what may be heard out of Petty Sessions, 696.
Publicity of proceedings, and when examinations may be in private, 696.
Contempt of Court, how punished, *ib.*
Informations and complaints generally, as to offences within and outside his
jurisdiction: when to be verbal, and when in writing, 697, &c.

3 K

TIMBER:
conveying on roads, streets, &c., 414.

TIME:
when, may be given to pay penalties, 717.

TITLE:
question of, where it arises, 276.

TOBACCO:
smuggling, *see* CUSTOMS.

TOLLS (*see* TURNPIKE), 424

TOWNS COMMISSIONS ACT, 414.

TOWNS IMPROVEMENT ACT, 414.

TRADE DISPUTES, 50.

TRADE MARKS, 285.

TRADES UNIONS, 415.

TRANSFER OF LICENCE:
of dogs, 96.
publican's transfers, 260.
form of, 697.

TRANSMITTING INFORMATIONS, 767.

TRANSPORTATION, 604.

TREASON, 604.
treasonable felony, 604.
no bail in, but by order of Lord Lieutenant, 710, &c.

TREASURE-TROVE, 605.

TREES, PLANTS, &c.:
larceny of, 232.
malicious injury to, 272.

TRESPASS:
of persons, 416.
of animals, 341.

TROUT, *see* FISHERIES.

᠌   ᠌mary Index, 417–424.

᠌   ᠌ow recovered, 431.

WINE LICENCE:
how obtained, 375.

WINNOWING:
on roads, 450.

WITNESSES:
bound to give evidence, 450.
payment in civil cases, *ib.*
protection from arrest for debt, 705.
as to payment of medical witnesses, 788.

WOOD:
see LARCENY and MALICIOUS INJURIES.

WORKMEN, 451.
and *see* EMPLOYERS AND WORKMEN.

WORKSHOP:
Regulation Act (30 & 31 Vic., c. 146), 451.
and *see* BAKEHOUSES, FACTORIES.

WORSHIP:
disturbing, &c., 44, 495.

WRECK AND SALVAGE, 452, 610.

WRITING:
when complaint should be in, under Petty Sessions Act, 699.
in depositions should be legible, 705.

YOUNG PERSONS, between 12 and 16, charged with certain indictable offences,
punishable summarily under Summary Jurisdiction over Children (Ireland) Act, 1884, 35, &c.
see also Child.

THE END.

Printed by PONSONBY AND WELDRICK, *Dublin.*